PSYCHOLOGY

PSYCHOLOGY

E. BRUCE GOLDSTEIN

University of Pittsburgh

BROOKS/COLE PUBLISHING COMPANY
PACIFIC GROVE, CALIFORNIA

Brooks/Cole Publishing Company
A Division of Wadsworth, Inc.

Printed in the United States of America
10   9   8   7   6   5   4   3   2   1

Library of Congress Cataloging-in-Publication Data
Goldstein, E. Bruce, [date]
    Psychology/E. Bruce Goldstein.
    p.   cm.
    Includes bibliographical references and indexes.
    ISBN 0–534–13608–7
    1. Psychology. I. Title
BF121.G62   1994
150—dc20   93–37954
                                                                              CIP

Sponsoring Editor: *Marianne Taflinger*
Project Development Editor: *John Bergez*
Editorial Assistant: *Virge Perelli-Minetti*
Production Editor: *Kirk Bomont*
Manuscript Editor: *Pamela Evans*
Permissions Editor: *Linda Rill*
Cover Photo: *Copyright H. Mark Weidman, "Austrian Staircase"*
Art Coordinator: *Lisa Torri*
Interior Illustration: *Precision Graphics* and *Seventeenth Street Studios*
Photo Coordinator and Digital Photo Designer: *Larry Molmud*
Photo Researcher: *Laurel Anderson, Photosynthesis*
Indexer: *Do Mi Stauber*
Typesetting: *TSI Graphics*
Cover Printing: *Phoenix Color Corporation*
Printing and Binding: *Rand McNally & Company*

Credits continue on page C-1.

To Barbara Baker, for her constant loving support,
John Bergez, for his dedication and loyalty,
and Ken King, for having faith in me.

ABOUT THE AUTHOR

E. Bruce Goldstein is Associate Professor of Psychology at the University of Pittsburgh. He received his bachelor's degree in chemical engineering from Tufts University, his Ph.D. in experimental psychology from Brown University, and, before joining the faculty at the University of Pittsburgh, was a post-doctoral research fellow in the biology department at Harvard University. Bruce is the author of the best-selling text *Sensation and Perception* (also published by Brooks/Cole) and has published articles on perception and visual physiology in journals such as *Journal of Experimental Psychology, Vision Research, Archives of Ophthalmology,* and *Nature.* He teaches introduction to psychology as a natural science, sensation and perception, the psychology of gender, and the psychology of art.

BRIEF CONTENTS

1   The Science of Psychology   2

2   Understanding Psychological Research   32

3   The Biology of Behavior   72

4   The Senses and Perception   124

5   Consciousness and Behavior   172

6   Basic Learning Processes   220

7   Memory   272

8   Thought and Language   320

9   Physical, Perceptual, and Cognitive Development   362

10 Language and Social Development   402

11 Motivation   440

12 Emotion   482

13 Stress and Health   514

14 Intelligence   550

15 Personality   588

16 Psychological Disorders   630

17 Therapy   676

18 Social Cognition and Attitudes   712

19 Interpersonal Relations   752

CONTENTS

Chapter 1

The Science of Psychology   2

What You Do and Don't Know About Psychology   4

Psychology as Science   6

The Growth of Scientific Psychology   8

 Psychology's Philosophical Heritage   8

 Prelude to Scientific Psychology   10

 Wundt and Titchener   11

 James   12

 Gestalt Psychology   13

 Watson's Behaviorism   14

 Freudian Psychology   16

 The Humanistic Approach   17

 The Cognitive Revolution   17

 New Developments in Physiology   18

 Contemporary Psychology   19

Integrating the Field of Psychology   21

 Levels of Analysis   22

 Measurement & Methodology   24

 Connections   25

 Interdisciplinary Dimensions   25

 Follow-Through/Diversity   26

Reprise: The Challenge of Psychology   26

Follow-Through/Diversity: Diversity in the History of
 Psychology   28

Chapter 2

Understanding Psychological Research   32

Asking Questions of Nature: The Logic of Scientific Research   34

 Observation   35

 Experimentation   37

 Theory Building   38

Posing Questions About Behavior: Methods of Psychological
 Research   40

 Observational Methods   41

 Experimental Studies   43

 Causation and Correlation in Psychological Experiments   50

 Bias in Psychological Research   54

Drawing Conclusions from Psychological Research   57

Descriptive Statistics   58
Inferential Statistics   60
Ethical Issues in Psychological Research   62
Research on Human Subjects   62
Research on Animal Subjects   64
Reprise: Science as a Refinement of Everyday Thinking   66
Follow-Through/Diversity: The Lens of Culture and the Psychological
Study of Women and African Americans   68

Chapter 3
The Biology of Behavior   72

The Neuron: Building Block of the Nervous System   76
The Structure of the Neuron   77
The Action Potential   77
The Synapse   80
The Body's Communication Networks: The Nervous and
Endocrine Systems   87
The Central Nervous System   87
The Peripheral Nervous System   90
The Endocrine System   91
The Brain: Localized Functions Working Together   94
Localization of Function in the Brain   94
Organization on the Left and Right   103
Beyond Localization of Function   109
The Dynamic Nervous System: Changing with Development
and Experience   110
The Changing Brain: Transformation Through Maturation   110
The Changing Brain: Transformation Through Experience   111
Heredity and Behavior   115
Evolution and Behavior   116
Interdisciplinary Dimension: Evolution
Natural Selection and Sociobiology   117
Reprise: Levels of Analysis and Behavior   119
Follow-Through/Diversity: Sex Hormones, Brain Structure, and
Behavior   120

Chapter 4
The Senses and Perception   124

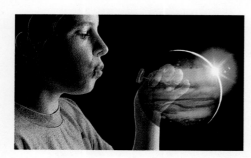

Two Questions About Perception   127
How Is Information in the Environment Represented in
the Nervous System?   127
How Do We Use Information from the Environment to
Create Perceptions?   129
Vision: Seeing Forms and Colors   129
The Stimulus for Vision   130
The Structure of the Visual System   130
The Sensory Code for Vision   131
What Perception Tells Us About the Environment   137
Hearing: Perceiving Pitch   138
The Stimulus for Hearing   138
The Structure of the Auditory System   140
The Sensory Code for Pitch   142
Interdisciplinary Dimension: Medicine
Cochlear Implants   144

The Skin Senses: Touch, Temperature, and Pain   146
    The Stimuli on the Skin   146
    The Structure of the Skin   146
    The Sensory Code for Skin Sensations   146
The Chemical Senses: Taste and Smell   148
    The Stimuli for Taste and Smell   149
    The Structure of the Taste System   149
    The Sensory Code for Taste   150
    The Structure of the Olfactory System   150
    The Sensory Code for Smell   151
How Do We Differentiate Objects in the Environment?   152
How Do We Perceive Depth?   156
    Oculomotor Cues   156
    Pictorial Cues   157
    The Movement-Produced Cue   158
    The Binocular Cue   158
How Do We Perceive the Sizes and Shapes of Objects?   160
    Size Constancy   160
    Shape Constancy   161
Why Do We Sometimes Misperceive?   162
    The Ames Room   163
    The Ponzo Illusion   163
    The Moon Illusion   164
How Do Expectations Influence Perception?   164
Reprise: The Creativity of the Brain and the Commonality
   of the Senses   167
Follow-Through/Diversity: Perception and Culture   168

Chapter 5
Consciousness and Behavior   172

Probing Inner States: The Scientific Study of Consciousness   175
Daily Variations in Consciousness: Circadian Rhythms   176
    Biological Clocks   177
    The Nucleus That Sets the Clock   178
    Jet Lag   180
    Work Shifts   181
Sleep: The Active Brain at Night   181
    The Stages of Sleep   182
    The Biological Control of Sleep   185
    Why Do We Sleep?   185
    Sleep Disorders   189
Dreams: Images During Sleep   192
    Common Questions About Dreams and Dreaming   192
    Theories of Dreaming   194
Hypnosis: The Power of Suggestion   197
    The Scientific Study of Hypnosis   198
    What Happens to a Person Who Is Hypnotized?   198
    Hypnotism as Paradox   200
    Theories of Hypnosis   201
Interdisciplinary Dimension: Criminal Justice
    Hypnotism and the Law   203
Drugs: Changing Consciousness at the Synapse   205
    What Kinds of Drugs Are There?   205
    Why Do People Use Drugs?   208
    Why Do People Sometimes Increase the Amount
      of Drugs They Use?   208

What Is the Physiological Basis of Drug Action?   209
What Is the Relationship Between Drug Dosage and
    Drug Effects?   209
Are All Drug Effects Caused by Their Chemical Action
    on Neurons?   211
How Describing Our Experience Can Shape Our Conception
    of Reality   212
Reprise: Consciousness and Levels of Analysis   214
Follow-Through/Diversity: Dreams and Culture   216

Chapter 6
Basic Learning Processes   220

Learning and Behavior   222
Habituation   224
Principles of Classical Conditioning   224
    Ivan Pavlov   226
    John B. Watson   228
    Elements of Classical Conditioning   230
    Modern Approaches to Understanding Classical
        Conditioning   234
    Applications of Classical Conditioning   239
Interdisciplinary Dimension: Public Health
        Conditioning, Drug Tolerance, and Cigarette Smoking   240
Principles of Operant Conditioning   242
    Edward Thorndike   243
    B. F. Skinner   244
    Elements of Operant Conditioning   246
    Refinements to the Traditional Account of Operant
        Conditioning   256
    Applications of Operant Conditioning   257
Interactions Between Classical and Operant Conditioning   260
Cognitive Processes in Simple Learning   263
    Edward Tolman   263
    Wolfgang Köhler   264
    Albert Bandura   265
Reprise: The Fruits of Behaviorism   266
Follow-Through/Diversity: Learning Gender Roles   268

Chapter 7
Memory   272

On the Trail of Memory: The Development of Memory Research   275
    Hermann Ebbinghaus   275
    William James   276
    The Rise of Cognitive Psychology   277
How Memory Works: An Information-Processing Model   278
    The Multistore Memory System   278
    Information Processing in Memory   278
Sensory Memory: The Sparkler's Trail   279
Short-Term Memory: Information in Action   280
    Working Memory   281
    Encoding   282
    Storage   283
    Retrieval   285
    Forgetting in STM   286
    Transferring Information from STM to LTM   288

Long-Term Memory: Information in Storage 289
    Encoding 290
    Storage 291
    Retrieval 295
    Forgetting in LTM 300
How the Brain Remembers: The Physiology of Memory 303
    Memory as a Change in Neural Processing 303
    Memory as Localized in Specific Brain Structures 304
    Memory as Requiring Time to Become Established
        in the Brain 305
Real-World Memory 306
    Long-Lived Memories 306
    Remembering Meaningful Stimuli 308
Interdisciplinary Dimension: Criminal Justice
    Memory in the Courtroom 311
Memory and Studying 312
Reprise: Memory and Cognitive Psychology 315
Follow-Through/Diversity: Gender Schemas and Memory 316

Chapter 8
Thought and Language  320

Categorization: A Basic Mechanism of Thinking 323
    The Process of Categorization 323
Reasoning: Thinking Logically—and Illogically 326
    Deductive Reasoning 327
    Inductive Reasoning 329
Making Decisions: Choosing Among Alternatives 330
    Elimination by Aspects 331
    Heuristics 331
    Framing Effects 334
Solving Problems: Overcoming Obstacles to Reach a Goal 335
    Obstacles to Problem Solving 336
    How Problem Solving Is Affected by the Way the
        Problem Is Stated 340
    Cognitive Operations During Problem Solving 342
    Problem Solving by Experts and Novices 345
Interdisciplinary Dimension: Artificial Intelligence
    Soar: An Intelligent Computer Program 347
Using and Understanding Language 350
    Problem Solving in Conversations 350
    Thought and Language 354
Reprise: Levels of Analysis in the Study of Learning and
    Cognition 357
Follow-Through/Diversity: Thinking in Traditional Cultures 358

Chapter 9
Physical, Perceptual, and Cognitive Development 362

Basic Issues in Developmental Psychology 365
    Stability Versus Instability 365
    Continuity Versus Discontinuity 368
    Nature Versus Nurture 369
Interdisciplinary Dimension: Anthropology
    Socialization and Children's Behavior: The Six-Cultures Study 372
Physical and Perceptual Development 373
    Prenatal Development 374

Infancy and Toddlerhood   375
Childhood   378
Adolescence   378
Adulthood   380
Cognitive Development   382
Piaget's Theory of Cognitive Development   382
Evaluating Piaget   389
The Information-Processing Approach   391
Cognitive Development in Adulthood   393
Reprise: What You Look at Determines What You See   396
Follow-Through/Diversity: Cross-Cultural Perspectives on Piaget   398

Chapter 10
Language and Social Development   402

The Development of Language   404
The Conditions Necessary for Language   404
The Course of Language Development   405
Theories of Language Acquisition   407
Social Development: Infancy, Childhood, and Adolescence   408
Erikson's Psychosocial Theory of Development   409
Attachment in Infancy and Childhood   409
Development of the Self in Childhood   414
The Self in Adolescence   418
Interdisciplinary Dimension: Anthropology
Identity Formation in Inner-City Gangs   420
The Development of Moral Reasoning   423
Social Development: Adulthood   427
Adult Behavior and Early Experience   427
Life Events in Adulthood   429
Reprise: Linkages Among Physical, Cognitive, and Social Abilities   434
Follow-Through/Diversity: Culture, Economic Stress, and Child
Development   436

Chapter 11
Motivation   440

General Theories of Motivation   444
The Instinct Approach   444
The Ethological Approach   445
The Biological Approach   445
Sigmund Freud's Approach   446
The Humanistic Approach   447
The Hunger Motive   448
The Biology of Hunger   449
Psychological Influences on Hunger Motivation   452
Hunger and Weight Problems   454
Sexual Motivation   460
Biological Factors in Sexual Motivation   461
Interdisciplinary Dimension: History
Sexuality and Society in Western Culture   463
Psychological Factors in Sexual Motivation   464
Sexual Orientation   468
Achievement Motivation   471
Early Research on Achievement Motivation   471
Expectancy-Value Theory   473

The Cognitive Approach to Achievement Motivation   474
Reprise: Multiple Causes of Behavior   476
Follow-Through/Diversity: Gender and Achievement Motivation   478

Chapter 12
Emotion   482

The Nature of Emotions   484
    The Components of Emotional Experience   485
    Classifying Emotions   485
The Behavioral Effects of Emotion   487
    Emotion and Memory   487
    Emotion and Judgment   488
    Emotion and Helping Behavior   488
    Emotion and Person Perception   489
    Emotion and Reacting to Threatening Information   489
The Expression of Emotion   490
    Body Language   491
    Facial Expressions   491
    Display Rules and Emotional Expression   492
Interdisciplinary Dimension: Medicine
    Managing Emotions in Medical School   493
Behavioral Explanations of Emotion   495
    Conditioned Emotional Responses   495
    Observational Learning   495
Physiological Explanations of Emotion   496
    The Evolutionary Approach to Emotion   496
    Bodily Changes and Emotion   497
    Brain Activity and Emotion   502
Cognitive Explanations of Emotion   505
    Schachter and Singer   505
    Richard Lazarus   507
Reprise: The Ebb and Flow of Scientific Understanding   508
Follow-Through/Diversity: Emotion and Culture   510

Chapter 13
Stress and Health   514

Health Psychology   517
    Health Psychology and AIDS   517
    Behavior and Health   519
What Is Stress?   520
Links Between Stress and Health   522
    Life Stress and Health   523
    How Stress Affects Health   527
Interdisciplinary Dimension: Immunology
    Conditioning the Immune Response   530
Social Support and Health   533
Personality and Health   536
Applying Health Psychology: Coping with Stress   539
    Attacking the Problem   540
    Rethinking the Problem   542
    Lessening the Effects of the Problem   542
Reprise: Biology and Behavior, a Two-Way Street   543
Follow-Through/Diversity: Hypertension Among African
    Americans   546

Chapter 14
Intelligence   550

The Measurement of Intelligence: Quantifying the Mind   553
    Early Intelligence Tests   553
    Modern Intelligence Tests   555
The Range of Intelligence: Giftedness and Mental Retardation   557
    Giftedness   558
    Mental Retardation   559
Interdisciplinary Dimension: Education
    Mainstreaming the Mentally Retarded   562
The Structure of Intelligence: Maps of the Mind   564
The Mechanisms of Intelligence: Looking at Mental Processes   567
    Processing Speed and Adult Intelligence   567
    Measuring Infant Intelligence   568
    Information Processing During Problem Solving   569
The Sources of Intelligence: The Roles of Heredity and the
    Environment   571
    The Role of Heredity   572
    The Role of the Environment   574
Intelligence and Society: The Uses and Abuses of Intelligence Tests   575
    Test Reliability and Validity   576
    Intelligence as a Cultural Construct   577
    The Uses of Intelligence Tests   578
Real-World Intelligence   579
Reprise: Intelligence—A Socially Relevant Construct   582
Follow-Through/Diversity: Measuring Intelligence in
    Minority Groups   584

Chapter 15
Personality   588

The Psychodynamic Approach   592
    Freud's Psychosexual Theory of Development   593
    The Id, Ego, and Superego, and People's Responses
        to Anxiety   595
    Evaluating Freud's Approach   597
    Other Psychodynamic Theorists   599
The Humanistic Approach   602
    Self-Actualization and Positive Regard   602
    Evaluating Rogers's Approach   604
The Behaviorist Approach   605
The Trait Approach   606
    Gordon Allport   606
    Raymond Cattell   607
    Hans Eysenck   608
    The Five-Factor Model   609
    The Origin of Traits   609
    The Trait-Situation Controversy   611
    Interactionism   612
Interdisciplinary Dimension: History
    Psychobiography   613
The Cognitive Approach   616
    Personal Constructs   616
    Locus of Control   616
    Perceived Self-Efficacy   617
    Self Schemas   618
    Possible Selves   619
Personality Assessment   620

Objective Personality Tests   620
Projective Personality Tests   622
Reprise: Theories and Multiple Theoretical Approaches   624
Follow-Through/Diversity: Freud and Women   626

Chapter 16
Psychological Disorders   630

What Are Psychological Disorders?   634
Deviance   634
Maladaptiveness   635
Distress   636
Classifying Psychological Disorders   636
The *Diagnostic and Statistical Manual of Mental Disorders*   637
Levels of Analysis and the Search for Etiology   639
Behavioral   639
Biological   639
Cognitive   640
Contextual   640
Anxiety Disorders   641
Types of Anxiety Disorder   641
The Search for Etiology   643
Dissociative Disorders   648
Types of Dissociative Disorder   648
The Search for Etiology   649
Interdisciplinary Dimension: Criminal Justice
The Expert Witness and Abnormal Behavior   650
Somatoform Disorders   652
Types of Somatoform Disorder   652
The Search for Etiology   653
Mood Disorders   654
Types of Mood Disorder   654
The Search for Etiology   655
Schizophrenia   662
Characteristics of Schizophrenia   662
Types of Schizophrenia   664
The Search for Etiology   665
Personality Disorders   669
Types of Personality Disorder   669
Reprise: Battling Misconceptions   671
Follow-Through/Diversity: Gender Differences in the
Prevalence of Psychological Disorders   672

Chapter 17
Therapy   676

How Therapy Evolved   679
Therapy as Expelling Evil Spirits   679
Therapy as Treating Illness   680
The Birth of Psychotherapy   680
Therapy Today   681
Psychodynamic Therapies   684
Freudian Psychoanalysis   684
Contemporary Psychodynamic Therapies   686
Interdisciplinary Dimension: Art
Art Therapy with Children   686
Client-Centered Therapies   687
Cognitive Therapies   689
Rational-Emotive Therapy   689

Beck's Cognitive Therapy   690
Behavior Therapies   692
        Therapies Based on Classical Conditioning   692
        Therapies Based on Operant Conditioning   694
Group Therapy   695
Biomedical Therapies   696
        Drug Therapies   697
        Electroconvulsive Therapy   700
Issues in Therapy   701
        The Trend Toward Eclecticism   701
        How Effective Is Psychotherapy?   702
        The Issue of Institutionalization   704
Reprise: Levels of Analysis and the Treatment of Psychological
        Disorders   706
Follow-Through/Diversity: Cultural Issues in Therapy   708

Chapter 18
Social Cognition and Attitudes   712

What Is Social Cognition?   715
Person Perception: Forming Impressions of Others   716
        Picking Up Cues   717
        Paying Attention to Appearance   718
        Schemas   719
        The In-Group/Out-Group Dynamic   721
Attribution: Cognitions About Causes   721
        Why Do We Make Attributions?   722
        Types of Attributions   723
        Kelley's Model of Attribution   723
        Attributional Errors and Biases   726
The Self: Knowing and Accepting Ourselves   728
        Representing the Self   729
        Self-Verification and Self-Handicapping   732
Attitudes: Evaluating Objects, Events, and People   733
        What Are Attitudes?   733
        When Do Attitudes Predict Behavior?   735
        How Are Attitudes Acquired?   736
        How and When Do Attitudes Change?   738
Interdisciplinary Dimension: Marketing
        The Social Psychology of Advertising   741
Reprise: Processing Information About Ourselves and Others   747
Follow-Through/Diversity: Prejudice and Racism   748

Chapter 19
Interpersonal Relations   752

Attraction: Liking and Loving Others   755
        Sources of Attraction   756
        From Liking to Loving   759
Prosocial Behavior: Helping Others   763
        When Do People Help in an Emergency?   763
        Why Do People Help Others?   764
Aggression: Hurting Others   765
        Biological Level   766
        Behavioral Level   767
        Contextual Level   768
        Cognitive Level   769
        Combining Context, Behavior, and Cognition   769

Conformity: Keeping in Step with Others   772
    Asch's Conformity Experiment   772
    When Do People Conform?   773
Interdisciplinary Dimension: Sociology
    Conformity, Deviance, and Social Bonds   776
Compliance and Obedience: Bowing to Pressure from Others   778
    Compliance   778
    Obedience   780
Groups: Behaving in Conjunction with Others   782
    Working in Groups   782
    Making Decisions in Groups   784
    Deindividuation   785
Reprise: Social Psychology and Social Change   786
Follow-Through/Diversity: Communication Between Women and Men
    About Sex   788

Glossary   G-1
References   R-1
Name Index   I-1
Subject Index   I-9

PREFACE

Goals of This Text

The mission foremost in the minds of many teachers of introductory psychology is to expose students to the theories and research that form the scientific background of psychology and to present this material in a way that students will find applicable to their own lives. However, in the process of providing this overview of psychology, it rapidly becomes apparent that the sheer multiplicity of studies, research areas, and approaches works against any coherent sense of psychology as a whole. What is needed is a way to integrate the subject matter of psychology that, by highlighting the connections between different research areas, enables students to appreciate the value of specialized studies while perceiving the coherence of psychology as a discipline.

My aim in this book is to accomplish this goal while also giving students an enduring sense of the *process* of psychology—of what scientific thinking about behavior is like—because it is this process that endures when specific findings are supplanted or specific theories outgrown. Thus, after reading this book, students should not only know about the specific content of psychology but also be able to question the basis for assertions, to appreciate the complexity of our attempts to understand behavior objectively, and to integrate information both *within* psychology and *between* psychology and other areas of study.

An additional goal of this book is to show how psychology can be brought to bear on the issue of diversity—the multicultural nature of our society, issues of gender and race, the widening rifts between different groups. These are issues that face us now and that will become increasingly important as we move into the 21st century. Psychology has a lot to say about these issues, and I take diversity seriously in this book by including in every chapter sustained explorations of what psychology, as a science, has to say about it.

How can we accomplish these goals within the context of an introductory psychology course? The first step is to present the facts, theories, and general principles of psychology in an engaging style that communicates clearly. The next step is to create a framework that will help (1) achieve integration, (2) develop an appreciation of the process of scientific thinking about behavior, and (3) cultivate an understanding of diversity. I will now consider in detail how this book works to achieve these goals.

Achieving Integration

The goal of achieving integration poses one of the greatest challenges to teaching introductory psychology. Human behavior is so complex and has so many facets that there is inevitably a tendency for psychology to become fragmented into many easier-to-handle parts. So we typically talk about such topics as development, perception, biology, and social relationships as disparate areas of study. But in breaking the study of behavior into so many parts we make it difficult for students to see two aspects of the bigger picture: (1) Although development, perception, biology, and social relationships may be separate chapter headings in texts, in reality they are aspects of whole people, and (2) underlying the many parts of psychology is a coherent science.

Let's consider integration in more detail by posing some specific problems and then looking at the solutions offered by this text.

Integration **Within** *Subareas of Psychology*

Problem: Each chapter describes many studies of highly specific topics.

Solutions: (1) Studies are selected judiciously rather than encyclopedically, and summaries and transitions within chapters create a coherent story. (2) In most chapters a concept called Levels of Analysis (discussed below) is used to show the logic underlying psychologists' approach to solving problems within an area. (3) A **Reprise** at the end of each chapter reflects on the larger message of the chapter.

Integration **Across** *Subareas of Psychology*

Problem: Psychology is divided into areas of study corresponding roughly to the chapter headings in introductory texts.

Solution: Three features, *Levels of Analysis, Connections,* and *Follow-Through/Diversity,* help students synthesize information and break down the divisions between chapters.

- **Levels of Analysis:** The idea of levels of analysis is used throughout the text to explain how psychologists arrive at a fuller understanding of behavioral phenomena by employing several complementary approaches. Levels of analysis is introduced in Chapter 1, using the following common-sense description, easily understood by students: *Humans behave in ways that we can observe (behavioral level), and they think, remember, imagine, and solve problems (cognitive level). This behavior and thinking involves biological mechanisms (biological level), and all of these activities—behavior, thinking, and biological processes—take place within a physical and social context (contextual level). This context includes such aspects as the physical environment, the availability of social support, economic conditions, and society as a whole.* The underlying philosophy behind the levels of analysis approach is that (1) to fully understand a particular phenomenon we must study it at a number of levels, and (2) the levels interact with one another.

Levels of analysis is discussed at the beginning of each chapter, is reinforced as appropriate within the chapter (often with summary tables), and serves as the point of departure for a number of the chapter Reprises. The chapter on Stress and Health, for example, opens by describing how AIDS research has been approached not only at the biological level but at the behavioral, cognitive, and contextual levels.

- **Connections:** The Connections feature is used to show how the study of various topics cuts across chapter lines. To achieve this, a "connection indicator" like the one shown beside this paragraph appears in the margin to indicate that "the research you are reading about here is related to work described in another chapter." For example, when students read in the learning chapter about how learning principles are used in treating certain forms of psychological disorders, a connection indicator tells them that this material is related to material discussed in Chapter 17, Therapy. As students encounter these connection indicators throughout the book, they will begin to appreciate the interconnections between different lines of research.

17   THERAPY

- **Follow-Through/Diversity** is a standard section at the end of each chapter. In addition to highlighting psychology's contribution to the understanding of diversity, this feature shows how studies in a number of subareas work together to contribute to our understanding of issues relevant to culture, ethnicity, and gender. This feature is described in more detail below.

Integration Between *Psychology and Other Disciplines*

Problem: Psychology is itself a sprawling, multifaceted discipline, and yet it is not the only window on human life and behavior. Just as students have a hard time connecting the subareas of psychology, they also have a hard time seeing across disciplinary lines in their college education.

Solution: The **Interdisciplinary Dimensions** feature highlights linkages between psychology and other disciplines in the natural and social sciences, humanities, and professional studies. A one- to two-page interdisciplinary section is integrated into most chapters. All of the Interdisciplinary Dimensions are highlighted in the table of contents.

Developing an Appreciation of Scientific Thinking in Psychology

Problem: Many students come into the course believing that psychology is "only common sense" and have little appreciation of the logical subtleties of psychological research.

Solution: To help students appreciate the intricacies of achieving accurate, unbiased psychological knowledge, a clear and thorough introduction to the scientific method is presented in Chapter 2. This discussion highlights the logic of scientific thinking by relating examples within psychology to illustrations from other areas of study, such as physics, evolutionary biology, and medicine. The lessons in this chapter are then reinforced by a feature called **Measurement & Methodology** in each of the following chapters. This is a boxed feature that points out specific issues in measurement, experimental design, or methodology where appropriate. There are one to three Measurement & Methodology features in each chapter.

Cultivating an Understanding of Diversity

Problem: Although today's students are more diverse than ever, many do not fully appreciate the nature of the diversity within which they live. In today's society, discussions of human diversity are often both ideological and ill-informed. Students need and deserve something more than a superficial understanding of diversity.

Solution: As the science of behavior, psychology has more than slogans to offer about issues related to diversity. To avoid giving them only token recognition or an oversimplified treatment, this text considers these questions in a sustained and serious manner that does not slight the complexities. In addition to appropriate discussions within the chapters, we focus specifically on psychology's contribution to an understanding of the diversity afforded by culture, ethnicity, and gender with a two–page feature called **Follow-Through/Diversity** at the end of each chapter. For example, in the Follow-Through for the biology chapter we consider gender ("Sex hormones, brain structure, and behavior"); for cognition we consider culture ("Thinking in traditional cultures"); and for stress and health we focus on ethnicity ("Hypertension among African Americans"). Sometimes discussions in one chapter are linked to discussions in another. (For example, "Learning about gender roles" in the learning chapter is closely related to "Gender schemas and memory" in the memory chapter.) Since this feature "follows through" in every chapter, it contributes to our goal of integration by showing that our understanding of the psychological aspects of ethnicity, culture, and gender is the summation of work in many subfields. The Follow-Throughs are highlighted in the table of contents.

Other Pedagogical Aids

Since "pedagogy" means everything we do to teach a subject, the features described above all qualify as pedagogical aids. But I believe that the most powerful pedagogical aid in any book is clear, accessible, and interesting writing. To this end, I have tried to reflect my attitude about psychology in my writing. I see psychology as a story to be told, and any good story should be told in a way that engages the reader. I have, therefore, written this book in a conversational style that poses questions and then answers them, that uses everyday examples to illustrate principles, and that talks directly to the student. In addition, the following study aids are included:

Summary: A concise and structured summary of the chapter's main points, presented under the headings that introduce them in the text, appears at the end of each chapter.

Key Terms: A listing of all boldfaced terms appears at the end of the chapter.

Glossary: Definitions of the key terms appear at the end of the text.

If I have achieved my purpose in this preface, I have made clear my goals for this book and the features that I have used to achieve these goals. But the real test of my success in achieving these goals is how these parts work together. I invite you to decide this for yourself as you read the book.

Acknowledgments

Although the author is the central figure in the drama called "creating an introductory psychology text," many others must play their roles in order for the project to succeed. I am pleased to thank all of those who worked on this book, from its initial conception through the writing, design, production, and marketing processes. Certain of these people stand out in my mind because I was privileged to interact with them on a personal basis. I am therefore particularly pleased to acknowledge them here.

Ken King was my editor at Wadsworth from 1976 until 1992. He shepherded me through three editions of *Sensation and Perception* and was responsible for bringing *Psychology* to Wadsworth (the sister company of Brooks/Cole, which eventually became the publisher of this book). My debt to Ken is enormous because he always believed in my abilities as a psychologist, teacher, and writer and he helped motivate me to translate these abilities into books. I have missed you, Ken.

Barbara Baker, my partner for over 13 years, knows what it is like to be in a relationship with someone who spends a great deal of time in isolation, writing. She has not only been understanding of my book writing efforts, but as my best friend and confidant she has supported me in all areas of my life. Her support helped me persevere through some of the more trying times during the creation of this book.

John Bergez, my developmental editor, worked masterfully with my writing, teaching me a great deal in the process, and also worked long hours on the illustration program. I owe John a tremendous debt for his work on this book. The fact that I had his home phone number and called him many times on weekends and late at night is testament to his dedication to this project. John is a one-in-a-million person who I feel honored to have known.

Pamela Evans and Kirk Bomont are the two people who, next to John, I worked with the most. Pamela was officially my "manuscript editor," but her contribution went far beyond editing the manuscript. She truly cared about this book and was a source of encouragement and strength as she worked with John and me during the grueling revision process. It is relevant to note that I also have her home phone number. Kirk never gave me his home phone number, but we talked so much while he was at the office, I didn't need it. He made the potentially stressful process of turning the manuscript into a book almost relaxing and enjoyable. We talked almost every day during the long production process, and I really appreciated his relaxed, can-do attitude. Thanks, Kirk.

I also thank Marianne Taflinger, my sponsoring editor, for her untiring efforts to keep the many facets of this project on track and for supporting my efforts by obtaining timely reviews and dealing with my concerns about the book. And a special thanks to Marianne's editorial assistant, Virge Perelli-Minetti, whose ever-cheerful voice was such a pleasure to hear and who never hesitated to offer her help. I can see her smile now, as I write this.

I also appreciate Lisa Torri for her art direction, Vernon Boes and Katherine Minerva for their design, the wonderful designers at Seventeenth Street Studios who created some of the original graphic concepts for this book, Larry Molmud for his computer magic on the chapter opening photographs, Faith Stoddard for her effervescent approach to the ancillaries, Laurel Anderson for her creative photo research, and Linda Rill for gathering the permissions. Two people who worked on earlier stages of this project also deserve thanks. Maggie Murray, who did developmental work on some of my early drafts, left her mark on this book and was a pure pleasure to work with, and Jonathan Cobb, who was involved with this book before it reached Wadsworth and Brooks/Cole, invested many hours on an early phase of the book's development.

Finally, I express my sincere appreciation to Craig Barth, vice president, acquisitions at Brooks/Cole, for his clear vision and sensitive guidance, and to Bill Roberts, the president of Brooks/Cole, whose decision to commit substantial resources to this book is what ultimately made it possible for me and all of the others acknowledged here to create this, the finished product.

E. Bruce Goldstein

REVIEWERS

An essential part of writing any textbook is receiving feedback from both teachers and experts in specific areas. I am pleased to thank the people listed below who, in their roles as reviewers, provided invaluable information that helped shape both the form and content of this book.

James Aiken
California Polytechnic State University

Thomas Alley
Clemson University

Virginia Andreoli Mathie
James Madison University

Hal Arkowitz
University of Arizona

Robert Baron
University of Iowa

Richard Block
Montana State University

David Bjorklund
Florida Atlantic University

Michael Botwin
California State University, Fresno

Frederick M. Brown
Pennsylvania State University

Celia Brownell
University of Pittsburgh

James Calhoun
University of Georgia

John Campbell
Franklin and Marshall College

Etzel Cardeña
Trinity College

Alice Carter
Yale University

Robert Castleberry
University of South Carolina

John Cavanaugh
University of Delaware

Stephen L. Chew
Samford University

Steve Clark
University of California, Riverside

Richard Colker
University of the District of Columbia

Kathleen Connor
Concord College

Gene Elliott
Glassboro State College

Robert Emmons
University of California, Davis

Matthew Enos
Harold Washington College

Ralph Erber
DePaul University

Joseph R. Ferrari
Cazenovia College

Frances Friedrich
University of Utah

Perilou Goddard
Northern Kentucky University

James Gonzales
DeKalb College

Marvin Gordon-Lickey
University of Oregon

Jeff Greenberg
University of Arizona

Ranald Hansen
Oakland University

Allan Hobson
Harvard University

Erika Hoff-Ginsberg
University of Wisconsin–Parkside

Mark Hoyert
Indiana University–Northwest

Elaine Hull
SUNY at Buffalo

Philip V. Hull
University of California, Berkeley

Vivian Jenkins
University of Southern Indiana

James J. Johnson
Illinois State University

Nancy King-Hunt
Lewis and Clark College

Randy Larsen
University of Michigan

Richard Lore
Rutgers University

Marta Laupa
University of Nevada at Las Vegas

Joseph Lowman
University of North Carolina

Richard Marrocco
University of Oregon

David Matsumoto
San Francisco State University

CHAPTER

I

What You Do and Don't Know About Psychology

Psychology as Science

The Growth of Scientific Psychology
Psychology's Philosophical Heritage
Prelude to Scientific Psychology
Wundt and Titchener
James
Gestalt Psychology
Watson's Behaviorism
Freudian Psychology
The Humanistic Approach
The Cognitive Revolution
New Developments in Physiology
Contemporary Psychology

Integrating the Field of Psychology
Levels of Analysis: A Way of Thinking About Psychology
Measurement & Methodology: The "How" of Psychology
Connections: Linking Areas of Psychology
Interdisciplinary Dimensions: Linking Psychology to Other Disciplines
Follow-Through/Diversity: Psychological Perspectives on Human
    Diversity

Reprise: The Challenge of Psychology

Follow-Through/Diversity
Diversity in the History of Psychology

The Science of Psychology

The purpose of psychology is to give us a completely different idea of the things we know best.

Paul Valéry (1871–1945)
French poet

When you walk into a classroom for the first time, what do you know about the course material you will be covering? In many cases, the answer is "Very little." If you have never taken calculus, there is little chance that you know how to calculate integrals or differentiate equations. Similarly, if you have never taken biology or chemistry, it is unlikely that you know the chemical reactions that occur during photosynthesis.

However, when you begin an introductory psychology course, you already know something about psychology. The very fact that you function in the world shows that, at least in a practical sense, you already know a lot about what psychologists study—the mind and behavior. As B. F. Skinner (1904–1990), one of psychology's most famous observers of human behavior, once stated, "We all know thousands of things about behavior. Actually there is no subject matter with which we could be better acquainted, for we are always in the presence of at least one behaving organism" (Skinner, 1953, p. 14).

By the time we reach adulthood, most of us have become skilled in such matters as having give-and-take conversations with others, negotiating our way through the physical environment, doing the "correct" thing in social situations ranging from business meetings to dates, and knowing that a distinctive baby's cry means "change me" whereas another means "feed me." We can "read" other people's unspoken reactions and often influence them to see us in a positive light, grant us a favor, or cooperate in some task. And some of us have remarkably shrewd perceptions of people's motivations, wishes, and fears.

If you know so much about psychology already, why should you spend time studying it? Is psychology just what an early and rather cynical definition claims—"the science of what everybody knew beforehand, anyway"? (Sanford, 1906). Let's take a closer look.

What You Do and Don't Know About Psychology

Do we really know as much about psychology as we think we know? The answer depends in part on what we mean by knowledge. At one level, knowing about human psychology means having accurate information about facts concerning behavior. Often we feel confident that we know the answers to psychological questions when in reality our confidence is unwarranted. Consider, for example, the following statements. Are they true or false?

1. A schizophrenic is someone with a split personality.
2. The more highly motivated you are, the better you will do at solving a complex problem.
3. Under hypnosis, people can perform feats of physical strength that they couldn't otherwise.
4. Fortunately for human babies, human mothers have a strong maternal instinct.

When psychologist Eva Vaughn (1977) tested her introductory psychology students' ability to answer these questions and others like them some 20 years ago, she found they were right only about half of the time—the success rate we would expect if they simply guessed. It is doubtful that the results would be much different today. (All four statements are false.)

At the level of factual statements most of us are walking encyclopedias of information and misinformation about behavior. Our "knowledge" comes from a hodgepodge of sources: family and cultural beliefs we have absorbed, claims we have heard other people make (with or without valid evidence), ideas we have picked up from (often sensationalized) news stories, images gleaned from movies and fiction, and our own experience of ourselves and others.

As none of these sources of knowledge is entirely reliable, it should be no surprise that the "common sense" that serves us well in much of everyday life contains many unsupported beliefs and outright inaccuracies. For example, many parents and caretakers of children have subscribed to the adage "Spare the rod and spoil the child," meaning that physical punishment encourages desirable behavior. In fact, however, research suggests that children who are physically punished often become overly aggressive as adults (Eron, 1982, 1987)—hardly the result their punishers had in mind.

Furthermore, many of us are quite happy to tolerate contradictions in what we "know" about behavior. Consider the case of interpersonal attraction. Is it true that "opposites attract"? Or do "birds of a feather flock together"? At different times we may confidently quote both sayings, even though they express contradictory "truths." But research tends to show that the second one is more accurate than the first: successful marriage partners tend to be much more alike than different, and people who are similar tend to be attracted to one another (Buss, 1985).

One reason our beliefs about psychology are often in error is that our own experience is both selective and subject to bias. For example, consider a recent poll in which drivers were asked to rate their own driving habits and those of others (*U.S. News and World Report*, 1989). Fully 92% gave good or excellent marks to *themselves* for "being courteous to other drivers," but only 40% gave good or excellent marks to *other drivers* for being courteous. Again, 86% felt that they "maintained the proper distance," but only 36% felt that other drivers did. On every question, the drivers gave themselves substantially higher ratings than they gave other drivers.

What's wrong with this picture? Simply that it is impossible for both ratings to be correct. If 92% of drivers are courteous (as they claim to be), it cannot be true that only 40% of them are (as rated by others). Apparently we evaluate ourselves differently than we evaluate other people (Dunning, Milojkovic, & Ross, 1989). This is only one of many sources of bias in our "knowledge" about human social behavior—a topic we will return to in Chapters 18 and 19.

So far we have been considering individual items of factual knowledge. But at another level, the test of knowledge is whether we can predict how people will behave in a particular situation. For example, knowing the laws of physics allows scientists to predict in detail how objects in motion—two cars on a collision course, say—will "behave" in a given set of circumstances. The fact that their predictions are borne out by observation and experiment reinforces their belief that the "laws" they have formulated are correct. But what about human behavior? Even if we are astute observers of ourselves and other people, does

Are these people attracted to each other because of qualities that differ ("opposites attract") or qualities they share ("birds of a feather flock together")?

Why is this woman unhappy? Is she annoyed at another driver? Most people rate their own driving skills as being much better than the skills of other drivers.

our everyday knowledge of psychology allow us to generalize accurately about how people will behave in a given situation?

One experiment explored this question in an ingenious way. Richard Nisbett and Timothy Wilson (1977) had subjects read descriptions of situations that occurred in actual psychological research. They asked the subjects to predict how they or others would behave in that situation and then compared their predictions with what actually occurred in the research studies. Try this yourself with the following description.

> You are sitting in a room with six other people waiting to participate in an experiment, when you hear a crash in the next room followed by the screams of a woman calling for help. As far as you can tell she seems to have fallen off of a stepladder and hurt herself badly enough so that she can't walk. What are the chances that you, or any of the other people in the room, will help the woman?

When presented with this description, most people claim that the chances are close to 100% that they, or someone else in the room, would offer to help the woman. But when this situation was created in an actual experiment, the woman received help only 40% of the time.

The original experiment, by Bibb Latané and John M. Darley (1970), is one of psychology's classics, in part because its result violates our expectations. It shows that objective investigation may reveal that what we *think* we know about human behavior—even our own—isn't always reliable. This finding means that we need a more objective and reliable way of knowing about behavior than by relying on our individual experiences and "common sense." That way of knowing is what scientific psychology seeks to provide.

But psychology aims to do more than establish facts and make it possible to generalize accurately about behavior. It seeks to *explain* human behavior by discovering the underlying influences that shape the way we think, feel, and act. Thus, although you know something about psychology before taking a psychology course, the study of psychology can give you new and more accurate information, suggest patterns you had not seen before, and, most important, give you new insight into what you thought you knew. Such knowledge has profound practical implications, ranging from ways to use rewards and punishments for controlling a person's behavior to how to treat mental illness. But for many people the study of psychology is also intrinsically rewarding, for the intellectual and emotional satisfaction of achieving a better understanding of human behavior.

Psychology's claim to establishing this understanding rests on its scientific nature. Exactly what this means will emerge as you read this book, because the purpose of this text is to introduce you not only to *what* psychologists have discovered but also to *how* they have arrived at their conclusions and theories. After all, you should not be asked to take on faith what you read in a psychology text, or any other book. In fact, basing your belief on someone's authority is the antithesis of the scientific approach. Let's pursue this point a little further by taking a look at what it means to say that psychology is a science.

Psychology as Science

What do you associate with the word *science*? Perhaps among the images that come to mind are laboratories filled with beakers and test tubes, white-coated researchers using elaborate instruments to make precise measurements, and books full of complex mathematical equations. Or perhaps the word *science* makes you think of a vast storehouse of scientific "facts" like those you learned in school: the speed of light is about 186,000 miles per second, water is two parts hydrogen and one part oxygen, living things are made up of structures called cells, and $e = mc^2$.

Certainly these things are all associated with science, but they do not get to the heart of what science is all about. Most scientists are not interested in simply cataloging more and more facts. As the great French mathematician Jules-Henri Poincaré remarked, "Science is built up with facts, as a house is with stones. But a collection of facts is no more a science than a heap of stones is a house" (1913).

Poincaré's point was that scientists ultimately seek to go beyond the mere accumulation of facts, and that their real goal is to understand the laws that govern the way the world works. To achieve this goal, science has developed a *way of thinking* that has proved to be the most effective means humans have invented for describing and explaining the natural world. One way to convey this way of thinking is to describe the methods science uses to study the natural world. Chapter 2 will cover this aspect of science, and of psychology in particular. But an even more fundamental way to describe the scientific way of thinking is to consider the attitudes that underlie the methods of science. If we take a scientific approach to a subject—whether it be the motions of the planets or the mysteries of human attraction—we are guided by a set of attitudes such as the following four suggested by B. F. Skinner (1953).

Galileo Galilei, whose observations of Jupiter's moons challenged the idea that the earth was at the center of the universe

1. *Cultivating intellectual honesty*: being willing to accept facts, even when they contradict our beliefs or wishes. A good example is the famous case of Galileo Galilei (1564–1642). By making observations through his homemade telescope, Galileo discovered four of Jupiter's moons, among other features of the night sky. These discoveries were profound, because they called into question the accepted idea that the earth is unique and situated at the center of the universe, with everything in the heavens revolving around it. An entire philosophy and theology were bound up in that conception of the universe, which was backed by the powerful authority of the Catholic church. In fact, so threatening were Galileo's discoveries that many learned men of his day simply refused to look through his instrument, and others chose to disbelieve what they saw with their own eyes. One scholar went so far as to say that he had tested Galileo's telescope "in a thousand ways" on both terrestrial and heavenly objects, and that it worked "wonderfully" for objects on earth, but "deceived" when turned to the sky! (Boorstin, 1983, pp. 315–316). Whereas Galileo's intellectual honesty led him to abide by his observations, others sacrificed evidence to their cherished—but incorrect—belief.

2. *Avoiding premature conclusions*: being willing to remain without an answer until a satisfactory one can be found. You will see in this book that, though our knowledge of psychology is vast, a tremendous number of questions remain to be answered. What brain mechanism controls eating behavior? Why is about 5% of the population homosexual? What causes schizophrenia? These questions, among others, psychology cannot yet fully answer. Often psychologists possess facts that tempt them to propose answers, but when the facts are incomplete they must resist the urge to proclaim the problem solved.

3. *Searching for orderly, lawful relationships among events*: going beyond simply collecting facts to determining rules or scientific "laws" that explain how one event causes another.

4. *Asking questions that are potentially answerable using currently available measuring techniques*: understanding that some questions can potentially be answered by present-day science and others can't. For example, a present-day astronomer would not ask "Does heaven exist?" or "What is the purpose of the universe?" and expect to find the answer through astronomy. (Of course, like anyone else, astronomers might have *beliefs* about those questions, based on sources other than their profession.) Instead, an astronomer asks "How far away is the farthest observable star?" and "Is there enough mass in the universe to keep it from expanding forever?" Similarly, a psychologist would not ask "What

is the nature of the soul?" but rather "How does the brain process input from the senses?" (Stanovich, 1989).

Accepting these four attitudes as the starting point for the study of behavior is the first step toward achieving a scientific psychology. In addition, as scientists, psychologists are committed to using the methods and techniques of scientific empiricism. **Empiricism** refers to making observations. Testing ideas by observing the motions of the plants, the life cycles of animals, or the helping behaviors of humans are all examples of empiricism. **Scientific empiricism** involves making observations that meet the following criteria.

1. They are *objective.* That is, they are not influenced by any preconceived ideas about how the results "should" turn out.
2. They are *systematic.* Observations or experiments should be carried out in an orderly way; for example, when observing behavior, experimenters should know exactly what behaviors they are looking for and how to record them accurately.
3. They are *replicable.* That is, the observations can be repeated by others, with the same results. Even if an observation is done objectively and systematically, the results are suspect if they cannot be obtained by others.

Do these criteria seem obvious to you? If so, it is probably because you have grown up in a culture that has been heavily influenced by the methods of Western science. We have learned how researchers and theoreticians working in fields such as astronomy, physics, and medicine have explained such previously mysterious phenomena as lunar eclipses, magnetism, and the transmission of disease—phenomena that earlier generations had explained in terms of gods, spirits, and even black magic. But even as Western science was explaining the previously unexplicable, it was not clear that the scientific way of thinking could be applied to human experience as well. Were there discoverable regularities in everything, from the way people think to the occurrence of dreams? What "telescope" could be turned on the human mind?

How scientific psychology was born a little over a century ago and then evolved into a dynamic science capable of dealing with many previously unanswered questions about human experience is the subject of the next section.

The Growth of Scientific Psychology

Most of us are so accustomed to using the scientific method to investigate the world that we may find it hard to appreciate that there is nothing obvious about using it to explore psychological questions. Yet for many centuries the study of the mind and behavior was largely the work of philosophers. Although this route to understanding behavior ultimately led to a dead end, the philosophers' legacy included one essential ingredient for a science of psychology: the belief that logic and reason can be applied no less to the mysteries of the mind than to other aspects of the natural world.

Psychology's Philosophical Heritage: An Emphasis on Logic and Reasoning

The origins of Western science and philosophy are often traced to the ancient Greeks. While other cultures were still dominated by traditional, mythological, and magical thinking, the Greeks asked questions about the world that no one had thought to ask before—furthermore, they believed in the power of human reason to answer them.

It was in this spirit that philosophers like Plato and Aristotle began to raise questions about psychology. While others sought explanations of human experience and behavior in the whims of gods, Plato (428–347 B.C.) asked what the connection was between behavior and physiology. He speculated that different abilities were located in different parts of the body: reason in the head, courage in the chest, and appetite in the abdomen. From this line of reasoning, he proposed that differences in people's characteristics could be determined by measuring the size of their body parts. Aristotle (384–322 B.C.), Plato's most illustrious student, suggested that anger was caused by the boiling of blood around the heart, and that the heart (not the brain) was the seat of thought.

Neither philosopher was correct, but both were doing something very important: they were establishing the idea that behavior and the mind were as accessible to reasoned investigation as other natural phenomena. Centuries later—after a long period in which religious dogma and belief in the teachings of authority eclipsed such speculations—philosophers in Europe took up this idea and helped prepare the way for a science of psychology.

For example, the great French philosopher René Descartes (1596–1650) believed that the light of reason could penetrate the inner workings of the mind. He proposed that the human ability to comprehend such truths as geometrical proofs or the existence of God depended on having certain thoughts implanted in our minds before birth. He reasoned as follows: I am imperfect, yet I can think perfect ideas. Because something perfect cannot come from something imperfect, these ideas must have been placed in my mind by God.

The difficulty with the philosophers' attempts to answer psychological questions through logic and reasoning was that there was no way to resolve a dispute between equally plausible positions. For instance, the English philosopher John Locke (1632–1704) disagreed with Descartes, believing instead that our thoughts originated in our sensory experience of the world. A newborn's mind, he claimed, is as blank "as white paper, void of any characters, without any ideas" (Locke, 1706/1974, p. 89). If the mind contained innate ideas, he argued, then all humans inevitably would have them—but not everyone does. Thus, all ideas come from experience, and the task is to discover how we derive abstract and other ideas from sensory impressions.

How could such disagreements be resolved? What capacities *does* a newborn infant possess? Does thinking take place in the head, as Plato maintained,

Raphael's *The School of Athens* (1510–1511) depicts Plato and Aristotle at the center of a group of famous Greek philosophers.

What capacities do newborns possess? Ancient philosophers speculated using logic and reasoning; modern psychologists collect relevant data using experimental procedures, as in this experiment in which an infant's vision is being tested.

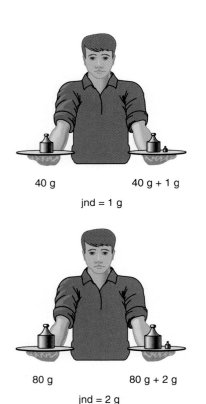

40 g   40 g + 1 g

jnd = 1 g

80 g   80 g + 2 g

jnd = 2 g

FIGURE 1.1

The just noticeable difference (jnd). A person can detect the difference between a 40-gram weight and a 41-gram comparison weight but cannot detect a smaller difference, so the jnd is 1 gram. With an 80-gram weight, the comparison weight must be 82 grams before a person can detect a difference, so the jnd is 2 grams. Note that for both the 40- and 80-gram weights, the ratio of jnd to weight is the same.

or in the heart, as Aristotle believed? The philosophers at least tried to answer such questions through logic and reason rather than by consulting a traditional authority, but progress in achieving more definitive answers would come only when the power of reasoning was combined with the kind of systematic observation that scientists in other fields were using to understand the movements of planets, the trajectories of cannonballs, the circulation of the blood, and other aspects of the natural world.

Before this empirical approach could be applied to psychological questions, however, the questions would have to be reformulated so that they could be answered by scientific techniques of observation and experiment—and techniques would have to be invented that could probe psychological phenomena. The impetus for this development came not from the philosophers but from physiologists, who were devising new ways of exploring age-old questions about the connections between physiology and behavior.

Prelude to Scientific Psychology: Nineteenth-Century Physiology and Psychophysics

In the early 1800s, physiologists were beginning to answer many of the questions regarding the connection between physiology and behavior that philosophers had been debating for centuries, replacing the philosophers' speculations with systematic observations. They studied the functioning of animals' brains by surgically removing parts of the brain and observing the resultant behavior. They studied the functioning of the human brain by observing the behavior of people with damage to various areas of the brain, and they studied the mechanisms of perception by systematically observing the relationship between stimuli in the environment and people's perceptual reports.

One of the pioneers in this quest to understand the connection between physiology and behavior was Hermann von Helmholtz (1821–1894), considered the foremost physiologist of his era. He not only carried out basic research on the functioning of the nervous system but also formulated theories to explain how we perceive the colors of lights and the pitches of tones. Helmholtz's theories of sensory functioning are important because they proposed a link between physiology and experience.

As Helmholtz and others were pursuing their physiological investigations, Ernst Weber (1795–1878), an anatomist, was carrying out one of the first experiments in a new area called **psychophysics**—the study of quantitative relationships between physical stimuli and the psychological responses to them. In one experiment, Weber had subjects lift a small "standard" weight and then a slightly heavier "comparison" weight and judge which was heavier. When the difference between the standard and comparison weights was small, subjects found it difficult to tell the two apart, but larger differences were easily detected. That much is not surprising, but Weber went further. He was able to determine the *just noticeable difference (jnd)*, the smallest difference between two stimuli that a subject can detect. For example, Weber found that the jnd for a 40-gram weight was 1 gram (see Figure 1.1). That is, a subject could tell the difference between 40 and a 41 grams, but smaller differences went undetected. Weber also found that the jnd for an 80-gram weight was 2 grams. In these two examples, the size of the jnd divided by the standard weight is constant (1/40 = 2/80), and Weber found this constant ratio to hold over a wide range of stimulus intensities.

Weber's experiments are important because they showed that the relationship between a physical stimulus and a psychological experience could be measured precisely—and that this relationship obeyed mathematical laws. Achieving such measurements was a major accomplishment and refuted the claims of those, such as philosopher Immanuel Kant (1724–1804), who said it was impossible to measure the products of the mind with any precision. Moreover, together with Helmholtz's physiological investigations of the senses, the experiments of Weber and other early psychophysical researchers set the stage for Wilhelm Wundt's founding of the first laboratory of experimental psychology.

Wundt and Titchener: The First Psychology Laboratory and the Rise of Structuralism

Wilhelm Wundt (1832–1920) had studied with world-renowned physiologists and in 1858 had been Hermann von Helmholtz's assistant. He published a number of books before publishing *Principles of Physiological Psychology* in 1874. In those days physiological was synonymous with experimental, so Wundt's book was one of the first about the experimental approach to psychology. In his preface to the book Wundt stated, "The book which I here present to the public is an attempt to mark out a new domain of science." Wundt was making no bones about it: he was founding the *science* of psychology!

After publication of his book, Wundt became a professor at Leipzig where, in a single room, he set out the brass measuring instruments that were to serve as equipment for the first laboratory dedicated to experimental psychology. Using these instruments, Wundt and his many graduate students began a program of psychological research based on the idea of presenting external stimulation to subjects and observing the resulting mental processes. Wundt accomplished this in two ways. First, he carried out psychophysical experiments like those of Weber. He measured such capacities as the eye's ability to perceive brief flashes, the skin's ability to perceive different qualities (hot, cold, touch, and pain), and people's ability to react rapidly to tones and lights. Second, Wundt used a technique called **introspection,** relying on a person's description of the sensations and feelings experienced in response to specific stimuli. By identifying as many of those experiences as possible, Wundt hoped to discover the "elements" of consciousness, much as physicists were endeavoring to discover the basic elements of matter.

A memorable example of an introspective experiment that illustrates extreme dedication is one in which subjects took ipecac syrup to induce vomiting and reported on the resulting sensations. One subject reported, 15 minutes after taking the ipecac and just before vomiting, "Dizziness. Pressure sensations in stomach—a dull pressure, unpleasant, slightly nauseating, a sort of gnawing sickish character . . ." (Boring, 1915). Other introspective experiments investigated people's responses to more benign stimuli. For example, subjects were asked to listen to a musical chord and determine how many notes it contained, or to report the feelings accompanying emotions such as disappointment or anger.

Wilhelm Wundt (third from left) and a few of his students in his laboratory at Leipzig

Wundt's founding of the first psychology laboratory took dedication and courage, for he was criticized by colleagues who doubted that psychology could be studied experimentally. Some even expressed fear that allowing students to examine their inner experience would drive them to insanity! (Hothersall, 1990).

But Wundt's importance extends beyond his daring to announce the founding of a new science and establishing a laboratory. He trained a large number of graduate students, many of whom established similar psychology laboratories elsewhere. One, Edward Titchener (1867–1927), became head of the psychology department at Cornell in 1892. Titchener was Wundt's champion in the United States and, like his mentor, was interested in determining the elements of consciousness through the method of introspection. Titchener originated the term **structuralism** to describe his introspective approach to the study of the structure of the conscious mind. He saw this approach as a natural extension of the methods of physical science into the realm of psychology. Titchener proposed that just as chemists use the methods of physical science to divide the world into various chemical elements, psychologists should use the method of introspection to divide mental experience into a number of "elementary mental processes" (Titchener, 1910).

In the hands of people like Wundt and Titchener this approach to the study of consciousness helped lead psychology from its associations with philosophy to a new status as an independent scientific discipline subscribing to the same principles that guided research in the physical sciences. By the turn of the 20th century, many psychology laboratories were being founded in the United States, and the voluminous writings of Wundt and Titchener had made structuralism highly influential. Not everyone agreed, however, that psychology had found its identity as a science in the methods of structuralism. In the turbulent years ahead new voices arose to question the structuralists' account of consciousness—and even their definition of psychology's subject matter. One of those voices belonged to William James (1842–1910), the first American psychologist, who championed an approach to psychology called *functionalism*.

James: The Functions of Behavior

William James stressed the importance of function over structure in the study of consciousness.

William James received his medical degree from Harvard in 1869 but never practiced medicine. Instead he joined the faculty of the physiology department at Harvard, where, in 1874, he offered the first American psychology course, "The Relations between Physiology and Psychology." James himself later recalled the first lecture of this course as being the first psychology lecture he had ever attended—a reference to the fact that James had no formal training in psychology (Hothersall, 1985). His book *The Principles of Psychology* (1890) quickly became a standard text in the United States and Europe and was even translated into Russian. This book, which owed its popularity as much to James's literate and accessible writing style as to its contents, cemented James's reputation as "Mr. American Psychology."

James's approach to psychology was very different from the structuralism of Wundt and Titchener. Although he shared their interest in consciousness, he believed that the structuralist's goal of dissecting consciousness into its "elements" was misguided. The following excerpt from James's *Principles of Psychology* illustrates both his conception of consciousness and his beautiful writing:

> Consciousness . . . does not appear to itself chopped up in bits . . . A "river" or a "stream" are the metaphors by which it is most naturally described. . . . As the brain changes are continuous, so do all these consciousnesses melt into each other like dissolving views. Properly they are but one protracted consciousness, one unbroken stream (From chapter 9).

The proper way to study consciousness, according to James, was to analyze its characteristics and to study its functions. This concern for function reflects the influence of Charles Darwin's (1859) theory of natural selection, which states that animals that are better adapted to their environment will survive to pass their characteristics on to their offspring. According to James, human consciousness, as a product of this evolutionary mechanism, must have evolved to maximize humans' ability to survive. This emphasis on the functions of consciousness stimulated the founding of **functionalism**—the school of psychology that was concerned with studying the *functions* of consciousness rather than its structure. This position gained a number of adherents, especially a group that flourished at the University of Chicago. Although few psychologists today call themselves functionalists, the idea that the functions of behavior are important is an integral part of modern psychology.

James's lack of support for structuralism was shared by a German psychologist and philosopher, Max Wertheimer (1883–1943), who was one of the founders of an approach that came to be known as Gestalt psychology.

Max Wertheimer, one of the founders of Gestalt psychology

Gestalt Psychology: Another Blow to Structuralism

Wertheimer challenged an idea put forth by the structuralists that perceptions are built up by the addition of numerous elementary sensations. According to this idea, each of the dots that makes up the face in Figure 1.2 results in a sensation, and the sum of those sensations creates a perception—a face, in this case—much as a physical object is made up of countless atoms.

Wertheimer countered this account of perception with the following argument. Consider the situation diagramed in Figure 1.3. A light on the left is flashed on and off, followed by 50 milliseconds of darkness. Then the light on

FIGURE 1.2

According to the structuralists, perceptions are created from numerous elementary sensations, represented here by dots, which "add up" to our perception of a meaningful whole.

FIGURE 1.3
Apparent movement. If one light is flashed, followed by a short interval of darkness, and then another is flashed nearby, the resulting perception is of a single light moving from left to right across the empty space.

Flash on left   50 ms darkness   Flash on right   Resulting perception

the right is flashed on and off. This sequence of flash–darkness–flash causes a phenomenon called *apparent movement*. That is, an observer perceives the light as moving from left to right through the dark space separating the two. How, asked Wertheimer, can individual sensations explain our perception of a light moving through dark, empty space? As there is no stimulation whatsoever in that space, no sensations can create the perception of a moving light—but movement is, nonetheless, perceived. Whereas the structuralists thought that they could break down perception into constituent elements, Wertheimer maintained that, in perception, *the whole is different than the sum of its parts.*

Having rejected the idea that perceptions are constructed from the building blocks of sensations, Wertheimer and his followers called the "whole" of perception a *Gestalt*, and their approach came to be known as **Gestalt psychology.** Their argument that the stimulus must be considered as a whole was embraced by many perception researchers and was one nail in the coffin of structuralism. Meanwhile, in the United States a brash young psychologist, John B. Watson, was mounting a more radical attack—one that called into question structuralism's definition of psychology as the scientific study of the conscious mind.

Watson's Behaviorism: Narrowing the Field to Observable Behavior

Whereas the Gestalt psychologists questioned structuralism's approach to studying perception, John Watson (1878–1958) based his rejection of structuralism largely on the premise that the method of introspection was completely unscientific. Introspection, Watson argued, violated a central principle of empiricism because it relied on reports from one subject that could not be verified by others. For example, your description of what it feels like to be sick or to perceive the color red cannot be confirmed by anyone but yourself. This inability to verify subjects' reports, combined with the fact that people's introspective descriptions varied tremendously, meant that the results of introspective research were not replicable from laboratory to laboratory. Watson felt that no self-respecting scientist had any business studying phenomena that were inherently unobservable and unverifiable.

But if a science of consciousness was a contradiction in terms, was there anything left for psychology to do? Watson's answer was that psychologists should not study consciousness but should focus instead on *behavior* that could be publicly observed—a viewpoint that came to be known as **behaviorism.** He set forth this idea in a paper titled "Psychology as the Behaviorist Sees It," published in 1913.

> Psychology as the Behaviorist sees it is a purely objective, experimental branch of natural science. Its theoretical goal is the prediction and control of behavior. Introspection forms no essential part of its methods, nor is the scientific value of its data dependent upon the readiness with which they lend themselves to interpretation in terms of consciousness. . . . What we need to do is start work upon psychology making behavior, not consciousness, the objective point of our attack (Watson, 1913, pp. 158, 176).

With this manifesto Watson advanced a new conception of psychology, one destined to be hugely influential in shaping the course of the young science. As we have seen, the structuralists thought of psychology as a kind of theoretical

Ivan Pavlov, one of his subjects (the dog), and members of his laboratory

physics of the mind that would analyze consciousness into its irreducible elements. In contrast, Watson's approach was closer in spirit to that of an engineer designing a bridge. The engineer needn't be concerned with the secrets of the atom to make use of the observable properties of materials like iron and steel. In fact, a technology of bridge building was developed before we knew anything at all about the atom's inner structure. In a similar way, Watson maintained that psychologists could construct a useful and valid science—one that would discover the general laws governing human behavior—without ever delving into the unobservable reaches of the mind.

This view of psychology's mission may seem strange at first. After all, isn't whatever happens in the mind the source of the behavior that others observe? Don't you behave the way you do because you *decide* to do so? How, then, can human behavior be "predicted and controlled" if psychology has nothing to say about what goes on in the mind?

For Watson, the answer was provided by a series of experiments that had been conducted early in the century by the Russian physiologist Ivan Pavlov (1849–1936). While investigating the physiology of digestion, Pavlov observed that dogs in his experiment would start salivating as soon as the lab assistant who fed them entered the room. What was triggering salivation before the dogs tasted their food? Curious, Pavlov pursued this question and in the process discovered a simple type of learning that came to be called *classical conditioning*. For example, Pavlov showed that if he repeatedly paired the ringing of a bell with the presentation of food, the dogs would eventually begin to salivate at the sound of the bell alone. The ringing bell had become a *conditioned stimulus* that elicited salivation, a *conditioned response*.

What was so striking about the dogs' new "behavior" of salivating when a bell was rung? To Watson, it suggested a process whereby animals—perhaps including humans—acquired new behaviors. This process, moreover, could be described and predicted in entirely observable terms, without any appeal to what was going on in the organism's mind. The conditioned response was exactly the kind of directly observable psychological phenomenon that Watson was looking for.

Watson proceeded to demonstrate classical conditioning in a human in his famous "Little Albert" experiment (Watson & Rayner, 1920). Little Albert, an 11-month-old child, was repeatedly presented with a white rat (which he had previously liked) followed by a loud noise that caused the child to cry and crawl away. Eventually, Albert began to cry and crawl away whenever the rat was presented, even without the frightening noise. The rat had become a conditioned

John B. Watson, Rosalie Raynor, and Little Albert, the first human to be classically conditioned in a laboratory experiment

B. F. Skinner, one of the most influential proponents of behaviorism

stimulus that elicited the conditioned responses of crying and crawling away. Triumphantly, Watson announced that he had demonstrated how a fear response could be conditioned in humans and confidently predicted that similar processes would eventually be shown to explain all kinds of human behavior.

Watson wrote many articles extolling the virtues of behaviorism, emphasizing that its primary concerns were (1) the objective measurement of behavior and (2) the study of *learning*—that is, how behavior is influenced by experience. In the spirit of the philosopher John Locke, Watson maintained that everything we do is shaped by our experience of our environment—specifically by the rewards ("satisfying events") and punishments ("unsatisfying events") that accompany behavior. Watson's emphasis on the importance of learning from experience was propelled further into the spotlight by the arrival on the scene of B. F. Skinner, who was to become behaviorism's champion beginning in the 1930s.

When Skinner arrived in Cambridge, Massachusetts, to begin his graduate studies at Harvard in 1928, he bought books by Pavlov and Watson and proceeded to label himself a behaviorist (Skinner, 1979). By focusing on a different type of conditioning (operant conditioning, discussed in Chapter 6), Skinner's research extended the range and power of behaviorism and solidified its status as a major force in psychology. Indeed, to many psychologists in the middle decades of this century, behaviorism *was* psychology. For them, psychology's subject matter was observable behavior and its method primarily laboratory research with animals. But once again there were contrary winds blowing from across the Atlantic.

Freudian Psychology: The Unconscious and Behavior

As scientific psychology was being born in Leipzig, Sigmund Freud, a Viennese physician, was formulating ideas that would revolutionize people's thinking about the functioning of the human mind. His work was carried out at the same time the structuralists, the Gestalt psychologists, and the behaviorists were studying psychology in the laboratory. Freud's focus, however, was not on laboratory research but on treating patients with psychological problems. His method of treatment, *psychoanalysis,* was based on the idea that the causes of patients' symptoms could be discovered by getting in touch with painful memories that lay within their *unconscious,* a level of the mind that Freud believed to be beyond the patient's awareness (Erdelyi, 1985). The goal of psychoanalysis was to help the patient retrieve those unconscious memories and to identify the reason they had been pushed into the unconscious.

Freud's idea that behavior is determined largely by unconscious forces was no less revolutionary than Watson's redirection of psychology to the study of observable behavior. Ironically, at the same time that the behaviorists were rejecting the study of *conscious* experience, Freud was maintaining that psychology should study something even less observable, the *unconscious* mind. Needless to say, his views were roundly rejected by behavioral psychologists, though they had a great impact on the treatment of mental disorders and made their way into popular culture through literature, plays, and films. But even though Freud's work was dismissed by many psychologists as speculative and unscientific, the concept of the unconscious was eventually accepted as a valuable concept by research psychologists. (We will describe Freud's ideas about the unconscious in more detail in Chapter 15.)

Another current in psychology, which developed alongside Freud's emphasis on the unconscious and behaviorism's emphasis on observable behavior, was an approach called humanistic psychology, pioneered by Carl Rogers and Abraham Maslow.

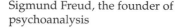

Sigmund Freud, the founder of psychoanalysis

The Humanistic Approach: Psychology's "Third Force"

When Carl Rogers began his career as a therapist he based his therapy on principles established by Freud. However, as he worked with more and more patients Rogers became disenchanted with the Freudian approach. One source of this disenchantment was Freud's pessimistic view of people. Freud saw the unconscious as a battlefield on which good and bad influences clashed, sometimes with beneficial results for the person, often not. This negative view was not to Rogers's liking, and he also couldn't accept behaviorism's mechanistic approach, which saw behavior as being controlled by rewards and punishments. Therefore, along with Abraham Maslow, he proposed a different, more "human" way of thinking about people and their development.

People, according to Rogers and Maslow, are naturally good and naturally strive toward realizing their full potential. This way of thinking about people, which is known as the humanistic approach, was incorporated by Rogers into a new form of therapy called client-centered therapy, in which the therapist provides a warm, caring environment designed to help the patient reach his or her full potential.

Humanistic psychology became recognized as an alternative to the Freudian approach and behaviorism and became known as the third force in psychology. Later in this book we will see that the humanistic approach has contributed to our understanding of personality and has formed the basis for a number of widely used psychological therapies.

Carl Rogers, a pioneer in the humanistic approach, proposed that the goal of therapy should be to help patients reach their full potential.

The Cognitive Revolution: The Reappearance of the Mind

For many years the behaviorists' idea that mental processes are unobservable and therefore beyond the scope of scientific investigation dominated academic psychology, particularly in the United States. Although some psychologists in the 1930s and 1940s did research on such mental processes as thinking and problem solving (Köhler, 1925; Tolman, 1932), most research psychologists thought of psychology as the science of behavior. As such, scientific psychology made a number of advances and spawned many practical applications in education, therapy, and other fields.

Recall that behaviorism's objection to the study of the mind was not that people don't do things like solve problems, make decisions, dream, or invent new ways of doing things—obviously they do. Rather, behaviorists had declared such mental processes "off limits" for psychology because they could not be observed objectively. Moreover, they maintained that the principles they were discovering would, in the long run, be able to explain even things like problem solving and decision making without looking "inside" the mind.

In the 1950s and 1960s, however, a growing number of psychologists began to question these tenets of behaviorism. For one thing, they argued that conditioning processes could not fully explain such activities as problem solving and decision making. For another, they began to question whether it was indeed impossible to study mental processes empirically. Slowly but surely, a revolution began to take shape around the emerging field of cognitive psychology—the study of such mental processes as memory, problem solving, language, and decision making.

The cognitive revolution was fueled in part by the growing popularity of a new invention, the electronic computer. What caught the imagination of researchers was an analogy between a computer's "behavior" and that of a human performing a cognitive task. Computers, they noted, process information—and so does the mind. Propelled by this suggestive metaphor of the mind as information processor, the cognitive revolution was off and running (Hilgard, 1987).

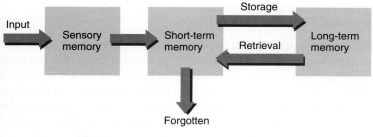

FIGURE 1.4

The memory processes involved in such tasks as studying have been described by cognitive psychologists in terms of information processing that occurs in several stages.

One reason the cognitive approach to psychology became so successful was that it not only opened the door to studying mental processes but also provided a new way to think about those processes. For example, the "information-processing" description of how we remember suggested that information is taken in from the outside world and passes through a series of identifiable stages of processing before being either forgotten or transferred to long-term memory storage (Figure 1.4). With models like this in hand, cognitive psychologists were able to devise experiments to test the validity of their ideas and thus to open mental processes to objective investigation. (We will discuss their methods in later chapters.) Their research has proved so fruitful that today cognitive research is one of the dominant areas in psychology.

New Developments in Physiology: Exploring the Nervous System with the Aid of Technology

With the cognitive revolution, research psychologists "welcomed back" one of their original concerns—the study of mental processes, which was championed by early psychologists like Wundt and Titchener. In the past few decades, new developments have given renewed emphasis to another of psychology's oldest concerns—the study of the *physiological processes* that underlie behavior.

You have already seen that the roots of scientific psychology extend to the work of 19th-century physiological researchers such as Helmholtz. The main goal of this early physiological research was to understand how our perceptions and other aspects of behavior are shaped by the brain and nervous system. This line of investigation continued to be pursued by physiological researchers, and progress accelerated in the early 20th century with the development of devices for recording electrical signals generated in the nervous system.

It wasn't until the 1950s, however, that research on the biological aspects of behavior began to grow into one of the most significant areas of psychological research. An important reason for this growth was the development of complex new technologies such as devices for measuring the electrical activity of single cells called neurons—which, as you will see in Chapter 3, are the building blocks of the nervous system. More recently, medical technology has produced instruments such as the Positron Emission Tomography (PET) scanner (Figure 1.5), which makes it possible to monitor brain activity as humans think, perceive, or experience emotions. The net result of these technological advances has been an increasingly sophisticated understanding of the biological processes involved in a wide range of human behaviors. We will summarize the findings of this research in Chapter 3, and the biological aspects of behavior will be referred to throughout this book.

FIGURE 1.5

The PET scanner is among the technological innovations that have led to greater understanding of the brain's role in thought, perception, and emotion.

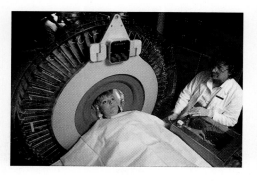

Contemporary Psychology: Many Complementary Approaches

By now you can appreciate that in its short history as a science, psychology has invented, used, discarded, and sometimes rediscovered many influences, approaches, and points of view. As they have worked to refine their science over the last hundred plus years, psychologists have sometimes disagreed not only on how they should go about their studies but on what they should be studying. What, then, is the picture today? How can we describe the science of psychology on the eve of the 21st century?

The answer to that question, in two words, is "large" and "varied." In 1892 the first convention of the American Psychological Association (APA) was attended by 18 of its 31 members. One hundred years later, in 1992, the association had grown to over 65,000 members, with 47 divisions representing the members' varied interests as researchers, educators, and therapists. In addition to the APA, numerous other psychological societies serve special interests within the field. One of the largest of these is the American Psychological Society, which focuses on psychological research.

Looking at psychology as a whole, we can differentiate three types of activities: research, teaching, and providing services to people or organizations. Psychologists engaged in research, who usually work in a university setting, add to our basic knowledge of psychology by carrying out research studies. Research psychologists also often supervise the training of graduate students. Psychologists who teach, also in the university setting, create courses such as the one you are now taking, as well as more advanced undergraduate and graduate courses.

Psychologists who provide services to people or organizations may be therapists who work in a private office, in a social service agency, in an elementary or secondary school, or in a university clinic. They may be involved in developing better educational practices to be used in teaching, or they may apply psychology to the needs of business or industry. Although we can distinguish the research, teaching, and service functions of psychologists, it is not unusual for psychologists to engage in more than one of these activities. For example, many psychologists both teach and carry out research; research psychologists may apply their findings to the service of people; and psychologists who practice therapy might also teach or participate in a research project.

The variety of psychologists is evident when we look at the large number of psychology's specializations (Table 1.1). Figure 1.6 indicates that the largest of them is clinical psychology—psychologists providing therapy or doing research

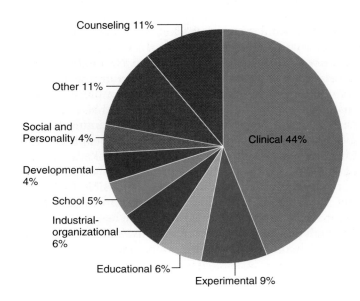

FIGURE 1.6
Specialties in the field of psychology

TABLE 1.1
Psychologists' major specialties

Research Psychologists		
Title	*Research Interest*	*Typical Research Questions*
Biological psychologist (or behavioral neuro-scientist or psychobiologist)	The physiological mechanisms underlying behavior and mental disorders	What is the physiological mechanism responsible for emotional experience?
Clinical psychologist (research emphasis)	The diagnosis, causes, and treatment of abnormal or maladaptive behavior (Note that many clinical psychologists focus not on research, but on helping through therapy; see "Psychologists Who Provide Services.")	What is the most effective treatment for depression?
Cognitive psychologist	Mental processes like thinking, memory, problem solving, and decision making	How do experts in a field go about solving problems in that field? How does their behavior differ from that of novices in the field?
Developmental psychologist	Process of change during the life span, primarily during infancy and childhood but also during adolescence and adulthood	What forces influence a child's social interactions with other children?
Educational psychologist	The application of psychological principles to educational practice, including classroom teaching methods, testing, and curriculum design	How does computer-aided instruction promote learning?
Experimental psychologist	Processes involved in perceiving, learning, motivation, and the emotions (The term *experimental psychologist* actually conveys little information, because psychologists of all kinds do experiments. It is therefore important to ask whether a particular experimental psychologist studies perception, learning, motivation, or the emotions.)	How do learning mechanisms contribute to drug addiction? What are some of the mechanisms that enable us to perceive depth?
Personality psychologist	Factors that make individuals unique, causing them to behave with some consistency in many different situations	How consistent is a particular person's behavior in different situations?
Psychometrician (or quantitative psychologist)	The theory and practice of testing to measure personality, intelligence, and various mental abilities; statistical procedures for analyzing data	Do the scores on intelligence tests accurately reflect a person's capabilities?
Social psychologist	How the presence of another person or groups of people influences a person's behavior	How does being in a group influence how hard a person will work at a task?

related to mental illness—which accounts for 40% of psychologists in the United States.

One of the interesting things about contemporary psychology is that of the major approaches that have been proposed since Wundt opened the first psychology laboratory in 1879, all but structuralism are still in use today. They are still with us because each provides a window on a different aspect of the complex phenomenon we call human behavior. For example, a psychologist studying the mechanisms responsible for depression would be using a behavioral approach if she focused on how environmental stimuli trigger depressive behaviors; a cognitive approach if she looked at how people's thought processes contribute to depression; a biological approach if she asked how depression is related to brain chemistry; or a Freudian approach if she focused on the unconscious memories and conflicts that might be responsible for depressive symptoms. Usually, a particular researcher focuses on and becomes expert in one approach to the study of behavior, but all approaches contribute to our understanding. Although this multiplicity of perspectives makes psychology complex, it also makes it a rich and fascinating discipline—as diverse and multifaceted as human behavior itself.

A social psychologist interviewing in a shopping mall

A biological psychologist measuring a sleeping subject's brain waves

A developmental psychologist studying children's behavior

*Psychologists Who Provide Services**

Title	Description
Clinical psychologist (therapy emphasis)	Diagnoses and treats people both with severe mental disorders and less severe psychological problems. Clinical psychologists may work in private practice or in clinic settings.
Counseling psychologist	Like clinical psychologists, counseling psychologists help people deal with psychological problems, working in both private practice and clinic settings.
School psychologist	Works with students in elementary through high school to help them with their academic performance, social adjustment, and career choices.
Industrial and organizational psychologist (I/O psychologist)	Often works in industrial or organizational settings, running personnel departments or designing training programs, for instance. I/O psychologists are usually trained as psychometricians or social psychologists, and some do research on organizational behavior in university departments.

*The focus of this book is on the results obtained by research psychologists. But psychologists who provide services to people or organizations also play an important role in the field of psychology.

Integrating the Field of Psychology

Psychology's diversity and multifaceted approach to studying behavior make it a challenging subject—not only for beginning students but for psychologists themselves, most of whom specialize in one of the discipline's many research areas or concentrate on only a few of the several approaches to understanding behavior. In this book you will read about the results of many kinds of research conducted from various angles of inquiry, ranging from biological studies of the brain to the psychology of conformity. How can you begin to form a coherent picture of so many lines of investigation, each focusing on a specific aspect of human behavior?

This book provides several tools to help you identify common threads and integrate what you learn as you progress through your introductory psychology course. Perhaps the most important is the simple but powerful concept of *levels of analysis.*

Levels of Analysis: A Way of Thinking About Psychology

The idea of **levels of analysis** simplifies the multiplicity of approaches in psychology by focusing attention on four main ways of looking at behavior. We can summarize these perspectives as follows: Humans behave in ways that can be directly observed (*behavioral* level), and they think, remember, fantasize, and solve problems (*cognitive* level). This behavior and thinking involve biological mechanisms, such as activity in various areas of the brain (*biological* level). Finally, all of these activities and processes—behavioral, cognitive, and biological—take place within a physical and social *context (contextual* level). This context includes aspects of the physical environment and social environment that affect behavior, such as the living conditions in a person's neighborhood and the interactions people have with one another, ranging from encounters with strangers to group activities to intimate relationships.

Figure 1.7 illustrates the levels of analysis approach as applied to psychology. The biological, cognitive, and behavioral approaches are all linked together and occur within a context. To see how these different ways of analyzing behavior are complementary, let's briefly apply each level of analysis to a single psychological phenomenon, the changes that take place as a person makes the transition from childhood into adolescence.

The biological level.   The **biological level of analysis** emphasizes the relationship between the brain, nervous system, and behavior; it also includes the study of how heredity and evolution influence behavior. When applied to adolescent development, the biological level might consider how increases in male and female hormone concentrations trigger physical changes such as increases in height and weight, the development of the genitals, growth of the beard in boys and of breasts in girls, and the beginning of menstruation in girls.

The cognitive level.   The **cognitive level of analysis** explores the study of mental processes. Applied to the study of adolescence, the cognitive level might study ways in which adolescents think, focusing on their ability to reason scientifically and think abstractly and on their deepening awareness of their own thought processes. In addition, the cognitive level might consider how adolescents deal with questions such as "Who am I?" and how they make decisions about schooling and future occupation. Any consideration of how unconscious processes might influence adolescent behavior also falls within the cognitive level of analysis.

FIGURE 1.7
The levels of analysis approach to psychology. Behavior can be studied at four levels—behavioral, biological, cognitive, and contextual. The first three levels contribute individually to our understanding of behavior while being linked within the fourth—the contextual level.

The behavioral level. The **behavioral level of analysis** involves research done in the spirit of behaviorism, in which the focus is on measuring observable behavior. Applied to the study of adolescence, the behavioral level might focus on how the adolescent's social behavior is affected by the rewards associated with acceptance by peers and by the punishment of being excluded. In addition, the behavioral level might consider how the adolescent's behavior is influenced by simply observing the behavior of his or her peers or by paying attention to the models for adult behavior presented by the media.

The contextual level. The **contextual level of analysis** has to do with looking at how behavior is influenced by the overall physical and social context or situation in which it occurs. To study adolescent development at this level we might look at how the cultural environment created by society affects adolescent behavior. For example, we could study how societal influences such as the media—particularly magazines, television, and film—create standards of "ideal" male and female behavior that many adolescents strive to live up to.

The preceding examples of how we can apply each of the levels of analysis illustrate the following principles.

1. Only by studying a behavior at all levels can we fully understand it. Information gained at each level helps fill in part of the total picture, or—to put it another way—provides a piece of the jigsaw puzzle that, when completed, creates a complete explanation of the behavior (see Figure 1.8).

2. We can study a behavior by focusing on just one level. In fact, most researchers devote their energy to studying one level in depth.

3. The levels interact with each other. For example, the biological, behavioral, and cognitive levels interact when a male who matures early due to biologically triggered hormone increases (biological level) experiences the social rewards of increased popularity (behavioral level), which in turn may shape the way he thinks about himself as a person (cognitive level). In a similar way, the contextual and behavioral levels interact, as the values of an adolescent's society (contextual level) influence the way the adolescent behaves with friends (behavioral level).

4. Each level of analysis answers a different type of question about an aspect of behavior, but no one level is intrinsically more fundamental or important

At the cognitive level of analysis, psychologists investigate the emergence of scientific reasoning in adolescence. At the behavioral level of analysis, psychologists investigate how adolescents' behavior is influenced by rewards provided by peers.

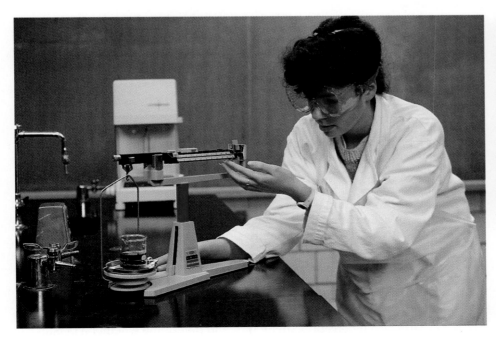

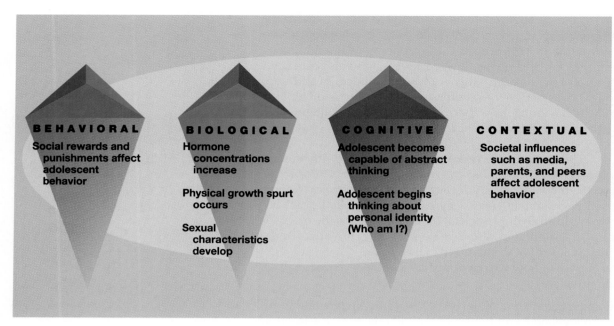

FIGURE 1.8
Levels of analysis applied to the study of adolescence. Similar diagrams appear throughout the book, illustrating how levels of analysis can be applied to different topics.

than another. For example, biological changes define the beginning of adolescence, causing an impressive growth spurt and the development of sexual changes. But the culture in which the adolescent lives is just as important as these biological changes, because that culture can influence, for example, the nature of the adolescent's family life, educational opportunities, possible occupations, and leisure-time activities, and can even influence the age at which biological changes take place.

Throughout this book we will use the concept of levels of analysis as a framework for organizing our thinking about psychology and relating specific research topics to one another. This common thread is one way of combating the segmentation of psychology into the different areas represented by the chapters in this book. Keeping in mind the concept of levels of analysis can help you appreciate how similar modes of thinking can be applied to psychology's different areas.

Although the concept of levels of analysis runs through the text, there are several special features in the book that are also designed to encourage you to connect ideas and focus on the "big picture" as you study specific topics. These features include Measurement & Methodology, Connections, Interdisciplinary Dimensions, and Follow-Through/Diversity.

Measurement & Methodology: The "How" of Psychology

This chapter has already introduced an important unifying theme that runs through all the various approaches and specialties in psychology—namely, that psychology is an empirical science. Thus, psychology's unity as a discipline stems not just from *what* it studies, but from *how* it accumulates knowledge. For this reason, understanding what psychology is all about requires some acquaintance with the particular methods psychologists use in pursuing their science.

Chapter 2 will introduce the tactics of psychological research. From that point on, you will also encounter one to three "Measurement & Methodology" features in each chapter. These brief discussions spotlight ingenious methods psychologists have devised for applying the ideal of empiricism to questions about the mind and behavior, or examine questions about what constitutes valid research. So you will see, for example, how psychologists create pictures of the brain, measure visual perception in infants, and determine whether a person has

At the biological level of analysis, psychologists watch the rapid physical changes triggered in adolescence. At the contextual level of analysis, psychologists study how adolescent behavior is affected by culture.

stress-prone behavior patterns. You will explore some of the problems psychologists have encountered in determining how frequently adolescents argue with their parents and why tall people who are nearsighted tend to be more intelligent than short people who have normal vision. Being exposed to some basic issues in psychological measurement and methodology will not only give you more of a feeling for what makes psychology a science, it will also help you develop your ability to critically evaluate claims about behavior.

Connections: Linking Areas of Psychology

At many points in this book, what you are reading will be related to a topic covered in more detail in another chapter. The relationships between different areas in psychology will be signaled by a "connection" symbol in the margin similar to the example shown here, indicating the topic to which the discussion you are reading is related and the chapter in the book that covers it. Since there are almost 200 such symbols in this book, it quickly becomes apparent that there is a great deal of cross-talk between different areas of psychology.

3 BIOLOGY

Interdisciplinary Dimensions: Linking Psychology to Other Disciplines

As you learned in the history section of this chapter, psychology achieved independence as a scientific discipline both by refining the kinds of questions it asked and by concentrating on empirical methods of answering those questions. Many other avenues to exploring human experience differ from psychology in the nature and scope of their questions or in the methods used to answer them. Just as it is important not to lose sight of the connections and common themes within psychology, it is also important to be able to forge links between psychology and other complementary areas of study.

Consider, for example, the study of literature. Questions such as the following attest to the fact that literary works often explore psychological issues: Was Hamlet insane? Why did he wait so long to avenge his father's death? Did Ophelia drown herself on purpose or was it an accident? Or consider the study of art. When the Renaissance painters developed perspective in the 15th century, they found a way to create a perception of three-dimensionality on a two-dimensional canvas. In an important sense, artists such as Leonardo da Vinci (1452–1519) were early perceptual psychologists, and understanding why their techniques work touches on of the principles of perception studied in psychology.

There are many such links between the material you will study in this course and other fields, whether they neighbor psychology (such as the biological sciences and the social sciences of sociology and anthropology) or are more remote from it (such as literature, art, and architecture) (Figure 1.9). To encourage you to make these links, each chapter, beginning with Chapter 3, will include a discussion called "Interdisciplinary Dimensions" that focuses on a specific point of intersection between psychology and another discipline.

Follow-Through/Diversity:
Psychological Perspectives on Human Diversity

As should be clear from the discussion of levels of analysis, to fully understand behavior it helps to look at a particular subject from a number of viewpoints. To illustrate this, a "Follow-Through/Diversity" feature at the end of each chapter focuses on one constant theme—human ethnic and sexual diversity—and discusses it from the perspective of that chapter. For example, the Follow-Through for the chapter on biology addresses how sex hormones have different effects on male and female behavior; in the chapter on intelligence, it describes special problems in measuring intelligence in minority children. In the chapter on cognition, the Follow-Through explores differences in the way people from various cultures think. In each chapter, you will see how a different area of psychology makes its own contribution to the understanding of psychological issues involving different cultures and the two genders.

Reprise: The Challenge of Psychology

The story of psychology is the story of the intellectual quest to arrive at a scientific understanding of behavior. As we have seen in this chapter, studying human behavior is no simple task. Although psychology has successfully tackled many of the problems that in earlier centuries people could only speculate about, its success has not come easily. In fact, psychology is one of the most challenging of the sciences.

Psychology is difficult because the subjects it studies—humans—are so amazingly complex and varied. The "control center" that directs our behavior, the human brain, has been called "the most complex structure in the known universe" (Thompson, 1985), and no two brains are exactly alike. Moreover, when we realize that studying the brain represents only one level of analysis relevant to behavior, the challenge of applying scientific thinking to psychological issues begins to become clear.

The unique challenge of psychology is perhaps more meaningful to me because my first training was in chemistry and engineering. The summer after receiving my undergraduate degree in chemical engineering, I had a job working at the Naval Research Laboratory outside of Washington, D.C. I was a member of a team that was precisely measuring the melting point of potassium at a number of different pressures. The laboratory where we made these measurements was impressive. It included a high-technology furnace, exquisitely sensitive measuring instruments, lots of electronics and dials, and banks of computers. Using all of this impressive technology, we determined the melting point of potassium to a number of decimal places. This result was valuable because the measurements we made were valid for all other equally pure samples of potassium, anywhere in the world.

Obtaining results in psychology does not usually pose such technological challenges, but it does involve other thorny issues. For one thing, psychologists can't generalize from just one person's behavior the way we can establish the universal melting point of potassium by measuring a purified sample of the substance. Because individuals are unique, measuring one person's behavior

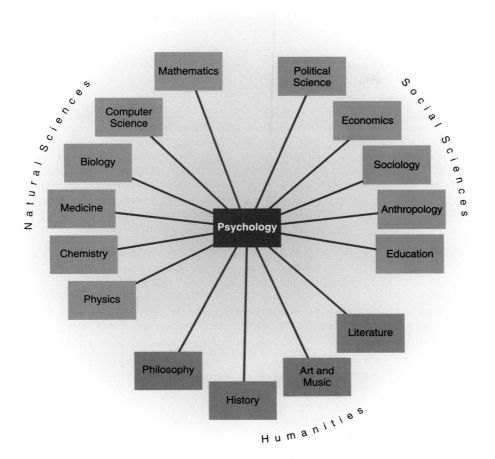

FIGURE 1.9
Psychology is linked in varying degrees to numerous other disciplines. The Interdisciplinary Dimensions feature in each chapter discusses an aspect of the interaction between psychology and one of these disciplines.

doesn't necessarily reveal what is true about another, let alone about people in general. In addition, psychologists are constantly confronted with problems of definition and measurement. What is aggression? Attraction? Intelligence? Emotion? Unlike "melting point," which is easily defined and measured, these concepts can be defined in many different ways, and each definition implies different ways to measure them. Intelligence, for example, may be measured by performance on an IQ test, but does the test really measure all that we mean by intelligence? What about creativity, or the knack of knowing how to respond to someone in distress, or the ability to succeed in the world of business? And what if the test measures what a certain culture values as intelligence but overlooks skills and aptitudes valued in a different culture? (We pursue these issues in Chapter 14.)

Finally, psychology is challenging for the very reason it is so fascinating to many of us, because it attempts to study what we think we know best. None of us comes to the study of psychology free of opinions, attitudes, and even deep-seated beliefs about ourselves and others. Reading this book will, therefore, challenge you to reexamine some of your assumptions about human behavior and your preconceptions about how psychologists go about studying it. It will challenge you to compare the way you have thought about behavior in the past with the scientific approach to behavior behind the findings documented here. You may find that some of the assumptions you have made about behavior are false—that psychology is much more than the cynic's definition, "the science of what everybody knew beforehand, anyway."

As you experience the challenge of studying psychology I hope you will find that the rewards of learning what psychology is really about are worth the effort. Speaking for myself, although studying behavior presents many more difficulties than measuring the melting point of potassium, I have never regretted giving up engineering to become a psychologist.

Diversity in the History of Psychology

You may have noticed that the history of psychology described in this chapter has focused on a rather narrow sample of human beings: European and American white males. One reason for this is that scientific psychology was very much a product of Western culture and its view of what constituted science. Furthermore, within this culture psychology developed at a time when white males had far greater access to education and to faculty positions in prestigious universities than did women or nonwhites. Thus, the science of human behavior was dominated in its formative years by a small subset of human beings. Fortunately, this picture is changing, and more and more viewpoints are coming into play within psychology.

Consider, for example, the representation of women and African Americans in the ranks of psychologists. When the first American Psychological Association (APA) convention was held in 1892, no women or African Americans were present. At the second convention, in 1893, one woman attended. Slowly, over the years, more women began entering the profession, and some became recognized as distinguished researchers or teachers. Even so, women generally remained in the background when it came to receiving credit for furthering the science of psychology. The situation for African Americans was even worse, as there were no African-American Ph.D.'s in psychology until the 1920s.

Women fared better than African Americans in terms of access to education but still faced attitudes such as those held by G. Stanley Hall, the founder of the American Psychological Association. Hall felt that education endangered women's health. The reason? It would disrupt their menstrual period and cause them to neglect their maternal urges (Russo & Denmark, 1987).

Remarks such as Hall's had their effect on women. Martha Thomas—who, despite Hall's remarks, eventually became president of Bryn Mawr College—reported that when she was a young woman, reading his pronouncements made her "terror struck lest she and every other woman . . . were doomed to live as pathological invalids . . . as a result of their education" (Ehrenreich & English, 1978, p. 117).

One result of male attitudes was a lack of opportunity for women to earn degrees and fellowships. For example, Mary Calkins (1863–1930) was denied a Ph.D. at Harvard in 1895, even though she had completed all of the requirements and was unanimously recommended for the degree by the professors in the psychology department. Unfortunately, Harvard's administrators stuck by their policy of not awarding advanced degrees to women.

Eventually, however, women began receiving advanced degrees in psychology. To its credit, the APA freely admitted women from the beginning. Mary Calkins attended the second APA convention and, having distinguished herself by developing a technique called paired associate learning that is still used today in memory research, was elected the first female president of the APA in 1905.

Margaret Washburn (1871–1939), the first woman to receive a Ph.D. in psychology (from Cornell, in 1894), became the second female president of the APA in 1921. In recognition of her work in animal psychology, which produced *The Animal Mind*, the first text on animal psychology, she became the second woman in *any* field

to be elected to the prestigious National Academy of Sciences, in 1932.

By 1923, 18% of the APA members were women. However, while women were increasingly taking their place in psychology during the first two decades of the 20th century, African Americans remained invisible. It was not until 1920 that Francis Sumner became the first African American to receive a Ph.D. in psychology, from Clark University. Up until that time only 11 of 10,000 recipients of Ph.D.'s in *all* fields in the United States were African American. The lack of African-American psychologists was primarily due to dismal educational opportunities. As late as 1940 only four of the hundreds of African-American colleges offered an undergraduate psychology major (Guthrie, 1976). One of them was Howard University, where Sumner served as department chairman and faculty member from 1928 to 1954.

Representation of women and African Americans within psychology is much better today than it was in the early days of the discipline. Largely due to the perseverance of early pioneers

Mary Calkins, although denied a Ph.D. at Harvard in 1895 because of her gender, distinguished herself in research and was elected president of the APA in 1905.

Margaret Washburn, elected president of the APA in 1921 and to the National Academy of Sciences in 1932

and the gains won by the women's rights and civil rights movements in the 1960s and 1970s, the percentage of Ph.D.'s in psychology earned by women rose from 15% in 1950 to 56% in 1989 (Ostertag & McNamara, 1991). Since 1972, five women have been elected president of the APA. One measure of the prominence of women's contributions to modern psychology is the large number of female researchers cited throughout this book. Another is the emergence of a new field—the psychology of women—exemplifying how increased diversity can affect the growth of the science itself.

Growth in the representation of African Americans in psychology has also accelerated, but it still lags behind the gains made by women. This reflects the situation in society as a whole. Even when more African Americans began earning Ph.D.'s in psychology, most could obtain positions only in "teaching" colleges. Those who did do research tended to focus on dispelling some of the myths about African Americans that existed in psychology (see the Follow-Through in Chapter 2). One of the most eminent African-American psychologists is Kenneth Clark, who received his bachelor's degree from Howard University and his Ph.D. from Columbia University in 1940, becoming a professor at the City University of New York. Clark is another example of how diversity within psychology opens up new issues for investigators, sometimes with important social consequences. His writings on racial discrimination were cited by the U.S. Supreme Court in its momentous 1954 *Brown* v. *Board of Education* decision, outlawing segregation in the public schools on the grounds that segregated education was inherently unequal. In 1970 Clark became the first African-American president of the APA.

What do the gains made by women and African Americans mean? Although the numbers of women and men in psychology are nearly equal, there are still more male faculty members in psychology departments of major universities. However, if present trends continue, women will eventually participate on an equal footing with men in psychology. African Americans still represent only a small fraction of psychology Ph.D.'s—accounting for about 3% of those awarded between 1975 and 1981 (Houston, 1990)—but are becoming increasingly visible in both research and clinical areas of psychology.

Looking at the overall picture today in psychology we see a field that has come a long way from the all-white male establishment of the early days. With the increased representation of women and African Americans in psychology, plus recent increases in the participation of Hispanics (Comas-Diaz, 1991), psychology has not only gained more participants but has expanded its research agenda to include work on subjects such as gender, ethnicity, discrimination, and attitude formation and change. But perhaps the most important effect of psychology's greater diversity of professionals is a wider view of what psychology *is*, which has opened the field to more approaches and ideas (Jacklin & McBride-Chang, 1991; Lewin & Wild, 1991; Morawski & Agronick, 1991).

Francis Sumner, the first African American to receive a Ph.D. in psychology (1920)

A scene from the early days of school desegregation, an important social change that was supported by psychological research that indicated that segregated schools are inherently unequal.

Kenneth Clark, the first African-American president of the APA (1970)

What You Do and Don't Know About Psychology

- One property of psychology is that you know something about the subject, based on your experience in living, even before taking your first course. In reality, however, much of that "commonsense" knowledge about psychology is unreliable. The "general public" does not necessarily possess correct factual information about psychology and often fails to correctly predict the outcome of psychological experiments.

Psychology as Science

- Science goes beyond the accumulation of facts in its quest to understand the laws that govern the way the world works. To achieve this goal science has developed a way of thinking that includes maintaining intellectual honesty, avoiding premature conclusions, searching for lawful relationships, and asking questions that are potentially answerable using currently available techniques.

- Scientific empiricism is a process by which observations are made that are objective, are done systematically, and are replicable.

The Growth of Scientific Psychology

- Before the establishment of scientific psychology, the study of the mind and behavior was largely the work of philosophers such as Plato, Aristotle, Descartes, and Locke. These philosophers often relied on logic and reasoning to reach their conclusions. This was an improvement over mythology or magical thinking, but there was no way to resolve disputes between equally logical positions.

- In the early 1800s physiologists began answering many of the questions about physiology and behavior previously debated by philosophers. Hermann von Helmholtz's research on sensory functioning proposed a link between physiology and experience. Ernst Weber, in one of the first psychophysical experiments, showed that the just noticeable difference is constant over a wide range of stimulus intensities. His experiments showed that the relationship between physical stimuli and psychological experience can be measured precisely and that the relationship obeys mathematical laws.

- Wilhelm Wundt founded the first laboratory of experimental psychology in 1879. He performed experiments using the techniques of psychophysics and introspection. His student Edward Titchener originated the term *structuralism* to describe his introspective approach. Titchener's goal was to study the structure of consciousness by analyzing experience into its simplest components.

- William James disagreed with the structuralists' attempts to dissect consciousness into simple components. James's emphasis on describing the functions of consciousness and behavior stimulated the formation of functionalism.

- Max Wertheimer's founding of Gestalt psychology was based on his rejection of the structuralist idea that perceptions are created by the addition of sensations. He focused instead on perceptions as "wholes."

- John Watson founded behaviorism because he felt the method of introspection was unscientific. Watson proposed that consciousness is not a proper subject of psychological inquiry and stated that psychologists should study only observable behavior. He used Pavlov's classical conditioning procedure to demonstrate how learning can be studied objectively. Following Watson, B. F. Skinner's pioneering work on operant conditioning made him the main spokesperson for behaviorism.

- Sigmund Freud's method of treatment, psychoanalysis, was based on discovering memories hidden in his patients' unconsciousness. Freud felt that behavior is determined largely by unconscious forces.

- Carl Rogers and Abraham Maslow founded the humanistic approach to psychology as a reaction to the Freudian and behavioral approaches. They created an approach to therapy based on the idea that people are naturally good and strive toward realizing their potential.

- In the 1950s and 1960s a number of psychologists began to question the behaviorists' idea that it was not possible to study mental processes empirically. Rejection of that idea led to the establishment of cognitive psychology and a new way of studying mental processes. The cognitive psychologists analyzed mental processes in terms of information processing: information is taken in from the outside world and processed through a series of stages, each of which can be studied empirically. The cognitive approach is one of the most dominant today.

- In the 1950s research on the biological aspects of behavior began to grow into one of the most significant areas of psychological research. The development of new technologies has made it possible to record electrical signals from the nervous system and to create images depicting the structure and functioning of the brain.

- Contemporary psychology consists of a large number of people employing varied approaches. Activities of psychologists include research, teaching, and providing services to people and organizations.

Integrating the Field of Psychology

- The diverse nature of psychology adds to its challenge. This book employs a number of ways of integrating that diversity, one of which is a way of thinking about psychology called levels of analysis. We consider four levels: biological, cognitive, behavioral, and contextual.

- We can summarize the levels of analysis as follows. Biological looks at the relationship between physiological processes and behavior; cognitive explores the operation of mental processes; behavioral focuses on measuring observable behavior; and contextual looks at how behavior is influenced by the context or situation in which it occurs.

- The idea of levels of analysis is used as a way of thinking about psychology throughout the text. In addition, the following features are included to help connect ideas across the field of psychology and between psychology and other fields. "Measurement & Methodology" features are short discussions that spotlight the methods psychologists have devised for applying empiricism to the study of the mind and behavior. "Connections" indicate places in the text where the discussion is linked to another area in psychology. "Interdisciplinary Dimensions" discuss a point of intersection between psychology and another discipline. "Follow-Through/Diversity" features are discussions of an aspect of human diversity from the perspective of each chapter.

Reprise: The Challenge of Psychology

- Psychology is challenging not so much because of its technological complexity as because the subject it studies—human behavior—is amazingly varied. Not only are individual humans complex, but each one is different, adding to the challenge of formulating general laws that hold for all humans or even for subgroups of humans. In addition, psychologists have to deal with problems of definition and measurement. Psychology is also challenging because its methods and findings often change our preexisting beliefs about psychology and human behavior.

Key Terms

behavioral level of analysis
behaviorism
biological level of analysis
cognitive level of analysis
cognitive psychology
contextual level of analysis
empiricism
functionalism

Gestalt psychology
humanistic approach
introspection
levels of analysis
psychophysics
scientific empiricism
structuralism

CHAPTER

2

Asking Questions of Nature:
  The Logic of Scientific Research
      Observation: Describing the Phenomena
      Experimentation: Testing for Causal Relationships
      Theory Building: Creating Models Based on the Data

Posing Questions About Behavior:
  Methods of Psychological Research
      Observational Methods: Ways to Describe Behavior
      Experimental Studies: Procedures for Determining Causation
      Causation and Correlation in Psychological Experiments
      Bias in Psychological Research

Drawing Conclusions from
  Psychological Research
      Descriptive Statistics: Describing the Results
      Inferential Statistics: Interpreting Differences

Ethical Issues in Psychological Research
      Research on Human Subjects
      Research on Animal Subjects

Reprise: Science as a Refinement
  of Everyday Thinking

Follow-Through/Diversity
      The Lens of Culture and the Psychological Study of Women
          and African Americans

Understanding Psychological Research

The real purpose of the scientific method is to make sure Nature hasn't misled you into thinking you know something you don't actually know.

Robert Pirsig, Zen and the Art of Motorcycle Maintenance *(1974)*

In Chapter 1 science was described as a set of attitudes, as a commitment to drawing conclusions based on systematic and objective empirical observations that can be repeated by others. That chapter addressed the question "What *is* scientific research?" This one answers the question "How do psychologists *do* scientific research?"

Why is it important for you to learn about the methods psychologists use in research? One reason is that you will be reading about the results of psychological research throughout this book. Understanding how psychologists arrive at those results will help you interpret their findings. But in addition, understanding the process of scientific research is useful because evaluating claims about behavior is something you are called on to do nearly every day.

Consider, for example, some claims I have recently been exposed to:

- Psychic readers can predict your future. (source: Television advertisement for "Psychic Friends Network")
- Eighty-three percent of the brain is unconscious. (source: A public talk)
- If given a choice, people will always choose to be in a relationship in which they are praised rather than criticized. (source: Conversation with a friend)

Are these assertions true? How can we tell? One way is to get into the habit of asking what evidence supports them—and to be able to evaluate the quality of that evidence. Simply taking on faith what we hear from the media, supposed authorities, or friends can mean basing our beliefs and actions on misinformation. As it turns out, all three statements listed are either unproved or untrue.

The methods of psychological research described in this chapter illustrate a way of looking at the world in a critical and discerning manner. Understanding the logic behind psychologists' thinking may make you more likely to question some of the "facts" you are presented with every day—and to recognize which claims people make about behavior are worthy of your belief. Let's begin by reviewing the process of scientific research in general. We will then see how it has been applied to answering questions in psychology.

Asking Questions of Nature: The Logic of Scientific Research

There is more than one way to do scientific research. The procedures used depend, among other things, on the types of questions being asked (are we asking questions about the inner workings of the brain or about mob behavior?), the subject being studied (are we interested in animal behavior or human behavior,

The H.M.S. *Beagle* (left) and Charles Darwin (right)

the behavior of infants, or the behavior of adults?), and the relative sophistication of our knowledge about the topic (is our knowledge about the topic limited or does the topic have a rich history of prior research?). However, no matter what procedures are used, the basis of all research is *observation.*

Observation: Describing the Phenomena

The first task in any scientific investigation is describing the phenomenon to be studied. Through careful, accurate, and objective observation, scientists try to see the world with fresh eyes and to purge from their vision, as far as possible, presumptions and expectations concerning what they *think* the world is like.

Observation is used to *define phenomena* to be studied, and to *identify relationships* between different phenomena. When we note that the moon goes through regular phases, that animals can be classified according to their physical similarities, that objects fall to the ground when we release them, and that people go through a cycle of sleep and wakefulness about every 24 hours, we are defining the basic fabric of the world we are trying to understand.

But most scientists are not content to simply catalog facts. They seek to identify relationships between phenomena so they can *explain* what they observe. As we will see, science insists that these explanations be based on the *data* provided by careful and accurate observation. Scientists are trained to be skeptical of explanations based on hunches, plausible guesses, or articles of faith without a foundation of well-established data to support them. That is why you will often hear people with scientific training challenging statements with questions like "Where are the data to support this?" or "Are the data reliable?"

The history of science abounds with examples of how carefully gathered data have revealed relationships between phenomena that were always there but had gone unnoticed. A dramatic example of the power of careful observation is the way Charles Darwin (1809–1882) arrived at his theory of evolution.

Shortly after receiving his bachelor's degree from Cambridge University, Darwin secured an appointment as the naturalist on the HMS *Beagle*, which was about to embark on a five-year, around-the-world voyage. Darwin's role on the voyage was to collect animal and plant specimens, which he would send back to England for study. Little did his sponsors—or Darwin himself—imagine that his task would lead to observations that would revolutionize the way humans think about their biological world.

FIGURE 2.1
The three types of finches observed by
Charles Darwin on the Galapagos Islands

The *Beagle* set sail two days after Christmas in 1831. Darwin made observations of living species at different sites during the voyage, sending numerous boxes of specimens back to England as he collected them. But his crucial observations occurred on the Galápagos Islands off the coast of South America. There he observed that the same species of bird—the finch—existed in slightly different forms on islands separated by as little as 50 or 60 miles. His curiosity aroused, Darwin proceeded to refine his observations. On each island, he noticed, the finches had different types of beaks, which seemed to be matched to the island's food supply. On an island rich in nuts and seeds, the finches had strong, thick beaks, well suited to cracking nuts and seeds; on an island with an abundance of insects, they had smaller beaks; and on an island with abundant vegetation, they had beaks well suited to feeding on plants and flowers (Figure 2.1). At this point an idea began to take shape in Darwin's mind: perhaps the finches' beaks differed because each subspecies had become *adapted* to its particular environment.

Darwin's observation put him on the trail of a general explanation of the characteristics of species, known as the *theory of natural selection.* The theory states that species can change in response to environmental pressures, and that change occurs when particular members of a species are better adapted to survive and reproduce in a competitive environment. For example, finches with thick beaks would be better adapted than finches with thin beaks to compete for a scarce food supply consisting mostly of nuts. If more thick-beaked finches survive to pass their characteristics to their offspring, then, over many generations, all finches living in that environment will eventually have thick beaks. Although Darwin's conclusion may seem familiar today, it was truly revolutionary when he proposed it because most people of his day believed, on the basis of their interpretation of Scripture, that the species had simply been created differently and didn't change over time.

Let's consider what Darwin did. His first observation, which was obvious to everyone, was that the world is populated with many species. He refined that observation by noting that in the Galápagos, finches existed in slightly different forms. He then made the crucial observation that linked the finches' beaks with their food supply; finally, he was able to pull all of those observations together into a general theory. The generality of Darwin's theory provided him with a powerful tool—he could now see whether other species fit the theory. Thus, Darwin went on to make many additional observations to test the validity of his idea about natural selection.

As we will see throughout this book, Darwin's theory has had important implications for psychology. It became the driving force behind the idea that psychology should focus on behavior, and it continues to suggest a fruitful perspective from which to analyze biological aspects of behavior. But the main point of this example is that his theory—which gave the world a new way of understanding nature—grew out of his keen observational skills. The "facts" were there for all to see, but it was Darwin who saw them with fresh eyes.

An example of a psychological observation that led to a landmark discovery is one that took place not on a remote island, but in a sleep laboratory at the University of Chicago. A graduate student, Eugene Aserinsky, sat watching a person sleep. His adviser, Nathaniel Kleitman, had asked him to watch for the rolling eye movements that begin when a person first falls asleep. But about 90 minutes after his subject had fallen asleep, Aserinsky observed something unexpected and very strange: the eyes started jerking rapidly back and forth. No sleep researcher had ever noted these *rapid eye movements* (*REMs*) before. Aserinsky's discovery would have meant little, however, if he and Kleitman hadn't made some additional observations: (1) periods of REM, called *REM sleep*, occurred at periodic intervals about five times during the night; (2) the person's brain waves during REM sleep resembled waking brain waves; and (3) persons awakened from REM sleep invariably reported dreaming. In contrast, when awakened from non-REM sleep, subjects were usually not dreaming (Dement, 1972; Dement & Kleitman, 1957).

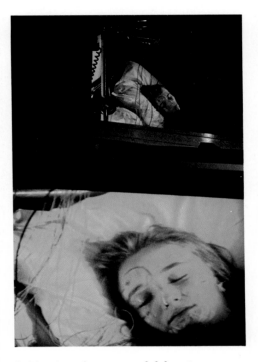

Subject in a sleep research laboratory

The discovery of REM sleep opened a window on something that had been extremely difficult to observe, the process of dreaming. (Prior to the discovery of REM sleep, the study of dreams was limited largely to people's reports of dreams they had just before they awoke in the morning.) We will have more to say about what REM sleep can tell us about dreaming in Chapter 5. For now our concern is with how REM sleep was discovered. First came the observation of the existence of REMs, then further observation of their periodic nature, and finally observation of the connections between REM sleep and waking brain waves and between REM sleep and dreams. Just as Darwin first observed the differences in finch beaks and then gave those differences meaning by linking them with the birds' food supply, Aserinsky and Kleitman began by observing rapid eye movements and then gave them meaning by linking them to specific brain waves and to dreaming.

Both examples illustrate that as the starting point of scientific discovery, observation often leads not only to greater understanding, but also to new questions that we couldn't have known to ask before the observations were made. For example, questions such as "Why does REM sleep occur?" and "What is its function?" derive directly from Aserinsky's observations.

How can we answer questions like these? In some cases answers can be proposed based solely on observations but, when possible, scientists usually take another step and move from observation to experimentation. Psychologists, for example, have increased their knowledge about REM sleep by doing experiments to find out what happens if people are deprived of it. They find that when they deprive people of REM sleep by awakening them every time they show rapid eye movements during the night, people experience longer periods of REM sleep on subsequent nights. What these experiments do is to take control of the situation by manipulating the amount of REM sleep the subject experiences. As we are about to see, experimentation transforms researchers from passive observers of what is happening into active participants in the questioning of nature.

Experimentation: Testing for Causal Relationships

Observation is a passive science, experimentation an active science.

Claude Bernard (1865)

Science is more than simply describing phenomena. Another of its goals is to explain natural events by determining relationships between causes and effects. For example, Darwin was not content to note just the *effects*, the differences in finches' beaks; he was motivated to puzzle out what the *causes* of those differences might be. Though observation alone might suggest where to look for causes, it cannot prove that a cause-and-effect relationship exists. To accomplish this scientists need to use **experimentation,** a method in which observations are made under controlled conditions designed to test specific ideas about causal relationships.

A compelling illustration of the need for experimentation in establishing cause and effect is provided by Joseph Goldberger's investigations into the causes of pellagra in the early 1900s. Pellagra, a disease characterized by dizziness, vomiting, running sores, and severe diarrhea, was responsible for hundreds of thousands of deaths in the southern United States. Because the disease struck only families lacking indoor plumbing, observation alone could easily suggest that pellagra was caused by poor sanitary conditions, which is what health experts concluded (Stanovich, 1989).

But was poor sanitation really the culprit? Goldberger had a different idea. He suspected that pellagra was caused by the low-protein, high-carbohydrate diet of poor people in the South—the same people who lived with poor sanitary conditions. To test this idea, Goldberger conducted a study that followed the **basic rule of experimentation:** *To determine a cause-and-effect relationship, change one variable while keeping every other relevant variable constant.* A **variable** is a property or condition that can be measured. If only one variable is changed and some effect is observed, the effect must be due to the change in that variable.

The variable Goldberger was interested in was diet. Using two groups of pellagra-free prisoners as subjects, he placed one group on a high-carbohydrate, low-protein diet (corn, grits, and "mush") and the other on a more balanced diet (including meat, eggs, and milk). All the other relevant factors—including sanitary conditions—were the same for both groups. The result: the low-protein group got pellagra and the other group didn't.

Goldberger's study illustrates the basic logic of an experiment. The experimental tactic of changing one variable (protein in the diet), keeping everything else constant, and measuring the changes that result (the contraction of pellagra by the low-protein-diet group) accomplishes something very important: it establishes a **cause-and-effect relationship.** The results of Goldberger's experiment allowed him to conclude that a low-protein diet, not poor sanitation, caused pellagra (Figure 2.2.).

Before moving on we should note, however, that Goldberger's experiment, in which he subjected people to a diet that he suspected would make them sick, would be considered unethical today.

Poverty led to dietary deficiencies that caused pellagra.

Theory Building: Creating Models Based on the Data

We have seen that by manipulating one variable and holding all others constant, as Goldberger did in his pellagra study, researchers can determine cause-and-effect relationships between variables. But in some cases scientists can take a step beyond determining specific causal relationships to proposing theories that explain a large body of relationships.

Theoretical physicist Stephen Hawking defines a **theory** as "a model of the universe, or a restricted part of it, and a set of rules that relates quantities in the model to observations we make" (1988, p. 9). Hawking's main interest is creating theories that explain the origin and structure of the universe, but his definition holds for psychology as well. Psychologists are interested in that part of the universe that has to do with behavior and the mind.

According to Hawking, a good theory must satisfy three requirements:

1. It must accurately describe a large body of observations as simply as possible.
2. It must make definite predictions of the results of future observations.
3. It must be stated in such a way that it can be disproved if it is incorrect.

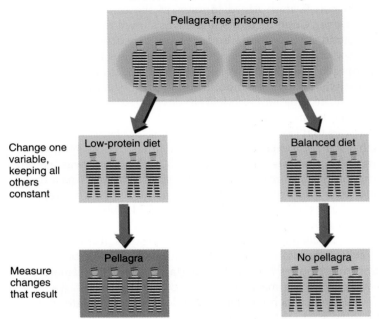

Q: Does low-protein diet cause pellagra?

Pellagra-free prisoners

Change one variable, keeping all others constant

Low-protein diet

Balanced diet

Measure changes that result

Pellagra

No pellagra

FIGURE 2.2
The key to the design of Goldberger's pellagra experiment was that only one variable, diet, was changed and everything else was held constant. The result—the prisoners who consumed the poor diet got pellagra—enabled Goldberger to conclude that there is a cause-and-effect relationship between diet and pellagra.

Notice that all three requirements link theory to actual or potential observations. This dependence on observation is what we mean when we say a science is empirical.

According to Hawking's criteria, a theory may be plausible, elegant, and intellectually satisfying, but its ultimate test is whether it *explains* observations that have already been made, *predicts* future observations, and is capable of being *disproved* by observations that fail to support it. Does this mean that if a theory meets all of these requirements it provides a true and correct representation of that part of the universe it is attempting to explain? The answer to this question is "Not necessarily." A theory can meet all three requirements and still be incomplete or incorrect.

Consider, for example, the theory of the universe proposed by Claudius Ptolemy in the second century A.D. Ptolemy proposed that the earth was situated at the center of the universe and that the other planets, sun, and stars revolved around the earth. This model of the universe made perfect sense when it was proposed. For one thing, it explained the data from people's senses, which certainly indicated that the earth stayed stationary while the other celestial objects moved. Didn't the planets, sun, moon, and stars move across the sky? In addition, the theory did a good job of predicting the movements of the heavenly objects as they were observed by the naked eye. This predictive power was, in fact, accurate enough to be used as a basis of navigation for explorers such as Columbus. True, some astronomers did report irregularities in the motions of the planets that weren't predicted by Ptolemy's theory. In principle, enough contrary observations would have disproved the theory (Hawking's third criterion). However, subsequent astronomers were able to explain the known inconsistencies by introducing correction factors that left the essence of the theory intact.

Ptolemy's model of the universe was therefore a "good theory" based on Hawking's criteria, although the need for more and more correction factors began to make it less elegant and simple. Eventually, Nicolaus Copernicus (1473–1543) attacked the very basis of the theory by asserting that the earth moves through space and is not, therefore, the center of the universe. At first this theory was not significantly better at explaining observations than Ptolemy's, and it had the added disadvantage of seeming to conflict with religious and philosophical beliefs that placed humans at the center of the universe. In the long run, however, Copernicus's scheme was shown to do a better job of explaining and predicting observations, and Ptolemy's theory was abandoned.

The story of Ptolemy and Copernicus illustrates that the role of a theory is to do the best job possible of explaining and predicting observations—but that theories are always subject to modifications and even abandonment as new observations or more satisfying models are developed.

The same is true in psychology. Like other scientists, psychologists adopt and use theories that later are modified or replaced. For example, for years it was believed that schizophrenia, a severe mental illness whose symptoms include experiencing hallucinations and losing touch with reality, was caused by conditions in the family. According to this idea, schizophrenia was a disorder caused by mothers who were cold and uncaring toward their children. However, researchers probing schizophrenia at the biological level of analysis have uncovered more and more evidence that schizophrenia is genetically determined and that it causes defects in the operation of the person's brain. Today the dominant theory of schizophrenia maintains that the disease has a biological origin—an explanation that implies a very different approach to treatment of the disease than if it were caused primarily by family conditions.

You will see in this book that psychological theories are continually evolving. Nevertheless, at each stage theories help us impose order on what would otherwise be a body of confusing data, even if those theories are sometimes disconfirmed, modified, or rethought in light of new observations, disconfirming results, or new ways of thinking.

We will also be discussing theories that differ in the scope of what they attempt to explain. Some, like Sigmund Freud's theory, which we will discuss in Chapter 15, attempt to explain the vast scope of human behavior. But most psychological theories are narrower than Freud's. By focusing on explaining a restricted set of behaviors such as color vision, decision making, or memory, they lend themselves more readily to being tested empirically. Whatever their scope, however, psychological theories share with other scientific theories the goal of placing many individual facts into a larger framework, suggesting predictions that lead to further research and stating propositions that can, in principle, be disproved.

Like other sciences, psychology sometimes advances ideas that challenge accepted ways of thinking. At times we—no less than the people of Western Europe in Copernicus's day or in the time of Darwin—may find some of our beliefs challenged by the results of psychological research. Psychology's commitment is to submit ideas about behavior to the demanding logic of science, and to abide by the verdict of observation. How psychologists go about this work is our next topic.

Posing Questions About Behavior: Methods of Psychological Research

Although psychology shares a common outlook with other scientific disciplines, it has some unique procedures and concerns. This uniqueness stems from psychology's specific subject matter—human behavior in all its variability and complexity—and the fact that behavior can be studied at the various levels of analysis introduced in Chapter 1. To apply the logic of the scientific approach to human behavior, psychologists have had to develop their own tactics for conducting research. These tactics fall into two broad categories: (1) observational methods, used to describe behavioral phenomena, and (2) experimental methods, used to probe cause-and-effect relationships.

Observational Methods: Ways to Describe Behavior

You can observe a lot by just watching.

Yogi Berra

Baseball player and coach Yogi Berra's statement is funny because of its choice of words, but it is also true. Watching what is going on can uncover important facts about behavior. Of course, there is much more to scientific observation than *just* watching. Careful, accurate observation requires special techniques designed to reveal specific aspects of phenomena. In psychology the most important of these are naturalistic observation, case studies, and surveys.

Naturalistic observation.   In **naturalistic observation** a researcher systematically observes behavior without intervening directly in it. The word "naturalistic" is used because behavior is allowed to unfold in the setting in which it would normally occur. An example of naturalistic observation is an experiment set up by Mary Main and Carol George (1985). These researchers were interested in the effects of physical abuse on children's reactions to another, distressed, child. For the purpose of research, they refined their interest to one specific question: "Are young children who have been battered less likely to show concern for a distressed child?" To answer this question, they observed two groups of children 1 to 3 years old. One group came from a day-care center for battered children, the other from a center serving disadvantaged families. All the children came from similarly disadvantaged families, but only those in the "battered" group had been abused.

To be useful, scientific observations must be as precise and objective as possible. In this case trained raters, each observing an individual child, carefully recorded the child's social behaviors. Based on a number of such observations for each child, Main and George were able to determine how the children responded to other children's distress (crying or other signs of fright or panic). The results, shown in Figure 2.3, indicate that there was a significant difference between the groups: abused children often responded to another child's distress with fear and aggression, whereas nonabused children rarely responded in that way.

The value of naturalistic observations like those of Main and George is that the results are firmly grounded in the richness of everyday behavior. These observations can define real-world variables that psychologists may want to probe further with experimental studies. Naturalistic observation is also the source of ideas for theories. We only have to remember Darwin's observations in the Galápagos to appreciate how keen observation can lead to important theoretical ideas. For example, Main and George's research revealed that young children who have been abused respond to distress in much the same way that abusing adults do, suggesting the hypothesis that these children's experiences with abuse may predispose them to become abusers themselves.

In addition, naturalistic observation is the only way certain behaviors can be studied. Clearly, Main and George could not ethically study the effects of battering on children by taking two groups of children and arranging to have one group battered, while holding all other variables constant. They could, however, use observation to study the effects of battering as it occurs in real life. Thus, naturalistic observation is a tool for studying behaviors that researchers cannot manipulate in the laboratory. At the same time, it shares with all other observational

Naturalistic observation of children's behavior in a preschool setting

FIGURE 2.3
Results of the Main and George experiment on how abused and nonabused children respond to other children in distress. Not only were the abused children much more likely than the nonabused children to respond with distress, aggression, or anger, but they never showed concern.

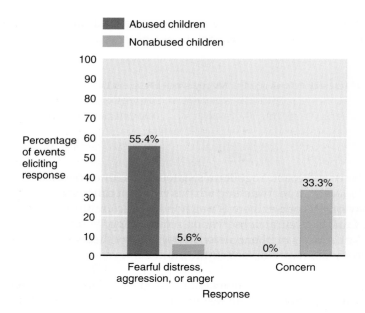

Jean Piaget, whose observations of young children led to his influential theory of cognitive development

techniques the limitation that it cannot establish cause-and-effect relationships (recall the health experts' ideas about the causes of pellagra).

Case studies.   **Case studies** are in-depth observations of the history and behavior of an individual subject. This type of observation is widely used in clinical settings to develop detailed information that can be used to diagnose and treat persons with psychological disorders. These clinical case studies usually include information about one patient's past history, her or his complaints, the results of psychological tests and interviews, and the course of therapy. But case studies are not only used in describing clinical patients; they also play an important role in the advancement of psychological knowledge. For example, Sigmund Freud's theory of personality and his conception of the role of the unconscious in human behavior were based on intensive case studies of a small number of his patients. Another example of case studies that led to a theory is the work of the Swiss developmental psychologist Jean Piaget, whose influential theory of cognitive development was based largely on his careful observations of his three children as they were growing up. Here, for example, is his description of his daughter Jacqueline's behavior at the age of 7 months, 28 days:

> Jacqueline tries to grasp a celluloid duck on top of her quilt. She almost catches it, shakes herself and the duck slides down beside her. It falls very close to her hand but behind a fold in the sheet. Jacqueline's eyes have followed the movement, she has even followed it with her outstretched hand. But as soon as the duck has disappeared—nothing more! It does not occur to her to search behind the fold of the sheet, which would be very easy to do [Piaget, 1937/1954, p. 36].

From observations such as this one Piaget proposed that children do not develop what he called *object permanence*, the realization that a hidden object still exists, until around their second birthday. This is just one part of Piaget's wide-ranging theory that relates biological age to changes in the way children think.

Case studies, in narrowing their focus to one person, go into more depth than naturalistic observation and are, therefore, well suited to probing questions about the details of individual behavior. As applied to research, case studies both suggest hypotheses for further study and provide information from individual cases that can be used to test the predictions of an existing theory. A specific limitation of such studies is their lack of generalizability: because individuals are so different, conclusions that hold for one don't necessarily hold for others.

Surveys and inventories.   Whereas case studies allow researchers to study just a few individuals in depth, **surveys** and **inventories** permit them to collect information from large numbers of people about their attitudes and behavior. Public opinion polls asking how people intend to vote are examples of surveys, as are the Kinsey Institute's studies asking people to describe their sexual behavior (Kinsey, Pomeroy, & Martin, 1948; Kinsey et al., 1953). Inventories usually refer to instruments such as personality tests that measure people's traits, or tests designed to measure people's abilities or attitudes about themselves.

Surveys and inventories are well suited to determining the basic characteristics of populations of people. The data they generate can be used to identify variables for further study and to test the predictions of theories. Like all observational methods, they may suggest ideas about causal relationships by uncovering associations between variables (for example, a Kinsey survey might find an association between sexual behavior and marital satisfaction), but they cannot establish that a causal relationship exists. To test ideas about direct causes, psychologists—like other scientists—turn to experiments.

Experimental Studies: Procedures for Determining Causation

Earlier in this chapter we saw how Goldberger solved the riddle of what was causing pellagra by following the basic rule of experimentation: he changed one variable while keeping all other relevant variables constant. The need to observe this basic rule accounts for most of the complexities you will encounter as you read about the results of psychological experiments. The logic underlying this research is, however, straightforward. To appreciate what psychologists are up to when they design and report on experiments, let's dissect a typical experimental study.

The anatomy of an experiment.   Does playing violent video games cause children to behave more aggressively? To explore this question, Nicola Schutte and her co-workers (Schutte et al., 1988) designed an experiment that would allow them to isolate the effect of playing violent video games on children's behavior. To generate the basic plan of the experiment, called the **experimental design,** the researchers had to make a number of decisions. The steps they followed in creating their experiment illustrate the principal elements in experimental studies.

Step 1: Formulating the problem.   The first step in any research effort is to define a problem for study. Noting the pervasiveness of video games in American culture (over 93% of children sometimes play them [Dominick, 1984]), Schutte wondered what effect these games might have on children's behavior. To find out, she needed to refine her question into a specific idea—called a *hypothesis*—that she could test experimentally.

Step 2: Stating the hypothesis.   The **hypothesis** is a precise statement of the predicted outcome of an experiment. It is often derived from the experimenter's "hunch" about what will happen and from the results of other experiments. Noting that a number of previous experiments had shown that children imitate aggressive models (Bandura, Ross, & Ross, 1961) and that watching television can affect children's behavior (Comstock et al., 1978), Schutte formulated the follow-

Does playing violent video games influence children's subsequent behavior?

ing hypothesis: *Aggressive behavior will be more likely to occur following the playing of a violent video game than a nonviolent video game.*

Step 3: Identifying the relevant variables.   The variables relevant to a particular experiment can usually be determined by referring to the relationship described by the hypothesis. For example, for Schutte's hypothesis that playing violent video games will increase aggressive behavior in young children, the relevant variables are the violence of the video games and the aggressiveness of the children's behavior.

All experiments involve two different types of variables. The **independent variable** is the variable controlled by the experimenter in order to observe what happens when that variable is changed. In Goldberger's study of pellagra, the independent variable was protein in the diet. In the video game experiment the independent variable was the violence of the video game. The **dependent variable** is the variable that is hypothesized to change as a result of manipulations of the independent variable (it *depends* on changes in the independent variable). In Goldberger's experiment, the dependent variable was the occurrence of pellagra. In Schutte's study, the dependent variable was the level of the children's aggressive behavior. In general, independent variables in psychological experiments are usually the conditions controlled by the experimenter, and dependent variables are the resulting behaviors.

Step 4: Operationally defining the variables.   Having determined the relevant variables, the researcher must determine their operational definitions. An **operational definition** is a statement of the procedures used to create the independent variable or to measure the dependent variable. Operationally defining the variables is one of the most crucial steps in psychological research, because the way they are defined determines what the subject experiences and how the subject's behaviors are measured. Most important, precisely specifying operational definitions makes it possible for other experimenters to repeat an experiment using the same procedures and for us to better evaluate exactly what the results mean. (See Measurement & Methodology, "Operational Definitions and the Outcome of Experiments.")

For her experiment, Schutte decided to operationally define the independent variable as "playing the violent Karateka video game for five minutes" or "playing the nonviolent Jungle Hunt video game for five minutes." In Karateka, the "hero" kills villains by hitting or kicking them; in Jungle Hunt, the child's task is to make the hero swing from one vine to another at exactly the right time. Schutte operationally defined the dependent variable, aggressive behavior, as "the number of 30-second intervals during the five-minute play period in which each child pushes another child or hits or kicks toys."

Step 5: Selecting subjects.   Experimenters are usually interested in studying a particular type of subject: children, adults, or animals, for example. To create an experiment, it is also necessary to specifically define the **population** to which the researcher wants the results to apply. For example, if a researcher were interested in the effects of video games on children aged from 5 to 7 in the United States, the population would be all children of those ages in the United States. As often happens, this population is much too large for all of its members to be included in an experiment. In such cases researchers must pick a representative sample from the population to study.

Ideally, to make the sample representative of the population as a whole, the researcher selects subjects by means of **random sampling,** a procedure that ensures that any person in the population is equally likely to be chosen for the experiment. Using the random sampling technique increases the chances that the results obtained from the sample can be generalized to the population from which the sample was drawn. For the population of all U.S. children between ages 5 and 7, subjects would have to be selected from all areas of the country. This type of random sampling is often used in large-scale survey research such as national political polls and the surveys of TV-viewing behavior used to generate the ratings of television shows.

Although random sampling is the ideal, in psychological experiments it is often impossible to adhere strictly to this procedure. Think of the expense and time involved in randomly selecting subjects from different parts of the country and then flying them to one place to participate in an experiment. Because of such practical difficulties, experimenters must often use subjects not randomly sampled from a population, which makes it more difficult to know whether the results generalize to the larger population. There is always the chance that the subjects in the experiment have some special characteristics that affect the results obtained. One way to deal with this problem is to **replicate** the experiment, to repeat it using other subjects. Obtaining the same results in a number of replications increases confidence—not only in the results but also in their generalizability to a larger population.

In the video game study, Schutte decided to select her subjects from 5- to 7-year-old children in a day-care center. The fact that her sample cannot be guaranteed to be representative of all similarly aged children needs to be considered when interpreting her results.

Step 6: Creating experimental and control groups.   There are usually at least two groups in psychological experiments: an **experimental group,** which experiences the independent variable, and a **control group,** which does not. Because

MEASUREMENT & METHODOLOGY

Operational Definitions and the Outcome of Experiments

A researcher is designing an experiment to test the hypothesis that frustration leads to aggression. To test this hypothesis she needs to create operational definitions for the independent variable, frustration, and for the dependent variable, aggressive behavior. Operational definitions describe the *procedures* researchers use to create the independent variable and to measure the dependent variable. The independent variable should be described as a clearly stated procedure that can be easily repeated by other researcheres. Assuming that our researcher has created a good operational definition for frustration that enables her to create a group of highly frustrated experimental subjects and a group of unfrustrated control subjects, let's consider her next task: operationally defining the dependent variable.

The dependent variable should be specified as a behavior that can be precisely measured. With this criterion in mind, our researcher might consider three possible ways to define aggressive behavior:

Aggressive behavior can be measured by determining

- the number of aggressive words a subject remembers from a previously read list of both aggressive and neutral words

- the force with which a subject pounds a nail into a board
- the intensity of a subject's voice as he or she responds to questions asked by another person

Which of these operational definitions should the researcher choose? The success of her experiment—if we define success as demonstrating a relationship between the indenpendent and dependent variable—may depend on her choice. What if only one of these measures was affected by manipulating the independent variable? People in the experimental group might pound nails harder than those in the control group yet not talk louder or remember more aggressive words. If this were the case, choosing the intensity of nail pounding as the operational definition for aggression would demonstrate a relationship between frustration and aggression, but choosing loudness of speech or memory for aggressive words would not. Deciding on an operational definition is, therefore, one of the most important decisions an experimentor can make when designing an experiment.

the subjects in the control group have the same experience as those in the experimental group, except for experiencing the independent variable, comparing the results from the two groups indicates the effect of the independent variable. In this case, the experimental group plays a violent video game and the control group a nonviolent one.

When researchers set up experimental and control groups they follow the basic rule of experimentation by making sure that the only difference between them is whether or not the subjects are exposed to the independent variable. To do this, researchers place subjects in groups using **random assignment.** For example, each subject is given a number from a random number table. Those with odd numbers are assigned to one group, those with even to the other. Random assignment means that each person in the *sample* has an equal chance of being in the experimental or the control group.

Don't confuse random assignment with random sampling. Random sampling means picking people from the population to form the representative sample that will be used in the experiment. Random assignment means assigning subjects in the sample to the experimental and control groups (see Figure 2.4).

You can appreciate why random assignment is important if you consider that in any experiment the individual subjects will differ in a number of ways. For example, the children in Schutte's experiment differed in height, gender, hair color, and aggressiveness, among other things. Some of those variables, such as height and hair color, probably will not influence how aggressively the children behave after they play the video game. However, other variables, such as aggressiveness and perhaps gender (as boys are generally more aggressive than girls), could affect the children's behavior. These are called **extraneous variables—** variables in addition to the independent one that could influence the results of the experiment. Thus, if more naturally aggressive children were in the experimental group than in the control group, this extraneous variable would contaminate the results obtained.

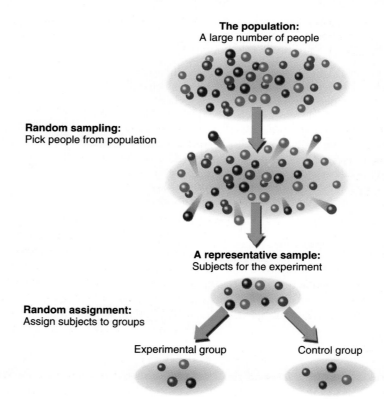

FIGURE 2.4
Random sampling and random assignment of subjects. Random sampling from the population results in a representative sample that is smaller than the population but contains a similar mix of people. Random assignment from the sample is used to create experimental and control groups.

Random assignment reduces the chances that the results will be affected by extraneous variables by ensuring that each subject has an equal chance of being in either group. Thus, any extraneous variables should be present in both groups to an approximately equal degree, effectively canceling each other out. In her experiment Schutte used random assignment to guard against the possibility that a large number of aggressive children would be assigned to one of the groups.

Although random assignment minimizes differences between the experimental and control groups, there is still a possibility that extraneous variables could differ between the groups. For example, in Schutte's experiment, half of the subjects were girls and half were boys. If the children were assigned randomly to the experimental and control groups regardless of gender, it is unlikely that an equal number of boys and girls would be assigned to each group. To appreciate this, consider the classic example of a random process, flipping a coin. Even though each flip has an equal chance of being heads or tails, we would not be surprised if, after 30 flips, we happened to have flipped 18 heads and 12 tails. Only in the very long run would the number of heads and tails even out. Similarly, if Schutte had used only random assignment in her experiment, she would probably have ended up with an unequal number of boys and girls in each group.

Because gender seemed to be a key extraneous variable, Schutte decided to ensure that an equal number of boys and girls were assigned to the experimental and control groups by using *matching*. Matching is a procedure in which subjects with the same qualities are paired, one subject from each pair being randomly assigned to the experimental group and the other to the control group. In Schutte's experiment, boys were paired and then randomly assigned to the groups, and girls were similarly paired and randomly assigned. In this way an equal number of girls and boys ended up in the experimental and control groups.

Step 7: Running the experiment and measuring the dependent variable.   Once subjects are assigned to their groups, it is time to run the experiment. In the video game experiment, subjects played either the violent or the nonviolent game and were then observed by trained raters who recorded their aggressive behaviors during the subsequent play period. The aggressiveness score—the dependent variable in this experiment—was the result.

Although we have been focusing on the single dependent variable of aggressive behavior in describing Schutte's experiment, it is possible to measure more than one dependent variable. For example, playing video games might have effects in addition to increasing aggression. In fact, Schutte hypothesized that playing the Jungle Hunt game might cause children to play more with a jungle swing toy that was available during their play period. She therefore had raters measure an additional dependent variable—frequency of playing with the jungle swing—and found that children in the control group did play with it more than the children in the experimental group.

Step 8: Analyzing the data and drawing conclusions.   The final step in an experiment is to analyze the raw data to see what conclusions can be drawn from them. In Schutte's experiment, the results indicated a difference in aggressiveness between the experimental and control groups (Figure 2.5). This would seem to support her hypothesis that playing violent video games increases children's aggressiveness. We will see in the next main section, "Drawing Conclusions from Psychological Research," that before we can be certain that the difference observed between groups is meaningful, we must run statistical tests to analyze the data further.

Schutte's video game experiment illustrates a relatively simple experimental design. Many variations on this design are possible, including experiments having more than one independent variable (for example, we could investigate

FIGURE 2.5

Results of Schutte's video game experiment. Children who played the violent game behaved much more aggressively afterward than did children who played the nonviolent game.

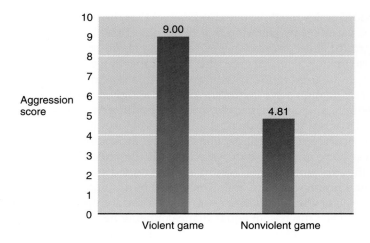

how the video game "sound track" affects aggression by having some subjects play the games with the sound turned off), and some in which subjects are used as their own controls (for example, we could have the same subject play both the violent and nonviolent games and compare aggressiveness after each game). The key point is that the same logic underlies all experiments regardless of the complexity of the experimental design. Figure 2.6 summarizes the eight steps in experimental design.

Field experiments.   The power of experimental studies lies in the experimenter's ability to precisely control the independent variable and to determine cause-and-effect relationships. But with this ability to control comes some artificiality. People do not carry out their day-to-day behavior in psychology laboratories, and the behavior that *can* be studied in the laboratory is obviously abstracted from the rich complexity of real-world behavior. For these reasons, some researchers have taken the experimental method outside of the laboratory in the form of field experiments. **Field experiments** combine experimental logic with the study of events as they take place in the natural environment.

Such an experiment was Alice Isen and Paula Levin's (1972) research, designed to investigate the hypothesis that if people are in a good mood they will be more likely to help others. In this experiment, which took place in a shopping mall, the independent variable was the subjects' mood and the dependent variable their helping behavior. To manipulate the subjects' mood, Isen and Levin placed a dime in the coin return of a pay phone used by subjects in the experimental group. (Phone calls cost ten cents in 1972.) Subjects in the control group also made a phone call but did not receive the unexpected dime. To test their subjects' willingness to help, the researchers had a female assistant drop a manila folder full of papers in the subject's path as he or she walked away from the phone.

What result would you predict? Do you think that a little good fortune like finding a dime would affect people's willingness to help a stranger? Of the 16 subjects in the experimental group who found the dime, 14 helped the woman pick up her papers. In contrast, only 1 of the 25 subjects in the control group helped the woman (Figure 2.7).

Isen and Levin's results were not new; others had shown that people are more likely to help when in a good mood (Aderman & Berkowitz, 1970). Previous experiments, however, had been done in a laboratory setting. Isen and Levin succeeded in showing that the laboratory results do, in fact, generalize to the real world.

Although field experiments provide results that are easier to generalize to the real world than are the results of laboratory experiments, field experiments

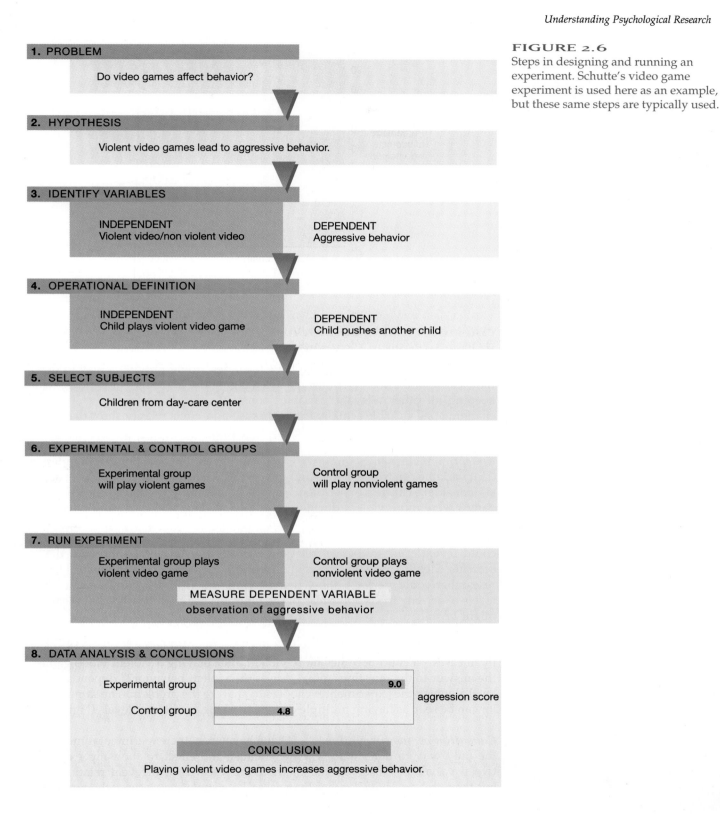

FIGURE 2.6
Steps in designing and running an experiment. Schutte's video game experiment is used here as an example, but these same steps are typically used.

have their limitations. The most serious is that it is difficult to control extraneous variables in field experiments. For example, Isen and Levin had no control over who used the pay phone in their experiment. Thus, more women than men may have used it, since there are more women in shopping malls during the day. Laboratory experiments, in contrast, enable the experimenter to control the variables in the experiment more easily.

FIGURE 2.7
Results of Isen and Levin's (1972) helping experiment. Subjects who found money in the pay phone were more likely to help the woman pick up her paper than were subjects who didn't find money.

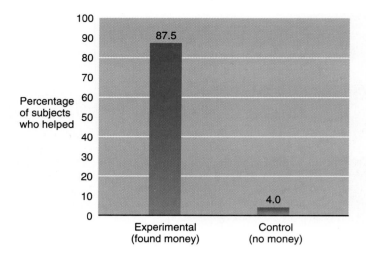

Percentage of subjects who helped

Experimental (found money): 87.5
Control (no money): 4.0

Field experiments are carried out in natural environments, such as shopping malls.

Causation and Correlation in Psychological Experiments

The experimental procedures we have been describing provide a way to determine cause-and-effect relationships by changing the independent variable while keeping all other relevant variables constant. It is important to realize that changing one variable actually triggers cause-and-effect relationships that can be studied at a number of different levels of analysis.

Causation and levels of analysis.   To understand how changing an independent variable can trigger cause-and-effect relationships at several levels of analysis, consider Schutte's experiment, in which children who played violent video games were more violent during a play period. This is a cause-and-effect relationship at the behavioral level of analysis, because Schutte was looking at how changing the video game affected observable behavior. But the same experiment could reveal cause-and-effect relationships at other levels of analysis if the researcher chose to measure different dependent variables. At the biological level a researcher could perhaps show that playing violent video games causes high levels of activity in specific areas of the brain. At the cognitive level a researcher might be able to show that playing violent video games makes young children think about fighting, or perhaps makes them angry.

The important point here is that whereas the ultimate *behavior* is the same in all cases—a child becomes more violent after playing a violent video game—the answer to the question "What causes the violent behavior?" depends on the level at which the experimenter chooses to analyze the problem. The same behavior can be seen as having multiple causes, working at different levels (Figure 2.8).

Causation versus correlation.   As we have seen, the experimental method is the only way to determine whether a cause-and-effect relationship exists between variables. Observational methods of research also reveal relationships, but they are *correlational* rather than *causal*. A **correlation** occurs when two variables are related to each other so that specific values of one are associated with specific values of the other. (See Measurement & Methodology, "The Correlation Coefficient" on pp. 52–53.) Some correlational relationships do in fact turn out to be ones of cause and effect, but others do not.

To appreciate the difference between correlation and causality, take another look at Goldberger's study of the causes of pellagra. Before Goldberger solved the puzzle of pellagra, the experts had noted that people with pellagra did not have indoor plumbing. This observation led them to conclude that poor sanitary

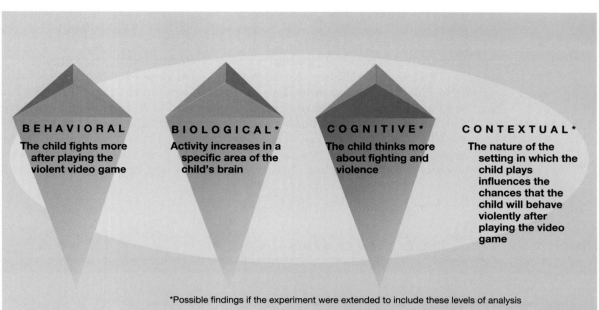

FIGURE 2.8
Levels of analysis applied to aggression in Schutte's video game experiment

BEHAVIORAL

The child fights more after playing the violent video game

BIOLOGICAL*

Activity increases in a specific area of the child's brain

COGNITIVE*

The child thinks more about fighting and violence

CONTEXTUAL*

The nature of the setting in which the child plays influences the chances that the child will behave violently after playing the video game

*Possible findings if the experiment were extended to include these levels of analysis

conditions caused pellagra. In reaching that conclusion, the experts committed the error of inferring cause and effect from a correlational relationship. The problem is that the existence of a relationship between two variables does not guarantee that one variable *causes* the other. Although poor sanitary conditions are correlated with pellagra, the real cause of pellagra is poor diet, which also happens to be correlated with poor sanitary conditions (Figure 2.9). The only way to confirm that a relationship is one of cause and effect is to do an experiment in which one variable is changed and all other relevant variables are held constant.

Can you think of correlational relationships from your everyday experience that are not cause-and-effect relationships? How about umbrellas and rain: have you ever noticed that on days when people carry umbrellas it is more likely to rain? You certainly would not conclude that carrying umbrellas *causes* rain. People are carrying umbrellas because they have listened to a weather report or looked at the sky. The real cause-and-effect relationship in this case is "the threat of rain causes people to carry umbrellas."

Another of my favorite correlational relationships is the relationship be-

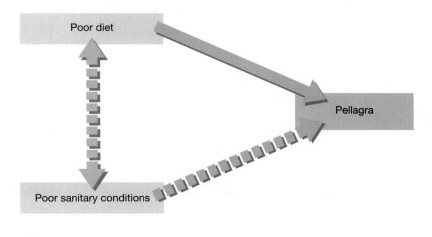

FIGURE 2.9
Relationships between variables in the Goldberger pellagra experiment. Correlational relationships are indicated by a dashed arrow; the solid arrow signifies a cause-and-effect relationship.

tween the number of people waiting at a bus stop and the time it takes for the bus to come. Generally, the more people at the bus stop, the more quickly the bus comes. Does this mean that increasing the number of people at a bus stop will *cause* the bus to come? How could you experimentally test this hypothesis?

As a final illustration, consider Main and George's study of battered children. This study demonstrated a relationship between children who were battered and the tendency to respond to another child's distress in an aggressive, nonsupportive way. Does this mean that battering causes children to respond aggressively to others' distress? It is certainly possible that a cause-and-effect relationship exists between these two variables. But it is also possible that the cause lies elsewhere. For example, children might react negatively to others' distress if

MEASUREMENT & METHODOLOGY

The Correlation Coefficient

When two variables are related to each other so that changes in one tend to be associated with changes in the other, there is a correlation between them. You can get an intuitive idea of the meaning of correlation by looking at the left scatterplot in Figure A. This graph plots hypothetical data relating intelligence quotient (IQ) to grade point average (GPA). Each point represents the IQ and GPA scores of one individual. By plotting the data for many individuals, we can see that there is a relationship between IQ and GPA. Reading from left to right, the upward slope of the scatterplot indicates that people with higher IQs tend to have higher GPAs. If this relation-

ship did not exist, the points on the scatterplot would tend to be "all over the map" instead of showing the definite grouping and slope we see on the left in Figure A.

The relationship between IQ and GPA is an example of a positive correlation. A **positive correlation** indicates that *increases* in one variable are associated with *increases* in the other. It is also possible for variables to show a negative correlation. A **negative correlation** indicates that *increases* in one variable are associated with *decreases* in the other. For example, there is a relationship between IQ and the number of errors a person makes on a test, but

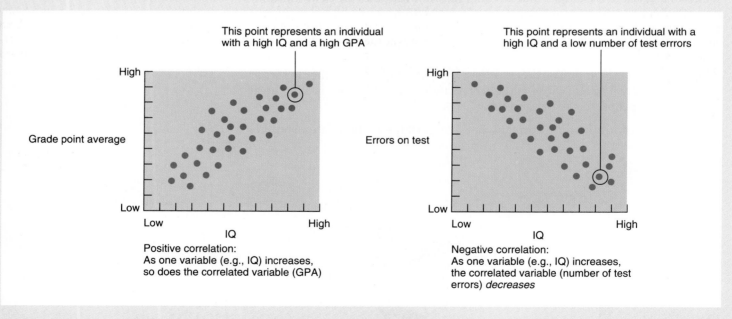

This point represents an individual with a high IQ and a high GPA

Positive correlation:
As one variable (e.g., IQ) increases, so does the correlated variable (GPA)

This point represents an individual with a high IQ and a low number of test errrors

Negative correlation:
As one variable (e.g., IQ) increases, the correlated variable (number of test errors) *decreases*

FIGURE A

they have watched their father abuse their mother for acting distressed (Figure 2.10). This interaction between the father and mother, which could occur in households in which the father also abuses the child, might be the real cause of the behavior measured by Main and George.

The distinction between correlation and causation is a key to interpreting the results of psychological research, and one that is often obscured in accounts of research you encounter in the popular news media. Keep in mind that, though both observational and experimental studies provide valuable information about behavior, only experimental studies allow us to infer cause and effect. It is therefore important to avoid the mistake the pellagra "experts" made, of inferring cause from a correlational relationship.

the relationship is *inverse:* people with higher IQs would tend to make *fewer* errors on a test, as indicated by the downward slope of the right scatterplot in Figure A.

When two variables are related to each other, that relationship, indicated by the correlation between them, can be more or less strong. The weaker the correlation, the more "exceptions to the rule" there are in the data (for instance, some people with high IQs will make many test errors, despite the general tendency to the contrary). The strength of the relationship between two variables can be precisely calculated by means of a mathematical formula and expressed in a number called the **correlation coefficient** (denoted by the letter *r*) You will encounter this number when you read about the results of correlational research in this text.

Correlation coefficients can have values of between +1.00 and –1.00. When you read these numbers, keep in mind that the *sign* (plus or minus) indicates whether the correlation is positive or negative, whereas the *magnitude* of *r* (ignoring the sign) indicates how strong the relationship is. The closer *r* is to either +1.00 or –1.00 (that is, the farther away it is from zero), the stronger is the relationship between the variables (Figure C). Thus, correlation coefficients of +.75 and –.75 denote relationships that are *equally strong, but opposite in direction.* By the same token, a correlation of –.75 is *stronger* than a correlation of +.50.

In psychological research, most correlations of interest fall in the range of plus or minus .30 to .80. It is rare for correlations to approach "perfect" correlations of +1.00 or –1.00, because there are usually exceptions to any relationship that decrease the magnitude of the correlation. For example, the correlation between people's height and weight is about +.60. This means that tall people tend to be heavier than short people, but not always—there are some thin, tall people and some short, heavy people. Similarly, the correlation coefficients for the hypothetical data in Figures A and B are about +.50 and –.50, respectively—indicating moderately strong tendencies for IQ to be associated with higher GPA and lower numbers of test errors.

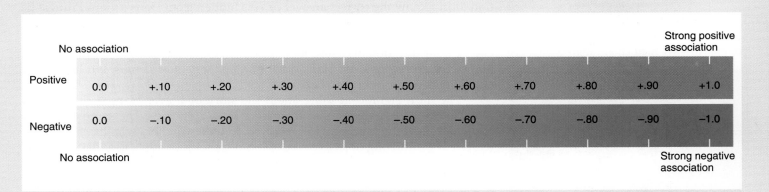

FIGURE B

FIGURE 2.10

What causes a child from an abusive home to respond aggressively to another's distress? Main and George's result suggests that this response is caused by the child having been battered by the father, but there are other possibilities. For example, the response could be caused by the child having watched the father abuse the mother. The relationships between all these variables are correlational, as indicated by the dashed arrows. To determine cause and effect, we would have to design and run an experiment.

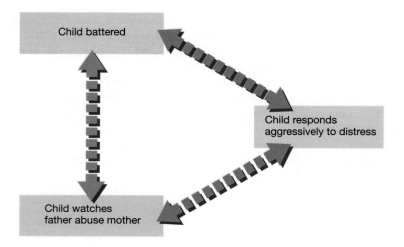

Bias in Psychological Research

In addition to being careful not to mistake correlation for causation, researchers also must take precautions to avoid errors that can occur during the experiment. Two ways these errors can occur are by the presence of researcher bias or by the presence of subject bias.

Researcher bias.   The results of research are determined by more than just the research design. They are also determined by the way the researcher runs the experiment. The reason is that even in well-designed research, the researchers' behavior can potentially affect their results—for example, researchers may emit cues that influence their subjects' behavior.

One of the most famous cases of such a situation is the horse who, at the turn of the century, earned the name "Clever Hans" by his ability to do arithmetic (Figure 2.11). When his master posed a problem, Hans began tapping the ground with his hoof and would stop at exactly the correct number. People were amazed at Hans's abilities, especially because he could not only add but could also subtract, multiply, and divide with equal ease.

What was behind Hans's amazing performance? This question was answered after a series of investigations by the German psychologist Oscar Pfungst (1911). Pfungst found that Hans's ability decreased if the person asking the question didn't know the correct answer or was hidden from Hans's view. Pfungst finally discovered the visual cues that tipped off Hans about the correct answer. Hans began tapping just after his questioners tilted their heads forward at the end of their question and stopped tapping as they straightened up in anticipation of the correct answer. Hans was not a mathematical genius, but he was an excellent observer of human behavior.

The most significant thing about the story of Clever Hans is that Hans's questioners were unaware that they were providing cues. The same thing can happen in modern psychological research. Even researchers who have every intention of conducting objective research can sometimes emit cues that bias their results. For example, consider a hypothetical investigation to determine whether the drug imipramine helps people who are suffering from depression. The experimenter uses two groups of depressed people: the experimental group receives daily doses of the drug, whereas the control group receives a *placebo*, a pill containing no active ingredients. The placebo is used because it has been shown that taking *any* pill—even one with no active ingredients—often alleviates a person's symptoms (Weisenberg, 1977). The test of the effectiveness of the imipramine, then, is whether it provides more relief than the placebo.

Clever Hans, the horse that was reputed to be able to solve mathematical problems

Of course, the experimenter also needs a way of measuring depression. How does she determine just how depressed each subject is? One way might be to rate the subjects' degree of depression based on their responses to interview questions such as "Has there been any change in your sleep patterns lately?" or "Tell me about some of the things that have happened to you in the last week." There is a danger here, however, that the interviewer might unintentionally influence the results. If, for example, she knows that John received the drug, she may unintentionally smile more and ask the questions in a happier, more upbeat tone of voice than when interviewing Sam, whom she knows received the placebo. Research has shown that even subtle differences in a researcher's behavior can have a great effect on a subject's responses (Rosenthal, 1966). If John's responses are caused by the interviewer's upbeat manner he will appear less depressed, as the hypothesis predicts, when in fact he may not be.

One solution to this problem is to standardize procedures across all conditions. For example, having subjects respond to tape-recorded questions rather than to a live experimenter would ensure that the same tone of voice was used for the experimental and control groups. Another solution is to use a **blind interviewing procedure,** in which the interviewer doesn't know which group the subject is in. **Blind scoring procedures** have also been used to eliminate bias. The experimenter might, for example, decide to evaluate the effect of the drug and placebo by having a trained observer watch videotapes of subjects interacting with people in a small group and score their behavior on such dimensions as how animated they are or how they smile in response to others. To prevent bias, the person observing the video should be "blind" to which subjects received the drug and which didn't.

Because of these considerations, well-designed psychological research always takes into account the possibility of researcher bias and institutes procedures such as blind interviewing and blind scoring to prevent it.

FIGURE 2.12
The setup used for Perky's experiment. Subjects did not realize that a faint image was being projected onto a screen, so they thought they were imagining what they saw.

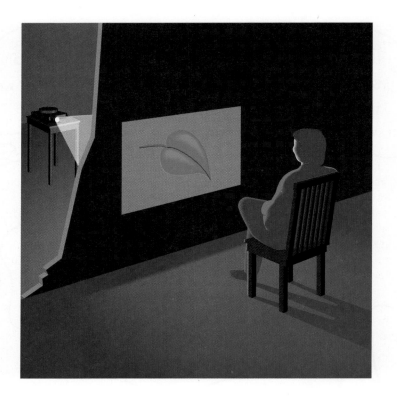

Subject bias.   Just as researchers' expectations can bias the results of a study, so can the subjects'. One form of subject bias occurs when subjects try to figure out the purpose of a study and then, based on what they think the purpose is, behave in either a cooperative or an uncooperative manner. This can occur in an experiment, in which subjects may alter their responses to the experimental conditions; during observational research, if subjects alter their behavior because they know they are being watched; or in surveys, in which subjects may tailor their answers to what they think the researcher wants to hear.

The most common source of subject bias is caused by **demand characteristics**— characteristics of the situation that suggest how the subject *should* behave. A subject who detects these demand characteristics will often heed that message and try to be a "good subject." For example, suppose a researcher wants to determine how alcohol affects people's inhibitions. If one group of subjects drinks an alcoholic-tasting beverage, its members may decide that they are supposed to act drunk. Demand characteristics are a particularly troublesome problem in hypnosis research, as some subjects may pretend to be hypnotized in order to make the experiment "work."

To prevent demand characteristics from affecting the results, researchers often use **deception** to hide the purpose of the research. For example, experiments on the effects of alcohol on behavior often use vodka mixed with orange juice or some other beverage that masks the faint vodka taste. If precautions such as this are taken so the subject doesn't know which group he or she is in and if, in addition, the experimenter doesn't know what group the subject is in, the procedure is called a **double-blind procedure.** Such a procedure guards against both experimenter and subject bias. Once the data are collected, of course, the experimenter does have access to information indicating the group to which each subject belongs.

Because of the problem of subject bias, deception is often essential to the success of psychological research. To achieve this deception psychologists may create cover stories to mask the real purpose of the study. For example, in an early experiment in cognitive psychology, Cheves Perky (1910) demonstrated that people can confuse mental images with actual visual images. She did this by seating subjects in a room facing what appeared to be a white wall. She asked them to imagine images such as a tomato, a banana, and a leaf while looking at the wall. In reality, the wall was a rear-projection screen onto which Perky's assistant projected extremely faint slides of the objects the subject was trying to imagine (Figure 2.12). As the assistant slowly increased the brightness of the images, the subjects began to report that they were, in fact, imagining images. In fact, not one of Perky's 24 subjects became aware that the images were being projected on the screen. They all thought they were creating the images in their minds, thereby supporting Perky's hypothesis that people can confuse mental images with those created by actual visual stimuli.

Looking back through this section, it becomes clear that our original description of the steps involved in designing and running an experiment was only a starting point. There is much more to psychological research than simply deciding on experimental and control groups, assigning subjects to those groups, and running the experiment. Within each step, psychologists must take great care to guarantee that procedures are designed so as to uncover relationships that may exist as well as that the basic rule of experimentation is followed. If an experimenter wants to change *only* the independent variable, she or he must be sure that the subject's behavior is not affected by either researcher bias or subject bias. (Similar issues can occur in observational research. For an example, see Measurement & Methodology, "Observing Behavior Without Influencing It.")

Drawing Conclusions from Psychological Research

We have described how data are collected in psychological research. But without analysis and interpretation, the data have no meaning. How do researchers decide what conclusions can be drawn from their data? Usually they follow a two-step process. First they *describe* the data, using descriptive statistics, and then they *draw conclusions* about what the data mean, with the aid of inferential statistics.

MEASUREMENT & METHODOLOGY

Observing Behavior Without Influencing It

Because psychologists seek to understand behavior as it occurs naturally, they must design their studies so that the results can be generalized to the "real world." This is always a concern of psychologists who do laboratory research, as the laboratory environment is always more or less artificial. But researchers who make naturalistic observations must also take care to ensure that the very act of observing behavior doesn't change it. People who know they are being observed often become self-conscious and change their behavior.

One example of how researchers take these precautions is a study by I. Eibl-Eibesfeldt (1973). The study was designed to discover whether there is a signaling code—a language without words—common to people of all cultures. To find out, Eibl-Eibesfeldt decided to film people in many different cultures as they interacted with one another. The danger was that people would act for the camera instead of behaving naturally. To get around this problem, Eibl-Eibesfeldt used an "angle camera" with a special lens that was actually taking pictures off to the side instead of in the direction it appeared to be pointing. With this camera, he was able to film people without their knowledge.

With the aid of the angle camera, Eibl-Eibesfeldt was able to demonstrate many similarities in people's facial expressions across cultures. For example, he showed that Europeans, South American Indians, Balinese, and African Bushmen all use an "eyebrow flash" as a form of greeting.

FIGURE 2.13
Data from hypothetical SAT experiment

Scores of the Experimental Group

436 455 463 474 477 481 482 496 496 497 501 507 517 523 523 527 527 529 532 535 543 545 545 549 551 555 557 557 568 572 579 580 588 607 609

Scores of the Control Group

422 440 442 452 462 464 469 471 472 472 479 483 492 494 500 506 506 507 512 514 515 518 520 528 531 535 540 540 545 550 551 565 578 583 602

Descriptive Statistics: Describing the Results

Consider a hypothetical experiment designed to see whether taking a special SAT preparatory course improves a person's score on the College Boards. Everyone in the experimental group takes the course and studies from a book, and everyone in the control group studies from the book only. Both groups then take the SAT test, with the results shown in Figure 2.13. How can we make sense of these raw data? The first step is to calculate **descriptive statistics**, statistics that organize and summarize the data. The two most commonly used types of descriptive statistics are measures of central tendency and measures of variability.

Measures of central tendency.   **Measures of central tendency** result in a single number that is representative of an entire set of scores. Two important measures of central tendency are the mean, or arithmetical average, and the median. The **mean** is the sum of the scores divided by the total number of scores. The mean for the two groups in our experiment is 528.1 for the experimental group and 507.4 for the control group (Figure 2.14).

The **median** is the middle score when all scores are listed in numerical order from highest to lowest. The score halfway down the list—so that half of the scores are higher than that score and half lower—is the median. In our experiment the medians are 529 and 507 for the experimental and control groups, respectively.

Calculating the mean and the median reduces a large mass of data into a single number that can be used to compare two or more groups. The mean is more commonly used, except when a few scores are very different from any of

FIGURE 2.14
Determining the median and mean from raw data

		Scores = 35
		Sum = 18,485
Scores of the Experimental Group	↓ *Median* = 529	Mean = $\frac{18,485}{35}$ = 528.1

436 455 463 474 477 481 482 496 496 497 501 507 517 523 523 527 529 529 532 535 543 545 545 549 551 555 557 557 568 572 579 580 588 607 609

		Scores = 35
		Sum = 17,760
Scores of the Control Group	↓ *Median* = 507	Mean = $\frac{17,760}{35}$ = 507.4

422 440 442 452 462 464 469 471 472 472 479 483 492 494 500 506 506 507 512 514 515 518 520 528 531 535 540 540 545 550 551 565 578 583 602

the others. For example, replacing the three lowest scores in the experimental group with 300 would reduce the mean from 528.1 to 515.1, while leaving the median unchanged. In a situation like this, researchers use the median, which is less affected by extreme scores and therefore results in a number more representative of the overall data.

Measures of variability. **Measures of variability** indicate how scattered the data are. Data are scattered because people are different from one another, so they differ in their responses when measured under the same conditions. Just as students in a class typically earn a wide range of grades on an exam, people in psychological experiments typically respond in a variety of ways.

The simplest measure of variability is the **range,** which is the difference between the highest and lowest scores. In the SAT example, the range for the experimental group is 609 – 436 = 173. If the high and low scores were more extreme, the range would be larger, reflecting the greater variability.

Another measure of variability is the **standard deviation,** which is calculated using a mathematical formula that takes into account the extent to which each score in a group differs from the group mean. If most of the scores are close to the mean, the standard deviation is small. If the scores vary widely from the mean, the standard deviation is larger. The standard deviation is the most popular measure of variance. One of its advantages over the range is that it is not as affected by extreme scores.

Measures of central tendency and measures of variability enable researchers to describe their results in a few easy-to-understand numbers. Another way to describe results is to create a **frequency distribution,** such as the one in Figure 2.15, which indicates how many subjects fall within narrow ranges of scores. These distributions are much easier to understand than all of the individual scores, and plotting the frequency distributions in a graph (Figure 2.16) makes it possible to visualize the differences between the experimental and control groups. The graph indicates that the scores from the experimental group tend to be slightly higher than the scores for the control group, but that there is a great deal of overlap between the scores of the two groups.

Having calculated descriptive statistics and plotted distributions for our

Number of Subjects

Scores	Experimental	Control
410–429	0	1
430–449	1	2
450–469	2	4
470–489	4	5
490–509	5	6
510–529	6	6
530–549	6	5
550–569	5	3
570–589	4	2
590–609	2	1

FIGURE 2.15
Frequency distribution of hypothetical SAT data indicating the number of subjects in the experimental and control groups that fall within each interval of scores

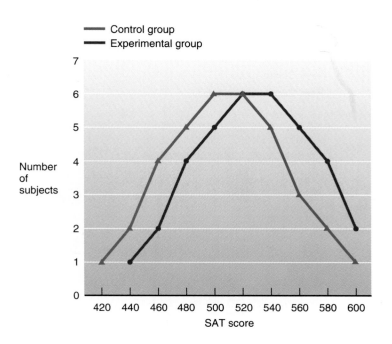

FIGURE 2.16
Graph of the frequency distributions for experimental and control groups in the SAT experiment

two groups, what can we conclude? Because the mean SAT score for the experimental group is higher than the mean score for the control group, we might be tempted to conclude that the preparatory course caused the higher SAT scores. But it is also possible that the difference between the two groups could have occurred by chance.

You can appreciate how two groups can differ just by chance if you imagine the following demonstration: Write numbers from 1 to 20 on 20 pieces of paper and mix them up. With your eyes closed, create two piles by picking out half of them. Then add up the numbers in the two piles. When I tried this, one pile totaled 120, the other 90. When I tried it again, one pile totaled 101, the other 109. Just by chance—the way the ten papers happen to be picked—there is likely to be some difference between the two sums. The same thing can occur in an experiment. For example, if neither group took the preparatory course, it is likely that, just by chance, one would have a slightly higher average score on the test.

Because of the operation of chance factors, researchers cannot be sure, based on the data alone, that a difference measured between two groups is actually due to the experimental manipulation (taking the preparatory course, in our example) rather than to chance. Psychologists therefore use inferential statistics to help them decide how likely it is that the effects they observe could be due to chance.

Inferential Statistics: Interpreting Differences

Inferential statistics are statistical methods for interpreting data and drawing conclusions from them. For example, statistical tests have been developed to answer the question "How likely is it that the differences observed between two groups have occurred by chance?" These statistical tests take into account both the size of the difference between the two groups and the variability of the two groups.

You can get an intuitive idea of how this works by contrasting the distributions of scores in our SAT experiment with a pair of distributions that are more obviously different. Panel A of Figure 2.17 shows the distributions for two groups that have the same mean as our SAT data (replotted in Panel B), but that are less variable and hence overlap less. By just looking at these two distributions you would probably conclude, based on their lack of overlap, that it is unlikely that the difference between them is due to chance.

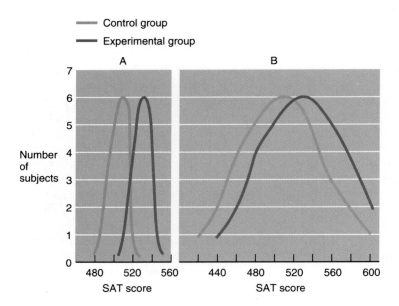

FIGURE 2.17

The distributions in A and B have the same means. The distributions in A are less variable, however, so they overlap less; most of the scores from the experimental group are higher than most of the scores from the control group.

In contrast, the distributions from our SAT experiment (Panel B), with their higher variability, overlap a great deal. Because of this large overlap between groups we cannot be certain that the differences between the groups are not due to chance.

Statistical tests give precision to these impressions by providing a *probability statement* of exactly how likely it is that observed differences are due to chance. For example, the probability statement $p < .01$ means that there is less than a 1 in 100 chance that the difference between two groups could have occurred due to chance. Thus, the lower the value of p, the greater the likelihood that a difference in *not* due to chance. Psychologists have adopted the convention that p must be .05 or less for the difference between two groups to be considered **statistically significant**—that is, unlikely to be due to chance. This is usually stated in psychological journals by saying that "the difference between the groups is significant at the .05 level." In this book we will only report differences that are statistically significant at least at the .05 level.

A statistical test of our SAT data indicates that the difference between the experimental and control groups is, in fact, significant at the .05 level. We can, therefore, conclude that the difference between these groups is statistically significant; that is, there is only a small chance that the difference we observe between these two groups has occurred due to chance.

In summary, to interpret the results of an experiment researchers first describe the data by means of descriptive statistics and then use inferential statistics to assess the likelihood that the difference between groups occurred simply because of chance. Only when a difference is probably *not* owing to chance is a researcher in a position to claim that there is a relationship between the independent and dependent variables. Because a statistical test of our SAT data does indicate that the difference between the groups is significant at the .05 level, we can say that the preparatory course did, in fact, cause an increase in SAT scores.

You might think that, having used statistical procedures to determine that the difference between two groups is statistically significant, the experiment has accomplished its goal. On one level it has: the experiment has shown that changing the independent variable had an effect. However, thoughtful researchers go beyond simply demonstrating differences between groups. In addition, they ask, "Is the difference I have measured a *meaningful difference?*"

Let's look again, for example, at the difference between the two distributions in our SAT experiment. Even though the difference between these two distributions is statistically significant, the large overlap between the two indicates that many people in the control group scored higher on the SAT test than many of the people in the experimental group. Thus, if there is a lot of overlap between two groups, a statistically significant difference may not be very meaningful in a practical sense. In fact, even if there isn't much overlap between groups, as in Panel A of Figure 2.17, a small difference in the means may not be very meaningful. Would you feel it was worth it to spend $200 and your time to take the SAT preparatory course if you knew that doing so would only guarantee scoring 20 points higher on the SAT? That improvement might be statistically significant yet still of little practical value in terms of helping you get into college. You might well decide not to take the course. This same standard can be applied to psychological experiments in general. In evaluating the meaningfulness of a result, we need to consider both whether the difference is statistically significant and whether it is large enough to have any *practical* significance.

Whether a difference is meaningful or not is an important issue, because the way people interpret research results can have significant implications for social issues. Consider, for example, the question of gender differences. Are there differences in males' and females' abilities? A large body of research has shown that females and males differ in certain abilities (Basow, 1992; Halpern, 1986; Hyde, 1991). For example, research has shown that males perform better than females on some tests of mathematical ability. These results have generated many newspaper reports of a "significant" male-female difference. Females, it is reported, are inferior to males in terms of mathematical ability.

Although these newspaper reports may be correct in terms of the average scores of males and females, there are two facts that such accounts often overlook: (1) the average difference is small, and (2) there is considerable overlap in the distributions of the male and the female scores (Figure 2.18). Many females outscore males on mathematics tests. Thus, although there may be a statistically significant difference between male and female mathematics performance, it is not meaningful enough to prevent many females from qualifying for careers in science and engineering that require mathematical ability. Unfortunately, the publicity about this difference in the popular press could have the effect of discouraging females from taking mathematics courses or from aspiring to careers that require mathematical skills.

The idea that the results of psychological research have social implications is one that we will encounter repeatedly in this book. As the science of human behavior, psychology is naturally relevant to many areas of our lives. The next section addresses some social issues involved in the way psychological research is conducted. These issues, which have to do with the ethics of psychological research, deal with how both human and animal subjects are treated in psychological experiments.

Ethical Issues in Psychological Research

The ethics of scientific research has been increasingly in the news. Controversies have raged over whether a laboratory in the United States or one in France should receive credit for discovering HIV, the virus that causes AIDS. Congressional committees have investigated allegations that data published in scientific literature have been faked. Issues such as stealing other people's ideas and honesty in reporting data have been a part of science in general since long before the present controversies, and they have occasionally surfaced in psychology as well. One of the most famous cases in psychology is the case of Sir Cyril Burt, one of England's foremost researchers in intelligence. Many years after his death, it was discovered that he had changed some of his data to more closely fit his theory of intelligence (Kamin, 1974). Fortunately, cases such as Burt's are rare. The ethical issues of most concern among psychologists involve how human and animal subjects are treated in psychological experiments.

Research on Human Subjects

Research on human subjects, particularly experimental research, raises ethical issues related to guaranteeing the subject's safety, how much the subject should be told about the experiment beforehand, the subject's freedom to terminate participation in the experiment, and the confidentiality of information collected about subjects. Underlying these specific issues is the general question of how much risk to the subject is tolerable in the cause of advancing scientific knowledge. To explore this question I will focus on the specific issue of deception, the creation of cover stories to mask the real purpose of the experiment from the subjects.

The first question to consider is whether deception is necessary in psychological research. Psychologists disagree on this issue, with some arguing that as deception means lying to subjects it is unethical and moreover could cause them harm (Baumrind, 1964, 1979, 1985; Kelman, 1967; Sieber, 1982). Others argue that some types of research require deception and that most deception used in psychological experiments is harmless: recall Perky's mental image experiment or experiments in which the taste of alcohol is masked.

A classic and controversial 1963 study by Stanley Milgram, however, raised

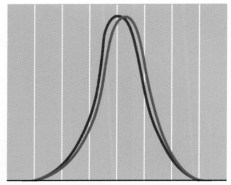
Mathematical ability

FIGURE 2.18
Distributions of scores on mathematical ability tests for males and females (from Hyde, 1991). This graph, which is based on the results of many experiments, shows the large overlap between male and female mathematics ability.

the issue in a dramatic way. More generally, the experiment led many psychologists to ask what the ethical limits are for research on human subjects. Milgram's topic was an important one, with significant implications for human life. Disturbed by the apparently blind obedience of many people in Nazi Germany during World War II, Milgram wanted to study the factors that influence the extent to which people will obey authority figures.

To mask the true purpose of his experiment, Milgram told his subjects that they were in an experimental study of learning. Milgram's subjects were given the task of testing another person, the "learner" (who was actually an accomplice of the experimenter), on a memory task. Each subject was instructed to deliver shocks to the learner for incorrect answers and to increase the intensity of the shock every time the learner answered incorrectly. In actuality, no shocks were given, but the subject was made to think that throwing the switch on the control panel delivered a shock to the learner. The idea that the learner was experiencing shocks was made particularly compelling by the learner's screams of pain and pleas that the experiment be stopped as the shock intensity level was increased. These screams and pleas were actually played from a prerecorded tape, but the subjects didn't know this.

FIGURE 2.19
Subjects in Milgram's experiment used this "shock generator." Markings of shock intensities ranging from 10 volts to 450 volts indicate that the highest voltages are "extremely dangerous." In actuality, no shocks were generated.

When confronted with the learner's screams, some of the subjects became upset and told the experimenter that they didn't want to deliver any more shocks. The experimenter, however, told them that they had to continue, and 65% continued to the end, administering what they thought were 450-volt shocks (marked "extremely dangerous" on the control panel—see Figure 2.20). These disturbing results suggested that ordinary people will go to surprising lengths, even in violation of their own conscience, to obey an authority figure.

Milgram's experiment produced highly meaningful results, but at the price of using a number of levels of deception. Subjects were given a false impression of the overall purpose of the experiment, because knowing that it was about obedience would have affected their behavior. They were also led to believe that the learner was a fellow subject and that they were giving the learner painful and possibly dangerous shocks.

Following the experiment, the subjects were thoroughly debriefed; that is, they were told the actual purpose of the experiment and were reassured that they had not actually inflicted shocks on anyone. Nevertheless, for many of them the experiment had been a harrowing experience, and for this reason critics have questioned the ethics of the study.

The basic criticisms of Milgram's experiment are that his subjects could have been harmed because (1) they often became emotionally upset during the experiment; (2) those who obeyed the experimenter and administered what they thought were high-intensity shocks may have learned things about themselves that they did not want to know; (3) the debriefing at the end of the experiment, during which its purpose was explained, may have humiliated some subjects; and (4) the entire experience could have had long-term effects beyond the duration of the experiment.

One of Milgram's responses to these criticisms was that psychology should study the full range of human behavior. Behaviors that involve stress, conflict, and emotions are important parts of human experience that should not be ignored by psychologists. Understanding why people obey orders to do things they normally wouldn't do is the first step toward eliminating such horrors as the blind obedience that led to the murder of more than six million Jews under Nazi rule in World War II.

Does the quest to gain useful and important knowledge justify subjecting people to a harmful experience? Many psychologists say "No." But others ask whether subjects in experiments that involve deception are actually harmed by the deception. Research on this issue has generally failed to uncover harmful aftereffects. For example, in a questionnaire completed after the experiment, 84% of Milgram's subjects reported that they were glad to have participated. Only

FIGURE 2.20
Results of the Milgram experiment.
Sixty-five percent of the subjects continued
to the highest level on the shock generator.

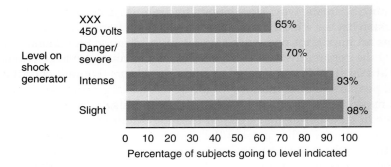

1.3% reported any negative feelings. In follow-up interviews of Milgram's subjects one year later, a psychiatrist found no evidence that the subjects had been harmed by their experience.

Most psychological experiments that involve deception are much less stressful than Milgram's. Studies of subjects' reactions to these experiments have also shown that the vast majority report that they were not disturbed by the deception and, in fact, that they often enjoyed being in the experiments and found them educational (Christiansen, 1988). Thus, the idea that subjects have been harmed by participating in experiments using deception is not supported by research.

Nevertheless, deception remains a controversial issue in psychology. Many psychologists feel that deception is justified only if it is necessary and precautions are instituted to safeguard subjects. Similar considerations apply to other issues involving the treatment of human subjects in research. Today most universities ensure that subjects' rights are respected by requiring that all experiments using human subjects be reviewed by special committees. Because of this review process, subjects can be assured that they will not be subjected to any procedures that jeopardize their welfare; in fact, it is unlikely that such committees would approve an experiment similar to Milgram's today. In addition, the American Psychological Association has formulated ethical principles to guide psychological research involving both humans and animals (Figure 2.21).

Research on Animal Subjects

Who are the cruel and inhumane ones, the behavioral scientists whose research on animals led to the cures of the anorexic girl and the vomiting child, or those leaders of the radical animal activists who are making an exciting career of trying to stop all such research and are misinforming people by repeatedly asserting that it is without any value?

Neal Miller (1985)

Like other scientists, psychologists sometimes carry out experiments on animals that could not be performed on people. For example, a standard technique in biological psychology is to perform operations on animals to determine the functioning of various parts of the brain. The rationale is that it is justifiable for animals to be used in the service of the betterment of human life. Indeed, animal research by both medical researchers and psychologists has led to many significant developments: vaccines for human and animal diseases; procedures for organ transplants and other surgical techniques; techniques to teach retarded or learning disabled children; drugs for relieving anxiety, depression, psychoses, and Parkinson's disease; treatments enabling premature infants to gain weight more rapidly; important advances in understanding the mechanisms responsible for learning; and knowledge about the mechanisms of drug addiction, among others (Miller, 1985).

Some animal rights activists, working from the premise that animals have the same rights as humans, contend that animals should never be used in research. Groups supporting this idea have often circulated "horror stories" about animals that have been starved or tortured in the name of science. However, a survey of all research published in American Psychological Association journals over a

The American Psychological Association has set forth a code of ethics to guide psychologists in their practice of psychology on both human and animal subjects. The *Ethical Principles of Psychologists and Code of Conduct* (1992) sets forth standards to be followed both by psychologists who work as therapists and those who conduct research. The following excerpts cover some of the key principles that apply to research on humans and animals.

Research with Human Subjects
- Psychologists conduct research competently and with due concern for the dignity and welfare of the participants.
- Psychologists inform participants of the nature of the research, that they are free to participate or to decline to participate or to withdraw from the research, of significant factors that may be expected to influence their willingness to participate (such as risks, discomfort, adverse effects, or limitations on confidentiality), and they explain other aspects about which the prospective participants inquire.
- Psychologists do not use deception unless they have determined that the use of deceptive techniques is justified by the study's prospective scientific, educational, or applied value and that equally alternative procedures that do not use deception are not feasible.
- Psychologists never deceive research participants about significant aspects that would affect their willingness to participate, such as physical risks, discomfort, or unpleasant emotional experiences.
- Any other deception that is an integral feature of the experiment must be explained to participants as early as feasible.
- Psychologists provide participants with information about the nature, results, and conclusions of the research, and attempt to correct any misconceptions that participants may have.

Research on Animals
- Psychologists who conduct research involving animals treat them humanely.
- Psychologists trained in research methods and experienced in the care of laboratory animals supervise all procedures involving animals and are responsible for insuring appropriate consideration of their comfort, health, and humane treatment.
- Psychologists make reasonable efforts to minimize the discomfort, infection, illness, and pain of animal subjects.
- A procedure subjecting animals to pain, stress, or privation is used only when an alternative procedure is unavailable and the goal is justified by its prospective scientific, educational, or applied value.
- Surgical procedures are performed under appropriate anesthesia; techniques to avoid infection and minimize pain are followed during and after surgery.
- When it is appropriate that the animal's life be terminated, it is done rapidly and with an effort to minimize pain.

FIGURE 2.21
Ethical Principles of the American Psychological Association

four-year period found no evidence to support this claim (Coile & Miller, 1984).

The strong emotions raised by some protests against using animals in research may lead to the impression that the use of animals in psychological research is more widespread than it actually is. In fact, less than 10 percent of psychological research involves animals, and most of these animals are rodents or birds. The following statement by Neal Miller (1985) gives us some perspective on the extent to which animals are used in psychological research.

> At least 20 million dogs and cats are abandoned each year in the United States; half of them are killed in pounds and shelters, and the rest are hit by cars or die of neglect. Less than 1/10,000th as many dogs and cats were used in psychological laboratories (p. 427).

Most of the people concerned with animal welfare feel it is permissible to use animals for research as long as the animals are not subjected to unnecessary pain or distress. Guidelines regulating the use of animals have been established by the American Psychological Association, the Society for Neuroscience, and animal care committees at each university in which animal research occurs. The idea that animals should not be subjected to pain or distress is a central tenent of these guidelines. In addition, the guidelines specify that if experiments are proposed that do cause animals to experience pain or distress they should be carried out only if it is likely that the research will yield information that will improve the lives of humans or other animals.

Reprise: Science as a Refinement of Everyday Thinking

The whole of science is nothing more than a refinement of everyday thinking.

Albert Einstein (1936)

This chapter has focused closely on how psychologists conduct their research, and on the care and ingenuity necessary to produce results that are objective and trustworthy. Yet despite the complexities involved in doing good research, Einstein's statement is as true of psychology as of other sciences: scientific psychology is nothing more than a refinement of everyday thinking. To see why this is so, consider how we go about making sense of the world in our everyday lives. For example, developmental psychologists point out that infants act like "little scientists" as they play: they push a toy and it moves; they let go and it falls. By repeating these "experiments" they learn that certain actions reliably lead to specific reactions.

As people grow older they continue this process of observing and experimenting with nature. As was noted in Chapter 1, by the time you reach adulthood you have learned quite a bit about psychology from direct experience. But you also saw that some of the things people think they know about psychology are not true. In other words, informal observations and experiments sometimes lead us to erroneous conclusions about human behavior. Among the reasons for our mistakes is the fact that we live in a complex world in which many variables are changing at the same time. The "experiments" we do as part of our everyday life often do not follow the basic rule of experimentation; we normally don't have the means or the sophistication to isolate a single variable and observe its effects. Moreover, we usually aren't paying attention to the extraneous variables that might affect our results. So, for example, when your friend becomes upset with something you say, you might conclude that your statement caused the upset. In reality, however, another event you were unaware of might be the real cause of your friend's distress.

In everyday life we do not normally take special precautions to remove sources of bias from our observations and experiments; we may also take our own experiences as being typical of other people's, whereas in reality our experiences may not be representative.

It is here that Einstein's refinement of everyday thinking comes in. Controlled scientific experiments and systematic observations such as the ones described in this chapter refine everyday thinking by (1) simplifying problems until everything remains constant except for one variable (2) focusing our attention on extraneous variables that could affect our results, (3) taking precautions to remove potential sources of bias, and (4) making sure our results are representative of a larger population than the subjects observed in the experiment.

Thus, Einstein's "refinement" simply means creating the conditions and maintaining the awareness that enable us to channel our everyday thought processes into the basic rule of experimentation, so that nature doesn't mislead us into thinking we know something we don't. As we study the biology of behavior in the next chapter, and then topics ranging from perception to abnormal behavior in the chapters that follow, we will be looking at how the refinement of everyday thinking called scientific psychology has opened windows of understanding on why we behave as we do.

The Lens of Culture and the Psychological Study of Women and African Americans

Science, we are often lead to believe, is an objective way to determine "truth." For example, if researchers want to test for a causal relationship between two variables, be they protein in the diet and pellagra or playing violent video games and aggressive behavior, they might get valid results if they take care to follow the basic rule of experimentation. Provided that the experiment is sound, we can have a high degree of confidence that it has revealed something about the world.

But though it is true that using the scientific method is an excellent way to develop an accurate picture of the world, it is not true that science is totally objective and always discovers the truth. Like everyone else, scientists look through a lens colored by the culture in which they live. Cultural attitudes affect both the way scientists think and what they think about.

History is replete with examples of educated people whose cultural "blinders" prevented them from achieving the ideal of scientific objectivity. When Roger Bacon (1220–1292), the most famous European scientist of the Middle Ages, proposed to study light and the rainbow and a process for making gunpowder, some of those "educated" people accused him of black magic. Galileo's championing of Nicolaus Copernicus's theory, which placed the sun and not the earth at the center of the universe, led to his trial by the Inquisition and the banning of his books.

Today we sometimes witness similar clashes between cherished beliefs and scientific findings and ideas, such as the movement on the part of some religious believers to ban or qualify the teaching of Darwin's theory of evolution in the schools. But we should realize that science, too, is affected by cultural beliefs. For example, consider the history of psychology's view of women and of African Americans. Early work in psychology reflected the cultural assumption of the early 1900s that both of these populations were inferior. Some psychologists supported the idea of African American inferiority by proposing the *mulatto hypothesis*, that mental abilities were proportional to the amount of "white blood" a person of mixed blood had, a greater proportion of white ancestry resulting in higher intelligence. Once the hypothesis was proposed, many studies in the 1920s and 1930s reported a relationship between white ancestry and intelligence test scores of African American children (Guthrie, 1976). Even after a number of respected scientists refuted these findings in the 1930s (Herskovits, 1934; Kleinberg, 1931), a survey of white psychologists indicated that 23% felt that the data supported the mulatto hypothesis (Thompson, 1934).

We see a similar picture of psychology reflecting cultural values when we look at the attitudes of early psychologists toward women. Belief in the inferiority of women was particularly strong in the late 1800s, when scientific psychology was just beginning. Given their unquestioned belief in female inferiority, early psychologists proposed a hypothesis to explain it. The *variability hypothesis* stated that men were superior because they were biologically more variable. Support for that variability came from data showing that there were more low-achieving and retarded males than females but, at the other end of the scale, many more males than females who had achieved positions of eminence in science and the arts. Females, on the other hand, were clustered more toward the middle.

This line of reasoning seems suspect today, because it is obvious that one reason women were clustered toward the middle was that they had little opportunity to achieve eminence, consigned as they were to their roles as wives and mothers (Hollingworth, 1914). However, the early psychologists were looking through cultural lenses that emphasized biological explanations. Social factors seemed unimportant to them, so they ignored them (Shields, 1975). What is perhaps more important, they took female inferiority so much for granted that they were more inclined to look for explanations of this supposed "fact" than to question whether it was actually true. Indeed, in an earlier version of the variability hypothesis, Mechel, an early 19th-century anatomist, proposed that women were *more* variable than men and therefore inferior, as variability is a sign of inferiority (Ellis, 1903; Shields, 1975)!

In reaction to these examples, you might say that the problem with an idea like the variability hypothesis is simply biased reasoning and that modern science is not as susceptible to such biases. To a certain extent this is true. Present-day scientists are more aware of potential sources of bias and can make more accurate measurements than their predecessors. These facts notwithstanding, there is still room—even today—for culture's lens to distort the questions asked by scientists, the methods they use to answer those questions, and the way they interpret their results.

For example, even modern scientists have been influenced by a number of societal ideas about women. One of them is that women are unstable because they are "at the mercy" of monthly variations in their hormonal levels. Thus, some research on women's monthly cycles has focused on the idea that women's changing hormonal balance causes them to experience *premenstrual syndrome* (PMS), a condition characterized by anxiety, irritability, and depression.

Most research on PMS has been based on the biological level of analysis and ignores important social factors that may contribute as much as hormones to women's experience of PMS. At the cognitive level, the belief, prevalent in Western culture, in the negative moods of PMS could itself account for some of the negative symptoms that women experience (Clarke & Ruble, 1978; McFarland, Ross, & De Courville, 1989). Further, whereas a large body of research has accumulated on mood changes in women, little research has been done on how moods vary in men. Only recently has research shown that males' moods vary just as much as females' (Alagna & Hamilton, 1986; McFarlane, Martin, & Williams, 1988). The very fact that researchers are finally studying men's mood changes suggests a shift in cultural beliefs that opens up new questions.

Another phenomenon that has been interpreted in terms of women being "slaves of their hormones" is menopause, the "change of life" that women in middle age experience as hormonal changes cause the end of menstruation. Until recently most research on menopause focused almost solely on the biological level of analysis. Physicians treating women for physical symptoms such as "hot flashes" (abrupt changes in body temperature) and psychological symptoms such as depression and difficulty in concentrating explained the symptoms in terms of hormonal changes. But there is another model for menopause that works at the cognitive and contextual levels of analysis. This model has shown that some of the symptoms of menopause can be explained by social factors such as the psychological stress associated with growing older in our youth-oriented culture and the fact that women have been told what symptoms to *expect* when they experience menopause. This more recent way of looking at menopause represents a widening of the point of view from the biologically based medical model to one that sees menopause in terms of both biological and social factors, as shown in Figure 2.22 (Fausto-Sterling, 1985).

The examples of medical research on menstruation and menopause illustrate how looking through a biological lens has blinded researchers to possible social causes of women's symptoms. Psychologists' early ideas on the causes of the mental illness schizophrenia illustrate a case of looking through a social lens that blinded researchers to possible biological causes. Sigmund Freud's idea that mental illness is caused by a person's early experiences—and especially by the dynamics within the family—focused psychologists' attention on the patient's mother. The term *schizophrenogenic mother* was coined to describe mothers whose cold personality supposedly caused schizophrenia in their children. Unfortunately, the possibility that biology could be involved was not considered. Not until recently, when the biological approach was applied to research on schizophrenia, did attention shift from the mother's behavior to consideration of the patient's genetics and abnormal brain chemistry. Now, schizophrenia researchers have abandoned the idea of the schizophrenogenic mother in favor of more biologically based explanations.

These examples all show that cultural pressure can lead researchers to study a behavior at only one level of analysis, thereby creating a form of biased science. The chances of uncovering a more complete and therefore truer explanation for any phenomenon increases as more levels of analysis are brought into play.

Bias in psychology can, however, go beyond what aspects of a problem psychologists decide to look at. It can also occur when psychologists interpret their data. Consider an experiment in which students were asked to estimate their performance on an exam they had just taken. The males' estimates were higher than the females'. How can we interpret these results? One interpretation, which fits the cultural stereotypes that females are more timid and less assertive than males, is that females have less confidence in their ability than males. But another interpretation becomes more reasonable when we compare the students' estimates to the grades they actually received. We then find that the females estimated their scores fairly accurately, but the males *overestimated* their scores. This opens the door to the interpretation that perhaps males set unrealistically high expectations for their performance (Hyde, 1991). This example illustrates that even if researchers take precautions to eliminate bias in the design and execution of an experiment, social values can still influence how they interpret its results.

It is clear that there are many ways in which a cultural lens can narrow scientists' perspectives and thus influence the questions they ask, how they go about asking them, and the conclusions they reach. Does this mean that science is useless? Far from it. As you will see in the pages of this book, the science of psychology has provided many valuable insights into human behavior. It is important to be aware, however, that because of culture's influence, areas of research may have been left unstudied, ways of looking at problems may have been unimagined, and alternative interpretations may have not been made. While appreciating the power of science we need to be aware of the limitations of the fallible humans who practice it.

FIGURE 2.22

The symptoms of menopause are most accurately seen as being caused by both biological and social factors.

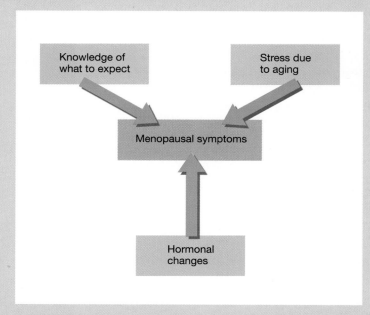

Asking Questions of Nature:
The Logic of Scientific Research

- The first step in any scientific investigation is observing the phenomenon to be studied. Through observation, researchers describe behavior and seek to identify relationships between phenomena.

- In an experiment, observations are made under controlled conditions that lead researchers to follow the basic rule of experimentation: To determine a cause-and-effect relationship, change one variable while keeping every other relevant variable constant.

- Theories are models that describe a large body of data, can predict the results of future observations, and can be disproved if incorrect. Psychological theories are often proposed and accepted only to be later modified or replaced in response to new observations or better models.

Posing Questions About Behavior:
Methods of Psychological Research

- Three major observational methods are (1) naturalistic observation, in which a researcher systematically observes behavior without intervening directly in what is going on; (2) case studies, in-depth observation of the history or behavior of an individual subject; and (3) surveys and inventories such as public opinion polls or instruments that measure a person's characteristics. A common feature of observational methods is that they can suggest relationships between variables but cannot prove cause-and-effect relationships.

- These eight steps are followed when creating and running experiments: (1) formulating the problem, (2) stating the hypothesis, (3) identifying the independent and dependent variables, (4) operationally defining the variables, (5) selecting subjects by random sampling from a population (often not strictly followed), (6) creating experimental and control groups by using random assignment to place subjects in them, (7) running the experiment and measuring the dependent variable, and (8) analyzing the data and drawing conclusions.

- The cause of any behavior can be analyzed at the biological, behavioral, cognitive, or contextual level of analysis. The level used depends on the level at which the experimenter chooses to analyze the behavior.

- It is important to distinguish between cause-and-effect and correlational relationships. Correlational relationships may not be cause and effect. To determine whether a cause-and-effect relationship exists, it is necessary to do an experiment.

- Researchers seek to prevent bias from affecting their results. Researchers can cause bias, which can be avoided by blind interviewing and scoring procedures, and subjects can cause bias, especially if demand characteristics are present in an experiment. Double-blind procedures are used to prevent both researcher and subject bias. This procedure can involve deception of the subjects.

Drawing Conclusions
from Psychological Research

- Researchers use descriptive statistics to describe their results. Measures of central tendency include the mean and median. Measures of variability include the range and standard deviation. Although descriptive statistics may indicate differences between the experimental and control groups, they could be due to chance factors. Inferential statistics are used to determine whether a difference is statistically significant by creating probability statements indicating how likely it is that the difference could be due to chance.

- Even if a difference is statistically significant, it may not be meaningful. Small differences may have little practical significance. There is a danger that small statistically significant differences can be misinterpreted as being meaningful when in a practical sense they aren't.

Ethical Issues in Psychological Research

- Research on human subjects raises ethical issues related to guaranteeing the subjects' safety and dignity. The central issue in the debate over ethics—whether deception should be used—is a source of disagreement among psychologists. Research on psychological experiments that have used deception indicates that subjects generally are not disturbed by deception. University committees and APA guidelines have been created to ensure that experiments will not be harmful to subjects.

- Some psychologists do research on animals. These experiments are based on the rationale that it is justifiable for animals to be used in the service of the betterment of human life. Many discoveries with significant practical applications have resulted from animal experimentation. The APA and other organizations have created guidelines to ensure the humane treatment of animals in research.

Reprise: Science as a Refinement
of Everyday Thinking

- According to Einstein, science is nothing more than a refinement of everyday thinking. What Einstein meant was that scientific procedures refine normal thinking by ensuring that only one variable changes during an experiment, that we take procedures to remove bias, and that we use procedures that make our results generalizable to a larger population. In short, science creates the conditions and awareness that enable us to follow the basic rule of experimentation.

Key Terms

basic rule of experimentation
blind interviewing procedure
blind scoring procedure
case study
cause-and-effect relationship
control group
correlation
correlation coefficient
deception
demand characteristics
dependent variable
descriptive statistics
double-blind procedure
experimental design
experimental group
experimentation
extraneous variable
field experiment
frequency distribution
hypothesis

independent variable
inferential statistics
inventory
mean
measures of central tendency
measures of variability
median
naturalistic observation
negative correlation
operational definition
population
positive correlation
random assignment
random sampling
range
replicate
standard deviation
statistically significant
survey
theory
variable

CHAPTER

3

The Neuron: Building Block of the Nervous System
   The Structure of the Neuron
   The Action Potential
   The Synapse

The Body's Communication Networks:
   The Nervous and Endocrine Systems
   The Central Nervous System
   The Peripheral Nervous System
   The Endocrine System

The Brain: Localized Functions Working Together
   Localization of Function in the Brain
   Organization on the Left and Right: Lateralization of Function
   Beyond Localization of Function

The Dynamic Nervous System:
   Changing with Development and Experience
   The Changing Brain: Transformation Through Maturation
   The Changing Brain: Transformation Through Experience

Heredity and Behavior

Evolution and Behavior

Interdisciplinary Dimension: Evolution
   Natural Selection and Sociobiology

Reprise: Levels of Analysis and Behavior

Follow-Through/Diversity
   Sex Hormones, Brain Structure, and Behavior

The Biology of
Behavior

As long as the brain is a mystery, the universe . . .
will also be a mystery.

Santiago Ramón y Cajal (1852–1934)
Spanish anatomist

It is early in 1975, and neurologist Oliver Sacks enters Jimmie G.'s hospital room for the first time. He meets a handsome, calm, cheerful 49-year-old man who had been admitted to the Home for the Aged accompanied only by a transfer note that described him as "helpless, demented, confused, and disoriented." As he talks with Jimmie, Dr. Sacks hears about some events of Jimmie's childhood, his experiences in school, and his days in the navy. But Dr. Sacks notices a puzzling thing—Jimmie talks as if he were still in the navy, even though he was discharged ten years earlier. Their conversation continues, as recounted by Dr. Sacks.

"What year is this, Mr. G.?" I asked, concealing my perplexity under a casual manner.

"Forty-five, man. What do you mean?" He went on, "We've won the war, FDR's dead, Truman's at the helm. There are great times ahead."

"And you, Jimmie, how old would you be?"

Oddly, uncertainly, he hesitated a moment, as if engaged in calculation.

"Why, I guess I'm nineteen, Doc. I'll be twenty next birthday."

Looking at the grey-haired man before me, I had an impulse for which I have never forgiven myself—it was, or would have been, the height of cruelty had there been any possibility of Jimmie's remembering it.

"Here," I said, and thrust a mirror toward him. "Look in the mirror and tell me what you see. Is that a nineteen-year-old looking out from the mirror?"

He suddenly turned ashen and gripped the sides of the chair. "Jesus Christ," he whispered. "Christ, what's going on? What's happened to me? Is this a nightmare? Am I crazy? Is this a joke?"—and he became frantic, panicked.

"It's okay, Jimmie," I said soothingly. "It's just a mistake. Nothing to worry about. Hey!" I took him to the window. "Isn't this a lovely spring day. See the kids there playing baseball?" He regained his color and started to smile, and I stole away, taking the hateful mirror with me.

Two minutes later I re-entered the room. Jimmie was still standing by the window, gazing with pleasure at the kids playing baseball below. He wheeled around as I opened the door, and his face assumed a cheery expression.

"Hiya, Doc!" he said. "Nice morning! You want to talk to me—do I take this chair here?" There was no sign of recognition on his frank, open face.

"Haven't we met before, Mr. G.?" I said casually.

"No, I can't say we have. Quite a beard you got there. I wouldn't forget *you*, Doc!" . . .

"You remember telling me about your childhood, growing up in Connecticut, working as a radio operator on submarines? And how your brother is engaged to a girl from Oregon?"

"Hey, you're right. But I didn't tell you that. I never met you before in my life. You must have read all about me in my chart."

"Okay," I said. "I'll tell you a story. A man went to his doctor complaining of memory lapses. The doctor asked him some routine questions, and then said, 'These lapses. What about them?' 'What lapses?' the patient replied."

"So that's my problem," Jimmie laughed. "I kinda thought it was. I do find myself forgetting things, once in a while—things that have just happened. The past is clear, though" (Sacks, 1987, pp. 25–26).

Jimmie suffers from Korsakoff's syndrome, a condition caused by a prolonged deficiency of vitamin B_1, usually as a result of chronic alcoholism. The deficiency leads to the destruction of a tiny area near the base of the brain and to severe impairments in memory. The damage to Jimmie's memory makes him incapable of assimilating or retaining new knowledge. He cannot recognize people he has just met, follow a story in a book, find his way to the corner drugstore, or solve problems that take more than a few moments to figure out. Because of this damage to his brain, Jimmie will spend the rest of his life in an institution. His is not an isolated case; tens of thousands of Americans each year are severely disabled by brain damage.

Cases like Jimmie's highlight a simple but profound truth: all behaviors—including those you take for granted, such as walking, breathing, reading this book, creating a shopping list, and remembering where you parked your car—are ultimately traceable to biological processes. Thus, one approach to understanding both normal and impaired behaviors is to probe the biological processes that underlie them.

The material in this chapter focuses on one of the levels of analysis introduced in Chapter 1, the biological level. As you recall, human behavior can be studied from a number of angles, including observable behavior, cognitive processes, and factors in the physical and social context. This chapter illustrates how a great deal of knowledge can be gained by narrowing our focus temporarily to a single level of analysis. It is important to remember, however, that behavior is multifaceted and that the processes we study in this chapter interact with processes at the behavioral, cognitive, and contextual levels of analysis. For in-

A scene from the film *Awakenings*, in which Robert De Niro (center) plays a patient who awakens temporarily from a sleeplike state caused by a brain disease

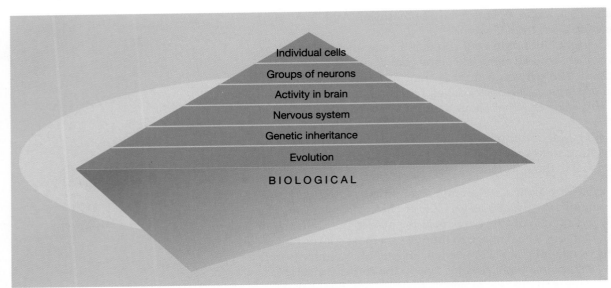

FIGURE 3.1
Within the biological level of analysis we can focus on levels of explanation ranging from individual neurons to genetics and the process of evolution.

stance, a complete treatment program for a brain-damaged patient could include not only biological interventions such as surgery or drugs, but also cognitive therapy (such as training the person in special memory techniques), behavioral therapy (such as providing rewards for correct behavior), and contextual interventions (such as helping to create a warm and supportive family environment). Similarly, a complete understanding of normal behavior requires attention to all four levels of analysis and their interaction.

This chapter also illustrates another important principle: *within* a given level of analysis there can be a number of levels of explanation that focus on different aspects of a behavior. For example, consider the simple behavior of turning your head in response to a tap on your shoulder. The first step in studying this behavior is to realize that, since the stimulus is applied to one place on the body (the shoulder) yet the action occurs at another (the neck), there must be communication between parts of the body. We can then study that communication by focusing on different aspects of the nervous system—the network of cells responsible for communication throughout the body. We do this by starting at the microscopic level of cells called neurons and then expanding our view to how neurons work within the nervous system, looking especially at activity in the brain (Figure 3.1). In addition, we describe the body's other communication system—the endocrine system, with its network of glands that secrete chemicals called *hormones.* Finally, we extend our biological analysis in time by looking at the processes of genetic inheritance and evolution.

The Neuron: Building Block of the Nervous System

Early anatomists saw the brain as a solid, homogeneous structure, in which communication was effected by waves of activity that sometimes encompassed the whole structure. This conception of the brain persisted until the development of the microscope in the 18th century and a technique called *staining* in the 19th century. The microscope enabled scientists to see structures invisible to the naked eye, and chemicals called **stains,** which selectively color one kind of structure and ignore others, enabled them to differentiate one structure from another.

As stains and the staining technique were perfected, it became clear that the brain is made up of billions of small structures called **cells,** which typically

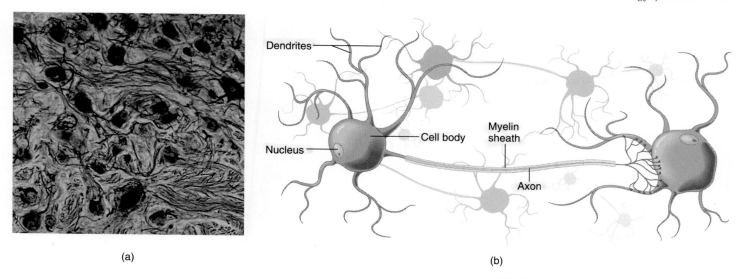

Dendrites

Nucleus

Cell body

Myelin sheath

Axon

(a)

(b)

FIGURE 3.2
(a) Stained neurons, showing cell bodies and their axons. (b) Components of neurons

contain protoplasm—the basic material of living things—plus structures to keep the cell alive, all enclosed within a membrane called the cell wall. There are many kinds of cells in the body—fat cells, supporting cells, muscle cells, and nerve cells, to name but a few. Of particular interest to us are the nerve cells, or **neurons:** cells that are specialized to conduct electrical signals. Neurons are found everywhere in the body, from the eyes to the tips of the fingers and toes; in internal organs such as the heart and intestines; and—most important of all—by the tens of billions in the brain. By responding to stimuli and transferring information to other neurons, these remarkable cells transmit messages throughout the brain and between the brain and the rest of the body.

The Structure of the Neuron

How do neurons transmit information? A step toward answering this question was achieved in 1875 when the Italian physician Camillo Golgi (1844–1926) developed what has come to be known as the *Golgi stain*. This stain has two remarkable properties: (1) it stains an entire neuron (previous stains would color only certain parts of the neuron), and (2) it randomly stains only about 5% of the neurons, allowing individual neurons to stand out. (Figure 3.2a).

Golgi's stain revealed the basic parts of the neuron: (1) the **cell body,** which contains a nucleus and other metabolic mechanisms needed to keep the cell alive, (2) **dendrites,** which branch out from the cell body to receive electrical signals from other neurons, and (3) the **axon,** a hollow tube that conducts electrical signals.

There are variations on the basic neuron shown in Figure 3.2b. Some neurons have long axons; others have short axons or none at all. Many neurons' axons are covered with a fatty coating called a *myelin sheath* that insulates the axon and increases the speed with which it can conduct electricity. Some neurons are designed to receive signals not from other neurons but from the environment. These neurons, which respond to environmental stimulation such as light, pressure, chemicals, or sound waves, are called **receptors.** They receive the environmental stimuli and transform them into electrical signals (Figure 3.3). This process of transforming environmental energy into electrical energy, which is called **transduction,** is the primary function of the receptors.

The Action Potential

What kinds of electrical signals are transmitted by neurons? When most people think of electrical signals they imagine signals conducted along electrical power

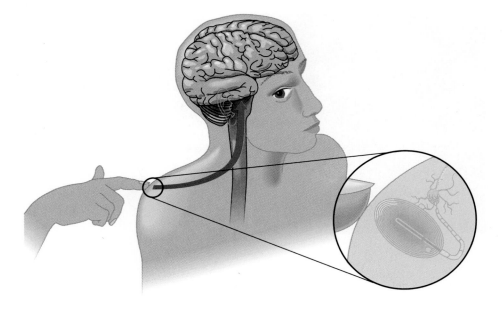

lines or along the wires used for household appliances. Unlike the electrical cord
of your television set, however, neurons are bathed in liquid. What kinds of electrical signals can exist in this liquid environment?

The key to understanding the "wet" electrical signals transmitted by neurons is to look at the neuron's liquid environment. Neurons are immersed in a
solution rich in **ions,** molecules that carry an electrical charge. Ions are created
when molecules gain or lose electrons, as happens when compounds are dis-
solved in water. For example, adding table salt (sodium chloride, or $NaCl$) to
water creates positively charged sodium ions (Na^+) and negatively charged chlo-
rine ions (Cl^-). The solution *outside* the axon of a neuron is rich in positively charged sodium ions (Na^+), while the solution *inside* the axon is rich in
positively charged potassium ions (K^+) and also contains a number of different
negatively charged ions.

How do these ions create electrical signals in the neuron? To answer this
question let's focus on one segment of an axon that is connected to a touch receptor in a person's shoulder (see Figure 3.4). We will observe (1) the ions inside and
outside the axon, and (2) the electrical charge created by these ions.

We begin by observing the electrical charge of an axon at rest—when it is
not conducting electrical signals. We observe that the inside of the axon has a
negative electrical charge compared to the outside. This negative charge exists
for two reasons: (1) any time there is a difference in the concentration of charged
molecules across a membrane, as there is for sodium and potassium across the
membrane of the axon, a difference in charge is created; and (2) there are negatively charged ions inside the axon.

We now stimulate the touch receptor by pushing on the person's shoulder.
When we do this we observe sodium ions rushing into the axon. Since sodium
has a positive charge, this causes the inside of the axon to become more positive
than it was when the axon was at rest. After the sodium has been rushing into
the axon for less than 1/1000 second, the sodium stops flowing into the axon and
the potassium begins flowing out. Since potassium is a positive ion, this outward
flow causes the inside of the axon to become more negative, and the charge inside the axon eventually returns to its original resting level.

The rapid increase in positive charge inside the axon followed by the rapid
return to the resting level is called the **action potential.** This potential, which
lasts about 1/1000 second at any one segment of the axon, travels all the way

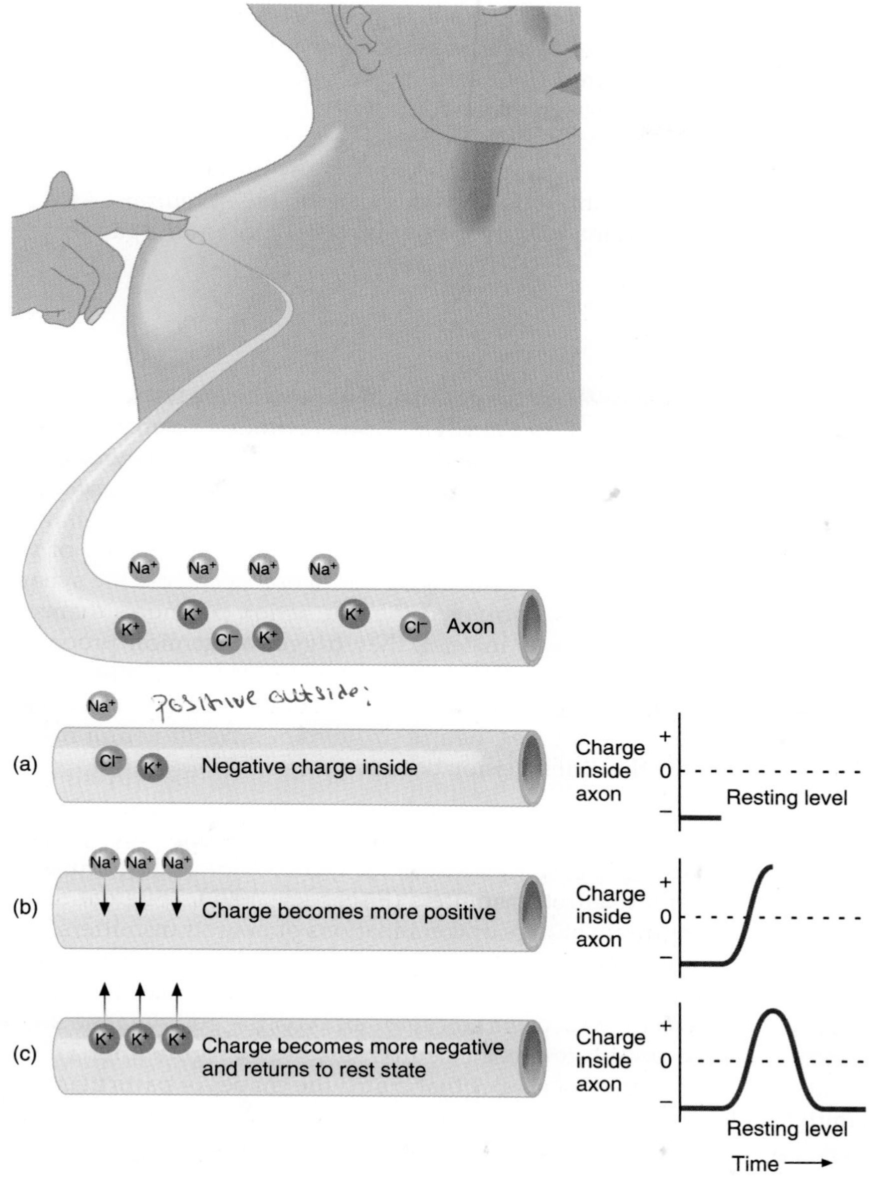

FIGURE 3.4
How the flow of ions creates the action potential. We begin with the axon at rest (a). A push on the shoulder triggers the action potential; positively charged sodium ions rush in, causing the charge inside the neuron to become positive (b). Then positively charged potassium ions rush out; the inside of the axon becomes more negative and returns to its resting level (c).

down the axon, enabling the neuron to communicate with other neurons, located at the end of the axon.

Another property of the action potential is the way it responds to increases in stimulation. If we push harder on the person's shoulder and observe the resulting action potentials, we see that the action potentials remain the same size as when we pushed more gently, but that more travel down the axon. That is, increasing stimulus intensity increases the *rate* of nerve firing without increasing the *size* of the action potential.

What does this property of the action potential mean in terms of its function for a person? In our example, the increased rate of nerve firing carries information that the intensity of the push on the shoulder has been increased. But this information has no meaning unless it is *transmitted* to other neurons, and eventually to the brain or other organs that can react to it.

This idea that the action potential in one neuron must be transmitted to other neurons poses the following problem: once the action potentials reach the end of the axon, how is the message transmitted to other neurons? One idea, put

Santiago Ramón y Cajal, who received the Nobel prize in 1906 for his research on the nature of the synapse

forth by Golgi, was that neurons make direct contact with each other so that a signal reaching the end of one neuron passes directly to the next. But his contemporary, the Spanish anatomist Santiago Ramón y Cajal, used Golgi's staining technique to show that there is a microscopic space between the neurons. Cajal's discovery earned him the Nobel Prize in 1906 (he shared it with Golgi, as the discoverer of the stain). It also raised the question of how the electrical signals generated by neurons are transmitted across this space to other neurons. As we will see, the answer lies in a remarkable process that takes place at the gap that separates neurons.

The Synapse

The place where one neuron communicates with another neuron is called the **synapse** (from a Greek word for "junction"). For neurons to communicate, the information carried by an action potential in one neuron (the **presynaptic neuron**) must cross this space and generate a signal in another (the **postsynaptic neuron**). If this does not occur, the message will stop at the terminal button of the presynaptic neuron—like a messenger who comes to a large body of water and lacks a boat to get across. But how does information get across the synapse?

Early in the 1900s it was discovered that the action potentials themselves do not travel across the synapse. Instead, they trigger a chemical process that bridges the gap between neurons. What happens is this. When the action potential reaches the end of the axon, it causes the release of a chemical called a **neurotransmitter.** As their name implies, neurotransmitters *transmit* neural information. Let's look at how this transmission occurs.

Neurotransmitters and receptor sites.   Neurotransmitters are stored in **synaptic vesicles** in the presynaptic neuron (see Figure 3.5b). At last count, there were nearly 50 different neurotransmitters (Fischbach, 1992). Different neurons contain different neurotransmitters or combinations of neurotransmitters.

When the action potential reaches the synaptic vesicles at the end of the axon, the vesicles release a neurotransmitter (Figure 3.5b). The neurotransmitter molecules flow across the synapse to **receptor sites** on the postsynaptic neuron, small areas that are sensitive to specific neurotransmitters (Figure 3.5c). These receptor sites exist in a variety of shapes that match the shapes of particular neurotransmitter molecules. When a neurotransmitter makes contact with a receptor site matching its shape, it activates it and triggers a voltage change in the postsynaptic neuron. Thus, a neurotransmitter is like a key that fits a specific lock. It has an effect on the postsynaptic neuron only if its shape matches that of the receptor site.

The effects of neurotransmitters on the receptor sites normally last only the fraction of a second that it takes to produce a change in voltage in the postsynaptic neuron. Once neurotransmitters have done their job, most are either deactivated by an enzyme or taken back up into the presynaptic neuron, a process called **reuptake.** If reuptake did not occur, receptor sites on the postsynaptic neurons would be continuously stimulated. An example of such a situation is the effect of the drug cocaine, which blocks transmitter reuptake. This blocking of reuptake prolongs the transmitter's action and causes the stimulating effect of this drug.

Excitation and inhibition.   At the synapse, then, an electrical signal generates a chemical process that, in turn, triggers a change in voltage in the postsynaptic neuron. This is not to say, however, that the neurotransmitter's action in the receptor site automatically generates a new action potential in the postsynaptic neuron. Instead, when a neurotransmitter molecule makes contact with a receptor site that matches its shape, it can have one of two effects:

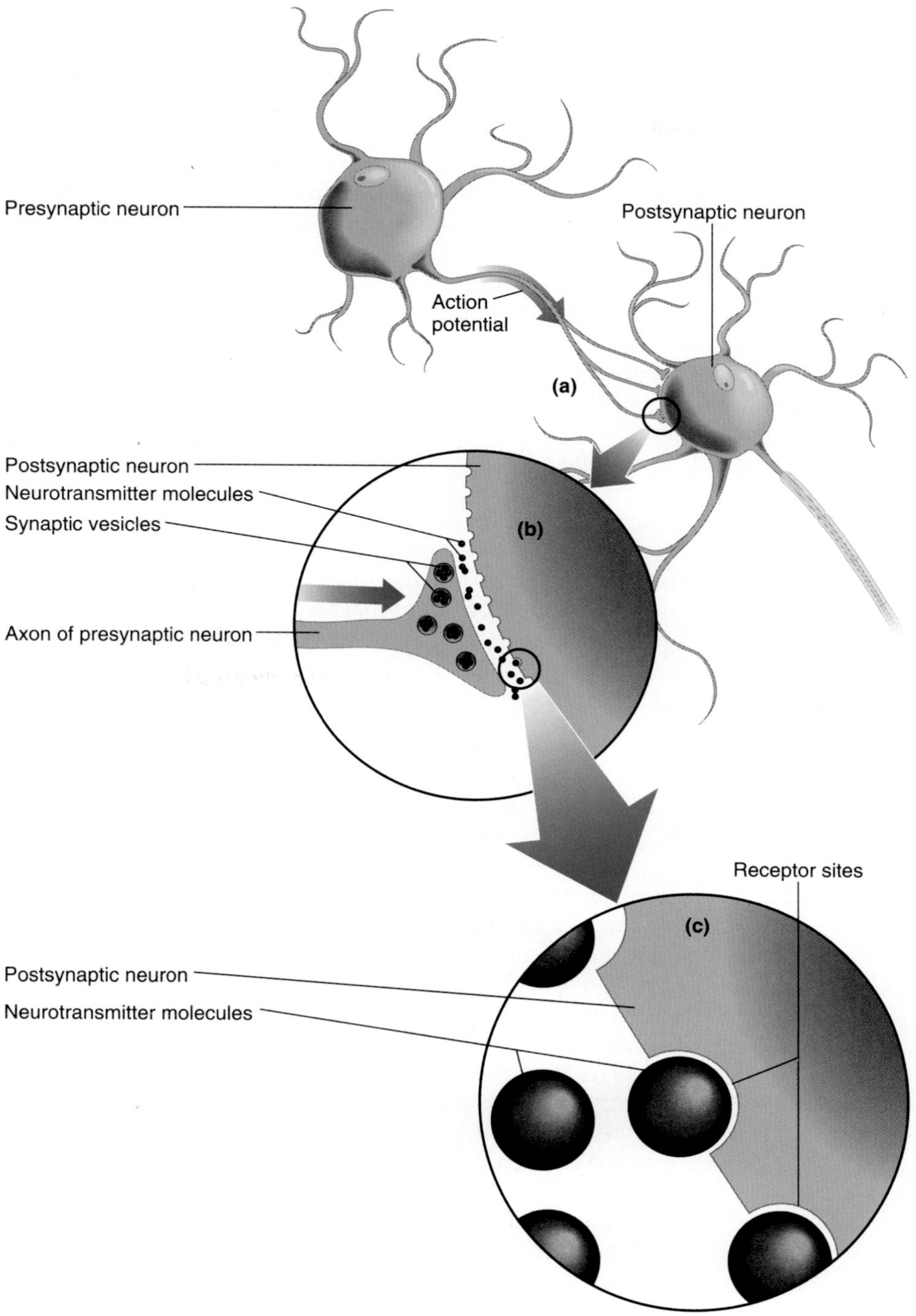

FIGURE 3.5
The transmission of information from one neuron to another

- It can generate an excitatory postsynaptic potential (EPSP). An EPSP is a small decrease in the charge inside the neuron, resulting in a greater positive charge inside the neuron.
- It can generate an inhibitory postsynaptic potential (IPSP). An IPSP is a small increase in the charge inside the neuron, resulting in a greater negative charge inside the neuron.

Transmitters that generate EPSPs are called **excitatory transmitters;** those that generate IPSPs are called **inhibitory transmitters.** Excitatory transmitters increase the probability that an action potential will be generated in the postsynaptic neuron, whereas inhibitory transmitters decrease that probability.

We say that transmitters released from a particular neuron affect the "probability" that the next neuron will fire because the firing usually depends not on the action of just one other neuron but on the summed effect of transmitters released from a large number of neurons. A typical neuron in the brain, for example, receives input from an average of 1000 other neurons. Thus, neurons do not "fire" (generate an action potential) in response to each message individually. Instead, they *integrate* the information being received from hundreds or even thousands of neurons only if the overall excitatory signal compared to the overall inhibitory signal is large enough that the inside of the axon becomes positive enough to reach its threshold for firing.

Figure 3.6 illustrates the principle that whether or not a neuron fires depends on the relative amounts of excitation and inhibition it receives. When there is insufficient excitatory input, as in Figure 3.6b, the neuron does not fire. With sufficient excitation, the neuron reaches threshold and fires, as in Figure 3.6c. If, however, inhibition cancels the excitation, either the neuron slows down its firing or its signal falls below the threshold and it stops firing altogether (Figure 3.6d).

Inhibition may seem counterproductive at first, since it seems to impede the generation of action potentials and therefore to prevent the transmission of messages. In fact, however, it is an essential part of the process of communication that makes behavior possible. Consider what would happen if only excitation occurred at synapses. Because each neuron *receives* signals from many other neurons, and each neuron *sends* signals to many other neurons, the following scenario would unfold in response to a stimulus such as a touch on the shoulder.

Nerve impulses generated by a pressure-sensitive receptor travel to the

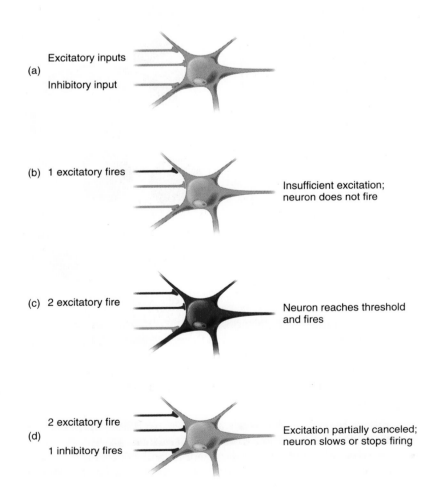

FIGURE 3.6

How excitation and inhibition interact. A neuron receives both excitatory and inhibitory inputs. Low levels of excitation do not cause the neurons to fire. Higher levels do cause it to fire, but the presence of inhibition can stop firing from occurring.

synapse and release excitatory transmitters that excite other neurons. These other neurons, in turn, release excitatory transmitters that trigger impulses in hundreds of other neurons. These neurons, in turn, send their signals to hundreds more neurons, and so on. A simple stimulus, touching a person's shoulder, rapidly generates enough neural activity to engulf the nervous system in waves of excitation. This is clearly not a desirable situation, especially if this uncontrolled excitation reaches the muscles, causing wild contractions. Inhibition prevents such a chaotic response by limiting the uncontrolled spread of excitation.

Perhaps as important as the moderating effect inhibition has on the spread of nerve impulses is the way inhibition enables us to take control of our actions. To understand what this means, consider what happens if you touch a hot stove. You draw your finger back within a fraction of a second. Your behavior, in this case, is automatically determined by a mechanism called the **reflex arc,** which operates as shown in Figure 3.7. The mechanism is so called because the impulses flow in an arc from the finger into the spinal cord and then back to the muscles, without traveling to the brain first, as they normally would in response to milder, less damaging, stimulation.

The reflex arc between receptors in your fingers and muscles in your arm serves an important protective function by bypassing the brain and rapidly sending excitatory signals to keep you from burning yourself. If, however, all of

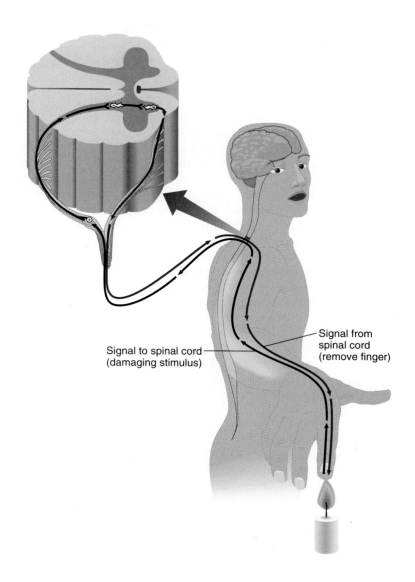

Signal to spinal cord (damaging stimulus)

Signal from spinal cord (remove finger)

FIGURE 3.7
The reflex arc is a mechanism whereby impulses bypass the brain to allow a rapid reaction to potentially dangerous stimulation.

TABLE 3.1
Some common neurotransmitters

Transmitter	Functions and Characteristics
Acetylcholine (ACh)	Movement (activation of skeletal muscles) Attention, arousal, memory Decreased levels found in brains of Alzheimer's patients Drug effects: ACh receptors are stimulated by nicotine, blocked by curare Botulism prevents ACh release; black widow venom causes release
Adenosine triphosphate (ATP)	Activation of smooth muscles such as the heart and such as those found in the intestines and other internal organs
Dopamine	Voluntary movement Decreased levels associated with Parkinson's disease Increased levels associated with symptoms of schizophrenia Drug effects: Chlorpromazine blocks dopamine receptors and therefore decreases symptoms of schizophrenia
Endorphin	Stucture and effects resemble opiate drugs (see Chapter 5) Associated with pain and pleasurable emotions
Epinephrine	Also called adrenaline; also acts as a hormone Causes physiological arousal in autonomic nervous system in response to excitement and emergencies
Gamma-aminobutyric acid (GABA)	A major inhibitory transmitter that is widely distributed in the body Lower-than-normal concentrations associated with anxiety
Norepinephrine	Also called noradrenaline; like epinephrine, associated with autonomic nervous system arousal
Serotonin	Sleep and wakefulness Affected by drugs such as LSD, Ecstasy (see Chapter 5)

our behaviors were controlled in this way, with all stimuli automatically triggering excitatory responses, we would be automotons—we would react to stimuli in the same way every time with no possibility of variance or creativity.

The fact that we don't react in the same way to all stimuli is due, at least in part, to inhibition, and it is this inhibition that enables us to take control of our actions. Imagine, for example, that you are serving guests at a dinner party. You pick up a hot serving tray with two potholders, but as you are carrying the tray across the room you realize that there is a thin spot in one of the potholders and that the fingers of your right hand are rapidly getting very hot. Do you immediately drop the tray, bouncing the turkey across the dining room floor? Probably not. More likely you grin and bear it, getting the turkey to the table as fast as possible even if it means experiencing some discomfort.

Your conscious suppression of the initial urge to drop the serving tray is made possible by inhibitory signals in your nervous system. You created these signals by choosing to hold onto the tray, and those signals prevented your hand from reflexively dropping the tray (Graham, 1990).

We have seen that neurons generate action potentials, communicate with other neurons, and integrate excitatory and inhibitory inputs from many neurons. This integration occurs where neurons come together at the synapse. Let's look more closely at how the neurotransmitters that are released at the synapse influence behavior.

Neurotransmitters and behavior.   One way neurotransmitters influence behavior is by specializing: each neurotransmitter serves a limited number of functions. Table 3.1 lists a few of the major transmitters and their functions. Neurotransmitters have been linked to specific functions in a number of ways. One way has been to note how behavior is influenced by higher- or lower-than-normal concentrations of a specific transmitter. Consider the case of Peter W., a patient with **Parkinson's disease,** a condition characterized by difficulty in initiating voluntary movements.

Patients with Parkinson's disease have difficulty initiating voluntary movements.

Shortly after he turned 53, Peter W. began to notice a slight tremor in his right hand. Within a year he was having difficulty performing everyday tasks such as buttoning his shirt. Later he found it hard to change his facial expression and to gesture with his hands, and began to walk with slow, shuffling steps. He was diagnosed as having Parkinson's disease and given a drug called L-DOPA. After taking it, Peter experienced an almost immediate improvement: he could walk smoothly again and had little trouble buttoning his shirt. Unfortunately, after three years the drug became less effective, and Peter began experiencing hallucinations and periods of out-of-control emotionality. To prevent these side effects it was necessary to discontinue the use of the drug for periods of time.

Peter's treatment was based on the fact that Parkinson's patients often have decreased levels of the neurotransmitter **dopamine,** suggesting that dopamine plays a role in controlling voluntary movements. Additional evidence for this conclusion comes from research in which the brain is treated with stains that mark specific neurotransmitters. Stains that highlight dopamine in the rat brain have shown that it is localized near nerve pathways that control movement.

Discovery of this link between dopamine, movement, and Parkinson's disease led to the development of L-DOPA as a therapy for the disease. This drug, when ingested, is transported in the bloodstream to the brain and converted by the body into dopamine. (Dopamine cannot be given directly, because it is blocked from entering the brain by a membrane called the blood-brain barrier. L-DOPA can, however, pass through that barrier.) By elevating patients' dopamine level, L-DOPA allows them to regain much of the control they had lost over their muscular movements.

When L-DOPA was introduced in 1968, it was hailed as a miracle drug. Unfortunately, adverse side effects, like the hallucinations and emotionality experienced by Peter, have limited the drug's usefulness. But those side effects in themselves provide further insight into the link between neurotransmitters and behavior.

In the search for the cause of L-DOPA's side effects, researchers noticed that they resembled some of the symptoms of schizophrenia, a severe mental disorder marked by hallucinations and disturbed thoughts and emotions. Furthermore, the symptoms of schizophrenia have been linked to an *excess* of dopamine

16   DISORDERS

Left: Cocaine affects behavior by influencing neurotransmitter activity at the synapse. **Right:** Curare, a chemical used by South American Indians on poisonous darts, causes paralysis and death by its action at the synapse.

in an area of the brain associated with emotions. Thus, increasing dopamine in the brain areas responsible for movement, which occurs in L-DOPA therapy for Parkinson's disease, might also act on other brain areas that are associated with emotions, to create symptoms resembling those of schizophrenia.

Although this explanation of Parkinson's disease and its side effects sounds reasonable and is backed by considerable evidence, questions still remain. For example, why don't the side effects appear immediately? Why does L-DOPA work well on some patients but not on others? Obviously, there is a strong link between neurotransmitters and behavior, but many details of this relationship are still unclear.

The example of Peter W. shows that neurotransmitters are more than just vehicles to help the action potential jump the synapse. Many neurotransmitters are associated with specific brain areas or parts of the body and therefore have specific effects on behavior. For example, acetylcholine (ACh) is the transmitter released onto muscles that causes them to contract. Disrupting the action of ACh can therefore have disastrous effects, as demonstrated by what happens when an animal is poisoned by the chemical curare. Curare, which is placed on the tips of arrows by native hunters in South America, blocks receptors that are usually stimulated by ACh. When those receptors are blocked, ACh can't stimulate them and movement becomes impossible. Thus, if an animal has the misfortune of being hit by a curare-tipped arrow, paralysis results, making breathing impossible and leading to the animal's death.

A more familiar drug, nicotine, affects acetylcholine receptors in a different way. Rather than blocking them, nicotine stimulates ACh receptors, thereby causing people to become highly active, especially when the concentration of nicotine is high. Drugs can also affect behavior by enhancing or preventing the release of a neurotransmitter or, as in the case of cocaine, by blocking a neurotransmitter's reuptake into the synaptic vesicles. These drug effects, which we'll discuss in detail in Chapter 5, graphically illustrate the link between neurotransmitter action at the synapse and behavior. The action of drugs at the synapse can potentially disrupt behavior by upsetting the normal balance of excitation and inhibition there.

It is clear that we can learn much about behavior by studying biological mechanisms that operate at a microscopic level of the neuron, synapse, and neurotransmitter. We now expand our field of view by looking at how messages travel through the body as a whole.

5   CONSCIOUSNESS

The Body's Communication Networks: The Nervous and Endocrine Systems

The body has two communication networks. The first is the **nervous system,** which consists of billions of neurons. The nervous system comprises two subsystems, the *central nervous system* and the *peripheral nervous system.* The body's second communication network is the endocrine system, which transmits messages through the bloodstream by means of chemicals called hormones. We will first describe the nervous system and then the endocrine system.

The Central Nervous System

The **central nervous system** is made up of neurons that comprise the brain and the spinal cord (Figure 3.8a). Of central importance to this system is the brain, the control center for behavior.

The brain.   The centerpiece of the central nervous system, the **brain,** is the amazingly complex network of neurons contained in the skull that directs behavior; creates our perceptions, emotions, and thoughts; and oversees the bodily functions that keep us alive. Although it weighs only about 3 pounds, the human brain has been called "the most complex structure in the known universe" (Thompson, 1985). For one thing, there are almost as many neurons in the brain—about 100 billion—as there are stars in the Milky Way galaxy (Fischbach, 1992). But even more indicative of the brain's complexity is that each of these 100 billion neurons receives signals from about 1000 others. The number and complexity of these connections parallels the complexity of human behavior.

If we look at the brain from the top (see Figure 3.8b), we immediately see a key feature of its anatomy. From this viewpoint, it resembles the two halves of a walnut. These two halves are called the **left** and **right hemispheres.** They are connected to each other by a bundle of nerve fibers called the **corpus callosum,** which sends messages between them. Later in this chapter we will see the functional significance of the brain's division into hemispheres. Note that both have a wrinkled covering, or outer layer. This top portion of the brain, called the *cerebral cortex,* contains the machinery for our senses, thinking, and movement.

The cerebral cortex.   The term *cortex* comes from the Latin for "bark" or "rind." The cortex of any organ is hence its outer layer. The **cerebral cortex** is a 3-millimeter-thick layer of neurons containing mechanisms that enable us to coordinate our movements, perceive the environment, and carry out higher mental functions such as language, problem solving, and planning for the future.

As shown in Figure 3.8c, the cerebral cortex is divided into four **lobes** governing different functions: the **occipital lobe** (seeing), the **temporal lobe** (hearing), the **parietal lobe** (touch), and the **frontal lobe** (thinking, planning, and motor coordination). The "wrinkles" of the cortex, called *convolutions,* provide a way of packing a large amount of cortex into a small area. If the cortex were flattened out it would cover a surface over 6 square feet in area (Mountcastle, 1978).

Subcortical nuclei.   If we look beneath the cerebral cortex, into the center of the brain, we find a vast array of different structures, called *nuclei*—places in which many neurons synapse. **Subcortical** (beneath the cortex) **nuclei** serve functions such as sexual behavior, hunger, thirst, memory, and emotional behavior (Figure 3.8d). The following four structures are of particular importance.

1. The **amygdala** is one of the places in the brain in which memories are stored; the amygdala specializes in memories about things to approach and avoid. As you'll see later, it also plays a role in emotion.

2. The **hippocampus,** another structure involved in memory and emotion, stores memories for events.

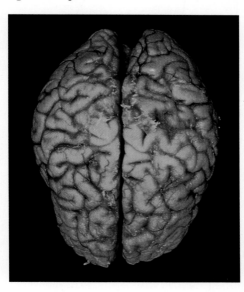

Top view of the brain, showing left and right hemispheres

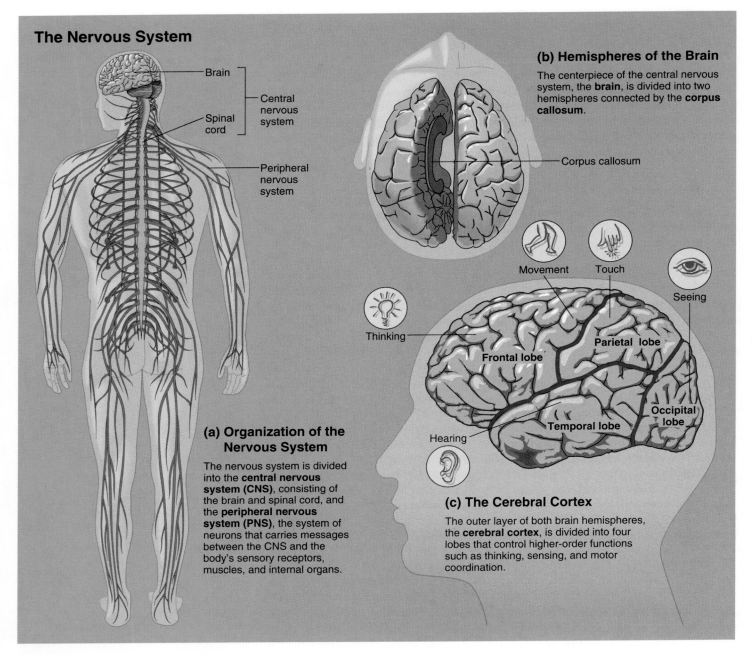

The Nervous System

Brain
Spinal cord
Central nervous system
Peripheral nervous system

(a) Organization of the Nervous System

The nervous system is divided into the **central nervous system (CNS)**, consisting of the brain and spinal cord, and the **peripheral nervous system (PNS)**, the system of neurons that carries messages between the CNS and the body's sensory receptors, muscles, and internal organs.

(b) Hemispheres of the Brain

The centerpiece of the central nervous system, the **brain**, is divided into two hemispheres connected by the **corpus callosum**.

Corpus callosum

Thinking
Movement
Touch
Seeing
Frontal lobe
Parietal lobe
Temporal lobe
Occipital lobe
Hearing

(c) The Cerebral Cortex

The outer layer of both brain hemispheres, the **cerebral cortex**, is divided into four lobes that control higher-order functions such as thinking, sensing, and motor coordination.

FIGURE 3.8
The nervous system

3. The **thalamus,** which is located almost exactly at the center of the brain, is the switching station for sensory information. Neurons from all sensory systems pass through the thalamus on their way to areas in the cerebral cortex. This structure, too, like the amygdala and hippocampus, has a role in storing memories.

4. The **hypothalamus** is divided into many smaller nuclei that serve different functions. Within the hypothalamus are groups of neurons that regulate temperature, hunger, thirst, sexual arousal, and the emotions. In addition, the hypothalamus controls the nerve circuits that regulate internal organs such as the heart and digestive system; it also regulates the endocrine system—the second communication system of the body—which controls many aspects of our behavior by secreting chemicals into the bloodstream. For a structure about the size of a small pea, the hypothalamus has an astounding number of functions.

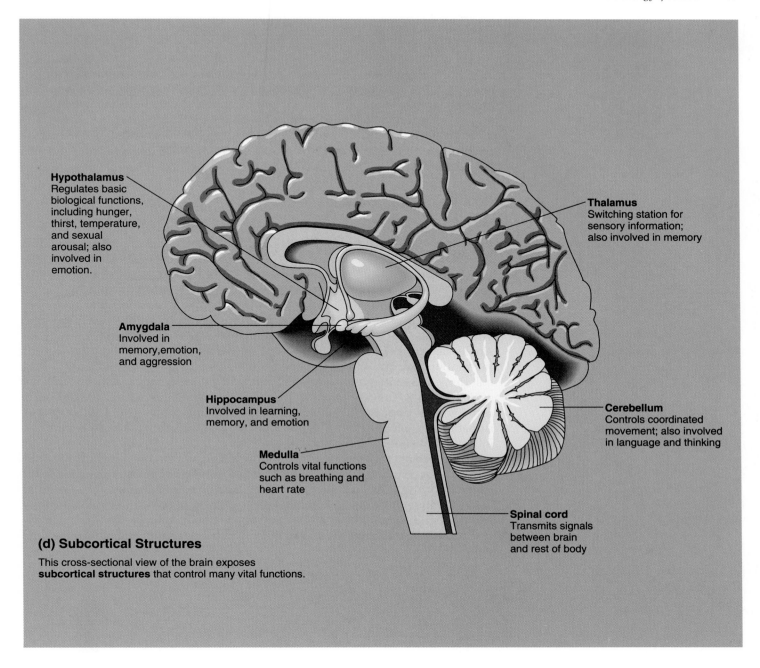

Hypothalamus
Regulates basic biological functions, including hunger, thirst, temperature, and sexual arousal; also involved in emotion.

Thalamus
Switching station for sensory information; also involved in memory

Amygdala
Involved in memory, emotion, and aggression

Hippocampus
Involved in learning, memory, and emotion

Cerebellum
Controls coordinated movement; also involved in language and thinking

Medulla
Controls vital functions such as breathing and heart rate

Spinal cord
Transmits signals between brain and rest of body

(d) Subcortical Structures

This cross-sectional view of the brain exposes **subcortical structures** that control many vital functions.

The cerebellum.   The small, wrinkled, brainlike structure nestled under the back of the brain is called the **cerebellum** (which means "little brain" in Latin). One of its major functions is to control coordinated movement. In addition, parts of the cerebellum are important for language and thinking, as evidenced by the fact that damage to the cerebellum is associated with memory problems and with learning disorders in children (Leinen et al., 1989).

The brain stem and spinal cord.   The brain and the cerebellum sit atop a long, roughly cylindrical tube called the **spinal cord.** The spinal cord transmits signals from the sense organs and muscles that are below the level of the head to the brain, and funnels signals from the brain to the rest of the body. (Signals at the level of the head enter the brain through separate *cranial nerves* that do not travel in the spinal cord. For example, signals from the eyes enter the brain through the optic nerve.)

As signals traveling up the spinal cord enter the skull, the spinal cord becomes the **brain stem,** which contains the **medulla,** a group of neurons that controls vital functions such as breathing, heart rate, salivation, coughing, and sneezing. Fatal heroin, cocaine, or amphetamine overdoses occur when those drugs, acting on the medulla, disrupt the body's vital functions.

Also contained in the medulla are the **reticular formation** and the **raphe system,** collections of neurons that play important roles in controlling sleep and wakefulness.

The Peripheral Nervous System

The central nervous system usually holds center stage in descriptions of the biology of behavior, because it includes the body's central computer, the brain. It is important, however, not to lose sight of the **peripheral nervous system**—the system of neurons outside the brain and spinal cord that carries nerve impulses between the brain and the sensory receptors, muscles, and internal organs (Figure 3.9). Consider, for example, what life would be like if signals could no longer reach the brain or be transmitted from the brain. With no input to the brain from your senses, you would be totally isolated in utterly silent darkness, with no smells, tastes, or sensations from your skin. With no input from receptors in your internal organs, you would experience no feeling inside your body. You could still think and remember past events and perhaps feel hunger and thirst or have sexual feelings, but you wouldn't be able to talk or move, because the brain could send no signals to the muscles. The communications achieved by the peripheral nervous system are essential for translating the workings of the brain into consciousness and behavior.

The peripheral nervous system is divided into autonomic and somatic divisions. The autonomic division (or **autonomic nervous system**) is responsible for communicating between the brain and the body's internal organs. These internal organs include the heart, stomach, lungs, tear ducts, glands, and blood vessels—and the smooth muscles found in the stomach and intestines. The somatic division (or **somatic nervous system**) is responsible for communicating between the

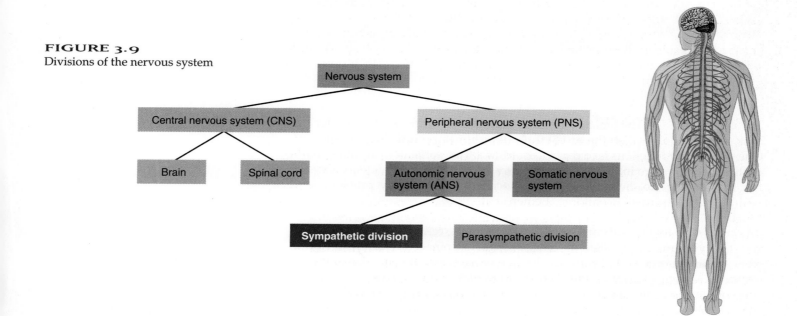

FIGURE 3.9
Divisions of the nervous system

brain and the rest of the body, including the senses and the skeletal muscles responsible for moving the arms, legs, torso, and head.

The somatic and autonomic nervous systems transmit signals both toward and away from the brain. When you are touched on the shoulder and respond by turning your head, signals are sent via the somatic nervous system from your shoulder to your brain so that you sense the touch, and from your brain to your neck muscles so that you turn your head. Similarly, stomach contractions occur in response to signals sent via the autonomic nervous system from the brain to stomach muscles, and you sense those contractions only when receptors in your stomach send signals back to your brain.

An important organizing feature of the autonomic nervous system, from a behavioral point of view, is its division into *sympathetic* and *parasympathetic divisions*. The sympathetic and parasympathetic divisions are connected (with a few exceptions) to the same internal organs, but their effects on those organs are different (Figure 3.10). The **sympathetic division** mobilizes the body for emergencies, whereas the **parasympathetic division** maintains the body at a more normal level. For example, in an emergency sympathetic neurons send signals that cause our heart rate to increase and breathing to speed up. Once the emergency is over, signals from parasympathetic neurons bring our heartbeat and respiration back to normal. One way to remember the functions of the sympathetic and parasympathetic divisions is to associate the *S* in sympathetic with Speed or Stress; another is to consider that the sympathetic division is "sympathetic" to the emotions.

Although they are distinct, the somatic and autonomic nervous systems and the sympathetic and parasympathetic divisions often act simultaneously under the direction of the brain. Consider the following scene in a basketball game. As she dribbles down the court, the player's brain is sending signals along neurons in her somatic nervous system to the muscles involved in running, dribbling, and looking up at the basket. Meanwhile, her eyes are sending signals along neurons that connect her visual receptors to the brain, so that she sees the basket, the crowd, and the other players. When she is ready to shoot, signals from her brain to her arm and hand muscles help her loft the ball toward the basket. These functions are all handled by the somatic nervous system as it receives information from the environment and sends signals to the muscles.

But there is more to the game of basketball than the somatic nervous system's perceiving, running, and shooting. There is also an emotional component, served by the autonomic nervous system. As tension and excitement mount, with the score tied and only seconds to go, our player's heart rate increases. When she shoots the game-winning basket at the buzzer, her heart is pounding wildly and her energy is sky-high; she is energized by the sympathetic neurons of the autonomic nervous system. Eventually, however, her body begins to calm down as the parasympathetic division of the autonomic nervous system takes over and helps return her heart rate and other functions to normal.

12   EMOTION

The Endocrine System

We have seen how nerve impulses communicate along neurons, the transmission lines of the nervous system. There is, in addition, another communication system in the body. The **endocrine system** consists of **endocrine glands** that secrete chemicals called **hormones** into the bloodstream (Figure 3.11). We can appreciate the difference between the way the two systems communicate by likening the nervous system to a telephone network and the endocrine system to a radio transmission tower.

In a telephone network signals follow specific wires to reach their destination. In contrast, a radio transmission tower broadcasts signals widely through the air over a large area, and those signals are picked up only by radios tuned to the frequency of the signal. In our analogy, neurons correspond to the wires of the telephone network, coursing through the body. The endocrine system is sim-

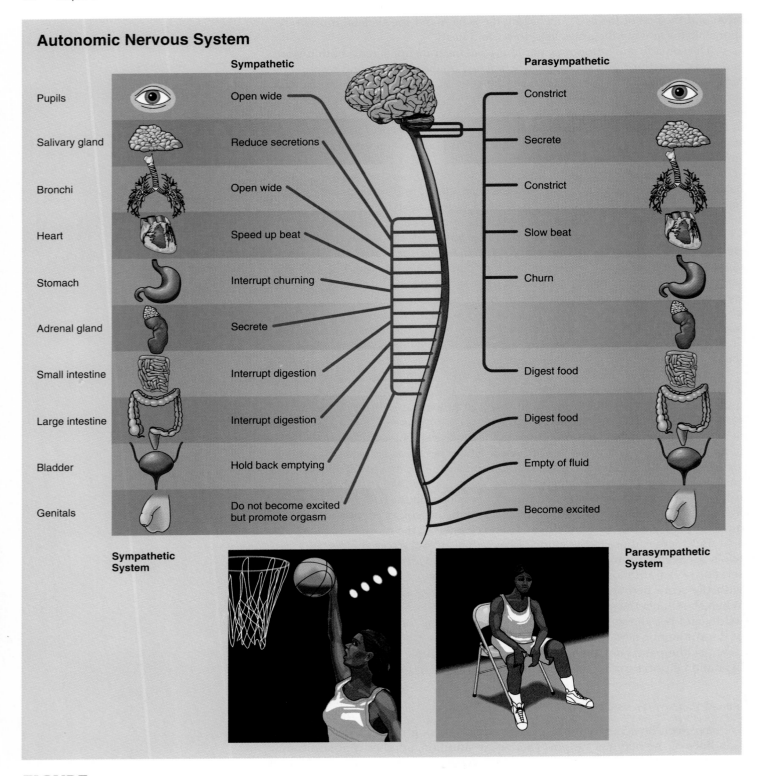

Autonomic Nervous System

	Sympathetic		**Parasympathetic**	
Pupils	Open wide		Constrict	
Salivary gland	Reduce secretions		Secrete	
Bronchi	Open wide		Constrict	
Heart	Speed up beat		Slow beat	
Stomach	Interrupt churning		Churn	
Adrenal gland	Secrete			
Small intestine	Interrupt digestion		Digest food	
Large intestine	Interrupt digestion		Digest food	
Bladder	Hold back emptying		Empty of fluid	
Genitals	Do not become excited but promote orgasm		Become excited	

Sympathetic System

Parasympathetic System

FIGURE 3.10

The autonomic nervous system, showing what happens when the sympathetic or parasympathetic divisions are active

ilar to the radio transmission tower, because it sends messages over a wide area by releasing hormones that travel throughout the bloodstream. Just as radio signals are only picked up by radios tuned to that signal's frequency, these hormones have an effect only at places possessing *receptor sites* sensitive to them.

The hormones released by the endocrine system serve a variety of functions, playing a role in regulating digestion, metabolic function, growth, and reproduction. For example, hormones secreted from the ovaries (for women) and

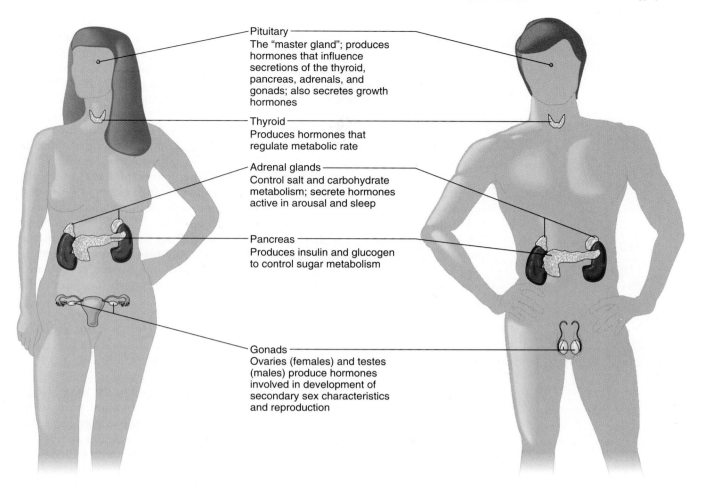

Pituitary —
The "master gland"; produces hormones that influence secretions of the thyroid, pancreas, adrenals, and gonads; also secretes growth hormones

Thyroid —
Produces hormones that regulate metabolic rate

Adrenal glands —
Control salt and carbohydrate metabolism; secrete hormones active in arousal and sleep

Pancreas —
Produces insulin and glucogen to control sugar metabolism

Gonads —
Ovaries (females) and testes (males) produce hormones involved in development of secondary sex characteristics and reproduction

FIGURE 3.11
The major glands in the endocrine system. The adrenal glands sit atop the kidneys.

11   MOTIVATION

the testes (for men) help establish female and male secondary sex characteristics and regulate reproduction. Hormones secreted from the adrenal glands help increase activation and mobilize a person for action in response to danger. Hormones secreted from the thyroid gland help regulate metabolic rate.

The importance of these hormones for maintaining our body becomes apparent when an endocrine gland malfunctions and secretes too little or too much hormone. For example, people whose thyroid glands produce too little hormone often become tired, sensitive to the cold, and, in extreme cases, have difficulty thinking. People whose glands produce too much thyroid hormone usually become nervous and irritable and lose weight. People with these conditions often take medication to achieve the proper hormone concentration.

Although the endocrine system operates differently than the nervous system, the two systems are closely linked. The major link is between the hypothalamus—the subcortical structure responsible for regulating temperature, hunger, thirst, sexual arousal, and the emotions—and the pituitary gland. The pituitary has been called the master gland of the endocrine system because it contains at least eight hormones, some of which stimulate other glands in the endocrine system.

We can grasp the link between the hypothalamus and the pituitary gland by returning to our basketball game. The high stress and physical exertion of the game generate signals throughout our player's brain, some of which reach the hypothalamus. The hypothalamus responds to this stimulation by signaling the pituitary, which in turn releases hormones into the bloodstream that mobilize other endocrine glands. The adrenal gland, for example, is stimulated to secrete epinephrine into the bloodstream to provide the extra energy needed to deal with the stress and exertion of the game.

Another link between the nervous system and endocrine glands is the signals sent by the autonomic nervous system to the glands. Just as glands can be triggered into action by hormones released by the pituitary gland, they can be triggered by neural signals from the autonomic nervous system. Thus, during the basketball game the adrenal gland receives signals from the sympathetic division of the autonomic nervous system that also causes it to release epinephrine.

The neurons of the nervous system and the glands of the endocrine system therefore work together to achieve a common goal: communication of information throughout the body. The nervous system's speed makes it ideal for directing immediate action such as perception, movement, and thinking, and it also has the storage capability to serve memory. The endocrine system is slower but serves essential functions such as regulating growth and reproduction, maintaining the body's chemical environment, and regulating metabolism. Later in this book, in the chapter on stress and health, we will see that endocrine function plays an important role in determining the body's response to stressful stimuli.

Having described the body's two communication systems, we are now ready to focus in more detail on the functioning of the master structure of the nervous system—the brain.

The Brain: Localized Functions Working Together

One of the things you will have observed while learning about the brain's organization and the function of its various structures is that different parts of the brain have different functions. This idea—that different functions are located in specific areas—is called **localization of function.** Localization of function is now accepted as an important principle of brain function, but researchers did not always accept this principle.

Early brain researchers felt that the brain operated according to the principle of *holism*—that is, that it functioned as a whole. According to this view, the whole brain is involved in the activities it controls so that activities such as thinking, seeing, or memory would each generate activity in all lobes and areas of the brain. Prior to 1800, holism was the accepted mechanism of brain functioning, but thereafter research providing evidence for localization began in earnest. This research helped us to understand that one way that the brain accomplishes its amazing feats is through specialization, specific areas specializing in specific behaviors.

Yet research has also established that, as specialized as specific brain areas may be, behavior is rarely determined by one area working in isolation. Even the simplest behavior involves the simultaneous operation of many specialized brain areas. For example, you have just learned that memory is served by a number of different subcortical structures, and that movement is controlled by an area in the frontal lobe of the cerebral cortex as well as by the cerebellum. Thus, the modern view of brain operation is that *many areas specialized for specific functions work together as a system* to determine behavior. Before investigating how numerous structures work together as a system, we will examine the idea of localization.

Localization of Function in the Brain

One of the most prominent challenges to holism was put forward in the late 18th century by the Austrian anatomist Franz Joseph Gall, who tried to trace specific abilities and behavioral tendencies to particular parts of the brain. For example, Gall thought he observed that people with good memories had large protruding eyes, so he hypothesized that the person's eyes were pushed forward by a large brain area located directly behind the eyes. Based on this kind of reasoning and

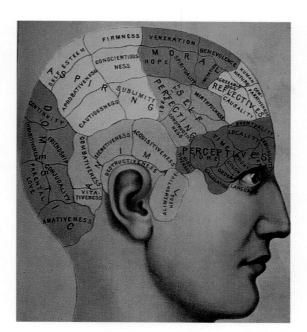

FIGURE 3.12
A phrenology map, showing the supposed locations in the brain of various human characteristics

the knowledge that damage to specific parts of the brain seemed to affect specific behaviors, Gall developed maps of the cortex in which he assigned characteristics such as cautiousness, self-esteem, and parental love to specific brain areas (Figure 3.12).

Besides drawing maps of brain areas, Gall also formulated a procedure, called *phrenology,* for determining the development of specific characteristics in individuals. His procedure was simple enough: he felt the bumps and depressions on a person's skull and used them to gauge the amount of a certain personality characteristic. So, for example, a sizable bump on the skull over the "self-esteem" area of the brain indicated that the person had high self-esteem, whereas a bump over the "parental love" area indicated that a person had a high capacity to love children.

Gall's proposal is a good example of a pseudoscientific theory, one based on no empirical evidence. The lack of actual correlations between the shape of the skull and specific personality characteristics, combined with scientists' skepticism that a bump or depression on the brain would cause a corresponding bump or depression in the skull, led Gall's contemporaries to reject his theory.

The ironic thing about Gall's theory of phrenology is that although it was both wrong and unscientific, the basic idea that specific brain areas served specific functions *was* correct. But it took a long time for this idea to overcome the ridicule heaped upon Gall and other phrenologists by holists in the scientific establishment. Holists referred even to legitimate scientific evidence for localization of function as the work of the "diagram makers." Nonetheless, later in the 1800s convincing evidence began accumulating to support the idea that different functions are localized in different areas of the brain.

We will look first at evidence for localization in the cortex, the 3-millimeter-thick covering of the brain. We will begin with language—because it was one of the first functions to be studied—and will then consider the closely related function, thinking. Continuing our consideration of cortical localization, we will describe research showing how the senses and our ability to move are served by specific cortical areas. Finally, we will look within the brain at subcortical evidence for localization of functions such as memory and the emotions.

Language: Broca's and Wernicke's areas.   Beginning in the mid-1800s, a number of investigators reported that damage to a specific area in the left frontal lobe of the brain results in *aphasia,* a condition in which those afflicted have difficulty

8   LANGUAGE

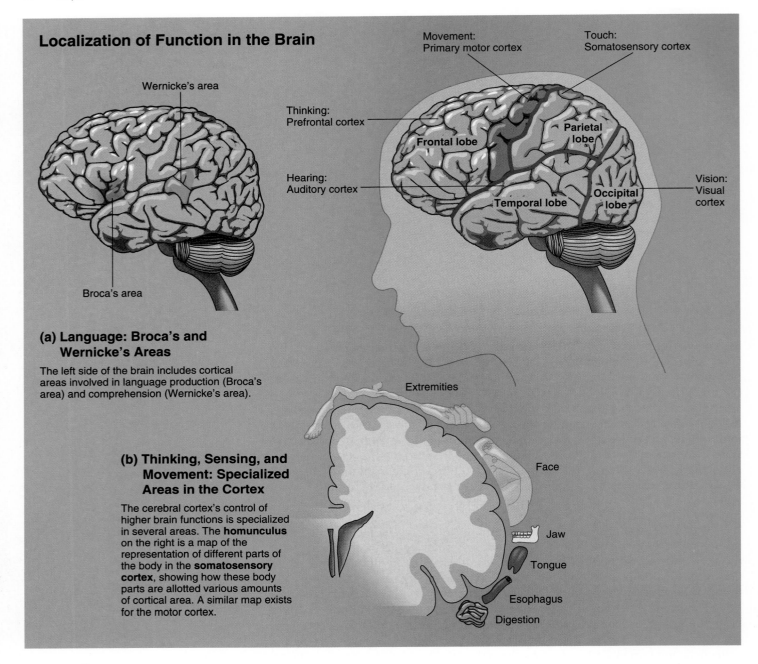

Localization of Function in the Brain

Wernicke's area

Broca's area

Movement:
Primary motor cortex

Touch:
Somatosensory cortex

Thinking:
Prefrontal cortex

Parietal
lobe

Frontal lobe

Hearing:
Auditory cortex

Temporal lobe

Occipital
lobe

Vision:
Visual
cortex

(a) Language: Broca's and Wernicke's Areas

The left side of the brain includes cortical areas involved in language production (Broca's area) and comprehension (Wernicke's area).

Extremities

Face

Jaw

Tongue

Esophagus

Digestion

(b) Thinking, Sensing, and Movement: Specialized Areas in the Cortex

The cerebral cortex's control of higher brain functions is specialized in several areas. The **homunculus** on the right is a map of the representation of different parts of the body in the **somatosensory cortex**, showing how these body parts are allotted various amounts of cortical area. A similar map exists for the motor cortex.

FIGURE 3.13
The localization of function in the brain

producing speech even though they can understand other people's. In 1863, the renowned French surgeon Paul Broca described eight patients who had damage in what is now called **Broca's area** (see Figure 3.13a). Their major symptom, Broca reported, was labored and disjointed speech. A modern example is a patient who was asked by neurologist Norman Geschwind (1979) about his dental appointment. The patient answered, with great difficulty, "Yes . . . Monday . . . Dad and Dick . . . Wednesday nine o'clock . . . ten o'clock . . . doctors . . . and . . . teeth." This way of speaking, which omits many linking words, is called *telegraphic speech* and contains mostly nouns, verbs, and short familiar phrases. People with this condition can still comprehend speech and, as they are aware that they often can't find the correct word, can become extremely frustrated in their attempts to communicate.

Not long after Broca's report was published, Carl Wernicke found another area, this one in the left temporal lobe, that also plays a role in language. Patients

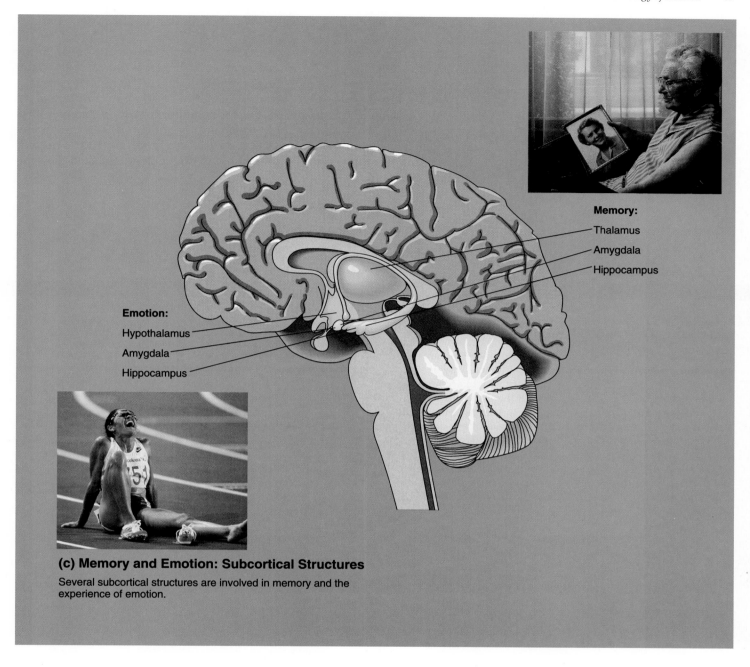

Memory:

Thalamus

Amygdala

Hippocampus

Emotion:

Hypothalamus

Amygdala

Hippocampus

(c) Memory and Emotion: Subcortical Structures
Several subcortical structures are involved in memory and the experience of emotion.

with damage to this area, now known as **Wernicke's area,** have difficulty *understanding* speech. This difficulty in understanding speech is reflected in their own speech, which though fluently produced makes little sense. Consider, for example, the following ramblings that a patient produced during an interview with a psychologist:

> Oh, sure, go ahead, any old think you want. If I could I would. Oh, I'm taking the word the wrong way to say, all of the barbers here whenever they stop you it's going around and around, if you know what I mean, that is tying and tying for repucer, repuceration, well, we were trying the best that we could while another time it was with the beds over there the same thing . . . (Gardner, 1976).

The nonsensical nature of this patient's speech is due to the fact that he does not comprehend the meaning of the speech sounds he is producing.

More recently, further studies of people with damage to various parts of the cortex have indicated that certain areas of the brain are specialized for the production of different parts of speech. Patients with damage to areas in the frontal and parietal lobes have trouble using verbs, whereas patients with damage to areas in the temporal lobe cannot produce nouns (Damasio & Damasio, 1992). Some patients suffer from even more specific deficits; for example, one patient with temporal lobe damage lost the ability to produce proper nouns, such as people's names, but could still produce other types of nouns. This modern research, which has located brain areas that serve very specific functions, extends the pioneering work of Broca and Wernicke that originally established the principle of localization.

MEASUREMENT & METHODOLOGY

Imaging the Brain

Drawing connections between damage to a specific area of the brain and a patient's symptoms is a time-honored way of studying brain function. But until recently the only way to accomplish this was to observe patients' symptoms and then wait for them to die so an autopsy could be performed. The time between observing a patient's symptoms and determining the site of the damage was therefore often lengthy. But within the past few decades, new technology has made it possible to create images of the living brain. These images of the working human brain enable researchers to determine not only the site of brain damage, but also the neural activity that occurs as the brain directs different behaviors. The fol-

lowing four techniques are used both in brain research and for the medical diagnosis of brain problems.

CAT (Computerized Axial Tomography) Scan

The **CAT scan,** the most widely used imaging technique, combines X-ray technology with computer processing. The patient's head rests inside a large cylinder (Figure A) while an X-ray tube is rotated around it, taking pictures of a horizontal "slice" of the brain. Computer processing of these X rays creates pictures like the one shown in Figure B.

FIGURE A

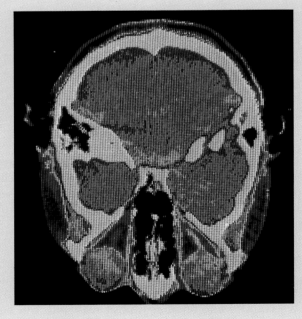

FIGURE B

Thinking: The prefrontal cortex.   Thinking, problem solving, and planning for the future appear to be localized in the **prefrontal cortex** (see Figure 3.13b), the part of the frontal lobe toward the front of the head (Goldman-Rakic, 1984; Roland, 1984). P. E. Roland and L. Freiberg (1985) demonstrated this by measuring *regional cerebral blood flow (RCBF)* in humans engaged in various types of thinking tasks. (See Measurement & Methodology, "Imaging the Brain.") They observed increased cortical activity in the prefrontal lobe when subjects were solving a subtraction problem or a problem that involved imagining walking along a route in the neighborhood near their house. During the "route" task, Roland and Freiberg also observed activity in the occipital and temporal lobes.

The finding that a number of different areas in the brain are activated during thinking illustrates that, though specific areas of the brain serve specific

MRI (Magnetic Resonance Imaging)

MRI, like the CAT scan, creates pictures of the brain's structure. MRI pictures are created by placing the patient in a strong magnetic field and sending radio waves through the brain. These radio waves activate hydrogen atoms inside brain structures and cause them to emit harmless radiation. Because different structures emit different amounts of radiation, they become sharply differentiated, as shown in Figure C. These pictures are much sharper than CAT scan images, and it is also possible to create three-dimensional representations of the brain with MRI. Its drawback at the present time is its high cost and the limited availability of MRI machines (Elliot, 1986).

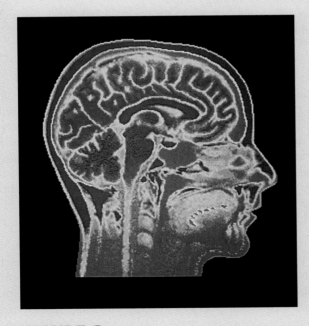

FIGURE C

PET (Positron Emission Tomography) Scan

The **PET scan** is used to determine the biochemical *activity* of the brain as a person behaves. The person is typically injected with an isotope of carbon, nitrogen, or oxygen that has been radioactively labeled. These isotopes are incorporated into brain structures to the degree that the structure is active, with more active structures taking up more isotope. The resulting radioactivity, which is extremely weak and of no danger to the person, is picked up by radiation detectors placed around the head and turned into images. The PET scan image is much fuzzier than those produced by CAT scans or MRI. But because it records the brain's *functioning*, it can often detect changes that are not visible from simply looking at the brain's structure. For example, PET scan images can show the brain activity of a person who is alternating between manic (euphoric and highly active) and depressive mood states. Large increases of brain activity in the manic state, indicated by a red color on a PET scan record (Phelps & Mazziotta, 1985), would not be visible in a CAT scan or MRI record.

RCBF (Regional Cerebral Blood Flow)

The **RCBF** technique described in the text also measures the brain's activity during behavior. Radioactively labeled xenon is injected into the blood. Because increases in brain activity cause increases in blood flow, areas of the brain that are more active take up the xenon and give off more radiation. This radiation is picked up by detectors surrounding the cerebral cortex. RCBF imaging is similar to PET scans in that both measure radiation given off by active brain structures. They differ in that the PET scan can measure activity both on the brain's surface and deep inside the brain, whereas the RCBF technique can measure activity only in the 3-millimeter-thick cerebral cortex, on the surface of the brain.

The brain imaging techniques described here have not only become part of the physician's arsenal of tools for the diagnosis of health problems, but have also created new ways for researchers to uncover the secrets of the living human brain.

functions, most behaviors require a number of brain areas to work together. This concept will resurface soon, when we examine the idea that the brain operates as a system.

Touch: The somatosensory cortex.   The area on the parietal lobe that is specialized to respond to touch is called the **somatosensory cortex** (Figure 3.13b). Just as the brain as a whole is organized into different areas with different functions, the somatosensory area of the cortex is organized so that specific parts of the cortex correspond to specific locations on the body. Researchers have demonstrated this by showing that touching a particular point of a monkey's body generates electrical signals at a specific small area of the somatosensory cortex (Nelson et al., 1980; Woolsey, Marshall, & Bard, 1942). This correspondence between points on the body and points on the cortex has been demonstrated in humans by two neurosurgeons, Wilder Penfield and Theodore Rasmussen (1950). Penfield and Rasmussen's patients were undergoing operations to remove tumors in the brain suspected of causing epileptic seizures. Before performing the surgery, Penfield and Rasmussen applied low-voltage electrical stimulation to different points on the surface of the somatosensory cortex. The following case report illustrates what happens when specific points in the somatosensory cortex are stimulated.

> Sally R. has been diagnosed as having a tumor located near the parietal lobe of her cortex. Prior to her operation for its removal she is given a mild sedative, but she remains awake. Local anesthesia is applied to areas of the skull covering the parietal cortex. A piece of skull is removed, exposing the surface of the parietal cortex and the surrounding area. The surgeon, Wilder Penfield, instructs Sally to report any sensations she feels in her body. The dialogue between Penfield and Sally proceeds as follows:
>
> *Penfield:* (positioning stimulating electrode at a point on the parietal lobe) "Tell me if you feel anything."
> *Sally:* "I feel a tingling sensation in the fingers of my right hand."
> *Penfield:* (moves electrode about half a centimeter) "OK, ready again."
> *Sally:* "It feels like someone is touching my arm."
> *Penfield:* (moving electrode some distance on the parietal lobe) "Ready, again."
> *Sally:* "Now there's a prickling feeling on my leg."
> *Penfield:* (moving electrode back to its original position) "Ready."
> *Sally:* "A tingling sensation in the fingers of my right hand" (Adapted from Penfield & Rasmussen, 1950).

Penfield and Rasmussen's observations, based on a large number of patients, indicate that each point on the somatosensory cortex is associated with a specific part of the body. This relationship between the body and the somatosensory cortex is shown as the "map" in Figure 3.13b. This map, which is called a **homunculus** (Latin for "little man"), illustrates the amount of cortical area allotted to various parts of the body. It is no coincidence that the hands, fingers, face, mouth, feet, and toes are the parts of the body most sensitive to touch stimuli. More cortical area is allotted to them than to other (less sensitive) parts of the body such as the legs or back.

Vision and hearing: The visual cortex and the auditory cortex.   The picture that emerged from Penfield and Rasmussen's studies is that the body's communication system transmits signals from the body to the brain in an organized way, with communications from each part of the body reaching their own specific area in the somatosensory area of the parietal lobe. Similar localization has also been demonstrated for other senses. For example, each point in a person's field of view causes signals at a specific location in the **visual cortex,** on the occipital lobe. Similarly, tones with different pitches activate specific locations in the **auditory cortex,** on the temporal lobe (Goldstein, 1989).

Movement: The motor cortex.   The map of the body that Penfield and Rasmussen measured on the parietal cortex is repeated in a strip of frontal cortex located just across the central sulcus, the groove in the brain that divides the somatosensory area from the frontal lobes (refer to Figure 3.13b). The map in this area of frontal cortex describes the organization of the **motor cortex,** the area of cortex that causes movement by sending nerve impulses to the muscles.

The location of the motor area of the cortex was determined by Gustav Fritsch and Eduard Hitzig who, in 1870, found that electrical stimulation of points on a strip of frontal cortex just in front of a dog's parietal lobe caused movement of various parts of the dog's body. Fritsch and Hitzig showed that each point on the motor cortex corresponded to a particular point on the dog's body. So, for example, stimulating one point caused the dog's left rear leg to move, and stimulation at another caused its left front leg to move. Fritsch and Hitzig's work thus localized motor functioning in the motor area of the cerebral cortex. As we have already noted, the *coordination* of movement is controlled by the cerebellum. The cerebellum and motor cortex work together to create smooth, coordinated movements.

Memory: The hippocampus, amygdala, and thalamus.   Recall from the earlier discussion of the brain's anatomy that the hippocampus, amygdala, and thalamus all play a role in memory (Figure 3.13c). The importance of these subcortical structures for memory is dramatically illustrated by instances of memory loss following surgery. An example is the tragic case of H. M., which has contributed greatly to psychologists' understanding of the physiology of memory.

> H. M. had severe epilepsy, centered in his temporal lobes, which could not be controlled by medication. He underwent an operation which removed most of his left and right temporal lobes. Following the surgery, H. M.'s I.Q. was slightly higher than before, and his convulsions were gone. However, he lost the ability to form any new memories (although he did remember the details of much of his life from before the operation). Ten months after moving into a new house, he still had not learned his new address even though he remembered the old one perfectly. He could not find his way home alone, did not know where objects in constant use were kept, and he would read the same magazines over and over again without finding their contents familiar . . . forgetting occurred as soon as H. M. shifted his attention (Milner, 1965).

Additional observations of other patients have led investigators to the conclusion that H. M.'s problem was due mainly to the removal of his hippocampus (Zola-Morgan, Squire, & Amaral, 1986). Jimmie G.'s memory loss, described at the beginning of this chapter, was even more severe than H. M.'s in that he both lacked the ability to form new memories *and* lost memory for many of the years prior to being hospitalized. Memory loss in Korsakoff patients like Jimmie appears to be caused by damage to part of the thalamus (Victor, Adams, & Collins, 1971; von Cramon, Hebel, & Schuri, 1985). Memory thus seems to be localized in both the hippocampus and the thalamus. In addition, studies on animals show that the amygdala is also important for forming memories (Mishkin & Appenzeller, 1987).

More recent research has also shown that a particular aspect of memory, called working memory, is serviced by an area in the frontal lobe of the cerebral cortex. *Working memory* is the memory we use to guide ongoing behavior, such as retrieving the fingerings of a piece of music when playing the piano. Patricia Goldman-Rakic (1992) has studied patients who have essentially normal intelligence and ability to store information in memory but who, because of injuries to their frontal lobe, have trouble using their knowledge to guide their everyday behavior. Thus memory, like thinking, provides an example of the idea that functions are localized in the brain but that most behaviors involve a number of different areas of the brain working together.

MEASUREMENT & METHODOLOGY

Brain Stimulation and Lesioning

How can researchers determine the function of a particular brain structure? Two methods often used in animal research are **brain stimulation**—presenting an electrical or chemical stimulus to a brain structure—and **brain lesioning**—destroying a brain structure.

Brain Stimulation

The rationale behind brain stimulation is that stimulating a structure causes neural activity, which in turn elicits the behavior controlled by that structure. The first step toward achieving electrical stimulation is to use a *stereotaxic device* to precisely position the tip of a small *electrode* in a specific structure in an anesthetized animal's brain (see figure). Once accurately positioned, the electrode is permanently implanted in the brain. When the animal recovers from its anesthesia it behaves normally, apparently unaware of the implanted electrode. A structure's function is determined by passing electrical stimulation through the electrode and observing the animal's behavior. For example, electrical stimulation of a nucleus in the rat's hypothalamus causes the rat to begin eating. This lends support to the idea that the hypothalamus is involved in the control of feeding behavior. The brain can also be stimulated chemically. A small metal tube, called a cannula, is inserted into a target structure, and a stimulating chemical is injected into the structure through the cannula.

Lesioning

Like brain stimulation, lesioning also uses an electrode positioned with its tip inside a specific brain structure. An electric current is passed through the electrode, intense enough to destroy nearby brain tissue. Larger areas of the cortex can be removed surgically. Once a structure is lesioned or removed surgically, the animal is observed for possible behavioral changes. For example, lesioning the same area in the hypothalamus that when stimulated caused the rat to eat will cause it to stop eating (Anand & Brobeck, 1951; Hoebel & Teitelbaum, 1962). Lesioning usually has the opposite effect of stimulation, because lesioning destroys the structure and stimulation excites it.

Some Potential Problems

There are many reasons to be cautious when interpreting the results of stimulation or lesion studies. For example, although it is assumed that stimulation mimics the normal electrical activity of a structure, this isn't always the case. Stimulation can sometimes block the structure's normal activity and produce effects similar to lesioning (Solomon et al., 1983).

As for lesioning, suppose we lesion structure A and observe a change in the animal's behavior. Does this mean that structure A controls that behavior? Not necessarily. Perhaps the animal's change in behavior is caused by the interruption of a neural pathway that runs through A to another structure, B, which really controls that behavior.

Despite problems like these, stimulation and lesioning studies have provided much valuable information about the functioning of specific areas in the brain. Although these techniques are most commonly used in animals, human brains have on occasion been stimulated or lesioned, usually in conjunction with a radical medical procedure.

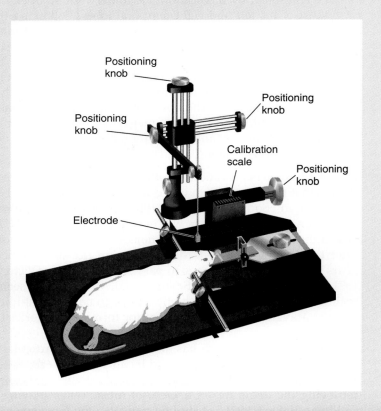

Emotion: The hypothalamus, amygdala, and hippocampus.   Fear, anger, and anxiety are localized in a number of different subcortical brain structures, the predominant ones being the amygdala, the hippocampus, and the hypothalamus. The evidence that supports this conclusion comes from studies in which the brain is stimulated and in which areas of the brain are removed. (See Measurement & Methodology, "Brain Stimulation and Lesioning.")

12   EMOTION

In an early study linking the amygdala to emotion, Klüver and Bucy (1938) found that a rhesus monkey whose amygdala had been removed became docile and friendly toward humans, in marked contrast to the aggressive behavior these monkeys usually display. Other studies have shown that the electrical stimulation of the amygdala causes cats to hiss and snarl (Egger & Flynn, 1963; Moyer, 1976) and humans to feel fear and anxiety (Chapman et al., 1954).

Similar results have been obtained when the hippocampus or hypothalamus is stimulated. Both of the these structures appear to be involved in the emotions of anger and fear. For example, a human epilepsy patient became extremely angry and violent the whole time that his hippocampus was stimulated but was able to describe his experience in a calm and collected way once the stimulation was turned off (Heath, 1981).

The amygdala, hippocampus, and hypothalamus are not only involved in "negative" emotions like fear and anger. The fact that animals will spend long hours pressing a bar to electrically stimulate other areas within these same structures suggests that the stimulation may also be pleasurable (Olds & Milner, 1954; Olds & Olds, 1963). This conclusion is supported by the finding that humans who are stimulated in these areas report feelings of well-being and euphoria (Heath, 1963).

So far we have looked at localization of function in specific structures and areas of the brain. A closely related idea is that the two halves of the brain—the left and right hemispheres—serve different functions. We'll consider this kind of specialization in the brain next.

Organization on the Left and Right: Lateralization of Function

The idea of "left-brained" and "right-brained" thinking has now become part of our culture. Most people think of a person described as "left brained" as someone who thinks logically and analytically, whereas one described as "right brained" is artistic or good at expressing feelings and emotions. This awareness of left- and right-brain differences has caused educators to bemoan the fact that our schools teach left-brain skills such as mathematics, science, and analyzing literature, while ignoring right-brain skills such as art and music. This concern has sometimes been translated into programs designed to train people to use their neglected right-brain skills, and books such as *Drawing on the Right Side of the Brain* (Edwards, 1989) have appeared on the best-seller lists.

How much truth is there in the popular view of left- and right-brain thinking? Although the popular obsession with the left and right brain has sometimes pushed the idea of hemispheric differences too far, there is no question that there are differences between left- and right-brain functioning.

Differences between the functioning of the left and right hemispheres began to be recognized as early as the 1800s. The first scientific report of differences between the brain's hemispheres was presented in 1836 by the physician Marc Dax at a meeting of a medical society in Montpellier, France. Dax reported the interesting finding that whereas 40 of his patients who suffered from an inability to speak had damage to the left hemisphere of the brain, not one with this condition had damage to the right hemisphere. Despite its importance, Dax's report was ignored. He died the next year, and it wasn't until 25 years later, in 1861, that the French surgeon Paul Broca reported a result similar to Dax's to the French Society of Anthropology. Broca autopsied two patients who had suffered

8   LANGUAGE

from loss of speech and found that both had damaged left hemispheres. Whereas scientists had ignored Dax's report 25 years earlier, they reacted enthusiastically to Broca's report. Either they were now ready to accept the idea of localization of language, or they were impressed by Broca's status as a medical professor, founder of the French Anthropological Society, and a renowned scientist.

The positive reaction to his report encouraged Broca to collect more data, and in 1864 he concluded that there was a definite link between the left hemisphere and speech. This marked the beginning of research on **lateralization of function,** the idea that some functions are based in either the right or the left hemisphere.

Additional evidence for lateralization of function has come from people who have suffered from stroke, a disruption of the blood supply to part of the brain. Stroke patients often become paralyzed on only one side of the body; if the paralysis is on the right side, they often experience difficulty in speaking. What does this mean? As each hemisphere has an independent blood supply, a stroke usually affects only half of the body. Moreover, each half of the brain controls *the opposite side of the body* (Figure 3.14). Thus, paralysis on the right side indicates damage to the left hemisphere—exactly what we would expect, if speech is localized in the left hemisphere. This evidence, and other research, indicates that speech is localized solely in the left hemisphere in about 90% of right-handed people and in about 65% of left-handed people (Kupferman, 1981).

The hemisphere that controls speech also appears to control the gestures that we make when speaking. A person whose speech is controlled by the left hemisphere gestures primarily with the right hand (which is controlled by the left hemisphere), whereas a person whose speech is controlled by the right hemisphere uses predominately left-handed gestures (Kimura, 1973).

The predominate location of language in the left hemisphere, combined with the importance of language in our society, has led to the idea that the left hemisphere is the **dominant hemisphere.** Does this mean that the right, or minor, hemisphere has little function? Not at all. Consider the following case report.

> Patricia, a 39-year-old high school teacher, suffered a stroke on the right side of her brain. At first she was paralyzed on the left side of her body, but within a month she was able to get around well enough to return to teach-

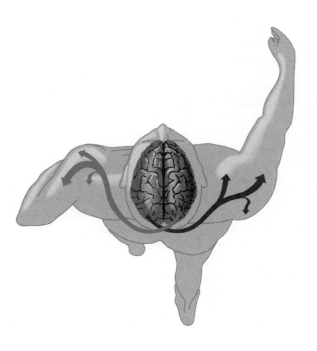

FIGURE 3.14
The left hemisphere controls the right side of the body and the right hemisphere controls the left side of the body.

ing. She couldn't, however, express her emotions by varying the tone of her voice, or by making gestures with her arms and hands. She could speak only in a monotone, her speech lacking the rise and fall in intensity, changes in tone, and sometimes musical quality of normal speech. This made it difficult for her to control her students, since saying "I'm really mad" in a monotone did not capture her students' attention. She also lost the ability to laugh or cry. Although she felt these emotions, she couldn't express them. Eventually, Patricia's ability to express her emotions returned (Adapted from Ross & Mesulam, 1979).

This case and many others like it demonstrate the important role of the right hemisphere in the experience of emotion. Because of the damage to the

MEASUREMENT & METHODOLOGY

Presenting Information to One Hemisphere

The goal of many of the experiments carried out on split-brain patients is to test the capacities of a particular hemisphere. We can do this by selectively presenting information to either the left or the right hemisphere. For touch information this is straightforward: Stimulation of the right hand sends signals to the left hemisphere; stimulation of the left hand sends signals to the right.

Does an analogous situation exist for vision, so that information presented to the left eye goes to the right hemisphere and information presented to the right eye goes to the left? Students are often surprised to hear that the answer to this question is "No." We can understand why this is so by looking at the neural pathways leading from the eyes to the visual cortex (see figure). Looking at the pathways leading from either eye to the brain, we see that fibers from the *nasal* side of the retina (near the nose) cross over to the other side of the brain at the *optic chiasm* and therefore end up in the opposite hemisphere. However, fibers from the *temporal* side of the retina (away from the nose) do not cross over. Thus, information presented to either eye can reach either the left or right hemisphere, depending on where on the retina the information is imaged.

To achieve our goal of presenting information to only one hemisphere, therefore, we need to present stimuli to the left or right *visual field.* The left visual field is, roughly, the area in space to the left of the nose when the person is looking straight ahead; the right visual field is the area to the right of the nose. A stimulus presented to the right visual field is imaged on the temporal retina of the left eye and the nasal retina of the right eye, both of which transmit neural signals to the left hemisphere. A similar result occurs when information is presented to the left visual field, with information reaching the right hemisphere. Thus, where visual stimuli are presented *in space,* not which eye is stimulated, determines whether the left or right hemisphere receives the information.

In addition to paying attention to where stimuli are presented in space, researchers must also be sure that their subjects' eyes remain stationary. A stimulus positioned to send information to the right hemisphere when the person is looking straight ahead will send information to the left hemisphere if the person looks to the left. For this reason, subjects are instructed to look steadily at a point in front of them, and stimuli are usually flashed rapidly so that subjects don't have time to move their eyes while the stimuli are present.

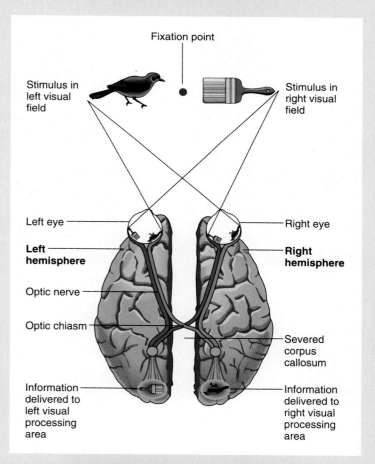

12   EMOTION

right hemisphere of her brain, Patricia was unable to *express* her emotions, although she could *recognize* the emotions of others. Other patients with right-hemisphere damage find it very difficult to correctly recognize the emotions expressed by other people. For example, a patient with a damaged right hemisphere might have trouble differentiating between "You haven't watered your flowers" spoken in an irritated tone of voice and the same sentence spoken in a questioning tone. In contrast, a patient with left-hemisphere damage, though perhaps unable to talk, will be able to interpret speakers' emotions from their tone of voice. These observations underscore the conclusion that the right hemisphere is responsible for our ability to both express and understand emotions.

Other research with patients with right-hemisphere damage indicates that the right hemisphere is also important in spatial tasks. For example, patients with right-hemisphere damage often have difficulty solving puzzles or finding their way around familiar environments.

Studies like the ones just described, involving primarily stroke patients, have firmly established the idea of lateralization of function. These studies were well known to brain researchers for many years, but it wasn't until the 1960s that a procedure called the **split-brain operation** or commissurotomy, in which a person's left and right hemispheres are separated by cutting a bundle of nerve fibers called the corpus callosum, produced results dramatic enough to capture the popular imagination. The following case study is an example.

> James S. suffered from severe epileptic seizures. Although various drugs had been tried, none was effective in quieting the seizures, which were both frequent and violent. As a last resort, James underwent a commissurotomy operation. Following this operation his seizures stopped and he was able to lead a normal life.

Severing the corpus callosum cuts off communication between the brain hemispheres. This has the effect of preventing the out-of-control brain activity associated with seizures from traveling from one hemisphere to another, and thereby stops the seizures that epilepsy patients experience. Surprisingly, patients who undergo this operation show few if any side effects. Their intelligence, personality, and general behavior remain unchanged.

FIGURE 3.15
When the words *key* and *chain* are presented to a split-brain patient, information about the word *key* reaches the right hemisphere and information about *chain* reaches the left hemisphere. In (a), the left hemisphere produces a verbal response. In (b), the right hemisphere produces a nonverbal response with the left hand.

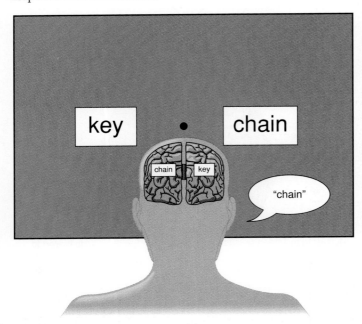

(a)

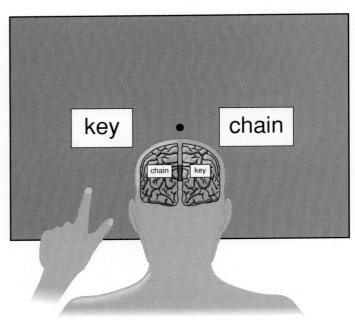

(b)

The story does not end here, however. Roger Sperry (1966) devised ways to test split-brain patients in the laboratory that uncovered some amazing behavioral effects not obvious in the patients' everyday experience. Consider the following experiment. A split-brain patient looks straight ahead at a small dot on a screen while two words are flashed briefly onto the screen. The display is designed so that the word on the left, *key*, reaches only the right hemisphere and the word on the right, *chain*, reaches only the left hemisphere. (See Measurement & Methodology, "Presenting Information to One Hemisphere," on page 105.) When the subject is asked "What did you see?" he answers, "Chain" (Figure 3.15a). If asked "Did you see anything else?" he answers, "No, that's all I saw." Why does the subject deny seeing the word *key*? Because when a subject responds verbally to a question, the response comes from the left hemisphere, the one responsible for language. The only information the left hemisphere received was the word *chain*, so that is the only word the patient acknowledges seeing.

Does the fact that the subject denies seeing anything other than the word *chain* literally mean that he saw nothing else at all? Not necessarily. The experimenter can show that the split-brain subject actually saw the word *key* by using a nonverbal test that enables the *right* hemisphere to respond. If the subject is asked to pick the word he saw from a list by pointing with his left hand (which is controlled by the right hemisphere), he points to the word *key* (Figure 3.15b). Thus, we know that the word *key* reached the right hemisphere, but, lacking capacity for speech, the right hemisphere simply can't communicate this information in words.

This result seems very strange to most people. It is important, however, not to forget that the split-brain subject has had his left and right hemispheres separated. When the brain is intact, the corpus callosum allows the left and right hemispheres to share information. With the corpus callosum cut, however, the information that the word *key* was presented to the right hemisphere was not automatically transmitted to the left hemisphere and was, therefore, not available to the patient's language system.

This experiment confirms the results of studies of the effects of stroke and brain damage, that language is located in the left hemisphere. Other research with split-brain patients confirms another result derived from the stroke studies: the right hemisphere is important in tasks involving spatial orientation.

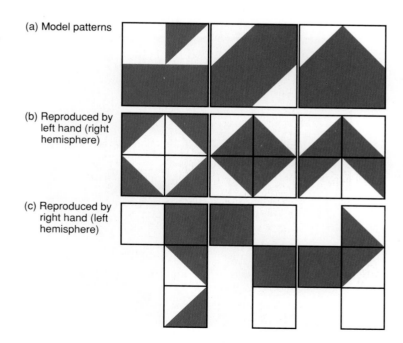

(a) Model patterns

(b) Reproduced by left hand (right hemisphere)

(c) Reproduced by right hand (left hemisphere)

FIGURE 3.16
Results of left- and right-hemisphere attempts to match the model patterns in the top row. Neither hemisphere alone succeeds but the right hemisphere comes closer.

8 —— THINKING

5 —— CONSCIOUSNESS

In one test of a split-brain patient's spatial ability (Gazzaniga & LeDoux, 1978), the experimenter asked the patient to arrange colored blocks to copy patterns like the ones in Figure 3.16a. The patient's performance of this task depended on the hand he used. Although he made frequent errors using either hand, the patient's left-handed arrangements in Figure 3.16b are better copies of the patterns than the right-handed ones in Figure 3.16c, which bear little resemblance to the originals. In other words, the right hemisphere (controlling the left hand) does better on spatial tasks than the left hemisphere (controlling the right hand). However, either hemisphere operating independently does less well than the two working together in an intact brain.

Split-brain research has implications that go beyond confirming the findings of previous lateralization research. The behavior of split-brain patients demonstrates the existence of two different realities within the brain. One of these, the "left-brain reality," can be easily brought into awareness because it can be verbalized; the other, the "right-brain reality," is more hidden from view because it is much more difficult to put into words. Thus, split-brain patients are much more aware of information that is presented to their left hemisphere because they can talk about it, and they are much less aware of information presented to their right hemisphere, because they cannot express it in words.

This difference in awareness between the left and right hemispheres is dramatically illustrated in a film of a split-brain experiment carried out by Michael Gazzaniga and Roger Sperry (see Springer & Deutsch, 1989). In the film, a split-brain patient is asked to perform a colored-block task like the one just described. When the patient is asked to perform the task with his left hand (controlled by the "spatial" right hemisphere), he completes the task easily. However, when the patient is asked to use his right hand (left hemisphere), he rearranges the blocks over and over with little success. Furthermore, as the right hand struggles unsuccessfully to solve the problem, the patient's left hand (which he was told to keep under the table) suddenly appears from under the table and starts arranging the blocks in the correct pattern. Apparently the right hemisphere, seeing an easy solution to the problem, can't bear watching the right hand's inept performance and sends the left hand to the rescue.

At this point, the experimenter reprimands the patient, reminding him that he is to use only his right hand, and tells him to put his left hand back under the table. But as the right hand continues its struggle to solve the problem, the left hand again appears and tries to help. When asked to explain what is going on,

FIGURE 3.17
Reading a word out loud activates a number of different areas in the brain, including (1) the visual cortex, for seeing the word; (2) an area adjacent to Wernicke's area, for matching the word's visual form with its spoken sound; (3) Wernicke's area, for understanding the word; (4) Broca's area, for producing the word; (5) the motor area, for moving the muscles of the lips, tongue, and mouth in order to actually speak the word; (6) the somatosensory cortex, for feeling the movement of the lips, tongue, and mouth; and (7) the auditory cortex, for hearing the word as it is being spoken.

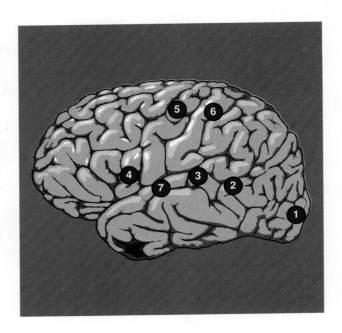

the patient (responding with his left hemisphere, which had nothing to do with the right hand's illegal actions) cannot offer a plausible explanation. The patient's left hemisphere is unaware of the reasons for the right hemisphere's actions. Thus, the left and right hemispheres, with their separate worlds of awareness, can create behaviors that appear extremely strange to someone observing a person behave.

One possible reaction to the results we have been reviewing is that they are interesting but apply only to split-brain patients. But researchers argue that split-brain research has much to tell us about the workings of intact brains. For example, one of its implications is that at any given time we are aware of some of the things that the brain is doing (such as making us aware of what we are sensing and thinking at the moment), but that we are unaware of many other things it's doing. We will encounter some examples of this in the next section when we look at how the brain processes information, and we will again pursue the idea that much of the brain's work occurs behind the scenes when we consider the experience of consciousness in Chapter 5.

Beyond Localization of Function

We have seen that specific behaviors are associated with activity in specific areas of the brain. We have also seen examples of behaviors such as thinking, memory, and reacting to touch that activate a number of areas of the brain. Thus, while the old idea of holism gave way to the idea that functions are localized in specific parts of the brain, modern researchers do not view the brain as made up of a number of independent areas, each taking care of its own business. Instead, they emphasize that the brain is a system of interconnected areas.

The brain as a system.   Modern brain researchers continue to look for connections between brain areas and functions, but their emphasis has shifted from trying to localize a function completely in a specific structure to trying to determine the *overall neural system* associated with specific functions. They emphasize that most behaviors involve activity in numerous areas of the brain interacting with one another. To illustrate how the brain works as a system, let's look at two relatively simple behaviors that sometimes occur together: reading and speaking.

Early brain researchers had no way to monitor activity simultaneously occurring in many brain areas. But recently developed techniques of brain imaging make this possible. For example, by using PET scans, researchers have been able to visualize the pattern of blood flow in large areas of the brain (Lassen, Inguar, & Skinhøs, 1978). These PET scans show, as we would expect, that listening to speech increases blood flow in two areas: the auditory area in the temporal lobe, which is involved in hearing sound, and Wernicke's area, which is important for understanding speech (areas 7 and 3, respectively, in Figure 3.17).

To make things more interesting, we can look at what happens when a person reads aloud. This activates still more areas. Because reading involves vision, the primary area in the occipital lobe (1) becomes active as does the *visual association area* (2), an area involved in perceiving complex visual stimuli. Also active are Wernicke's (3) and Broca's (4) areas, because the person is producing *and* understanding speech. In addition, activity occurs in the motor cortex (5) and the somatosensory cortex (6) (because the person *feels* the movement of the face, tongue, and mouth that occurs as he or she speaks), and the auditory cortex (7) (because the person *hears* the words he or she is speaking). These two examples make it clear that, though functions are localized in the brain, large areas of the brain are involved in even simple activities.

Parallel processing in the brain.   The fact that numerous brain areas are active as a person reads aloud is an example of **parallel processing,** simultaneously taking into account a number of different types of information. That is, the

4 ——— PERCEPTION

brain carries out many operations in parallel—seeing, the motor movements of speech production, hearing, and feeling touch are all happening simultaneously in different brain areas.

An example of parallel processing at the behavioral level can be found in typing. A trained typist typing the word *vacuum* hits the *v, a,* and *c* in rapid succession with the fingers of the left hand. But before the *c* is typed, the index finger of the right hand has moved over the *u*. The right finger moves in parallel with the left fingers, anticipating the *u* and increasing typing speed. At the neural level, parallel processing means that a number of individual nerve circuits work in parallel.

One example of nerve circuits working in parallel is the way signals are processed in the visual system. After visual signals reach the primary visual receiving area in the occipital lobe, separate neural circuits stretching into the temporal and parietal lobes simultaneously process information about form, color, movement, and depth (Livingstone & Hubel, 1987; VanEssen, 1979; VanEssen & Mavensell, 1983; Zeki, 1992). Eventually, the information in each of these circuits must be combined, because we perceive all of these qualities at once when we look at something. For example, when we see a round, red ball rolling away from us we don't see "round," "red," and "rolling" separately, nor do we see a succession of smaller and smaller images. We process and integrate all the inputs into a single perception of a red ball rolling away.

A simple act of memory also involves parallel processing. When you want to find your special red pen and you remember that you put it in your desk drawer, you are simultaneously remembering a specific object and its location. These two pieces of information, however, are processed in two different parts of the brain. Memory for remembering *what* an object is involves neurons in the temporal lobe, whereas remembering *where* an object is involves neurons in the parietal lobe (Figure 3.18) (Mishkin & Appenzeller, 1987; Mishkin, Ungerleider, & Macko, 1983; Ungerleider & Mishkin, 1982). What and where are determined simultaneously in these two areas, and the information is then shared, to enable us to remember both the object and its location.

From our discussion in this section it is clear that the brain is not simply a collection of identical neurons, nor is it merely a number of separated areas, each carrying out its own specialized function. The brain is a system of specialized components working together and often carrying out their separate processing tasks in parallel, eventually combining their information to create coordinated behaviors and a unified picture of the world.

The Dynamic Nervous System: Changing with Development and Experience

The brain's ability to create the amazing diversity of human behavior is dependent on its complexity and the remarkable properties of the nervous system. But the brain has still another remarkable property: the capacity to change its structure as it develops and interacts with the environment. Let's look at some of these changes, focusing first on how the brain changes during the early stages of its development.

The Changing Brain: Transformation Through Maturation

The most dramatic changes in brain structure occur during the early years of life, as the brain develops from its primitive embryonic beginnings to its complex adult state. Consider the fact that the brain, little more than a fluid-filled neural tube at 3 weeks after conception, develops within a little over 30 months into a structure that creates the 2-year-old's endless chatter, ability to navigate through

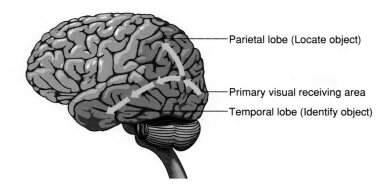

Parietal lobe (Locate object)

Primary visual receiving area

Temporal lobe (Identify object)

FIGURE 3.18
Visual information reaches the primary visual receiving area and is transmitted to the temporal and parietal lobes, which separately determine what the object is and where it is located. This information is then combined elsewhere in the brain.

the environment, and emotional outbursts. What is behind this amazing process of development?

The brain at birth is one-quarter the size of an adult brain. Despite its small size the newborn's brain contains all of the cortical areas and nuclei present in the adult brain, and essentially all of its neurons (although they are much smaller than the adult's neurons). At birth, however, a crucial process remains to be completed: formation of the complex web of synapses that link these billions of neurons together. Synapse formation, the major event of brain development over the first two years of life, underlies the dramatic perceptual and cognitive changes of infancy. During the first six months of life, the infant's ability to see details (visual acuity) increases from legal blindness at birth to near-adult acuity at six months (Banks & Salapatek, 1978; Dobson & Teller, 1978). In addition, depth perception and the ability to perceive complex forms begin to appear, accompanied by cortical changes that are never again equaled in magnitude (Trevarthen, 1987). At about eight months, talking begins, signaling the maturation of Broca's area, and between eight months and two years language and other cognitive skills develop, all in concert with increases in the number of brain synapses (Goldman-Rakic, 1987).

This process of creating synaptic connections is programmed genetically and reflects the normal process of maturation. However, the brain is shaped by more than genetically programmed maturation. The stimuli the brain experiences as it develops play an important role in shaping its structure and functioning.

The Changing Brain: Transformation Through Experience

To understand what it means to say that the brain's structure is shaped by experience, consider the process of acquiring a skill. Learning a skill, whether solving mathematical problems or shooting three-pointers in basketball, usually involves practice. As you solve more math problems or shoot more baskets, your skill improves. Underlying these improvements in your ability are changes in the structure of your brain.

The idea that the brain's structure changes may seem strange. After all, the architecture of the brain—its wiring and organization of structures—is genetically fixed. The lobes of the cerebral cortex, the subcortical nuclei, and the connections between them are organized in essentially the same way in all normally functioning brains. But if we look beneath this similarity in general organization, we find that at the synaptic level the brain is amazingly plastic. The number of synapses, their structure, and the way they function are affected by the nature of the tasks the brain is required to perform.

Experiencing enriched environments: Enhancing neural wiring.   The idea that the brain's structure could change in response to experience was first suggested by the Canadian psychologist Donald Hebb. Hebb (1949) proposed that repetition of a particular stimulus activates a series of interconnected neurons. As this group of neurons continues to be activated during learning, the synaptic connections between them are strengthened, so that in the future this group is more likely to fire together. This group of neurons that is likely to fire together, which Hebb called a *cell assembly,* formed the centerpiece of his explanation of the physiological basis of learning and memory.

Although some of the details of Hebb's proposal are not accepted today, his basic hypothesis that experience causes changes in the brain has been confirmed in experiments by E. L. Bennett and Michael Rosenzweig, which showed that the structure of synapses in rats' brains can be affected by the environment in which they are raised.

Bennett and Rosenzweig's experiments are now considered classics in psychology. In these experiments, one group of rats was raised in barren, isolated lab cages and another group was raised in an "enriched" environment with other rats and access to complex toys (Figure 3.19). The effect of the enriched environment was dramatic. The brains of the environmentally enriched rats were thicker and had more dendrites and more synapses per neuron. Moreover, the individual synapses were larger and had more synaptic vesicles (Bennett et al., 1964; Rosenzweig, Bennett, & Diamond, 1972; Squire, 1987; Turner & Greenough, 1983). These studies were the first to show that the brain's structure changes in response to environmental conditions.

④   THE SENSES

Sensory experience: Changing the sensory map.   The enriched environment studies demonstrate large generalized changes in brain structure associated with enriching an animal's overall environment. Other research has focused on how experience can affect the size of a specific sensory area in the cerebral cortex.

We saw earlier, in the description of Penfield and Rasmussen's work on the somatosensory cortex, that "maps" exist on the cortex. Thus, when Penfield and Rasmussen determined the area of the brain that becomes active when a particular area on the skin is touched, they created a homunculus, a picture of the body on the brain. One of the most significant things about the homunculus is that areas on the body like fingers, hands, toes, and feet—which are more sensitive to touch and which are used most frequently for touching—are allotted large areas on the cortex.

FIGURE 3.19
Bennett and Rosenzweig's enriched environment, which enhanced the development of the rats' brains

The fact that allocation of area on the somatosensory cortex is proportional to how much a part of the body is used suggests the following question: If we increase the *usage* of a particular part of the body, will the amount of cortical space devoted to that area increase?

To answer this question, M. M. Merzenich and co-workers (Merzenich et al., 1988) first measured the area on the brain associated with the stimulation of a monkey's fingertip (Figure 3.20). Then, after having the monkey engage in a task that heavily stimulated its fingertip, they remeasured the area. The result showed that the brain area associated with the active fingertip got larger. Thus, the homunculus is not a permanent map but can change in response to how much we use a particular part of the body.

Traumatic stress: Damaging neurotransmitter receptors. The studies we have described so far have used animals as subjects. Researchers have little doubt, however, that the basic findings of these studies generalize to humans. An example of how human brain functioning may be affected by the environment is provided by recent research on the effects of traumatic events on human behavior and physiology. An illustration of the effects of trauma is provided by the following case report on a soldier who participated in the Gulf War in 1991.

> Roger, stationed somewhere in the Saudi Arabian desert, was sitting on a crate playing cards with his buddies when a shrieking sound—as it turned out, that of a Scud missile—was followed by a succession of terrifying explosions as the camaraderie of the card game turned into a blazing conflagration. By some miracle, Roger escaped with minor cuts and bruises. Everyone else in the card game was killed and many others in the barracks were seriously wounded. Now, two years later, Roger still wakes up in a sweat in the middle of the night, reliving the shrieking sound of the missile followed by the screams of his comrades. He has also found it difficult to focus his attention on daily tasks, suffers from depression, becomes easily irritated with his wife, and feels detached from others.

Roger is experiencing the symptoms of *posttraumatic stress disorder (PTSD)*. This disorder sometimes occurs following exposure to catastrophic or traumatic threats to life or safety over which a person has no control. Survivors of airplane crashes, natural disasters, wartime trauma, and rape often experience long-lasting symptoms of PTSD (Foy et al., 1987; Helzer, Robins, & McEvoy, 1987). Accompanying the behavioral symptoms of PTSD are biological changes such as large increases in heart rate and blood pressure in response to stimuli similar to the original traumatic event (Blanchard et al., 1982; Pallmeyer, Blanchard, & Kolb, 1986).

These biological reactions have been traced to changes in the brain—specifically, decreases in the number of alpha-2 receptors in some brain areas (Perry, Southwick, & Giller, 1990). One of the functions of alpha-2 receptors is to limit the release of epinephrine, the endocrine hormone that energizes the body to

16   DISORDERS

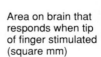

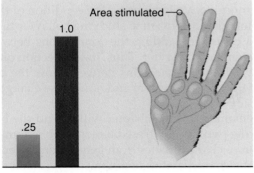

Area stimulated

1.0

Area on brain that responds when tip of finger stimulated (square mm)

.25

Before   After

FIGURE 3.20
Extensive stimulation of the monkey's fingertip can cause an enlargement of the area of the brain that responds to fingertip stimulation.

Psychological trauma after a Scud missile
attack in the Persian Gulf War

help it deal with emergency situations. The reduced number of alpha-2 receptors
causes those with PTSD to respond to even mild stress with excessive epinephrine, so they overreact to situations that most people would not find threatening.

The finding that at least some of the symptoms of PTSD may be caused by
changes in the biology of the brain shouldn't be surprising, especially in view of
our knowledge that physiological processes in the brain underlie all of our behaviors. Yet, before the recent evidence showing brain changes in PTSD patients
was uncovered, most descriptions of the disorder focused on explanations at the
level of cognition or behavior. For example, in analyzing Roger's condition, attention might be focused on the possibility that he feels guilty because he survived whereas others did not, an emotional reaction often experienced by survivors of catastrophes. A behavioral approach to evaluating Roger's condition
would be to evaluate how he was functioning prior to leaving the States for
Saudi Arabia. This information might help in predicting his chances of recovery,
as there is evidence that being well adjusted before a trauma increases a person's
chances of recovery (Carson & Butcher, 1992).

These cognitive and behavioral approaches to PTSD are valuable in their
own right. But the biological research that linked the effects of PTSD to reduced
numbers of alpha-2 receptors in the brain provides important information that
until then was missing from psychologists' understanding of PTSD. To truly understand this disorder, we must approach it from the cognitive, behavioral, *and*
biological levels of analysis. Not considering the biological level of analysis is
like analyzing an automobile's performance by describing how difficult it is to
start in the morning while ignoring the condition of the battery.

The biological approach to studying behavior that we have described so far
has focused on understanding the connections between the functioning of the
nervous system and behavior. Thus, in this section on the dynamic nervous system we have drawn connections between how the environment can affect the
structure of the nervous system and how those changes in structure in turn affect
behavior.

The remainder of this chapter will extend the biological approach in time
by considering two closely related biological phenomena: heredity, the biological
transmission of characteristics from generation to generation, and evolution, the
shaping of the characteristics of organisms over many generations.

Heredity and Behavior

Each person is constructed according to a biological "blueprint" created by genetic contributions from his or her parents. At the time of conception, 23 chromosomes from the father's sperm combine with 23 chromosomes from the mother's egg to form a *zygote* (fertilized egg) containing 46 chromosomes that specify the plans for creating a unique human being (Figure 3.21).

Exactly what do these chromosomes look like, and how do they orchestrate the creation of a person? If we look closely at a chromosome, we see that it is made up of about 20,000 **genes.** These genes are molecules of deoxyribonucleic acid (DNA), helical-shaped strings of smaller molecules that control the synthesis of proteins. These protein molecules are the building blocks of the body, and it is by controlling their manufacture that genes influence physical characteristics as well as the characteristics of the brain and the rest of the nervous system.

The idea that heredity shapes the way people appear is obvious to anyone who has observed the resemblance between members of the same family and the uncanny similarity of identical twins, who have identical genes. But how do genes shape a person's behavior? Genes influence behavior in the same way that they determine physical characteristics—by determining the structure of protein molecules. The protein molecules most essential for behavior are those that make up the cells that create the various systems in the brain. For example, the trait of emotionality may be determined by the development of an area such as the hypothalamus that controls the emotions. Each part of the brain is shaped by thousands of genes that control creation of the protein molecules that are the essential components of neurons.

The genetic blueprint contained in a person's chromosomes and genes, that creates her or his physical and behavioral characteristics, is called the person's **genotype.** Although this genotype exerts a powerful influence, it is not the only thing that shapes that individual. This is so because the environment in which the person develops affects the way the genotype is expressed. The *expression* of

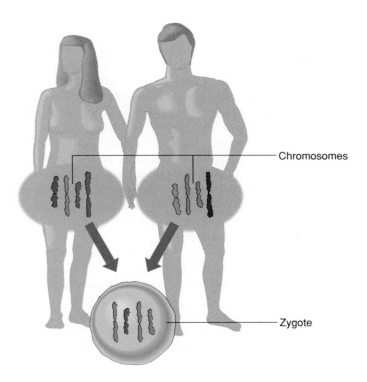

FIGURE 3.21
The male and female each contribute half of their 46 chromosomes to create a zygote with 46 chromosomes. (Only 4 chromosomes for the male, female, and zygote are shown here.)

Chromosomes

Zygote

Similarities in physical features are transmitted genetically from parents to children.

9   DEVELOPMENT

the genotype—the person's characteristics and behavior that actually develop—is called the **phenotype.**

We can understand how the phenotype is formed by the environment by considering a pair of identical twins separated at birth. Being created from identical genetic specifications, the twins have the same genotype. Suppose that one twin develops in a deprived environment marked by poor nutrition, poor schooling, and a tumultuous home life, while the other enjoys a healthy, happy upbringing. The deprived twin will most likely be underdeveloped both physically and intellectually compared with the other, more fortunate twin. Even though their genetic heritage is exactly the same, these twins' phenotypes—*their actual characteristics and behavior*—are likely to be significantly different. Thus, our characteristics are determined by an interaction between our genetic makeup and the environment within which we develop. We will review this principle in more detail in the chapter on Physical, Perceptual, and Cognitive Development.

As we have examined the interaction of heredity and the environment, we have been focusing on how particular individuals acquire their characteristics. But we can take a larger view of this issue by focusing not on what determines the characteristics of individuals, but on what determines the characteristics of entire species. We'll prepare for this larger view by reviewing some basic principles of evolution.

Evolution and Behavior

Our brain is the product of many tens of thousands of years of **evolution,** the process by which organisms change from their ancient ancestors into their present form. When we consider how these biological changes have come about we are explaining the biology of behavior at a far more global level than when we look at the operation of individual neurons, the way genetics determines an indi-

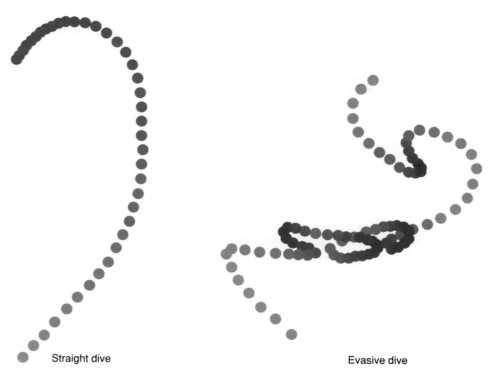

Straight dive

Evasive dive

FIGURE 3.22
Flight paths of moths in reaction to hearing
a simulated bat cry. The moth on the right,
which takes evasive action, is more likely to
survive.

vidual's characteristics, or even the operation of the brain as a whole. When we look at brain and behavior from an evolutionary point of view we are considering not the specific mechanisms of the brain's operation but rather how behaviors produced by thousands of prior generations of brains have literally shaped the form and functioning of the brains we possess today.

The general idea of evolution has suggested a number of lines of inquiry concerning how evolutionary forces have shaped behavior. One of the most controversial is that of **sociobiology,** a recently developed branch of evolutionary biology that applies evolutionary theory to the explanation of social behavior (Barash, 1977; Wilson, 1975). We look at this idea in the following "Interdisciplinary Dimension."

INTERDISCIPLINARY DIMENSION EVOLUTION

Natural Selection and Sociobiology

To begin to understand how sociobiology explains social behavior, we can profitably return to Darwin's observations of finches on the Galápagos Islands, discussed in Chapter 2. As you recall, Darwin observed that finches on different islands had beaks suited to the different food sources on those islands: strong, thick beaks for cracking open nuts and seeds or smaller beaks better suited to eating insects. To explain his observation, he formulated the *theory of natural selection,* based on the following line of reasoning.

1. All living things have a tendency to produce more offspring than are needed to replace themselves. If all of these offspring survived, the earth would be rapidly overrun. However, this has not occurred. The population of most species has remained relatively constant.

2. Because of the overproduction of offspring, there is a struggle for survival within each species, with many individuals competing for finite food resources.

3. Hereditary variations within each species result in some members being better adapted for survival than others. For example, among hunting animals, strength, speed, and good eyesight are important for procuring food. Animals with these characteristics will win the competition for food and will survive. This is called **survival of the fittest.**

Sociobiologists explain the altruistic behavior of the screeching prairie dog in terms of kin selection.

 19   SOCIAL

4. Characteristics that increase the chances of surviving also increase the chances that the animal will live long enough to reproduce and to pass the genes for those characteristics on to the next generation. Animals with less adaptive characteristics are less likely to live long enough to reproduce, and so do not pass their characteristics along. Thus, animals with more adaptive characteristics survive, a process called **natural selection.** Because of natural selection, succeeding generations will be more likely to have characteristics better suited for survival. The change in the characteristics of a species over many generations is what we mean by evolution.

The evolutionary mechanism of natural selection can explain the origin not only of physical characteristics, such as the thickness of a finch's beak, but of behavior as well. It is easier to appreciate this when we grasp the importance of behavioral characteristics to survival. Consider the behavior of a moth pursued by a bat. Figure 3.22 shows flight tracks of two moths immediately after hearing a simulated bat cry. The moth on the left dives straight down, whereas the one on the right dives with a more evasive series of irregular loops and turns (Roeder & Treat, 1961). Which moth is more likely to escape the bat? By filming many interactions between moths and bats, Roeder and Treat determined that evasive moths are almost twice as likely to escape than are straight-diving moths. All else being equal, the more evasive moths stand a better chance of surviving to pass their characteristics to their offspring.

The principle of survival of the fittest thus offers a logical explanation of how evolution can influence behavior, based on the connection between adaptive behavior and an individual animal's ability to survive. However, this principle runs into problems when applied to behaviors that do *not* seem to promote survival. An example is **altruistic behavior,** behavior that is good for the survival of the group but not for the survival of an individual. For example, when a prairie dog spots a coyote, it signals other prairie dogs with a high-pitched screech. In a similar way, deer sensing danger emit warning snorts to warn other deer. In both these cases, the animal giving the warning signal puts itself at risk by making itself more obvious. Such behavior seems to violate the basic idea of survival of the fittest. If animals who give warning signals are more vulnerable to being killed by predators, how has the trait of giving warning signals been passed on to succeeding generations instead of dying out?

Sociobiology proposes an answer to this question. As its name implies, *socio*biology tries to explain such problems by suggesting that evolutionary biology has a *social* dimension. That is, the principle of survival of the fittest can apply to the group as well as to individual animals.

But what mechanism could account for the persistence of characteristics that foster the survival of the group? To explain altruistic behavior, sociobiologists propose the principle of **kin selection.** According to this principle, characteristics selectively survive that increase the chances of survival of the animal's relatives (which, because they are related, share some genes). So although animals that sound the warning signals are more likely to be killed, their nearby blood relatives, who share the "calling" trait, survive, so the genes that determine calling are passed to future generations. Sociobiology, then, emphasizes the survival of *genes* rather than of *individuals.* The important point, as far as sociobiologists are concerned, is that an individual has an interest in the survival of its genes, and that this interest is served by social behaviors that ensure the survival of its close relatives.

Another example of altruistic behavior in animal society is that of a communal flock of scrubjays. A typical flock includes a breeding pair and as many as six other birds—usually older offspring of the pair—who help feed and protect their parents and younger siblings. Although these older offspring may never reproduce, they help perpetuate some of their genes by working for the survival of their immediate family.

Sociobiology thus seems to offer a plausible explanation for the evolution of behaviors that otherwise would be inexplicable according to the principle of survival of the fittest. What makes sociobiology controversial is its claim to explain a wide range of *human* behaviors as the products of the same kind of evolutionary processes as the altruistic behavior of prairie dogs, deer, and scrubjays. For example, sociobiologists have proposed an evolutionary explanation of the sexual "double standard"—the fact that it is more acceptable for males in our society to have numerous sexual partners than it is for females.

In behavioral terms the double standard means that many males strive to have multiple sexual partners, whereas females more commonly seek out monogamous relationships. Most people would probably see the double standard as a cultural and psychological phenomenon—for instance, as the product of our male-dominated society. According to sociobiologists, however, the basis of the double standard is evolutionary and biological. They argue that the behaviors that give rise to the double standard evolved as ways for males and females to maximize their contribution to the genes of future generations. The male faces the problem that he can never be certain that a female's children are his. Consequently, his best strategy for ensuring that his genes will populate future generations is to impregnate as many females as possible. A female, on the other hand, is normally limited to producing only one or two children at the end of each nine-month pregnancy. She can, however, be certain that 50% of each child's genes are hers. Therefore, it is important to her to maximize the chances that her children will survive to pass her genes to future generations. She achieves this by devoting her energies to child care and attempting to enlist the help of a male to supply protection and food.

Is the sociobiologists' explanation correct? Critics of sociobiology argue that it ignores the powerful influences of learning and culture on human social behavior. If we look at social behavior at the behavioral, cognitive, and contextual levels of analysis, it seems apparent that our social behavior is powerfully affected by many variables, including the values we are taught by our religion, parents, groups we belong to, and our culture as a whole. No one denies that genetics and evolutionary forces have affected humans both structurally and behaviorally. Indeed, we will often have occasion to point out the strong influence of genetic inheritance in human behavior in future chapters. But to say that evolution and genetic inheritance are part of the mix of influences on behavior is not to say that all behavior can be explained in purely evolutionary terms. In particular, many psychologists question sociobiology's claim that *social behavior*—the type of human behavior most heavily influenced by cognitive and contextual variables—can be explained primarily in terms of evolutionary biology.   ■

Reprise: Levels of Analysis and Behavior

This chapter has been an exercise in applying one level of analysis to the study of behavior. As such, it has provided an opportunity to examine the meaning of levels of analysis in more detail. We have seen that there are many sublevels, even within the biological level. We can look at molecular events in neurons and at synapses, at the way the brain organizes information, or at the broad sweep of behavioral evolution. These levels have time scales ranging from thousandths of a second for molecular events at the synapse to thousands of generations for behavioral evolution.

But one thing that all of these sublevels of the biological level have in common is a commitment to explaining *behavior*. This may seem like an obvious point, but it is an extremely important one. Consider, for example, the fact that many researchers have dedicated themselves to studying the chemistry of synaptic transmission. This research has resulted in much valuable information about how synapses operate, but the mechanisms of synaptic transmission become relevant to psychologists only when they are related to behavior. Thus, talking about how neurotransmitters are released at a synapse has little meaning for psychology unless it is related to a specific behavior, whether it is observable, like turning the head in response to a touch on the shoulder, or more interior, like experiencing a thought or an emotion. The same is true of the other levels of analysis: whether we are working from a biological, behavioral, cognitive, or contextual level of analysis, our ultimate goal is to understand behavior.

In the next several chapters we will be describing how psychologists have studied behaviors such as perceiving, dreaming, learning, and memory. We will look for biological explanations for those behaviors and, in addition, will ask questions like the following: "What mental processes underlie these behaviors?" (cognitive level), "What can we learn by observing the characteristics of these behaviors without concern for biological or mental processes?" (behavioral level), and "How does a person's overall environment affect these behaviors?" (contextual level). The important thing to remember is that behavior is part of every level of analysis, and each level has its contribution to make toward the understanding of behavior.

Sex Hormones, Brain Structure, and Behavior

The effects of sex hormones on brain organization occur so early in life that from the start the environment is acting on differently wired brains in girls and boys.

Doreen Kimura (1992)

The existence of body differences between males and females—technically called **sexual dimorphism**—is obvious to everyone. But in addition to the easily observable external differences in male and female bodies, there are also differences in the structures of male and female brains that cause differences in sexual functioning and other behaviors. What causes these brain differences, and what is the evidence that they lead to different male and female behaviors?

Let's begin by looking at how differences between males and females originate, beginning just after conception. About three weeks after conception, an embryonic sex gland called *gonads* is formed. At this point, the gonads have both male and female properties; they contain genetic instructions capable of directing their development into either a male or a female organ. Thus, initially, the potential exists for the development of female ovaries or male testes. Not until six weeks after conception is the "decision" made whether development will proceed in the male or the female direction. This decision is controlled by the sex chromosomes, a pair of chromosomes on one of the 23 pairs of genes.

There are two types of sex chromosomes, an X chromosome and a smaller Y chromosome. If the chromosome pair is XY, the gonads develop into testes that secrete **testosterone,** the male hormone. If the chromosome pair is XX, the gonads develop into ovaries that secrete **estrogens,** the female hormones. From this point of development on, these hormones direct **prenatal sexual differentiation,** the differentiation between males and females that develops in the womb prior to birth. If a high concentration of testosterone is present in the bloodstream, male genitals develop. If low concentrations are present, female genitals develop. In other words, female genitals develop *unless* testosterone is present.

The development of male or female genitals is, however, only one of the manifestations of sexual dimorphism. A large amount of evidence suggests that sexual dimorphism exists in the brain as well. Many studies have demonstrated structural brain differences between male and female rodents such as rats, mice, and hamsters (Hines, 1982). Differences between male and female brains have also been observed in monkeys (Ayoub, Greenough, & Juraska, 1983) and in humans (Allen et al., 1989; deLaCoste-Utamsing & Holloway, 1982). For example, when Laura Allen and her co-workers autopsied 11 male and 11 female brains, they found that a nucleus in the hypothalamus that regulates sexual behavior was almost three times larger in the male brain.

It appears that the same mechanism that causes the sexual dimorphism of male and female genitals also causes sexual dimorphism in the brain. Studies of guinea pigs and rats have shown that the presence of testosterone during prenatal development influences the size of a number of brain nuclei (Gorski et al., 1980;

Hines et al., 1985). Based on animal research, it is assumed that human brain differences are also caused by prenatal hormones. Evidence supporting this conclusion comes from studies showing that prenatal hormones can influence a person's behavior.

Aggression is the behavior most clearly different in males and females. Not only is most of the violence in our society perpetrated by males, but young human and animal males play much more aggressively than do young females. Is this greater male aggression related to the high concentration of testosterone in males? In animals, exposure to excess testosterone prenatally leads to more aggressive behavior in adults (Reinisch, 1981). Does this effect also occur in humans? June Reinisch investigated this question by studying the children of mothers who had been treated with synthetic hormones called progestins to prevent miscarriages during pregnancy. Because **progestins** have effects similar to testosterone, Reinisch hypothesized that children who had been exposed to this hormone during prenatal development would be more aggressive than children who had not.

To test her idea, Reinisch gave children, who averaged 11½ years of age, a paper-and-pencil test to measure the likelihood of their reacting with physical aggression in a number of different conflict situations. One group of children (the experimental group) had been exposed to progestin during their mother's pregnancy. The other group (the control group) were those children's brothers or sisters, who had not been exposed to progestin. Males in the experimental group were compared with their brothers, females with

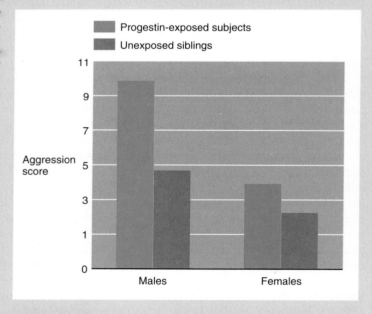

FIGURE 3.23

The potential for aggression is higher in subjects who were exposed to progestin prenatally.

their sisters. The results (Figure 3.23) show that (1) males had higher aggression scores than females, whether or not they received the hormone; and (2) both male and female subjects in the experimental group, who were exposed to the hormone prenatally, had higher aggression scores than their brothers or sisters in the control group.

The relation between hormones and behavior has also been demonstrated by looking at the relationship between adults' hormone levels and their performance on various tasks. Males and females tend to excel at different types of tasks. For example, on the average, males perform better than females on spatial tasks such as the mental rotation task, in which subjects are asked to determine which object on the right in Figure 3.24a would match the one on the left. Females outperform males on tests of perceptual speed, in which subjects are asked to rapidly identify matching items such as the houses in Figure 3.24b (Kimura, 1992).

To determine whether such differences are related to different hormone concentrations in males and females, Doreen Kimura (1992) measured testosterone concentrations in her subjects' saliva and then measured their spatial ability and perceptual speed, using tests like the ones in Figure 3.24. Although she found no relationship between testosterone levels and performance on the perceptual speed task (on which women usually do better), she found an effect for the spatial task. Men with low testosterone scored higher than men with high testosterone, and women with high testosterone scored higher than women with low testosterone (Figure 3.25). On the basis of these results, Kimura concluded that

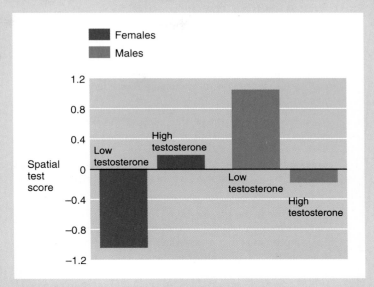

FIGURE 3.25
Scores on a spatial test vary as a function of gender and testosterone level.

the optimal testosterone level for spatial performance may be in the low male range (which is still higher than the top of the female range, as males have higher testosterone levels than females).

Data such as these indicating a relationship between hormones and behavior, as well as the finding that prenatal hormones can affect brain development, have led Kimura to conclude that "men's and women's brains are organized along different lines from very early in life." Her conclusion is bolstered by her finding that damage to the front of the brain is more likely to cause the speech disorder called *aphasia* in women, whereas damage to the back of the brain is more likely to cause it in men.

All of these results taken together indicate that some of the differences we observe between men and women are biologically determined. This does not, however, mean that *all* such differences are biologically determined. In the chapters that follow we will see that there is also strong behavioral evidence linking many gender differences to differences in the learning boys and girls experience as they grow up. Just as our general characteristics are determined by the interaction between our heredity and our environment, differences between males and females are caused by the interaction between their biological makeup and their experiences.

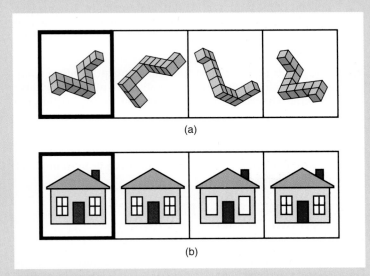

FIGURE 3.24
Males perform better on the mental rotation task (a), determining which object can be rotated to match the object at left. Females perform better on the perceptual speed task (b), determining which object exactly matches the object at left.

The Neuron:
Building Block of the Nervous System

- Neurons—cells specialized to conduct electrical signals—are the building blocks of the nervous system. The neuron's main components are the cell body, dendrites, and axon. Neurons specialized to receive environmental stimuli have receptors that transform environmental energy into electrical energy.

- When the neuron is at rest, the inside of the axon has a negative electrical charge compared to the outside. When an action potential is generated, the charge inside the axon becomes more positive as sodium ions rush into the axon and then returns to resting level as potassium ions rush out of the axon.

- The synapse is the place where two neurons connect. When neurotransmitters released from the presynaptic neuron contact receptor sites that match their shapes, the result is either an excitatory or inhibitory electrical potential in the postsynaptic neuron. An action potential occurs only if the summed excitatory responses are strong enough to cause the postsynaptic neuron to exceed the threshold for generating a nerve impulse.

- Each neurotransmitter serves a limited number of functions. For example, one of the functions of the neurotransmitter dopamine is to help control voluntary movement.

The Body's Communication Networks:
The Nervous and Endocrine Systems

- The central nervous system consists of the brain and the spinal cord. The brain has numerous components: The cerebral cortex contains mechanisms that create our ability to move, to perceive the environment, and to carry out higher mental functions; and subcortical nuclei such as the amygdala, hippocampus, thalamus, and hypothalamus are responsible for functions such as memory, emotion, temperature regulation, thirst, hunger, sexual arousal, and the processing of sensory information.

- The cerebellum is important for coordinating movement and for some aspects of language and thinking. The brain stem consists of the medulla—which controls vital functions such as breathing, heart rate, and salivation—and the reticular formation and raphe nucleus, which play important roles in controlling sleep and wakefulness.

- The peripheral nervous system is composed of all the neurons outside of the central nervous system. It is divided into somatic and autonomic divisions. The autonomic nervous system is divided into sympathetic and parasympathetic divisions: The sympathetic division mobilizes the body for emergencies; the parasympathetic division maintains the body at its normal level.

- The endocrine system communicates by means of glands that secrete hormones into the bloodstream. The glands of the endocrine system are controlled by the pituitary gland, which is itself controlled by the hypothalamus. The glands also receive signals from the autonomic nervous system.

The Brain:
Localized Functions Working Together

- Early brain researchers thought that the brain operated according to the principles of holism. Beginning in the 1800s, research began establishing the principle of localization of function.

- Paul Broca and Carl Wernicke showed that there are areas in the left frontal and temporal lobes that are specialized for speech. Other evidence for localization has come from research in which activity in the prefrontal cortex and other brain areas is measured as a person solves problems. In addition, brain activity in response to touch has been measured in the somatosensory cortex in the parietal lobe. The "map" of the body in the somatosensory cortex is called a homunculus. There is a similar map of the body on the motor cortex, an area in the frontal lobe that causes movement when stimulated.

- Functions are also localized in subcortical structures. Memory is served by the hippocampus, amygdala, and thalamus. Emotions are served by the hippocampus, amygdala, and hypothalamus.

- Lateralization of function refers to the left and right hemispheres of the brain serving different functions. Language is usually located in the left hemisphere, and the expression of emotions and performance on spatial tasks are served by the right.

- The results of research on split-brain patients confirm many of the conclusions of earlier lateralization research and also illustrate the existence of two different realities within the brain.

- Modern researchers emphasize the idea that most behaviors involve numerous brain areas interacting with one another. This activation of a number of brain areas is an example of parallel processing.

The Dynamic Nervous System:
Changing with Development and Experience

- The brain has the capacity to change its structure as it develops and interacts with the environment. Synapse formation is the major process that occurs as the brain matures during the first years of life.

- The brain's structure changes not only with maturation, but with experience. Raising animals in enriched environments increases the complexity of the neural wiring in their brains; increasing the usage of one part of the body increases that part's representation in the somatosensory cortex; and exposure to traumatic events can cause structural changes in the brain that are associated with post-traumatic stress disorder.

Heredity and Behavior

- Each person is constructed according to a biological blueprint created by genetic contributions from his or her parents. This genetic blueprint is called the person's genotype. The expression of the genotype is called the phenotype.

Evolution and Behavior

- Evolution is the process by which organisms have changed from their ancient ancestors to their present form. Darwin's theory of natural selection applies to both physical and behavioral characteristics. However, this principle encounters a problem when we consider altruistic social behaviors. For instance, emitting signals to warn other animals of danger reduces the warning individual's chances of survival.

- Sociobiologists propose the principle of kin selection to explain the problem posed by altruistic social behavior. Critics of sociobiology argue that this principle is inadequate to explain human social behavior, which is heavily influenced by learning and culture.

Reprise: Levels of Analysis and Behavior

- There is a wide range of sublevels within the biological level of analysis, from molecular events at the synapse to the organization of the brain to behavioral evolution. All these sublevels, as well as the other main levels of analysis, have in common a commitment to explaining behavior. Whether we are working at a biological, behavioral, cognitive, or contextual level of analysis, our ultimate goal is to understand behavior.

Follow-Through/Diversity: Sex Hormones, Brain Structure, and Behavior

- Differences in prenatal hormones in males and females may be responsible for differences in male and female brains. These brain differences may, in turn, be responsible for differences in male and female adult performance on various tasks. Such performance differences have also been related to differences in the concentrations of various hormones in adult males and females. Some of the differences we observe between males and females are, therefore, biologically determined.

Key Terms

action potential
all-or-none principle
altruistic behavior
amygdala
auditory cortex
autonomic nervous system
axon
brain
brain lesioning
brain stimulation
brain stem
Broca's area
cells
cell body
central nervous system
cerebellum
cerebral cortex
computerized axial tomography (CAT) scan
corpus callosum
dendrite
dominant hemisphere
dopamine
endocrine glands
endocrine system
estrogens
evolution
excitatory transmitter
frontal lobe
genes
genotype
hippocampus
homunculus
hormones
hypothalamus
inhibitory transmitter
ions
kin selection
lateralization of function
left hemisphere
lobes
localization of function
magnetic resonance imaging (MRI)
medulla
microelectrode
motor cortex
natural selection
nervous system
neurons
neurotransmitter
occipital lobe
parallel processing
parasympathetic division
parietal lobe
Parkinson's disease
peripheral nervous system
phenotype
positron emission tomography (PET) scan
postsynaptic neuron
prefrontal cortex
prenatal sexual differentiation
presynaptic neuron
progestins
raphe system
receptor
receptor sites
reflex arc
regional cerebral blood flow (RCBF)
resting potential
reticular formation
reuptake
right hemisphere
sexual dimorphism
sociobiology
somatic nervous system
somatosensory cortex
spinal cord
split-brain operation
stains
subcortical nuclei
survival of the fittest
sympathetic division
synapse
synaptic vesicles
temporal lobe
terminal buttons
testosterone
thalamus
transduction
visual cortex
Wernicke's area

CHAPTER

4

Two Questions About Perception
How Is Information in the Environment Represented
in the Nervous System?
How Do We Use Information from the Environment
to Create Perceptions?

Vision: Seeing Forms and Colors

Hearing: Perceiving Pitch

Interdisciplinary Dimension: Medicine
Cochlear Implants

The Skin Senses: Touch, Temperature, and Pain

The Chemical Senses: Taste and Smell

**How Do We Differentiate Objects
in the Environment?**

How Do We Perceive Depth?

How Do We Perceive the Sizes and Shapes of Objects?

Why Do We Sometimes Misperceive?

How Do Expectations Influence Perception?

**Reprise: The Creativity of the Brain
and the Commonality of the Senses**

Follow-Through/Diversity
Perception and Culture

The Senses and Perception

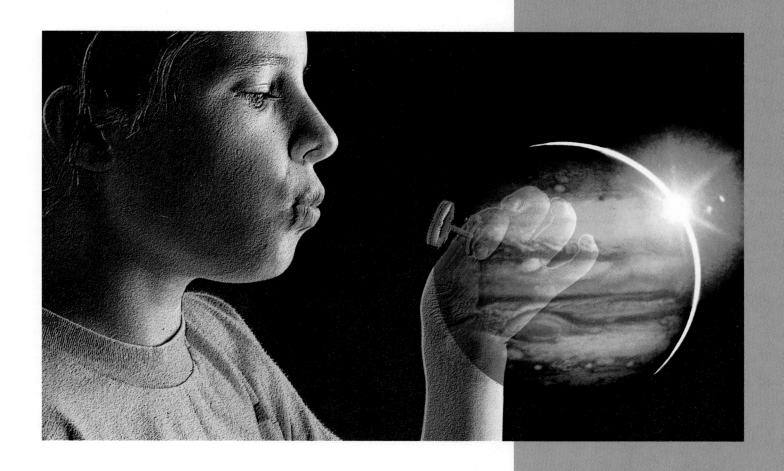

"You have been in Afghanistan, I perceive."

Sherlock Holmes, *in* A Study in Scarlet

Sherlock Holmes, master detective

Sherlock Holmes, the fictional detective created by Sir Arthur Conan Doyle, was famous for his ability to deduce startling conclusions from seemingly meager clues. One such example occurs when Holmes is introduced to his future sidekick, Dr. Watson, in London. Without prompting, Holmes immediately observes that Watson has just come from Afghanistan. Amazed, Watson naturally assumes that someone must have told Holmes that he had been an army doctor serving in Afghanistan. "Nothing of the sort," Holmes protests. He goes on to explain:

> I *knew* you came from Afghanistan. From long habit the train of thoughts ran so swiftly through my mind that I arrived at the conclusion without being conscious of intermediate steps. There were such steps, however. The train of reasoning ran, "Here is a gentleman of a medical type, but with the air of a military man. Certainly an army doctor, then. He has just come from the tropics, for his face is dark, and that is not the natural tint of his skin, for his wrists are fair. He has undergone hardship and sickness, as his haggard face says clearly. His left arm has been injured. He holds it in a stiff and unnatural manner. Where in the tropics could an English army doctor have seen much hardship and got his arm wounded? Clearly in Afghanistan." The whole train of thought did not occupy a second. I then remarked that you came from Afghanistan, and you were astonished.

Doyle's readers are amused and entertained when Holmes claims that he performed such an elaborate chain of reasoning so instantaneously that he wasn't even "conscious of intermediate steps." Only in detective fiction, we think, do people so effortlessly put together theories from fragmentary clues. Yet this is just what we do every time we open our eyes or listen with our ears: without realizing it, we perform complex, instantaneous feats of organizing and integrating information and make inferences from it. As you will see in this chapter, **perception**—the process that creates our sensory experiences—is as remarkable as the exploits of the greatest fictional detectives. Every waking moment, you and I are engaged in an active creative process of *constructing* our perceptual world from many sources of sensory information.

Two Questions About Perception

There is no way to understand the world without first detecting it through the radar-net of our senses.

Diane Ackerman (1990, p. xv)

In this chapter, we will actually be following two detective stories. One story is about how our perceptual system sifts and combines many types of information to create our experience of perceiving. The other is about how researchers have devoted themselves to figuring out how the perceptual system does this. This way of looking at perception—through a detective's eyes—can be applied to many areas of psychology, but it is especially well suited to perception because of the perceptual system's task: the perceptual system must determine what is out there in the environment, based on clues contained in the firing of neurons, images on the retina, properties of the physical environment, and the prior experience and knowledge of the perceiver. In addition, looking at perception from the point of view of how researchers have studied it offers some compelling examples of the sometimes detectivelike process of scientific research.

As most detective stories begin with questions to be answered, we can pose two central questions that will guide our discussion in this chapter: (1) How is information in the environment represented in the nervous system? and (2) How do we use information from the environment to create perceptions? Let's consider each of these questions in turn.

How Is Information in the Environment Represented in the Nervous System?

We are immersed in an environment that is filled with energy: light energy from the sun and other sources, mechanical energy from pressure changes in the air and pressure on our skin, chemical energy from liquids and airborne molecules. Yet when we perceive this energy-filled environment, what we actually experience is not energy but objects, colors, smells, tastes, sounds, touch, tickle, and pain. All our sensory experiences come from environmental energy, but we somehow transform that energy into the *experiences* that we call seeing, hearing, tasting, smelling, and touch.

How can we explain the transformation of physical energy in the environment into the perceptions that we experience? Chapter 3 provided a starting point for our answer: Physical energy (such as light) impinges on our sensory receptors (for example, in the eye). Those receptors transduce the physical energy into electrical energy that, through a complex process, creates action potentials (which we refer to as nerve impulses in this chapter). Those nerve impulses travel through a network of neurons to the brain, and we perceive (Figure 4.1).

So, working at the biological level of analysis, we can ask, How can different nerve impulses—all of which are simply electrical energy generated by the movement of charged molecules across nerve membranes—lead us to "see" in response to some forms of stimulation, to "hear" in response to others, and to "taste" in response to still others? Part of the answer is that nerve impulses from different senses travel to different parts of the brain. Impulses from the eye reach the visual receiving area in the occipital lobe of the cortex; impulses from the ear reach the auditory receiving area in the temporal lobe; and impulses from the skin reach the somatosensory area in the parietal lobe. Thus, the brain "knows" when the eye, ear, or skin has been stimulated by the area of cortex that is receiving nerve impulses.

3   BIOLOGY

FIGURE 4.1
As Sherlock Holmes investigates the evidence, he takes in several kinds of physical energy: (a) visible light (electromagnetic energy); (b) pressure changes in the air (mechanical energy); (c) airborne molecules (chemical energy); and (d) pressure on the skin (mechanical energy). Receptors in the eye, ear, nose, and skin, respectively, convert this energy into electrical impulses, which travel to the brain to be transformed into perceptions.

But this explanation leads to another, more challenging question. How does the brain know which *specific stimulus* has been presented to a given sense? How can some nerve impulses produce the taste of a sour lemon, whereas others create a jumble of blues, reds, and greens, and still others signal the presence of bitterly cold wind? This is the problem of **sensory coding,** how the information contained in nerve impulses represents different qualities of the environment. Sensory coding will be a central concern of the first part of this chapter, as we survey the senses and ask what it is about the neural signals generated by each sense that enables us to detect various qualities in the environment.

But explaining how basic properties of the environment are represented in the nervous system is only one part of our detective story. The other part is how those basic properties, those *clues*—bits of information that might stand for "yellow" or "sour," for example—eventually lead us to perceive objects in the environment. Constructing an *object* like "lemon" from "yellow" and "sour" is like Holmes inferring that Dr. Watson had been in Afghanistan. And that brings us to the second main question we want to answer about perception.

How Do We Use Information from the Environment to Create Perceptions?

Consider the patterns of white and black in Figure 4.2. What do they represent? The answer is not obvious to many people when they first look at these pictures. The key to perceiving these patterns is to *organize* them into meaningful units. Once you organize the patterns correctly, pictures that originally appeared meaningless become recognizable. (For an explanation of the images in Figure 4.2, see Figure 4.3.)

The processes involved in solving picture puzzles like these are similar to those used in everyday perception. In both cases we encounter stimuli and try to figure out their meaning. Usually this process of figuring out happens so smoothly and quickly that, like Sherlock Holmes, we are unaware of the complex activity we have just performed. It is only when our normal perceptual processes are frustrated by unusual or complicated stimuli that we realize how many steps intervene between receiving stimuli through our senses and perceiving a coherent and meaningful environment.

How can we understand the processes involved in transforming the stimulation received by our senses into perceptions? Working at the behavioral level, we can observe people's responses to the *physical properties* of stimuli. For instance, we can measure how well people can estimate the sizes of objects, under conditions ranging from close up to far away, and from sharply visible on a clear day to partly obscured by morning fog. Working at the cognitive level, we can focus on the relation between the *meanings* people assign to stimuli and their perception of them. For instance, we can ask how people's expectations about what they are going to see actually influence what they do see. Working at the contextual level, we can ask how the *context* in which people learn to perceive influences their perceptions. For example, we can compare how people from different cultures perceive pictures, visual illusions, the shapes and sizes of objects, and even internal experiences like pain.

We begin our study of perception by returning to our first question: How is information in the environment represented in the nervous system? Working at the biological level of analysis, we will examine each of the five major senses—vision, hearing, the skin senses, taste, and smell—and trace the path of sensory information from physical stimulus to encoded data in the brain. Then we will turn to our second question and, working at the behavioral, cognitive, and contextual levels of analysis, we will consider how the perceptual system transforms those sensory clues into a meaningful and orderly perceptual world.

FIGURE 4.2
What do these pictures represent?

Vision: Seeing Forms and Colors

The greatest thing a human soul ever does in this world is to see something.

John Ruskin (1819–1900)
English writer and artist

Imagine that you are looking out over a valley stretching from a farmhouse in the foreground to gray-blue hills in the distance. Above you, white clouds move slowly against an azure blue sky, casting shadows on the ground below. In the valley are hundreds of trees decked out in brilliant fall colors, their leaves fluttering gently in the breeze. The scene contains a myriad of colors, shapes, and sizes; it has variety, depth, and movement. All these qualities are detectable by your perceptual system only because your sense of vision allows you to transform the light energy reaching your eyes into encoded signals that reach your brain.

FIGURE 4.3
The map of Europe and the cow were difficult to perceive in Figure 4.2 because they were either presented with colors reversed and in an unfamiliar orientation (the map) or degraded (the cow). But once recognized, it is not only easy to perceive them, but it becomes difficult *not* to see the black and white patterns as objects.

The Stimulus for Vision

Our environment is filled with electromagnetic radiation, energy radiated as waves produced by the movement of electric charges. The many different forms of electromagnetic energy can be arranged along an **electromagnetic spectrum,** which shows the range of wavelengths of different forms of energy, from the extremely short gamma rays and X rays (having wavelengths of about 10^{-12} meters) to the long radio waves (having wavelengths of about 10^{+4} meters) (Figure 4.4).

Electromagnetic energy is the *physical stimulus* for vision. Although most of it is invisible to humans, within the vast electromagnetic spectrum is a narrow band of wavelengths that our sense of sight *can* detect. **Visible light**—the light we can see from the sun, from biological sources such as luminous minerals and lightning bugs, and from artificial sources such as light bulbs—has wavelengths ranging from about 400 to 700 nanometers (a nanometer is 10^{-9} meter). We perceive different wavelengths across this band as different colors: the short ones appear as blue, those in the middle of the visible spectrum appear as green, and long ones appear as yellow, orange, and red. We see different wavelengths in this way because of the structure and function of our visual system.

The Structure of the Visual System

Like all our senses, our visual system consists of receptors, a network of neurons, and structures in the brain that receive the information transmitted by nerve impulses (Figure 4.5a). Our eyes, as our window to the world, are the part of the visual system that accepts light energy, focuses it into images, and transforms it into the electrical energy of the nervous system. As shown in Figure 4.5b, light entering the eye passes through the **cornea,** the transparent front of the eye, before proceeding through a hole called the *pupil* and then the **lens.**

The cornea and lens in combination focus light so that—if things are working properly—an image of the objects from which the light originated is formed on the **retina,** a thin layer of neurons that contains the receptors for vision, **rods** and **cones** (Figure 4.5c). These receptors are distributed differently on the retina. A small area on the retina called the **fovea** contains only cones, whereas the rest of the retina, called the **peripheral retina,** contains some cones but mostly rods. Besides being distributed differently on the retina, rods and cones have different functions: the cones are responsible for detail vision, whereas rods register details poorly. Thus, when you look directly at something, its image is focused on the all-cone fovea to take advantage of the cone's excellent detail vision. This is why, when you want to find a friend's face in a crowd, you have to scan the crowd until you are looking directly at the person. Only when your friend's face is imaged on your fovea can you see it clearly.

Rods and cones also differ in another important way that affects our perception. The cones control our vision in high-illumination situations such as daylight and produce the neural code for color that causes different wavelengths of light to appear colored. The rods, however, control vision in dim illumination and do not produce a sensory code for color. That is why, as dusk approaches and your vision begins to shift from cones to rods, colors in the environment begin to fade. Eventually, when the illumination has become very dim, you are seeing only with your rods and you perceive only shades of gray. Shortly we will see in more detail how the cones produce the sensory code for color.

Once the rod and cone receptors transform incoming light energy into electrical signals, those signals travel in the form of nerve impulses out of the back of the eye along the optic nerve. They reach a nucleus in the thalamus called the **lateral geniculate nucleus (LGN)** and from there reach the occipital lobe of the cortex, also called the **visual receiving area** of the brain (Figure 4.5d). The journey of these nerve impulses does not, however, end in the occipital cortex. As we will see later, these signals also reach areas in the parietal and temporal lobes.

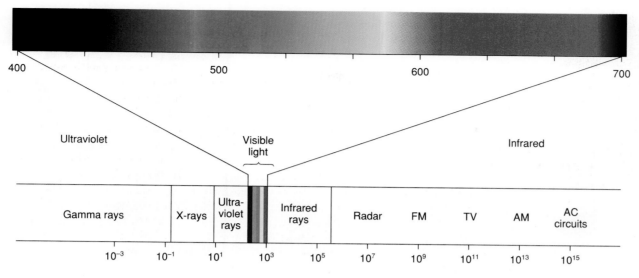

FIGURE 4.4
Visible light—electromagnetic energy with wavelengths between about 400 and 700 nanometers (nm)—accounts for only a small portion of the entire electromagnetic spectrum.

The Sensory Code for Vision

So far we have described the visual system in fairly simplified terms: light enters the eyes through the pupil, electrical signals leave the eye in the optic nerve, those signals reach the occipital cortex and other areas of the brain, and we see. We are now ready to look at this process in more detail by describing the sensory code—the properties of neural signals that give rise to various visual qualities. As we focus on two qualities, form and color, we will see that the discovery of the sensory codes for those qualities resulted from some scientific detective work.

The code for form.   The search for the sensory code for form led researchers to study the responses of single neurons in the visual system. The researchers who began, in the 1950s, to record from neurons in the visual system asked the following question: What kinds of stimuli presented to the retina cause neurons in the three major structures of the visual system—the retina, LGN, and the cortex—to fire? Their tactic for answering this question was to use a recording electrode to pick up signals from a single neuron and then to present different stimuli to the retina to see which ones were most effective at causing the neuron to fire.

Applied to neurons in the optic nerve and the LGN, this tactic revealed that neurons in those structures responded weakly, if at all, when the entire retina was flooded with light, but that they responded vigorously when a small spot of light was presented to a particular area of the retina.

But our perception of the complex shapes and forms we encounter in everyday life cannot be explained simply by neurons that respond to small spots of light. To find neurons that respond to more complex stimuli, we need to move from the optic nerve and LGN to the visual receiving area of the cortex. Recording from neurons in the occipital cortex reveals a number of types of neurons that respond best to more complex stimuli. Some cortical neurons respond best to lines *oriented* in a particular direction, others respond best to lines that *move* in a particular direction, and others respond best to lines of a *specific length* that move in a particular direction.

The researchers primarily responsible for determining the properties of these cortical neurons, David Hubel and Thorsten Wiesel, received the 1981 Nobel Prize in physiology and medicine for this research (1959, 1961, 1965). They

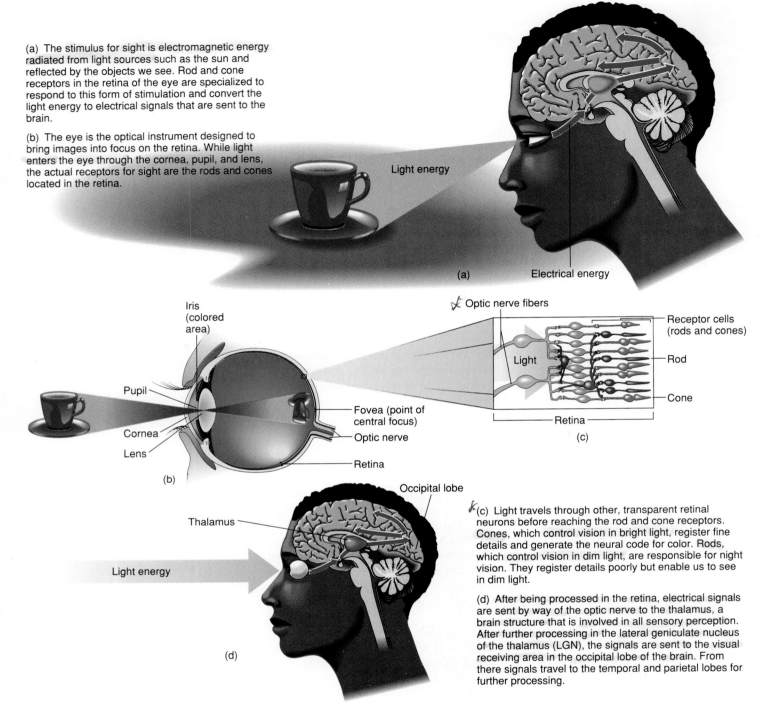

(a) The stimulus for sight is electromagnetic energy radiated from light sources such as the sun and reflected by the objects we see. Rod and cone receptors in the retina of the eye are specialized to respond to this form of stimulation and convert the light energy to electrical signals that are sent to the brain.

(b) The eye is the optical instrument designed to bring images into focus on the retina. While light enters the eye through the cornea, pupil, and lens, the actual receptors for sight are the rods and cones located in the retina.

Light energy

Electrical energy

(a)

Iris (colored area)

Pupil

Cornea

Lens

(b)

Fovea (point of central focus)

Optic nerve

Retina

Optic nerve fibers

Light

Receptor cells (rods and cones)

Rod

Cone

Retina

(c)

Occipital lobe

Thalamus

Light energy

(d)

(c) Light travels through other, transparent retinal neurons before reaching the rod and cone receptors. Cones, which control vision in bright light, register fine details and generate the neural code for color. Rods, which control vision in dim light, are responsible for night vision. They register details poorly but enable us to see in dim light.

(d) After being processed in the retina, electrical signals are sent by way of the optic nerve to the thalamus, a brain structure that is involved in all sensory perception. After further processing in the lateral geniculate nucleus of the thalamus (LGN), the signals are sent to the visual receiving area in the occipital lobe of the brain. From there signals travel to the temporal and parietal lobes for further processing.

FIGURE 4.5
The visual system

and other researchers created a picture of the visual system in which neurons at early stations in the system, such as the optic nerve and LGN, respond best to simple stimuli such as spots of light. In contrast, neurons in later stations, such as the cortex, respond best to more complex types of stimuli, such as lines of a particular length moving in a particular direction.

Cortical neurons that respond best to more specific stimuli are called **feature detectors.** We can see that they might offer a partial explanation for how we perceive forms by considering how a large number of feature detectors might respond to a form such as the chair in Figure 4.6. The chair's image on the retina would cause feature detectors that respond to lines of different orientations to fire. Information from all of those detectors would then have to be combined to create a perception of the chair.

This explanation glosses over a crucial step, because researchers still don't know how the information from many feature detectors is combined in the brain. But they *have* found neurons that receive inputs from many other neurons, and so respond to stimuli that are more complex than moving lines. Many of these neurons are located, not in the visual receiving area in the occipital lobe, but in other lobes of the cortex. For example, there are neurons in a monkey's temporal lobe that respond best to pictures of monkey and human faces (Bruce, Desimone, & Gross, 1981) (Figure 4.7).

The fact that neurons outside of the visual receiving area play an important role in form perception has also been demonstrated by experiments that show that removing an area in a monkey's temporal lobe makes it difficult for the monkey to *identify* objects it has seen before and that removing an area in the parietal lobe makes it difficult for monkey to *find* objects it has seen at a particular location. Thus, the neurons in the temporal lobe are involved in *identifying* objects and neurons in the parietal lobe are involved in *locating* objects (Mishkin, 1986; Mishkin, Ungerleider, & Macko, 1983.)

Thus, feature detectors in the visual receiving area, plus neurons in other areas of the cortex, represent the beginning of the solution to the problem of form perception at the biological level of analysis. However, as we will see later on, the problem of how we combine the sensory clues of sight to perceive forms can also be studied at the behavioral, cognitive, and contextual levels of analysis.

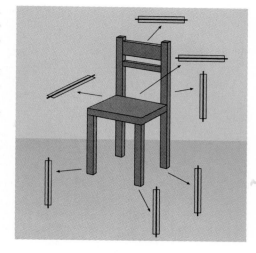

FIGURE 4.6
Cortical neurons called feature detectors respond to lines with specific orientations. The edges of this chair, therefore, would cause neurons to fire that respond to horizontal lines, vertical lines, and angled lines.

The code for color. Like our perception of form, our ability to discriminate between different colors depends on having a sensory code. The story of how researchers have tracked down the code for color begins in the 1800s, long before the development of techniques for recording from single neurons. The challenge facing early color researchers was to explain how people can perceive hundreds or even thousands of different colors. Because the means for studying this question at the biological level were not available in the 1800s, researchers attacked the question via experiments at the behavioral level of analysis. They did this by studying people's observable response to colors, using a technique called **color matching.**

In a color-matching experiment subjects are asked to match the color of one wavelength of light by combining three other wavelengths. For example, the subject might be asked to match the color of a 500-nanometer light presented in the test field by mixing together 420-, 560-, and 640-nanometer lights in a comparison field. These experiments revealed that subjects with normal color vision could match *any* wavelength in the test field by combining three other wavelengths in the appropriate proportions. They could not, however, match every test wavelength if they were provided with only two other wavelengths. For example, if a subject was given only the 420- and 640-nanometer lights to mix in the comparison field, there would be some colors that she couldn't match.

Why should we need a minimum of exactly three wavelengths to match all wavelengths in the spectrum? This question prompted Thomas Young (1801) and Hermann von Helmholtz (1852) to develop a theory that Sherlock Holmes might have admired. Their **trichromatic theory of color vision** (also known as the Young-Helmholtz theory of color vision) hypothesized that color vision results from the action of three receptors that respond best to light in different regions of the spectrum. Figure 4.8a plots *response curves* for those three receptors—each one responding best to short-wavelength, medium-wavelength, or long-wavelength light.

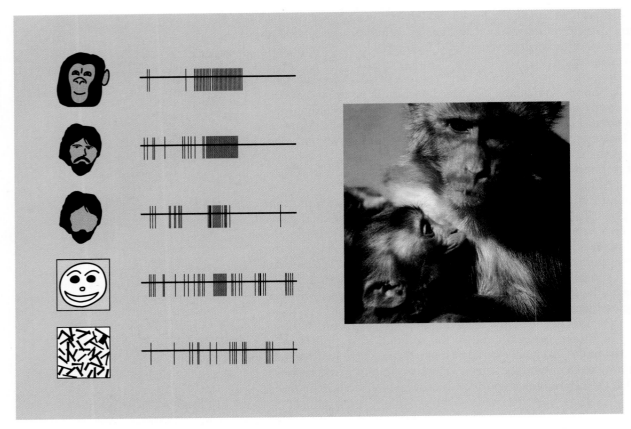

FIGURE 4.7
The records illustrated here are from a neuron in a monkey's temporal lobe that responds with a vigorous burst of impulses to a monkey's or a man's face but responds more weakly to a face without features, a cartoon face, or an array of lines.

Figure 4.8b shows how the three receptors of trichromatic theory might respond to a short-wavelength and a long-wavelength light. The short-wavelength light causes a large response in the short-wavelength receptor and smaller responses in the other two. The long-wavelength light causes a large response in the long-wavelength receptor and smaller responses in the other two. The important point is that the *pattern of firing* of the three receptors is different for the two wavelengths. That pattern, according to this theory, is the sensory code for color. Each color has its own pattern that the brain can read.

But trichromatic theory was not the only theory of color vision in the 1800s. Like a rival detective, another researcher, Ewald Hering (1878, 1964), created another theory based on completely different evidence. Hering's evidence consisted of the following perceptual observations:

- Blue and yellow cannot exist together in the same color. Nor can red and green. Can you imagine, or find an example of, a yellowish blue or bluish yellow? How about a reddish green or a greenish red? Most people find it difficult to imagine any of these colors but can easily imagine, say, a bluish red (purple) or a greenish blue (turquoise).

- If gray material is surrounded by a red background, it takes on a slightly greenish tint. Similarly, a blue background makes gray material look slightly yellow. This effect, in which one color changes our perception of an adjacent color, is called *simultaneous contrast.*

- Exposing the eye to red light results in a green *afterimage,* whereas exposing the eye to blue light results in a yellow afterimage. You can demonstrate this effect for yourself by staring at the center of Figure 4.9 for about 45 seconds and then looking at the white space on the right. You should see an afterimage in which the green and red squares have changed places and the blue and yellow squares have changed places. Looking at red causes a green afterimage (and vice versa), and the afterimages of blue and yellow are similarly paired.

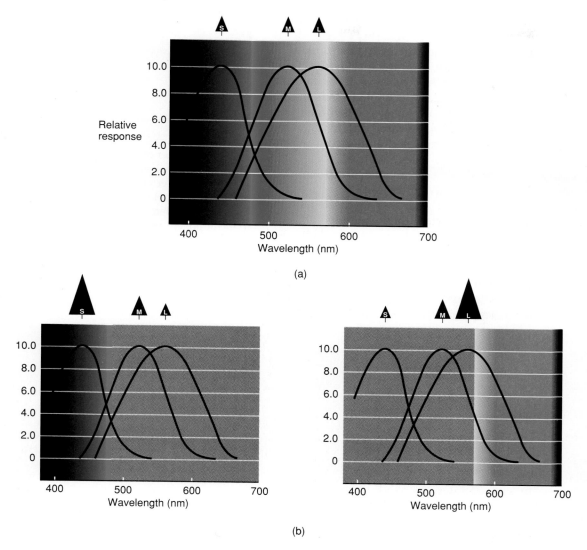

(a)

(b)

• People who are color-blind to red are also blind to green, and people who can't see blue can't see yellow either.

All of these observations pointed Hering to the conclusion that blue and yellow are paired with each other in the perceptual system, and that red and green are, as well. This conclusion led him to propose the **opponent-process theory of color vision,** which states that there are opponent mechanisms in the retina that respond in opposite ways to blue and yellow and to red and green. The *blue-yellow mechanism* responds negatively to blue light and positively to yellow light, and the *red-green mechanism* responds positively to red light and negatively to green light. According to Hering, the response of these opponent mechanisms was the sensory code for color. A blue light would cause a negative response in the blue-yellow mechanism; a red light would cause a positive response in the red-green mechanism; and so on.

Let's stop for a moment to consider the state of the proposed sensory code for color near the end of the 19th century. Young, Helmholtz, and Hering all hypothesized possible physiological mechanisms for color vision that they deduced from perceptual observations. Because they lacked the tools to study the physiology of vision directly, their physiological hypotheses were based on evidence gathered at the behavioral level of analysis. But these attempts to infer the

FIGURE 4.8
There are three types of cone receptors. (a) Response curves show that each responds best to light in one part of the spectrum. (b) According to the trichromatic theory of color vision, each color is signaled by these receptors firing in a distinctive pattern. At left, short-wavelength light causes more firing in the short-wavelength receptor than in the medium- and long-wavelength receptors. This pattern of firing, symbolized by the sizes of the cones, results in a perception of "blue." At right, long-wavelength light causes more firing in the long-wavelength receptor than in the other two, resulting in a perception of "red."

sensory code for color produced two quite different theories, both apparently supported by good evidence. Which theory was right?

In a good mystery, there comes a point when the detective masterfully reconstructs the crime, reconciling all the apparently contradictory evidence that had bewildered slower-witted rivals. In the case of the sensory code for color, the ending to the story had to await the arrival of modern technology that enabled researchers to look directly at the visual system's physiology. When they were able to do this, beginning in the 1960s, they discovered three different types of visual receptors, each sensitive to a particular part of the spectrum, just as trichromatic theory had proposed. These receptors, which were all cone receptors, contained different chemicals called *visual pigments* that absorbed light best in different parts of the visual spectrum (Brown & Wald, 1964).

But what about opponent-process theory? It, too, was vindicated by the physiologists, who found neurons in the visual system that responded with opposing excitatory and inhibitory responses to wavelengths perceived as blue and yellow and those perceived as red and green (DeValois & Jacobs, 1968, 1984) (Figure 4.10). Thus, both trichromatic and opponent-process theories are correct. Trichromatic theory describes the activity of the cone receptors, and opponent-process theory describes the activity of neurons that receive signals from those cone receptors, (Figure 4.11). Color perception, therefore, depends both on

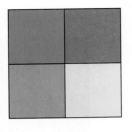

FIGURE 4.9
Stare at the center of this grid for about 45 seconds, then look at the white space on the right. You will see an afterimage with the red and green and the blue and yellow reversed. This demonstration lends support to the opponent-process theory of color vision.

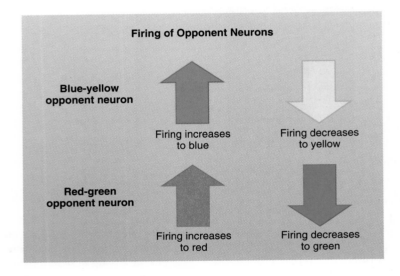

FIGURE 4.10
Opponent neurons respond in opposite ways to blue and yellow and to red and green. Some blue-yellow opponent neurons respond with an increase in firing to blue and a decrease to yellow, others with an increase to yellow and a decrease to blue. Red-green neurons follow a similar pattern.

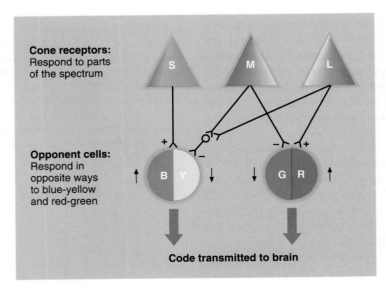

FIGURE 4.11
Color vision can be explained by the trichromatic and opponent-process theories working together. The trichromatic components, the receptors, fire in different patterns for different wavelengths, as in Figure 4.8. The opponent-process components are neurons that receive either excitation (which increases firing) or inhibition (which decreases firing) from the receptors. The red-green neuron receives excitation from the medium-wavelength receptor and inhibition from the long-wavelength receptor. The blue-yellow neuron receives excitation from the short-wavelength receptor and inhibition from the added responses of the medium- and long-wavelength receptors.

receptors sensitive to three different parts of the spectrum *and* on the way those receptors are connected to other neurons to create color-opponent neurons. The information contained in the firing of these opponent neurons transmits information to the brain about the wavelength of light presented to the retina.

The story of how Young, Helmholtz, and Hering deduced *physiological mechanisms* from *behavioral observations* shows how, by starting with an observable result—the person's color perception—researchers can work backward to deduce the cause—the underlying physiological mechanism. The reason researchers can "backtrack" in this way is that physiological processes sometimes leave clues in the perceptions they create.

These perceptual clues are sometimes right out in the open, as with the opponent nature of afterimages. Red and green afterimages had been observed by many people before Hering proposed the opponent-process theory, but Hering correctly figured out what those afterimages implied for physiology. In other cases, perceptual clues are more difficult to discover. For example, the fact that we can match any wavelength in the spectrum by combining a minimum of three other wavelengths is not obvious from everyday perceptual experience. Helmholtz needed to carry out color-matching experiments to uncover this perceptual clue to the underlying physiology.

In discussing the sensory code for vision we have considered form and color separately. Form and color are, in fact, processed in separate pathways in the brain, as we learned in Chapter 3. In that chapter we saw how separate neural circuits simultaneously process information about form, color, movement, and depth (Livingstone & Hubel, 1984, 1987, 1988; Zeki, 1992). It is important to remember, however, that the information in each of these circuits must eventually be combined, as we perceive all of these qualities as a whole when we look at something. We noted in Chapter 3 that when we see a round, red ball rolling away from us we don't see "round," "red," and "rolling" separately—we see all of those qualities as part of one object. Although processed separately, each of those qualities must eventually be combined in the brain so that we can experience them as combined in our perception. Exactly how these qualities are combined is under investigation in a number of laboratories.

What Perception Tells Us About the Environment

The story of the sensory code for color, with its conclusion that physiological mechanisms leave clues in our perceptions, makes an important point about perception's relation to the environment. It tells us that perception is not simply a "copy" of the environment. We don't see wavelengths; we see *colors,* and the colors we see depend on the particular structure of our visual system. As you have seen, a green afterimage follows a red flash because you have neurons that respond in opposite ways to the wavelengths that signal red and green. And the reason you need *three* wavelengths to match any other color in the spectrum is that you have three kinds of cones. There are people with only two types of functioning cones who perceive fewer colors than people having all three types. Other people, who have only rods, experience the world in shades of gray. Perception is therefore most accurately described as a *record* of the environment, shaped by physiological mechanisms poised between external stimuli and our perceptual experience.

Let's take our consideration of this connection between perception and physiology one step further by asking this question: Why do we experience blue in response to a 450-nanometer light? Why don't we experience red, green, orange, or magenta? One possible answer is that electromagnetic energy with a wavelength of 450 nanometers is colored blue; but in fact that is not the case. Electromagnetic energy is simply energy—it is colorless. There is nothing in the energy itself that would enable us to predict that a 450-nanometer light would appear as blue.

Our experience of "blueness" is *created* by the brain. It would make just as much sense to experience a 450-nanometer light as red, or even as a high-pitched tone. Imagine, for example, a being from another planet whose perceptual system is wired completely differently from ours and who experiences wavelengths as smells, chemical stimuli as sounds, and different patterns of vibration in the air as delectable tastes. Although this might seem like science fiction, there are many examples in our own animal kingdom of what we might consider strange ways of sensing: flies that taste with their feet (Roeder, 1963); bats that are blind to what we call visible light but that can detect radar waves (Simmons, 1971, 1979); and fish that can detect electrical fields (Crawford, 1991). In each of these cases of animal perception it is not obvious what "experience" should go with the fly's taste, the bat's radar waves, or the fish's electrical fields. But the important thing about these sensory systems is not the quality of the experiences they create but that they signal important information about the animal's environment.

We now turn to the sense of hearing, a sense that endows pressure changes in the air with the experience we call sound. Although it is not obvious why air pressure changes should be experienced as *sound,* it is clear that our sense of hearing helps us detect important information about our environment.

Hearing: Perceiving Pitch

You ain't heard nothin' yet…

Al Jolson, in the first talking picture, *The Jazz Singer* (1927)

On the first day of my perception class I pose the following question to my students: "If you had to lose either your hearing or vision, which one would you choose?" Of course, no one wants to lose either sense, but when forced to choose, more of my students say they would prefer to lose their hearing. But Helen Keller, who was both deaf and blind, disagreed: "Deafness is a much worse misfortune. For it means the loss of the most vital stimulus—the sound of the voice that brings language, sets thoughts astir and keeps us in the intellectual company of man" (Keller, 1910). In addition to connecting us intellectually with others, hearing warns us of approaching dangers (such as an onrushing car) and brings us the unique pleasure of music. Yet it does all these things on the basis of a quite simple physical stimulus: changes in air pressure.

The Stimulus for Hearing

The stimulus for hearing has been described by Diane Ackerman (1990) as "an onrushing, cresting and withdrawing of air molecules that begins with the movement of any object . . . and ripples out in all directions." The sound stimulus is created when objects move or interact with one another so as to create pressure changes in the air. These pressure changes are invisible, but you can understand them by considering how waves of pressure changes are produced by the vibrations of your stereo's loudspeaker.

People have been known to turn up their stereos loud enough so that vibrations can be felt through the floor. Even at lower levels, however, you can feel vibrations if you place your hand on your stereo's speaker. These vibrations affect the surrounding air, creating the physical stimulus for the music you hear. When the diaphragm of the speaker moves out, it pushes the surrounding air molecules together, increasing their density near the diaphragm. When the diaphragm moves back in, it pulls the air molecules apart, decreasing their density. By repeating this process hundreds or thousands of times a second, the speaker creates a pattern of alternating high and low pressure in the air that travels outward from the speaker, in much the same way that ripples travel outward from a pebble dropped in a quiet pool of water (Figure 4.12a). This pattern of air pressure changes, which is called a **sound wave,** is simplest in the case of **pure tones**—tones in which the air pressure changes follow the top pattern shown in Figure 4.12b, which we call a sine wave. These sine-wave pressure changes are produced by tuning forks or by a flute playing a high-pitched tone. In the case of music or speech, the pattern of sound waves is far more complex. It is that complexity that provides us with the richness of sounds that we experience.

Most research on hearing has used the sine-wave pressure changes of pure tones as stimuli. A characteristic that specifies the nature of a particular sine wave is the wave's **frequency,** the number of times per second the pressure wave goes through one cycle, from one peak and back to the next. Different tones can be differentiated in terms of their frequency in units called *Hertz (Hz)*. One Hertz is the same as one cycle per second; thus, a 1000-Hz tone is a pure tone that goes through 1000 cycles per second.

Why is frequency important? Because it is related to the experience of **pitch,** the highness or lowness of tones. Low-frequency tones have low pitches (the lowest note on the piano keyboard has a frequency of 27.5 Hz), whereas high-frequency tones have high pitches (the highest piano note has a frequency of 4186 Hz).

As with vision, our perceptual system for hearing allows us to perceive only a fraction of the stimuli that can be produced by different frequencies. Figure 4.13 shows the **audibility curve,** a plot of the threshold for hearing a tone versus frequency. (See Measurement & Methodology, "Measuring the Audibility Curve," on page 142.) This curve shows that the range of human hearing extends from about 20 Hz to 20,000 Hz. It also indicates that we require more sound en-

FIGURE 4.12
The stimulus for hearing is pressure changes in the air, illustrated here as the pressure wave emitted by a loudspeaker. The dark areas represent regions of high air pressure (the molecules are pushed closer together) and the light areas represent regions of lower air pressure. When these pressure changes occur smoothly from high to low pressure, as shown by the sine-wave pattern, a pure tone results. The pressure changes are more complex for most commonly encountered sounds, such as in music, speech, or noise.

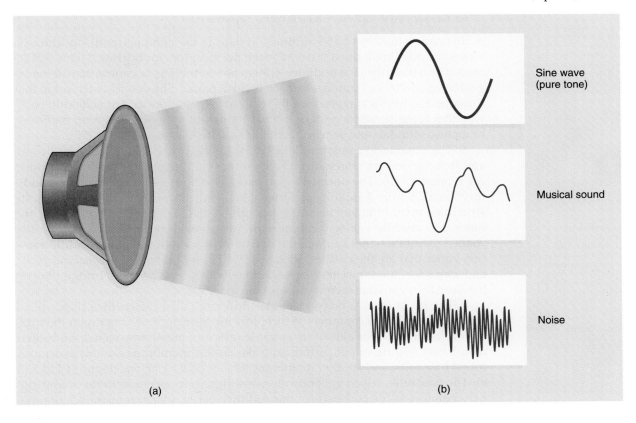

Sine wave (pure tone)

Musical sound

Noise

(a)   (b)

FIGURE 4.13

The audibility curve is a plot of the lowest sound pressure level at which we can hear a tone at different frequencies. This curve indicates that we are most sensitive to frequencies between 1000 to 4000 Hz, the frequencies of conversational speech. The upper curve shows the threshold of feeling, the sound pressure levels at which we actually "feel" the sound—a situation that might, for example, occur at a rock concert. Sustained exposure to these high levels can cause damage to the ear.

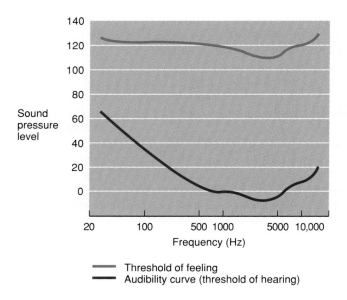

Threshold of feeling
Audibility curve (threshold of hearing)

very low or very high frequencies, and that we are most sensitive to frequencies between 1000 and 4000 Hz—exactly the frequencies of conversational speech. The perceptual systems of other organisms are attuned to a different range of frequencies, which is why a dog, for example, responds to the high-frequency stimulus of a dog whistle.

We will focus on pitch perception in this discussion of the sensory code for hearing, because changes of pitch play such an important role in creating the sounds of speech and music. For the same reason, pitch has been the subject of a great deal of research. The first step toward understanding pitch perception is to describe the structure of the auditory system (Figure 4.14).

The Structure of the Auditory System

A distinctive feature of the auditory system is the complex pathway through which sound stimuli must travel to reach the receptors for hearing. Diane Ackerman (1990) describes the auditory system as resembling "a contraption some ingenious plumber has put together from spare parts." She describes the route that the sound stimulus traverses on its way to the receptors as "an elaborate pathway that looks something like a maniacal miniature golf course, with curlicues, branches, roundabouts, relays, hydraulics and feedback loops" (p. 177).

The "maniacal miniature golf course" Ackerman is describing is the ear, and it is divided into three sections: the outer ear, the middle ear, and the inner ear (Figure 4.14b). The **outer ear** consists of the pinna, or earlobe, and the **auditory canal,** a tube 3 millimeters long whose function is to protect the delicate structures inside the ear from the hazards of the outside world. Dividing the outer and middle ear is the **tympanic membrane** (or eardrum), a conically shaped membrane that contacts the first of the three **ossicles** of the **middle ear**—tiny bones that are the smallest in the body. The ossicles, called the *malleus, incus,* and *stapes* (or, more popularly, the hammer, anvil, and stirrup), bridge the gap between the tympanic membrane and the inner ear.

The **inner ear** is a bony, snail-like structure called the **cochlea** that is filled with liquid and that contains the receptors for hearing. Running down the middle of the cochlea, for almost its entire length, is a membrane called the **basilar membrane** (Figure 4.14c). Sitting atop the basilar membrane are tiny receptors, called **hair cells,** and another membrane, the *tectorial membrane* (Figure 4.14d and e). The hair cells, which generate electrical signals in response to the sound signals, connect to fibers that form the auditory nerve, which transmits action po-

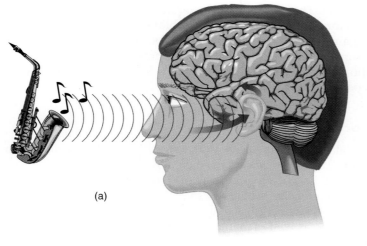

The stimulus for hearing is pressure changes in the air (sound waves), which receptors in the inner ear convert to neural impulses that carry a code representing various auditory qualities such as loudness and pitch (a).

The complex anatomy of the ear (b) is designed to transmit vibrations created by sound waves to the receptors for hearing, located in the cochlea in the inner ear.

The cochlea (c) is a bony, snail-like structure filled with liquid. It is shown in cross-section in (d). The vibrations transmitted to the cochlea generate vibrations in the fluid, which in turn cause the basilar membrane to vibrate.

The hair cells, the receptors for hearing, sit atop the basilar membrane (e). When the basilar membrane vibrates, the hair cells rub against the tectorial membrane. This rubbing bends the hair cells and electrical signals are transmitted along the auditory nerve to the brain.

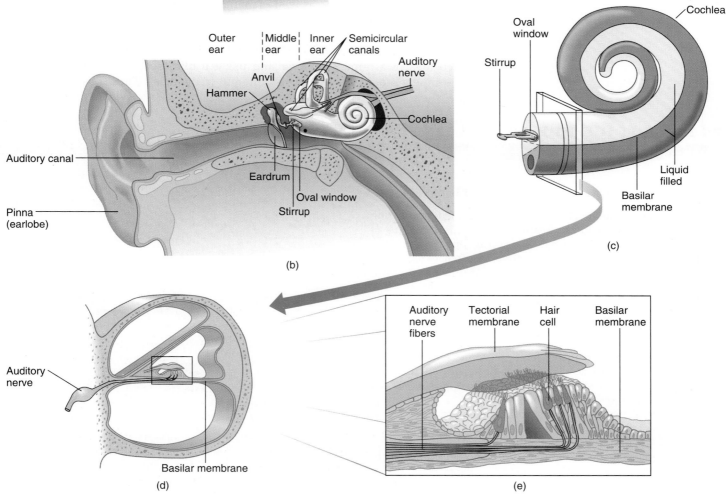

FIGURE 4.14
The auditory system

tentials out of the inner ear, through a number of nuclei, and finally to the auditory receiving area in the temporal lobe of the cortex.

Now that we have described the structure of the auditory system, let's return to the ear and observe how its structures react to the introduction of a sound stimulus. The stimulus for sound is vibration, and the ear's structures are engineered to transmit those vibrations. The first structure to vibrate, in response to the pressure changes of the sound stimulus, is the eardrum. Its vibration sets the three ossicles into motion, and the last bone in the chain, the stirrup, pushes gainst the oval window—the opening into the cochlea—and sets the liquid in the cochlea into vibration. The vibration of the liquid sets the basilar membrane into vibration. This vibration of the basilar membrane causes the hair cells to bend as they rub against the tectorial membrane. As the hair cells bend, they generate electrical signals. Thus, a relay system of vibrations ultimately leads to the hair cells' creation of an electrical signal, which is later translated by the auditory system into perceptions of different pitches.

The Sensory Code for Pitch

If vibration of the basilar membrane causes the hair cells near the basilar membrane to bend and generate electrical signals, then one way to search for the sensory code for pitch would be to determine how the basilar membrane vibrates in response to different frequencies. This was the tactic adopted by Georg von Békésy (1960), who, in a series of studies that began in 1928, determined how the basilar membrane vibrates, as well as many other facts about the operation of the auditory system, and won the 1961 Nobel Prize in physiology and medicine for his efforts.

Békésy determined how the basilar membrane vibrates by drilling a hole in the cochlea of a human cadaver and using a microscope to observe how the membrane vibrated in response to different frequencies. These observations led

MEASUREMENT & METHODOLOGY

Measuring the Audibility Curve

The audibility curve defines the frequency range of human hearing by plotting the threshold for hearing (the smallest amount of sound energy it takes to just barely detect a sound) versus frequency. To determine the audibility curve, researchers use an instrument that electronically produces tones of different frequencies. The subject sits in a sound-attenuated room wearing earphones and gives a specific response (raising a hand or finger) when he hears a tone. The tone is first presented at an inaudible level and the intensity is slowly increased until the subject indicates that he just barely hears the tone. This "just-heard" intensity is the threshold for that frequency. This procedure is then repeated at a series of frequencies across the range of hearing (20 to 20,000 Hz) to obtain a relationship between the threshold for hearing and frequency like the one shown in Figure 4.13.

For clinical evaluation, an instrument called an *audiometer* is used to present tones over the range of frequencies between 250 and 8000 Hz. The results are plotted on a graph called an *audiogram*, which plots the degree of hearing loss across the range of audible frequencies. The figure here shows an audiogram for a normal subject having essentially no hearing loss (Curve A), for a subject who has a loss of hearing at high frequencies (B), and for one with a severe hearing loss at all frequencies (C).

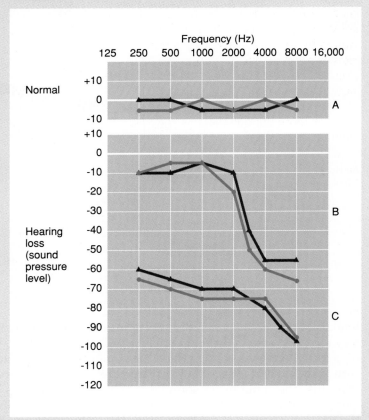

Audiograms for three subjects. The two lines in each curve represent hearing in the left and right ears.

him to conclude that the frequency of the stimulus determines the place along the basilar membrane that vibrates the most. High-frequency tones cause maximum vibration of the membrane at the beginning of the cochlea near the stapes, whereas low-frequency tones do so at the other end of the cochlea.

Békésy's theory is called the **place theory of pitch perception,** because it proposes that each frequency causes (1) maximal vibration of a particular place along the basilar membrane, and (2) maximal neural firing of the hair cells located at that place (Figure 4.15).

If the sensory code for pitch is *which* hair cells are firing the most vigorously, then the auditory system needs a way to keep track of which hair cells are firing. It does so by having hair cells that are near each other in the cochlea send their fibers to the brain together. This creates a map of frequencies on the brain, so that a specific frequency causes electrical activity at a specific place on the structure. Thus, the place information that originates in the receptors creates place information in the brain.

Békésy's place theory does not, however, provide the complete answer to the question "How do nerve impulses in the auditory system indicate the frequency of a tone?" The auditory system also uses the *pattern* of neural firing to transmit information about frequency. For example, a pattern in which neurons fire in closely separated bursts indicates a higher-frequency stimulus than a pattern in which they fire in widely separated bursts (Rose, Brugge, Anderson, & Hind, 1967). This method of indicating frequency is responsible for our perception of pitch at low frequencies (below 1000–2000 Hz), whereas Békésy's place mechanism is responsible for our perception of pitch at higher frequencies.

Our description of neural firing in the auditory system reinforces the idea that important information about the stimulus is coded by the way the receptors fire. We saw that this was the case for the visual system, in which each *wavelength* of light causes different patterns of firing of the three cone receptors. We now see that a similar situation exists for the auditory system, in which each *frequency* of sound causes different hair cells to fire. In both cases, our perceptions are determined by the information contained in the firing of neurons. Just as our perception of color is created by neurons of the visual system, our perception of sound is created by the neurons of the auditory system. (See Measurement & Methodology, "Distinguishing Between Physical Stimuli and Perceptual Experience.")

The discovery of the connection between neural firing and our experience is of far more than intellectual interest. This information has been used to create devices called *cochlear implants* that enable deaf people to hear.

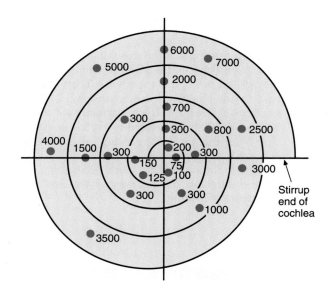

FIGURE 4.15
Schematic view of the cochlea, showing locations at which the hair cells' vibration and firing is strongest for different frequencies. The numbers, which represent frequencies, indicate that high frequencies cause greater vibration and firing at the stirrup end of the cochlea, and low frequencies cause greater vibration and firing at the cochlea's other end—deep inside its snail-like coil.

INTERDISCIPLINARY DIMENSION MEDICINE

Cochlear Implants

At the age of 45 Jack Troutman's previously normal hearing began to fade, until eventually he had trouble hearing courtroom testimony and had to resign his position as an associate circuit judge. A few years later, after he had become profoundly deaf, he withdrew from his family and friends, began communicating by writing notes, and became severely depressed.

Then Jack underwent an operation in which a cochlear implant was placed in his left ear. One month after the operation, he returned to the hospital to have the device activated. The audiologist, standing behind Jack so he couldn't lip-read, said, "Mr. Troutman, can you hear me?" "Yes," Jack replied, "I can!" Jack Troutman was able to hear again (Cochlear Corporaton, 1989).

Jack Troutman's story illustrates a situation faced by many people: normal hearing early in life, followed by progressive hearing loss and eventual deafness. During the initial stages, when some hearing is present, a hearing aid to amplify sounds is helpful. However, when hearing loss becomes profound, usually due to damage of the hair cell receptors in the inner ear, a hearing aid is of little use. The hair cells are not able to generate electrical signals, and no degree of amplification can help.

One solution is the **cochlear implant,** a device developed over the last 30 years that bypasses the damaged hair cells and stimulates auditory nerve fibers directly. The following are the basic components of a cochlear implant (shown in Figure 4.16):

- The *microphone*, which is worn behind the person's ear, receives the speech signal and transforms it into electrical signals, and sends these signals to the speech processor.
- The *speech processor*, which looks like a small transistor radio, shapes the signal generated by the microphone to emphasize information needed for the perception of speech by splitting the range of frequencies received by the microphone into a number of frequency bands. These signals are sent in the form of an electrical code from the processor to the transmitter.
- The *transmitter* is mounted on the mastoid bone, just behind the ear. It transmits the coded signals received from the processor, through the skin, to the receiver.

MEASUREMENT & METHODOLOGY

Distinguishing Between Physical Stimuli and Perceptual Experience

You have probably heard the question "If a tree falls in the forest and no one is there to hear it, is there any sound?" The answer hinges on what we mean by "sound." If we define sound as "the experience we have when we hear," the answer is "No." The tree may fall and create the *stimulus* for sound—pressure changes in the air—but if no one is around to receive those pressure changes and transform them into the experience of hearing, no sound occurs. If, however, we define sound as "pressure changes in the air," the falling tree creates sound whether or not someone is there to hear it.

Which definition is correct? The answer depends on whom you talk to. Physicists usually favor the second one (sound as a physical stimulus); psychologists are more likely to endorse the first (sound as an experience).

The example of the tree falling in the forest is based on the distinction between the physical stimulus (pressure vibrations in the air) and perceptual experience (hearing a sound). We have already made this distinction for vision, in which we saw that our *perceptual experience* of color is actually not contained in the wavelengths of light but is created by the visual system. The same principle holds true for hearing. Adopting the psychological definition of sound, we would say that there is no "sound" in pressure changes in the air, but that sound occurs only when these pressure changes stimulate our auditory system and cause the perceptual experience of hearing.

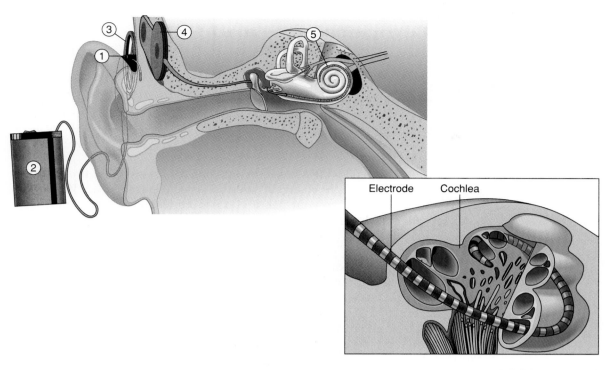

FIGURE 4.16
A cochlear implant device, consisting of (1) a microphone worn behind the ear, (2) a speech processor, (3) a transmitter attached to the bone behind the ear, (4) a receiver under the skin, and (5) an electrode coiled inside the cochlea. The electrode, shown in the inset, stimulates nerve fibers along the cochlea.

- The *receiver* is surgically mounted on the mastoid bone, beneath the skin. It picks up the coded signals from the transmitter and converts the code into signals that are sent to electrodes implanted inside the cochlea.

The implant makes use of Békésy's observation that low frequencies are represented by activity near the base of the cochlea and high frequencies by activity at its end. Low-frequency signals from the transmitter are therefore directed to the electrodes nearer the base and high-frequency signals to electrodes near the end. This electrical stimulation of the cochlea then causes signals to be sent to the auditory area of the cortex, and hearing results.

What does a person using this system hear? It depends on the person. Most patients are able to recognize a few everyday sounds, such as horns honking, doors closing, and water running. In addition, many patients are able to perceive speech. In the best cases, patients can perceive speech on the telephone, but it is more common for cochlear implant patients to use the sounds perceived from their implant in conjunction with lipreading. In one test 24 patients scored 54% on a test of lipreading alone, and 83% when lipreading was combined with sound from the implant. In addition, the implant enabled patients to track speech much more rapidly—an average of 44 words per minute compared with just 16 using lipreading alone (Brown, Dowell, & Clark, 1987; Owens, 1989).

By 1993 thousands of people had received cochlear implants. The best results occur for *postlingually deaf* individuals, people like Jack Troutman who were able to perceive speech before they became deaf. These people are most likely to be able to understand speech with the aid of the implant, because they already know how to connect the sounds of speech with specific meanings. Thus, these people's ability to perceive speech often improves with time, as they again learn to link sounds with meanings.

Cochlear implantation is an impressive demonstration of how basic research in a field can yield practical benefits. The technology of cochlear implants has transformed Békésy's discovery of the place principle of hearing into a procedure that has improved the lives of thousands of people. ■

The Skin Senses: Touch, Temperature, and Pain

Our skin is what stands between us and the world. . . . For most cultures, it's the ideal canvas to decorate with paints, tattoos, and jewelry. But, most of all, it harbors the sense of touch.

Diane Ackerman (1990, p. 68)

We often take the perceptions sensed by our skin for granted. But imagine how your ability to write might change if your hand were anesthetized. Would you know how firmly to grasp your pen if you had no feeling in your hand? Consider, too, all of the other things you do with your hands. How would losing feeling in your hand affect your ability to play a musical instrument, grasp a baseball bat, or give another person a backrub? We know that a complete loss of our ability to feel via the skin is dangerous—people who have this problem suffer constant bruises and burns in the absence of the warnings provided by touch and pain. And consider for a moment what sex would be like without the sense of touch. Perhaps a better way to put this is to ask whether, without the sense of touch, people would care about sex at all.

We often use the sense of touch as a metaphor for being in contact with external reality, as if touching were believing. Yet, as with all the senses, being "in touch" really means experiencing a perception that is the product of an interaction between physical stimuli and our physiological receptors.

The Stimuli on the Skin

The skin stands between us and the world and thus is exposed to everything with which we come in contact. The stimuli that touch the skin include light-pressure stimuli, which cause us to perceive gentle touch or tickling, and intense-pressure stimuli, which can damage the skin and cause us to perceive pain (Figure 4.17a). In addition, the skin is sensitive to temperature, eliciting perceptions ranging from the freezing sensation of touching an ice cube to the burning sensation produced by a flame.

The Structure of the Skin

When you look at your skin, you see its outer layer—the **epidermis**—the top layers of which are tough, dead skin cells. Skin protects us by keeping dirt and moisture from penetrating our bodies; at the same time it allows sweat to escape, to help our bodies maintain a stable internal temperature. But the main function we are concerned with here is the skin's ability to provide *information* about the various stimuli that contact it.

The sun's rays heat our skin, and we feel warm; a cold wind chills our skin, and we feel cold; a pinprick hurts us; and a backrub feels great. These perceptions originate in receptors located just under the surface of the skin. These receptors, which come in many different shapes and sizes (Figure 4.17b), send their axons (which we will call fibers in the discussion below) to the thalamus and then to the somatosensory area in the parietal lobe of the cortex. The search for the sensory code for skin sensations has focused on studying the firing of these fibers.

The Sensory Code for Skin Sensations

Researchers have identified nerve fibers in the skin that respond to specific types of stimulation. For example, *cold fibers* respond best to a temperature of 30°C and

Our skin is sensitive to several kinds of stimuli, including pressure, temperature, and chemical energy. These forms of energy are transduced by receptors in the skin into electrical signals that are sent into the spinal cord and to the brain (a).

A cross-sectional view of the skin (b) shows the skin's inner layer, the dermis, which contains many different nerve endings and receptors specialized to respond to different kinds of stimulation. Electrical recordings from nerve fibers in the central nervous system reveal fibers that respond to specific kinds of stimulation.

Touch signals travel to the somatosensory cortex in the parietal lobe of the brain (c). Because a disproportionate area of the somatosensory cortex is allotted to signals from the fingers, lips, and tongue, these parts of the body are particularly sensitive to touch stimuli.

(a)

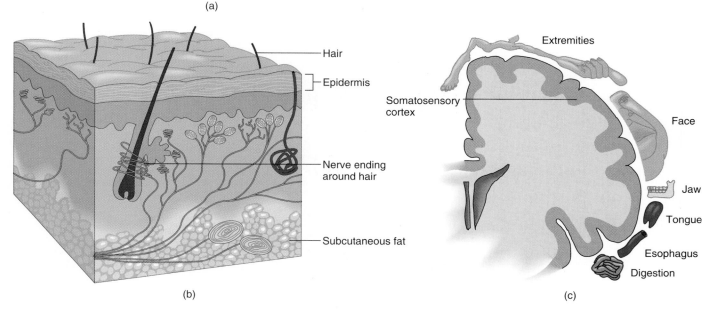

(b)

(c)

FIGURE 4.17
The system for sensing stimulation on the skin

respond with a burst of firing when the temperature is decreased, whereas *warm fibers* respond best to a temperature of 44°C and respond with a burst of firing when the temperature is increased (Duclaux & Kenshalo, 1980; Kenshalo, 1976).

Other fibers respond best to pressure on the skin, and are probably responsible for the sensation of touch. Still others respond to high heat, intense pressure, or chemicals that damage the skin; these are probably responsible for the perception of pain.

This description of the code for skin sensations, as contained in the activity of nerve fibers that fire in response to specific stimuli on the skin, is correct as far as it goes. But it cannot explain one important fact: the same stimulation on the skin does not always cause the same psychological effect. Pain provides the most dramatic example of this. Damage to the skin can cause intense pain, but the same damage in another situation may cause little pain. For example, H. K. Beecher (1972) observed that only 25% of men seriously wounded in battle requested a narcotic for pain relief, even though their injuries would normally be considered extremely painful. One reason for the soldiers' seeming indifference to pain is that their wounds were seen as positive, providing an escape from the hazardous battlefield to the safety of a behind-the-lines hospital.

This and many other examples support the idea that cognitive and contextual factors influence the perception of pain (see this chapter's Follow-Through on perception and culture). But how do our thoughts change the amount of pain we experience? Researchers have proposed that these cognitive factors

FIGURE 4.18
According to the gate control theory of pain, our cognitions can open and close a gate to regulate the flow of incoming pain signals. The closing of the gate is symbolized here as a physical blockage. In reality, however, the gate is closed by neural inhibition.

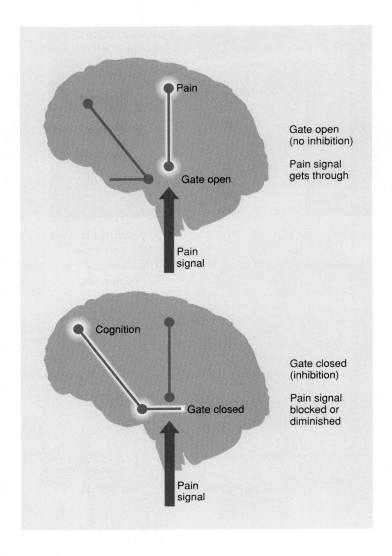

work by influencing neural firing. This idea, called the **gate control theory of pain,** is diagrammed in simplified form in Figure 4.18. The theory is that cognitions can control a "gate" that determines what proportion of the signals from fibers responding to painful stimulation gets transmitted to the brain. If the gate is opened, the maximum amount of activity from those fibers gets through, and pain increases; if the gate closes, less activation gets through, and pain decreases.

This idea, which was proposed by Ronald Melzak and Patrick Wall (1983), provides a link between activity at the biological and cognitive levels. As we will see more fully later on, a complete account of perception must include the interaction of factors working at several levels of analysis.

The Chemical Senses: Taste and Smell

Hit a tripwire of smell, and memories explode all at once.

Diane Ackerman (1990, p. 5)

7   MEMORY

Smell generates not only memories, but also a vast array of emotionally charged experiences. People seek out some smells—flowers, perfume, simmering soup—

and avoid others—spoiled foods, irritating chemicals. Taste is the most public of all the senses. When people get together at meals they often share their taste experiences, especially if they are visiting a new restaurant or trying new food. Smell and taste also play a part as aids to survival. We can often detect spoiled or poisonous foods from their taste or smell, and the smell of smoke or gas can alert us to potential danger. In the following discussion, however, we will focus not on the emotional, social, or survival aspects of taste and smell, but on the basic problem of sensory coding. How do the taste and smell systems signal the identity of the liquid molecules that stimulate the tongue or the molecules of gas that enter the nose?

The Stimuli for Taste and Smell

Taste and smell respond to *chemical* stimuli: liquid solutions for taste and molecules in the air for smell (Figure 4.19). In fact, taste and smell have been called "molecule detectors," because they respond to the chemical properties of different molecules by creating different perceptual experiences (Cain, 1988; Kauer, 1987).

The Structure of the Taste System

The receptors for taste are the **taste buds,** which are located in ridges and valleys called **papillae** on the tongue (Figure 4.19). There are four kinds of papillae.

1. Filiform papillae, shaped like cones, are found over the entire surface of the tongue, giving it its rough appearance.
2. Fungiform papillae, shaped like mushrooms, are found at the tip and sides of the tongue.
3. Foliate papillae are a series of folds along the sides of the back of the tongue.
4. Circumvallate papillae, shaped like flat mounds surrounded by a trench, are found at the back of the tongue.

All of these papillae except the filiform contain taste buds, with the human tongue containing a total of about 10,000 taste buds (Bartoshuk, 1971). As the

FIGURE 4.19
The taste system

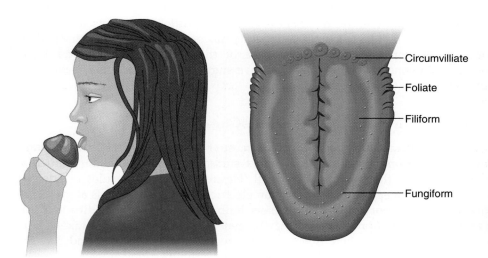

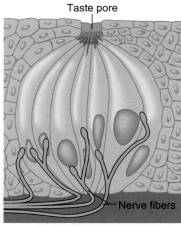

The stimuli for taste are chemical substances that dissolve in saliva. Receptors in the tongue (taste buds) respond to these substances by generating neural signals that are sent to the parietal lobe of the cortex through the thalamus.

The more than 10,000 taste buds on the human tongue are located in papillae on the tongue's surface. Different parts of the tongue are sensitive to different tastes. Taste stimuli contact the receptor cells of taste buds at the taste pore. This contact generates electrical signals that are transmitted along the fibers leaving the taste bud.

filiform papillae contain no taste buds, stimulation of the central part of the tongue, which contains only those papillae, causes no taste sensations. Other areas of the tongue are most sensitive to specific kinds of tastes. Salty and sweet tastes are sensed best at the tip and sides of the tongue, sour along the sides, and bitter along the back. Wine tasters take this distribution of taste sensitivities into account by rolling wine around in their mouth, allowing it to contact all areas of the tongue.

Signals generated in the taste receptors travel through various nuclei, then to the thalamus (where neurons from the other senses also synapse), and from there to the parietal lobe of the cortex.

The Sensory Code for Taste

How do the signals generated by taste receptors convey the presence of different chemical stimuli? One answer to this question is called **labeled line theory.** According to this theory, each of the four basic taste qualities—sour, salty, sweet, and bitter—is signaled by activity in specific nerve fibers (the "labeled lines"). Evidence supporting this theory is that, although each neuron in the taste system responds to a number of qualities, we can group neurons according to the quality to which each responds best.

For example, researchers have made recordings from the taste system of the hamster showing that a particular nerve fiber responds best to one quality, but also responds to others (Frank, 1973). Thus, "salty-best" fibers respond best to salt, less well to sour, and very slightly or not at all to sweet and bitter. Similar types of response profiles have been found for bitter and sweet.

This way of thinking about taste can explain the fact that most substances elicit a mixture of the four basic tastes. A salty substance might, for example, also have some sour and bitter taste. According to labeled line theory, the salty substance would cause vigorous firing in the "salty-best" fibers, which would result in a strong perception of saltiness. However, the salty substance would also cause smaller responses in the "sour-best" and "bitter-best" fibers, and the activity in those fibers would add slight sour and bitter tastes to the salty compound (Bartoshuk, 1978).

Although there is evidence for different types of taste neurons, this doesn't mean that the neural signal for taste qualities must depend on the firing of individual neurons. We know, for example, that color vision depends on three types of cone receptors that are maximally sensitive to different regions of the spectrum. However, color perception depends not on the responses of individual neurons but on the *pattern of response* of the short-, medium-, and long-wavelength cones. Some researchers have suggested that taste may work in a similar fashion (Erickson, 1963, 1982).

The Structure of the Olfactory System

Our perception of smell begins with the nose (Figure 4.20a). Smell stimuli enter the nose and find their way to a moist surface called the **olfactory mucosa,** which contains the receptors for smell (Figure 4.20b,c). Molecules of odorant contact those receptors and produce an electrical signal that travels along nerve fibers to the **olfactory bulb.** The olfactory bulb is analogous to the retina in that it is where the initial processing of signals generated in the receptors takes place; the olfactory bulb is where fibers from the receptors first synapse, and, like the retina, contains many additional synapses and complex connections.

From the olfactory bulb, fibers travel in two circuits to a cortical area in the frontal lobe just above the eyes. One circuit passes through the thalamus, where all the other senses also synapse; the other passes through the amygdala, the hippocampus, and the hypothalamus, structures deep inside the brain that play a role in regulating feeding, drinking, reproductive behavior, memory, and

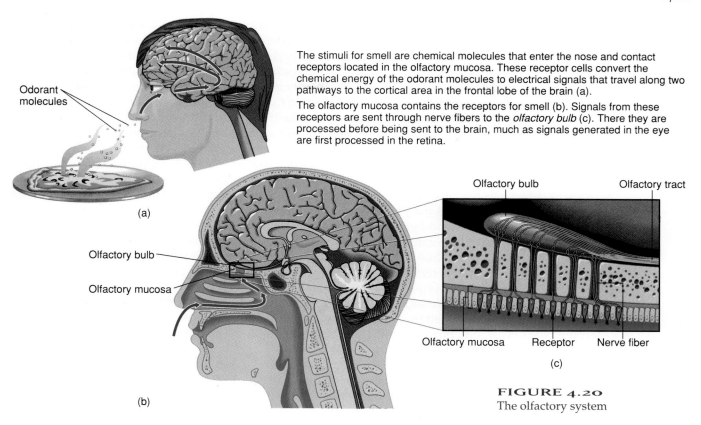

The stimuli for smell are chemical molecules that enter the nose and contact receptors located in the olfactory mucosa. These receptor cells convert the chemical energy of the odorant molecules to electrical signals that travel along two pathways to the cortical area in the frontal lobe of the brain (a).

The olfactory mucosa contains the receptors for smell (b). Signals from these receptors are sent through nerve fibers to the *olfactory bulb* (c). There they are processed before being sent to the brain, much as signals generated in the eye are first processed in the retina.

FIGURE 4.20
The olfactory system

emotion. It has been suggested that the pathway through the thalamus is primarily responsible for our perception of specific odors, whereas the pathway through the hypothalamus may help determine whether a particular odor smells "good" or "bad" (Cain, 1988; Takagi, 1980).

The Sensory Code for Smell

Researchers have only a rudimentary knowledge of the sensory code for smell, but they do know that different areas on the olfactory mucosa are more sensitive to specific chemicals. For example, the chemical amyl acetate causes large responses in receptors near the front and back of the mucosa, whereas the chemical camphor causes large responses in the middle of the mucosa (Kauer & Moulton, 1974; MacKay-Sim, Shaman, & Moulton, 1982). Although these results are promising, scientists have a long way to go before they understand the olfactory code that signals the thousands of different odors we can distinguish.

When we consider our perception of odors, we encounter a situation similar to the one for pain. Pain perception cannot be explained simply as the firing of fibers that respond to damaging stimuli, because cognitive factors may come into play. Cognitive factors also influence smell, as becomes apparent when we try to identify unknown aromas. When blindfolded subjects are presented with familiar substances like coffee, bananas, or motor oil, they can identify only half of them correctly (Desor & Beauchamp, 1974). However, telling subjects what the substance is the first time they smell it greatly increases their ability to identify it the next time it is presented.

This finding suggests to William Cain (1979, 1980) that we have difficulty identifying unknown odors not because we don't smell them "correctly," but because we can't retrieve the odor's name from our memory. The amazing thing about the role memory plays in odor identification is that knowing the correct label for the odor actually seems to transform our perception into that odor. Cain (1980) gives the example of an object initially identified by a subject as "fishy-

12   EMOTION

8   THINKING

7   MEMORY

goaty-oily." When the experimenter told the subject that the fishy-goaty-oily smell actually came from leather, the smell was transformed into that of leather.

I recently had a similar experience. A friend gave me a bottle of Aquavit, a Danish drink with a very interesting smell. As I was sampling this drink with some friends, we tried to identify its smell. Many odors were proposed ("anise," "orange," "lemon"), but it wasn't until someone turned the bottle around and read the label on the back that the truth became known. She read aloud, "Aquavit ('Water of Life') is the Danish national drink—a delicious, crystal-clear spirit distilled from grain, with a slight taste of caraway." As we heard the word *caraway*, our previous hypotheses of anise, orange, and lemon were instantly transformed. Caraway seemed the obvious scent as soon as we knew the answer.

Evidence of how cognition affects pain and smell indicates that we must go beyond the physiology of receptors, nerve fibers, and neural firing to truly understand perception. A complete picture of how we perceive must include factors operating at the behavioral, cognitive, and contextual levels of analysis.

Thus far, we have viewed the perceptual system as a *physiological* detective that determines properties of the environment based on clues provided by neural impulses. As we move to new levels of analysis, we will view it as a *cognitive* detective that determines properties of the environment based on clues provided by external stimuli. In other words, we now focus on the second question posed at the beginning of the chapter: How do we use information from the environment to create perceptions? There is no one simple answer, but we can begin to glimpse how our perceptual world is created by asking a number of more specific questions that researchers have investigated. Their work, which has emphasized the sense of vision, has demonstrated dramatically how tireless and clever a detective our perceptual system really is.

How Do We Differentiate Objects in the Environment?

The question in the heading may sound like one that would be easy to answer. After all, as we move through the environment we easily differentiate one object from another: here is a chair on the rug in front of the stereo system. Why should our ability to differentiate these things be seen as a mystery to be explained? We can appreciate the nature of the problem by remembering that in the initial stages of the process of perception there is no "chair," "rug," or "stereo"—there

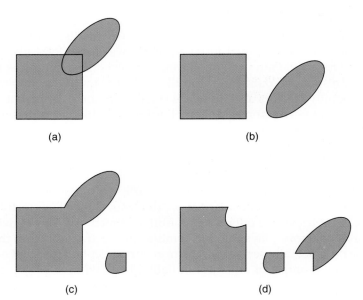

(a)   (b)

(c)   (d)

FIGURE 4.21
Although we naturally perceive the shape in (a) as being made up of a square and an ellipse, as shown in (b), this shape might actually be a square with a bulge at the corner plus a small, half-rounded shape as in (c) or the three shapes shown in (d). The fact that we usually perceive this as two regular shapes is consistent with the Gestalt law of simplicity.

is merely light energy of different wavelengths and patches of light and dark. From these basic elements of stimulation, the visual system must create our perception of separate objects.

One way that the perceptual system solves the problem of transforming environmental stimuli into objects was proposed at the behavioral level of analysis by Gestalt psychologists. You may remember from Chapter 1 that Gestalt psychology developed partly in reaction to the structuralists' idea that perceptions are created from elementary sensations. Gestalt psychologists took a broader view of perception, asking "What properties of stimuli cause us to group elements of a scene together?" They answered this question by proposing the **laws of organization,** which describe what perceptions will occur given certain stimulus arrangements (Helson, 1933; Hochberg, 1971). Let's look at some of these laws.

The law of simplicity.   How do you perceive Figure 4.21a? It could be a square and an elliptical object (b), or it could be perceived as shown in (c) and (d). Gestalt psychologists proposed that the answer lay in the **law of simplicity:** *Stimulus patterns are seen in such a way that the resulting structure is as simple as possible.* According to this law, you should perceive the figure as a square and an elliptical object because that is simpler than some of the other possible perceptions. Similarly, we perceive Figure 4.22 as a triangle overlapping a rectangle and not as a complicated 11-sided figure.

The law of similarity.   What do you see when you look at Figure 4.23a? Most people perceive this figure as horizontal rows of circles, vertical columns of circles, or both. But what happens to your perception when some of the circles are changed to squares, as in Figure 4.23b? Most people now perceive vertical columns of squares and circles. The change in our perception illustrates the **law of similarity:** *We perceive similar things as being grouped together.* Thus, we group the circles with other circles and the squares with other squares. Grouping can also occur on the basis of similarity of size, hue, orientation, or lightness (Figure 4.24).

The law of similarity also applies to auditory stimuli. This was common knowledge to composers in the Baroque period (1600–1750), whose compositions often included sequences of rapidly alternating high and low tones, as in the composition by J. S. Bach shown in Figure 4.25. When this passage is played rapidly by a single instrument, the low notes sound as if they are a melody played by one instrument, while the high notes sound like a different melody played by another instrument. This grouping, which occurs because of similarity of pitch, is called *compound melodic line* by musicians and *auditory stream segregation* by psychologists (Bregman & Campbell, 1971).

The law of nearness.   Do you perceive Figure 4.26a as horizontal rows of circles, or as vertical rows of circles? If you see horizontal rows, you are being influenced by the **law of nearness:** *We tend to group together things that are near to each other.* Even when every other circle is changed to a square, as in Figure 4.26b, we still perceive horizontal rows; in this case, the law of nearness overpowers the law of similarity.

This law also works for auditory stimuli. Consider, for example, what you would hear if two notes close to each other in pitch, such as A and B, were played alternately, with a long pause between them. Even though the notes are close together in pitch, you would hear two separate notes, slowly alternating. Now consider what would happen if the notes were alternated rapidly, so that they were near in time. You would hear a "trill": the notes would be heard not as

FIGURE 4.22
Is this a rectangle and a triangle or an 11-sided figure? According to the Gestalt law of simplicity, perception as a rectangle and triangle wins out over the more complicated alternative.

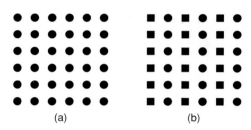

(a)   (b)

FIGURE 4.23
We can perceive the pattern in (a) either as rows or as columns, but (b) is usually seen as alternating columns of squares and circles, illustrating the law of similarity.

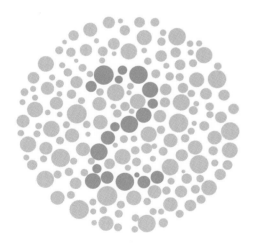

FIGURE 4.24
Darkening some of the dots causes perceptual grouping as described by the law of similarity, which creates the perception of a "2."

FIGURE 4.25
Two measures from a composition by J. S. Bach illustrating perceptual grouping according to similarity of pitch.

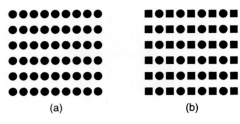

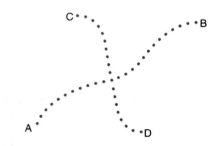

FIGURE 4.26
In (a), we see horizontal rows of circles because objects that are near to each other tend to be perceived as grouped together. If we continue to perceive horizontal rows in (b), the law of nearness is still determining our perception; if we see vertical columns, then the law of similarity is determining our perception.

FIGURE 4.27
According to the law of good continuation, you see this as two smoothly curved lines, one flowing from A to B, the other flowing from C to D. You are less likely to see this as two "curved angles," A–D and C–B, because the sharp angles violate the law of good continuation.

separate units, but as grouped together. (You can try this for yourself if you have access to a piano.)

The law of good continuation.   Where does the series of points starting at A in Figure 4.27 go? If you see them as flowing smoothly to B rather than going to C or D, your perception is following the **law of good continuation:** *Points that, when connected, result in straight or smoothly curving lines are perceived as belonging together, and lines are seen in such a way as to create the smoothest possible path.* Pissarro's painting *The Great Bridge at Rouen* (Figure 4.28) contains a number of examples of good continuation. Can you find them?

In the painting, the smoke cuts the bridge in two and cuts the smokestack into three pieces. Confronted with disconnected bits of color, we assume, because of the law of good continuation, that the various parts belong together; the bridge and smokestack do not, therefore, fall apart.

Good continuation also works for tones. When bursts of tone are interrupted by gaps of silence, listeners perceive both the tones and the silence between the tones. If, however, the silent gaps are filled in with a hissing sound, called *noise* by researchers, listeners perceive the tone as continuing under the noise. Just as Pissarro's smokestack is perceived as continuous even though it is twice interrupted by smoke, an interrupted tone can also be perceived as continuous if the interruptions are filled in with bursts of noise.

The law of common fate.   Why do you perceive the dancers in Figure 4.29 as a group rather than as separate dancers? Maybe because of their nearness and similar orientation, but perhaps more important is their "common fate," the fact that they are moving in the same direction. The **law of common fate** states that *We tend to group together things that are moving in the same direction.*

The law of meaningfulness or familiarity.   Look at the picture in Figure 4.30. At first glance the scene appears to contain mainly trees, rocks, and water. But can you see some faces in the trees in the background, and in the various groups of rocks? There are, in fact, a total of 13 faces in this picture. Once you perceive them it is extremely difficult *not* to perceive them as faces, even though a moment before you did not organize your perceptions in that way. The images

FIGURE 4.28
The law of good continuation is illustrated in this painting, Camille Pissaro's *The Great Bridge at Rouen*. Notice how the bridge, smokestacks, and buildings appear to continue behind the smoke.

FIGURE 4.29
These dancers are grouped perceptually because they are moving in the same direction, illustrating the law of common fate.

become permanently organized into faces because of the **law of familiarity**: *We are more likely to form things into groups if the groups appear familiar or meaningful.*

The Gestalt laws are simple but important illustrations of how links between basic elements of the environment and perception reflect, to some extent, the way the world is constructed. For example, many objects have the same colors or patterns throughout, and perceiving all of those similar elements as belonging together (the law of similarity) helps us to correctly perceive the object as a unit. Or consider the branch behind the tree in Figure 4.31. Although it is possible that this perception could be created by two branches, it is much more likely that only one is involved. Thus, the law of good continuation, by causing us to perceive one branch, usually makes an accurate prediction about the way the world is constructed.

Occasionally, however, the Gestalt principles can deceive us. For example, if the colors or patterning of an object match those in the environment, we may fail to differentiate an object from its context—an example of *camouflage.* In this case, the Gestalt laws work against us, leading us to group parts of the object with the environment. The fact that many insects and animals use principles of camouflage that hide them from both humans and potential predators suggests that humans and other animals may make use of similar principles of perceptual organization.

A camouflaged moth, its colors and wing pattern minimizing perceptual cues that would distinguish it from its background

FIGURE 4.30
The Forest Has Eyes by Bev Doolittle (1985). Can you find the 13 faces in this picture?

FIGURE 4.31
By the Gestalt law of good continuation, we assume that the scene on the left is a tree with a single branch behind it. It is also possible that two different branches could create this perception. In general, the law of good continuation results in perceptions that accurately reflect the most likely physical reality.

As valuable as the Gestalt laws are, they give an incomplete picture of object perception. For one thing, they employ simple examples such as circles and squares, but only rarely deal with how we perceive the complexity of our actual environment. In addition, the laws ignore an important aspect of our environment that helps us differentiate objects from one another: the fact that objects exist at different distances from us. We now turn to this aspect of the environment, and as we do, we will see that depth perception raises puzzles of its own.

How Do We Perceive Depth?

Just as we perceive most objects effortlessly, we have little trouble perceiving their relative distance from us. We look at a scene and know what is in the foreground and what is in the background. But exactly how do we accomplish this perceptual feat? Recall from our discussion of the sense of vision that visual stimuli produce two-dimensional images on the retina. The major question posed by our ability to see depth is "How do we transform two-dimensional information into the three-dimensional environment that we perceive?" Or, to put it another way, "Why doesn't everything we see look flat and seem to be at the same distance from us?"

One approach to answering this question is to look for connections between the stimulus patterns imaged on the retina and depth within the scene. By doing this, psychologists have identified a number of **depth cues,** properties of visual stimuli that provide information we interpret to create the perception of depth. Depth cues can be classified into four groups: oculomotor, pictorial, movement produced, and binocular. Our use of these cues is one of the clearest illustrations of how our perceptual system actively participates in constructing the world we experience.

Oculomotor Cues: Sensing Changes in the Eye

Look at your finger at arm's length, and then slowly move it toward your nose. As it gets closer, can you feel your eyes turning inward and an increasing tension in them? These feelings are caused by *convergence*, as your eye muscles cause your eyes to turn inward, and by *accommodation*, as the lens of your eye bulges to focus on a nearby object. Although you are not usually aware of it, in normal perception the brain uses convergence and accommodation as **oculomotor cues** to depth (*oculo-motor* means, roughly, "eyeball movement"). These cues suggest depth because the shape of the lens and the position of the eyes are correlated with the distance of the object we are observing. The cues are, however, effective only for objects that are relatively near (within 10 feet) (Liebowitz, Shina, & Hennessy, 1972).

Pictorial Cues: Deducing Depth from a Flat Image

Another way the brain translates two-dimensional information into three-dimensional perception is through **pictorial cues**—cues that can be represented in a flat picture like the one formed on the retina. Figures 4.32 and 4.33 display a variety of pictorial cues. Let's look at how we use each one to perceive depth.

Which fish in Figure 4.32a do you perceive as close to you? This figure illustrates the cue of *overlap*: if object A covers part of object B, we perceive object A as being in front of object B. Note that this cue does not provide information about an object's distance from us; instead, it indicates *relative depth*, simply one object being closer than another.

In Figure 4.32b, compare the radio telescope antennae in the foreground with those in the background. Why do the background antennae appear to be more distant? Here the cue is *size in the field of view*: an object that takes up less of the field of view appears to be farther away.

Relative distance can also be indicated by *height in the field of view* (Figure 4.32c). The effect of this cue depends on the object's position with respect to the horizon. Below the horizon line, objects *higher* in the field of view (such as the mountains) are seen as being more distant than those lower in the field of view (such as the flowers). Above the horizon line, objects *lower* in the field of view (the clouds at the sides of the mountains) are seen as being more distant than objects higher in the field of view (the clouds above the mountains).

Next, look at Figure 4.33a. Why do we see objects that are blurred as being distant? When we look at distant objects, we are looking through the air and the particles suspended in it that lie between us and the objects. The farther away the objects are, the more air and particles we have to look through, which makes far objects look less sharp than close ones. This difference in the clearness of near and far objects gives us the depth cue of *atmospheric perspective*.

In addition to making far objects look fuzzy, the atmosphere also makes them look blue. This blueness of distant objects was emphasized by 15th- and 16th-century artists, who often painted mountains in the background even bluer than they appeared in the actual scene (Figure 4.33b). Thus, atmospheric perspective is a clear example of how prior knowledge—in this case, our experience with atmospheric effects—influences our perception of depth.

Figure 4.33c shows that our perception of depth is also influenced slightly by *familiar size*, our knowledge of the sizes of objects. Knowing that elephants are large, we interpret the small image of the elephant at right to mean that it is far away.

All the cues we've considered help solve the perceptual system's problem of how to represent three dimensions on the flat surface of the retina. Those cues are clearly also applicable to the artist's task of creating an impression of depth on the two-dimensional surface of a canvas. This challenge has concerned artists as far back as ancient Greece, but it wasn't until the 1400s that Renaissance painters discovered a drawing system that enabled them to convincingly depict depth (Hagen, 1979, 1986; Kubovy, 1986; White, 1968). Their system made use of the depth cue of *linear perspective*: Lines that are parallel in a scene (such as the sides of the ceiling windows in Figure 4.33d) seem to converge as they get farther away. The greater the distance, the greater the convergence, which provides information about depth. If you have ever looked at railroad tracks stretching away from you into the distance, you have experienced this depth cue.

FIGURE 4.32

(a) *Overlap:* Fish that overlap other fish appear closer. (b) *Size in the field of view:* Objects that take up less of our field of view tend to appear farther away. This is especially evident when comparing the two radio telescopes at far left. (c) *Height in the field of view:* Objects higher in the visual field appear farther away if they are below the horizon and closer if they are above the horizon.

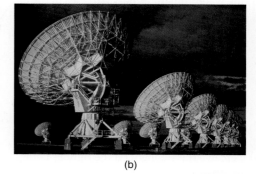

(a)

(b)

(c)

FIGURE 4.33

(a, b) *Atmospheric perspective:* In (a), fog on the water illustrates how particles in the air, or even the air itself, causes objects to appear increasingly indistinct in the distance. Distant objects often also appear slightly blue, though this effect is seldom so pronounced as in (b), the painting *The Rest on the Flight to Egypt* by Gerard David; also note the artist's use of other perceptual cues—of relative size (the man against the houses) and overlap (the donkey behind the tree). (c) *Familiar size:* We should perceive the elephant on the right as being far away even without a closer elephant for comparison; we know that elephants are huge, so an elephant this small must be far away. (d) *Linear perspective:* Parallel lines appear to converge as they stretch into the distance. (e) *Texture gradient:* The pattern of cracks in the mud appears smaller and more closely packed together with increasing distance.

A final pictorial cue makes use of information in textured surfaces. Textured surfaces that extend from the foreground into the background create a *texture gradient,* a pattern in which elements on the surface appear to become packed closer and closer together as the surface stretches into the distance (Figure 4.33e). This gradient pattern creates an impression of depth (Gibson, 1950, 1979).

The Movement-Produced Cue: How Movement Creates Depth

In some cases our perception of depth is enhanced when we move or when objects in the environment move. Imagine that you are walking along a country road, looking off to the side at a nearby pasture and at a farmhouse in the distance. As you walk, small bushes near the side of the road pass rapidly across your field of vision, but the farmhouse in the distance appears hardly to move at all. This effect is particularly apparent when you look out the side window of a moving car. Nearby objects appear to speed by in a blur, whereas those on the horizon move very slowly (Figure 4.34). This effect creates the **movement-produced cue** of *movement parallax:* objects that move across an observer's field of view more rapidly in response to the observer's movement are closer than objects that move more slowly.

The Binocular Cue: Comparing the Images on the Two Retinas

Many people learn as children that one reason we have two eyes is to enable us to see depth. Each eye sees the world from a slightly different point of view, a

FIGURE 4.34
Movement parallax. Moving objects that are closer (such as the blurred racers) pass across our field of view more rapidly than those that are farther away. This also occurs if the observer is moving and the near and far objects in the environment are stationary.

fact that produces the **binocular cue** of *binocular disparity*, a difference in the locations of images on each retina.

You can demonstrate this double view to yourself by closing your left eye and holding one finger upright about 6 inches in front of you. Then position a finger from your other hand about 6 inches farther back, so that it is completely hidden by your front finger. You should now be able to see only your front finger. If you now close your right eye and open your left eye, you can see your rear finger. You have "looked around" your front finger by changing your point of view.

How does the brain translate this difference in images into a perception of depth? The full answer to this question is complicated, but we can approximate it with another demonstration. Close your right eye and position your fingers as you did before, but only a few inches apart. Then blink back and forth between the left and right eyes and notice how the front finger seems to jump to the left every time you open your right eye. Now do this again, holding your fingers farther apart. Notice that the front finger jumps much farther to the left than it did when your fingers were closer together. What this demonstration tells us is that increasing the separation between two objects increases the difference, or *disparity*, between their images on the two retinas. The amount of disparity thus indicates the distance between the objects: the greater the disparity, the greater the distance.

When you look into a stereo viewer, the depth you perceive is created by the fact that you are looking at *stereoscopic photographs*. These two pictures—one presented to the left eye and the other to the right—are slightly different because they have been created by a stereoscopic camera, which has two lenses separated by the same distance as our eyes. The difference between the images mimics the disparity that would be created if you viewed the actual scene. In this way, two flat images create an impressive illusion of depth—a clear demonstration of the brain's active participation in the perceptual process. You can experience this process yourself without the aid of a special viewing device, by looking at Figure 4.35 and following the directions in the legend above it.

In summary, we use a number of cues to create the perception of depth, no one of which is crucial. Even people who lose sight in one eye, and therefore lose binocular disparity, can perceive depth (though not as well as they could with two healthy eyes). However, if enough depth cues are eliminated, as might occur

FIGURE 4.35
To create binocular depth without a stereoscope, place a 4 × 6 card vertically, long side up, between these two pictures and place your nose against the card so you are seeing the left-hand drawing with just your left eye and the right-hand drawing with just your right eye. (Blink back and forth to confirm this.) Then *relax* and wait for the two drawings to merge. When the drawings form a single image, you should see the stairs in depth, just as you would if you looked at them through a stereoscope.

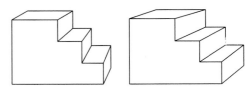

on a foggy morning, our ability to perceive depth suffers. In the next section, we will see that changes in our ability to perceive depth can have a great effect on our ability to perceive size and shape.

How Do We Perceive the Sizes and Shapes of Objects?

The puzzle of depth perception is how we arrive at a three-dimensional perception given the two-dimensional image on our retina. It turns out that we *infer* depth by taking into account the information provided by many different cues, much as a detective pieces together a crime from a number of clues. What about the important characteristics of size and shape? Do we perceive them directly, or do we infer them?

Size Constancy

Most of us are quite skilled at judging size. We can, for instance, estimate someone else's height within a few inches, and we have little trouble estimating the sizes of objects even some distance from us. But how do we do this? A straightforward answer might be that large objects produce large images on the retina, and small objects produce small images. But a simple demonstration shows that this cannot be the answer.

Hold your hand in front of your face, about 6 inches away. Then move it to a distance of 12 inches from your face. What happens to your perception of your hand's size? Does it appear to shrink to half its size? That would be the result if size perception were determined solely by the size of your hand's image on your retina, because doubling your hand's distance reduced the size of its image on your retina by half. But this is probably not what you perceived. Moving an object away usually has little effect on its perceived size. And just as your hand doesn't appear to shrink by half when you move it away, this book doesn't appear to shrink to the size of a postage stamp when you view it from across the room. Your perception of the sizes of objects remains fairly constant when you view them at different distances. This stable perception of an object's actual size, no matter what its distance or what the size of its retinal image, is called **size constancy.**

Size constancy depends on our ability to perceive depth. This connection becomes obvious when we note what happens to our perception of an object's size when we decrease our ability to perceive its distance from us. Close one eye (to eliminate binocular disparity) and observe what happens as you again move your hand away from your face. This time your hand may appear to get slightly smaller as you increased its distance. By reducing your ability to perceive depth, you have also decreased size constancy. Research has shown that when *all* depth information is eliminated, size constancy no longer holds: when we move an object from nearby to far away, its size appears to decrease as the size of its image on our retina decreases (Holway & Boring, 1941). Thus, under conditions of no depth perception, doubling an object's distance will cause it to be perceived as half as large.

The close connection between our perception of size and our perception of depth has led researchers to propose a **size-distance scaling** mechanism (Gregory, 1973). According to this idea, we arrive at *perceived size* by taking into account both an object's *retinal size* and its *perceived distance*. Consider, for example, the demonstration with your hand. When it is close, its retinal size is large and its perceived distance small. As you move it away, its retinal size decreases while its perceived distance increases. According to the idea of size-distance scaling, the decrease in retinal size is compensated for by the increase in perceived dis-

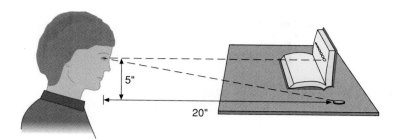

FIGURE 4.36
Viewing procedure for shape constancy demonstration

tance, so your perception of your hand's size remains constant no matter what its distance. If, however, you perceive distance inaccurately because you have closed one eye, the calculation of the size-distance scaling mechanism is upset and your hand appears to become smaller at greater distances.

This taking into account of both retinal size *and* distance illustrates an important perceptual principle: *perception depends on multiple sources of information.* The fact that our perception of depth depends on many depth cues also illustrates that principle.

Shape Constancy

Our perception of the shape of objects also depends on the ability to combine multiple sources of information. Try a simple demonstration: Place a coin on your desk, then view it from a height of 5 inches and a distance of 20 inches, as shown in Figure 4.36. While viewing the coin, decide which shape in Figure 4.37 (viewed straight on, as shown in Figure 4.36) most clearly matches your perception of the coin. Stop now to do this before reading further.

To understand the rationale behind this demonstration, consider that when you view a circular object like a coin straight on, it casts a circular image on your retina. However, when you view the object at an angle, as you just did, it casts an elliptical image on your retina. The purpose of our demonstration was to see whether your *perception* of the coin's shape is as elliptical as the shape of its image on your retina. If you picked stimulus number 1 from Figure 4.37, your perception matches the elliptical shape of the coin's image on your retina. If you picked number 6, your perception matches the actual physical shape of the coin. Most people pick numbers 3, 4, or 5, because they perceive the coin to be elliptical, but less elliptical than the image of the coin on the retina.

This tendency to see the coin as close to its true circular shape is an example of **shape constancy**—the tendency for our perception of an object's shape to remain constant even when we view it from different angles. Research has shown that shape constancy occurs under conditions that allow us to perceive an object's slant. Just as we take depth into account when perceiving size, we take slant into account in perceiving shape (Thouless, 1931).

The "corrections" we make in our perceptions of size and shape are so automatic that it is easy to take them for granted. But try to imagine what the world would be like if your perceptions were determined exclusively by the images produced on your retinas. As you walked through a room, things would change in size as you approached or moved farther away from them. At the same time, shapes would be changing with your every movement—circular objects becoming elliptical, square and rectangular objects becoming trapezoidal. You live in a stable perceptual environment only because of perceptual processes that silently and continually "correct" the sensory input received through your eyes.

FIGURE 4.37
Which shape matches your perception of the coin?

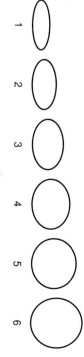

Why Do We Sometimes Misperceive?

"There is nothing more deceptive than an obvious fact."

Sherlock Holmes, in *The Boscombe Valley Mysteries*

So far we have been considering perception as a process by which environmental information is transformed into representations in the nervous system to create *veridical* perceptions, perceptions that correspond to the physical reality of the environment. Thus, normally we correctly perceive a 6-foot-tall man to be 6 feet tall, whether he is standing next to us or across the room. However, like a detective misled by false clues, our perceptual systems can be fooled. What makes perceptual errors so interesting is the light they shed on how our perceptual system works.

One kind of error depends on misperceiving one of the sources of information that the perceptual system takes into account in constructing its perceptions. For example, because size perception depends on depth perception, a misperception of depth can lead to a misperception of size. An illustration of this effect is provided by the kinds of perceptual problems encountered by workers at an Antarctic research base during a condition known as whiteout.

> The most treacherous weather phenomenon is something known as a whiteout, in which light is reflected from a thick cloud cover and back up from the snow, obscuring the horizon and surface definition, and surrounding one with a dazzling whiteness. Someone flying a helicopter during a whiteout can't tell up from down. Pilots have been known to drop smoke grenades to determine their altitude only to find that they were a few feet above the ground. Others have flown at full power directly into the ice. What one can see is distorted—a discarded matchbox may look like a tent or a vehicle (*The New Yorker*, 1981).

How could a tiny matchbox be mistaken for a tent or a vehicle? In the poor visibility of a whiteout, the features of objects become unclear and the lack of depth cues can make the nearby matchbox appear to be far away. When this hap-

FIGURE 4.38
Ames room. Although the boy is actually shorter than the woman, he appears taller because the distorted Ames room fools us into thinking they are about the same distance from us. Actually, the woman is twice as far away as the boy.

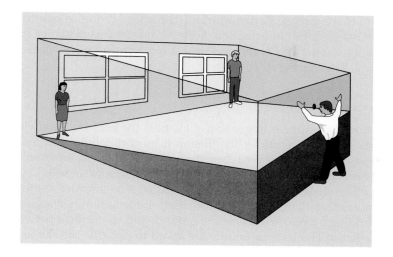

FIGURE 4.39
The Ames room, showing its true shape. The woman is actually almost twice as far away, but when the room is viewed through the peephole this difference in distance is not seen. The left side of the room is enlarged, so it appears normal when viewed through the peephole.

pens, the erroneous perception of distance creates the illusion that the small matchbox is much larger than it really is. This illusion results from our perceptual system's attempt to judge size in the absence of accurate information about distance. Similar mechanisms are at work in three other well-known illusions of size: the Ames room, the Ponzo illusion, and the moon illusion.

The Ames Room

Figure 4.38 shows the famous **Ames room,** constructed by Adelbert Ames to explore the connection between our perception of size and our perception of depth. The woman in the picture is actually taller than the boy, yet the boy appears much taller. The reason for this illusion lies in the distorted shape of the room and the misleading depth cues that are built into the design of the room. The shapes of the wall and windows at the rear of the room are constructed so that the room will look like a normal rectangular room when it is viewed from a particular observation point. When, however, we are allowed to view the room from other vantage points, we can see that it is extremely distorted, with the left corner of the room almost twice as far away from the observation point as the right corner (Figure 4.39). The reason we misperceive the people's sizes is that we see the two as being at the same distance from us when, in fact, the woman is much farther away. Because of the misleading distance cues, our size-distance scaling mechanism doesn't take the woman's greater distance into account, and we misperceive her size.

The Ponzo Illusion

Look at the two rectangles in Figure 4.40. Does the top one seem slightly larger than the bottom one? If so, you are experiencing the **Ponzo illusion** (also called the railroad track illusion): the rectangles are actually the same size (measure them). What accounts for this illusion? Richard Gregory (1966) explains the Ponzo illusion in terms of size-distance scaling by pointing out that the top rectangle appears larger because it seems to be located farther down the railroad tracks. The size-distance scaling mechanism takes the apparently greater distance of the top rectangle into account, and you see it as slightly larger. Of course, in reality both rectangles are actually on the flat surface of the page, at the same distance from the viewer.

Other evidence supporting the idea that this illusion depends on the depth information in the picture comes from cross-cultural studies. These studies show that people who have more experience perceiving depth in the environment

FIGURE 4.40
The Ponzo (or railroad track) illusion. The black bars are actually the same length.

FIGURE 4.41
The moon illusion. The moon seen on the horizon is perceived as larger than the moon at the zenith (high in the sky).

experience a more intense Ponzo illusion than those living in environments in which there is less depth information. We will discuss this evidence in more detail in the Follow-Through at the end of this chapter. (Also see Measurement & Methodology, "Measuring an Illusion.")

The Moon Illusion

Why does the moon appear larger when it is near the horizon than when it is directly overhead, at its zenith? This illusion is so compelling that many people think the moon is actually *closer* when it is near the horizon, when in fact it is at the same distance on a given night no matter where it is in the sky. One explanation of the **moon illusion** (Figure 4.41) is based on size-distance scaling. This explanation notes that there is much more depth information between us and the horizon (buildings, trees, texture on the ground, and so on) than between us and the sky overhead. Thus, when people are asked to imagine the sky as a surface, they usually judge that the surface appears farther away at the horizon than at the zenith (Kaufman & Rock, 1962a, b). Since the size of the moon's retinal image is the same whether on the horizon or at its zenith, our size-distance scaling mechanism compensates for the *apparent* greater distance of the horizon moon by making the moon seem larger. In support of this idea, Lloyd Kaufman and Irving Rock (1962a, b) have shown that when people view the horizon moon over a far-away horizon they see a bigger moon illusion than when they see the moon over a nearby horizon, just as the size-distance scaling mechanism would predict (Goldstein, 1989).

Visual illusions illustrate general points about perception. First, the fact that the Ames, Ponzo, moon, and other illusions depend on both retinal size and perceived distance reinforces the idea that our perceptions are constructed from multiple sources of information. Second, the fact that these illusions represent a misperception of the physical situation shows that what we perceive does not always reflect objective reality. Third, illusions demonstrate how our perceptions are influenced by context. The depth information provided by railroad tracks, the strange construction of the Ames room, and the terrain reaching out toward the horizon moon all provide contexts that influence our perception of size. When the context creates an accurate perception of depth, we tend to perceive size accurately. But when the context creates an inaccurate perception of depth, we experience illusions that create misperceptions by size. Finally, illusions illustrate that even our everyday perceptions are the product of complex interactions between physical stimuli and physiological, cognitive, and contextual factors.

How Do Expectations Influence Perception?

At several points in our discussion of perception we have noted the role that cognitive factors play in helping create our perceptual experience. Our discussion of size-distance scaling, for example, involves the cognitive level of analysis, because size-distance scaling is a hypothesized mental process. In this section we will expand our application of the cognitive level by looking at some examples of how people's expectations based on prior knowledge can influence what they perceive.

Our knowledge can affect our perceptions in a number of ways. Perception can be affected by knowledge that a person has just acquired, as when an event happens that changes a perception that occurs moments later. Perception can also be affected by knowledge acquired through the experiences of a lifetime spent in a particular environment or culture.

An example is provided by the British art historian E. H. Gombrich (1956) in the following description of his World War II experience, when his job was to monitor enemy radio transmissions.

Some of the transmissions which interested us most were often barely audible, and it became quite an art, or even a sport, to interpret the few whiffs of speech sound that were all we really had on the wax cylinders on which these broadcasts had been recorded. It was then we learned to what an extent our knowledge and expectation influence our hearing. *You had to know what might be said in order to hear what was said* (italics added, p. 204).

Gombrich's last sentence highlights a key point: our expectations can influence what we perceive. Psychologists call this phenomenon **perceptual set.**

I demonstrate perceptual set to my classes by playing the Rolling Stones' rendition of the song "Tumbling Dice." So far, of the thousands of my students who have listened to the recording, none has been able to decipher more than a few words of Mick Jagger's singing. However, when I replay the tape while simultaneously projecting the lyrics on a screen, students instantly recognize the words they are hearing. *Expecting* what the words will be transforms the muddled sound into meaningful lyrics.

To demonstrate perceptual set to yourself, look at the drawing in Figure 4.42. Afterward, close your eyes, turn the page, and open and shut your eyes rapidly to briefly expose the picture in Figure 4.45. Decide what the picture is and then open your eyes to read the explanation below it. Do this before reading further.

Did you identify Figure 4.45 as a rat (or mouse)? If you did, you were influenced by the rat- or mouselike figure you observed initially. But people who first see Figure 4.43 (on page 166) usually identify Figure 4.45 as a man (try this

FIGURE 4.42
Look at this drawing, then close your eyes, turn the page, and look at the same place on the page directly beneath this one. Then open and shut your eyes rapidly.

MEASUREMENT & METHODOLOGY

Measuring an Illusion

When we look at the Ponzo illusion, we perceive two physically identical stimuli as being different. A similar effect is shown in the figure to the right, which is called the *Müller-Lyer illusion*. Both horizontal lines are the same length, but because of the "fins," the line on the bottom appears longer. You can measure the magnitude of this effect by means of a matching procedure that you can use on yourself or on others.

The first step in carrying out the matching procedure is to create some stimuli. To do this, create a "standard stimulus" by drawing a line 30 millimeters long on an index card and adding outward-going fins, as in the bottom Müller-Lyer figure. Then, on separate cards, create "comparison stimuli" by drawing lines 28, 30, 32, 34, 36, 38, and 40 millimeters long with inward-going fins, as in the top figure. Then ask your subject to pick the comparison stimulus that most closely matches the length of the standard stimulus. The difference in length between the standard stimulus and the comparison stimulus chosen by the subject (typically between 10% and 30%) defines the size of the illusion. Try this procedure on a number of people to see how variable this illusion is.

Also try answering this question: "Is the size of the illusion affected by the subject's knowledge of the illusion?" Show the subject that the lines in the figure are actually the same size; then use the matching procedure to measure the size of the illusion.

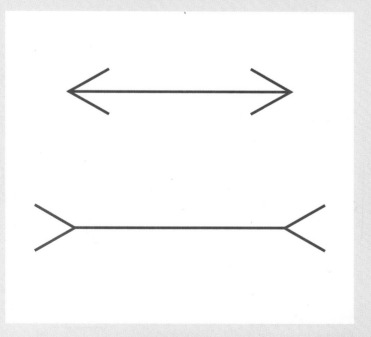

FIGURE 4.43
Manlike version of the rat/man stimulus.

demonstration on some other people). This demonstration, called the *rat/man demonstration,* sets up an expectation, or *set,* for you to see Figure 4.45 as a rat. If you had first seen the man's head, you would have been perceptually "set" to see the figure as a man's head (Bugelski & Alampay, 1961).

Perceptual set shows that object perception depends in part on the observer's mental predisposition to see things in a certain way, and that this predisposition can be changed by experiences that happen just prior to perception. But our perceptions can also be affected by experiences that extend over longer periods of time. For example, we become skilled at identifying objects in our environment because we have learned, through long experience, where objects belong in environment. Irving Biederman (1981) showed how we make use of this information via the following experiment: He flashed a picture like that in Figure 4.44 on a screen and asked subjects to identify an object located at a particular place in the scene. (They were told where to look immediately before seeing the picture.) For this picture, they were asked to identify the fire hydrant. Biederman found that subjects made more errors when the hydrant was in a strange location—such as on top of the mailbox—than when it was located where it belonged, on the sidewalk. Subjects' knowledge of where fire hydrants belong influenced their ability to recognize it.

Perceptual set is a phenomenon that would be instantly recognized by any detective who has ever been predisposed to see a particular person as the guilty (or innocent) party, thereby missing the "obvious" clues that point to the facts. As we have seen, our analogy between the process of perception and detective work is an apt one. All through the perceptual process—from the decoding of neural signals, to taking multiple sources of environmental information into account, to being influenced by our prior knowledge—the perceptual system does the "detective work" necessary to create our perception of the world around us. And perhaps the most amazing thing about this detective work is that we are usually unaware of this behind-the-scenes drama. We are too busy perceiving the world.

As we continue the story of psychology in the chapters that follow, we will see that our behaviors, experiences, and thoughts are often determined by processes that we are unaware of.

FIGURE 4.44
One of the stimuli used in Biederman's experiment. In this picture, subjects were asked to identify the fire hydrant.

Reprise: The Creativity of the Brain and the Commonality of the Senses

This chapter is a celebration of the creativity of the human brain. We have seen how environmental stimuli are transformed into neural messages that travel to the brain, encoded so that they stand for perceptual qualities such as colors, forms, pitches, tastes, and smells. We have also seen that from the sensory clues it receives, the brain not only identifies what those impulses stand for, but also creates the different experiences for each quality and combines those experiences into an orderly perceptual world.

When we look at the qualities that make up sensory experience, we see that although they are all created by the brain, we can divide them into two categories. Galileo classified qualities as primary and secondary. **Primary qualities,** such as quantity, shape, size, position, and movement, have a basis in physical reality—we can use measuring instruments to confirm our perception. Our observation of a tennis ball, by vision or by touch, indicates that it is round, and we can confirm its roundness with a measuring instrument. In contrast, **secondary qualities,** such as color, sounds, temperature, smell, and taste, are primarily psychological and have no counterparts in the physical world. Secondary qualities are, according to Galileo, only names that we use to describe our perceptual experience (Hergenhahn, 1992).

We can relate Galileo's observation about secondary qualities to our discussion of the idea that there is no objective reason that we should perceive a 450-nanometer light as "blue." "Red" or "green" would make just as much sense, but the interaction of that light and the structures of our visual system causes us to experience blueness. It is as if the brain contains a "wavelength detector" creating experiences we call "color," and then pairs these experiences with specific wavelengths. Similarly, the brain contains a "frequency detector" that creates experiences we call "pitch" and pairs those pitches with specific frequencies.

The similarity of the two examples cited from two different senses—vision and audition—point to a more general similarity that exists among all of the senses. The senses of smell and taste also create "arbitrary" experiences from physical stimuli when molecules are endowed with smells and tastes.

But the similarities among the senses go beyond the creation of experiences from physical stimuli. For example, in our discussion of Gestalt psychology, we saw that similar organizational principles hold for vision and hearing. Each of the senses is also affected by cognitive influences. We cited examples of perceptual set for vision; the effect of the situation on pain perception; and the role of memory in helping us identify smells. Hearing is likewise affected by cognition, especially as one of its major uses is to understand language. Thus, when we listen to someone speak, we "hear" breaks between individual words—a process called *speech segmentation*—even though there are actually no breaks in the sound stimulus. This lack of actual breaks between words is why an unfamiliar language often sounds like an unbroken string of sounds. The reason we don't hear the breaks in the foreign language is that we don't know the meanings of the words. Our knowledge of meaning causes segmentation.

There are many similarities among the senses besides those described in this chapter. For example, just as neurons in the visual cortex called feature detectors respond to specific visual stimuli, feature detectors in the auditory cortex respond only to certain types of sounds.

The commonalities among the senses may seem surprising, as the experiences associated with each sense are so different. But those different experiences simply reflect the wide variety of environmental stimuli to which our senses respond. All of the senses use similar mechanisms because they all share the same nervous system. The diversity of experience that the brain creates using such similar mechanisms is all the more reason to marvel at its creativity.

FIGURE 4.45

Did you see a rat or a man? Looking first at the more ratlike picture in Figure 4.42 increased the chances that you would perceive this one as a rat. But your perceptions probably would have been different if you had first seen the manlike version of the picture in Figure 4.43.

8   LANGUAGE

Perception and Culture

What do you see when you look at the moon on a clear night? Most people in our culture probably see the "man in the moon." But Native Americans report seeing a rabbit; Chinese see a lady fleeing her husband; and Samoans see a woman weaving (Samovar & Porter, 1991). As we know from the rat/man demonstration described earlier, when presented with an ambiguous stimulus people tend to see what they expect to see. If different cultures attach different stories to the appearance of the moon, people from various cultures will *expect* to see different things when they look at the moon, so it is not surprising that they do.

There is a good deal of evidence for such cultural influences on perception. One widely researched effect concerns people's perception of pictures. Cross-cultural psychologists have explored how people with limited experience in looking at pictures see them. Consider, for example, the picture in Figure 4.46. What do you see? Most Western observers see a family gathered inside a room, which has a window located behind the young woman's head. But many rural East Africans see the "window" as a tin bal-

anced on the woman's head. You can appreciate why they might do so if you cover up the markings that represent the corner of the room. Those markings provide a perspective cue, indicating that the family is inside a room. Apparently East African subjects either see those markings as a tree or simply are not sensitive to the pictorial depth information that they provide (Deregowski, 1980).

Another way to determine how people perceive pictures is to use the Hudson test, which uses stimuli like the ones in Figure 4.47 (Hudson, 1960, 1967). A subject is shown the picture and asked, "Which is closer to the man, the elephant or the duiker?" Comparison of subjects from the Bantu tribe in Africa and Europeans indicates that the Bantus are more likely to say the elephant is closer to the man than are the Europeans (who almost unanimously say the duiker is closer). The Bantu subjects evidently perceive the picture as a two-dimensional display, whereas the Europeans perceive it as a depiction of a three-dimensional scene (Deregowski, 1980; Gregory, 1973). Apparently, lack of prior experience in perceiving pictures makes it more difficult to perceive the pictorial depth cues of overlap, relative size and height, and linear perspective that create an impression of depth for observers accustomed to those cues.

People in different cultures also vary in how much they are affected by visual illusions. Hershel Liebowitz and his co-workers (1969; Liebowitz & Pick, 1972) demonstrated that subjects from Guam experience a less pronounced Ponzo illusion in response to a stimulus like the one in Figure 4.40 than do American subjects. Guam is a hilly country, with no railways or straight roads. The fact that residents of Guam rarely look into the far distance across terrain apparently makes them less susceptible to illusions that depend on interpreting the depth information in pictures.

Culture also affects perception in senses other than vision. For example, members of different cultures give widely varying reports of the intensity of pain they experience when presented with the same stimuli. One study presented electric shocks to a group of Westerners and a group of Nepalese subjects (Clark & Clark, 1980). Although all the subjects had identical pain thresh-

FIGURE 4.46
Westerners and East Africans view this picture quite differently.

FIGURE 4.47
One of the stimuli used in the Hudson test to determine how people of different cultures perceive depth in pictures

olds, the Nepalese endured much higher stimulus intensities before reporting "faint pain" and "extreme pain" (Figure 4.48).

What explains these results? Further experiments, which used procedures too complex to describe here, ruled out the possibility that the Nepalese *experience* less pain than Westerners (see Goldstein, 1989). Apparently, both groups experienced the shocks in the same way, but the Nepalese subjects simply withstood higher levels of pain before reaching what they considered faint or extreme pain. It may be that Nepalese culture teaches people to withstand pain without complaining.

In fact, comparison of two groups of American subjects supports the idea that the ability to tolerate pain may be socially learned. Evelyn Hall and Simon Davies (1991) had female varsity track athletes and female nonathletes immerse their hands and arms in freezing ice water and rate the level of pain they experienced on a scale of 0 ("no pain sensation") to 150 ("the strongest sensation I can imagine"). Although both groups experienced the same pain stimuli, the athletes rated the pain as less intense (their average rating was 76) than the nonathletes (whose average was 130). One reason the athletes gave lower pain ratings may be reflected by the sports slogan "No pain, no gain." Athletes' ability to withstand pain may be something they learn during painful training workouts. Another reason could be that people who can withstand pain might be the ones attracted to athletics. Whatever the reason, there is no question that two groups that are, in a sense, from different "cultures" (athletic versus nonathletic) show a different tolerance for pain.

A more graphic demonstration of how culture affects pain perception is the hook-swinging ceremony practiced in some parts of India (Kosambi, 1967). This ritual has been described as follows.

> The ceremony derives from an ancient practice in which a member of a social group is chosen to represent the power of the gods. The role of the chosen man (or "celebrant") is to bless the children and crops in a series of neighboring villages during a particular period of the year. What is remarkable about the ritual is that steel hooks, which are attached by strong ropes to the top of a special cart, are shoved under his skin and muscles on both sides of his back. The cart is then moved from village to village. Usually the man hangs on to the ropes as the cart is moved about. But at the climax of the ceremony in each village, he swings free, hanging only from the hooks embedded in his back, to bless the children and crops. Astonishingly, there is no evidence that the man is in pain during the ritual; rather, he appears to be in a "state of exaltation" (Melzak & Wall, 1983, p. 20).

As the celebrant's skin is clearly damaged by the steel hooks, nerve fibers that respond to skin damage must be firing, but he apparently experiences little or no pain. Researchers don't know exactly what is going on here, but perhaps it is similar to the phenomenon of wounded soldiers leaving the battlefield being less likely to ask for pain relievers than we would expect. Perhaps a similar kind of cognitive effect, or attaining a trance state during the ceremony, dulls the celebrant's perception of pain.

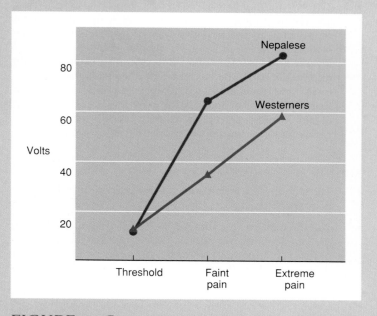

FIGURE 4.48
Voltages for shock stimuli at which Westerners and Nepalese subjects reported threshold for feeling, faint pain, and extreme pain. The Nepalese withstood much higher levels of pain than the Westerners.

Thus, although all people have basically the same physiological makeup, their cultures—which affect what they learn, determine how they are supposed to behave, and create the physical environment within which they grow up—differ greatly, and those differences can cause differences in perception.

"Celebrant" in the Indian hook-swinging ceremony

Two Questions About Perception

- Two key questions are asked by perceptual researchers. They answer the first—How is information in the environment represented in the nervous system?—by determining the sensory code for different perceptual qualities (biological level of analysis). They answer the second—How do we use information from the environment to create perceptions?—by looking for relationships between stimuli and perception (behavioral level of analysis), by exploring how the meaning of stimuli affects perception (cognitive level), and by investigating how culture affects perception (contextual level).

Vision: Seeing Forms and Colors

- The stimulus for vision is the visible part of the electromagnetic spectrum.

- The three major structures of the visual system are the eye, the lateral geniculate nucleus (LGN), and the visual receiving area of the cortex. Electrical signals generated by rod and cone receptors in the retina travel from the eye to the LGN and cortex.

- Researchers have studied the sensory code for form by determining the responses of neurons in the different structures of the visual system. Single neurons in the retina and LGN respond best to small spots of light. Cortical neurons called feature detectors respond best to lines oriented in specific ways.

- A possible physiological mechanism for form perception could involve combining information from all of the feature detectors that fire to various parts of an object. Exactly how this occurs is not yet known.

- Two theories of the sensory code for color were proposed by early researchers on the basis of behavioral studies: the trichromatic theory and the opponent-process theory. Modern physiological research shows that both theories of color vision are correct. Color perception depends on receptors sensitive to three different parts of the spectrum and on the activity of color-opponent neurons.

- Perception is not a "copy" of the environment—it is a "record" of it, reflecting the fact that the environment is filtered through physiological processes before it is perceived.

Hearing: Perceiving Pitch

- The stimulus for hearing is pressure changes in the air. The frequency of sound waves is related to the perception of pitch. The frequency range of human hearing extends from 20 to 20,000 Hz.

- The auditory system is a complex pathway through which vibrations travel. Vibrations traveling through the outer, middle, and inner ear eventually stimulate the hair cells, which in turn generate electrical signals in the nervous system.

- The sensory code for pitch is a combination of place (the place in the cochlea where the basilar membrane vibrates the most depends on frequency) and the timing of nerve firing.

- Cochlear implants bring hearing to deaf people by stimulating the hair cells through electrodes inserted inside the cochlea.

The Skin Senses: Touch, Temperature, and Pain

- The skin serves as the receptor surface for sensations such as touch, temperature, and pain. The code for these sensations appears to be the firing of neurons called cold fibers, warm fibers, and other fibers that respond to specific types of stimulation on the skin.

- Pain is influenced by cognitive factors, a phenomenon addressed by the gate control theory of pain, which proposes that people's cognitions can control a gate that modulates the incoming impulses from pain fibers.

The Chemical Senses: Taste and Smell

- Taste receptors are located in papillae on the tongue. The labeled line theory proposes that the four taste qualities—sour, salty, sweet, and bitter—are signaled by activity in specific fibers. It is also possible that the code for taste may be determined by the pattern of responses of these fibers.

- The receptors for smell are located in the olfactory mucosa. Different substances cause activity in different areas of the mucosa.

- Being able to retrieve an odor's name from memory increases our ability to identify odors, which shows there is a cognitive component to odor identification.

How Do We Differentiate Objects in the Environment?

- The Gestalt laws of organization specify what perceptions will occur given a certain stimulus configuration. Six of these laws are the laws of simplicity, similarity, nearness, good continuation, common fate, and familiarity. These laws are applicable to both visual and auditory stimuli.

How Do We Perceive Depth?

- We perceive depth by using the information contained in depth cues. There are four major classes of depth cues: (1) oculomotor cues; (2) pictorial cues; (3) the movement-produced cue of movement parallax; and (4) the binocular cue of binocular disparity. Depth perception illustrates how the brain's activity interacts with sensory information to create perceptions.

How Do We Perceive the Sizes and Shapes of Objects?

- Size constancy refers to the tendency for our perception of an object's size to remain constant, no matter what its distance from us or the size of its image on the retina. It depends on the observer's ability to perceive depth. Thus, when depth cues are not available, size constancy breaks down and perceived size changes as the size of the retinal image changes.

- According to the idea that there is a size-distance scaling mechanism, perceived size is determined by both an object's retinal size and its perceived distance. This illustrates the principle that perception depends on multiple sources of information, from which the brain actively constructs perceptions.

- Shape constancy refers to the tendency for our perception of an object's shape to remain constant, even when we view it from different angles. Its accuracy depends on our ability to take slant information into account.

Why Do We Sometimes Misperceive?

- Misperceptions can occur when a person misperceives one of the sources of information that the perceptual system takes into account in constructing its perceptions. For example, misperceptions of depth can cause errors in the perception of size, as illustrated by the Ames room, the Ponzo illusion, and the moon illusion. Illusions are important because they show that what we perceive is not always a reflection of objective reality.

How Do Expectations Influence Perception?

- Perception can be affected by knowledge that a person has just acquired or by knowledge acquired through the experiences of a lifetime spent in a particular environment or culture. The fact that our expectations can influence what we perceive is the basis for the phenomenon of perceptual set.

Reprise: The Creativity of the Brain and the Commonality of the Senses

- The brain creates our perceptions. Of particular interest are perceptual qualities Galileo called secondary qualities (color, pitch, smell, and taste), which are psychological and have no counterparts in the physical world. We can think of the brain as containing "detectors" that differentiate qualities in stimuli by creating distinct experiences for different qualities.

- There are many commonalities among the senses. The brain creates a diversity of experiences but often uses similar mechanisms, because the senses all share the same nervous system.

Follow-Through/Diversity: Perception and Culture

- Growing up in a particular culture can influence perception in a number of ways. Culture influences people's ability to perceive depth in pictures, to see visual illusions, and to withstand pain.

Key Terms

Ames room
audibility canal
basilar membrane
binocular cue
cochlea
cochlear implant
color matching
cones
cornea
depth cues
electromagnetic spectrum
epidermis
feature detectors
fovea
frequency
gate control theory of pain
hair cells
inner ear
labeled line theory
lateral geniculate nucleus (LGN)
law of common fate
law of familiarity
law of good continuation
law of nearness
law of similarity
law of simplicity
laws of organization
lens
middle ear
moon illusion
movement-produced cue
oculomotor cues

olfactory bulb
olfactory mucosa
opponent-process theory of
    color vision
ossicles
outer ear
papillae
perception
perceptual set
peripheral retina
pictorial cues
pitch
place theory of pitch
    perception
Ponzo illusion
primary qualities
pure tone
retina
rods
secondary qualities
sensory coding
shape constancy
size constancy
size-distance scaling
sound wave
taste buds
tectorial membrane
trichromatic theory of color
    vision
tympanic membrane
visible light
visual receiving area

CHAPTER

5

Probing Inner States: The Scientific Study of Consciousness

Daily Variations in Consciousness: Circadian Rhythms
Biological Clocks
The Nucleus That Sets the Clock
Jet Lag
Work Shifts

Sleep: The Active Brain at Night
The Stages of Sleep: A Night in a Sleep Laboratory
The Biological Control of Sleep
Why Do We Sleep?
Sleep Disorders

Dreams: Images During Sleep
Common Questions About Dreams and Dreaming
Theories of Dreaming

Hypnosis: The Power of Suggestion
The Scientific Study of Hypnosis
What Happens to a Person Who Is Hypnotized?
Hypnotism as Paradox
Theories of Hypnosis

Interdisciplinary Dimension: Criminal Justice
Hypnotism and the Law

Drugs: Changing Consciousness at the Synapse

How Describing Our Experience Can Shape Our Conception of Reality

Reprise: Consciousness and Levels of Analysis

Follow-Through/Diversity
Dreams and Culture

Consciousness and Behavior

Consciousness is the "front page" of the mind.

Robert Ornstein (1986, p. 62)

I am thinking about the day that my grandfather died. I was at junior high school and Bill walked into the office. I was in the office and I was crying and I didn't really care if he, if he cared that I was crying. I walked outside. I remember walking down by the football field. It was a long, curvy driveway sort of and I remember looking over through my tears at them playing football. Now I'm thinking about my coach in junior high school. He was Mr. Thomas and he used to beat up all of, all of these kids, but he liked me. And I'm still thinking of Mr. Thomas. I'm thinking of his big nose and bald head. Now I'm thinking of this pillow and it reminds me of something but I can't tell what it is. I'm looking at the sack on the wall. I'm looking at my coat again. I'm looking at this piece of cellophane on the floor. It's from a cigarette package. I'm thinking of Susan and our pollution club in junior high school. I was vice president and she was president . . .

Transcript of a male college student's stream of consciousness, recited into a tape recorder (adapted from Pope, 1978, p. 288)

I found myself walking to a class with one of my former professors, a man in his late 30s or early 40s. He was explaining that his class was being held in a large auditorium and that he was having some trouble with snakes in the room. We reached the building and I stood in the background while he opened the side door to see if the snakes were still there. At first nothing happened, but gradually snakes began appearing in increasing size and number. The next thing I remember, I was jumping from one table to another trying to escape snakes of all sizes, a good many of them very large. They were coming very close but apparently never reached me as I awakened with no particular feeling of anxiety. The only question left in my mind was how I got away.

Female college student's written record of a dream (Hall, 1963, p. 8)

These two narratives—a report of the thoughts going through a person's mind and remembrances of a dream—are examples of the contents of consciousness. **Consciousness** is what you are *aware* of, and what is accessible to you at any given moment. Your consciousness at this very moment therefore contains the words you are reading but also other things you are simultaneously perceiving—sounds, colors, perhaps smells—and any other thoughts, memories, or feelings that you might be having.

In addition to the perceptions, thoughts, and feelings you are aware of at any moment, consciousness includes your *knowledge* that you are having those experiences. This idea that consciousness includes both what we are experiencing *and* our awareness that we are experiencing it has led some researchers to

States of consciousness vary greatly with time of day and type of activity. Here, consciousness varies from sleep to intense concentration to heightened awareness.

distinguish two different kinds of consciousness. **Perceptual consciousness** includes the perceptions, thoughts, and feelings we are experiencing (in short, what we are aware of), and **reflective consciousness** is our awareness that those mental events are occurring (Humphrey, 1983, 1987; Natsoulas, 1978, 1988).

The two quotes that begin this chapter illustrate both types of consciousness. The narratives themselves report the students' perceptual consciousness, the experiences they had while talking into the tape recorder and remembering a dream. Their description of those experiences to others represents reflective consciousness, their awareness of their conscious experiences. Many researchers feel that reflective consciousness is what distinguishes humans from other animals (Blakemore & Greenfield, 1987; Griffin, 1992), but others feel it's possible that other animals have some form of reflective consciousness (Griffin, 1992).

Our main concern in this chapter is perceptual consciousness and, specifically, the idea that an important property of this aspect of consciousness is *change*. Consciousness varies throughout the day, from wide-eyed alertness to extreme tiredness; from aimless daydreaming to focused thinking; and, most dramatically, from wakefulness to sleep. Even in quiet moments our thoughts and perceptions are constantly changing, as they are for you right now with each new sentence and with each fleeting thought about matters other than psychology. As we will see, one of the most fascinating discoveries about consciousness is that this restless change continues even when we are fast asleep.

In addition to these natural, ongoing changes in consciousness we will consider the changes that people deliberately try to bring about by agreeing to be hypnotized or by taking "mind-altering" drugs. Among the questions we will explore are whether being hypnotized is an "altered state" and how drugs produce the effects that people experience when they take them. At the end of the chapter, we'll return to the distinction between perceptual and reflective consciousness and explore some of its implications for behavior.

Probing Inner States: The Scientific Study of Consciousness

Because the study of consciousness is the study of what is going on "in our minds," it may seem that consciousness is what psychology is all about. And in fact conscious experience was one of the first subjects to seize the attention of the pioneers who established psychology as a discipline separate from physiology. In particular, conscious awareness was central to the thinking of Wilhelm Wundt, founder of the first psychology laboratory, and to William James (1892), the foremost American psychologist at the turn of the century.

From the start, however, psychologists' study of consciousness ran into serious difficulties. Most American psychologists accepted the argument of behaviorist John B. Watson that there was no scientific way to study mental processes because they could not be objectively observed. Nor was there any need to study consciousness, according to the behaviorists, because the behavior of any organism could be explained in terms of its observable responses to changes in the environment.

Watson's behaviorist definition of psychology's mission reigned in the United States, and as a result words such as *consciousness, awareness,* and *mind* all but disappeared from the discourse of research psychologists from the 1920s to the 1950s. Yet it was hard to deny the psychological reality of awareness. The problem was how to study it objectively.

A step toward objectifying the study of consciousness was taken in 1953, in a surprising place—the sleep research laboratories at the University of Chicago. There researchers stumbled on the discovery that an objectively measurable response—brain waves recorded from a subject's scalp—could be used to identify the times during the night when the subject was dreaming. Suddenly, researchers had a "window" into a state of awareness that had previously been inaccessible except through subjective reports. This discovery stimulated intensive research into sleep and dreaming, with intriguing results that we will review later in this chapter. Ironically, the impetus for this development occurred at the same university from which Watson had received his Ph.D. 50 years earlier.

Other research on awareness was stimulated by the growing popularity of "consciousness-expanding" drugs like marijuana and LSD in the 1960s and, later, by the realization that alcohol and cocaine addiction were major national problems. In response to these societal changes, psychologists, often in collaboration with physiologists, began studying the psychological and biological mechanisms of drug action and drug addiction.

The research on consciousness described in this chapter thus owes a great deal to efforts undertaken at the biological level of analysis. The pioneering sleep research of the 1950s depended on the availability of physiological techniques to measure brain waves, and research on how drugs affect behavior was built on new knowledge about how neurotransmitters act at the synapse. Research on consciousness has also drawn heavily on the idea that there are biological rhythms that influence how consciousness changes throughout the course of the day. We begin our study of consciousness by looking at those rhythms.

Daily Variations in Consciousness: Circadian Rhythms

If you've ever had your campsite invaded by foraging raccoons in the middle of the night, you know that raccoons operate on a different schedule than humans. Unlike raccoons and other nocturnal animals, most humans sleep at night and are very active during daylight hours. But one thing humans have in common with many other animals is a tendency to begin a period of sleep once every 24 hours. This behavioral cycle of wakefulness and sleep is an obvious "rhythm" in our lives.

More detailed observation reveals, in addition to the sleep/wakefulness cycle, over 100 other cycles in the human body. Body temperature, for example, varies with the time of day, typically reaching a high in the late afternoon and a low at about 4:00 A.M. (Graeber, 1989). As body temperature changes, so does the ability to remain alert, which is one reason you may hit a pronounced "low" at about 4:00 A.M. when you try to stay up all night to cram for an exam (Figure 5.1). Interestingly, a number of accidents that have been traced to human error—such as the nuclear power plant accidents at Three Mile Island, Pennsylvania,

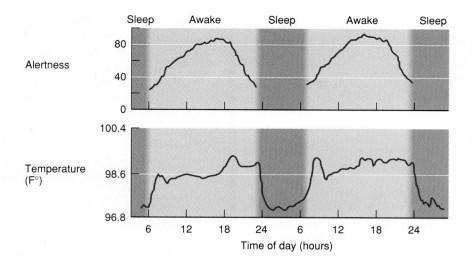

FIGURE 5.1
Body temperature and alertness change throughout the day, the lowest points coming during hours when most people are asleep.

and Chernobyl, Russia, and the release of poisonous gas at the Union Carbide plant in Bhopal, India—occurred in the early morning hours, around 4:00 A.M. (Coleman, 1986). Many other body functions, such as blood pressure, heart rate, and the frequency of cell division, oscillate between maximum and minimum values every 24 hours (Dement, 1972). Even the time babies are born is affected by these cycles: women are most likely to go into labor and give birth between midnight and 6:00 A.M. (Coleman, 1986).

Biological Clocks

These 24-hour rhythms are called **circadian,** which means "about a day"; they are controlled by a **biological clock** within our bodies. But what sets the clock to the 24-hour rhythm? Is the clock's timekeeping controlled by some inner mechanism, or does it respond to cues from the environment, such as the daily cycle of light and dark?

In 1729, the French astronomer Jean de Mairan asked this question about a plant called the heliotrope that normally opens its leaves during the day and closes them at night. It would be logical to assume that the plant is responding to light or temperature, but when de Mairan placed it in complete darkness, he found that it continued to open and close its leaves (Figure 5.2). Later observations showed that the plant also continues to cycle if kept in continuous light, the length of the cycle being 22 hours. The heliotrope apparently has an internal clock that operates independently of the 24-hour light/dark cycle (Coleman, 1986).

Our own biological clocks also operate in the absence of environmental prompts. Experiments in which people descend to live in caves without any clues about the time of day show that the cycle of sleep and wakefulness, as well as that of most physiological functions, continues to repeat on a regular daily schedule. Interestingly, though, this schedule, which is called the **free-running cycle** because it occurs in the absence of environmental cues, is about 25 hours long rather than 24 (Figure 5.3).

The fact that our free-running cycle doesn't match the 24-hour cycle of light and dark means that our 25-hour biological clock must be reset every day to be synchronized with the environment. This setting is controlled by **zeitgebers** (German for "time givers") such as the light/dark cycle and the ringing of your alarm clock on weekday mornings. Many species in our 24-hour world have free-running cycles. Flying squirrels, for example, have a 23-hour biological day and monkeys a 24.5-hour one (Coleman, 1986). Like the 25-hour human cycle, these cycles are reset by zeitgebers in the environment.

3   BIOLOGY

FIGURE 5.2
When de Mairan placed a heliotrope plant in complete darkness, it continued to open and close its leaves according to its internal biological clock.

Sometimes this resetting does not take place. A 28-year-old blind man's biological clock continued to run on a schedule of 24.9 hours, despite the fact that his alarm clock went off at exactly the same time every morning. Unfortunately for him, his sleep/wakefulness cycle became more out of sync with everyone else's with each passing day. As a result, he felt sleepy during the day, when his body felt it should be asleep, and couldn't sleep at night for two to three weeks out of every month (Miles, Raynal, & Wilson, 1977).

The Nucleus That Sets the Clock

Why couldn't the blind man adjust to a 24-hour schedule? The answer to this question may be located deep in the brain, in a small nucleus in the hypothalamus called the **suprachiasmatic nucleus (SCN).** When this nucleus is destroyed in a rat, its sleep/wakefulness cycle is disrupted, so the animal sleeps for the normal amount of time every day but in small spurts, rather than on a regular cycle. Researchers have also shown that this nucleus receives inputs from the retina and is more active when the animal is in the light rather than in the dark (Rusak & Groos, 1982; Rusak & Zucher, 1979). Taken together, this evidence suggests that the SCN sets the free-running sleep/wakefulness cycle, but that zeitgebers such as the light/dark cycle reset it so that the animal's behavior is synchronized with the length of its day (Schwartz & Gainer, 1977). Accordingly, we can guess that the blind person's reset mechanism was not functioning, perhaps due to the absence of light signals from the retina to the SCN. In addition, his reset mechanism would have to be insensitive to other zeitgebers, which presumably are used by the majority of blind people whose biological clocks are reset every day despite their blindness.

Humans normally function well on a 24-hour schedule, although our urge to sleep in when freed from the alarm clock on weekends may be the body's way of reminding us of its natural 25-hour cycle. But what if the day lasted only 18 hours or was extended to 30? This can happen when people fly across many time zones and the body refuses to adjust immediately to those drastic changes in the length of the day.

Since space shuttle astronauts do not experience the normal 24-hour light-dark cycle, they depend on ground control to regulate their sleep periods.

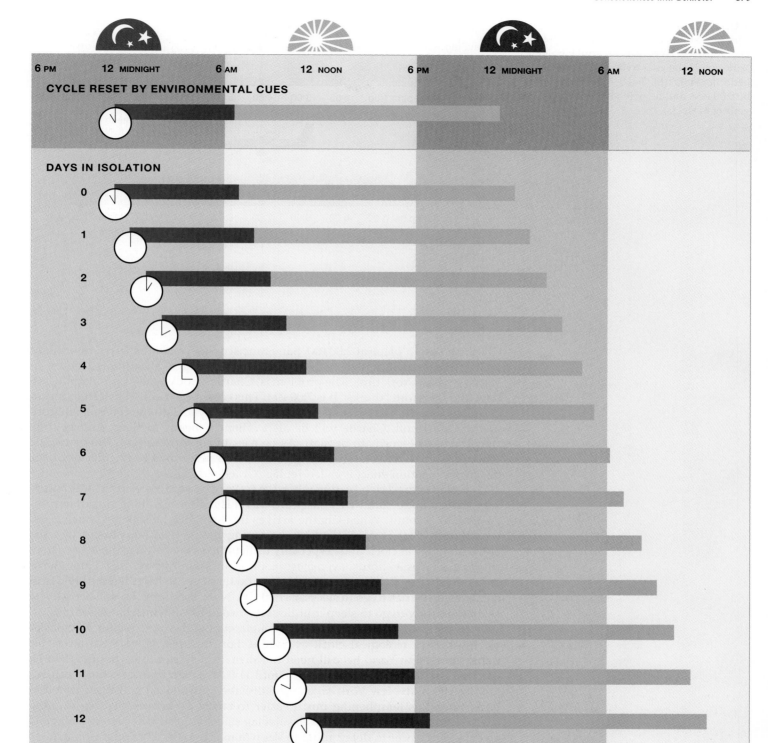

CYCLE RESET BY ENVIRONMENTAL CUES

DAYS IN ISOLATION

FIGURE 5.3

Periods of sleep and wakefulness for someone in isolation, away from clues about the time of day. Note that at first the person sleeps during normal sleeping hours. However, since the person's overall cycle is 25 hours, he goes to sleep an hour later every night, eventually sleeping in the middle of the day.

Time to bed   **Sleep periods**   **Waking periods**

FIGURE 5.4
Charlie leaves San Francisco at 2:00 P.M. and arrives in New York at 10:00 P.M. New York time. If he goes to bed at his usual bedtime, 11:00 P.M., his body time will only be 8:00 P.M. and he will have difficulty getting to sleep.

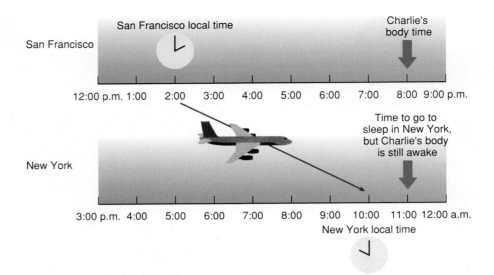

Jet Lag

Charlie boards a plane at 2:00 P.M. San Francisco time, and after a five-hour flight arrives in New York, where he resets his wristwatch ahead three hours to 10:00 P.M. New York time. The problem is, Charlie's body is still on San Francisco time and therefore "thinks" it is 7:00 P.M. This condition is called **external desynchronization:** the body's biological clock is out of sync with the external environment. As a result, Charlie will be alert when he needs to sleep, and he'll be sleepy when he needs to be alert. As he tries to conform to New York time, he will probably become fatigued and be unable to perform at peak efficiency. This desynchronization effect is called **jet lag** (Graeber, 1989).

Jet lag is most debilitating when we travel eastward, as Charlie did (Figure 5.4). We can understand why eastward travel is harder by taking circadian principles into account. When Charlie arrives in New York he sets his watch *ahead* three hours. This is equivalent to shortening the day, an adjustment that the body's biological clock finds especially difficult to make because the body's free-running cycle is 25 hours, even *longer* than the normal 24-hour day. Thus, shortening the day goes against the body's natural tendency to lengthen the biological day. If Charlie tries to go to sleep at 11:00 P.M. New York time, he will actually be asking his body to go to sleep four hours ahead of its own internal schedule.

In contrast, traveling westward lengthens the day and is therefore easier for the body's biological clock to handle. For example, when Charlie travels home from New York, he will need to set his watch *back* three hours when he reaches San Francisco. If he stays up until 11:00 P.M. San Francisco time (equivalent to 2:00 A.M. New York time), he will have experienced a 27-hour day. The body finds this lengthening much easier to adapt to, because its free-running clock is already set for a 25-hour day. Jet lag aside, your own experience may tell you that it is easier to delay going to sleep than it is to try to go to sleep early.

Once we've been in a new time zone for a while, we eventually adapt to the prevailing schedule. But this adaptation takes time, and it takes longer after eastward than westward travel. To complicate this situation, different cycles within the body adapt at different rates. As a result, various cycles are not only out of sync with local time (external desynchronization), but are also out of sync with each other, a condition called **internal desynchronization.** For example, if you travel across six time zones in a westward direction, your body temperature cycle takes 11 or 12 days to readjust, but your reaction time (the time it takes you to react to a briefly presented stimulus like a tone or light) takes only 6 days to adjust. After eastward travel across the same number of time zones, adjustment time is longer—14 or 15 days for body temperature and 9 days for reaction time

(Graeber, 1989). Thus, even after you have adjusted your sleep schedule to the new time zone (usually in just a few days), it may take over a week before all of your body cycles begin functioning in harmony.

Work Shifts

Before the advent of electricity in 1883, the pace of life typically slowed appreciably after sunset. But with the ready availability of artificial light, people created "cities that never sleep" and industries that operate on a 24-hour basis. In industries such as steel production, shift work was introduced to keep mills and plants operating around the clock.

Until the 1920s many people worked 12-hour shifts that left them drained and with shortened life expectancies. Eventually, 8-hour shifts became the norm, but even with these reduced hours workers often experienced problems sleeping and remained tired much of the day. One of the reasons for the drain on workers was the way the shifts were programmed. The typical shift-work pattern featured three 8-hour shifts—a day shift from 8:00 A.M. to 4:00 P.M., an evening shift from 4:00 P.M. to midnight, and a night shift from midnight to 8:00 A.M.

A worker who stays on one of these shifts will eventually adjust to the new schedule. However, few people want to be continuously on the evening or night shift, as that eliminates most contact with family and friends. This problem was solved by rotating shifts every few weeks, but the way this was typically done created even more problems. The typical rotation schedule was in a "counterclockwise" direction, so that a worker would rotate from the night shift to the evening shift and then to the day shift (Figure 5.5a). Consider what that pattern means for workers whose biological clocks have adapted to the evening shift. They leave the plant at midnight and get to bed around 2:00 or 3:00 A.M. After three weeks on this schedule, it is their turn for the day shift. Now they get off work at 4:00 P.M. and try to get to sleep by 10:00 P.M., four or five hours *earlier* than the bedtime they had adapted to.

A better way to alternate work schedules is to shift them in a clockwise fashion, as shown in Figure 5.5b. Now our evening workers, who are used to 3:00 A.M. bedtime, rotate to the night shift and can begin sleeping around 10:00 A.M. This rotation to a later bedtime, which is equivalent to creating a *longer* day, is an easier adjustment for their biological clocks. Experiments comparing counterclockwise shift rotation with clockwise rotation have found that workers on the clockwise rotation are more productive, rate their jobs as more satisfying, and have better health (Coleman, 1986).

Research on jet lag and shift work shows that biological rhythms underlie some of the normal changes in consciousness and that disruption of those rhythms can adversely affect alertness and the ability to perform effectively. The intimate connection between physiology and consciousness is also evident in the discoveries of researchers who have probed the changes in consciousness that occur while we sleep.

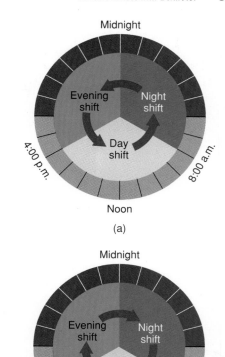

FIGURE 5.5
Counterclockwise (a) and clockwise (b) work shift changes. (The arrows indicate the direction of the shift changes.) The body adapts more easily when shifts are rotated in the clockwise direction.

Sleep: The Active Brain at Night

Sleep that knits up the raveled sleave of care, . . .
Chief nourisher in life's feast.

William Shakespeare, *Macbeth*

People often think of sleep as a "blank-out" period during which nothing happens, except for occasional dreaming. Modern sleep researchers, however, have uncovered a dramatically different picture (Dement, 1972, 1992; Kleitman, 1963). In sleep, as in the waking state, change is the rule.

The Stages of Sleep: A Night in a Sleep Laboratory

Imagine that you have agreed to spend the next four nights in a sleep laboratory as a subject in a sleep experiment. When you arrive on the first night, the experimenter attaches electrodes to your head, arms, and on either side of your eyes. (See Measurement & Methodology, "Physiological Measures of Sleep.") You are then invited to lie down for your first night's sleep.

Your first night in the laboratory is a little uncomfortable. The electrodes don't hurt, but they feel strange to you, and the bed is different from yours, so you have some trouble getting to sleep. During the night you awaken a few times without the prompting of the experimenter. Your dreams are also different than usual—you recall dreaming about electrodes, electronic equipment, and being "plugged in." This uneasiness and dreaming about being in the laboratory is part of the *first night effect* that usually occurs at the beginning of a sleep experiment. Because of this effect, the experimenter disregards the data collected during the first night.

MEASUREMENT & METHODOLOGY

Physiological Measures of Sleep

In a sleep laboratory measures are often taken of numerous physiological functions, such as body temperature, heart rate, skin resistance, eye movements, brain waves, and muscle tension. The three most commonly used—and the ones most relevant to our discussion in this chapter—are eye movements, brain waves, and muscle tension. All of these provide physiological evidence reflecting the experiences a sleeper is having.

Eye Movements

Eye movements are measured by attaching two small electrodes to the face on either side of the subject's eyes. Eye movements generate a difference in charge between the two electrodes, called the **electrooculogram (EOG):** when the eyes move, the EOG changes.

Brain Waves

Brain-wave electrodes attached to the scalp pick up the summed activity of the millions of cortical neurons that are near the electrodes. The response picked up by the electrodes, called the **electroencephalogram (EEG),** is very small, only thousandths of a volt. Once amplified, however, these signals are large enough to indicate changes during the various stages of sleep.

Muscle Tension

Muscle tension is usually measured in sleep laboratories by placing electrodes on the arm or neck muscles. The resulting electrical response is called the **electromyogram (EMG).**

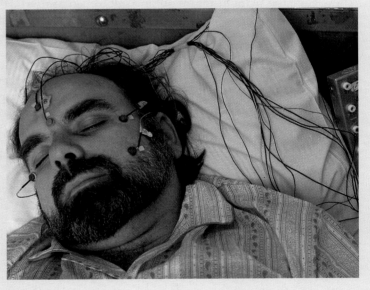

Subject in a sleep laboratory, showing electrodes for recording the electrooculogram (eye movements) and electroencephalogram (brain waves)

By the second night you feel more relaxed. After being hooked up to the electrodes, you lie in bed for a while and then feel yourself slowly drifting off to sleep. This feeling—that your transition from being awake to being asleep is gradual—is, however, an illusion. The transition from wakefulness to sleep is actually very sudden, as the following experiment shows: A subject lies in bed in a sleep laboratory with her eyes taped open and is instructed to press a switch every time a brief flash of light goes off. This is an easy task, which she has no trouble performing. However, after a few minutes she suddenly stops pressing the switch. One second she is awake, seeing and responding to the light; the next second she is functionally blind and asleep.

The sudden onset of sleep is confirmed by the fact that as soon as the subject stops pressing the button, her eyes start moving in a slow, rolling pattern and the electroencephalogram, or EEG (see the Measurement & Methodology), suddenly changes from awake brain waves—either the rapid, low-voltage **beta waves** of alert thinking or the more rhythmical **alpha waves** of relaxed wakefulness—to the small, fast waves characteristic of **stage-one sleep** (Figure 5.6). As sleep researcher William Dement notes, "Awareness stops abruptly, as if 10 billion furiously communicating brain cells were suddenly put on 'stand-by' status" (1976).

The sudden transition from wakefulness to stage-one sleep marks the beginning of your descent to deeper and deeper stages of sleep. Researchers have identified five stages of sleep, each characterized by its own brain-wave pattern. After about 5 or 10 minutes of stage-one sleep, you go through stages two and three until you reach stage four, about 30 minutes after falling asleep. The brain waves of these stages change in a systematic way: **stage-two sleep** is identified by rapid waves called **sleep spindles** and **stage-three sleep** by the appearance of large, low-frequency waves (one to four per second) called **delta waves.** In **stage-four sleep,** the deepest stage, these delta waves dominate your sleep records. (To remember that delta waves increase as you fall more deeply asleep, associate the *d* in *d*elta with *d*eep sleep.)

A second characteristic change in brain waves during the descent toward stage-four sleep is the increasing regularity of the waves, with fewer sudden bursts of activity such as the sleep spindles of stage two. This regularity is called *synchrony,* because it occurs as the thousands of neurons that are generating these waves begin firing more in step with one another.

As you approach stage-four sleep, your blood pressure, heart rate, and body temperature decline and you become harder and harder to waken. Small children, who spend much more of their time in stage-four sleep than do adults, are almost impossible to waken when in this stage. It is during this stage that people walk and talk in their sleep and small children are most likely to wet their beds.

9 DEVELOPMENT

After about 30 minutes in stage-four sleep, you begin to go through the sleep stages in reverse—passing through stages three, two, and finally back to stage one. This retracing begins a repeated cycling through these stages throughout the night. However, as you first cycle back to stage one, a number of things happen for the first time since you feel asleep. Your eyes start jerking rapidly back and forth; your muscles—which up to this point have been helping you change your position during the night—go completely limp; and your heart rate becomes irregular. Meanwhile, your brain waves become *desynchronized,* indicating that the neurons are now firing out of synchrony with each other, and they appear fast and irregular, like waking brain waves. What's going on?

That was the question confronting Eugene Aserinsky and Nathaniel Kleitman (1953) when they discovered this abrupt change in sleep in the University of Chicago sleep laboratory. Aserinsky, a graduate student of Kleitman's, was watching the slow, rolling eye movements that begin when a person first falls asleep. About 90 minutes later, Aserinsky noticed that the subject's eyes started moving rapidly back and forth. At first Aserinsky couldn't believe what he was

FIGURE 5.6

Brain waves for wakefulness (top two records) and for the five stages of sleep. The brain waves of REM sleep are like the beta waves of alert wakefulness, but the body's muscles are relaxed, making body movement impossible.

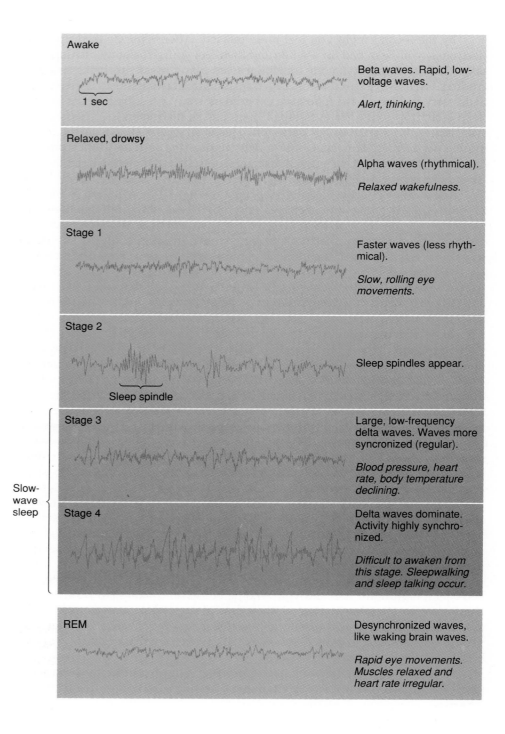

observing. As William Dement, also a student of Kleitman's, puts it, "These eye movements, which had all the attributes of waking eye movements, had absolutely no business appearing in sleep" (1976, p. 25).

These eye movements defined a fifth stage of sleep, called **rapid eye movement (or REM) sleep.** Stages 3 and 4 are called **slow-wave sleep (SWS)**, because of the slowness of their EEG waves compared with the rapid, disorganized waves of REM sleep.

REM sleep would have remained an interesting but relatively unimportant discovery if it hadn't been for Aserinsky and Kleitman's next observation. When they awakened subjects during REM sleep, the subjects usually reported that they had just been dreaming; yet when they awakened subjects during SWS, they usually reported that they weren't dreaming. Subsequent research has shown that subjects report dreams on about 80% of REM awakenings, but on only about 20% of SWS awakenings (Carskadon & Dement, 1989; Dement, 1976). Furthermore, REM dreams are usually more visual, vivid, emotional, and bizarre than SWS dreams. As William Dement points out in his highly readable *Some Must Watch While Some Must Sleep*, REM sleep is as different from slow-wave sleep as sleep is from wakefulness.

After the first period of REM sleep you resume the cycle, again descending toward stage-four sleep. As shown in Figure 5.7, you go through this cycle four or five times before you awaken, although as the night progresses you stop descending to stages three and four and spend most of your time alternating between stage two and REM sleep. Notice that the final REM stages are the longest of the night. If you sleep about seven and a half hours, you will have spent one and a half to two hours in REM sleep and will most likely wake up during the last REM period.

You may awaken under the illusion that your night of sleep was uneventful. As we have seen, however, it was continually active, with alternating periods of relative calm and great activity. Researchers have asked many questions about this activity during sleep: What causes the fluctuations between stages? Are separate brain mechanisms responsible for REM and slow-wave sleep? What is the purpose of each type of sleep? What is the purpose of sleep in general? What causes the sleep disorders that some people experience? We will now consider some of these questions.

The Biological Control of Sleep

3   BIOLOGY

We saw earlier that the suprachiasmatic nucleus (SCN) is involved in controlling our sleep/wakefulness cycle. But many other brain structures are involved in controlling sleep. One of the most important structures is the **reticular formation** (RF), a network of about 100 small nuclei that runs from the spinal cord into the thalamus at the base of the brain (Figure 5.8 on p. 188). Its name refers to its net-like appearance (the Latin *reticulum* means "little net"). Particularly important for sleep is that part of the reticular formation just below the thalamus called the **midbrain reticular formation** (**MBRF**). The conclusion that this area is responsible for triggering *activation* or *arousal* of the brain comes from experiments in which electrical stimulation of a sleeping cat's MBRF awakens the cat and causes the desynchronized brain waves of alertness (Moruzzi & Magoun, 1949).

Signals from the senses trigger the MBRF to send arousal messages to the brain. In addition to sending arousal signals *to* the cortex, the MBRF receives signals *from* the cortex. For example, excessive worrying just before going to bed can send signals from the cortex to the MBRF, causing the MBRF to send activation back to the brain and making it difficult to sleep.

Why Do We Sleep?

We have described the stages of sleep and the nuclei in the brain that control sleep. But these observations don't explain *why* we sleep. One answer is provided by Macbeth's description of sleep as the "chief nourisher in life's feast." Modern researchers call this view the *restorative theory of sleep*—the idea that we need sleep to recharge and repair the body and the brain. We will see that there is some evidence to support this idea, but that the restorative theory may not be the whole answer.

The restorative theory of sleep.   The **restorative theory of sleep** has been tested by looking at (1) how exercise affects the amount of sleep we need and the kind of sleep we experience and (2) how sleep deprivation affects physical and cognitive performance.

FIGURE 5.7
Sleep cycles throughout the night. Notice how REM periods get longer after the initial short period. Eye movements and vivid dreaming occur during REM periods.

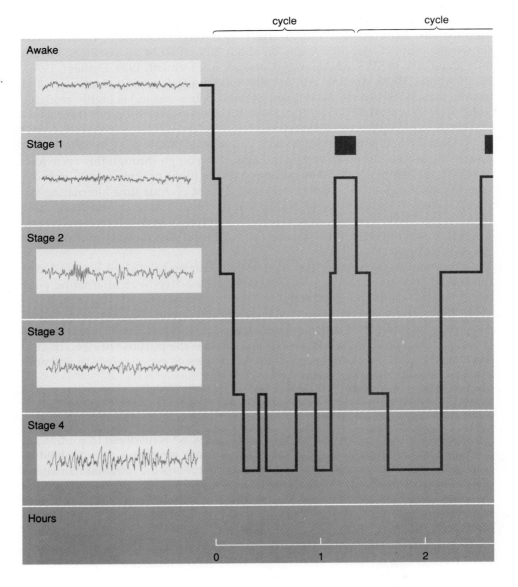

The effect of exercise. According to the restorative theory, exercise, which uses up the body's resources, should increase a person's need to sleep. Consistent with this idea, Colin Shapiro and his co-workers (1981) found that six marathon runners increased their sleep by about one and a half hours per night for a few nights following a marathon. Even more significant, this increase in sleep time was accompanied by a doubling of the proportion of time devoted to slow-wave sleep. Before the marathon, SWS accounted for 20 percent of their sleep time; but for a few nights after the marathon this proportion increased to 40 percent. Perhaps, Shapiro suggests, it is during SWS that the body's resources are restored.

The effect of sleep deprivation. If the restorative theory of sleep is correct, being deprived of sleep should cause a breakdown in our physical abilities and in our ability to think. However, depriving people of sleep for long periods of time causes much less severe effects than we might expect. Depriving people of

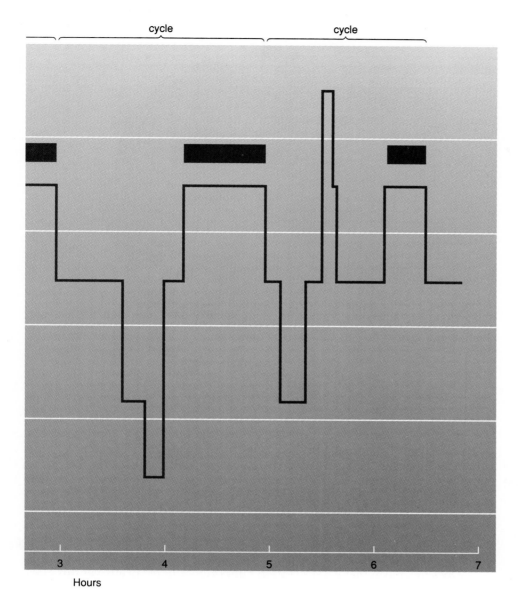

Hours

sleep for two or three days has little effect on their ability to perform complex or novel tasks. The main effects are an increase in irritability and a tendency to become disinterested in simple, repetitive tasks. A sleepy person may be capable of performing these tasks well, but just doesn't feel like it.

Some deprivation experiments have lasted far longer than two or three days. Randy Gardner, a high-school student who stayed up for 264 hours as part of a science project (and to get into *The Guinness Book of World Records*), did experience severe tiredness and could stay awake only by continued activity. However, he was able to perform many tasks quite well, including beating well-rested sleep researcher William Dement in over 100 consecutive games of pinball on the last day of his 11-day deprivation. When finally allowed to sleep, Randy slept only 14 hours and then returned to his normal 8-hour schedule the following night. (In 1977, Maureen Werton broke Randy Gardner's record by staying up for 18 days 17 hours in a rocking chair marathon!)

So far it would seem that sleep deprivation experiments provide little sup-

FIGURE 5.8
Cross section of the brain, showing the reticular formation, which is responsible for triggering activation of the brain, and the suprachiasmatic nucleus, which sets the free-running sleep-wakefulness cycle.

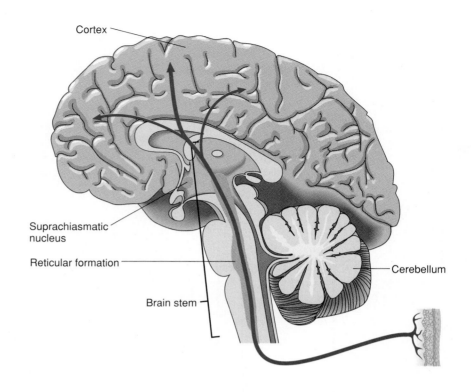

Jane Fonda props up her partner in this scene from the film *They Shoot Horses, Don't They?*, about dance marathons in the 1930s.

port for the restorative theory of sleep. However, other sleep deprivation evidence does tend to support it. When subjects are allowed to sleep after long deprivation, they tend to stay in slow-wave sleep longer than usual (Borbely et al., 1981). Also, people who normally sleep less than most tend to get as much stage-three and stage-four sleep as people who sleep longer (Webb & Agnew, 1977). These results, which parallel the results of Shapiro's study of marathon runners, have led some researchers to suggest that the restorative theory may have some merit, and that this restoration may take place primarily during slow-wave sleep (Cohen, 1979).

Does this mean that REM sleep isn't important? To try to answer this question, researchers have selectively deprived people of REM sleep by waking them every time they go into it. These studies show that people deprived of REM sleep tend to experience more and more REM periods (Webb & Agnew, 1967). Also, on the first nights following REM deprivation, a **REM rebound** occurs, in which subjects experience much more REM sleep than normal. The body clearly possesses a mechanism dedicated to triggering REM sleep; however, the function of REM sleep is not well understood.

The evolutionary theory of sleep.   Another view of why we sleep is the **evolutionary theory of sleep,** which proposes that sleep is an adaptive response of a particular species to its environment (Webb, 1974). For example, an animal with poor night vision would be safer asleep in a cave than being awake in the woods, where it could be attacked by larger animals with good night vision. For this animal, sleeping at night would serve a protective function.

How close this linkage of sleep with survival is depends on how vulnerable the animal is when sleeping. Ground squirrels sleep 14 hours a day in a safe burrow, bats 19 hours a day in caves. But animals such as deer and sheep, which are often prey and don't have a safe place to sleep, spend only about 3 hours a day sleeping. In contrast, predators, like members of the cat family, sleep 14 hours a day (Allison & Chichetti, 1976). Food needs are also linked to sleep patterns: for instance, elephants, who need lots of time to search for food, sleep only 2 hours per night (Figure 5.9).

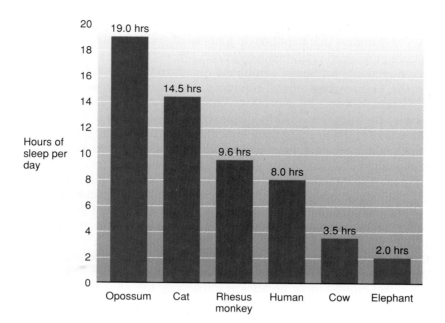

Although the evolutionary theory of sleep may help explain the natural sleep patterns of many animals, the sleep patterns of modern-day humans are influenced by numerous factors in addition to those established by evolutionary pressures. Although we have no way of knowing how well our distant ancestors slept, there is no question that today, given the availability of artificial light and the stressful lifestyles many of us lead, large numbers of people have at least occasional trouble sleeping. And some suffer from *sleep disorders,* which can be extremely disruptive and even dangerous to human health.

Sleep Disorders

In spite of natural rhythms of sleep and wakefulness, a significant population suffers from sleep-related problems—temporary or habitual. In this section we cover what researchers have discovered about three types of sleep disorders: *insomnia, narcolepsy,* and *sleep apnea.*

16   DISORDERS

Insomnia. The majority of Americans with sleep disorders suffer from **insomnia,** an inability to get enough sleep to feel rested the next day. From 15 to 30% of adults suffer from various degrees of insomnia, with females generally having higher rates of insomnia than males (Coleman, 1986; Kripke & Simons, 1976).

Many people try to deal with insomnia by taking sleeping pills—a solution that is unsatisfactory for at least two reasons. First, the sleep you experience under the influence of sleeping pills differs from normal sleep in an important way: drug-induced sleep contains reduced periods of rapid eye movements. Second, users of sleeping pills usually develop a tolerance for the pills, so they have to take progressively more to get to sleep. The combination of tolerance and lack of REM sleep only compounds the insomniac's problems.

Consider a hypothetical patient, Susan. After an upsetting experience made it difficult for her to sleep, Susan obtained a prescription for sleeping pills from her doctor. At first the pills seemed to be working, although Susan noticed that she didn't feel as rested as she should, even after a full night's sleep. Soon she found that to get to sleep she needed to increase the dosage from one pill to two and then from two pills to four. Eventually Susan felt that she was becoming too dependent on the pills (and besides, she was sure her sleep was more restful before she began taking them), so she decided to stop. The next night she had terrifying nightmares that kept her up half the night. To avoid these nightmares Susan started taking the pills again (Figure 5.10).

What accounts for Susan's troubles? She didn't feel rested during the day because the brain waves of drug-induced sleep are different from the brain waves of normal sleep. She experienced nightmares after stopping the sleeping pills because the suppressed REM sleep caused REM rebound. Besides these effects, the action of the sleeping pills sometimes continued past the ringing of the alarm clock in the morning, causing Susan to feel less alert than usual.

If sleeping pills are not the answer, how should insomnia be treated? According to most sleep researchers, the cure for insomnia is to eliminate its underlying psychological causes. This may not be easy, because in most cases insomnia is a symptom of depression or psychological stress, but in the long run dealing with these psychological problems is much more effective than becoming addicted to sleeping pills.

One tactic that sleep therapists sometimes use is called **paradoxical intention:** they instruct the patient to go to bed and try to *remain awake* as long as possible. This technique works because it eliminates the anxiety that overcomes some people as soon as they lie down and start thinking they won't be able to get to sleep.

Although insomnia is a genuine problem, some people who think they have insomnia actually get a full night's sleep. The case of Barry G. illustrates this curious problem. He came to a sleep laboratory complaining that he always felt fatigued during the day because he had trouble falling asleep, and that even after getting to sleep, he awoke many times during the night. However, two nights of monitoring in the sleep laboratory showed that Barry was actually a normal sleeper. He fell asleep in less than 10 minutes and awoke for only 20 minutes throughout the night. Barry G.'s case of **pseudoinsomnia** is not uncommon.

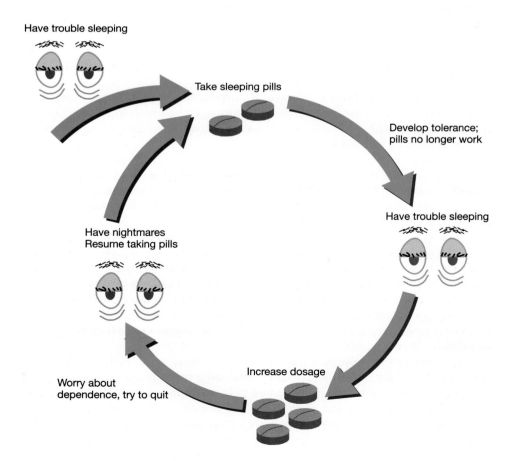

FIGURE 5.10
The vicious circle of sleeping-pill use. Tolerance causes the need for increased dosage. If the person stops taking the pills after tolerance builds up, nightmares result and the person may begin taking the pills again.

People with this problem may feel that they aren't getting much sleep because they may selectively remember the times they were awake, or because when they are sleeping they dream that they are awake, thereby turning a good night's sleep into an illusion of insomnia. Luckily, just finding out that they are actually sleeping through the night is often enough to eliminate these people's feeling of tiredness during the day (Mitler et al.,1975).

Narcolepsy.   Over 100,000 Americans suffer from **narcolepsy,** a condition causing numerous daytime "sleep attacks," during which a person falls asleep and sometimes goes completely limp (Dement et al., 1972, 1973). These attacks can occur while the person is passive (reading or watching TV) or active (walking, eating, or riding a bicycle) and can last from a few minutes to an hour. So Ralph steps up to bat, swings at a pitch, and falls down in a heap. Or worse, he falls asleep at the wheel of his car.

Researchers are beginning to understand something about the nature of narcolepsy. EEG records of narcoleptics indicate that when they go to sleep at night they immediately enter REM sleep (Rechtschaffen et al., 1962). This suggests that the narcoleptic's experience of daytime sleep attacks combined with going limp are actually attacks of REM sleep, which makes sense when we remember that one characteristic of REM sleep is a complete relaxation of the muscles.

One promising development is the discovery of several poodles that exhibit symptoms similar to narcolepsy and also have lower-than-normal levels of the neurotransmitter dopamine (Mefford et al., 1983; Mitler et al., 1974). These findings have led to the hypothesis that a drug that increased dopamine in humans might reduce a narcoleptic's sleep attacks. So far, however, no completely effective treatment has been developed. Although some drugs do alleviate the symptoms of narcolepsy, it remains a very disabling condition (Guilleminault, 1989).

Sleep apnea.   **Sleep apnea,** a condition in which a person's breathing is repeatedly interrupted during sleep, may affect as many as one out of every 200 Americans (U.S. Department of Health and Human Services, 1987). A person with sleep apnea falls asleep rapidly and then begins to have respiratory problems. The trachea (windpipe) partly closes down and the sleeper stops breathing for 30 to 60 seconds, until receptors in the brain sense the lack of oxygen, which wakens the person. After briefly awakening, he or she goes back to sleep and begins the cycle again. The result of this constant cycling of no breathing–awakening–no breathing, which occurs 400 to 500 times a night, is that the sufferer remembers nothing about stopping breathing or waking up but does feel sleepy the next day.

Another characteristic of this disorder is the loud snoring that occurs as the person struggles to push air through the closed trachea. Frequently, patients appear at a sleep clinic not because they feel tired, but because their spouses bring them in to treat their snoring. Many treatments exist. Depending on the severity, it may be treated with medication, tongue-restraining devices to prevent choking, or tracheotomy, a surgical procedure in which a small hole is cut and a tube is inserted in the trachea, which the patient opens at night to bypass the closed-off trachea.

All three of the sleep disorders we have described have something in common: no completely satisfactory cure. This situation reflects the fact that researchers still have much to learn about sleep. The brain mechanisms responsible for sleep are extremely complex and incompletely understood. We are faced with a similar situation when it comes to dreaming: it is something everyone does, but no one fully understands.

Dreams: Images During Sleep

To sleep: perchance to dream: ay, there's the rub . . .

William Shakespeare, *Hamlet*

A dream is something to look at while you are asleep.

Child's definition (Hall & Van de Castle, 1966)

Dreams can be entertaining and mystifying, exhilarating and frightening. They have inspired great poetry and been seen as signs from the gods. The early Greeks thought dreams were delivered by gods, who entered the sleeper's bedroom through a keyhole and delivered their message standing at the head of the bed before exiting the same way (Van de Castle, 1971). Psychologist Carl Jung offered a more modern interpretation, calling dreams "the small hidden door in the deepest and most intimate sanctum of the soul" (1934, p. 46).

It is clear that dreams have been accorded great importance throughout the ages. Even today people who do not view dreams as divine messages still seek hidden meanings in them, sometimes consulting psychics or "dream books" that purport to decode them. Despite such claims, there is no scientific basis for such dream interpretation.

Another way to look at dreams is to study them empirically: to ask questions that can be answered by objective observation. Approaching dreams in this way, psychologists have asked a number of questions. Does everyone dream? Why do we forget our dreams? How does time pass in dreams? What do people typically dream about? We will first look at these questions and then consider some of the theories that have been proposed to explain dreams.

Common Questions About Dreams and Dreaming

Does everyone dream?   Sleep researchers have explored the question of whether everyone dreams by awakening people during REM sleep. When they do so, even people who claim they never dream report—much to their surprise—that they were indeed dreaming. So it appears that we all dream at night, but not everyone *remembers* dreaming on awakening. One reason some people don't remember their dreams is that they typically wake up slowly. To understand why this is true, we need to consider how memory works.

7   MEMORY

Why do we forget dreams?   If someone tells you his telephone number, you will forget it within about 30 seconds unless you repeat the number over and over to yourself. You forget the number because it is in *short-term memory*. As you will see in Chapter 7, short-term memory is rapidly lost from consciousness unless you rehearse it. The same forgetting may occur when you wake up slowly. Unless you wake up fast enough to begin rehearsing your dream while it is still in short-term memory, by the time you are fully awake your memory of it will have vanished, just as that telephone number did.

Supporting this idea is the finding that people remember more dreams if they are awakened suddenly from REM sleep than if they are awakened gradually (Goodenough, 1978). This explanation in terms of short-term memory does not, however, explain the fact that a 10- or 15-minute dream stays in our memory as we sleep, and only begins to vanish as we awaken.

How does time pass in dreams?   Many people believe that the experiences that take place in a dream are compressed into the few seconds just before waking. Experiments have shown, however, that time passes in dreams at about the same rate as it does when we are awake. Thus, when people are awakened from REM sleep, the length of the dream they report is related to the length of the REM period just before they awoke. Short REM periods result in short dream reports, and long REM periods result in long dream reports (Dement, 1976).

William Dement and Edward Wolpert set up an experiment in which they took advantage of the fact that we sometimes incorporate external stimuli into our dreams. Ten minutes after a REM period began, they sprayed cold water onto a sleeper's back, waited 30 seconds, and then awakened the subject. The subject described a dream about acting in a play, which ended as follows:

> I was walking behind the leading lady when she suddenly collapsed and water was dripping on her face. I ran over to her and felt water dripping on my back and head. The roof was leaking. I was very puzzled why she fell down and decided some plaster must have fallen on her. I looked up and there was a hole in the roof. I dragged her over to the side of the stage and began pulling the curtains. Just then I woke up (1958, p. 550).

The time between the appearance of water in the dream and the end of the dream corresponded fairly well with the 30 seconds that actually passed between spraying water on the subject's back and the end of the dream. Thus, it appears that *dream time,* the time that appears to pass in the dream, and *real time,* the actual time that elapses, are the same.

It is worth noting that the incorporation of external stimuli into dreams is another illustration of the fact that sleep is a far from passive activity. We do not, however, necessarily incorporate all external stimuli into our dreams. Some people are extremely proficient at remaining unaware of the loud blasts of their alarm clock. But when those same people become parents, they may report that they are easily awakened by their baby's quiet whimpering.

What do we dream about?   We often think of dreams as having exotic settings and fantastic characters and events. In reality, however, Calvin Hall's (1951) analysis of thousands of dreams indicates that most have commonplace

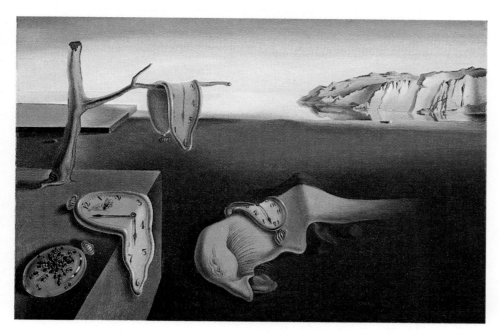

Surrealistic art, such as the painting *The Persistence of Memory* (1931) by Salvador Dali, often contains dreamlike images.

TABLE 5.1
Various dream events and the percentage of people reporting them

Event	Percentage Reporting It
Falling	83
Being attacked or chased	77
Trying again and again to do something	71
School teachers; studying	71
Sexual experiences	66
Arriving too late	64
Eating	62
A loved person is dead	56

settings. Bizarre or exotic environments are rare, whereas settings such as living rooms, automobiles, streets, fields, and grocery stores are common. The characters in the dreams analyzed usually included the dreamer, and 85% included characters in addition to the dreamer. Of those characters 43% were strangers (though they may have *represented* someone the dreamer knew), 37% were friends or acquaintances, and 19% were family members. Hall also found that when emotions were remembered from dreams 64% were negative (apprehension, anger, sadness) and only 18% positive (happiness). Paradoxically, when people were asked to rate their dreams as a whole, they rated more as pleasant (41%) than unpleasant (25%).

Both commonplace activities and threatening or frustrating situations are often found in the dreams of college students. Griffith and his co-workers (1958) asked 250 college students to answer "Yes" or "No" to statements like "Have you ever dreamed of eating?" Some of the more common responses, showing the percentage of students answering "Yes," are shown in Table 5.1.

What can we conclude from these data? One conclusion is that the characters and settings in dreams are much more commonplace than we might have supposed. Perhaps we are more likely to remember our fantastic dreams, so we erroneously think that most dreams have these qualities. These data do not, however, address an important characteristic of many dreams. Even though settings and characters in most dreams may be commonplace, the elements of the dream's story often follow each other in a strange and illogical progression. This quality of dreams, more than their actual content or setting, may be responsible for our feeling that many dreams are bizarre.

Theories of Dreaming

Having explored some of the characteristics of dreams, we still need to know why they occur. A number of theories pose intriguing explanations, but none can be regarded as proved. Let's take a brief look at some psychologists' suggestions.

8   THINKING

Dreams as information processing or problem solving.   Dreams are clearly a form of mental activity, a fact that has led to some cognitive theories of dreaming. Some propose that dreams serve an *information-processing function,* helping us sort out memories of the day's events (Foulkes, 1985; Palumbo, 1978), or that they serve a *problem-solving function,* helping us creatively work through problems (Adler, 1936; Cartwright, 1977, 1978; Dreistadt, 1971).

Dreams as responses to neural signals.   According to a number of theories, dreams are the brain's attempt to make sense of the bursts of electrical signals that occur during sleep (Lavie & Hobson, 1986). Allen Hobson and Robert

McCarley hypothesized that the cortex "makes the best of a bad job in producing . . . partially coherent dream imagery from the relatively noisy signals sent up to it from the brain stem" (1977, p. 1347). According to this idea, the cortex creates dreams from basically meaningless random neural discharges originating in the brain stem. Any meaning that the dream has is created by the cortex from these random discharges.

Martin Seligman and Amy Yellen (1987), who share the same assumptions, point out that the rapid eye movements that occur during dreaming are often accompanied by activity in the visual cortex. They suggest that the brain creates dreams in an attempt to make sense of visual hallucinations created by those bursts of cortical activity.

Dreams as wish fulfillment.   Sigmund Freud (1900/1953) explained dreams as **wish fulfillment**—wishes that the dreamer would like to see fulfilled. For example, when a young man whose girlfriend has been in another city for a few weeks dreams that he and his girlfriend are together, he is expressing his wish to be with her. In this example, the wish is expressed in a straightforward way in the dream. In many dreams, however, wish fulfillment is a far less obvious feature. Thus, Freud devised a way to explain dreams with less obvious meanings. His explanation is worth exploring in some detail, not because it is any more correct than more recent theories of dreaming, but because it has been highly influential in our culture. Moreover, an explanation of Freud's theory serves to introduce an important idea: just because a theory is ingenious does not mean that it is correct.

Freud's explanation of hard-to-interpret dreams.   How does Freud explain dreams that are confusing, disjointed, and difficult to understand? According to Freud, these dreams occur because the dreamer's thoughts are unacknowledged wishes that are unacceptable and therefore potentially dangerous to her or him. Examples of such thoughts are wishes to harm another person, wishes to have a relationship with someone who is unattainable, or wishes to leave a present relationship. Because of the dangerous nature of these thoughts, they are pushed out of the conscious part of the mind into the **unconscious,** where they are hidden from awareness. Our ability to push dangerous material into the unconscious, which Freud called **repression,** is strong enough to keep it there during waking hours, but during sleep the repressed material surfaces in our dreams. Before these thoughts appear in a dream, however, they are transformed by a process called **dream work** into a distorted form that protects us from becoming aware of the dangerous material.

According to Freud, then, dangerous thoughts exist in their original form in the unconscious and appear in disguised form in dreams. It follows that dreams have two levels of meaning. The surface level is the content of the dream as we would describe it to another person. Freud called this the **manifest dream.** The dream's deeper meaning consists of the unconscious thoughts that underlie the dream we remember. Freud called these thoughts the **latent dream.** It follows that if we could decode the "language" of dream work, we could uncover the *latent content* of a dream and in this way expose the thoughts that lie hidden in the unconscious. It was for this reason that Freud called dreams "the royal road to the unconscious" (see Figure 5.11).

How did Freud determine a dream's latent content? In two ways. One is through a process called **association,** in which the dream is broken into small components and the dreamer asked to think of as many associations with each component as possible. For example, if a man dreamed about riding a horse, Freud would ask him what things he associated with horses. As the man talked about those thoughts, he might remember, for example, a situation in which he met a young woman while horseback riding. This woman was someone he fell in love with, but who rejected him. Through the process of association, it would

FIGURE 5.11
Freud's method of determining a dream's content. Association: The dreamer creates associations for parts of the dream. A dream with a manifest content about horses may have a latent content about love. Symbolism: The therapist determines what the dream symbols represent. The examples shown here are symbols for male and female sex organs.

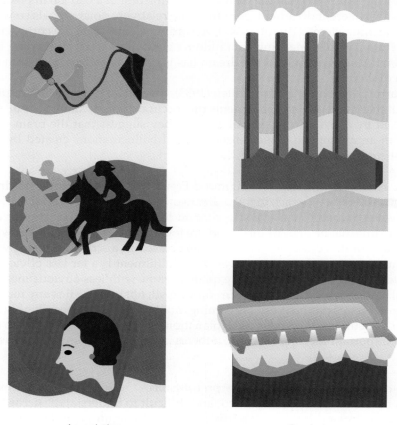

Associations   Symbols

eventually become clear that the man's dream about horses was really a dream about his unrequited love for this woman.

The second way to decode the latent content is through an analysis of the manifest dream's symbolism. The manifest content contains many symbols, which represent the dream's latent content. Freud proposed that many of these symbols are erotic, because he believed that hidden thoughts are often erotic wishes. Thus, Freud interpreted sharp weapons and long objects such as trees, sticks, and chimneys as symbolizing the male genital organs; hollow objects such as cupboards, boxes, or ovens as representing the female genital organs; and staircases, running upstairs, or riding horses as representing sexual intercourse. Applying these symbols to the man's dream about riding horses, Freud might hypothesize that the man's dream about the woman also indicated that he had a desire to have sex with her.

What if the meanings of the symbols that appear in dreams aren't so obvious? When this happens, we fall back on the process of association to decode the symbols in the dream. Freud (1900/1953) gives as an example a woman who dreamed that she saw her sister's only surviving child lying dead, in the same surroundings where years earlier she had seen the dead body of her sister's first child. How does a dead child symbolize an erotic wish? By eliciting the woman's associations to parts of the dream, Freud concluded that the dream was really about her love for a man with whom she had spoken at the first child's funeral many years before. Her wish was to see that man again, something that could occur at the funeral of the second child. This illustrates how association can be used to understand symbols with nonobvious meanings.

Testing Freud's theory.   Freud's wish fulfillment theory offers both a rationale for the strangeness of many dreams and a way to determine the meanings of those dreams. In addition, Freud's dream theory fits nicely into his overall theory that the mind is divided into conscious and unconscious components.

But how can we judge whether Freud's theory is correct? As the "dead child" dream shows, Freud's dream analysis could be extremely clever. However, someone with a different theory might propose a completely different interpretation that seems equally plausible. Thus, Freud's ability to devise clever dream interpretations does not in itself prove the correctness of his theory. What we need is some means of determining whether the dream really means what the interpretation says it means.

One way to evaluate Freud's theory would be to design an experiment to determine whether there is a relationship between people's unconscious wishes and their dreams. The difficulty with this proposal should be readily apparent. If dangerous wishes are hidden in the unconscious and the meaning of dreams disguised, we have no objective way of determining either the person's wishes *or* the latent meaning of the dream. In other words, we have no way of measuring the variables. Freud's theory has proved so difficult to test that there have been very few attempts to do so during the more than 90 years since he proposed it. Other than some experiments showing that people tend to dream about what they are deprived of (hungry people dream about food, for example) (O'Neil, 1965), no one has been able to provide evidence that supports or refutes Freud's theory.

Freud's idea that unconscious processes influence our lives, and in particular our dreams, has influenced many types of psychological therapies, as well as fields outside of psychology such as painting and literature. It is important to distinguish, however, between people's readiness to accept and use an idea and the existence of persuasive evidence to support it. Today most psychologists do not accept Freud's theory—even if they admire its cleverness—because of the lack of evidence for it.

The fact that there are a number of theories of dreaming—none of which is widely accepted—is a testament to the difficulty of studying a response (the cognitive activity of dreaming) that occurs while a person is asleep. Dreams, like many other behaviors, are cognitive processes that can be studied at a number of levels of analysis: behaviorally, by describing people's dreaming activity; biologically, by looking for connections between physiology and dreaming; and cognitively, by attempting to understand the mental processes that occur during dreaming. In the Follow-Through at the end of this chapter, we will see that context, in the form of the dreamer's culture, also influences dreams. Unlocking the secret of dreaming will require research at each of the four levels of analysis.

From our discussion so far we have seen that consciousness is synonymous with change. The changes we have focused on so far—those associated with circadian cycles and the stages of sleep—are naturally occurring changes that everyone experiences. We now look at a variation in consciousness that all people have *not* experienced: hypnosis.

Hypnosis: The Power of Suggestion

I vividly remember my first contact with hypnosis. I was about 11 or 12, attending summer camp. The evening program featured a hypnotist. He brought a volunteer up to the stage and somehow put him into what seemed to be a trance. The amazing thing to me was that the hypnotized boy did whatever the hypnotist requested. I distinctly remember being both amused and disturbed as my camp mate imitated a dog, convincingly crawling around on all fours and barking, without seeming the slightest bit embarrassed.

FIGURE 5.12
A 17th-century hypnotist "mesmerizing" a patient, in this case without the aid of iron rods.

I came away from that program confused about what had happened that night. Questions such as the following went through my mind: "Is what I saw real or was the volunteer an accomplice of the hypnotist?" "If it is real, what does it feel like to be hypnotized?" "Can I be hypnotized?" "If I learned the technique, could I get people to do whatever I wanted them to do?"

The questions I thought of occur to many people after observing someone being hypnotized, and researchers have asked them as well. In our discussion of hypnosis we will look at *how* psychologists have addressed these questions as well as what they have found out.

The Scientific Study of Hypnosis

Scientific interest in hypnosis can be traced back to the 1700s (Figure 5.12). Often as many as 30 people would stand in a trough filled with iron filings and glass bottles as Anton Mesmer (1734–1815), a Viennese physician, "magnetized" them by touching them with an iron rod, by placing his hands on their bodies, and by staring at them. Mesmer was applying a principle he called *animal magnetism*, reflecting his belief that magnetic forces could cure physical and psychological ailments. The results of this "treatment," which came to be called *mesmerism*, were apparently dramatic to behold: many of Mesmer's patients reacted with violent convulsions, hysterical laughter, and trancelike states.

Although Mesmer's procedures were highly questionable and were much ridiculed by the scientific community, the fact that many of his patients went into a trancelike state impressed the Scottish physician James Braid. Braid felt that these trances represented a state of "nervous sleep," which could be achieved by simply having patients concentrate their attention on a single point. When he had patients do this, Braid found that they became very responsive to his suggestions. He named this phenomenon **hypnosis,** after Hypnos, the Greek god of sleep.

Braid's modification of Mesmer's techniques, which brought respectability to hypnosis, became known as a way to induce a state of consciousness in which the subject became highly suggestible. A modern definition of hypnosis emphasizes both this suggestibility and the interaction between the hypnotist and subject: *"Hypnosis may be defined as a social interaction in which one person (designated the subject) responds to suggestions offered by another person (designated the hypnotist) for experiences involving alterations in perception, memory, and voluntary action"* (Kihlstrom, 1985, pp. 385–386).

Following the organization we used for dreams, we will first look at some of the basic phenomena of hypnosis, focusing primarily on what happens to a person who is hypnotized. We will then consider theories that purport to explain hypnosis, and will see that, as for dreams, no one explanation has been accepted by all researchers.

What Happens to a Person Who Is Hypnotized?

What exactly are the alterations in perception, memory, and voluntary action that occur as the result of hypnosis? How are those alterations achieved? A person being hypnotized is often told to concentrate on an object such as a swinging watch, a spot on the wall, or something the hypnotist is holding in his or her hand. The hypnotist offers a suggestion, such as "You are feeling sleepy; your eyelids are getting heavy." The main goal is to get the subject to relax, to let his or her barriers down, and to accept the hypnotist's suggestions.

People show varying degrees of responsiveness to this procedure; only about 10% become highly hypnotized. (See Measurement & Methodology, "The Hypnotic Susceptibility Scale.") Subjects who are susceptible to hypnosis reliably exhibit behaviors such as the following:

1. *Involuntary movements.* Hypnotist's suggestion: "Hold your arm straight

out in front of you. Imagine that a string is tied to your hand and that this string is pulling your arm up toward the ceiling." In response to this suggestion the subject's arm rises, even though the person doesn't feel as if he or she is causing the movement.

2. *Positive hallucinations.* Suggestion: "You see a small green dog sitting on the chair next to you." Subjects "see" the dog without questioning the reasonableness of seeing something as strange as a green dog.

3. *Negative hallucinations.* Suggestion: "There is no one sitting in the chair next to you. It is completely empty." Even though there is, in fact, someone in the chair, subjects see an empty chair.

4. *Age regression.* Suggestion: "You are at your eighth birthday party." Subjects feel as if they are present at the party.

5. *Hypnotic analgesia.* Suggestion: "You have no feeling in your hand. No matter what happens to it you will feel no pain." Subjects show no outward signs of pain even when their hands are placed in a normally painful ice bath. When questioned later, subjects often say that although they felt the pain when under hypnosis, they didn't feel the distress that usually accompanies it. The pain reduction achieved through hypnosis enables some people to undergo surgery without anesthesia (Hilgard & Hilgard, 1983). (Note: *analgesia* means "insensibility to pain.")

MEASUREMENT & METHODOLOGY

The Hypnotic Susceptibility Scale

Not everyone can be hypnotized, and of those who can, some can be hypnotized more deeply than others. Numerous scales have been developed to measure how susceptible people are to hypnosis. One of the most popular is the **Stanford Hypnotic Susceptibility Scale (SHSS)** (Weitzenhoffer & Hilgard, 1959, 1962, 1963), which defines **susceptibility** as *the depth of hypnosis achieved under standard conditions of hypnotic induction* (Hilgard, 1965).

This SHSS was developed by subjecting groups of students to a standard induction procedure such as the eye closure method. In this method, subjects are told to stare at a small target while the hypnotist suggests that they relax, that they are feeling drowsy, and that their eyes will involuntarily close. Following induction, subjects are presented with 12 different suggestions. For example, they are asked to hold their arms in front of them at shoulder height, hands a foot apart, palms inverted. Then it is suggested that the hands are moving involuntarily together as though being moved by an external force. About 70% of college students do this. Harder items include an instruction to place their hands together, intertwining the fingers, followed by the suggestion that the hands have become so tightly locked together that they can't be pulled apart. Only 30% are unable to open their hands. These students are therefore considered more deeply hypnotized, and therefore more highly susceptible, than those who pulled their hands apart. One of the hardest items on the scale is *negative hallucination*, in which subjects are presented with three small boxes and told that they will see only two. Less than 10% of subjects achieve this hallucination.

Scores on the SHSS range from 0 (not hypnotizable) to 12 (strongly hypnotizable). The accompanying figure shows a distri-

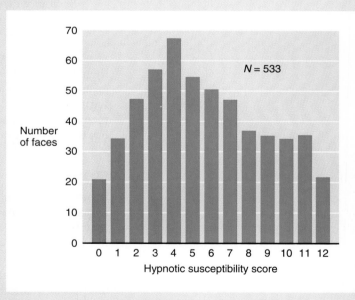

The number of people who earn scores from 0 to 12 on the Stanford Hypnotic Susceptibility Scale. Higher scores indicate greater susceptibility to hypnosis (from Hilgard, 1965).

bution of the scores of 806 students (Hilgard & Hilgard, 1975). The scores indicate that there is a wide variation in hypnotizability, with only a small percentage of people at either extreme.

Two hypnotized men in a carnival show, their bodies rigid in response to the hypnotist's suggestion.

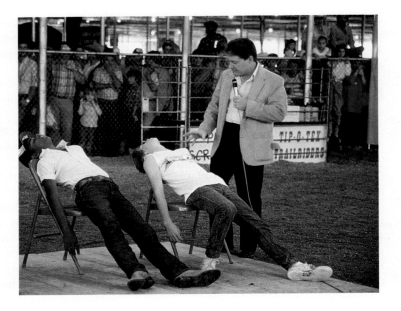

6. *Posthypnotic amnesia.* Suggestion: "When you come out of the trance you will forget everything you have done while under hypnosis. Then when I clap my hands, you will remember everything that happened." Subjects forget everything they have done until they hear the hand clap.

7. *Posthypnotic suggestion.* Suggestion: "After you have come out of the trance I want you to return to your seat. When I say the word *hot*, I want you to take off your jacket." Subjects will remove their jackets in response to the word *hot* without realizing why.

8. *Trance experience.* Many subjects report feeling as if they had been in a state of consciousness different than normal, but they can't explain exactly what they mean by this.

Many of these behaviors certainly appear strange. How can we understand them? Martin Orne (1951), one of the pioneers of modern hypnosis research, suggests that hypnosis creates a type of paradoxical behavior, which he calls **trance logic.** Trance logic enables subjects to be oblivious to paradoxes that they would recognize immediately in everyday experience. Let's consider some of the paradoxes of a hypnotized person's behavior.

Hypnotism as Paradox

Some of the most compelling examples of trance logic occur when subjects are regressed to an earlier age. When Orne regressed subjects to the age of 6 years, they began acting very uninhibited and childlike and drew pictures with childlike characteristics (Figure 5.13). But in many cases their responses did not match those of a 6-year-old. One subject wrote (in childlike printing) "I'm conducting an experiment that will access my psychological capacities" without misspelling one word. In another case, a person who lived in Germany as a child and didn't learn English until he arrived in the United States in his teens described all of the events at his sixth birthday party in English.

Trance logic, in short, is illogical. Does this mean that subjects aren't really hypnotized? On the contrary, the very nature of this illogical behavior makes it unlikely that subjects are "faking" being hypnotized, because we would expect someone who was faking to recognize logical inconsistency and avoid responding in those ways. One way to test this idea is to ask unhypnotized subjects to fake being hypnotized. These subjects, called *simulators,* are told to try to fool the experimenter by pretending to be hypnotized. It turns out that simulators are less likely to exhibit illogical responses than subjects who are actually hypnotized (Spanos et al., 1985).

FIGURE 5.13
Drawings made by a person at age 6 (a) and as a college student hypnotized and regressed to age 6 (b, c, d). Notice that the drawings created under hypnosis are more complex than the drawings made as a child.

Another difference between hypnotized subjects and simulators shows up in their response to the command that they hallucinate an object (positive hallucination). Hypnotized subjects often report that the hallucinated object appears transparent, so they can see things located behind the object. This effect apparently occurs because it is very difficult to create perfectly realistic hallucinations. Simulators, on the other hand, are more likely to report solid hallucinations. In trying to mimic what they think a hypnotized person *would* see, they report perfect rather than imperfect hallucinations (Nash, 1987; Stanley, Lynn, & Nash, 1986).

These examples show that the behavior of hypnotized subjects differs from the behavior of people faking being hypnotized. But if hypnotized subjects aren't faking, what *are* they doing? What, exactly, is the mechanism behind hypnosis?

Theories of Hypnosis

The mechanism responsible for hypnosis remains a matter of debate among researchers. Unlike sleep, for which physiological responses in the form of brain waves have been identified, no specific physiological response has been associated with hypnosis. Hypotheses about the nature of hypnosis therefore work at the behavioral and cognitive levels of analysis, as they look at the *behaviors* that occur during hypnosis and the *cognitions* that may accompany those behaviors. These hypotheses range from the idea that hypnosis creates an altered state of consciousness to the idea that people who are hypnotized are playing a role designed to please the hypnotist (Kihlstrom & McConkey, 1990).

Hypnosis as an altered state of consciousness.   Is hypnosis an altered state of consciousness? As we saw earlier, hypnotized people report *feeling* they are in a trance state. However, as we have no direct access to people's feelings, these reports are not conclusive. More convincing evidence for the idea that hypnosis is an altered state of consciousness is the fact that hypnotized subjects can undergo major surgery without feeling pain (Hilgard & Hilgard, 1983).

Hypnosis as dissociation.   We often carry out well-practiced behaviors without thinking about what we are doing. For example, people who drive a car with a stick shift rarely think about shifting—they just do it, often while listening to the radio, talking to someone else, or thinking about something totally unrelated to driving. In fact, many drivers have had the experience of driving many miles while lost in thought and then suddenly realizing their lack of consciousness of the road and traffic conditions.

Hilgard (1973) and others before him (Janet, 1889) have called phenomena such as this **dissociation,** in which a set of mental processes becomes separated from the rest of the person's mind and functions independently. Hilgard argues that dissociation of a stronger sort occurs in hypnosis, with one part of the person's mind carrying out the hypnotist's commands and another part—which Hilgard calls the **hidden observer**—watching what is happening. Hilgard maintains that the following experiment demonstrates this dissociation effect.

1. A hypnotized subject is told that she will feel no pain in her left hand and arm.
2. The subject is then told that she will be completely unaware of her right hand.
3. The subject's *left* hand and forearm are immersed in circulating ice water for 45 seconds. In response to the ice water the subject's heart rate goes up—the normal physiological reaction to this painful stimulus. The subject, however, remains passive and shows no sign that she is feeling pain. If asked, she will say that the ice water is not painful. According to Hilgard, this is the hypnotized part of the person's mind talking.
4. The subject is told to signal how much pain there is by pushing a button with her *right* hand.
5. The right hand indicates, by pushing the button, that the left hand is experiencing a substantial amount of pain. As the subject has been told that she will be unaware of her right hand, this response is the subject's hidden observer talking.

About 40 to 50% of highly hypnotizable subjects have access to this hidden observer. For these subjects, hypnotism appears to create a "split" or "dissociation" of the mind into two parts, one that is hypnotized and one that is observing the results of the hypnotism. For example, one subject explained after the ice water experiment that the water was so cold that it ordinarily would have been very painful, but that it didn't bother her at all (Hilgard, 1977; Hilgard & Hilgard, 1983).

Hypnosis as a social role.   Most hypnosis researchers accept one or both of the two descriptions just outlined. Some, however, offer a sociopsychological explanation. They see hypnotic behavior as the subject's response to the *demand characteristics* of the situation (see Chapter 2). According to this idea, subjects want to please the hypnotist by being "good" hypnotic subjects, so they enact

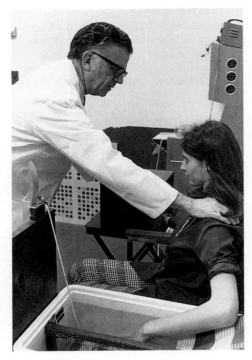

Ernest Hilgard carrying out a dissociation experiment in which the subject's left hand and arm are immersed in a painful ice bath.

18   SOCIAL

the social role of "being hypnotized" to the best of their ability. This does not mean that they are faking being hypnotized, because they may be totally convinced they are.

A group of researchers headed by Nicholas Spanos (1986) has conducted many experiments designed to support this explanation. One such experiment studied hypnotic amnesia, in which subjects are instructed to forget something they have previously learned. Subjects highly susceptible to hypnosis not only became unable to recall material when asked to repeat it, but persisted in their amnesia even when experimenters gave them clues to help them remember, exhorted them to be honest, and hooked them up to lie detectors and asked them to recall the material (Spanos, De Groot et al., 1985).

According to the role-playing hypothesis of hypnosis this persistent amnesia occurs because subjects *believe* that deeply hypnotized subjects do not recall material they have been told to forget. To support this idea Spanos, with Lorraine Radtke and Lorne Bertrand (1985), had subjects learn six words and then told them to forget them while under hypnosis. When asked to recall the words, the subjects were unable to do so, even when asked to be honest. But then Spanos took the experiment a step farther by using a variation on Hilgard's "hidden observer" procedure. He told the subjects they possessed a hidden self that was aware of everything in their minds, even the words they had been told to forget. When Spanos then told the "hidden self" to speak, the subjects repeated the words with 100% accuracy. Why did they suddenly remember what they could not recall before? According to Spanos, they did because the hypnotist led them to believe that good hypnotic subjects have hidden selves that have access to information.

Despite these results, many researchers disagree with the role-playing explanation of hypnotic effects. As they point out, it is hard to imagine that someone undergoing major surgery with hypnosis as their only anesthetic would report feeling no pain just to please the hypnotist (Orne, 1987). So far, then, there is no agreement on the mechanism responsible for hypnotic behavior. There is agreement, however, that whatever the mechanism responsible for hypnotism, it represents yet another way that our consciousness can vary from our already variable "normal" waking consciousness. In addition, hypnosis has found practical application in both medicine, where it has been used in place of chemical anesthesia, and criminal justice, where (as we will see in the Interdisciplinary Dimension) the use of hypnosis has proved sometimes useful and sometimes controversial.

INTERDISCIPLINARY DIMENSION CRIMINAL JUSTICE

Hypnotism and the Law

Chowchilla, California, July 15, 1977: Twenty-six schoolchildren and a bus driver are abducted at gunpoint by masked men driving vans. The driver and the children, many of them hysterical, are herded into the vans and transferred to a remote rock quarry, where they are sealed inside an underground tomb. After much frantic effort, the driver and two of the children dig their way out.

After this harrowing experience, the bus driver was questioned by the police to see if he could remember anything that might lead them to the kidnappers. Although the driver had tried to memorize the license numbers of the vans, his memory was hazy and he couldn't recall them. Eager to help apprehend the kidnappers, the driver agreed to be hypnotized to see whether it could help him remember what he saw. While under the influence of hypnosis, the driver was age-regressed back to the afternoon of the kidnapping and asked to imagine himself sitting in his favorite chair watching the events unfold as a documentary film on a TV screen. As he was doing this he suddenly called out two license plate numbers. One, with the exception of one digit, matched the number of one of the vans, thereby helping solve the case. The kidnappers were caught, convicted, and sentenced to life imprisonment (Kroger & Douce, 1979).

7   MEMORY

In the Chowchilla case, hypnosis was used successfully as an investigative tool to uncover clues that led to the apprehension of criminals. This is not, however, the only way that law enforcement officials have used hypnosis. Hypnosis has been used in situations in which some aspects of the crime are known, a suspect has already been identified, and a witness, whose memory about the crime is unclear, is trying to remember more details about what happened. In this kind of application there is a real danger that hypnosis can lead to misinformation and perhaps a miscarriage of justice.

One danger lies in the common perception that hypnotized people always tell the truth, and that the new memories uncovered while subjects are under hypnosis are always accurate. The fact is that people can and do create inaccurate information when under hypnosis, and many of their new "memories" often prove erroneous.

Jane Dywan and Kenneth Bowers (1983) conducted an experiment in which they showed that newly recalled material elicited under hypnosis is often inaccurate. They had subjects view a series of slides and then try to recall as many as possible. On the average, subjects recalled only 38 of the 60 slides they were shown. Dywan and Bowers then hypnotized the subjects and tried to get them to recall more slides. The subjects did, in fact, recall an average of five additional slides under hypnosis; however, an average of four of those five were incorrect. This result is analogous to what happens when nonhypnotized eyewitnesses are prodded to remember more details about a crime. Eyewitnesses prompted in this way *do* remember more details, but many are inaccurate (Hilgard & Loftus, 1979). Apparently, memories retrieved under hypnosis work the same way.

Perhaps the most dangerous thing about the use of hypnosis in court cases is the possibility that the hypnotist's suggestions will create erroneous **pseudomemories**— events the hypnotized person "remembers" as having happened but that never actually did. Consider the following scenario suggested by Martin Orne (1979): On the evening of February 17 a crime was committed outside of Esther's window. The police believe that two shots were fired at about 4:00 A.M. in connection with the crime. It would be helpful to their case if the occurrences of those shots could be verified by a witness. When questioned, Esther can't remember hearing anything, but she agrees to undergo hypnosis in the hope that she will be able to remember what, if anything, she heard during that night.

The hypnotist age-regresses Esther back to the night of February 17, and she begins reliving it. The hypnotist then asks Esther whether at 4:00 A.M. she heard any loud noises. She answers "Yes" and proceeds to describe, in great detail, how she got out of bed and went across the room to the window to see what was happening. After that, Esther is brought out of hypnosis and she is questioned about her memories of the night of February 17. When questioned this time, she now remembers hearing some loud noises during the night, and when asked when she heard those noises, she answers "At 4:00 A.M."

But did Esther really hear the shots? Her sense that she heard some noises may have come not from actually hearing noises and remembering them with the aid of hypnosis, but rather from a pseudomemory created by the hypnotist's question.

There is good experimental evidence that this effect can occur. Jean-Roche Laurence and C. Perry (1983) put 27 subjects under hypnosis and asked them to try to remember the events of a previous night. Just as in the case of Esther, they asked each subject whether they had heard some loud noises during the night. Although it had been determined beforehand that each of the subjects had slept soundly through the night in question, after coming out of hypnosis 13 of the 27 claimed that they had really heard loud noises during the night. Even when told that these "noises" had been suggested by the hypnotist, many of them stuck steadfastly by their story. One subject stated, "I'm pretty certain I head them. As a matter of fact, I'm pretty damned certain. I'm positive I heard these noises" (p. 524).

It's easy to imagine a witness in a real court case testifying in the most convincing way that she really did hear shots, when in fact the "memory" of the shots was planted by a hypnotist's suggestion. In an article titled "The Use and Misuse of Hypnosis in Court," Martin Orne (1979) cites a number of examples of actual court cases in which the misuse of hypnosis almost resulted in a miscarriage of justice.

Clearly, the Chowchilla case shows that hypnosis has proved a valuable investigative tool. But as a way to improve witnesses' memories, it must be used with extreme caution (Greene, 1986; Mingay, 1987). For this reason, a task force of the American Medical Association (1986) has recommended that it is appropriate to use hypnosis as part of the investigative process, but that it should not be used to influence subjects who may later testify in court.

Hypnosis illustrates a change in consciousness that has been fruitfully studied at the cognitive and behavioral levels of analysis. Because no physiological changes have been found in hypnotized subjects, the explanation of hypnosis apparently lies in cognitive processes, situational influences, or their combination. The case is different with another type of change in consciousness—the "mind-altering" effects of certain drugs. Researchers working at the biological level of analysis have been able to discover many of the physiological mechanisms that underlie the experiences drugs produce. Thus, considering drug effects gives us a chance to look at how events at the synapse can change a person's consciousness.

Drugs: Changing Consciousness at the Synapse

Drugs, more than any other way to change consciousness, elicit strong reactions from people. The reason for these reactions is that drugs are a major social problem. Drugs are the second leading cause of suicide in the United States; half of our highway fatalities can be traced to alcohol or drug use; 80% of lung cancer can be traced to cigarette smoking; and, as anyone who keeps up with the news is aware, crime due to the use of drugs such as cocaine, crack cocaine, and heroin has long been a major problem in our cities (Sarafino, 1990).

The social implications of drug use make it all the more important that we understand drugs from a psychological point of view. As we did with dreams, we'll organize our discussion by answering some common questions about drugs.

What Kinds of Drugs Are There?

There are a number of types of drugs. Drugs such as antibiotics fight disease, drugs like aspirin or cold remedies control disease symptoms, and drugs such as alcohol or cocaine have an effect on people's mental processes and behavior. This last class, called *psychoactive drugs,* is what we are concerned with here. A **psychoactive drug** is "any chemical that alters the workings of the human mind" (Goode, 1984). This definition embraces illegal substances such as cocaine, heroin, and marijuana as well as legal substances such as nicotine, caffeine, and alcohol: they all alter the workings of the mind.

The many types of drugs in use today can be grouped in five major categories based on their action on the central nervous system and their behavioral effects.

Stimulants.   Drugs that increase activity in the nervous system are **stimulants;** examples are amphetamine, cocaine, nicotine, and caffeine. Amphetamines were once popular as diet pills. However, tolerance rapidly develops, so dosages must be increased to levels that cause agitation. This effect, combined with the fact that their use has been severely restricted by the federal government, has essentially eliminated amphetamines as a hunger suppressant. Amphetamine is abused under the street name "speed."

Cocaine, once widely used as a local anesthetic, was contained in Coca-Cola until the 1920s and was thought to be a relatively harmless drug in the 1960s and 1970s. Recent evidence, however, indicates that cocaine use can cause heart and liver problems, and that a single large dose of cocaine can cause death even in occasional users.

Nicotine and caffeine, the most widely used psychoactive drugs, are potent drugs when ingested in high concentrations. Nicotine has been linked to increased incidences of birth defects and lung cancer.

Depressants.   **Depressants** decrease activity in the nervous system; they include alcohol, barbiturates, and tranquilizers. Alcohol, used as an anesthetic until the late 19th century, is one of the most destructive drugs both because of its health effects (heavy use can lead to heart and liver problems and the permanent memory loss described in the opening to Chapter 3) and because it leads to increased risk of driving accidents—seven out of ten males killed in traffic accidents are legally drunk (Goode, 1984).

Barbiturates such as Nembutal and Seconal are prescribed as tranquilizers to reduce anxiety and as sleeping pills to induce sleep. The sleep induced by barbiturates contains less REM, so discontinuing barbiturate use can lead to REM rebound, which causes difficulty in sleeping and irritability. Withdrawal from high doses of barbiturates can be extremely dangerous, leading to life-threatening convulsions.

The tranquilizers Valium and Librium, which are used to reduce anxiety, are two of the most widely prescribed drugs in the United States. These drugs have been commonly used in suicide attempts, a disproportionate number of them by women (Julien, 1981).

Opiates.   **Opiates** are "hard" narcotics: heroin, morphine, and opium, for instance. These drugs are derived from the opium poppy. Opium and its derivatives, morphine and heroin, have been used for thousands of years; opium cakes and candies were commonly available on the streets of ancient Greece. The wide use of morphine for pain relief in the Civil War caused many soldiers to become addicted. Opiates were common ingredients in many of the patent medicines and tonics popular in the late 19th and early 20th centuries, until they were outlawed in 1914. These drugs create an extremely pleasurable "rush" of sensation followed by feelings of contentment.

Hallucinogens.   Other drugs have the potential to cause hallucinations. **Hallucinogens** such as LSD (lysergic acid diethylamide) and mescaline became popular in the 1960s, when they were commonly referred to as *psychedelic* drugs and were said to have "mind-expanding" properties. The psychological effects of LSD were discovered in 1943 when it was accidentally ingested by chemist Albert Hoffman, who, in his diary entry for April 16, 1943, described his experience as causing "a peculiar sensation of vertigo and restlessness. Objects, as well as the shape of my associates in the laboratory, appeared to undergo optical changes. . . . With my eyes closed, fantastic pictures of extraordinary plasticity and intensive color seemed to surge toward me" (LeDain, 1970). These drugs can sometimes have fearful effects, such as those experienced by Dr. Hoffman when

Distorted colors and an other-worldly feeling are typically experienced under the influence of hallucinogenic drugs such as LSD or mescaline.

he ingested a second, larger dose of LSD. He was overcome by a fear that he was going out of his mind, and thought that he had died. The potential for these kinds of experiences often discourages repeated usage of this drug. Other hallucinogens such as mescaline are used in more moderate quantities in religious ceremonies of North, Central, and South American Indians.

Marijuana.   Marijuana is derived from the hemp plant *cannabis sativa;* its active ingredient, THC, is responsible for its mind-altering effects. Because THC is a powerful hallucinogen, marijuana is sometimes classed as a hallucinogen. However, since typical dosages of marijuana usually do not cause hallucinations, it is often placed in a class by itself (Abadinsky, 1989; Goode, 1989). Marijuana is the most frequently used of the illegal psychoactive drugs. Its effects are relatively weak compared with those of many other drugs, and research regarding its effects on health has been contradictory, some studies reporting adverse effects and others not (Akers, 1992; Goode, 1989). Studies of long-term marijuana use in Jamaica, Costa Rica, and Greece have failed to find evidence for physical or psychological damage (Rubin & Comitas, 1976; Stefanis, Dornbush, & Fink, 1977), but there is some evidence that chronic use of marijuana can cause lung damage (Goode, 1989) and that high doses of marijuana can impair driving performance.

Table 5.2 indicates the primary behavioral effects of typical drugs in each

TABLE 5.2
Characteristics of drugs

Drug	Behavioral Effects	Physical Dependence	Tolerance
Stimulants			
Amphetamines	Alertness, euphoria, increased energy; high-dosage/long-term: extreme euphoria, manic behavior, delusions, hallucinations, psychosis	Yes	Yes
Cocaine	Increased energy, self-confidence, euphoria; high-dosage/long-term: similar to amphetamines; "cocaine bugs": feeling that bugs are crawling under the skin	No[*]	Yes[†]
Nicotine	Increased arousal and alertness possible, but also increased relaxation	Maybe	Yes (slight)
Caffeine	Increased energy, alertness, motor and mental efficiency	No	No (at usual dose)
Depressants			
Alcohol	Relaxation, release of inhibition, reduced anxiety (at low doses), loss of motor control, decrease in judgment, stupor (at higher doses)	Yes	Yes
Tranquilizers	Decreased anxiety and emotional responsiveness	Yes[†]	Yes
Barbiturates	Mild euphoria, reduced anxiety, drowsiness, impaired speech and motor function, sleep	Yes[†]	Yes
Opiates			
Morphine, heroin	Initial euphoric rush followed by relaxation and feeling of contentment; pain reduction	Yes	Yes
Hallucinogens			
LSD, mescaline	Hallucinations; changes in perception of taste, odor, color, light, and sound, changed time perception, feelings of well-being, panic, or fear (depending on situation)	No	Yes
Marijuana			
Marijuana	Mild euphoria, light-headedness, sensory changes, altered time perception, slower reaction time, impairment of short-term memory	No	No

[*] Although cocaine has been pictured in the media as causing physical dependence, research indicates that it doesn't, because withdrawal symptoms do not occur (Akers, 1992). Nonetheless, there is a great deal of evidence that cocaine has a high potential for abuse, that some users have great difficulty quitting, and that there is a danger of death from cardiac seizures even if use is only occasional.

[†] At high doses and/or with prolonged use

category, whether the drug creates a physical dependence, and whether tolerance develops to the effects of the drug. We will consider physical dependence and tolerance in more detail as we answer some further questions about drugs.

Why Do People Use Drugs?

There is no simple answer to the question of why people use drugs. Actually, there are so many answers that one publication of the National Institute on Drug Abuse devoted 488 pages to describing the major views on this question (Lettieri, Sayers, & Pearson, 1980).

One theory states that people use drugs because they become physically dependent on them. **Physical dependence,** which is associated with many of the drugs in Table 5.2, occurs when the drug causes changes in the body's cells so that the body must have periodic doses of the drug to function normally. Physiological dependence is indicated when stopping use of the drug results in **withdrawal symptoms:** nausea, disorientation, hallucinations, or convulsions. The physical dependence theory of drug usage states that people continue using drugs to avoid experiencing the withdrawal symptoms. This idea is, however, not accepted as a complete explanation for drug usage, because withdrawal is actually not that bad for many drugs—in some cases it resembles no more than a bad case of the flu—and because, despite the unpleasantness of withdrawal, many drug users take "vacations" from drug use and then return to it again.

Other theories of drug use emphasize people's social situation. The fact that drug use is more prevalent among people with few family ties has led some to link drug usage to a person's lack of societal values and respect for the law (Elliott, Huizinga, & Ageton, 1985). Another hypothetical social factor is people's desire to be accepted by groups. To obtain social approval, a person who is rejected by peers who are not drug users may turn to groups who do use drugs. Drug usage, according to this view, is tied to a search for acceptance and self-esteem (Gottfredson & Hirschi, 1990; Kaplan et al., 1986). Or a person might be attracted to the personal values or political beliefs of people in drug-using groups, and associating with those people naturally leads to drug use. A theory favored by many psychologists is the *social learning theory* of drug usage (Akers, 1985). That theory states that people use drugs because of the rewards they derive from doing so. One reward is the pleasurable effect of the drug (notice in Table 5.2 how many drugs result in positive behavioral effects); other rewards are tied to social factors such as being accepted by peers (Akers, 1992; White, Bates, & Johnson, 1990). Which of these theories is correct? Probably all of them. As James Inciardi (1986) points out, "There are as many reasons for using drugs as there are individuals who use drugs." Thus, no one theory is likely to explain the behavior of all drug users.

Why Do People Sometimes Increase the Amount of Drugs They Use?

It is a common observation that people who are habitual drug users take larger and larger doses as they continue their drug use. The reason is that they have developed a tolerance for the drug. **Tolerance** is a state of progressively decreasing responsiveness to a drug, so a user requires more of it to achieve the same effect. Thus, some habitual drug users may take doses that are 10 to 20 times greater than those taken by occasional users. In fact, sometimes these dosages are high enough to kill an occasional user.

Why does tolerance occur? Answers to this question have come from the biological, contextual, and behavioral levels of analysis. At the biological level, research has shown that drug usage can cause an increase in the concentration of enzymes that deactivate drugs, so continued drug usage can cause neurons in the brain to respond less to the drug. Because of these physiological mechanisms, the user must increase the dose of the drug to get the desired effect. At the contextual and behavioral levels, it has been observed that always taking a drug in the same setting can lead to tolerance. This effect of the setting, which can be explained by learning principles, will be discussed further in Chapter 6.

What Is the Physiological Basis of Drug Action?

3   BIOLOGY

Not all drugs have the same mode of action, but many cause their effects by their action at synapses. To understand how this works, we need to briefly review the basics of synaptic transmission from Chapter 3. When the action potential reaches the end of the axon, it triggers the release of a neurotransmitter. This transmitter, which can be either excitatory or inhibitory, travels across the synapse and stimulates receptor cites on the postsynaptic neuron's cell body. After the transmitter has its effect, it is either deactivated by an enzyme or taken back into the synaptic vesicles, a process called reuptake (Figure 5.14).

Drugs can act at the synapse in a number of ways. The stimulant amphetamine achieves its activating effect by inducing the release of the transmitter norepinephrine (NE). Another stimulant, cocaine, achieves its activating effect by blocking the reuptake of NE, thereby prolonging its existence at the synapse and increasing excitation.

Depressants such as alcohol or barbiturates have an effect opposite to that of the stimulants: they depress synaptic transmission, particularly in the reticular formation, which is responsible for wakefulness. People often wonder why alcohol is classified as a depressant, because they observe that having one or two drinks decreases their inhibitions and makes them more willing to openly express themselves. The reason for this effect is that at low dosages alcohol's depressive effects act mainly on inhibitory synapses in the brain. The result of this suppression of inhibition is excitation, so people become more activated and less inhibited. However, at higher doses, alcohol's depressant effect spreads to excitatory neurons and begins causing the physiological depression that can lead to passing out, coma, and death.

What Is the Relationship Between Drug Dosage and Drug Effects?

This is an important question, because drugs can have vastly different effects at low and high dosages. For example, 10 mg of amphetamine taken as a pill by an occasional user would cause a mild tingling sensation and enhanced alertness, whereas 500 mg injected intravenously causes a "rush" that has been described as an intense, full-body sexual orgasm. These pleasurable effects at high dosages are often followed by fatigue, depression, and feelings of paranoia. We can see from this example that it is important to specify a drug's dosage when we talk about its effects.

Another example of how drug effects depend on dosage is provided by alcohol. We have already described how alcohol can have "stimulant" effects at low doses and "depressant" effects at high doses. Figure 5.15 shows the relationship between the percentage of alcohol in the blood and its behavioral effects.

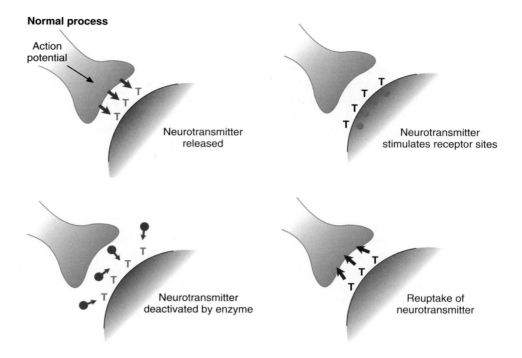

Normal process

Action potential

Neurotransmitter released

Neurotransmitter stimulates receptor sites

Neurotransmitter deactivated by enzyme

Reuptake of neurotransmitter

Action of Amphetamine

No amphetamine

NE NE NE

Norepinephrine released

With amphetamine

NE NE NE NE NE

Increase in norepinephrine released

Action of Cocaine

No cocaine

NE NE

Reuptake of norepinephrine

With cocaine

NE NE

Reuptake of norepinephrine blocked

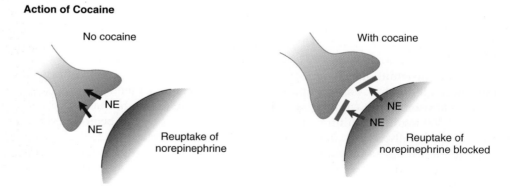

FIGURE 5.14

Synaptic transmission, showing normal processes and how transmission is affected by amphetamines and cocaine.

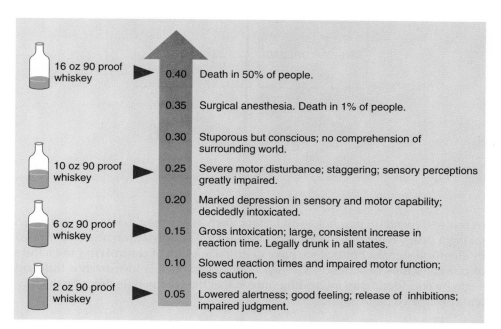

FIGURE 5.15
Behavioral effects of alcohol as a function of dosage

Are All Drug Effects Caused by Their Chemical Action on Neurons?

Although it is clear that the chemical action of drugs on neurons is the primary reason for their effects, there is also a great deal of evidence that psychological factors operating at the behavioral and cognitive levels can affect a person's drug experience. It is well known, for example, that the social setting in which alcohol is consumed can influence its effect. Drinking two or three beers with a group of friends who are having a good time might cause you to become happy and uninhibited, whereas drinking those same two or three beers alone at home might cause you to become thoughtful and introspective. Similarly, it has been reported that the same dose of barbiturate can provide either relief from anxiety or depression or stimulate aggression, depending on the setting in which it is taken (Goode, 1989; Julien, 1981).

Drug effects can also depend on a person's mental set, a cognitive factor. This has been demonstrated by Alan Marlatt and Damaris Rohsenow (1981), who had some of their subjects drink vodka and tonic water and others drink only tonic water. A crucial variable in this experiment was what subjects *thought* they were drinking, because some were misled by the experimenters. Half of the subjects who drank the vodka and tonic water were told they were drinking just tonic water, whereas half of the subjects who drank only tonic water were told that they were drinking vodka and tonic water (because the tonic water masked the vodka taste, those drinking vodka plus tonic water could not tell there was vodka in the drink). As it turned out, the subjects' behavior was determined not by what drink they consumed, but by what drink they *thought* they had consumed. Subjects who thought they were drinking alcohol acted more aggressively and became more sexually aroused than the subjects who thought they were drinking just tonic water. Since the higher aggressiveness and sexual arousal depended on the subjects' belief that they were drinking alcohol—even if they weren't—Marlatt and Rohsenow call their findings the *think-drink* effect.

Our survey of drug effects indicates that drugs, by affecting chemical events at the synapse, can have powerful effects on consciousness. But drug ef-

FIGURE 5.16
A split-brain subject verbally reports seeing only words presented to the right of the fixation dot, because these words are received by the left hemisphere, which in most people is responsible for language.

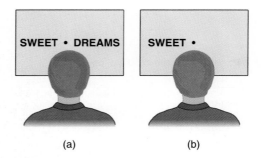

(a)   (b)

fects also depend on psychological factors, such as a person's state of mind when taking a drug. What this means is that we are not simply automatons controlled by chemical signals, but that we have a certain amount of control over the nature of our conscious experience. We will now reflect on this idea from a different angle by considering an interesting outcome of the way people describe the contents of their consciousness.

How Describing Our Experience Can Shape Our Conception of Reality

We opened this chapter by defining reflective consciousness as people's knowledge of their own awareness. In this section, we consider the possibility that this knowledge, which people express when they describe their conscious experience to themselves or others, can itself influence their consciousness.

To understand how this might occur, let's return to a topic we considered in Chapter 3—research on split-brain patients. Recall that people who have undergone a split-brain operation have their left and right hemispheres separated and so are controlled by two separate mental systems with different capabilities. Of particular importance for our discussion is the fact that the mental system in the left hemisphere can create language (so it can talk), whereas the one in the right hemisphere cannot create language (so it is mute). Also remember that the left hemisphere receives information from the right visual field and the right hemisphere receives information from the left visual field. This means that if a split-brain subject were presented with the two words in Figure 5.16a, he would report seeing the word *dreams,* because *dreams*—on the right—is the information being received by the left hemisphere. But when presented with the stimulus in Figure 5.16b, which contains no words in the right visual field, he would say "I don't see anything." What is happening in both of these cases is that the left hemisphere is truthfully reporting the information it received from the right visual field.

This special way that split-brain patients behave, with each hemisphere only registering stimulation in half of the visual field, was used by Michael Gazzaniga, Diana Steen, and B. Volpe (1979) to show how the behavior of a split-brain subject can be influenced by events that occur outside of the subject's awareness. Gazzaniga set up a situation in which the subject's left hemisphere was asked to explain the right hemisphere's actions. First Gazzaniga flashed two pictures onto a screen (see Figure 5.17). The picture of the snow scene, on the left, was received by the right hemisphere; the picture of the chicken's claw, on the right, was received by the left hemisphere. After seeing these pictures, the subject was asked to look at another group of pictures and *point* to the one most

FIGURE 5.17
The split-brain subject points to the snow shovel with his left hand, because the shovel goes with the snow scene, which he saw with his right hemisphere (controls left hand). He points to the chicken with his right hand, because the chicken goes with the claw, which he saw with his left hemisphere (controls right hand).

closely related to the one he saw on the screen. The correct response for the snow scene was a picture of a snow shovel; the correct response for the chicken claw was a picture of a chicken.

The subject accomplished this task easily, but his response depended on which hand did the pointing. With his left hand, controlled by the right hemisphere (which saw the snow scene), he picked the snow shovel. With his right hand, controlled by the left hemisphere (which saw the chicken claw), he picked the chicken.

When Gazzaniga asked him, "Why did you pick the chicken?" the subject, *answering this question verbally with the left hemisphere, which saw the chicken claw,* had no trouble explaining that he had picked the chicken because it went with the chicken claw. But when Gazzaniga asked him why he had picked the snow shovel, the subject's left hemisphere, which must answer because it is the hemisphere that controls language, had a problem: although it had observed the left hand pointing to the shovel, it knew nothing about the snow scene. The left hemisphere solved its problem by saying "I saw a claw so I picked the chicken, and you have to clean out the chicken shed with a shovel." An ingenious solution indeed! The left hemisphere first talked about the picture it saw ("I saw a claw so I picked the chicken"), and then used that information to fabricate a story that would explain why the left hand picked the shovel ("shovels are used to clean chicken sheds"). The left hemisphere, upon observing the right hemisphere's behavior, made up a story to explain it.

What is happening in this split-brain example is that the person's left hemisphere creates an explanation based on the information available to it, and thereby creates a reality that the person believes. But what does this have to do with the consciousness of people who have normal brains? To answer this question let's look at two examples from this chapter. Pseudoinsomnia: A man believes he has been up all night because he has dreamed it, and this belief causes him to be tired all day, even though he had slept soundly. Pseudomemories created by hypnosis: A hypnotist suggests to a woman that she heard shots at 4 A.M., she repeats that assertion when she awakens from the hypnosis, and from that point on, she believes she heard the shots—even though they never happened. In both of these examples the person's reality ("I was awake all night"; "I heard the shots") is determined by their interpretation of the information they have available. This is also the situation for our split-brain subject—interpreting the information available, the split-brain subject made up a story that became part of his reality.

These observations suggest that what we are conscious of is created by the stimuli around us, by what happens to us, *and* by the explanations we create about these stimuli and experiences. Sometimes we may not have complete or accurate information about what is going on, but we nonetheless make up an explanation that seems reasonable, and then that explanation becomes part of our consciousness. As we will see later in this book, this is typical of the way we think in many situations. We often create explanations based on incomplete information, and these explanations, which may sometimes be incorrect, then become part of our reality.

Reprise: Consciousness and Levels of Analysis

As the study of "what goes on in our minds," research into consciousness would seem most appropriately conducted at the cognitive level of analysis. In fact, however, our study of consciousness has made use of each of our four levels. Circadian rhythms have been studied at the behavioral level—in terms of what they mean for our performance—and at the biological level—by asking what brain nuclei control this 24-hour cycling. Sleep has been studied behaviorally by observing people's sleeping behavior and recording their reports of dreams; physiologically, by monitoring brain-wave and other changes; cognitively, by looking at how people's thoughts influence their experience of sleep problems; and contextually, by bringing evolutionary theories to bear on the question of why we sleep.

But perhaps the most dramatic example of how all four levels of analysis can be applied to a single topic is provided by our discussion of drugs. You might have thought at first that drug effects would be explained only in terms of biological mechanisms, because drugs are chemicals that act on the nervous system. But we have seen that such an explanation is far from complete. In addition to molecular events at the synapse (biological level), the effects of drugs can be studied in terms of the kinds of experiences that result from taking different types of drugs (behavioral level), the way people's expectations influence the effects they experience (cognitive level), and how social environments influence whether or not people become drug users (contextual level). Thus, the study of the variations of consciousness created by drugs runs the gamut from the molecular events at the synapse to the societal conditions in which a person lives (Figure 5.18).

Looking at how these different levels of analysis have been applied to variations in consciousness helps us appreciate how far scientific psychology has come since Wundt's and Titchener's attempts to study it via introspection. One reason that the study of consciousness fell into disrepute during the first half of

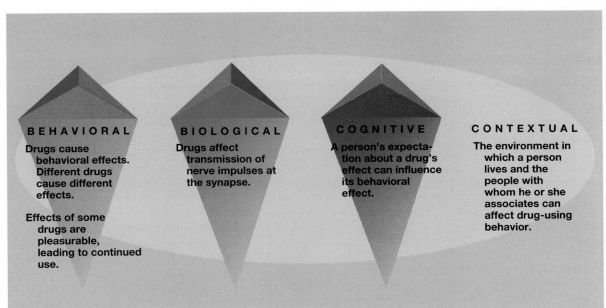

FIGURE 5.18
Levels of analysis applied to the effects of drugs.

this century was that psychologists had not yet figured out how to approach the subject with a variety of tools. "Objectivity" was associated with a single level of analysis, the biological. We now study consciousness at all four levels of analysis, each of which is accepted as making its own contribution to our overall understanding.

Dreams and Culture

Most discussions of the psychology of dreams are based on studies of people in the United States or other Western cultures. But what about dreaming in "traditional" cultures like those of the American Indian and African tribes? How do their dreams compare with ours? What can they tell us about their culture? What is the significance of dreaming in these cultures?

Questions such as these are studied by psychological anthropologists. **Psychological anthropology** is a subfield within anthropology that focuses on how people think, feel, and perceive the world in different cultures (Bourguignon, 1979). Psychological anthropology is closely related to cross-cultural psychology, a subfield of psychology that is also concerned with studying behaviors like thinking, feeling, and perception in different cultures. One difference between these two subfields is the approach they take. Psychological anthropology favors field research, whereas cross-cultural psychology favors experimentation. Thus, a psychological anthropologist might observe people within different cultures and create detailed descriptions of their living patterns. A cross-cultural psychologist would be more likely to administer psychological tests or measure people's performance in behavioral experiments.

The studies of psychological anthropologists are our main source of information about dreams in different cultures. There is, however, only a small amount of information available on this topic. We can appreciate why this is so by imagining the difficulties anthropologists face as they try to be accepted into a culture so they can observe living conditions, food preparation, rituals, and other aspects of cultural life. These difficulties are multiplied many times over when dealing with dream material that is hidden within individuals and that, in some cultures, may have spiritual significance. Despite these difficulties, psychological anthropologists have succeeded in uncovering the following facts about dreaming in different cultures.

Symbolism Occurs Across Cultures, but the Symbols Differ

Just as Freud and others in Western cultures have placed great importance on the symbolic nature of dreams, people in other cultures also use symbols to interpret dreams. However, the symbolism differs from culture to culture. For example, among the *mestizo* peasants of Colombia, dreams about the deaths of relatives, tombs, and flowers are said to predict happiness, and a dream about someone else's death to predict wealth. Similar dreams among the Nuer of Africa and in many other cultures are, however, considered bad omens (Bourguignon, 1979). Among the Hopi Indians in America, dreaming of a water serpent is interpreted as evidence of the dreamer's transgressions or those of others in the dream. In contrast, a snake in Western-culture dreams is often interpreted as a phallic symbol.

Dreams Are Institutionalized in Some Cultures

In North America we may tell a friend about a particularly interesting or meaningful dream, but no societal rules require that we do so. In some cultures, however, dreams are considered so important that the culture creates rules to govern them. In the Hopi Indian culture a person experiencing a bad dream is supposed to immediately awaken a relative and tell him or her about the dream. The dreamer then goes outside and spits four times to be cleansed of the dream. The Navajo treat bad dreams as an illness, using religious ceremonies and medicine to cure the dreamer (Eggan, 1961).

In some cultures the content of a person's dreams determines the person's role in that culture. For example, to become a priest or shaman in some cultures a person must have made dream contact with supernatural powers (D'Andrade, 1961). Another example of the cultural use of dreams occurs among the Trobriand Islanders, who use magic to induce people to have dreams so that the dream will *produce* wishes in the dreamer (Eggan, 1961). This is an interesting reversal of Freud's view of dreams as *indicating* a person's wishes. In contrast, the Trobriand Islanders see dreams as *causing* a person's wishes!

Dreams Reflect the Society the Dreamer Comes From

The environment in which people are raised is obviously going to affect the content of their dreams. City dwellers may dream of automobiles and tall buildings, forest dwellers of wild animals. Robert LeVine's (1966) study of the relationship between dream content and cultural characteristics illustrates the basic tactic of much anthropological research. The goal of research in psychological anthropology is to deduce relationships between some aspect of the culture and behavior. The basic data are a description of the culture and a description of people's behavior. The description of the culture includes child-rearing practices, the economic system, marriage customs, and the nature of the family group. The description of behavior, in this case, would be accounts of people's dreams.

LeVine hypothesized that people in cultures most conducive to individual advancement—where hard work is rewarded—would be more likely to have "achievement dreams" (dreams about making discoveries, being advanced in society, and winning contests) than are people in cultures less conducive to individual advancement. To test this hypothesis he compared the dreams of males in two African tribes: the Ibo, a society in which a person's ability and work is rewarded, and the Hausa, a society in which advancement is based more on political considerations and family connections. LeVine found that achievement dreams were experienced by 43% of the Ibo dreamers but by only 17% of the Hausa

Dream symbolism is found in many cultures, but the meaning of the symbols differs from culture to culture. For example, snakes are often interpreted as a phallic symbol in Western culture but can have many other meanings in other cultures.

dreamers. This supports his prediction of a connection between opportunities for advancement in a culture and the person's dream content.

Studies of such connections between aspects of a culture and dream content can be highly ingenious, as evidenced by Roy D'Andrade's (1961) study of the relationship between family living arrangements and dream content. D'Andrade hypothesized that people in societies that require that newly married couples take up residence in a group separated from the male's parents or in another village would become anxious about being on their own. He further hypothesized that people in these societies would have more dreams about seeking and controlling supernatural powers. His reasoning was that the comfort or aid of supernatural powers would be needed to help the person deal with the anxiety.

To test his hypothesis, D'Andrade surveyed the characteristics of 57 different cultures, using data collected by other researchers, and found that these "supernatural dreams" were common among males in 80% of societies in which the newly married male and his wife moved away from the husband's parents, but in only 27% of cultures in which the couple lived in the family home after marriage.

In evaluating studies like D'Andrade's, it is important to remember that the relationship he observed is correlational. We can't, therefore, say anything about a cause-and-effect relationship between cultural customs about living arrangements and dream content. Another factor, such as the nature of the culture's religion, may be the real cause of the supernatural dreams. Whatever the cause-and-effect relationship in this particular case, there is undoubtedly a relationship between the dreams people have and the culture they live in—a fact that any theory of dreaming must take into account.

- Consciousness is what you are *aware* of; it is accessible to you at any given moment. Some researchers distinguish between perceptual consciousness—perceptions, thoughts, and feelings that are experienced—and reflective consciousness—the awareness that those mental events are being experienced.

Probing Inner States: The Scientific Study of Consciousness

- Conscious experience was one of the first topics of study of the early psychologists. With the rise of behaviorism, research on consciousness waned until, in the 1950s, new research on sleep, an interest in drug effects, and research on biological rhythms revived interest in this area.

Daily Variations in Consciousness: Circadian Rhythms

- Circadian rhythms affect many of our bodily processes. These rhythms are controlled by a biological clock that sets our free-running sleep/wakefulness cycle at about 25 hours. Environmental signals called zeitgebers reset the clock to 24 hours each day. There is some evidence that the clock may be set by the suprachiasmatic nucleus in the hypothalamus.

- Jet lag, due to travel through numerous time zones, causes the body's time to be out of sync with local time (external desynchronization) and various body cycles to be out of synchrony with each other (internal desynchronization). Desynchronization causes tiredness and decreases performance efficiency. Changing work shifts also causes desynchronization and its behavioral effects. These effects can be minimized by changing work shifts in a clockwise fashion.

Sleep: The Active Brain at Night

- During sleep people pass through five stages, characterized by different brain waves. A number of times each night, the sleeper experiences rapid eye movement (REM) sleep, during which brain waves resemble rapid, waking brain waves. Dreaming is most common during REM sleep. The sleep stages that immediately preceed REM sleep are called slow-wave sleep (SWS), because the brain waves during them are slower. The midbrain reticular formation is one of the most important brain structures for controlling the sleep/wakefulness cycle.

- Two theories that have been proposed to answer the question "Why do we sleep?" are the restorative theory of sleep (we sleep to recharge and repair the body and brain) and the evolutionary theory of sleep (sleep is an adaptive response of a particular species to its environment). Neither theory seems to offer a complete explanation of why we sleep, or why we experience the kinds of sleep we do.

- Many people suffer from sleep disorders, ranging from common insomnia to narcolepsy and sleep apnea. Although all these conditions can be treated, the lack of completely satis-factory treatments reflects how much remains to be learned about sleep.

Dreams: Images During Sleep

- Several questions about dreams can be investigated empirically. Research suggests that everyone dreams, even if some people typically don't remember their dreams; that people may forget dreams because the dreams are lost from short-term memory on awakening; that "dream time" is about the same as real time; that most dreams have commonplace settings; and that the actions in dreams often include frustrating situations, such as being attacked or trying unsuccessfully to do something.

- Theories of dreaming have proposed that (1) dreams serve an information-processing function, helping sort out memories of the day's events; (2) dreams have a problem-solving function, helping us creatively work through problems; (3) dreams are the brain's attempt to make sense of the bursts of electrical signals that occur during sleep; and (4) dreams are an expression of wishes we would like to fulfill.

- Freud's theory that dreams are an expression of wish fulfillment is based on the idea that we push dangerous thoughts into our unconscious through a process called repression. These thoughts may appear in a distorted form in dreams after being transformed by "dream work." This distorted form of the dream is the manifest dream. The hidden thoughts that are the basis of the manifest dream are the latent dream. The thoughts of the latent dream can be determined through the technique of association and by analysis of the dream's symbolism. Freud's wish fulfillment theory has been influential, but because it is extremely difficult to test, it is not accepted by most psychologists.

Hypnosis: The Power of Suggestion

- Hypnosis is a social interaction in which a person becomes highly suggestible. People differ in the degree that they can be hypnotized. Those who can be hypnotized deeply exhibit behaviors such as involuntary movements, positive and negative hallucinations, age regression, hypnotic analgesia, trance experiences, posthypnotic amnesia, and posthypnotic suggestion.

- Hypnotized people often exhibit trance logic, in which they are oblivious to paradoxes they would recognize immediately in everyday experience. Trance logic is more likely to be evident in people who are hypnotized than in those who are faking.

- Theories of hypnosis include (1) hypnosis is an altered state of consciousness that causes people to feel as if they are in a trance state; (2) hypnosis is a form of dissociation, in which one part of the person's mind carries out the hypnotist's commands and another part, the hidden observer, watches what is happening; (3) hypnosis is the playing out of a social role, in which hypnotized subjects are influenced by the demand characteristics of the situation.

- Hypnosis has been used to help witnesses remember details connected with crimes. A danger in using hypnosis in this way is the possibility that suggestions made under hypnosis might create pseudomemories that then become part of the subject's memory. Hypnosis is best used as an investigative tool, and should be used only with caution for improving witnesses' memories.

Drugs: Changing Consciousness at the Synapse

- Psychoactive drugs are chemicals that alter the workings of the mind. There are five categories of psychoactive drugs, based on how the drugs affect the nervous system and behavior: (1) stimulants, such as amphetamine, cocaine, nicotine, and caffeine; (2) depressants, such as alcohol, barbiturates, and tranquilizers; (3) opiates, such as opium, morphine, and heroin; (4) hallucinogens, such as LSD and mescaline; and (5) marijuana.

- People use drugs for any of a number of reasons, ranging from influences in their social situation to the desire to experience positive drug effects to the need to avoid withdrawal symptoms associated with physical dependence.

- Habitual drug users typically develop a tolerance for the drug and therefore need to increase their dose to experience the same effects.

- Drugs create behavioral effects by altering the release or reuptake of neurotransmitters at synapses. Higher dosages of drugs cause more intense effects.

- The effect of a drug is determined not only by the drug's chemical action at the synapse but also by psychological factors, such as the user's thoughts and expectations.

How Describing Our Experience Can Shape Our Conception of Reality

- The way we describe our conscious experience to ourselves or to others can influence the contents of our consciousness. Experiments on split-brain subjects suggest that behavior can be influenced by processes that are hidden from awareness. When we create explanations for our behavior, those explanations often become part of our reality, even if our explanation was based on incomplete or erroneous information.

Reprise: Consciousness and Levels of Analysis

- The idea of levels of analysis is especially applicable to the study of drugs, which cause effects at the biological level but which can also be studied at the behavioral, cognitive, and contextual levels. Modern psychology's access to the tools of all four levels of analysis has made scientific study of consciousness possible.

Follow-Through/Diversity: Dreams and Culture

- Psychological anthropologists studying dreams in various cultures find that (1) symbolism occurs across cultures, but the symbols differ; (2) dreams are institutionalized in some cultures; and (3) dreams reflect the society the dreamer comes from, in terms of dream content.

Key Terms

alpha waves	physical dependence
association	pseudoinsomnia
biological clock	pseudomemories
circadian rhythm	psychoactive drug
consciousness	psychological anthropology
delta waves	rapid eye movement (REM)
depressants	sleep
dissociation	reflective consciousness
dream work	REM rebound
electroencephalogram (EEG)	repression
electromyogram (EMG)	restorative theory of sleep
electrooculogram (EOG)	reticular formation
evolutionary theory of sleep	sleep apnea
external desynchronization	sleep spindles
free-running cycle	slow-wave sleep (SWS)
hallucinogens	stage-four sleep
hidden observer	stage-one sleep
hypnosis	stage-three sleep
insomnia	stage-two sleep
internal desynchronization	Stanford Hypnotic
jet lag	Susceptibility Scale (SHSS)
latent dream	suprachiasmatic nucleus (SCN)
manifest dream	susceptibility
midbrain reticular formation (MBRF)	tolerance
	trance logic
narcolepsy	unconscious
opiates	wish fulfillment
paradoxical intention	withdrawal symptoms
perceptual consciousness	zeitgebers

CHAPTER

6

Learning and Behavior

Habituation

Principles of Classical Conditioning
Ivan Pavlov: Conditioned Reflexes
John B. Watson: Applying Conditioning to Human Learning
Elements of Classical Conditioning
Modern Approaches to Understanding Classical Conditioning
Applications of Classical Conditioning

Interdisciplinary Dimension: Public Health
Conditioning, Drug Tolerance, and Cigarette Smoking

Principles of Operant Conditioning
Edward Thorndike: The Law of Effect
B. F. Skinner: Learning Begins with a Response
Elements of Operant Conditioning
Refinements to the Traditional Account of Operant Conditioning
Applications of Operant Conditioning

Interactions Between Classical and Operant Conditioning

Cognitive Processes in Simple Learning
Edward Tolman: Cognitive Maps in Rats
Wolfgang Köhler: Insight in Chimpanzees
Albert Bandura: Learning by Observation

Reprise: The Fruits of Behaviorism

Follow-Through/Diversity
Learning Gender Roles

Basic Learning
Processes

For the things we have to learn before we can do them,
we learn by doing them.

Aristotle (384–322 B.C.)

A marine snail, subjected to a stream of water, retracts its gill. The stream repeats. The gill retracts again, but less forcefully. After a number of repetitions, the water elicits little reaction from the snail.

Sam eats a delicious meal of fish bathed in a rich cream sauce. After 90 minutes he becomes ill from the rich food. A week later he is served fish but can't eat it. In fact, just thinking about fish makes him a little queasy.

A chimpanzee roaming through a rain forest spies a large nut under a Panda tree. The chimp walks 80 yards to another Panda tree and returns with the piece of granite he had used to crush open a similar nut a few days before. He places the nut on a root and smashes it open with the granite.

Susan had a scary experience when, while climbing a steep cliff, her foot became wedged in a crevice. She was stranded for over an hour high on the face of the cliff. Now, when Susan visits a friend who works on the 25th floor of an office building, she gets goose bumps and feels anxious if she looks out of the window toward the street below.

At first, these anecdotes may appear to have little in common. But if you read them again, you will see that in each case an organism's response reflects a *change* in behavior resulting from interactions with the environment. The marine snail's reflex response to being squirted with water begins to disappear after several exposures to this stimulus (Kandel, 1976). Sam avoids fish—a food he used to like—because he experienced sickness in conjunction with it. The chimpanzee learned from past attempts at opening Panda nuts that only a hard rock would do the job (Boesch-Ackerman & Boesch, 1993; Griffin, 1992). Susan feels anxious when looking out of the window because of her scary rock-climbing experience. All of these examples involve **learning**—relatively long-lasting changes in behavior that are based on past experience. As you will see in this chapter, learning is one of the most important concepts in psychology.

Learning and Behavior

One reason learning is important is that it helps us *survive*: in fact, our lives and the lives of other animals may depend on it. Although much animal behavior is biologically programmed and therefore does not have to be learned, a great deal of it is learned adaptations to environmental stimuli. Most of the behaviors you need for survival—from securing a meal to avoiding oncoming traffic—were not in your behavioral repertoire when you were born. They result not from instinctive programming but from learning.

In fact, can you think of many behaviors you did *not* acquire through learning? (Breathing is one.) This should suggest why learning is a central concept in psychology. Clearly, one way to explain behavior—from normal, everyday actions like getting up in the morning and getting dressed to many kinds of maladaptive or abnormal behavior like fear of flying or a person's need to wash their hands constantly—is to explain how those responses were created from previous interactions with the environment.

Our opening examples also suggest two provocative questions. First, if learning is pervasive in the animal world, is it possible that the same basic principles account for learning in all species, from snails to humans? If so, then we should be able to understand human learning by studying changes in animal behavior, which are much easier to examine under controlled conditions than are changes in human behavior, which are much more complex. Second, if most behavior is learned, can we understand behavior in general simply by staying at the behavioral level of analysis and relating people's learned responses to events in the environment?

Two men in particular, John B. Watson and B. F. Skinner, answered "Yes" to both of these questions. They believed that learning was the centerpiece of psychology, the key to explaining human behavior. Further, Watson and Skinner believed that the way to study learning was to focus entirely on the relationship between the organism's response and events in the environment. Thus, looking at processes such as thoughts or biological mechanisms "inside" the organism is unnecessary. Behavior can be completely understood, according to Watson and Skinner, by simply studying the behavior itself.

Watson and Skinner's approach, *behaviorism,* is a beautiful illustration of single-minded devotion to one level of analysis. The behavioral level of analysis,

MEASUREMENT & METHODOLOGY

Measuring Learning: The Learning/Performance Distinction

When you learn something, it may not be obvious to someone else. Your new knowledge may not have changed you in any visible way, because the cognitive changes that occur in learning are internal and can't be observed directly. We often measure learning with tests, but there is no guarantee that tests will accurately measure the learning you have achieved. You can probably identify with this idea if you have ever performed poorly on an exam even though you felt you knew the material. Of course, maybe you didn't know the material as well as you thought you did, but it is also possible that you knew quite a lot but were so tired from studying all night that you had trouble concentrating during the exam. Or perhaps you got sick right before the exam, took it anyway, and had trouble remembering what you had learned before you got sick.

In such a situation, your *learning*—the knowledge you possessed—may have been high, but your *performance*—the score you earned on the exam—was low. It is important to be clear about the distinction between learning and performance, because it conveys the fact that observable performance does not always provide an accurate measure of learning. For this reason, some psychologists define learning as the *potential for performance*, and most psychologists try to ensure, by measuring under optimal conditions, that the performance they measure accurately reflects the learning that actually took place.

Does this jockey's failure to stay on his horse mean he is a poor rider? Not necessarily. His spill, which may be caused by his horse, the condition of the track, or other factors, lowers his performance in this particular race, but in general he may be an excellent jockey.

In addition to pigeons, rats, and monkeys, the animals most commonly used in learning research, many others have been used. Here, a parrot picks a stimulus.

in their hands, led to a wealth of research, much of it laboratory studies of animals. This research has revealed some of the most important influences on our behavior and spawned applications in a number of areas, including education and psychotherapy. The voluminous research generated by the behaviorists is testament to how behaviorism caught the imagination of many psychologists and dominated American psychology from the 1920s into the 1950s.

This chapter is largely the story of behaviorism and the research it generated. It begins with a brief consideration of the very simple form of learning illustrated by our marine snail. We then examine in detail two forms of learning that, though quite distinct, both go by the name of *conditioning*. Finally, we will see how psychologists ultimately came to supplement the behavioral approach by looking to the cognitive and biological levels of analysis for a more complete picture of learned behavior.

Habituation

Our opening example of the marine snail illustrates a kind of learning called *habituation*. **Habituation** is a *gradual decrease in the size of a response to the repeated presentation of a particular stimulus* (Kandel, 1976). Thus, the snail's reaction to the stream of water diminishes with repeated exposure to the stimulus.

Habituation occurs in all animals, including humans (see Measurement & Methodology, "Using Habituation to Measure Perception in Infants"). As I write in my study, I am almost unaware of the ticking of the clock on my desk, the noise of planes flying overhead, or the sound of the dog barking next door. Because I have become habituated to these sounds, I can focus my attention on what is important to me without being distracted by stimuli that don't matter.

We take habituation for granted, but imagine what life would be like for animals and humans alike if we lacked the ability to ignore unimportant stimuli. The woods are filled with noises: the rustling of leaves blown by the wind, trees creaking as they sway, small animals scurrying about. If an animal inhabiting those woods were to notice every one of those noises, it would constantly be shifting its attention among relatively unimportant events and might miss the important sound of an approaching predator. Habituation has clear survival value, then, in eliminating irrelevant distractions and enabling animals to focus on the infrequent stimuli that signal danger (Wyers, Peeke, & Herz, 1973).

Although being able *not* to respond to familiar, repetitious stimuli serves an important function, it is also important that we be able to form new responses to stimuli. This ability is typical of most learning and is at the heart of the two types of learning we focus on for most of this chapter. As we will see, these two types of learning can account for an extraordinary range of behavior. Ironically, however, our story begins not with a behavioral psychologist, but with a fortuitous discovery by a Russian physiologist who was investigating digestion in dogs.

Principles of Classical Conditioning

You cannot create experience. You must undergo it.

Albert Camus, French author

Winning the Nobel Prize obliges the recipient to give a public address in Stockholm describing the research for which the prize was awarded. When, in 1904, physiologist Ivan Pavlov acknowledged the prize for his research on digestion in

MEASUREMENT & METHODOLOGY

Using Habituation to Measure Perception in Infants

Habituation—the decrease in the response to repeated presentations of a stimulus—provides a way to answer questions about the capacities of nonverbal animals such as young human infants. One question researchers have been interested in is what infants see. Infants cannot answer this question verbally, but they can answer it by the way they habituate. Suppose, for example, that we want to know whether an infant can tell the difference between sets of vertical and horizontal lines. We first present the vertical lines to the child and time how long she looks at them. Initially the lines catch the child's attention and are observed for most of a 20-second trial. As we continue to present the lines on succeeding trials, however, the child habituates to the stimulus, looking less and less, until by trial 6 her looking time has decreased to half of its original duration (see the figure below).

To determine whether the infant can tell the difference between the vertical and horizontal lines, we switch to the horizontal lines on trial 7. If the infant *cannot* tell the difference between vertical and horizontal lines, her looking time should decrease further as she continues habituating to the stimulus. If, however, the infant *can* tell the difference, the horizontal lines will catch her attention and her looking time will increase. This increase in looking time is *dishabituation*, the reemergence of a previously habituated response that occurs when a novel stimulus is presented. This procedure is ideal for determining the perceptual capacities of very young infants, as it doesn't require language (Slater, Morrison, & Rose, 1984). Habituation has been used to measure a number of infant capacities, including depth perception, color vision, and detail vision (Goldstein, 1989).

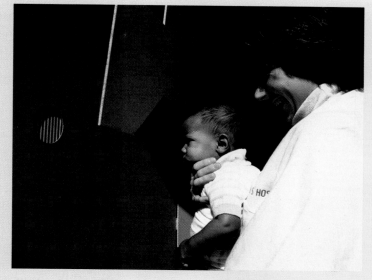

Above: A baby being tested using the habituation procedure. An experimenter looking through the small peephole to the right of the striped target watches to see how long the baby looks at the target before looking away. **Below:** Habituation record for a human infant. On trial 7 the lines the infant is observing are switched from vertical to horizontal. Continued decreases in looking time (red) indicate that the child didn't perceive the change. An increase in looking time (purple) indicates the child did perceive the change.

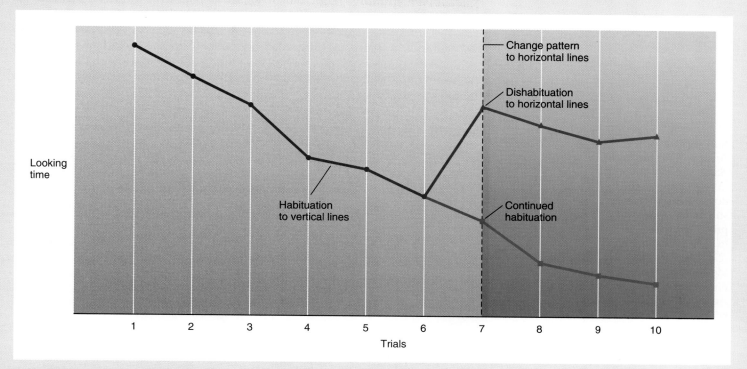

dogs, he departed from custom. Instead of describing the work for which he won the prize, he talked about an interesting observation he had made in the process of his research on digestion.

Pavlov described how, in his digestion research, he customarily placed some meat powder in a dog's mouth and recorded the amount of saliva produced by this stimulus. He then recounted how, after a dog had been exposed to the experimental situation for a while, it would often begin salivating when it heard the experimenter approaching the room. The sounds the experimenter made apparently were causing the dog to salivate in anticipation of being fed the meat powder. Pavlov called this salivation *psychic secretions*, because the stimulus was not physical—meat powder—but rather *psychological*—the anticipation of it.

Ivan Pavlov: Conditioned Reflexes

Pavlov's Stockholm audience was more interested in his Nobel Prize research on digestion than in these so-called psychic secretions, but Pavlov saw psychic secretions as offering a new way to understand the workings of the brain. With this idea in mind, he proceeded to spend the rest of his life researching them (Pavlov, 1927).

The research program that grew out of Pavlov's observations was the first investigation of **classical conditioning** (also sometimes called Pavlovian conditioning), a procedure in which a previously neutral stimulus is paired with one that elicits a response. Eventually, the neutral stimulus elicits the same response by itself. Pavlov used the basic procedure illustrated in Figure 6.1 and diagrammed in Figure 6.2. The steps are as follows:

1. Determine an existing unlearned reflex in which the presentation of a certain stimulus is always followed by a specific response. In Pavlov's experiment this reflex was the presentation of meat powder followed by salivation. The reflex (meat powder→salivation) is called the **unconditioned reflex,** because it occurs before any conditioning has taken place. The meat powder is the **unconditioned stimulus (US)**, which elicits salivation, the **unconditioned response (UR)**.

2. Determine a **neutral stimulus (NS)**, one that does not elicit the response. For example, initially the dogs did not salivate to the sound of the experimenter's footsteps as he approached the room. For his experiment, Pavlov chose the ringing of a bell as his neutral stimulus, as dogs do not normally salivate to the ringing of a bell.

FIGURE 6.1
An apparatus for classically conditioning salivation in a dog. The dog, trained to remain still in the harness, is presented with meat to elicit salivation. The dog's saliva is collected by a tube and recorded on the paper drum. An initially neutral stimulus such as a bell is presented immediately before the meat. After a number of such pairings, the bell alone elicits salivation.

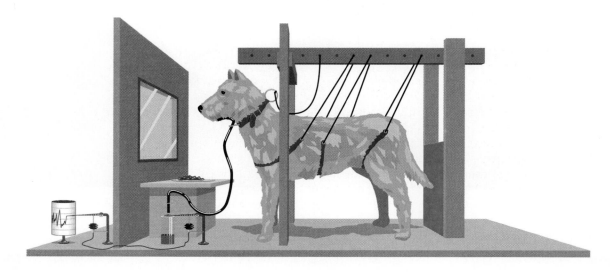

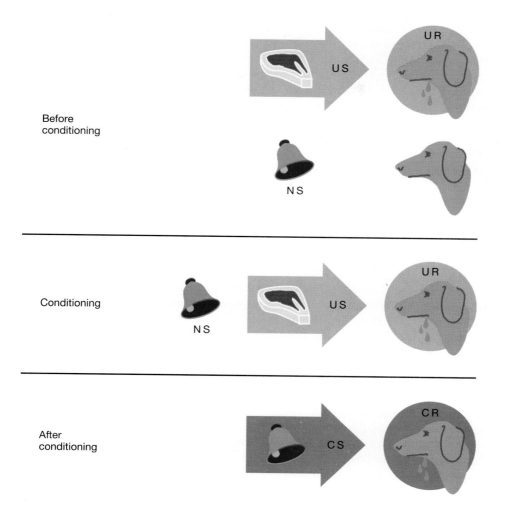

FIGURE 6.2
Steps in the classical conditioning procedure. In this figure (and others that illustrate classical conditioning), stimuli that elicit a response are shown inside an arrow pointing to the response elicited. Before conditioning (top panel), the meat (the US) elicits salivation (the UR), and the bell (the NS) elicits no salivation. During conditioning (middle panel), the bell is paired with the meat. After conditioning (bottom panel), the bell (shown inside the arrow because it now elicits salivation) has become the CS and the salivation the CR. The CS and the CR are shown in purple to indicate that conditioning has occurred.

3. Pair the neutral stimulus (the bell) with the unconditioned stimulus (the meat powder) a number of times. The NS (bell) is presented first and followed, about half a second later, by the US (meat powder).

4. Now present the bell alone. If conditioning has taken place, the dog will salivate on hearing the bell, without the presentation of the meat powder. The bell, originally a neutral stimulus, has become a **conditioned stimulus (CS)** that elicits the **conditioned response (CR)** of salivation. In other words, salivation, an unconditioned response to meat powder, has now been "conditioned" also to occur in response to a bell.

Using this procedure, Pavlov showed that a neutral stimulus took on new properties after being paired repeatedly with a stimulus that elicits a response. The bell, which originally was not followed by any response, was now followed by salivation. What he had demonstrated was one way in which a behavioral change—that is, a form of learning—could be brought about simply by manipulating events in the dog's environment.

Pavlov's conditioning experiments initially met with great skepticism from his colleagues: they either didn't believe his result or didn't appreciate its importance. The test of time has, however, shown that the dogs' "psychic secretions" were in fact real and that they tell us much about behavior in general.

The phenomena that Pavlov studied were obviously psychological phenomena, but as a physiologist, Pavlov had little interest in associating himself with the psychologists of his time. As far as he was concerned, the "psychic" secretions must have a physiological basis. He theorized that the connection between the bell and food reflected the formation of new neural connections in the cortex between neurons that fire to the sound of the bell and neurons in the "food center" of a dog's brain. Creation of this neural connection explained why ringing the bell elicited the same response as presenting food.

In short, Pavlov thought that the explanation of conditioning should be sought at the biological level of analysis. In fact, he saw his ideas about physiology as his most important contribution. (In the next chapter we will see that present day explanations of the physiology of learning and memory *do* include the notion of new neural connections forming in response to experience.) However, Pavlov was destined to be remembered not for his theories of brain functioning but for his discoveries about behavior. Despite his contempt for psychology, events were occurring in the United States that would ensure that his discoveries would have a major impact on psychology, whether he liked it or not.

3   BIOLOGY

John B. Watson:
Applying Conditioning to Human Learning

In 1903, just about the time Pavlov was beginning his research on conditioned reflexes, John B. Watson was in the process of becoming the youngest student ever to get a Ph.D. from the University of Chicago. Ten years later, Watson heard about Pavlov's procedures and used them to lay the foundation for a new school of psychology called behaviorism.

The origins of behaviorism.   As you know from Chapter 1, Watson was unhappy with the method of introspection used by most psychologists of his day. He believed it to be unscientific because it relied on subjective reports that were unreliable and incapable of being verified. When Watson received his Ph.D., he began to search for a more objective method of studying psychology—one whose results could be objectively verified.

A brilliant and articulate scientist, Watson rose quickly in the ranks of academic psychology, becoming chairman of the psychology department at Johns Hopkins University in 1908 and being elected president of the American Psychological Association in 1915. By the time Watson delivered his presidential address to the American Psychological Association, he had decided that Pavlov's classical conditioning was the method that would objectify American psychology. With Pavlov's procedures in hand, Watson (with Rosalie Rayner) began some experiments that led to the publication, in 1920, of his famous paper, "Conditioned Emotional Reactions." The experiment reported in this paper was notable because it was the first report of conditioning in humans. The star of Watson's experiment was an 11-month-old child whom Watson identified as Albert B., but who is now generally referred to as Little Albert.

Classically conditioning a human: The Little Albert experiment.   One of Little Albert's characteristics was his calm disposition. He hardly ever cried and, most important for the purposes of Watson's experiment, he appeared totally unafraid of rats, rabbits, and other furry animals. Watson did find, however, that he could make Albert cry by striking a hammer against a steel bar held right behind his head. Watson now wondered whether that sound could be used to condition Albert's startle response to a neutral stimulus, such as the presentation of a furry animal. Watson's procedure for conditioning Little Albert is shown in Figure 6.3.

The situation prior to conditioning was that the loud noise (the unconditioned stimulus) produced crying (the unconditioned response) whereas the rat (the neutral stimulus) did not produce crying. To create conditioning, Watson paired the rat with the loud noise. After seven pairings of the rat and the noise, the rat was presented alone. This time the sight of the rat caused Albert to cry and "to crawl away so rapidly that he was caught with difficulty before reaching

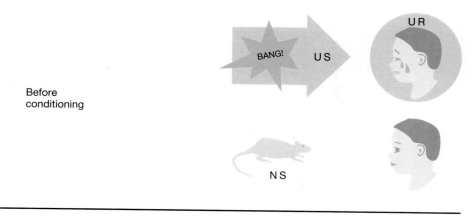

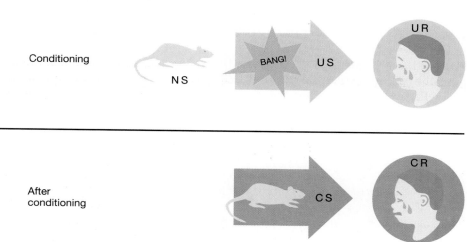

FIGURE 6.3
Watson and Rayner's Little Albert experiment. Before conditioning, the loud noise (US) causes Albert to cry, and the rat (NS) does not. During conditioning the rat is paired with the noise. After conditioning, the rat (now the CS) elicits the CR (Albert's crying).

the edge of the table" (Watson & Rayner, 1920, p. 5). Clearly, Albert's reaction to the rat had changed from an initial positive reaction to a very negative one, simply by pairing it with the noise.

Watson was triumphant; he had succeeded in conditioning a new emotional response in Little Albert. Unfortunately, we know nothing about what happened to Albert later, because shortly after the experiment Albert's mother removed him from the hospital where Watson had been conducting his research. We might wonder whether, as an adult, Albert still cringed in fear at the sight of white rats or other white, furry animals. The possibility of such an outcome, plus the obvious mental distress suffered by Albert during the experiment, are reasons that a present day researcher would never consider repeating Watson's procedure; it would be considered unethical. Nevertheless, his was a landmark study that showed how principles of conditioning could be applied to human behavior.

In classical conditioning, Watson believed he had found the key to learned behavior. More important, his work led him to believe that virtually *any* behavior could be conditioned by manipulating an organism's environment. Given a dozen healthy infants, he proclaimed, he could pick any one at random "and train him to be any kind of specialist I might select—doctor, lawyer, artist, merchant-chief, and yes, even beggar-man and thief, regardless of his talents, penchants, tendencies, abilities, vocations, and race of his ancestors" (Watson, 1926, p. 10).

As we will see, Watson's ambitious claims for the power of classical conditioning were overstated. Both learning and behavior are too complex to be explained by classical conditioning alone. Nevertheless, his observation held a kernel of truth. Classical conditioning *can* account for a number of behavioral

12 EMOTION

9 DEVELOPMENT

responses that otherwise would be puzzling, including emotional reactions like Little Albert's acquired response to rats.

But how, exactly, does classical conditioning work? To answer this question we first need to understand the elements at work in this type of learning.

Elements of Classical Conditioning

> *He who has been bitten by a snake,*
> *fears a piece of string.*
>
> Persian proverb

Pavlov's discovery of classical conditioning, and Watson's introduction of this procedure to the United States, stimulated extensive research into the properties of conditioning. What happens in classical conditioning? Under what conditions does it work? Let's consider some of the findings of this research.

Pairing the NS and US. Any description of classical conditioning emphasizes the *pairing* of a neutral stimulus (NS) and an unconditioned stimulus (US). But what exactly constitutes pairing? Four methods are shown in Figure 6.4.

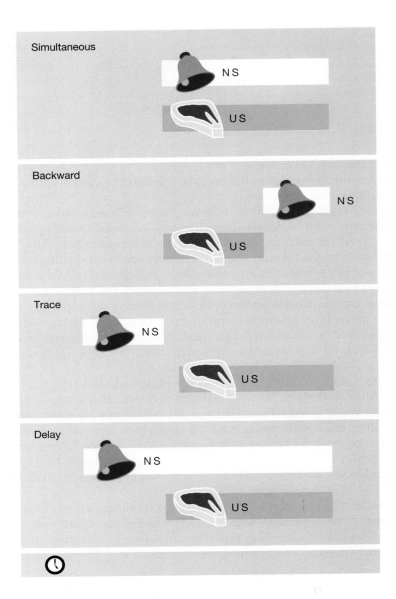

FIGURE 6.4
Four ways to pair a neutral stimulus (a bell in this example) with an unconditioned stimulus (the meat). Simultaneous: NS and US are presented at the same time (weak conditioning effect). Backward: NS is presented after the US (weak effect). Trace: NS is presented first and stops before the US begins (good effect). Delay: NS is presented first and then continues as the US is being presented (best effect).

You might think that presenting the NS and US together (for example, sounding the bell at the same time the meat powder is given to the dog) would create strong conditioning. In fact, researchers have discovered that such **simultaneous conditioning** produces an extremely weak effect, as does **backward conditioning,** in which the NS is presented *after* the US (Rescorla, 1981).

Conditioning is much stronger with **trace conditioning,** in which the NS is presented first, then terminates before the US is presented (for example, the bell is sounded briefly before the meat powder is presented). However, this procedure works best when the interval between the NS and the US is brief.

Pavlov and subsequent researchers found the most effective procedure to be **delay conditioning,** in which the NS is presented first and remains on while the US is presented. Thus, in the salivation experiments, the bell would be sounded first and would continue to ring while the meat powder was presented. Further, optimal conditioning occurs when the interval between the onset of the NS and the onset of the US is about half a second (Ross & Ross, 1971).

Extinction and spontaneous recovery.   To establish conditioning, experimenters repeatedly pair the NS with the US until presenting the NS alone elicits a response, indicating that the NS has become a conditioned stimulus (CS). Does this mean that the conditioned response (CR) is permanent? That is, will a dog conditioned to salivate to the sound of a bell continue to do so for the rest of its life? As you might suspect, the answer is "No." If, after conditioning is established, we repeatedly present the CS alone, the conditioned response will decrease with each trial until it eventually decreases to zero (Figure 6.5). This is **extinction**—repeatedly presenting the CS alone until the CS ceases to elicit a response.

As an example of conditioning followed by extinction, consider the following situation: A driver has a frightening accident at an intersection he habitually drives through on his way to work. He escapes without serious injury, but is emotionally shaken. A few days later, when he next approaches the intersection, he begins to feel anxious and emotional, just as he felt immediately after the accident. The previously neutral intersection has become a conditioned stimulus by being paired with the accident and feelings of anxiety. On subsequent drives through this intersection the driver continues to feel anxious, but his anxiety decreases with each encounter. This is a case of the CS being presented alone (without an accident) so that extinction proceeds, until eventually it is complete and the driver passes through the intersection with no feelings of anxiety at all.

However, extinction is not always permanent, because of a phenomenon called **spontaneous recovery**—the reappearance of the previously extinguished conditioned response following a rest period during which the CS is not presented (Figure 6.5). For example, when Pavlov extinguished his dog's salivation

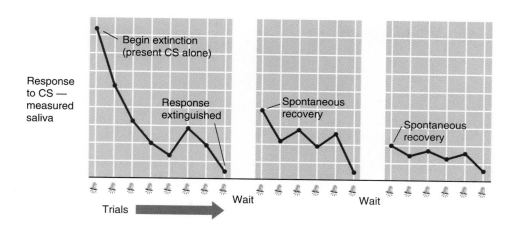

FIGURE 6.5

Extinction and spontaneous recovery. If the conditioned stimulus is presented repeatedly, the conditioned response, salivation in this example, gets smaller (extinction). After a wait, the response recovers somewhat (spontaneous recovery). After a second wait, spontaneous recovery occurs again, but the response is small.

to the bell and then waited a few days and rang the bell again, the dog's salivation reappeared. This spontaneous recovery effect might occur for our driver if, after his anxiety response to the intersection is extinguished by repeated journeys through it without an accident, he takes another route to work for a few weeks. When he approaches the intersection again, he might be surprised to re-experience the anxiety he used to feel: spontaneous recovery has occurred. Extinction can again be accomplished by again experiencing the CS alone (the bell without the meat powder, or the intersection without an accident). However, extinction following a spontaneous recovery takes less time than it did originally.

Generalization.   When Watson and Rayner conditioned Little Albert's startle response to the rat, they discovered another effect of conditioning. Little Albert began to show a similar emotional reaction to other stimuli that were furry and consequently similar to the rat, even though they had not been conditioned. A white rabbit, cotton wool, a fur coat, and even Watson wearing a Santa Claus beard elicited emotional reactions from Albert. This phenomenon, in which a conditioned response is elicited by stimuli that are similar to the original CS, is called **generalization.**

I can relate personally to this idea of generalization because of an experience I had as a newspaper carrier when I was in junior high school. While delivering my papers I was attacked by barking dogs on a number of occasions. Barking dogs, therefore, became a conditioned stimulus for fear, and that fear generalized to dogs in general. Because of generalization, I am still very wary of dogs—especially ones that bark.

Laboratory experiments have, in fact, shown that the more similar the stimulus is to the original CS, the greater the response due to generalization. This is illustrated by the results of an experiment by G. V. Anrep (1923), an English psychologist working in Pavlov's laboratory. Anrep used Pavlov's procedure but, instead of sounding a bell before presenting the meat powder, he presented a touch stimulus to the dog's leg. The response to this CS, a touch at point C on the dog's leg, was 71 drops of salivation. Following conditioning, touching other points also caused salivation, with points closer to C causing a larger response (Figure 6.6).

Discrimination.   One way we can prevent generalization from occurring is by establishing a *discrimination.* Consider the dog in Figure 6.6. Every time we touch the dog it salivates, even if we touch it at a point far from C. Suppose we now want to train the dog to salivate when we touch point C, but not to salivate when we touch everywhere else. To do so we would use a procedure called **dis-**

FIGURE 6.6
The results of Anrep's generalization experiment. Anrep conditioned the dog to salivate when touched at point C (response = 71 drops). Salivation also occurred when the dog was touched at other points (generalization), with stimulation closer to the original location causing larger responses.

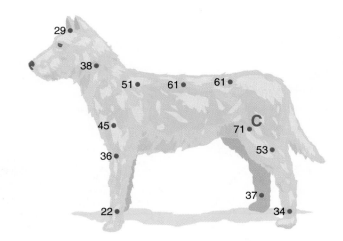

crimination training. This procedure is simple: Every time we touch point C, we present meat, as we did in the original conditioning. However, every time we touch other places, we do not present meat. Thus, we are continuing to condition salivation at point C while *simultaneously extinguishing* the response at other locations. At first, generalization causes some salivation when we touch the other locations, but eventually the dog salivates only when touched at point C. The dog has developed a discrimination between point C and other points on its body.

This process of discrimination has helped me in my relationships with dogs over the years. Although I still become uneasy around dogs that resemble the ones I encountered on my paper route, I have learned through repeated non-threatening experiences to relax around dogs that are friendly. I have developed a discrimination between loud, threatening dogs and gentle, friendly dogs.

Second-order conditioning.   So far, the conditioning we have described has involved establishing a link between a neutral stimulus and an unconditioned stimulus, as when Pavlov turned the ringing of a bell into a conditioned stimulus by pairing it with the unconditioned stimulus, food. But once the bell elicits salivation, can we use it as an unconditioned stimulus? For example, what if we pair the bell with a new neutral stimulus, such as a light, as shown in Figure 6.7? When we do this, the light becomes a conditioned stimulus and also elicits salivation, even though it was never paired with the food.

Using one conditioned stimulus to create another is called **second-order conditioning.** Although second-order conditioning does work, it is neither very

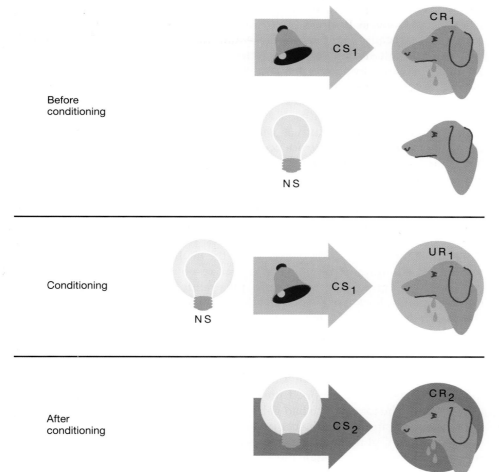

Before conditioning

Conditioning

After conditioning

FIGURE 6.7
Second-order conditioning. Here the bell, which became a conditioned stimulus from a previous conditioning experiment, elicits salivation, whereas the light does not. Pairing the light and bell causes the light to become a conditioned stimulus. This is called second-order conditioning because one conditioned stimulus is used to create another.

strong nor long lasting. After a number of presentations the salivation response to the bell extinguishes—but the response to the light extinguishes even faster. Nonetheless, the fact that second-order conditioning is possible means that a stimulus can take on new properties by being paired with a previously conditioned stimulus. Second-order conditioning is another way, besides generalization, in which the effects of conditioning can extend to stimuli other than those directly associated with the original US→UR reflex. It differs from generalization in involving a new pairing of stimuli and in not depending on the stimuli being similar.

Second-order conditioning occurs often in everyday life. For example, after Alice exercises at the health club, she feels much more relaxed and contented. The health club therefore becomes a conditioned stimulus that elicits feelings of relaxation even when Alice doesn't exercise during her visits there. Second-order conditioning occurs when Alice meets someone new at the club. Her acquaintance becomes paired with the health club and may take on some of the positive feelings elicited by the club, so that Alice feels positively toward him. Her new friend may think it's his winning smile, but another reason for Alice's regard may be second-order conditioning.

Modern Approaches to Understanding Classical Conditioning

Based on what you know so far about classical conditioning, what words would you use to describe the process? Two of the top candidates—*pairing* and *automatic*—say a lot about researchers' conceptions of classical conditioning in the first half of the century.

It should be clear why we might pick the word *pairing*. Conditioning occurs when we pair an NS and US with the right timing. The word *automatic* also makes sense, because of the automatic way that the US always elicits the UR and because of the automatic bond that forms between the NS and US. In the decades following Pavlov's and Watson's pioneering work, classical conditioning was seen as involving an automatic reflex achieved through pairing, or *contiguity* (nearness in time), between the NS and US. Furthermore, it was believed that conditioning would work with *any* stimulus, as long as it was made contiguous with the US. This idea, which is called the **contiguity hypothesis,** began to change in the 1960s because evidence from a number of laboratories challenged both the idea of contiguity and the idea that a response could be conditioned to any stimulus.

Robert Rescorla: Contiguity is not sufficient.   Robert Rescorla (1966, 1968), while a graduate student at the University of Pennsylvania, experimented with the role of contiguity in the conditioning of rats. The design of his experiments is shown in Figure 6.8. Rescorla paired tones (the neutral stimulus) with shock (an unconditioned stimulus that elicited a fear response). Two groups of rats, a contiguity-only group and a contiguity-plus-random group, received the same number of tone-shock pairs. However, the rats in the contiguity-only group were shocked only during the tones, whereas rats in the contiguity-plus-random group received additional shocks during the intervals between tones.

To test the effects of pairing the shock and the tone, Rescorla trained the rats in both groups to press a bar for food. As they were pressing, he then sounded the tone. For the rats in the contiguity-only group this tone had an immediate effect—the rats stopped pressing—a phenomenon called **conditioned suppression.** The tone, which had gained its negative properties by being paired with the shock, suppressed the bar pressing. However, sounding the tone as rats in the contiguity-plus-random group pressed the bar had no effect—they kept pressing the bar even though the tone was sounding. This means that even though the rats in the contiguity-plus-random group experienced many pair-

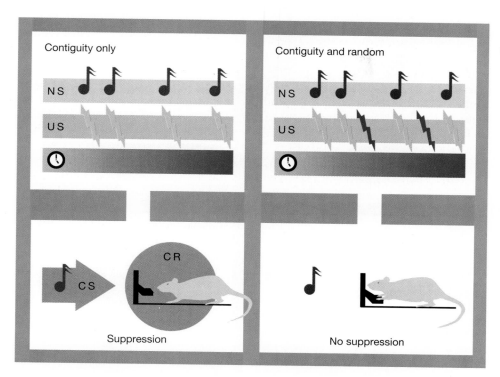

FIGURE 6.8
Rescorla's experiment that showed that contiguity—pairing an NS and a US—does not always result in conditioning. The rats in the contiguity-only group (left panel) experience the usual conditioning procedure: Pairing a tone and shock causes the tone to take on properties of the shock. Thus, presenting the tone during bar pressing suppresses bar pressing (lower left panel). The rats in the contiguity-and-random group experience the same tone-shock pairing as the contiguity-only group but, in addition, also get extra shocks (in blue), which are presented when there is no tone. For this group, the tone does not suppress bar pressing (lower right panel).

ings of the tone and the shock, the tone had not taken on the shock's negative properties.

Pairing alone, therefore, does not automatically create a connection between a neutral stimulus and an unconditioned stimulus. Apparently what is important is not pairing but *predictability.* The animals in the contiguity-only group had learned that the tone (NS) *always* predicted the shock (US), so they formed a connection between tone and shock. But since the rats in the contiguity-plus-random group were equally likely to be shocked during the silent interval as during the tone, they did not learn to associate the tone with the shock (Rescorla, 1972, 1988).

Leon Kamin: Blocking.   Another experiment that raised doubts about the contiguity hypothesis was carried out by Leon Kamin (1969). Like Rescorla, Kamin used a conditioning procedure followed by a measurement of conditioned suppression. With his control group, he repeatedly presented both a noise and light together (NS) to each of the rats, followed by a shock (US). Then, in the suppression test, the rats stopped pressing the bar for food when the light was turned on (Figure 6.9). This is exactly the result we would expect from the contiguity hypothesis, as the light was paired with the shock during conditioning.

With his experimental group, Kamin used exactly the same procedure, pairing the noise and light together with the shock. But he added a pretraining session, in which the noise alone was paired with the shock; he then found that the experimental group showed no suppression when the light was subsequently presented during bar pressing. Why did this occur? If conditioning depended only on contiguity we would expect the light, which was always paired with the shock, to cause suppression in both groups. What happened was that the pairing of the noise and shock during the pretraining caused **blocking,** the prevention of the conditioning of one stimulus pair (in this example, the light-shock pair) by the prior conditioning of another stimulus pair (in this example, the noise-shock pair).

We can understand why blocking occurs if we remember Rescorla's result.

FIGURE 6.9

Kamin's blocking experiment. The rats in the control group (at left) experience the usual conditioning procedure: The noise and light (the NS) are paired with the shock (the US). The light then takes on properties of the shock, so it suppresses bar pressing (lower left). The rats in the experimental group (at right) are treated in exactly the same way, except they are first exposed to a pretraining session in which just the noise is paired with the shock (upper right). For this group, the light does not suppress bar pressing (lower right).

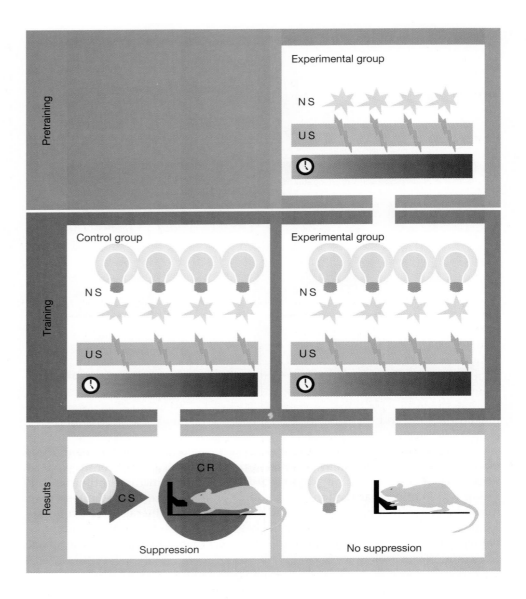

In his experiment, the tone caused suppression only if it *predicted* the shock. The animals in Kamin's experimental group learned during the pretraining session that *noise* predicted shock. Adding the light during the next conditioning session provided no new information, so conditioning to the light didn't occur.

Kamin's and Rescorla's results left the contiguity theory in shambles. Another experiment reported at about the same time similarly undermined the idea that any response can be conditioned to any stimulus.

John Garcia: Conditioned taste aversion.   When John Garcia submitted a paper describing some results of his research to scientific journals, his results were so unbelievable to the journals' reviewers that the paper was rejected by the major journals that publish research on learning and conditioning. Eventually, Garcia's results were published (Garcia, Hankins, & Rusiniak, 1974; Garcia & Koelling, 1966), but many people remained skeptical. The reason for their skepticism was that Garcia's results directly contradicted the idea that conditioning should occur any time two stimuli are paired.

Conditioning, remember, was supposed to be an automatic process. But Garcia's results demonstrated that the effect of pairing two stimuli depends on *which* stimuli are paired. Some pairings result in conditioning; others do not.

TABLE 6.1

Garcia's conditioned taste aversion experiment

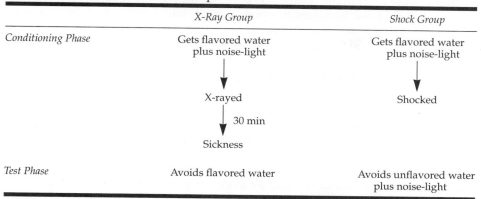

	X-Ray Group	Shock Group
Conditioning Phase	Gets flavored water plus noise-light	Gets flavored water plus noise-light
	↓	↓
	X-rayed	Shocked
	↓ 30 min	
	Sickness	
Test Phase	Avoids flavored water	Avoids unflavored water plus noise-light

In the conditioning phase of Garcia's experiment, two groups of rats were given access to a drinking tube. When the rats licked the tube they received water plus two other stimuli: (1) a *flavor stimulus* added to the water and (2) a *noise-light stimulus*—a brief noise together with a flash of light. As the rats were being exposed to the flavor and the noise-light stimulus, those in the "X-ray" group were irradiated with X rays that made them ill about 30 minutes later, whereas those in the "shock" group were shocked (Table 6.1).

In the test phase of the experiment, the rats in both groups were given separate access to water that was either (1) flavored or (2) unflavored but accompanied by the noise-light stimulus. During this phase the rats were neither irradiated nor shocked. The results? The rats in the X-ray group, who had been made sick during the conditioning phase, avoided the flavored water but drank the plain water that was accompanied by the noise-light stimulus. For this group, the conditioning trials had produced a link between sickness and *flavor,* so the rats avoided the flavor. We saw this phenomenon, which is called **conditioned taste aversion,** in the example at the beginning of the chapter in which a person who got sick after eating fish subsequently avoided eating fish.

In contrast, the rats who had been shocked drank the flavored water but avoided the water that was accompanied by the noise-light stimulus. For those rats the conditioning trials had produced a link between the shock and the *noise-light* stimulus, so the rats avoided this stimulus.

Notice that the most important result in this experiment is what *didn't* happen. During the conditioning trials, the flavor, noise, and light were all simultaneously paired with either the X rays or the shock. Yet the irradiated rats did not learn to associate the noise and light with sickness, and the shocked rats did not learn to associate the flavor with shock.

How can we explain such "selective" conditioning effects? Garcia's results led Martin Seligman (1970) to introduce the concept of **preparedness.** According to this idea, animals are *prepared* to associate certain NS-US combinations. As Garcia demonstrated, rats are biologically prepared to associate taste with sickness, an ability that is of great practical importance to a rat. Consider the rat that eats a piece of poisoned bait put out by an irritated homeowner. If it eats enough so that it gets sick 30 minutes later but then lives, it will learn to avoid any bait with the same taste. This phenomenon, which had been observed long before Garcia did his experiments, is called **bait shyness.** It makes sense that evolution would have prepared rats to associate taste and sickness, because rats eat at night and have poor vision. Therefore, in its natural environment it would be difficult for the rat to associate what the bait *looks* like with its later sickness. However, rats do have highly developed chemical senses, so they are well prepared to associate the *smell* or *taste* of the bait with later sickness.

Rats have poor vision but a good sense of smell; quails rely heavily on vision. So rats associate sickness with the taste of food and quails associate sickness with the visual properties of food.

4   THE SENSES

If that reasoning is correct, animals with a highly developed visual sense should be able to learn the connection between the sight of food and getting sick. This, in fact, is what happens. Suppose a quail, which relies heavily on vision, drinks water that tastes sour and is dark blue and then becomes sick a half-hour later. When tested later, the quail will not drink unflavored dark blue water but *will* drink uncolored sour water (Wilcoxon, Dragoin, & Kral, 1971). The highly visual quail is therefore biologically programmed to associate the *color* of the water with sickness but not the *taste.*

3   BIOLOGY

That different species are "prepared" to associate different stimuli was not anticipated by Pavlov. Another result Garcia obtained also might have surprised Pavlov. He showed that stimuli don't always have to immediately follow one another to cause conditioning. The rats in Garcia's experiment that were exposed to X rays while drinking did not get sick until about 30 minutes after they tasted the water, yet they still developed an aversion to the flavor. In another experiment, Garcia, Ervin, and Koelling (1966) showed that the connection between flavor and sickness can be established with delays lasting over an hour. These findings mean that conditioning need not always be "stamped in" by immediate pairing.

Results such as Garcia's, Rescorla's, and Kamin's, all published in the 1960s, transformed psychologists' ideas about the nature of classical conditioning. Classical conditioning is no longer thought of as simply an automatic response to a pairing of stimuli. Instead, it is seen as one of many mechanisms that help organisms identify meaningful relationships between events in their environment. This way of thinking about classical conditioning brings notions associated with both the biological and cognitive approaches to the study of behavior. The idea of biological preparedness indicates that we need to take into account the species of animal that is learning. The idea that the way stimuli *predict* each other determines whether conditioning occurs has cognitive implications. Apparently, mechanisms exist within any given organism to extract information that predicts pairings specifically useful to it.

8   THINKING

In addition to creating bridges between learning, biology, and cognition, modern research on classical conditioning has led to a number of applications of the conditioning process. Let's examine a few of the practical results that have been derived from the line of research begun by Pavlov.

People who have a phobia for heights become afraid when looking down from a high place, even if there is no real danger.

Applications of Classical Conditioning

From its earliest days, classical conditioning was promoted as having a large role in shaping human behavior. Although modern psychologists do not take seriously Watson's claim that conditioning can totally shape a person's life, classical conditioning does shape our reactions in ways we may not be aware of.

Examples of classical conditioning in everyday life.   Examples of classical conditioning in everyday life are easy to find. Many of our emotional and physiological responses are elicited by stimuli that have been paired in the past with specific experiences. The fragrance of a perfume or after-shave, paired with a particularly enjoyable date, may trigger pleasant feelings when encountered at a later time. The taste of coffee in the morning may wake someone up even though decaffeinated coffee has been substituted for the usual brew. Women who breast-feed their babies often notice that the *milk let-down reflex,* the milk ducts' release of milk to the nipple that is triggered by the baby's sucking, is eventually elicited even before the baby begins to nurse. In fact, just thinking about breast feeding can cause the milk to be released.

Classical conditioning has also been used to explain **phobias,** fears of specific stimuli or situations that are out of proportion to the true danger. For example, a construction worker who was left dangling 100 feet above the ground after slipping on a high beam developed such an intense fear of high places that he became afraid to cross bridges or fly in airplanes (Levine & Sandeen, 1985). In this case, being high above the ground was the neutral stimulus, as it did not originally cause fear for the construction worker. Dangling 100 feet above the ground was the US, and fear was the UR. After the accident, being high above the ground became the CS, which led to the CR of fear. That fear then generalized to other situations involving height. A similar thing happened to Susan, our rock climber from the beginning of the chapter, whose fear from her rock-climbing scare generalized to fear of looking out of windows in tall buildings.

These links between classical conditioning and people's experiences illustrate the relevance of classical conditioning to everyday life. However, modern researchers have gone beyond simply noting the presence of classical conditioning in common experiences. Among the practical applications of the principles of classical conditioning is the development of new therapy techniques.

Behavior therapy: Systematic desensitization.   Therapy based on the principles of conditioning is called **behavior therapy.** We have discussed how phobias might be acquired through the pairing of a stimulus with a fearful situation. If conditioning can create the anxiety or fear that accompanies a phobic stimulus, perhaps conditioning can be used to *eliminate* it. That is, perhaps a new response can be conditioned to the stimulus that arouses anxiety or fear—a procedure called **counterconditioning.**

This was the reasoning behind the pioneering experiment Mary Cover Jones (1924) carried out on a boy named Peter, who was terrified of rabbits. To cure Peter of his fear of rabbits, Jones decided to pair the rabbit with eating, an activity that Peter found pleasurable. Jones realized, however, that abruptly introducing the rabbit during a meal might simply stop Peter from eating. Consequently, she introduced the rabbit slowly over several meals, first keeping it at a distance and then moving it closer over a period of days. This pairing of the rabbit with a pleasurable activity not only eliminated Peter's fear of rabbits, but eventually enabled boy and rabbit to become the best of friends.

Although Jones demonstrated how classical conditioning could be used to eliminate an irrational fear, little further work was done with this technique until the 1950s, when Joseph Wolpe described **systematic desensitization,** a technique in which a phobia is eliminated by training a subject to relax in the presence of stimuli similar to the feared stimulus. Consider how Peter Lang and David Lazovik (1963) used desensitization to eliminate snake phobias in college students.

Mary Cover Jones

16   DISORDERS

17   THERAPY

A snake phobic person would probably become anxious just by looking at this picture. The people in this picture obviously don't qualify.

Many people dislike snakes, but among them about 3 of every 100 are *snake phobics*, who become excessively anxious around snakes. For example, they won't go into the reptile section of the zoo, even though they know the snakes are safely behind glass, and they even feel anxious looking at pictures of snakes.

The rationale behind desensitization therapy is to condition a response to the anxiety-provoking stimulus that is associated with reduced anxiety. Anxiety is usually accompanied by muscle tension and its absence by muscle relaxation. Lang and Lazovik, therefore, sought to eliminate their subjects' anxiety by pairing snake stimuli (the NS) with *muscle relaxation* (the US).

The subjects first were trained in the technique of muscle relaxation. Next, they constructed an **anxiety hierarchy,** a list of about 20 situations involving snakes, ordered according to the severity of the anxiety associated with them. The list starts with situations that are not very frightening, such as "writing the word *snake*," and progresses through increasingly frightening situations, such as "seeing a picture of a snake," "seeing a snake in a glass case at the zoo," and "accidentally stepping on a dead snake." The final item in this case, "contact with a live snake," is the most anxiety producing of all.

After learning the muscle relaxation technique and constructing their anxiety hierarchies, Lang and Lazovik's subjects visualized the first item on their list while practicing muscle relaxation. As the first item causes only mild anxiety, they were able to learn to relax while, say, visualizing the word *snake*. This process was continued over a number of sessions, working up the hierarchy, until the subjects felt relaxed even while visualizing contact with a live snake. Eventually Lang and Lazovik's subjects became much less anxious, and some were even able to hold a live snake. This type of therapy has been used successfully to eliminate many other types of phobias, including fear of flying and fear of closed spaces (Martin & Pear, 1983; Wilson, 1982).

Conditioning is clearly not a phenomenon that occurs only in psychological laboratories. In fact, research on drug addiction indicates that conditioning may play a role in establishing some effects associated with drug addiction. We consider the link between conditioning and addiction in the following "Interdisciplinary Dimension."

INTERDISCIPLINARY DIMENSION PUBLIC HEALTH

Conditioning, Drug Tolerance, and Cigarette Smoking

The field of public health is concerned with safeguarding the public from hazards and improving their health. One way this is accomplished is through educational programs such as those that publicize the dangers of drug abuse, smoking, and unsafe sex (Stone, 1987). Learning psychologists have contributed to the field of public health through research that has identified the connection between principles of learning and health hazards. Two areas in which psychologists have made significant contributions are drug abuse and smoking.

Classical Conditioning and Drug Tolerance

As we saw in Chapter 5, people who take drugs often find that the drug's effect decreases with repeated administrations. This phenomenon, which is called *drug tolerance*, means that the drug user must increase the dosage to maintain the same effect. Thus, long-term users of heroin typically inject doses of the drug that would kill an inexperienced user.

Tolerance is caused partly by the drug's physiological effect on the body. For example, neurons may become less sensitive to the drug, or the body may metabolize the drug differently (Pratt, 1991). However, there is also evidence that tolerance can be cause by classical conditioning. To understand how this works we need the concept of **homeostasis,** the body's tendency to keep its internal environment constant. The body maintains homeostasis by using compensating mechanisms such as the shivering that generates body heat when a person gets cold. These compensating mechanisms also come into play when a person takes drugs. When a person injects heroin, one of its effects is to depress the respiratory system. To compensate for this *decrease* in respiratory function, the

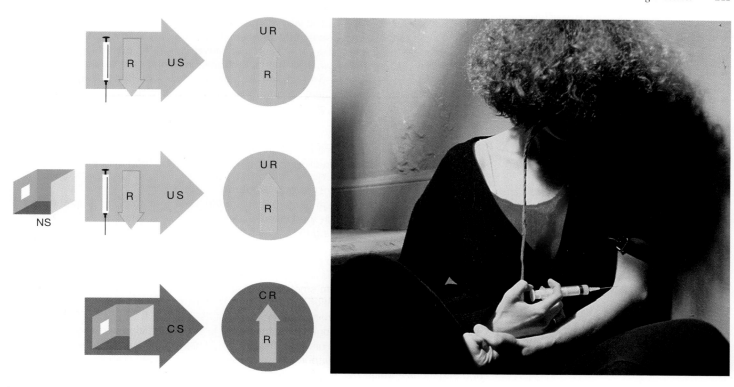

FIGURE 6.10
Conditioned drug tolerance. **Upper left:** Injecting heroin causes decreased respiratory activity. The heroin injection and decreased respiratory activity, which together are the unconditioned stimulus, trigger the body's compensatory response, increased respiratory activity, which is the unconditioned response. **Center left:** Heroin is injected in the same surroundings (the room) repeatedly. The room is the neutral stimulus. **Lower left:** The room alone causes increased respiratory activity. The room has become a conditioned stimulus and the increased respiratory activity the conditioned response. This response to the room creates tolerance for the drug, so a larger dose needs to be used to obtain the same effect.

body sets into motion compensating mechanisms that *increase* it. We can think of the compensatory response as the body's bracing itself to absorb the effect of the heroin.

Let's now apply conditioning principles to a situation in which a drug is repeatedly administered in the same surroundings. When this occurs, *environmental cues,* such as the smells, sights, and sounds associated with the room and the drug user's paraphernalia, become *predictors* of the administration of the drug. With repeated pairings of the cues and the drug, the cues become a CS that elicits the body's compensatory response (the UR) of increased respiratory activity even *before* the heroin is injected (Figure 6.10). Thus, conditioning causes the body to brace itself for the heroin injection when the drug is administered in familiar surroundings.

This triggering of the compensatory response by familiar surroundings is called **conditioned drug tolerance** because the compensatory response *decreases* the drug's effect on the body. As administration of the drug continues, the ability of the environmental cues to elicit the compensatory response becomes stronger, thereby increasing the body's tolerance and causing the addict to administer larger and larger doses of the drug to achieve the same effect.

Evidence supporting this conditioning explanation of drug tolerance is found in an experiment by Shepard Siegel and his co-workers (Siegel, 1986; Siegel, Hinson, Krank, & McCully, 1982; Siegel, Krank, & Minson, 1987; Siegel & MacRae, 1984). Siegel injected rats with doses of heroin every other day for 30 days, in increasing doses, until the final injection was eight times as large as the first. He then injected them with a dose twice as high as any they had ever received. Half of the rats received their final injection in the same environment in which they received the series of injections, and half received the final injection in a different environment. The result was that twice as many of the rats that were injected in the different environment (64% versus 32%) died from a heroin overdose. A third group of rats (the control group), which never received any heroin until the high-dose injection, suffered a 96% mortality rate.

Why did the rats in the same-environment group have a higher survival rate? Even though all the rats received the same high-dose injection of heroin, conditioned tolerance enabled the ones injected in the same environment to resist the effect of the drug. The rats injected in the different environment didn't experience the environmental cues that normally trigger the body's compensatory response and consequently had less tolerance for the drug. The rats in the control group, of course, had no tolerance at all, as they had never been injected.

Siegel's results may explain why many heroin addicts die each year from drug overdoses. Some of these overdoses may be caused by taking an overly potent dose of the drug. But many drug users die after giving themselves the same dose they injected the previous day. To determine whether the lack of environmental cues could explain such deaths, Siegel (1984) interviewed ten former heroin addicts who had suffered near-fatal heroin overdoses. Seven of them reported that when they overdosed they had administered the drug under different conditions than usual. For example, one of the victims, who had used heroin for ten years, reported injecting the drug with a large group of people in his living room, whereas he had usually taken the drug alone in another room. Reports such as these, combined with the experimental evidence provided by the rat studies, support the idea that classical conditioning plays a role in creating drug tolerance.

11   MOTIVATION

Classical Conditioning and Cigarette Smoking

Even though the U.S. Surgeon General declared in 1964 that smoking is dangerous to health, about 30% of adults in the United States still smoke (DiMatteo, 1991). Although many people have quit smoking (53% of adults smoked in 1955), millions have not. Why haven't they quit?

One reason that people continue to smoke is that a stimulant, nicotine, is contained in cigarette smoke. Nicotine is an addictive chemical that creates dependence, so when people attempt to abstain from smoking they experience mild withdrawal symptoms (see Chapter 5). However, in addition to the chemical effect of nicotine, smoking behavior is also maintained by classical conditioning.

Smoking, the unconditioned stimulus, leads to the unconditioned response: physiological stimulation caused by nicotine. If a person usually smokes in the presence of certain people or in certain environments or situations, then those people, environments, and situations—which began as neutral stimuli—eventually become conditioned stimuli and elicit the physiological stimulation usually caused by nicotine. This physiological stimulation, in turn, creates a desire to smoke.

It is because of this conditioning that smokers often find themselves "lighting up" in specific situations. Some smokers, for example, tend to smoke under stress. One reason they do so is to experience the calming effect they derive from the nicotine, but the initial urge to smoke may be triggered by the fact that because of past experience the stress has become a conditioned stimulus for smoking. ■

Looking back on the history of classical conditioning research, we can see that Pavlov's work, which began as a way to understand the brain, evolved into research that has led to a greater understanding of basic learning processes, to practical applications, and to a better understanding of many everyday behaviors. But learning in everyday situations also occurs through another type of conditioning, *operant conditioning*, which has even more far-reaching implications for behavior.

Principles of Operant Conditioning

Nothing is worth doing unless the consequences may be serious.

George Bernard Shaw (1856–1950)
British playwright

Many classical conditioning experiments were like Pavlov's original experiment with dogs: the experimenter presented stimuli to a passive animal. But in real life, animals are rarely passive. They are constantly initiating behaviors and seeking out their own stimuli from the environment (think of a dog who is allowed to run free in a park). This kind of active behavior is the focus of **operant conditioning,** in which the animal operates on its environment to gain rewards or avoid negative stimuli. As we will see, operant conditioning introduces new principles that help explain many common behaviors. The starting point for our discussion is an experiment involving a cat in a device called a puzzle box.

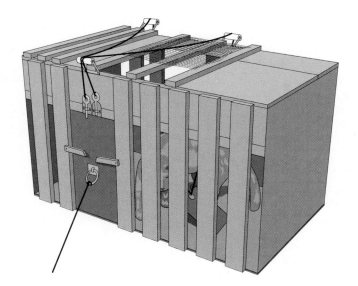

FIGURE 6.11
Thorndike's puzzle box. The cat can escape by depressing the pedal.

Edward Thorndike: The Law of Effect

What will a cat do if placed in a box that keeps it from reaching a dish of food placed just outside? This question was answered by Edward Thorndike (1898), who was experimenting in the United States at about the same time Pavlov was beginning his conditioning experiments in Russia. Thorndike's "puzzle box" held the cat captive until it activated a mechanism for opening the door. In the box shown in Figure 6.11, the mechanism is activated by depressing a pedal.

When a cat was placed inside one of these boxes, it typically tried to reach the food by clawing and biting various parts of the box and by pushing its paws through the openings between the boards. In the process of this random clawing and biting, it would eventually accidently depress the pedal that opened the box. Thorndike's most important finding was that if a cat was repeatedly placed inside such a box, *it took progressively less time to escape on each trial.* The results for one cat are shown in Figure 6.12. On the first trial, this cat took 448 seconds to escape from the box, but by the 40th trial it escaped within 15 seconds. The cat's behavior had changed in a way that was both durable and measurable. In short, it had *learned.*

Notice that the cat's learning is quite different from that of the dog in Pavlov's conditioning experiments. The response of depressing the pedal is not a reflexive response to a stimulus, like the dog's salivation response to the meat powder. Instead, it is a new behavior that the cat "stumbles on" and then learns to repeat in order to escape the box. In this case, the animal takes an active role in its own learning.

What explains the learning demonstrated by Thorndike's cat? One explanation is that the cat, on seeing the connection between depressing the pedal and escaping from the box, "figured out" that pulling on the wire opened the door. But the data in Figure 6.12 suggest another explanation. If the cat had suddenly figured out how to escape from the box, we would expect a sudden decrease in the time it took to escape. However, no such sudden decrease occurs. Instead, the cat's learning is gradual. To explain this result, Thorndike proposed the **law of effect**: Behaviors that are followed by satisfying effects are strengthened and are therefore more likely to occur again; behaviors that are followed by unsatisfying effects are weakened and are therefore less likely to occur again. Thus, every time depressing the pedal allowed the cat to escape from the box and gain access to the food outside, the response of clawing on the loop became more likely to occur and occurred faster on the next trial. According to the law of effect, the behavior of pulling on the wire is gradually strengthened every time the cat does it.

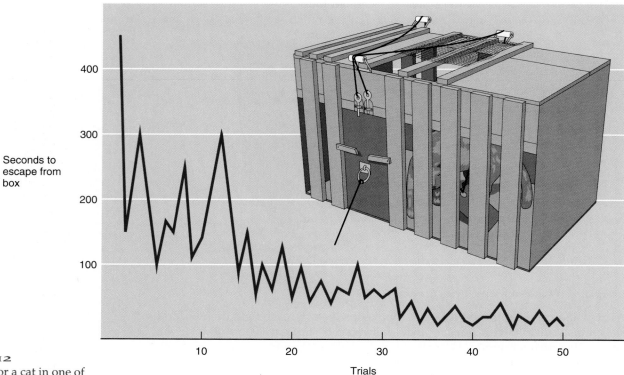

FIGURE 6.12
Learning curve for a cat in one of Thorndike's puzzle boxes. The cat generally takes less and less time to escape from the box as the number of trials increases.

The key to understanding the law of effect is to focus on the idea that the behavior that is strengthened is the behavior *followed by* the satisfying effect. Or, to put it another way, the behavior that is strengthened is the behavior that occurs *immediately before* the satisfying effect. So, if the cat depresses the pedal and the door immediately opens, the behavior of depressing the pedal will be strengthened and will occur more rapidly the next time.

Again, note the contrast with Pavlov's classical conditioning. In classical conditioning, the response comes after the stimulus (conditioned stimulus→ conditioned response). In the kind of learning studied by Thorndike, the response comes first (response→satisfying effect). It's what happens *after* the response that governs the subsequent frequency of the response.

The idea that behavior is governed by its consequences has proved to be one of the most important ideas in the psychology of learning. However, it wasn't until almost 40 years after Thorndike's experiments that the law of effect received widespread recognition. Much of the credit for this development belongs to B. F. Skinner, who was born in 1904, six years after Thorndike proposed the law of effect.

B. F. Skinner: Learning Begins with a Response

Although Skinner's research was very closely related to Thorndike's, he was more influenced by Pavlov and Watson, whose books he bought upon beginning his graduate studies at Harvard University in 1928 (Skinner, 1979). Following Watson's lead, Skinner called himself a behaviorist and committed himself to finding ways to objectively measure behavior.

Skinner's first project was a study of eating behavior in rats. To measure this behavior he designed a box with a small bar protruding from the wall. When the rat pressed the bar, two things happened: (1) the rat received food, and (2) a record was made of the rat's response. With this apparatus, which eventually came to be known as the **Skinner box,** Skinner had found a way to get the rat to feed itself and to create a continuous record of the rat's feeding behavior. (See Measurement & Methodology, "The Cumulative Record.")

MEASUREMENT & METHODOLOGY

The Cumulative Record

Skinner's box provides a way to automatically reinforce an animal for specific responses such as pressing a bar. But how can we record those responses? Skinner solved this problem with the *cumulative recorder,* a device that creates a plot of an animal's responses over time (see figure below). The cumulative recorder's pen writes on a strip of continuously moving paper. Every time the animal responds, the pen moves upward, so the animal's response is recorded as a "step" in the record. The result is a **cumulative record,** which has the following properties: (1) when the animal is not responding, the movement of the paper under the stationary pen creates a horizontal line, and (2) when the animal emits a number of responses, the upward movement of the pen creates a sloping line. The faster the animal responds, the steeper the slope of the line. The figure at right shows the record created by one rat as it changes its response rate. At first the rat is not pressing the bar at all (a). Then it begins at a slow rate (b), presses faster (c), and finally begins to slow down (d). After that the rat presses every so often, and then, as indicated by the horizontal line, eventually stops altogether (e).

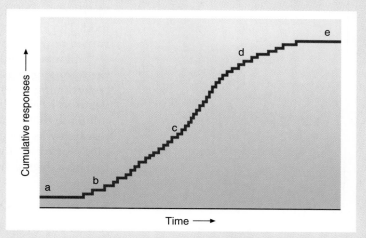

A cumulative record. A steeper slope indicates faster responding.

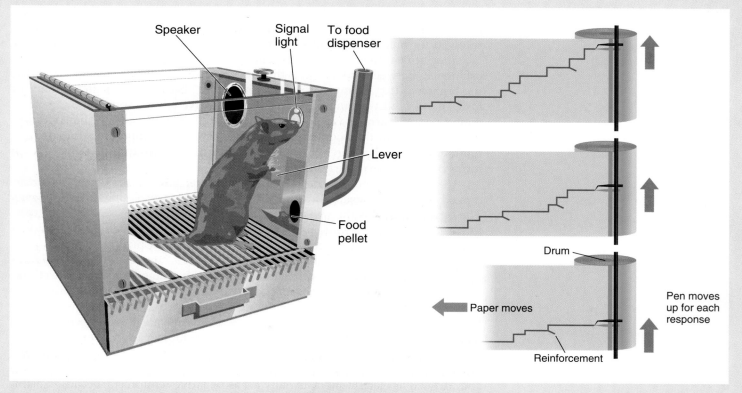

A rat in a Skinner box. Each time the rat presses the bar, the pen on the recorder moves up one notch. This creates a cumulative record of the rat's response on the moving chart.

Just as Thorndike found that a cat depressed the pedal more quickly if depressing it was followed by access to food, Skinner found that the rat pressed the bar more rapidly if each bar press was followed by the delivery of food. There is, however, an important difference between Thorndike's and Skinner's procedures. In Thorndike's puzzle box, depressing the pedal removes the cat from the experiment (because the cat leaves the box). In Skinner's box, pressing on the bar does not remove the rat from the experiment. The rat remains close to the bar, and as soon as it has eaten its reward, it can immediately press the bar again. This feature of Skinner's method was extremely important, because instead of having to put the animal back into the box after every trial as Thorndike did, Skinner was able to let the rat continue behaving, with only brief pauses to eat its food. The Skinner box therefore enabled Skinner to study the relatively uninterrupted flow of the rat's behavior.

Skinner used **operant behavior** to specifically indicate behavior in which the animal *operates* on its environment. In many years of research on operant conditioning, from his initial work on rat feeding behavior in 1928 until his death in 1990, Skinner studied how the *consequences* of an organism's behavior influence that organism's future behavior. Note that although most of Skinner's research was done on animals, he felt that he was discovering universal principles of learning that could be generalized from animals to humans. We will see that, to a degree, his assumption was correct.

Elements of Operant Conditioning

Just as Pavlov spent years determining the basic characteristics of classical conditioning, Skinner and those who followed his line of research determined the basic characteristics of operant conditioning.

Reinforcement: Increasing the rate of responding.   Skinner used the term *reinforcer* rather than *reward* to designate the food and other stimuli that organisms received for making a response. Why did Skinner prefer that term? On the surface they appear to mean the same thing, but as we will see, there are important differences between them. One is that a reward implies a subjective effect within the organism (for example, food is "rewarding" because it satisfies hunger or tastes good). But we can't observe these subjective effects, so using them to explain operant learning would violate one of the cardinal rules of behaviorism: psychologists should study only observable behavior. Skinner therefore defined reinforcing stimuli (or reinforcers) not in terms of their reward value, but in terms of their observable effect on behavior.

Skinner defined a **reinforcer** as a stimulus that, when presented or removed after a response, raises the rate of that response above its baseline level. The **baseline level** is the rate of a response prior to the introduction of the reinforcer. For example, a rat in a Skinner box has a high baseline level for sniffing and standing on its hind legs and a low baseline level for pushing the bar.

Reinforcers can be either positive or negative. A stimulus is a **positive reinforcer** if the rate of a response increases above its baseline level when the stimulus is *presented* after the response. Food, therefore, usually acts as a positive reinforcer, because the animal's response rate increases when a response is followed by the presentation of food. Other positive reinforcers are water, access to a sexual partner, and praise (an especially powerful reinforcer for humans). A stimulus is a **negative reinforcer** if the rate of a response increases above its baseline level when the stimulus is *removed* after the response. Aversive (unpleasant) stimuli such as electric shock usually act as negative reinforcers, because an animal's response rate increases when a response is followed by the removal of electric shock.

A trap that students sometimes fall into is to associate "negative" with a *decrease* in the rate of response. But remember that reinforcers, whether positive or

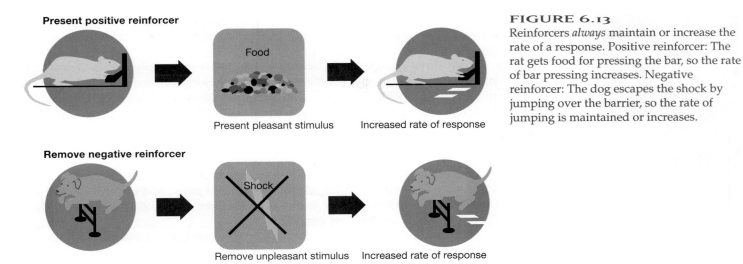

Present positive reinforcer

Present pleasant stimulus Increased rate of response

Remove negative reinforcer

Remove unpleasant stimulus Increased rate of response

FIGURE 6.13
Reinforcers *always* maintain or increase the rate of a response. Positive reinforcer: The rat gets food for pressing the bar, so the rate of bar pressing increases. Negative reinforcer: The dog escapes the shock by jumping over the barrier, so the rate of jumping is maintained or increases.

negative, always *increase* the rate of response. The key is that the response rate increases when positive reinforcers are *presented* but when negative reinforcers are *removed* (Figure 6.13).

An example of how a negative reinforcer can increase the frequency of a behavior is provided by a procedure called **escape-avoidance training.** Suppose we place a dog on one side of a **shuttle box** like the one shown in Figure 6.14. Initially the box is illuminated, but then the light goes off. Ten seconds later, the dog receives a shock through the grid floor. At first the dog whines, runs around the compartment, and acts disturbed, but after a few shocks the dog tries jumping to the other side of the box, where it is not shocked. Soon the dog jumps to safety on the other side of the box as soon as the shock begins. The jumping response increases because it *removes* the negative reinforcer, shock. This part of the escape-avoidance training is called *escape training,* because the dog learns to escape the shock (Solomon & Wynne, 1953). If the procedure continues, the dog eventually learns to avoid the shock altogether by jumping *before* the ten-second "lights-out" period is over. Most responses to negative reinforcers involve escape, avoidance, or both.

What kinds of stimuli can function as reinforcers? In addition to distinguishing between positive and negative reinforcers, we can distinguish between

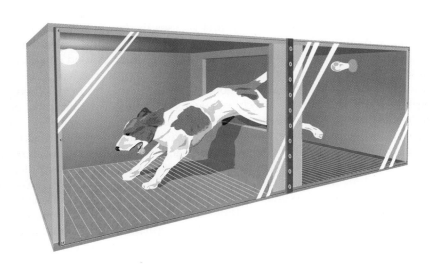

FIGURE 6.14
Shuttle box used for escape-avoidance training. When the light goes off the dog has ten seconds to jump to the other side. If it jumps before the ten seconds are up it *avoids* the shock; if it jumps after the shock has started, it *escapes* the shock. The shock is a negative reinforcer because its removal maintains or increases the rate of jumping.

FIGURE 6.15
Chimpanzee working to receive poker chips (a secondary reinforcer) that can be exchanged for food (a primary reinforcer).

primary and secondary reinforcers. A **primary reinforcer** is one that is unlearned. Examples of primary reinforcers are food, water, access to sex, and painful stimuli.

In addition to these reinforcers, which are obviously of great biological significance, another group, **sensory reinforcers,** was established by researchers beginning in the 1950s. They discovered that monkeys will work to be allowed to look out a window into the experimental room (Butler, 1954) and that humans will work at a button-pushing task to turn on a display of lights in a dark room (Jones, Wilkinson, & Braden, 1961). As these sensory reinforcers are apparently unlearned, they are classed as primary reinforcers.

A category of reinforcers that is especially important for humans and for some animals as well is **social reinforcers,** such as praise and attention. Social reinforcers are effective in very young infants (Lieberman, 1990), suggesting that they also qualify as primary reinforcers.

In contrast to primary reinforcers, a **secondary reinforcer** is learned. Grades, for example, are a secondary reinforcer. They have little worth in themselves, but they lead to other reinforcers such as praise, admission to graduate school, and perhaps a better chance at a job. Money is another example of a secondary reinforcer. Essentially worthless in itself, money has gained its reinforcing properties because it has been paired with obtaining primary reinforcers. That is, it can be exchanged for biological, sensory, and social reinforcers. Using a secondary reinforcer as a medium of exchange to obtain a primary reinforcer is not a behavior restricted to humans. A chimpanzee, for example, can be conditioned to work for "money." The chimpanzee in Figure 6.15 is working to receive small poker chips that he has learned can be inserted into a vending machine to obtain food (Wolfe, 1936).

The shaping of behavior.   We have defined a reinforcer as a stimulus that, when presented or removed after a response, raises the rate of a response above its baseline level. But what if the baseline level is zero? If an animal never makes a response, we can't reinforce it. This is a problem if we have chosen to reinforce a rat for pressing a bar, because the rat's baseline level for this activity is often zero. Our problem, therefore, is to get the rat to press the bar for the first time so that we can reinforce it. Psychologists have solved this problem by using a technique called *shaping.*

Shaping is a technique of establishing a desired behavior by rewarding successive approximations to the behavior. To shape a rat to press a bar, at first we reinforce the rat with food whenever it turns toward the bar. Soon the rat is turning toward the bar more (remember the law of effect), but once that behavior has increased, we require that it come closer to the bar before it receives a reinforcement. We then require the rat to move even closer, then to touch the bar, and finally to actually press it. After the rat first presses the bar, it soon returns and presses again. At first the rate of response is fairly slow, with pauses between each press, but shortly the pressing becomes fairly regular as food continues to be delivered after each press. We have shaped the rat to press the bar.

The technique of shaping is commonly used by animal trainers. When you see dolphins flying through hoops, chimpanzees riding bicycles, and most other animal "tricks," you are witnessing the results of shaping.

Shaping works on people, too. A story is often told of students in an introductory psychology class who used shaping to get their professor to walk either to the far left or far right of the classroom. They achieved this by reinforcing the professor every time he moved even slightly toward a predetermined side of the room. The reinforcement was smiling and nodding their heads as if interested in his lecture. Eventually, the story goes, they had him lecturing against one wall of the classroom and then, by reinforcing small movements in the other direction, moved him to the other wall!

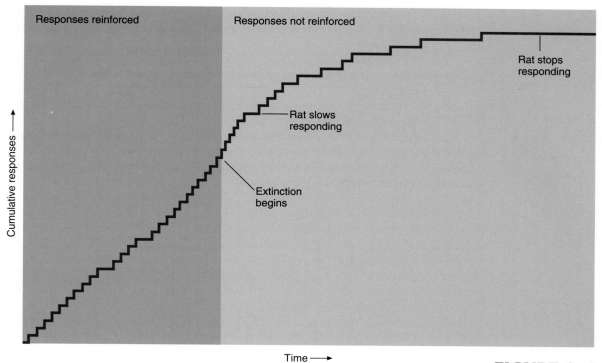

Time ⟶

FIGURE 6.16
Cumulative record showing a fairly steady rate of response when responding is being reinforced. When reinforcers are no longer presented (beginning at the vertical line), the rat's responding eventually slows and then stops. When the rat stops responding altogether the response has been extinguished.

Extinction.   Up until now, we have been discussing how to increase a certain response by presenting positive reinforcers or removing negative ones. Once a behavior has been acquired, what happens if we discontinue the reinforcement altogether? Skinner answered this question by accident. One of his rats was pressing a bar to receive food pellets when the automatic pellet dispenser jammed. Skinner was not there at the time, so the dispenser remained jammed, and the rat received no food for bar pressing. When Skinner returned, he inspected the record of the rat's responding and found that right after the reinforcers stopped, the rat briefly increased its rate of responding. Following this burst of responding, however, the rat began pressing the bar less and less frequently and eventually stopped altogether (Figure 6.16). This decrease in responding is similar to what happens when the unconditioned stimulus is discontinued in classical conditioning—and, as in classical conditioning, this decrease in response is called extinction.

Now that we have covered the basic concepts of reinforcement, shaping, and extinction, we can consider the dynamic aspects of operant conditioning by looking at how the way reinforcers are presented influences behavior. We begin with the timing of reinforcers.

The timing of reinforcers.   Our ability to shape a rat's behavior so that it eventually presses the bar demonstrates the importance of the timing between the reinforcer and the behavior. The behavior that is strengthened is the behavior that occurs *just before* the reinforcer is presented. If we reinforce looking at the bar, the rat looks at the bar more often. If we reinforce moving toward the bar, the rat moves closer to the bar. For this shaping procedure to work, the experimenter must carefully observe the animal's behavior and deliver a reinforcer only after behaviors that lead the rat toward the bar.

What if we don't pay attention to what the animal is doing when we present our reinforcers? When Skinner set a timer that presented food to pigeons at regular intervals no matter what they were doing at the time, he found that each bird developed its own strange behavior. One pigeon turned around in a circle two or three times between reinforcers, another continually thrust its head into an upper corner of the cage, and another rocked back and forth like a pendulum (Skinner, 1948).

The cause of these bizarre behaviors can be traced to the timing of the pigeons' reinforcers. If a pigeon happens to be turning around when the first reinforcer is presented, it will be more likely to turn around again. If another reinforcer coincidentally happens to come right after another turn, more turning occurs, until the pigeon is executing a dizzying sequence of turns.

Skinner called this **superstitious behavior,** because the organism is behaving as if there is a causal relationship between the response (for example, turning) and delivery of the reinforcer, when in reality the behavior is only related to the reinforcer by chance. We don't have to look far to realize that humans, too, are susceptible to superstitious behavior. Baseball players, for example, are notorious for developing superstitious habits. George Gmelch (1978), a minor league baseball player, tells of the time that he ate fried chicken every day at 4:00 P.M., kept his eyes closed during the national anthem, and changed sweatshirts for seven consecutive nights until a hitting streak ended. Of course, superstitious behavior is not restricted to pigeons and baseball players. Perhaps you can think of a superstition of your own that may have originated from a chance pairing between a behavior and a reinforcer.

If the timing of reinforcers influences operant conditioning, what happens when we deliberately change that timing? We can answer this question by looking at schedules of reinforcement.

Schedules of reinforcement.   So far we have assumed that we present or remove a reinforcer every time an animal makes a response. This way of presenting reinforcers, which is called a **continuous reinforcement schedule (CRF),** is usually used to initially train an animal. Presenting a reinforcer for every response results in a fairly steady rate of responding, but it has the disadvantage of using up reinforcers rapidly, and if we are reinforcing with food the animal may become full and lose interest in responding.

Instead of reinforcing an animal for every response, what happens if we reinforce only some of its responses? The answer to this question was discovered by Skinner because of a food shortage in his laboratory. Today, an experimenter who wants to do an operant conditioning experiment can purchase reinforcers (usually food pellets, for rats) from a number of companies. However, when Skinner was the only person doing this research, he had to make his own food pellets. One Friday afternoon he found himself with only a few pellets on hand and didn't want to spend part of the weekend making more. So he decided to conserve pellets by reinforcing the rat for only some of its bar presses. In doing so, Skinner discovered **partial reinforcement,** the reinforcement of only some of the animal's responses.

If we are not going to reinforce every response, then we have to decide when responses are going to be followed by reinforcers. There are two general types of partial reinforcement schedules, *ratio* schedules and *interval* schedules. A **ratio schedule** is tied to the *number of times* the animal responds (that is, a reinforcer is delivered after a certain number of responses). An **interval schedule** is tied to the *amount of time* that elapses between reinforced responses (that is, a reinforcer is delivered when a response occurs after a certain amount of time since the last reinforcer).

With both types of schedule, the number of responses or the amount of time between reinforcers can be either *fixed* or *variable*. This results in four possible reinforcement schedules, each of which produces its own characteristic effect on behavior (Figure 6.17).

Fixed ratio.   In the **fixed-ratio (FR) schedule,** the animal is reinforced every time it makes a certain number of responses. On a fixed-ratio 10 (FR 10) sched-

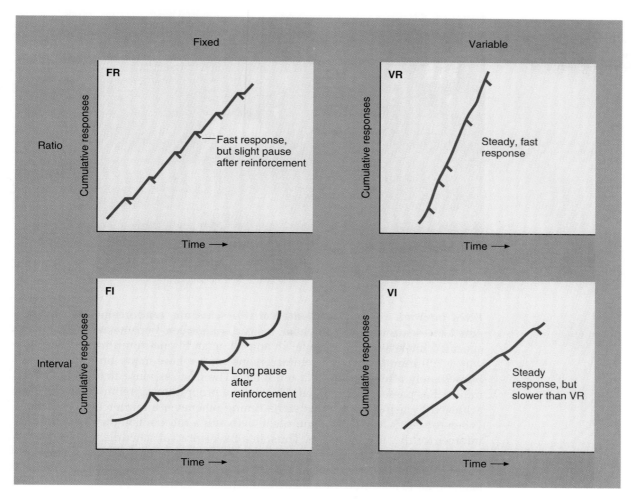

FIGURE 6.17
Cumulative records for the four most common partial reinforcement schedules. The timing of reinforcers, indicated by the short angled lines, determines the pattern of responding.

ule, for example, the animal receives a reinforcer every tenth time it presses the bar. Like continuous reinforcement, this schedule results in a fairly high rate of response, though the animal typically slows down a bit immediately after receiving a reinforcer. A human example of a fixed-ratio schedule is working on a piecework basis. Getting paid $10 for every 5 cars you wash represents work on a FR 5 schedule.

Variable ratio.   The **variable-ratio (VR) schedule** is the same as the fixed-ratio schedule, except that the number of responses required for a reinforcer varies. For example, an animal on a VR 20 schedule receives reinforcers *on the average* every 20 responses, but the number of responses between any two reinforcements might be 7, 28, 15, and so on. The rates of response for VR schedules are very high, because more responding results in more reinforcers; as the animal has no way of predicting when the next reinforcer will be presented, it does not pause after receiving one.

A human example of a behavior controlled by a VR schedule is playing slot machines. These machines are programmed to pay off for a certain average number of plays, but there is no way of telling when the next payoff will come. (That's why it's called gambling!) As a result it is common to see people pulling the handles of "one-armed bandits" at very high rates. Another example of human behavior on a variable-ratio schedule is selling insurance. The salesperson needs to pay a large number of calls to make only a few sales, and there is no way to predict which people will buy and which will not. This unpredictability is a property of VR schedules.

People tend to pull the lever of slot machines at a high rate because the machines are programmed to deliver payoffs on a variable-ratio schedule of reinforcement.

Fixed interval.   In a **fixed-interval (FI) schedule,** reinforcement is not triggered by the number of responses. Instead, reinforcers become available only at specified intervals. For example, an animal on an FI one-minute schedule has to wait a full minute between reinforcers, no matter how many times it responds immediately after it receives a reinforcer. The first response that occurs *after* a minute has passed is reinforced. This way of programming reinforcers is usually achieved by using a clock that starts timing whenever a reinforcer is presented. When the clock reaches one minute, it activates a mechanism that presents a reinforcer for the next bar press. Thus, in a fixed-interval schedule it does the animal no good to respond before the one-minute interval is up, but it will get a reinforcer for the first response *after* one minute. For this reason, animals who have been on an FI schedule for a while usually slow down or stop responding right after being reinforced, and slowly begin responding as the end of the interval approaches. This creates an effect called **scalloping** in the cumulative record.

Fixed-interval schedules are created whenever events are scheduled at specific times and separated by the same interval, such as weekly examinations or a favorite TV program. The effect of FI schedules is the same for humans as for rats. For example, many students show scalloping in their studying behavior: exerting great effort just before an exam but studying little in the days immediately following it..

Variable interval.   In a **variable-interval (VI) schedule,** the presentation of reinforcers is again governed by time, but the interval between reinforced responses changes instead of remaining fixed. Thus, on a VI two-minute schedule, the interval between reinforced responses may be as short as a few seconds or as long as five minutes, but the *average* interval is two minutes.

Because the delivery of reinforcers is unpredictable, this schedule results in a steady rate of responding, though usually slower than for the variable-ratio schedule. An example of a behavior controlled by a VI schedule is looking down the street while waiting for a bus that operates on an unknown or irregular schedule. Eventually the looking behavior is reinforced by the sight of the bus, and you are likely to repeat that behavior with some frequency the next time you have to wait for the bus. On the other hand, looking down the street is not like playing slot machines, as no amount of looking will make the bus come any faster. (If the bus always ran on time, and always came at the same interval, chances are you would start looking for it only as the time for it to arrive approached—the pattern of responding that results from a fixed-interval schedule.)

From these descriptions of reinforcement schedules you can see that there is a very important difference between ratio and interval schedules of reinforcement. To increase the chances of getting reinforced for making a response on a ratio schedule, you must *respond more* (wash more cars, play the slot machine more). To increase the chances of getting reinforced for making a response on an interval schedule, you must *wait more* (wait until the bus arrives). This important difference explains why responding differs on the two different types of schedules.

The effect of schedules of reinforcement on responding also extends to extinction. This is particularly apparent when we compare extinction following continuous reinforcement with extinction following partial reinforcement.

The partial reinforcement effect.   It may seem logical that extinction should occur more readily following partial reinforcement than continuous reinforcement, as the animal receives fewer reinforcers on a partial reinforcement schedule. However, the opposite is true: extinction is much slower following partial reinforcement, a phenomenon called the *partial reinforcement effect*. This slower extinction following partial reinforcement is illustrated by an experiment in which a pigeon pecked about 200 times following the termination of a continuous reinforcement schedule, but pecked over 5,000 times following termination of a VI schedule (Ferster, Culbertson, & Boren, 1975).

We can better understand the partial reinforcement effect if we look at what happens right at the beginning of extinction for continuous and partial reinforcement schedules. Consider, for example, what happens when you put money in a soft drink machine. If it is working properly, the machine reinforces you with a beverage every time you feed it money. But suppose the machine suddenly stops giving you a soft drink when you insert your coins. You might chance inserting money one more time, but if you fail to get the drink you're more likely to express your feelings toward the machine with your foot than continue putting money in it. Extinction is therefore complete after only two trials.

If, however, you are playing a one-armed bandit in a gambling casino, you don't *expect* to be reinforced every time you put in a coin. If the machine reinforces you on a VR 15 schedule, you win money every 15 tries, on the average—but you may not win for 30 or 40 tries. If, unknown to you, the machine jams and stops giving reinforcers altogether, you may continue responding until you have pulled the lever many times without winning anything. Thus, it takes a much longer time for your response to extinguish following partial reinforcement than it does following continuous reinforcement.

Partial reinforcement, then, tends to lead to more durable conditioning than continuous reinforcement, a fact that many of us fail to appreciate in real-life situations. The behavior of many children who accompany their parents to the supermarket provides a good example of how hard it can be to extinguish responses established through partial reinforcement. As small children are being wheeled around the store in the shopping cart, they often ask their parents again and again to buy things like potato chips, cookies, and ice cream. If the parent consistently refrains from reinforcing this behavior by ignoring the child's requests, there is some chance that the child's asking behavior will eventually extinguish. If, however, the parent gives in at some point (as many often do), he has created a partial reinforcement schedule—the child asks many times before getting reinforced. The parent may feel proud of himself for giving in only once, but by rewarding the child on a partial reinforcement schedule he has increased the chances that the child will continue to ask for things in the supermarket. In other words, it will be extremely difficult to extinguish the child's asking behavior. The same principle holds for dogs begging for food at the dinner table. Give in just once or twice, and it becomes extremely difficult to extinguish the response.

Air traffic controllers are constantly on the lookout for a signal that indicates a dangerous air traffic situation, such as two planes in the same air space. This signal is a discriminative stimulus which indicates that an immediate response (notifying the planes to correct their altitude) is necessary.

Discriminative stimuli.   Although it is difficult to extinguish responding following partial reinforcement, we can find a way to speed up this process by considering why extinction is so rapid following continuous reinforcement. Remember the soft drink machine. Nondelivery of just one beverage is an unmistakable signal that something has changed. Missing just one reinforcer on a continuous reinforcement schedule signals that extinction has begun. However, when reinforcement is stopped following partial reinforcement, no such signal is ordinarily present, because it is normal not to regularly receive reinforcers on a partial reinforcement schedule. But suppose we provide a stimulus that signals the beginning of extinction. This signal, which is called a **discriminative stimulus,** can cause responding to stop almost immediately.

We can illustrate how a discriminative stimulus works in the laboratory by using a process called **differential reinforcement.** In differential reinforcement we reinforce a behavior performed in the presence of one stimulus and extinguish the same behavior performed in the presence of another. For example, we might reinforce a pigeon for pecking when a green light is illuminated but not reinforce it for pecking when a red light is illuminated. Thus, "green light" signals reinforcement and "red light" signals no reinforcement. Once the pigeon has learned to make this discrimination, its pecking behavior will extinguish almost immediately in the presence of the red light, even if it has previously been on a partial reinforcement schedule.

The importance of discriminative stimuli extends far beyond the world of the laboratory rat or pigeon, for they play a major role in controlling much of our daily behavior. They serve as signals that tell us when to engage in certain behaviors. Many children swear around their friends but learn to avoid swearing around their parents. Their parents are discriminative stimuli for not swearing. Similarly, many an employee has learned to use the boss's mood as a discriminative stimulus to indicate when to ask for a raise or a day off.

Generalization.   The opposite of discrimination is generalization. You may recall that in classical conditioning, *generalization* occurs when a conditioned response (for example, Little Albert's crying) is elicited by a stimulus that is different from the original conditioned stimulus (the white rat) but still similar to it (for example, a rabbit). A similar phenomenon happens if we change the discriminative stimulus in operant conditioning. Let's go back to our pigeon who pecks only when the green light is illuminated. If we trained this pigeon to peck when the light was green, what would happen if we changed the light to blue? The pigeon, which has good color vision, will still peck, but at a slower rate than

in a shuttle box only with great difficulty; it takes over 100 trials for some rats. However, a rat can learn to avoid shock by running in a wheel in only 40 trials. It takes only 6 trials for the rat to learn to run down an alley, and just 1 to learn to jump out of a box. On the other hand, if you try to get a rat to avoid shock by pressing a bar, it won't do it—it simply freezes on the bar when it is shocked. Pigeons have the same problem. They can be trained to peck at a target key to avoid shock only with great difficulty (Hineline & Rachlin, 1969), but they can easily avoid a shock by flying away. The pigeon's species-specific defense reaction is flying, not pecking on keys.

Animals react differently to the same learning situations because different animals have different ways of dealing with the environment. This observation is consistent with the idea of *preparedness,* which we encountered in our discussion of conditioned taste aversion. In both operant and classical conditioning, the biologically programmed predispositions of animals influence whether learning will occur in a specific situation.

Applications of Operant Conditioning

The term *conditioning* may imply to some people a procedure carried out on subjects in a laboratory. Conditioning does, of course, take place in laboratories, as psychologists study its mechanisms under controlled conditions. But principles of conditioning have also proved highly useful in modifying human behavior outside of the laboratory and in helping us better understand everyday behavior. Following are a few examples of those applications of operant conditioning, beginning with some illustrations of how it has been used to help children with a condition called *autism.*

Operant conditioning as therapy.   In Chapter 17 we will see how principles of operant conditioning have been used to treat a number of different mental conditions. Here, we will focus on one particular mental condition, childhood autism, because work done by Ivar Lovaas at the Neuropsychiatric Institute at UCLA illustrates how both positive reinforcement and punishment have been used to treat children with this condition.

Childhood autism affects 4 in 10,000 children under the age of 15 (Ritvo et al., 1989). Its symptoms include an inability to interact with people, little or no speech, repetitious activity such as rocking, and self-destructive behavior such as head banging. Lovaas (1987) used shaping and positive reinforcement to teach autistic children to speak. The children were first reinforced

Operant conditioning procedures have been used to teach autistic children to talk.

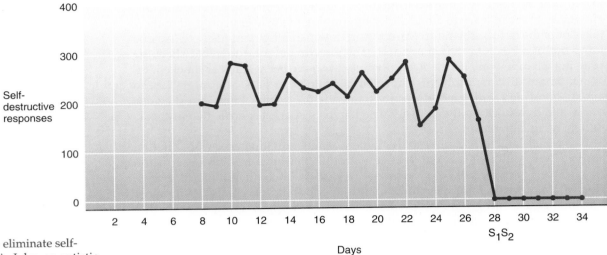

FIGURE 6.19
Using punishment to eliminate self-destructive behavior in John, an autistic child. Self-destructive responses were recorded beginning on the eighth day after admission to the clinic. Shocks (S_1 and S_2) presented on days 28 and 29 eliminated self-destructive behavior.

(often with small candies) for imitating one-syllable sounds made by the therapist. The therapist then reinforced them for making more complex sounds and simple words. Eventually, after a year-long program of daily training sessions, some children were able to have conversations. No other therapeutic technique has come close to operant conditioning's success in changing the behavior of autistic children, and it has also proved effective in treating many other disorders (Rachman & Wilson, 1980).

Here is another example of Lovaas's work. With James Simmons (1969), he used punishment to eliminate the self-destructive behavior of an autistic child named John. John had limited speech and social behavior when he was admitted to the clinic, and he had multiple scars all over his head and face caused by banging his temple and forehead with his knuckles. Due to his self-destructive behavior, for the prior six months John had continuously worn restraints on his arms and legs.

To eliminate John's self-destructive behavior, Lovaas and Simmons presented punishment in the form of a painful shock every time John hit himself. Figure 6.19 shows the results of this procedure. Each data point represents the number of self-destructive responses during a ten-minute testing period, when John was in a small dormitory room with two or three adults. On the day marked S1, John received a painful one-second shock immediately after a self-destructive response. He received another shock on the day marked S2. These two shocks eliminated self-destructive behavior in the dorm room, and presentation of a few shocks in other areas of the hospital effectively freed John from his self-destructive behavior.

People are sometimes dismayed that psychologists would present shocks as a way to control a retarded boy's behavior. But consider the alternatives. One way to eliminate self-destructive behavior is through drug therapy, but in John's case this was not effective. Another way might be to use extinction, because self-destructive behavior is sometimes a way to get attention. Terminating the positive reinforcement of attention might therefore extinguish the self-destructive behavior. Before resorting to the shock punishment procedure, therefore, Lovaas and Simmons tried to *extinguish* John's self-destructive behavior.

The researchers placed John in a small room, unfastened his restraints, and left him alone for one and a half hours at a time. An observer, whom John could not see, recorded every act of self-destructive behavior. During the first 90-minute session John hit himself 2,750 times. Although his self-destructive behavior ultimately extinguished, John had hit himself over 9,000 times during the course of extinction. Moreover, though he no longer hit himself in the room where the extinction took place, his behavior remained unaffected everywhere else.

Extinction clearly was not the answer for John, because it allowed him to hit himself thousands of times and was only effective in one room. In this situation, punishment was actually the fastest and kindest therapy for changing John's behavior. However, before jumping to the conclusion that punishment should be used any time we want to discourage a behavior, we need to take a number of factors into account.

1. Punishment can result in hostility toward the person doing the punishing. This hostility can be minimized if it is made clear that there is a good reason for the punishment.

2. Timing is important. Punishment works best if it is delivered immediately after the response to be eliminated. If your dog chases a car and you yell at her when she comes home, you are punishing coming home, not chasing cars. If you are dealing with a person, you can usually explain that a deferred punishment is for something that happened earlier—nonetheless, even for humans, punishment is more effective if it occurs immediately. The long delay between the commission of a crime and punishment for the crime (plus the chance that punishment may not occur at all) has often been cited as a possible reason for the seeming ineffectiveness of our criminal justice system.

3. Punishment may lead to escape behavior. A child punished for talking in class may escape the situation by skipping class the next day.

4. Punishment tells the person being punished only what not to do. If the result you want is a change in behavior, you should attempt to reinforce the desirable behavior as well as to punish the undesirable behavior.

5. What we think is a punishment may not be punishing at all. Consider a child who is usually ignored by his parents but is soundly scolded when he misbehaves. Rather than the punishment the parents intend, the scolding may actually be reinforcing to the child, because it is a form of attention. Unfortunately, this fact is often lost on the parents, who continue to ignore the child *except* when he misbehaves and then wonder why the misbehavior keeps happening. A similar effect happens in school. In a study of kindergarten behavior, it was found that boys disrupt class three times more than girls, even though teachers respond almost every time the boys disrupt class, often with a loud reprimand, but respond only occasionally to girls (Serbin et al., 1973). What's going on here? It seems likely that being loudly reprimanded may actually be reinforcing the boys' disruptive behavior. After all, when the teacher screams at Johnny after he bonks Ralph over the head with a toy truck, all eyes turn to Johnny. Both the teacher's and the class's attention is likely to be highly reinforcing for Johnny, who may, later in the day, go looking for someone else to assault with his truck. It is clear that though punishment is a powerful way to eliminate unwanted behavior, it only works well when used intelligently (Azrin & Holz, 1966; Walters & Grusec, 1977).

Operant conditioning has also been used to shape desirable behavior in classrooms, mental institutions, and prisons by using a technique called *token economy*. In the token economy system the student, patient, or prisoner earns tokens for appropriate behavior (working, not fighting, paying attention, handing in homework on time, and so on). These tokens, which function like money, can then be cashed in for rewards (Kazdin, 1977).

Operant conditioning in everyday life.   As important as operant conditioning has been in therapeutic settings, its major importance lies in its pervasiveness in our everyday lives. We've already seen numerous examples of the role of positive and negative reinforcement in everyday behavior. Consider your own behavior. What do you find particularly reinforcing? Money? Food? Social approval? Think about how your behavior is influenced by your attempts to obtain your favorite reinforcers. Do you go out of your way to be with other people or to please them, so they will like you? Are food and eating important to you? Are you afraid that if you eat too much, you might not be thin enough to gain the social approval you seek? Whatever questions might be relevant for you, your answers provide information about the kinds of reinforcers that are important in your life.

10   DEVELOPMENT

In addition to influencing your day-to-day behavior, reinforcement played an important role in your early development. Reinforcement is one of the mechanisms responsible for socialization—the process by which you learned the rules of correct behavior as you were growing up. Young boys and girls often experience *differential reinforcement*; that is, they are reinforced for different behaviors. Boys are often reinforced for aggression and competitiveness and girls for caretaking and cooperation. Later in life, this differential reinforcement is translated into differences in the way they behave as men and women (Hyde, 1991).

Differential reinforcement also occurs in school. For example, boys generally receive more attention from their teachers than girls do for their efforts in math and science classes. This has been cited as a factor responsible for boys' greater interest in math and science, compared with girls', and for their higher scores on the math section of the SAT (Meece et al., 1982; Sherman, 1982). We pursue the possible role of reinforcement in shaping our behaviors as men and women in the Follow-Through at the end of this chapter.

Interactions Between Classical and Operant Conditioning

Operant and classical conditioning are different kinds of learning that can be distinguished from one another in a number of ways. Table 6.2, which compares the properties of the two, highlights some of their differences. However, just as processes at different levels of analysis interact in our behavior, classical and operant conditioning often work together. For example, consider my own responses when, as a young paper carrier, I was bitten by a dog and came to fear dogs. My emotional response was established by *classical* conditioning: the sight of dogs came to elicit fear. That emotional response, however, also influenced my behavior: I began to *avoid* dogs. This was operant behavior (I was "operating" on my environment). That behavior was then maintained by *operant* conditioning, as my "dog-avoiding" behavior was followed by the *removal* of the unpleasant feeling of fear caused by the classical conditioning. My avoidance of dogs was thus negatively reinforced, and I continued to avoid dogs into adulthood. In this example, classical conditioning explains my emotional response, whereas operant conditioning explains why I learned to avoid dogs (Figure 6.20).

Secondary reinforcement provides another example of interaction between classical and operant conditioning. A secondary reinforcer is created by being paired with a primary reinforcer. This association between two stimuli, with one taking on the properties of the other, is classical conditioning. For example, Donald Zimmerman (1957) exposed rats to a buzzer for two seconds and then gave them some water. After a number of buzzer-water pairings, Zimmerman's rats would press a bar to hear the buzzer, which they wouldn't do before it was paired with water. Through classical conditioning the buzzer had become a secondary reinforcer by being paired with the primary reinforcer of water; it could, therefore, reinforce the operant behavior of bar pressing.

Conditioned suppression is established by a similar mechanism. Earlier in this chapter we discussed Robert Rescorla's and Leon Kamin's use of conditioned suppression. After they paired a tone with shocks, presentation of the

TABLE 6.2
Basic properties of classical and operant conditioning

	Classical Conditioning	*Operant Conditioning*
Key Researchers	Pavlov, Watson, Rescorla, Kamin, Garcia	Thorndike, Skinner
Types of Response	Reflexes, emotional reactions	Voluntary responses emitted by the organism
Goal	To create a new response to a stimulus	To increase the rate of a response
Basic Procedure	Pair the stimulus to be conditioned (NS) with a stimulus (US) that elicits a response (UR). Eventually, the NS elicits the response (CR), so NS becomes CS.	Present a positive reinforcer or remove a negative reinforcer immediately after an organism makes a response.
Examples	• Dog's salivation to bell • Emotional responses elicited by environmental stimuli • Conditioned drug tolerance • Establishment of phobias • Desensitization: elimination of phobias	• Rat pressing bar for food • Humans seeking social approval • Elimination of destructive behavior in autistic children • Establishing speech in autistic children • Token economy: reinforcing desirable behavior with tokens
Key Concepts	*Contiguity.* Old idea: contiguity between NS and US is crucial for best conditioning. Delay conditioning is most effective. Reformulation: contiguity is not always sufficient; important factor is how well NS *predicts* UR. Contiguity is not necessary in conditioned taste aversion. *Extinction.* Response elicited by the CS decreases as the CS is repeatedly presented alone. *Spontaneous recovery.* If the extinction procedure is stopped and CS is presented again after a time interval, the response is larger than on last extinction trial. *Discrimination.* To establish discrimination, present NS and US together and present other, similar stimuli without US. *Generalization.* Response occurs to stimuli other than the CS. The more similar stimuli are to the CS, the larger the response.	*Reinforcement.* Behavior is controlled by consequences. Reinforcers are most effective if presented or removed immediately after a response. Rate and pattern of response depend on schedules of reinforcement. *Extinction.* Rate of response emitted by animal decreases when the response is no longer reinforced. *Partial reinforcement effect.* Extinction takes longer following partial reinforcement than following continuous reinforcement. *Discrimination.* To establish a discriminative stimulus, reinforce responding in presence of the stimulus; don't reinforce responding in presence of other stimuli. *Generalization.* Animal responds in presence of stimuli different than the discriminative stimulus. Response rate is faster if stimuli are more similar to the discriminative stimulus.

tone suppressed ongoing bar pressing. Here, too, classical conditioning endows a previously neutral stimulus (the tone) with properties that are then used to influence operantly conditioned behavior (bar pressing).

A particularly interesting example of the interaction between classical and operant conditioning comes from the experiences of two colleagues of Skinner, Keller Breland and Marian Breland (1961, 1966), who used their expertise in operant conditioning to train animals for circus, TV, and film stunts. In the process of training 38 species and over 6,000 animals, they observed a few interesting breakdowns in the animals' behavior that are difficult to explain on the basis of operant conditioning alone.

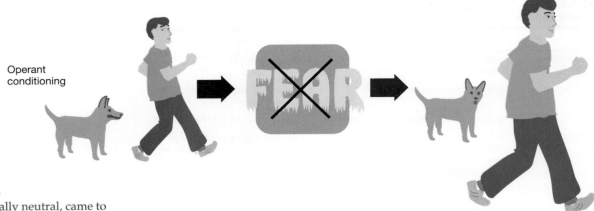

Operant
conditioning

FIGURE 6.20

Dogs, although initially neutral, came to elicit fear when the author was bitten by one. Pairing "biting" and "dog" to create fear of dogs is an example of classical conditioning. The fear of dogs then controlled operant behavior as illustrated here. The author avoids dogs, and since it eliminates the fear this behavior is negatively reinforced, so he continues to avoid dogs. Compare this diagram with the one at the bottom of Figure 6.13 on page 247. Both are examples of how negative reinforcers influence behavior.

In one of their projects, the Brelands' goal was to train a raccoon to pick up two coins and drop them into a piggy bank. They began by reinforcing the raccoon with food for picking up a single coin. They then used shaping to get the raccoon to drop the coin into a metal container. Having accomplished this (although with some trouble, as the raccoon insisted on rubbing the coin on the side of the container before dropping it in), the Brelands put the raccoon on a fixed-ratio 2 schedule; to get the reinforcer it had to pick up two coins and drop them into the container. Unfortunately, at this point the raccoon's performance broke down altogether. Instead of dropping the two coins into the container, the raccoon began rubbing them together, dipping them into the container, and rubbing them some more. This behavior was so persistent that the Brelands abandoned their attempts to condition the raccoon.

Why wasn't the raccoon cooperating? According to what we know about operant conditioning, if a behavior is reinforced it should become more likely to happen again. But if we consider how classical conditioning works, we can solve this puzzle. Because the coins were *paired* with food, they apparently took on the properties of food. Once this occurred, the raccoon's biological makeup took over and it started treating the coins as if they were food. What do raccoons normally do with food? They wash freshly caught crayfish by rubbing them together or on rocks to remove their external shell.

The Brelands coined the term **instinctive drift** to describe behavior like that of the raccoon and other species, because the animal's "instinctive" or biologically built-in behaviors were interacting with conditioning. The raccoon's instinctive drift created a situation in which a classically conditioned response

3   BIOLOGY

Raccoons are used to rubbing crayfish together to open their shell, a biologically programmed behavior that proved disastrous to the Brelands' attempt to condition them to drop two coins into a container.

(coins taking on the properties of food) interfered with an attempt to create an operantly conditioned behavior (dropping coins into the container).

From these examples it is clear that although classical and operant conditioning are different, they often interact, with classical conditioning creating new properties for stimuli that then act as reinforcers to control operant behavior.

Cognitive Processes in Simple Learning

We have seen that early behaviorist researchers viewed learning as a fairly simple, automatic process that could be studied exclusively at the behavioral level of analysis. Most researchers, and especially Watson and Skinner, totally disavowed any interest in studying cognitive processes. This attitude becomes especially apparent when we look back at how the behaviorists defined reinforcement and punishment: strictly in terms of their observable effects on behavior. Reinforcement increases the rate of response; punishment decreases the rate of response. There is no need to hypothesize about anything going on inside the organism's mind if all we have to do is look at its rate of responding.

But even as Watson and Skinner were extolling the benefits of focusing exclusively on the behavioral level of analysis, other psychologists were suggesting that many learned behaviors cannot be fully explained by conditioning. One of these psychologists was Edward Tolman, an early proponent of the idea that conditioning alone cannot explain how animals solve many learning problems.

Edward Tolman: Cognitive Maps in Rats

As far back as the 1920s, some researchers were following a cognitive trail in their explanation of learning. Notable among them was Edward Tolman, who 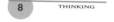 carried out a number of clever experiments in which rats had to run through a maze to receive food. One of these mazes offered a rat three pathways from the starting box to the food box (Figure 6.21). When placed in the maze the rats moved about and explored it. After this exploration, the rats chose path 1, the shortest route to the goal area. When Tolman blocked that path (block A), they chose path 2, the next-shortest route (Tolman & Honzik, 1930).

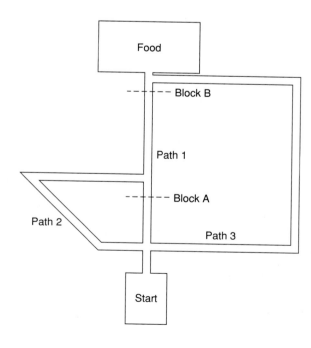

FIGURE 6.21

Top view of the maze used by Tolman and Honzik to test the idea that rats form cognitive maps.

Why did the rats choose the shortest available path when the best route out of the maze was blocked? According to reinforcement theory, the rats picked path 2 because, as they explored the maze, they had learned that turning left out of the start box led more quickly to rewards than turning right. Tolman, however, suggested that the rats picked path 2 because they had formed a **cognitive map** of the maze during the initial exploration. To prove this point, Tolman and Honzig blocked the maze at B. Reinforcement theory predicts that the rats should still pick path 2, as they would still associate turning left with more immediate reward than turning right. In contrast, Tolman predicted that the rats would consult their cognitive map of the maze, determine that path 2 would be blocked by the barrier at B, and then pick path 3. This is, in fact, what they did. Fully 93% of the rats picked path 3 on the first trial.

This kind of result convinced Tolman that cognitive maps play an important role in animal learning (Tolman, 1948). Others disagreed, however—partly because some researchers had trouble replicating Tolman's results and partly because of the strong grip that behaviorism had on psychology in the 1930s and 1940s. Remember the behaviorist view that it is inappropriate to invoke unobservable mental processes in explaining behavior. Because the formation of cognitive maps is a mental process, Tolman's proposal at the height of behaviorism's popularity did not gain wide acceptance (Lieberman, 1990). Researchers generally preferred to look for explanations that relied solely on behaviorist principles.

By the 1960s, however, psychology was ready to explore ideas like cognitive maps, and many researchers provided further evidence for their existence (Olton, 1979). For example, R. G. M. Morris (1981) found that after rats were trained to swim from one starting place to an underwater platform that they could not see, they were able to immediately find the platform when they were released from other starting places, something they could not have done if they had learned only how to get from the original starting point to the platform. The rats had apparently created a cognitive map indicating the location of the platform.

The idea of cognitive maps, which is now well accepted, pointed to one of the cognitive components of learning that was ignored by early researchers studying conditioning. Another type of learning that clearly involves cognitive components is learning that involves **insight**—the sudden realization of the solution to a problem. Like cognitive maps, this topic was ignored by most early researchers; however, Wolfgang Köhler (1927) was an exception. His studies of problem solving in chimpanzees have become classics in psychological literature.

Wolfgang Köhler: Insight in Chimpanzees

Köhler's research on chimpanzees was to some extent created by World War I. In 1913 Köhler went to the Spanish island of Tenerife in the Canary Islands to study chimpanzee behavior. Shortly after he arrived World War I broke out, stranding him on the island. Undaunted, Köhler undertook a series of research projects that culminated in his classic book, *The Mentality of Apes* (1927).

Köhler's book immortalizes the behavioral exploits of a number of chimpanzees. One of them, Sultan, was given the problem of retrieving fruit from a basket that was out of reach, far overhead. Sultan first tried knocking the fruit down with one of the sticks in his cage. After a number of attempts with a stick that was too short and some attempts with another stick that was too heavy, Sultan became frustrated with the task and appeared to give up. Then all of a sudden he ran over to a box that was in the cage, pushed it to the place where the basket was hanging, jumped up on it, and used the short stick to knock down the fruit.

FIGURE 6.22
Köhler's chimp Sultan stacking boxes to retrieve bananas.

Köhler was struck with the way Sultan solved this problem and others like it (see Figure 6.22). For example, one task required Sultan to use two short sticks to pull in a long stick that could reach the fruit. In each case, Sultan arrived at a solution suddenly, in a way that demonstrated the operation of insight, or what has been called an "Aha" experience.

"Aha" experiences are familiar to most people. A solution to a problem may not be obvious, but then all of a sudden it comes to us. This is clearly different from the simple responses of the operant conditioning experiments we have described. There is no doubt that solving a problem that yields a banana is highly reinforcing for a chimpanzee. But how can we understand the *processes* involved in determining how to obtain that reinforcement? Many psychologists today feel that a logical place to look for the answer to this question is within the organism's brain. We will see how modern psychologists go about doing this in the chapters that follow.

Albert Bandura: Learning by Observation

Finally we consider a type of learning that we all participate in, often without realizing it. **Observational learning** is a change in behavior that occurs after observing someone else's behavior. For example, as young children we observe and often mimic the behavior of our parents or other adults.

The classic laboratory demonstration of this effect is Albert Bandura's "Bobo doll" experiment (Bandura, Ross, & Ross, 1963). In it, children observed a film of an adult repeatedly hitting a large, plastic doll. After this observation, the children played much more aggressively than children who hadn't observed the aggressive adult. This effect became particularly powerful when the children not only observed the adult model being aggressive but also saw the adult receive praise for the aggressive behavior (Bandura, 1965). In this case, therefore, observation and reinforcement work together to influence behavior.

Observational learning is sometimes called **modeling** because it involves observing a "model" whose behavior is imitated. A major contrast between observational learning and conditioning is that in observational learning the subject's behavior is changed even though the subject never directly receives reinforcements, whereas conditioning requires that at least some of the subject's responses be followed by reinforcers. Observational learning is extremely important in the process of socialization, or learning the rules of correct behavior in our society. We look at this role of observational learning in the socialization of male and female roles in the Follow-Through at the end of the chapter.

Reprise: The Fruits of Behaviorism

This chapter has primarily been about the application of the behavioral level of analysis to understanding behavior. A nice thing about the behavioral level of analysis is that it generally deals with phenomena that can actually be observed. They are not hidden away in some nucleus in the brain or in some subconscious cranny of the mind. This means that you can apply the knowledge you have gained from this chapter toward increasing your awareness of some of the mechanisms responsible for your own behavior. Your knowledge of classical conditioning might, for example, help you trace the source of an emotion to a past experience that occurred in a similar situation. Or consider, for example, the following simple illustration of how knowing about the principles of conditioning can be used to influence one's own behavior.

I had gotten into the habit of playing a certain tape every time I drove to a hiking trail in the woods. After playing it on a number of these trips I noticed that I became very relaxed when I played the tape while driving around the city, and recognized this as a clear case of classical conditioning. The music had been paired with an unconditioned stimulus (the peacefulness of the woods) that elicited an unconditioned response (relaxation). Thus, the music became a conditioned stimulus that elicited the conditioned response of relaxation. My realization that this is classical conditioning, combined with my knowledge of extinction, makes me very careful not to play the tape too often in the city. The last thing I want is for my conditioned relaxation response to the music to extinguish because I listened to the tape too many times in the absence of the unconditioned stimulus.

You can probably think of situations in your own life in which your response can be explained by either classical or operant conditioning. Being more aware of the causes of your behavior makes it possible to take more control of your behavior. You can use reinforcement in a number of ways—by placing yourself in situations that are likely to be reinforcing, and intelligently using your ability to dispense reinforcements to others. (Don't reinforce undesirable behavior, though, especially on a partial reinforcement schedule!) For example, many weight control programs are built on principles of conditioning, by using periodic weigh-ins to reinforce weight loss.

The fact that we can relate many of the principles introduced in this chapter to everyday behavior says a great deal about the importance of the behaviorist approach. But we need to give behaviorism credit for more than simply discovering some principles that we can apply to everyday behavior. Behaviorism was responsible for nothing less than revolutionizing psychology. There is no doubt that behaviorism's emphasis on objectively measurable behavior played an essential role in the evolution of scientific psychology from its crude beginnings to its present stature as an objectively based science.

At the same time, we have seen that we need to go beyond the principles established by the behaviorists if we are to fully understand behavior. As the later refinements to classical and operant conditioning illustrate, we need to broaden our scope to include the biological and cognitive levels of analysis. In the chapters that follow we will see how the cognitive approach, in particular, has become a powerful force in present day psychology. But before we leave behaviorism in favor of the cognitive approach it is important to acknowledge the debt that present day cognitive psychologists owe behaviorism.

Even though cognitive psychologists are studying the "mind" and "mental processes"—two subjects avoided by the behaviorists—they base their research on the *objectively measurable responses* that the behaviorists held so dear. One reason the study of cognition has become such a powerful force within current psychology is that the cognitive psychologists found ways to use those objectively measurable behaviors to draw conclusions about what is going on "inside the head." As we study this approach in the next chapter we will begin to appreciate how both the behaviorist and cognitive approaches enrich our understanding of behavior.

Learning Gender Roles

Since ancient times, when people have thought about the differences they observe in the behavior of their fellow humans, they have often explained the differences in terms of biology. Thus, many people explain differences in the behavior of men and women in terms of the obvious differences in the biological makeup of the sexes. According to this idea, it is natural for women, who are biologically constructed to give birth and to nurse, to be responsible for child care. Women, also being slighter of build than men, are often deemed to be unqualified for jobs that require physical strength. And, as we saw in the Follow-Through at the end of Chapter 2, intellectual differences between males and females have sometimes been explained by hypothesized (although often not true) differences between male and female brains.

But what of the increasing number of people who reject the idea that people's behavior and roles are predetermined by their biology? These people often support equal opportunity for women in employment, and an equal sharing of housework and child care by men and women. So far, despite the growing movement toward equality in our society, true equality in employment or at home is not a reality: 97% of the top executives of the largest U.S. companies are males (Saltzman, 1991), and females do the vast majority of housework and child care, even when they have full-time jobs (Belsky et al., 1984; Lewis, 1989). Male and female behaviors also differ—most obviously in terms of aggression. Males are much more aggressive and account for most of the world's violent crime.

What we are talking about here is differences in **gender roles,** the behaviors considered appropriate for males and females in our society. In this chapter we have surveyed information that might lead us to question whether those different behaviors are determined by biological differences between men and women. We have seen that learning—behavioral change resulting from experience with the environment—is an immensely powerful force. Could it be that learning, rather than biology, is the preeminent force responsible for many of the differences we observe between males and females in our society?

The idea that learning plays an important role in determining male/female differences is reflected in the concept that gender roles are largely established through **socialization**—the process by which we learn the rules of "correct" behavior as we grow. According to this idea, as we grow up we are taught by **socializing agents**—our parents, our peers, the media, and our schools—how boys and girls and men and women should behave. Is it true that, as boys and girls grow up, the learning they experience socializes them to play different roles? To answer this question we will first look at the socializing influences of parents and the media.

Socializing Influences in Children's Lives

There is no question that some differences between males and females are biologically determined. Boys are more active and aggressive than girls from birth (Hyde, 1991), and hormone and brain differences may be involved in determining these and other behavioral differences. (See the Follow-Through for Chapter 3, "Sex Hormones, Brain Structure, and Behavior.") But most psy-

chologists consider socialization to be the major factor responsible for differences in the way males and females behave. Socialization works by exposing boys and girls to different experiences.

Parents as socializing agents. Parents often treat boys and girls differently, based on differences in the way they view boys and girls. When J. Z. Rubin and co-workers (1974) interviewed parents during the 24 hours following the birth of their first child, both mothers and fathers tended to describe the boys as being firm, alert, and strong; girls were more likely to be described as little, beautiful, pretty, and cute. As in reality there was no difference between the babies, except for gender, the differing descriptions reflected the parents' attitudes about boys and girls rather than the babies' actual characteristics.

These stereotypes find their way into the decorating schemes and toys found in young children's rooms. A survey of 96 preschoolers' bedrooms revealed that boys' rooms contained significantly more vehicles and sports equipment and girls' rooms were more likely to be decorated with "flowered patterns and ruffles" and to contain more dolls (Rheingold & Cook, 1975). Moreover, as children grow up, parents, and particularly fathers, treat sons and daughters differently. Fathers play more roughly with sons than with daughters, and usually give them more independence (Hyde, 1991; Parke, 1979, 1981; Power, 1981).

The media as socializing agent. The media are another powerful socializing agent for young children, with television heading the list. As children watch TV they see that the males act more aggressively than females, and that females are more likely to understand other people's needs and feelings (Hodges, Brandt, & Kline, 1981). You don't have to read the research literature, however, to know that there are large differences in the way males and females are portrayed on TV. All of the children's shows in the 1991 Saturday morning TV lineup had male lead characters, and even on public TV's "Sesame Street," most of the Muppet characters were identified as males (Carter, 1991). The message children get from watching TV is clear: males and females not only behave differently, but males are dominant.

Mechanisms of Gender Role Learning

The differences we have noted in the messages boys and girls receive from their parents and TV become important only if they are translated into differing gender roles for males and females. Psychologists have proposed that a number of different mechanisms help to translate these messages into male and female roles.

Reinforcement. When a child behaves in a gender-appropriate way (a boy acting aggressively, a girl playing with dolls), that behavior is often reinforced by the child's parents. Conversely, gender-inappropriate behavior (a boy playing with dolls, or crying) is often punished (Langlois & Downs, 1980). This reinforcement of gender-appropriate behavior and punishment of gender-inappropriate behavior is handed out not only by parents, but also by the child's nursery-school classmates (Fagot, 1984, 1985a, b).

If this boy continues to play with dolls as he gets older, his parents or friends may label him a "sissy."

Levels of Analysis and Gender Role Learning

From our discussion thus far, it is clear that to achieve a full understanding of gender role learning we must consider it from both the behavioral and contextual levels of analysis. At the behavioral level, we have considered how reinforcement and observational learning shape gender roles; at the contextual level, we have considered how society—which surrounds boys and girls with expectations from parents and powerful media images—can point boys and girls in different directions.

Additional evidence for the effect of context comes from cross-cultural studies, which show that, despite the fact that males may be biologically predisposed to be more aggressive than females, in some cultures they are not. The anthropologist Margaret Mead (1935) found tribes in New Guinea in which males and females were equally aggressive (the Mundugumor), in which neither males nor females were aggressive (the Arapesh), and in which females were aggressive but the males passive (Tchambuli). Differences in how various cultures view aggression is also apparent when we compare Western cultures. For example, boys raised in the United States receive much more encouragement to behave aggressively than do boys in Scandinavia (Basow, 1992; Block, 1973).

But what of the cognitive level of analysis? We will look at how gender roles have been approached from a cognitive level in the Follow-Through in Chapter 7, on memory. There we will see how what children learn about male and female roles influences how they *think* about males and females and on the roles they play.

Observational learning. Psychologists have proposed that observational learning influences socialization as children observe same-sex models. Boys observe males; girls observe females—and then they imitate the model's behavior. However, research shows that modeling doesn't occur exactly as proposed by this theory. Boys and girls do imitate the behaviors of others, but don't focus exclusively on a same-sex model (Maccoby & Jacklin, 1974).

If boys and girls observe and model *both* male and female behaviors, why do they end up engaging primarily in behavior considered "appropriate" for their own gender? One answer is found in the child's everyday environment. Susan may learn to imitate her father as he pounds nails in his carpentry shop, but her brother, not her, is invited to work alongside the father. Just because a behavior is learned doesn't mean it will be used; it must be both practiced and perceived as appropriate before it is used.

This idea—that children must perceive a role to be appropriate before they take it on—becomes particularly important when we realize how many environmental cues teach children which behaviors are considered appropriate for males and females. When asked which occupation they associated with males and females, 67% of 2- to 3-year-olds responded by picking a male doll to go with "doctor" and 78% to go with "construction worker." In contrast, only about one-third of the children picked the male doll to go with "secretary" or "dancer" (Gettys & Cann, 1981). Young children not only know which professions are most likely to be filled by males or females; they also know about male and female behaviors. In another study, 94% of kindergarten children said that males are more likely to fight, and 66% said that females are more likely to say "Thank you" (Williams & Bennett, 1975).

Although young children learn at an early age that most construction workers are males, there are many exceptions to this "rule."

Learning and Behavior

- Learning is any relatively long-lasting change in behavior that is based on past experience. Learning occurs in different forms in all animals and is essential to survival.

- The pervasiveness of learning suggests two questions: (1) do the same basic principles of learning hold for all species? and (2) can we understand behavior in general by describing the processes that govern learning? John B. Watson and B. F. Skinner, two psychologists whose names are linked with behaviorism, answered "Yes" to both questions.

Habituation

- Habituation is a simple form of learning that occurs when the size of a response decreases with repeated presentation of a stimulus.

Principles of Classical Conditioning

- Ivan Pavlov pioneered research on classical conditioning using dogs as subjects. Classical conditioning involves pairing a neutral stimulus (NS) with an unconditioned stimulus (US); the neutral stimulus eventually comes to elicit a conditioned response (CR) that it had never elicited before. John B. Watson applied Pavlov's conditioning technique to a human when he conditioned Little Albert to be afraid of a rat.

- Pavlov and other researchers described a number of different properties of classical conditioning. They found that the strength of conditioning is affected by the way the NS and US are paired. The strongest conditioning occurs with delay conditioning, in which the NS is presented first and continues as the US is presented.

- Other classical conditioning phenomena include extinction, spontaneous recovery, generalization, discrimination, and second-order conditioning.

- Modern approaches to classical conditioning have challenged the contiguity hypothesis of classical conditioning by showing that contiguity doesn't automatically cause conditioning (Rescorla), and by showing that blocking can prevent subsequent conditioning of contiguous stimuli (Kamin).

- Garcia's conditioned taste aversion experiments showed that biological preparedness also influences classical conditioning, with different animals being "prepared" to associate different NS-US combinations. These experiments also showed that conditioning can occur even when the interval between presentation of the NS and US is very long. The results of Rescorla's, Kamin's, and Garcia's experiments led to the idea that classical conditioning is not an automatic response to pairing but rather a mechanism that helps organisms identify meaningful relations between events in their environment.

- Classical conditioning plays an important role in shaping behavior. It has, for instance, been implicated as a possible cause of phobias. The technique of systematic desensitiza-tion, which is based on classical conditioning, has been used to eliminate phobias. Classical conditioning can also explain drug tolerance and contributes to cigarette addiction.

- Conditioned drug tolerance occurs when environmental cues become the conditioned stimulus and the body's compensatory response becomes the conditioned response. Classical conditioning of cigarette smoking occurs when certain environments or situations become the conditioned stimulus and the physiological response to smoking becomes the conditioned response.

Principles of Operant Conditioning

- Operant conditioning is learning in which an animal operates on its environment to gain rewards or avoid negative stimuli. Early research on operant conditioning was carried out by Edward Thorndike, who proposed the law of effect. Later, B. F. Skinner created the Skinner box, which made it possible to reinforce animals for a specific response and to create a record of the animal's responding over time. Most of Skinner's early experiments involved rats pressing bars.

- Reinforcers control operant behavior. Both positive and negative reinforcers cause an increase in the rate of response. We can also distinguish primary (unlearned) reinforcers and secondary (learned) reinforcers. Secondary reinforcers gain their reinforcing properties by being paired with primary reinforcers.

- Some additional principles of operant conditioning are shaping, extinction, the timing of reinforcers, the effects of different schedules of reinforcement, the partial reinforcement effect, discriminative stimuli, generalization, and punishment.

- Two important refinements of operant conditioning are the Premack principle—the idea that any response can be reinforced by a more preferred response—and the role of species-specific defense reactions, which show that operant conditioning can be influenced by biological factors.

- Operant conditioning has many practical applications. For example, positive reinforcement has been used to teach autistic children to talk and punishment to eliminate their self-destructive behavior. To effectively use punishment to control behavior we need to use it intelligently to avoid negative side effects. Operant conditioning has also been used to create token economies to encourage socially desirable behaviors in schools, prisons, and mental institutions. It is a pervasive element of our everyday lives and a useful tool for self-knowledge.

Interactions Between Classical and Operant Conditioning

- Operant and classical conditioning often interact. For example, emotional responses established by classical conditioning can influence operant behavior; secondary reinforcers in operant conditioning are established by classical conditioning; and the "misbehavior" of trained animals sometimes occurs when a classically conditioned behavior interferes with operant responding.

Cognitive Processes in Simple Learning

- Although conditioning can explain many phenomena, additional explanations are needed to explain many cognitively based behaviors. The work of Edward Tolman and others has shown that animals often seem to base their responding not on reinforcement but on cognitive maps. And Wolfgang Köhler's chimpanzees solved problems after what appeared to be flashes of "insight." Further, the phenomenon of observational learning—or modeling—shows that behavior can be influenced in the absence of directly presented reinforcement.

Reprise: The Fruits of Behaviorism

- Knowledge of the principles of classical and operant conditioning can help people gain more control over their own lives. Historically, behaviorism not only brought psychology more into the scientific mainstream, but also paved the way for cognitive psychologists' use of observable behavior to study mental processes.

Follow-Through/Diversity: Learning Gender Roles

- Gender roles—the behaviors considered appropriate for males and females in a society—are determined largely by socialization. Parents and the media serve as socializing agents, and gender role learning occurs through reinforcement and observational learning. Cross-cultural studies also emphasize the importance of context in determining gender roles.

Key Terms

anxiety hierarchy
backward conditioning
bait shyness
baseline level
behavior therapy
blocking
classical conditioning
cognitive map
conditioned drug tolerance
conditioned response (CR)
conditioned stimulus (CS)
conditioned suppression
conditioned taste aversion
contiguity hypothesis
continuous reinforcement schedule (CRF)
counterconditioning
cumulative record
delay conditioning
differential reinforcement
discrimination training
discriminative stimulus
escape-avoidance training
extinction
fixed-interval (FI) schedule
fixed-ratio (FR) schedule
gender roles
generalization
habituation
homeostasis
insight
instinctive drift
interval schedule
law of effect
learning
modeling
negative reinforcer
neutral stimulus (NS)
observational learning
operant behavior
operant conditioning
partial reinforcement
phobias
positive reinforcer
Premack principle
preparedness
primary reinforcer
punishment
ratio schedule
reinforcer
scalloping
secondary reinforcer
second-order conditioning
sensory reinforcers
shaping
shuttle box
simultaneous conditioning
Skinner box
socialization
socializing agents
social reinforcers
species-specific defense reactions
spontaneous recovery
superstitious behavior
systematic desensitization
trace conditioning
unconditioned reflex
unconditioned response (UR)
unconditioned stimulus (US)
variable-interval (VI) schedule
variable-ratio (VR) schedule

CHAPTER

7

On the Trail of Memory: The Development of Memory Research

How Memory Works: An Information-Processing Model
The Multistore Memory System
Information Processing in Memory

Sensory Memory: The Sparkler's Trail

Short-Term Memory: Information in Action
Working Memory: STM as a Dynamic System
Encoding
Storage
Retrieval
Forgetting in STM
Transferring Information from STM to LTM

Long-Term Memory: Information in Storage
Encoding
Storage
Retrieval
Forgetting in LTM

How the Brain Remembers: The Physiology of Memory

Real-World Memory
Long-Lived Memories
Remembering Meaningful Stimuli: Memory as Constructive

Interdisciplinary Dimension: Criminal Justice
Memory in the Courtroom

Memory and Studying

Reprise: Memory and Cognitive Psychology

Follow-Through/Diversity
Gender Schemas and Memory

Memory

> *Every thought, every action, our very conception of personal identity, is based on memory. . . . Without memory, all experience would be useless.*
>
> F. W. Edridge-Green (1900)

What would life be like without memory? One way to find out is to examine the experiences of people who have lost their ability to form memories. Remember Jimmie G., the man with Korsakoff's syndrome, whom we described at the beginning of Chapter 3? He could remember events from his distant past but couldn't assimilate any new knowledge. He couldn't recognize people he had met just moments before; he would reread the same newspaper endlessly without remembering anything he had read. Without his memory, Jimmy was a man suspended in a small window of time, living such a hollow existence that he said he didn't even feel alive (Sacks, 1987).

The case of Jimmie G. illustrates how central the ability to remember is to our experience and even our identity. What would your life be like if you couldn't retain what you read, recall how to find your way to school, or recognize the voices and faces of loved ones? What if you could no longer bring to mind vacations, friendships, or things you had learned? Clearly, virtually everything you do depends on your mysterious capacity to store and retrieve many kinds of memories.

How exactly do you do it? How do you preserve images of your fifth birthday, recognize the smell of baking bread, recall a melody, and remember how to ride a bicycle or read French? To put it another way, why don't you immediately forget an experience the moment it is past? And are all kinds of memory really the same, or does remembering who founded scientific psychology involve a different kind of memory than remembering your first day in kindergarten or how to play the piano? Finally, if you remember so many things without effort, why do you ever *forget*—and why does forgetting often affect the very things you are trying hardest to remember, like the information you study the night before an exam or the phone number of that attractive person you met yesterday?

By now you might suspect that the answers to these questions must be sought at several levels of analysis. We can approach memory from a *behavioral* level, by studying people's observable performance on memory tasks under different conditions. But memory is clearly a *cognitive* process—one that involves both unconscious and conscious mental activities, such as suddenly recalling the answer to a problem or actively searching our memories for the name of the movie that won the Oscar for best picture last year. So a second approach to studying memory is to probe what happens in people's minds as they sort incoming information, register it, and recall it later on. This is the approach taken by a great deal of recent work that treats memory as a form of *information processing*. Work at this cognitive level of analysis will occupy most of our attention in this chapter.

Of course, underlying any behavioral or cognitive activity is the physiology of the brain. The case of Jimmie G. illustrates that our ability to form and re-

How do you remember things that have happened to you?

trieve memories depends on the proper functioning of the brain. What happens at the level of neurons when we create memories? To answer this question we need to work at the biological level of analysis, probing the physical mechanisms that underlie not only disruptions of memory like those experienced by Jimmie G. but also the everyday ability to remember that most of us take for granted.

In this chapter we will explore each of these levels of analysis, and in the process retrace the steps of the psychologists who have explored the fascinating terrain of human memory. At the end of the chapter we will apply some of their research results to a practical problem you are facing right now: how to use memory more effectively while learning.

On the Trail of Memory: The Development of Memory Research

The story of scientific research on memory mirrors the development of psychology itself. We saw in previous chapters that the psychologists of the late 1800s sought ways to make the study of the mind as objective as the study of the physical sciences. One of those pioneers was Hermann Ebbinghaus, who was so dedicated to the study of memory that he spent countless hours doing something extremely tedious—memorizing nonsense syllables.

Hermann Ebbinghaus: Making Memory Measurable

In the 1880s German psychologist Hermann Ebbinghaus became intrigued with the process of *forgetting*. Why, he wondered, should information we have learned be forgotten with the passage of time? Why is it available to us at one moment but "gone" a week later?

Ebbinghaus felt the first step toward answering this question was to compile accurate data that described the precise course of remembering and forgetting. But how could psychologists obtain such data? As Ebbinghaus asked in his 1885 book *Memory,* "By what possible means are we to measure numerically the mental processes which flit by so quickly and which on introspection are so hard to analyze?" (1885/1964, p. 7).

The key word in this quotation is *numerically,* because what Ebbinghaus sought was a way to *quantify* mental processes—specifically, the processes involved in memory. Ebbinghaus believed that remembering must involve some kind of *memory trace,* formed when we learn something. Whether we can remember what we learned depends on the strength of the memory trace; at some point the trace is too weak, and we forget. The key to quantifying the processes of remembering and forgetting, therefore, was to measure the changing strength of the memory trace. But, asked Ebbinghaus, how can we measure the strength of something we can't remember?

To answer this question, Ebbinghaus devised the following *relearning procedure.* He first determined how long it took him to learn lists of nonsense syllables such as XIG, KAZ, or MAJ. Why did he use nonsense syllables? Because they lack meaning, Ebbinghaus found them to be a purer test of memory than poetry or prose, in which certain passages might be more memorable than others. Ebbinghaus would repeat lists of 12 to 16 nonsense syllables until he could recite them perfectly. He then waited a period of time ranging from 20 minutes to a month and measured how many repetitions it took him to relearn the same lists. Even though Ebbinghaus had "forgotten" the nonsense syllables between sessions, relearning them always took less time than the original learning. This fact provided him with a way of measuring the strength of the memory trace for ap-

FIGURE 7.1
Ebbinghaus's revolutionary forgetting curve, representing the first quantitative information about a mental process

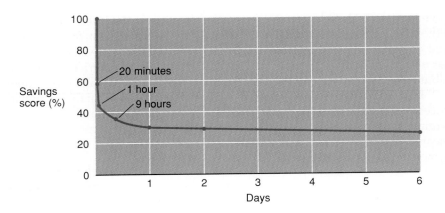

parently forgotten information. He defined the strength of the memory trace by the *savings score*, the difference between the number of repetitions needed for the original learning and the number needed for relearning. For example, if it took 10 repetitions to learn a list the first time and 4 repetitions to relearn it, the savings would be 10 − 4 = 6, or 60%. If relearning took only 3 repetitions, the savings would be 7, or 70%.

Once Ebbinghaus quantified *how much* remembering (and forgetting) had taken place for a particular piece of information, the next step was to show how the amount of remembering changed with the passage of time. To accomplish this he plotted savings scores against the time intervals between different learning and relearning sessions. Figure 7.1 shows the result: a *forgetting curve* that graphically portrays the decrease of memory over time. With his technique Ebbinghaus succeeded in providing exact quantitative information about a mental process *as it occurred*. This was a revolutionary accomplishment in 1885, when most people believed there was no way to measure mental processes.

Ebbinghaus's pioneering studies led him to a number of discoveries about the workings of memory over time. For example, he found that forgetting was most rapid during the first few hours after a learning experience and then slowed, and that meaningful material was (as you might expect) easier both to memorize and to retain than nonsense syllables. *Why* these effects occurred, however, remained to be explained by later researchers working at other levels of analysis.

William James: Different Kinds of Memory

At about the same time that Ebbinghaus was demonstrating the measurability of at least one type of memory, the American psychologist William James (1890) was formulating his own observations about memory, based on his own experiences. James hypothesized two different kinds of memory. One kind, which he called *primary memory,* is for information that has just been presented and that is, therefore, still lingering in conscious awareness. Your memory for the last few words you've read or for a telephone number you've just looked up is of this kind. The other kind, which James called *secondary memory,* occurs when you "bring back" information that has long been forgotten, as when you expend some effort to recall a telephone number you used to know or to recollect what you were doing a year ago today. These two kinds of memory seemed to call for distinct explanations.

James's idea that there is more than one kind of memory is well accepted today. As we will see, the two kinds of memory he identified are very similar to what contemporary psychologists call short-term memory and long-term memory. However, 60 years went by before researchers showed how the two forms of memory proposed by James operate. The culprit responsible for this delay was behaviorism, with its exclusive devotion to the study of observable behavior. The mental experiences described by James were exactly the kinds of internal processes that behaviorists believed could not be studied objectively. Thus, with very few exceptions, researchers abandoned the investigation of the mechanisms responsible for memory until the 1950s brought a new approach to the study of mental processes.

The Rise of Cognitive Psychology

As we saw in Chapter 1, cognitive psychology, the area of psychology concerned with the study of mental processes, began to come into its own in the late 1950s. One reason for this development was that some psychologists questioned whether behaviorism, with its emphasis on conditioning processes, could explain complex activities like remembering and problem solving. A second reason for the growth of cognitive psychology was the advent of the digital computer, which provided a new model for thinking about how the mind works. The key to the analogy between computers and the mind is the theory of **information processing,** because both computers and the mind analyze and transform information.

Once psychologists began conceiving of the mind as a *processor of information,* a whole new avenue of inquiry opened. To describe how the mind processes information, psychologists began constructing models that looked very much like the flowcharts used by computer programmers (Figure 7.2). Thus, the question of how we remember became viewed as the question of what happens to information as it is taken into the mind, sorted, stored, and retrieved. This line of attack has proved so fruitful that cognitive psychology has grown into a major subschool of psychology. Among its many achievements is the information-processing explanation of how memory works.

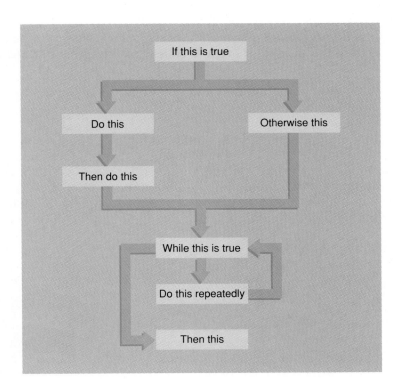

FIGURE 7.2
Computer flowcharts organize the steps involved in computer programs. Cognitive psychologists have created similar flowcharts to describe how the mind processes information.

How Memory Works: An Information-Processing Model

One of the most influential of the new models of the mind developed by cognitive psychologists was Richard Atkinson and Richard Shiffrin's (1968, 1971, 1977) model of memory. As we will see, this model elaborates on William James's distinction between types of memory.

The Multistore Memory System

The Atkinson and Shiffrin model of memory is outlined in Figure 7.3. It is called a **multistore model,** because it proposes three types of memory stores that hold information for different periods of time. The first type, *sensory memory*, holds information for only a brief period—a few seconds at most. The next type, *short-term memory*, holds small amounts of information for immediate use. Short-term memory is what you use when you are dialing an unfamiliar phone number that you forget a moment later. The third type of memory, *long-term memory*, holds voluminous amounts of information for long periods of time—sometimes as long as a lifetime. For example, your memories of yesterday's events as well as of childhood events are contained in long-term memory.

This model indicates that information flows from sensory memory to short-term memory to long-term memory. In the pages that follow, we will see that information is transferred by "rehearsal" from short- to long-term memory and by "retrieval" from long- to short-term memory, as we examine how information is processed in each of the stores. Before we do this, however, we will briefly consider what it means to say that information is *processed* in memory.

Information Processing in Memory

We process information by taking it in, transforming it, and analyzing it. But exactly what kinds of analysis and transformation does information undergo when it is processed in memory? In answering this question, psychologists have found it convenient to separate the **memory process** into the **three stages of** *encoding*, *storage*, and *retrieval*.

Encoding.   Before you can remember anything, it must enter your mind. This means that the object, sound, or event to be remembered must be transformed

FIGURE 7.3
The multistore model of memory. According to this model, information, such as a telephone number, is held for a fraction of a second in sensory memory, is transferred to short-term memory—where it is held for 10–20 seconds (longer if rehearsed)—and then may be transferred to long-term memory, where it can be stored for as long as a lifetime.

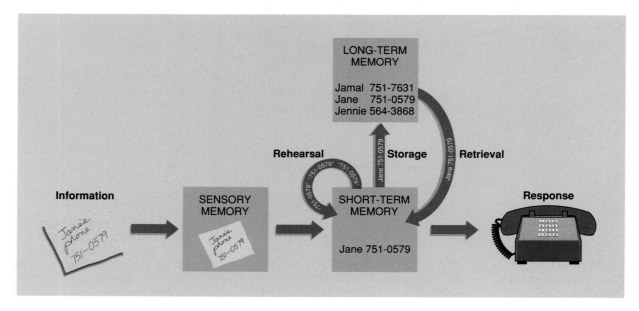

into a *mental representation*—an image, sound, or meaning contained in the mind. This formation of the mental representation is called **encoding,** because the actual object, sound, or event is represented by a **memory code.** For example, a rocking chair you have just seen can be represented in your mind by an image of a rocking chair (a visual memory code), by the sound of the words *rocking chair* (an acoustic code), or by a thought about the chair, such as "I used to have a rocking chair just like that" (a semantic, or meaning, code). In this way the chair itself becomes represented in the form of one or more memory codes that remain in your mind long after you've left the actual chair behind.

Storage.   Once information is encoded, it must be placed in **storage** if we are to remember it later. As we will see later in this chapter, our ability to remember information depends on *how* it is stored. For example, information filed away in an organized manner (like cataloged books in a library) is easier to remember than information filed away haphazardly.

Retrieval.   To remember something you have stored, you need to get it out of storage. This process is called **retrieval.** Sometimes retrieval is easy—for example, you can easily retrieve your present telephone number. But sometimes retrieval is more difficult. How easy is it to remember your last telephone number, or the telephone number of your first girlfriend or boyfriend? This information is probably not lost completely—you would recognize it if you saw it again—but you might not be able to retrieve it at will. This is one of the puzzles of memory: if the information is stored in your memory, why can't you retrieve it whenever you want to? As we will see later, your ability to retrieve information from memory depends on how it was encoded and stored and on "hints" that may help you find where it is stored.

The three steps of encoding, storage, and retrieval help illuminate the transformations that information goes through in the memory system, as you will see when we examine short- and long-term memory. (Sensory memory is so fleeting that there is no need to break it into these steps.) However, each type of memory has its own distinguishing characteristics and its own role to play in the process of remembering. Let's take a closer look at how each kind of memory operates.

Sensory Memory: The Sparkler's Trail

Why does light from a sparkler appear to leave a trail as it is waved about in the dark (Figure 7.4)? At any given instant, the light for the sparkler is a *point.* When you see the curved trail of light, you are seeing where the sparkler *has been*, not where it is. In other words, the trail of light is actually a lingering image in your mind. This image is the result of **sensory memory,** the stage of memory that automatically registers any stimulus to hit the sensory receptors and that holds that stimulus information there for a few seconds or fractions of a second.

People have known for centuries that a rapidly moving light seems to leave a trail, but it wasn't until 1960 that George Sperling related this fact to sensory memory. Sperling demonstrated the existence of sensory memory in a study in which he flashed an array of twelve letters like the array in Figure 7.5 for 50 milliseconds (50/1000 of a second). Sperling's subjects often stated that they briefly saw the whole array of letters, but that some of the letters seemed to fade away before they could report them. Thus, Sperling's subjects were able to report only four or five of the twelve letters.

Was it true that Sperling's subjects briefly saw all of the letters of the array? To answer this question, Sperling asked them to report which letters were present on only one line of the array. He accomplished this by signaling the relevant

FIGURE 7.4
The sparkler's image lingers in the mind, creating the perception of a trail.

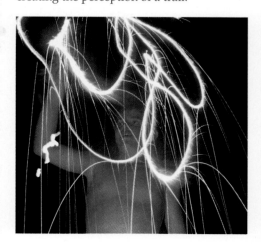

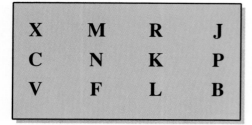

FIGURE 7.5
Sperling's stimulus array for measuring sensory memory

line of letters with a cue tone that sounded immediately after he presented the entire array. A high-pitched tone indicated that the subjects should report the letters in the top row, a medium-pitched tone signaled the middle row, and a low-pitched tone signaled the bottom row. Since these cue tones were presented *after* the letters were turned off, the subjects' attention was directed not to the actual stimulus (which was no longer present) but to whatever mental trace remained after the stimulus was turned off (Figure 7.6).

The results of this procedure confirmed the subjects' reports that most of the letters in the array lingered briefly visually and then faded. No matter which row the subjects were instructed to report, they remembered at least three of the four letters in that row. This means that *immediately after the stimulus was turned off*, the subjects saw three stimuli in each row, or a total of nine of the twelve.

But what do subjects see at longer intervals after the stimulus is extinguished? Sperling answered this question by delaying the cue tone: he found that his subjects' ability to report letters in each row worsened rapidly, as shown in Figure 7.7. By one second after the flash, they could report slightly more than one letter in a row, or a total of about four letters for all three rows. This was the same number they had reported in the first experiment, when they viewed the whole array of twelve.

Sperling concluded that a short-lived sensory memory registers all or most of the information that hits our visual receptors. That information decays, however, within less than a second. This brief sensory memory for *visual* stimuli is called **iconic memory** (icon means "image"). Other experiments (Darwin et al., 1972) have shown that sensory memory also occurs for *auditory* stimuli, with the information presented in a brief auditory stimulus persisting for several seconds. This brief memory for auditory stimuli is called **echoic memory.**

Why is sensory memory important? Because it holds information long enough so that we can take it in and encode it. Without sensory memory, information would not register in the memory system and would be immediately lost. Sensory memory is an example of a psychological process that occurs so rapidly that we are not conscious of it. With the next type of memory, however, we enter the realm of conscious awareness.

Short-Term Memory: Information in Action

The second type of memory is **short-term memory (STM),** in which we store the small amount of information that we are currently using. For example, the beginning of this sentence is now in your short-term memory, but it won't stay for long unless you continually focus on it or process it further until it is transferred to long-term storage.

When STM is represented as a box, as in Figure 7.3, there is a danger that we might mistakenly see it as simply a passageway through which information journeys on its way to more durable storage in long-term memory. Or we might see it as a storage bin, which holds some information while letting other information leak out. Although there is some truth to both of these conceptions of

FIGURE 7.6
Left: An array of letters is presented to the subject. **Right:** After a short delay, the letters are no longer present on the screen, but the subject can still see a faint mental trace of the stimulus.

Actual letters   Mental image

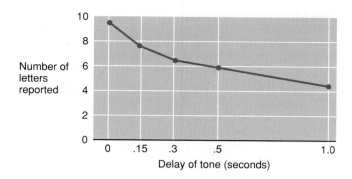

FIGURE 7.7
The number of letters subjects can report after seeing arrays such as the one in Figure 7.6 decreases from 9 to about 4 in the first second after the stimulus is presented.

STM, they leave out its major function. STM is a place where *work* is accomplished. Information doesn't just pass through STM—it is *processed* there. Further, STM receives information not only from sensory memory, such as your visual image of the words on this page, but also from *long-term memory (LTM)*, such as your memory of the meanings of the words used in this sentence. As we will see, information travels both from STM to LTM and from LTM back to STM. Because of short-term memory's quality of being active and always involved any time we bring any memory to conscious awareness, it has also been called **working memory** (Baddeley, 1992; Baddeley & Hitch, 1974).

Working Memory: STM as a Dynamic System

We can appreciate the active nature of STM by looking at some of its functions.

1. *Attention.* We are aware of only a small fraction of the information that enters sensory memory. STM helps us to *selectively attend* to information that is important to us; it therefore keeps us from becoming overloaded with extraneous information. For example, you are attending to the words you are now reading but not to the other words in your field of view, all of which were briefly contained in your sensory memory.

2. *Rehearsal.* Most people have to repeat a phone number over and over until they dial it, or else they forget it. This *rehearsal* is a control mechanism that allows us to hold information in STM and, as we will see later, to transfer some of it into long-term memory.

3. *Problem solving.* Try multiplying 24 × 14 in your head. The solution to such a problem doesn't come instantaneously to most people. Instead, they arrive at the solution through a step-by-step process in which they have to rehearse what they did at each previous step, perhaps by *visualizing* the numbers. This quality led one writer to describe STM as "a kind of blackboard where the mind performs its computations" (Waldrop, 1987, p. 1565).

4. *Communicating with long-term memory.* Consider what happens as you read this sentence. To understand it, you need to know the meanings of each individual word. Those meanings are stored in your long-term memory, so you must retrieve each one from LTM and then put those meanings together in STM. Just about everything we do involves taking information from storage in LTM and using it in STM.

The fact that STM carries out a number of different functions has led some researchers to suggest that it is itself divided into a number of distinct components (Baddeley, 1988, 1990, 1992; Baddeley & Hitch, 1974). This may be so, but for the purposes of simplicity we will consider STM as a whole. We begin our description of information processing in STM by considering how information is encoded in this system.

8   THINKING

A birdwatcher uses short-term, or working, memory, selectively attending to specific aspects of the environment and drawing on past knowledge to interpret them.

Encoding

How do we encode information in STM? Despite the blackboard analogy just cited, two experiments by R. Conrad (1964) support the idea that the code, or mental representation, of information in STM is *auditory* in form.

In Conrad's first experiment, his subjects listened to recordings of strings of target letters (for example, X M L C R G) presented against a background of white noise, a meaningless sound similar to what you hear when you tune in a nonfunctional TV channel. The subjects' task was to write down the letters in the order in which they were presented. Although this may sound easy, the white noise made it difficult to hear the letters clearly, so the subjects made some errors. It was the errors that Conrad was interested in.

When errors occurred, the subjects were most likely to misidentify the target letter as one that *sounded like* the target. For example, F was most often misidentified as S or X, two letters that sound similar. This result is not surprising, since subjects *heard* the letters. But what would happen if they *saw* the letters instead? In Conrad's second experiment, he presented letters to the subjects visually. Even though they saw the letters, subjects still made the same type of *auditory* errors they made when they heard them. For example, they confused the letter F with the similar-sounding S, but they rarely identified it as P or T, which both *look* similar to it.

From these results Conrad concluded that the code for STM must be auditory (based on the sound of the stimulus) rather than visual (based on the appearance of the stimulus). This fits our common experience with telephone numbers. Even though our contact with them in the phone book is visual, we remember them by repeating their sound over and over rather than by visualizing what they looked like in the phone book (also see Wickelgren, 1965).

Do Conrad's results mean that STM encoding is *always* auditory? Not necessarily. Some tasks, such as remembering the details of a diagram or architectural floor plan, require visual codes (Kroll et al., 1970; Posner & Keele, 1967; Shepard & Metzler, 1971). This use of visual codes in STM was demonstrated in an experiment by Guojun Zhang and Herbert Simon (1985) that presented Chinese-language symbols to native Chinese subjects. The stimuli for this experiment were radicals and characters (Figure 7.8). Radicals are symbols that have no oral name and consequently cannot be given an auditory code. In contrast, every character (which is made up of a radical plus another part) has a one-syllable pronunciation (the soundless radicals are used to look up characters in Chinese dictionaries). The subjects looked at either a list of radicals or a list of characters that contained the radicals. When they were asked to write down as many of the radicals or characters as possible, they were able to recall an average of 2.7 radicals and 6.4 characters. Notice that the subjects' ability to remember the radicals must be due to *visual* memory, because no sound or meaning is associated with each radical. But the subjects' superior memory for the characters demonstrates the importance of acoustic coding, since each character represents

FIGURE 7.8
Subjects can recall more Chinese characters than radicals at least in part because the characters are linked to sounds and the radicals aren't.

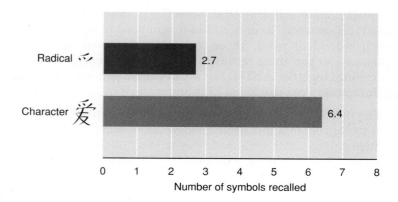

a sound. In short, information can be encoded in STM in *both* visual and acoustic forms.

Storage

Material encoded into STM must be stored there, so it will be available to be used. As we will see, STM has limited storage space, and information is usually stored there for only brief periods of time. There are, however, ways to increase both the amount of time information is held in STM and the amount of information that can be held there.

Rehearsal.   Even a small amount of information, such as a telephone number or a short list of words, must be repeated over and over to keep it in STM. Without rehearsal, the information is rapidly forgotten. But even with rehearsal, STM's storage capacity is small.

Capacity.   The Zhang and Simon experiment with Chinese radicals and characters illustrates the limited capacity of STM storage, because the subjects were often able to recall only a few of the stimuli presented. You can demonstrate the limited capacity of STM to yourself by reading each of the following rows of letters to another person, one at a time, and asking the person to repeat the letters in each row in the correct order.

Stimulus	Number of Letters
M L C D R F	6
G M R L T C F	7
C G B Z T R S Q	8
D B K S Q Y G T M	9
F N T W C G D H S L	10
R V O M A I W X T Y D	11

Tasks like this are used to determine a person's **memory span,** the longest sequence she or he can recall. Most people are able to repeat the first and second rows, with six and seven letters each, but then begin having difficulty. Why? Because most people have a memory span for seven items, plus or minus two (Miller, 1956).

Chunking.   Although it seems straightforward to say that the capacity of STM is about seven items, we run into a complexity when we try to define what we mean by an item. Consider the following sequence of fifteen letters:

F B I P H D T W A I B M N B C

Most people can't remember this string of letters, because it is considerably larger than their seven-item memory span. However, suppose we arrange the letters as follows:

FBI PHD TWA IBM NBC

Now the string is simple to remember, because the letters have been grouped into meaningful units. Instead of remembering fifteen items, we only have to remember five, which is well within the average memory span (Bower & Springston, 1970). This tactic of combining a number of smaller units to create a larger one is called **chunking** (Miller, 1956).

In our example, fifteen letters became five chunks that could be remembered easily. We can carry this chunking process further by combining letters into words

BOAT   MONEY   RADIO   TABLE   IDEA   LOVE   STORE

or by creating sentences

AFTER STUDYING ALL NIGHT FOR HIS EXAM, JIM FELL ASLEEP WITH HIS FACE IN HIS BOOK.

The reason most people can remember letters that spell words or words that make up a sentence is that they are not remembering single letters, in the case of the words, or single words, in the case of the sentence. Instead they are remembering the *meanings* created by combining letters into words and words into sentences. Memory experts often use this technique of creating meaningful chunks as a *mnemonic device,* or memory aid.

Researchers at Carnegie-Mellon University demonstrated the chunking technique by training a college student with average memory ability until he was capable of amazing feats of memory. Their subject, S. F., was asked to repeat strings of random digits that were read to him. His starting point was the typical memory span of seven digits. However, after 230 one-hour sessions, he was able to repeat much longer strings of digits without error. How did he do it? S. F.'s secret was to recode the digits into *meaningful sequences.* For example, he recoded 3492 as "3 minutes and 49 point 2 seconds, near world-record mile time" (S. F. was on the track team); 893 became "89 point 3, very old man." S. F. also developed additional techniques that eventually enabled him to remember strings as long as 79 digits (Ericsson, Chase, & Faloon, 1980). His techniques illustrate the basic principle behind **mnemonic devices**: memory is aided by associating material to be remembered with something meaningful and familiar.

People use numerous mnemonic devices to remember facts. Two of the most familiar are "Thirty days hath September . . ." for remembering the number of days in each month and "Every Good Boy Does Fine" for remembering the names of the notes on each line of the treble clef (E G B D F). If you should ever need to remember the first 15 digits in π, just recite the sentence "How I want a drink, alcoholic of course, after the heavy lectures involving quantum mechanics." If you count the number of letters in each word, you get 3.14159265358979.

Another example of chunking can be found in the prodigious memory of chess masters. William Chase and Herb Simon (1973) demonstrated this by asking chess players with different levels of skill to reproduce chess positions they had seen for five seconds (Figure 7.9). When they compared the performance of a chess master who had played or studied chess for over 10,000 hours with that of a beginner who had less than 100 hours of experience, they found that the chess master placed 16 out of 24 pieces correctly on his first try, compared with the beginner's 4 out of 24 (Figure 7.10a). Moreover, the master required only four trials to reproduce the positions exactly, whereas even after seven trials the beginner was still making errors.

Why does the chess master's superior performance illustrate chunking? Because it occurs only when the chess pieces are arranged in positions *from an actual chess game.* When the pieces were arranged *randomly,* as in Figure 7.10b, the

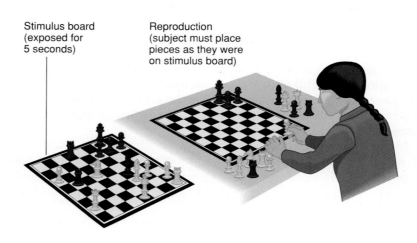

FIGURE 7.9
In Chase and Simon's experiment, subjects were asked to reproduce the positions of chess pieces after observing a stimulus board for 5 seconds.

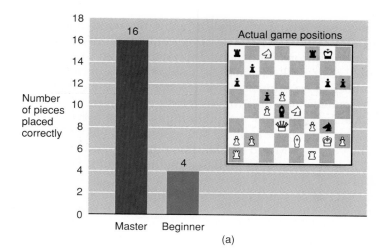

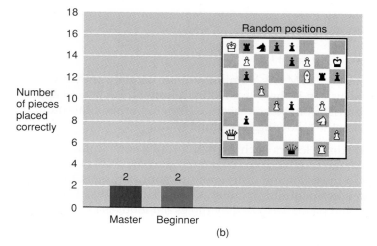

FIGURE 7.10
Chess masters' memory for chess positions
is far superior to beginners' for real game
positions (a) but is the same for random
positions (b).

chess master performed as poorly as the beginner. Chase and Simon concluded
that the chess master's advantage was due not to a more highly developed short-
term memory, but to his ability to group the pieces into meaningful chunks. Because he had learned to perceive familiar patterns that occur in real games, he
saw the layout of chess pieces not in terms of individual pieces but in terms of
four to six chunks, each made up of a group of pieces that formed familiar,
meaningful patterns. When the pieces were arranged randomly, the familiar patterns were destroyed and the master's advantage vanished (also see de Groot,
1965).

Chunking is an essential feature of STM, because it enables this limited-
capacity system to deal with the large amount of information involved in many
of the tasks you perform every day, such as chunking letters into words as you
read this, remembering the first three numbers of familiar telephone exchanges
as a unit, and transforming long conversations into smaller units of meaning.

Retrieval

Based on our experience, it appears that we can retrieve information from STM
instantaneously. For example, repeat the numbers 3, 7, 1, and 8 to yourself. Then
look at the number in the box at the top of the next page, and decide whether it is
one of the numbers you are holding in STM. Do this now.

How quickly were you able to make your decision? It takes most people

9

only a fraction of a second to decide whether the target number matches the numbers in STM. Although retrieval of the contents of STM is so fast that it appears to be instantaneous, Saul Sternberg (1966) showed that it isn't, by using a more precisely controlled version of the task you just performed.

In Sternberg's experiment, subjects were given some digits to remember and then responded "Yes" or "No," as rapidly as possible, if a test digit flashed on a screen matched or did not match the digits in STM. His results indicate that the subjects' reaction time was about 400 milliseconds (400/1000 of a second) if there was one item in STM and that reaction time increased by about 40 milliseconds for each item added to STM. Based on these results, Sternberg concluded that retrieval from STM involves *memory scanning.* Each item held in STM is rapidly scanned and compared with the test digit before the subject makes his or her decision. (See Measurement & Methodology, "Reaction Time and Mental Processes.") Sternberg's results not only point to an important property of STM but also illustrate how controlling the presentation of stimuli and precisely measuring reaction times can uncover mental processes that operate outside of our awareness.

Forgetting in STM

We have seen that STM has a limited storage capacity of about seven items and that those items can be held in STM by rehearsal. But what happens if we prevent this material from being rehearsed? You can answer this question by testing a subject using the following procedure:

1. Pick three letters such as FQZ or any other combination that has no meaning (don't use combinations like ABC, NFL, or USA).
2. Read the following instructions to your subject: "I'm going to read you three letters of the alphabet. Right after I do this, I want you to start at 100 and count backward by threes out loud, as fast as you can."
3. Read the letters and then, after the subject has counted backward for 18 seconds, say "Stop" and ask him or her to repeat the three letters.

When Lloyd and Margaret Peterson (1959) tried this, they found that their subjects had difficulty remembering the letters they had heard only 18 seconds before. (You may have to run a number of trials to get this effect, since subjects sometimes do better in the first few trials.) Peterson and Peterson were able to measure how quickly information is lost by having subjects count backward for times ranging from zero to eighteen seconds. As shown in Figure 7.11, their sub-

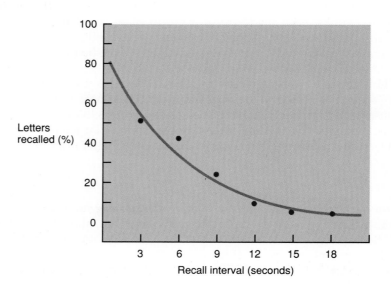

FIGURE 7.11

Peterson and Peterson demonstrated that memory for three letters decreases rapidly if the subject counts backward after hearing them.

jects' performance dropped to nearly 60% incorrect in the first six seconds! Although this result surprises most people, it shouldn't: just consider how we have to continuously rehearse new telephone numbers to keep them in memory.

What causes us to rapidly forget the information in STM? Peterson and Peterson assumed that the forgetting in their experiment occurred because counting backward kept people from rehearsing and allowed the memory trace to decay. Later experiments have shown, however, that counting backward does more than simply prevent rehearsal. Apparently it also creates **interference,** which disrupts subjects' memory for the letters.

Richard Atkinson and Richard Shiffrin (1971) conducted an experiment

MEASUREMENT & METHODOLOGY

Reaction Time and Mental Processes

One of the behaviorists' arguments against studying the mind was that reports generated by introspection were subjective, unverifiable, and extremely variable from subject to subject. Modern cognitive psychologists have, however, been able to quantify subjects' reports by using objectively measurable responses such as reaction time. Sternberg's use of reaction time to discover memory scanning in STM is a good example of how a subject's behavior can be used to uncover extremely rapid mental processes that he or she isn't even aware of.

But Sternberg went beyond using reaction time to demonstrate memory scanning. He also used it to differentiate between the two ways in which this scanning could be occurring.

1. Scanning could be *self-terminating:* the subject scans STM until a match occurs between one of the digits in STM and the test number flashed on the screen. Once a match occurs, scanning stops.
2. Scanning could be *exhaustive:* the subject compares all the digits to the test digit, even if an early comparison yields a match.

Which of these two processes is occurring? Sternberg answered this question by comparing reaction times for trials in which there was no match between the STM digit and the test digit with trials in which there was a match. As illustrated in the figure, if scanning is exhaustive we would expect reaction times to be the same in both conditions; if scanning is self-terminating, we would expect faster reaction times for trials in which a match exists. Sternberg's data indicate that reaction times were identical in both conditions. He concluded, therefore, that scanning of STM is exhaustive—once it starts it goes to completion.

Although this isn't what we might have expected, it does make sense if we consider the high speed of the scanning. It might be more efficient to always scan all the way through than to have to stop scanning at different places on different trials. The important point here, however, is that an objectively measurable response like reaction time can be used to probe a mental activity such as scanning.

Exhaustive scanning (left) and self-terminating scanning (right) for a match and a nonmatch

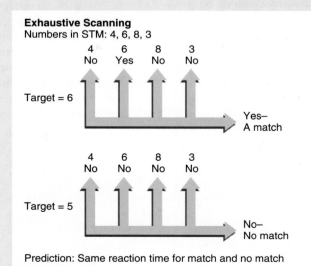

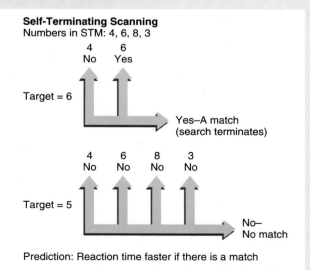

that supports this idea by substituting another task for the counting. Instead of having subjects count backward after hearing the letters, Atkinson and Shiffrin had them press a key every time they heard a tone. Even though this task kept the subjects from rehearsing, it did not create interference, because pressing a key is a completely different type of task than remembering letters. Subjects could still accurately remember the letters even after pressing the key for 40 seconds. Thus, the forgetting that Peterson and Peterson thought resulted from a decay of memory was actually caused by interference. Other experiments have confirmed this conclusion by showing that increasing the amount of interference increases the amount of forgetting (Waugh & Norman, 1965).

Transferring Information from STM to LTM

We have been focusing on how information can be lost from STM. But not all of the information that enters STM is lost. Some of it is *transferred* to long-term memory. How does that transfer take place, and why is some information more likely than others to get transferred to long-term storage?

To answer these questions, B. B. Murdock (1962) conducted an experiment in which he read a list of words to his subjects and then asked them to write down as many words as they could remember. The results of this experiment are plotted in Figure 7.12 as a *serial position curve,* in which the proportion of subjects who got each word correct is plotted against the word's position in the list.

Notice that memory for the words depends on their position: words presented at the beginning or end of the list are most likely to be remembered. Why should position matter? Let's first consider the better memory for words at the end of the list. This is called the **recency effect,** because these words were presented most recently. What if the better memory of the recency effect occurs because the most recently presented words are still in STM? If this is true, then we should be able to decrease memory for those words by both waiting and taking steps to prevent the subjects from rehearsing before testing their memory. Murray Glanzer and Anita Cunitz (1966) accomplished this by doing an experiment similar to Murdock's, but having the subjects in one condition count for 30 seconds before starting their recall. The result was that memory for words at the end of the list decreased to the same level as memory for words in the middle of the list—in other words, the curve in Figure 7.12 flattened out. Thus, the recency effect is due to storage of recently presented items in STM.

But what about the words at the beginning of the list? Superior memory for stimuli presented at the beginning of a sequence is called the **primacy effect.** How do we explain it? We can conclude that the words at the beginning of the list are not in STM, because they are still remembered even after counting for 30 seconds. One possibility is that the words were moved to long-term memory. But how did they get there? Perhaps, since those words were at the beginning of the list, the subjects had more time to rehearse them. To test this idea Glanzer and Cunitz presented the list at a slower pace, leaving more time between each word and thereby giving subjects more time to rehearse. Just as we would expect if the

FIGURE 7.12
A serial position curve. Words at the beginning and end of a list are more likely to be remembered than words in the middle.

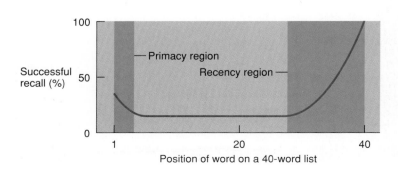

primacy effect is due to rehearsal, increasing the time between each word increased memory for words at the beginning of the list, as indicated by the higher initial part of the serial position curve (also see Rundus, 1971).

Rehearsal, therefore, not only keeps information in STM but also transfers it into LTM. This effect will show up again when we consider long-term memory.

Long-Term Memory: Information in Storage

A memory is what is left when something happens and does not completely unhappen.

Edward de Bono, British writer

Whereas short-term memory is what we work with in the present moment, long-term memory is our link with the past. **Long-term memory (LTM)** is an essentially permanent storehouse of our knowledge about the world (Klatzky, 1980). When we remember events such as a conversation that took place a half-hour ago or a family outing in childhood, we are retrieving information from LTM. Similarly, when we perform a task such as riding a bicycle or recall a fact such as the capital of Idaho, we are using information from LTM. Without long-term memory, our lives would be a succession of unrelated, fleeting events.

These examples—memories of events, ways to do things, and facts or ideas—suggested to Endel Tulving (1983, 1984) that three different kinds of

Memory of a childhood birthday party is episodic memory; memory for skills such as engine repair is procedural memory; and memory of facts in a quiz show is semantic memory.

memories are stored in LTM. **Episodic memory** contains the kinds of information you would include in your life story, such as the names of the schools you attended, where you have lived, and a description of your most memorable vacation (and the others, too). **Procedural memory** stores skills and procedures, such as how to drive a car or buy food at the supermarket. Finally, **semantic memory** contains your knowledge of words, rules for putting them together, and all the facts, ideas, and concepts you have learned about the world. Your knowledge of state capitals, sports or movie trivia, and the titles of current hit songs all come from semantic memory.

Are these three types of memory served by separate memory systems? Tulving's feeling that they are is based on his hunch "that there is basically something different about the way people remember their own past and how they store and retrieve general information about the world" (Tulving, 1986, p. 308). Evidence supporting the idea that long-term memory includes a number of separate memory systems is found in the behavior of people with brain damage. For example, some of them can learn facts (semantic memory) without remembering *when* or *how* they learned those facts (episodic memory) (Claparede, 1911/1951; Schacter, Harbluk, & McLachlan, 1984). However, other researchers argue that, though episodic and semantic memories may represent two different types of information, they are served by a single memory system (McKoon, Ratcliffe, & Dell, 1986; Ratcliffe & McKoon, 1986).

Whether or not LTM should be subdivided into distinct systems, research has uncovered some of the basic characteristics of LTM as a whole. As we did with STM, we'll look at how long-term memory works by examining the three processes of encoding, storage, and retrieval.

Encoding

We have seen that the contents of STM are usually encoded in terms of *sounds*. In contrast, the contents of LTM are encoded in terms of *meanings*. Evidence for this conclusion again comes from the kinds of errors subjects make, this time on a recall test of long-term memory. Many of these errors involve incorrectly recalling a word whose meaning is similar to one that was originally presented. For example, the word *tree* might be incorrectly recalled as *bush* (Kintsch & Buschke, 1969).

An experiment by Jacqueline Sachs (1967), which used sentences as stimuli, also supports the idea that encoding in LTM is based on meaning. In her experiment, subjects heard a tape recording of a passage such as the following:

> There is an interesting story about the telescope. In Holland, a man named Lippershey was an eye-glass maker. One day his children were playing with some lenses. They discovered that things seemed very close if two lenses were held about a foot apart. Lippershey began experimenting and his "spyglass" attracted much attention. *He sent a letter about it to Galileo, the great Italian scientist.* Galileo at once realized the importance of the discovery and set about to build an instrument of his own. He used an old organ pipe with one lens curved out and the other in. On the first clear night he pointed the glass toward the sky. He was amazed to find the empty dark spaces filled with brightly gleaming stars! (p. 438).

After a subject heard the passage, which was actually about twice as long as this, Sachs presented the following test sentences and asked the subject to decide which were "identical" or "changed" compared with one of the sentences in the original passage (italicized in the passage).

1. He sent a letter about it to Galileo, the great Italian scientist.
2. Galileo, the great Italian scientist, sent him a letter about it.
3. A letter about it was sent to Galileo, the great Italian scientist.
4. He sent Galileo, the great Italian scientist, a letter about it.

The results showed that sentence 2, whose meaning differs from that of the original sentence, was easily identified as changed. However, sentences 3 and 4, which have the same meaning as the original (sentence 1) but are different in form, were often incorrectly identified as being identical to the original sentence. Thus, subjects did not remember the exact *form* of the sentence from the original passage, but they did remember the *meaning*.

But the fact that much of the material in LTM is coded in terms of meaning does not mean that everything is. For example, you can identify a woman you know based on your memory of her appearance (a visual code), the sound of her voice (an auditory code), or the smell of her perfume (an olfactory code). As we will see, however, one way to improve our ability to retrieve information is to encode it in terms of meanings. Later on we will translate this finding into practical advice on improving your memory for academic material.

Storage

In contrast to STM, with its limited capacity, LTM's storage capacity is essentially limitless. It seems that we never reach a point at which we can't learn another fact because our memory is "full." But how does information get into LTM storage? Earlier we saw that one way is through rehearsal. However, just saying that rehearsal transfers information to LTM doesn't go far enough, because sometimes rehearsal is effective in adding that information and sometimes it isn't. We need to distinguish between two kinds of rehearsal: maintenance rehearsal and elaborative rehearsal.

Maintenance rehearsal. How many of the hundreds of phone numbers you've repeated after looking them up have you been able to remember much later? Most people remember very few, in spite of having rehearsed them. Why? Because repeating phone numbers is an example of **maintenance rehearsal**—rehearsal by mere repetition rather than by associating the repeated material with information already in long-term memory.

Maintenance rehearsal was studied by Fergus Craik and Michael Watkins (1973) in an experiment in which they showed that holding material in STM longer doesn't necessarily lead to better memory. Craik and Watkins's subjects were instructed to listen to a list of words and to pay particular attention to those starting with a "critical letter." When the presentation ended, they would be asked to repeat the most recent word they had heard starting with that letter. For example, for the list in Figure 7.13, the critical letter is G. Consequently, the subjects start rehearsing the word *garden* as soon as they hear it—but before having a chance to rehearse it much, they hear *grain* and begin rehearsing that word. *Grain* gets rehearsed until the word *giraffe* appears; then the list ends and the subjects should report *giraffe*.

The point of this procedure is that it results in more rehearsal time for *grain* than for *garden* or *giraffe*. If the *time* of rehearsal alone determines transfer to LTM, *grain* should be remembered best. However, when subjects were later asked to recall as many words as possible, the words that had been held in STM longer had no such advantage. Craik and Watkins therefore concluded that simply maintaining information in STM by rehearsal doesn't automatically transfer it to LTM (also see Glenberg & Bradley, 1979).

Elaborative rehearsal. Craig and Watkins's result shows that to transfer information to LTM we must do more than simply repeat it. One technique for more effective transfer is **elaborative rehearsal,** in which meaningful associations are formed between new information to be remembered and information already in LTM.

We can illustrate this technique by looking at a *paired-associate learning* experiment. In this type of experiment, the subjects' task is to associate two words, so that when one of the pair is presented, they can remember the other. To investigate ways of transferring information to LTM, Gordon Bower and David

FIGURE 7.13

The Craik and Watkins experiment. Words were presented in the order shown. In this example, "G" was the critical letter, so subjects rehearsed words starting with G. Of the three "G" words on this list, "grain" was rehearsed the most, but a later memory test showed no advantage for this word.

List	Silent Rehearsal
daughter	—
oil	—
rifle	—
garden*	garden
grain*	grain
table	grain
football	grain
anchor	grain
giraffe*	giraffe

*Critical word.

FIGURE 7.14

In Bower and Winzenz's experiment, subjects remembered word pairs better if they used the words in a sentence or if they visualized the objects represented by the words—more than twice as well as when they simply repeated the word pair.

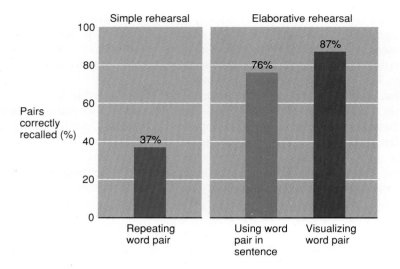

Winzenz (1970) had subjects learn paired associates using three different techniques. Subjects were told to (1) just repeat the pairs, (2) make up a sentence using the two words, or (3) visualize the objects signified by the two words (Figure 7.14). The results show that subjects remembered 37% of the repeated pairs, 76% of the pairs used in sentences, and 87% of the pairs visualized.

One interpretation of the Bower and Winzenz result is that it isn't rehearsal as such that transfers information from STM to LTM, but *how the information is programmed into the mind.* This is the basic principle behind mnemonic devices like the one used by the subject S. F., who was able to remember strings of up to 79 digits by converting them into running times and ages.

The idea that transfer to long-term memory is enhanced by meaningful associations explains why we remember information about ourselves better than information about others. N. A. Kuiper and T. B. Rogers (1979) demonstrated this difference by presenting personal adjectives such as *intelligent, handsome,* and *short* to subjects and having them answer one of two questions: "Does this word describe the experimenter?" or "Does this word describe you?" The purpose was to influence the way the subjects processed the words. After the subjects answered the questions, they were asked to recall as many of the adjectives as possible. The subjects remembered only 9% of the adjectives they associated with the experimenter but 42% of the adjectives they associated with themselves.

Why do we have better memory for words associated with ourselves? According to Kuiper and Rogers, it is because we "hook" these words to ourselves as we are encoding them into memory, and their association makes them memorable. This is essentially what happens in elaborative rehearsal, in which we form associations between the information to be remembered and information already in long-term memory. As we will see next, distinguishing maintenance rehearsal from elaborative rehearsal is closely related to an idea called *levels of processing,* which distinguishes two different ways of processing stimuli to be remembered.

Levels of processing.   The idea that memory depends on the way information is programmed into the mind forms the basis of **levels of processing theory,** proposed by Fergus Craik and R. S. Lockhart (1972). This theory states that the memory system's processing of a stimulus can be "shallow" or "deep." In **shallow processing,** we pay little attention to a stimulus (such as a word) and process it only in terms of its physical features (for example, whether the letters are capitals or lowercase). In **deep processing,** we pay close attention to the stimulus and process its meaning, relating it to other things we know. For example,

18   SOCIAL

shallow processing occurs when, as you read this book, your mind wanders so that you "read" the words without really taking in their meaning. Deep processing occurs when you read carefully, stopping to think about what each section means and perhaps how the material relates to your own experiences.

Two hypotheses that follow from this theory are that (1) deeper processing takes longer than shallow processing, and (2) deeper processing results in better memory. To test these predictions, Craik and Tulving (1975) devised the following experiment. Subjects were presented with a question about a word, saw the word for 200 milliseconds, and then responded "Yes" or "No" to the question, as quickly as possible.

The point of this procedure is to vary the subjects' level of processing. To do this the researchers manipulated the independent variable in this experiment, the subjects' level of processing, by asking three different types of questions about the word presented.

1. *Shallow processing:* questions about the physical structure of the word
   Example: "Is the word printed in capital letters?"

2. *Deeper processing:* questions about the phonemic (sound) properties of the word
   Example: "Does the word rhyme with *train?*"

3. *Deepest processing:* questions about the semantic (meaning) properties of the word
   Example: "Would the word fit into the sentence 'He met a _____ on the street'?"

The researchers then measured two dependent variables: how long it took the subjects to respond to the question and how many words they recognized after answering these and similar questions for 60 different words. The results (Figure 7.15) confirmed the theory's predictions. Deeper processing resulted in (1) longer reaction times to answer the questions and (2) better recognition.

The idea of levels of processing stimulated a large amount of research, much of it confirming the predictions of the theory (Hyde & Jenkins, 1973). Although more recent criticisms of the theory have led to a decrease in research on it, its major message remains: it is *how* we process information that determines whether we will be able to remember it later.

Organization. So far in our discussion of long-term memory storage, we have been exploring how information comes to be stored in LTM. We've seen that the elaboration of information—tying it to other information already in

FIGURE 7.15
Craik and Tulving's levels of processing experiment. When deep levels of processing were needed to answer a yes/no question about a word, (a) it took longer for subjects to answer, and (b) subjects recognized more words, compared to when shallow levels of processing were used.

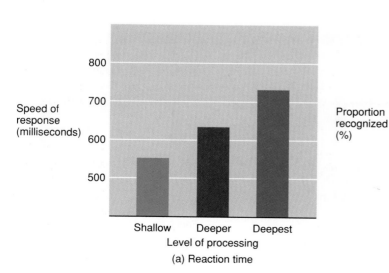

(a) Reaction time

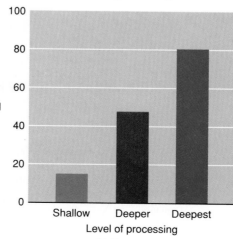

(b) Recognition

memory—helps place that information in storage. But what happens to the bits of information we store? Are our memories like attics, into which we haphazardly stuff new information? Or are they more like tidy library catalogs, in which information is sorted and filed away?

A great deal of evidence indicates that memory storage is not haphazard. Rather, we store memories in an organized way that makes them easier to find later. Consider, for example, an experiment by James Jenkins and Wallace Russell (1952), who presented subjects with a list of words to remember. Although they presented the words in random order, the subjects tended to recall meaning-related words together (for example, *knife* and *fork; man* and *woman; black* and *white*). Thus, in this experiment, the words presented in random order were spontaneously organized when they were being recalled.

There is some evidence that, given enough time, we organize stimuli *as we are storing them.* When subjects are asked to rehearse a list of words out loud as the words are being presented, they tend to group the words and rehearse them by category. For example, presenting the word *horse* triggers rehearsal of *dog, cat,* and *cow* (Ashcraft, Kellas, & Needham, 1975).

If information that is presented randomly becomes organized in the mind, what happens if we present information in an organized way? Gordon Bower and his co-workers (1969) answered this question by presenting material to be learned in a "tree" that organized a number of words according to categories. For example, one tree organized the names of different minerals by grouping together precious stones, rare metals, and so on (Figure 7.16). One group of subjects studied trees for "minerals," "animals," "clothing," and "transportation" for one minute each and were then asked to recall as many words as they could from all four trees. In the recall test, these subjects tended to organize their responses in the same way as the trees were organized, first saying "minerals," then "metals," then "common," and so on. Subjects in this group recalled an average of 73 words from all four trees. Another group of subjects also saw four trees, but the words were randomized, so that each tree contained a random assortment of minerals, animals, clothing, and transportation. These subjects were able to remember only 21 words from all four trees. Thus, organizing material to be remembered results in substantially better recall.

In summary, the results of these experiments support the idea that memory depends largely on how information is programmed into the mind. One way of improving this programming is to form associations between the information to be remembered and other information already in memory. A second way is to organize information by grouping similar items together.

FIGURE 7.16
"Stimulus tree" used to organize minerals in Bower and co-workers' experiment. Recall was much higher when information was organized logically (as shown here) than when it was randomized.

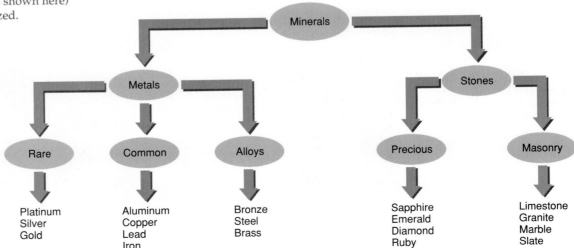

A further illustration of the importance of the way information is programmed into the mind is an experiment performed by John Bransford and Marcia Johnson (1972). You can play the part of a subject in this experiment by reading the following passage:

> If the balloons popped, the sound wouldn't be able to carry since everything would be too far away from the correct floor. A closed window would also prevent the sound from carrying, since most buildings tend to be well insulated. Since the whole operation depends on the steady flow of electricity, a break in the middle of the wire would also cause problems. Of course, the fellow could shout, but the human voice is not loud enough to carry that far. An additional problem is that the string could break on the instrument. Then there would be no accompaniment to the message. It is clear that the best situation would involve less distance. Then there would be fewer potential problems. With face to face contact, the least number of things could go wrong (p. 719).

Now, without looking back at the passage, try to reproduce it as accurately as possible. How much of it can you recall?

As you can probably appreciate, subjects in Bransford and Johnson's experiment had a difficult time reproducing the passage when all they had been exposed to was the passage itself. Other subjects, however, were shown the picture in Figure 7.17 before hearing the passage. Seeing the picture doubled the subjects' amount of recall. A third group was shown the picture *after* reading the passage. This group recalled far less than the group that saw the picture first.

What does this experiment show? The stimulus material (the passage) was the same in all cases, but those subjects who saw the picture beforehand had a *context* that enabled them to *organize the incoming information* and give it meaning. Notice that it was important that the context be present as the passage was read so that information could be organized *as it was being presented* rather than after the fact.

You may have experienced an effect similar to reading the passage without the picture if you have ever tuned in to the middle of a TV movie and found it difficult to figure out what was going on. Without the context provided by the beginning of the movie, it can be difficult to figure out the meaning of what you are seeing.

Retrieval

Suppose I am silent for a moment, and then say, in commanding accents: "Remember! Remember!" Does your faculty of memory obey the order and reproduce any definite image from your past? Certainly not. It stands staring into vacancy, and asking, "What kind of a thing do you wish me to remember?" It needs, in short, a cue.

William James (1890/1981, pp. 117–118)

Our long-term memory contains an astonishing amount of information. How do we retrieve it from storage when we need it? We have seen that memories are easier to retrieve when they have been stored in an orderly way. William James's observation introduces a second idea concerning retrieval: We retrieve information more easily when a *retrieval cue* is available.

Retrieval cues.   A **retrieval cue** provides information that helps us retrieve other information from memory. For example, I recently experienced the familiar phenomenon called the **tip-of-the-tongue (TOT) effect.** A friend asked me to help him remember the name of a large department store chain. It was, according to him, nearly as big as Sears Roebuck and, like Sears, did a large proportion of its business through catalog sales. As he posed this problem, I felt sure I knew

FIGURE 7.17
Picture used in the Bransford and Johnson experiment

the answer—it was on the tip of my tongue—but it wouldn't come to me. This was a case of memory stuck in storage. The information had been encoded and stored, but I couldn't retrieve it (Brown & McNeil, 1966; Meyer & Bock, 1992). He then said, "It has two words," and I immediately replied "Montgomery Ward." This added information was the retrieval cue I needed.

To appreciate the effectiveness of retrieval cues, try the following demonstration (Bransford & Stein, 1984). Get two blank sheets of paper and a pencil. Then spend three to five seconds reading each of the sentences in Figure 7.18. Read through them only once. As soon as you are finished, cover the sentences and write down as many as you can remember on one of your sheets of paper (you don't have to write "can be used" each time). Continue reading after you have written all your sentences. Begin now.

After you've recalled as many sentences as you can, take your second sheet of paper and try the exercise again, this time using the following list of words as retrieval cues (be sure not to look back at Figure 7.18). Once more, write down as many sentences as you can remember. Continue reading when you have completed your list. Begin now.

flashlight	sheet	rock	telephone
boat	dime	wine bottle	board
pen	balloon	ladder	record
TV antenna	lampshade	shoe	guitar
scissors	leaf	brick	knife
newspaper	pan	barrel	rug
orange	bathtub		

A brick can be used as a doorstop.	A TV antenna can be used as a clothes rack.
A ladder can be used as a bookshelf.	A sheet can be used as a sail.
A wine bottle can be used as a candleholder.	A boat can be used as a shelter.
A pan can be used as a drum.	A bathtub can be used as a punch bowl.
A record can be used to serve potato chips.	A flashlight can be used to hold water.
A guitar can be used as a canoe paddle.	A rock can be used as a paperweight.
A leaf can be used as a bookmark.	A telephone can be used as an alarm clock.
An orange can be used to play catch.	A knife can be used to stir paint.
A newspaper can be used to swat flies.	A pen can be used as an arrow.
A barrel can be used as a chair.	A rug can be used as a bedspread.
A scissors can be used to cut grass.	A board can be used as a ruler.
A balloon can be used as a pillow.	A shoe can be used to pound nails.
A dime can be used as a screwdriver.	A lampshade can be used as a hat.

FIGURE 7.18
Read this list of sentences once, then cover them and write down as many as you can remember. (It isn't necessary to write "can be used" each time.)

If you have completed the exercise, compare the number of sentences you were able to recall on each trial. How much better was your recall on the second try?

As you can see from this demonstration, having cues available greatly increases your ability to remember. Because of this power of retrieval cues to help us find "lost" memories, some researchers have suggested that we never actually lose *any* information from LTM. Our inability to remember, they argue, occurs not because the information has been lost but because we can't retrieve it.

Consider, for example, Willem Wagenaar, a Dutch psychologist who kept a diary in which he recorded one or two incidents every day for five years. He recorded *what* happened, *who* was involved, *where* it happened, and *when* it happened. After recording 2400 incidents, he tested his memory for each item by presenting one cue (what, who, where, or when) and attempting to remember the rest. Wagenaar (1986) found that he couldn't remember many of the incidents, given just one retrieval cue. However, by using more retrieval cues, he was eventually able to remember almost every incident, even those that had seemed irretrievably lost.

Apparently, even information hidden away in the recesses of long-term memory can eventually be found. With the help of retrieval cues, you may be able to remember anything you have ever stored in LTM—things like old phone numbers, what you did on your twelfth birthday, and the name of your fourth-grade teacher. Although not all researchers take this view (see Loftus & Loftus, 1980, and Zaragoza & McCloskey, 1989, for a discussion of this issue), there is no doubt that retrieval can uncover previously lost information.

The effect of context.   Retrieval is enhanced if the context in which remembering takes place matches the context in which the material was originally encoded. An example of enhanced retrieval caused by similar learning and retrieval contexts is provided by the **state-dependent learning effect,** the idea that recall is better if we are in the same mental state or setting during encoding and recall. One way this has been demonstrated is by having people learn material when intoxicated with alcohol. When tested later, the subjects were more likely to remember the material if tested while intoxicated than if tested when sober.

(Recall was best, however, when subjects were sober both while learning and during testing.) (Parker, Birnbaum, & Noble, 1976). Another experiment that tested this effect had divers learn lists of words either underwater or on land and then tested them either underwater or on land. The divers learned the lists better when tested in the setting in which learning had occurred (Godden & Baddeley, 1975). This finding has implications for test taking: one way to improve your memory for information to be tested is to study in the room in which the test will be given!

Why is it easier to remember information when the learning and testing contexts match? According to some researchers, the context functions as a retrieval cue (Nadel & Willner, 1980; Spear, 1978). This idea was tested by Carolyn Rovee-Collier and her co-workers (1985) in a memory experiment with 3-month-old infants. The infants were first taught to move a mobile by kicking with one of their legs, which was connected to the mobile with a strap (Figure 7.19). For context, there was a colorful crib bumper inside the crib during the testing. Two weeks later, infants who were simply placed back in the same crib did not remember the kicking response they had learned. However, infants given a retrieval cue did remember the kicking response. The retrieval cue, given 24 hours before the test, was a three-minute exposure to the same bumper that was in the crib when they originally learned to kick the panel. A control group of infants, exposed to a different crib bumper 24 hours before the test, did not remember the kicking response.

This study shows that the use of retrieval cues is not limited to older children or adults. In fact, Rovee-Collier suggests that context may be a major way that very young infants make sense of their environment (also see Shields & Rovee-Collier, 1992; Rovee-Collier, 1993).

FIGURE 7.19

In Rovee-Collier's (1985) experiment, infants who learned to move the mobile in the presence of a crib bumper were more likely to remember how to do it when tested later if they saw the same bumper again the day before testing.

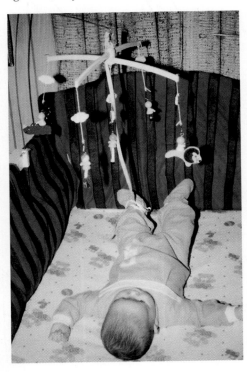

Retrieving semantic memories: A network model.   We have already seen that our efforts to retrieve information are aided by organization. Let's consider this idea by looking at a *model* that has been proposed to explain how organization helps us retrieve semantic memories, memories having to do with our knowledge of the world.

The model, proposed by Allan Collins and Ross Quillian (1969), states that our memory is organized in a network like the one in Figure 7.20. This network is similar to the one Bower and his co-workers used to organize the stimuli in their experiment (Figure 7.16), in that the most general category is at the top of the tree ("animal"), with categories becoming more and more specific ("bird," then "canary") down the tree. However, the network in Figure 7.20 adds a new feature. The categories, which are located at *nodes*, are described by a number of properties. Thus, "bird" is described as "has wings," "can fly," and "has feathers." Since "canary" comes under "bird" in the structure, we can also state that canaries have wings, can fly, and have feathers. The point of organizing the tree in this way is to save storage space. Thus, we don't have to list all the properties of canaries, because canaries share many properties with birds in general.

One assumption behind this model of memory organization is that when we want to retrieve information from memory we will start with the nodes at the bottom of the tree and work up. This assumption leads to the prediction that the amount of time it takes to decide whether a statement is true or false depends on how far we have to search up the tree to find the answer. For example, we can determine whether the statement "A canary can sing" is true or false by starting at the node "canary" and retrieving the property "can sing" stored at that node. However, to determine whether "A canary can fly" is true or false, we must move up one level to the node for "bird" before we can retrieve the property "can fly" at that node. Therefore, we should require more time to decide whether "A canary can fly" than whether "A canary can sing." And it should take even longer to decide whether "A canary has skin," because that property is stored on the node for "animal," which is nearer the top of the tree.

9   DEVELOPMENT

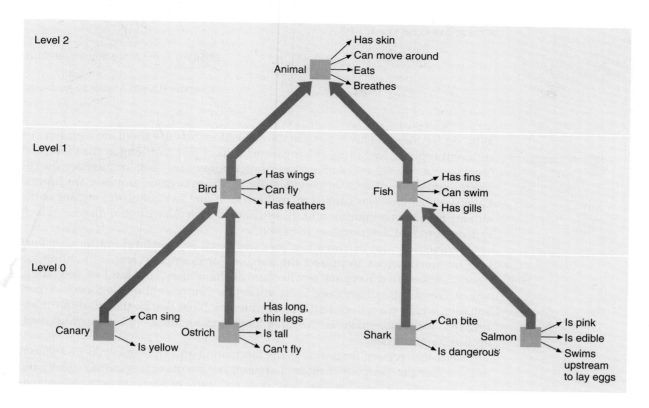

FIGURE 7.20
The network model of memory organization proposed by Collins and Quillian

To test these predictions, Collins and Quillian presented statements to subjects and measured how long they took to push one key for "True" or another for "False." Their results for the three questions about canaries (Figure 7.21), fit their prediction.

Collins and Quillian's model of memory organization is only one of many that have been proposed. Most of the other models are, however, similar in that they are networks in which closely related nodes are connected (Anderson & Bower, 1973; Collins & Loftus, 1975). But whatever model of memory organization proves most satisfactory, we can be certain of one thing: without the organization built into our memory system, retrieving anything from memory would be extremely difficult.

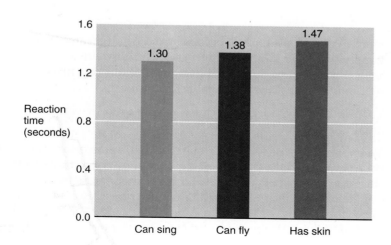

FIGURE 7.21
Collins and Qullian's results. Reaction time to answer three questions about canaries increased as the questions tapped knowledge contained higher up in the network.

Forgetting in LTM

Memory is the thing you forget with.

Alexander Chase, American journalist

3   BIOLOGY

Why do we forget? This is a fascinating question, because there are a number of different types of forgetting (Weingartner et al., 1983). Working at the biological level of analysis we encounter cases of *organic amnesia*—loss of memory due to brain damage. Examples of people suffering from organic amnesia are Jimmie G., whose damage was caused by malnutrition due to alcoholism; victims of accidents or wartime injuries; and those afflicted with Alzheimer's disease, which causes a gradual deterioration of memory.

Forgetting also occurs when an early event is so painful that it is pushed into the unconscious to protect the person. For example, victims of childhood sexual abuse often have no recollection of the abuse. This kind of forgetting, which Freud called *repression,* is an important component of his theory of personality, which we will describe in Chapter 15. Note that in this kind of forgetting the "forgotten" material is still in long-term memory—it is simply unavailable to consciousness.

Another type of forgetting is the fascinating and still-unsolved problem of *infantile amnesia,* people's inability to remember events that occurred during the first three or four years of life. Why does this type of amnesia occur? Explanations at the cognitive level have proposed that young children encode, store, and retrieve information differently than adults do (Meudell, 1983) and that they don't begin using adult modes of storage until about 3 years of age (Nelson, 1988). Thus, childhood experiences are not "lost," but rather cannot be retrieved because of the way they have been encoded and stored.

Information-processing explanations of forgetting.   Although infantile amnesia remains a puzzle, the possible explanations proposed for it illustrate an important point: the information-processing model of memory suggests there are several ways to forget. Let's consider this idea, focusing on how normal, everyday forgetting—forgetting things such as where you put your keys, material you memorized for an exam, and acquaintances' names—might occur during encoding, storage, or retrieval.

- *Encoding.* We may "forget" because of a failure to encode (Figure 7.22). For example, if we fail to pay attention when someone is being introduced to us, we never encode or store the person's name. Technically this isn't forgetting, because the material was never remembered in the first place; but it is a mechanism that short-circuits memory right at the beginning of the process.

- *Storage.* We may also forget because we didn't rehearse material deeply enough to transfer it into long-term storage. Or we may forget because of the way we organized material in storage. If it is organized in a haphazard manner, it may not be available for retrieval.

- *Retrieval.* We may "forget" because we can't retrieve information that is actually stored in LTM.

These explanations of forgetting suggest that information doesn't "leak" out of LTM or fade with the passage of time. Instead, forgetting results from a failure in the processing of information within the memory system. In LTM, as in STM, one of the major causes of failure in memory processing is interference.

Interference in LTM.   We begin our discussion of interference in LTM by re-

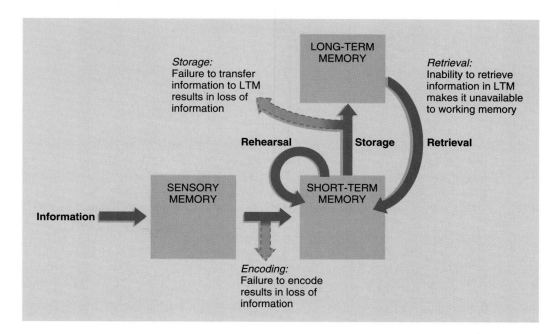

Storage:
Failure to transfer
information to LTM
results in loss of
information

Retrieval:
Inability to retrieve
information in LTM
makes it unavailable
to working memory

LONG-TERM
MEMORY

Rehearsal   Storage   Retrieval

SENSORY
MEMORY

Information

SHORT-TERM
MEMORY

Encoding:
Failure to encode
results in loss of
information

FIGURE 7.22
In the multistore model of memory,
information can be forgotten because of
failure to encode, failure to transfer material
from short-term memory to long-term
memory, and failure to retrieve material
from long-term memory.

turning to Ebbinghaus's forgetting curve (Figure 7.1). From the way his memory curve plunged downward with increasing time, Ebbinghaus concluded that this forgetting was due to the *decay* of memories with time. But later research has shown that, just as for STM, *interference* rather than decay is the major mechanism responsible for forgetting in LTM. Interference in LTM can occur in two ways: (1) old memories can interfere with the formation of new ones, a process called *proactive interference*, or (2) new memories can interfere with old ones, a process called *retroactive interference*.

Proactive means "acting forward." **Proactive interference** occurs when learning from the past interferes with new learning. For example, assume you are to learn the associations in list 1.

> *List 1*
> table—fox
> clock—pipe
> heater—keys
> pencil—raincoat

Once you have learned these associations, the word *table* elicits *fox,* *clock* elicits *pipe,* and so on. Now suppose you are required to learn the new associations in list 2.

> *List 2*
> table—can
> clock—paper
> heater—sun
> pencil—radio

Now the word *table* is supposed to elicit *can* instead of *fox.* However, you might have difficulty remembering the new associations, because you have already stored the old ones. In this case, prior learning interferes forward—*pro*actively— with new learning (Figure 7.23).

Retroactive means "acting backward." **Retroactive interference** occurs when new learning interferes with memories from the past. For example, assume that you have overcome the proactive interference of list 1 and have succeeded in learning list 2. Now you are asked to recall the associations not from

FIGURE 7.23

The effects of proactive and retroactive interference on memory performance

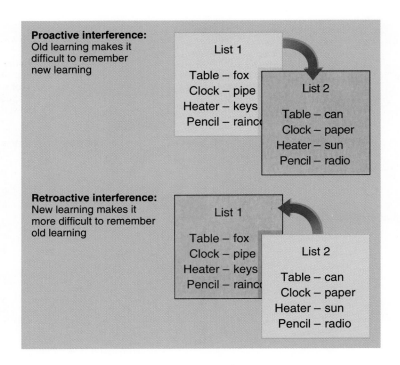

Proactive interference:
Old learning makes it difficult to remember new learning

List 1

Table – fox
Clock – pipe
Heater – keys
Pencil – rainc[oat]

List 2

Table – can
Clock – paper
Heater – sun
Pencil – radio

Retroactive interference:
New learning makes it more difficult to remember old learning

List 1

Table – fox
Clock – pipe
Heater – keys
Pencil – rainc[oat]

List 2

Table – can
Clock – paper
Heater – sun
Pencil – radio

list 2 but from list 1. Possibly you'll find it difficult to recall the old ones because of the interfering effect of learning list 2. In this case, learning interferes in reverse—*retro*actively. Thus, if you previously learned a modest number of German words and are now taking French, your new French learning might make it more difficult for you to remember your old German vocabulary.

What does interference interfere with? Both proactive and retroactive interference disrupt performance on long-term memory tasks. But what exactly causes this disruption of performance? That is, at what step in information processing is interference taking place?

It seems likely that interference works by affecting our ability to *retrieve* information. Consider, for example, your friend Susan's phone number, which you have known for years. When Susan moves and gets a new number your life becomes more difficult for a while, because every time you want to call Susan you think of her old number. This is a case of proactive interference. From the point of view of retrieval cues, we can consider "Susan's phone number" to be the cue that elicits Susan's number from your memory, but the strong link between that cue and her old number keeps leading you to her old number, still stored in your memory. Her new number is stored as well, but you have trouble *retrieving* it.

In giving us a picture of memory as a system, the information-processing approach has also provided a new picture of forgetting. For information that has entered the memory system, forgetting appears to be due largely to interference. In the case of LTM, interference causes forgetting by disrupting the process of retrieval. For a general summary of the properties of both short-term and long-term memory, see Table 7.1.

We have, for the bulk of this chapter, been focusing on the cognitive approach to the study of memory. An outcome of this approach has been the multi-store model of memory and an understanding of many of the mechanisms that operate within each of the stores. This model attempts to explain memory in terms of the cognitive processes involved when we encode, store, and retrieve information. We are now ready to move to another level of analysis by looking at the biology of memory.

TABLE 7.1
Properties of short- and long-term memory

Process	Short-Term Memory	Long-Term Memory
Encoding	Auditory and visual	Mainly in terms of meaning (but visual, auditory, etc., also possible)
Storage	Capacity of about seven items, but chunking can increase amount of information held	Maintenance rehearsal: simple repetition
		Elaborative rehearsal: forming meaningful associations
		Organization: storage is more efficient if information is organized as it is programmed into the mind
Retrieval	Occurs rapidly, via memory scanning	Network models describe how organization aids retrieval
		Aided by retrieval cues
		Encoding specificity functions as a retrieval cue
Forgetting	Caused mainly by interference	Can occur through psychological or organic trauma or through interference
		Proactive interference: old learning interferes with new
		Retroactive interference: new learning interferes with old
		Interference disrupts retrieval

How the Brain Remembers: The Physiology of Memory

Research on the biology of memory has focused on determining processes within the brain that are responsible for forming and storing memories. What is happening at the physiological level when we remember? Researchers have explored this question by conceiving of memory in the following three ways:

1. memory as a change in neural processing
2. memory as localized in specific brain structures
3. memory as requiring time to become established in the brain

Memory as a Change in Neural Processing

Our discussion of memory at the cognitive level has focused on how people process information such as words and sentences. At the biological level we look at how neurons process the information provided by action potentials. How might neural impulses be translated into information that indicates the presence of memories?

One possibility is that when a neuron or group of neurons fires in response to a particular stimulus (which could be an apple, some words, an idea, or a series of events), changes occur at the synapses that increase the chances that the same group of neurons will fire together. The firing of this *group* of neurons therefore comes to *represent* the stimulus in the brain (Figure 7.24). In line with this idea, researchers have searched for evidence that stimulation can strengthen connections between neurons. Several types of evidence point to the fact that such strengthening does occur.

Electrical changes in neurons: Long-term potentiation.   When a neuron is repeatedly stimulated, it shows an enhanced response. This change in the way the neuron responds is called *long-term potentiation* (LTP) (Bliss & Gardner-Medwin, 1973; Goddard, 1980).

FIGURE 7.24
If the group of neurons shown in green fires every time the apple is presented, the connections between these neurons will be strengthened, increasing the likelihood that the apple will be remembered.

One way researchers have demonstrated LTP is by presenting a rapid burst of electrical stimulation to one area of a rat's brain and then measuring how an adjacent area, which receives input from the stimulated area, responds. The results indicate that LTP can increase a neuron's firing rate for as long as months (Teyler & Discenna, 1984). Whereas enhancement that lasts for months cannot explain the longevity of memories that last for decades, this enhancement may be an initial stage in a process that eventually creates very long-lived memories.

Anatomical changes in neurons: The effects of experience.   In Chapter 3 we saw evidence indicating that our experiences can change the physical structure of the brain. Extensive structural changes in the brain as a function of experience were demonstrated in a series of now-classic experiments by Mark Rosenzweig and his co-workers (Rosenzweig, 1984, 1986; Rosenzweig & Bennett, 1984; Rosenzweig, Bennett, & Diamond, 1972; also see Greenough, 1984a, 1984b; Squire, 1987; Turner & Greenough, 1985). In those experiments, the brains of animals raised in enriched environments showed increases in the total number of synapses as well as changes in the structures of individual synapses. For example, experience causes an increase in the density of synaptic vesicles and in the size of synaptic endings.

If experiences cause structural changes in the brain, might those changes explain how the brain records memories? Recent research supports this idea by showing that drugs that block the structural changes caused by experience also prevent the formation of long-term memories (Rosenzweig, 1984). The fact that these drugs work by inhibiting the synthesis of proteins, a major structural component of nerve membranes, has led many researchers to suggest that protein synthesis plays an important role in the formation of memories.

Protein synthesis and memory formation.   Injecting a drug that inhibits protein synthesis prevents rats from forming long-term memories (Rosenzweig & Bennett, 1984). In addition, other studies show that learning leads to an increase in the concentration of specific proteins within brain structures that are important for memory. In one experiment, rabbits were classically conditioned to blink their eyes in response to a tone. After the rabbits learned this association, researchers detected an increase in an enzyme called *protein kinase C* within the hippocampus (Olds et al., 1989), which is one of the structures involved in the formation of memories in humans.

Memory, then, may represent changes in neural processing. A second way to explore the physiology of memory is to identify specific brain structures that play a role in memory.

Memory as Localized in Specific Brain Structures

If our memories are stored in the brain, where in the brain can we find them? Recall from our discussion in Chapter 3 that early researchers were able to show that specific brain areas are associated with functions such as vision, hearing, movement, emotions, and language. Among those functions is memory, which involves several brain structures (Figure 7.25). One of these is the hippocampus, as was illustrated by the case of epileptic patient H. M. Following bilateral removal of his hippocampus (removing it on both the left and right sides), H. M. lost the ability to form new long-term memories (Corkin, 1984; Milner, Corkin, & Teuber, 1968; Scoville & Milner, 1957). Like Jimmie G., the Korsakoff patient we also described in Chapter 3, H. M. could remember experiences from before the operation but could not remember new experiences for longer than a few minutes.

The fact that H. M.'s old memories remained after the operation means that the hippocampus cannot be the place where memories are *stored*. If it were the site of storage, no memories would have remained. But the fact that he could not

6   LEARNING

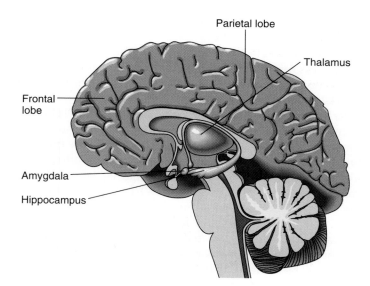

FIGURE 7.25
Cross section of the brain, showing structures that play a role in memory

form new memories suggests that the hippocampus is involved in the process of storing *newly formed* memories (Eichenbaum, 1992; Zola-Morgan, Squire, and Amaral, 1986).

Bilateral removal of the hippocampus results in severe amnesia for newly formed memories, but removing only the left or the right hippocampus does not cause complete amnesia. Instead, it causes specific forms of less serious amnesia, depending on the side removed. Removing the left hippocampus affects a person's performance on the *repeating digits test,* which tests long-term memory for digits that are repeated many times. Removing the right hippocampus has little effect on the digit test but decreases a person's ability to learn to tap a sequence of blocks in a specific order. The results of the digit and block-tapping tests indicate that the left hippocampus is more important in forming memories of verbal material, the right in forming memories of visual and spatial material (Kolb & Whishaw, 1985). This finding fits what we learned about the functions of the left and right hemispheres in Chapter 3: language ability usually depends on the left hemisphere, spatial ability on the right.

The hippocampus is not the only brain structure involved in memory. Damage to a number of other structures, including areas in the parietal and frontal lobes and parts of the thalamus, causes memory deficits. Although memory is localized in specific structures, then, there are clearly a number of areas responsible for our ability to remember (McCormick & Thompson, 1984; Mishkin & Appenzeller, 1987; Squire, 1986; Squire & Zola-Morgan, 1988; Thompson, 1986).

Memory as Requiring Time to Become Established in the Brain

We have seen evidence that the formation of memories is accompanied by physical changes in brain structures. The **consolidation hypothesis** states that these structural changes need to remain undisturbed for a period of time before long-term memories become firmly established. The period of time necessary for that stabilization is called the **consolidation period.**

The existence of such a period is supported by the observation that accident victims who suffer trauma to the head often experience *retrograde amnesia,* a loss of memory for the events just preceding the accident. According to the consolidation hypothesis, the trauma of an accident interrupts consolidation of the memory traces that were present just before the trauma. As a result, those traces are never consolidated and so are lost.

17   THERAPY

Retrograde amnesia also occurs in people who are given shock treatments—called *electroconvulsive therapy (ECT)*—to help relieve severe depression. In these treatments a brief electrical current is passed through the brain, causing loss of consciousness for a few minutes. These patients typically suffer from retrograde amnesia on awakening—they can't remember things that happened just before the shock (Squire, 1977).

How much time is needed for consolidation to occur? The evidence from accident victims and ECT patients suggests that the consolidation period is short, since events that happened several minutes before the trauma are remembered. However, other evidence suggests that consolidation can take much longer, in some cases as long as several years (Squire, 1986). For example, Larry Squire and his co-workers (1975) found that ECT patients lost their memories for TV programs that were on the air for one TV season about a year or two before their treatment. The patients' memory for programs that were on the air many years earlier was not, however, affected by the ECT (also see Squire & Cohen, 1979). Thus, though long-term memories may form rapidly after an event is experienced, they may be liable to disruption by trauma for a number of years.

It should be clear from our description of the biology of memory that the complexity we observed when studying memory at the cognitive level is mirrored at the biological level. There is nothing simple about how neural events represent our past experiences. It is also clear that our understanding at the biological level is more primitive than our understanding at the cognitive level. Our present understanding of the biology of memory enables us to make general statements about possible mechanisms, but we are far from being able to explain the biology behind cognitive processes such as interference and retrieval. How memories as diverse as multiplication tables and last summer's vacation are represented by neural discharges remains a tantalizing mystery.

Real-World Memory

Memory is the diary that we all carry about with us.

Oscar Wilde (1854–1900)
English playright

We've seen how researchers, beginning with Ebbinghaus, have studied memory in experimental and laboratory conditions, and how they've looked at the physiological underpinnings of memory. One of the great achievements of the cognitive revolution was to devise ingenious experimental procedures to help researchers gain access to internal processes like remembering and forgetting. Still, such procedures usually require creating artificial memory situations, such as Ebbinghaus's nonsense syllables task, memorizing lists of numbers or words, or paired-associate learning. An important step, then, is to take the study of memory outside the laboratory to see how we form memories of the things we try to remember in real life. Psychologists working at the cognitive level have been able to do just that for things such as remembering past acquaintances, significant events, and meaningful prose passages (Neisser & Winograd, 1988).

Long-Lived Memories

A number of studies have found that we have an impressive ability to remember things we were exposed to many years ago. For example, Harry Bahrick and his co-workers (1975) tested people's ability to remember the names and faces of members of their high school graduating class. When they tested people ranging from recent graduates to people who had graduated 48 years earlier, they found that the ability to *recall* their classmates' names declined from about 80% to 20% over a 47-year period. Recall is, however, a stringent test of memory that doesn't uncover everything in our memory stores (see Measurement & Methodology, "Recognition Versus Recall"). By also using a *recognition* test, Bahrick showed that people are able to recognize, with 90% accuracy, their classmates' names for as long as 15 years after graduating from high school and their high school yearbook photographs for as long as 35 years. In another study, Bahrick (1984) found that people retained much of what they learned in high school Spanish over a 50-year period, as shown in Figure 7.26 (also see Bahrick & Phelps, 1987).

How is it possible to remember people's faces and Spanish vocabulary for many decades? One reason for this impressive memory is that you learn this information over a long period of time. You see many of the people in your high school class on an almost daily basis for four years and may spend many hours studying Spanish. These conditions, which involve both meaningful material and extremely intensive learning, are much more resistant to forgetting than are nonsense syllables or lists of words that are studied only briefly.

Long-lived memories are also associated with events that have special significance. Do you remember what you were doing when you heard about the bombing of Baghdad that marked the beginning of the Persian Gulf War (January 16, 1991), the explosion of the space shuttle *Challenger* (January 28, 1986), or,

MEASUREMENT & METHODOLOGY

Recognition Versus Recall

Two of the most widely used measures of memory are recognition and recall. A **recognition test** requires that a person pick the correct answer from a list of alternatives, as in the following multiple-choice question:

Information you might include in your life story would be retrieved from

   a. semantic memory
   b. episodic memory
   c. procedural memory

A **recall test** requires that the person supply the answer without seeing any alternatives, as in this fill-in-the-blanks question:

Information you might include in your life story would be retrieved from _____.

Although both methods measure memory, the results of recall and recognition tests are very different (as you can probably testify from your own experience with exams). Luh (1922) demonstrated this difference by testing subjects' memory for the same material with both kinds of tests. His subjects studied lists of nonsense syllables such as *funt, loke,* and *muld* and were then tested by either a recognition test (pick the syllables you learned from this list) or a recall test (write down the syllables you learned) at various times after they had memorized the lists. The figure shows that although performance on the recognition test is still high after two days, performance on the recall test has fallen to less than 10% during this time.

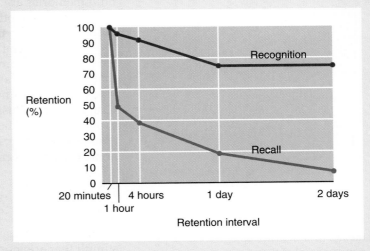

Why are the results of the recognition and recall tests so different? One reason is that the recognition format provides *retrieval cues*—subjects see the answers, and this helps them retrieve the items from memory. In contrast, the recall test contains no retrieval cues, so even though information about the syllables exists in LTM, it isn't retrieved (also see Haist, Shimamura, & Squire, 1992).

FIGURE 7.26
Retention of vocabulary from a Spanish high school course stays remarkably high for 25 years or more after graduation.

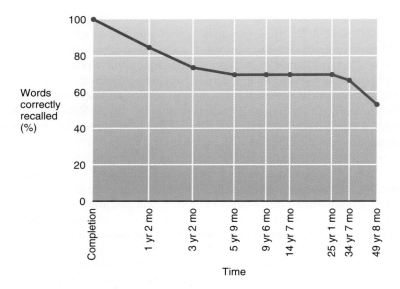

if you are old enough, the assassination of John F. Kennedy (November 22, 1963)? The fact that people can often recall where they were and what they were doing when they heard of shocking and emotionally charged events caused Roger Brown and James Kulick (1977) to call these memories **flashbulb memories.**

Brown and Kulick argue that there is something special about the mechanisms responsible for flashbulb memories. Not only do they form under highly emotional circumstances that are remembered for long periods of time, but they are especially vivid and detailed. Although not all researchers agree that flashbulb memories are formed by special memory mechanisms (McCloskey, Wible, & Cohen, 1988), others concur with Brown and Kulick (Schmidt & Bohannon, 1988). This issue remains for future memory research to resolve.

Of course, not all real-world memories are so long-lived. You need only try to remember commonplace events from a few weeks or months ago to realize that many everyday memories are difficult to retrieve. Wagenaar's (1986) diary study of episodes from his own life (see "Retrieval Cues" in the section on long-term memory) illustrates that retrieval cues can trigger recall of many everyday events (also see Thompson, 1982). But memories are more likely to persist, and are more easily retrieved, when events are repeated or are associated with emotional or highly significant circumstances.

Remembering Meaningful Stimuli: Memory as Constructive

Another way of approaching real-world memory is to use meaningful, complex stimuli that are more like the stimuli we encounter in our day-to-day lives than are lists of words or nonsense syllables. We have already seen one such example in Jacqueline Sachs's 1967 study, in which she tested subjects' memory for the content of stories like the one about Galileo and found that subjects remember the general meanings but not the exact wording. A major conclusion of many studies that use meaningful stimuli is that our recall of complex materials is influenced by the knowledge we already possess.

The *Challenger* disaster created a flashbulb memory for many people, who clearly remember what they were doing when they heard about the explosion.

Schemas: Bartlett's "War of the Ghosts" experiment.   The importance of prior knowledge to memory for complex stimuli was demonstrated in a study that was far ahead of its time. In 1932 F. C. Bartlett described a study he had conducted in England prior to World War I, in which he had subjects read a strange story called "The War of the Ghosts." Take a moment to read the story (Figure 7.27).

FIGURE 7.27
Passage read by subjects in Bartlett's memory experiment

The War of the Ghosts

One night two young men from Egulac went down to the river to hunt seals, and while they were there it became foggy and calm. Then they heard war cries, and they thought: "Maybe this is a war party." They escaped to the shore, and hid behind a log. Now canoes came up, and they heard the noise of paddles, and saw one canoe coming up to them. There were five men in the canoe, and they said:

"What do you think? We wish to take you along. We are going up the river to make war on the people."

One of the young men said: "I have no arrows."

"Arrows are in the canoe," they said.

"I will not go along. I might be killed. My relatives do not know where I have gone. But you," he said, turning to the other, "may go with them."

So one of the young men went, but the other returned home.

And the warriors went up the river to a town on the other side of Kalama. The people came down to the water, and they began to fight, and many were killed. But presently the young man heard one of the warriors say: "Quick, let us go home: that Indian has been hit." Now he thought: "Oh, they are ghosts." He did not feel sick, but they said he had been shot.

So the canoes went back to Egulac and the young man went ashore to his house, and made a fire. And he told everybody and said: "Behold I accompanied the ghosts, and we went to fight. Many of our fellows were killed, and many of those who attacked us were killed. They said I was hit, and I did not feel sick."

He told it all, and then he became quiet. When the sun rose he fell down. Something black came out of his mouth. His face became contorted. The people jumped up and cried.

He was dead.

After his subjects read this story, Bartlett had them try to remember the story as accurately as possible. He then used the technique of *repeated reproduction*, having the same subjects come back a number of times to try to remember the story at longer and longer intervals after their initial exposure to it. Not surprisingly, subjects forgot much of the information in the story. Most subjects' reproductions of the story were shorter than the original and contained many omissions and inaccuracies. But what interested Bartlett the most were the kinds of changes the subjects made. In particular, he noticed that the changes tended to reflect the subjects' own culture. Thus, the original story, which came from Canadian Indian folklore, was transformed by many of Bartlett's subjects to make it more consistent with the culture of Edwardian England. One subject remembered the two men who were out hunting seals as being involved in a sailing expedition, the "canoes" as "boats," and the man who joined the war party as a fighter that any good Englishman would be proud of: ignoring his wounds, he continued fighting and won the admiration of the natives. In short, the story was transformed in memory from a rather strange folktale to a story that Bartlett's British subject could relate to.

Bartlett's study points to an extremely important characteristic of memory. Memory is not simply a playback of information that the mind has passively received; rather it is a constructive, active process. The process of remembering involves an interaction between the information we take in and our existing store of knowledge, our past experiences, and our culture. In studying real-world memory it is important to consider the context within which memories occur. An important component of this context, your knowledge of the world, causes you to develop a number of **schemas,** or ways of interpreting information, about particular concepts. Thus, the subject whose reproduction was just described may have been tailoring his memory of the story to fit into his "Englishman-going-to-battle" schema.

There are as many schemas as there are interests. Someone with a strong interest in politics would pay particular attention to political developments and therefore be likely to remember events related to politics and to interpret many events in political terms. In the Follow-Through at the end of this chapter, we will see how people with strong gender schemas tend to interpret events in terms of gender.

Scripts: Going to a restaurant.   Forty-five years after the publication of Bartlett's book, Roger Schank and Robert Abelson (1977) introduced an idea closely related to Bartlett's schemas. They suggested that our knowledge of everyday life is organized around stereotypical situations and routine activities that take the form of *scripts*. **Scripts** are sequences of actions that describe common activities such as going to a restaurant, having someone over for dinner, or going out on a date. For example, most people, having eaten in restaurants many times, know that certain rules are normally followed in that situation. You usually wait to be seated, you give your order to the waitress, and you leave a tip after paying the bill. A complete "restaurant script" is shown in Figure 7.28.

Scripts are, therefore, one way we express our schemas. Schemas and their scripts are relevant to memory because they set up expectations about what usually happens in a particular situation, and those expectations may influence our memory of a situation. This idea has been tested by Gordon Bower and his coworkers (1979), who determined how well a subject could remember short passages like the following:

The Dentist
Bill had a bad toothache. It seemed like forever before he finally arrived at the dentist's office. Bill looked around at the various dental posters on the wall. Finally the dental hygienist checked and x-rayed his teeth. He wondered what the dentist was doing. The dentist said that Bill had a lot of cavities. As soon as he'd made another appointment, he left the dentist's office.

The subjects read a number of similar passages, all of which were about familiar activities like going to the dentist, going swimming, or going to a party. After a delay period, the subjects were given the titles of the stories they had read and were told to write down what they remembered about each one as accurately as possible. The recalled stories included material that matched the original stories, but they also included a specific kind of error: material that

FIGURE 7.28
Script based on the responses of subjects who were asked what people do when they go to a restaurant. Items in capital letters were listed by most subjects; items with first letters capitalized were listed by fewer subjects; and items in lowercase letters were listed by fewer subjects.

1. open door	9. LOOK AT MENU	17. Finish Meal	
2. Enter	10. Discuss Menu	18. Order Dessert	
3. Give Reservation Name	11. ORDER MEAL	19. Eat Dessert	
4. wait to be seated	12. Talk	20. ask for bill	
5. go to table	13. drink water	21. bill arrives	
6. BE SEATED	14. Eat Salad or Soup	22. PAY BILL	
7. Order Drinks	15. meal arrives	23. Leave Tip	
8. put napkins on lap	16. EAT FOOD	24. get coats	
		25. LEAVE	

wasn't presented in the original story but that is part of the "script" for the activity described. For example, for the dentist story some subjects "recalled" that "Bill checked in with the dentist's receptionist." This element is part of most people's "going to the dentist" script, but it was not included in the original story.

In both Bartlett's and Bower's experiments, memory was affected by their subjects' prior knowledge of their environment. These results illustrate the **constructive nature of memory.** What we recall is not a mental photograph of reality but rather a *construction* from a combination of information stored in memory and other information we have on hand.

The way psychologists discovered the constructive nature of memory shows that uncovering human capacities often depends on the way those capacities are tested. Most of the early memory experiments, which used nonsense syllables, single words, or numbers as test stimuli, were designed to eliminate the possibility of creativity on the part of the subject. The subject either did or did not remember the stimuli. It wasn't until researchers designed experiments in which subjects were given an opportunity to be creative that the constructive nature of memory became evident.

We now turn to a practical application of memory research—evaluating the trustworthiness of crime witnesses' memories for events. As we will see, the constructive nature of memory may, within the context of the police station or courtroom, result in "memories" that are not accurate representations of past events.

INTERDISCIPLINARY DIMENSION CRIMINAL JUSTICE

Memory in the Courtroom

It is mid-February 1931. Two men burst into a New York speakeasy and demand money from the cashier. Two policemen follow, a gun battle ensues, and one of the robbers and a policeman are killed. When 19-year-old Harry Cashin, a former employee of the speakeasy, is called into the police station for questioning, none of the robbery's eyewitnesses identify him. A few months later a prostitute who says she was at the speakeasy identifies Cashin. He is arrested for murder and placed on trial. Although Cashin had what seemed like an airtight alibi—a number of people testified that he was far from the speakeasy when the robbery occurred—he was convicted of first-degree murder based on the prostitute's eyewitness identification (Wells, 1984).

Cashin's conviction was reversed, but others haven't been so lucky. David Webb was sentenced to up to 50 years in prison for rape, attempted rape, and attempted robbery based on eyewitness testimony. He was released after serving ten months when another man confessed to the crimes. Charles Clark went to prison in 1938 for murder because of eyewitness testimony that 30 years later was proved inaccurate. He was released in 1968 (Loftus, 1979). Lenell Gertner served 16 months for robbing a fried chicken restaurant; there were five "positive" eyewitness identifications. Later, four of the five eyewitnesses identified a different person, and Gertner was released (Wells, 1984).

These miscarriages of justice and many others, some of which have undoubtedly never been discovered, are based on judges' and jurors' assumptions that people see and report events accurately. But this is an erroneous assumption. We already know that people don't remember things perfectly—they forget more and more with the passage of time. Even more disturbing, considering the role memory plays in testimony in criminal cases, people often construct their own memories. This was demonstrated long ago by Bartlett's "War of the Ghosts" experiment.

One problem with relying on eyewitness testimony is that people often do not perceive events correctly in the first place. Especially if events are rapid, perception can be inaccurate. This was demonstrated by an experiment in which the stimulus was televised on the NBC nightly news. On December 19, 1974, viewers saw a reenactment of a mugging, staged by actors, in which the mugger's face was visible for a second or so as he ran directly toward the camera. Viewers of the program were then shown a lineup of six men who resembled the mugger. They were asked to call a special number if they thought they could pick out the mugger from the lineup. Of over 2000 calls, only 14% correctly

4 — PERCEPTION

identified the attacker (Buckhout, 1975; Loftus, 1979). Perception of rapid events is notoriously inaccurate.

Errors of memory occur not only because of inaccurate perception but also because memories can be affected by what happens after the event. Imagine, for example, that after witnessing an incident you heard others talk about it and read newspaper stories about it. Eventually, you might have trouble sorting out what you actually saw from the information you took in afterwards. This is common in criminal cases when witnesses are asked "leading questions" by the police. A question like "Was the car a white sedan?" imparts information to the witness that may become part of a subsequent "memory." (See the Interdisciplinary Dimension in Chapter 5, "Hypnosis and the Law.")

This "leading question" effect was demonstrated experimentally by Elizabeth Loftus and her co-workers (1978). They had subjects view a film of an automobile accident and then asked a misleading question like "How fast was the white sports car going when it passed the barn on the country road?" (The subjects actually saw no barn.) A control group of subjects saw the same film and were asked "How fast was the white sports car going on the country road?" A week later all the subjects were asked whether they had seen a barn. Of the subjects who heard the question about the nonexistent barn, 17% reported seeing it. Only 3% of the subjects in the control group "remembered" the barn.

In one of Loftus's most widely reported experiments (Loftus & Palmer, 1974), she showed subjects a film of an automobile accident. One group was then asked "About how fast were the cars going when they smashed into each other?" and another, "About how fast were the cars going when they hit each other?" Although both groups saw the same film, the average speed estimated by subjects who heard the word *smashed* was 41 miles per hour and that by subjects who heard *hit,* 34. Even more interesting were the subjects' responses one week later to the question "Did you see any broken glass?" Although there was no broken glass in the film, 32% of the subjects who heard *smashed* reported seeing broken glass; only 14% of those who heard *hit* reported seeing the glass.

Results such as Loftus's indicate that our memories are constructed from two kinds of information: (1) the information supplied by the actual event and (2) externally presented information such as leading questions (Loftus, 1992). This external information, though often supplied by people such as police interrogators, can also be supplied by the person doing the remembering. Consider the following situation: A witness is asked to identify a robbery suspect from a lineup. She sees a person she thinks might be the robber, but she isn't positive. She says, "I'm not sure, but I think it might be Number 5." Later, when again asked to identify the suspect, the witness is more confident in her choice because she has seen the person before and perhaps has been rehearsing her original decision in her mind. Eventually, she is certain it was him. In this case, the witness's initial guess creates information about the suspect that eventually becomes transformed into a confident identification.

It is clear that eyewitness testimony isn't always reliable. On the other hand it can't be banned as evidence, because accurate eyewitness testimony often plays a crucial role in bringing criminals to justice. The message here for police, judges, and juries is that the validity of an eyewitness report must be evaluated according to the circumstances under which the witness saw the crime and what intervened between seeing the crime and the actual identification. ■

Memory and Studying

One of your goals in reading this chapter on memory is to commit its key facts to memory! Do the principles we have discussed in this chapter have any implications for the way you try to study and remember material? Let's take a look at some practical suggestions based on what psychologists have learned about memory.

Two of the major principles for remembering established by research are (1) the importance of elaborative rehearsal and (2) the importance of organization. You can apply those principles to studying academic material by using Francis Robinson's (1970) SQ3R method of studying. SQ3R stands for a five-step process: (1) Survey, (2) Question, (3) Read, (4) Recite, and (5) Review (Figure 7.29). As we examine this method of studying, note how it relates to some of the principles of memory we have discussed in this chapter.

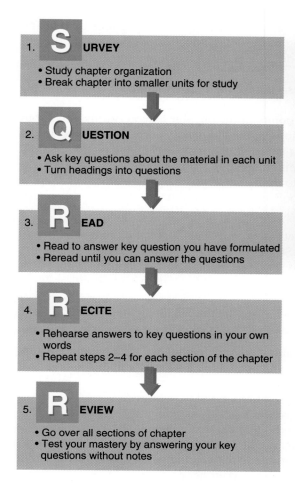

FIGURE 7.29
Steps in the SQ3R method of studying

1. *Survey.* The first step helps you perceive the overall organization of a chapter. Before beginning each chapter, look at its chapter outline. Get a feel for its main topics and how they are organized. Then break the chapter into smaller units for more intensive studying.

By surveying the overall picture, you are creating an organizational scheme that will help you more efficiently file what you have read into LTM. By studying in small units you are taking into account the limits on your ability to remember large chunks of information. The idea is to master smaller chunks and then combine them later.

2. *Question.* Create questions about the material within one of the smaller units you have chosen. One way to do this is to change section headings into questions. So the heading "Elaborative Rehearsal" might become "What is elaborative rehearsal?"; "Why is elaborative rehearsal important?"; "How is elaborative rehearsal different from maintenance rehearsal?" By creating questions you are setting the stage for the next step, reading the material.

3. *Read.* You are now ready to read the section of the chapter for which you have created questions. As you read, be sure to achieve your goal of answering the questions you formulated. Answering questions forces you to process the material in terms of its meaning and therefore to achieve a deep level of processing.

4. *Recite.* Once you have read the section with the goal of answering the questions in mind, you need to *rehearse* your answers. One of the most common mistakes students make at this point is to use maintenance rehearsal. They look at the book or the answer they've written down and simply repeat what they see. This type of rehearsal is superficial and therefore unlikely to be an effective way

to memorize the material. The key is to achieve *elaborative* rehearsal by rehearsing your answers without looking at the book. Most important, create the answers *in your own words*. Only by doing this can you achieve true elaborative rehearsal.

Repeat steps 2 to 4 for each section of the chapter and then proceed to the final step.

5. *Review.* Go over the key points in the chapter as you did in step 4, but this time test yourself on all sections of the chapter at once. At this step in the process, or perhaps at step 4, you could enhance your elaborative rehearsal by thinking of ways to relate what you are reading to examples from your own life. Although this might be difficult to do in, say, a physics or chemistry class, psychology presents numerous opportunities for drawing connections between textbook learning and your own experiences.

As you can see, the SQ3R method is simply an application of the principles established by memory research. Students who, in the past, have studied inefficiently by means of maintenance rehearsal often find that applying the SQ3R technique substantially improves both their understanding and retention of the material.

In addition to the principles related to the SQ3R method, the following study principles follow from the results of memory research:

- Minimize interference while studying. Although some students claim they can study efficiently while watching TV or listening to music, it is likely that these extraneous stimuli cause interference, which makes it more difficult to commit relevant material to memory.
- Rehearse, rehearse, rehearse. We mentioned elaborative rehearsal in conjunction with the SQ3R method, but rehearsal is such a basic tool for improving memory that it bears repeating. And there are a number of different ways to rehearse. You can repeat things out loud, write them down, or silently rehearse them in your head.
- Spread studying out over time rather than cramming at the last minute. Memory for material is much better when studying is spaced—preferably with 24-hour breaks between study sessions—than when it is all done in one intensive session (Dempster & Farris, 1990; Underwood, 1961, 1970) (Figure 7.30).
- Study under conditions that most closely approximate the conditions you will be tested under. If you chew a particular flavor of gum while

FIGURE 7.30
When children studied lists of words four times, they remembered them better if the study sessions were spaced over time (distributed practice) than if they occurred immediately after one another (massed practice).

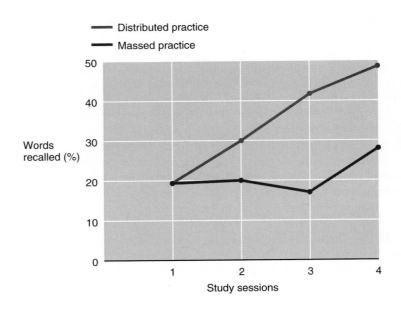

studying, you might try chewing the same flavor during the exam. The more retrieval cues you have working for you, the better!

- Create mnemonic devices to aid in remembering hard-to-remember material. Just as subject S. F. made up running times to help him remember strings of numbers, you can create meaningful material to help you remember specific facts. One way to do this is to form *acrostics*—phrases in which the first letter of each word functions as a memory aid. For example, if you were having trouble remembering the names and locations of the lobes of the cerebral cortex, you could create an acrostic such as "Thin Oars Pull Freely" to stand for Temporal, Occipital, Parietal, and Frontal (the order of the lobes as we move around the cortex in a counterclockwise direction).

- Organize material to be learned. A good example of organizing material is provided by the tables that appear in this chapter and throughout the book. These tables summarize and organize material that is spread over many pages. Writing down the headings of a table and then filling in the blanks without looking at the table can help you organize the material in your mind (and is also a form of rehearsal). Better yet, create your own tables. When you do this you are taking an active role in organizing the material—a powerful way to improve your memory.

Reprise: Memory and Cognitive Psychology

Let's look back at the ground we've covered since the beginning of Chapter 6, the chapter on learning. Beginning with Pavlov's salivating dogs and Skinner's bar-pressing rats, we observed how the behaviorists, with their emphasis on objectively measurable responses, focused on observable behaviors. We then saw how psychologists began to question the behaviorists' idea that only observable behavior was relevant to psychology. Perhaps, the cognitive psychologists suggested, we might gain some important understandings about behavior by looking at the mental processes that underlie behavior. In this chapter we have been immersed in these mental processes, specifically looking at how psychologists have gathered evidence to support their conception of the human mind as an information-processing unit whose functions can be broken down into different stages having different properties.

Our description of the mind as an information processor has introduced some of the methods and conclusions of the "cognitive revolution" that swept through psychology beginning in the late 1950s. This approach to psychology has taken its place alongside behaviorism as an important way to study behavior. In fact, the idea that we must study mental processes to truly understand behavior has pervaded every area of psychological research. In the next chapter we will look further at research on mental processes as we consider how people make decisions, solve problems, and learn language. And the influence of the cognitive approach will also be evident as we consider psychologists' ideas about topics such as development, intelligence, personality, and social psychology in the chapters that follow.

Gender Schemas and Memory

As we grow up we learn about the nature of our world and create schemas that lead to scripts, such as the restaurant and dentist scripts discussed earlier. These scripts lead us to expect that in certain situations certain things are going to happen; those expectations in turn influence our memory for events. Sandra Bem (1981, 1985) has suggested that we not only have schemas about visits to restaurants and dentists, but that we also have schemas about what it is like to be a male or a female. She calls these **gender schemas** and hypothesizes that they influence the way we think about ourselves and others, causing us to interpret many of the events in our lives in terms of gender.

To understand what she means by this, let's return to the idea of gender socialization that we introduced in the last chapter's Follow-Through, "Learning Gender Roles." As children grow up they are taught what behavior is appropriate for males and females; they also learn, by observing adults in their culture, that there are differences between males and females. They learn, for example, that girls wear dresses but boys don't; that boys should be strong and girls pretty; that boys grow up to be daddies and girls grow up to be mommies. They also learn that some occupations tend to be dominated by females and others by males. Children see that nurses, secretaries, child care workers, and salespeople in dress shops are usually females and that football players, CEO.s of large corporations, tractor-trailer drivers, and U.S. presidents are usually males. As children learn these things, they create gender schemas that contain information about the appearance, behavior, and professions associated with males and females.

Once gender schemas are learned they affect behavior, as girls and boys begin patterning their behavior after the schema for their gender. Behaviors ranging from career choice to book-carrying style to the physical distance maintained in a conversation are determined by these schemas. In addition to influencing outward behaviors, they influence the way we think about gender.

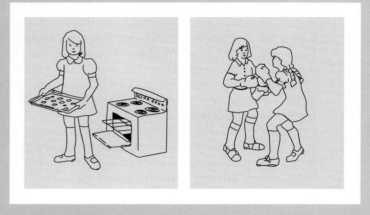

FIGURE 7.31
Gender-appropriate (left) and gender-inappropriate (right) pictures used by Martin and Halverson

This influence on thinking thus affects our memory for gender-related information.

Martin and Halverson (1983) demonstrated the effect of gender schemas on memory by showing pictures like the ones in Figure 7.31 to 5- and 6-year-old children. Some of these were of "gender-appropriate" behaviors, like the one on the left, and others were of "gender-inappropriate" behaviors, like the one on the right. A week after seeing the pictures, the children were asked to describe as many as possible. When they did this, something interesting happened. They accurately described the gender-appropriate pictures, but when describing the others they switched gender to make them "appropriate." If the original picture was of a girl sawing wood, they described a boy sawing wood.

Just as the restaurant script influences a person's memory for a story about a restaurant visit, the gender schemas we learn as we grow up influence the way we deal with gender information. One way to interpret Martin and Halverson's results is to hypothesize that their subjects filtered out incoming information that was inconsistent with their gender schema and reinterpreted it to be consistent with their schema. Gender schema theory, therefore, provides a way of thinking about gender role socialization in addition to the ones we discussed in the last chapter.

Gender schema theory also hypothesizes that different people have different gender schemas. Bem predicted that gender schemas would be stronger and more central to the lives of highly gender-typed people (very masculine males or very feminine females). In an experiment designed to test this idea, Bem (1981) first measured the strength of her subjects' gender typing. A person with many qualities associated with one gender (such as being aggressive, forceful, and self-reliant for males or understanding, tender, and sensitive to the needs of others for females) but with few qualities associated with the other gender, is strongly gender typed. In contrast, someone who has an equal number of male and female qualities is weakly gender typed.

Male and female styles of carrying books

Until recently, a woman shooting a pistol was incompatible with most people's gender schemas.

After determining the strength of each person's gender typing, Bem presented her subjects with a list of 61 words to remember. Some of the words were "feminine" (*butterfly, blushing, bikini*), some "masculine" (*gorilla, hunting, trains*), and some "neutral" (*ant, stepping, sweater*). On a recall test presented later, both strongly and weakly gender-typed subjects recalled the same number of words. However, the strongly gender-typed subjects tended to recall the words in clusters based on the word's gender. This means that once a strongly gender-typed individual recalls a feminine item, he or she is more likely to recall another feminine item. This result suggests that people who are strongly gender typed are more likely to organize their world in terms of gender. Thus, strong gender schemas affect not only their behavior but how they take in, organize, and remember information.

The idea that the strength of people's gender schema influences their memory for gender-relevant information has also been demonstrated in experiments on young children. Bruce Carter and Gary Levy (1988) interviewed children between 3 and 5 1/2 years of age to determine the strength of their gender schema. They then presented pictures similar to the ones in Figure 7.31, depicting gender-appropriate or gender-inappropriate behaviors. Later, in the memory test, those drawings were shown to the children along with similar pictures they had never seen, and they were asked to pick the pictures they had seen before.

As in the study with 5- and 6-year-olds, the children showed a bias toward picking gender-appropriate pictures, even if they had originally seen the gender-inappropriate ones. And another interesting result emerged: children who had stronger gender schemas were less likely to remember the gender-inappropriate pictures and more likely to "remember" a *transformation* of a gender-inappropriate picture. For example, they would pick a picture of a male doctor even though they had previously seen a picture of a female doctor.

Gender schemas, therefore, exert a powerful influence on information processing and memory among children in the process of learning about the role of gender in our society. Thus, gender schemas and socialization processes such as reinforcement and observational learning that we discussed in the last Follow-Through work together to shape our conceptions of gender as we are growing up.

Who is in charge here? Many people's gender schemas about "hard hat" environments would lead them to say that the man is in charge. It isn't clear in this picture, however, that this is the correct answer.

On the Trail of Memory:
The Development of Memory Research

- Memory is the ability to store information we have been exposed to and to reproduce that information at a later time. Ebbinghaus carried out the first scientific memory experiments by using his relearning procedure to measure a forgetting curve. James, in his theorizing about memory, proposed that there are two different types of memory.

- Cognitive psychology, which began to be a force in psychology in the late 1950s, has led to information-processing models of memory.

How Memory Works:
An Information-Processing Model

- The multistore model of memory proposes that three types of memory stores hold information for different periods of time: sensory memory, short-term memory, and long-term memory. We can understand how information is processed in these stages in terms of the cognitive processes of encoding, storage, and retrieval.

Sensory Memory: The Sparkler's Trail

- Sensory memory automatically registers any stimulus that hits the sensory receptors and holds that information there very briefly (less than 1 second for visual stimuli, a few seconds for auditory stimuli).

Short-Term Memory: Information in Action

- Short-term memory (STM) is where we store the small amount of information we are currently using. STM has been called working memory, because we are constantly using it and because of its dynamic nature. The functions of STM include regulating attention, rehearsing information, serving as a "bulletin board" for doing computations, and communicating with long-term memory.

- Information is encoded in STM based on the sound of the stimulus, though visual encoding is also possible. The storage capacity of STM is about seven items. The use of chunking can, however, increase the amount of information that can be stored. Information is retrieved rapidly from STM by a process called memory scanning.

- Forgetting material held in STM is caused by interference, in which the presentation of new stimuli interferes with memory for stimuli already stored there. Information that is not lost from STM through forgetting is transferred to long-term memory. This transfer takes place primarily because of rehearsal.

Long-Term Memory: Information in Storage

- Long-term memory (LTM) is our storehouse of information from our past. According to Tulving, there are three kinds of LTM: episodic memory, procedural memory, and semantic memory. Some researchers feel that these types of memory are served by separate memory systems; others disagree.

- Research suggests that information is encoded in LTM primarily in terms of meanings. Information becomes stored in LTM through rehearsal, with elaborative rehearsal being much more effective at creating storage than maintenance rehearsal.

- Levels of processing theory says that deep processing (processing a stimulus by associating it with other things we know) results in better memory than shallow processing (processing a stimulus based only on its physical features). Some research has supported this idea, but criticisms have decreased its influence.

- Organization plays an important role in the storage of information in LTM. Given enough time during learning, we will organize stimuli as we store them. Presenting information in an organized way increases a person's ability to remember material, so memory depends on how information is programmed into the mind.

- Retrieval of information from LTM is aided by retrieval cues. Retrieval is also enhanced if the conditions in which remembering takes place are similar to the conditions in which the material was originally encoded. This encoding specificity effect may occur because the original conditions of learning function as a retrieval cue. Models for the retrieval of material from LTM have been proposed, based on the idea that memory organization is a network of closely related nodes.

- One of the major mechanisms of forgetting in LTM is interference. Proactive interference occurs when old learning interferes with new learning. Retroactive interference occurs when new learning interferes with old learning. Interference apparently disrupts the process of retrieval.

How the Brain Remembers:
The Physiology of Memory

- Researchers have taken a number of different approaches to determine what brain processes are responsible for forming and storing memories. Three of those approaches are (1) linking memory to changes in neural processing, (2) linking memory to specific brain structures, and (3) determining the consolidation period for memory (the period required for any structural changes associated with the establishment of long-term memories to become permanently established).

Real-World Memory

- We have an amazing ability to remember everyday events from long ago. A special type of long-lived memory is associated with events that have special significance, such as national or personal disasters (the flashbulb memory effect).

- Memory for meaningful stimuli involves an interaction between the information we take in and our existing knowledge and past experiences. Memory is a constructive process that depends to some extent on the schemas we have learned (for example, schemas that describe specific types of events such as going to a restaurant).

- Memory research suggests reasons why eyewitness testimony can be faulty, leading to miscarriages of justice. Eyewitnesses may not perceive events correctly in the first place, and their memories can be affected by events that occur after the significant one. Leading questions posed by law enforcement officers can also affect what such witnesses "remember."

Memory and Studying

- The SQ3R method of studying incorporates several principles gleaned from memory research. Elaborative rehearsal is extremely helpful, for instance. In addition, studying efficiency can be enhanced by minimizing interference, spreading studying over time, and studying under conditions similar to those under which you will be tested.

Reprise: Memory and Cognitive Psychology

- Research on memory, and specifically the information-processing approach to the study of memory, has enabled the cognitive approach to psychology to take its place alongside the behavioral approach as an important way to study behavior.

Follow-Through/Diversity: Gender Schemas and Memory

- Gender schemas are our ideas about what it is like to be male or female; they can influence the way we think about ourselves and others. Some research on children shows that these schemas encourage thinking in terms of stereotypical male and female roles. People with stronger gender schemas tend to have greater memory for gender-relevant information than do people with weak gender schemas.

Key Terms

chunking
consolidation hypothesis
consolidation period
constructive nature of memory
deep processing
echoic memory
elaborative rehearsal
encoding
episodic memory
flashbulb memories
gender schema
iconic memory
information processing
interference
levels of processing theory
long-term memory (LTM)
maintenance rehearsal
memory code
memory span
mnemonic device

multistore model
primacy effect
proactive interference
procedural memory
recall test
recency effect
recognition test
retrieval
retrieval cue
retroactive interference
schema
script
semantic memory
sensory memory
shallow processing
short-term memory (STM)
state-dependent learning
storage
tip-of-the-tongue (TOT) effect
working memory

CHAPTER

8

Categorization: A Basic Mechanism of Thinking
    The Process of Categorization

Reasoning: Thinking Logically—and Illogically
    Deductive Reasoning
    Inductive Reasoning

Making Decisions: Choosing Among Alternatives
    Elimination by Aspects
    Heuristics
    Framing Effects

**Solving Problems: Overcoming Obstacles
  to Reach a Goal**
    Obstacles to Problem Solving
    How Problem Solving Is Affected by the Way the Problem Is Stated
    Cognitive Operations During Problem Solving
    Problem Solving by Experts and Novices

Interdisciplinary Dimension: Artificial Intelligence
    Soar: An Intelligent Computer Program

Using and Understanding Language
    Problem Solving in Conversations
    Thought and Language

**Reprise: Levels of Analysis in the Study
  of Learning and Cognition**

Follow-Through/Diversity
    Thinking in Traditional Cultures

Thought and
Language

What is the hardest task in the world? To think.

Ralph Waldo Emerson (1803–1882)
American essayist and poet

The cognitive revolution that swept psychology beginning in the 1950s shifted psychologists' attention away from the behaviorist doctrine that mental processes should be ignored. Psychology's agenda changed from the study of animals pressing bars in Skinner boxes to the study of humans solving problems and making decisions, and the information-processing model found favor as a way of understanding the operation of the mind. The information-processing approach was applied most successfully to the study of memory. But mental activities include much more than memory: every day you engage in such cognitive acts as reasoning, making decisions, solving problems, and using language. In this chapter we expand our survey of cognitive psychology to include how psychologists have studied each of those activities (Table 8.1).

Reasoning, decision making, problem solving, and understanding language all involve **thinking,** the active transformation of existing knowledge to create new knowledge that can be used to achieve a goal (Glass & Holyoak, 1986, p. 333). The key words in this definition are *transformation* and *goal.* Each of the tasks we will consider in this chapter begins with the presentation of information that is transformed to reach a goal. In reasoning, information is used to reach a conclusion; in decision making, choices are transformed into a decision; in problem solving, components of a problem are manipulated to create a solution; in conversation, words that are heard are transformed into meanings.

Cognitive psychologists are interested in the mental processes responsible for these transformations. They typically study these mental processes in two ways. First, they describe how people accomplish thinking tasks by asking ques-

Problem solving is a cognitive activity common in everyday life.

TABLE 8.1
Cognitive actions in everyday life

Cognitive Actions	Definition	Example
Reasoning	Using logical thinking to draw a conclusion from information	"Charles must have been the person who took my ruler, because he was looking for a straightedge and he has taken things from me in the past."
Decision making	Choosing between two or more alternatives	"Should I go to the state university or a private college?"
Problem solving	Overcoming obstacles to change the present state of affairs to the desired state	"My usual route to the airport has just been shut down, and the traffic is terrible. How can I get to the airport in 30 minutes to catch my plane?"
Using and understanding language	Using language to express meaning; determining what another person's utterances mean	"When John said 'Do you want to see a movie?' he really meant that he wanted to see a movie with me."

tions such as "What strategies do people use?" "Do they follow particular rules?" and "Do different people use different approaches?" Second, they look at the *mistakes* people make. Sometimes we reason illogically, make irrational decisions, fail to find the solution to a problem, or misinterpret what someone says. Just as perceptual illusions can shed light on normal perception, studying cognitive mistakes can reveal the mental processes involved in reasoning, decision making, problem solving, and how we use language.

In this chapter we will consider each of these tasks in turn, beginning with the processes involved in reasoning. Before proceeding to specific tasks, however, we need to look at a process that underlies all of them—*categorization*.

Categorization: A Basic Mechanism of Thinking

The world is made up of countless components. We can perceive over 7 million different colors (Goldstein, 1989), and the objects in our environment—chairs, tables, vehicles, articles of clothing—come in a multitude of shapes, sizes, and configurations. What would happen to our ability to think and communicate about the world if we had to consider every separate object and event as a unique entity? Thinking would grind to a halt, because we would have no way of representing general ideas or of referring to collections of things in terms of their common characteristics. A thought like "watch out for dogs; some of them bite" would be impossible, because we would have no way of forming the idea "dog." Instead, we would be limited to thoughts like "watch out for Fido; he bites," "watch out for Spot; he bites," and so on, for every four-legged biting thing in our experience. In short, we would lack an ability that is fundamental to thinking and language—the ability to form *categories*.

The Process of Categorization

Categories are groups of objects or events having similar properties. Categories can be broad ("animal," "furniture"), specific ("dogs," "chairs"), or even more specific ("German shepherds," "rocking chairs"). It is these categories that enable us to think about our world—for example, to formulate the ideas that "dogs are four-legged animals of the family *Canis familiaris*, which sometimes bite" or "a chair is something to sit on" (Figure 8.1).

Our ability to categorize not only reduces the number of items we need to deal with in the environment to a manageable level, but it also reduces the need for constant learning (Bruner, Goodnow, & Austin, 1956). If we encounter an object we have never seen before, but we know its category—"chair," for instance—we immediately know something about the object—"it is something to sit on."

FIGURE 8.1
These objects all obviously belong in the category "chair" even though they look very different from one another.

FIGURE 8.2
Vase or drinking glass? Sometimes what an object is used for determines the category in which we place it.

Cognitive psychologists are interested in how we go about placing objects into categories. One explanation is that we categorize things based on how they are *defined*. According to this idea, an item is placed in a particular category if it meets the definition for that category. Thus, a four-legged animal that is warm blooded, has large canine teeth and a tail, and is typically domesticated qualifies for the category "dog."

Although the definitional approach sounds reasonable, it faces a problem: it is difficult to propose adequate definitions for many categories because the boundaries between them are often fuzzy. For example, on my desk is a vase holding some flowers. But when I bought this "vase" I thought it was a drinking glass. What is it, a vase or a drinking glass? (Figure 8.2). What definition can I use to explain how I place objects in the category "drinking glass" or "vase"? This fuzziness of category boundaries is illustrated by the results of an experiment by Labov (1973). Labov asked subjects to describe pictures similar to the drawings in Figure 8.3 as either a cup or a bowl. When presented with this task, most subjects labeled objects 1, 2, and 5 as cups and objects 3 and 4 as bowls. But when Labov's subjects imagined the objects as being filled with mashed potatoes and placed on a table, they were much more likely to classify all the containers as "bowls." Changing what the object is used for shifts the borders that separate one category from another.

FIGURE 8.3
Bowls or cups? Labov (1973) found that subjects who imagined these containers filled with mashed potatoes tended to see them as "bowls."

If we don't categorize by means of definitions, how do we do it? Eleanor Rosch (1975) suggests that we place objects in categories based on how closely

TABLE 8.2
Subjects' ranking of objects as examples of categories

Item	Furniture	Fruit	Vegetable	Weapon
1	chair	orange	peas	gun
2	sofa	apple	carrots	knife
3	table	banana	string beans	sword
4	dresser	peach	spinach	bomb
5	desk	pear	broccoli	hand grenade
6	bed	apricot	asparagus	spear
7	bookcase	plum	corn	cannon
8	footstool	grapes	cauliflower	bow and arrow
9	lamp	strawberry	Brussels sprouts	club
10	piano	grapefruit	lettuce	tank
11	cushion	pineapple	beets	tear gas
12	mirror	blueberry	tomato	whip
13	rug	lemon	lima beans	ice pick
14	radio	watermelon	eggplant	fists
15	stove	honeydew	onion	rocket
16	clock	pomegranate	potato	poison
17	picture	date	yam	scissors
18	closet	coconut	mushroom	words
19	vase	tomato	pumpkin	foot
20	telephone	olive	rice	screwdriver

their features match the features of *prototypes*—objects that are considered to be the best examples of a category. Rosch and Mervis (1975) tested this idea by asking people to rate objects in terms of how well they represented a particular category. The results, shown in Table 8.2, indicate that people rank some objects as better examples of a category than others (Mervis & Rosch, 1981; Rosch, 1973, 1975, 1977; Rosch & Mervis, 1975).

Inspection of these lists reveals that items ranked near the top of a category share many features with other members of the category. For example, items at the top of the "furniture" category, like chairs and sofas, have features in common with many of the other items on the list (they have legs and rest on the floor). However, items at the bottom of the list, like vases and telephones, share fewer features with other items in that category. Thus, objects that have many features associated with a certain category are considered good examples of the category, whereas objects that have fewer features associated with the category are considered poor examples of the category.

Rosch (1973) also found that when both adults and children were asked to answer questions like "Is an orange a fruit?" their reaction times were faster for good examples of the category than for poor examples (Figure 8.4).

Although not all researchers agree with Rosch's interpretation of her results in terms of her feature theory (see Armstrong, Gleitman, & Gleitman, 1983), her results do give us some insight into how people think about categories. Categorization is more complex than simply deciding whether or not something belongs in a particular category based on a definition. Moreover, categorization affects other cognitive processes. For example, the results displayed in Figure 8.4 show that facts about items that are good examples of a category are retrieved more rapidly from long-term memory than are facts about items that are poor examples. Recall also from Chapter 7 that our ability to retrieve information from long-term memory is affected by how that information is organized. When we organize information, we often use categories.

The creation of categories simplifies our dealings with the world. We now consider a number of types of thinking that depend heavily on the use of categories, beginning with reasoning.

FIGURE 8.4
Reaction times for children and adults to answer questions like "Is an orange a fruit?" Adults answered more rapidly than children, but both adults and children answered more slowly for nonprototypical fruits.

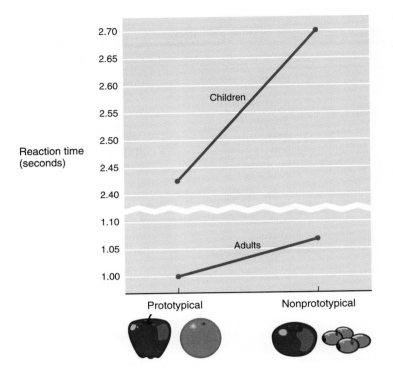

Reasoning: Thinking Logically—and Illogically

> *"Contrariwise," continued Tweedledee, "if it was so, it might be; and if it were so, it would be; but as it isn't, it ain't. That's logic."*
>
> Lewis Carroll, *Alice's Adventures in Wonderland*

Reasoning, the ability to think logically, is the process by which we draw conclusions from information. In the example from Table 8.1, you are reasoning when, in evaluating available information about your ruler's disappearance, you suspect Charles. Since Charles was just looking for a straightedge, and since he has a past history of borrowing things without asking, he is a prime suspect.

Cognitive psychologists are interested in how people go about reasoning. They ask questions such as "What are the processes involved in drawing conclusions from information?" and "In what situations do these processes lead to errors in reasoning?" They address these questions by using two models of reasoning. The *descriptive model* describes how people *actually* perform reasoning tasks. The main goal of cognitive psychology is to develop descriptive models of reasoning and other cognitive tasks. Thus, in the last chapter we were concerned with how cognitive psychologists have developed a descriptive model of memory and forgetting.

The *normative model* describes how people *should* perform reasoning tasks to achieve optimal performance. That is, it specifies the correct answers to reasoning problems. Normative models of reasoning, which have been developed by logicians and statisticians, provide a benchmark against which psychologists can compare people's actual performance. In this section we will see how psychologists have applied the descriptive and normative models to study two types of reasoning, *deductive* and *inductive* reasoning.

Deductive Reasoning

A **deduction** is a judgment that, when certain assertions are true, a conclusion *must* follow. For example, from the two assertions "If Mars is a planet, then it revolves around the sun" and "Mars is a planet" we can deduce that "Mars revolves around the sun." Note that the conclusion—that Mars revolves around the sun—follows logically from the assertions on which it is based.

Cognitive psychologists have studied **deductive reasoning** by presenting subjects with a sequence of assertions and a conclusion that allegedly follows from them. They ask the subjects to indicate whether the conclusion does in fact follow. They then compare the subjects' judgments with the correct answers, determined by the normative model of reasoning.

The assertions and conclusions are presented as a *syllogism*, a form created by the Greek philosopher Aristotle in which two assertions, the *premises*, are followed by a conclusion. The sequence of statements ending in the conclusion "Mars revolves around the sun" is an example of a syllogism.

The advantage of using syllogisms to study people's reasoning processes is that there are well-defined rules for judging whether a syllogism is *valid*—that is, whether the conclusion does follow logically from the premises. To illustrate how cognitive psychologists use the rules of valid syllogisms to study people's reasoning processes, we will look at a type of deductive reasoning called conditional reasoning. We will look at the logical rules involved and then at how people actually reason when presented with syllogisms.

Our opening syllogism about Mars is an example of *conditional reasoning*, reasoning in which the first premise has the form "If P then Q," where P and Q can be replaced with meaningful statements. For example, in our Mars example above, "Mars" is P and "revolves around the sun" is Q. Logicians have formulated two *inference rules* that enable us to determine whether the conclusion of a conditional syllogism is valid. The first rule, called *modus ponens*, states that when premise 2 has the form "P is true," the conclusion follows that "Q is true," as shown below:

The philosopher Aristotle (left), the creator of the syllogism

Syllogism valid according to modus ponens:

Premise 1:	If P is true, then Q is true.
Premise 2:	P is true.
Conclusion:	Therefore, Q is true.

According to *modus ponens*, our conclusion that "Mars is a planet" is a valid deduction. The second rule, called *modus tollens*, is trickier. It states that when premise 2 is "Q is false," as in the example below, then the conclusion necessarily follows that "P is false."

Syllogism valid according to modus tollens:

Premise 1:	If P is true, then Q is true.
Premise 2:	Q is false.
Conclusion:	Therefore, P is false.

For example, consider the following argument:

If it is sunny on Tuesdays, then we play baseball.	If P, then Q.
We did not play baseball.	Q is false.
Therefore, it was not sunny on Tuesday.	P is false.

Think about this syllogism for a moment. How obviously does the conclusion follow from the premises? Most people have to think for a while to convince

FIGURE 8.5
Two syllogisms with the same first premise.
Are the conclusions true or false?

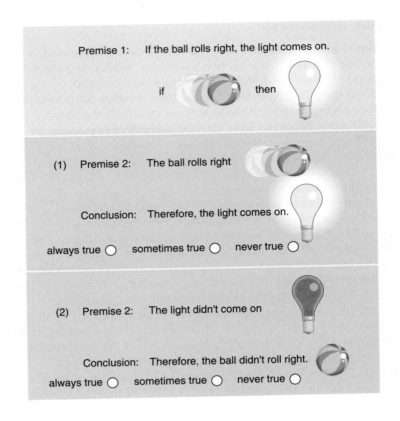

themselves of the validity of conclusions reached through applying *modus tollens*.

With these rules of logic in mind, we can now ask how people actually perform on tasks involving conditional reasoning. To what extent do people's actual mental processes reflect the rules of logic? Lance Rips and Sandra Marcus (1977) explored this question by presenting a number of syllogisms to subjects and asking them whether the conclusion was always true, sometimes true, or never true. Two of the syllogisms presented by Rips and Marcus are shown in Figure 8.5.

After you have made your own decisions about the two syllogisms in Figure 8.5, check the results in Table 8.3, which reports the percentage of subjects giving each answer. All subjects evaluated syllogism 1 correctly, as specified by the rule *modus ponens*. However, 43% of subjects made errors on syllogism 2, which relies on the rule of *modus tollens*. You might identify with this result if the validity of the syllogism about the baseball game was not immediately obvious to you. Thus, in some cases (when arguments are based on *modus ponens*) people can easily evaluate a deductive argument, and in other cases (when arguments

TABLE 8.3
Rips and Marcus results

Syllogism	Always True	Sometimes True	Never True	Explanation
1. If the ball rolls right, then the light comes on. The ball rolled right. Therefore, the light came on.	<u>100</u>	0	0	*modus ponens*
2. If the ball rolls right, then the light comes on. The light did not come on. Therefore, the ball didn't roll right.	<u>57</u>	39	4	*modus tollens*

Note: Numbers are the percentage of subjects picking that answer. Percentages for the correct answers are underlined.

are based on *modus tollens*) the correct outcome of a deductive argument is not obvious.

Although people sometimes make errors, an important property of deductive reasoning is that we can always determine with certainty whether a conclusion follows from a set of premises, provided we apply logic correctly. Although deductive reasoning has its place, most of the reasoning we use in everyday life involves considerable *un*certainty. This form of reasoning is called *inductive reasoning*.

Inductive Reasoning

Inductive reasoning is the process of drawing the conclusion that a given statement is probable, based on our past experiences (Glass & Holyoak, 1986). Consider your reaction if, when driving along the highway, you were assaulted by a skunklike odor. You might conclude that a skunk was hit by a car. Though your conclusion might be correct, it isn't the only possible explanation—perhaps the skunk was fighting off an enemy and just happened to be near the road (Best, 1989). You judge it *probable* that a skunk was hit by a car, but you might not be willing to wager a week's salary on this conclusion.

Everyday thinking such as this is thus based on probabilities rather than on logical certainties. We make an *inference* based on often incomplete facts and our past experiences. The probability that our inference is correct depends on the number and quality of the observations that support it. For example, my judgment that the sun will rise every day is an **induction** based on my lifelong observation of the sun rising every day in the past. Whereas there is no *logical* necessity for the sun to rise tomorrow, my past experiences give me a very high degree of confidence that it will.

Inductive reasoning plays a large role in scientific research, particularly in creating hypotheses. Recall, for example, our discussion in Chapter 2 of Joseph Goldberger's research on pellagra. Goldberger's hypothesis, that pellagra was caused by poor nutrition, was an induction based on observation. His explanation had a higher probability of being correct than the previous hypothesis (that pellagra was caused by sanitary conditions) because Goldberger used experimental evidence to support his conclusion, not because it was inherently more logical. Remember, too, that scientific experiments usually involve drawing conclusions about a large population based on observations of a small sample. There is no logical necessity for what is true of the sample to be true of the whole population. Rather, researchers induce a general rule that has a greater or lesser probability of being correct, depending on the number and quality of their observations.

Most of our everyday reasoning is like induction in science, in that it involves reaching more or less probable conclusions based on the evidence of our experience. And just as psychological factors can influence our ability to reason deductively, they can also influence our ability to reason inductively.

A major roadblock to successful inductive reasoning is **confirmational bias**—our tendency to selectively look for information that confirms our hypothesis and to overlook information that argues against it. This effect was demonstrated by P. C. Wason (1960), who presented subjects with the following instructions:

> You will be given three numbers which conform to a simple rule that I have in mind. . . . Your aim is to discover this rule by writing down sets of three numbers together with your reasons for your choice of them. . . . After you have written down each set, I shall tell you whether your numbers conform to the rule or not. . . . When you feel highly confident that you have discovered the rule, you are to write it down and tell me what it is (p. 131).

After Wason presented the first set of numbers—2, 4, and 6—the subjects

People's existing beliefs about an issue can cause them to focus on information that supports their belief and ignore information that does not.

began creating their own sets of three numbers and receiving feedback. Note that Wason told subjects only whether their numbers fit his rule. The subjects did not find out whether their *rationale* was correct until they felt confident enough to actually announce their rule. The most common initial hypothesis was "increasing intervals of two." Since the actual rule was "three numbers in increasing order of magnitude," the rule "increasing intervals of two" was incorrect, even though it created sequences that satisfied Wason's rule.

The secret to determining the correct rule was to create sequences that did *not* satisfy the person's current hypothesis but *did* satisfy Wason's rule. Thus, determining that the sequence 2, 4, 5 was also correct would have allowed subjects to reject the "increasing intervals of two" hypothesis and formulate a new one. The few subjects whose rule was correct on first guess followed the strategy of testing a number of hypotheses by creating sequences that were designed to *disconfirm* their current hypothesis. In contrast, subjects who didn't guess the rule correctly on their first try tended to keep creating sequences that confirmed their current hypothesis.

The confirmational bias acts like a pair of blinders: we see the world according to rules we think are correct and are never dissuaded from this view, because we seek out only evidence that confirms our rule. This is why the hypothesis that linked pellagra and sanitation persisted for so long. Everywhere scientists looked they found evidence for this hypothesis, but they didn't bother looking anywhere else.

This bias is so strong that it can affect people's reasoning even when the relevant information is literally staring them in the face. Charles Lord and his co-workers (1979) demonstrated this in an experiment that tested how people's attitudes are affected by exposure to evidence that contradicts them.

By means of a questionnaire, Lord identified one group of subjects in favor of capital punishment and another group against it. Each subject was then presented with descriptions of research studies on capital punishment. Some of the studies provided evidence that capital punishment had a deterrent effect on murder; others provided evidence that it had no deterrent effect. When the subjects reacted to the studies, they voiced the same attitudes they held at the beginning of the experiment. For example, an article presenting evidence that supported the deterrence theory was rated as "convincing" by proponents of capital punishment and "unconvincing" by opponents. This is confirmational bias at work: people's prior beliefs cause them to focus on information that agrees with their beliefs and to disregard information that doesn't.

In summary, though we are capable of being highly logical, our reasoning processes are often influenced by various logical lapses and cognitive biases. The same is true of the kind of cognitive activity involved in making decisions such as which school to attend, what car to purchase, or whom to marry. In the next section, we look at some of the strategies people use when making decisions—and at some mechanisms that lower the efficiency of the decision-making process.

18   SOCIAL

Making Decisions: Choosing Among Alternatives

"To be, or not to be: that is the question."

William Shakespeare, *Hamlet*

We make decisions every day, from relatively unimportant ones (what clothes to wear, what movie to see) to those that can have a great impact on our lives (what college to attend, whether to end a relationship). Confronted with important decisions, most of us would like to feel assured that we will make the right choice, and we often try various strategies we hope will help. Let's consider some common decision-making strategies people use and the cognitive pitfalls awaiting the prospective decision maker.

Elimination by Aspects

Elimination by aspects is a decision-making strategy in which a choice is eliminated if it does not meet a minimum requirement for some consideration. For example, if you are trying to decide which college to attend and have limited financial resources, you might eliminate all Ivy League schools because they share the aspect of costing too much. Similarly, perhaps you have used elimination by aspects to winnow your field of potential romantic partners, ruling out those who fall short on some specific criterion (looks, intelligence, religious belief, and so on).

Elimination by aspects has a number of advantages. It is easy to apply, it involves no computations, and the decision you reach is easy to justify to yourself and defend to others. When 6-foot, 3-inch Mark picks a new car because it is the only two-seater in his price range with enough leg room, his decision sounds reasonable. However, sometimes we pay a price for simplicity. Consider the following example of elimination by aspects in a television commercial for a computer programming school:

> There are more than two dozen companies in the San Francisco area which offer training in computer programming. (*The announcer puts some two dozen eggs and one walnut on the table to represent the alternatives.*) Let us examine the facts. How many of these schools have on-line computer facilities for training? (*The announcer removes several eggs.*) How many of these schools have placement services that would help find you a job? (*The announcer removes some more eggs.*) How many of these schools are approved for veteran's benefits? (*This continues until the walnut alone remains. The announcer cracks the nutshell, which reveals the name of the company.*) This is all you need to know in a nutshell (quoted in Tversky, 1972, p. 297).

The commercial tries to simplify your choice of schools by encouraging you to use elimination by aspects. Yet eliminating a school because it doesn't have a placement service might be a mistake. What if the eliminated school's reputation is so good that a placement service isn't necessary? Elimination by aspects would rule out this school in favor of one that might have a placement service but also a poor reputation. Thus, elimination by aspects can sometimes lead to faulty decision making (Tversky, 1972).

Heuristics

Another tactic that sometimes leads people astray in decision making is using **heuristics**—"rules of thumb" that are often helpful in decision making or problem solving but sometimes are not. We can appreciate the nature of heuristics by comparing them with algorithms, another problem-solving aid. **Algorithms** are procedures that are guaranteed to result in the solution of a problem. The procedures for multiplication and division are algorithms because, if you follow them, you will always arrive at the correct answer. Similarly, Aristotle's rules for syllogisms are algorithms that unfailingly determine the validity of deductive arguments.

To compare algorithms and heuristics, let's consider how you might use them to look for your missing cat, which you know is hiding somewhere in your house. An algorithm for finding the cat would be to systematically look in every conceivable place in every room of the house, starting at the front and working back. If the cat is in the house, you are sure to find it using this procedure, though it may take a long time (a disadvantage of algorithms). A heuristic for finding the cat would be to look first in the places where you have found the cat before—in front of the heat registers, behind the furnace, and behind the clothes in your closet. Looking in these places doesn't guarantee that you'll find your cat but, based on your knowledge of its habits, there's a high probability that it's in one of these places. Starting with them eliminates the need to look in places you know your cat never goes, like the shower.

Heuristics are often used in decision making because they save time and because most decisions must be made based on limited information. When we cannot gather all the information we need, we are likely to resort to the heuristics we think will lead to the best decision. They often work, but sometimes they don't. We will consider two of the heuristics that have been most widely studied by psychologists, the *availability heuristic* and the *representativeness heuristic*.

The availability heuristic. People use the **availability heuristic** when they judge events that are more easily remembered as being more probable than other events (Tversky & Kahneman, 1973a). This heuristic often works because events that occur frequently (and so are more probable) are usually easier to remember than events that occur infrequently. For example, if you remember seeing many Hondas but few BMWs on your street, you might correctly predict that you will, in the future, see more Hondas than BMWs.

But sometimes using the availability heuristic leads to errors. Paul Slovic and his co-workers (1976) presented subjects with two causes of death (for example, suicide and drowning) and asked them to indicate which one they thought caused more deaths. In the case of suicide and drowning, 70% correctly answered that suicide caused more deaths (in fact, about ten times as many people die by suicide as by drowning). But some pairs were seriously misjudged. In these cases the cause of death that was incorrectly thought to be the most prevalent was the one most publicized by the media. For example, 58% thought that more deaths were caused by tornados than by asthma; in reality, 20 times more people die from asthma than from tornados. Table 8.4 lists some other examples of these misjudgments (from Slovic et al., 1976; also see Slovic, 1987).

Particularly striking is the fact that 41% of the subjects thought that botulism (a particularly deadly form of food poisoning that occurs when foods are not properly canned) caused more deaths than asthma, though in reality 920 times more people die of asthma. The reason for this is clear. When someone dies of botulism it is front-page news, whereas deaths from asthma go virtually unnoticed by the general public (Lichtenstein et al., 1978).

Although tornadoes give rise to dramatic pictures in the newspaper, far fewer people die from tornadoes than from other, less publicized causes of death.

TABLE 8.4
Errors of judgment about causes of death

More Likely	Less Likely	True Ratio (More Likely/ Less Likely)	Percentage of Subjects Who Picked the Less Likely Alternative
Diabetes	Breast cancer	1.25	77
Appendicitis	Pregnancy	2.00	83
Lightning	Botulism	52.00	63
Asthma	Botulism	920.00	41

The representativeness heuristic. In discussing categorization, we saw that people tend to create prototypes for different categories. Cats are more prototypical pets than are sharks or aardvarks. This tendency to create prototypes can affect how people judge the probability of certain events. People use the **representativeness heuristic** when they judge events to be more likely if they more closely match a prototype.

We can understand how the representativeness heuristic operates by considering the following problem:

> We randomly pick one male from the population of the United States. That male, Robert, wears glasses, speaks quietly, and reads a lot. Is it more likely that Robert is a librarian or a farmer?

When presented with this question, more people guessed that Robert was a librarian (Tversky & Kahneman, 1973b). Obviously, the description of Robert as wearing glasses, speaking quietly, and reading a lot matches our prototype of a librarian. However, in 1973, when this study was conducted, there were many more male farmers than male librarians in the United States, so it was actually much more likely that Robert was a farmer (remember that he was randomly chosen from the whole population). People who picked librarian were seduced by the representativeness heuristic into basing their judgment on Robert's characteristics, whereas a more rational choice would have been based on the relative proportion of farmers and librarians in the population.

Representativeness can also lead us to violate the **conjunction rule,** which states that the probability of a conjunction of two events (A and B) cannot be more than the probability of the single constituents (A alone or B alone). For example, the probability that Anne has a red Corvette cannot be greater than the probability that she has a Corvette, because the two constituents together (red and Corvette) define a smaller number of cars than one constituent (Corvette *or* red) alone. Violation of the conjunction rule, which is called the **conjunction fallacy,** is illustrated by subjects' responses to the following problem:

> Linda is 31 years old, single, outspoken, and very bright. She majored in philosophy. As a student, she was deeply concerned with issues of discrimination and social justice and also participated in antinuclear demonstrations. Which of the following alternatives is more probable?
>
> 1. Linda is a bank teller.
> 2. Linda is a bank teller and is active in the feminist movement.

When presented with this problem, 85% of the subjects picked the second choice, a clear violation of the conjunction rule, as there are fewer feminist bank tellers than bank tellers. To put it another way, stating that Linda is a bank teller *includes* the possibility that she is a feminist bank teller. Statement 2 *cannot* be more probable than statement 1 (Tversky & Kahneman, 1990).

People tend to commit the conjunction fallacy even when it is clear that they understand the conjunction rule. The culprit is the representativeness heuristic; in the example just cited, the subjects saw Linda's characteristics as more representative of a feminist bank teller than of a bank teller.

Librarian or farmer? After reading a description of such a person, most subjects in a 1973 experiment used the representative heuristic and guessed "librarian."

The use of heuristics like availability and representativeness can affect decision making by leading us to use invalid information in making decisions. Consider the following situation:

> Six doctors in white hospital coats approach your bed. No one is smiling. The results of the biopsy are in. One doctor explains that the cells were irregular in shape; they appeared abnormal. It seems that the tumor was not clearly malignant, but not clearly normal either. They probably removed the entire tumor. It's hard to be certain about these things. You have some choices. You could leave the hospital this afternoon and forget about this unpleasant episode, except for semiannual checkups. There is an above-average chance, however, that some abnormal cells remain and will spread and grow. On the other hand, you could choose to have the entire area surgically removed. While this would be major surgery, it would clearly reduce the risk of cancer (from Halpern, 1989, p. 307).

How might you go about making this very important decision? The problem here is that you don't have enough information to feel certain of your choice. Even the doctors can't tell you with certainty what to do. You do, however, remember an acquaintance who, in a similar situation, elected not to have surgery and survived. Should you base your decision on this information, which just happens to be available to your memory? If you do, then you are falling prey to the availability heuristic and may be making a mistake. A more rational course of action would be to search out additional information to help you make your decision.

Framing Effects

We have seen that decisions are not always made rationally. Sometimes the strategy of elimination by aspects leads us to pick the less desirable choice, and sometimes using availability or representativeness heuristics can bias our judgment and lead to faulty decisions. Another factor standing in the way of rational decision making is the way choices are stated, or *framed*.

Consider the following problem that Tversky and Kahneman (1981) posed to college students:

> Imagine that the United States is preparing for the outbreak of an unusual disease that is expected to kill 600 people. Two alternative programs to combat the disease have been proposed. Assume that the exact scientific estimates of the consequences of the programs are as follows:
>
> - If program A is adopted, 200 people will be saved.
> - If program B is adopted, there is a one-third probability that 600 people will be saved, and a two-thirds probability that no people will be saved.
>
> Which of the two programs would you favor?

Program A was chosen by 72% of the students and program B by 28%. The choice of program A represents a **risk aversion strategy.** The idea of saving 200 lives with certainty is more attractive than the risk that no one will be saved. Now consider the following alternative proposals for combating the same disease:

> - If program C is adopted, 400 people will die.
> - If program D is adopted, there is a one-third probability that nobody will die, and a two-thirds probability that 600 people will die.

When Tversky and Kahneman presented these alternatives to another group of students, 22% picked program C and 78% picked program D. This represents a **risk-taking strategy.** The certain death of 400 people is less acceptable than a 2-in-3 chance that 600 people will die. Tversky and Kahneman conclude

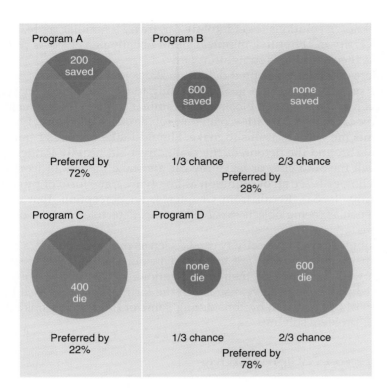

FIGURE 8.6
In this diagram it is clear that programs A and C are equivalent and B and D are equivalent. But people's reactions to them were very different, depending on how the programs were presented.

that, in general, when a choice is framed in terms of gains (as in the first problem, which is stated in terms of saving lives), people use a risk aversion strategy, and when a choice is framed in terms of losses (as in the second problem, which is stated in terms of losing lives), people use a risk-taking strategy.

But if we look at the four programs together, we can see that they are identical pairs (Figure 8.6). Programs A and C both result in 200 people living and 400 people dying. Yet 72% of the subjects picked program A and only 22% picked program C. Similarly, if we compare programs B and D, we find that both lead to the same number of deaths, yet one was picked by 28% of the subjects and the other by 78%. These results show that decisions are influenced both by the objective outcome of the decision and by how the problem is stated.

In discussing decision making, we have touched on cognitive processes that are also used in solving problems. In fact, all the types of thinking we have been considering—categorizing information, reasoning, and arriving at decisions—can be seen as forms of problem solving. We turn now to research that has focused specifically on the cognitive processes at work when people solve problems.

Solving Problems: Overcoming Obstacles to Reach a Goal

If we can really understand the problem, the answer will come out of it, because the answer is not separate from the problem.

Jiddu Krishnamurti (1895–1986)
Indian philosopher

What is a problem? One definition is any present situation that differs from a desired goal (Bransford & Stein, 1984). By this definition, the fact that I am now at home but need to get to the university is a problem. "Problems" such as this that have well-known solutions (I get into my car, travel a familiar route, and arrive at the university in about five minutes) aren't usually perceived as problems at all, because their solution is straightforward.

A more commonly accepted definition states that a problem is an obstacle between a present state and a goal. According to this definition, an obstacle—such as a construction project blocking my familiar route to the university or the fact that my car refuses to start—creates a problem for me to solve. Of course, it also presents me with decisions to make. Should I take the longer but less congested route around the detour, or the more direct but heavily trafficked route? Should I call the auto club or leave my car and take the bus to work? In fact, many psychologists see all of cognition as involving some form of problem solving (Waldrop, 1988a). Recall from Chapter 4, on perception, that even basic processes such as seeing objects involve complex detective work by our perceptual systems.

Although all cognitive activity can be seen as problem solving, a number of cognitive psychologists who are interested in determining how people think have narrowed the scope of their investigations by presenting subjects with well-defined problems to solve, usually in the form of puzzles. We'll begin our exploration of this research by considering some of the mechanisms that create obstacles to problem solving.

Obstacles to Problem Solving

Just as various difficulties sometimes get in the way of efficient reasoning or decision making, we often encounter obstacles that hinder our ability to solve problems. Of particular importance are obstacles caused by perceptual assumptions and by our past experiences.

Obstacles created by perceptual assumptions.   Many puzzles are visual in nature. Sometimes we make perceptual assumptions about these problems that block our ability to reach the solution. You may be familiar with the two problems shown in Figure 8.7. If not, try to solve them before reading further.

People who find these problems difficult (and many do) usually create difficulties for themselves by making erroneous assumptions about the problem. In thinking about the nine-dot problem, many people perceive the dots as defining a square and therefore assume that the four lines must fit within the boundaries of the square. Similarly, assuming that the matches must be arranged on a flat

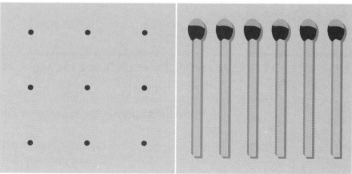

FIGURE 8.7
Nine-dot (left) and six-matches (right) problems

Draw four straight lines that pass through each of the nine dots without removing your pencil from the paper.

Arrange six matches so that they form four triangles with all sides equal to the length of one match.

surface keeps people from finding the solution to the six-matches problem (see Figure 8.9). In both cases, erroneous perceptual assumptions block the solution of the problem.

Obstacles caused by past experience.   Sometimes what we have learned in the past influences our thinking in ways that keep us from seeing the solution to a problem. Consider the following situation:

> Imagine that it's two o'clock in the morning. Your doorbell rings; you get up, startled, and make your way downstairs. You open the door and see a man standing before you. He wears two diamond rings and a fur coat, and there's a Rolls Royce behind him. He's sorry to wake you at this ridiculous hour, he tells you, but he's in the middle of a scavenger hunt. His ex-wife is in the same contest, which makes it very important to him that he win. He needs a piece of wood about three feet by seven feet. Can you help him? In order to make it worthwhile he'll give you $10,000. You believe him, he's obviously rich. And so you say to yourself, how in the world can I get this piece of wood for him? You think of the lumber yard; you don't know who owns the lumber yard; in fact you're not even sure where the lumber yard is. It would be closed at two o'clock in the morning anyway. You struggle but you can't come up with anything. Reluctantly, you tell him, "Gee, I'm sorry."
>
> The next day, when passing a construction site near a friend's house, you see a piece of wood that's just about the right size, three feet by seven feet— a door. You could have just taken a door off its hinges and given it to him, for $10,000 (Langer, 1989, pp. 9–10).

What went wrong here? Last night it didn't occur to you to sell your door because you classified it as a "door" and not as a "3-by-7-foot piece of wood." This phenomenon is called **functional fixedness**—our preconceived notions about an object's function can cause us to ignore its other possible uses.

Karl Duncker (1945) showed how functional fixedness can hinder problem solving by asking subjects to mount three lighted candles on a wall using the materials shown in Figure 8.8. Think about how you might go about solving this problem before reading further.

The solution to this problem, shown in Figure 8.10, involves using the boxes as supports for the candles rather than as containers. Robert Adamson (1952) showed that presenting boxes to the subjects as containers decreases the chances that subjects will think of using them as supports. Only 12 of the 29

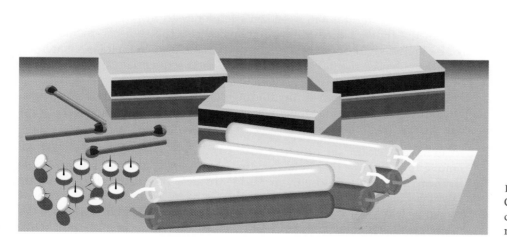

FIGURE 8.8
Can you figure out how to mount these candles, lighted, on a wall using the materials shown?

FIGURE 8.9
Answers to the nine-dot and six-matches problems

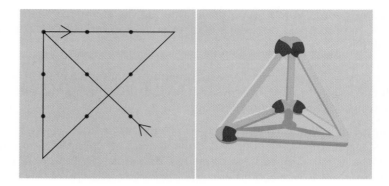

FIGURE 8.10
Solution to Duncker's candle problem

subjects who were presented with the boxes containing the candles and matches solved the problem, whereas 24 of the 28 subjects who were presented with empty boxes solved the problem.

Another example of functional fixedness is provided by Maier's (1931) two-string problem (Figure 8.11). The subject's task is to tie together two strings that are separated so that it is impossible to reach one of them while holding the other. Other objects available for solving the problem are a chair, a pair of pliers, and some tacks, but the solution requires only that the pliers be tied to one of the strings to create a pendulum that can be swung within the person's reach. Most subjects (60%) failed to solve this problem because they were influenced by their past experiences of using pliers as a tool and didn't think to use it as a weight.

Another way to show how past experience can get in the way of problem solving is to have subjects solve one set of problems that influences their attempts to solve another. This procedure was used by Luchins (1942) in his classic water-jug problem. Subjects were given three jugs of different capacities and were required to use them to measure out a specific quantity of water, as shown in Figure 8.12.

Problem 1 is solved by first filling the 127-cup jug B and then filling jug A once and jug C twice from it, thereby subtracting 27 cups and leaving 100 cups in jug B. This solution, which can be stated by the formula B – A – 2C, works for all the problems in Figure 8.12. However, problem 6 can also be solved using the simpler method of filling jug A and then using it to fill jug C once (A – C), leaving the desired 20 cups in A. Problem 7 can be solved simply by filling jugs A and C (A + C = 18). Nonetheless, most of Luchins's subjects who solved these problems in sequence stuck with the more complex B – A – 2C solution when they came to problems 6 and 7.

Both the functional fixedness experiments and Luchins's water-jug experiment demonstrate **mental set,** a person's tendency to respond in a particular manner. In the functional fixedness demonstrations the subjects' mental set is created by knowledge about objects' functions in the past; in Luchins's water-jug problem the subjects' mental set is created by their sequential exposure to a series of problems.

Mental set works against our finding solutions in many problems, especially when we focus on one strategy and ignore others that may work. For example, consider the following situation:

> You have a flat tire on a country road. You begin changing the tire. You remove the five lugs that hold the tire onto the axle, and place them in the hubcap so you won't lose them. Suddenly a car zooms by, hits the hubcap (which you had placed on the road), and propels the lugs into a nearby swamp, where they sink out of sight. You are now without tire lugs. How can you fasten your spare tire onto the axle so that it won't fall off while you drive to the nearest town?

FIGURE 8.11
How can this man tie the two strings together without help from anyone else?

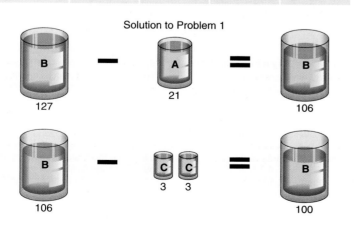

FIGURE 8.12
Luchins's water-jug problem. Subjects were asked to use the three jugs to measure out the quantities of water on the right.

Capacities (cups)

Problem	Jug A	Jug B	Jug C	Desired quantity
1	21	127	3	100
2	14	163	25	99
3	18	43	10	5
4	9	42	6	21
5	20	59	4	31
6	23	49	3	20
7	15	39	3	18
8	28	59	3	25

Solution to Problem 1

B 127 − A 21 = B 106

B 106 − C 3 C 3 = B 100

Stop for a moment and try to think of a solution before reading further.

Many people working on this problem focus on finding substitutes for the tire lugs. By focusing on this approach they forget that other tire lugs are in fact available. There are five lugs on each of the other three wheels. Removing one from each wheel produces three lugs, which can be used to fasten the spare securely enough to drive slowly to the next town. Sometimes focusing on an inappropriate strategy keeps us from seeing the solution.

In fact, the solutions to many problems often appear obvious *once we see the solutions*. Problems that are difficult are often stated so that our attention is not directed toward the "key," as we can see from the pairs of problems discussed in the next section. Each pair is logically equivalent, but the problems are stated differently, so that one is difficult and the other easy to solve.

How Problem Solving Is Affected by the Way the Problem Is Stated

Figure 8.13 contains two problems. The first one is difficult, the second one easier. Try the first problem before the second. Do this now, before reading further.

Most people find the matchmaker problem easier because they see that, since a marriage consists of one male and one female, the answer must be "No." We can apply the reasoning behind the solution to the matchmaker problem to the mutilated checkerboard problem by realizing that in both problems there are 32 *pairs*. The checkerboard has pairs of black and white squares and the Russian village has pairs of males and females. When two males die in the village, 30 couples and two single women remain. Similarly, when two black squares are removed from the checkerboard, 30 black/white pairs and two extra white squares remain. The key to solving the checkerboard problem is to realize that a domino must always cover a black/white pair. As there is no way that two extra white squares can be covered by the dominos, the answer to the checkerboard problem is also "No." Changing the problem representation from the black and white

FIGURE 8.13
The mutilated checkerboard (left) and matchmaker (right) problems. Try the checkerboard problem before reading the matchmaker problem.

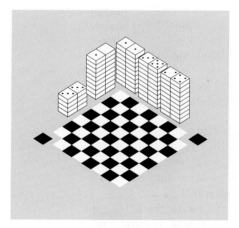

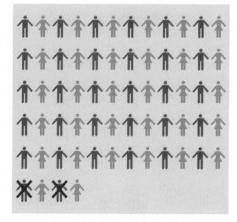

A standard checkerboard has 64 squares, 32 black squares and 32 white squares. If you are given 32 dominos, each of which can cover two squares on the checkerboard, you can cover every square on the checkerboard with the 32 dominos. But what if we mutilate the checkerboard by removing a black square at the two corners? Is it now possible to cover the remaining 62 squares of the checkerboard with 31 dominos? Spend a few minutes thinking about this problem before reading the second problem.

In a small but very proper Russian village, there were 32 bachelors and 32 unmarried women. Through tireless efforts, the village matchmaker succeeded in arranging 32 highly satisfactory marriages. The village was proud and happy. Then one drunken Saturday night, two bachelors, in a test of strength stuffed each other with pirogies and died. Can the matchmaker, through some quick arrangements, come up with 31 satisfactory marriages among the 62 survivors? (Hayes, 1978, p. 180)

An old monk leaves the monastery at exactly 6 a.m. to climb a trail that leads to a mountain peak. He arrives at 4 p.m. After a night of sleep and meditation, he leaves the mountain peak at 6 a.m. and starts down the same trail he climbed the day before. He walks faster going down than climbing up, but stops at a few places along the way to rest and enjoy the views. Is there some point on the mountain trail that he passes at exactly the same time each day? Think about this problem for a few minutes before you try the next problem.

Assume that Charley leaves the base of the mountain at exactly 6 a.m. to climb to the peak. At exactly the same time, Susan leaves the peak and begins climbing down the same trail. Charley reaches the peak at 4 p.m. and Susan reaches the base of the mountain at 4 p.m. Is there some point on the mountain trail that Charley and Susan pass at exactly the same time?

FIGURE 8.14
The monk-and-mountain (left) and two-hikers (right) problems. Try the monk problem before reading about the hikers.

squares of the checkerboard to male/female couples focuses our attention on the importance of the *pairing* of two dissimilar items, which is the key to the problem's solution.

Another example of how changing the representation affects our ability to solve a problem is shown in Figure 8.14. Again, try these two problems before reading further.

Whereas the monk-and-mountain problem is difficult, the answer to the two-hikers problem is so trivial that it isn't really much of a problem. Of course Charley and Susan must pass each other at some point, because they are walking on the same trail. Returning to the monk problem, we can think of the monk's ascent as equivalent to Charley's ascent, and the monk's descent as equivalent to Susan's descent. Clearly, just as Charley and Susan must pass the same point at a particular time, the monk must also be at a particular point at the same time each day.

Finally, stop and consider the two problems in Figure 8.15. A common response to the numbers and vowels problem is to suggest that the "E" needs to be turned over. This choice makes sense, because uncovering an odd number would tell us that the rule is untrue. But which other card did you pick? Many of the subjects in an experiment by P. C. Wason (1968) picked the "4." This answer is incorrect, because if a nonvowel is on the other side, the rule could still be true. The other card that needs to be turned over is the "7," because if it has a vowel on the other side, we can reject the rule.

When subjects were presented with the ages and drinking problem, most of them easily identified "beer" and "16" as the cards that needed to be turned over (Griggs & Cox, 1982). In this task it seems obvious that we need to check whether the 16-year-old is drinking beer or soda. Evidently, creating a *context* that people can easily relate to makes the reasoning task much easier than a noncontextual, abstract content like letters and numbers.

The message of these examples, as well as of the examples of perceptual set, is that many problems are problems because of the way they are stated.

There are four cards below, each with a letter on one side and a number on the other. Select the two cards that must be turned over to discover whether the following rule is true: "If a card has a vowel it also has an even number."

There are four cards below, each with a drink on one side and an age on the other. Select the two cards that must be turned over to discover whether the following rule is true: "If a person is drinking beer, he or she must be over 19 years of age."

FIGURE 8.15
Numbers-and-vowels (top) and drink-and-ages (bottom) problems. Try the top problem before reading the bottom one.

Thus, when we read the mutilated checkerboard problem, we don't focus on the fact that a domino always covers a black/white pair; when we read the monk-and-mountain problem, we may not think to visualize the monk's upward and downward journeys as occurring simultaneously.

Looking at problem solving in this way leads to the conclusion that the reason we experience some problems as difficult is because the way they are stated influences our cognitive processes. Taking their cue from this idea, many cognitive psychologists have begun to approach the study of problem solving by attempting to observe the cognitive operations that occur while a problem is being solved.

Cognitive Operations During Problem Solving

What is going on in a person's mind as a problem is being solved? This question is particularly important to cognitive psychologists, who view problem solving as information processing.

In the last chapter we saw how the information-processing approach can be applied to memory, and that psychologists investigate memory by asking how information is taken in, stored, and retrieved. Applied to problem solving, the information-processing approach asks how we manipulate information in solving a problem.

Alan Newell and Herbert Simon (1972), two of the leading proponents of the information-processing approach to problem solving, describe problems in terms of a **problem space** that consists of the various elements of the problem. The four elements of the problem space are as follows:

1. The **initial state:** the conditions at the beginning of the problem.
2. The **goal state:** the condition at the end of the problem.
3. The **intermediate states:** the various conditions that exist along the pathways between the initial and goal states.
4. The **operators:** permissible moves that can be made toward the problem solution.

A schematic diagram of the problem space, shown in Figure 8.16, represents the problem space as a maze of pathways between the initial and goal states. According to this conception, solving a problem requires finding a path

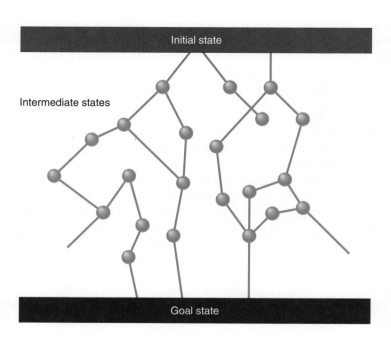

FIGURE 8.16
According to the information-processing approach to problem solving, solving a problem is a matter of finding a pathway between the initial state and the goal state.

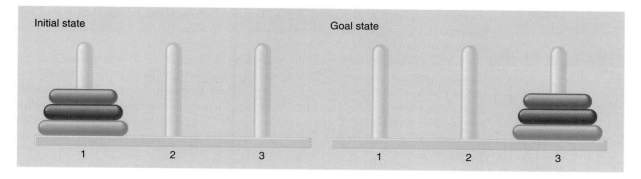

FIGURE 8.17
Initial and goal states of the tower of
Hanoi problem. See Measurement &
Methodology, "Thinking Aloud Protocols"
for a solution.

from one intermediate state to another that eventually leads to the goal state. If
this path is efficient, a problem is solved in a small number of steps.

How do people go about solving problems? Which pathways do they take?
Newell and Simon propose that we solve many problems using a strategy called
means-end analysis. The primary goal of means-end analysis is to reduce the
difference between the initial and goal states. This is usually achieved not by
jumping directly from the initial to the goal state but by creating subgoals—intermediate states that are closer to the goal.

We can illustrate this process by considering the "tower of Hanoi" problem
shown in Figure 8.17. In this problem, the initial state consists of a large, a
medium, and a small disk stacked on the left peg. The goal state is all three disks
moved to the right peg. Our solution is constrained by the following operators:
(1) disks must be moved from one peg to another; (2) only one disk can be
moved at a time; (3) a disk can be moved only when there are no others on top of
it; and (4) a large disk can never be placed on top of a smaller one.

This problem is named for a legend claiming that monks in a monastery
near Hanoi are working on this problem. Their version of it is, however, vastly
more complex than ours, with 64 disks on peg 1. According to the legend, the
world will come to an end when the problem is solved. Luckily, this will take
close to a trillion years to accomplish, even if the monks make one move every
second and every move is correct (Raphael, 1976).

Now let's apply means-end analysis to our three-disk version of the problem. The first thing we see is that there is a difference between the initial state (all
disks on peg 1) and the goal state (all disks on peg 3). Our goal is to reduce the
size of this difference. However, if we are to obey the operators, we can't accomplish this in just one step (we can't move more than one disk at a time). Thus, we
first set a subgoal—to move the large disk onto peg 3—and proceed to determine
what needs to be done to achieve that subgoal. But before we can move the large
disk we need to remove the other two. Thus, we establish an additional subgoal:
to remove the small and medium disks. The first step toward this subgoal is to
remove the small disk. Once this is done, the medium disk can be removed, completing one of our subgoals. We continue in this way, setting subgoals and
achieving them, until we reach our final goal. (See Measurement & Methodology, "Thinking Aloud Protocols" for one solution to this problem.)

Means-end analysis is important for two reasons. First, it is one way that
people actually go about solving problems. When your car needs service, your
goal is to get it fixed. However, to achieve your goal you need to meet subgoals,
such as making an appointment with the mechanic and arranging to have a
friend follow you over to the service station. Second, means-end analysis forms
the basis for a computer program called the General Problem Solver, developed
by Alan Newell and Herbert Simon (1972). Using means-end analysis, this program has been able to solve many different types of problems.

Unfortunately, means-end analysis does not always work. Sometimes the
most efficient path from the initial to the goal state requires some backtracking,

thereby temporarily *increasing* the difference between the current state and the goal state. This occurs in the problem shown in Figure 8.18. Try solving it before reading further.

The solution to this problem is shown in Figure 8.19. When we look at the solution we can see that the first three trips to the right bank reduces the difference between the initial and goal states. Trip 1 leaves four creatures on the left bank, trip 2 leaves three creatures, and trip 3 leaves two creatures. However, following trip 3, two creatures return to the left bank, increasing the population to

MEASUREMENT & METHODOLOGY

Thinking Aloud Protocols

The goal of much research on problem solving is to determine what mental processes are occurring as people solve problems. We've seen that one way to get at mental processes is by measuring how rapidly people can respond to stimuli (see the Chapter 7 Measurement & Methodology, "Reaction Time and Mental Processes"). Another way is to ask people to relate into a tape recorder what they are doing as they are solving a problem. The resulting description is called a **thinking aloud protocol**. The following is a hypothetical example of such a protocol for the tower of Hanoi problem:

> There are three disks on peg 1. I want to get the large disk onto peg 3, but I can't move it yet, because the other two disks are on top of it. Thus my first move has to be the small disk, I'll put it onto peg 2. Then I have to move the medium disk. The only place it can go is onto peg 3. But there's a problem here: I want to move the large disk onto peg 3, but the medium disk is already there (Figure A). I have to get it off. I'm going to start over. Move the medium disk back to peg 1, and then the small disk. Now, put the small disk on peg 3 and the medium disk on peg 2. I can now move the small disk onto the medium disk to free up peg 3 (Figure B). OK, move the large disk to peg 3. Now my goal is to get the medium disk onto the large disk, but I have to move the small disk first, onto peg 1. This frees up the medium disk (Figure C). I move it onto the large disk. Then I put the small disk on top. It's done!

Descriptions such as this have been widely used in comparing how experts and novices solve problems. From these descriptions researchers have found, for example, that when solving physics problems, experts proceed from the beginning of the problem toward the end. They begin with the variables given and work through a series of equations toward the answer. Novices, on the other hand, work backward, starting with the unknown and trying to find equations to solve for it. In other words, experts and novices choose different pathways between the initial and goal states. Thinking aloud protocols therefore enable researchers to look beyond the subject's *response* to uncover the *process* that leads to the response (Chi, Glaser, & Rees, 1982; Ericsson & Simon, 1980).

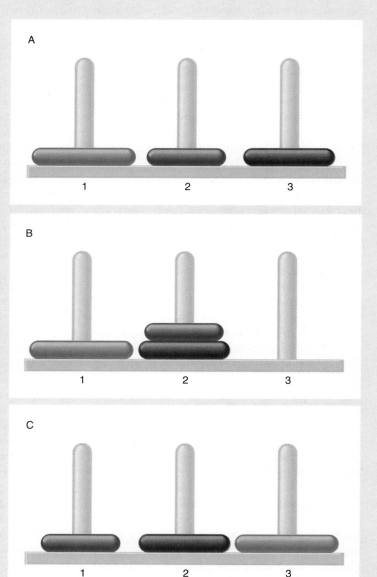

A

B

C

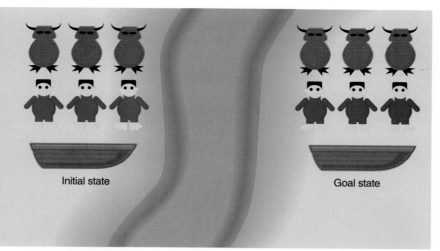

On the left bank of a river are three hobbits (gentle, humanlike creatures) and three orcs (beasts). They have a boat on their side that is capable of carrying two creatures at a time across the river. The goal is to transport all six creatures across to the right side of the river. At no point on either side of the river can orcs outnumber hobbits, because if that happens the orcs will kill the hobbits. The problem is to find a method of transporting all six creatures across the river without the hobbits ever being outnumbered. Remember that in order to cross the river the boat must be piloted by at least one creature.

Initial state

Goal state

FIGURE 8.18
The hobbit-and-orc problem

four; and after trip 4, two creatures remain on the left bank—the same number as were left after trip 3. Thus, to reach our final goal it is necessary to violate the means-end rule—that we should strive to reduce the difference between the initial and goal states. Subjects trying to solve this problem often make errors just after trip 3, because they resist making a move that seems to be increasing the distance to the solution (Greeno, 1974).

In this section we have seen how psychologists have used various puzzles to investigate the factors that influence problem solving and the processes involved in problem solving. But how much does an analysis of how people perform on puzzles tell us about problem solving in the real world? Problems encountered in the real world differ from problems posed by puzzles in a number of important respects. In real-world problems, the goal state is often not well defined, and specific operators are not given. That is, the "rules of the game" (such as "only two creatures can travel across the river at once") are often not specified. Also, the solution of real-world problems usually involves the application of a person's knowledge. Most puzzle problems, in contrast, require little knowledge beyond the rules specified in the puzzle. Because of these differences, a number of researchers have begun studying how people solve problems that more closely approximate those we encounter in everyday life. One of the tactics they use is to compare the problem solving of people who are experienced in a field (experts) with that of people who are relative newcomers (novices).

Problem Solving by Experts and Novices

How do experts and novices in a field differ? Obviously experts have much more experience, and with that experience comes a greater store of knowledge. But how is that greater knowledge translated into differences between the way experts and novices solve problems?

One way cognitive psychologists have studied this question is by using the "thinking aloud" protocol. Thinking aloud records gathered from experts and novices indicate that, because novices have less knowledge, they often start out by proposing the wrong strategy for solving a problem. But perhaps even more important than differences in knowledge is a difference in the way experts' and novices' knowledge is *organized.* This difference in organization was illustrated by Michilen Chi and her co-workers (1982; also see Chi, Feltovich, & Glaser, 1981). They posed 24 physics problems to a group of experts (physics professors) and a group of novices (students with one semester of physics) and asked them to sort the problems into groups based on their similarities.

FIGURE 8.19
Solution to the hobbit-and-orc problem. The symbols on the banks indicate which creatures are present either just after the boat has left or just after it has arrived. The numbers indicate the number of trips to the right bank.

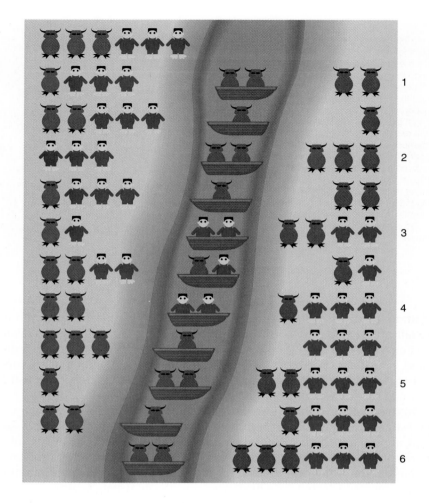

Figure 8.20 shows diagrams of physics problems that were grouped together by an expert and by a novice. The difference is striking. The novice sorted problems based on how similar the *objects* in the problem were. Thus, two problems that included inclined planes were grouped together, even though the physics principles involved in the problems were quite different. The expert, in contrast, sorted the problems based on general principles. The expert perceived two problems as similar because they both involved the principle of conservation of energy, even though the objects in the problems differed. Thus, novices categorized problems based on their *surface structure* (what the objects looked like), whereas experts categorized them based on their *deep structure* (the underlying principles involved).

These results tell us that experts' knowledge is organized by principles, whereas novices' knowledge is organized by the way objects in the problems appear. We encountered this same difference in the last chapter, on memory. Do you remember the studies in which chess masters and beginning players were tested for their ability to reproduce the positions of pieces on a chessboard? Experts were able to recall many more positions because they organized the chess pieces into "chunks" based on configurations they had seen in previous games. The beginners, in contrast, simply focused their attention on individual pieces. This ability to organize knowledge has been found to be important not only among chess masters and physics experts, but in other fields as well (Egan & Schwartz, 1979; Reitman, 1976).

The idea that experts approach problems differently than novices has implications for an endeavor that has been receiving recent attention from cogni-

7   MEMORY

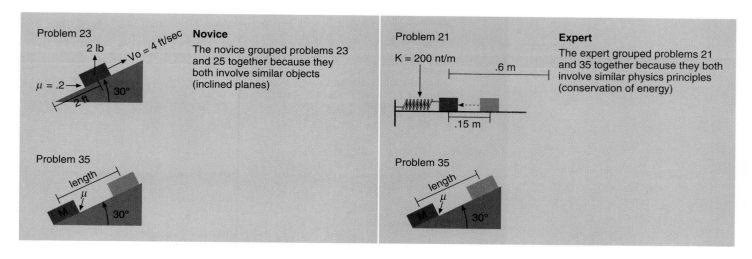

FIGURE 8.20
Physics problems grouped together by a novice and by an expert

tive psychologists: creating a computer program that enables a computer to become an expert at solving problems. One approach to achieving this is described in the following Interdisciplinary Dimension.

INTERDISCIPLINARY DIMENSION ARTIFICIAL INTELLIGENCE

Soar: An Intelligent Computer Program

The computer HAL-9000 plays a main role in *2001: A Space Odyssey,* a film based on a book by Arthur C. Clarke. As the spacecraft in Clarke's story hurtles toward Saturn, HAL, the on-board computer, begins to malfunction. To deal with this problem, David Bowman, the ship's captain, begins disconnecting HAL's memory unit. When HAL realizes what is happening it says, "Stop, Dave. I'm afraid, Dave. Dave, my mind is going; I can feel it."

HAL is clearly a very special computer—one that not only can perform rapid calculations but also can think creatively and, like humans, feel fear and other emotions. No computer today feels emotions, but some can solve problems creatively. The creation of "intelligent" computer programs is the goal of researchers in **artificial intelligence** (**AI**), an interdisciplinary field combining the work of cognitive psychologists and computer scientists.

14   INTELLIGENCE

Numerous "expert systems" programs have been developed that can perform specific tasks. A program called Deep Thought plays chess well enough to beat grand masters. The programs Mycin and Neomycin diagnose diseases (Clancey & Letsinger, 1981; Shortliffe, 1976). Though these programs are excellent at what they do, they have two limiting characteristics: (1) they are specific to one field only; and (2) they are knowledge based—that is, their operation is based on knowledge fed them by humans.

Recently, however, AI researchers have begun developing computer programs that not only handle many kinds of problems but also learn from experience. One of these programs, called Soar, was developed by a team of researchers from Carnegie-Mellon University, the University of Michigan, and the University of Southern California (Newell, 1990; Waldrop, 1988a, 1988b). Soar's name provides a hint regarding its operation: it stands for State, Operate, And Result (we encountered these terms when we looked at the information-processing approach to problem solving). Soar solves problems by starting with an initial *state* and then applying *operators* until the *result* is achieved.

Observe how Soar deals with the "block problem" shown in Figure 8.21. The goal is to transform the initial state to the final state in the fewest moves. The operators that govern this problem are (1) you can move only one block at a time; and (2) you can move blocks onto another block or onto the table.

Soar's first task is to decide on the first move. There are three possible moves: (1) move A onto C, (2) move A onto the table, or (3) move C onto A. Which is best? The first time it encounters this problem, Soar has no way of telling. With no basis for deciding,

In *2001: A Space Odyssey,* the computer HAL-9000 (in background) eavesdrops on the astonauts' conversation by reading their lips.

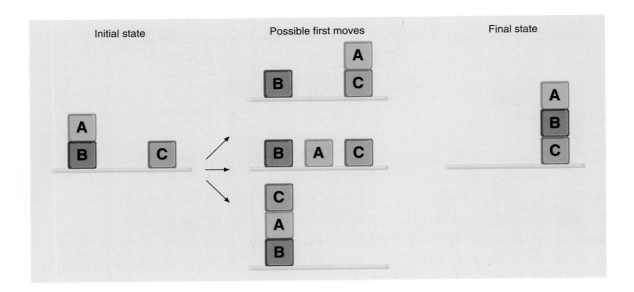

FIGURE 8.21

The block problem. The computer must choose among three possible first moves as it attempts to get to the final state. After evaluating the situation, Soar determines that moving A onto the table is the best move.

Soar has reached an *impasse.* But rather than stopping at the impasse, as other computer programs might (for example, if asked to divide by zero, most programs generate an error message and shut down), Soar works to solve it by going into its *evaluation mode.* It evaluates the possible outcomes of moving blocks A and C by trying out each move and working ahead for enough moves to see which one achieves the final goal in the fewest moves. When it does this it finds that moving A onto the table works best, so it makes that move. Thus, when Soar gets to an impasse it simply takes a detour, much like a driver who encounters a traffic jam and turns off onto an alternative route.

One of Soar's strengths is this ability to find its way around impasses. Another is its ability to learn from experience. Once it has dealt with an impasse, it stores the problem configuration that existed just before the impasse and the final result in its memory, so if it ever encounters a similar configuration it can jump directly to the result. This process, which is called *chunking,* enables Soar to cut down considerably on the time it takes to solve subsequent problems. For example, when Soar was applied to a complex task that involved determining how to link together various computer components, it took 1731 steps to solve the problem with its learning function turned off, so no chunking could occur. However, when the learning function was turned on, the program took only 485 steps to complete the task. This great decrease in the number of steps means that Soar created chunks as it was working on the problem and then used them during later stages of the task. Even more impressive, once Soar had completed the task it needed only 7 steps to solve it the next time. Chunking learned from working on one task also speeds up performance on other tasks, so when Soar is given a series of different tasks, it takes less time to complete each succeeding one.

The development of Soar is exciting not only because its design enables it to solve a wide variety of problems much more easily than earlier programs, but because Soar behaves similarly to a problem-solving human. When faced with obstacles to problem solving, both humans and Soar find a way around them, and both are capable of learning from

FIGURE 8.22

How Soar (left) and a human (right) improve their performance as they do the same task over and over. Each data point represents one attempt to perform the task.

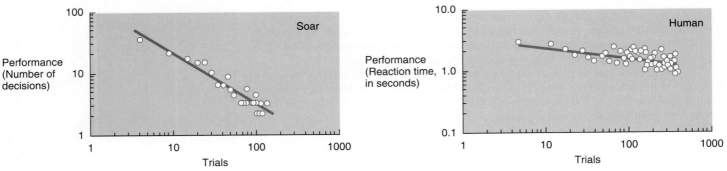

the experience. Also, humans and Soar generate similar learning curves. Figure 8.22 compares how a human's performance of a task improves from trial to trial with how Soar's performance improves on the same task. Although the slopes of the curves are different (Soar shows greater improvement over trials), both curves are described by the same type of mathematical function.

Despite its strides toward human thinking, Soar is far from human. Unlike HAL, it experiences no emotions, has no feelings, and can experience no images. Nevertheless, the way Soar goes about solving problems makes it a pioneer in the area of artificial intelligence. As several research teams are now working on updated versions of Soar, it promises to gain in power and to be used in more applications in the future. ■

Our discussion of cognitive processes has revealed a number of cognitive traps that can lead us to reason illogically, make incorrect decisions, or fail to see the key to solving a problem. These traps, summarized in Table 8.5, show that our thinking can be led astray both by the characteristics of the problems and the decisions we are presented with and by what we bring to cognitive tasks from our past experiences.

TABLE 8.5
Psychological sources of error in reasoning, decision making, and problem solving

Deductive Reasoning	
Errors in applying logical rules	Difficulty in applying modus tollens
Inductive Reasoning	
Confirmational bias	Selectively looking for information that confirms a hypothesis
Decision Making	
Misapplying elimination by aspects	Allowing one aspect to dominate a decision when other aspects are just as important
Misapplying the availability heuristic	Wrongly judging the most easily remembered events as the most frequently.
Misapplying the representativeness heuristic	Allowing the representativeness of characteristics of events to obscure other relevant information
	Violating the conjunction rule, which states that the probability of the conjunction of A and B can't be higher than the probability of A or B alone
Framing effects	Being influenced by the way choices between outcomes are stated
Problem Solving	
Obstacles created by perceptual assumptions	Allowing perceptual assumptions to obscure the solution to a problem
Obstacles created by past experience	Functional fixedness: allowing preconceived notions about an object's function to obscure its other possible uses
	Mental set: staying with a single problem-solving strategy that has worked before, even though a more efficient strategy is available.
Effect of problem representation	Failing to see the key aspect necessary for solving a problem because of the way the problem is stated
Novice effects	Formulating inefficient problem-solving strategies because of insufficient or poorly organized knowledge

At this point you may be tempted to conclude that our thinking is hopelessly infected by one error after another (this would be the availability heuristic at work—what you recall right now is our focus on sources of error in thinking). Keep in mind that much of the time we do reason logically, make good decisions, and successfully solve problems—especially when those thinking processes occur within the context of familiar situations.

An excellent example of thinking that occurs within the context of familiar situations is conversation. As we are about to see, this everyday behavior requires highly sophisticated problem solving.

Using and Understanding Language

"The time has come," the Walrus said,
"To talk of many things:
Of shoes—and ships—and sealing wax—
Of cabbages—and kings—
And why the sea is boiling hot—
And whether pigs have wings."

Lewis Carroll, *Through the Looking Glass*

Producing and understanding language is an astoundingly complex behavior, but we do it so effortlessly that we take it for granted. Undoubtedly we sometimes misunderstand each other (Tannen, 1990), but much of the time we communicate clearly and successfully. Moreover, language is an important component of virtually all the other kinds of thinking we engage in. In this section we explore the processes involved in understanding and using language. In Chapter 10 we will explore how, beginning in infancy, we acquire and develop linguistic skills.

Problem Solving in Conversations

Even the most routine conversation poses a number of cognitive problems for both speaker and listener. The speaker must solve the problem of how to transfer ideas into words that the listener can understand. The listener must solve the problem of how to transform the speaker's words into the ideas that the speaker is trying to transmit (Figure 8.23). Within these problems lurk others: How does a speaker present ideas without losing the listener? How does a listener place breaks between the speaker's words, understand ambiguous sentences, and infer things that are left unsaid? How do listeners understand statements that don't mean what they appear to mean? Let's consider how we go about solving these problems.

4 PERCEPTION *Perceiving breaks between words.*   A good example of a problem most people are unaware of is the need for listeners to create breaks between words, a process called **speech segmentation.** "What's the problem?" you might ask. We *hear* breaks as the speaker pauses briefly between words, don't we? Actually, we don't: in normal conversational speech, the speaker *doesn't* pause between words. As the speech spectrogram in Figure 8.24 shows, the sound energy in the speech stimulus is continuous.

If the speech spectrogram doesn't convince you of the continuous nature of the speech stimulus, recall from Chapter 4 that this is how you perceive speech

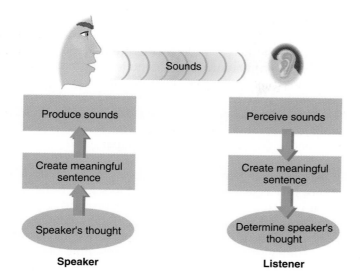

FIGURE 8.23
Steps in communicating a thought. The speaker changes thoughts into a sentence and produces sounds. The listener perceives the sounds and translates them into a sentence containing the speaker's thoughts.

in a foreign language. If you're unfamiliar with the language, the sounds of that language seem to speed by in an unbroken string. To a speaker of that language, however, the words seem separated, just as English words seem separated to you.

How do we accomplish speech segmentation? Our knowledge of the *meanings* of words must help us create perceptual breaks between them. Consider, for example, pairs of words that flow together. *Big girl* can be heard as *Big Earl*—the interpretation you pick depends on the meaning of the sentence in which these words appear. As a child, did you chant "I scream, you scream, we all scream for ice cream"? The different segmentations of *ice cream* and *I scream* are created by the meaning of the sentence, not by a difference in sound.

Even after we have used meaning to help us perceive the individual words in a conversation, we are still faced with the task of *interpreting* the sentence as a whole. One way to appreciate this task is to look at ambiguous sentences.

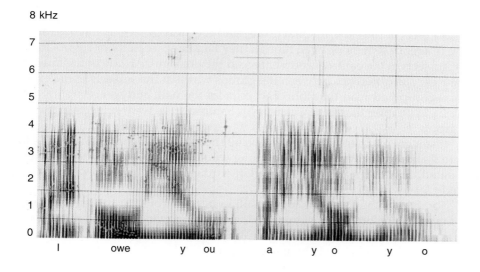

FIGURE 8.24
Speech spectrogram. The dark areas indicate the presence of sound energy at the frequencies shown on the left axis. Note that the sound energy does not stop even though there are five separate words.

Understanding ambiguous sentences.   Perhaps the link between language and problem solving is most obvious when a listener is confronted with an ambiguous sentence, such as "The mayor ordered the police to stop drinking in the park." Three possible interpretations of this sentence are that (1) the mayor ordered the police not to drink in the park anymore; (2) the mayor ordered the police to stop other people from drinking in the park; and (3) while the mayor was in the park, he ordered the police to stop their drinking. Or consider the sign used to encourage conservation during World War II, "Save Soap and Waste Paper," which can mean (1) *save* soap but *waste* paper or (2) save both *soap* and *waste paper.*

Although there are many ambiguous sentences, there are far fewer ambiguous conversations. Just as listeners use meaning to segment the speech stimulus into individual words, they use the information provided by the rest of the conversation to determine the correct meaning of ambiguous sentences. For example, if all we hear is "The sailors enjoyed the port," we may assume that the sailors had a great time visiting bars and other entertaining places during their shore leave. But if we also heard the beginning of the conversation, which was about some sailors ordering wine in a restaurant, then we would know that the word *port* refers not to a place where ships dock but to a type of wine. Or consider this sentence: "George thinks vanilla." It sounds meaningless out of context, but makes sense if it is heard after the question "What kind of ice cream does Vivian like?" (Haviland & Clark, 1974).

Making inferences.   As we hear sentences, we are constantly using knowledge we already have, plus knowledge we have gained from the conversation, to help us interpret what is being said. Sometimes interpretation requires that we fill gaps by inferring things implied by the conversation but not said directly. Marcia Johnson, John Bransford, and Susan Solomon (1973) demonstrated this inference process in an experiment in which subjects read sentences such as the following:

> *Experimental group:* John was trying to fix the birdhouse. He was pounding the nail when his father came out to watch him do the work.
> *Control group:* John was trying to fix the birdhouse. He was looking for the nail when his father came out to watch him.

After reading a number of sentences, all subjects were given a recognition test containing some sentences that exactly matched those they had read and some "inference sentences" that they had never seen before. The following sentence is the inference sentence that goes with the preceding two sentences:

> John was using the hammer to fix the birdhouse when his father came out to watch him and to help him do the work.

Subjects in the experimental group said they recognized an average of 62% of the inference sentences, even though they had never seen them before. In contrast, subjects in the control group only said they recognized 22% of the inference sentences. The difference between the groups was that the subjects in the experimental group had read that John had *pounded* the nail, and so apparently were more likely to infer that John was using a hammer than were subjects in the control group.

Listeners make inferences like this all the time without realizing it. It's fortunate that they do; otherwise, everything would have to be described in unending detail. Instead, many details are left to the listener, who fills in what the speaker leaves out.

Sometimes the listener's need to fill in information that the speaker leaves out slows down comprehension. Consider Susan Haviland and Herbert Clark's (1974) idea that effective communication involves a contract between the speaker and listener called the **given-new contract.** According to this contract, the speaker constructs sentences so they include two kinds of information:

(1) *given information*, information that the listener already knows; and (2) *new information*, information that the listener is hearing for the first time. For example, consider the following two sentences:

(1) "For his birthday Ed was given a new stereo."
Given information (repeated from previous conversation): Ed had a birthday.
New information: He got a new stereo.
(2) "The stereo was his favorite present."
Given information (from sentence 1): Ed got a stereo for his birthday.
New information: It was his favorite present.

Notice how new information in the first sentence becomes the given information in the second sentence (Figure 8.25a). We can appreciate how the presence of this new information makes understanding the second sentence easier by considering the following two sentences:

(3) "For his birthday Ed was given lots of things."
Given information: Ed had a birthday.
New information: He got lots of things.
(4) "The alligator was his favorite present."
(All new information)

A listener hearing sentence 4 is at a momentary disadvantage, because this is the first mention of the alligator (Figure 8.25b). To fill the missing information, the listener needs to make the assumption "One of the presents Ed got was an alligator." Haviland and Clark call an assumption such as this, which provides the missing information necessary to connect two sentences, a *bridging assumption*. Creating bridging assumptions takes time, so it takes slightly longer for a person to comprehend sentence 4 than sentence 2. Haviland and Clark demonstrated this effect by presenting pairs of sentences and asking subjects to press a button when they felt they understood the second sentence in each pair. They found that it took longer for subjects to comprehend the second sentence in pairs like this:

"We checked the picnic supplies. The beer was warm."

than it took to comprehend the second sentence in pairs like this:

"We got some beer out of the trunk. The beer was warm."

Thus, comprehending a sentence takes more time if the listener has to infer missing information.

Understanding indirect statements. Sentences do not always mean what they appear to mean. Imagine that, during a barracks inspection, a sergeant says to a soldier "Do you see that cigarette butt there, soldier?" What thought is he trying to transmit to the soldier? It would be clear to the soldier that the sergeant is not really asking whether or not he can see the cigarette butt; rather, he is telling him to shape up and not leave cigarette butts lying around in the future. Similarly, when Rodney Hammersmith III, sitting in the drawing room of his mansion, says "It's stuffy in here, Jeeves," he is doing more than commenting on the

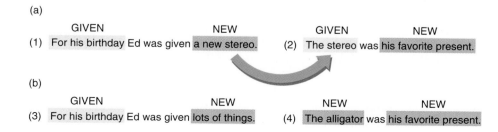

(a)

GIVEN	NEW		GIVEN	NEW
(1) For his birthday Ed was given	a new stereo.		(2) The stereo was	his favorite present.

(b)

GIVEN	NEW		NEW	NEW
(3) For his birthday Ed was given	lots of things.		(4) The alligator was	his favorite present.

FIGURE 8.25
In (a), the given/new contract is honored, so the second sentence is easy to comprehend. In (b), the given/new contract is not honored, so the second sentence is more difficult to understand.

When a speaker makes an indirect statement, the listener uses a conversational rule to determine the real meaning.

atmosphere in the drawing room. Rodney's statement, translated into its true meaning, is "Open the window, Jeeves" or "Turn up the air conditioning, Jeeves." Jeeves, being an intelligent listener, knows exactly what Rodney means. Both Rodney and the sergeant are making **indirect statements**—statements whose literal meaning is not the meaning the speaker intends to convey.

According to Herbert Clark and Peter Lucy (1975), in many instances listeners must go beyond the *literal* meaning of a sentence to determine its true, or *conveyed,* meaning. D. Gordon and G. Lakoff (1971) propose that listeners accomplish this by taking the following three steps:

1. The listener must first comprehend the literal meaning of the sentence. For example, when Ruth asks Anne "Would you mind opening the door?" she is *literally* asking Anne how she feels about opening the door.

2. The listener then considers the context in which the statement is being made. Anne, taking her knowledge of Ruth and the general situation into account, reasons that because Ruth already knows she would be glad to open the door, she must mean something else.

3. The listener then uses a **conversational rule** to determine the real meaning of the sentence. The conversational rule Anne calls on might go something like this: "If a speaker questions a listener's willingness to do something when the listener's willingness is already known, then the speaker is actually requesting that the listener do something." In this case, therefore, Anne figures out that the conveyed meaning of "Would you mind opening the door?" is "Would you please open the door?"

The conveyed meaning of a sentence differs from the literal meaning in so many situations that we have become experts in figuring out what is really behind what a person is saying. So when someone asks "Do you have the time?" you don't have to go through an elaborate reasoning process to know that the person is really asking "What time is it?"

The use of indirect statements is not unique to speakers of English. In Asian cultures it is often customary to use statements even more indirect than those used by most Americans. Whereas someone in the United States might say "The door is open" to mean "Please shut the door," in Japan a person might say "It is somewhat cold today" to accomplish the same result. The Japanese statement is more indirect because it does not even refer to the door (Yum, 1991). Someone who doesn't understand the implicit "rules" of Japanese conversation—an American business traveler, for instance—might not understand the meaning the speaker intended to convey.

In summary, communication between people involves more than simply understanding the meanings of strings of words. Cognitive processes—taking the context of a statement into account, making inferences and assumptions, and following conversational rules that have been learned over years of practice— help us communicate clearly and with a minimum of uncertainty. But if cognitive processes are involved in language use, the reverse is also true: language is central to thinking.

Thought and Language

The many examples of thinking processes we have presented in this chapter— formulating syllogisms, stating decision choices, and solving problems—all involve the use of language. But is language *necessary* for thinking? Some psychologists and linguists have proposed that it is, but others suggest that language only *influences* thought. Let's consider each of these ideas.

Is language necessary for thought?   Do we always use language when we think? It is tempting to answer this question affirmatively, because most of our thinking is accompanied by language (as exemplified by "thinking aloud" protocols), and we use language to express our thoughts to other people. However, the following evidence shows that thinking and using language are not synonymous.

1. Animals such as Köhler's insightful ape, which we discussed in Chapter 6, can solve problems.
2. Young children with very limited verbal abilities solve complicated problems.
3. We often find it difficult to translate thoughts into words. Donald Hebb (1980) asks us to consider "how far it is from knowing something about electricity to communicating the knowledge to someone else" (p. 24).
4. Some thought can be visual. For example, if you are asked how many windows are on the front of your house, what do you do? Most people solve this problem by visualizing the front of the house and counting the windows they "see."

It thus seems that not all thinking involves language. Nevertheless, many kinds of thinking do. For example, even though we may be able to point to examples of reasoning in animals or preverbal children, there is no question that our ability to use language greatly enhances our ability to reason and, for that matter, to carry out all the other thinking processes we have discussed in this chapter.

Does language influence thought?   Is it possible that the language we speak can affect the way we think and even how we perceive reality? That's the suggestion made by Benjamin Whorf's (1956) **linguistic relativity hypothesis,** which states that the structure of a culture's language strongly influences the way people in the culture think and perceive the world. According to Whorf, an expert on North American Indian languages, the fact that the Eskimo language has over 20 different words for "snow" whereas English has only one means that Eskimos *perceive* snow differently than English speakers. Whereas English speakers see only snow, Eskimos see different *kinds* of snow. Similarly, Hopi Indians have only one word for all flying things that are not birds. According to Whorf's hypothesis, they might see more similarity between insects and airplanes than would a person whose language distinguishes between those objects (Cole & Scribner, 1974). If Whorf is correct, speakers of different languages live to some extent in different realities.

Although Whorf's hypothesis about the effects of Eskimo and Hopi language is intriguing, there is little evidence to support it. His hypothesis has been most extensively tested by comparing the color perception of people whose language distinguishes only a few colors with that of people whose language distinguishes many. If English-speaking people are presented with small color chips that cover the entire range of human color vision and are asked to pick the "best" example of each color, they pick chips representing 11 basic colors: red, orange, yellow, brown, green, blue, purple, pink, black, white, and gray (Brown & Lenneberg, 1954). These "best colors," which are distinguished by short, simple names, are called *focal colors.* Interestingly, focal colors appear to maintain their special properties even in cultures that have no names for them.

For example, Eleanor Rosch (1973), whose research on categories we described at the beginning of this chapter, compared English speakers with people in the Dani tribe, a culture in New Guinea that has only two basic words for colors: *mili* for dark or "cold" colors, and *mola* for bright or "warm" colors. When people from both cultures learned nonsense words for many different colors, speakers of English and speakers of Dani both found it easier to remember the labels for the focal colors. This result does not support the Whorfian hypothesis, which would predict that focal colors would not have special properties for the Danis, who lack special names for them.

Another study supporting the special status of focal colors is a survey of 98 different languages by Brent Berlin and Paul Kay (1969). Berlin and Kay found a

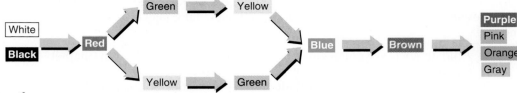

FIGURE 8.26
Color names in different cultures follow the pattern shown here, with colors being added in the order shown.

pattern in the way different cultures have developed names for those colors. If a culture has two color names, they are used for white and black; additional color names are added in the same order in all cultures. If three color names are used, red is the next one added, then green or yellow, then blue, then brown, and finally purple, pink, orange, and gray (Figure 8.26). Apparently, all cultures divide the world of color up in the same way, but some languages, like English, go into more detail.

Berlin and Kay's study, like Rosch's, does not support Whorf's hypothesis. Apparently, people in all cultures perceive colors in the same way. On the basis of studies such as these, most researchers have rejected the linguistic relativity hypothesis.

The Whorf hypothesis has, however, received some support from more recent experiments that study the effect of the "generic he"—when the pronoun "he" is used to indicate people in general, as in the sentence "A pedestrian must be careful when he crosses the street." Although the generic he is supposed to stand for both males and females, it has been argued that using "he" favors males and ignores females. To test this idea, John Gastil (1990) had subjects read sentences in one of the following three forms.

1. The average American believes he watches too much TV.
2. The average American believes he/she watches too much TV.
3. Average Americans believe they watch too much TV.

After reading one of these sentences, subjects were asked to verbally describe any images that came to mind. For example, one subject responded to sentence 1 with the description, "I see a fat guy sitting on a couch with a remote control. TV's sitting in front of him."

The results, shown in Figure 8.27, show that "he" is far from neutral. For female subjects it generates a much larger number of male images than either "they" or "he/she" and for male subjects it generates more male images than "they." This example of how language can influence thinking would be particu-

FIGURE 8.27
Number of male images generated by the use of "he," "they," or "he/she" in sentences. Using "he" is far from neutral, especially for females.

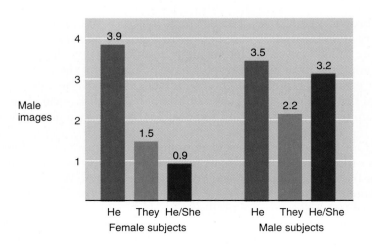

larly significant if people continued using the generic he when referring to people in general, because it reinforces the male dominance of our society at a time when many people are working toward achieving equality for women. However, most writers now use a nonsexist pronoun such as "they," or use "he" and "she" equally throughout an article or book.

Considering all of the evidence, we conclude that in a few specific cases, such as the generic he (see Hoffman, Lau, & Johnson, 1986, for another example), language influences thought, as Whorf suggested. However, most researchers do not accept Whorf's idea that different languages cause widespread differences in the way people perceive and think about the world.

Reprise: Levels of Analysis in the Study of Learning and Cognition

All that we are is a result of what we have thought.

Abraham Lincoln

The end of this chapter marks the end of a story we have been developing since Chapter 6, the one on learning. This story began with Pavlov conditioning dogs, Thorndike challenging cats to get out of his puzzle box, and Watson causing Little Albert to become very uneasy around white, furry animals. In the learning chapter we discovered how the behaviorists, by studying psychology at the level of behavior, demonstrated the enormous impact of both classical and operant conditioning on our lives. But by the end of that chapter we saw how psychologists came to appreciate that understanding the complexity and creativity of human behavior required broadening their horizons to include the level of cognition, the study of how the mind operates.

We have been working at the cognitive level in both this chapter and the preceding one on memory. These two chapters illustrate that researchers have found a number of ways to make "unobservable" cognitive processes observable and measurable. These techniques include measuring recall, recognition, and reaction time to understand how information flows through various stages of the human information-processing system. Other techniques are asking people to evaluate the validity of syllogisms, to make decisions, and to solve problems in order to discover the strategies people use as they work on problems and the biases that hinder effective thinking.

The sum of these efforts at the behavioral and cognitive levels has been a greater understanding of both the external forces that control our behavior and the internal workings of the mind. The picture that emerges of our behavior is a complex one. We are sometimes influenced by forces we are unaware of, yet we also actively direct much of our learning and problem solving. We can be misled by our biases and by faulty reasoning; but we can also be creative and ingenious in the way we solve seemingly mundane—but actually very complex—problems such as understanding spoken language. And we have seen once again that multiple perspectives are often needed to give us a more accurate view of complex human behavior. Perhaps one lesson to take away from these chapters is the need to guard against one of the most common of all our cognitive biases—oversimplification.

Thinking in Traditional Cultures

It begins to look as though formal logic, as we know it, is an attribute of the group of Indo-European languages with certain grammatical features.

Percy W. Bridgman (1958)

In this chapter we have described some experiments showing that people sometimes don't think logically. Most of the subjects in those experiments were college educated. But what about people from traditional cultures, cultures isolated from Westernization and in which many people lack formal schooling? In the 1950s and 1960s many anthropologists and cross-cultural psychologists felt that these "tribal" subjects had underdeveloped powers of thinking. In 1977 an experiment carried out by Michael Cole generated results that might seem to confirm this idea. Cole's subjects were adults of the Kpelle tribe of Liberia. Two subjects were seated at a table, separated by a barrier, and each was given ten sticks made of different kinds of wood in different shapes and sizes. One of them was told to choose a stick and to describe it. His task was to describe the stick accurately enough so that the other subject could pick the identical stick from his pile.

A sample result, shown in Table 8.6, compares the "English description" (the way Cole would describe the sticks) with a Kpelle description. It is clear that the Kpelle description does not give enough information to enable the other subject to pick out the correct stick. In fact, the Kpelle descriptions are roughly equivalent to what might be expected from a 6-year-old American child. Does this experimental result mean that Kpelle adults operate at the intellectual level of a 6-year-old child? From his observations of the Kpelle outside the laboratory, it was clear to Cole that their intelligence was far from childlike. He explains this conclusion by noting that outside the experimental situation, the Kpelle communicate very adequately, and about the time they con us into buying them a couple of bottles of beer, we are uncertain about just what was going on back in that room."

As suggested Cole, measurements made in the psychology laboratory don't adequately represent the everyday thinking of these people. Evidence supporting this idea came from Cole's colleague Sylvia Scribner (1977), who

People in traditional cultures may do poorly on Western tests of logic but function extremely well in their own culture.

studied how the Kpelle and other traditional people deal with syllogisms. She presented two premises of the syllogism and then asked a question that could, logically, be answered given the premises. For example,

Premise 1: All people who own houses pay a house tax.
Premise 2: Boima does not pay a house tax.
Question: Does Boima own a house?

Her results showed that unschooled subjects answered correctly about 60% of the time, only slightly better than chance performance (50%). In contrast, subjects from the same tribe who had attended school answered correctly over 80% of the time.

Does this result mean that the unschooled Kpelle don't reason logically? One way to answer that question is to look at the following conversation between an experimenter (E) and a Kpelle farmer (the subject, S). The conversation begins with the experimenter's statement of the problem.

E: If Sumo or Saki drinks palm wine, the Town Chief gets vexed. Sumo is not drinking palm wine. Saki is drinking palm wine. Is the Town Chief vexed?
S: People do not get vexed with two persons.
E: (*Repeats the problem.*)
S: The Town Chief was not vexed on that day.
E: The Town Chief was not vexed? What is the reason?
S: The reason is that he doesn't love Sumo.
E: He doesn't love Sumo? Go on with the reason.
S: The reason is that Sumo's drinking is a hard time. That is why when he drinks palm wine, the Town Chief gets vexed. But sometimes when Saki drinks palm juice he will not give a hard time to people. He goes to lie down to sleep. At that rate people do not get vexed with him. But people who drink and go about fighting—the Town Chief cannot love them in the town (p. 487).

Kpelle Description
one of the sticks
one—a large one
one of the sticks
piece of bamboo
one stick
one piece of bamboo
one of the bamboo
one of the thorny
one of the thorny sticks

Scribner observed that the man gave the wrong answer to the question, if the question were considered purely in terms of formal logic. However, he *did* use logic in justifying his answer. In logical format, the subject's reasoning was as follows:

Sumo's drinking gives people a hard time.
Saki's drinking does not give people a hard time.
People do not get vexed when they are not given a hard time.
The Town Chief is a person.
Therefore, the Town Chief is not vexed at Saki.

What is happening here is that the subject is using evidence from his own experience with Saki and Sumo (*empirical* evidence) and is ignoring evidence presented in the syllogism (*theoretical* evidence). That traditional subjects base their responses on empirical evidence becomes clear when we ask them to explain their answers. For example, consider the following problem, presented to an illiterate woman from a remote area in Central Asia called Uzbekistan (Scribner, 1977).

Premise 1: In the far north, all bears are white.
Premise 2: Novaya Zemyla is in the far north.
Question: What color are the bears there?

The subject's response to this problem was "You should ask the people who have been there and seen them. We always speak of only what we see, we don't talk about what we haven't seen." The woman's response makes it clear that she has a style of thinking that puts a high value on what one can know through direct experience. She did not see the question as a logical puzzle, but as a question to be answered empirically.

Studies like these suggest that traditional peoples are far from stupid. Their apparently poor performance on logic tasks stems from the fact that they relate to the data presented differently than does a person with schooling. But why should education make people focus on the data presented in the syllogism? Here we might draw an analogy with a typical problem posed to elementary school students: "John has one apple and Mary has two apples. How many apples do John and Mary have together?" When presented with a problem such as this, very young students might first think the problem is about a "real" John and Mary. But they quickly learn that they cannot obtain the answer by looking around the room to see if anyone has apples. Instead, they must focus on the information presented by the teacher. With exposure to schooling, they learn to pay attention to the kind of theoretical data presented in syllogisms, and they therefore do well on tests of logical thinking.

An important conclusion to draw from these cross-cultural experiments is that when a group of people does poorly on a particular test, we should resist the urge to automatically downgrade our evaluation of the group's intelligence. The construction of the test itself or the group's lack of specific training in the kind of task being evaluated may be causing the low scores. We will return to this problem in Chapter 14 when we discuss how different cultural groups perform on intelligence tests.

Categorization: A Basic Mechanism of Thinking

- A process fundamental to thinking and language is categorization, which involves placing objects and events into groups based on their characteristics. Researchers have tried to explain how we form categories. The explanation that we categorize things based on how they are defined has been rejected, because of the difficulty of creating adequate definitions for many categories. Eleanor Rosch suggests that we place objects in categories based on their features. According to this idea, objects that have many of the features associated with the category are "good" examples of the category, whereas objects with fewer features are "poor" examples. Experiments show that people do, in fact, consider some items to be better examples of a category than others.

Reasoning: Thinking Logically—and Illogically

- Reasoning, the ability to think logically, is the process by which we draw conclusions from information. Deductive reasoning involves making a judgment that when certain assertions are true, a specific conclusion must follow. Psychologists study deductive reasoning by presenting syllogisms and asking people whether or not the conclusion follows from the premises.

- Conditional reasoning involves statements of the form "If P is true, then Q is true." Logicians have formulated two inference rules, *modus ponens,* and *modus tollens,* to determine whether or not a syllogism starting with the premise "If P, then Q" is valid. When people are asked to evaluate the validity of syllogisms, they have no trouble applying *modus ponens* but make errors when applying *modus tollens.*

- Inductive reasoning is the process of drawing the conclusion that a given outcome is probable, based on our past experiences. This type of reasoning plays a large role in everyday thinking and in scientific research as well. A major roadblock to successful inductive reasoning is the confirmational bias.

Making Decisions: Choosing Among Alternatives

- We make decisions when we choose among alternatives. Psychologists have identified several strategies people use in making decisions, including elimination by aspects, the availability heuristic, and the representativeness heuristic. Although these strategies are often useful, each can lead to errors in decision making.

- Framing effects arise from the way decision choices are stated. How choices are framed can affect the decision-making process.

Solving Problems:
Overcoming Obstacles to Reach a Goal

- A problem exists when there is an obstacle between the present state and a goal. Cognitive psychologists often use puzzles to study how people go about solving problems.

- Among the psychological obstacles to successful problem solving are perceptual assumptions and the effects of past experience, including functional fixedness and mental set.

- Problem solving is also affected by the way the problem is stated. Often a complex problem becomes simple when it is restated in a different way. Sometimes problems are difficult because the way they are stated keeps us from noticing the aspect of the problem that is crucial for arriving at a solution.

- The information-processing approach to the study of problem solving asks how we manipulate information in solving a problem. Problems are described in terms of a problem space having an initial state, intermediate states, a goal state, and operators that specify moves that can be made toward a solution. Means-end analysis, a common strategy used to solve problems, is often successful, but this strategy must sometimes be violated to solve certain problems.

- Experts are better at solving problems than novices are, because they have more knowledge and so are more likely to propose the correct strategy. In addition, experts and novices organize their knowledge differently. Whereas novices organize knowledge about physics problems based on the way the problem appears (surface structure), experts organize that knowledge based on basic principles of physics (deep structure).

- A computer program called Soar has been developed that can use the knowledge it gains while solving a problem to solve the problem more efficiently on subsequent presentations. Soar's behavior in problem solving is similar to that of humans.

Using and Understanding Language

- Understanding language can be seen as a series of problems to be solved. One problem is speech segmentation—the need to put breaks between words, though in reality there are none in the speech signal. We achieve this by taking the words' meanings into account. We also use the context of the overall conversation to help us understand ambiguous sentences. Another process that occurs during conversations is making inferences: we fill in information that may not have been directly stated. Effective communication occurs when the speaker follows the given-new contract.

- Listeners understand indirect statements by going beyond the literal meaning of a sentence to determine its true, or conveyed, meaning. They accomplish this by considering the context of a statement and then applying a conversational rule.

- Language is an important component of thinking, but we don't always have to use language when we think.

- According to Whorf's linguistic relativity hypothesis, our language affects the way we think and perceive reality. Tests of this hypothesis using color perception have not confirmed the hypothesis, though there is some evidence that language may have some influence on thinking about gender when the generic "he" is used.

Reprise: Levels of Analysis in the Study of Learning and Cognition

* Both this chapter and the previous one, on memory, have illustrated how cognitive psychologists have found ways to observe and measure mental processes. Although we are unaware of some of the things that influence our behavior, what we are aware of plays an important role in our ability to actively direct much of our learning and thinking.

Follow-Through/Diversity: Thinking in Traditional Cultures

* Subjects from traditional cultures often perform poorly on problems that are solved easily by people from Western culture. This poor performance does not, however, reflect low intelligence, but instead reflects an approach to problem solving that is different from the Western approach.

Key Terms

algorithms
artificial intelligence (AI)
availability heuristic
categories
confirmational bias
conjunction fallacy
conjunction rule
conversational rule
deduction
deductive reasoning
elimination by aspects
functional fixedness
given-new contract
goal state
heuristics
indirect statements
induction
inductive reasoning
initial state
intermediate states
linguistic relativity hypothesis
means-end analysis
mental set
operators
problem space
reasoning
representativeness heuristic
risk aversion strategy
risk-taking strategy
speech segmentation
thinking
thinking aloud protocol

CHAPTER

9

Basic Issues in Developmental Psychology
Stability Versus Instability: Do Characteristics Remain Consistent over Time?
Continuity Versus Discontinuity: A Smooth Progression, or Steps?
Nature Versus Nurture: How Do Heredity and the Environment Interact?

Interdisciplinary Dimension: Anthropology
Socialization and Children's Behavior: The Six-Cultures Study

Physical and Perceptual Development
Prenatal Development
Infancy and Toddlerhood
Childhood
Adolescence
Adulthood

Cognitive Development
Piaget's Theory of Cognitive Development
Evaluating Piaget
The Information-Processing Approach
Cognitive Development in Adulthood

Reprise: What You Look at Determines What You See

Follow-Through/Diversity
Cross-Cultural Perspectives on Piaget

Physical, Perceptual, and Cognitive Development

When I was a child, I spake as a child, I understood as a child, I thought as a child: but when I became a man, I put away childish things.

I Corinthians 13:11

I recently attended a friend's wedding. As I sat there observing the service, I asked myself, "What path did these two adults, who are vowing to share the remainder of their lives together, travel to get to this point in their lives?"

They started like everybody else, as small infants being cared for by their parents. But how were they influenced, I wondered—as they progressed through infancy, childhood, and adolescence—by their family life, by their different cultures (one was of English descent, the other, eastern European), and by the qualities they inherited from their parents?

As I mused, I began looking around the congregation and was struck by the differences among the people. The group attending this wedding was particularly diverse, differing in age, race, appearance, and social standing. But even as I noticed these differences, I realized that these varied people had experienced many things in common. Many of them had participated in a ceremony similar to this one; most had traversed the sometimes rough seas of adolescence, experienced their first date, coped with relationships, and made decisions about schooling and careers. In what ways were their experiences alike, and in what ways were they different? How had each person come to be the adult she or he was that day?

What I was thinking about was the process of **development**—the lifelong process of change stretching from conception to death. And as the bride and groom took their vows—proclaiming that they would stay with each other "for better or for worse, for richer or for poorer, in sickness and in health, as long as you both shall live"—I became acutely aware that the process of change all of us experience as we mature continues past childhood and into adulthood. The bride and groom were both in their 40s (it was his second marriage, her first). They were embarking on a journey in which, despite their status as "middle-aged" adults, they would experience continuing change.

The questions that occurred to me during this wedding are just a few of the issues of interest to **developmental psychologists**—psychologists who study the process of human development. In this chapter and the next we will be focusing on their research. Some of it seeks to describe the changes that take place as people develop; but most developmental research goes beyond simply describing the process of development to asking *why* development proceeds as it does. How is development affected by our biological heritage and by our environment? How do we learn what it means to be a boy or a girl? How do we develop the ability to talk and hold conversations, to think and solve problems, to view ourselves as unique individuals, and to cope with the changes that occur as we grow older?

Our survey of development will consider questions such as these by looking at the processes of physical, perceptual, and cognitive development in this chapter and at language and social development in the next one. We will, therefore, be following five "streams" of development, each having its own course. However, studying aspects of development as separate streams should not mislead you into thinking they are independent of one another. As we will see, these aspects of development overlap and interact. Consider a boy who is one of the first in his age group to experience the physical growth spurt of adolescence. These physical changes lead to social changes (his peers may look up to him because of his more adult appearance), and they may also lead to cognitive changes (his new appearance, and the way his friends relate to him, may influence the way he thinks about himself). And all the aspects of development are affected by contextual factors, including a person's family, society, and social network.

The different streams of development can thus be studied at all four levels of analysis: biological, cognitive, behavioral, and contextual. In this chapter we will focus primarily on the biological and cognitive levels as we consider the physical, perceptual, and cognitive changes that take place from infancy through old age. Before we begin to describe these changes, however, we will consider three basic issues in developmental psychology that are relevant to all aspects of development.

Basic Issues in Developmental Psychology

So far we have spoken of development as a process of change. But what exactly does it mean to say that people "develop" as they grow older? Three basic issues provide a framework for understanding development.

1. **Stability versus instability:** How stable are personal characteristics? Do qualities present early in childhood persist into later childhood, adolescence, and adulthood? For example, does a person who is shy as a child necessarily develop into a shy adult? Do childhood intelligence scores predict adult intelligence scores?

2. **Continuity versus discontinuity:** Is development best described as a smooth, continuous process in which gradual changes build on one another—or as a sequence of distinct stages, each of which is a qualitative "leap" from the one before? For example, is the development of thinking best described in terms of a gradual increase in the child's reasoning abilities, or in terms of a series of jumps, each adding a new ability?

3. **Nature versus nurture:** Is the unfolding of people's lives affected more by their genetic inheritance (nature), or by the environment in which they grow up (nurture)? For example, can we attribute a person's high verbal intelligence to an inherited ability to use language, or to the fact that his mother talked to him a lot and read him bedtime stories every night when he was a child?

Research in a number of areas has contributed to developmental psychologists' understanding of each of these issues. Let's briefly consider some of this research.

Stability Versus Instability:
Do Characteristics Remain Consistent over Time?

How constant are a person's characteristics over time? Do shy babies always grow up to be shy adults? If we could look back at the childhood of extremely aggressive adults, would we see that they were also aggressive as children?

One way to approach questions like these is to compare the same behavioral characteristics at different ages. Psychologists typically use two different methods to create these comparisons. In the **cross-sectional method** psychologists test a number of groups of people, with each group differing in age. In the

longitudinal method psychologists measure particular behaviors at an early age and then repeat those measurements as the same subjects grow older. (See Measurement & Methodology, "Measuring Changes over Time: The Cross-Sectional and Longitudinal Methods.") Psychologists usually use the longitudinal method to answer the kinds of questions posed by the stability-versus instability issue.

12   EMOTION

Consider Jerome Kagan's (1984) longitudinal studies of shyness. Kagan observed that about 10% of 2-year-olds are shy, or "inhibited." Such toddlers cease their play and become quiet when they experience a new event such as an unfamiliar adult talking to them. Other infants, however, are not inhibited—they respond to the unfamiliar adult by smiling, talking, and allowing the adult to play with them.

Through longitudinal studies, Kagan and his co-workers have shown that three-quarters of the children who were classified as extremely inhibited at 21

MEASUREMENT & METHODOLOGY

Measuring Changes over Time: The Cross-Sectional and Longitudinal Methods

How can researchers measure changes that occur with age? One way is the cross-sectional method: assemble a number of groups of people, with each group representing a certain age (Figure A). Each group of same-aged people, which is called a **cohort,** can be tested to yield an average score for that age. The scores can then be compared to show changes that occur with age. Figure B, which was derived using this method in a study of intelligence, shows that intelligence declines from age 25 on (Green, 1969).

These results seem to lead to the conclusion that individuals reach their maximum intelligence at age 25 and then begin a downhill slide. However, this conclusion is flawed. Why? Because

the cohorts differ in ways other than just age. Consider, for example, two people from different cohorts: Susan, born in 1924, from the 70-year-old cohort, and Jessica, born in 1964, from the 30-year-old cohort. In addition to differing in age, Susan and Jessica differ in their years of education. After graduating from high school in 1942, Susan married and devoted herself to raising her children, a typical practice at that time. After Jessica graduated from high school in 1982, she chose to attend college, a practice far more common today for both sexes than it was in the 1940s. In general, because people born in 1964 are more likely to have a college education than those born in 1924, individuals in the 70-year-old cohort have, on the average, less education than those in the 30-year-old cohort.

This educational difference is shown in Figure C. The similarity of the education and IQ curves supports the idea that the apparent decline in intelligence with age measured cross-sectionally is actually due to the lower level of education in the older cohorts. In fact, similar studies that have controlled for educational level at each age show that intelligence actually *increases* until about 65 years of age (Green, 1969).

One way to avoid cohort differences that distort data derived by the cross-sectional method is to use the longitudinal method, in which the same individuals are repeatedly tested as they get older (Figure D). By continually retesting the same people, this method not only avoids cohort differences but also enables researchers to follow changes that occur in individual subjects.

The advantages of the longitudinal method do, however, come with a cost. Deriving a curve like the one in Figure B using the longitudinal method would require tracking people over a 35-year span—a large portion of an experimenter's lifetime! Furthermore, as time passes, some of the subjects in the study inevitably drop out. Often those who drop out have different characteristics than the ones who continue, a phenomenon called *selective attrition.* Typically, the people who drop out are the ones in the poorest health, leaving the healthier ones to be tested. This obviously changes the characteristics of the sample (Schaie, 1977).

In the cross-sectional method, age groups are created by selecting people born at different times. In this example, all age groups are tested in 1995; people born in 1990 comprise the 5-year-old group, people born in 1980 comprise the 15-year-old group, and people born in 1970 comprise the 25-year-old group.

months of age were still inhibited at age 4. Conversely, none of the children who were extremely *uninhibited* at 21 months became inhibited by age 4. (Garcia-Coll, Kagan, & Resnick, 1984; Kagan, 1984). Similar results were obtained when the children were retested at age 5½ (Reznick et al., 1986). These studies, which approach the study of development at the behavioral level of analysis by focusing strictly on behavior, show that the personality trait of extreme shyness remains relatively constant through early childhood.

But is there any evidence of traits that remain consistent from childhood all the way into adulthood? The most impressive examples of such consistency are intelligence and aggression. We will see in Chapter 14 that once most people reach the age of 6 years their intelligence, as measured by intelligence tests, remains fairly stable into adulthood. The results are similar for aggression, as illustrated by a longitudinal study that spanned 22 years.

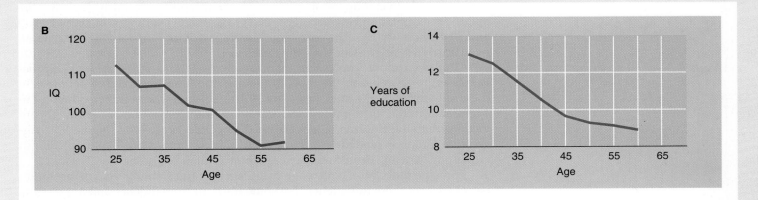

Curve B, from a study that used the cross-sectional method, indicates that the intelligence of the older cohorts is lower. This appears to be related to the fact that the older cohorts received less education, as indicated by curve C.

Knowing the advantages and disadvantages of the cross-sectional and longitudinal methods enables psychologists to pick the method best suited for their research. A longitudinal study is usually picked to study how individual subjects change over time. Cross-sectional studies are often used to compare subjects of different ages. As developmental psychologists often focus on a particular stage of development, such as the preschool years or the grade school years, the age range of their subjects is narrow enough so that distorting cohort effects are usually not a problem. Often, to take advantage of the positive features of both the cross-sectional and longitudinal methods, developmental psychologists combine the two, following some people over a short period of time and also testing groups of different ages at the same time.

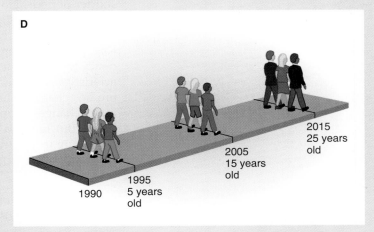

In the longitudinal method, the same people are followed over time. In this example, people born in 1990 are tested in 1995 (when they are 5 years old), 2005 (15 years old), and 2015 (25 years old).

FIGURE 9.1

Children who were rated high in aggression at age 8 are more likely to have committed crimes by age 30. This result holds for both males and females, but the female crime rate is much lower.

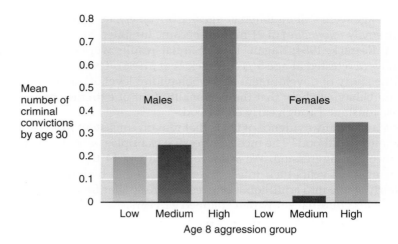

L. Rowell Huesmann and his co-workers (1984) first determined aggression ratings of 8-year-olds by having their third-grade classmates rate their tendency to engage in aggressive behaviors. The researchers then determined aggressiveness, using a number of different methods, at ages 19 and 30. The correlations between aggressiveness at different ages were fairly high for the males: the correlation between aggression at 8 and 30 years was .50; between 19 and 30 years it was .85. The correlations were lower for females who, in general, were much less aggressive than the males.

But even more impressive than these correlations is the relationship between aggressiveness in the third-grade classroom and aggressive behavior in the adult world. By the time they were 30, the children who were rated highest in aggression in the third grade had received over three times more criminal convictions than the children who were rated lowest in aggression (Figure 9.1). Aggressive children tended to become adults who were more likely to commit crimes, drive while drunk, and severely punish their children.

So where do these data leave us in terms of the stability-versus-instability issue? Clearly, there is evidence that some traits, like intelligence and aggression, are fairly stable over long periods and that others, like shyness, are stable over shorter periods. However, it is important to remember that change is also possible for many individuals. The results of the shyness research were, for example, based on children who were extremely inhibited. The majority of the children in Kagan's study, even those who were somewhat shy, did not show as strong a tendency to remain the same as they grew older. The fact is that even if certain characteristics remain fairly stable in some people, development by its very nature implies change. Thus, our emphasis in this chapter and the next one is on the many changes people experience physically, cognitively, and socially as they develop. But how do these changes take place? Does change occur in a series of "quantum leaps" from one discrete stage to another, or does it occur in a smooth progression?

Continuity Versus Discontinuity: A Smooth Progression, or Steps?

Two possible courses of development are illustrated in Figure 9.2. The curve in Figure 9.2a depicts development as gradual and continuous change. The step-like curve in Figure 9.2b depicts development as occurring in a series of abrupt leaps.

Psychologists who subscribe to the idea of sudden changes see children as passing through a series of stages, each a more advanced level of functioning than the one before (Shaffer, 1989). Proponents of the stage idea point to the dif-

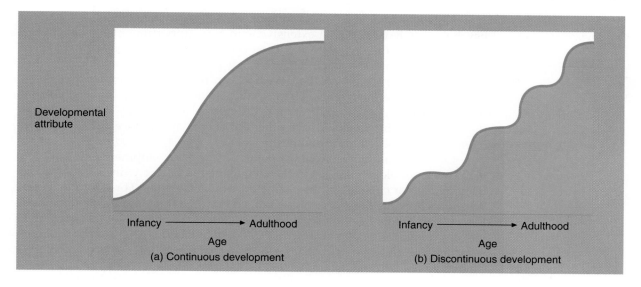

Infancy ⟶ Adulthood
Age
(a) Continuous development

Infancy ⟶ Adulthood
Age
(b) Discontinuous development

FIGURE 9.2
Development as (a) a process of gradual and continual change, and (b) a series of abrupt changes.

ferent quality of the processes that occur at different points in development. For example, when asked to remember a list of words, adolescents not only remember *more* words than 7-year-olds, they also use a different *strategy* for remembering them. Whereas adolescents group similar words together as they rehearse them, 7-year-olds, if they rehearse at all, do so in no particular order, or in the order in which they heard the words. This tells the stage theorist that the adolescent has achieved a qualitatively distinct stage of development.

There are a number of prominent stage theories of development, including the stage theories of social and moral development that we will discuss in the next chapter. In this chapter we will focus on the stage theory of cognitive development proposed by Jean Piaget, probably the most influential developmental psychologist. Piaget portrayed children as achieving changes in the basic nature of their thinking as they proceed from one stage to another. His theory asserts, for example, that an adolescent who can think about abstract concepts like "justice" and "love" is in a later stage of development than a younger child who is not yet cognitively equipped to think in terms of abstract ideas.

Piaget's stage theory of cognitive development has been extremely influential. Nevertheless, we will see other evidence that children move to new levels of cognitive development in a gradual progression rather than by abrupt leaps between discrete stages.

Nature Versus Nurture:
How Do Heredity and the Environment Interact?

The third basic developmental issue concerns a debate that dominated psychology for many years: the *nature-nurture controversy*. Those on the nature side of the controversy believed that people's capacities are determined primarily by their biological makeup. Those on the nurture side believed that people's capacities are determined primarily by the environment in which they are raised.

You may recall from our discussions of behaviorism in earlier chapters that many early American psychologists argued strongly that learning and the environment are far more important than genetic inheritance in determining behavior. This belief in the power of the environment is nowhere more strongly stated than in John B. Watson's assertion that he could mold any healthy infant to be "any kind of specialist I might select—doctor, lawyer, artist, merchant-chief, and yes, even beggar-man and thief" (Watson, 1925, p. 82). This statement typifies the early behaviorists' conviction that any person's characteristics can be shaped by rewarding "desirable" behavior and punishing "undesirable" behavior.

3   BIOLOGY

Watson's confidence in the role of learning notwithstanding, present-day psychologists have gathered extensive evidence supporting a large role for genetics. Much of this evidence has been obtained by comparing *identical twins,* who develop from the same fertilized egg and therefore share 100% of their genes, with *fraternal twins,* who develop from two separate fertilized eggs and share only 50% of their genes. These studies, which we will describe in detail in the "Intelligence," "Personality," and "Abnormal Psychology" chapters, show that identical twins resemble each other not only in appearance but also in intelligence, personality, and mental health.

Of particular interest from the point of view of development is that as identical twins get older, changes in the characteristics of one twin are often paralleled by similar changes in the characteristics of the other. For example, Figure 9.3 shows how intelligence scores changed between three months and six years for one pair of identical twins. The similar patterns of change for these two individuals are typical in identical twins but not in fraternal twins. Genetic programming apparently contributes to the similar changes in intelligence scores over time observed in these twins (Wilson, 1978, 1983).

The evidence from twin studies and other research clearly indicates that genetic inheritance is an important factor in development. Yet learning is obviously important as well. Consider, for example, how a child learns language. Children learn a particular language because they grow up around other people who speak that language. The question for present-day psychologists is not whether nature *or* nurture determines our characteristics, but how both nature—our genetic heritage—and nurture—our upbringing—*interact* to shape our physical, perceptual, cognitive, and social abilities.

One way to understand this interaction is to reexamine the concepts of genotype and phenotype that were introduced in Chapter 3. Remember that the genotype is a person's biological heritage as specified by his or her genes. The phenotype is the *expression* of the genotype: the characteristics and behaviors that *actually develop* as the person is affected by the environment and by experiences he or she has while growing up. Thus, a particular person's genotype specifying a potential for high intelligence may not be realized in the phenotype if that person grows up in an impoverished environment.

Heredity and environment thus interact with each other in complex ways. Examples of this interaction are plentiful, including the following:

• *Language learning:* All normal children learn a language, a fact that reflects its genetic basis. However, the specific language children learn is determined by their environment. French children speak French because they are exposed to the French language, not because they have "French-language" genes.

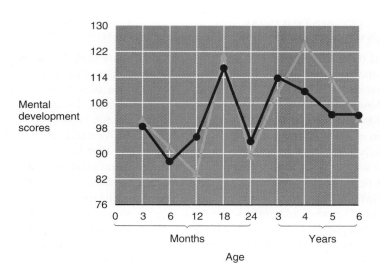

FIGURE 9.3
Intelligence scores measured at different times between three months and six years of age in one pair of identical twins. The scores for these twins change in similar ways, but similar measurements on fraternal twins do not show this degree of correspondence.

The differences in behavior among people growing up in different cultures argue for the role of learning and the environment in determining behavior.

• *Sexual behavior*: Most people who have gone through puberty are capable of sexual activity, but the nature of a particular person's sexual activity is greatly influenced by such environmental factors as society's rules, the individual's religious beliefs, and peer pressure. For example, a person who grows up in societies that have strict rules governing sexuality—such as the Amish of Pennsylvania—is much less likely to engage in premarital sexual behavior than a person who is exposed to the sexual images of modern American culture.

• *Alcoholism*: A person may be genetically predisposed to alcoholism, but that biological predisposition does not doom him or her to being an alcoholic. If a child grows up in a family that strongly discourages drinking, or if witnessing the effects of alcoholism as a child leads the person to shun alcohol, he or she may never become addicted to alcohol.

Sandra Scarr and Kathleen McCartney (1983) have taken the idea that heredity and the environment interact with each other a step beyond these examples by showing how a person's genetic makeup can help *determine* her or his environment. They point to the *evocative influence of genetics* on the environment—the fact that a person's genetically determined characteristics can *evoke* reactions from other people. For example, babies who are active and smile frequently usually receive more attention than babies who are passive. Activity and smiling, two traits that in babies are largely determined by genetics, affect the environment the infant experiences, which in turn influences the baby's subsequent behavior.

Scarr and McCartney also point to the *active influence of genetics* on the environment—people *actively select* aspects of the environment that fit their genetically determined characteristics. A person with good coordination is likely to seek out sports; her brother, with high mathematical ability, might take advanced mathematics courses. Thus, two people who come from the same family but have different inherited capabilities may self-select very different environments. This self-selection of environments is called **niche building**—people select the part of the environment they want to experience.

This idea of niche building helps to explain why children from the same family who are similar when they are young tend to diverge as they grow older (Scarr & Weinberg, 1983). When the children in a family are young, they are all exposed to similar environments created by the parents. However, as the children get older, the active influence of their genetic makeup becomes stronger and they begin selecting their own niches to create an environment that suits them. Genetic differences, according to this view, create environmental differences, which serve to magnify the effect of the genetic differences as the person gets older (Scarr, 1992).

3   BIOLOGY

In considering the complex interplay of genetic inheritance and environmental influence, we need to bring into the picture some of the factors that work at the contextual level to influence development. In the following Interdisciplinary Dimension we look at an important anthropological study that illustrates how environmental factors help determine child-rearing practices that influence children's behavior.

INTERDISCIPLINARY DIMENSION ANTHROPOLOGY

Socialization and Children's Behavior: The Six-Cultures Study

An anthropological study called the Six-Cultures Study was conducted to determine whether differences in child-rearing practices are associated with differences in children's behavior (Whiting, 1963; Whiting & Whiting, 1975). Teams of researchers were sent to live in small communities in the United States, India, Kenya, Okinawa, the Philippines, and Mexico. During their stay the researchers (1) carried out an *ethnographic survey,* a description of the economic and political situation and living arrangements in each community; (2) compiled a description of child-raising practices; and (3) recorded the children's typical day-to-day behavior.

The basic assumptions of the study were that characteristics of a culture affect the way children are *socialized*—the way they are taught the knowledge, values, and social skills of the culture within which they are raised—and that differences in socialization affect children's behavior. To show how the study examined these relationships between characteristics of a culture and its children's behaviors, we will focus on the results from two very different cultures studied in the project: the culture of Orchard Town, a small community in New England, and the culture of Nyansongo, a small village in eastern Kenya.

One of the most obvious differences between these cultures is their economic structure. Orchard Town, with its industry and modern conveniences, has a complex economic structure. In contrast Nyansongo, with its primitive farming and herding economy, has a simple economic structure (Table 9.1). These differences in complexity influence a child's socialization by affecting how much work the children are expected to do to help their parents. The simple nature of Nyansongo culture places a great burden on the mother. Not only does she cook and clean house without the aid of any modern conveniences, but she also takes care of children and spends many hours every day gardening and herding cattle. Because of the mother's work load, Nyansongo children are recruited to help with chores beginning at an early age. It isn't unusual for young girls to be caretakers for infants, or for boys and girls alike to help with the gardening, cooking, herding, and other chores. The children are, therefore, socialized to take care of others and to act in a responsible manner.

Orchard Town culture places little burden on children to help with chores. In fact, Orchard Town children are used to being cared for and learn to seek help when they need it. Also, in response to the sophisticated society in which they live, they are taught to be competitive so that as adults they will be able to achieve in their materialistic, status-conscious society.

The differences in childhood socialization in the two cultures lead to differences in behaviors. These behaviors were measured by systematically observing children's social

Scenes from communities similar to Orchard Town (top) and Nyansongo (bottom), two of the six cultures studied.

TABLE 9.1

Comparison of the economic structures of Orchard Town and Nyansongo

Orchard Town (Complex)	*Nyansongo (Simple)*
• Many occupations.	• Mostly agricultural occupations (subsistence farming).
• People's social status varies depending on job, salary, etc.	• People don't differ in social status.
• Wife is responsible for cooking and child care. Has modern conveniences (heat, running water, stove).	• Wife is responsible for cooking, child care, gardening, herding, and fetching wood and water. Has no modern conveniences.

TABLE 9.2
Connections between socialization and behavior related to economic structure

Orchard Town		Nyansongo	
Socialization	*Behavior*	*Socialization*	*Behavior*
Used to being cared for	Dependent	Help with chores	Responsible
Taught to be competitive	Dominant	Take care of infants	Nurturant

interactions with other children and with their parents. Based on these observations, Beatrice Whiting and John Whiting (1975) described the behavior of Nyansongo children as "nurturant and responsible." That is, they were willing to help others whom they perceived to be in a state of need (for example, by offering food to a crying baby) and were willing to do chores to help the family (fetching water from the stream, for instance). In contrast, Orchard Town children were described as being "dependent and dominant." That is, they sought their parents' attention (by calling out for their mother) and tried to control others (by fighting with their brothers or sisters, for example). Table 9.2 shows the connections that Whiting and Whiting made between socialization practices in the two cultures and the children's behaviors.

Comparisons like this suggest how cultural characteristics may affect childhood socialization and how that socialization, in turn, affects the children's behavior. Although the relationships observed in this study are all correlational, so that we cannot draw any conclusions regarding cause and effect, it is significant that similar connections between cultural characteristics, socialization, and social behaviors were also observed in the other four cultures studied. Whatever the actual causes of the children's behavior, the Six-Cultures Study documents differences in children's behavior across cultures. The study also illustrates that controlled experiments are not the only way to study behavior. Naturalistic observations of behavior, in the setting in which it occurs, are an alternative to experimentation. ■

One of the themes in our discussion so far is that the process of development and the idea of change go together. People's behavior is changed by the environment in which they grow up, and even if some of their characteristics remain stable as they get older, people change in countless ways as they mature. In the next section, we look at how people's physical characteristics and perceptual capacities change as they grow from conception into adulthood.

Physical and Perceptual Development

What creature walks in the morning on four feet, at noon upon two,
and at evening upon three?

The riddle of the Sphinx

The most obvious changes that occur as a person ages are physical. These changes are crucial for survival. Babies, helpless at birth, become self-sufficient as they develop the muscle strength and coordination that enables them to manipulate objects and to walk, at first haltingly, and then with greater confidence. This physical growth, which continues throughout infancy and into childhood and adolescence, not only has survival value, but often plays a role in determining a person's thoughts and behaviors. For example, when we discuss the physical changes that occur in adolescence we will see that these changes influence the way other people view the adolescent as well as the adolescent's conception of himself or herself.

Physical development begins prenatally—before birth—when a sperm and egg combine, and it continues throughout life. We begin our examination of the course of physical development with the moment of conception.

Prenatal Development

3   BIOLOGY

The union of sperm and egg produces a **zygote,** an egg that has been fertilized by a sperm cell. At conception the zygote is microscopic—about 1/175 inch in diameter—and weighs about 30 billionths of a pound. Nine months later, the process of cell division (*mitosis*) has created a baby made of 2 million cells and weighing about 7 pounds. At no other time in life is development so breath-takingly rapid.

The course of prenatal development, shown in Figure 9.4, proceeds through three periods.

1. The **germinal period** begins when cells begin to divide, within hours of fertilization. Occasionally the first division of the zygote creates two identical cells that separate and develop two individuals: identical twins, called *monozygotic (MZ)* because they develop from the same cell. Sometimes two eggs are fertilized separately, producing fraternal twins, called *dizygotic (DZ)* because they develop from two different zygotes.

2. The **embryonic period** lasts from the second through eighth week. The developing organism, now called an *embryo,* begins to form arms, legs, a face, a beating heart, lungs, and a brain. By six weeks all the basic organs of the body have taken shape, and the nervous system has developed to the point at which the embryo responds to stimulation and can move.

3. The **fetal period** extends from the second month to birth. The body's proportions change and the *fetus,* as the baby-to-be is now called, begins to look more like a miniature newborn. The organs, limbs, muscles, and other systems of the body become functional during this period. Higher functioning of the brain begins to develop at four to five months (Figure 9.5). About nine months after conception the infant, now weighing about 7 pounds, is born.

Although prenatal development occurs within the isolated confines of the womb, the environment begins to affect the child-to-be even before birth. The primary pathway for the interaction between the fetus and the environment is

FIGURE 9.4
Stages of prenatal development.
Left: Germinal period (week 4–5 in photo).
Center: Embryonic period (week 7).
Right: Fetal period (month 4).

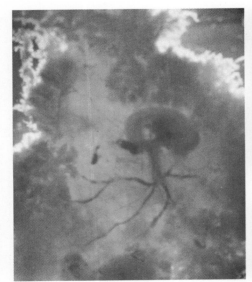
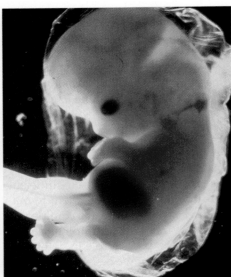

the *umbilical cord,* which provides the developing fetus with oxygen and nutrients from the mother. But the umbilical cord can also be a pathway for harmful substances, called **teratogens,** which can cause drastic disruptions in the normal developmental process.

An example of a teratogen is the drug thalidomide, which was prescribed in Europe, Japan, and Canada between 1956 and 1961 to control nausea in the early stages of pregnancy—the very period during which the embryo and fetus are most susceptible to damage. The tragic result for thousands of children was to be born without arms or legs and to have hands and feet attached to their bodies like flippers.

Cigarette smoke and alcohol are also teratogens. Although smoking has not been shown to cause birth defects, it does increase the probability of low-weight births and stillbirths (in which the baby is born dead) (Bolton, 1983). Alcohol consumption by the mother during the first three months of pregnancy can cause fetal alcohol syndrome, in which babies are born with small heads and underdeveloped brains and are severely retarded (Figure 9.6). Mothers who use drugs such as heroin and cocaine can give birth to babies who are addicted to those drugs. These babies also have lower birth weights, shorter length, and smaller heads than average infants (Coles et al., 1992; Lester et al., 1991; Strauss et al., 1975). They begin life suffering the pangs of withdrawal symptoms from the drugs they have ingested in the womb.

In addition to the umbilical cord, the developing fetus has other means of contact with the outside world. One of the most obvious is sound, as any mother knows who has felt the fetus kick when she enters a noisy room.

A startling demonstration of the fetus's ability to both hear sounds and remember them was an experiment carried out by Anthony DeCasper and William Fifer (1980) that showed that newborns have already learned the distinctive sound of their mother's voice. Using an operant conditioning procedure, DeCasper and Fifer were able to show, by recording their pattern of sucking on a nipple, that 2-day-old infants distinguish between their mother's voice and that of a stranger.

DeCasper and Fifer used the fact that infants usually suck in bursts separated by pauses to establish the following reinforcement contingency: a long pause in sucking activated a recording of the mother's voice, and a short pause activated a tape recording of a stranger's voice (Figure 9.7). (For half of the infants these conditions were reversed, with the short pause activating the mother's voice.) DeCasper and Fifer found that the babies regulated pauses in their sucking so that they heard their mother's voice more than the stranger's voice. This is a remarkable accomplishment for a 2-day-old, especially when we consider that after birth most of them had been with their mothers for only a few hours prior to the experiment.

DeCasper and Fifer suggest that newborns prefer their mother's voice because as fetuses they have heard their mother talking. This suggestion is supported by the results of another experiment, in which DeCasper and Melanie J. Spence (1986) had one group of pregnant women read from Dr. Seuss's book *The Cat in the Hat* and another group read the same story replacing the words *cat* and *hat* with *dog* and *fog.* Newborns regulated their sucking pattern to hear the version of the story they heard before they were born. Apparently, even in the womb the fetus becomes familiar not only with the intonation and rhythm of the mother's voice but also with the sounds of specific words.

Infancy and Toddlerhood (Birth to 3 Years)

Infancy—usually considered to be the first one and a half to two years of life, ending when the infant has begun learning language—is a period of extremely rapid growth. Indeed, if the child's growth were to continue at the rate typical of the first six months of life, the average 10-year-old would be approximately 100

100 days

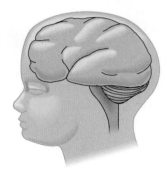

7 months

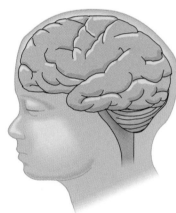

9 months

FIGURE 9.5
Growth of the brain during prenatal development.

FIGURE 9.6
A child with fetal alcohol syndrome.

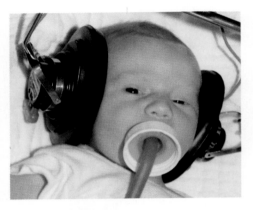

FIGURE 9.7
This baby, a subject in DeCaspar and Fifer's study, can control whether she hears a recording of her mother's voice or a stranger's voice by the way she sucks on the nipple.

feet tall and weigh roughly 240,000 tons (McCall, 1979)! The rate of growth begins to slow down toward the first birthday, but continues to be relatively rapid before starting to taper off by about the third birthday (Figure 9.8).

Just as impressive as this increase in size is the development of physical skills. These physical skills are particularly evident during the toddler stage, which lasts from $1\frac{1}{2}$ to 3 years of age. Toddlers may start out by "toddling"—walking punctuated by frequent falling down—but they are soon able to walk more rapidly. The progression from the fetal posture at birth to accomplished walking is shown in Figure 9.9, together with the development of motor skills.

The emergence of motor skills is biologically programmed, but it can be affected by extreme environmental conditions. One such environmental effect on physical development was documented by Wayne Dennis (1960), who observed infants being raised under conditions of extreme deprivation in a "foundling home" in Iran. During their first year, these infants were placed in their cribs and then, except for being bathed every other day, were almost totally ignored. Even when they were being fed, handling was kept to a minimum. Very young infants were fed with a bottle supported by a small pillow. Because the infants were rarely handled and received little attention from their caregivers, these children's motor development was extremely retarded; only 8% between the ages of 12 and 21 months were able to walk alone. Compare that with Figure 9.9, which shows that a normally developing child walks alone at about 14 months.

Infancy is also a period of rapid perceptual development. Most 19th-century psychologists believed newborns' experience to be a chaotic stream of sights, sounds, and sensations making little sense. We know this can't be true from DeCasper's studies, which show that even within the womb the fetus distinguishes the mother's words. Similarly, research using new methods of measuring visual capacity shows that infants see much more than a meaningless blur. Not only can newborns perceive contours, such as the border between their mother's hairline and forehead, but they also have some color vision (Adams, Maurer, & Davis, 1986). Moreover, infants can distinguish different tastes and smells, as shown by their visible reactions to such stimuli as sweet and sour tastes.

Although their vision is extremely limited compared with normal adult vision, infants can see well enough to mimic adult facial expressions, as shown in Figure 9.10 (Field, 1990; Meltzoff & Moore, 1989; Reissland, 1988). This imitative ability not only demonstrates the infant's ability to see but also shows that infants can make the connection between vision and the sense of proprioception. *Proprioception* is the ability to sense the position of parts of one's own body in space. Your ability to tell where your hands are right now is an example of pro-

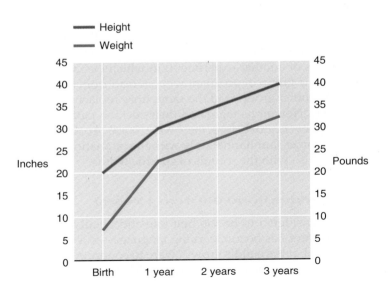

FIGURE 9.8
Increases in height and weight occur at a rapid rate during the first three years of life.

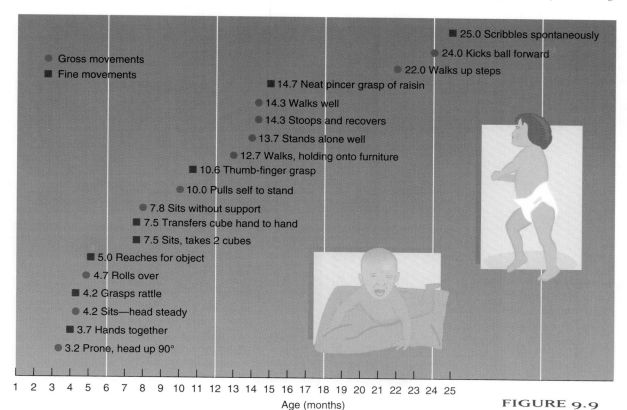

● Gross movements
■ Fine movements

■ 25.0 Scribbles spontaneously
● 24.0 Kicks ball forward
● 22.0 Walks up steps
■ 14.7 Neat pincer grasp of raisin
● 14.3 Walks well
● 14.3 Stoops and recovers
● 13.7 Stands alone well
● 12.7 Walks, holding onto furniture
■ 10.6 Thumb-finger grasp
● 10.0 Pulls self to stand
● 7.8 Sits without support
■ 7.5 Transfers cube hand to hand
■ 7.5 Sits, takes 2 cubes
■ 5.0 Reaches for object
● 4.7 Rolls over
■ 4.2 Grasps rattle
● 4.2 Sits—head steady
■ 3.7 Hands together
● 3.2 Prone, head up 90°

1 2 3 4 5 6 7 8 9 10 11 12 13 14 15 16 17 18 19 20 21 22 23 24 25

Age (months)

FIGURE 9.9

The course of motor development over the first two years of life. Numbers indicate the average age in months at which these abilities appear.

prioception. Infants who imitate a facial expression are not only able to see the adult's face but, in order to imitate it, must also be able to sense the positions of parts of their own face.

In addition to their visual proprioceptive abilities, infants can discriminate between different speech sounds (Bertonici et al., 1988). This ability has been demonstrated in infants only a few days old by using an operant conditioning procedure that capitalizes on *habituation,* the fact that an infant's willingness to work to hear a sound decreases as that sound is repeated. An infant sucks on a nipple to hear a recording of the syllable *ba*; eventually, he becomes habituated to hearing the sound and slows his sucking. When this decrease in sucking rate occurs, the experimenter changes the syllable so that the infant hears *da* when he sucks. If the infant were unable to distinguish the new *da* sound from the old *ba* sound, his sucking rate would continue to decrease. A decrease is not, however, what is observed: changing the sound causes an increase in sucking, indicating that the infant perceives the difference between *ba* and *da.*

The amazing thing about infant perception is not just that some capacities are present at birth, but that these capacities develop so rapidly that they almost reach adult levels before the infant is a year old. Detail vision improves to almost adult levels in 9-month-olds, and infants are able to perceive depth and three-dimensional forms by 4 months of age (Fox et al., 1980; Held, Birch, & Gwiazda, 1980; Kellman & Short, 1987; Shea et al., 1980). This achievement is remarkable in light of the sophisticated nature of depth and three-dimensional perception that we saw in Chapter 4.

Equally impressive is the infant's ability to go beyond such basic perceptual capacities as detail, color, and depth perception. Six-month-old infants know that male faces go with male voices and female faces go with female voices (Francis & McCroy, 1983), and 6- to 7-month-old infants can recognize a face

8 LANGUAGE

6 LEARNING

FIGURE 9.10
The fact that 2- to 3-week-old infants can imitate adults' facial expressions indicates that they can see the adults' faces and that they can sense the positions of parts of their own faces.

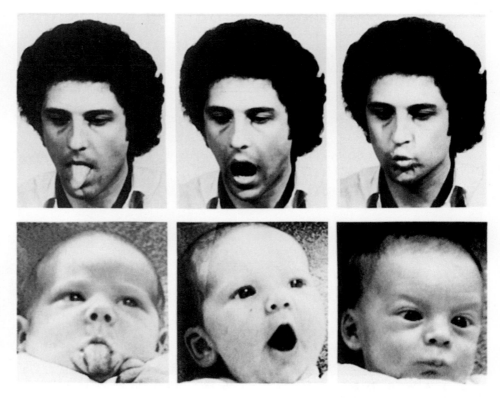

from different viewpoints (Fagan, 1976). This development of perceptual abilities to near-adult levels during the last half of the first year of life is important, not only because these abilities enable infants to experience more of the perceptual world, but also because they prepare them for the cognitive development that becomes increasingly important as they approach their first birthday.

Childhood (3 Years to Puberty)

After the first years' spurt in physical development, the child settles down to a steady rate of growth of 2 to 3 inches and 4 to 6 pounds every year during childhood—the period between 3 years of age and the sexual changes associated with puberty. Between 3 and 6, children lose the roundness of infancy and toddlerhood and take on a more slender, athletic appearance, as body proportions become increasingly adultlike (Figure 9.11).

Along with physical growth come improved motor skills. For example, a 3-year-old can walk in a straight line but can't stop suddenly. A 5-year-old can run fast, like an adult, and can stop and execute turns. Skills that develop later include skipping (age 6), the ability to balance on one foot (age 7), and such skills as running, jumping, and throwing that are important for participation in games and sports (Cratty, 1979).

Adolescence

> *I'm sixteen years old,*
> *And every day something happens to me . . .*
> *I am special*
> *I am special*
> *Please, God, please—*
> *Don't let me be normal!*

Luisa, in *The Fantasticks*, by Tom Jones and Harvey Schmidt

Head size as proportion of total body length

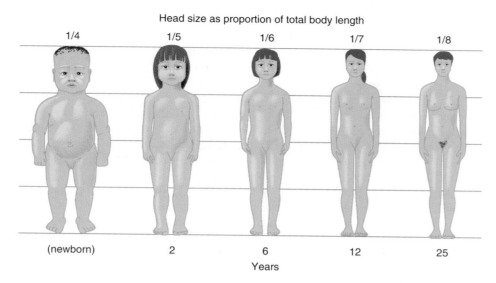

| 1/4 | 1/5 | 1/6 | 1/7 | 1/8 |

(newborn)   2   6   12   25

Years

FIGURE 9.11

As people develop, their body proportions change, with their head size becoming smaller relative to the rest of the body.

The word **adolescence** is derived from the Latin verb *adolescere,* which means "to grow up" or "to grow into maturity." Adolescence begins with the onset of **puberty,** the period during which the reproductive organs become functional, and its overall course is marked by physical changes that occur more rapidly than during any other time of life (with the exception of the prenatal period and the period immediately following birth). These changes include rapid increases in height for boys and girls, increases in body fat for girls, and numerous changes related to sexual development. Boys' testes and penis grow larger, and ejaculation becomes possible; hair appears on the face and in the armpits and genital area. Girls produce hair in the armpits and genital area; their hips widen and their breasts grow. A dramatic change for girls is menstruation: **menarche,** the first menstruation, is often considered the mark into adult sexual status.

    One thing that makes adolescence a unique period in life is that the rapid physical changes that occur are actively observed by the individuals themselves. This fact is stated by Tanner (1971), who observes that

> For the majority of young persons, the years from twelve to sixteen are the most eventful ones of their lives so far as their growth and development is concerned. Admittedly during fetal life and the first year or two after birth, developments occurred still faster . . . but the subject himself was not the fascinated, charmed or horrified spectator that watches the developments, or lack of developments, of adolescence (p. 907).

The rapid developments that mark adolescence don't occur at exactly the same time for everyone. One 14-year-old boy may have adult characteristics while his peer is still clearly a boy. This disparity in maturation is accentuated by the fact that girls mature, on the average, two years sooner than boys, so that 12-year-old girls can be more mature physically than boys two or three years older.

    The effects of the timing of physical maturity are a good illustration of the interaction between the various aspects of development. Boys often like being early maturers because being larger and physically stronger not only makes them more popular with the already matured girls but also enhances their athletic prowess and status among their peers (Petersen, 1988). Thus, biological development can significantly influence social development. In fact, there is evidence that individual differences in the maturation of boys can have effects that persist into adulthood. A longitudinal study that followed a group of males from elementary school age into their 40s found that boys who matured early and had

These two children are both in the fifth grade, but the difference in their physical maturation is striking.

more masculine physiques at an early age became more responsible and sociable adults who easily made a good impression on others. The late maturers were more talkative and more flexible (Jones, 1965). What does this mean? One possibility is that the difference in the way early and the late maturers experience their high school years affects their personality development. This idea is supported by interviews in which men who were late maturers reported memories of being inept, shy, and rejected by their peers in high school. There was, however, some advantage to being a late maturer, because they became more playful adults who found it easier to cope with ambiguous situations. Perhaps these late-maturing males developed those qualities as they coped with their early social hardships.

Whereas boys often see early maturation as positive, girls often have the opposite reaction. One early-maturing girl said that she "didn't like being early. A lot of my friends didn't understand." Another girl confessed, "I tried to hide it. I was embarrassed and ashamed" (Petersen, 1987, p. 30). This unhappiness about being different is, however, transitory: by eighth or ninth grade, the other girls catch up.

However, even when everyone has reached the same level of maturation, girls have other reasons to be unhappy about their newfound maturity. For one thing, once girls mature they find themselves saddled with adults' expectations that they engage in traditional gender-role behavior (Basow, 1992). More value is placed on being feminine and ladylike, less on participating in the "male" activities that many girls enjoyed during childhood. In addition, girls often suffer more severe restrictions than boys, such as earlier curfews.

The pressure on girls does not, however, come only from parents. The culture of junior and senior high school places a premium on female attractiveness. Attractive girls are more popular and get more dates, whereas attractiveness isn't as important for boys (Berscheid et al., 1971). There is also pressure to be thin, so many girls are unhappy with their bodies (Offer, Ostrov, & Howard, 1981). In a survey of adolescents in which teenagers affirmed many positive, upbeat statements about themselves, girls' responses to statements about their bodies stand out as exceptions. Only 51% answered "Yes" to the statement "I am proud of my body," compared with 80% of the boys. While 42% of the girls said they frequently felt ugly or unattractive, only 21% of the boys felt this way (Offer, Ostrov, & Howard, 1981).

You may have noticed that our discussion of the physical changes of adolescence has taken a decidedly cognitive and behavioral turn. It is clear that physical changes have consequences both for how adolescents think about themselves and for how others view them. These thoughts, in turn, lead to behaviors. For example, unhappiness with their bodies leads most girls to diet. Some diet so excessively that they are diagnosed as having eating disorders such as *anorexia nervosa*, in which dieting results in weights 20% or more below normal, or *bulimia*, in which binge eating is followed by vomiting to avoid gaining weight. (We explore eating disorders further in Chapter 11, "Motivation.") Thus, the physical changes of adolescence affect more than just appearance—they also affect thinking and behavior.

11   MOTIVATION

Adulthood

Until very recently adulthood was largely "uncharted territory" for developmental psychologists. Most limited their attention to the changes completed by the end of adolescence, and even today most developmental psychologists study infancy or childhood. A few focus on aging and the elderly, but even fewer are concerned with the broad age range of 20 to 65 years that lies in between (Levinson, 1990).

It has, however, become more and more difficult to ignore adulthood, if only because of sheer numbers. As people's life expectancies increase, adults ac-

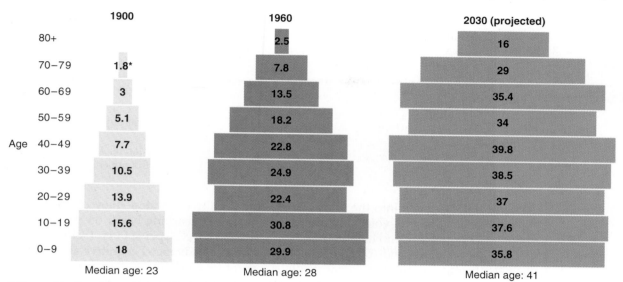

Age	1900	1960	2030 (projected)
80+		2.5	16
70–79	1.8*	7.8	29
60–69	3	13.5	35.4
50–59	5.1	18.2	34
40–49	7.7	22.8	39.8
30–39	10.5	24.9	38.5
20–29	13.9	22.4	37
10–19	15.6	30.8	37.6
0–9	18	29.9	35.8
	Median age: 23	Median age: 28	Median age: 41

* Those older than 79 are included in the figure for those aged 70–79

FIGURE 9.12
Changing population patterns in the United States. Each bar indicates the number of people in each age group (in millions). Early in the century younger people dominated the population, creating a pyramidal distribution. By the year 2030, higher life expectancies and lower birth rates will have created a much larger population of older people, creating a more rectangular distribution.

count for a greater and greater proportion of the population. In 1800 one-half of the population was older than 16; now more than three-fourths of the population is. The distribution of age groups in our society used to resemble a pyramid, with a large number of young people supporting a smaller population of older people. But by the year 2030, the distribution will resemble a rectangle, with more people over 70 than under 10 (Figure 9.12).

A key developmental task in adulthood is adapting to the gradual physical changes that aging brings. People reach their peak of physical power in their middle 20s; after that, physical ability slowly decreases. For example, cardiac output decreases about 1% per year beginning at about age 20 (Kohn, 1977). After 30, strength begins to decline, with decreases in muscle mass becoming noticeable by the 40s. Deaths due to heart disease, cancer, and stroke increase appreciably in the 50s. The incidence of arthritis, which makes movement more difficult, increases in the 60s and 70s. Sensory abilities, such as the ability to taste, to see details, and to perceive speech, all begin declining in the 40s but decline more rapidly in the 50s and 60s.

This description of gradual physical decline may make it seem that our bodies begin falling apart shortly after adolescence. It is true that no one yet knows how to control the aging process, yet modern health care, improved diet, and increased physical fitness have enabled many people in our society to enjoy a vigorous adult life span until they reach their 70s or—increasingly—80s (Labouvie-Vief & Blanchard-Fields, 1982). Moreover, the declines that do occur as adulthood progresses are generally so gradual that they are often difficult to notice. And when changes do become noticeable, it is often possible to compensate for them. Thus, as people's ability to read small print begins to erode in their 40s, reading glasses can eliminate that "deficit." Furthermore, physical decline can be slowed by exercise (Emery & Blumenthal, 1991; Pfaffenbarger et al., 1986; Thomas & Rutledge, 1986). A person who works out a few times a week can rival the physical condition of a younger, more sedentary person.

While it may not be literally true that "you're only as old as you feel," the physical changes of adulthood *are* inextricably entwined with psychological factors. People who take good care of their bodies and deal with physical changes constructively often age more slowly than those who neglect their bodies or adopt a fatalistic attitude about physical decline. As comedian Groucho Marx

For many people, vigorous physical activity continues well into old age.

said, "Old age is simply a question of mind over matter. If you don't mind, it doesn't matter."

Cognitive Development

Our life is what our thoughts make it.

Marcus Aurelius (121–180)
Roman emperor

Infants come into the world with some cognitive abilities—they can recognize their mother's voice and are capable of simple learning based on principles of conditioning and habituation (Bjorklund, 1989; DeCasper & Fifer, 1980)—but our survival depends on the development of more advanced cognitive abilities. We begin our study of cognitive development by considering the work of Jean Piaget (1896–1980), a Swiss psychologist whose observations of children led to ideas that have greatly influenced the field of developmental psychology.

Piaget's Theory of Cognitive Development

Soon after receiving his Ph.D., Piaget started work in the laboratory of Theodore Simon, developer of one of the first intelligence tests. Simon gave Piaget the task of testing Parisian elementary school students. As he was scoring the students' tests, Piaget noticed that students of the same age usually made the same kinds of mistakes. His curiosity aroused, Piaget began interviewing the students to determine why they chose the incorrect answers. The results of this questioning led him to what was to become his life's work—getting inside children's minds to discover how they think. Over the course of his career Piaget would write more than 35 books on how children develop intellectually.

Piaget's investigations into children's thought processes combined the behavioral and cognitive levels of analysis. He observed children's behavior and then interpreted his observations in terms of what was going on in their minds. By respecting children's uniqueness instead of seeing them as imperfect, miniature adults, Piaget was able to show that children's thinking has its own distinctive qualities.

We can appreciate Piaget's interview method by considering this segment of a conversation between Piaget and a 5-year-old child.

Jean Piaget, whose pioneering observations of children's behavior led to his influential theory of cognitive development.

> *Piaget:* Where does the dream come from?
> *Child:* I think you sleep so well that you dream.
> *Piaget:* Does it come from us or from outside?
> *Child:* From outside.
> *Piaget:* What do we dream with?
> *Child:* I don't know.
> *Piaget:* With the hands? . . . with nothing?
> *Child:* Yes, with nothing.
> *Piaget:* When you are in bed and you dream, where is the dream?
> *Child:* In my bed, under the blanket. I don't really know. If it was in my stomach the bones would be in the way and I shouldn't see it.
> *Piaget:* Is the dream there when you sleep?
> *Child:* Yes, it is in my bed beside me (Piaget, 1929, p. 97).

In addition to interviewing children, Piaget observed them carefully. Such observations provided Piaget with a rich source of information about children's behavior that formed the basis for his theory of cognitive development. But Piaget's work was rejected by the behaviorists, because they felt that his observational methods did not meet the rigorous scientific standards of their own learning experiments. Piaget's work was not accepted in the United States until the 1960s, when a book about his research was published (Flavell, 1963) and the climate within psychology had become more open to his observational approach.

Once Piaget's work took hold in the United States, developmental psychologists enthusiastically embraced many of his ideas. One of the appealing things about Piaget's approach was that he saw children as learning about the world by *interacting* with it. Piaget believed that as children encounter new situations and information, they eventually come to understand them, thereby developing more sophisticated ways of thinking about the world. One of the concepts Piaget used to describe development is the idea of the **scheme** (sometimes translated as *schema*)—an organized pattern of actions that guides children's interactions with the environment.

Schemes and their development.   Schemes typically observable in infants are those for sucking and grasping. The sucking scheme comprises all the actions the child engages in when sucking, and the grasping scheme comprises the sequence of movements that the child uses to grasp objects. Both schemes are primitive and rather simple. However, schemes are not static. As the infant gains more experience with the world his schemes can change by means of what Piaget called **adaptation,** which consists of *assimilation* and *accommodation.*

Assimilation is the process by which children apply existing schemes to new situations. For example, a child might apply her sucking scheme, first elicited by the mother's breast, to a new stimulus—her own thumb—by adjusting the way she holds her thumb so she can suck on it. However, sometimes attempts to apply existing schemes to new uses will result in failure. For example, when an infant first tries to apply his grasping scheme—which has been used primarily to grab his blanket—to the task of grasping his rattle, he may be unsuccessful. It is here that accommodation comes in. **Accommodation** is the process of modifying the existing scheme to fit new challenges. Thus, through trial and error the infant accommodates his blanket grasping so that it also works for picking up the rattle. Piaget underscored the close relationship between assimilation and accommodation when he stated that "there is no assimilation without accommodation" (Piaget, 1970). The two work together to change schemes so that they will become applicable to a wider range of uses.

An example of how an older child's scheme might evolve through the complementary actions of assimilation and accommodation is the process by which the child might learn subtraction. What happens when a child who has developed a scheme to solve simple subtraction problems such as 7 minus 3 is confronted with a more complex problem, such as 11 minus 5 (Figure 9.13)? If the child doesn't know the technique of "borrowing from the tens column," she may erroneously apply the rule that worked for 7 minus 3 (subtract the smaller number from the larger one) and conclude, by subtracting 1 from 5 in the far right column, that 11 minus 5 equals 4, or perhaps 14. This initial attempt to apply an existing rule to a new problem is an example of assimilation.

After it becomes clear that the child has made an error, accommodation comes into play to help her change the way she thinks about subtraction problems. Once instruction in the technique of "borrowing" has broadened the child's knowledge of how to subtract, her original subtraction scheme has become *accommodated* to the new situation. She now has a subtraction scheme that works for a wider variety of problems.

Another process that helps children adapt their schemes to new situations is **organization,** the formation of more complex schemes by combining simple ones. For example, the infant's initial sucking scheme is later combined with looking and grasping schemes to form a nursing scheme. Complex behaviors, according to Piaget, are the result of this organization of smaller parts into larger units.

FIGURE 9.13
The process of learning how to solve subtraction problems that involve "borrowing from the tens column" illustrates how assimilation and accommodation combine to create new skills from old ones.

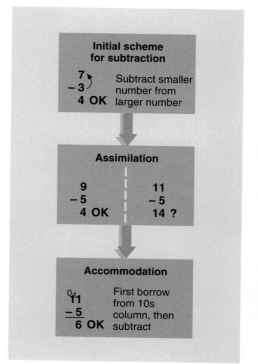

As this 9-month-old learns to walk, he simultaneously learns about properties of the environment.

FIGURE 9.14

Hiding an object from an infant who has not yet developed object permanence causes the infant to act as if the object no longer exists.

The proposal that adaptation and organization are the mechanisms underlying cognitive development was one outcome of Piaget's extensive observations of children's behavior. Another was his proposal that children's thinking develops through four distinct stages as they mature from birth through adolescence. Piaget proposed a stage theory of development because he felt development was a process in which a series of *qualitative* changes take place.

In other words, children develop different *ways* of thinking as they grow older. To appreciate what this means, we need to look at the nature of children's thinking at each stage.

The sensorimotor stage (birth to 2 years).   In 1936 Piaget published *The Origins of Intelligence in Children,* a book that focused on the first two years of life. The title reflected Piaget's belief that during those first two years children develop the intellectual abilities that differentiate humans from lower forms of animals. He called this period the **sensorimotor stage,** because of the rapid development of the child's sensory and motor capabilities during the period.

The rapid cognitive development that occurs during the first years of life is every bit as impressive as the simultaneous rapid physical development. This becomes clear when we compare the newborn and the 2-year-old. At birth, infants have only a limited ability to think. They respond reflexively to a variety of stimuli—for example, newborns turn their heads in response to a brush on their cheek—and are capable of simple learning, based on classical and operant conditioning. In contrast, 2-year-olds have learned to use language, to pretend during play, and to solve problems such as finding out-of-sight objects or retrieving an out-of-reach object with a stick.

Piaget emphasized the idea that children are active participants in their own development, an insight that has led developmental psychologists to describe infants as "little scientists." For example, infants may carry out "experiments" by manipulating objects in their crib, in which they determine that thin objects placed in the correct orientation can be slipped through the crib bars.

By the end of the sensorimotor stage, infants begin to understand basic principles of space, time, and causality (Piaget, 1954). A young infant watching a toy train disappear into a long tunnel would not be surprised if the train instantly emerged at the other end. A 2-year-old, however, would be surprised, because she understands that if the train continues to traverse the tunnel at the same speed, it is impossible for it to instantly emerge at the other end.

During the sensorimotor stage children also develop the concept of **object permanence**—the realization that an object still exists when it is not being perceived (Figure 9.14). The absence of object permanence is illustrated by an 8-month-old's reaction when a favorite toy she is playing with falls out of sight behind a fold in a sheet. Rather than search for the toy, she acts as if it no longer exists. The concept of object permanence develops slowly, but before their second year most children know that a hidden object still exists; they are able to represent it *mentally,* even though they can't see it. This is an example of the child's developing ability to think symbolically.

Another example of symbolic thinking is language, a skill that begins developing during the second year. The 2-year-old's ability to use words like *dog* or *cat* as symbols for real animals is an important step in the development of the ability to think symbolically. This ability ushers in Piaget's next stage of development, the preoperational stage.

The preoperational stage (2 to 7 years).   One of the most impressive accomplishments of the **preoperational stage** is the child's continuing mastery of language. But even as children become adept at manipulating the symbols of language during this stage, their thought processes often lead them to incorrect conclusions about the world around them. This stage, therefore, has the interesting quality of being described by researchers almost entirely in terms of abilities that the child lacks or of deficiencies in the way the child thinks. Among these "deficiencies" are *egocentrism*, *lack of conservation*, and *animism*.

Egocentrism.   Preoperational children are **egocentric;** that is, they interpret the world in terms of their own vantage point, without taking another person's point of view into account. It would not be unusual, for example, for a young child to point to a disabled person and loudly exclaim, "Look at that man—he can't walk." The embarrassed parent may not realize that the child's "bad manners" simply reflect the fact that the child doesn't understand how his comments can affect others.

Children's egocentrism also places them at the center of the universe—an attitude exemplified by statements such as "The moon is following me home" or "The sun is rising for me." Consider this age group's performance on a task called the *three-mountain problem*. A child presented with this problem views a display like the one in Figure 9.15 from one position, while a doll is placed in each of the other positions. The child's task is to indicate which view the doll is seeing, either by picking a drawing of the correct view or by constructing the doll's view with cardboard cutouts. Preoperational children typically pick the view they themselves are seeing, irrespective of where the doll is. Not until the age of 9 or 10—after the preoperational period is over—can a child solve the problem (Inhelder & Piaget, 1955).

Lack of conservation.   If you were to pour water from a drinking glass into a narrow beaker, it would be obvious to you that the same amount of water is in the beaker as was in the glass, even though the water rises to a much higher level in the narrow beaker. Similarly, you realize that molding a ball of clay into a long, cylindrical shape does not change the amount of clay you have. This realization that changing an object's shape doesn't change its volume is called **conservation** of volume.

When preoperational children are presented with a test of conservation, they react differently than adults or older children do. In a typical conservation task the child is shown two identical containers filled to the same level with water (Figure 9.16). One of the containers is then poured into a taller, thinner container, and the child is asked whether the two contain the same or different amounts of water. Preoperational children presented with the conservation task

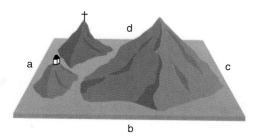

FIGURE 9.15
In the preoperational stage of development, children viewing the three-mountain stimulus from position b cannot indicate what a doll placed in positions a, c, or d would see.

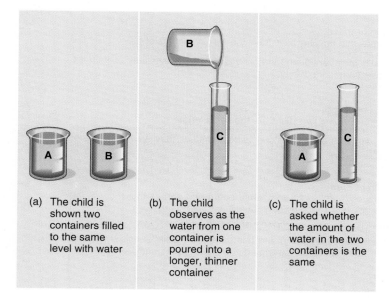

(a) The child is shown two containers filled to the same level with water

(b) The child observes as the water from one container is poured into a longer, thinner container

(c) The child is asked whether the amount of water in the two containers is the same

FIGURE 9.16
When preoperational children are asked whether containers A and C contain the same or different amounts of water, they usually say container C contains more, even though they saw the water being poured from B to C. This response indicates a lack of understanding of conservation of volume.

are likely to say that the two containers contain different amounts of water (they usually say the taller one contains more), illustrating the absence of the concept of conservation.

Animism.   In their thinking, preoperational children exhibit **animism,** the attribution of conscious life to inanimate objects. They believe these objects can experience the same thoughts and emotions that we can. Consider, for example, two conversations with preoperational children:

Child: Oh, the sun is moving. It's walking like us . . .
Piaget: Where is it walking?
Child: Why, on the sky. The sky's hard. It's made of clouds (Piaget, 1962, p. 252).

Piaget: Is a stone alive?
Child: Yes.
Piaget: Why?
Child: It moves.
Piaget: How does it move?
Child: By rolling (Piaget, 1929, p. 199).

Although preoperational children are egocentric in their thinking, lack the concept of conservation, and see inanimate things as alive, a great deal of development takes place during this stage. Between the ages of 2 and 7 children's ability to use language grows dramatically. At the same time, their thought processes are changing. For example, at the beginning of the preoperational stage, children believe that all objects are alive; later they believe that only objects that move are alive; and by late in this period they begin to restrict their definition of life to objects that adults consider living.

We close our discussion of this stage of development by asking why preoperational children fail when faced with, for example, the three-mountain prob-

FIGURE 9.17
Children in the concrete operations stage can solve a number of different conservation problems. Conservation ability occurs when the child becomes aware that a property remains constant even when other changes are made. A child who has mastered conservation would, for example, realize that changing the length of the row of marbles does not change the number of marbles in the row.

	Task	Approximate age of mastery
	Conservation of number The child agrees that each row contains the same number of marbles	6–7
	One row is spread out and the child is asked whether the rows contain the same or different numbers of marbles	
	Conservation of mass The child agrees that the clay balls have the same amounts of clay	7–8
	One of the balls is flattened, and the child is asked whether they contain the same or different amounts of clay	
	Conservation of length The child agrees that the two sticks are the same length	7–8
	One stick is moved, and the child is asked whether they are the same or different lengths	
	Conservation of area The child sees colored blocks on a white board and agrees that there is the same amount of white space on each board	8–9
	The blocks are moved on one of the boards and the child is asked whether the amount of white space on the two boards is the same or different	

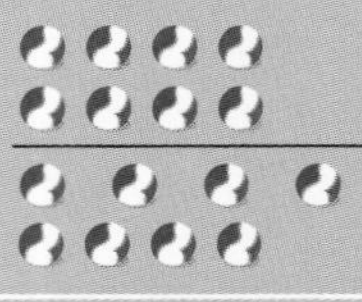

lem or the conservation problem. Piaget would answer that these children lack the necessary *mental operations*. For example, the conservation of volume problem requires carrying out the mental operation of taking into account both the height *and* the width of the containers. Once children can perform these operations, they have entered Piaget's third stage, concrete operations.

The concrete operations stage (7 to 11 years).   Although preoperational children make great strides in thinking between 2 and 7 years of age, they rarely think logically; that is, they don't use general rules to guide their thinking. In contrast, children in the **concrete operations stage** develop the ability to think logically. Logical thinking becomes possible when a child has acquired **cognitive operations,** ways of mentally transforming information. When the child can transform information, a number of basic abilities emerge:

   • *Reversibility*: **Reversibility** is achieved when the child realizes that situations can be reversed to a previous state. For example, pouring part of the water out of a jar can be reversed by pouring the water back into the jar.

   • *Decentration*: Instead of focusing on just one aspect of an object or event, the child can simultaneously focus attention on several attributes and realize that those attributes can be separated. The child realizes, for example, that although a balloon may be large, it can also be light. Piaget called this ability to focus on multiple attributes **decentration.**

   • *Conservation*: The child responds correctly to a number of conservation tasks (Figure 9.17). The realization that pouring water from one container to another doesn't change the amount of water requires both reversible thinking (reasoning that if the water were poured back to its original container it would look the same as before), and decentration (taking into account both the height and width of the containers).

   • *Seriation*: **Seriation** is the ability to arrange objects in order along quantitative dimensions such as weight, length, or size. A concrete operational child can arrange a series of dolls in order of height, whereas a preoperational child might alternate tall and short dolls, or arrange them more randomly (Figure 9.18).

   • *Transitivity*: **Transitivity** is the ability to recognize relations among a number of ordered objects. According to the transitivity principle, if Susan is taller than Ruth and Ruth is taller than Grace, then Susan must also be taller than Grace.

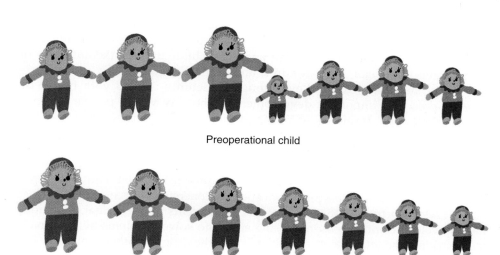

Preoperational child

Concrete-operational child

FIGURE 9.18
Seriation. When children are asked to arrange dolls in order of height, the preoperational child only partially succeeds, whereas the concrete operational child arranges all of the dolls in the correct order.

A visit to an aquarium exposes a child to tangible objects, which children in the concrete operations stage can understand. Abstract thinking comes later, in the formal operations stage, when adolescents are able to explore hypothetical ideas such as those that might arise in a mock government workshop.

Adolescents' rebellion and questioning of social norms reflect an important advance in their thinking ability.

Along with acquiring these cognitive operations, children in the concrete operations stage exhibit two other significant changes in their way of thinking.

• *Diminished egocentrism*: The child's thinking becomes less egocentric. The child can now envision other people's points of view in order to solve the three-mountain problem.

• *A shift in moral thinking*: The concrete operational child approaches moral judgments differently than the preoperational child does. Whereas the preoperational child tends to base moral judgments on the *outcome* of a person's actions (breaking ten of mother's best plates accidentally is more "wrong" than breaking a single plate on purpose), the concrete operational child relies more on *intentions* (breaking the single plate on purpose is more serious).

It is clear that concrete operational children, in developing the ability to think logically, have made great strides compared with the preoperational child. However, according to Piaget, there are still limitations to the way concrete operational children think. Although they can think logically, their thinking tends to be based on *concrete objects* (hence the term *concrete operations*), such as the amount of water in a glass or sticks of different lengths. Children in this stage have difficulty thinking about abstract and hypothetical ideas. This type of thinking develops in Piaget's last stage, which coincides with the beginnings of adolescence.

Formal operations stage (11 to 15 years). One of the most obvious characteristics of adolescence is rebellion. Adolescents often begin to question many of the basic ideals and values they learned as young children, from the authority of their parents to societal norms for dress and even hair color.

These new ways of thinking, though sometimes viewed with horror by parents, reflect an important development in the way young people think. A characteristic of the **formal operations stage** is the ability to think abstractly and hypothetically. This ability leads to abstract thoughts regarding issues such as morality, justice, and the adolescent's own place in the world. Dreaming about the future, imagining different occupational roles, debating moral and philosophical issues, and interpreting literature in symbolic terms all require manipulating concepts that are detached from specific, concrete instances.

In addition to hypothetical thought, adolescents in the formal operations stage develop scientific reasoning—the ability to solve problems by systematically varying one attribute of a problem while holding the others constant. For example, in the *pendulum problem* (Figure 9.19), subjects are shown a pendulum made of a metal weight tied to the end of a string. They are then given different sizes of weights and different lengths of string and are asked to find out which factor determines the speed at which the weight swings to the top of its arc. Is it the length of the string? The size of the metal weight? The height at which the weight is released?

Most subjects in the formal operations period determine the correct answer to the pendulum problem (the length of the string is what matters) by systematically varying the weight, the string length, and the height at which the weight is released. For example, they might test for the effect of weight by trying a number of different weights while keeping the string length constant and releasing the weights at the same height. This systematic way of approaching a problem is an advance over the methods of concrete operational children. The latter usually change the weight, length, and height in a haphazard way, thereby making it difficult to arrive at a correct solution (Inhelder & Piaget, 1955/1958).

As we have already noted, the adolescent's ability to think abstractly and hypothetically can lead to questioning parental values and to rebellious behavior. This is an example of how a cognitive change can affect social behavior. Another example is the phenomenon of adolescent egocentrism.

When we described childhood egocentrism, we saw that preoperational children may not only think that the moon is following them as they walk at night, but also find it difficult to take another person's point of view. When childhood egocentrism fades, children come to realize that everything in the world hasn't been created for their personal benefit, and they become able to take another person's point of view.

But egocentrism reappears in a different guise during the formal operational stage in the form of **adolescent egocentrism**—adolescents' belief that other people share their own preoccupation with themselves (Elkind, 1967). The emergence of this belief can be traced to adolescents' newfound capacity to think not only about the nature of their own thought processes, but also about the thought processes of others. Preoccupied with their own appearance and behavior, adolescents imagine how they look to others and assume that others are always watching and evaluating them. In this way, adolescents' ability to consider others' points of view paradoxically leads to extreme self-consciousness and the creation of an *imaginary audience* (Elkind, 1967).

Whereas heightened self-consciousness usually fades by age 15 or 16, another type of egocentric behavior, the creation of a personal fable, lasts longer. The **personal fable** is the idea that one's own experiences and thoughts are unique. Adolescents believe that no one else could ever have felt the pangs of love or the shattering disappointments that they feel. This type of thinking declines somewhat in adulthood but may never completely vanish. Even adults may think their experiences are unlike any one else's.

These ideas about how adolescents' social behavior can be affected by the way they think illustrate the far-reaching implications of Piaget's description of cognitive development (summarized in Table 9.3). And the vast amount of research that has been carried out on many aspects of Piaget's theory attest to his influence on developmental psychology. But how do current developmental psychologists evaluate Piaget's theory? We consider this question next.

FIGURE 9.19

The pendulum problem. Given several sizes of weights and lengths of string, children are asked to figure out what determines the amount of time it takes for the pendulum to swing from one side to the other. Formal operational children solve this problem by systematically varying the amount of weight, the string length, and the height at which the weight is released.

Evaluating Piaget

There is no question that Piaget's observations changed the face of developmental psychology. Before Piaget, developmental psychologists were interested primarily in cataloging children's abilities without regard to the thinking processes underlying them. After Piaget, psychologists saw even young children as being active problem solvers and became interested in studying how children of all ages think.

Though Piaget's ideas have been extremely influential, his whole system is not uncritically accepted. Ironically enough—since it was Piaget who cham-

TABLE 9.3
Piaget's stages of child development

Stage	Characteristics
Sensorimotor (birth to 2 years)	Learns about world through assimilation and accommodation Carries out `experiments" as "little scientist" Develops concept of object permanence Begins to acquire language
Preoperational (2 to 7 years)	Develops language Exhibits egocentrism (has difficulty with three-mountain problem) Lacks concept of conservation Exhibits animistic beliefs
Concrete operational (7 to 11 years)	Develops a number of cognitive operations: (1) reversibility; (2) decentration; (3) conservation; (4) seriation; (5) transitivity Learns to take another's point of view (decrease in egocentrism)
Formal operations (11 to 15 years)	Shifts to more complex moral thinking Develops the ability to think abstractly and hypothetically Develops the ability to reason scientifically Displays adolescent egocentrism (imaginary audience and personal fable)

pioned the idea that children have cognitive capacities far beyond what they had previously been given credit for—many researchers feel that Piaget underestimated children's abilities. For example, the ability to conserve volume, which Piaget had used as one of the criteria for entry into the concrete operations stage at about 7 or 8 years of age, has been demonstrated in children as young as 4 years old (Botvin & Murray, 1975).

One way researchers have demonstrated the presence of cognitive capacities prior to the ages reported by Piaget is by using special training procedures. For example, Robert Siegler, Diane Liebert, and Robert Liebert (1973) showed that 10-year-olds, who would be classified as being in the concrete operations stage by Piaget, can solve the pendulum problem if they are first trained in the basic scientific procedure of varying one factor while holding the others constant. The fact that children as young as 10 can solve this problem after some training contradicts Piaget's assertion that children of this age are not "cognitively ready" for such problems.

Another way researchers have uncovered cognitive capacities at an early age is by using special testing procedures. By testing children on the three-mountain problem with a model of a scene more familiar to children, and having the "Sesame Street" character Grover view it from different angles as he travels around it in his car, Helene Borke (1975) was able to show that children as young as 3 or 4 have some ability to take another person's point of view. Young children are apparently not as egocentric as Piaget thought. Additional evidence supporting the idea that young children are not completely egocentric is that 4-year-olds talk differently to 2-year-olds than they do to adults (Gelman & Shatz, 1978).

Criticizing Piaget for underestimating children's abilities may sound like simply quibbling over the exact time that children's capacities emerge. But the implications of these research results go deeper. They call into question the idea that development proceeds from one discrete stage to the next. For example, consider the finding that 3- or 4-year-olds can take another person's point of view when tested appropriately. Piaget stated that this ability doesn't emerge until the child acquires the necessary mental operations in the concrete operations stage, which begins at 7 years of age. An alternative way of conceptualizing the development of this ability is that it develops gradually, beginning at an early age. When the child is 3 or 4 some evidence of this ability can be found, with the right testing procedure. Later—by 7 or 8—the ability is better developed and therefore easier to demonstrate. The course of development according to this conception does not proceed in discrete stages but unfolds gradually.

Another target for criticism in Piaget's theory is his treatment of formal operational thinking. Piaget saw formal operational thinking as the end of a natural progression of development reached by all young adults. However, cross-cultural studies indicate that many adults in non-Western cultures are not capable of formal operational reasoning (see the Follow-Through, "Cross-Cultural Perspectives on Piaget," at the end of this chapter), and other research indicates that even in Western culture many adults do not reach the formal operations stage (Muuss, 1982; Neimark, 1982). Also, as we will see when we discuss cognitive development in adulthood, there is evidence that some adults reach a stage that goes beyond formal operational thinking.

Thus, critics of Piaget contend that some people never reach his "final" stage and that some surpass it. Others criticize the idea of stages in general. These researchers, who feel that cognitive ability unfolds gradually rather than in discrete stages, have analyzed children's thinking using the information-processing approach.

The Information-Processing Approach

As we discussed in Chapters 7 and 8, the information-processing approach to cognition sees the brain as a processor and transformer of information. For example, incoming information is processed by the memory system as it passes through the three memory stages: sensory memory, short-term memory, and long-term memory. This view of how the brain operates has also been applied to cognitive development.

7   MEMORY

There is no one information-processing theory of development. A large number of researchers are, however, using the information-processing approach to study mental processes in children, in part because many psychologists feel that some of the mechanisms proposed by Piaget are too vague to be useful. This sentiment was expressed by David Klahr as follows:

> For 40 years now we have had assimilation and accommodation, the mysterious and shadowy forces of equilibration, the Batman and Robin of the developmental process. What are they? How do they do their thing? Why is it after all this time, we know no more about them than when they first sprang on the scene? What we need is a way to get beyond vague verbal statements of the nature of the developmental process (1982, p. 80).

To illustrate how psychologists have tried to use information-processing concepts to understand children's cognitive operations, let's consider a few examples of research based on this approach.

Encoding in children's problem solving.   In Chapter 7 we saw that one of the first steps involved in remembering something is to create a mental representation of it, a process called *encoding*. Robert Siegler (1976) investigated the encoding process in children by testing them on a balance task, in which they were presented with a set of scales with pegs onto which different sizes of weights could be placed (Figure 9.20). Their task was to predict which side of the balance would go down for a given configuration of weights. Most of Siegler's 5- and 8-year-olds based their decision on the amount of weight present; they invariably said that the side with more weight was the one that would go down, irrespective of how the weights were distributed along the beam. After obtaining their judgments Siegler showed the children how the scale worked, using different combinations of weights, and then retested them. The 5-year-olds stayed with their old rule: the side with the most weight goes down. In contrast, the 8-year-olds showed they had learned something from the demonstration, and began

8   THINKING

FIGURE 9.20
In Siegler's balance experiment, weights were placed on the pegs while the balance was held in place. Subjects were asked to predict which side would go down when the balance was released.

using a more advanced rule that took into account the distance of the weights from the fulcrum.

From an analysis of his results, Siegler concluded that the crucial difference between 5- and 8-year-olds was the way they encoded information. Even after the training session, the 5-year-olds did not encode the distance of the weights from the fulcrum, so they couldn't use that information to solve the problem. In contrast, the 8-year-olds learned from the training to encode the distance information and therefore were more likely to propose correct solutions to the problem.

Strategy selection in children's thinking.   One of the most active areas of research using the information-processing approach to development looks at the strategies children use to perform cognitive tasks such as solving mathematics problems or remembering words. (See Measurement & Methodology, "Determining Children's Problem-Solving Strategies: Sometimes Asking Helps.")

Two memory strategies we discussed in Chapter 7 were organization and rehearsal—people remember information better if they organize it into categories and if they rehearse it. Developmental research has shown that the ability to use organization and rehearsal as memory aids increases with age. When children younger than 6 years old are given memory tasks, they typically do not rehearse at all. By age 7 or 8, children begin rehearsing to remember, but it isn't until adolescence that rehearsal becomes organized. When presented with a list of words such as *dog, table, red, lamp, blue,* and *cat,* young children simply rehearse the words in the order presented. Adolescents, however, greatly increase their memory capacity by grouping the words into categories—for example, pairing *dog* with *cat* and *red* with *blue.* Thus, developmental change in this instance can be described as changes in the information-processing strategies children use in memorizing (Folds et al., 1990; Schneider & Pressley, 1989).

Another example of the use of information-processing strategies in memorizing is *elaboration.* Elaboration is the strategy of combining to-be-remembered

7   MEMORY

MEASUREMENT & METHODOLOGY

Determining Children's Problem-Solving Strategies: Sometimes Asking Helps

G. Groen and J. Parkman (1972) proposed a model called the *min model* to explain how young children solve addition problems. They hypothesized that a child identifies the larger number ("7" for the problem "7 plus 3"), and then counts upward from this point for the number of counts indicated by the smaller number. (The child would think, "seven, eight, nine, ten"). This model was accepted as correct because experiments indicated that the solution time needed by first-graders depended on the size of the smaller number, just as the model would predict. For example, children would take longer to add 7 plus 4 than to add 8 plus 3 (Ashcraft, 1982; Kaye et al., 1986), because the former involved four "counts" but the latter only three.

Although the min model was supported by empirical results, it ran into trouble when mathematics teachers reported that children used other strategies to solve addition problems. Following up on this information, Robert Siegler (1987) asked 5- to 7-year-olds how they solved addition problems. The children reported that they broke difficult problems down into simpler ones—for example, 12 plus 3 would become 10 plus 2 plus 3—and also counted from 1, memorized the answers, guessed, *and* used the min strategy.

If children were using other strategies, why had the solution time data fit the min model? Siegler answered this question by determining solution times for solving specific problems *and* asking children what strategy they used on each problem. When they used the min strategy, which they did on 36% of the trials, the solution times fit the min model even better than they had in previous studies. But when they used other strategies, the solution times did not fit the model. Thus, the min model is correct for some children, some of the time. But when researchers went beyond simply testing children and asked them what they were doing, they found out that the min model was only part of the picture.

items in a meaningful way (Siegler, 1986). For example, in order to remember to buy sliced cheese, hot dogs, and rolls, a person might conjure up an image of hot dogs in rolls flying through the air on wings made of cheese slices.

Older children are much more likely to use elaboration as a memory device than are younger children. For example, Michael Pressley and Joel Levin (1977) found that 47% of 10-year-olds used the elaboration strategy, whereas 94% of 14-year-olds used it (also see Lodico et al., 1983).

Stages versus continuous development.   An important difference between Piaget's approach and the information-processing approach is that the information-processing psychologists see development as the gradual learning of new ways to process information. Development, according to this idea, is a continuous curve rather than a sequence of steps or stages. Thus, although sampling behaviors at two very different ages, as Piaget did, may reveal very different types of mental processes (for example, no rehearsal for a 6-year-old and elaborative rehearsal for an adolescent), those processes may be linked by a smooth developmental pathway.

Some evidence supporting the idea that development follows a smooth course is provided by Robert Kail (1991), who measured the speed at which people ranging from 7½ to 21 years of age were able to execute different types of tasks. Some of Kail's tasks were *perceptual-motor* in nature: the *pegboard task* required subjects to move ten pegs from holes in one side of a board to holes in the other side of the board. Other tasks were *cognitive* in nature: the *mental addition test* required subjects to indicate whether addition statements such as "8 plus 9 equals 16" are true or false.

Kail's results are shown in Figure 9.21. One obvious feature of these curves is their smoothness; there are no sudden jumps in performance of the sort that might be predicted by a stage theory. Even more interesting, the *shapes* of the curves are exactly the same for both the perceptual-motor and cognitive tasks. The similarity of the shapes led Kail to propose that the same psychological mechanism controls processing speed for both types of tasks.

We have seen that researchers approaching cognitive development from the information-processing viewpoint are concerned less with describing *what* children can do at different ages and more with *how* they do it.

Cognitive Development in Adulthood

The research we have considered so far, on Piaget's stage approach and the information-processing approach, has focused on the span between early childhood and adolescence. But what about cognitive development in adulthood? We will consider this question in two ways. First, we will look at some research on how intelligence changes as people age; second, we will consider the idea that

FIGURE 9.21

Subjects ranging from 7½ to 21 years of age accomplish pegboard and mental addition tasks more rapidly as they get older. The functions show a smooth decline and follow the same mathematical function for each task.

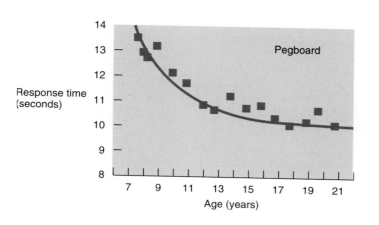

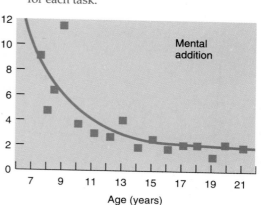

some adults may attain a stage of cognitive development beyond Piaget's formal operations stage.

Intelligence through the life span.   Earlier in this chapter, in the Measurement & Methodology discussion of cross-sectional versus longitudinal methods, we saw that intelligence tends to remain fairly constant during most of adulthood and begins to decline only later in life. Other research looks more closely at how intelligence changes with age by proposing that there are two types of intelligence, *crystallized intelligence* and *fluid intelligence*, and that these two types are affected differently by aging.

Crystallized intelligence is based on information aquired from previous experience and education, such as vocabulary and historical knowledge. The ability to use this type of knowledge stays the same or increases with age. **Fluid intelligence,** which is based on basic information-processing skills that do not depend on past experience, such as problem solving through reasoning or manipulating numbers, usually declines in parallel with the decline of a person's physical abilities (Horn and Donaldson, 1976; Horn, 1982) (Figure 9.22).

Although not all researchers accept the idea of crystallized and fluid intelligence, research on memory supports the idea that adulthood brings declines in some capacities and increases in others. For example, Marion Pearlmutter (1986) has found that adults' memory performance is worse than that of younger subjects on tasks that require memory for information that has just been presented, such as lists of words, but that adults perform better than younger subjects on memory tests that depend on remembering information acquired through past experiences.

We can think of aging, therefore, as being accompanied by a *decrease* in memory *capacity*—a decrease in the effectiveness of the machinery system that helps us record and retrieve information form short- and long-term memory. On the other hand, aging is also accompanied by an *increase* in memory *contents*—an increase in the data in the memory system, consisting of the person's accumulated knowledge of the world.

The picture that emerges from research on adult memory is that as people age, the cognitive abilities that decrease are compensated for by others that remain constant or increase. The net result is that there is little or no overall decline in cognitive functioning over most of adulthood. Schaie (1981) puts it this way:

> Aging is not synonymous with intellectual incompetence. It is only as the 80's are reached that age-related decrement becomes evident in many persons, and even then to a lesser extent than previous literature has led us to believe (p. 211).

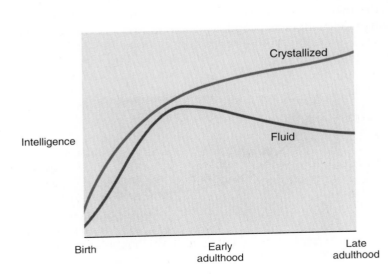

FIGURE 9.22
Change in crystallized and fluid intelligence as a function of age

The data we have been looking at have been derived by quantitatively measuring various mental abilities. Another approach to studying cognition in adulthood is to consider *qualitative* changes that may occur in the way people reason. Some researchers who have looked at these qualitative changes have concluded that cognitive development continues beyond the formal operations stage described by Piaget.

Post-formal reasoning in adulthood.   The mental systems of formal operational thought are what enable people to use scientific reasoning to solve problems. Faced with the pendulum problem, for instance, they can dissect the problem into its component parts and vary each one to determine what controls the pendulum's movement. Problems such as this and others used in research on formal operations reasoning are called closed systems—well-defined problems with definite answers.

But many problems are not so well defined and don't have straightforward, correct solutions. Real-life problems, such as whether to end a relationship or move to a new city, are difficult to solve because they involve *open systems*— they have a large number of variables, many of which are unknown or ambiguous.

Some researchers have suggested that open-system problems require a type of thinking called *dialectical thinking,* which goes beyond formal operations. This type of thinking is able to handle contradictions and makes it possible to see the merits of many different viewpoints. Accordingly, these researchers propose a stage following the stage of formal operations; they call it the **post–formal operations stage,** or sometimes the *stage of dialectical operations* (Labouvie-Vief, 1985). To appreciate how reasoning operates in this stage, consider the following problem:

> John is known to be a heavy drinker, especially when he goes to parties. Mary, John's wife, warns him that if he comes home drunk one more time, she will leave him and take the children. Tonight John is out late at an office party. John comes home drunk. Does Mary leave John?

This hypothetical problem was one of many that Giesela Labouvie-Vief (1985) presented to subjects ranging from 10 to 40 years old. As they worked to solve these problems, different patterns of problem solving emerged for the younger and older subjects. The younger subjects usually solved the problem as if it were the following exercise in logic.

> If John comes home drunk, Mary will leave him.
> John comes home drunk.
> Therefore, Mary will leave him.

Older subjects, however, went beyond the logical statement of the problem to consider other factors that might apply in a real-life situation. In this situation, they would consider the nature of John's behavior on returning (whether he was nasty or apologetic); the possibility that if Mary were economically dependent on John, she might not follow through with her threat; and the possibility that Mary's threat really wasn't meant seriously, but was a cry for help and understanding. This type of thinking, therefore, takes into account what the world is really like and recognizes that people's behavior cannot always be understood in terms of logic alone.

The kind of advanced thinking characteristic of dialectical operations is enhanced by education. William Perry (1970, 1981) has looked at how the thinking of many college students evolves over their college years by interviewing them about their experiences in school. From these interviews Perry found that at the beginning of college many students use the *duality principle:* everything is stated in terms of good and bad or right and wrong, and "authorities" know what is right. Later they begin to realize that sometimes there aren't always "right" answers, and finally they begin to accept the basic contradictions of life's dilemmas

FIGURE 9.23
How college students' reasoning evolves, according to Perry

Authorities know what is correct.

↓

But even authorities admit they don't
know all the answers yet.

↓

There are so many things the authorities
don't know the answers to.

↓

Where authorities don't know the right
answers, everyone has a right to his or her
own opinions; no one is wrong!

↓

I'm going to have to make my own
decisions in an uncertain world.

↓

I can't make logical sense out of life's
dilemmas. This is how life will be. I must be
wholehearted while tentative, fight for my
values yet respect others, believe my deepest
values yet be ready to learn.

and begin thinking dialectically—realizing that there are often no "pat" answers to life's problems (see Figure 9.23).

Perry's research led the way for other researchers' descriptions of how thinking evolves from an initial absolutist position in adolescence and young adults (there is only one correct solution to the problem) to a relativistic position in young and early middle-aged adults (there are many sides to any issue), to the final position, dialectical thinking (different viewpoints can be synthesized into a workable solution) (Cavanaugh, 1993; Kramer, 1989). The more we study cognitive development in adulthood the more obvious it becomes that, especially for people who continue their education past high school, cognitive development continues well into adulthood.

Reprise: What You Look at Determines What You See

One of the themes of this book has been that any given behavior can be studied from a number of different angles and that the angle we select can determine what we see and what we learn about the behavior. In this chapter we have looked at development from the biological and cognitive angles, seeing how physical capacities and thinking processes change as people get older, and how those changes contribute to changes in behavior.

The idea that what we look at determines what we see has significant implications for the basic questions about development that were posed at the beginning of this chapter. The research reviewed in this chapter suggests that these questions do not have straightforward answers, and that the answers we arrive at may be influenced by how we go about collecting evidence. For example, in looking for evidence relevant to the first question, "Do people's characteristics remain constant over time?" we saw that there is evidence that children who are particularly shy tend to be shy later in their lives. But we also saw that this constancy does not necessarily hold for the majority of children, who fall somewhere between being extremely shy and extremely outgoing. When we considered aggression, however, we saw that there is stronger evidence for constancy—many people who are aggressive as children become aggressive adults. The answer to our question about constancy is, therefore, "it depends on what characteristic you are talking about."

Or consider our second question, on whether development proceeds in a smooth curve or in stages. The answer depends to some extent on how often we sample a child's behavior. Looking at behavior at frequent intervals favors seeing small changes and supports the idea of smooth, continuous development. Looking at behavior at larger intervals emphasizes large differences and supports the idea of stages of development. Thus, the answer may lie somewhere between the two extreme positions. Children separated by a number of years may indeed think in very different ways, but those large differences may have evolved gradually.

In response to the statement that large differences may evolve gradually, someone favoring the stage approach might say, "But look at the large and rapid shift that takes place at puberty, when children enter adolescence. Isn't that clearly a discrete stage?" The evidence for this point is clear when we look at physical growth. There is no doubt that a growth spurt occurs suddenly between the ages of about 11 and 15. There is also no doubt that a person on the adolescent side of the growth spurt looks quite different from one who hasn't yet changed. However, even in this case, the metamorphosis of child into adolescent takes place over a period of years, starting in junior high school and extending into college.

And the changes of puberty are not only physical, but also cognitive and social. The major physical changes occur relatively rapidly once they begin, spanning only a few years. But the cognitive and social changes may be just picking up steam as the physical changes are completed. Not only do adolescents begin thinking differently—focusing on the more abstract and hypothetical thinking that they have become capable of—but they also have to negotiate a new, complex, and sometimes confusing social environment. They must deal with issues of sexuality, relationships, and thinking about their future that take many years to work out. If we just focus on the more obvious and dramatic physical changes that usher in adolescence, we can be misled into concluding that the shift from childhood to adolescence is more stagelike than it may in fact actually be.

Finally, when we considered our third question, regarding the relative roles of nature and nurture for development, we became aware of the interplay between the environment and heredity. We saw that even though physical development is obviously genetically programmed to a large degree, environmental influences begin even before birth and continue to have effects all through the course of development. Consider, for example, the age of menarche, the first menstruation that marks the beginning of puberty in girls. If we focus on the biological level, we will see that this event is biologically programmed. If, however, we look at menarche from a contextual level, we see that factors such as family relations and conflict within a family affect the age of menarche (Moffitt et al., 1992; Surbey, 1990).

Someone just beginning their study of development might be tempted to strive for simplicity by saying that personal characteristics are highly stable (or unstable), or that development occurs in discrete stages (or continuously), or that biology (or the environment) is mainly responsible for development. But we have seen that simple explanations such as these are simply not accurate. When we look at development from a number of angles and sample behavior in different ways, we come to appreciate the complexity of development, to see the need to qualify our answers, and to recognize the interaction of factors working at different levels of analysis. In the next chapter, on language and social development, we will see even more clearly how the various components of development interact with each other in complex ways.

Cross-Cultural Perspectives on Piaget

Although Piaget's theory of cognitive development is based largely on observations of Swiss children, one of his basic assumptions is that all children, no matter what their culture, achieve the concepts and abilities of the sensorimotor, preoperational, concrete operational, and formal operational stages of development. What Piaget is saying is that by virtue of being human, we all develop the same mental mechanisms. Culture, according to Piaget, might affect the age at which a person enters each stage, but not whether a stage is achieved.

This idea has been tested by psychologists who have presented Piagetian tasks to people from both a Western, industrialized culture and traditional cultures. One of the main tasks used in these studies is a conservation test, such as the one in which the experimenter pours water from a wide container into a narrow, taller container, or rolls clay from a ball into a sausage shape. Children who have acquired the concept of conservation indicate that pouring the water or molding the clay does not affect the amount of water or clay present. According to Piaget, acquisition of the concept of conservation marks the child's entry into the concrete operations stage of development, an event that occurs around the age of 6 or 7 for most Western children.

The possible outcomes of cross-cultural studies are shown graphically in Figure 9.24, which plots the percentage of people who have mastered a given task (in our example, conservation) versus age (Dasen & Heron, 1981). Curve *w* represents the performance of subjects from a Western, technologically advanced background. As these children get older, more and more master the task until eventually 100% can do it.

Curves *a*, *b*, and *c* represent hypothetical data that might be collected for other cultures. Children in cultures *a*, *b*, and *c* all eventually master the task, with children in culture *a* mastering it earlier than the Western children, *b* at the same time, and *c* later. In culture *d*, performance is not only delayed, but never reaches 100%. For example, only about half of children in culture *d* eventually develop the concept of conservation.

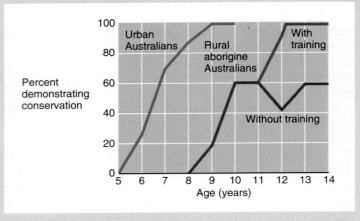

FIGURE 9.25

A large percentage of rural aborigine Australians do not acquire the concept of conservation. However, with training, all acquire the concept, although about three years later than urban Australians.

All four of these curves have been obtained in cross-cultural research, with the typical result for the conservation task being like curve *c*—all children eventually master the concept, but a year or so later than Western children. However, there have also been reports of performance similar to curve *d* (Dasen, 1982). For example, when Patricia Greenfield (1966) tested 10- to 13-year-old children from the Wolof tribe in the West African nation of Senegal, she found that only 50% of them understood that the quantity of liquid doesn't change when the liquid is poured from a wide container into a narrow one. Results such as these led some researchers to conclude that people from traditional cultures may never acquire the concepts of the concrete operations stage of development. Thus, Greenfield concluded that in the Wolof culture, "Intellectual development . . . ceases shortly after age nine."

But can this be? Is it reasonable to suppose that a society could function if people with the most highly developed intellect only reached the level of a Western 9-year-old? Other cross-cultural researchers have suggested that perhaps poor performance such as that observed by Greenfield is caused not by inferior intellect, but by the way tribes are tested. Perhaps the problem is simply that subjects from traditional cultures don't understand the questions they are being asked.

More recent cross-cultural research supports this idea. For example, when Pierre Dasen and his co-workers (1979) compared the performance of Australian children from the city of Canberra with that of aboriginal children from rural Australia on a conservation task, they found that many of the aborigines did not acquire the concept of conservation (Figure 9.25). However, when the aborigines were given some training to help them understand the test, all of them mastered the concept, with the aboriginal children's acquisition of conservation lagging behind the urban children's by about three years.

FIGURE 9.24

Possible outcomes of cross-cultural studies on conservation tasks. Curve *w* represents Western culture, and curves *a*, *b*, *c*, and *d* represent possible results for other cultures.

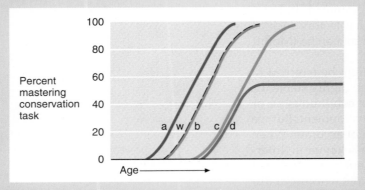

Another approach to testing subjects from traditional cultures is to ensure they understand the nature of their task by using researchers who speak their language and are from their own cultural group. Raphael Nyiti (1982) did this for two groups of 10- and 11-year-old Canadian children: one group came from a European background and lived in an industrialized town; the other was from the Micmac Indian tribe and lived on a reservation. When these groups were presented with the conservation tasks by an English-speaking European descendant, the results mirrored past cross-cultural results: the European-origin children did much better than the Indian children. However, when the Indian children were tested in their own language by a member of their tribe, their performance was nearly identical to that of the European children (Figure 9.26). Nyiti concluded that, given proper testing procedures, concrete operations concepts such as conservation are observable in people of all cultures.

The research we have considered so far has focused on the conservation task that signals entrance into the concrete operations stage. What about the formal operational thinking that Piaget saw as the pinnacle of cognitive development? Most studies that present Piagetian tests to people from rural, technologically unsophisticated societies have failed to find much evidence of formal operational thinking (Dasen, 1977; Jahoda, 1980; Laboratory of Comparative Human Cognition, 1983).

Does this mean that people who are raised in these traditional cultures are not capable of formal operational thinking? In Chapter 8's Follow-Through, "Thinking in Traditional Cultures,"

FIGURE 9.26

When Micmac Indian children are tested by someone from their own culture and in their own language, their conservation performance is identical to that of the European children.

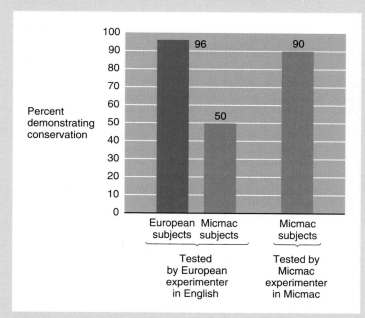

FIGURE 9.27

we saw that adults who fail Western tests of thinking often demonstrate impressive skills in their everyday lives. The achievement of formal operational thinking *as defined by performance on Piaget's tests* may require the Western-type schooling that teaches logical thinking and the scientific method. But if a person knows how to solve problems by systematically changing variables, does this mean his or her mental capacities are more highly developed than another person's, who doesn't solve problems in this way? One way to answer this question is to look at the intellectual accomplishments of people from non-Western cultures. Consider, for example, the sailors of the Micronesian Islands in the South Pacific. Before they had access to such modern navigational aids as the magnetic compass, Micronesian sailors navigated small outrigger canoes (Figure 9.27) across many miles of ocean to get from one island to another. Their navigation system was complex, using a "star compass" based on the paths that 14 stars travel throughout the night (Gladwin, 1970; Goodenough, 1953; Hutchins, 1983).

Micronesians' ability to develop such a complex system shows that they are capable of thinking at the formal operational level. However, when presented with a Piagetian test for formal operational thinking, they performed poorly. When they were given poker chips of different colors and asked to find all possible combinations of the colors, most of the sailors succeeded in determining only a few of the color pairs—far below the performance of a Western child in the formal operations stage (Gladwin, 1970). Interestingly enough, a few Micronesian adults who had attended high school showed some aptitude for this test; however, these men were not able to use the navigational system!

Was Piaget right in stating that his stages are universal? A fairly strong case can be made that people in all cultures are capable of concrete operational thinking if they are given some training or are tested correctly. The case for universality is harder to make for formal operational thinking. Entrance into Piaget's formal operations stage requires an ability to think according to Western rules of logic and to be able to use scientific methods of reasoning. These skills develop through formal schooling, so people without it often do not meet Piaget's requirements. This does not mean that people from other cultures are not cognitively advanced. Examples like the Micronesian system of navigation testify to the impressive cognitive capacities of people from non-Western cultures.

Basic Issues in Developmental Psychology

- The question of stability versus instability concerns whether a person's characteristics remain constant or change over time. Examples of traits that are stable are shyness in some people during early childhood, and intelligence and aggression from childhood into adulthood.

- The question of continuity versus discontinuity is whether the changes that happen during development occur as a sequence of discrete stages or in a smooth progression. Piaget's theory of cognitive development is an example of a stage theory. Most developmental psychologists today favor the idea of continuous development.

- Both heredity and the environment contribute to a person's characteristics, but rather than thinking about these two factors as acting separately, it is more accurate to think of them as interacting.

- The results of the Six-Cultures Study indicate that children's environment, as defined by socialization practices of their cultures, influence the way they interact socially with their parents and with other children.

Physical and Perceptual Development

- Prenatal development begins with the zygote and proceeds through the germinal, embryonic, and fetal periods. This course of development can be disrupted by teratogens such as cigarette smoke or alcohol.

- During infancy, from birth to 3 years, physical growth proceeds at its most rapid rate, as motor skills such as walking emerge. During childhood physical growth settles down to a steady rate.

- Newborns have limited vision but can perceive contours and facial expressions. They can also discriminate speech sounds. During the first nine months of life, basic perceptual capacities like color vision, acuity, and depth perception develop extremely rapidly.

- Childhood is a period of slow but steady physical development. The onset of adolescence is marked by rapid physical changes and the development of sexual characteristics. These changes do not occur at the same time for everyone.

- Adulthood is a period of declining physical capacity. Yet this decline is so gradual that it is often possible to compensate for the changes that occur.

Cognitive Development

- Piaget saw cognitive development as proceeding through four periods. The sensorimotor stage (birth to 2 years) introduces such basic mechanisms as schemes, assimilation, accommodation, and organization and sees the emergence of the concept of object permanence. The preoperational stage (2 to 7 years) is characterized by language development, egocentrism, lack of conservation, and animism. In the concrete operations stage (7 to 11 years), children learn to think logically. Reversible thinking, decentration, conservation, seriation, transitivity, diminished egocentrism, and a shift in moral thinking are typical abilities achieved in this stage. In the formal operations stage (11 to 15 years), abstract and hypothetical thinking, adolescent egocentrism, and higher moral development are observable.

- Piaget has been criticized for underestimating children's capabilities. Research showing that children can do some things earlier than Piaget stated calls into question his idea of stage-like development.

- The information-processing approach sees development as a smooth progression rather than as stages. It focuses on processes such as encoding, rehearsal, and retrieval. Experiments show that young children and older children encode information differently when working on the balance task, and that they use different rehearsal strategies in memory tasks.

- There are two types of intelligence that are affected differently by aging. Crystallized intelligence stays the same or may increase with age. Fluid intelligence usually declines in parallel with the decline of a person's physical abilities. Some psychologists have proposed that there is a stage following formal operations called the stage of post–formal operations, in which people are able to engage in dialectical thinking. This ability increases with age and education.

Reprise: What You Look at Determines What You See

- The answers to questions about development can depend on how we look at developmental changes. For example, some characteristics change during development and others remain relatively stable; sampling behavior frequently is more likely to yield data supporting the idea of gradual development, whereas sampling behavior at larger intervals is more likely to support the idea of stagelike development.

Follow-Through/Diversity: Cross-Cultural Perspectives on Piaget's Theory of Cognitive Development

- Children in traditional cultures eventually master conservation tasks, but usually at a later age than children from Western cultures. People in all cultures can master conservation if proper testing procedures are used. The case for universality of Piaget's stages is harder to make for formal operations tasks; apparently, people must undergo formal schooling before they can master these tasks.

Key Terms

accommodation
adaptation
adolescence
adolescent egocentrism
animism
assimilation
cognitive operations
cohort
concrete operations stage
conservation
continuity versus discontinuity
cross-sectional method
crystallized intelligence
decentration
development
developmental psychologists
egocentric
embryonic period
fetal period
fluid intelligence

formal operations stage
germinal period
longitudinal method
menarche
nature versus nurture
niche building
object permanence
organization
personal fable
post–formal operations stage
preoperational stage
puberty
reversibility
scheme
sensorimotor stage
seriation
stability versus instability
teratogens
transitivity
zygote

CHAPTER

10

The Development of Language
    The Conditions Necessary for Language
    The Course of Language Development
    Theories of Language Acquisition

Social Development: Infancy, Childhood, and Adolescence
    Erikson's Psychosocial Theory of Development
    Attachment in Infancy and Childhood
    Development of the Self in Childhood
    The Self in Adolescence
    The Development of Moral Reasoning

Interdisciplinary Dimension: Anthropology
    Identity Formation in Inner-City Gangs

Social Development: Adulthood
    Adult Behavior and Early Experience
    Life Events in Adulthood

Reprise: Linkages Among Physical, Cognitive, and Social Abilities

Follow-Through/Diversity
    Culture, Economic Stress, and Child Development

Language and Social Development

Each ten years of a man's life has its own fortunes, its own hopes, its own desires.

Johann Wolfgang von Goethe (1749–1832)
German poet and novelist

Normal babies who experience a normal childhood say their first words some time during their second year of life. Those words and the many that follow are an amazing cognitive achievement, for they are more than simply sounds: they are symbols combined in sequences to create language, the communication system that greatly enhances the infant's ability to interact with others. More than any other cognitive achievement, the acquisition of language allows young children to interact socially with others, and that interaction in turn facilitates further cognitive growth.

In this chapter, we will take a strongly cognitive and behavioral view of development as we consider linguistic and social development. At the cognitive level, we will be considering what children *know* and how they *think* as they begin to use language to interact socially in the world. At the behavioral level we will see how children develop language and how they change socially with age. By its very nature the study of social development also involves the contextual level of analysis, because social behaviors develop in the context of an environment populated by other people and created by institutions such as family and school, as well as cultural influences.

The Development of Language

An essential property of language is that it provides the means for expressing indefinitely many thoughts and for reacting appropriately in an indefinite range of new situations.

Noam Chomsky, American linguist

Much infant-mother interaction occurs through speech and facial expressions.

Because most of our interactions with others depend on language, linguistic development and social development are inextricably entwined. Moreover, the acquisition of language involves the development of many other abilities. A variety of physical, perceptual, cognitive, and even social conditions must be satisfied before a child's first words can be spoken.

The Conditions Necessary for Language

An infant can make a variety of sounds, yet we don't think of infants as "talking" until they are over a year old—and from then on it seems they never stop. What happens in the first 18 months or so of life to make this development possible? To put the question another way, why can't babies talk?

One reason babies can't talk is that they don't yet have the vocal apparatus necessary for creating speech. It isn't until about 6 months of age that the baby's vocal cords, oral cavity, and muscle control are developed enough to support the creation of speech sounds. A second reason is that additional brain development is necessary for language. As the baby is preparing physically for the emergence of speech, the language areas of the brain are beginning a process of development that continues for the first two years—exactly the point at which the development of language begins (Goldman-Rakic, 1987; Goldman-Rakic et al., 1983).

Learning to speak also depends on being able to hear oneself talking. All normal children begin cooing and babbling in their cribs at about 2 months old and utter syllables at about 4 months. These vocalizations eventually stop in hearing-impaired children, however, as they can't hear themselves. (These children can learn to talk, but only after special training over a long period of time.)

But possessing the necessary physical ability and perceptual equipment to create speech isn't enough to ensure the development of language. Children must also have achieved a certain level of cognitive understanding. For example, to understand the meaning of the word *gone*, a child must first master the concept of object permanence—that when an object is hidden from view it still exists. Similarly, to use plurals, children must understand the concept of "greater than one."

A final condition for normal language development is interaction with other people. Arlene Moskowitz (1978) reports the case of a child with normal hearing who was confined to his home due to an asthmatic condition. His parents were deaf and communicated only with sign language, so the child's only exposure to spoken language was through TV. Apparently that wasn't enough, because by the age of 3 the child could communicate with sign language but could neither speak nor understand English. The problem with learning language from TV, according to Moskowitz, is that although the TV set can ask questions, it can't respond to the child's answers.

If the necessary conditions are present, however, children's language development follows a predictable course from babbling to adultlike speech. We will first review the course of language development and then turn to some theories that attempt to explain how this development occurs.

The Course of Language Development

Language development proceeds rapidly, from early vocalizations at birth to adultlike speech by the age of 4 or 5. The milestones in language development are summarized in Figure 10.1 (based on Wood, 1981). Let's briefly examine each of them.

Early vocalizations.   At birth babies cry; at about 2 months of age they coo; and by about 5 or 6 months they are expert babblers who produce almost all the sounds needed to speak English—plus some that aren't needed. Because of the wide variety of sounds produced, it has been said that babbling often sounds

FIGURE 10.1
Milestones in language development

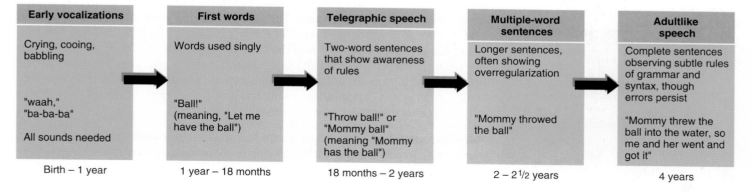

Early vocalizations	First words	Telegraphic speech	Multiple-word sentences	Adultlike speech
Crying, cooing, babbling	Words used singly	Two-word sentences that show awareness of rules	Longer sentences, often showing overregularization	Complete sentences observing subtle rules of grammar and syntax, though errors persist
"waah," "ba-ba-ba"	"Ball!" (meaning, "Let me have the ball")	"Throw ball!" or "Mommy ball" (meaning "Mommy has the ball")	"Mommy throwed the ball"	"Mommy threw the ball into the water, so me and her went and got it"
All sounds needed				
Birth – 1 year	1 year – 18 months	18 months – 2 years	2 – 2½ years	4 years

Tactile and visual communication between infant and father

like an effort to communicate in a foreign language (Liebert, Wicks-Nelson, & Kail, 1986). At the babbling stage a baby is both beginning to learn the sounds that he will shortly put to use in communication and learning how to use changes in *intonation*—falling or rising pitch patterns—to convey meaning. Adults use intonation to distinguish statements such as "You're in love?" and "You're in *love*." Infants begin modulating their babbling with these pitch variations at between 4 and 6 months of age.

The production of different intonations means that even before words are spoken, the interactive nature of language—in which one person is transmitting information to another—is apparent. That quality is also evident in the beginnings of turn taking between caregivers and infants. This turn taking results in **pseudodialogues** in which the infant vocalizes, the adult responds, the infant vocalizes back, and so on. This behavior, which marks the beginnings of conversation, begins at about 3 months of age (Schaffer, 1979).

The first words.   A child's first isolated words occur between 12 and 18 months of age; they usually refer to objects in the child's immediate environment. At this early stage of development, children are faced with the problem of learning how to attach appropriate labels to objects. Their initial labels often demonstrate **overextension,** the overinclusion of objects in a particular category. For example, all men may be called "Daddy"—or cats, cows, and horses may all be "doggies." However, sometimes the opposite—**underextension**—occurs, as when a child uses the word *car* to refer only to the family car.

As young children learn the meanings and pronunciation of new words, they learn how to use more than one word at a time. Within a few months after saying their first words, they begin saying them in pairs.

Telegraphic speech and multiple-word sentences.   The use of "shorthand sentences" or **telegraphic speech**, such as "throw ball" or "no eat," marks the beginning of a child's understanding of the rules of **syntax**— how to combine words to form grammatically correct sentences (Clark & Clark, 1977). A key point here is that even these primitive two-word "sentences" appear to follow some rules. For example, in English syntax, word order is important for meaning. Children may have a rudimentary understanding of this principle even at the stage of telegraphic speech. If a person or object is performing an action, that person or object comes first in the word pair. Thus, children will say "Mommy throw" to mean "Mommy throws the ball," rather than "throw Mommy." Another rule is that if a person or thing is being *acted upon*, it comes last in a word pair: "throw ball" for "throw the ball" rather than "ball throw."

Thus, at this stage of language learning it appears that children are not simply memorizing phrases but are learning *rules* for new word combinations. Further evidence of this rule learning surfaces at about age 2 or $2^1/_2$, as children learn to produce increasingly sophisticated, multiple-word sentences and begin learning word endings that turn a word into the past tense or plural form. Rather than memorizing these endings, children appear to learn rules for applying them. This can be inferred from the mistakes they make. For example, the rule for constructing the past tense of most verbs is to add the ending *-ed*. Sometimes, however, this rule doesn't apply. The verb *hit* has the same form in both present and past tense, and the past tense of the irregular verb *go* is *went*. Thus, when 3-year-olds say things like "I hitted the ball" or "I goed home," they are not repeating what they have heard adults say. Instead, they are applying the *-ed* rule to all verbs, including the exceptions. This tendency, called **overregularization,** eventually stops when children learn which words have irregular forms; but it may still creep into the speech of children as old as 5 or 6.

Once children learn language, they often seem to chatter away nonstop.

Adultlike speech.   By the time children are about 4 years old, they have become proficient speakers. Although they may occasionally create strangely constructed sentences and still have a limited vocabulary, they are capable of adultlike speech that observes many subtle rules of grammar and syntax.

As children get older, they continue to refine their use of grammar and rapidly increase their vocabularies. The average 6-year-old has a vocabulary of about 14,000 words (Carey, 1978) and learns about 22 new words a day! According to George Miller (1981), "Nobody teaches them 22 words a day. Their minds are like little vacuum pumps designed by nature to suck up words" (p. 119). This process continues into adolescence, culminating in an average high school graduate's vocabulary of about 80,000 words (Miller & Gildea, 1987).

Theories of Language Acquisition

> *Why do children talk? The ultimate reason is that they are biologically designed to do so.*
>
> Catherine Garvey (1984, p. 2)

The progression from babbling to meaningful sentences is well documented, but how do children accomplish this remarkable transformation? What mechanisms enable them to progress from making meaningless sounds to engaging in adult conversation? These questions have inspired much debate among psychologists. Three basic approaches to the explanation of language acquisition have been offered: the behaviorist approach, the nativist approach, and the cognitive approach.

The behaviorist approach. In 1957 B. F. Skinner articulated the behaviorist approach to language development in a book titled *Verbal Behavior*. Skinner sought to explain language learning in terms of the mechanisms he believed to be responsible for all learning—namely, reinforcement and punishment. The parents first reinforce babbling with attention and then selectively reinforce the production of wordlike sounds. As a child begins talking, parents begin focusing on rewarding the child for producing grammatically correct sentences. The process of reinforcement therefore shapes language just as it would shape any other behavior. Observational learning also promotes language learning, as children imitate the speech of the more practiced speakers they hear.

In offering this explanation of language learning Skinner was, in part, trying to show how behaviorist theory could explain a particularly complex behavior. If he succeeded, he would not only have explained language learning but would also have scored an impressive coup for his general theory of behavior. Unfortunately for Skinner, his explanation almost immediately drew heavy fire.

The nativist approach. Noam Chomsky (1959), a well-known linguist, responded to Skinner's book with a scathing review. How, asked Chomsky, can imitation and reinforcement possibly explain the huge number of words and sentences children learn? Children are continually creating new sentences that they have never heard and for which they have never been reinforced. Furthermore, parents don't consistently reinforce good usage or punish bad usage. In fact, most parents correct their children only when they state incorrect *facts*. Thus, the grammatically correct statement "I have two fingers" would be more likely to elicit a negative comment from a child's mother than would the grammatically incorrect statement "Daddy goed bye-bye in the car." Parents view conversations not as occasions for teaching grammar, but as occasions for interacting with their children (Miller, 1981).

The behaviorist idea that children learn by observational learning and imitation runs into problems for other reasons, as well. First, when children are overregularizing, they blatantly ignore all the correct examples of irregular tense forms provided by older children and adults in favor of their own incorrect constructions. Second, even when adults try to coerce children into imitating them, their attempts are often futile, as indicated by this conversation:

6   LEARNING

Child: Nobody don't like me.
Mother: No, say nobody likes me.
Child: Nobody don't like me.
[*eight repetitions of this dialogue*]
Mother: No, now listen carefully. Say, nobody likes me.
Child: Oh! Nobody don't likes me (McNeil, 1966, p. 67).

3   BIOLOGY

As an alternative to Skinner's theory, Chomsky proposed that language learning is a biologically programmed process controlled by a **language acquisition device (LAD)** in the brain. This device, which is specially adapted to language learning, specifies rules for grammar and sentence construction that guide the development of language. As evidence for this idea, Chomsky cited the finding that all languages share certain structural characteristics and that language learning progresses through the same stages in all cultures.

Recent evidence supporting the idea that language learning is biologically programmed is provided by Simon, a 9-year-old hearing-impaired boy. Simon learned grammatically correct sign language even though his only contact with sign language was through his parents, who signed using incorrect grammar because they didn't learn the signs until adulthood. The fact that Simon had in-

8   THINKING

dependently figured out grammatical rules that his parents could not grasp supports Chomsky's idea that children can learn rules of language that they are never explicitly shown (Kolata, 1992).

The cognitive approach.   Though language does seem to have some biological basis, other psychologists have pointed out the need to take cognitive factors into account. They note that at any given time children's speech depends on their cognitive development. Thus, when children are acquiring the concept of object permanence, they are learning words such as *see, all gone,* and *bye-bye.* Later, when they become concerned with belongings, they begin learning how to use possessives: *my truck, Daddy's hat.*

Another way of looking at the connection between cognition and language development emphasizes the social aspect of language—the fact that the purpose of language is communication and that parents (particularly mothers) spend a great deal of time practicing language with their infants. Language acquisition, according to this view, depends heavily on the *interaction* between infant and adult (Bruner, 1983).

What is the current status of theories of language development? Most psychologists see Skinner and Chomsky's views as opposite extremes, both contributing to our understanding of language development but neither view completely explaining it. The current view is that language development is propelled by inborn biological forces combined with reinforcement, punishment, and imitation and nurtured by the constant communication that occurs between parents and their children.

Social Development: Infancy, Childhood, and Adolescence

When people talk they are necessarily also performing social acts.

Catherine Garvey (1984, p. 5)

In considering language development, we have been discussing social development as well, because learning language depends on other people and using it creates connections with them. In this section, we broaden our explanation of the ways that people make connections by considering such issues as how infants and caregivers interact emotionally; how males' and females' conversations sometimes take on the characteristics of cross-cultural communication; how people connect with others within social groups; and how people develop a sense of themselves through social experiences. To set the stage for these topics, we will first describe a general theory of social development that resembles Jean Piaget's approach to cognitive development in proposing that development proceeds through a series of stages. This theory, proposed by Erik Erikson, one of Sigmund Freud's most famous students, provides a useful overview of social development.

Erikson's Psychosocial Theory of Development

Erik Erikson's **psychosocial theory of development** is notable not only because it is a stage theory, but also because it follows development from birth to death. As one of the first theorists to see development as continuing into adulthood, he led developmental psychologists to consider development a lifelong process.

Erikson (1963) postulated that development proceeds through a series of eight stages, each marked by a specific crisis. Each of us must resolve those crises successfully in order to continue on a course of healthy development. As you can see from the description of Erikson's stages in Figure 10.2, each crisis involves a conflict between two poles that represent positive and negative outcomes. For example, in Erikson's first stage, the infant is faced with a conflict between trust and mistrust. If the infant's caregivers are supportive and supply the infant's needs, then it is likely that the infant will learn to trust people. If, on the other hand, the caregivers do not support the infant, he or she may not trust them, and that mistrust may generalize to other people and to the self, as well.

According to Erikson, resolving each conflict in the positive direction helps create a well-adjusted personality that can deal with life's successive crises. His description of adulthood and old age is especially noteworthy for its emphasis on the positive. It pictures aging as a time of continued challenges that, when met, lead to further growth even in late adulthood. Erikson emphasizes, however, that even when a person has "conquered" a particular stage's conflicts, this doesn't mean that the person will never have to deal with those conflicts again (Erikson, 1980). Erikson sees life as a continual process of confronting issues that have surfaced in earlier stages. Even in adulthood we sometimes need to cope with the fear of abandonment we first faced as young children. Similarly, as people negotiate the pathway that leads through adulthood toward old age, they are often still redefining their identity as they change careers or retire. They may also have to readdress issues of intimacy as they experience divorce, new relationships, and the death of loved ones. Our journey through life, therefore, means both confronting new challenges and revisiting old ones.

Having examined Erikson's life-span approach to development, we now focus on a fact of early development that he saw as extremely important: the development of the relationship between infant and caregiver.

Attachment in Infancy and Childhood

Researchers have studied the development of infants' first relationship by focusing on a process called **attachment**—the formation of bonds between infant and caregivers. Early research on attachment was carried out by Harry and Margaret Harlow, using infant rhesus monkeys as subjects. The Harlows (Harlow, 1958; Harlow & Harlow, 1962) removed newborn monkeys from their mothers and reared them with two "surrogate mothers"—one a wire mother, which contained a bottle for feeding, the other a terry cloth mother that contained no bottle but was soft and comfortable to hold onto (Figure 10.3).

The Harlows found that even though these monkeys were being fed on the wire mother, they spent most of their time clinging to the cloth mother, and that

Stage	Infancy (0–1 year)	Early childhood (1–3 years)	Play age (3–6 years)	School age (6–11 years)
Developmental challenge	**Trust versus mistrust** If infants receive support and nurturance from caregivers, trust develops. This trust generalizes to others as well as to the infants themselves. Infants who do not receive adequate support develop mistrust and become suspicious of others and themselves.	**Autonomy versus shame and doubt** During early childhood, children's strivings to become independent are encouraged by developing abilities such as walking, talking, eating independently, and gaining control over their bladder and bowels. Developing a sense of the ability to handle tasks alone results in a feeling of autonomy and good self-esteem. Experiencing repeated failures or overly harsh criticism results in shame and doubt.	**Initiative versus guilt** Children who successfully take initiative in planning activities gain confidence in their abilities. When children's attempts at initiative fail, they may experience guilt and become less likely to initiate action in the future.	**Industry versus inferiority** As children encounter the challenges of school, functioning as a member of a family, and relating to friends, positive outcomes lead to a valuing of personal accomplishments and a sense of competency, or industry. Negative outcomes lead to a sense of failure and inferiority.

FIGURE 10.2
Erikson's stages of development

12   EMOTION

FIGURE 10.3
Monkeys in the Harlows' experiments preferred the cloth mother even though they were fed on the wire mother.

they went to the cloth mother for reassurance when confronted with a threatening situation. This result showed that contact comfort is extremely important to these monkeys, and since the behavior occurred in infants who had been isolated from other monkeys, some researchers saw the clinging response as being biologically programmed (Bowlby, 1969, 1973, 1980). Following up on this result, other researchers began to study attachment in human infants, focusing not only on contact comfort but also on the communication that occurs between infant and parent.

Emotional communication between infants and adults. A newborn's first task is to adapt to the environment of others (Lewis, 1987). One of the ways infants achieve this adaptation is by communicating with their parents or caregivers through their emotions. Crying, for example, sends the signal "Come change what's happening; take care of me." This cry for attention, when responded to by parents with food or a change of diaper, marks the beginning of the development of both social abilities and the connection between infant and adult.

By 4 to 6 weeks of age the infant begins to smile in response to specific stimuli in the environment (Izard, 1982). This response sends a signal to the other: "I like what you're doing; keep it up." Smiles are joined later by facial expressions and vocalizations (see Figure 10.4) that show anger, surprise, and sadness (3 to 4 months old) and fear (5 to 7 months) (Izard, 1982).

These early emotional responses are important because they establish communication that conveys information to the adult. Recent research shows, for example, that parents are sensitive to variations in the pitch of infants' cries. Philip Zeskind and Timothy Marshall (1988) found that parents respond more urgently to cries that are more high pitched than usual. A baby's normal cry, which indicates mild hunger or a wet diaper, has a pitch slightly above middle C on the piano. Higher-pitched cries usually indicate more distress—one comparable in pitch to the whistle of a teapot signals a possibly serious problem.

Stage			
 Adolescence	 Young adulthood	 Middle adulthood	 Old age

Developmental challenge	**Identity versus role confusion**	**Intimacy versus isolation**	**Generativity versus stagnation**	**Integrity versus despair**
	The main task of adolescence is determining one's identity. This may involve deciding on values, aspirations for the future, and sexual orientation. Adolescents who fail to reach these decisions experience role confusion and become unsure about who they are and their eventual role in life.	In this stage, the developmental task is to establish meaningful relationships with other people. Experiencing successful friendships and a committed relationship results in the creation of intimacy. Failure to achieve these relationships results in a feeling of isolation.	During this stage, adults become established in their careers, but they also shift attention to helping others through caring for children or otherwise working for the benefit of others. The result is generativity—a feeling of continuity with the next generation. People who become too self-absorbed and do not connect to coming generations experience feelings of boredom and meaninglessness.	When people enter old age able to look back on a lifetime of accomplishment and positive resolutions of past challenges, they experience a sense of integrity—the knowledge that their lives have had meaning and that they have done the best they could given their circumstances. Those who have not resolved past conflicts successfully and who look back at their lives with disappointment experience despair—a sense of bitterness and helplessness.

Emotional communication occurs in both directions, however. Caregiver-to-infant communication begins when infants become able to perceive their parents' emotions, at about 10 weeks of age. Jeanette Haviland and Mary Lelwica (1987) documented this ability by having infants' mothers display happy, sad, or angry facial expressions while saying "You make me happy (sad, angry)" in a voice that matched their expression. Each of these emotional expressions elicited different reactions from the infants. Infants looked interested in response to the mother's smiles; looked off to the side in response to her expressions of anger; and exhibited "mouthing" behavior (sucking the lip and tongue and pushing the lips in and out) in response to her sad expression. This ability to react to adult emotions continues to develop as infants grow older. By the middle of the first year, infants react differently to a wide range of emotions (Johnson et al., 1982; Lester, 1984).

FIGURE 10.4
Long before infants can talk they use facial expressions and vocalizations to communicate with their caregivers.

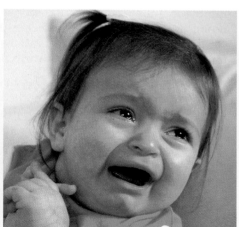

FIGURE 10.5
An infant at the edge of a visual cliff

Once they have learned to perceive adults' emotions, infants can begin to use information about those emotions to regulate their own behavior. Consider, for example, the following situation, which occurred in James Sorce's laboratory (Sorce et al., 1985) but can easily be generalized. A 12-month-old infant is perched on the edge of what would be a 1-foot drop if it weren't for the sheet of glass covering the drop (Figure 10.5). This arrangement, called a **visual cliff,** has been used to demonstrate infants' depth perception by testing their reactions to being placed on the edge of the "cliff" (Gibson & Walk, 1960).

The infant is on one side of the cliff and the mother is on the other side next to a toy. Will the infant venture onto the glass to retrieve the toy? The answer depends on the mother's emotional expression. If, without saying anything, the mother looks fearful, the infant won't cross over; but if the mother looks joyful or interested, the infant is more likely to crawl across the glass to retrieve the toy. The infant's behavior in Sorce's experiment is called **social referencing**—faced with an uncertain situation, the infant "refers to" the mother's emotional expression before determining a course of action.

Social referencing occurs not only between infants and mothers but between infants and other familiar people. However, the degree to which infants use social referencing depends on the nature of their relationship with the other person. For example, Susan Dickstein and Ross Parke (1988) have shown that the strength of an infant's social-referencing response to the father depends on how satisfied the *father* is with his marriage. When placed in an uncertain situation, infants of fathers who were dissatisfied with their marriage looked at their fathers for information less than half as often as did infants of fathers who were satisfied with their marriage.

What does this result mean? One possibility is that infants of the dissatisfied fathers have found that their fathers are not as available to them, so they do not depend on them so much. If this is true, it means infants are sensitive to the kinds of interactions they have with their caregivers and that they modify their behavior based on the quality of those interactions.

Establishing communication with caregivers is the first step toward developing an attachment bond with them. Why is this bond important? To answer this question, we need to look at how researchers have distinguished different degrees of attachment and their consequences.

Consequences of attachment.   The standard procedure for measuring infant-caregiver attachment is called the **strange situation.** In this procedure, developed by Mary Ainsworth (Ainsworth, 1982; Ainsworth & Wittig, 1969), a mother and her 12- to 20-month-old infant are initially together in a room. Over the next 15 to 20 minutes the infant experiences being just with the mother, being with the mother and a stranger, being just with the stranger, and being alone. During these episodes, the experimenter observes the child's behavior, especially noticing the infant's reaction to the mother when she returns after being out of the room, the infant's reaction to being picked up, and his or her reaction to the stranger. Based on these observations, researchers have defined the following four types of attachment (Ainsworth, 1982; Main & Solomon, 1990):

1. **Securely attached:** The infant seeks out the mother and reacts positively to her when she reenters the room. The mother can comfort the infant, who shows a preference for the mother over the stranger. About 65% of infants in the United States are classified as securely attached.
2. **Insecurely attached/avoidant:** The infant avoids the mother when she reenters the room and treats the mother and stranger in the same way. About 20 to 25% of U.S. infants are avoidant.
3. **Insecurely attached/ambivalent:** The infant seems angry at the mother and may push her away. The mother can't comfort the child. About 10 to 15% of U.S. infants are ambivalent.

4. **Insecurely attached/disorganized:** The infant's behavior toward the mother is confused, sometimes positive and sometimes negative. The mother cannot comfort the infant. About 5% of U.S. infants show disorganized attachment.

What is the significance of being securely or insecurely attached? A large number of studies have tested the hypothesis that children who become securely attached in infancy will later be more competent socially and cognitively than will insecurely attached children. This is accomplished through longitudinal studies in which infants' attachment is measured at an early age (usually during the second year) and their behavior assessed a few years later. For example, Michael Lewis and his co-workers (1984) classified 1-year-old boys and girls as being secure or insecure, based on their behavior in the strange situation. When the children were 6 years old Lewis asked their parents a series of questions designed to identify behavior problems. They found that only 5% of the securely attached boys had behavior problems, whereas 40% of the insecurely attached boys had some behavior problems (also see Cohn, 1990; Erikson, Sroufe, & Egeland, 1985). For reasons that aren't clear, Lewis found no relationship between attachment and later behavior problems for girls. In another study, Adriana Bus and Marinus van Ijzendoorn (1988) found that children who were securely attached at 2 years of age showed more interest in reading at the age of 5 than did insecurely attached children. Still other studies have shown the following:

- Securely attached children are better liked by peers at 6 years old; insecurely attached children tend to be more aggressive (Cohn, 1990).
- Securely attached 4-year-olds play with their friends more harmoniously; insecurely attached children are more likely to grab and take possessions (Park & Waters, 1989).
- Securely attached preschoolers are less emotionally dependent on their teachers. They seek help by asking directly and then play at a distance from the teacher. Insecurely attached children stay near the teacher but don't directly ask for help. Instead, they wait for the teacher to act (Sroufe, Fox, & Pancake, 1983).

These results support the idea that the quality of the early relationship between infant and caregiver is related to the child's later development. Remember, however, that showing an association between attachment and later behavior doesn't by itself establish a *causal* relationship between these variables. For example, a child's naturally pleasant disposition might help him establish a secure attachment to his mother, and might also explain why he is well liked by his peers and less emotionally dependent on his teachers.

It is also important to realize that the correlation between attachment and later behavior is far from a perfect one. Although 40% of the insecurely attached boys in the Lewis study experienced behavior problems at age 6, remember that 60% did *not*. Attachment can predict later behavior, but other factors are also important.

Determinants of attachment.   What causes children to be securely or insecurely attached? Remember that Erikson felt that an infant develops trust if he or she experiences support and nurturing from caregivers. In fact, research has shown that an important factor appears to be how the mother responds to the child—specifically, how *sensitive* the mother is to the infant's needs.

Susan Crockenberg (1981) found that children are more likely to be securely attached if their mothers are supportive. "Mothers of securely attached infants are more responsive to the infant's cries, hold their babies more tenderly and carefully . . . and exhibit greater sensitivity in initiating and terminating feeding" (p. 857). From these positive interactions infants develop an expectation that their needs will be met, and their attachment thus becomes secure.

Fathers' interactions with children tend to involve more physical play than do mothers' interactions.

Other studies have shown not only that secure attachment is fostered by mothers who are responsive to their children's cries, are more affectionate, and interfere less with their infants' behavior, but also that insecure attachment is fostered by *extremes* of mothering. Mothers who respond to their children so vigorously that they become intrusive might "turn off" the child and increase the chances of avoidant attachment. At the other extreme, mothers who hardly respond at all, or who are inconsistent in the way they respond, increase the chances of resistant attachment (Isabella & Belsky, 1991). Other influences on attachment—and differences in attachment across cultures—are discussed in this chapter's Follow-Through.

The research on attachment has focused on mothers, because they are most likely to be the infant's primary caregiver; but Michael Lamb (1977) has shown that infants are also attached to their father. Lamb found that mothers and fathers interact with their infants differently: mothers tend to hold babies while performing caretaking functions such as changing diapers or feeding; fathers tend to hold babies while playing with them. Fathers, Lamb suggests, are not simply "mother substitutes," but provide their children with qualitatively different experiences than the mother does.

We have seen that during the brief period of infancy many changes take place in the infant's social world. Newborns enter the world with only a biological relationship to their parents, and they communicate mainly by crying. Shortly, however, they become able to express emotions and to recognize the emotional displays of others. As their physical and cognitive capacities mature, they begin using language to establish relationships with parents and other caretakers, gradually developing the ability to take other people's points of view. These relationships prepare the way for others, as children's social world expands to include peers and adults outside the home.

As children develop these relationships with others, an important insight occurs—they begin to realize that they are separate from others and have qualities that define them as unique individuals. This realization is the development of the self.

Development of the Self in Childhood

When you think about yourself, what comes to mind? Perhaps you make positive judgments about yourself: you feel you have accomplished a lot in school or socially, or you are simply pleased about the type of person you are. Perhaps you make some negative judgments: you feel you could work harder, do better, or be more sure of what you want to do in the future. Or perhaps you might simply describe yourself in terms of characteristics such as height, weight, religion, gender, ethnic background, and occupation.

Whatever specifics come up when you think about yourself, the fact that you *can* see yourself as a distinct person separate from others—with your own qualities, abilities, feelings, and thoughts—is the result of a learning process that started early in your life and continues today. From the perspective of Erikson's stages of development, this process begins in early childhood, as young children strive to achieve autonomy (stage 2); it peaks in adolescence, as teenagers strive to determine their identity (stage 5).

As we discuss the development of a sense of self, we will see that it is based on an interesting paradox: the process of learning to see yourself as an *individual* is created largely through social interactions with *others*. The development of this sense of self begins with self-awareness.

Self-awareness.   Infants lack **self-awareness,** an awareness of the boundaries that separate them from others. The first behavioral evidence of this awareness surfaces in the middle of the second year. By this time children have developed from their helpless beginnings to being mobile beings who are not only capable of "getting into things" but are also rapidly developing a will of their own. Two-year-olds begin asking other people for things (pointing to the cookie jar and saying "want cookie") and describing their own behavior ("I fix"). Awareness of the self is also indicated by the child's ability to appreciate others' feelings; during the last part of the second year, children begin showing concern for someone who is hurt with hugs or kisses, or by comforting the person in some way (Dunn & Kendrick, 1982: Radke-Yarrow, Zahn-Waxler, & Chapman, 1983). These actions, which show that children can identify the inner feelings of others, suggest that they are becoming aware of their own inner feelings as well.

An important ability that develops during the second year is **self-recognition,** the ability to recognize oneself. One way to test for the development of self-recognition is to notice how children react to seeing their image in a mirror. At 4 months of age babies will reach out to touch their mirror image. At 10 months they will reach behind themselves if a toy is lowered behind them while they are watching in the mirror. These demonstrations show that infants will react when they see their image in a mirror, but they do not prove that the infants actually *recognize* that image as being themselves. To test for *self-recognition,* George Gallup (1970) developed a procedure that was first used on chimpanzees.

⑤ CONSCIOUSNESS

When Gallup exposed chimpanzees to a mirror, he observed that for the first few days they reacted to their image as if it were another chimp, making threatening gestures and vocalizations. But by about the third day, the chimps began looking into the mirror as they groomed themselves. To determine whether chimps actually recognized themselves in the mirror, Gallup anesthetized one and placed a red dye on the ridge of one eyebrow and on the opposite ear. When the chimp woke up and looked at himself in the mirror he immediately began touching the places on his face where the spots were located. The important point here is that the chimp touched *himself,* not the image of the spot he saw in the mirror. Gallup interpreted this behavior as showing that the chimp recognized that he was seeing himself in the mirror.

Michael Lewis and Jeanne Brooks-Gunn (1979) used Gallup's procedure with children by placing a spot of red rouge on their noses. Those younger than 18 to 21 months did not touch their noses when they saw their image in the mirror, but two-thirds of 24-month-olds did. They pointed to their own red nose (not to the image in the mirror), asked what it was, and sometimes tried to rub it off. Within a few months after they became capable of passing the rouge test, children began using the pronouns *I, me,* and *you*—a sign that they had a sense of themselves as separate from other people.

Self-concept.   As children grow older they move beyond self-awareness and begin developing a **self-concept**—a sense of who they are and what their unique qualities are. Until the age of about 7, children describe themselves primarily in terms of their physical characteristics and their possessions. Asked to respond to the open-ended question "Who am I?" young children typically will say something like "I have brown hair and I have a teddy bear." Older children typically describe themselves on a more abstract level, referring to their future occupation, their beliefs, and how they feel or think (Montemayor & Eisen, 1977). A typical response from an older child would be "I plan on becoming a doctor, because I think it is important to help people." Increasing age creates other, more subtle, shifts in self-concept as well. When children between 10 and 18 were asked to describe their traits, 10-year-olds focused on *character* traits (honest, brave) or emotions (happy, cheerful), whereas older youths were more likely to focus on *interpersonal* traits (friendly, shy, well liked, sociable, attractive to others). By 17 or 18, adolescents commonly focus on internal psychological states such as emotions, attitudes, wishes, and secrets.

Self-esteem.   The formation of the self is accompanied by a process of *evaluation,* in which people decide how they *feel* about who they are. They ask such questions as "How attractive am I?" "How intelligent am I?" "Am I likable?" "How well am I doing at my job?" Answers to questions such as these determine a person's **self-esteem**—the overall value that the person assigns to the elements that make up his or her identity.

The development of self-esteem is one of the main outcomes of Erikson's fourth stage of social development, in which the crisis is *industry versus inferiority*. During this stage, which lasts from 6 to 11 years of age, children are faced with the challenges of achieving in school, making friends, and fitting into a family. If a child succeeds in these tasks, he or she achieves *industry*, which translates into high self-esteem.

Susan Harter (1982) has measured self-esteem in young children by presenting them with 28 statements like the one shown in Figure 10.6. The child is asked to pick the statement that is "most like me" and then to decide whether that choice is "really true for me" or "sort of true for me." This scale results in self-esteem ratings in the following four areas:

1. *Cognitive competence:* Doing well at school, feeling smart, remembering what I read.
2. *Social competence:* Having a lot of friends, being popular and well liked.
3. *Physical competence:* Doing well at sports, being chosen early for games.
4. *General self-worth:* Feeling sure of myself, liking the way I am, feeling like a good person.

By the time children are 8 years old their evaluations of themselves tend to coincide with the way they are evaluated by others. Thus, teachers give ratings that correlate well with the ratings students give to themselves.

What causes high or low self-esteem in children? Parenting style is an important factor. Children with high self-esteem tend to have parents that (1) demonstrate acceptance by being supportive or affectionate; (2) set clearly defined limits on the child's activity; and (3) show respect by taking the child's point of view into account (Coopersmith, 1967). Self-esteem also develops as children compare themselves with others in a number of ways. They look at others' test scores in school, notice who is the most popular and has the most popular friends, and compare their performance in sports with that of their classmates (Frey & Ruble, 1985).

The development of self-esteem becomes a part of a child's self-concept. Another important part of children's self-concept is their awareness of their gender and their understanding of what being a male or a female means. The process of gaining this awareness is called gender identification.

Gender identification.   Just as a sense of self takes time to develop, so too does an understanding of the categories "male" and "female." By the time children are between 2 and 3 years of age they have heard their parents and others repeatedly refer to them as a boy or a girl, and they can perceive differences between other boys and girls. Children therefore acquire **gender identity**—the knowledge that they are a boy or a girl—between 2 and 3 years of age (Fagot, 1985c).

We saw in the Follow-Through in Chapter 6 that children 2 or 3 years old

FIGURE 10.6

A sample item used to measure self-esteem in young children. Children pick the statement "most like" themselves and then decide whether it is "really" or "sort of" true for them.

Really true for me	Sort of true for me	Some kids often forget what they learn	but	Other kids can remember things easily	Sort of true for me	Really true for me
☐	☐				☐	☐

not only are aware of their own gender but also know a lot about the kinds of things males and females typically do. But even though young children know their own gender and have a developing picture of differences between males and females, they still do not totally understand gender. One of their main confusions is whether they will always be a boy or a girl. It is not unusual for a 3- or 4-year-old to think that it is possible to grow up to be the other gender. This is illustrated by the following conversation between Steve, who is 4$^1/_2$, and Jimmy, who is 4.

> *Steve:* I'm going to be an airplane builder when I grow up.
> *Jimmy:* When I grow up, I'll be a mommy.
> *Steve:* No, you can't be a mommy. You have to be a daddy.
> *Jimmy:* No, I'm going to be a mommy.
> *Steve:* No, you're not a girl; you can't be a mommy.
> *Jimmy:* Yes, I can (adapted from Kohlberg, 1966, p. 95).

In this example, Steve has achieved **gender constancy**—the knowledge that one's gender is permanent—whereas Jimmy has not. Children acquire the concept of gender constancy between the ages of 4 and 7 (Hyde, 1991; Intons-Peterson, 1988).

Gender socialization.   As they are learning their gender identity, children are also learning what it *means* to be a boy or a girl. As we saw in Chapter 6's Follow-Through, children's early assimilation of how males and females are "supposed" to behave is a part of **socialization**—the process by which children are taught the values, rules of behavior, and social roles deemed appropriate by their culture. Socialization includes teaching such rules as how to behave at the dinner table, how to interact with others, and how to dress for different occasions (Saarni, 1989, 1990).

Though some of the rules learned through socialization apply to everyone, **gender socialization** teaches rules specific to gender. For example, most girls in our society are socialized to behave in a "ladylike" fashion and to be interested in caring for young children and becoming a mother. Boys, on the other hand, are socialized to be independent, to play roughly with other boys, and to be interested in having a career that will enable them to support a family.

Socialization is carried out by **socializing agents**—people or institutions that teach children the behaviors deemed appropriate in a particular culture. At the end of Chapter 6 we saw that parents treat boys and girls differently, and that males and females are depicted differently in the media.

In addition to being socialized by their parents and the media, children are socialized by their peers. Beginning in preschool, usually boys play mostly with boys, and girls play mostly with girls, a situation called **gender segregation** (Maccoby & Jacklin, 1987). This segregation establishes two different "cultures" with different environments and rules, as indicated in Table 10.1. For example, boys tend to play in larger groups than girls, and their play tends to be rougher and to occur farther away from adults. Boys and girls are, therefore, socialized to act differently by virtue of their membership in these gender-segregated groups.

Girls and boys also encounter different experiences in school. Observational studies of school classrooms indicate that preschool teachers most often respond to girls when they are nearby but respond to boys no matter where they are. In all grades, boys receive more attention than girls (Fagot, 1985b; Sadker & Sadker, 1985; Serbin & O'Leary, 1975).

The different treatment of girls and boys teaches them different behaviors. For example, if girls receive attention only when they play near the teacher, they learn to be dependent, a trait often associated with females in our society. Boys, on the other hand, receive the teacher's attention even when playing far away, thereby allowing them to be more independent, a trait often associated with males in our society.

19   SOCIAL

By acting out male and female roles, these children are learning about their own gender.

TABLE 10.1
Characteristics of boy and girl "cultures"

Activity	Boys	Girls
Play	In large groups; in public places away from adults; rough, with fighting	In groups of two or three; nearer adults; gentle
Social interaction	Likely to have a leader who issues commands	Likely to interact as equals, taking turns talking or deciding what to do
Friendships	Based largely on activities	Based on intimacy; self-disclosure common; conflicts more distressful
Speech	Used to attract attention and assert position	Seldom used to interrupt each other; often used to agree; used to create close and equal relationships

Source: Maccoby and Jacklin, 1987.

The Self in Adolescence

Although children become aware of themselves as individuals early in childhood, the process continues as they get older, and it becomes extremely important with the onset of the physical and cognitive changes of adolescence. In adolescence a major concern is defining oneself in relation to others; most adolescents place a high priority on having same-sex friends and on being accepted by the other sex. Adolescents' social relations also involve interactions with their parents, which sometimes become strained as adolescents begin asserting their independence (Steinberg, 1987). (See Measurement & Methodology, "Do Parents and Adolescents Argue? A Question of Measurement.")

Social development entails not only interacting with others but also learning to function independently. Asserting independence is one of the central tasks of adolescence. As we saw in our depiction of Erikson's psychosocial theory earlier in this chapter, he views the conflict of adolescence as one of *identity versus role confusion*. Adolescents' main developmental focus, according to Erikson, is discovering their identity by answering the question "Who am I?" If they fail in this task, they end up being confused about the roles they will fill as adults.

Identity formation.   Although young children do play "identity games"—as they pretend to be particular characters or pick occupations like fireman or ballet dancer—we usually do not picture 8-year-olds thinking in any serious way about their future occupations or being concerned with politics or religious beliefs. It is easy, however, to imagine 17-year-olds as extremely concerned with such questions. According to James Marcia (1966, 1980), it is just these issues—career, politics, and religion—that are critical in forming an identity.

By focusing on how people make occupational choices and form ideological beliefs, Marcia has observed that different people go through the process of identity formation in different ways. He classifies people into four different *identity statuses* based on their responses to questions about their choice of occupation and their religious and political views. Marcia's four identity statuses are:

1. **Identity achievement:** This person has gone through a decision-making process and has defined his or her own occupational and ideological goals.
2. **Identity foreclosure:** This person has settled on occupational and ideological goals, but they have been defined by others—usually the person's parents. This type of solution to the identity problem is most typical of individuals who feel pressured to conform to family values. For example, Don's father and older brothers are all doctors, so it is assumed that he will become a doctor. George's father is a building contractor, so it is assumed that he will work with his father and eventually take over the family business. In the past, young women's occupational identities have often been defined by strong social pressures to devote themselves to taking care of a home and children.

3. **Identity moratorium:** This person is having an **identity crisis;** he or she is struggling with the decision process. Such a person is more likely to change college majors than are peers whose status is one of identity achievement or identity foreclosure.

4. **Identity diffusion:** This person has not yet defined his or her occupational or ideological identity.

The differences in the four categories of identity status can be illustrated by the following answers to the question "Have you ever had any doubts about your religious beliefs?" (Marcia, 1966, p. 553):

1. *Identity achievement:* "Yeah, I even started wondering whether or not there was a God. I've pretty much resolved that, though. The way it seems to me is . . ." (Thoughts on religion are defined by the person.)
2. *Identity foreclosure:* "No, not really. Our family is pretty much in agreement on these things." (Thoughts on religion are defined by others.)
3. *Identity moratorium:* "Yes, I guess I'm going through that right now. I just don't see how there can be a God and yet so much evil in the world . . ." (Thoughts on religion are in flux.)

MEASUREMENT & METHODOLOGY

Do Parents and Adolescents Argue? A Question of Measurement

A popular picture of the adolescent-adult relationship is one of conflict. According to this conception, it is a fact of life that adolescents and adults will be "at" each other, as the adolescent's need for independence conflicts with the adult's need to set boundaries for the adolescent's behavior.

But is this conception of adolescent-adult relations correct? According to a number of studies, it isn't. These studies have reported surprisingly little conflict between most adolescents and their parents (Bath & Lewis, 1962; Offer, 1969; Rutter et al., 1976). When Michael Rutter and his co-workers (1976) asked 14- and 15-year-olds and their mothers if they argued, only 18% of the moth-

ers and 36% of the teenagers reported that they did. Two aspects of Rutter's results are interesting. First, the teenagers' reports of conflict are twice as high as the adults'. One reason for this discrepancy might be that the mothers are more reluctant to report conflict. Another possible reason is that adolescents *perceive* more conflict. Thus, when the mother says "Pick up your clothes," she may not perceive any conflict, whereas the adolescent might feel resentment. The second aspect of interest is that most of the adults and teenagers—82% of the mothers and 64% of the adolescents—reported little or no conflict.

Are parent-adolescent relationships really as tranquil as these data suggest? Raymond Montemayor (1983) argues that, in fact, a substantial amount of conflict can be detected if researchers change the way they ask the questions. Rather than ask parents and adolescents to report the *general* level of conflict in the relationship, as was done in the studies we have discussed so far, it is necessary to ask whether conflict has occurred during a *specific period of time*. Montemayor (1982) did this by telephoning adolescents on three randomly selected evenings over a three-week period. The adolescents were asked to recount the events of the previous day, including conflicts with parents. When asked about conflicts in this way, adolescents reported an average of one argument every three days, mostly with mothers and especially between mothers and daughters. The adolescents reported that many of these arguments were moderately upsetting to them.

The results of Montemayor's research indicates that all is not peaceful between parents and adolescents. Thus, parent-teen conflict may not be as severe as many people think, but some conflict is apparently the norm. The important point for our purposes is that the answers we get to questions about behavior depend on the method we use to gather information about that behavior.

4. *Identity diffusion:* "Oh, I don't know. I guess so. Everyone goes through some sort of stage like that. But it really doesn't bother me much. I figure one's about as good as another." (Thoughts on religion are not defined.)

Marcia points out that although we can place people in different identity statuses, and though we know that adolescence and the college years are the key period for identity formation, we know little about how identity actually develops. One of the least understood aspects of identity formation is how the process occurs for women. Some research suggests that it proceeds differently for women than for men. For example, Dan Schiedel and Marcia (1985) found that the proportion of females in the achievement and moratorium stages—the stages that represent the most active thinking about identity—remains constant between 18 and 24 years, but the proportion of males increases. This difference may be due to the fact that males receive a strong message from our society that one of their primary roles as adults is choosing a career and advancing in that career, wheras contemporary women are sent the double message that they should seek a career *and* get married and devote considerable time and energy to caring for a family (Houston-Stein & Higgens-Trenk, 1978). This double message from society may make it more difficult for young women to decide on an identity and also affects how women *evaluate* the elements that make up their identity.

A number of studies have demonstrated a relationship between identity status and behavior. People who have achieved their identity have higher grade point averages (Cross & Allen, 1970), perform better under stress (Muuss, 1982), are better at engaging in intimate interpersonal relationships (Fitch & Adams, 1983; Orlofsky, Marcia, & Lesser, 1973), and are more self-assured (Adams, Abraham, & Markstrom, 1987).

The studies on identity formation that focus on how people feel about politics and religion and how they choose a career have been carried out primarily on middle-class people. Is the process different for individuals in other subcultures in our society? A fascinating glimpse into this question is provided by research on young males who become members of urban gangs.

Urban gangs have become an increasingly visible feature of our cities. It is estimated that Los Angeles alone has 750 gangs with up to 100,00 members (Majors & Billson, 1992). Because of the prevalence of gangs, some researchers have studied this "culture" by interviewing gang members and, in some cases, participating in gang activities. The following Interdisciplinary Dimension explores the implications of some of this research for the issue of identity formation.

INTERDISCIPLINARY DIMENSION ANTHROPOLOGY

Identity Formation in Inner-City Gangs

Anthropologist James Diego Vigil (1988a, 1988b) has conducted a study of youth gangs in Chicano (Mexican-American) areas of Los Angeles. Vigil, an anthropologist at UCLA, is uniquely qualified to study Chicano youth gangs, because along with his anthropological training he has had the experience of growing up in a Chicano neighborhood, or *barrio*. This not only gave him an insider's view of life in the barrio but made it possible for him to gain the trust of gang members in a number of East L.A. gangs. He sought not only to observe gang activities but to determine the purpose the gang served for its members.

Vigil's study spanned five years, during which he interviewed gang members and was an observer-participant in gang activities. One of the questions he addressed is "What makes a person join a gang?" This is an important question, because only about 3 to 10% of barrio youth join gangs" (Morales, 1982). Vigil found that the youths attracted to gang life were the most deprived in terms of home life and school achievement. Their poor home life, often characterized by parental fighting or by a single mother overwhelmed by too many children to care for, pushes them into the streets, where they face the reality of street violence. The threat of violence and the presence of gang members on the street encourages some to join the neighborhood gang. A 24-year-old gang member puts it this way:

Gangs offer many barrio youths not only protection, but acceptance by others and a sense of identity.

> I was born into my barrio. It was either get your ass kicked every day or join a gang and get your ass kicked occasionally by rival gangs. Besides, it was fun and I belonged (Vigil, 1988b, p. 427).

Thus, the gang provides protection plus fun and a sense of belonging. Much of the fun comes from hanging out, joking, drinking, playing games, and sometimes fighting with other gangs. Underlying these activities is the attainment of identity, through being both *macho*—a strong male—and through being a member of the group. Being identified as *macho* is achieved by performance in areas ranging from handball games (in which players endure friendly catcalls such as "*Juegas como chavala*" ("You play like a girl"), to the gang initiation ceremony, to street fighting.

The initiation ceremony often involves enduring a physical beating by gang members. This ritual is not restricted to Chicano gangs: Richard Majors and Janet Billson (1992) report that the PGBs, a black L.A. gang, require prospective members to engage in a ritual called a "jump in," in which the initiate chooses three gang members and "jumps in" to fight them all at once. If he remains standing after 10 minutes, he belongs.

By taking the beating, the new member shows he is tough enough to engage in street fighting with the gang. As one 17-year-old interviewed by Vigil put it, "I guess I took an ass whipping to be able to back up the barrio." This macho idea of toughness is reinforced in fights with individuals outside of the gang, as described by this 22-year-old:

> If anybody threatens a member we had to get together and beat the guys near to death. That's when you show how tough you are because you have to be tough to make it in this world (Vigil, 1988b, p. 428).

This idea of toughness may be doubly important to gang members who grow up in female-headed families: the gang may provide a substitute for the absent father. Older members serve as male role models, and street fighting provides a way to affirm maleness by being tough. A 16-year-old recalls his transition from the female world of home to the male world of the gang as follows:

> I remember my Mom used to comb my hair. . . . She would play some Spanish music on radio KALI and she would get dressed and cook breakfast, comb our hair. I remember she used to comb it to the sides. So one day I took the comb from her and started combing it back. That's when I started thinking I was all *chingón* (tough guy, in control) (Vigil, 1988b, p. 430).

In addition to demonstrating toughness, which affirms their identification as strong males, these adolescents also identify themselves as gang members by adopting the street style of manners and dress called *cholo*—speaking a mixed Spanish-English slang, wearing khaki pants and Pendleton shirts, adopting a conservative, combed-back hair style, and affecting a type of body language that Vigil describes as "controlled, deliberate and methodical." In black gangs, members often adopt a style called "Cool Pose," a ritualized form of masculinity that includes a masked facial expression—betraying no emotion, even in dangerous situations—and a distinctive swaggering, springy walk—one arm swinging at the side, hand slightly cupped, the other hand slipped into the pocket (Majors & Billson, 1992).

These anthropological observations suggest that youth gangs serve purposes similar to other adolescent groups that affirm their members as individuals and help them achieve an identity. In groups legitimized by society, the adolescent's identity is achieved in the context of activities like playing organized sports, organizing the school homecoming dance, or participating in church activities. In the case of youth gangs, identity is achieved within a more antisocial context, which in its extremes includes street fighting, killing members of rival gangs, and shooting that may involve innocent bystanders as well. It is within this antisocial context that the gang affirms its members' status as important people. The gang, according to Vigil, takes on the responsibility of "doing what the family, school, and other social agencies have failed to do—provide mechanisms for age and sex development, establish norms of behavior, and define and structure outlets for friendship, human support, and the like" (1988b, p. 168).

When gang members begin moving out of adolescence and into adulthood, many of them "mature out" of the gang. Once out of the gang, in their early or middle 20s, they are forced to cope with survival in the adult world. Some obtain jobs and succeed; others remain unemployed, hold marginal jobs, or engage in criminal activities such as robbery or drug dealing. Although it might be said that the gang does not prepare its members for adult life, it does give adolescents who are experiencing an identity moratorium an identity, at least for a time.   ■

Self-esteem in adolescence.   We have seen that self-esteem begins to form at an early age, with 8-year-old children being able to accurately evaluate their own capacities. How does self-esteem change as a person progresses through adolescence? The answer to that question is different for males and females. Girls' self-esteem tends to be slightly lower than boys' in elementary school. Then, after elementary school, girls' self-esteem drops appreciably, whereas boys' drops only a little (American Association of University Women, 1991; Basow, 1992). For example, the percentage of boys and girls who agree with the statement "I'm happy the way I am" drops as they progress from elementary school to high school, but the drop is greater for girls than for boys (Figure 10.7).

This difference in how males and females feel about themselves persists through high school and beyond, with males' self-esteem either staying the same or increasing, especially if they do well in college and obtain a high-status job. Among females, not only does self-esteem drop more sharply than for males at the beginning of adolescence, but it may drop even further in college (Hesse-Biber & Marino, 1991; Widnall, 1988).

We can understand the reason for this drop by contrasting females' situation with that of males. Males' self-esteem is based largely on their ability to make progress toward educational and career goals. This straightforward equation doesn't work as well for females. Beginning in junior high or high school,

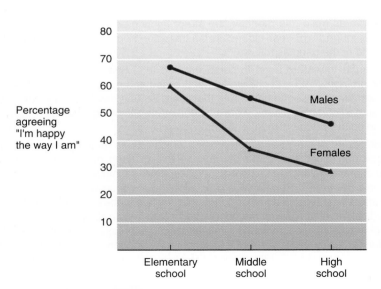

FIGURE 10.7
Self-esteem drops for both males and females as they get older, but the drop is much greater for females, especially between elementary and middle school.

girls become concerned about being popular with boys, and then later become focused on finding a marriage partner. One problem girls face is that high career aspirations are often incompatible with popularity. Jane might want to be a nuclear physicist, but the boys she knows may not be interested in having a relationship with a future nuclear physicist. As a result, some adolescent girls sacrifice career aspirations for popularity (Basow, 1992; Petersen, 1987).

Another issue that is important for girls' self-esteem in high school is appearance. Although personal appearance tops the list of concerns in high school for both boys and girls (Eme, Maisiak, & Goodale, 1979), it is especially important for girls. For example, Richard Lerner and his colleagues (1976) had high school girls and boys rate their self-esteem and then rate 24 parts of their bodies for physical *attractiveness* and physical *effectiveness*. The results indicate that attractiveness was more important to girls, effectiveness more important to boys. The importance of effectiveness for boys isn't surprising, considering the emphasis our society places on male physical prowess and participation in athletics.

The importance of appearance to girls is also not surprising, given the emphasis our society places on physical beauty in women. At least initially, attractiveness is the major concern of males looking for a partner (Deaux & Hanna, 1984; Smith, Waldorf, & Trembath, 1990). The resulting pressure for girls to be attractive appears to be one of the major reasons for the increase in depression that occurs in girls at about 12 years of age. Prior to 12 years, the rate of depression is the same for boys and girls. After 12 years of age, depression is twice as high in girls (Basow, 1992). It is probably no coincidence that when high school girls are surveyed, the most common problem they report is feeling ugly or unattractive (American Association of University Women, 1991).

Society's emphasis on attractiveness (Garner et al., 1980; Silverstein et al., 1986) puts so much pressure on girls to be thin that most girls think they weigh too much even if their weight is normal. For example, in one survey, three-quarters of teenage girls of normal weight wanted to weigh less (Eisle et al., 1986; also see Hesse-Biber & Marino, 1991). As we mentioned in Chapter 9, this pressure to be thin causes some girls to take such drastic steps to control their weight that they are diagnosed as having eating disorders such as anorexia nervosa—a condition in which people starve themselves—and bulimia—a condition in which people go on eating binges and then throw up to avoid gaining weight. These disorders affect 5 to 10% of adolescent girls, and 95% of the people who suffer from them are females (Muuss, 1986; Schwartz, Thompson, & Johnson, 1985).

A key statistic with regard to eating disorders is that women with an eating disorder or who are overweight have lower self-esteem than either normal-weight women or those without eating disorders (Hesse-Biber & Marino, 1991; Rodin, Silberstein, & Striegel-Moore, 1985). Thus, the development of self-esteem is particularly complex for females. Young girls learn that they must be good-looking to attract boys. They also learn that attractiveness means being thin, in part because of models they see in magazines, on TV, and in movies who provide ideals difficult to match. *Feeling* overweight (even irrationally) leads to low self-esteem and sometimes eating disorders.

It is clear that self-esteem depends on both a person's actual characteristics *and* pressures from society. Another area in which society plays an especially prominent role is moral development—the development of the reasoning behind a person's conception of right and wrong.

The Development of Moral Reasoning

We don't expect a baby or a young infant to know right from wrong. But as children grow older, they are socialized by parents, teachers, and society to follow certain rules of acceptable behavior. The study of moral development goes beyond simply determining when people behave "correctly" or know "right" from

16   DISORDERS

11   MOTIVATION

One of the symptoms of the eating disorder anorexia nervosa is the perception of being fat when in reality weight is normal or even below normal.

People at the postconventional level of morality tend to question society's rules.

"wrong." The study of moral development is concerned with determining the *beliefs and values* that underlie people's judgment of rightness or wrongness. This is what Piaget was studying when he asked children which was more wrong, accidentally breaking ten of their mother's best plates, or breaking one plate on purpose. We saw in Chapter 9 that whereas preoperational children (from 2 to 7 years) base their judgment on the *outcome* of the actions (breaking ten plates is more wrong), concrete operational children (from 7 to 11 years) base their judgment on the person's *intentions* (whether the action was accidental or intentional).

Lawrence Kohlberg (1963, 1981, 1984) extended Piaget's work by analyzing moral development in more detail and studying it as it progresses into adolescence. His analysis is based on how people respond to moral dilemmas such as the following:

> In Europe, a woman was near death from a special kind of cancer. There was one drug the doctors thought might save her. It was a form of radium that a druggist in the same town had recently discovered. The drug was expensive to make, but the druggist was charging ten times what the drug cost him to make. . . . The sick woman's husband, Heinz, went to everyone he knew to borrow money but he could only get together about $1,000, which is half of what it cost. He told the druggist that his wife was dying, and asked him to sell it cheaper or let him pay later. But the druggist said, "No, I discovered the drug and I'm going to make money from it." Heinz got desperate and broke into the man's store to steal the drug for his wife. Should the husband have done that? (1963, p. 18)

Once people respond "Yes" or "No" to this problem, Kohlberg asks them to explain their answer. It is this explanation, rather than the actual response, that Kohlberg uses to place people at one of three levels of moral judgment: preconventional, conventional, or postconventional.

Preconventional level.   People in the preconventional level give reasons that emphasize satisfying desires or avoiding punishment. For example, a preconventional response to Heinz's dilemma might be that someone in his position should steal the drug because "if your wife dies, you will be in trouble" or that he should not steal the drug because "if you get caught, you will go to jail." Kohlberg finds that most children under the age of 10 give preconventional responses.

Conventional level.   At the conventional level, people give reasons that are based on obeying the law and receiving social approval. Reasons that justify stealing the drug might be "People would think you are a good person for help-ing your wife" or "You should help your wife, because marriage is an obligation, like a legal contract." Reasons for not stealing the drug might be "You can't be blamed if your wife dies if you've done everything you legally can" or "The law has no exceptions." Many people reach the conventional level in late childhood, and most adolescents and adults reason at the conventional level of morality.

Postconventional, or principled, level.   Moral reasoning at this level is based on questioning the underlying basis for society's rules. A postconventional re-sponse defending Heinz might be "Stealing is wrong, but under these circum-stances stealing is justified to prevent a greater harm." A principled argument against stealing the drug might be "Laws become meaningless if we allow peo-ple to decide when to obey them." Only a small minority of adolescents and about 15% of adults reach the postconventional stage.

Kohlberg's theory is actually more complex than this description suggests, because he divides each level into two stages and uses a complicated scoring system to classify people as being in either the first or second stage within each level. (See Table 10.2 for a description of each stage.) For example, though some

TABLE 10.2
Kohlberg's theory of the development of moral reasoning

Level/Stage	Examples of Moral Reasoning	
	For Stealing Drug	*Against Stealing Drug*
Preconventional Level: Self-Interest		
Stage 1 Punishment and obedience orientation: Obey rules to avoid punishment.	"If you let your wife die, you'll get in trou-ble."	"You shouldn't steal the drug because you'll get caught and sent to jail."
Stage 2 Instrumental and exchange orientation: Do what will pay off for you; be nice to others so they will be nice to you.	"If you do happen to get caught, you could give the drug back and you wouldn't get much of a sentence. "	"He may not get much of a jail term if he steals the drug, but his wife will probably die before he gets out so it won't do him much good."
Conventional Level: Conventional Laws and Values		
Stage 3 Conformist, "good boy/good girl" orienta-tion: Act so as to get others' approval.	"No one will think you're bad if you steal the drug, but your family will think you're an in-human husband if you don't."	"It isn't just the druggist who will think you're a criminal; everyone else will too."
Stage 4 Law-and-order orientation: Don't break the rules.	"If you have any sense of honor, you won't let your wife die because you're afraid to do the only thing that will save her."	"You'll always feel guilty for your dishonesty and lawbreaking."
Postconventional Level: Abstract Moral Principles		
Stage 5 Social contract orientation: Generally follow rules, because they are rational and necessary for social order; but in some instances keep-ing one's own and others' respect means breaking the rules.	"If you let your wife die, it would be out of fear, not out of reasoning it out. So you'd just lose self-respect and probably the respect of others too."	"You would lose your standing and respect in the community, and violate the law."
Stage 6 Universal ethical principle orientation: Act in accordance with your personal conscience, based on what you believe would be right for anyone to do.	"If you don't steal the drug and let your wife die, you wouldn't be blamed and you would have lived up to the outside rule of the law but you wouldn't have lived up to your own standard of conscience."	"If you stole the drug you'd condemn your-self because you wouldn't have lived up to your own conscience and standards of hon-esty."

Source: Adapted from Kohlberg, 1981.

adults reach the first stage of the postconventional level, only extraordinary individuals such as Mahatma Gandhi or Martin Luther King, Jr., reach the highest stage of postconventional morality, in which the ultimate determinants of a person's behavior are the standards set by his or her conscience.

Kohlberg's model of moral development provides a theoretical picture of how people's moral reasoning develops. But do people actually follow the course of development described by the theory? Longitudinal research using Kohlberg's moral dilemmas shows that many individuals do continue to move to higher stages of development throughout adolescence and into adulthood (Colby et al., 1983) (Figure 10.8). However, despite its position as the pioneering work in the field of moral development, Kohlberg's research has not gone unchallenged. Some have criticized it for being culturally biased, because responses corresponding to Kohlberg's higher levels of moral reasoning are commonly observed only in Western, industrialized societies (Snarey, 1985). A second criticism, advanced by Carol Gilligan (1982), claims that Kohlberg's theory is biased against women.

Gilligan argues that because women are socialized to focus their energy on relationships and on being connected to others, they approach Kohlberg's moral dilemmas differently than men. A woman addressing a particular dilemma would tend to emphasize the relationships between the people involved, whereas a man would tend to downplay relationship issues. For example, when Gilligan presented the Heinz dilemma to an 11-year-old girl, the girl's responses focused on the idea that Heinz and the druggist should sit down and talk the matter over again, so that stealing wouldn't be necessary. This approach to the problem would not be given as much credit as the more male-oriented responses on which Kohlberg's scoring system is based.

Although Gilligan's ideas have been widely publicized, some researchers have failed to find differences between how men and women are classified in Kohlberg's system (Walker, 1984); others argue that there is, in fact, evidence for gender differences in moral reasoning (Baumrind, 1986). The issue of whether Kohlberg's model is biased against women remains to be settled.

There are obvious parallels between the reactions of researchers to Kohlberg's stage theory of moral reasoning and to Piaget's stage theory of cognitive development. Both Piaget and Kohlberg proposed theories that have revolutionized the way people think about development. Also, in both cases criticism of the theories by other researchers has led to additional research—some of it bolstering the theories, some of it calling them into question. It would be com-

FIGURE 10.8
As people get older they tend to reach higher stages of moral development. However, even by age 36 many people still have not reached stage 4 or 5.

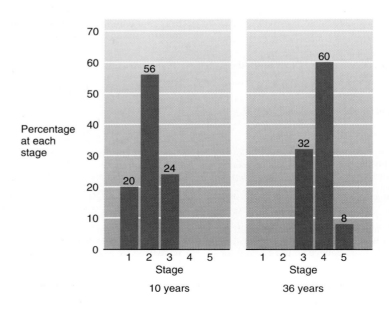

forting if all theories provided clear-cut answers to the questions they are supposed to answer, yet this rarely happens. But good theories provide new ways of thinking about the world that generate new directions in research. In this sense both Piaget's theory of cognitive development and Kohlberg's theory of moral development have been fruitful as well as influential.

Social Development: Adulthood

One of the signs of passing youth is the birth of a sense of fellowship with other human beings as we take our place among them.

Virginia Woolf (1882–1941)
English novelist

We have seen that people develop socially in dramatic ways from infancy through adolescence. This process does not, however, stop in adulthood. Social development in adulthood involves both continuity and change. In this section we will see that early experiences continue to influence social behavior in adulthood, and that change occurs in response to new experiences and challenges. We begin by considering how adults' behavior is related to their experiences as children.

Adult Behavior and Early Experience

When we discussed attachment we saw evidence that an infant's attachment classification, measured at 12 to 24 months of age, predicts, to some extent, later behavior in children. One of the significant things about these results is that an infant's attachment classification—whether secure, avoidant, ambivalent, or disorganized—depends to some extent on how she or he is parented. There is, in fact, some evidence that the way a child is parented, as well as other aspects of their socialization experiences, can affect their behavior as adults.

Adult social accomplishment and early parenting.   One of the most dramatic pieces of evidence supporting the idea that early parenting can affect a person's later characteristics is a study done by Carol Franz and her co-workers (1991). This study was a follow-up of one originally published in 1951 (Sears, Maccoby, & Levin, 1951). In the earlier study, the researchers asked 379 mothers of 5-year-old children questions about their parenting practices and those of their husbands. In 1987, 36 years later, Franz located 76 of the people who were children in the 1951 study.

Franz's subjects, now 41-year-old adults, were interviewed to determine their degree of social accomplishment and the warmth of their relationships with others. Combining the results from these 1987 interviews with the parenting practices documented in the 1951 study, Franz concluded that having a "warm" mother and father at the age of 5 increased the chances of being socially accomplished (having close friends that are seen often) and of being in a warm relationship with a significant other as an adult.

This demonstration of a relationship between events in early childhood and behavior 36 years later is impressive. However, we need to interpret these results cautiously, for two reasons. First, we are dealing with *correlations*. Therefore, although there is a *relationship* between parental warmth and later social accomplishment, *correlations do not demonstrate cause and effect*. It is possible that some other aspects of the home environment related to parental warmth might be the real causal factor. For example, perhaps "warm" parents went out of their way to expose their children to other young children. Or the causal factor could be biological, if characteristics that lead to "warmth" are genetically transmitted from parent to child.

Second, it is important to keep in mind the size of the correlations, which are on the order of .25 to .35. This means that the relation between early childhood experiences and adult behavior is not that close. Having a warm father does not guarantee later social success, just as having a distant one doesn't doom a person to social ineptness. Behaviors as complex as "relating" are influenced by many different environmental and biological factors in addition to parenting styles.

Differences in male and female communication.   Another connection between past experiences and adult social behavior has been suggested by linguist Deborah Tannen (1990), who sees a parallel between how girls and boys are socialized and the perspectives from which men and women approach conversations. Men, according to Tannen, use talk to preserve their independence, win "contests," and avoid failure. Women, in contrast, use talk to create connections between people, give information and support, and reach a consensus.

Tannen's data, which she presents in a book titled *You Just Don't Understand: Women and Men in Conversation,* consist mainly of descriptions of situations in which men's and women's differing conversational styles became a roadblock to clear communication. Here's one example.

> When Josh's high school buddy announced he would be visiting Josh's city on business, Josh immediately invited him to spend the weekend at his house. When he got home that evening, Josh informed his wife, Linda, that his friend would be spending the weekend. Linda was not pleased that Josh had made plans that affected both of them without checking with her. Josh's response was, "I can't say to my friend, 'I have to ask my wife for permission'!" (p. 26).

What's going on here? For Josh, checking with his wife makes him feel he isn't independent—it takes him back to his childhood, when he wasn't free to act on his own. For Linda, checking with Josh in similar circumstances is a way of establishing intimacy—it makes her feel more involved with him. According to Tannen, the conflict between Josh and Linda isn't a case of one of them being "wrong," but an illustration of different male and female perspectives: the male asserts his independence while the female stresses her need for intimacy.

What accounts for differences in the way males and females converse? Tannen answers this question by describing how boys and girls are socialized. Early in life, boys receive messages from parents, the media, and school that they should be independent, in charge, and not outwardly emotional. Girls receive messages that they should be concerned with taking care of other people and relating to others. This socialization is reflected in the way boys and girls talk to each other when playing. Jacqueline Sachs (1987) observed that when 2- to 5-year-old girls and boys played doctor, the girls *proposed activities* by saying "Let's do this . . ." whereas the boys *issued orders* such as "Lie down" and "Gimme your arm." The girls' way of relating creates a feeling of community through language that includes others in the decision-making process. The boys' way establishes dominance through language calculated to get others to follow their wishes. The boys also achieve dominance by insisting on being the doctor; girls, who aren't as concerned with dominance, are happy to be the patient, baby, or mother (Sachs, 1987; Anderson, 1977).

Looking again at adult conversation, we can see that males and females are simply continuing the behaviors they practiced as boys and girls. Josh asserts his independence from Linda by inviting his friend to stay without asking her, but Linda interprets his behavior as reflecting a lack of intimacy and concern for her wishes. Each has approached the exchange from the standpoint of what they learned about interacting with others as children.

According to Tannen, these differences reflect such different expectations that male-female conversation often amounts to cross-cultural communication. Thus, many of the misunderstandings that occur between men and women stem from the fact that, because of their childhood training, they approach conversation from such different perspectives.

We have seen how early experiences can leave their mark on later adult behavior. Another approach to adult social development is to consider the impact of some of the important events that take place during adulthood.

Life Events in Adulthood

Social development occurs throughout adulthood, often in response to specific life events such as marriage, having children, divorce, and retirement. One way to appreciate the nature of these changes is to remember Erikson's three stages of adult development described in Figure 10.2:

> *Young adulthood*: Dealing with intimacy; establishing relationships
> *Middle adulthood*: Continuing work in a career; helping the next generation
> *Older adulthood*: Coming to peace with life; resolving old conflicts

With this framework in mind, we will look at some of the important changes that occur in adulthood, beginning with a major task of young adulthood—dealing with intimacy and, for most people, getting married and having children.

Marriage and children.   Although there is a slight trend away from marriage and having children, over 90% of American adults marry, and most of these marriages result in children (Cavanaugh, 1993). The median age at which people get married has increased between 1960 and 1990, from 23 to 26 years for men and from 20 to 24 years for women (U.S. Bureau of the Census, 1991). Looking at marriage from a developmental perspective, we find that couples who have been together for many years experience changes across time both in the importance of different components of the relationship (Reedy, Birren, & Schaie, 1981) (Figure 10.9) and in overall satisfaction with the relationship (Rhyne, 1981) (Figure 10.10).

Apparently children are one of the important determinants of marital satisfaction, with satisfaction decreasing during child-raising years, particularly for women, who usually bear the brunt of child-rearing responsibilities (Harris, Ellicott, & Holmes, 1986). When the children begin leaving home, marital satisfaction begins to increase, a fact that contradicts the once widely held idea of the

Some misunderstandings between men and women result from differences in the way they learned to communicate while they were growing up.

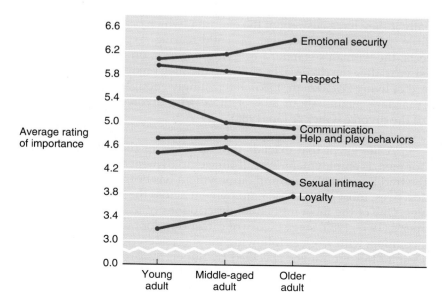

FIGURE 10.9
How different-aged adults rate the importance of components of a relationship. The importance of loyalty and emotional security increases with age, while that of sexual intimacy and communication decreases.

FIGURE 10.10
Marital satisfaction as a function of the stage of the relationship. Satisfaction decreases during child-rearing years.

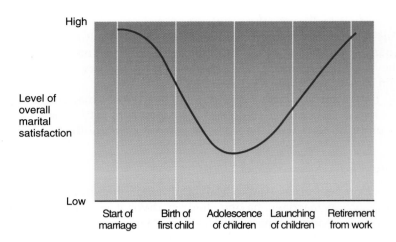

empty nest syndrome—a period of stress during which the mother is unhappy because her children have left home. Recent research indicates, however, that the opposite is true. When the children leave, women generally become happier and experience an increase in marital satisfaction (Reinke, Holmes, & Harris, 1985). Apparently, it is a relief to be free of the responsibility of raising children and their absence makes it possible for the husband and wife to spend more time together.

Although most people do marry, it is becoming more common in our society for people to remain single. The decision to remain single may be involuntary, because of an inability to find a suitable partner, or deliberate, because of a conscious choice to remain single. Years ago, a person who remained single was considered abnormal. Now there is less of a stigma on remaining single, especially since the high rate of divorce means that many married people will at some point return to single status.

Divorce.   Although most people enter marriage with the intention that the marriage will be permanent, about one out of every two marriages that occur in the 1990s will end in divorce (Fisher, 1987). If divorce does occur, it is most likely that it will be early in the marriage, since half of all divorces occur within the first seven years of marriage (Fisher, 1987).

The effect of divorce on both men and women can be devastating at first, especially if the marriage was a long one (Chiriboga, 1982) and if children are involved. Although men suffer more psychological and physical stress immediately after the divorce (Bloom & Caldwell, 1981), women suffer more financially, especially if they have custody of the children (which occurs in 90% of divorces) and little job training. Because of child-rearing expenses and low wage prospects, the woman's standard of living declines, on the average, by 73% in the first year after the divorce. In contrast, the men enjoy a 42% increase in their standard of living (Weitzman, 1985). Interestingly enough, most people are eager to try marriage again. About 80% of those who divorce remarry within three years of the divorce (Glick & Lin, 1986).

Work.   A life event that extends through most of the adult life span, especially for men, is employment. As full-time employment outside of the home has been the traditional male role, and employment has been seen as a central focus in males' lives, most research on employment across the life span has been done on males. One of the most influential descriptions of male employment is Donald Super's (1957, 1980) stage theory of career development. Super sees people's first encounters with work as following the stages described in Table 10.3.

Despite the age ranges specified by Super, research shows that there are large individual differences in the ages at which people enter the various stages. Susan Phillips (1982) found that 37% of 36-year-old males (who should be in

TABLE 10.3
Super's stages of occupational development

Stage	Description	Age Range
Exploration	First jobs; searching for a career	15–24
Establishment	Critically evaluating career choice; stable period of work and career advancement	25–44
Maintenance	Maintain job; less striving for advancement	45–65
Decline	Retire and adapt to leaving work force	over 65

Source: From Super, 1957, 1980.

Super's establishment stage) viewed their jobs as exploratory—they were evaluating their jobs to see if they really liked a particular field of work. Thus, even at age 36 over one-third of these men had not yet determined their adult career. This wide variation in the ages at which men enter the establishment stage means that adult development is not as fixed by age as Super's age ranges might imply.

Research also indicates that the idea that work dominates men's lives may not be valid for all men. Consider, for example, the study done by Douglas Bray and Ann Howard (1983), in which they measured men's attitudes about work from when they started as beginning managers at AT&T into middle age. They found that the degree to which work dominated the men's lives was a function of their success within the company (Figure 10.11). Those who became higher-level managers were satisfied with their jobs and saw work as a central focus of their lives. In contrast, those who became only middle- or lower-level managers were less happy in their jobs and tended to focus their energy more on their family, friends, and outside interests.

What about women and work? As over two-thirds of women between the ages of 18 and 64 hold jobs (U.S. Department of Labor, 1988), employment clearly plays a major role in many women's lives. It is a popular stereotype that most women work to supplement the family income, but that the husband provides the main support. However, in reality most women work out of economic necessity. Nearly two-thirds of women in the labor force are single, widowed, divorced, separated, or have husbands who earn less than $15,000 a year. Thus, for most women, work is crucially important to the support of their family, and they remain in the labor force for the majority of their adult lives. In 1980, women spent an average of 29.3 years of their lives in the labor force (U.S. Department of Labor, 1988).

Although employment plays an important role in many women's lives, the nature of women's employment differs from men's, because most jobs are

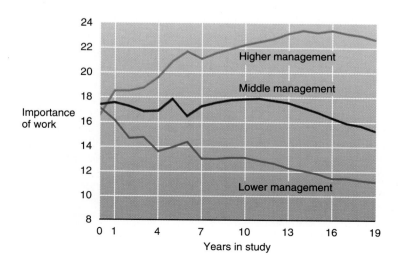

FIGURE 10.11
Importance of work as a function of years of employment. All subjects started at the same management level. Those who reached higher levels of management saw work as more important.

Many women in the work force are single mothers who must support their families.

gender segregated—they are populated predominately by males or females (Table 10.4). Thus, even though opportunities are opening up for women in fields that have been dominated by men, women are still likely to wind up employed in female-dominated occupations, which, on the average, are lower paying than male-dominated occupations.

What does employment mean for women's lives? One result is the "second shift": women who are employed full-time are also responsible for the bulk of the housework and child care, even if they are married. Nonetheless, women who want careers report being happier when employed full time, despite the second-shift stresses (Pietromonaco et al., 1987; Repetti et al., 1989). In fact, one survey found that only one in five employed mothers would leave their jobs to stay at home with their children if they had that option (DeChick, 1988).

Is there a midlife crisis?   One of the most hotly debated facts of adult development has been whether or not there is a **midlife crisis**—a period, usually around the age of 40 to 45, during which men, and perhaps women, experience a questioning of their lives that results in a change in how they view themselves.

One argument for the existence of the midlife crisis comes from the results of studies of men in their 40s (Gould, 1972, 1980; Levinson, 1990; Levinson et al., 1978; Vaillant, 1977; Vaillant & McArthur, 1972). For example, Levinson and his co-workers extensively interviewed a group of 40 men between the ages of 35 and 45. The idea was to collect complete biographies of each man and, based on this information, to describe the major events and issues that occur as men develop from their late teens through their late 40s. Over 80% of the men in Levinson's study reported experiencing a "crisis" around age 40, which caused some of them to take steps such as changing occupations, getting divorced, or moving to new cities.

Is the midlife crisis real? A number of studies that have followed both men and women through midlife have failed to confirm the earlier studies' reports of a specific time of crisis or upheaval. For example, when Michael Farrell and Stanley Rosenberg (1981) interviewed 300 middle-aged men, they found that only 12% felt they had experienced a midlife crisis. Similarly, when Robert McCrae and Paul Costa (1990) measured "emotional instability" by surveying over

TABLE 10.4
Gender segregation in occupations, 1989

Occupation	Women in Occupation (%)
More Males	
Auto mechanic	0.7
Carpenter	1.2
Airline pilot	3.8
Welder	6.6
Dentist	8.6
Telephone installer, repairer	10.8
Physician	17.9
Lawyer, judge	22.3
College/university teacher	38.7
Editor, reporter	49.2
More Females	
Bus driver	54.8
Social worker	68.1
Elementary school teacher	84.7
Librarian	87.3
Data entry keyer	87.8
Telephone operator	89.8
Registered nurse	94.2
Child care worker	97.1
Dental assistant	98.9

Source: U.S. Bureau of Labor Statistics (1990).

10,000 men and women, they found no evidence of a crisis around the age of 40 (Figure 10.12). Perhaps, as McCrae and Costa (1984) point out, one of the reasons for the popularity of the concept of midlife crisis is that it has been publicized by the media. Knowing that they are supposed to experience a crisis in their 40s, some people do. However, the bulk of scientific evidence indicates that although crises do occur in people's lives, they appear to be distributed throughout the life span.

Retirement and inactivity are not synonymous. Many retired people lead busy, active lives.

Retirement.   One of the biggest changes of adulthood is retirement, when people leave a work force in which they have spent the majority of their lives. Although some view retirement as a privilege that they have worked long and hard to achieve, others see it as a loss. Our society tends to view retired people as having lower status than those who are employed (Streib, 1983), and many working people associate retirement with decreased activity. However, in reality there is a wide range of reactions to actual retirement. Although as many as 30% of retired people are never satisfied with retirement, fewer than 10% miss their jobs (Atchly, 1980). A good adjustment to retirement is correlated with financial security and the availability of other activities to replace work (Parker, 1982).

Responses to death and dying.   The comedian Woody Allen's quip, "I'm not afraid to die. I just don't want to be there when it happens," is funny while at the same time capturing the fact that death is something that many people have a great deal of trouble thinking about.

Sometimes death occurs suddenly, such as when a person dies in an accident or from a fatal heart attack. But when a person finds out that they have a terminal disease, such as cancer or AIDS, then they must deal with the knowledge that they have only a limited time to live. When this occurs, the way the individual deals with the approach of death can be viewed in developmental terms. This is what Elizabeth Kübler-Ross (1969) did when she interviewed hundreds of dying patients to determine the process by which people adapt to the idea of their impending death. From these interviews, she concluded that people's reactions to their impending death occurs in the following five stages:

1. *Denial*: The person doesn't believe the news, feeling that there must be a mistake.
2. *Anger*: The person becomes angry with the hospital, friends, and family. "Why me?" is a typical reaction at this stage.
3. *Bargaining*: The person tries making "deals" such as "I'll be a better person if I'm allowed to live."
4. *Depression*: In this stage the person becomes depressed, a sign of self-mourning.
5. *Acceptance*: A person who gets through the depression stage accepts the situation and begins peacefully detaching from the outside world.

Although Kübler-Ross's ideas are credited with the founding of the "death awareness movement," many researchers now feel that her five stages

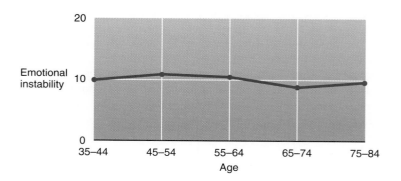

FIGURE 10.12
Emotional instability as a function of age. McCrae and Costa found no evidence of a midlife crisis.

FIGURE 10.13
In this three-stage process, the dying person gradually comes to terms with death.

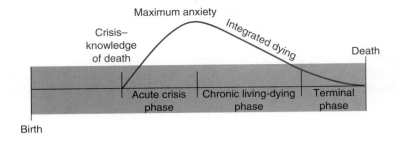

oversimplify the process. For example, some people never reach the acceptance stage, or they may be in a number of stages simultaneously—perhaps accepting their fate, yet clinging to a hope that it won't happen, while feeling anger that it is happening to them (Stevens-Long, 1988).

Other researchers describe the process of reacting to impending death as having three phases: an acute phase, in which the person first becomes aware that they have a terminal condition; a chronic living-dying phase, during which the person adjusts to the idea of being terminally ill; and a short terminal phase, when the person begins withdrawing from the world (Figure 10.13) (Pattison, 1977; Weisman, 1972). This way of looking at the dying process is similar to Kübler-Ross's in that it sees the process as a gradual coming to terms with death.

Whether or not the details of these descriptions are totally accurate, the general approach of describing people's reactions to their impending death is valuable because it emphasizes that even as life approaches its end, development continues. This idea that death is part of the process of life has focused attention on how death has generally been viewed in our society and has led to the concept of a "good death"—one that occurs without prolonged pain and suffering and in a setting that enables the person to maintain contact with family and loved ones.

Unfortunately, modern medicine, which can keep people alive with complex life-support systems, works against achieving a good death. Many people die in hospitals while attached to machines, and most people die alone or among strangers (Aries, 1981). One effort at making death more humane is the hospice movement, founded in London in the 1950s. A hospice is a place where terminally ill people can go to die in a homelike environment that supplies medical care but avoids "heroic measures" to prolong life. Only a small percentage of people can currently take advantage of hospices, however. Another alternative is for the dying person to spend his or her last days at home, treated by visiting doctors and nurses and cared for by family members who can provide the necessary time and dedication.

Reprise: Linkages Among Physical, Cognitive, and Social Abilities

In this chapter and the one before it we have seen that development describes a series of changes that occur throughout a person's lifetime. Sometimes the changes are momentous—as during the early years, when a helpless infant matures into a walking, talking child, or as adolescence begins, with its considerable physical and cognitive changes. Sometimes the changes are more subtle—as when an adult gradually loses physical power or slowly gains educational and life experiences that enhance her or his ability to think dialectically.

Whether changes are dramatic or subtle, it is clear that changes in one capacity have effects on other capacities. Some of these interactions are shown in Figure 10.14. Linkages between an adolescent's physical, social, and cognitive abilities begin in infancy: the infant's ability to interact socially with others de-

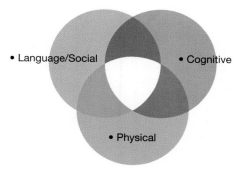

Infancy	Childhood	Adolescence	Adulthood	Old age
Infant's ability to sense environment and to locomote is important for optimum cognitive development	Child's cognitive ability to take another's point of view enhances social interaction with others	Adolescent's opposite-sex relations affected by physical change of puberty	Cognitive ability may affect job achievement and satisfaction, which may in turn affect family relationships	Physical decline in old age can decrease social activity. This varies greatly from person to person

• Language/Social   • Cognitive

• Physical

Developmental areas

FIGURE 10.14
Although our discussion of development has been organized around the areas of physical, cognitive, language, and social development, it is more accurate to think of development not as occurring in separated areas but as being integrated, with overlap and close linkages between areas. The overlapping circles here symbolize this integration, and examples of linkages are provided above.

pends on physical developments such as perceptual and motor skills and cognitive developments such as the ability to talk and understand language. Similar processes also occur later in the life span. For example, research has shown a relationship between a person's educational attainment—as measured by the number of years of school completed—and the person's level of moral development—as measured by Kohlberg's stages. Those who have completed more schooling generally progress to a higher stage of moral development (Rest & Thoma, 1985).

The reason for the link between educational attainment and moral development is not clear—it could be that greater cognitive attainment causes a shift in moral thinking, or perhaps people who seek out more education were raised in a social environment that influenced their moral thinking. Whatever the reason for this connection, the important fact for our purposes is that moral development does not occur in isolation; it is linked to other aspects of life. We cannot, therefore, truly understand people by studying them in isolated categories such as "physical," "perceptual," "cognitive," or "social." A person is an integrated whole in which the physical, perceptual, cognitive, and social realms are all interrelated.

Culture, Economic Stress, and Child Development

For most children development occurs within the context of a family. This family provides a number of things that can affect a child's development: education, religion, economic resources, siblings, and perhaps most important, parents. Most of our discussion of social development in this chapter has been about children who grow up in American families and in families that provide an environment that supports their growth and psychological development. But what about children who grow up in families in other cultures or in families in which there is economic stress? In this Follow-Through we will consider this question by examining how parents are affected by their culture and by economic stress and then by looking at how those effects on parents in turn affect their children.

One way culture can affect children's development is by influencing infants' attachment to their caregivers, as measured by how they respond in the strange situation. Table 10.5 shows the percentage of infants classified as secure, avoidant, or ambivalent in a number of countries. Notice that though the results for some countries are similar, Israel and Japan stand out as having smaller percentages of infants classified as avoidant.

What is it about these cultures that creates fewer-than-usual numbers of avoidant infants? Helen Bee (1992) suggests some possibilities based on the fact that one of the things that determines attachment is the nature of the interaction between caretaker and infant. Culture, therefore, could affect the infant's development through the chain of events depicted in Figure 10.15.

What is it about child rearing in Israel and Japan that might affect the interaction between infant and caretaker? The Israeli children who were tested in the strange situation grew up in a *kibbutz*, a communal settlement. Children in *kibbutzim* are cared for in a group during the day by one or more caretakers. These children see their parents regularly during the day and for a longer period in the evening. What this means is that if the mother is feeling depressed or feels like rejecting the child—a behavior that often leads to avoidant attachment—the child would be exposed to this behavior for only part of the day. According to this idea, the diversity of care the child receives protects the child's attachment status from being overly influenced by any one person.

The situation in Japan is different: the mother is in almost constant contact with her infant, especially in the early months.

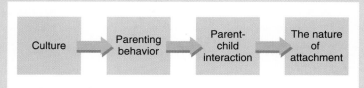

FIGURE 10.15
Culture can affect parent-child attachment by influencing parenting behavior.

The Japanese cultural ideal that mothers should be extremely sensitive to their infant's needs and the intense bond that develops between Japanese children and their mothers may explain why so few Japanese children are classified as avoidant. It is possible that Japanese children's strong dependence on their mother could lead them to cry more when separated from their mother in the strange situation, and that this crying could cause them to be classified as ambivalent.

These explanations for why Israeli and Japanese children show different attachment patterns than other cultures are speculative, but the important point for our purposes is that culture does affect attachment. It is likely that variations in the pattern are caused by culture's effect on parent-child interactions.

Another influence on parent-child interactions is the parents' economic situation. One way this factor might affect children is through the chain of events depicted in Figure 10.16, which suggests that stress caused by economic hardship affects the way parents deal with their children.

A research program to study how parents are affected by economic hardship and how those effects are translated into parenting behavior was carried out by Glen Elder (1974), who studied the effects of the Great Depression of the 1930s on parents. He found that fathers who had experienced heavy income losses tended to become more emotionally unstable, tense, and explosive

Left: A child and his caregiver in an Israeli kibbutz. **Right:** A Japanese child accompanies his mother in a ritual bow.

TABLE 10.5
Attachment of infants in six countries as measured by the strange situation

Country	Secure (%)	Avoidant (%)	Ambivalent (%)
Netherlands	67	26	6
West Germany	57	35	8
Great Britain	75	22	4
United States	65	21	14
Israel (kibbutz-reared)	65	7	29
Japan	68	5	27

Figures may not add up to 100 because of rounding.
Source: From van Ijzendoorn and Kroonenberg, 1988.

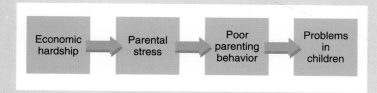

FIGURE 10.16
Economic hardship can cause stress in parents, which leads to poor parenting behavior.

(Elder, Liker, & Cross, 1984; Liker & Elder, 1983). These fathers were also more likely to punish their children and to be arbitrary in handing out punishment. Young children in these families were more likely than others to be irritable and experience temper tantrums (Elder, Caspi, & Nguyen, 1987; Elder et al., 1984).

The results of Elder's studies have led researchers to conclude that there is a connection between the effects of stress on parents and developmental problems experienced by their children. Parents living in poverty—especially female heads of households—must deal with a great deal of stress. As shown in Figure 10.17, female heads of households in the United States have substantially lower incomes—and a correspondingly more difficult time meeting the family's material needs—than either single male parents or two-parent families. Evictions, assaults, illness, poor housing, dangerous neighborhoods, and the struggle to obtain enough money to pay the rent and put food on the table are among the stressors these parents have to face daily. This stress makes it difficult to be a good parent. Vonnie McLoyd (1990) puts it this way: "Rewarding, explaining and negotiating with the child re-

quires patience and concentration—qualities typically in short supply when parents feel harassed or overburdened" (p. 322).

The idea that there is a connection between poverty and how parents relate to their children is supported by research showing that poor mothers value obedience more, are more likely to use physical punishment, and are less likely to reward their children (Conger et al., 1984). In addition, it has been shown that economically stressed parents are less likely to nurture their children (for example, by giving them attention, praise, or rewards) and more likely to be inconsistent in discipline (for example, by making rules and then not enforcing them). These parental behaviors have been linked to effects on the children that include feelings of depression and loneliness and an increased probability of delinquency and drug use (Lempers, Clark-Lempers, & Simons, 1989).

Although the connection between economic hardship, parental stress, and problems in child development holds for children of all races, it is particularly relevant for African-American children in the United States, because of the disproportionate number of African-American children living in poverty. Fully 51% of African-American children less than 6 years old—compared with 18% of white children—live in poverty (Slaughter, 1988), and almost 90% of persistently poor children are black (U.S. House of Representatives, Committee on Ways and Means, 1985).

Perhaps the most disturbing aspect of the connection between poverty and childhood development is that many low-income families appear doomed to remain in poverty (Reischauer, 1986). This situation is particularly true in African-American families because of the generally more limited resources, the large number of female-headed families, and the fact that it is often difficult for low-income or unemployed African Americans to get new jobs. Because of this situation, many experts feel that the main way to help children of these families is to provide resources to the parents to help reduce their stress and then improve their parenting skills (Halpern, 1990). Although this may sound simple, poverty is a persistent social problem with no easy solutions.

FIGURE 10.17
The extremely low income of female heads of households creates added stress, making effective parenting more difficult.

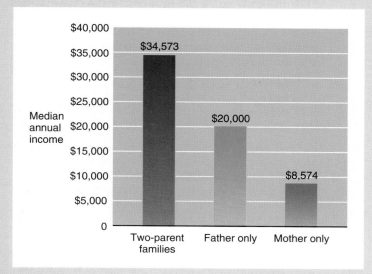

CHAPTER TEN SUMMARY

The Development of Language

- Normal language acquisition depends on (1) development of the vocal apparatus, (2) the ability to hear oneself talking, (3) the achievement of a level of cognitive understanding that masters object permanence, and (4) interaction with other people.

- Language development proceeds from babies' early vocalizing to adultlike speech by the age of 4 or 5. Babies babble at 5 to 6 months and say their first words during their second year. Overextension and underextension are typical language errors during this time, and children begin using more than one word at a time. As children begin forming sentences, telegraphic speech develops. As they apply rules to their speech, they sometimes make mistakes such as over-regularization.

- The behaviorist approach to language acquisition attempts to explain language development as the result of parental reinforcement and punishment. The nativist approach proposes that language learning is a biologically programmed process controlled by a "language acquisition device" in the brain. The cognitive approach proposes that cognitive factors, such as the level of cognitive development and social interactions with adults, must also be taken into account.

Social Development: Infancy, Childhood, and Adolescence

- Erikson's psychosocial theory of development describes social development as a series of stages featuring eight crises to be resolved over the life span.

- The newborn's ability to communicate, first by crying and then by smiling, marks the beginning of the development of social abilities. At about 10 weeks of age they can perceive others' emotions. Social referencing occurs between infants and people they have relationships with, beginning at about 12 months.

- Infants can be classified as securely or insecurely (avoidant, ambivalent, or disorganized) attached to caregivers by using the strange situation procedure. Securely attached infants are later more likely to perform better and be better adjusted than insecurely attached ones, but the relationship between attachment and later childhood characteristics is far from perfect. Attachment has been linked to the nature of the relationship between infant and mother, with responsive, warm mothering fostering secure attachment.

- The first appearance of self-awareness begins in the middle of the second year. Most 2-year-olds exhibit self-recognition by recognizing themselves in a mirror. As they grow older they develop a self-concept. The formation of the self is also accompanied by a process of evaluation that leads to the development of self-esteem.

- Gender identity develops between 2 and 3 years of age, gender constancy between 4 and 7. Children learn what it means to be a boy or a girl through the process of gender socialization, taught by socializing agents and experienced by gender segregation among their peers.

- Identity formation is one of the major tasks of adolescence. People can be classified as being in one of the following identity statuses: identity achievement, identity foreclosure, identity moratorium, or identity diffusion. Identity formation proceeds differently in males and females because of the different demands society places on the two genders.

- Youth gangs appeal to some adolescents in search of identity, especially to those that come from very deprived home environments. Although their activities are sometimes anti-social, urban youth gangs serve a purpose similar to other adolescent groups that affirm their members as individuals and help them achieve an identity.

- The development of self-esteem differs for adolescent girls and boys, in that girls' self-esteem drops in high school and often drops further in college. An important self-esteem issue for girls is appearance, and the higher incidence of depression and eating disorders in females compared to males is related to societal pressure for girls to be attractive.

- Lawrence Kohlberg has differentiated three levels of moral development: the preconventional, conventional, and post-conventional (or principled) levels. Individuals generally move towards higher stages of development throughout adolescence and into adulthood.

Social Development: Adulthood

- Longitudinal research has demonstrated a relationship between the quality of parenting given young children and their adult social accomplishment levels 36 years later.

- Differences in the way adult males and females converse with one another has been linked to the different socialization expressed by girls and boys.

- Most Americans marry and have children. As the marriage continues, changes occur both in the importance of different components of the relationship and in overall satisfaction. Satisfaction with the marriage is usually high at the beginning, decreases during the child-raising years, and increases as the children leave home.

- About half of all present-day marriages end in divorce. Men suffer more psychological and physical trauma, but women suffer more financially.

- Full-time employment outside the home extends throughout adulthood, especially for males. According to Super's stage theory of occupational development, people go through the following stages: exploration, establishment, maintenance, and decline. The importance of work is a function of a person's job. Women are more likely than men to be employed in lower paying, gender-segregated jobs.

- There is some evidence for the existence of a midlife crisis in males, around the age of 40, but the bulk of research indicates that crises that people do experience seem to be distributed throughout the life span.

- An important social change in older adulthood is retirement. Though few retirees miss their jobs, satisfaction with this change depends on financial security and alternative activities to work.

- Elizabeth Kübler-Ross has suggested that people's reactions to their impending death progress through five stages: denial, anger, bargaining, depression, and acceptance. According to another description, people experience three phases: an acute phase, a chronic living-dying phase, and a terminal phase. Attempts to achieve a "good death" are complicated by medicine's ability to prolong life.

Reprise: Linkages Among Physical, Cognitive, and Social Abilities

- Since physical, cognitive, and social abilities are interlinked, we can't fully understand people by studying them solely in one of these categories or another.

Follow-Through/Diversity: Culture, Economic Stress, and Child Development

- Culture influences parenting behavior, which in turn influences parent-child interactions. The closeness of parent-child attachment is one example. Economic hardship causes parental stress, and the poor parenting that results can lead to adjustment problems in children.

Key Terms

attachment
empty nest syndrome
gender constancy
gender identity
gender segregation
gender socialization
identity achievement
identity crisis
identity diffusion
identity foreclosure
identity moratorium
insecurely attached/ ambivalent
insecurely attached/avoidant
insecurely attached/ disorganized
language acquisition device (LAD)
midlife crisis

overextension
overregularization
pseudodialogues
psychosocial theory of development
securely attached
self-awareness
self-concept
self-esteem
self-recognition
socialization
socializing agents
social referencing
strange situation
syntax
telegraphic speech
underextension
visual cliff

CHAPTER

II

General Theories of Motivation
The Instinct Approach: Behavior as Genetically Determined
The Ethological Approach: Instincts in the Natural Habitat
The Biological Approach: Motives as Drive Reduction
Sigmund Freud's Approach: Motives as Unconscious
The Humanistic Approach: Behavior as Striving for Self-Actualization

The Hunger Motive
The Biology of Hunger
Psychological Influences on Hunger Motivation
Hunger and Weight Problems

Sexual Motivation
Biological Factors in Sexual Motivation
Psychological Factors in Sexual Motivation
Sexual Orientation

Interdisciplinary Dimension: History
Sexuality and Society in Western Culture

Achievement Motivation
Early Research on Achievement Motivation
Expectancy-Value Theory
The Cognitive Approach to Achievement Motivation

Reprise: Multiple Causes of Behavior

Follow-Through/Diversity
Gender and Achievement Motivation

Motivation

Why do you do the things you do?
Why do you do these things?

asked of Don Quixote in The Man of La Mancha

Imagine that you are on an ocean liner. On the fifth day of your cruise a violent storm rages around the ship, and it appears that all will be lost as the crew starts lowering the lifeboats. You don't remember much of what happens after that, but you find yourself miraculously washed up onto a beach of what appears to be a deserted tropical island. The island is lush, teeming with vegetation and animal life. What would you do?

People answer this question in a number of ways. Some say they would search for other people; some say they would begin looking for shelter; others talk about setting up signals to alert rescuers. Most say that one of the first things they would do is look for food and water.

People's tendency to talk about taking action when confronted with the tropical island scenario is an example of **motivation**—the process that drives an organism to act and that determines what direction the action takes. In the case of our island scenario, we might say that seeking shelter or devising rescue signals is motivated by a desire to survive; that searching for food and water is motivated by the prospect of hunger; and that looking for other people is at least in part motivated by a need for human contact. This simple example demonstrates that there are many kinds of motivation.

Psychologists have studied motivation by looking at the different kinds of forces that initiate and direct specific behaviors. As we see how different levels of analysis come into play in this research, we will come to appreciate the complexity of the forces that motivate people. This complexity is illustrated by the experiences of the English colonists who began exploring America in the 1600s. On arrival they found a land populated by Native Americans and bountiful animal and plant life—clearly an environment in which humans could flourish.

But not long after the settlers arrived, they began dying of malnutrition and starvation. Despite plentiful plant and animal life, the colonists spent little energy hunting, fishing, searching for edible native plants, or planting corn and other crops. Though surrounded by a bounty of available food, they preferred to subsist on what they had brought with them from England; when these supplies ran out, they could not or would not find other sources. Because of this course of action, about 80% of the colonists sent to Virginia between 1607 and 1625 died, mostly from lack of nutritious food (Sale, 1990).

Why would people behave in this way? When subjects are presented with our tropical island example, one of the first things they mention is searching for food. But the colonists, faced with a similar problem, took no action. Historians have speculated about why, in the midst of clearly adequate resources, the colonists starved. One hypothesis is that the English settlers were unwilling to recognize unfamiliar food as food, even though the Indians thrived on it. Another is that too many of the colonists were gentlemen, who thought it was beneath them to work for their food. A third posits that their feeling of disorientation in a "hostile" environment, far from "civilization," made them psychologically unable to cope with their situation (Sale, 1990). Perhaps all these factors came into play.

Whatever explanation is correct, the point for our purposes is that understanding an apparently simple motivation such as hunger is a complex undertaking. To comprehend the colonists' behavior we need to go beyond biological explanations of hunger motivation and consider such factors as the colonists' thought processes and the context of their behavior.

Confronted with the number and complexity of human motives, psychologists have taken two basic approaches to studying this broad subject. The first is to create general theories of motivation. Examples that we will discuss are biological theories, which emphasize evolutionary and physiological forces; Sigmund Freud's theory, which proposes that human motives are largely unconscious; and Abraham Maslow's humanistic theory, which includes such "higher" human motives as the desire to reach one's full potential.

These and other general theories have proved useful in organizing psychologists' thinking about motivation and in suggesting lines of research. However, in recent decades many psychologists have argued that such all-encompassing theories provide only incomplete explanations for many of the specific things we do. For example, when Freud's theory describes overeating as the result of unconscious forces, it fails to consider how a person's biology and conscious thoughts might influence eating behavior. For this reason, psychologists have moved away from constructing general theories of motivation and have taken to applying several levels of analysis to the study of specific motives.

The plan of this chapter mirrors that development. We begin by reviewing several general theories of motivation and then look at how psychologists have studied three specific kinds: hunger motivation, sexual motivation, and achievement motivation. These three types of motivation are interesting to study not only because they are extremely relevant to our lives but because they allow us to see how a number of levels of analysis can be brought to bear on the study of motivation. For example, an understanding at the biological level of analysis is obviously relevant to hunger and sexual motivation, but biology is not the whole story. As the history of the early English colonists illustrates, behavioral, cognitive, and contextual levels of analysis can all shed light even on hunger and eating behavior. Similarly, though sexual motivation obviously involves physiology, to understand how people satisfy this motive we have to consider how they think about sex, how they respond to different environmental factors, and how contextual influences, including cultural norms, affect their behavior. In the case of achievement motivation, cognitive, behavioral, and contextual forces play a

Biological explanations alone can't explain eating behavior. The tailgate party emphasizes the social aspects of eating, and Mahatma Ghandi's hunger fast shows that eating (or not eating) can even have political implications.

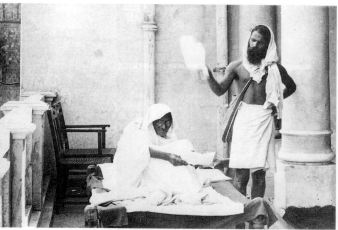

larger role than physiology, so we concentrate on factors operating at those levels of analysis.

General Theories of Motivation

General theories of motivation have tended to emphasize one or another kind of influence operating on our behavior. As we review these theories, ask yourself how well each one might account for a wide range of behaviors—from eating when you're hungry to studying hard to fulfill a goal, such as landing a good job or living up to others' expectations. Do all kinds of motivation have a common source, or are different motives distinct from one another?

The Instinct Approach: Behavior as Genetically Determined

3   BIOLOGY

An explanation of motivation popular early in the century viewed human behavior as controlled by instincts. **Instincts** control behavior that is genetically programmed and that requires no learning. The idea that such genetically programmed behavior could occur follows from Charles Darwin's (1859/1959) principle of natural selection. According to this principle, organisms that can best cope with the environment will survive to pass their characteristics on to future generations. Thus, animals that have protective coloration enabling them to blend into their environment will be more likely to survive and pass their coloration to their offspring (Figure 11.1); animals that do not have this protection will be less likely to survive and will eventually become rare or vanish altogether.

The same principle applies to behavior. If some members of a species tend to protect their young from attack more than other members do, more of the "protected" offspring will survive and, assuming they have the same protective tendencies as their parents, will protect their offspring who will, in turn, survive to produce more offspring with "protective" qualities. Thus, the idea that some behaviors can be genetically programmed is a reasonable one.

This possibility led psychologist William McDougall (1908, 1932) to propose that human behavior is also controlled by genetically programmed instincts. In fact, McDougall considered *all* human behavior to be instinctive. Some of the instincts he ascribed to humans are as follows:

combat	fearfulness	parental care
constructiveness	food seeking	protectiveness
curiosity	gregariousness	self-assertiveness
disgust	humorousness	sex
escape	mating	submission

An obvious difficulty with McDougall's list is that learning clearly plays a role in many if not all of these behaviors—yet instincts are by definition unlearned. But there is also a conceptual difficulty. Simply calling a behavior instinctive doesn't explain anything. For example, if we say that a team of explorers skied to the North Pole because of the human instinct to explore, all we have done is describe the explorers' behavior. We might just as well have said "They explored the North Pole because exploring is something humans are programmed to do." But what forces drove these *particular* people to explore the North Pole? McDougall's theory can't answer that question.

Because of the inadequacy of McDougall's theory, the early American psychologists rejected the idea that genetics or instincts play *any* role in behavior. European psychologists, in contrast, did not reject the role of instinctive behavior but approached it in a different way by carefully observing animals' behavior in their natural habitats.

FIGURE 11.1
A moth's coloration can serve to deceive, enhancing the moth's chances of survival.

The Ethological Approach: Instincts in the Natural Habitat

In the 1930s a group of European biologists called **ethologists** began to study behavior from a genetic point of view, not by simply listing instincts but by carefully studying the behavior of animals in their natural settings (Lorenz, 1952; Tinbergen, 1951). Ethologists developed the idea of the *key stimulus*, a stimulus that can trigger instinctive behavior. An example of a key stimulus is the red belly of a fish called the three-spined stickleback, which triggers an aggressive response in other male sticklebacks who have set up territories. Behaviors such as the stickleback's aggressive response are called *fixed-action patterns*. These fixed-action patterns are stereotyped, are seen in all members of the species, and require no learning.

Not only did these researchers observe and describe behaviors, but they also conducted experiments to determine under what conditions specific behaviors occurred. For example, Tinbergen (1951) determined that the stickleback's red belly was a key stimulus for aggression by exposing sticklebacks to models of fish of different sizes, shapes, and colors. This scientific approach to the study of instinctive behavior kept alive the idea that much animal behavior is genetically determined; in addition, it provided some evidence for genetically determined human behavior. For example, the work of ethologist Irenaus Eibl-Eibesfeldt (1972), which showed that people in many different cultures greet each other with a quick flick of the eyebrow called an eyebrow flash (discussed in Chapter 2), provides evidence for a genetically determined human behavior. In ethological language we would say that a person's friendly approach is the key stimulus for the eyebrow flash.

The ethological approach strengthened the argument for the importance of instinctive behavior in animals, but it is a long way from a simple response like an eyebrow flash to such complex behaviors as studying for exams or falling in love. Another biologically oriented theory that applies to a broader range of both human and animal behaviors is drive theory.

The Biological Approach: Motives as Drive Reduction

3   BIOLOGY

While the ethologists were investigating instinctive behavior in Europe, American psychologists were approaching motivation in a different way. They focused on the idea that a deficit within an organism, such as the absence of food, causes the buildup of a drive, such as hunger. A **drive** is an internal state of tension that

Predators hunt only enough to satisfy their hunger, a fact that fits well with drive theory. However, we need to look beyond biological drive to understand many facets of human motivation.

motivates behaviors capable of alleviating that tension. Thus, the hunger drive motivates eating behavior, which reduces the unpleasant feeling of hunger.

The drive concept is similar to the instinct concept in that both describe behavior as governed by biological mechanisms. There are, however, two major differences between the instinct and drive explanations of motivation. First, the instinct explanation describes stereotyped behaviors that are elicited by specific stimuli. The drive explanation relates behaviors such as eating, drinking, sleeping, and sexual activity to physiological changes occurring when an organism is deprived of food, water, sleep, or sex. Second, drive theory assigns great importance to learning, a process ignored by instinct theories. Learning, according to drive theory, is important in two ways. To begin with, it is often important in finding ways to satisfy a drive. An animal activated by its hunger drive to look for food has to learn how to obtain food in order to satisfy that drive. Furthermore, the satisfaction of a drive leads to **drive reduction,** which results in learning through reinforcement.

Thus, the drive concept combines biology and learning in an ingenious way: A state of deprivation causes an increase in drive. This increase in drive activates the animal. That activation leads to satisfaction of the drive. The satisfaction of the drive is reinforcing, and this increases the probability that when the drive is reactivated, responses that have been successful in the past will recur.

The concept of drive dominated thinking about motivation in the 1940s and 1950s, but then it began to be questioned. One question arose from the idea, central to the drive concept, that behavior triggered by a drive will act to reduce the drive. But how, then, can we explain the fact that in some situations eating food activates the desire to eat more food? This is exactly what happens when eating some salted peanuts (or potato chips, or other desirable food) leads to eating many more.

Drive theory also has difficulty accounting for the fact that people will work harder for some goals than for others. The theory states that motivation to reduce a drive is determined by an organism's deprivation. If that were the case, hunger should motivate any eating behavior that results in reducing the drive, whether the behavior is eating at a gourmet restaurant or in a school cafeteria. Clearly, however, some people may be much more motivated to work to earn a fancy meal than a plain one. Drive theory is therefore incomplete, because it does not take into account the desirability of the goals that motivate our behavior.

Both drive and instinct theories thus seem to be incomplete. A third general theory of motivation, proposed by Sigmund Freud, tried to explain motivation from a different direction. Freud's theory does share some features of the instinct and drive theories, because he felt that much of our behavior is determined by inborn drives (Freud, 1949/1915). However, his proposal focused on something missing from either the ethologists' fixed-action patterns or biological drive theory: the operating of unconscious forces in a person's mind.

Sigmund Freud's Approach: Motives as Unconscious

One of Freud's central ideas is that the motivations underlying our behavior may not be obvious, even to ourselves. He came to this conclusion in the course of treating patients with physical ailments that had no obvious physiological cause. The absence of a physiological cause led Freud to believe that the cause must be mental, and as his patients had no awareness of any mental cause, Freud postulated that it must be hidden within their unconscious.

As we have noted in earlier chapters, Freud believed that we are unaware of the majority of our mental processes, which take place in the unconscious. According to him, the unconscious is also where we must look for the motivations underlying many of our behaviors. When we offer an explanation for why we do something, our explanation comes from only the portion of our mind we are conscious of; therefore, it may not be the real reason for our behavior. For example, you might explain your behavior in an intimate relationship as being largely determined by how your partner reacts to you. Freud would respond that this may be partly true, but that many unconscious influences stemming from your childhood experiences—such as the way your parents related to you—are also affecting how you behave toward your partner. We will look at Freud's ideas about unconscious motivation in more detail when we cover his theory of personality in Chapter 15.

The Humanistic Approach: Behavior as Striving for Self-Actualization

The humanistic approach to motivation developed in part as a reaction to the other theories we have discussed. The other theories see motivation as being determined by instincts, drives, or unconscious processes—all forces outside of our conscious control. Humanistic psychologists, in contrast, believe that much of human motivation involves conscious choices, and that humans strive for loftier goals than simply reducing the tension of a drive state.

Humanistic psychologists emphasize the idea that one of the basic human motives is people's striving to reach their full potential. Abraham Maslow (1943, 1973), one of the most influential of these psychologists, incorporated this idea in the general motivational theory depicted in Figure 11.2, known as Maslow's **hierarchy of needs.** According to Maslow, motivation consists of needs ranging from those related to basic survival to "higher" psychological needs. An important feature of this theory is the idea that some needs are more fundamental than others and need to be at least partly satisfied before other needs become active. Thus, people must satisfy basic **physiological needs,** such as satisfying hunger and thirst, and **safety needs,** such as living in a secure environment that is sheltered from weather, before they will be motivated to satisfy needs higher up on the pyramid. Once physiological and safety needs are met, people begin striving to satisfy **love or belongingness needs** (the need to receive affection from others and to feel part of a group) and **self-esteem needs** (the need to feel positively about one self and to be esteemed by others). Finally, at the top of the pyramid, is the need for **self-actualization**—the desire to attain one's full human potential.

Much of Maslow's energy went into studying the characteristics of such people as Thomas Jefferson, Abraham Lincoln, and Eleanor Roosevelt, all of whom he classified as having achieved self-actualization. From this research he created lists of characteristics of self-actualized people. A few of them are acceptance of self, of others, and of nature; being spontaneous; having mystical experiences; feeling sympathy for humankind; enjoying close, interpersonal

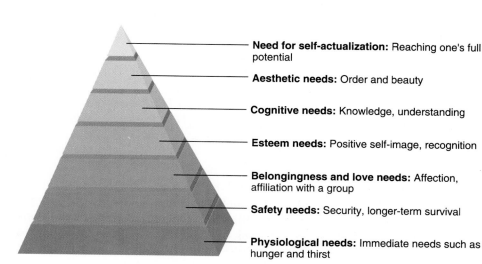

Need for self-actualization: Reaching one's full potential

Aesthetic needs: Order and beauty

Cognitive needs: Knowledge, understanding

Esteem needs: Positive self-image, recognition

Belongingness and love needs: Affection, affiliation with a group

Safety needs: Security, longer-term survival

Physiological needs: Immediate needs such as hunger and thirst

FIGURE 11.2
Maslow's hierarchy of needs. According to Maslow, needs at the bottom of the hierarchy must be satisfied before needs higher up.

TABLE 11.1
Summary of theoretical approaches to motivation

Theory	Description
Instinct	We are driven by instincts. There is a specific instinct for each type of behavior (McDougall). *Example:* We eat because of our "eating instinct."
Ethological	Behavior is controlled by stimuli that trigger instinctive behavior (Tinbergen). *Example:* People's "eyebrow flash" greeting.
Biological: drive reduction	Behavior is motivated by the need to reduce drives that build up over time. *Example:* People deprived of food experience a buildup of the hunger drive, which they will then work to reduce.
Unconscious motivation	Behavior is controlled by motives that we are not aware of. These motives are often determined by experiences in early childhood (Freud). *Example:* A person is shy with strangers because of a frightening encounter with a stranger in early childhood, of which the person is no longer aware.
Self-actualization	People strive to achieve a hierarchy of needs leading to self-actualization (Maslow). *Example:* A person works to satisfy hunger and safety needs in order to be free to achieve career goals.

relationships; and being creative. According to Maslow, fewer than 1% of people ever achieve this level of functioning, and those who do usually don't reach that level until they are over 60 years old.

But Maslow's theory has been criticized on several grounds. One criticism is that it is vague—it is unclear exactly how to classify someone as having achieved self-actualization, for example. A second criticism is that it is not clear that people must always satisfy lower-level needs before moving higher up the pyramid. A third criticism is that if so few people actually achieve self-actualization, maybe the theory doesn't hold for most of us (Petri, 1991).

Each of the general theories of motivation we have reviewed calls attention to a specific feature of human behavior (for a summary, see Table 11.1). However, as they try to explain all motivation by means of a few general principles, they all seem to fall short when it comes to explaining specific behaviors. For this reason, present day researchers have decided that a more fruitful way of trying to understand motivation is to study specific behaviors at different levels of analysis. In this way, we can begin to see how biological, cognitive, behavioral, and contextual factors all influence the motivation to act and the direction that action takes. We will use this approach as we describe how researchers have studied hunger, sexual, and achievement motivation.

The Hunger Motive

When the house burns one forgets even lunch.
Yes, but one eats it later in the ashes.

Friedrich Nietzsche (1844–1900)
German philosopher

Newborn rats will nurse as long as their mother's milk is available (Blass & Teicher, 1980). Bears eat almost nonstop during the few weeks that nuts and berries are available, so that they can go for weeks or months without eating (Herrero,

1985; Kalat, 1992). Horses eat by grazing for long periods each day. In contrast, most humans behave quite differently: they eat a meal and then wait for a few hours before eating the next meal. This property of human eating, which seems to be "turned on" for a while and then "turned off," is one of the facts that hunger researchers have focused on as they ask two questions about eating behavior: "What makes people start eating?" and "What makes people stop eating?"

Hunger motivation—motivation that induces a person to eat—has been studied at all four levels of analysis. At the biological level, researchers have attempted to identify physiological signals that turn eating on and off. At the behavioral level, they have shown how eating can be affected by classical and operant conditioning. At the cognitive and contextual levels, they have noted that eating behavior is affected by the presence of others and by messages people receive from society about how much they should weigh. Let's look at how each level of analysis contributes to an understanding of hunger motivation.

The Biology of Hunger

The principle that has guided much of the research on the biology of hunger motivation is that of **homeostasis**—the tendency to maintain some quality within a fixed range. The basic mechanism for achieving homeostasis is the *feedback loop*—the most familiar example of which is the thermostat that maintains the temperature of a room at a constant level. The thermostat accomplishes this control by means of a temperature sensor, which sends signals that (1) turn on the furnace when the room temperature drops below the thermostat's temperature setting and (2) turn off the furnace when the room temperature rises above that setting (Figure 11.3).

The homeostatic mechanism, as applied to hunger, works analogously. Rather than turning the heat on and off, the goal of the body's homeostatic mechanism is to turn hunger, and therefore, eating, on and off so that a person's body weight remains within a fairly narrow range. The challenge facing hunger researchers has been to determine the physiological signals and structures that accomplish this regulation. As we will see, they have identified signals in the blood and have implicated structures ranging from the stomach and liver to nuclei in the brain as playing a role in the regulation of hunger and eating behavior.

Hunger and stomach contractions.   In 1912 an experiment that John Pinel (1993) describes as "a perfect collaboration" was undertaken by Walter Cannon

3   BIOLOGY

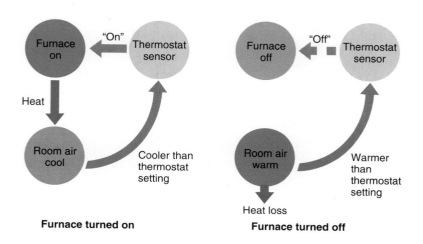

Furnace turned on   **Furnace turned off**

FIGURE 11.3
The functioning of a thermostat is an example of a feedback loop—a mechanism for maintaining homeostasis.

and A. L. Washburn. "Cannon had the ideas, and Washburn had the ability to swallow a balloon" (p. 302). Washburn's balloon swallowing was carried out to test Cannon's hypothesis that hunger was signaled by hunger pangs caused by contractions of the stomach. Washburn swallowed the balloon that, when inflated in his stomach, indicated when his stomach was contracting (Figure 11.4). He then pressed a key every time he felt a hunger pang. Comparing the records of stomach contractions and hunger pangs indicated that there was a close match between Washburn's experience of hunger pangs and the balloon's measurement of stomach contractions.

Cannon's conclusion that stomach contractions were the stimulus for hunger ran into difficulty, however, when confronted with evidence that people who have had their stomachs surgically removed still feel hunger and are able to regulate their food intake (Novin & VanderWeele, 1977). The failure of Cannon's theory led researchers to direct their attention to the brain.

Hunger and nuclei in the hypothalamus.   Recall from Chapter 3 that the hypothalamus (Figure 11.5) is involved in the regulation of several biological processes. Researchers implicated the hypothalamus as a center that controls hunger motivation by showing that lesioning (destroying) two nuclei in the hypothalamus had dramatic effects on a rat's feeding behavior. In this research, a structure called the **ventromedial nucleus of the hypothalamus (VMH)** was destroyed by passing an electrical current through an electrode situated in the nucleus. After rats have their VMH lesioned, they eat large quantities of food and become extremely obese (Figure 11.6). This condition is called **hyperphagia**. Rats who have the **lateral nucleus of the hypothalamus (LH)** lesioned simply stop eating. LH-lesioned animals die unless they are force-fed and then presented with extremely palatable food. This condition is called **aphagia**. With help the

FIGURE 11.4
In Cannon and Washburn's experiment, Washburn pressed a button when he experienced hunger pangs, and his stomach contractions were measured by the contraction of the balloon he had swallowed.

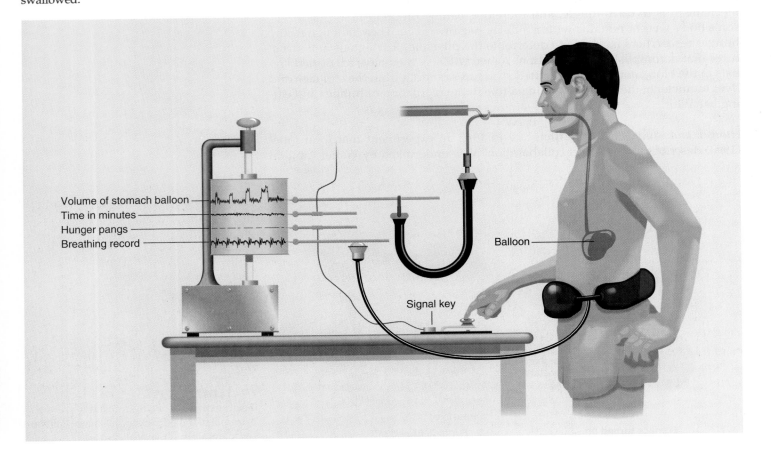

Volume of stomach balloon
Time in minutes
Hunger pangs
Breathing record

Balloon

Signal key

aphagic animals eventually do begin eating, but they maintain their weight at a low level (Teitelbaum & Stellar, 1954).

These results led to the **dual-center hypothesis,** the idea that the VMH and the LH are centers in the brain that control hunger and feeding behavior. The VMH was labeled the **satiety center,** because it appeared to turn off eating (hence, lesioning it causes eating to go out of control). The LH was labeled the **excitatory center,** because it appeared to turn on eating (hence, lesioning it causes eating to stop).

The dual-center hypothesis was the explanation hunger researchers had been looking for. Its particular appeal was the simplicity of two "switches" in the brain—one that turned eating on, another that turned eating off. But explanations of behavior are rarely simple, and hunger is no exception. It wasn't long before the dual-center hypothesis began to unravel.

One finding that led researchers to question whether the LH was the excitatory center was the observation that lesioning it creates animals that are underaroused and unresponsive to sensory stimuli (Marshall & Teitelbaum, 1974). LH-lesioned animals not only don't eat—they don't do much of anything else, either. This suggested that their decrease in eating was due not to the destruction of an "eating center" but to the destruction of an "arousal center." More recent research has shown that the LH does in fact play some role in eating behavior, but that other mechanisms—primarily chemicals in the blood—are also responsible for regulating hunger and eating.

Other observations cast doubt on the idea that the VMH was the satiety center. One such observation was that although hyperphagic animals eat large amounts, they are finicky eaters—they decrease their consumption when their food is made less tasty (Teitelbaum, 1955). In addition, hyperphagic animals don't work as hard as normal rats do to get food (Teitelbaum, 1957). These behaviors aren't consistent with the idea that lesioning the VMH makes the rats hungry. Because these rats weren't acting the way we would expect hungry rats to act, researchers began to doubt that the VMH was the satiety center.

Hunger and chemicals in the blood. Current research on hunger focuses not on the VMH and LH but on substances in the blood such as glucose and insulin. The importance of glucose has been demonstrated in a number of ways. If its concentration in the blood is increased, feeding decreases (Tordoff, Novin, & Russek, 1982). If we administer a drug that prevents glucose from signaling its presence by entering cells, feeding increases (Thompson & Campbell, 1977). Glucose therefore acts as a **satiety signal**—a signal that turns off hunger.

Insulin plays its role in controlling eating by increasing the ability of glucose to enter cells. The high concentration of insulin present after eating makes it easier for glucose to enter cells and send the signal that decreases hunger. As insulin concentration drops, less glucose enters cells, and hunger increases (Figure 11.7).

This interaction between insulin and glucose explains what happens to people with diabetes, who have abnormally low insulin levels. Diabetics' low level of insulin keeps glucose from entering their cells, so even though they may eat frequently, they remain hungry. Also, since less glucose is entering the cells, less of it is converted into fat, more is excreted by the body, and the person's weight declines.

In addition to glucose and insulin, another hormone, **cholecystokinin (CCK),** evidently acts as a satiety signal. CCK is released when food enters the small intestine, and its presence in the bloodstream has been shown to decrease food intake in humans (Pi-Sunyer et al., 1982). These chemical satiety signals apparently act on the brain and also on the stomach and liver. Yet another satiety signal has been proposed that is particularly significant, given the history of hunger research. Allan Geliebter and his co-workers (1987) have found that stretching the stomach decreases eating in rats. Apparently there are receptors in

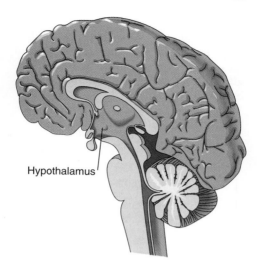

FIGURE 11.5
The hypothalamus has been suggested as a possible site of the control mechanism that regulates hunger.

Hypothalamus

FIGURE 11.6
A hyperphagic rat. This rat's excessive eating, following lesioning of the ventromedial nucleus of its hypothalamus, has caused it to weigh more than twice as much as a normal rat.

FIGURE 11.7

The amount of glucose in the body's cells is a sign for satiety (fullness). More glucose in the cells decreases hunger. The ability of glucose to enter cells is determined, in part, by the concentration of insulin.

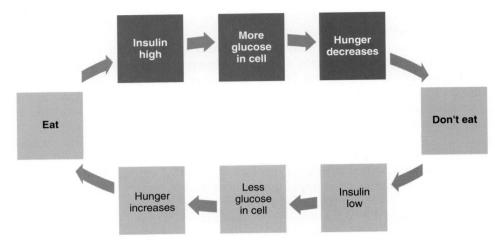

the stomach that signal this stretching and send a satiety signal to the brain. As often happens in science, an early finding that was rejected as incorrect returns in a modified form many years later. Thus, Cannon's idea, that hunger signals are caused by contractions of the stomach, has now reappeared in a different form. Cannon said that stomach *contractions* signal *hunger,* but we now know that stomach *stretching* signals *satiety.* The biological regulation of hunger, then, is a complex interplay of physiological mechanisms. As we turn to psychological influences on eating behavior, however, we will see that hunger is not determined by physiology alone.

Psychological Influences on Hunger Motivation

There is no question that biological signals play a large role in hunger motivation and eating behaviors. But we also know from our experience that what and when we eat is influenced by events in our environment not necessarily governed by homeostatic regulation. Consider the scene at a typical Thanksgiving dinner. There are so many different foods that even if you try only a little of each one you still stuff yourself far beyond your usual limits. Even so, you somehow find room for dessert.

Besides being influenced by the variety of food and the holiday atmosphere (which may give you "permission" to overeat even if you're supposed to be on a diet), the fact that the other people at the dinner table are eating large quantities of food may add to your motivation to eat. Rena Wing and Robert Jeffery (1979a) demonstrated this influence by showing that college students who eat together tend to eat the same amount, even if they eat different amounts when dining apart.

Eating can also be triggered by environmental stimuli, such as TV advertisements or a string of signs for fast-food restaurants. This ability of specific stimuli to trigger eating is an example of classical conditioning. Harvey Weingarten (1983) showed that classical conditioning endows a previously neutral stimulus with the power to trigger eating in a satiated animal, by presenting a buzzer and a light to rats for four and a half minutes immediately before each of their meals. Following 11 days of this pairing, rats who had already eaten began eating again when the buzzer-light stimulus was presented. Stimuli that have become signals for food—the buzzer-light for the rat or the "golden arches" of a McDonald's restaurant for a person—can trigger an eating response even when the organism wouldn't ordinarily eat.

Another approach to studying psychological factors that influence eating is to observe the behavior of people who are continually on diets. A common experience among such people is binge eating once the diet is over. We can gain some insight into this phenomenon by considering an experiment by Peter Herman

The environment abounds with stimuli that encourage eating.

and Deborah Mack (1975), in which they differentiated two classes of people: (1) *restrained eaters,* who are concerned about their weight and are, therefore, very conscious of how much they eat and often diet to control their weight; and (2) *unrestrained eaters,* who are not as conscious of how much they eat and rarely if ever diet to control their weight.

Herman and Mack demonstrated differences in the eating behavior of restrained and unrestrained eaters by first separating a group of women into these two categories based on their responses to questions about how often they dieted or thought about food. (For example, restrained eaters report frequent dieting and many thoughts about food.) They then divided each group into three subgroups who consumed different numbers of milkshakes (Figure 11.8). Both restrained and unrestrained subjects, thinking they were participating in a taste experiment (they were asked to rate the taste of the milkshakes), consumed either no milkshakes (these subjects were told they were in the control group), one milkshake, or two milkshakes. They were then given access to three 3-pint containers of ice cream and, still thinking they were in a taste experiment, were told that they could eat as much of the ice cream as they wanted within the 10-minute "taste test."

The results for the zero-milkshake condition are what we would expect. The restrained eaters ate less ice cream than the unrestrained eaters (Figure 11.9). However, the results of the two-milkshake condition were vastly different. The restrained eaters in the two-milkshake group not only ate more than the restrained eaters in the zero-milkshake group but more than the unrestrained eaters in the two-milkshake group. The results for the one-shake condition were similar to those for the two-shake condition.

Why do the restrained eaters—who diet often and should be more concerned about their food intake—eat *more* after drinking the milkshakes? Answering this question at the behavioral level, Herman and Mack suggest that restrained eaters are constantly depriving themselves of food in order to keep their weight down, and that binge eating can be "triggered" by the presence of an attractive food cue such as the milkshakes. Looking at it from the cognitive level, they suggest that drinking two milkshakes eliminates the subjects' determination to limit their eating; once that cognitive restraint is eliminated, these subjects eat more because they have been deprived.

The research we have reviewed so far shows that biological and psychological influences interact in hunger motivation. This interaction is highly relevant to an aspect of hunger that is of concern to many people—problems with weight.

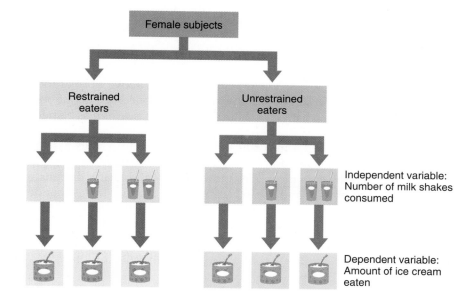

Independent variable: Number of milk shakes consumed

Dependent variable: Amount of ice cream eaten

FIGURE 11.8
Design of Herman and Mack's experiment that compared the eating behavior of restrained and unrestrained eaters. The results are shown in Figure 11.9.

FIGURE 11.9
Results of Herman and Mack's experiment. Surprisingly, in the two-shake condition, the restrained eaters ate more ice cream than the unrestrained eaters.

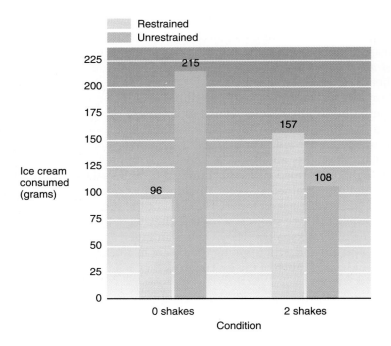

Hunger and Weight Problems

Almost any overweight person can lose weight. Few can keep it off.

Judith Rodin (1981)

Weight is a central concern for many people. Evidence for this assertion is easy to find: we need only count the diet and exercise books that appear regularly on best-seller lists, or tabloid stories about a new miracle diet or a celebrity who has just lost or gained a large amount of weight. Over 30 million Americans are obese (Lichtman et al., 1992), and Americans spend upward of $10 billion per year on weight reduction (Fitzgerald, 1981).

The fact that weight is a concern for so many people raises a number of questions. What is it about being "heavy" that motivates people to diet and exercise? Why are some people overweight and others not? Specifically, what biological and psychological factors contribute to being overweight? Before examining how excessive weight accrues, let's consider why weight is of concern in the first place.

The concern about body weight. **Obesity** is defined as an excess of body fat frequently resulting in an impairment of health (National Institutes of Health, 1985). In practice, people whose weight is at least 15% above normal for their height and age are considered obese. Why are people concerned about obesity? One reason has to do with what you've just read: obesity is *defined* as being detrimental to health.

Obesity has been called a major health problem because of its association with lower back pain, diabetes, and cardiovascular problems (Bray, 1986; Lichtman et al., 1992). But the data most relevant to obesity and health designate the relationship between obesity and life expectancy. The familiar tables that define the "normal" weight for a given age and height were constructed by Metropolitan Life Insurance Company, based on life expectancy data collected from millions of its policyholders. According to those data, a group of males 60% above average weight will experience twice the number of deaths as a group of average-weight males.

Even though the health hazards of obesity are well known, most people's concern about being overweight has less to do with potential health hazards than with the pressure in our society to be thin. From an early age, children prefer lean bodies and reject fat ones (Lerner & Gellert, 1969). When children and adults are shown pictures of an obese child and children with various disabilities, including deformities of the limbs, they rate the obese child as least "likable" (Goodman et al., 1963; Maddox, Back, & Liederman, 1968). To the extent that overweight individuals are perceived as unattractive, they are disadvantaged by the demonstrable bias in favor of attractive people. For example, elementary schoolteachers rate attractive children more favorably and have higher expectations of their performance (Adams & Cohen, 1974; Clifford, 1975), and employers are more likely to hire attractive people and to offer them higher starting salaries than they offer to unattractive people (Dipboyle, Fromkin, & Wiback, 1975, 1977).

The effects of this prejudice are felt most strongly by females, who learn the importance of being thin and beautiful from an early age. In earlier centuries, Western women's ideal body style was on the plump side by today's standards (Figure 11.10). Today the standard for beauty is thin, with many sources reinforcing the pressure to be thin, from the Barbie dolls that serve as a model of the "ideal woman" to which young girls should aspire, to television programs and magazine advertisements that depict the most desirable women as not only beautiful but thin (Rodin, 1985).

One well-documented cognitive effect of our society's obsession with thinness is a tendency for women to overestimate their weight. Kevin Thompson (1986) found that 95% of the women he tested overestimated their body size by an average of 25%; those who overestimated it the most had the lowest self-esteem. Psychological factors, therefore, are more important than biological factors in women's efforts to diet and exercise to control their weight. Men also diet and exercise for weight control, but are in general less concerned with weight, as society views overweight men much less negatively than overweight women (Rodin, Silberstein, & Striegel-Moore, 1984).

Biological factors in body weight. Why do some people become obese but not others? To answer this question researchers have considered a number of factors, both biological and psychological. On the biological side, they have

FIGURE 11.10

Changing standards of female beauty are reflected in these images: 16th-century painter Jacopo Palma's "Three Sisters," emphasizing "plump voluptuousness," and two extremely thin, modern-day fashion models.

Obesity often runs in families. Research indicates that this is due at least in part to genetics.

compared the weights of identical and nonidentical twins; they have looked for connections between body weight and metabolism; and they have suggested that a person's natural body weight may be determined by a biologically based factor called the set point.

Body weight in families.   Excessive weight runs in families. Lean parents tend to have lean children and obese parents tend to have obese children (Gurn, 1985). But what causes this? Is it due to the environment (perhaps overweight parents put more food on the table and encourage eating), or to genetics (perhaps parents pass on physiological characteristics that make their children prone to gaining weight)? Psychologists used to think that environmental factors were the major cause of obesity. One piece of evidence supporting an environmental cause was the relationship between obesity and a person's socioeconomic status, with lower status being associated with obesity. But recent evidence argues that genetics probably also plays a role in determining weight.

Albert Stunkard and his co-workers (1990) studied hereditary influences on body weight by comparing twins reared apart and twins reared together. They found a strong correlation between the body mass index (weight divided by the square of height) of identical (MZ) twins whether or not they were reared together, and a much lower correlation between the indices of fraternal (DZ) twins (Figure 11.11). Stunkard based his conclusion that genetics is important in determining weight on the following reasoning: (1) The correlations of MZ twins (who are identical genetically) are higher than the correlations of DZ twins (who have only 50% of their genes in common). (2) Disparate rearing conditions had little effect on the correlations.

In another study, Claude Bouchard and a team of researchers (1990) overfed 12 pairs of MZ twins for 84 days. The resultant weight gain varied from 4.3 to 13.3 kilograms (9.5 to 29.3 pounds), but each member of a particular pair of twins gained about the same amount and tended to put on weight in the same body areas. Based on this result, Bouchard came to the same conclusion as Stunkard: genetic factors are involved in determining a person's weight.

But exactly what does genetics influence? The physiological mechanisms for the regulation of weight and eating are so complex that any number of factors could be implicated. A primary candidate is the **resting metabolic rate,** the amount of energy the body needs to maintain itself when at rest.

FIGURE 11.11

The fact that MZ twins are more likely than DZ twins to have the same body builds, even when reared apart, supports the idea that genetics is an important determinant of body weight.

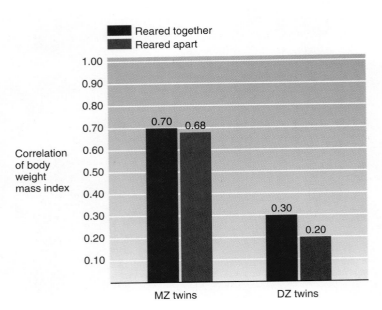

Body weight and metabolism.   What is the role of metabolism in determining a person's weight? If obese people had lower-than-normal metabolism, they would turn food into energy more slowly and would therefore gain weight more easily. A recent study of obese members of a Native American tribe in the Southwest has shown that, over a two-year period, subjects with a low resting metabolic rate were four times as likely to have gained more than 7.5 kilograms (16.5 pounds) than those with a high metabolic rate (Ravussin et al., 1988). This study was hailed, when it appeared, as providing convincing evidence of a link between obesity and low metabolism (Hirsch & Leibel, 1988).

Body weight and the set point.   Richard Keesey (1980, 1986) has proposed that weight is regulated by a physiological mechanism, probably located in the lateral nucleus of the hypothalamus, that establishes a **set point** for a particular body. This set point is the weight toward which the body naturally gravitates.

One observation on which Keesey based his proposal is that if people are starved until their body weight is substantially reduced, they return to their previous weight once adequate food becomes available (Keesey, 1986). Keesey also observed that people on stringent diets often lose much less weight than would be predicted from their decreased caloric intake. The reason? Dieting causes a 15 to 30% decrease in metabolism, making it harder to reduce the body's weight below its set point.

This decrease in metabolism makes dieting difficult; it also makes it difficult to avoid regaining weight after the diet is over. This is illustrated by an experiment in which rats were put on a diet to lose about 20% of their body weight (Boyle, Storlien, & Keesey, 1978). After the diet ended, the experimenters provided unlimited food to the rats and measured the amount of food eaten and the weights for the group that had "dieted" against those of a group of control rats that were not put on a diet. In the week following the diet, the rats that had dieted gained 30 grams, whereas the control rats gained only 1.6 grams, even though the control rats ate more than the rats that had dieted (Figure 11.12). This occurred because the depression of the dieting rats' metabolism persisted after the diet was over, making it possible for them to gain weight while eating less food.

Keesey interprets these results as evidence that the body attempts to keep its weight constant in the face of diminished food supplies, and that obesity is caused by a high set point. But though biology is an important determinant of body weight, psychological factors play a role as well.

Psychological factors in body weight.   A popular psychological explanation for obesity was proposed by Stanley Schachter (1971), based on experiments that

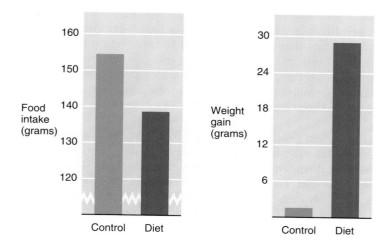

FIGURE 11.12
Even though rats that "dieted" ate less food after their diet ended than control rats that did not diet (left), they gained more weight (right).

showed that obese people are more likely than normal-weight people to increase their eating when presented with a large amount of food or food that smells good or is particularly tasty. Schachter's **externality hypothesis** stated that obese people's eating is controlled not by internal cues provided by the body, but by external cues such as the presence or appearance of food.

The externality hypothesis led to a large amount of research but did not live up to its promise, because later researchers failed to find a strong relationship between degree of obesity and degree of external responsiveness. In fact, some very obese people are almost completely insensitive to external cues. Thus, although many people do eat more in response to external cues, obese people do not do so substantially more than normal-weight people (Rodin, 1981).

What about other psychological factors that might be associated with obesity? One time-honored explanation is that overweight people increase their eating because they are unhappy or emotionally upset. This idea is usually supported by the results of case studies in which obese people with emotional problems seek help from therapists. But the overall picture, in which the mental health of large groups of obese and normal-weight people are compared, provides no evidence that the former are more psychologically distressed than the latter (Wadden & Stunkard, 1985). In fact, the suicide rate of obese people is lower than that of normal-weight people (Fitzgerald, 1981).

Although the mental health of obese people is essentially the same as that of lean people, there is some evidence from laboratory studies that obese people eat more than lean people when they are aroused (McKenna, 1972; White, 1973). This result, combined with the finding that obese people are more easily aroused than normal-weight people (Rodin, 1982), suggests that stressful, arousal-producing conditions might tend to trigger overeating in obese people.

A recent study points to another psychological factor that may contribute to obesity. Steven Lichtman and his co-workers (1992) studied a group of obese subjects who were unable to lose weight even when on stringent diets. When Lichtman asked them to record their food intake and their amount of daily exercise in a diary, he found that they underreported the amount of food they consumed and overestimated their daily exercise. (This result also occurs in normal-weight people and in obese people who are able to lose weight, but to a much lesser degree.) Lichtman's subjects reported that they consumed an average of 1028 calories per day, though they actually consumed an average of 2081.

Was this the result of purposeful misrepresentation by the subjects? Not according to Lichtman. His subjects were both surprised and distressed when presented with the results. Apparently, they were simply unaware of the discrepancy between their reported and actual eating and exercise (Danforth & Sims, 1992). Some as yet poorly understood mechanism is responsible for these subjects' unawareness of their food intake, and this behavior makes it difficult for them to lose weight when dieting.

We have seen that whereas people are strongly motivated to keep from being overweight, they are often fighting a battle against both biological and psychological factors that make it difficult to lose weight or to keep it off once they have lost it. Perhaps the most striking message of obesity research with regard to motivation is the persistence with which people work to lose weight in the face of these obstacles. We will now describe some of the programs that have been developed to help people lose weight.

Treatment for weight problems.   In 1958, Albert Stunkard made a bleak prediction based on his research: "Most obese people do not enter treatment for obesity. Of those that do enter, most will not remain. Of those who remain, most will not lose much weight. Of those who lose weight, most will regain it." In the more than 30 years since Stunkard's observation, many different techniques have been devised to help people lose weight. These techniques, involving approaches ranging from individual therapy to drugs to hypnosis, can measure their success in very small weight losses during treatment and weight gains following the termination of treatment. For many of the reasons we have discussed, researchers have yet to find a truly effective method to help people lose substantial amounts of weight and keep it off.

One method that shows promise is **behavior therapy,** which attempts to reduce eating by modifying clients' behavioral patterns in various ways. Three of the techniques used in behavior therapy programs for weight control are self-monitoring, stimulus control, and reinforcement.

1. *Self-monitoring:* Most overweight people are not aware of their individual pattern of food consumption. To determine this pattern, clients are asked to record all their eating and drinking and to note under what circumstances consumption occurs. The idea is to increase clients' awareness of the situations in which they eat.

2. *Stimulus control:* A program is developed to limit the clients' contact with stimuli that trigger eating. For example, suppose that a writer discovers from her self-monitoring record that when she works at home, she often goes to the kitchen to snack as a diversion from writing. One way to eliminate this behavior would be to do her writing away from home to remove the temptation of the kitchen refrigerator.

   In addition to individualized measures based on clients' **self-monitoring** reports, the following suggestions have proved useful for gaining control over stimuli that trigger eating (Abramson, 1982):

   - All food must be consumed while sitting at a specific place.
   - Food must be removed from any other place in the house and kept only in the kitchen or dining room.
   - Eating should not be done in conjunction with other activities. Conversation is allowed, but not reading or watching television.

3. *Reinforcement:* In the chapter on learning we saw that reinforcement is usually most effective when it immediately follows a behavior. This principle works against weight-loss programs, because the reinforcement for eating (good taste and satisfaction of hunger) occurs immediately or shortly after eating, whereas reinforcement for not eating (loss of weight) occurs days or even weeks later. Accordingly, behavior therapists have looked for ways to create other reinforcements for not overeating. For example, the client is asked to deposit a sum of money at a clinic and is refunded some of it every time he or she shows a weight loss on a return visit to the clinic.

6   LEARNING

How successful are such weight control programs? A survey of research studies evaluating different methods of treatment found that the weight losses achieved by current therapies average only about 12 pounds, with only one person in five losing 20 pounds or more (Wing & Jeffery, 1979b). No one treatment procedure seemed superior to others, though some research suggests that people in behavior therapy programs do better than others at keeping their weight off once the formal treatment program has ended. Linda Craighead and her co-workers (1981) compared people's weight loss in three different programs: (1) behavior therapy; (2) drug therapy, using an appetite suppressant; and (3) a combination of behavior therapy and drug therapy. People in all these programs achieved substantial weight loss, with those in the combined treatment losing the most. However, one year after the treatment had ended, the behavior therapy group had gained back the least amount of weight and so ended up with the largest net weight loss (Figure 11.13).

Why did the behavior therapy group do so well? One possibility is that the clients learned, as they underwent the treatment, that they personally had power

FIGURE 11.13
Drug therapy, behavior therapy, and a combination treatment all resulted in weight losses during treatment. A year after treatment ended, however, the behavior therapy group had gained back the least weight.

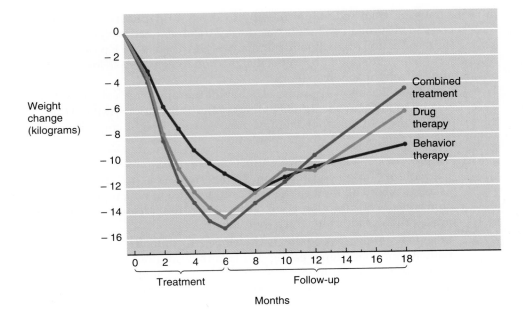

over their situation. And they saw their weight loss as achieved not by a drug but by their own effort. These people may have been motivated by the prospect of not only losing weight but also accomplishing something through personal effort. We will return to this kind of motivation later in this chapter, when we discuss achievement motivation.

Looking back on our study of hunger motivation, we can see that we have really been talking about two motives: (1) a motive to eat, which is driven by the body's internal mechanisms and by factors such as the taste of food, conditioning, external cues, and the social nature of eating; and (2) a motive to diet, which is driven by health concerns and by societal pressures to be thin. Both motives are powerful, and they work at cross purposes to one another. For that reason, hunger and dieting play a persistent and central role in the lives of many people.

Sexual Motivation

Is Sex Necessary?

Title of 1929 book by humorists James Thurber and E. B. White

Sexual motivation—the motivation to engage in sexual behavior—is, like hunger, strongly influenced by biology. But unlike hunger, it is not essential to an individual's life. An individual can, if he or she chooses, survive without ever engaging in any sexual activity. From an evolutionary perspective, however, a powerful sexual motivation makes sense in ensuring the propagation of the species and the survival of one's own genes. It is not surprising, therefore, that sexual motivation is a central part of life for many species, including our own.

From a psychological standpoint, sexual motivation is worth studying not only because of its importance in people's lives, but because it provides an excellent example of a biologically driven behavior that in humans is greatly influenced by behavioral, cognitive, and contextual factors. Just as hunger can be triggered by specific environmental stimuli, for example, sexual thoughts and feelings can be triggered by other people, by scents and sounds, by media images, and by music.

Environmental and contextual influences clearly contribute to the wide range of ways in which people express sexual motivation. In particular, cultural and social institutions, customs, and mores help shape sexual expression. In our society, films, advertising, and music often glorify sexual activity, whereas religious and family influences emphasize sexuality's place within a system of morality. From a scientific standpoint, we are not primarily concerned with whether one system of values or another is preferable, but rather with describing and explaining why people do what they do. Whatever personal beliefs we may have about how people *should* behave, it is informative to know what role biological and psychological factors—including cognitive ones, such as values— play in determining how they *do* behave. Accordingly, in our discussion we will first consider the biological mechanisms involved in sexual motivation and then look at the psychological factors that influence how it is expressed.

Biological Factors in Sexual Motivation

③   BIOLOGY

The biological basis of sexual motivation is established prenatally, as the developing embryo and fetus takes on either male or female characteristics. After that, sexual behavior is influenced by the action of hormones—although, as we will see, this effect is greater in the lower animals than in humans.

Sexual differentiation.   The biological starting point for human sexual behavior is the developmental process of *sexual differentiation*, which, during the sixth week after conception, begins endowing the initially sexless embryo with either male or female characteristics. As we saw in the Follow-Through for Chapter 3, embryonic sex glands called the gonads are formed about three weeks after conception. At this point the gonads can become either male or female sex organs. At six weeks after conception, differentiation begins. If the sex chromosomes are XY, differentiation proceeds in the male direction, with the gonads developing into testes and secreting **testosterone.** The resulting high concentration of testosterone causes male genitals to develop. If the sex chromosomes are XX, differentiation proceeds in the female direction, with the gonads developing into ovaries and secreting **estrogen.** In the absence of high testosterone, female genitals develop. This situation—in which the female develops *unless* testosterone is present, has been called the **Eve principle** because the male is, in a sense, derived from the female.

Sexual differentiation is manifested not only by the development of different sex organs, but also by the development of differences in the brains of males and females. These brain differences, like the gonadal differences, are determined by the different types of hormones present during prenatal development (Bancroft, 1987). One example of a brain difference is that some nuclei in the hypothalamus are larger in males (Swaab & Fliers, 1985).

These brain differences have important effects, especially later in life when males and females become able to reproduce. For example, we can demonstrate a brain difference related to reproduction by introducing estrogen, via an injection or a pill. This causes the females' hypothalamus to signal the pituitary gland to release the *luteinizing hormone,* which is involved in the female reproductive cycle but has no effect on the male hypothalamus.

Hormones and sexual desire.   The same hormones involved in the sexual differentiation of the genitals and brain are also involved in activating sexual behavior. Sexual behavior depends on the presence of a minimum level of sex hormones. Thus, removal of a male rat's testes or a female rat's ovaries causes a decline in sexual behavior because of a decline in the concentration of sex hormones in the blood.

Hormones play a greater role in determining sexual behavior in animals than they do in humans. Sexual behavior in humans is governed not only by biology, but by complex social and cognitive factors.

In many animals sexual receptivity follows the animal's hormonal cycle. For example, the increase in hormone levels that occurs just prior to a female dog's fertile period (called *estrus,* or being "in heat") causes her to be receptive to copulation. In humans, male sexual activity is influenced by testosterone concentration: sexual excitement is at its highest between the ages of 15 and 25, when testosterone concentrations are highest (Kalat, 1992). There is also some evidence for a link between hormone level and sexual activity in women. Females are more likely to initiate sexual activity during periods of ovulation, when estrogen levels are highest (Figure 11.14) (Adams, Gold, & Burt, 1978).

Although hormones have been shown to affect human sexual behavior, we are not at the mercy of our hormones, as are lower animals such as rats or dogs. Moving up the phylogenetic scale (from lower to higher animals), the effect of hormones on sexual behavior decreases. Human sexual activity can occur at any time, not just at certain times of the month. And high concentrations of testosterone do not guarantee sexual activity in males, as some males with normal testosterone levels are impotent (unable to achieve an erection), and giving them extra doses of testosterone doesn't change their condition (Carani et al., 1990).

Another variable that influences sexual activity is age. Male sexual activity peaks at about 18 years of age, whereas female sexual activity peaks at around 30 years (Griffitt, 1987; Griffitt & Hatfield, 1985). As these differences cannot completely be explained on the basis of hormones, it has been suggested that they reflect the fact that for females, traditionally, the majority of their sexual experience occurs within marriage. For males, on the other hand, sexual activity is not correlated with their marital status, so a high level of early sexual activity is common (Basow, 1992).

Psychological factors are so important in humans that it has been suggested—not entirely in jest—that our most important sex organ is the brain. Thus, in humans, sexual arousal is not simply an automatic response to hormones or to sensory stimulation; it also depends on many psychological variables, including our thoughts, feelings, and values. The importance of these psychological factors in determining sexuality is vividly illustrated by how sexuality has been viewed at different times in Western history. The following Interdisciplinary Dimension provides some historical perspective on the way humans have literally construed the meaning of sexuality.

FIGURE 11.14
Women who are not taking birth control pills tend to be more sexually active (as measured by their tendency to initiate sexual activity) during ovulation, when estrogen levels are high. The same effect does not occur for women taking birth control pills, which suppress variations in hormone levels.

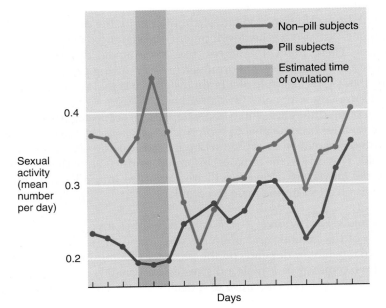

INTERDISCIPLINARY DIMENSION HISTORY

Sexuality and Society in Western Culture

> Just as the first step in understanding any clinical problem is in taking the patient's history, so the first step in understanding any area of basic human concern is looking at its history. Nowhere is this more true than in the area of human sexuality where past myths and misinformation often remain an integral part of the current belief structure of vast numbers of people (Bullough, 1987, p. 49).

Our attitudes about sex come largely from the society we grow up in and, as pointed out by historian Vince Bullough (1976, 1987), many of people's beliefs about sex are based on assumptions handed down from past generations. By looking at the history of Western attitudes toward sexuality, we can better understand both people's belief systems from the past and the basis of some of the beliefs still held by many in our culture today.

One way to approach the history of sexuality is to look at views held by the dominant institutions during various periods of history. We see that first the church and then the medical establishment were powerful forces in constructing society's definition of morally correct behavior. As we will see, both of these institutions reinforced negative attitudes about sexuality. For many centuries the Catholic church was the most powerful social institution in Western Europe. Saint Augustine (A.D. 354–430) was one of the early church fathers who, in his writings, set forth many of the church's views on sexuality. He saw sex as basically sinful, and felt that sexual intercourse should be allowed only for procreation. This meant that activities that did not result in procreation, such as "protected" sex, masturbation, and homosexuality, were sinful.

Church theoreticians who came after Saint Augustine generally reinforced his negative attitude. These attitudes were embraced many years later by 16th- and 17th-century physicians, who provided a medical rationale for labeling "excess" sexual activity as dangerous. One line of medical reasoning followed from the observation that males tend to become lethargic after having an orgasm. Some physicians therefore concluded that too many orgasms would cause severe damage, because the effect would be cumulative. Thus, Hermann Boerhaave (1668–1738), one of the early developers of modern medicine, stated that a "rash expenditure of semen brings on a lassitude, a feebleness, a weakening of motion, fits, wasting, dryness, fevers, a decay of the spinal cord, a fatuity, and other like evils" (Bullough, 1976, p. 496). Writings such as this led to the popularization of the idea that masturbation or engaging in intercourse for pleasure only led to physical problems and even madness (Tissot, 1766). These ideas persisted into the 19th and 20th centuries, as many physicians continued disseminating the myth that masturbation, particularly in adolescents, could lead to terrible consequences, including insanity (Bullough, 1980).

Another cultural influence on sexuality was the English Industrial Revolution of the 19th century. It was during this time that men went to work in factories and businesses and women's roles became more narrowly defined as homemakers. Whereas in the rural economy women had been seen as hardworking providers, society created a new image of women—at least among the upper classes—as fragile creatures, incapable of strenuous activity. Women, according to this idea, should be protected from the real world by having their reading material censored and by being sheltered from information about sex (Bullough, 1980). These ideas affected the way girls were socialized. The message they received as young girls—that they weren't supposed to be interested in sex—led many women to deny their sexual desires and needs. This behavior fit well with the ideas of people such as William Acton (1871), who theorized that God created women to be indifferent to sex so that men wouldn't waste their energy in senseless sexual activity.

Eventually, however, these ideas were challenged. In the 20th century, women became less willing to be sexually passive and began asserting their own sexual needs. And in 1948, with the publication of Alfred Kinsey's book *Sexual Behavior in the Human Male*, the American public became aware of how the realities of sexual behavior had changed. Kinsey's book, which was based on extensive interviews with 12,000 people, uncovered levels of sexual activity that startled many readers. For example, Kinsey reported that 37% of American males had had at least one homosexual experience and that the majority had masturbated. Apparently, not everyone was following the "socially correct" view of sexuality espoused by the church and other cultural institutions. Clearly, much more was going on in people's bedrooms than many had realized.

The prevalent view in the 19th century was that women were fragile creatures who needed to be sheltered from information about sex.

Kinsey's results, though praised by many (Ernst & Loth, 1948; Palmore, 1952), were also attacked. For example, *Life* magazine called it "an assault on the family as a basic unit of society, a negation of moral law . . ." (Wickware, 1948). And the reaction to Kinsey's second book, *Sexual Behavior in the Human Female,* which was published in 1953, was particularly harsh. Many church leaders and educators condemned Kinsey's findings as amoral and antifamily (Masters, Johnson, & Kolodny, 1988); his life was thoroughly investigated; his financial backers, threatened with congressional hearings, withdrew their support. Even in today's society, many segments of the population believe that dissemination of information about sexuality should be controlled.

We have seen that throughout history sexual motivation, with its immensely powerful biological component, has intersected with the attitudes, beliefs, and values held by both individuals and the culture as a whole. Any account of sexual motivation based only on biology cannot, therefore, hope to explain people's experience of sexuality or the sexual behavior that they engage in. ■

Psychological Factors in Sexual Motivation

There is a widely repeated story—perhaps true, perhaps not—about an incident that is said to have occurred as President Calvin Coolidge and his wife were making a campaign visit to a chicken farm.

> One day President and Mrs. Coolidge were visiting a government farm. Soon after their arrival they were taken off on separate tours. When Mrs. Coolidge passed the chicken pens, she paused to ask the man in charge if the rooster copulated more than once each day. "Dozens of times," was the reply. "Please tell that to the President," Mrs. Coolidge requested. When the President passed the pens and was told about the rooster, he asked, "Same hen every time?" "Oh no, Mr. President, a different one each time." The President nodded slowly, then said, "Tell that to Mrs. Coolidge" (Bermant, 1976, pp. 76–77).

This story gave the name the **Coolidge effect** to the finding that a sexually gratified male rat or hamster will become aroused when a new female is presented (Lester & Gorzalka, 1988). This effect is one illustration of how sexual motivation can be influenced by environmental stimuli.

In humans, the role of psychological processes in sexual behavior goes beyond the effects of environmental stimuli. Psychological influences on sexuality are closely tied to socialization processes that boys and girls of a particular culture experience as they grow up. For example, in Western culture boys and girls are trained from an early age to expect to eventually "fall in love" with a member of the other sex, to marry that person, and to settle down and have a family. However, in the Sambian culture of eastern New Guinea, normal sexual development includes a period in which all young boys participate in homosexual activity with older tribesmen before marrying and starting heterosexual activity. Although this may sound like deviant behavior from the perspective of our culture, *not* to engage in homosexual activity as a young boy would be considered deviant from the perspective of Sambian culture (Herdt, 1984; Money, 1987). Thus, it is important to recognize that, while sexual *motivation* is biologically based and in that sense both "natural" and universal, how that motivation is expressed in *behavior* depends a great deal on learning.

In this section, we will look at some examples of how psychological influences affect sexual behavior as practiced in our culture. We will consider early sexual experiences, attitudes about sex, and sexual response to erotica, focusing on similarities and differences between males and females. Then we consider the topic of sexual orientation—that is, the process involved in determining whether sexual motivation is directed to members of the same or the other sex.

Early sexual experiences.   Even though boys enter puberty two years later than girls on the average, they typically report having sexual experiences earlier

10   DEVELOPMENT

than girls. Teenage boys report being aroused several times daily, whereas girls report that they are aroused only once or twice a week. Boys are also more likely to engage in masturbation and start at a much earlier age than females (Hass, 1979; Kinsey et al., 1953; LoPresto, Sherman, & Sherman, 1985).

These differences in the early sexual experiences of males and females have important implications for heterosexual males' and females' first sexual experiences with each other. When this first sexual encounter occurs, males are usually more experienced sexually than females because of their previous experience with masturbation. This may place the female in a dependent position relative to the male, both because he knows more about his own sexuality than she does and because she depends on him for sexual arousal. The male, in contrast, has become aroused many times without the presence of a female, so he is not dependent on her for arousal.

This idea of females being sexually dependent and males being sexually independent falls in line with our society's general stereotype of males and females, according to which males are active, strong, and independent and females passive, nurturing, and dependent. Our society not only assigns different qualities to males and females but also creates different rules regarding appropriate behavior. It is considered more appropriate for males to initiate sex than for females to do so. Many people consider it normal for a male to have had many sexual partners (he would be considered "macho"), but not appropriate for a female (who would be considered "easy"). These differences between society's unwritten rules for male and female behavior is called the **double standard**—females are, in general, expected to behave less sexually than males.

Male and female attitudes about sexual activity. The differences in society's rules for male and female sexual behavior are reflected in the attitudes of males and females toward sexual intercourse. As shown in Table 11.2, most college males in one survey typically felt little need to be emotionally connected with their sexual partners; for college females, the opposite was true. This difference in attitudes is expressed in behavior: males are more likely than females to have sex with more partners (Carroll, Volk, & Hyde, 1985). Females are twice as likely as males to be in love with their first sexual partner (Leigh, 1989). When Janell Carroll and her co-workers (1985) asked females to describe their motives for sexual intercourse, they responded with answers such as the following:

- "Emotional feelings that were shared, wonderful way to express love!!"
- "My motives for sexual intercourse would all be due to the love and commitment I feel for my partner."
- "To show my love for my partner and to feel loved and needed."

18   SOCIAL

TABLE 11.2

Survey of college students' sexual behaviors and attitudes

	Males (%)	Females (%)
Number of sexual partners:		
None	6	20
Over 16	25	2
Need sex for emotional reasons	19	58
Emotional involvement is a prerequisite for sexual intercourse always or most of the time	40	85
Feel comfortable or relaxed about one-night stands	50	9

Males, on the other hand, typically responded as follows:

- "Need it."
- "To gratify myself."
- "For the pleasure or the love."
- "When I'm tired of masturbation."

In another survey, Carol Tavris and Carole Offir (1977) asked college men and women to list their problems with "any aspect of sexual functioning." The answers given by males and females differed greatly, as shown in Table 11.3. Note that women's concerns are dominated by fears of being hurt emotionally, whereas men's concerns are dominated by complaints about *women's* sexual behavior. Not surprisingly, women are more selective in both their sexual partners and the activities they choose to engage in. Such differences clearly reflect the role of learning in determining how sexual motivation is expressed.

The differences between male and female approaches to sexuality, and the observation that men are the primary consumers of "pinups" and erotic magazines, might seem to indicate that men and women would respond differently to erotic pictures or literature. But experiments designed to test this idea have yielded some surprising results.

Male and female responses to erotica.   From the data reviewed so far, one hypothesis we might formulate about male and female responses to erotica is that females will respond primarily to pictures or literature that emphasize romance, whereas men will be more likely to respond to explicit depictions of sex. This hypothesis is supported if we look at experiments in which women are given a choice of which type of stimuli they will be exposed to. When given a choice, they tend to pick soft-core ("loving") depictions of sexual activity over hard-core ("lustful") depictions, or nonerotic over erotic (Kendrick et al., 1980). However, contrary to what we might expect from females' rejection of "lustful" erotic material, they *do* become aroused when they are exposed to these materials (Fisher & Byrne, 1978; Harrell & Stolp, 1985).

An experiment by Julia Heiman (1975) investigated male and female responses to erotica by comparing (1) the subjects' rating of their own arousal with (2) a physiological measure of their arousal. Her subjects listened to tapes of either erotic material (containing explicit descriptions of sexual activity) or roman-

TABLE 11.3
Problems cited with "any aspect of sexual functioning"

Females' Concerns	Males' Concerns
• Fear of pregnancy • Fear of rape • Fear of being conquered and then regarded as of no further use • Accepting masturbation • Fear that their partners would be physically repulsed by them • Fear of losing self-respect • Fear of becoming too attached when the feeling was not mutual • Guilt feelings about premarital sex • Pressure to have sex even when they did not want to • Fear of not satisfying their partners • Embarrassment or concern over not being orgasmic	• Finding partners who were open to varying sexual experiences • Not being able to have sexual relations when they wanted to • Women who "tease" without wanting to engage in sexual activity • Women's refusal to take responsibility for their own sexuality • Women who use their sexual attractiveness in a manipulatory fashion • The excessive modesty of women (they wanted the lights off) • Passive women • Aggressive women • Necessity to say you love the woman even if it is not true • Always having to be on the hunt • Being expected to know all about sex • Inability to communicate feelings or needs during sex

tic material (containing no explicit descriptions). The male subjects' physiological arousal was measured by a strain gauge fitted around the base of the penis that measured blood volume, an indicator of excitement. Women's arousal was measured by a device called a photoplethysmograph, which is placed just inside the entrance to the vagina and that also measures blood volume. Subjects were fully clothed during the experiment and listened to the tapes in private listening booths. After hearing a tape they answered a series of questions designed to measure how arousing the tape was. (If you're wondering why anyone would submit to these procedures, see Measurement & Methodology, "Volunteer Bias in Selecting Subjects for Sexuality Studies.")

Both self-report and physiological measures showed that men *and* women were aroused by the erotic tapes, and that neither found the romantic tapes as arousing. Thus, contrary to what we might expect, men and women are both aroused by explicit erotica. Heiman did, however, observe one interesting difference between males and females. Every time the males were physically aroused they also *reported* being aroused. However, half of the time that females were physically aroused, they did not report being aroused. Apparently, women detect their own arousal less readily than do men. It is not hard to formulate a possible reason for this: when men are aroused, the resulting erection is difficult to miss. Women's physiological arousal, in contrast, is not as obvious.

Heiman also noted that the women who were the least accurate in reporting their arousal were among the few who became aroused by the romantic tapes and by tapes in a control condition that had no sexual content at all.

MEASUREMENT & METHODOLOGY

Volunteer Bias in Selecting Subjects for Sexuality Studies

What kinds of people volunteer to be subjects in psychological research? If volunteers differ from people in the general population, then we have to be careful before generalizing the results of psychological research to the population as a whole. This problem of potential **volunteer bias** is especially important in studies of sexuality, because these studies require that subjects violate societal norms by (1) divulging personal information; (2) observing erotic stimuli; and (3) allowing measuring instruments to be attached to their genitals in physiological studies.

How do subjects who are willing to do these things differ from those who aren't? Patricia Morokoff (1986) answered this question by first recruiting 92 unmarried undergraduate women to volunteer for an experiment titled "Films and Sexual Fantasies." Notice that this group of volunteers may already have been different from the general college population, since they were willing to participate in an experiment about sexuality. Morokoff's experiment sought to discover, *within this already select group of subjects*, whether there were differences between those who were willing to have their physiological arousal measured while watching an erotic film and those who were not.

The 92 women completed questionnaires designed to determine the nature of their sexual experiences. They were then told that in the second part of the experiment they would be required to view an explicitly erotic videotape, write out a sexual fantasy, and have their physiological arousal measured with a photoplethysmograph, a small tampon-shaped device inserted into the vagina. They were told to think about whether they wanted to participate in the second part, and that they would be contacted in one or two days for their decision. When contacted, 62 subjects agreed to be in the experiment, and 30 decided not to participate.

How did the subjects who volunteered for the second part of the study differ from those who didn't? When Morokoff compared the two groups' responses to the questionnaires, she found that those agreeing to be in the second part had more sexual experience, were more likely to masturbate, and were less inhibited sexually. Thus it seems likely that subjects who participate in sexuality experiments are different in relevant ways from those who don't. Whether these differences influence the results of an experiment depends on the particular experiment. It is important to be aware, however, that the effects of volunteer bias may be particularly large in sexuality studies. We must, therefore, be cautious about generalizing the results of these experiments to the population as a whole.

For the same reasons, we need to be cautious about how we interpret the results of surveys in popular magazines. These surveys are usually based not on a random sample of the population but on those among readers of a particular magazine who are interested enough to respond. The results of such surveys may make interesting reading, but are not necessarily generalizable to the population as a whole.

Perhaps, Heiman suggests, these subjects thought it might not be socially acceptable to be aroused by the sexually explicit tapes, so "their minds denied or ignored their bodies" (p. 94).

The research on responses to erotica points to the complex interweaving of biological and psychological influences, including learning, that shape sexual motivation and its expression. Currently a great deal of debate is given to the relative importance of biology and learning in determining whether people's sexual motivation is directed toward the same or opposite sex. We now look at the evidence on this issue, along with other questions about sexual orientation.

Sexual Orientation

Sexual orientation refers to the gender toward which a person feels sexual attraction. **Heterosexuality** is defined as a preferred sexual attraction to people of the other sex over a significant period of time. **Homosexuality** is defined as a preferred sexual attraction to people of the person's own sex over a significant period of time. Notice that these definitions say nothing about sexual *activity*. The key part of these definitions is to whom the person is *attracted*, not whether the individual is acting on that attraction. Persons of either orientation can decide to engage in or abstain from sexual activity. Attraction, therefore, not behavior, defines a person's sexual orientation.

In a class I teach on the psychology of gender I discuss research on homosexuality. The class discussion that ensues, along with papers I have my students write about their attitudes about homosexuality, uncovers a great deal of **homophobia**—negative feelings about homosexuals. My students' attitudes about homosexuals are typical of the attitudes of the population as a whole. Although many people are accepting of the homosexual lifestyle, it is no secret that there is a great deal of prejudice against homosexuals in our society. For example, in a 1987 survey, 75% of the respondents said that they felt sexual relations between two adults of the same sex is always wrong (Davis & Smith, 1987), and in a 1993 survey 45% said that homosexual relations between consenting adults should be illegal (Schmalz, 1993).

One of the interesting observations made by many of my students is that they don't know any homosexuals. This assertion is, however, often in error—chances are that they do know people who are homosexual, but that they are simply *unaware* of their acquaintances' orientation. The likelihood of knowing someone who is homosexual becomes apparent when we consider that the incidence of homosexuality in the United States has been reported to range from 4 to 10%, with the incidence being higher among people who have graduated from college (Fay et al., 1989; Kinsey, Pomeroy, & Martin, 1948). In fact, there are more homosexuals than left-handed people. How many left-handers do you know?

As with other issues involving sexual behavior, homosexuality invokes questions of values and mores as well as questions of fact. Too often, however, discussions of sexual orientation are simply ill informed—as exemplified by those of my students who underestimate the chances that they know someone who is homosexual. Thus, you may hear people make unwarranted conclusions about the "facts" of sexual orientation. To shed some light on this sensitive and often politicized topic, let's consider two questions: (1) "How have mental health practitioners viewed the relationship between sexual orientation and mental health?" and (2) "What causes homosexuality?" We will see that the first question is easy to answer, the second one much more difficult.

Sexual orientation and mental health.   Heterosexuality is clearly the norm in our society. But does that mean that another sexual orientation is "deviant," in the sense of stemming from some kind of psychological disorder? Let's examine how mental health professionals have answered this question—and, more important, what evidence they have given for their answers.

A lesbian couple. Research indicates that there is no difference between homosexuals and heterosexuals in adjustment or general personality characteristics.

The second edition of the *Diagnostic and Statistical Manual* (*DSM-II*) of the American Psychiatric Association (1968), used by mental health practitioners to identify and classify psychological problems, classified homosexuality as a mental disorder. The evidence supporting this classification consisted primarily of therapists' reports of homosexuals who were undergoing therapy.

The main problem these homosexuals-in-therapy had, in the view of their therapists, was that they were homosexuals. Their therapy was, therefore, usually designed to "cure" them of their homosexuality by turning them into heterosexuals (Ellis, 1965). Unfortunately, this cure rarely worked. Even homosexuals who would have been happy to join mainstream society by changing their sexual orientation remained attracted to their own gender after extensive psychotherapy. For many homosexuals, this gap between their sexual makeup and society's values caused considerable anguish. Some could accept their own sexual orientation but still suffered from other people's rejection or the shame of hiding their sexuality to avoid condemnation and discrimination. Others were torn because they were being told—and may have come to believe—that their sexual orientation was, in fact, a mental disorder.

But was the therapists' view of homosexuality based on fact, or on their own cultural values? In the 1950s Evelyn Hooker (1957), a psychologist at UCLA, began to question the evidence for homosexuality being a disorder. She approached the problem experimentally, by comparing groups of homosexual and heterosexual males drawn from the general population (not just from people in therapy). To make the comparison fair and accurate, she matched these groups on dimensions such as intelligence, economic status, and education and then measured their psychological adjustment and personality characteristics. Her results showed no differences between heterosexuals and homosexuals in terms of adjustment or general personality characteristics.

Based on Hooker's studies and on subsequent research that confirmed her results for both males and females (Reiss, 1980; Rosen, 1974), the American Psychiatric Association removed homosexuality from its list of mental disorders in 1973. Since that time, as therapists have become more educated about the nature of homosexuality, their focus has been not on "curing" homosexuality by eliminating it but on helping clients deal with the stress they experience because of society's attitude toward homosexuality, and on helping them accept their own identity.

What causes individuals' sexual orientation?   Concluding whether people's sexual orientation can or should be changed depends in part on what causes that orientation. Since heterosexuality is the norm, most psychologists who have addressed the question of what determines sexual orientation have focused on homosexuality.

One of the earliest—and most popular—explanations of homosexuality was based on Sigmund Freud's theory of development. For Freud, the crucial developmental events that shape sexual orientation occur in what he called the *phallic* stage of development. During this stage, the 4- or 5-year-old boy is in the thrall of the Oedipus complex, in which he becomes sexually attracted to his mother and sees his father as a competitor. Eventually, when the boy realizes that his father is too powerful to be beaten, he joins him, identifies with him, and thereby gains a strong male identity.

According to Freud, homosexuality occurs when this process is derailed because the father is weak and the mother dominating. When this happens, the boy doesn't identify with his father and so doesn't develop a normal male identity. He therefore becomes homosexual. Freud had much less to say about the development of lesbianism (female homosexuality). He hypothesized that female homosexuality occurs when the mother-daughter relationship is poor, so that, when grown, the daughter establishes relationships with other females to take the place of the unresolved mother-daughter relationship.

Freud's explanations are intuitively appealing to many people, but are they correct? According to research by Alan Bell and his co-workers (1981), they aren't. They interviewed nearly 1,000 homosexual men and women and nearly 500 heterosexual men and women, collecting detailed information regarding their family life and past sexual experiences. Based on these interviews, Bell concluded that boys whose mothers were dominating and fathers were weak had nearly the same chance of being homosexual as boys who grew up in an "ideal" family situation. For girls, parents were more influential in determining sexual orientation but much less so than Freud's theory suggests.

Other statistics revealed by this study show that many popular beliefs about homosexuality are untrue. The researchers found the following:

- For many people, sexual orientation is established by adolescence, often before any sexual contact has occurred.
- Homosexuals typically have a normal number of opportunities for heterosexual involvement as they grow up.
- Homosexuals are no more likely than heterosexuals to have had an early traumatic sexual experience.

In summary, Bell's research group failed to find any single social or psychological cause that could be linked to homosexuality. It therefore concluded that sexual orientation is probably caused by inborn, biological factors.

3 BIOLOGY

Is there any direct evidence that biological factors determine sexual orientation? We know that prenatal hormones can affect male and female brain structure. Could it be that these hormones might affect brain structure in such a way as to influence sexual orientation?

There is some evidence to support this idea. The daughters of mothers who took a synthetic estrogen drug during pregnancy were more likely than normal to become lesbians (Ehrhardt et al., 1985). Stress on the mother, which could influence her hormones, has also been suggested as a possible cause of male homosexuality. Subjecting pregnant rats to stress increases the chances of homosexual behavior in their offspring. And males born in Germany during and just after World War II, when their mothers were being exposed to the stressful wartime environment, were more likely than normal to be homosexual (Dorner et al., 1980; also see Dorner et al., 1983).

If stress or changed hormonal environment is affecting development of the brain, then we might expect to find differences in brain functioning between homosexual and heterosexual subjects. Brian Gladue and his co-workers (1984) found such differences by measuring the brain's response to increased estrogen concentrations. We have already seen that increased estrogen causes the release of the luteinizing hormone in females but not in males. However, male homosexuals did respond to increased estrogen with a release of luteinizing hormone, releasing hormones in concentrations between those of heterosexual males and heterosexual females.

Evidence such as this led Lee Ellis and Ashley Ames (1987) to state that "sexual orientation is mainly the result of neurological factors that are largely determined prenatally, even though they do not fully manifest themselves until adolescence or adulthood" (p. 248). Not all researchers are prepared to make such a strong statement in favor of a biological cause, but there is increasing evidence that biology plays an important role in determining sexual orientation. For example, Simon LeVay (1991) has shown that a small area in the hypothalamus that is associated with sexual behavior is only half as large in homosexual men as in heterosexual men, and that it is the same size as this area in females.

Additional evidence for genetic determination of homosexuality is provided by two twin studies, one on males (Bailey & Pillard, 1991) and one on females (Bailey et al., 1993). These studies determined the sexual orientations of members of pairs of identical (MZ) twins, nonidentical (DZ) twins, and pairs of siblings in which one was adopted (so they were not related genetically). The results show that greater genetic similarity in pairs of brothers or sisters increases the chances that both members of the pair will be homosexual. Thus, 52% of male and 48% of female identical twins were both homosexual in a pair, whereas only 22% of male and 16% of female nonidentical twins were both homosexual in a pair. The chances of the non–genetically related brothers or sisters both being homosexual was even lower (11% for males and 6% for females).

The possible biological determination of homosexuality suggested by these results has important implications because, if true, it would mean that people's sexual attraction to members of their own sex is not a matter of choice or even of environmental influence, but rather results from the way the brain is programmed during prenatal development.

Achievement Motivation

The secret of success is constancy to purpose.

Benjamin Disraeli (1804–1881)
British prime minister

All her life Evelyn has striven to work to capacity. In college, she studied hard in her courses and trained hard as a member of the track team. Now that she is a project engineer for an important engineering firm, she has her sights set on becoming a higher-level manager. But while she's waiting for her next promotion, she enjoys the day-to-day challenges that she has to deal with in her present position.

Evelyn is an example of a person with high **achievement motivation,** which has been defined as "the desire to do things rapidly and/or as well as possible . . . to accomplish something difficult . . . to overcome obstacles and attain a high standard" (Murray, 1938) and as "a disposition to approach success" (Atkinson, 1964).

Achievement motivation is a good example of a human motive that is not biologically based in the same way as hunger and sexuality but that has been studied at the behavioral, cognitive, and contextual levels of analysis. As we begin our discussion of research on achievement motivation, we will see how it was first conceived of in rather simplistic terms—as a personality characteristic that caused some people to seek success. This early work, which was carried out by David McClelland and his co-workers, culminated in a now-classic book titled *The Achievement Motive* (McClelland et al., 1953).

Early Research on Achievement Motivation

The first problem facing McClelland and his group was how to measure achievement motivation. They began by assuming that one way to get at people's motives is to look at their fantasies, reasoning that fantasies may be a more accurate indicator of individuals' motives than their actual achievements. One reason for this is that people can fantasize about things they might never do in real life (McClelland, 1985b). Thus, knowing that a girl dreams of being president of her class may be a better indicator of her desire to be important than whether she actually *is* president of her class. In fact, a girl who *is* president might have achieved her position not because she really wanted to be president, but because her friends pressured her into running for the office.

What accounts for the strong motivation some people have to succeed in a difficult endeavor?

To test the idea that measuring fantasies is a way to get at achievement motivation, McClelland made use of the **Thematic Apperception Test (TAT).** Psychologists administer the TAT by showing a picture like the one in Figure 11.15 to a subject and asking him or her to write a story about it in about 1 minute that answers the following questions:

1. What is happening? Who are the persons?
2. What led up to this situation? That is, what happened in the past?
3. What is being thought? What is wanted? By whom?
4. What will happen? What will be done?

The basic rationale behind the TAT is that the subject identifies with the main character in the picture and so writes about this character in ways that reveal himself or herself. Thus, there are separate sets of TAT pictures for males and females, with male and female main characters, respectively.

To determine whether this test could be used to measure achievement motivation, McClelland and his colleagues (1953) administered it to a number of groups of subjects under conditions calculated to arouse different levels of achievement motivation. To simplify our discussion, we will consider just two of them: the *relaxed condition* and the *achievement-oriented condition*. Before taking the TAT, both groups of subjects were asked to solve some word puzzles. In the relaxed condition the experimenter introduced himself as being a graduate student and gave the impression that the tests were of little importance. This was calculated to make subjects indifferent about whether or not they did well, so that their achievement motivation following the tests would be low. In contrast, in the achievement-oriented condition the experimenter presented himself in a very serious way and indicated that the tests measured intelligence and leadership ability. The seriousness of this presentation was calculated to arouse high achievement motivation in the subjects.

After completing the puzzle tests, both groups of subjects were asked to write stories about pictures like the one in Figure 11.15. These stories were then scored for achievement imagery by counting the number of times subjects mentioned goals concerned with the drive to achieve a standard of excellence. So, for example, statements such as "He wants to do well" or "He has been practicing every day for a week" would be given points for achievement imagery. The following two stories, written in response to the picture in Figure 11.15, illustrate high- and low-achievement imagery (McClelland et al., 1953).

High-achievement imagery
A boy is dreaming of being a doctor. He can see himself in the future. He is hoping that he can make the grade. It is more or less a fantasy. The boy has seen many pictures of doctors in books, and it has inspired him. He will try his best and hopes to become the best doctor in the country. He can see himself as a very important doctor. He is performing a very dangerous operation. He can see himself victorious and is proud of it. He gets world renown for it. He will become the best doctor in the U.S. He will be an honest man too. His name will go down in medical history as one of the greatest men.

Low-achievement imagery
A young fellow is sitting in a plaid shirt and resting his head on one hand. He appears to be thinking of something. His eyes appear a little sad. He may have been involved in something he is very sorry for. The boy is thinking over what he has done. By the look in his eyes we can tell that he is very sad about it. I believe the boy will break down any minute if he continues in the manner in which he is now going.

The results of this experiment confirmed McClelland's expectation that the TAT test could measure achievement motivation. The average achievement

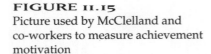
FIGURE 11.15
Picture used by McClelland and co-workers to measure achievement motivation

scores of 1.95 for the relaxed condition and 8.77 for the achievement-oriented condition show that when achievement motivation is aroused by experimental conditions, subjects tend to invent stories containing more achievement imagery.

Armed with the TAT, McClelland then showed that if a large group of people are tested under *identical* conditions, a wide range of scores results. McClelland concluded that achievement motivation, or the **need to achieve (nAch),** is a personality characteristic present in different strengths in different people (McClelland, 1985b; Spence & Helmreich, 1983). Perhaps you have made this same observation about people you know. Some people are very relaxed about achieving, whereas others are driven to reach difficult goals. What McClelland did was to develop a way to measure these differences.

Much of the research done by McClelland and other researchers focused on determining whether there were other differences between subjects with high and low nAch. Some of these experiments indicate that subjects with high nAch tend to perform better on a number of tasks (particularly ones that are difficult), are more innovative, find their jobs more interesting, and are more likely to do well in their professions than subjects with low nAch (McClelland, 1985).

McClelland's work on achievement motivation stimulated many others to become interested in this topic, though his procedures were not accepted by everyone. Some questioned the reliability of the TAT. Others felt that McClelland's conception of nAch was too simplistic, and that nAch was actually the result of a number of factors. John Atkinson's (1957) **expectancy-value model of achievement motivation** takes some of these complexities into account.

15   PERSONALITY

Expectancy-Value Theory

John Atkinson (1957), one of McClelland's early collaborators, proposed that nAch actually results from two tendencies, one to *approach success* and another to *avoid failure*. These tendencies, in turn, depend on three factors.

1. The strengths of the motive to achieve *and* the **motive to avoid failure.** Both motives are characteristics of a person's personality.
2. The probability (or expectancy) that a behavior will result in success or failure. Easy tasks have a high probability of success, difficult ones a high probability of failure.
3. The **incentive value** of success or failure. The incentive value is the degree of anticipated pride in succeeding or shame in failing, and depends on the difficulty of the task. For example, shame would usually be greater for failing at an easy task than for failing at a hard one.

Atkinson's model makes predictions about the types of tasks that people with high and low nAch will attempt. The model predicts that people with a high nAch will, more than people with low nAch, try tasks of *intermediate* difficulty—that is, tasks that are neither extremely easy nor extremely hard.

An experiment by Richard deCharms and V. Carpenter (1968) illustrates such a result. Both high- and low-nAch children were given a series of spelling words ranging from very easy to very difficult. After taking this test, each child was told that in the next test he or she could choose the level of difficulty of each item, and that more points would be awarded for correctly answering difficult items than for answering easy ones. As predicted by Atkinson's theory, children with high nAch tended to pick items of intermediate difficulty, whereas children with low nAch picked easier items.

Why does this result occur? High-nAch children apparently avoid the easy items because scoring well on them would give them little satisfaction. They avoid the difficult items, however, because seeking unrealistically high goals is unlikely to result in the success that people with high achievement motivation seek. In contrast, the low-nAch children were satisfied to do well on the easier items.

According to expectancy-value theory, landing a part in a play may be a highly desirable goal for this actor, but he may not be willing to work hard to achieve that goal if he believes that the chances of success are small.

The expectancy-value model is an advance over McClelland's original conception, because it takes into account that a person's behavior in achievement situations depends not only on the motive to achieve but also on the incentive value of success and cognitive factors such as the person's assessment of the likelihood of succeeding. Expectancy-value theory was also the starting point for a cognitive approach to achievement motivation that proposed that to fully understand this phenomenon we must take people's thought processes into account.

The Cognitive Approach to Achievement Motivation

8   THINKING

The cognitive approach to achievement motivation proposes that people's willingness to do things depends on their cognitive appraisal of the situation. We can illustrate this by considering (1) how people's behavior is affected by receiving external rewards, and (2) how they interpret the *causes* of behaviors and events.

Intrinsic and extrinsic motives.   **Intrinsic motivation** leads an individual to perform some activity for the satisfaction of doing the activity itself. **Extrinsic motivation** is the desire to gain some external reward. Thus, playing the piano is intrinsically motivating if you do it because you enjoy playing the piano but is extrinsically motivating if you do it just to get paid.

Extrinsic motivation is often used to encourage people to do things they wouldn't do if left to themselves. Thus, teachers often try to motivate their pupils to study by offering rewards such as prizes, good grades, and praise. Their attempts to motivate students assume that extrinsic incentives are necessary because the students are not intrinsically motivated to study. But what happens if extrinsic motivators are added to a task that people are already intrinsically motivated to perform? Will they then work twice as hard, because their motivation is doubled?

Rather surprisingly, the effect is just the opposite. Edward L. Deci (1975, 1978) demonstrated this by having two groups of subjects work on a difficult puzzle. Subjects in the experimental group were paid a dollar every time they solved the puzzle; subjects in the control group were not paid at all. After a session in which both the experimental and control subjects solved the puzzle a number of times, the experimenter left the room for eight minutes and told the subjects that they could do whatever they wanted. When he did this, he found that now that neither group was paid for solving the puzzle, the control subjects (who had never been paid) played with the puzzle more than the experimental subjects. Apparently, adding an external reward like money *decreases* a subject's tendency to work on a puzzle "just for the fun of it."

Deci suggests a cognitive explanation for this result. Perhaps, he suggests, people tend to look upon money as something you receive for doing what you wouldn't ordinarily do for free. Therefore, paying people for solving a puzzle makes them feel they wouldn't be interested in solving it if they weren't paid for it, and they lose interest in the task once the pay is withdrawn.

Deci's results led to two major conclusions. One is practical: If people are willing to do a task for its intrinsic properties, adding extrinsic motivation may actually decrease their willingness to do the task. In other words, don't pay people to do what they would willingly do for free. The other conclusion is theoretical: The reasons people do things can be affected by their cognitive appraisal of the situation.

Attribution theory.   One of the major proponents of the cognitive approach is Bernard Weiner (1972, 1974a, 1974b, 1985b), whose conception of achievement motivation is based on attribution theory. **Attribution theory** states that we all tend to attribute *causes* to our own behaviors and the behaviors of others. For example, assume that you have worked diligently for 90 minutes to solve a math problem but have failed to get the right answer. You will, according to Weiner, make a judgment about why you have failed—an **attribution.** Weiner identifies four basic factors that you consider when making this attribution.

1. *Ability:* You might decide you failed because you aren't good at math.
2. *Effort:* Since you tried hard, you probably would *not* attribute your failure to a lack of effort.
3. *Task difficulty:* You might decide you failed because the problem was very difficult.
4. *Luck:* This factor is most likely to come into play if you succeeded in solving the problem, in which case you could decide that you were fortunate to stumble across the correct solution.

The actual attribution you make in a given situation depends on cues that help you judge the causes of the event or behavior. One of the main cues is **social norms**—how other people do on the same task. If you found that almost everyone else in the class also failed to solve the problem, you might tend to attribute your poor performance to the difficulty of the task. If, on the other hand, you found that most people succeeded in solving the problem, you might feel that your poor performance was due to a lack of ability. In addition to using social norms to help you make attributions, you might also consider factors such as how much effort you expended on the task, your assessment of how competent you are in general, and how likely you thought it was that luck would play a role in the task (for example, luck is of minimal importance in solving math problems but makes a big difference in a game of dice).

18 SOCIAL

What do our attributions about the causes of events have to do with achievement motivation? To appreciate the connection, ask yourself how the attributions you make about your performance on a task might influence your motivation to continue performing the task. Most people would be more motivated to do more math problems if they felt they had solved previous ones because of their high ability rather than just luck.

The relevance of attribution theory to achievement motivation becomes even more obvious when we compare the attributions made by people with high and low nAch. The general results of these comparisons are that high-nAch subjects tend to attribute outcomes to *internal factors,* such as ability and effort, that they can control. Low-nAch subjects, on the other hand, attribute outcomes more to *external factors,* such as luck or task difficulty, that they can't control (Weiner, 1974a).

There is, therefore, a link between achievement motivation and the way people view the causes of their actions. Children who tend to see achievement-related events in their lives as being caused by other people view their achievements differently than children who see these events as being within their own control. Carol Diener and Carol Dweck (1980) demonstrated this by dividing children into a *helpless group* and a *mastery group* based on their answers to a questionnaire. The helpless group felt events were more controlled by others, whereas the mastery group felt that events were more controlled by themselves. Both groups were presented with a series of eight problems, which they all solved with equal ease. They were then asked to pick one of the following reasons for their success:

9 DEVELOPMENT

- It was easy.
- I was lucky.
- I am good at this.
- I am smart.

The results are exactly what we would predict. The helpless children, who saw events as being more out of their control, attributed their success much more to luck than did the mastery children. Because the helpless children did not give themselves credit for their success, they expressed less confidence than the mastery children that they could succeed if presented with similar problems in the future, even though both groups of children had performed equally well up to that point.

Achievement motivation provides an excellent example of theory building in psychology, in which an initial, rather simple proposal is elaborated on. McClelland's initial proposal of nAch as a simple aspect of a person's personality was expanded by a number of later researchers, so that we now think of people's achievement behavior as being affected by many different factors, including fear of failure, the types of rewards available, and the attributions made. What the other researchers added to McClelland's initial conception was cognition, the consideration of how people's thought processes influence behavior.

Reprise: Multiple Causes of Behavior

Faced with the question posed by the study of motivation—"Why do we do what we do?"—it is easy to come up with simple answers. Statements like "I eat because I'm hungry," "I have sex because it feels good," and "I work hard to get ahead" all sound simple and straightforward enough and may even be true. But under the surface of these "explanations" is a complex network of causes.

Nowhere is this complexity more evident than for hunger. The biological explanation of eating behavior put forth in this chapter may seem complicated, involving as it does a number of chemicals in the blood, a number of nuclei in the brain, and sites of action that include the brain, the stomach, and the liver. But the story told here is an extremely simplified version of what is happening behind the scenes that causes us to eat and to stop eating. For example, we briefly mentioned receptors that sense the stretching of the stomach. But in addition to this, there may also be receptors that sense the chemical composition of the food that reaches the stomach, so that drinking a cup of water and drinking a cup of orange juice have different effects (Kalat, 1992). And what about the taste

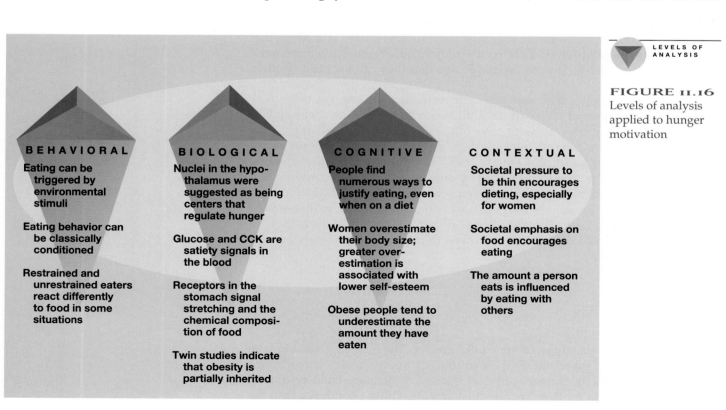

LEVELS OF ANALYSIS

FIGURE 11.16
Levels of analysis applied to hunger motivation

BEHAVIORAL

Eating can be triggered by environmental stimuli

Eating behavior can be classically conditioned

Restrained and unrestrained eaters react differently to food in some situations

BIOLOGICAL

Nuclei in the hypothalamus were suggested as being centers that regulate hunger

Glucose and CCK are satiety signals in the blood

Receptors in the stomach signal stretching and the chemical composition of food

Twin studies indicate that obesity is partially inherited

COGNITIVE

People find numerous ways to justify eating, even when on a diet

Women overestimate their body size; greater overestimation is associated with lower self-esteem

Obese people tend to underestimate the amount they have eaten

CONTEXTUAL

Societal pressure to be thin encourages dieting, especially for women

Societal emphasis on food encourages eating

The amount a person eats is influenced by eating with others

receptors in the mouth? The pleasure of eating derives not just from eliminating hunger, but from experiencing the flavors of food.

So, just at the level of biology, we are dealing with a system of such complexity that researchers still disagree on exactly how it operates. But multiple causation also refers to factors at other levels of analysis (Figure 11.16). The fact that we sometimes eat when we're not hungry attests to the powerful roles that behavioral and cognitive factors play in eating. When we walk into an ice-cream parlor at midnight after seeing a movie, classical conditioning and cognition both help us decide to get that hot fudge sundae. The ice-cream parlor, having been paired with hot fudge sundaes in the past, now elicits "have a hot fudge sundae." Being with friends who intend to eat may make you feel funny about not eating, which helps justify ordering that sundae. "Why not," you think, "everyone else is doing it." And your taste buds, in anticipation, second the motion.

Or consider sexual behavior. Although heavily influenced by biology, sexual behavior is also greatly affected by contextual factors. For example, for all the importance of the biological changes that makes adolescent sexual activity possible, the leading reason that teenage boys and girls have sex is peer pressure ("Teen Sex," 1989; Wilcox & Udry, 1986).

That even seemingly simple behaviors are complex when we look under the surface is an idea we will encounter again in the next chapter, on emotion. There we will see that feelings such as happiness, sadness, anger, and fear are created by a complex web of biological events plus a generous helping of cognitions that we create in response to the contexts in which we find ourselves.

Gender and Achievement Motivation

From an early age, children are expected to respond to the query: "What do you want to be when you grow up?" They soon learn that their gender is relevant to the question.

Hillary Lips (1993, p. 283)

Does a person's gender play a role in determining their achievement motivation? One way to approach this question is to look at what boys and girls learn about careers as they are growing up.

One way that boys and girls learn that gender is relevant to their career aspirations is by looking around them at the occupational roles currently filled by males or females. Although there is an increasing number of female doctors, lawyers, and business executives, many jobs in the work force are still gender segregated. Even young children know which gender goes with jobs such as nurse, secretary, construction worker, or bank president.

Another influence on the career aspirations of males and females is the way boys and girls are treated by their teachers. Elementary schoolteachers pay more attention to boys than girls, and they praise boys for good academic performance but girls for "being good" (Lips, 1993). Thus, early in their school careers boys and girls are taught to behave differently, with the behaviors that boys learn being more likely to result in high achievement motivation. It is not surprising, therefore, that as early as in the third grade boys begin to rate their potential for success more highly than do girls (Erkut, 1983; Vollmer, 1984). Boys also generally have higher self-esteem than girls even though girls' grades are higher, on the average, in high school (Freiberg, 1991).

We might expect that these differences between the way boys and girls are socialized and the way they feel about themselves might affect the way men and women react to achievement situations. A classic example of such an effect occurred as David McClelland and his co-workers (1953) began their pioneering research on achievement motivation in the 1950s. Early in his research, McClelland discovered a difference between male and female performance on his newly developed TAT tests of achievement motivation. He found that males' achievement scores increased in response to instructions that encouraged high achievement motivation, whereas females' achievement scores did not. Because McClelland did not understand why the females were responding this way, he focused his research exclusively on males.

Almost 20 years later, females became the center of attention in achievement motivation research when Matina Horner (1970) reported the results of some experiments that she interpreted as showing that women have a "fear of success." Her procedure paralleled that of most achievement motivation experiments, in that she asked her subjects to write a story in response to a stimulus. The stimulus for her story was, however, not a TAT picture as in McClelland's experiments, but the sentence "After first-term finals, Anne (or John) finds herself (himself) at the top of her (his) medical school class." Females were asked to react to the Anne sentence and males to the John sentence.

Rather than scoring these stories for achievement imagery, Horner scored them for "fear of success" (FOS) imagery by awarding a point every time any mention was made of negative feelings about success, of actions leading away from success, or of emotional conflict about success. High FOS scores indicated, according to Horner, the presence of a **motive to avoid success**. The results of Horner's studies were quite different for males and females. Only 9% of the male's stories had FOS imagery. Most males' stories, such as the following one, emphasized positive feelings toward success:

> John is a conscientious young man who worked hard. He is pleased with himself. John has always wanted to go into medicine and is very dedicated. . . . John continues working hard and eventually graduates at the top of his class.

In contrast, a striking 65% of the females' stories contained FOS imagery. In these stories Anne is depicted as unhappy, abnormal, or ambivalent about her success. Here are some typical stories written about Anne:

> Anne feels guilty. . . . She will finally have a nervous breakdown and quit medical school and marry a successful young doctor.

> Unfortunately Anne no longer feels certain that she really wants to be a doctor. She is worried about herself and wonders if perhaps she isn't normal. . . . Anne decides not to continue with her medical work but to take courses that have a deeper personal meaning to her.

> Anne starts proclaiming her surprise and joy. Her fellow classmates are so disgusted with her behavior that they jump on her in a body and beat her. She is maimed for life.

Differences between girls and boys in achievement motivation can be traced partially to differences in socialization. For example, elementary school teachers tend to pay more attention to boys than to girls.

These results were widely interpreted as indicating that women feared being successful because working toward success would lead to social rejection and a loss of femininity. However, a few years after Horner's research appeared, other researchers began to question both her results and her interpretation of them. Her results were questioned because many studies failed to repeat her findings (Tresmer, 1977). In fact, some studies reported that fear of success was as high in males as in females. (However, in such cases males and females often gave different reasons for their FOS. Males wondered whether the rewards of success were really worth it, whereas females focused on the negative social consequences of success.)

But what of the many experiments, including Horner's, that *did* elicit a large amount of FOS imagery from women? Most researchers interpret these results as follows: Most women (and men) observe their society and see that anyone who deviates from what society considers appropriate may suffer negative consequences. It is for this reason, and not because women grow up with a motive to avoid success as part of their personality, that women respond with FOS imagery. This way of thinking about the problem combines the cognitive level of analysis—considering people's thought processes—within the contextual level—in which we take into account the "rules" set by society.

To illustrate the idea that people's responses in FOS experiments may reflect their knowledge of what society considers appropriate, consider a hypothetical experiment suggested by J. Condry and S. Dyer (1976). Suppose you were asked to write a story in response to the following sentence: "Lucy Smith, a white woman from Philadelphia, and her husband, Sam Jefferson, who is black, have decided to live in a small rural town in Mississippi." It is likely that many people would write stories focusing on the fact that a rural town in Mississippi might not be a good place for an interracial couple to live. They would be likely to caution that if the couple went through with their plan, they would have some negative experiences.

Would a person writing such a story be accused of having a "motive to avoid the South" or a "motive to avoid mixed-race couples"? Unlikely, say Condry and Dyer. A more reasonable explanation is that the story reflects the writer's awareness of the probable consequences of violating the social norms of small rural towns in Mississippi. When viewed in this light, the negative stories written about Anne in Horner's experiment can be reinterpreted as reflecting not a personality characteristic called "motive to avoid success" but realistic expectations about the consequences of deviating from what society considers appropriate behavior for females.

What does this mean for the relationship between achievement motivation and gender in the 1990s? Our society is slowly changing to one in which specific careers are less likely to be labeled "male" or "female." As this transformation continues, we can expect that more and more females will be motivated to aspire to traditionally masculine careers (Geller, 1984). But will males in large numbers eventually aspire to traditionally female careers such as nurse, secretary, and kindergarten teacher? There is presently a slight trend in that direction, but realistically speaking, it will be many years before all careers in our society are equally populated by females and males.

Hillary Clinton's career achievements and independent views made her something of a lightning rod for debates about women's role in society even before her husband was elected president. Researchers argue that women who seem to manifest a "fear of success" trait are in reality responding to their observations of what happens when women challenge social norms.

- Motivation is the process that drives an organism to act and that determines what direction that action takes. Psychologists have taken two approaches to studying motivation: (1) creating general theories and (2) studying specific behaviors at a number of levels of analysis.

General Theories of Motivation

- Several early approaches to motivation focused on biology. Instinct theory proposed that all human behavior is controlled by instincts. The ethological approach to motivation is based on studying the behavior of animals in natural settings. The drive reduction approach sees behavior as motivated by a deficit within an organism that causes the buildup of a drive.

- Freud's theory of motivation sees behavior as being motivated by unconscious forces.

- The humanistic approach to motivation views people as striving to reach their full potential. Maslow's hierarchy of needs postulates that people must satisfy lower-order needs before they can aspire to needs higher up in the hierarchy.

- A problem with all the general theories of motivation is that in focusing on general principles they don't offer a complete explanation of specific behaviors.

The Hunger Motive

- The principle of homeostasis guides much of the research done in the biological approach to hunger. The goal of hunger research has been to find the mechanisms that turn hunger on and off.

- Early hunger researchers proposed that hunger is signaled by stomach contractions, and that the ventromedial and lateral hypothalamic nuclei are control centers for hunger and satiety. More recent research favors the idea that a number of substances in the blood—including glucose, insulin, and cholecystokinin—act as satiety signals. There is also evidence that stretching the stomach is a satiety signal.

- Eating is also influenced by psychological factors, such as the presence of other people, classically conditioned stimuli, and situations that eliminate a person's cognitive restraints on eating.

- Weight is an important concern for many people. Although one reason for this concern has to do with health, the principal reason has to do with societal pressure to be thin.

- Biological bases for being overweight include genetic predisposition (excessive weight seems to run in families), low metabolism, and a high set point—the weight toward which the body naturally gravitates.

- Psychological factors can also add to weight problems. People who are overweight do not have more psychological problems than people with normal weight, but obese people may eat more under anxiety-producing conditions. In addi-

tion, some obese people who are attempting to control their eating by dieting underestimate the amount of food they are eating and overestimate the amount that they are exercising.

- Although treatment for weight problems has generally not been very successful, behavior therapy shows promise of helping some people maintain a more desirable weight. This method uses the principles of self-monitoring, stimulus control, and reinforcement to help people control their eating behavior.

Sexual Motivation

- Sexual motivation is a good example of a strongly biological behavior that is also influenced by many psychological factors.

- The biological starting point for human sexual behavior is sexual differentiation. Whether a person becomes a male or female is determined by the individual's sex chromosomes, which determine whether or not testosterone is present in the prenatal environment.

- There is some correlation between hormones and sexual desire, but human sexual behavior is not rigidly controlled by hormones. Human sexual behavior is not an automatic response to sensory stimuli, but also depends on psychological variables.

- In Western culture, negative institutional attitudes toward any sexual activity not resulting in procreation within marriage have strongly influenced society's general attitudes toward sex. Although sexuality is more accepted in the 20th century, sexual motivation continues to be influenced by a complex set of cultural and personal values and beliefs.

- Psychological influences on sexuality are closely tied to the way girls and boys are socialized. Because of different developmental experiences, females may be in a dependent position relative to males during their first sexual encounters. Research with college students suggest that males and females also have different attitudes about sexual intercourse, with males seeking fun or pleasure and females seeking feelings of love and commitment.

- Despite their different attitudes about sexual intercourse, both females and males become aroused when exposed to erotic stimuli. Males, however, are more aware than females of their physical arousal.

- Homosexuality is defined as a preferred sexual attraction to one's own sex over a significant period of time. Although early mental health practitioners labeled homosexuality a mental disorder, controlled studies comparing homosexuals and heterosexuals reveal no differences between them in terms of adjustment or general personality characteristics.

- Current evidence regarding the cause of homosexuality is heaviest for homosexuality being biologically determined. This conclusion is supported by hormone studies, anatomical studies, and research on the prevalence of homosexuality in twins.

Achievement Motivation

- Achievement motivation—the desire to do things rapidly and as well as possible to accomplish something difficult, to overcome obstacles and attain a high standard—is a good example of a primarily psychological (that is, nonbiological) motive. McClelland's early research on achievement motivation used the Thematic Apperception Test (TAT) to measure people's need to achieve.

- Atkinson's expectancy-value model of achievement motivation states that the need to achieve results from tendencies to approach success and avoid failure. The model's prediction that people with a high need to achieve (nAch) are more likely to attempt tasks of intermediate difficulty than are people with a low nAch has been supported by research.

- The cognitive approach to achievement motivation proposes that people's willingness to attempt things depends on their cognitive appraisal of the situation.

- Research on intrinsic and extrinsic motivation indicates that adding an external reward for doing a task that a person would do for free decreases the person's motivation to do the task.

- Another cognitive factor in achievement motivation is the way people view the causes of their experiences. People with low nAch tend to attribute outcomes to external factors (such as luck or task difficulty), whereas people with high nAch tend to attribute outcomes to internal factors (such as ability and effort.).

Reprise: Multiple Causes of Behavior

- A complex network of causes underlies most motivations. This is especially true of hunger, which involves biological mechanisms in the brain, the stomach, the mouth, and the blood, as well as mechanisms that operate at the behavioral, cognitive, and contextual levels of analysis.

Follow-Through/Diversity: Gender and Achievement Motivation

- McClelland's early experiments on achievement motivation, in the 1950s, focused solely on males. In 1973 Matina Horner published results that she interpreted as showing that females have a "motive to avoid success." Later researchers have seen females' achievement motivation as influenced not by a motive to avoid success but by a realistic appraisal of what types of achievement society considers appropriate for women.

Key Terms

achievement motivation
aphagia
attribution
attribution theory
behavior therapy
Coolidge effect
double standard
drive
drive reduction
dual-center hypothesis
estrogen
ethologists
Eve principle
excitatory center
expectancy-value model of achievement motivation
externality hypothesis
extrinsic motivation
heterosexuality
hierarchy of needs
homostatis
homophobia
homosexuality
hunger motivation
hyperphagia
incentive value
instincts
intrinsic motivation
lateral nucleus of the hypothalamus (LH)
love or belongingness needs
motivation
motive to avoid failure
motive to avoid success
need to achieve (nAch)
obesity
physiological needs
resting metabolic rate
safety needs
satiety center
satiety signal
self-actualization
self-esteem needs
set point
sexual motivation
social norms
testosterone
Thematic Apperception Test (TAT)
ventromedial nucleus of the hypothalamus (VMH)
volunteer bias

CHAPTER

12

The Nature of Emotions
The Components of Emotional Experience
Classifying Emotions

The Behavioral Effects of Emotion
Emotion and Memory
Emotion and Judgment
Emotion and Helping Behavior
Emotion and Person Perception
Emotion and Reacting to Threatening Information

The Expression of Emotion
Body Language
Facial Expressions
Display Rules and Emotional Expression

Interdisciplinary Dimension: Medicine
Managing Emotions in Medical School

Behavioral Explanations of Emotion
Conditioned Emotional Responses
Observational Learning

Physiological Explanations of Emotion
The Evolutionary Approach to Emotion
Bodily Changes and Emotion
Brain Activity and Emotion

Cognitive Explanations of Emotion
Schachter and Singer: Interpretation of Arousal
Richard Lazarus: Cognitive Appraisal

Reprise: The Ebb and Flow of Scientific Understanding

Follow-Through/Diversity
Emotion and Culture

Emotion

Life is the enjoyment of emotion derived from the past and aimed at the future.

Alfred North Whitehead (1861–1947)
English philosopher

Emotions—what would life be like without them? Philosophers like the great Aristotle may define humans as "rational animals," yet much of the color and texture of human life comes not from our ability to reason but from our capacity to feel and to share our feelings with others. Someone who has lost the capacity to feel or express joy, excitement, tenderness, fear, and rage might be diagnosed as clinically depressed and in need of treatment.

Emotions are also of obvious importance to anyone who seeks to understand human behavior. Although much of our behavior involves rational thinking, most of us would readily admit that we do many of the things we do because of our emotional reactions to events. We give to others out of tenderness and love, we lash out in anger, we avoid the things that frighten us, and we strive for the things that will bring us joy.

At the same time, many of us are often puzzled or troubled by our emotions. We regret acting "emotionally," or we wonder why we feel as we do, or we try to hide our feelings from others. Often we think of our emotions as needing to be "managed" or "controlled," so that we don't get "carried away." This way of viewing emotions seems to suggest that they come from some source we don't control, that they somehow just *happen* to us, whether we want them to or not. Even the original Latin meaning of the word *emotion*—to "disturb" or "move away"—reflects this notion that we are passive victims who are moved by the mysterious force of our emotions.

In this chapter we will explore the mystery of emotions and shed some light on how and why they occur and how they affect our behavior. To do so we will look at emotions using all four levels of analysis: biological, behavioral, cognitive, and contextual. As we will see, influences operating at all these levels help explain how we experience and express emotions.

The Nature of Emotions

What exactly are emotions? Some important clues can be gleaned from the ways people describe emotional experiences. Consider, for example, the following common descriptions of emotion:

I was seething inside.	She shouted in anger	He was blind with rage.
My blood turned to ice.	His heart pounded with fear.	She froze in her tracks.
My heart overflowed.	She cried tears of happiness.	He leapt with joy.

These descriptions imply several points psychologists have focused on in studying emotion. In particular, they suggest that emotional experience has a number of components.

The Components of Emotional Experience

The following three key components of emotional experience are reflected in the common descriptions of emotion just listed.

Emotions as inner experiences.   Emotions are subjective, often intense, inner experiences. ("I was seething inside," "My blood turned to ice," "My heart overflowed"). This means that psychologists must be creative in finding ways to study these inner experiences, which they cannot observe or measure directly. It also suggests that a complete account of emotion must include cognitive elements—how we perceive and think about what we are experiencing.

Emotions are associated with inner experiences, behaviors, and physiological responses.

Emotions as behavioral events.   Despite being "inner" experiences, emotions are often manifested in behaviors observable to others ("She shouted in anger," "She cried tears of happiness"). Even when we describe our own emotions, we typically include both feelings and behavioral responses in our descriptions. For example, we might describe sadness both as a feeling ("I felt empty inside") and as a behavior ("I couldn't stop crying") (Davitz, 1969; Plutchik, 1984). The fact that emotions have an outward, observable aspect raises questions about how we express them. When and how do we use emotional displays to communicate? Is the expression of emotion essentially inborn and the same for everyone? If not, what factors influence how we display emotion? The expression of emotions is a significant behavior in its own right that has been closely studied by psychologists.

Emotions as physiological responses.   The experience of emotion has a strong physiological component ("He was blind with rage," "His heart pounded with fear"). Think of a time when you felt a strong emotion, and you will probably recall a powerful physical feeling associated with it—your stomach was "tied in knots," your heart "raced," or your head "swam." This aspect of emotions suggests that one way to grasp emotional experience is to study physiological events such as changes in heart rate that are observable and measurable. Moreover, it raises the question of the extent to which emotions are *caused* by physiological reactions. As we will see, psychologists have taken different positions on this question.

In addition to these components of emotional experience, notice that descriptions of emotions imply a *situation* in which the emotion is being felt. When you overhear a statement like "I was seething inside" or "My heart overflowed," you know there is a story behind the statement—the speaker is referring to some specific event or situation that triggered the emotional response. An **emotion,** then, is a complex experience involving subjective feelings, observable behavior, and physiological responses, all taking place in the context of a specific event or situation. Later in this chapter, we will see how these various aspects of emotion have all played a role in psychologists' investigations of what causes emotional experience.

Of course, "emotional experience" covers a lot of territory. The breadth of range of the experience we call emotion is illustrated by the fact that there are hundreds of English words referring to emotion, each with its own shade of meaning (see Table 12.1). Are all emotions truly distinct, or can we organize emotional experiences in some way that shows commonalities and differences among them? This questions has been addressed by psychologists, who have proposed ways of classifying emotions.

Classifying Emotions

Efforts to classify emotions have been spurred by evolutionary theories of emotion. As we will see later on, evolutionary theorists, taking their cue from the work of Charles Darwin, propose that emotions are largely innate reactions to

TABLE 12.1
A sampling of English words related to emotions

	Afraid	Angry	Happy
Descriptive Words	alarmed anxious apprehensive beside oneself fretful nervous panicky petrified startled terror-stricken	annoyed beside oneself displeased enraged frustrated furious indignant irate irritated offended piqued provoked resentful	beside oneself blissful contented delighted ecstatic glad gleeful joyous jubilant lighthearted peaceful pleased thrilled

Physical Feelings	blood running cold
	dizzy
	goosebumps
	heart racing
	ready to jump out
	  of one's skin
	shiver down the
	  spine
		blood boiling
		inflamed
		face flushed
		ready to burst
		seething
		surge of anger
			calm
			bursting with joy
			energized
			light-headed
			shiver of excitement
			  or joy
			walking on air
			warm

Behavioral Descriptions	cowering cringing eyes wide hands shaking lips trembling pale quaking rigid screaming shaking shivering sweating teeth chattering trembling	eyes blazing face flushed fists clenched nostrils flaring rigid scowling screaming shaking shouting teeth clenched trembling veins standing out	eyes alight face flushed giggling grinning hands clapping laughing jumping for joy radiant relaxed shouting smiling trembling

certain stimuli and that those reactions have adaptive value. These theorists have tried to identify a relatively small number of fundamental emotions that are universal in the human species and clearly valuable in terms of helping the species survive (Izard, 1977; Plutchik, 1984; Tomkins, 1980). Other emotions, these psychologists believe, represent either (1) blends of the fundamental emotions or (2) differences in the intensity of feeling associated with a particular emotion.

This line of reasoning is represented by the emotion wheel developed by Robert Plutchik (1980). Plutchik's wheel consists of eight **primary emotions:** fear, surprise, sadness, disgust, anger, anticipation, joy, and acceptance. These primary emotions are "pure" in the sense that they do not result from combinations of other emotions. In contrast, **secondary emotions** are produced by combinations of primary emotions that are adjacent on the emotion wheel. For example, Plutchik characterizes love as a combination of joy and acceptance, whereas submission is a combination of acceptance and fear (Figure 12.1). In Plutchik's scheme, additional emotions can be classified as representing different degrees of intensity of primary and secondary emotions. For instance, fear can range from mild apprehension to blind terror, anger can range from annoyance to rage, and so on.

Other psychologists have proposed classification systems that differ in detail from Plutchik's. All such efforts, however, assume that there is a small number of basic emotions from which others are derived. Often they also agree on at least some of the emotions they consider to be basic. For example, of the eight to ten basic emotions in the classifications of Plutchik (1984), Silvan Tomkins (1980),

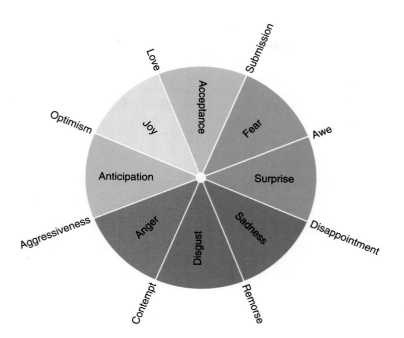

and Caroll Izard (1984), five occur in all three schemes: fear, anger, joy, disgust, and surprise.

As we will see later in the chapter, these basic emotions are universal—they can be used to describe the experiences of people in many different cultures. These emotions also have behavioral effects; they affect processes as diverse as memory, judgment, helping behavior, and perception.

The Behavioral Effects of Emotion

Emotions clearly have important behavioral effects. Not only do they affect physical performances and social behavior ("He froze in his tracks," "She shouted in anger"), but they also affect cognitive performances such as judgment ("He was blind with rage"). How emotions affect many aspects of our behavior is an important area of study for psychologists. Let's consider a few of these behavioral effects.

Emotion and Memory

Emotional states can affect the workings of memory. Consider, for example, the following conversation between a depressed patient and her therapist.

> *Therapist:* I see you brought your diary—and how did things go in the last few days?
> *Patient:* (Silence) Terrible. I didn't get anything done. The house is still filthy and I didn't cook—I don't know—I don't seem to be able to get anything done.
> *Therapist:* Let's see. (Takes diary) Well, it says here that on Monday you went to the supermarket and shopped for the week, and you took the kids to a party that evening and in the afternoon you made a number of phone calls and sorted the laundry and . . .
> *Patient:* (Silence) Well, maybe I did get some things done, but it wasn't much.

This conversation illustrates how depressed people tend to remember failures, inadequacies, and negative experiences much more than successes or positive experiences.

This link between emotion and memory also occurs in nondepressed subjects. Gordon Bower (1981) showed that if people are hypnotized and are told to

16   DISORDERS

7   MEMORY

feel "happy," they remember more positive things about a story than people who are hypnotized and are told to feel "sad." Bower calls the fact that our memory is better for things that match our mood the **mood congruity effect.** You have probably experienced this effect yourself. When you are "down" you may have a hard time remembering good things that have happened to you—and when you are on top of the world, your unpleasant experiences may fade into the background.

Emotion and Judgment

8   THINKING

Emotions also affect our ability to make judgments. Eric Johnson and Amos Tversky (1983) demonstrated this by having three groups of subjects read different stories. The "positive-mood" group read a story about a man who experiences a series of positive events, including being admitted to medical school and doing well on a difficult exam. The "negative-mood" group read a story about a man who had just broken up with his girlfriend, was under stress at his job, and was being pressured by his family. A control group read a neutral story designed to have no effect on mood.

After reading one of these stories, each subject was asked to estimate the frequency of undesirable events such as street crime, accidental falls, or bankruptcy. The results of this experiment (Figure 12.2) show that putting subjects in a positive mood decreased their estimate of risk, whereas putting subjects in a negative mood increased their estimate of risk. When questioned after the experiment, half of the subjects felt the story had influenced their mood, but only 3% felt it had influenced their judgment of risk. Hence, even as our emotions are influencing our judgments, we may be unaware of their influence. You may have observed this effect yourself if you have ever seen people in high spirits engage in risky behavior and downplay the dangers.

Emotion and Helping Behavior

19   SOCIAL

In Chapter 2 we looked at an experiment by Alice Isen and Paula Levin (1972) that showed that people who found money in a pay phone were more likely to help a stranger than people who didn't find the money. The relationship between emotional state and helping behavior has been demonstrated many times in a number of ways. Listening to soothing music, being on a winning team, and imagining enjoying a vacation all increase a person's tendency to help others (Carlson, Charlin, & Miller, 1988; Rosenhan, Salovey, & Hargis, 1981). So if you

FIGURE 12.2
Frequency of various negative events as estimated by people who read positive or negative stories, compared to estimates made by a control group that read a neutral story.

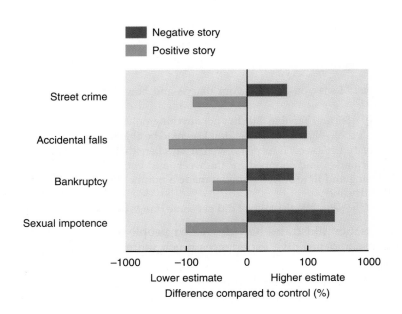

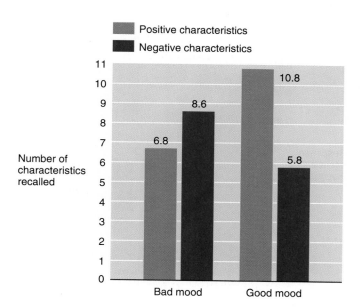

FIGURE 12.3
Number of positive and negative characteristics remembered by subjects in a bad mood and by subjects in a good mood.

want to solicit someone's help, it is a good idea to try to put the person in a positive mood before making your request.

Emotion and Person Perception

Just as our emotions can affect what we pay attention to when remembering events and making judgments, they can also affect how we learn about, judge, and remember the characteristics of others. We can illustrate this by considering a study by Joseph Forgas and Gordon Bower (1987). The subjects in Forgas and Bower's experiment first took a test and then were given feedback on their performance. This feedback, which was unrelated to how they actually did on the test, was positive to half of the subjects and negative to the other half. The purpose of the feedback was to encourage some subjects to feel happy (the positive-mood group) and the others to feel sad (the negative-mood group).

The subjects then read descriptions of other people that included both the positive and negative characteristics of each one. After a short break, they were asked to write down everything they could remember about each of these people. The subjects in the positive-mood group remembered more of the people's positive characteristics and fewer of their negative characteristics than subjects in the negative-mood group (Figure 12.3).

This result suggests that the way we evaluate others depends on our own emotional state as well as on people's actual characteristics. Have you ever formed a negative impression of a new acquaintance simply because you happened to meet the person when you were unhappy or angry?

Emotion and Reacting to Threatening Information

People sometimes experience traumatic events that have a number of after-effects. Being mugged or raped, surviving a terrible accident, or enduring the stress of the battlefield all can result in a condition called **posttraumatic stress disorder (PTSD).** People who suffer from PTSD may experience flashbacks (involuntarily reexperiencing their traumatic experience), have nightmares, and endure bouts of depression.

Edna Foa and Michael Kozak (1986) have proposed a link between PTSD and emotions by suggesting that people with PTSD develop cognitive "fear structures." These fear structures make people more attentive to information related to the experiences that caused their PTSD. Foa and her co-workers (1991) tested this idea by presenting colored word stimuli such as the ones in Figure 12.4 to rape victims with PTSD. Some of the words, such as *rape, stalker,* and

FIGURE 12.4
Stimuli for the Stroop task. The subject's task is to call out the color of the ink in which the words are printed. Starting at the top left and reading left to right, the correct responses are "blue," "red," "green," "red," and so on.

RAPE	MELON	ATTACK
PEAR	STALKER	SCREAM
BERRY	APPLE	PENETRATE

FIGURE 12.5
Results of the Stroop experiment. Rape victims with PTSD took longer to name the colors of the threatening words.

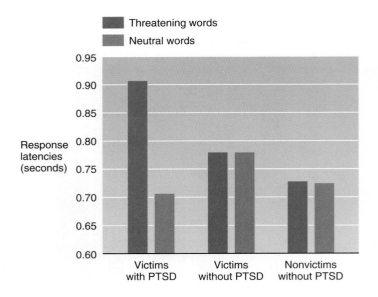

attack, were related to being raped; others were neutral, such as *melon*, *apple*, or *pear*. The subjects' task was to name, as quickly as possible, the *colors* in which the words were printed. To accomplish this task, which is called the *Stroop task*, subjects have to ignore the meanings of the words and focus on the colors. So, for the stimuli in Figure 12.4, the correct responses would be "blue," "red," "green," and so on.

If the meanings of the threatening words captured the subjects' attention because of their fear structures, we would expect that the subjects would take longer to name the colors for these words. This is exactly what happened. The rape victims with PTSD took longer to name the colors of the threatening words than the colors of the neutral words, whereas control groups of rape victims and non–rape victims who did not have PTSD showed no difference between the threatening and neutral words (Figure 12.5). In a similar experiment with Vietnam War veterans with PTSD, Richard McNally and his co-workers (1990) observed the same result.

From these examples, it is clear that emotions affect people's lives in ways that extend beyond simply adding "feelings" to their experience. Emotions affect people's ability to remember and to make judgments, their tendency to help others, their perceptions of others, and their sensitivity to threatening words. Humans may be rational animals, but the experience of emotions—especially strong ones—has a pronounced effect on their thinking and behavior.

So far we have been considering emotion as a subjective experience that also affects many other behaviors. We turn now to the second component of emotions—the behaviors associated with expressing emotions.

The Expression of Emotion

When angry, count four; when very angry, swear.

Mark Twain (1835–1910)

Being able to communicate our emotions to others serves an important social function. Letting others know when we are angry, sad, elated, or depressed can help us get the response we need or want ("Don't bother me now"; "Console me"). Similarly, the ability to recognize others' emotions has obvious advantages—you probably don't want to ask for a raise when your boss is furiously angry, even if it's at someone else.

This ability to recognize others' emotions is especially important because people often don't come right out and *say* what they are feeling, or how intensely they feel it. In fact, one thing most of us have learned quite well is that, when it comes to the expression of emotions, actions speak much louder than words. Let's look at the behaviors that are associated with emotions and at the social conventions that govern how emotions are expressed.

Body Language

Very often we express our emotions more truthfully through our body language than our words. When a man says "I'm not angry" but has his fist tightly clenched, the clenched fist is probably a more accurate barometer of his emotion than his words.

An experiment by Richard Walk and Carolyn Homan (1984) shows that people can accurately judge emotions based on seeing *only* a person's body movements. They accomplished this by placing points of light on a person's joints and darkening the room (Figure 12.6). These points of light form a meaningless pattern when the person is still, but are perceived as human movement as soon as the person moves. Walk and Homan had a mime wearing these lights act out emotions such as fear, surprise, happiness, and anger and asked subjects to identify the emotions being displayed. Based solely on the movement of the lights, subjects correctly identified different emotions with an accuracy ranging from 71% for fear to 96% for happiness.

Facial Expressions

The face can send many subtle signals. Raised eyebrows can express either a greeting or skepticism; a wink of the eye can signal sexual interest or a private joke. Similarly, a myriad of facial expressions—a smile of happiness, a frown of sadness or disapproval, the wide-open eyes of surprise, and a lip curled in disgust—all signal a wide range of emotions. Research by Paul Ekman (1972) has identified six basic emotions that people can identify from facial expressions with a high degree of accuracy (Figure 12.7).

But do facial expressions provide unambiguous information about a person's emotions? The answer is "Not always." Sometimes people try to deceive others: they may feel sad but "put on a happy face," or conceal excitement or satisfaction by assuming an expressionless "poker face." But do these efforts at deception work? Again, the answer is "Not always."

In one series of studies, Paul Ekman, Wallace Friesen, and Maureen O'Sullivan (1988) showed that they could distinguish the false smiles that people purposely manufacture from genuine smiles caused by feeling happy. The French anatomist Duchenne de Boulogne showed that false smiles activate muscles that pull up the corners of the lips, whereas genuine smiles—which Ekman calls *Duchenne smiles*, also activate muscles around the eyes that cause crow's feet in the corners of the eyes.

Ekman and his co-workers videotaped interviews with student nurses while they watched two kinds of films: one of nature scenes, the other showing amputations and burns. The nurses were told to react naturally to the nature film but to smile during the unpleasant film so that the interviewer would think they were watching the nature film. When observers viewed videotapes of the nurses' expressions they were able to tell, by noting which muscles were tensed, which film they were watching (Figure 12.8) (also see Ekman, Davidson, & Friesen, 1990).

The fact that real emotions cause different facial expressions than faked emotions tells us there is a special connection between the emotions we feel and specific muscles in the face. As we will see in the Follow-Through at the end of

FIGURE 12.6
With points of light attached to her joints, a mime acts out various emotions in the dark. Subjects in the Walk and Homan experiment, seeing only the motion of the lights, were able to identify the emotions expressed.

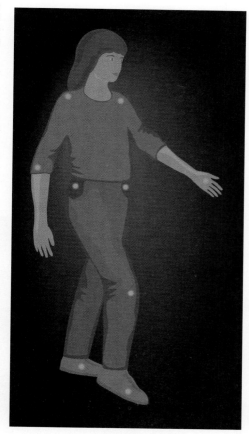

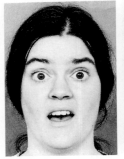
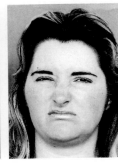

FIGURE 12.7

Facial expressions of the six basic emotions identified by Ekman: surprise, digust, fear, anger, happiness, and sadness

this chapter, people from a wide range of cultures can recognize which emotion goes with each facial expression. This suggests that emotions are biologically programmed to be expressed through the face in the same way for all humans. But what of situations in which humans fight this biological program and attempt to cover up their true emotions?

Display Rules and Emotional Expression

Why would people try to mask the emotions naturally signaled by their facial expressions? At times we have personal reasons for concealing our feelings, but often we try to mask them because of culturally determined **display rules**—rules that specify when it is appropriate to display certain emotions. A well-known display rule in American culture, for example, is the one that discourages males from crying in public, especially in professional settings. Display rules can also encourage the expression of emotion, as in cultures in which a public display of intense grief is encouraged at funerals.

Howard Friedman and Terry Miller-Herringer (1991) studied a situation in which people manage their true emotions by showing that people tended to conceal their happiness after winning a competitive game if the people they had defeated were present in the room. If, however, their vanquished opponents were in another room, they were more likely to show their happiness. The display rule they were following was "When adults are in competition, the loser should appear good-natured about the loss and the winner should be modest and self-effacing" (Mayo & LaFrance, 1978, p. 221).

Skater Brian Boitano followed this display rule after his gold medal performance in the 1988 Winter Olympics. A newspaper article described Boitano's behavior as follows:

> On finishing his wildly successful skating, the skillful and disciplined skater burst into tears of joy. Boitano was universally hailed by the press as

Compare the public display of grief in this Romanian funeral (left) with the more subdued emotions in the German funeral (right). Display rules for different countries and ethnic groups often govern people's public expression of emotions.

a "grand and classy champion." Why was this young competitor so well liked? Here is an insight: At the awards ceremony, Boitano stood, *stone-faced*, next to the runner-up—long-time rival Brian Orser of Canada. Why stonefaced? "I almost felt guilty," Boitano said. "I had to hold back. My facial expression could only make him [Orser] feel worse. I was not going to gloat" ("Brian Boitano," 1988, p. 3).

The cultural requirement that emotional displays be suppressed in certain situations does serve a purpose—in the Boitano example, acting subdued in victory is designed to protect the feelings of the loser. Another display rule, which requires that physicians be cool and professional even under stress, helps them reassure their patients that they are receiving competent care. But in some situations purposely masking emotions can have harmful effects, especially if people find themselves in situations in which they can't even acknowledge that their emotions exist. This situation is common in medical school, as described in the following Interdisciplinary Dimension.

FIGURE 12.8
Student nurses' smiles were genuine (left) when they watched a pleasant film but faked (right) when they watched an unpleasant film. The raised upper lip in the faked expression is a sign of disgust.

INTERDISCIPLINARY DIMENSION MEDICINE

Managing Emotions in Medical School

Many professions have unwritten rules regarding the relationship between professional and client. Professionals usually are not supposed to become "involved" with clients in a personal way, for instance. Thus, doctors offering professional care to their patients should be personable without being emotionally involved. In addition, though physicians may often see their patients unclothed and examine their "private" areas, they are not supposed to express sexual feelings or emotions such as disgust that might be normal if they were not acting as physicians. Expression of such emotions would not only be seen as unethical and detrimental to good medical practice, but would also undermine the physician's status as an authority figure.

This means that part of medical students' training involves learning to suppress the emotions they might feel when examining patients; if they can't suppress feeling these emotions, they learn at least to avoid expressing them. With these facts in mind, Allen Smith and Sheryl Kleinman (1989) undertook a two-year study of students as they made their way through medical school. They observed students as they were trained in situations that involved intimate contact with bodies—such as the dissection of cadavers, or breast, genital, and rectal examinations. In addition, they conducted in-depth interviews with medical students, physicians, and faculty members.

One of the first things Smith and Kleinman realized was that although students often experienced strong emotions in situations involving close contact with patients, this fact was ignored by the medical school curriculum. Not only were there no courses dealing with how to manage their emotions, but students did not discuss their discomfort or negative feelings for fear that they might be seen as unworthy of entering the medical profession. This "unwritten rule" against expressing emotions is described as follows by a first-year male student:

> It wouldn't be a problem if I weren't in medicine. But doctors just aren't supposed to feel that way. *(Interviewer)* How do you know? *(Student)* I don't know how, just sense it. It's macho, the control thing. Like, "Med student, get a grip on yourself." It's just part of medicine. It's a norm, expected (p. 60).

The unwritten rule notwithstanding, students *do* experience strong emotions during their medical training. Consider the following statements:

> I did my autopsy ten days ago. That shook me off my feet. Nothing could have prepared me for it. The person was my age. . . . She just looked asleep. Fluid, blood, smell. It smelled like a butcher shop. And they handled it like a butcher shop (second-year female; p. 58).

> When you listen to the heart you have to work around the breast, and move it to listen to one spot. I tried to do it with minimum contact, without staring at her tit . . . breast. . . . The different words show I was feeling both things at once (second-year male; p. 59).

Physicians are expected to subdue their emotional expression in the presence of patients.

One patient was really gross! He had something that kept him standing, and coughing all the time. Coughing phlegm, and that really bothers me. Gross! (second-year female; p. 59).

How do medical students deal with situations such as these? Smith and Kleinman found that they used a number of different strategies to manage their emotions. Two of these strategies are *transforming the contact* and *laughing about it*.

Transforming the contact.   Students mentally transform their contact with the body into something very different than their usual contact with bodies:

The patient is really like a math word problem. You break it down into little pieces and put them together. The facts you get from a history and physical, from the labs and chart. They fit together, once you begin to see how to do it. . . . It's an intellectual challenge (third-year female; p. 61).

[The pelvic exam] is pretty much like checking a broken toaster. It isn't a problem. I'm good at that kind of thing (second-year male; p. 61).

Laughing about it.   Students create humor about situations in which they feel uncomfortable. By doing this they acknowledge the problem and relieve their tension without having to confess any weakness.

When the others are talking it's usually about unusual stuff, like jokes about huge breasts (second-year male; p. 63).

The fact that medical students have emotions that they can't directly express may add to the already stressful nature of medical school and to the psychiatric problems that many medical students experience (Vitaliano et al., 1989). In addition, emotion-management strategies such as seeing the patient as a system of mechanical parts or something to joke about can have adverse effects on the patients (if doctors think of them as objects) and on the doctors themselves (if they lose touch with their ability to feel). One third-year student expressed his fears of losing the ability to feel as follows:

It's kind of dehumanizing. We just block off the feelings, and I don't know what happens to them. This is pretty important to me. I'm working to keep a sense of myself through all this (p. 68).

Is the situation in medical school unique? Smith and Kleinman argue that medical school's approach to emotions is simply an extension of the training that children receive as they are growing up. Boys in particular are socialized not to show their emotions—to "be a man"—particularly in situations that are stressful. Medical training, which until recently was dominated by males (and still is, at the faculty level), simply carries that tradition into the field of medicine. ∎

10   DEVELOPMENT

6   LEARNING

In the Follow-Through at the end of this chapter, we discuss research indicating that display rules differ in different cultures; these results are consistent with the idea that display rules for emotions are learned. Research also indicates that the learning of display rules may begin at a very early age. Carol Malatesta and Jeannette Haviland (1982) suggest that this learning may begin when infants are as young as 3 months old. When 3- and 6-month-old infants and their mothers were videotaped as they interacted, Malatesta and Haviland found that the infants made a wide range of both positive and negative facial expressions, but that the mothers responded—with facial expressions or words—predominately to the infants' positive expressions. Thus, mothers were more likely to respond to their infant's interested or happy face, and less likely to respond to their infant's sad or angry face.

From what we know about operant conditioning, we can hypothesize that the mother is selectively reinforcing the infant's positive expressions and extinguishing the negative ones. The fact that the 6-month-olds' expressions were more positive than the 3-month-olds' supports this idea (although just getting older, independent of selective reinforcement, could also be causing greater positive responding). Thus, mothers may begin teaching display rules to their children at an early age. In this case, the rule is "show positive emotions but not negative ones."

Our discussion of how emotions are expressed (or inhibited) has focused on the behavioral and contextual levels of analysis. We have seen how observable behaviors reveal emotions and how contextual influences, in the form of situations that cause people to follow display rules, affect emotional expression. In the rest of this chapter, we will focus on the question "What causes emotions?" We will see that answers have been sought at the behavioral, biological, and cognitive levels of analysis. Each of these approaches to the explanation of emotions has something to contribute to our understanding of the "why" of emotions.

Behavioral Explanations of Emotion

A burnt child fears the fire.

Proverb

The major assumption behind the behavioral approach to emotion is that the expression of emotion is learned and, in some situations, is governed by the situations in which people find themselves. In emphasizing the role of conditioning in determining emotions, the behavioral approach focuses on conditioned responses and observational learning.

Conditioned Emotional Responses

Experiments demonstrating that emotions can be conditioned date back to John B. Watson and Rosalie Rayner's (1920) famous Little Albert experiment, in which Albert began showing fear responses to the rat only after it had been repeatedly paired with a loud noise. This effect of classical conditioning, in which a neutral stimulus begins to elicit the response associated with an aversive stimulus, has been demonstrated in rats using the **conditioned emotional response** procedure developed by William Estes and B. F. Skinner (1941). This procedure is based on the fact that fear disrupts bar-pressing behavior in rats. Estes and Skinner demonstrated conditioned fear in rats by first training them to press a bar to receive food. They then paired a neutral stimulus (a tone) with an aversive stimulus (an electric shock). Later, when they presented the tone while the rat was bar-pressing to receive food reinforcements, the rat's activity slowed down appreciably. This result, which does not occur if the tone has not been previously paired with shock, indicates that the tone has become a fearful stimulus.

6   LEARNING

Many people can attest to similar experiences in which once-neutral stimuli have become frightening to them after being paired with an aversive experience. A dentist's or doctor's office and a state trooper's car are examples of stimuli that, because of conditioning, elicit fear responses from many people. Can you think of an upsetting incident that changed the way you react to stimuli that were present during that incident? Or how about a locale in which something positive happened, such as winning a sporting event or first meeting your girlfriend or boyfriend, so that you feel good every time you return to that place? Both positive and negative emotions can be affected by conditioning.

Observational Learning

We "learn" our emotions not only through experiencing them in specific situations, but also by observing others' emotions in specific situations. When we described the process of social referencing in Chapter 10, we saw how infants observe their parents' emotions to determine how they should behave. In a series of experiments Michael Cook and Susan Mineka (1989, 1990; Mineka & Cook,

Many emotional behaviors are learned through modeling.

1988) researched this process of observational learning by inducing laboratory-raised monkeys to become afraid of snakes.

Their research was stimulated by the observation that monkeys in the wild are afraid of snakes but laboratory-reared monkeys are not. This led to the idea that perhaps wild-reared monkeys are afraid of snakes because they have experienced them as being dangerous. Cook and Mineka wondered whether laboratory-reared monkeys could learn to fear snakes by observing wild-reared monkeys' reactions to them. Their experiments confirmed that this, in fact, can occur.

In a further experiment, Cook and Mineka had laboratory monkeys watch films that were edited to show other monkeys being afraid of snakes or being afraid of flowers. As in the earlier experiment, the laboratory monkeys who watched the fear response to snakes also became afraid of snakes. However, watching fear responses to flowers had no effect on these monkeys; they remained unafraid of flowers. This result fits the idea of *preparedness* introduced in Chapter 6, on learning. According to this idea, specific animals are biologically prepared to associate specific combinations of stimuli during learning. Apparently, monkeys are biologically programmed to become afraid of snakes but are not programmed to become afraid of flowers. This predisposition to develop a fear of specific stimuli may be why so many humans are afraid of the same stimuli—the dark, snakes, and spiders, for instance.

3   BIOLOGY

The demonstration that we can learn some emotional responses through conditioning and observation explains why we feel emotions in certain situations. However, observations at the behavioral level tell us nothing about the physiological mechanisms responsible for these emotions. To uncover those mechanisms we need to study emotions at the biological level of analysis.

Physiological Explanations of Emotion

We have already mentioned two connections between emotions and biology. We have suggested that facial expressions are biologically programmed and that organisms may be biologically prepared to react fearfully to certain stimuli. We now consider other aspects of the physiological approach to emotions by looking at the connection between evolution and emotion and between emotions and physiological processes in the body.

The Evolutionary Approach to Emotion

The starting point for the evolutionary approach to emotion is Charles Darwin's book *Expression of the Emotions in Man and Animals* (1872/1965). Darwin proposed that animals and humans express emotions in similar ways and that the facial expressions and body movements associated with emotions have evolved because they increase the organism's chances of survival. Thus, when a dog tenses its muscles and begins to bare its teeth at an attacker, the display both signals a warning and prepares the dog to attack (Figure 12.9).

A number of modern theorists follow a similar line of reasoning for humans when they say that human emotional feelings and behaviors are *adaptive*. The fear a man feels as he walks down a dark urban alley at 2:00 A.M. serves an alerting function: because of his fear, he is vigilant against danger and walks quickly through the alley to safety. Perhaps even more sensibly, fear of the situation might cause him to avoid the alley route altogether. If emotions did not exist, this person might foolishly expose himself to a dangerous situation.

But what about situations in which emotions seem to be maladaptive? For example, though fear can mobilize us for action, it can also prevent us from mobilizing, as when we "freeze" in response to danger. Although this may not seem like an adaptive behavior, we need to remember that our emotions evolved tens of thousands of years ago, long before the existence of modern culture. In the prehistoric environment in which emotions evolved, freezing in place in the forest—just as many animals do when they encounter danger—might be the best way to avoid being attacked by an animal.

Although evolution has undoubtedly played an important role in determining our emotions, most research at the biological level of analysis has focused not on evolution, but on the physiological processes that are responsible for emotions. As we look at how researchers have addressed this problem, we will see that mechanisms involving both the brain and structures outside the brain have been proposed to explain how we experience emotional feelings. We begin by looking at some explanations that focus on bodily changes that occur outside of the brain.

FIGURE 12.9
The fierce display of a dog meeting an attacker not only serves as a warning but also readies the dog for a fight.

Bodily Changes and Emotion

As we saw at the beginning of the chapter, emotions are associated with a number of bodily changes—we may cry, tremble, or shout in response to emotional situations, and we respond to specific emotions with specific facial expressions. A particularly influential early theory of emotion that focuses on these bodily changes is called the James-Lange theory of emotion.

The James-Lange theory.   Consider the following situation: You are awakened from sleep at 2:30 A.M. by the piercing sound of a smoke alarm. As your fogged mind struggles to awareness you detect the smell of smoke. You realize that this is not a false alarm—there actually is a fire somewhere in the house. You throw on some clothes and run to the phone to call the fire department. The phone is dead, and now the house is filling up with thick, white smoke. You panic, running out of the house as quickly as possible and dashing across the street to call for help.

If you were in this situation, exactly when do you think you would have felt fearful? Would you have felt fear the moment you heard the smoke alarm? Would it have hit you later, when you were already on your way out the door? Or would you have felt fearful sometime after hearing the alarm but before making your way out the door? Most people say that they would feel fearful immediately. But according to a theory advanced by the American psychologist William James (1884/1968), what comes first is not the fear, but the person's bodily response to the fearful situation. Perception of a situation, according to James, causes bodily changes, and these bodily changes are the feelings we call emotions. James puts it this way: "We feel sorry because we cry, angry because we strike, afraid because we tremble" (p. 450).

In James's theory of emotion, the autonomic nervous system (ANS)—the system responsible for communicating between the body's internal organs and the brain—takes center stage. James proposed that we feel emotions because of ANS activity, an idea that was also proposed at about the same time by the Danish philosopher David Lange (1885/1922). The resulting theory was called the **James-Lange theory** of emotion. We can understand how this theory explains emotions by looking at the following example for fear (Figure 12.10):

1. You perceive a threatening stimulus.

2. In response to the perceived threat, your autonomic nervous system mobilizes the body by speeding up your heart rate, decreasing activity in the digestive system, and triggering the secretion of the hormone epinephrine to provide extra energy. In addition to reacting to the stimulus with these *visceral responses*—responses of organs such as the stomach and intestines in the abdominal cavity—you would also react with *skeletal responses*—responses of the muscles that control your facial expressions and movement of your body. Arm and leg muscles are activated as you run away, and facial muscles are activated to create expressions consistent with the situation.

3. You sense these visceral and skeletal responses, and this causes you to experience an emotional feeling.

Thus, in our fire example, fear doesn't occur until *after* our heart is pounding, our stomach muscles have tightened up, and our face is contorted in response to perceiving the smoke and finding the phone dead. The James-Lange theory asserts—contrary to what most people believe—that emotion is the result of physiological arousal rather than the other way around.

The James-Lange theory emphasized the importance of ANS activity and visceral responses in determining emotion. However, early in his exploration of emotion, James also suggested that activity of the facial muscles is a source of information about emotions (Izard, 1990). He did not, however, emphasize facial expressions in his writings, so it was left to later researchers to explore the role of facial muscles. Later researchers proposed the facial feedback hypothesis of emotion.

Facial feedback.   According to the **facial feedback hypothesis,** we sense different emotions through feedback from the patterns of facial muscles that are

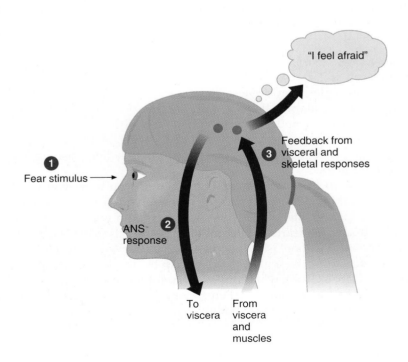

FIGURE 12.10
How we experience emotion, according to the James-Lange theory. The ANS response (2) triggers visceral responses. The feedback from both the visceral responses and skeletal responses from muscles (3) create the feeling of emotion.

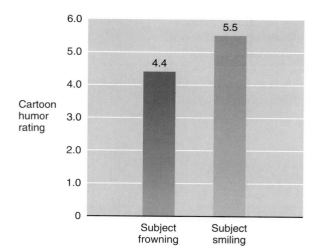

FIGURE 12.11
Subjects rated cartoons as funnier when they viewed them while smiling, suggesting that different facial expressions induce specific emotions.

tensed by the emotions (Izard, 1971; Leventhal, 1984; Tomkins, 1962). A particularly intriguing demonstration of the facial feedback hypothesis has been provided by James Laird (1974), who showed that emotional feelings can occur in response to tensing muscles even if the activation of these muscles is orchestrated by the experimenter. Laird demonstrated this in an experiment in which he had subjects look at cartoons while tensing their facial muscles to produce either a smile or a frown.

Laird's subjects were told that this muscle tensing was part of a study of facial muscle activity during perception. To make this "cover" story more convincing, electrodes were attached to each subject's face to measure muscle tension (in reality, the electrodes did nothing). When subjects rated the cartoons for funniness, they gave higher ratings to those viewed while they were smiling and lower ratings to those viewed while they were frowning (Figure 12.11). This result is what we would predict if different facial expressions led to specific emotional feelings (See Measurement & Methodology, "When Is a 'Smile' a Smile?"). Laird puts it this way: "Considering the importance of facial expressions in judgments of other people's moods, it certainly seems likely that facial expression is also one of the most important determinants of one's own feelings" (p. 915).

The link between feelings and facial expressions has been studied at the biological level by Paul Ekman, Robert Levenson, and Wallace Friesen (1983), who demonstrated a relationship between facial expressions and ANS activity. They demonstrated this relationship by training subjects to tense and relax different groups of facial muscles while they measured the subjects' heart rate and finger temperature. For example, the man in Figure 12.12 is simultaneously (a) raising his eyebrows and pulling them together, (b) raising his upper eyelids, and (c) stretching his lips toward his ears. The resulting expression, which duplicates the expression for fear, increases this person's heart rate and decreases his finger temperature (the decrease in finger temperature indicates that the flow of blood

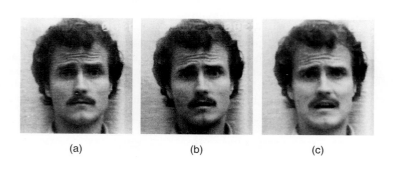

(a)   (b)   (c)

FIGURE 12.12
Subjects raised their heart rates and lowered their finger temperatures when they simulated fearful facial expressions.

to the finger is reduced). Similar measurements for five other emotional expressions showed that heart rate increases for anger, fear, and sadness but decreases for happiness, disgust, and surprise. The expressions that cause an increase in heart rate can be further divided into those that also increase finger temperature, such as anger, and those that decrease finger temperature, such as fear and sadness (Figure 12.13). Thus, these six emotions can be partly distinguished by differences in ANS activity (also see Levenson, 1992).

MEASUREMENT & METHODOLOGY

When Is a "Smile" a Smile? Demand Characteristics in Facial Expression Experiments

Imagine that you are a subject in Laird's (1974) experiment, described in the text. You are asked to draw the corners of your mouth back and up and then rate the funniness of cartoons. You are then asked to draw your eyebrows together and down and to rate some more cartoons. Do you think it might occur to you that drawing the corners of your mouth up creates a smile, and that the experimenter might expect this smile to cause you to give higher funniness ratings to the cartoons? Being a "good subject," might you then increase your funniness ratings while "smiling"?

If you did this, you would be responding to *demand characteristics* of the experiment. Demand charateristics, as we described in Chapter 2, are cues that indicate to the subject what results the experimenter expects. Since results influenced by demand characteristics are obviously invalid, researchers want to eliminate them by concealing the nature of the experiment.

That was the goal in an experiment designed by Fritz Strack, Leonard Martin, and Sabine Stepper (1988). Instead of asking subjects to tense their muscles, they had them hold a felt-tipped pen either between their lips (the nonsmile condition) or between their teeth (the smile condition) (see Figure A). They were told that the purpose of the experiment was to test people's ability to perform

FIGURE B

Subjects rated cartoons as funnier while writing with a marker held between their teeth, which caused them to "smile."

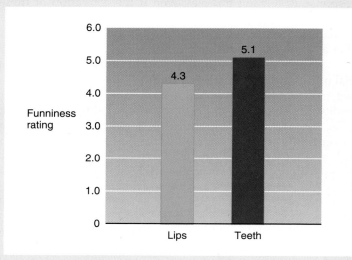

FIGURE A

By asking this woman to hold the pen in her teeth, the experimenter has created the facial expression for smiling. In contrast, holding the pen in her lips does not cause the "smile."

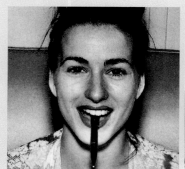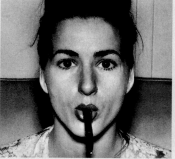

tasks using parts of their body they normally wouldn't use for such tasks, as might be required of individuals who couldn't use their hands or arms because of a birth defect or paralysis.

The subjects were asked to carry out a number of tasks with the pen in the two positions in their mouth and also in their hand. The experimenters were most interested in the task in which subjects were sked to rate the funniness of four cartoons by marking a scale ranging from 0 (not funny) to 9 (extremely funny) with the pen. The results, shown in Figure B, confirm Laird's findings: with their mouths in the "smile" position, subjects rated cartoons as funnier than they did by hand or with their mouths in the nonsmile position. Strack's clever procedure for getting the subjects to "smile" without considering it a smile minimized the chances that demand characteristics could contaminate the results of his experiment.

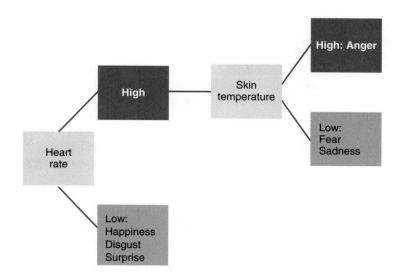

FIGURE 12.13
Tensing muscles to create expressions for different emotions can increase or decrease a person's heart rate. Among the emotions that result in an increase in heart rate, anger is associated with an increase in finger temperature, and fear and sadness are associated with a decrease in finger temperature.

How might different facial expressions lead to different patterns of physiological activity? One possibility is that signals sent from the motor cortex cause movement of the facial muscles; then, a feedback signal from the facial muscles reaches the brain centers that control ANS activity (Figure 12.14, left). Another possible explanation is that two signals are sent from the motor cortex. One causes movement of the facial muscles; the other activates the brain centers that control ANS activity (Figure 12.14, right) (Ekman, 1992).

A third way that facial expressions might affect physiological activity has been proposed by Robert Zajonc (1985) in the form of his **vascular theory of emotional efference (VTEE).** Before describing this theory, let's define some terms. *Vascular* refers to blood vessels; in the case of the VTEE, the blood vessels in the face are the ones that are important. *Efference* refers to neurons that carry signals to the muscles; in the case of the VTEE, efference refers specifically to the action of the facial muscles.

According to the VTEE, contraction or relaxation of facial muscles can control blood flow in the face by compressing or releasing veins or arteries. What does blood flow in the face have to do with emotions? Changes in blood flow can cool or warm the brain, and this cooling or warming can affect chemical reactions of neurotransmitters that affect a person's emotions (Figure 12.15).

FIGURE 12.14
Two possible explanations for facial expressions for different emotions leading to different patterns of physiological activity. In both, a signal (1) is sent from the motor cortex to move the facial muscles. At left, a signal from the facial muscles (2) activates the brain center that triggers ANS activity (3). At right, this signal (2) comes from the motor cortex.

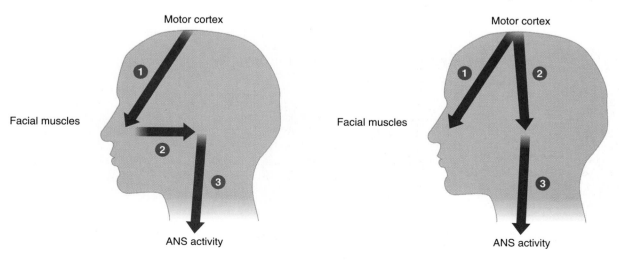

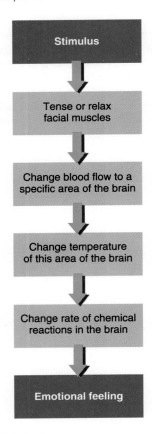

FIGURE 12.15
How facial expressions might affect physiological activity, according to the vascular theory of emotional efference. Tensing or relaxing facial muscles affects blood flow to the brain, which changes the temperature of specific areas of the brain. This change in temperature affects chemical reactions which, in turn, lead to emotional feelings.

Zajonc's proposal is intriguing, but is there any support for it? In a series of experiments, Zajonc and his co-workers (Zajonc, Murphy, & Inglehart, 1989) showed that relaxing or contracting certain muscles changes both facial temperature and the feelings of pleasantness or unpleasantness a person experiences. In one of these experiments subjects read two stories out loud. One story contained a sound that relaxes (slackens) one of the muscles used in smiling; the other story did not. The result was consistent with the VTEE: When reading the story that relaxed the smiling muscle, the temperature of the subject's face rose 0.3°C (compared to no temperature change for the other story), and 81% of the subjects said that they found that story less pleasant. Apparently, warming of the face causes negative feelings.

Zajonc admits that there is no proof that the warming and cooling he observed does, in fact, affect chemical reactions in the brain. But he does show that there is a connection between facial temperature and the tensing or relaxing of certain facial muscles. Does this mean that when you smile or say "cheese" for the photographer you are cooling your brain by changing the flow of blood and this is what makes you feel good? Perhaps. More research needs to be done before we can accept the VTEE. We do know, however, that whatever the mechanism linking facial expressions and emotions, it is safe to conclude that facial expressions are more than simply a response that accompanies a person's emotions—they also help the person to experience these emotions.

Brain Activity and Emotion

As with all behaviors, emotions are ultimately associated with activity in the brain. Throughout the years, researchers have proposed different sites for the brain activity that accompanies emotion. We begin our discussion of brain activity and emotion by describing a theory proposed early in the century by physiologists Walter Cannon and Philip Bard.

The Cannon-Bard theory.   The **Cannon-Bard theory,** which was championed by Cannon and based on experimental results obtained by Bard (1929), hypothesized that an emotion-producing stimulus elicits activity in the thalamus, which simultaneously (1) signals the cortex, causing us to feel emotions, and (2) triggers autonomic nervous system activity, helping us mobilize for action (Figure 12.16). In this account, the factor that determines emotions is the almost instanta-

FIGURE 12.16
How we experience emotions, according to the Cannon-Bard theory. Activation of the thalamus (2) simultaneously signals the cortex, causing emotional feeling and mobilizing the ANS.

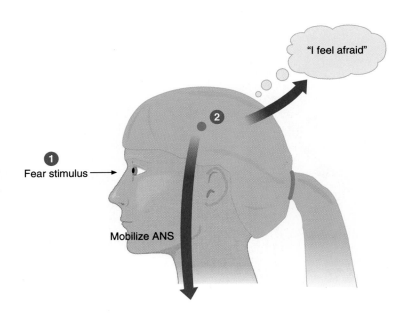

neous activity in the cortex. Unlike the James-Lange theory, which sees emotions as caused by ANS activity, the Cannon-Bard theory sees ANS activity as mobilizing us for action but not necessarily creating emotional feelings.

When Cannon presented his theory as an alternative to the James-Lange theory, he criticized the James-Lange theory on a number of grounds. He first pointed out that we are physiologically aroused by activities such as exercise without necessarily experiencing emotions. He also wondered why, even though the heart, lungs, and muscles take a number of seconds to reach their maximal activity in response to a stimulus, intense emotions can occur almost immediately in a threatening situation. Furthermore, Cannon reasoned that if emotions were the result of visceral activity, there would have to be a different pattern of visceral response for each emotion. The evidence available to Cannon at that time indicated, however, that this was not true—similar patterns of visceral activity had been reported for very different emotions. (We now know, from the research of Ekman and his co-workers, that we can, in fact, detect different patterns of ANS activity for different emotions.)

Modern evidence that calls into question the strong link between visceral activity and emotions proposed by the James-Lange theory is provided by Kathleen Chwalisz and her co-workers (1988). They asked the question illustrated by Figure 12.17: Do people feel emotions if they have suffered spinal cord injuries that prevent visceral signals from reaching the brain? She answered the question by asking people who had been paralyzed by spinal cord injuries to compare their emotional feelings before and after their injuries.

Contrary to what the James-Lange theory would predict, Chwalisz found that even subjects with injuries high in the spinal cord, which completely

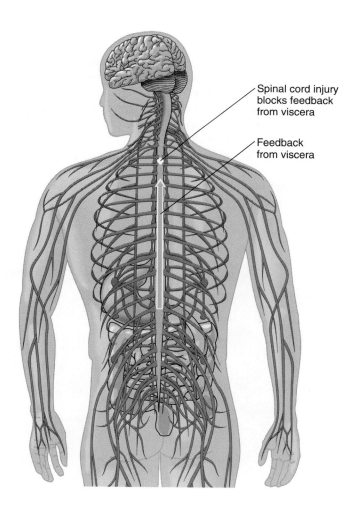

Spinal cord injury
blocks feedback
from viscera

Feedback
from viscera

FIGURE 12.17
Spinal cord injuries can block feedback from the viscera. If emotion is caused solely by this feedback, then such injuries would eliminate emotional feelings. Research indicates, however, that emotional feelings are still present even when people have injuries high in the spinal cord.

eliminated signals from the viscera, related stories of intense emotions: One subject reported being so angry that he wanted to run his wheelchair into a wall. Another subject described being in a "euphoric state" and crying "tears of joy and pride" following a tender moment with his family. The fact that these intense emotions occurred when signals from the viscera could not get to the brain argues that these signals are not as important as the James-Lange theory proposed. Another spinal cord study, published after Chwalisz's paper, came to the same conclusion (Bermond et al., 1991). Although these results show that ANS signals may not be as crucial for experiencing emotions as James and Lange proposed, they do not rule out the possibility that visceral signals might contribute to emotional feelings in people with intact spinal cords.

Cannon's criticisms of the James-Lange theory, combined with his proposal of an alternative theory that included the thalamus, caused the Cannon-Bard theory to be taken seriously by emotion researchers. As we will see, however, the crucial site for emotions in the brain is not the thalamus.

Modern brain research.   Modern research on the role of brain activity in determining emotions has searched in a number of different ways for the brain structures associated with emotion. In one approach, researchers observe emotional behavior in animals in response to **electrical stimulation of the brain (ESB).** ESB is achieved by lowering an electrode into the brain so that its tip is positioned near a structure to be stimulated. A weak electrical current is then passed through the electrode tip and the animal's behavior is observed. Stimulation of specific areas in the hypothalamus and the limbic system of cats and monkeys causes them to behave aggressively or to attempt to escape—behaviors usually associated with anger and fear, respectively, in humans.

Although such studies show that stimulation of the hypothalamus and limbic system can cause animals to *behave* as if they are angry or fearful, we don't really know what they are *feeling*. To study emotional feelings we must do research with humans, who can report what they are feeling in response to stimulation. In the few instances in which humans experienced ESB during brain operations, they reported feeling anger, depression, relaxation, or euphoria in response to stimulation of areas in the hypothalamus, amygdala, and hippocampus (Figure 12.18) (Delgado, 1969; Sem-Jacobson, 1968). Based on more recent research and new information about the anatomy of the brain, Joseph LeDoux (1989) has proposed that the amygdala is the central brain structure for determining emotion.

What can we conclude from the physiological research we have described? The situation today is clearly not one in which the two early theories—the

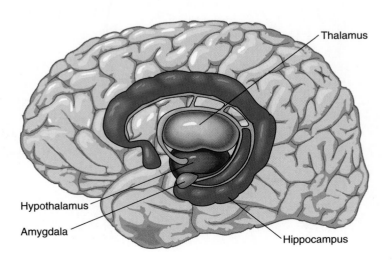

FIGURE 12.18
The colored structures—the hypothalamus, hippocampus, and amygdala—are involved in determining emotional feelings.

James-Lange theory and the Cannon-Bard theory—are in competition with each other. There is clear evidence that components of both theories are correct: Rapidly activated brain structures are responsible for our almost instantaneous emotional response to many situations, and information generated by tensing and relaxing facial muscles, and to some extent from activity of the ANS, contribute to our emotional experience over the longer term.

Physiological explanations of emotion emphasize the biological processes that underlie our experience of emotion. But as we have seen repeatedly in this book, human beings are complex creatures whose experiences involve a blending of physiological, behavioral, contextual, and cognitive factors. To complete our investigation of emotion, we move to the cognitive level of analysis and explore how a person's *thoughts* influence the experience of emotion.

Cognitive Explanations of Emotion

Anybody can become angry—that is easy; but to be angry with the right person and to the right degree, and at the right time, and for the right purpose, and in the right way— that is not within everybody's power and is not easy.

Aristotle (384–322 B.C.)

The idea that cognitions are important in determining emotions has been proposed by a number of different researchers. We begin our discussion with an experiment by Stanley Schachter and Jerome Singer (1962) that stimulated a great deal of research regarding the link between cognition and emotion.

 8 THINKING

Schachter and Singer: Interpretation of Arousal

Schachter and Singer hypothesized that subjects who experience physiological arousal will seek reasons for the arousal, and that their thoughts during that search will determine their emotional feelings. According to this idea, it is not arousal alone that explains the emotions we feel, but our *interpretation* of that arousal. If this is true, the same physiological state could give rise to different emotions, depending on what we *think* we are feeling. Schachter and Singer's experiment was designed to test this idea (Figure 12.19).

Schachter and Singer first stimulated physiological arousal by giving their subjects the drug epinephrine. One group of subjects, the *informed group,* was told the truth: that the drug would increase their heart rate, cause a tingling

FIGURE 12.19
Design of Schachter and Singer's experiment. All subjects received an injection of epinephrine, but the informed group was told the actual effects of the drug, whereas the misinformed group was given incorrect information. The subjects in each of these groups were then subjected to either the happy or the angry condition.

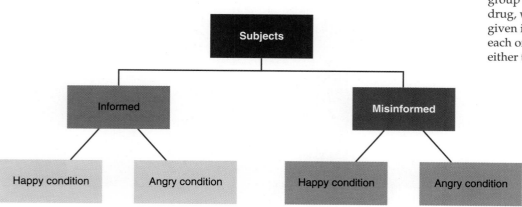

sensation in their hands, and bring a feeling of warmth to their face. Another group of subjects, the *misinformed group*, was told that the drug would cause numbness in their feet, an itching sensation over parts of their body, and perhaps a slight headache.

Having given their subjects the drug and either correct or incorrect information about its effects, the researchers had them each wait with a fellow subject while the drug began taking effect. The "fellow subject" was, however, a confederate of the experimenters.

While waiting in the room, the subjects experienced one of two conditions. Subjects in the *happy condition* were exposed to a confederate who cracked jokes, shot baskets with wadded-up paper, flew paper airplanes, and played with a hula hoop (which just happened to be in the room). Subjects in the *angry condition* were exposed to a confederate who complained about the experiment and about an insulting questionnaire that they both were asked to fill out. (The questionnaire asked them, for instance, to "List members of your family who do not bathe or wash regularly.")

What emotions might the subjects feel in the two situations? Schachter and Singer hypothesized that the answer to this question would differ between the misinformed and informed subjects. They reasoned that the misinformed subjects, in trying to find an explanation for their drug-induced arousal, would look to their situation. Thus, misinformed subjects in the happy condition would attribute their physiological arousal to the antics of the happy confederate ("My heart must be beating rapidly because I'm having fun with this funny guy"). Misinformed subjects in the angry condition would associate their arousal with the complaining of the angry confederate ("My heart must be beating rapidly because I agree with this angry guy"). The interpretations of the informed subjects, on the other hand, should be unaffected by the happy or angry environment, since the subjects already had decided that their arousal was caused by the drug.

The subjects' emotions were measured in two ways: (1) by asking how they felt (subject self-report) and (2) by observing whether they joined the confederates' activities (subject behavior). The results of this experiment (Figure 12.20) supported Schachter and Singer's hypothesis most strongly for the happy condition. As predicted, the misinformed subjects acted much happier than the informed subjects, as measured by both self-report and behavior.

Schachter and Singer concluded that emotion is determined by a combination of (1) physiological arousal and (2) cognitive attempts to explain the cause of this arousal (Figure 12.21). This idea became known as the **two-factor theory** of emotion, since emotion was said to be caused by *both* physiological arousal and cognition.

Schachter and Singer's original experiment has been criticized because it has been difficult to replicate (Marshall & Zimbardo, 1979; Maslach, 1979;

FIGURE 12.20
Results for subjects in the happy condition in Schachter and Singer's experiment. Subjects in the misinformed group reported being happier, and they copied the confederate's behavior more frequently.

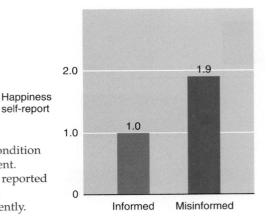

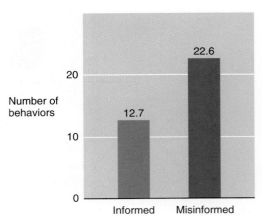

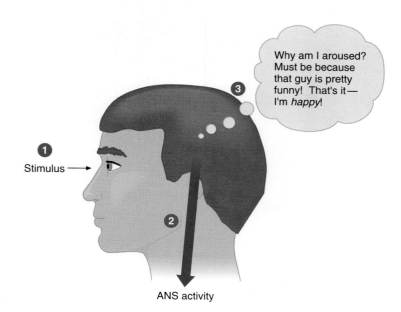

FIGURE 12.21
When the stimulus (1) causes physiological arousal (2) accompanied by cognitive attempts to explain it (3), emotion results, according to Schachter and Singer's two-factor theory of emotion.

Reisenzein, 1983) and because of doubts that all emotions are based on physiological arousal (Lazarus, Coyne, & Folkman, 1982). Thus, although Schachter and Singer's experiment hasn't withstood the test of time, it did influence other research, which has shown that when people become aroused, they do, in some cases, experience different emotions, depending on how they interpret the arousal (Reisenzein, 1983; Zillman & Bryant, 1974).

Richard Lazarus: Cognitive Appraisal

Another cognitive approach to emotion has been proposed by Richard Lazarus (1982, 1984, 1991a, 1991b). Lazarus argues that emotions occur only after a person carries out a process of **cognitive appraisal**—an assessment of the significance of a particular situation for the person's well-being. Consider, for example, what might happen if you returned home one twilight evening to find a large dog on your front steps. Your response to this animal would depend on your appraisal of its implications for your safety. If you recognized the animal as your faithful retriever, you would appraise the situation as "friendly animal," and you might feel happy. If you recognized it as a notoriously fierce Doberman that escaped from your neighbor's backyard, you would probably evaluate the situation quite differently, and might feel fearful. Lazarus's idea is that emotion is the result of a cognitive transaction between person and environment.

Lazarus also points out that the connection between cognition and emotion goes in both directions. That is, cognitive appraisal may be necessary to feel a specific emotion, but once that emotion is felt it becomes in turn something to think about and react to. For example, a woman might express anger if she interpreted another person's actions as slighting her. She might then feel guilty or ashamed for expressing her anger, if she regards showing anger as a personal weakness. There is, therefore, an interplay between cognition and emotion.

This connection can be seen not only in adults but in young children as well. For example, Lazarus cites the observation that infants begin to show fear when placed on a visual cliff (the transparent tabletop, discussed in Chapter 10, that creates the illusion of dangerous height) only when they have begun to crawl (Berthenthal, Campos, & Barrett, 1984). It is their experience while crawling, argues Lazarus, that teaches children about falling and being hurt and that enables them to appraise the potential danger of the visual cliff.

10   DEVELOPMENT

LEVELS OF
ANALYSIS

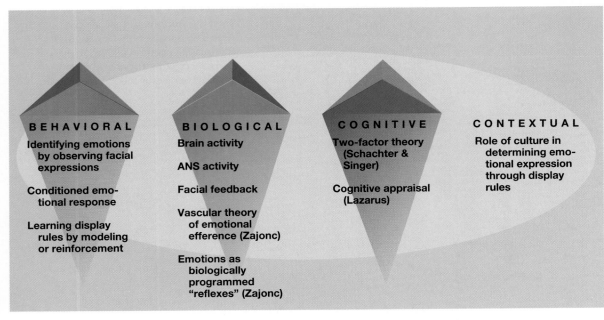

FIGURE 12.22
Levels of analysis
applied to emotion

Although Lazarus argues strongly that cognitive appraisal always occurs prior to the existence of an emotion, Robert Zajonc (1984) disagrees. Zajonc points out that emotional reactions to some stimuli can occur rapidly, such as to an object hurtling rapidly toward your face or to strong tastes or smells. In these cases, argues Zajonc, there is not enough time for cognitive appraisal to occur. According to this idea, in some situations we are biologically programmed to react emotionally, even in the absence of cognition. Lazarus (1984) answers Zajonc by saying that even rapid reactions involve cognitions, because an emotion cannot occur until a person decides whether or not a situation affects his or her well-being. In the case of these rapid reactions, cognitive appraisal may occur unconsciously, according to Lazarus. This controversy between Lazarus and Zajonc remains unsettled. We can say, however, that cognitive appraisal occurs in many emotional situations.

As we end our discussion of emotion, it should be clear that the factors that determine emotions are far from simple. One way to look at emotions is to think of each one as having a unique "signature"—a pattern of tensed and relaxed facial muscles, a pattern of ANS activity, the activation of specific brain structures, and certain thoughts or "appraisals." The complexity of emotion becomes obvious when we realize that these factors interact with one another. For example, the brain controls ANS activity, and the pattern of ANS activity may, in turn, signal specific emotions to the brain. Also, cognitions generated in the brain help channel physiological responses into specific feelings. Thus, the experience we call emotion is the result of a number of physiological responses and cognitions interacting with one another and operating at a number of levels of analysis (Figure 12.22).

Reprise: The Ebb and Flow of Scientific Understanding

In this chapter not only have we seen that our feelings of emotion are caused by many interacting factors, but we have also gotten a glimpse of the way science progresses. We have already examined instances of how scientific understanding ebbs and flows: a particular explanation is accepted by the scientific community;

that explanation is supplanted by another that is in turn replaced by another, which in some cases may resemble the first explanation, which had been rejected earlier. Consider, for example, the process we observed in Chapter 11, on motivation. Originally hunger was thought to be caused by peripheral factors like stomach contractions. Then attention shifted to the brain. Finally, evidence emerged indicating that peripheral factors (though not the stomach contractions posited earlier) are, in fact, important in causing hunger.

In this chapter we have described a similar situation. First James and Lange proposed that emotion is caused by signals sent from the viscera. This idea stood for many years, until Cannon and Bard questioned the James-Lange theory and redirected scholars' attention to the brain. Modern researchers have since concluded that both approaches contain elements of truth, and they have added a sprinkling of cognition to complete the picture.

What this ebb and flow in research and theorizing tells us is that the course of scientific discovery does not have to be a contest, in which acceptance of one explanation necessarily precludes all competing explanations. Nor is progress usually smooth or linear, with each new finding simply adding to our store of knowledge. It often turns out that there is truth in both of what initially appeared to be conflicting accounts. One of the reasons this is so is that even seemingly simple behaviors like "feeling happy" or "feeling sad" are actually highly complex and determined by a number of processes working simultaneously and often interacting with one another. In the next chapter, as we consider stress and health, we will encounter a similar situation, as we see that health is not determined by physiological processes alone but by their interaction with behavioral mechanisms.

Emotion and Culture

People from all cultures feel emotions, but do they express them in the same way? Do people from the United States, Japan, and Brazil all frown when they are sad and smile when they are happy? Charles Darwin (1872/1965) considered these questions and decided that the expression of emotions was determined by biological processes that are similar for all humans, and so emotional expressions should be similar for all people.

The evidence for Darwin's conclusion consisted of some observations indicating that facial expressions are basically the same in many different cultures. His hypothesis was challenged, however, by a number of researchers (Kleinberg, 1938; LaBarre, 1947) who criticized Darwin's unsystematic methods of data collection and presented data of their own that seemed to show that emotional expressions differ across cultures (also see Birdwhistell, 1970; Leach, 1972).

More recent research, however, shows that there is evidence for universal emotional expressions across cultures. Paul Ekman, Wallace Friesen, and a number of other researchers (Ekman & Friesen, 1971; Ekman et al., 1987) asked people from over a dozen countries, including the United States, Estonia, Germany, Turkey, Brazil, and Japan, to indicate which emotions were being expressed in a series of photographs. The similarity of these people's judgments, no matter where they came from, supports the idea that the expression of emotions is universal (Table 12.2).

But could it be that people from different cultures actually express their own emotions differently, but that when judging pictures they reflect what they have learned from watching American movies or TV? To dispose of this problem, Ekman and Friesen (1971) showed pictures of facial expressions (similar to those in Figure 12.7) to people in an isolated tribe in New Guinea called the South Fore who had never seen TV or movies and had little contact with the outside world. The subjects' task was to match the pictures with specific emotions. To ensure that their results were not distorted by language problems, Ekman and Friesen did not use simple labels like "angry" or "happy," but presented the following stories to be matched with the appropriate picture:

- *Happiness*: Her friends have come and she is happy.
- *Disgust:* She sees a dead pig that has been lying there for a long time.
- *Anger*: She is angry, is about to fight (p.126).

FIGURE 12.23
Facial expressions posed by a Fore man to match descriptions of situations that in Western culture would produce emotions of happiness, disgust, and anger

The Fore matched the pictures and stories the same way as a Westerner would. In addition, when other subjects were presented with the stories and were asked to show how their face would appear if they were the person in the story, the resulting facial expressions could be accurately identified by American college students (Figure 12.23) (Ekman, 1972).

Ekman and Friesen's cross-cultural studies, plus the fact that children who have been blind from birth exhibit the same facial expressions as sighted children in emotional situations (Goodenough, 1932; Eibl-Eibesfeldt, 1972), have led to the conclusion that the facial expressions accompanying emotions are, as Darwin suggested, a biologically programmed characteristic of all humans.

But all the data we have presented so far are at the behavioral level of analysis. Is there any biological evidence for universal biological programming of emotions? Robert Levenson and his co-workers (1992) have provided such evidence by measuring ANS activity in subjects from the Minangkabau culture of West Sumatra as they contracted their facial muscles into the configurations for anger, fear, sadness, disgust, and happiness.

You may remember that when Ekman, Levenson, and Friesen (1983) made similar measurements on American subjects, they found that heart rate increased when subjects posed expressions for anger, fear, and sadness but decreased for happiness, disgust, and surprise. In addition, they found that finger temperature increased for anger and decreased for fear and sadness.

Levenson decided to repeat these measurements on the Minangkabau—a culture very different from American culture. The Minangkabau culture is a Muslim culture of about 4.5 million people that places little emphasis on being in touch with emotional feelings and that socializes its members to diminish or mask the display of strong negative emotions such as anger.

Despite these large differences between the two cultures, Levenson found that the Minangkabau's autonomic nervous system responses to emotional expressions were very similar to the responses previously measured for Americans. This finding provides biological evidence to support the idea of universal biological programming of emotions.

But we have seen that there is more to emotional expression than biological programming. Emotional expression is also determined by the display rules that people learn as they grow up in a

TABLE 12.2
The universality of facial expressions of emotions

Emotion:	Happiness	Disgust	Surprise	Sadness	Anger	Fear
Culture	Percentage Agreeing with Predominant Judgment					
Americans	97	92	95	84	67	85
Brazilians	95	97	87	59	90	67
Chileans	95	92	93	88	94	68
Argentinians	98	92	95	78	90	54
Japanese	100	90	100	62	90	66

Source: Ekman, Friesen, and Ellsworth, 1972.

culture. Since these display rules differ in different cultures, people's responses in emotional situations may be different in different cultures. Wallace Friesen (1972; also see Ekman, 1972) demonstrated this by using a hidden camera to record Japanese and American subjects' responses to a stressful film. He found that they both reacted with the facial expressions associated with disgust, fear, and distress when they watched the film alone, but that the Japanese subjects smiled to mask their negative feelings when they viewed the films with an experimenter. This result reflects a display rule of Japanese culture: negative emotions should not be shown in public.

Researchers have also noted display rules in other cultures (Mesquita & Frijda, 1992). The Utku Inuits' expression of anger is limited to aggression toward their dogs (Briggs, 1970), and displays of aggression are frowned on by Tahitians, unless the person is drunk. The Utku also have a strong display rule against crying, which is taught to children beginning at a young age. Parents warn their child that "Your pants are all wet with tears. You mustn't cry. You'll make your pants wet and then you'll freeze" (Briggs, 1970, p. 172).

So far we have been considering cross-cultural similarities and differences in the *expression* of emotions. Another way to study cross-cultural differences in emotion is by looking at how people in different cultures react emotionally to specific situations. In general, people from different cultures say that they react in the same way to various events (Mesquita & Frijda, 1992). Thus, most people react with sadness to the loss of a loved one and with fear to a dangerous situation. However, there are some differences between cultures. For example, Elisha Babad (1986) asked Israelis and Europeans to describe events or situations that led to emotional reactions. She found particularly large differences for events associated with relationships: a greater percentage of Europeans than Israelis associated joy, sadness, and anger with relationships (Figure 12.24).

A particularly interesting reaction occurs in the Balinese culture in response to situations that are unfamiliar or frightening. According to Gregory Bateson and Margaret Mead (1942), the Balinese often react to these situations by falling asleep. Thus, "The older child who has lost or broken some valuable thing will be found when his parents return, not run away, not willing to confess, but in a deep sleep. . . . The thief whose case is being tried falls asleep" (Bateson & Mead, 1942, p. 39). This reaction helps achieve adherence to the Balinese display rule of avoiding emotional disruptions.

Most of the research on emotions and culture leads to the conclusion that because emotions are biologically programmed, people in all cultures have an initial tendency to express their emotions in a similar way. Research also indicates, however, that this initial tendency may be changed by display rules that regulate the degree to which people may express or inhibit their emotions and that determine the specific situations in which those emotions occur.

FIGURE 12.24
Israelis are less likely than Europeans to associate joy, sadness, and anger with events that occur in their relationships.

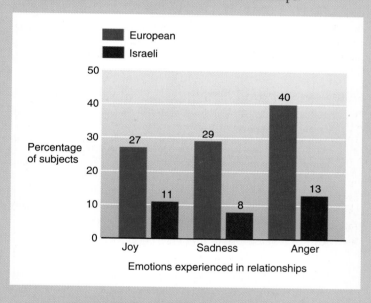

The Nature of Emotions

- The three components of emotions are subjective feelings, observable behaviors, and physiological responses.

- There are many labels for emotions, but some psychologists argue that a small number of emotions are fundamental, such as Plutchik's primary emotions: fear, surprise, sadness, disgust, anger, anticipation, joy, and acceptance.

- Emotions affect many aspects of cognition and behavior, including people's memory, their ability to make judgments, their tendency to help others, and their perception of others. Emotions also affect some people's reactions to threatening stimuli.

The Behavioral Effects of Emotion

- Emotions have numerous effects on behavior. Positive emotions tend to increase memory for positive events and for the positive characteristics of other people, cause people to underestimate risks, and increase helping behavior. Negative emotions tend to have the opposite effect.

- People with posttraumatic stress disorder experience negative emotions that lead to longer reaction times for naming the colors of threatening words in the Stroop task.

The Expression of Emotion

- Emotions can be expressed verbally or by body language or facial expressions.

- Body language is often a more accurate reflection of emotions than a person's verbal statements. Facial expressions do not always convey unambiguous information about emotions, since people sometimes create deceptive facial expressions. However, there is a detectable difference between genuine and faked facial expressions.

- Cultural display rules influence people's expression of emotion and often lead to the suppression of emotional displays.

- Medical students learn during their training to suppress emotions they may feel when examining patients. Since there are seldom courses in the curriculum that deal with this problem, students have to work out their own strategies to manage their emotions.

Behavioral Explanations of Emotion

- Behavioral approaches to emotion view emotional responses as learned behaviors. Behavioral research has shown that (1) emotions can be conditioned so that a previously neutral stimulus elicits an emotional response, and (2) emotions can be learned through observation.

Physiological Explanations of Emotion

- In the evolutionary approach, emotion is an adaptive response that serves to communicate what a person is feeling, and to motivate the person to avoid danger or escape from it.

- The James-Lange theory equated emotion with visceral and skeletal responses. According to this idea, emotion is the result of physiological arousal rather than the other way around. Modern evidence indicates that visceral responses may not be necessary for experiencing emotions, but it also indicates that feedback from facial muscles may play a role in determining emotions.

- A number of different ideas regarding the role of facial expressions in determining emotions have been proposed, including the facial feedback hypothesis and the vascular theory of emotional efference. It has also been shown that different facial expressions are associated with specific patterns of ANS activity.

- The Cannon-Bard theory focuses on activity in the thalamus. Modern brain research shows that key sites for emotion are the hypothalamus and amygdala.

Cognitive Explanations of Emotion

- Cognition plays a large role in determining emotion. Two prominent cognitive approaches to emotion are (1) Schachter and Singer's two-factor theory, which states that emotion is determined by physiological arousal plus our interpretation of the source of that arousal, and (2) Lazarus's idea that cognitive appraisal always precedes emotions.

- Zajonc argues that cognitive appraisal is not always necessary for emotions. While the controversy between Lazarus and Zajonc remains to be settled, it is accurate to say that cognitive appraisal occurs in many emotional situations.

Reprise: The Ebb and Flow of Scientific Understanding

- Scientific progress is not a simple linear progression. Scientific explanations replace one another and then—sometimes—previously discarded explanations reappear in a slightly changed form.

Follow-Through/Diversity: Emotion and Culture

- Darwin hypothesized that the expression of emotions is determined by biological processes that are the same in all people, and that facial expressions are therefore the same in different cultures. Modern cross-cultural research has confirmed Darwin's hypothesis. However, because of culturally determined display rules, people may inhibit or exaggerate their natural emotional expression in certain situations.

Key Terms

Cannon-Bard theory
cognitive appraisal
conditioned emotional
 response
display rules
electrical stimulation of the
 brain (ESB)
emotion
facial feedback hypothesis

James-Lange theory
mood congruity effect
posttraumatic stress disorder
 (PTSO)
primary emotions
secondary emotions
two-factor theory
vascular theory of emotional
 efference (VTEE)

CHAPTER

13

Health Psychology
    Health Psychology and AIDS
    Behavior and Health

What Is Stress?

Links Between Stress and Health
    Life Stress and Health
    How Stress Affects Health

Interdisciplinary Dimension: Immunology
    Conditioning the Immune Response

Social Support and Health

Personality and Health

Applying Health Psychology: Coping with Stress
    Attacking the Problem
    Rethinking the Problem
    Lessening the Effects of the Problem

Reprise: Biology and Behavior, a Two-Way Street

Follow-Through/Diversity
    Hypertension Among African Americans

Stress and Health

Gladness of heart is the very life of man, cheerfulness prolongs his days. . . . Envy and anger shorten the life, worry brings on premature old age.

Ecclesiasticus, 30:22, 30:24

T he best words to describe Roger would be intense or angry. He often seemed driven to work harder than his co-workers and rarely took time off to relax. Roger's anger flared up when least expected and often over things that seemed trivial to others. One day, on his way home from work, he suffered a heart attack that incapacitated him for months. He was lucky to have survived.

The news from the doctor shocked Rebecca. She had cancer, and less than a year to live. George, her husband of 50 years, was crushed, but he did his best to care for her as her illness progressed. After her death, he never really recovered, becoming sick himself and dying eight months after Rebecca's funeral.

Louise was at work when she heard some startling news on the radio. There had been some kind of accident at the nuclear reactor at Three Mile Island, Pennsylvania, near where she lived. Soon afterward officials announced that there was nothing to worry about, but then the governor ordered the 40,000 residents who lived near the reactor to evacuate. Eventually Louise and her family were able to return to their home, but she began suffering from anxiety attacks and constant headaches.

Men are at greater-than-normal risk of dying following the deaths of their wives.

What do these three descriptions have in common? They all describe health problems that could be connected to a person's lifestyle or to specific life events. Roger's friends suspected that his fast-paced lifestyle and his anger might have had something to do with his heart attack. It seemed more than a coincidence that George died just eight months after his wife, especially as he had been in relatively good health just before she became ill. And Louise's anxiety and headaches appeared to be connected to the accident at Three Mile Island.

This chapter is about cases such as Roger's, George's, and Louise's, in which health problems are linked to lifestyle or life events. By looking for explanations for health problems in people's behavior or experiences, we are taking an approach that is very different from the approach traditionally associated with "going to the doctor." In traditional medicine, when something is wrong with us, we fix it by taking medicine or, in more serious cases, by being treated in a hospital. Physicians have typically based their approach on the **biomedical model,** according to which all diseases or physical disorders can be explained by disturbances of physiological processes such as infection, injury, or inborn abnormality.

The biomedical model is based on the idea of **mind-body dualism** put forth by the French philosopher René Descartes (1596–1650), who believed that the mind and the body function separately from one another. According to this idea, illness is caused solely by biological processes uninfluenced by psychological processes. The biomedical model has therefore been described as an approach in which "the body is treated like a machine that is fixed by removing or replacing the ailing part or destroying the foreign body that is causing the problem" (McClelland, 1985a, p. 452).

The biomedical approach has been extremely successful. It has been responsible for eradicating many diseases and for increasing life expectancy from 50 years at the turn of the century to over 75 years currently (U. S. Department of Health and Human Services, 1987). This model analyzes health at the biological level and reasons that, since we are dealing with biological problems, we should use biological techniques to treat them.

However, the examples at the beginning of this chapter suggest that there may be more to health problems than just biology. Many health problems surface because of the way people behave, because of events in their lives, and because of the environment in which they live. This realization has led psychologists to become interested in connections between health and psychology, and to form a new discipline called health psychology.

Health Psychology

Health psychology is concerned with how psychological knowledge can contribute to promoting health, preventing and treating illness, identifying the causes of health problems, and operating a rational health system. The field of health psychology, which was established as a division of the American Psychological Association in 1978, is closely related to another field called **behavioral medicine**, which has similar goals but involves collaboration between psychologists, physicians, and biomedical scientists.

From the point of view of this book, we can state that health psychology supplements the biomedical model by adding the behavioral, cognitive, and contextual levels of analysis to understanding health and illness. To see how this might work, let's consider the case of acquired immunodeficiency syndrome (AIDS). This disease, which is acquired from the human immunodeficiency virus (HIV), will have claimed the lives of over 300,000 Americans by the end of 1994, according to the U.S. Public Health Service (Centers for Disease Control, 1993a). The virus itself has infected 8–10 million people worldwide, according to the World Health Organization (Centers for Disease Control, 1993b).

Health Psychology and AIDS

Researchers working on AIDS from a biomedical perspective have focused on identifying the mechanisms of action of the HIV virus and on developing treatments for the disease. This research has determined that AIDS is transmitted by body fluids through sexual activity, shared drug paraphernalia, and exposure to contaminated blood products. The biomedical perspective has, however, not yet developed a vaccine or a cure for AIDS.

Since the biomedical model has not yet developed a vaccine or cure, what can we do to curtail the spread of this epidemic? The answer hinges on the fact that AIDS primarily is behaviorally transmitted. Working at the behavioral level of analysis we can, therefore, ask how we can modify sexual activity and drug taking to stop the transmission of AIDS.

The fact that pleasurable and addictive behaviors such as sexual activity and drug taking are extremely difficult to regulate poses a serious problem. It is simply not realistic to expect most people to "just say no" to either of these activities. One solution is to attempt to get people to substitute lower-risk behaviors. Toward this end, programs have been instituted to convince people to clean shared needles with bleach and to practice safe sex by using condoms.

Social support for those testing HIV-positive increases their ability to cope with the diagnosis.

But making these programs work has not been easy. People must first be educated about the dangers of their behaviors and then realize that they are personally at risk (Cochran et al., 1992; Des Jarlais & Friedman, 1987). Neither of these tasks is easy, because even if people are given accurate information about how AIDS is transmitted, they often construct myths to support the idea that the problem doesn't apply to them. For example, an AIDS patient from Arizona explained that he and his friends hadn't protected themselves from AIDS by following safe sex guidelines because "there's only nine people in Arizona that have it and four of them are dead and two of them live in Tucson. So what are your chances? Even though we knew about it and we knew how awful it was, it was like, no, that's something that happens someplace else, not in Phoenix" (Weitz, 1991, p. 357).

In addition to studying ways to modify people's behavior, researchers have also studied AIDS from the behavioral perspective by looking at its side effects on mental health (especially the increases in depression and anxiety that occur in those stricken), how knowledge of the disease has altered sexual behaviors (practicing safe sex has increased, and promiscuous sex has decreased), and how childhood socialization can explain some people's resistance to changing dangerous behaviors. For example, Michael Kimmel and Martin Levine (1992) have shown that the ways in which males are socialized encourages the risk-taking behavior that has led some men to adopt the philosophy that "real" men don't worry about the risks associated with unsafe sex.

Health psychologists have also applied the cognitive level of analysis to the study of AIDS. Research has shown that gay men who are naturally optimistic experience less psychological distress, have fewer worries about AIDS, and use more effective coping strategies to deal with the possibility of AIDS infection compared with those who are not optimistic (Taylor et al., 1992).

Finally, researchers studying AIDS from a contextual point of view have shown how men testing positive for the HIV virus have been able to cope more effectively with their diagnosis if they have good social support from others and if they participate in the AIDS community in their city (Lesserman, Perkins, & Evans, 1992).

We can see from these approaches how health psychology has taken the study of AIDS beyond the biomedical model and the biological level of analysis (Figure 13.1). Similar stories can be told about other health problems such as can-

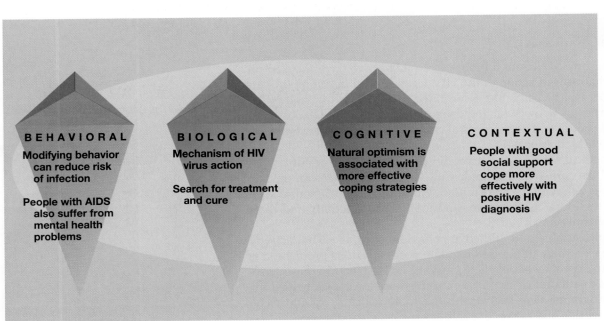

LEVELS OF ANALYSIS

FIGURE 13.1 Levels of analysis applied to AIDS research. In addition to medical research at the biological level of analysis, psychologists have identified a number of other approaches to studying AIDS at the behavioral, cognitive, and contextual levels.

BEHAVIORAL
Modifying behavior can reduce risk of infection

People with AIDS also suffer from mental health problems

BIOLOGICAL
Mechanism of HIV virus action

Search for treatment and cure

COGNITIVE
Natural optimism is associated with more effective coping strategies

CONTEXTUAL
People with good social support cope more effectively with positive HIV diagnosis

11   MOTIVATION

16   DISORDERS

9   DEVELOPMENT

cer, eating disorders, asthma, heart disease, and illnesses related to stress (Bennett, Weinman, & Spurgeon, 1990; Kaptein et al., 1990; Maes et al., 1988; Sheridan & Radmacher, 1992).

Behavior and Health

Health psychologists focus not only on specific health problems, but also on general behaviors that are connected with either good or poor health. For example, in a study that questioned nearly 7,000 people between 20 and 75 years of age about their activities, Nedra Belloc and Lester Breslow (1972) found that people's health was related to the following "healthful behaviors":

1. Sleeping seven to eight hours a day
2. Eating breakfast almost every day
3. Never or only occasionally eating between meals
4. Being at or near the appropriate weight for their height
5. Never smoking cigarettes
6. Never or moderately drinking alcohol
7. Regularly getting physical activity

The survey results indicated that older individuals who engaged in all seven of these practices had health similar to someone 30 years younger who engaged in few or none of them. In addition, as shown in Figure 13.2, the percentage of surveyed people dying in the nearly ten-year period following the initial survey was inversely related to practicing healthful behaviors (Breslow, 1983). Recently, in an extension of this study, Breslow found that good health habits decrease the chances of becoming disabled. Of those who practiced six or seven good health habits, 12.2% were disabled, whereas of those who practiced three or fewer good health habits, 18.7% were disabled (Breslow, 1993).

Health psychologists have also studied the connection between gender and health. One way to this—by looking at the statistics for males and females—reveals that males are more likely than females to die from violence (suicide and murder), accidents (motor vehicle and other), smoking (lung cancer, cancer of the mouth and pharynx, and heart attacks), drinking (cirrhosis of the liver), and aggressive, "hard-driving" behavior (heart attacks). These statistics, shown in Table 13.1, have something in common: they all represent definite links between behaviors and death. In contrast, conditions such as cerebral hemorrhage, diabetes, and arteriosclerosis that kill more women than men occur not so much because of behavior as because of old age.

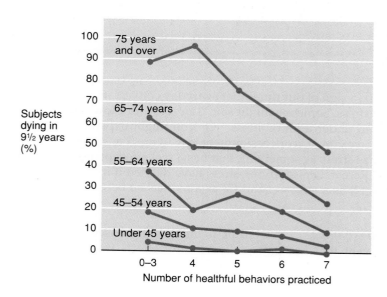

FIGURE 13.2

Belloc and Breslow found that, especially for older people, the likelihood of dying within a $9\frac{1}{2}$-year period was less for those practicing healthful behaviors.

TABLE 13.1
U.S. death statistics for males and females

Cause of Death	Male Deaths per 100 Female Deaths
Heart attack (ages 20–44)	400+
Homicide	366
Suicide	342
Auto accidents	278
Lung cancer	263
Cancer of the mouth & pharynx	250
Other accidents	218
Cirrhosis of the liver	193
Bronchitis, emphysema, & asthma	191
Heart attack (all ages)	149
Cerebral hemorrhage	89
Diabetes	73
Arteriosclerosis	69

Source: U.S. Department of Health and Human Services, 1987.

In describing the statistics for males, James Harrison and his co-workers (1992) noted something else that these behaviors have in common: they are all characteristic of the male gender role. Violence and aggression, the risk-taking behavior that leads to accidents, and daily behaviors such as smoking and drinking are all associated more with males than with females (though over the past 30 years females have been gaining in terms of smoking and drinking). Because of this connection, Harrison and his co-workers titled their article "Warning: Masculinity May Be Dangerous to Your Health."

It is clear that to fully understand health we need to go beyond the biomedical model and begin taking behavior into account. In fact, it has been estimated that behavior accounts for 40% of health statistics, and that health-related behaviors kill more people than murder, fires, suicides, and wars combined (Kaplan, Sallis, & Patterson, 1993).

In the remainder of this chapter, we will explore the relationship between behavior and health by focusing primarily on one of the most researched areas within health psychology—the nature, causes, and consequences of stress. Stress is important because it is an outcome of our modern environment that is experienced by large numbers of people, and because research has shown it to be connected with health in a number of ways. At the end of this chapter we will apply the findings of health psychology to the practical problem of coping constructively with stress.

We begin our discussion by asking exactly what stress is.

What Is Stress?

It is perhaps a sign of our times that everyday conversations are replete with references to stress. Someone might say, "I'm sorry for blowing up at you" or, "it's just that I'm under a lot of stress." Or you might explain your subpar performance on an exam or work assignment by saying "I'm stressed out." Clearly, we all recognize stress as something that has a real effect on our lives. But what exactly *is* it? Researchers studying stress have defined it in three main ways: (1) as a *stimulus*, (2) as a *response*, and (3) as a *transaction* between the person and the environment.

Stress as a stimulus.   According to the stimulus-based definition, stress is an external event that has potentially harmful effects (Jemmott & Locke, 1984). Richard Lazarus and J. B. Cohen (1977) have identified three kinds of stressful stimuli, which they call **stressors**. *Cataclysmic stressors* are powerful events such as earthquakes, floods, wars, or massive job layoffs that affect large numbers of people. *Personal stressors* are events such as failing a course, getting divorced, or losing a parent that affect individual people. *Background stressors* are day-to-day events such as being caught in a traffic jam, losing car keys, or meeting tight deadlines in a noisy workplace—things that constitute the daily hassles of life.

Stress as a response.   The response-based definition of stress focuses not on the stimulus but on its internal effects, "the emotional and biological responses to novel or threatening situations" (Riley, 1981, p. 1100). According to this definition, the sudden increase in heart rate that occurs when your car narrowly misses a pedestrian is an example of stress—not the event, notice, but the physiological response to it.

Both the stimulus-based and response-based definitions coincide to some extent with a commonsense concept of stress. However, as definitions they are inadequate, because they include situations that would not be considered stressful by everyone. For example, considering stress to be a stimulus ignores the fact that the same stimulus can elicit different responses in different people. John may feel very threatened by large dogs, whereas Roger might like them. Similarly, the response-based definition ignores the fact that some people *seek out* situations that will elicit an extreme physiological response. Riding roller coasters or taking a dip in a freezing river on New Year's Day usually causes a strong physiological response, but that response might be considered stressful by some and not others.

If stress can't be defined satisfactorily in terms of a specific stimulus or a specific response, how *can* we define it? Most psychologists subscribe to the transaction-based approach to stress that sees it as a process of interaction between the person and the environment.

Stress as a transaction.   The transaction-based approach defines stress as occurring when a person can't handle the demands of a situation. The advantage of this definition is that it allows for the fact that the same situation might be stressful for one person but not another. For example, consider how two people might react to highway construction that has traffic backed up for miles. Curt reacts by getting more and more impatient and tense. Janis, in the car next to him, realizes that there is nothing she can do about it, decides to relax, and pops a cassette into the tape deck. Of these two people, only one experiences stress.

The idea that different people react differently to the same situation led Richard Lazarus and Susan Folkman (1984) to describe the transaction between

8   THINKING

Handling snakes and shooting the rapids may be stressful to some people, but to others they are enjoyable activities.

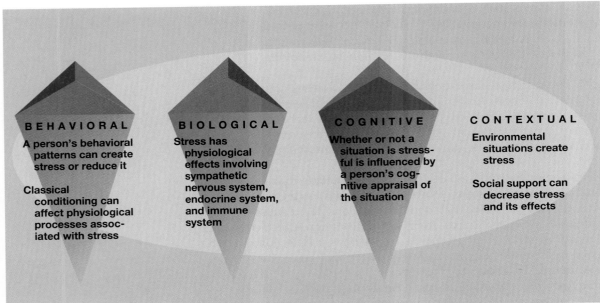

FIGURE 13.3
Behavioral, biological, cognitive, and contextual factors are associated with stress. Each of these factors is discussed in this chapter.

the person and the environment as a process of **cognitive appraisal.** This process consists of two components: primary and secondary appraisal. During *primary appraisal,* the person asks the question "How will this situation affect me?" During *secondary appraisal,* the person asks "How well can I handle this situation?"

To appreciate the difference between primary and secondary appraisal, let's consider how two people might react to a huge snowstorm. Sally's primary appraisal of the storm is positive, because it means she will get to go skiing this weekend. Her secondary appraisal is also positive, because she has plenty of food in the house and can walk to work, so she feels she will be able to handle whatever the storm brings. Ruth, however, appraises the storm negatively because one of its effects will be to make it hard for her to get to work; secondarily, when she thinks about what she will need to do to deal with the storm, she is not sure she can handle driving in the snow. As you can see from these examples, primary and secondary appraisals can interact with one another. Ruth's primary appraisal that she will have trouble getting to work is determined in part by her secondary appraisal that she will have trouble driving in the snow. The key point, however, is that Ruth's experience of the storm as stressful involves her judgment of whether she's up to dealing with the situation.

When we speak of the process of cognitive appraisal, we are describing stress at the cognitive level of analysis. But we can also examine stress at other levels of analysis: (1) at the biological level, when we look at how the body responds physiologically to stress; (2) at the behavioral level, when we see how principles of classical conditioning can affect the body's physiological response to stress; and (3) at the contextual level, when we see how the nature of a person's social environment can either increase or decrease stress (Figure 13.3). We will now explore the connections between stress and health at each of these levels of analysis.

Links Between Stress and Health

Stress can have powerful effects on many facets of behavior. The powerful emotions that often accompany stress are well known. Ending a relationship can be accompanied by sadness or depression; being confronted with a dangerous situation can result in fear; and wondering whether you will be laid off at work can cause anxiety. High levels of stress can also affect cognition by impairing people's memory and what they pay attention to (Cohen et al. 1986). Stress can also affect social behavior; for example, mothers who are under stress are less likely to provide stimulation for their children (Adamakos et al., 1986). But for our purposes the key point is the effects of stress on health. We begin our exploration of how stress affects health at the biological level of analysis by considering some research on animals.

Animal research has demonstrated a link between stress and disease by means of experiments that manipulate both the stressful stimuli and an animal's contact with a disease agent. For example, Vernon Riley (1975) injected two groups of rats with tumor cells. He then exposed one group to high stress (they were handled frequently and placed in a noisy environment) and another to low stress (they were handled rarely and placed in a quiet environment). The different levels of stress led to vastly different rates of tumor growth in the two groups. When half of the high-stress rats had developed tumors, few of the low-stress rats had, and tumor growth was slower in the low-stress rats. This result—one of the first to show a connection between stress and tumor growth—was followed by numerous other studies confirming this connection (Riley, 1981; Visintainer, Volpicelli, & Seligman, 1982).

Is there a similar connection between stress and health in humans? Since researchers can't ethically expose people to different degrees of stress and to disease agents, they have used correlational studies to look at existing relationships between stressful conditions and people's health.

Life Stress and Health

A central challenge facing psychologists who seek relationships between stress and health is how to measure the stress in people's lives. Thomas Holmes and Richard Rahe (1967) attempted to solve this problem by developing the **Social**

TABLE 13.2
Social Readjustment Rating Scale

Rank	Life Event	LCU	Rank	Life Event	LCU
1	Death of spouse	100	23	Son or daughter leaving home	29
2	Divorce	73	24	Trouble with in-laws	29
3	Marital separation	65	25	Outstanding personal achievement	28
4	Jail term	63	26	Wife begin or stop work	26
5	Death of close family member	63	27	Begin or end school	26
6	Personal injury or illness	53	28	Change in living conditions	25
7	Marriage	50	29	Revision of personal habits	24
8	Fired at work	47	30	Trouble with boss	23
9	Marital reconciliation	45	31	Change in work hours or conditions	20
10	Retirement	45	32	Change in residence	20
11	Change in health of family member	44	33	Change in schools	20
12	Pregnancy	40	34	Change in recreation	19
13	Sex difficulties	39	35	Change in church activities	19
14	Gain of new family member	39	36	Change in social activities	18
15	Business readjustment	39	37	Mortgage or loan less than $10,000	17
16	Change in financial state	38	38	Change in sleeping habits	16
17	Death of close friend	37	39	Change in number of family get-togethers	15
18	Change to different line of work	36	40	Change in eating habits	15
19	Change in number of arguments with spouse	35	41	Vacation	13
20	Mortgage over $10,000	31	42	Christmas	12
21	Foreclosure of mortgage or loan	30	43	Minor violations of the law	11
22	Change in responsibilities at work	29			

Readjustment Rating Scale (SRRS), shown in Table 13.2. The basic assumption on which this scale was constructed is that all life events involving change are potentially stressful, but that some are more stressful than others. Each of the "life events" on the scale is assigned a rating in *life change units (LCUs);* events requiring the most readjustment have the highest rating. Notice that not all the events on this scale are negative. Vacations, marriage, and outstanding personal achievements are usually seen as positive events, but they are included on the scale because they cause a change in the person's normal lifestyle. Thus, Holmes and Rahe suggested that *change itself* is a source of stress, even if the change is regarded as a positive one.

When the SRRS first appeared it attracted a great deal of attention, because it suggested a way to quantify stress and explain the connection between levels of stress and illness. And in fact a number of studies seemed to show that people with higher scores on the SRRS were somewhat more vulnerable to a variety of physical illnesses and psychological troubles. However, flaws in the way the scale was constructed and administered (see Measurement & Methodology, "The Social Readjustment Rating Scale: What Went Wrong?") led many researchers to question its value.

To replace the SRRS, Allen Kanner and his co-workers (1981) created scales that measure daily **hassles** and **uplifts**. The hassles scale is a list of 117 events that are negative in nature. The uplifts scale consists of 135 events that are seen as positive. The hassles scale was constructed on the assumption that more hassles would be associated with worse health. The uplifts scale assumes that experiencing uplifts would make hassles more bearable and would therefore be associated with better health. The most frequently mentioned hassles and uplifts from the possibilities listed in the scales are indicated in Table 13.3.

Although many of us experience some of the same hassles, we each have our own individual list. Younger people, for example, might be likely to list hassles related to social concerns or school. What would your hassles list include?

The most frequent finding of research using the hassles scale is that both the frequency and the intensity of hassles are correlated with psychological and

MEASUREMENT & METHODOLOGY

The Social Readjustment Rating Scale: What Went Wrong?

The Social Readjustment Rating Scale (SRRS) was greeted with great enthusiasm when it first appeared but was later criticized because of low correlations between life change units (LCUs) and illness. Why were these correlations so low? One reason may have been the choice of LCUs as the independent variable. Perhaps, some critics suggested, LCUs are a poor measure of stress, because stress is determined not by whether life events occur but by how people deal with them. For example, a comparison of smokers who had developed lung cancer with smokers who had not showed that both groups experienced the same LCUs, but the smokers with cancer *perceived* their life events to be more stressful than did smokers without cancer (Brody, 1983).

An even more damaging accusation levied against the SRRS was that the scale was biased. Two reasons cited for this bias are as follows:

1. *Faulty reporting:* People's memories are often faulty, or they may purposely distort their reports. People with many illnesses, for instance, might report more stressful life situations to explain their illness to themselves and others. If procedures are used to eliminate faulty reporting, correlations between LCUs and health drop nearly to zero (Schroeder & Costa, 1984).

2. *Health-related items on scale:* Items such as "personal injury or illness" or "major change in sleeping habits" are related to poor health, so it is not surprising that people who got points for those items also had the poorest health. It's a case of illness predicting illness (Rabkin & Streuning, 1976; Schroeder & Costa, 1984).

Despite all the attention the SRRS garnered when it was first proposed, it has largely been abandoned by researchers in favor of the hassles scale and others that are not as open to these weaknesses.

TABLE 13.3
The ten most frequently cited hassles and uplifts

Hassles	*Uplifts*
1. Concerns about weight	1. Relating well with spouse or lover
2. Health of a family member	2. Relating well with friends
3. Rising prices of common goods	3. Completing a task
4. Home maintenance	4. Feeling healthy
5. Too many things to do	5. Getting enough sleep
6. Misplacing or losing things	6. Eating out
7. Yard work or outside home maintenance	7. Meeting responsibilities
8. Property, investment, or taxes	8. Visiting, phoning, or writing someone
9. Crime	9. Spending time with family
10. Physical appearance	10. Home (inside) pleasing to you

physical health. These correlations, which range from about .25 to .35, are an improvement over those obtained with life change units, and they appear to be more valid (Delongis et al., 1982; Kanner et al., 1981; Weinberger, Hiner, & Tierney, 1987). Research with the uplifts scale, in contrast, has shown little correlation between uplifts and health (DeLongis et al., 1982).

Why do hassles predict health problems better than major life events do? Probably because hassles are a more accurate indication of the things that actually cause stress for people. Whereas divorce is near the top of the SRRS, its actual effect may vary for different people, depending on the degree of hassle connected with it. In addition to the possible emotional upset of a dissolving relationship, for some people divorce brings hassles such as the pressures of single parenthood and having to do things, such as cooking meals or maintaining the car, that the person rarely did during the marriage. For other people, this change in daily routine is less significant, or even positive, bringing more money, more free time, and new friends, for instance. What happens day in and day out, according to Lazarus, affects people more than do large, dramatic events, and it is therefore reasonable to assume that day-to-day hassles are better predictors of health problems.

Whereas Lazarus's hassles scale relates personal stressors to health, other studies have looked at the relationship between cataclysmic stressors and health, comparing the health of people who have experienced disasters with the health of people who have not. One such study followed up on the March 1979 accident at the Three Mile Island, Pennsylvania, nuclear power plant. Following the near-meltdown at the plant, people living near the reactor experienced serious stress because of concerns about the effects of possible radiation exposure. Figure 13.4 indicates that these people reported almost twice as many physical symptoms

FIGURE 13.4
Physical symptoms and depression scores of people living near the Three Mile Island nuclear reactor at the time of the accident were higher than those of people living near an undamaged nuclear plant or no plant.

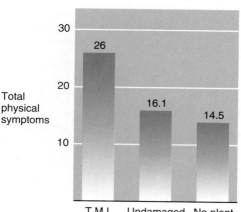

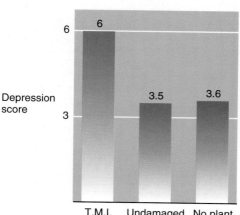

and were almost twice as high on a measure of depression as people who lived near undamaged nuclear plants or people who lived far from any plant (Baum, Gatchel, & Schaeffer, 1983).

Similar findings were obtained after the May 1980 eruption of Mount Saint Helens, in Washington State, which deposited large amounts of ash in the surrounding area. Problems in dealing with the fallen ash, plus the continuing threat of further eruptions, stressed the residents of the nearby town of Othello. As a result there were substantial increases in the use of mental health crisis lines, in hospital emergency room visits, and in reports of domestic violence, as shown in Figure 13.5 (Adams & Adams, 1984).

The link between stress and health has also been assessed by studying people in high-stress occupations. One job that can be extremely stressful is held by air traffic controllers, the people who guide planes to safe takeoffs and landings at airports. When Sidney Cobb and Robert Rose (1973) compared the medical records of air traffic controllers who worked at extremely busy airports (high stress) with those who worked at less busy airports (low stress), they found a greater prevalence of hypertension (prolonged high blood pressure) in the high-stress group (Figure 13.6). (In the Follow-Through at the end of the chapter we will also see that the stresses associated with being a member of a minority group may be partly responsible for the high prevalence of hypertension in African Americans.)

One reason that hypertension is a serious health problem is that it is one of the main risk factors for **coronary heart disease (CHD).** This disease encompasses a number of conditions that result from the narrowing or blocking of arteries that serve the heart. Two of the most common are (1) *arteriosclerosis*, in which the walls of the coronary arteries become hardened through the buildup of cholesterol-rich *plaques*, and (2) *myocardial infarction* (heart attack), which occurs when the blood supply to the heart is blocked for a prolonged period. Heart attacks are experienced by about 1.5 million people in the United States each year, and more than one-third are fatal (Krantz & Deckel, 1983).

What is the evidence for a connection between stress and CHD? One piece of suggestive evidence is that CHD is more prevalent in modern industrialized societies (Susser, Hopper, & Richman, 1983). However, modern industrialized societies bring with them many conditions in addition to possibilities for high stress. A more direct demonstration of the connection between stress and heart disease is the association between CHD and high work loads, job dissatisfaction, and high levels of job responsibility (Cottington & House, 1987).

FIGURE 13.5
Emergency room visits and calls to a mental health crisis line increased for the residents of Othello, Washington, following the eruption of Mt. St. Helens.

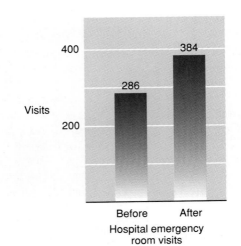

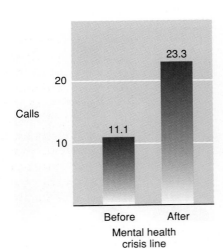

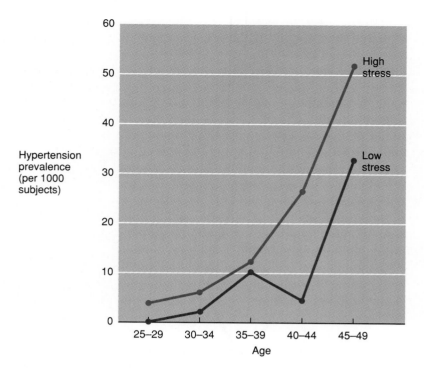

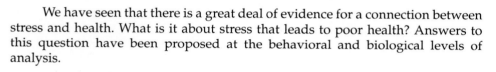

FIGURE 13.6
Air-traffic controllers who work in the high-stress environment of busy airports have a higher incidence of hypertension than do those who work in the lower-stress environment of less-busy airports.

We have seen that there is a great deal of evidence for a connection between stress and health. What is it about stress that leads to poor health? Answers to this question have been proposed at the behavioral and biological levels of analysis.

How Stress Affects Health

Stress can affect a person's health in a number of ways. Behaviorally, people under stress may be more likely to engage in unhealthful activities, such as consuming alcohol, smoking, and drinking coffee (Baer et al., 1987; Conway et al., 1981). They may also be more careless and therefore have more accidents (Lowenstein, 1991). Physiologically, stress affects systems that are designed to help the body cope with short-term stressors. The activation of these systems can result in health problems if stress is prolonged.

The basic physiological effects of stress are diagramed in Figure 13.7. Remember, from our description of the nervous system in Chapter 3, that the sympathetic nervous system is activated by situations such as emergencies in which the body is challenged. We saw that one of the responses of the sympathetic nervous system is to stimulate the adrenal gland to secrete the hormones *epinephrine* and *norepinephrine*, which in turn cause acceleration of the heart to help deal with the emergency. In addition, stress activates the endocrine system, triggering the release of the hormone *cortisol* into the bloodstream. This hormone helps reduce swelling that might occur in response to injury.

Thus, in situations perceived as threatening, these "stress hormones" are released to help the body deal with the short-term stressful emergency. If, however, the stress is sudden and extremely intense, large amounts of these hormones secreted into the bloodstream can cause erratic heartbeat and even death from a heart attack. Or, if the stress is prolonged, the continual presence of the stress hormones can cause the buildup of fatty patches, or plaques, on the artery walls. This can increase blood pressure and lead to heart problems (McKinney et al., 1984).

Besides these effects, the constant presence of stress hormones during long-term stress can interfere with the **immune system**—the system that protects the

3   BIOLOGY

FIGURE 13.7

Physiological effects of stress. In response to stress, the hypothalamus activates two pathways leading to the adrenal gland. In the endocrine system, the pituitary gland releases adrenocorticotropic hormone (ACTH) into the blood, which stimulates the adrenal gland to secrete cortisol. In the sympathetic nervous system, the neurons cause the adrenal gland to release epinephrine and norepinephrine.

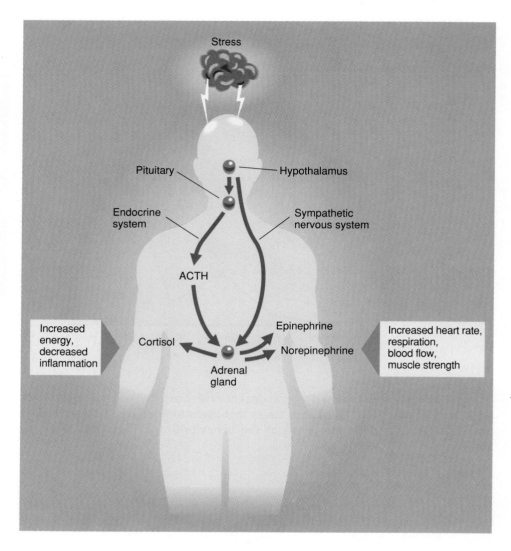

FIGURE 13.8

The immune system in action. A killer cell attacks a larger tumor cell.

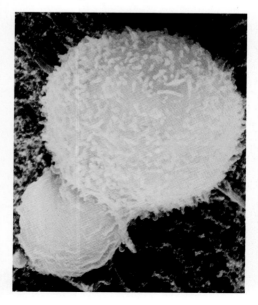

body from disease-carrying microorganisms. As shown in Figure 13.8, the immune system releases cells such as T-cells and NK (natural killer) cells to combat viruses and attack the foreign cells introduced by cancers. The study of the interaction between stress and the immune system is an extremely active area of research in health psychology. However, the discovery of this interaction came about from some experiments that were not concerned with the immune system at all. Let's look at those experiments, which were carried out by biologist Hans Selye.

In the 1940s and 1950s, Selye (1956, 1978) performed some classic experiments on how mice react to long-term stress. After exposing mice to prolonged low temperatures and other stressful situations, Selye found that they reacted to these stressors in three stages, which he called the **general adaptation syndrome** (Figure 13.9). In the first stage of the syndrome, the **alarm stage,** the autonomic nervous system (ANS) and endocrine system release hormones into the bloodstream, which energizes the body to help it deal with the situation. In the next stage, the **resistance stage,** the body continues to fight back as the stress continues. Eventually, if the stress continues for too long, the animal enters the **exhaustion stage,** becomes exhausted, and dies. When Selye autopsied the mice, he observed that their adrenal glands were enlarged and that their thymus glands and lymph nodes were shrunken. The significance of this finding lies in the fact that these are all key structures in the operation of the immune system.

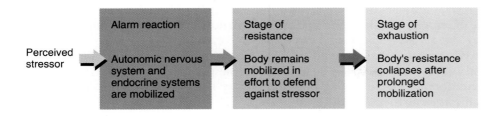

FIGURE 13.9
The response to long-term stress, which Selye called the general adaptation syndrome, consists of three stages: alarm reaction, resistance, and exhaustion.

Why does long-term stress affect immune system structures? The answer lies in the properties of the stress hormones—epinephrine, norepinephrine, and cortisol—released by the ANS and endocrine system in response to stress. Although these hormones help mobilize the body to deal with stressful situations, they are also **immunosuppressants**—substances that decrease the efficiency of the immune system. The resulting immune system suppression, which can leave the body open to attack by viruses and cancer cells, isn't a serious problem if the stress is short-lived. But it does become serious if the stress continues, as it did in Selye's experiments.

MEASUREMENT & METHODOLOGY

The White Coat Effect: False High Blood Pressure in the Doctor's Office

A physician measures Mary's blood pressure in his office and diagnoses her as being hypertensive, based on her high blood pressure reading. If, however, her blood pressure had been measured at home, the diagnosis would have been different: she has normal blood pressure there. What's going on here?

Mary is experiencing the **white coat effect,** a rise in blood pressure as measured in the physician's office compared with at home (Pickering & Friedman, 1991). This effect has been documented in many different situations in which a person's blood pressure is measured in the presence of an authority figure or high-status person. For instance, the blood pressure of army recruits is higher when measured by a captain than by a private (Reiser, Reeves, & Armington, 1958). Blood pressure rises twice as much when a male physician approaches a patient as when a female nurse approaches (Reiser et al., 1958). Even just talking to higher-status people causes many to experience a greater rise in blood pressure than does talking to lower-status people (Long et al., 1982).

How can we explain the white coat effect? According to Thomas Pickering and Richard Friedman (1991), the rise in blood pressure probably reflects the response of the body's defense mechanisms to threatening situations. The physician, seen as a bearer of bad news, activates those defense mechanisms. On subsequent visits, the white coat effect is maintained by classical conditioning, since the person associates not only the physician but the clinic setting itself with danger. Similiar considerations apply to other high-status figures who can be perceived as threatening.

What is the practical importance of the white coat effect? Researchers can take steps to minimize this effect when collecting data that involve measuring blood pressure. But what is more important than its potential to distort research findings, the white coat effect may be causing many basically healthy Americans to be misclassified as hypertensive and to be subjected to costly and unnecessary drug treatments that may cause undesirable side effects. One solution to this problem is for physicians to create a friendly atmosphere in their office and to have nurses measure their patients' blood pressure.

Many people experience a rise in blood pressure when confronted with authority figures, such as police officers and doctors.

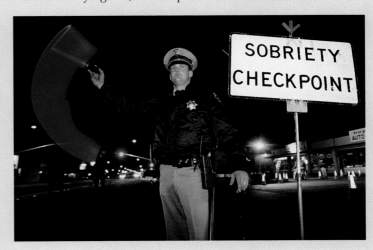

Having seen that prolonged stress can elicit a physiological reaction capable of crippling the immune system, we will now entertain a hypothesis that, before the 1970s, would have been considered radical. This hypothesis is that the body's immune system, whose functioning was once thought to be automatic and purely biological, can be affected by the psychological process of classical conditioning. The following Interdisciplinary Dimension recounts how that hypothesis came to be accepted.

INTERDISCIPLINARY DIMENSION IMMUNOLOGY

Conditioning the Immune Response

The immune system is constantly fighting off microorganisms that could cause disease. It surprises many people to hear this, because they think of the immune system as active primarily when a person is exposed to a specific disease that is "going around." But you are exposed to microorganisms all the time. They enter your body in your food, live in your intestines, are in the air you breathe, and enter your mouth when you touch your fingers to your lips.

You are unaware of the constant activity of the immune system because of its efficiency. Its battle against microorganisms is usually successful, so you take it for granted. But without the immune system, you would be sick all the time. When the immune system breaks down, as it does in AIDS, the eventual result is death from diseases such as pneumonia and other viral infections.

We now pose a question. Can the operation of the immune system be affected by psychological factors? The biomedical model's conception of the immune system solely in terms of physiological mechanisms is consistent with Descartes's idea that the mind and body are separate. But in the last few decades, evidence has been accumulating to support the idea that the mind can influence physiological processes. For example, we know that giving a sick person a **placebo**—a pill with no active ingredients—actually improves the person's condition in about 35% of the cases (Weisenberg, 1977). Since there is no physiologically active ingredient in the placebo, we can conclude that taking the pill triggers a psychological process that, in turn, activates a physiological mechanism that improves the person's condition.

One of the most fascinating pieces of evidence connecting psychological processes with physiological mechanisms is contained in a paper by Robert Ader and Nicholas Cohen (1975; also see 1984, 1985, 1993), which shows that the action of the immune system can be influenced by classical conditioning.

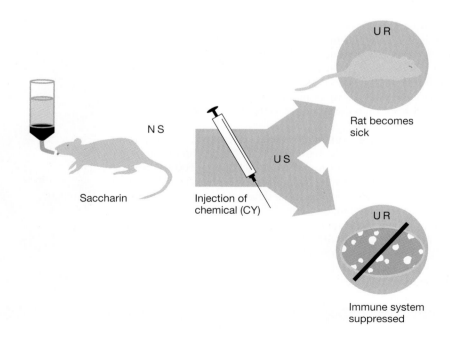

FIGURE 13.10
Ader paired the neutral stimulus (saccharin) with a CY injection that both made the rat sick and suppressed its immune system. This pairing caused the saccharin to become a conditioned stimulus, causing both sickness and immune system suppression.

In 1974 Ader was conducting a learning experiment using a conditioned taste aversion procedure to condition rats to avoid saccharin. Rats drank a saccharin solution and were then made sick by an injection of the chemical cyclophosphamide (CY). After only a few trials saccharin became a conditioned stimulus, so that when presented alone it caused the rats to become sick. The rats, therefore, stopped drinking the saccharin solution when they had a choice between plain water and water with saccharin. After establishing this avoidance of saccharin, Ader began forcing the rats to drink the saccharin (without the CY injections), to extinguish the avoidance. (Remember that a response extinguishes if the conditioned stimulus is repeatedly presented without the unconditioned stimulus.) Eventually, however, something strange started happening: the rats began dying!

At first, Ader was baffled about what could be causing these unexpected deaths. He came up with the answer when he realized that CY, the chemical injected to cause sickness, was an immunosuppressant. The CY injections presented during conditioning were, therefore, having two effects: (1) they made the animals sick, and (2) they suppressed the rats' immune systems. Thus, pairing the CY with saccharin had apparently transferred these two properties to saccharin (Figure 13.10). As a result of the conditioning, saccharin now made the rats sick *and* suppressed their immune system.

To test the idea that saccharin had triggered immunosuppression, Ader enlisted the help of Nicholas Cohen, an immunologist. Ader and Cohen ran an experiment using three groups of rats. On day 1 of the experiment the *conditioned group* drank saccharin and then received an injection of CY. The *unconditioned group* drank water and then received an injection of CY. The *control group* just drank water and received an injection of saline (Figure 13.11). On day 4 the conditioned and unconditioned groups were offered saccharin to drink and were then injected with red blood cells from sheep, which would normally cause their immune systems to produce antibodies to attack the foreign blood cells.

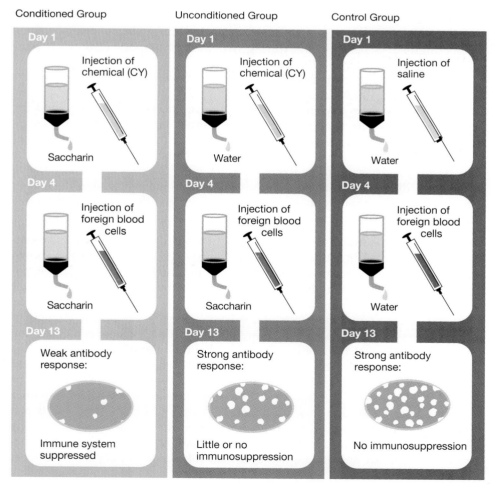

FIGURE 13.11

The design for Ader and Cohen's experiment, which showed that saccharin had become an immunosuppressant.

Based on the treatment these two groups received on day 1, how would you expect drinking saccharin on day 4 to affect the rats' immune systems? Since saccharin was paired with CY for the conditioned rats on day 1, we would expect the saccharin to be a conditioned stimulus and act as an immunosuppressant when consumed by the conditioned rats on day 4. These rats should, therefore, have weakened immune systems. This would not occur, however, for the rats in the unconditioned group or in the control group, which did not receive saccharin on day 1. Their immune systems should, therefore, function normally and mount an attack on the foreign red blood cells.

Ader and Cohen tested this prediction on day 13 by measuring the antibody response triggered by the red blood cells. As predicted, the unconditioned and control groups mounted a strong antibody response (see the white "antibodies" at the bottom of Figure 13.11). However, the antibody response of the conditioned group was weak—they produced only about a quarter of the antibodies that the other rats did. The saccharin solution had, as predicted, suppressed the conditioned group's immune system.

Ader and Cohen's result, which was considered a radical finding at the time, led to the founding of a new field—**psychoneuroimmunology**—the study of the effects of psychology and the nervous system on the immune system. Based on the research generated by this new field, physicians have become aware that curing illness may involve more than simply prescribing drugs or performing surgery. ■

After Ader and Cohen demonstrated that the rat's immune system can be affected by psychological processes, researchers began gathering evidence showing that stress suppresses the functioning of the immune system in humans. Here are some examples of that evidence.

• Skylab astronauts have decreased concentrations of T-cells after splashdown compared with preflight measures (Anderson, 1982; Kimzey et al., 1976).

• A study of dental students measured the concentration of an antibody that defends against upper respiratory infection immediately prior to three exams (high-stress periods) and during two vacation periods (low-stress periods). The results (Figure 13.12) indicate that antibody concentrations were low during the high-stress periods and high during the low-stress periods (Jemmott et al., 1983; Jemmott & Magloire, 1988).

• Several studies have demonstrated a connection between stress and the herpes virus infection. People who have the herpes virus may show no symptoms, since the virus usually lies dormant in the body in its inactive phase. However, when the virus becomes active it causes blisters and "cold sores" on the skin, and these sores are more likely to occur when the person is under stress. Apparently, during stressful periods the body's immune response to the herpes virus is decreased, thereby increasing the chances that these sores will appear (Cohen & Williamson, 1991).

All of these examples are of situations in which increased stress is accompanied by decreased immune system functioning. Researchers have also shown that lowering stress can improve immune system functioning. For example, patients who are infected with HIV have stronger immune systems and live longer if they relax or exercise regularly (Antoni et al., 1991). The effects of this relaxation and exercise equal the effects of the drug AZT, which is used to strengthen the immune systems of patients who are HIV positive. Or consider George, the husband described at the beginning of this chapter, who died shortly after his wife? The increased chances of death in husbands whose wives have just died has been documented (Bowling, 1987; Clayton, 1990) and appears to occur, at least in part, because the bereaved husband's immune system is impaired (Kiecolt-Glaser, 1986). But in a study of 23 spouses of female cancer patients, Robert S. Baron and his co-workers (1990) showed that those whose stress was alleviated by support from friends and relatives had immune systems that functioned more rapidly and at a higher level than subjects with poor social support networks.

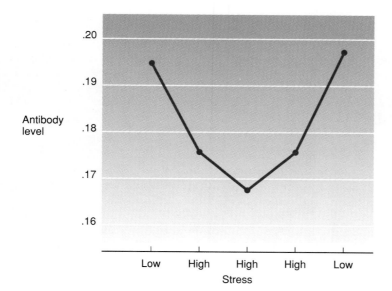

FIGURE 13.12
Dental students had high antibody levels during vacation periods and low levels during high-stress periods just prior to exams. The lowered antibody levels indicate a weakened immune system.

The important point about all of these links among stress, the immune system, and health is that psychological factors do play some role in the body's ability to ward off disease—a proposition that may seem self-evident today but that has gained acceptance only after careful research.

One of the implications of this link between stress and health is that we can exert some control over our health by controlling our stress. Norman Cousins, a magazine editor and author, took control of his stress when he was diagnosed with a connective tissue disease that in some cases is fatal. As part of his cure he watched videotapes of comedies, since his theory was that laughter reduces stress and helps cure illness. After Cousins conquered his illness he wrote a book, *Anatomy of an Illness,* describing his use of laughter, positive thinking, and other ways of taking control of his situation, as therapy. Although we do not know exactly how important Cousins's laughter was in effecting his cure (Sheridan & Radmacher, 1992), it is conceivable, based on the results of research in health psychology, that his unorthodox therapy may have done at least some good.

The effect of psychological interventions on disease has been demonstrated most clearly by studies that show that receiving social support can be beneficial to health. What is it about receiving support from others that enhances a person's health? Is it based purely on the good feelings associated with being with others, or is it that other people might provide practical help in dealing with specific problems? As we will see in the next section, there is evidence that social support provides both of these benefits, plus others as well.

Social Support and Health

In the aftermath of Hurricane Andrew, which devastated southern Florida in 1993, came stories of thousands of families left without food and shelter. But the stories were different for different people. Some described people being taken in by friends or relatives, or people using their savings to reconstruct their homes. Other stories described people being left alone with few resources to deal with the aftermath of this disaster. These stories illustrate differences in social support that, as we will see, have potential implications for health.

Social support, the resources provided to us through our interactions with other people (Sheridan & Radmacher, 1992), helps people in a number of different ways. *Tangible support* provides specific things we need to help solve the problem or to make life easier. After the Florida hurricane, the government pro-

19   SOCIAL

The aftermath of Hurricane Andrew, which struck Florida in 1992. The soldier helping a victim find clothing is an example of tangible support.

vided tangible support via temporary housing in tent cities. Similarly, relatives who provided places to stay were providing tangible support. If those relatives also expressed their concern and listened to their guests' feelings about their plight, they were also offering *emotional support*. Closely related to emotional support is *esteem support*, any activities that help people keep their self-esteem. Knowing that others love us is one source of self-esteem. Providing employment, which would be a form of tangible support, might also help build self-esteem. Finally, *informational support* provides advice on how to deal with the problem and feedback on how the person is doing.

Does social support accomplish more than helping people survive, making them feel better, and helping them cope with their problems more effectively? There is a great deal of evidence that, in addition to these benefits, social support has beneficial effects on health.

When Robert Hays and his co-workers (1992) had AIDS patients rate how satisfied they were with their social support, people who were more satisfied were also less depressed. One of the classic studies on social support, carried out by Lisa Berkman and Leonard Syme (1979), followed the health and social support systems of residents of Alameda County, California, for nine years. It found a clear relationship between social support and health. People who had more social ties in the form of church membership, marriage, contact with family and friends, and other affiliations were less likely to die in the nine-year period of the study than those with few social ties (Figure 13.13). The effect was especially pronounced for the oldest group (people in their 60s at the start of the study).

In response to the Alameda County study, some researchers raised the question of cause and effect. Could the relationship between low social support and poor health simply be that people who were less healthy in the first place tended to be the type of people who have fewer social relationships? James House, Cynthia Robbins, and Helen Metzner (1982) answered this question in a study similar to Berkman and Syme's but with an important addition: they carried out medical examinations of all the participants at the beginning of the study. They found that, even when health status at the beginning of the study was equal for participants with high and low social support, the participants with low social support were more likely to have died during the nine and a half years of their study. In a related study, House and his co-workers (1988) concluded that "more socially isolated individuals are less healthy, psychologically and physically, and more likely to die" (p. 540). This finding has been confirmed in studies of people suffering from a major illness or high levels of stress. For example, a study of women with advanced breast cancer found that women who were not members of cancer support groups lived an average of 18 months less than those who were, even though all the women were taking the same medications (Goleman, 1991).

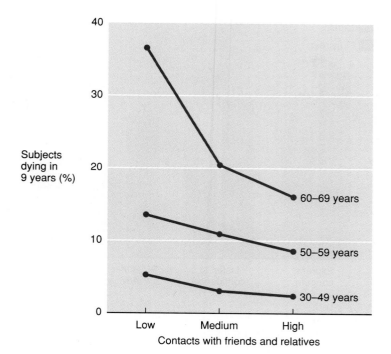

Subjects dying in 9 years (%)

60–69 years

50–59 years

30–49 years

Low   Medium   High

Contacts with friends and relatives

FIGURE 13.13
Results of the Alameda County study show that people with more social support, as measured by contacts with friends and relatives, were less likely to die within the nine-year period studied. This effect is greatest for older people.

How, exactly, does social support influence health? Two hypotheses have been proposed to explain how social support is physically beneficial to health: the *buffering hypothesis* and the *main effect hypothesis*. According to the **buffering hypothesis,** social support provides a buffer that protects people against high stress. This might occur in a number of ways. Receiving support might lead people to feel better able to deal with a stressful situation and might therefore change their cognitive appraisal so they are less likely to perceive the situation as stressful. Or perhaps receiving advice might help individuals cope more successfully with a stress-producing problem, thus diminishing the source of the stress.

In a study of college students, Carolyn Cutrona (1986) had subjects keep a diary of stressful events and social contacts over a two-week period. On the average, the students experienced a stressful event every two days, ranging from minor ones like arguing with their roommate to major ones like finding out that a parent had been diagnosed with cancer. (A result that surprised the researchers was that 20% of the students reported major stressful events over the 14-day period of the study.) Did these students use social support as a buffer against the effects of stress? Analysis of the students' diary entries suggests that they did. On days when they experienced a stressful situation, they also participated in more giving and receiving of social support (Figure 13.14).

The **main effect hypothesis** of social support says that a person's social network provides benefits both during stress and when there is no stress. Being married, attending a church or synagogue, and participating in organizations are all factors that can provide support and enhance a person's well-being, whether stress is present or not (Ganster & Victor, 1988). Berkman and Syme's Alameda County study provides evidence for the main effect hypothesis, since it demonstrates a relationship between social networks and health. Apparently, the beneficial effects of social support on health occur both because of continual support from a person's social network and from the buffering effects of support given in response to stress (Cohen & Wills, 1985).

Before you decide to improve your health by devoting a much larger proportion of your time to social activities, note that social support is not always beneficial to health. Joining a street gang might offer social support but might also endanger your health. Another, more likely, example of how social connections can have negative effects on health is the situation that sometimes occurs when women who have large, close-knit social networks of family and friends

FIGURE 13.14
When students experienced stressful situations, they were more likely to engage in social interactions. Simply initiating interactions with others, whether it involves giving or receiving support, may help some people relieve the effects of stress.

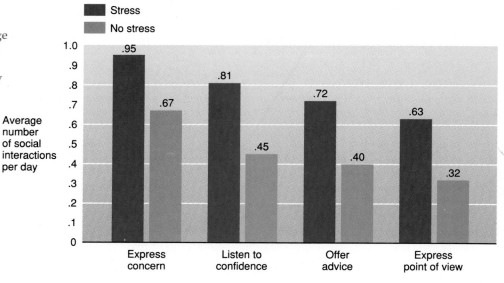

experience the stress of worrying not only about their own problems but about others' as well (Solomon, Mikulincer, & Hobfoll, 1987).

Our discussion so far has treated social support as something that happens to people—either you have it or you don't. But social support usually does not just "happen": people create it for themselves by their actions and, to some extent, by the nature of their personality. A person who is likable, sociable, and active in the community is much more likely to have a good social support network than a person who stays home and avoids interacting with others. We will now see how the effects of personality can extend to other behaviors that can have a large impact on health.

Personality and Health

Are some people more illness-prone than others due to their personalities? Research on the effects of personality on health have shown how various personality characteristics can lead to behaviors that are both beneficial and damaging to health.

15   PERSONALITY

One of the best-known links between personality and health is a negative one—the link between "Type A personality" and coronary heart disease (CHD). A person with a Type A personality demonstrates qualities such as competitiveness, hostility, and high energy. As we look at the history of research on the Type A personality we will see strong evidence that some of these Type A qualities are related to heart disease, whereas others are not.

What could be the physiological basis of a link between personality and CHD? One possibility is that people with certain characteristics may behave so as to subject themselves to high levels of stress. The link between stress and heart problems was noted by numerous early physicians. William Harvey, who did pioneering work on the operation of the cardiovascular system in the 17th century, stated that "every affection of the mind that is attended with either pain or pleasure, hope or fear, is the cause of an agitation whose influence extends to the heart" (1628). The 19th-century cardiologist Sir William Osler felt that heart diseases arose from "the high pressure at which men live and the habit of working the machine to its maximum capacity" (1892).

Modern research on possible links between stress and CHD was stimulated by the observations of two cardiologists, Meyer Friedman and Ray Rosenman (1974), who noticed that their patients tended to be agitated and always in a hurry. Their clients' impatience was reflected by the fact that when Friedman and Rosenman had the chairs in their waiting room reupholstered, the upholsterer noted that the fabric was selectively worn out on the front edges. The patients were apparently feeling so impatient that they were literally "sitting on the edge of their chairs."

At first Friedman and Rosenman called the pattern of behavior exhibited by their heart patients the "hurry up syndrome," but later they changed it to the more scientific-sounding **Type A behavior pattern (TABP).** People with TABP were generally observed to have the following characteristics:

- high competitiveness
- a sense of urgency and impatience
- a tendency to become angry or hostile
- difficulty relaxing
- an intense need for recognition and advancement
- a high energy level
- accelerated physical and mental activity
- a tendency to do two or more things at once

Friedman and Rosenman tested the idea that TABP is a risk factor for CHD by studying 3154 men between the ages of 39 and 59. These men, who were free of CHD at the beginning of the study, were classified as either Type A (with TABP) or Type B (no TABP) by means of the Structured Interview (see Measurement & Methodology, "Identifying Coronary-Prone Behavior"). Eight and a half

MEASUREMENT & METHODOLOGY

Identifying Coronary-Prone Behavior

How can we determine whether a person is impatient, hostile, and aggressive—and therefore at risk for coronary heart disease (CHD)? Friedman and Rosenman developed a way to answer this question, which they called the **Structured Interview**. In the Structured Interview, subjects are asked a series of questions about their behavior in various situations (Friedman & Powell, 1984; Rosenman,

People who engage in high-stress Type A behaviors often have little insight into their own behaviors.

1978; Rosenman, Swan, & Carmelli, 1988). Since people who engage in Type A behavior typically do not have much insight into their own behavior, their actual answers are of little importance. What counts are their *emotional reactions* during the interview.

To elicit these reactions, the interviewer behaves in a way designed to frustrate the subject, asking questions very slowly and sometimes stuttering. Subjects at risk for CHD tend to become impatient. This impatience is measured by noting the peron's style of speaking—speech that is loud, explosive, and rapid-fire indicates the Type A behavior pattern that puts subjects at risk for CHD. The point of this test, therefore, is to give subjects the impression that the interviewer is paying attention to *what* they are saying, whereas in reality the interviewer is noting *how* they are saying it.

The Structured Interview has proved to be reliable—that is, the ratings are fairly similar for different raters and fairly stable over time for a particular subject (Jenkins, Rosenman, & Friedman, 1968). But it is a difficult test to administer and requires that testers be trained. To dispense with these problems, alternative paper-and-pencil tests to measure risk for CHD have been developed (Jenkins, Rosenman, & Zyzanski, 1974). Although this kind of test is easier to administer than the Structured Interview, it predicts CHD less reliably because it rests on the ability of Type A people to do something they find difficult—answer questions about their own behavior. Since the Structured Interview does not depend on these answers, it remains the more accurate way to predict CHD in people with Type A behavior pattern.

FIGURE 13.15
Of the numerous characteristics that have been identified as part of the Type A behavior pattern, only a few—anger, hostility, and a tendency to distrust others—are linked to a higher risk for coronary heart disease.

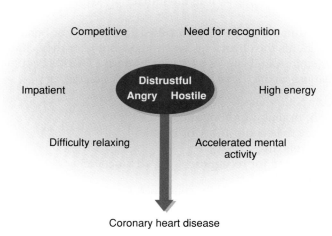

years after this initial classification, the Type A group was twice as likely to have experienced symptoms of CHD as the Type B group.

Based on this study and other research that followed it, a panel of scientists at the National Heart, Lung and Blood Institute concluded that TABP was a risk factor for CHD. For the first time, the medical community at large accepted that a psychological factor was implicated in a physical syndrome. High-energy, driven people (sometimes described as "workaholics") were urged to slow down or risk suffering heart attacks (Dembroski & Czajkowski, 1989).

But more recent research has shown that the energized, driven workaholic is not necessarily at high risk for CHD. Apparently, only certain characteristics of the Type A syndrome endanger health. People who are prone to hostility, who react to small frustrations with anger, and who distrust others are most at risk for CHD (Barefoot et al., 1983, 1987; Dembroski & Czajkowski, 1989; Weidner et al., 1987).

One study that supports this conclusion looked at the hostility scores on a personality test given to 255 medical students in the 1950s. When these subjects were recontacted 30 years after taking the test, those with hostility scores above the median were found to be five times more likely to have CHD (Barefoot et al., 1983). Apparently, of the many behaviors originally associated with TABP, hostility and anger are the primary risk factors for CHD (Figure 13.15).

What is it about being hostile, angry, and distrustful that might lead to heart disease? Robin DiMatteo (1991) points to one possible mechanism by drawing an analogy with a car driven with its accelerator floored and brakes on. She explains that when people are emotionally distressed, their accelerated heart is attempting to pump more blood through blood vessels that, because of the stress, are constricted. The end result is wear and tear on the arteries.

Another explanation is based on the hormones that are released as the autonomic nervous system responds to stress. Remember that the release of the hormones epinephrine, norepinephrine, and cortisol has the short-term beneficial effect of mobilizing the body to deal with stress. However, if a person is constantly reacting to even small incidents as if they were emergencies, then these hormones begin having harmful effects, including suppression of the immune system. A person who frequently becomes agitated—for instance, becoming enraged because a fellow shopper has 14 items in her shopping cart in the "12 items or less" checkout line—may be suppressing his immune system by constantly overreacting to trivial occurrences.

Whereas research on the Type A behavior pattern shows a negative connec-

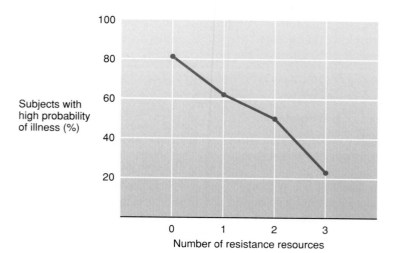

FIGURE 13.16
The resistance resources of exercise, social support, and hardiness all contribute to better health. In this study, executives with more resistance resources were less likely to become ill.

tion between personality and health, research on a personality characteristic called *hardiness* shows a positive connection. Suzanne Kobasa (1979) developed the idea of the **hardy personality**—a person who tends to be committed to work, relationships, and activities (rather than being apathetic or bored with these things); who takes control of situations (rather than acting powerless); and who sees change as a challenge and a possible opportunity for personal growth (rather than as a threat). Kobasa has found that people with these characteristics tend to be less affected by stress because they transform events that some people would consider stressful into challenges and opportunities, which are less stressful (Banks & Gannon, 1988).

When Kobasa and her co-workers (1982) studied a group of executives, they found that the ones with characteristics of the hardy personality suffered from only minor illnesses (such as colds and sore throats), whereas those without those characteristics had serious health problems (such as cancer and heart attacks). In another study, Kobasa and her co-workers (1985) studied the relationship between illness and three "resistance resources"—exercise, social support, and hardiness—in highly stressed business executives. They found that having more of these resources decreased the chances of becoming ill and that, of the three, hardiness was the most important (Figure 13.16).

In addition to reinforcing the relationship between psychological factors and health, Kobasa's studies of business executives and many of the other studies described in this chapter have important practical implications because they point to behavioral changes that can improve health. In the next section we explore some of these implications by looking at practical ways of coping with stress.

Applying Health Psychology: Coping with Stress

How do you cope with the stress in your life? Consider, for example, your behavior around exam time. Do you take steps to reduce the anxiety you may feel about the exam by finding a knowledgeable classmate to study with? Do you decide that grades aren't that important to you, so why study? Do you decide to go jogging to relieve the tension you are feeling?

Each of these approaches represents one of the following ways of dealing with a problem that is causing stress:

- Attacking the problem (finding a study partner)
- Rethinking the problem (deciding grades aren't a priority)
- Lessening the effects of the problem (going jogging)

Let's take a closer look at each of these ways of dealing with stress.

Attacking the Problem

In some cases we can alleviate stress by treating it as a problem to be solved and by taking appropriate action to solve it.

8   THINKING

Coping through problem solving.   A common reaction to a stressful situation is to solve the problem by changing it. Before an exam, you may feel stressed because you're having trouble understanding the material. You can change this situation in a number of ways: you can set aside more time to study; you can get help from a classmate who knows the material; you can ask the professor for help; or you can escape the situation by withdrawing from the course. This last way of dealing with stress is analogous to the tried-and-true way of dealing with physical danger—fleeing from the situation to avoid physical harm. Note that this particular solution, though excellent for avoiding physical harm, could be a poor option if overused in certain situations. Clearly, withdrawing from a course every time you are stressed by an exam will greatly decrease your chances of receiving your degree.

For most problems, there are numerous possible courses of action that minimize stress by changing the situation. In the examples just listed, the courses of action are *reactions* to the stress. In other cases, these courses of action can be of a *preventive* nature. Using time management to set aside time during the day for activities you want to accomplish is a way of keeping potentially stressful situations from occurring. For example, taking a few minutes in the evening to be sure you have gas in your car may make the morning rush to get to school or work on time a little less stressful. Similarly, planning your studying so that you keep up over the term is an obvious preventive antidote to exam-related stress.

Is there a particular type of person who might use problem-solving techniques to cope with stress? Michael Scheier and his co-workers (1989) showed that of a group of 51 middle-aged men who underwent coronary bypass surgery, those who were more optimistic were more likely to use problem solving than those who were pessimistic. The optimists were more likely to set goals for their recovery and to seek information regarding the best procedures to follow during it. The result was that the optimists recovered from surgery more quickly and felt that their quality of life was better.

FIGURE 13.17

Rats in group A, which could turn off shocks by touching their noses to the metal plate, had smaller ulcers than rats in group B, which had no control over the shocks they received.

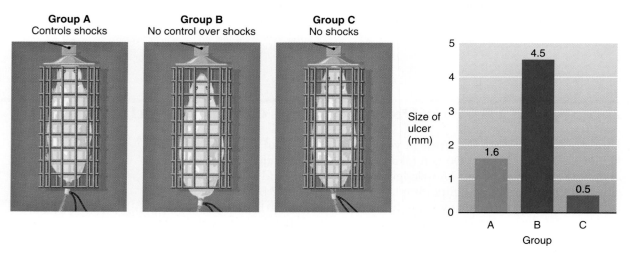

Why would optimists be more likely to use problem-solving strategies than pessimists? Consider Scheier and his co-workers' definition of optimism: the expectation that good outcomes will generally occur when confronting problems. Because optimists expect good outcomes, they are more likely to work toward achieving them, even under difficult or painful conditions. Pessimists, on the other hand, don't expect success, so are more likely to give up. Thus, the "power of positive thinking" (Cousins, 1979; Peale, 1952) gains its power not from the thinking alone, but from the way thinking influences behavior.

The importance of being in control.   When we use the tactic of "attacking the problem" we often create the feeling that we have *control* over it. Experiments with animals and humans have shown that simply having control over the circumstances that cause the stress can help relieve the effects of the stress-provoking situation. For example, Weiss (1968) created a situation in which one group of rats (group A) received shocks they could turn off by touching their nose to a metal plate. Another group of rats (group B) experienced exactly the same shocks as group A, but had no control over them, and a third group (group C) experienced no shocks at all (Figure 13.17). Rats in all three groups developed ulcers (lesions of the stomach), but even though groups A and B received exactly the same stimulation, the rats with control (group A) developed much smaller ulcers than the rats without control (group B). Group C, which had received no shocks, developed very small ulcers, presumably from the stress of being handled.

In an analogous human study, Jack Hokanson and his co-workers (1971) required that subjects engage in a task for 30 minutes, during which they received shocks for performing too slowly. Subjects received about one shock every 45 seconds, but those in the "in control" group were able to request rest periods whenever they wanted them. Subjects in the "no control" group could not request rest periods, but they received them at the same time as subjects in the "in control" group. Just as in the rat study, the humans in control experienced lower elevations of blood pressure in response to the shocks (Figure 13.18).

Having control over the stimulus not only affects physiological responses; it also affects health outcomes. For example, Madelon Visintainer and her co-workers (1982) injected rats with tumor cells and then divided them into three groups: (1) the *controllable shock group*, which received a series of 60 randomly timed shocks from which the rat could escape by pressing a bar; (2) the *uncontrollable shock group*, which received exactly the same sequence and duration of

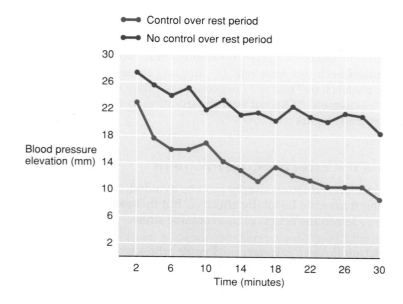

FIGURE 13.18
Subjects who could decide when to rest during a stressful task had less blood-pressure elevation than subjects who had the same rest periods but couldn't control when they would occur.

shocks as the first group but were unable to escape them; and (3) the *nonshock group*, a control group that received no shocks.

Thirty days after these treatments, 54% of the nonshock rats and 63% of the controllable-shock rats had rejected the tumor cells (that is, they were tumor free), but only 27% of the uncontrollable-shock rats had rejected the cells. Visintainer concluded that the low rate of tumor rejection in the uncontrollable-shock group was caused by the rats' lack of control over the shock.

Thus, one key to combating the negative effects of a potentially stressful stimulus is to gain control over it. Rats in the uncontrollable-shock group were unable to do this. These rats not only failed to reject their tumors, but they also developed the behavioral condition called **learned helplessness**—having learned that there was no way to escape the shocks, these rats had "learned" to be helpless even when they were put in another situation in which they could control the shocks (Maier et al., 1983). In Chapter 16, on abnormal behavior, we will see that learned helplessness has been proposed as a cause of depression in humans.

We can generalize these results to humans by considering a 15-year study of women with breast cancer, which showed a relationship between the women's way of dealing with the disease and their survival rate. Women who had a passive or helpless attitude ("There's nothing I can do about this") had lower survival rates than women who had a more positive attitude and decided to fight the disease (Greer, 1991).

The results of this cancer study are analogous in some ways to those from studies of people with hardy personalities, who tend to take control of situations and who also have better health. Remember that another characteristic of people with hardy personalities is that they often make a potentially stressful situation less stressful by reappraising it. This reappraisal is equivalent to another coping strategy—rethinking the problem.

The 15,000-meter gold medal winner in the 1992 Handicapped Olympics has combined two potential stress reducers: active control and exercise.

Rethinking the Problem

Many problems can be "rethought" to change a situation that initially appears negative into one with positive aspects. This stress-reduction tactic is embodied in the adage that "every cloud has a silver lining." For example, an engineer might see being fired from her job as a terrible disaster *or* as an opportunity to make the career change she was thinking about all along. A couple who escaped a fire that destroyed their house might be devastated by their loss, *or* they might see the experience as one that led them to appreciate the friends who helped out, to feel grateful for just being alive, and to realize that accumulating material possessions is not the most important priority in their life.

Another example of how rethinking can reduce stress is the technique used by some public speakers to cope with feelings of nervousness. Rather than labeling the "butterflies in the stomach" or "tingling sensations" that may occur before giving a speech as "fear" or "nervousness," they simply think of those sensations as "excitement." Often it isn't the situation so much as the way we think about it that leads to stress.

Lessening the Effects of the Problem

At times a stressful situation simply can't be avoided, and attacking the problem or rethinking it may not be totally effective. But there are still a number of tactics we can use to lessen the effects of unavoidable stress.

Stress reduction through exercise.   People who jog or engage in aerobic workouts often report that although exercising may be painful while it is happening,

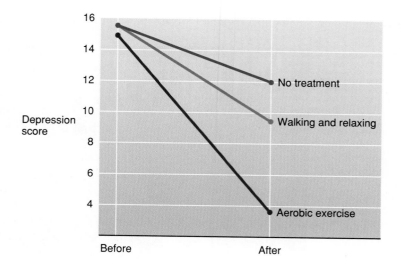

FIGURE 13.19
Participating in an aerobic exercise program caused a greater decrease in depression than either walking and relaxing or no treatment at all.

they experience a feeling of relaxation, power, and euphoria when it is over. This effect has been confirmed in studies in which the mood of people who exercise is compared with the mood of people who don't. For example, Lisa McCann and David Holmes (1984) found that depressed subjects who participated in an aerobic exercise program reported feeling less depressed than subjects in control groups who either walked and relaxed or did nothing at all (Figure 13.19).

Stress reduction through relaxation.   Another popular method of reducing stress is relaxation. The rationale for this method is that if stress involves an accelerated heart rate, tensed muscles, and autonomic nervous system arousal, then one way to combat it is to elicit the opposite of these physiological responses (Jacob & Chesney, 1986). In one relaxation technique, called **progressive muscle relaxation,** individuals typically listen to taped instructions designed to focus their attention on relaxing each part of their body in turn (Bernstein & Borkovec, 1973).

The results of studies on the effects of relaxation are mixed. Some show that relaxation reduces stress, but others do not. It's possible that stress reduction occurs not because of the relaxation technique used, but just because the person *expects* the procedure to reduce his or her stress (Jacob & Chesney, 1986). However, as far as the person is concerned, the exact mechanism responsible for stress reduction through relaxation may not be that important. A stressed person who feels better after relaxing is usually grateful for feeling better, no matter what caused it.

What do the ways of coping with stress that we have described mean to you personally? You may want to go beyond memorizing this material for the exam and actually apply some of these principles to your life. A number of practical hints for doing so are listed in Figure 13.20.

Reprise: Biology and Behavior, a Two-Way Street

One of the themes of this book has been that biological processes underlie behavior. Thus, in studying topics such as consciousness, the senses, memory, hunger motivation, and emotion, we have seen that specific behaviors are ac-

1. Get out of bed 15 minutes earlier to avoid the morning rushing around.
2. Prepare for the morning the evening before (set out clothes, breakfast, sack lunch, etc.)
3. Write things down: don't rely on your memory. (Trying to remember not to forget is stressful.)
4. Keep a duplicate car key in your wallet; bury a duplicate house key in your garden.
5. Practice "preventive maintenance" on your car, appliances, teeth, personal relationships, etc., so they won't break down at the worst possible moment.
6. Procrastination is stressful. Whatever you want to do tomorrow, do it *today;* whatever you want to do today, do it *now.* Hard work is simply the accumulation of easy things you didn't do when you should have done them.
7. Organize your home and work area so that everything has a place. You won't have to go through the stress of losing things.
8. Plan ahead. Don't let the gas tank get below one-quarter full; buy bus tokens and stamps *before* you need them, etc.
9. Schedule a realistic day. Allow ample time between appointments; make a "to do" list and cut it in half.
10. Relax your standards. The world will not end if the grass does not get mowed this weekend.
11. An *instant* cure for most stress: 30 minutes of brisk walking or other aerobic exercise.
12. Make friends with nonworriers.
13. Every day, find time for solitude and introspection. Seek out quiet places.
14. Say "No, thank you" to projects you don't have the time or energy for.
15. Always carry reading material to enjoy while waiting in lines or for appointments.
16. Remind yourself that Babe Ruth *struck out* 1,330 times.
17. For every *one* thing that goes wrong, there are 50 to 100 blessings. Count them.
18. Do nothing that, after being done, leads you to tell a lie.
19. Put brain in gear before opening mouth. Before saying anything, ask yourself if what you are about to say is (1) true, (2) kind, and (3) necessary. If it's not all three, K.M.S. (Keep Mouth Shut).
20. If an unpleasant task faces you, do it *early* in the day and get it over with.
21. Do one thing at a time.
22. Write your thoughts and feelings in a journal. This can help you clarify your ideas and put things in their right perspective.
23. The next time someone cuts you off in traffic, criticizes your work, and so on, don't get angry. Instead, think of instances when you've done the same.

Participating in a yoga class is another way to reduce stress.

24. Get enough sleep. Use an alarm clock to remind you to *go* to bed, if necessary.
25. To relax instantly, breathe as if you were trying to inflate an imaginary balloon in your stomach. Inhale slowly to the count of 10; then exhale slowly to the count of 10. Repeat.
26. Don't put up with things that don't work right. Get things fixed, or replace them.
27. Turn "needs" into preferences. Our body's basic needs are food, water, and keeping warm. Everything else is a preference.
28. Practice labeling situations differently. Are you really "furious" about something, or are you simple feeling *angry* or *annoyed?* Are you "crushed," or are you merely *let down* or *disappointed?* Resisting the temptation to exaggerate situations, and labeling situations with the apropriate word, can reduce stress.
29. Every day do at least one thing you really enjoy.
30. Be kind to unkind people—they probably need it the most.
31. Unplug your phone or switch on your phone answering machine while you take a bath, have dinner, etc.
32. Make promises sparingly and keep them faithfully.
33. Remember that the best things in life aren't things.
34. Using the TV or radio for background "company" can be surprisingly stressful. Learn to enjoy quiet.
35. Stop worrying. If something concerns you, do something about it. If you can't do anything about it, let go of it.
36. Forget about counting to 10. Count to 100 before saying anything that could make matters worse.

FIGURE 13.20
Three dozen stress reducers suggested by the Hope Heart Institute of Seattle, Washington

companied by activity in identifiable parts of the brain. Vision, for instance, is created by activity in the occipital cortex plus areas in the temporal and parietal lobes. And we have seen how emotions are linked to specific areas in the brain and to activity in the autonomic nervous system.

In this chapter, however, we have looked at another type of relationship between biology and behavior—one in which behavior (for example, learning through classical conditioning) produces changes in biology (for example, the functioning of the immune system). Another example is how the presence or absence of social support influences our longevity. Or consider an example from an earlier chapter—the description of gate control theory in Chapter 4, which proposes that our thoughts control a "gate" in the brain that determines whether signals from pain fibers reach the cerebral cortex.

The point of these examples is that the relationship between biology and behavior (which includes cognition, as in our pain example) is a two-way street. Although biological activity, particularly in the brain, forms the basis of our behaviors and thoughts, we now see that biology is itself influenced by the very behaviors and thoughts it makes possible.

Hypertension Among African Americans

Hypertension, an elevation of blood pressure in the arteries, is one of the major risk factors for coronary heart disease and a pervasive health problem in the United States. It is the leading reason that Americans visit doctors and consume prescription drugs: nearly 60 million Americans are currently diagnosed as hypertensive (Kaplan, 1986). Hypertension has been called the silent killer because there is no consistent pattern of symptoms and because some of them—dizziness, shortness of breath, and blurred vision—are also symptoms of other conditions.

Whereas hypertension is a serious problem in the population as a whole, it exists in near-epidemic rates in African Americans (Anderson, 1989). As shown in Figure 13.21, hypertension is about twice as prevalent among African Americans as among whites, for both males and females. In addition, the mortality rate for hypertensive heart disease is three times greater among African Americans than among whites (Johnson, 1987; Tischenkel et al., 1989).

Why should one group of people be at higher risk for hypertension? The search for reasons for the high rate of hypertension among African Americans has been carried out at several levels of analysis. At the biological level, researchers have found that African-American infants have a higher resting heart rate than white infants do (Schachter et al., 1974), although this difference does not persist into adulthood (Anderson, 1989). However, African-American adults do have higher blood pressure than whites, and there are also differences between African Americans' and whites' *blood pressure reactivity*, the tendency for blood pressure to increase in response to stress. Many studies have found

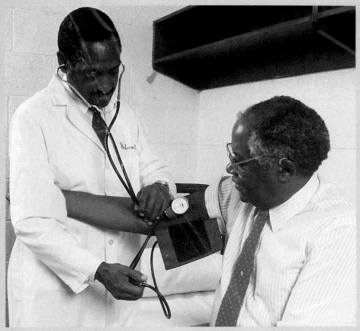

On the average, African-American adults have higher blood pressure and blood-pressure reactivity than whites.

that African Americans' reactivity is higher than whites'. This larger stress-induced increase in African Americans' blood pressure may be caused by the greater constriction of blood vessels that has been observed in them when they are subjected to stress (Anderson et al., 1988; Fredrickson, 1986).

But hypertension in African Americans is not caused by biology alone. At the contextual level of analysis we find a possible explanation in the stress caused by the harsher environmental conditions to which African Americans are often subjected. Living in high-stress, inner-city areas, under conditions of higher poverty, and having to deal with the effects of racial discrimination in school and at work all contribute to stress that could lead to hypertension (Harris, 1982).

To test the idea that stress associated with living in high-stress areas plays a role in hypertension, Harburg (1978) measured the blood pressure of residents of neighborhoods in Detroit defined as (1) high stress, because of low incomes, high unemployment rates, and high crime rates, and (2) low stress, because of high incomes, low unemployment rates, and low crime rates. The results of this study indicated that African-American males in the high-stress neighborhoods had higher blood pressure than those in the low-stress neighborhoods.

To test the idea that stresses associated with racism contribute to high blood pressure, Cheryl Armstead and her co-workers (1989) measured the blood pressure of African-American college students as they watched short film selections that (1) were neutral (for example, a song-and-dance scene), (2) depicted anger

FIGURE 13.21

Rates of hypertension are much higher for African Americans than for whites.

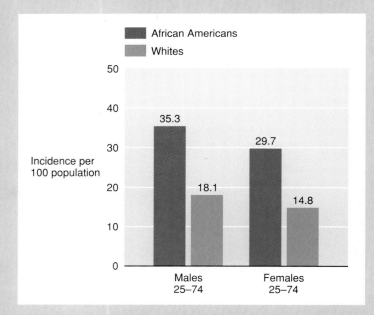

The high-crime inner-city environment creates stress, which can lead to high blood pressure.

(two soldiers fighting), or (3) depicted racism (white soldiers verbally and physically abusing an African-American soldier). As predicted, when viewing the scenes of racism, the subjects registered a greater rise in blood pressure than when viewing the anger film or the neutral film. Armstead concluded that "the racism that occurs in American society may pose a serious health hazard to its Black citizens" (p. 154).

Having added racist stimuli to the possible causes of the high incidence of African-American hypertension, let's move to the behavioral level and consider how hypertension may be re-

Situations in which anger must be concealed in order to avoid negative consequences are potential contributors to high blood pressure in African Americans.

lated to individuals' behavior patterns. We know that the way a person copes with stress can determine whether it becomes injurious to the person's health. Research confirms this conclusion for African Americans. A number of studies find that those who keep their anger in—who stay angry and harbor grudges against others without expressing how they feel—have higher blood pressure reactivity and are therefore at greatest risk for both high blood pressure in response to stress and for being diagnosed as hypertensive (Gentry et al., 1982, 1983; Harburg, Blacklock, & Roeper, 1979). This effect of keeping anger in is not only more pronounced for African Americans than for whites, but it can be more serious for those who live in regions of particularly overt discrimination and who have learned to hide their anger to avoid negative consequences.

The discrimination and poor living conditions suffered by many African Americans can lead to a paradoxical situation called John Henryism, named after the legendary African-American strong man who challenged a power drill to a contest and died, victorious, from exhaustion. **John Henryism** has come to mean a syndrome in which people feel that by working hard and showing determination they can overcome a stressful situation. Deciding to work hard to overcome stress sounds like a healthy response, but if the person is overestimating his or her capacity or the odds of success, devastating failure can result. Thus, when John Henry, "that steel-drivin' man," took on the steam pile-driver, he made a valiant effort but died in the process. This idea is supported by the results of a study in rural North Carolina, in which African-American males whose level of education was below the median and who scored high on a "John Henryism scale" had the highest levels of blood pressure compared with controls (James, Hartnett, & Kalsbeek, 1983). African Americans who feel they can overcome obstacles by hard work and determination but who have little power and opportunity because of their low social status may therefore be at high risk for hypertension (Anderson & Jackson, 1986).

We've seen that there is no simple answer to the question "Why do African Americans have a higher risk of hypertension than whites?" Though biology may be important, an individual's neighborhood and coping style also contribute to the risk of hypertension by increasing stress. Moreover, the effect of that stress is more dangerous for individuals who keep their anger in or who overestimate their ability to overcome obstacles. Thus, factors at all four levels of analysis help explain African Americans' elevated risk of hypertension (Table 13.4).

TABLE 13.4
Causes of hypertension in African Americans at each level of analysis

Behavioral	Biological	Cognitive	Contextual
Coping strategies such as keeping anger in	High blood pressure Higher blood pressure reactivity	Overestimating extent to which working harder can overcome obstacles	High-stress urban environment Racial discrimination

- The biomedical model of health views all diseases or physical disorders as the result of disturbances in physiological processes. There is evidence, however, that psychological factors can significantly influence health.

Health Psychology

- Health psychology is concerned with how psychological knowledge can contribute to our understanding of health. It supplements the biomedical model by adding the behavioral, cognitive, and contextual levels of analysis to understanding health and illness.

- The biomedical model has not yet developed a vaccine or cure for AIDS, so we must turn to behavioral approaches to stop the transmission of this disease. In addition, the cognitive and contextual approaches have been applied to the study of AIDS and its prevention.

- Individuals who practice many healthful behaviors show improved health and longevity over those who don't. The male gender role, with its emphasis on aggression and risk taking, may be responsible for the higher incidence of accidents and many diseases in males compared with females.

What Is Stress?

- Stress can be defined as a stimulus, as a response, or as a transaction between the person and the environment. Psychologists prefer the transaction-based definition, because it accounts for the fact that the same stimulus may be stressful for one person but not another.

- The transaction between the person and the environment that determines whether stress occurs has been described as a process of cognitive appraisal consisting of primary and secondary appraisal. A complete picture of stress, however, involves not only cognitive factors but also biological, behavioral, and contextual influences.

Links Between Stress and Health

- Evidence from animal studies of a link between stress and disease comes from experiments that show that tumor growth is higher in rats subjected to stress than in those not subjected to stress.

- Early evidence for the stress-disease connection in humans was provided by studies using the Social Readjustment Rating Scale (SRRS), which showed that greater life change was associated with poorer health. However, limitations of the SRRS led to the development of the hassles scale, which shows that poor health is associated with a greater number of everyday hassles.

- The incidence of poor physical and mental health is greater when people are exposed to disasters such as the Three Mile Island nuclear accident or the Mount Saint Helens volcanic eruption. Similarly, high job stress has been related to health problems such as hypertension and coronary heart disease.

- Research by Selye on the general adaptation syndrome demonstrated a link between long-term stress and damage to immune system structures. In response to threatening situations, the body releases hormones that help it deal with stress but that are also immunosuppressants. Suppression of the immune system by these hormones leaves the organism more susceptible to disease.

- Experiments done by Robert Ader and Nicholas Cohen have shown that the immune system can be influenced by classical conditioning. This finding has important implications, because it means that the functioning of physical systems can be influenced by psychological factors. A large amount of behavioral evidence indicates that stress can suppress the immune system in humans.

Social Support and Health

- Social support can take a number of forms: tangible, emotional, esteem, and informational. A relationship between social support and health has been demonstrated in longitudinal studies, which have shown that lower levels of support are associated with a greater likelihood of dying.

- Two hypotheses have been proposed to explain the effects of social support on health: the buffering hypothesis and the main effect hypothesis. There is evidence for both of them.

Personality and Health

- People exhibiting the Type A behavior pattern (TABP) are at risk for coronary heart disease. Recent research shows that hostility, distrusting others, and angry reactions to trivial matters are the specific characteristics of TABP implicated in this health risk.

- People with a "hardy personality" tend to be less affected by stress, because they transform potentially stressful events into challenges and opportunities. Research indicates that people who are under stress generally have less chance of experiencing serious health problems if they have a hardy personality.

Applying Health Psychology: Coping with Stress

- Three ways of coping with stress are (1) attacking the problem causing the stress; (2) rethinking the problem, so that a situation that appears negative is redefined as less negative or even positive; and (3) lessening the effects of unavoidable stress through such means as exercise and purposeful relaxation.

Reprise: Biology and Behavior, a Two-Way Street

- The relation between biology and behavior—which is usually approached by showing how biological processes affect behavior—has been reversed in this chapter, as we have shown that behavior can produce changes in biology.

Follow-Through/Diversity: Hypertension Among African Americans

- Hypertension is a serious health problem for African Americans. Possible reasons for African Americans' elevated risk include biological predisposition, the stress caused by discrimination and living in harsh environmental conditions, and personality factors such as keeping anger in and overestimating the degree to which obstacles can be overcome by hard work.

Key Terms

alarm stage
behavioral medicine
biomedical model
buffering hypothesis
cognitive appraisal
coronary heart disease (CHD)
exhaustion stage
general adaptation syndrome
hardy personality
hassles
health psychology
immune system
immunosuppressants
John Henryism
learned helplessness

main effect hypothesis
mind-body dualism
placebo
progressive muscle relaxation
psychoneuroimmunology
resistance stage
Social Readjustment Rating Scale (SRRS)
social support
stressors
Structured Interview
Type A behavior pattern (TABP)
uplifts
white coat effect

The Measurement of Intelligence
   Early Intelligence Tests
   Modern Intelligence Tests

The Range of Intelligence
   Giftedness
   Mental Retardation

Interdisciplinary Dimension: Education
   Mainstreaming the Mentally Retarded

The Structure of Intelligence

The Mechanisms of Intelligence
   Processing Speed and Adult Intelligence
   Measuring Infant Intelligence
   Information Processing During Problem Solving

The Sources of Intelligence
   The Role of Heredity
   The Role of the Environment

Intelligence and Society
   Test Reliability and Validity
   Intelligence as a Cultural Construct
   The Uses of Intelligence Tests

Real-World Intelligence

Reprise: Intelligence—A Socially Relevant Construct

Follow-Through/Diversity
   Measuring Intelligence in Minority Groups

Intelligence

Diana Cortez
Activities: Mathematics
club; glee club
Interests: Music, reading,
dancing
Goals: To teach at the
college level

Paul O'Brien
Activities: None listed
Interests: Automobiles
Goals: To get a job

Diana Cortez and Paul O'Brien—two very different people who graduated from the same high school over 20 years ago. Based on their record in high school, how would you rate their intelligence? Most people would say that Diana—college bound, member of the mathematics club, with a 3.85 grade point average—is clearly more intelligent than Paul, whose grades and test scores are in the lower half of the class and whose favorite courses are electronics and gym.

Our willingness to judge Diana as more intelligent than Paul illustrates the operation of an **implicit theory of intelligence,** a commonsense conception of what it means to be intelligent (Sternberg et al., 1981). Most of us use an implicit theory of intelligence to make everyday judgments about our own intelligence and that of others. Whether we base our judgments on evidence such as people's grades in school, the size of their vocabulary, evidence of intellectual accomplishment, or scores on standardized tests, we readily decide that one person is smarter, brighter, or "brainier" than another. The specific criteria we use to make these assessments reveal the nature of our particular implicit theory of intelligence.

Yet the nature and assessment of intelligence are among the most controversial areas in psychology. We can understand why this is so by looking at our two high school students 20 years after graduation. That Diana is now a mathematician at a well-known university comes as no surprise. Everyone knew Diana was intelligent enough to master a highly abstract subject such as mathematics. But Paul, who was a low achiever in high school and whose potential was considered average at best, surprises us. Now, 20 years after high school, he is a successful entrepreneur who runs his own computer sales and service business. Although he had never been one to shine in the classroom, after graduation he took a job selling electronic equipment and soon discovered that he had both business sense and a knack for working with people. Together with his understanding of electronics, these qualities helped make him a "star" in his chosen field.

Paul's success despite his supposedly low intelligence raises a number of questions. Should we conclude that Paul is an "overachiever," since he is doing much better than would be expected given his intelligence? Should we say that abilities like business sense, interpersonal skills, and an intuitive understanding of electronics reflect something other than intelligence? Or should we question our original assessment of Paul's intelligence? Should we conclude that grades in school and performance on tests are not necessarily the only ways to measure intelligence?

Behind these questions loom larger ones: What is intelligence? How can we measure intelligence? As we will see in this chapter, psychologists have proposed a variety of answers to these basic questions.

The issues of what intelligence is and how it can be measured can be approached at all four levels of analysis. At the behavioral level, we can construct various kinds of tests and assess people's performance on them. At the cognitive level, we can probe beneath the results of intelligence tests and look at the mental processes involved in different tasks. At the biological level, we can assess the contribution of genetics to intelligence. Finally, at the contextual level, we can look at how environmental conditions influence the development of intelligence—and more broadly, at how society shapes people's conceptions of intelligence by specifying what abilities are valued in a particular culture.

These issues are not of merely academic interest. As you know from your own experience, intelligence tests (and similar tests, like the Scholastic Aptitude Test) are used for a wide variety of purposes that are extremely relevant to our lives—from placing schoolchildren in classes according to their ability, to determining whether applicants should be admitted to college or offered a job. These uses have been questioned by those who fear that intelligence testing has too much power over our lives. Perhaps, some people suggest, we need to evaluate exactly what it is that intelligence tests measure and whether we need to create new ways of measuring different kinds of intelligence. We consider these issues at the end of the chapter.

We begin our exploration of intelligence by looking at how contemporary intelligence testing developed. As we will see, there has always been debate about the twin issues of what intelligence is and how it should be measured.

The Measurement of Intelligence: Quantifying the Mind

What, exactly, *is* intelligence? In 1921 fourteen experts were asked this question (Thorndike et al., 1921). Here are some of their answers:

- The ability to carry on abstract thinking
- The ability to adjust to one's environment
- The ability to adapt to new situations in life
- The capacity to acquire knowledge
- The capacity to learn or to profit from experience
- Good responses from the point of view of psychological truth or fact

Sixty-four years later, when the experts of 1985 were asked to define intelligence, they produced an equally wide range of answers (Sternberg & Detterman, 1986).

Although the experts cannot agree on an exact definition of intelligence, themes common to many of their definitions are that intelligence is (1) the ability to learn from experience and (2) the ability to adapt to the environment. These themes represent a good way to think about intelligence, even though we are not sure whether these abilities are what intelligence tests measure.

The experts' difficulty in finding a totally satisfactory definition of intelligence reflects the fact that intelligence is a **psychological construct**—an abstract attribute that is *inferred* rather than observed directly. One property of a construct is that it cannot be directly measured. We can appreciate the difficulty in measuring a construct like intelligence by comparing it with a well-defined and directly observable attribute such as height, which can be verified with a tape measure. Although specific well-defined skills such as the ability to add and subtract can be measured by simple tests, there is no "tape measure" for intelligence as such. The only way to measure intelligence is to measure observable characteristics that are thought to reflect intelligence. But which characteristics are good indicators of intelligence? Let's look at how psychologists have tried to answer this question.

Early Intelligence Tests: Measuring Skulls and Sensory Abilities

Nineteenth-century scientists began the quest for a measure of intelligence by picking characteristics that are easy to measure. One of the first methods

ANTHROPOMETRIC LABORATORY

For the measurement in various ways of Human Form and Faculty.

Entered from the Science Collection of the S. Kensington Museum.

This laboratory is established by Mr. Francis Galton for the following purposes:—

1. For the use of those who desire to be accurately measured in many ways, either to obtain timely warning of remediable faults in development, or to learn their powers.

2. For keeping a methodical register of the principal measurements of each person, of which he may at any future time obtain a copy under reasonable restrictions. His initials and date of birth will be entered in the register, but not his name. The names are indexed in a separate book.

3. For supplying information on the methods, practice, and uses of human measurement.

4. For anthropometric experiment and research, and for obtaining data for statistical discussion.

Charges for making the principal measurements: THREEPENCE each, to those who are already on the Register. FOURPENCE each, to those who are not:— one page of the Register will thenceforward be assigned to them, and a few extra measurements will be made, chiefly for future identification.

The Superintendent is charged with the control of the laboratory and with determining in each case, which, if any, of the extra measurements may be made, and under what conditions.

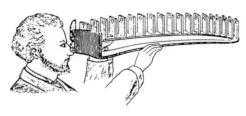

FIGURE 14·1
A description of Galton's anthropometric laboratory and one of the devices used to measure sensory capacities.

proposed for determining intelligence was *craniometry*, the measurement of skulls. The assumption behind this approach was that more intelligent people have larger brains and, therefore, larger skulls. Paul Broca (1861), the famous anatomist who discovered the brain area for speech (*Broca's area*, described in Chapter 3), asserted "Other things equal, there is a remarkable relationship between the development of intelligence and the volume of the brain" (p. 188).

Broca's statement notwithstanding, attempts to prove his hypothesis by measuring people's skulls had limited success. As it turns out, there are many cases of eminent scientists with small brains and marginally intelligent people with large brains. The bottom line is that systematic measurements of large numbers of people have failed to support Broca's statement (Gould, 1981).

Another 19th-century scientist who tried his hand at measuring intelligence was Sir Francis Galton. Galton was Charles Darwin's cousin and was famous in his own right for his many scientific discoveries both within and outside of psychology. For example, he introduced the method of correlation to psychology and invented weather maps and the teletype.

Galton (1883) unveiled his method of measuring intelligence in a display he called the "anthropometric laboratory" at the 1884 International Health Exhibition in London. (*Anthropometric* means "body-measuring.") For a small fee one of Galton's assistants determined people's intelligence by measuring their performance on a series of tests (Figure 14.1). Among them were visual acuity, the ability to see details; sensory discrimination, the ability to detect the difference between, say, two weights; and reaction time, the ability to react rapidly to a signal such as a tone (see Johnson et al., 1985). Galton reasoned that, since we obtain our knowledge of the environment through our senses, those with the most acute sensory abilities should have the highest intelligence.

One result of Galton's measurements was the discovery that measuring the attributes of large groups of people often results in a distribution of scores like the one in Figure 14.2. This distribution of scores is a **normal distribution**, or a "bell-shaped" curve, in which (1) most of the scores are grouped in the middle and (2) the distribution has two long tails, one extending to low scores and one to high scores. A common example of a normal distribution is height—most people tend to cluster around an average height, with the number of taller and shorter people tailing off to the extremes. Galton's results showed that the abilities he was measuring were "normally distributed," much as height is.

But were Galton's tests really measuring intelligence? At first James Cattell, an assistant in Galton's laboratory, thought so. In fact, he was so impressed with Galton's techniques that he constructed his own anthropometric laboratories in

FIGURE 14·2
The normal distribution. The vertical lines indicate standard deviations above and below the mean. The numbers between the lines indicate the percentage of the total scores that fall between each standard deviation line. (See Measurement & Methodology, "Determining the Deviation IQ.")

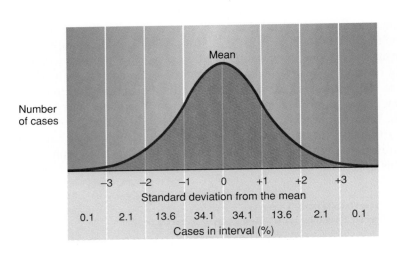

the United States, first at the University of Pennsylvania and then at Columbia University. At Columbia, Cattell tested Galton's idea that acuity and reaction time reflect intelligence by measuring the acuities and reaction times of Columbia students and comparing their scores with their grades in school. Although grades are a measure that we would expect to be closely related to intelligence, Cattell found no relationship between his scores and grades: students with good acuity and fast reaction times were no more likely than other students to get good grades. Cattell therefore concluded that sensory discrimination was not a valid measure of intelligence after all.

Broca's craniometry and Galton's anthropometric measurements illustrate the difficulty in finding measurable attributes that accurately reflect intelligence. However, just as these methods were being discredited, an alternative model for measuring intelligence was being developed that would provide the basis for modern intelligence testing.

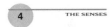

Modern Intelligence Tests: Measuring Intellectual Functioning

In 1904 the French Ministry of Education asked psychologist Alfred Binet to devise a method to identify children who would have difficulty keeping up in regular classes. In contrast to Broca and Galton, Binet reasoned that "if anyone wants to study the differences between two individuals, it is necessary to begin with the most intellectual and complex processes" (Binet & Henri, 1895). Binet produced a test based on this idea, designed to measure a person's ability to reason and use judgment. He created the test items by identifying questions that could be answered by average children of different ages. This procedure produced six questions for each age level. For example, 3-year-olds would be asked to point to their eyes or nose; 7-year-olds, to describe a picture.

In the resulting test, each child was interviewed individually by an examiner. The child was first asked questions slightly below his or her age level and was then asked questions of increasing difficulty. Testing stopped when the child failed to answer all the questions at a particular age level.

Binet's test was scored by noting the age level at which the child answered all the questions correctly and then adding two months' extra credit for each ad-

Age	Task
2	Where is your arm? See how high you can stack these blocks.
4	Why do people go to school? Boiling water is hot; ice water is _____ . Tell me which of these things have similar shapes.
6	What does "lamp" mean? What is the difference between a dog and a fish? Move these blocks so they make the pattern in the picture.
8	What is funny about this story: "John wore an eye patch because he broke his leg." If you had a cat and couldn't find it what would you do? Copy this design.
10	Repeat the following numbers: 4 7 2 9 4 6. Write down as many words as you can in the next minute.
12	Repeat the following numbers backward: 5 8 3 9 2. What does miserable mean? John went to a _____ to buy some food.
14	What is similar about "left" and "right"? If I punch a hole in this folded paper, how many holes will there be when I unfold it?
Adult	Repeat these numbers backward: 6 3 8 2 9 4. Create a sentence using the following words: grocery store, money, broken. Describe how merchant and athlete are similar.

FIGURE 14.3
Items similar to those on the Stanford-Binet tests for people of different ages

ditional answer at the next level. Thus, a child who correctly answered all the questions through age 9 plus three questions above the 9-year-old level was identified as having a "mental age" of 9 years, 6 months.

Binet's test was introduced to the United States by Lewis Terman (1916) of Stanford University. His revision of Binet's test, which is called the Stanford-Binet test, is still, in its modern form, one of the most widely used intelligence tests in the United States (Figure 14.3). In addition to revising the test for American use, Terman added a scale for adults and changed the way scores were reported. Instead of calculating mental age as Binet had done, Terman used a measure called the **intelligence quotient (IQ),** which had been introduced by the German psychologist William Stern in 1912. Stern calculated IQ by dividing mental age by chronological age and multiplying by 100. Thus, an 8-year-old child with a mental age of 10 years would have an IQ of 125 (10 divided by 8 equals 1.25; 1.25 times 100 equals 125). This way of calculating IQ was used until

FIGURE 14.4
Questions like those used in the adult and child versions of the Wechsler intelligence test. When two items are shown, the first corresponds to the children's test and the second to the adults' test.

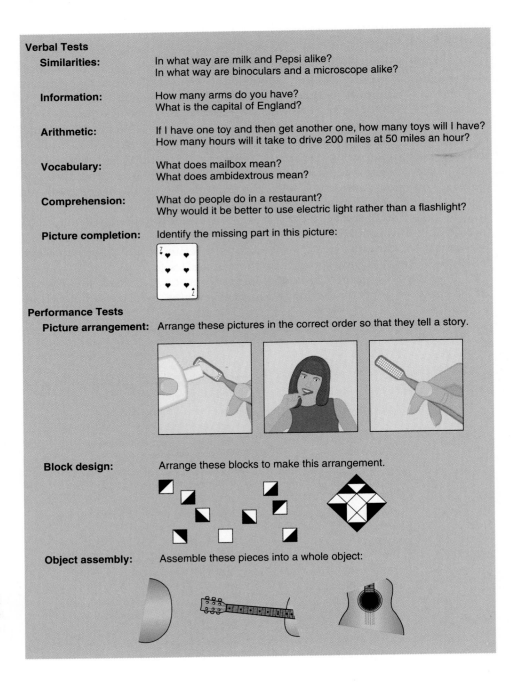

1960, when it was replaced by a measure called the *deviation IQ,* calculated by comparing a person's score with the distribution of scores obtained by the general population. (See Measurement & Methodology, "Determining the Deviation IQ.") An advantage the deviation IQ has over the old method, which gave the ratio of mental age to chronological age, is that the deviation IQ tells us where a person stands in relation to other people.

At about the same time that Terman was revising Binet's test for U.S. consumption, a major world event was unfolding that was to add another dimension to intelligence testing. Following the outbreak of World War I, the United States mobilized nearly 2 million army recruits. Faced with the task of assigning this huge number of soldiers to different jobs, the army sought a method to determine the job for which each recruit was best suited. However, Terman's revision of Binet's original test—which was administered to one person at a time by a trained examiner—was clearly not a practical way to test millions. The army therefore asked three of America's most well-known psychologists—Terman, H. H. Goddard, and Robert Yerkes—to create an intelligence test that could be given quickly to large numbers of people. Within three months they had created the U.S. Army Alpha and Beta tests. The Alpha test was a paper-and-pencil test designed for recruits who could read; the Beta test, which consisted mostly of picture questions, was given to recruits who couldn't read. These tests were the forerunners of the mass testing that is now familiar to all students.

The advent of group testing did not, however, spell the end of the individually administered test. In addition to the Stanford-Binet test, another widely used test that is individually administered by a trained examiner was developed by David Wechsler in 1939. Today two Wechsler tests are in use, the Wechsler Intelligence Scale for Children–Revised (WISC–R) and the Wechsler Adult Intelligence Scale–Revised (WAIS–R) (Wechsler, 1949, 1958). They differ from the Stanford-Binet in that they contain a number of subscales (Figure 14.4). These tests therefore enable the examiner to construct a profile indicating a person's strengths and weaknesses. The scales can also be combined to obtain two separate scores: a *verbal score,* which depends on knowledge accumulated in the past, and a *performance score,* which depends more on immediate problem-solving ability (Figure 14.5). These two scores make the WISC–R useful for identifying children with learning disabilities, who may achieve a good verbal score but a poor performance score (Sattler, 1988).

To what use do we put the scores that people earn on these tests? The army Alpha and Beta tests were used to place soldiers in different jobs. Today, intelligence test scores are used for a variety of purposes, as we will see later in the chapter. In the next section, we focus on how IQ scores have been used to place people in different categories of intellectual ability.

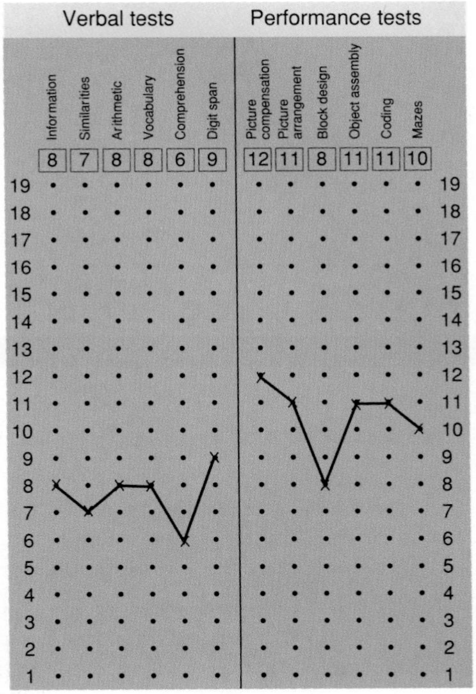

FIGURE 14.5

Profile of a child's score on the WISC IQ test. Each subtest is scored, and then the scores are connected to create the profile. This child has scored slightly higher on the performance tests.

The Range of Intelligence: Giftedness and Mental Retardation

Genius is one percent inspiration and ninety-nine percent perspiration.

Thomas A. Edison (1847–1931)

The intelligence tests we have been discussing accomplished something extremely important: They established, through testing, that people's performance varies over a wide range. This wide range of scores has been used as a starting point to classify people on a continuum stretching from "retarded" to "average" to "gifted." Let's consider some of the characteristics of people who fall at the high and low ends of the IQ scale.

Giftedness

At the high end of the distribution of IQ scores are people who are considered "gifted." It is common to think of giftedness in terms of a particular score on an IQ test. For example, admission to gifted classes in most high schools requires an IQ of 125 or 130, about the top 2–3% of the population.

MEASUREMENT & METHODOLOGY

Determining the Deviation IQ

The results of modern IQ tests are reported in terms of the deviation IQ—where a particular score falls within the distribution of scores obtained by the general population. The following procedure is used to determine the deviation IQ:

1. The intelligence test is given to a *norm group*—a group of people of a particular age that is representative of the general population of people of that age.
2. The scores obtained by the norm group are plotted as a distribution. Because the norm group is large and represents the general population, its distributions for each age approximate a normal distribution.
3. The mean score of this distribution is set equal to an IQ of 100. Thus, anyone taking the test later and obtaining that score has an IQ of 100.
4. To transform test scores that are above and below the mean into IQs, the standard deviation of the distribution is calculated. Remember from Chapter 2 that the standard deviation is a measure of variability that is large if the distribution is spread out and small if it is narrow.
5. The standard deviation is set equal to 15 IQ points (some

versions of IQ tests set it at 16 IQ points). This means that anyone whose score falls one standard deviation above the mean has an IQ of 115, and a score one standard deviation below reflects an IQ of 85.

6. To determine what a particular IQ score means in terms of how a person compares with the population as a whole, we can convert the IQs to percentiles. A property of the normal distribution is that a score one standard deviation above the mean falls in the 84th percentile—it is higher than 84 percent of the scores. Similarly, a score one standard deviation below the mean falls in the 16th percentile—it is higher than 16 percent of the scores. Figure A indicates the percentiles that correspond to some other IQ scores.
7. To determine individuals' deviation IQs, their scores are compared with the scores of the norm group for their age. So an 8-year-old's score is compared with the 8-year-old norm group, a 10-year-old's with the 10-year-old norm, and so on. Most tests use adult norms for all people above 15 to 18 years of age.

Distribution of scores determined by giving an intelligence test to a large norm group of a particular age. Notice that this distribution has a shape similar to the normal distribution of Figure 14.2.

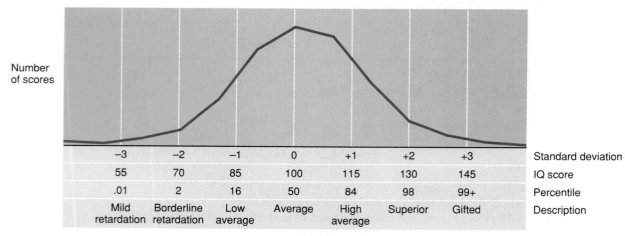

Standard deviation from the mean	−3	−2	−1	0	+1	+2	+3
IQ score	55	70	85	100	115	130	145
Percentile	.01	2	16	50	84	98	99+
Description	Mild retardation	Borderline retardation	Low average	Average	High average	Superior	Gifted

What are gifted people like? In a classic longitudinal study of giftedness, Lewis Terman (1925) studied over 1500 schoolchildren with IQs of more than 135. He followed this group, which had an average IQ of 151, over a period of 40 years and found that gifted people do not fit the stereotype of extremely intelligent people as being maladjusted and frail or not physically fit. Instead, Terman found his gifted subjects to be above average in health, adjustment, and success in their occupations.

But IQ is not the only criterion for giftedness. Many definitions of giftedness take into account both IQ *and* the person's accomplishments. Giftedness, according to John Feldhausen (1986), is a "predisposition for superior learning and performance in early years and high level achievement or performance in adulthood."

Thus, we think of people like Thomas Jefferson, Albert Einstein, Marie Curie, Charles Darwin, and Wolfgang Mozart as gifted because their intelligence was translated into observable achievements. Biographical studies of high achievers led Joseph Renzulli (1986) to propose a *three-ring conception of giftedness* (Figure 14.6). Giftedness, according to Renzulli, is present when there is (1) above-average ability; (2) a high degree of task commitment, with the person becoming deeply absorbed by specific problems for an extended period; and (3) creativity, or originality of thinking and a marked curiosity.

The idea that IQ is not the only important dimension for determining giftedness was confirmed by analyzing the 150 most and least successful of Terman's subjects. When Terman and M. H. Oden (1959) did this, they found that the people in the two groups did not differ in intelligence, but that they did differ in personality: the more successful people were generally better adjusted socially and emotionally and had a greater desire to achieve.

Terman's conclusion that "notable achievement calls for more than a high order of intelligence" supports the hypothesis that success in life reflects more than what intelligence tests measure. The IQ measured by intelligence tests interacts with other characteristics, such as personality and motivation, to determine a person's behaviors and achievements.

The idea that we need to take multiple factors into account to explain behavior was emphasized in Chapters 9 and 10, on development. There we saw that to truly understand development we need to consider how cognitive, social, and emotional factors interact with one another. As we consider mental retardation in the next section, we will see that a similar principle holds for understanding mentally retarded people, whose level of functioning depends on far more than their IQ.

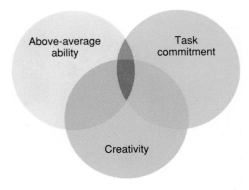

FIGURE 14.6
Renzulli's three-ring concept of giftedness. The dark area in the middle, in which all three qualities overlap, represents the presence of giftedness.

9 DEVELOPMENT

Mental Retardation

About 7 million people in the United States are classified as mentally retarded. Persons so classified meet three criteria: (1) they have an IQ below 70, in the lowest 2.5% of the population; (2) they exhibit difficulty in adaptation, usually in the form of behavior problems or an inability to take care of themselves; and (3) they exhibit these factors before the age of 18 (American Psychiatric Association, 1987). The last criterion is used to differentiate people who exhibit mental retardation from a young age from those whose normal intelligence has been lowered by brain damage or disease at an older age.

One feature of this definition, difficulty in adaptation, means that the number of people classified as mentally retarded at different ages varies. Prior to about 5 years of age, children who are mildly retarded can appear to be normal. With the beginning of school at 5 or 6, difficulties in schoolwork and the results of testing lead to some children being classified as mentally retarded. Mental retardation peaks at age 15 and then drops off, as people make use of school programs designed to help them adapt. Thus, many people who were diagnosed as mentally retarded as children may lose that classification as adults (Landsman & Ramey, 1989).

Many mentally retarded adults contribute to their own support by working.

FIGURE 14.7
This detailed picture was drawn by the "savant" Nadia when she was 5½ years old.

Levels of mental retardation.   Although the vast majority of mental retardation is mild, some people's intelligence falls below the mild range. Mental retardation is broken down into the following four levels:

1. *Mild retardation (an IQ of 50 to 70):* These people, who account for 85% of the retarded population, reach a sixth-grade educational level by adulthood. Their social adjustment is equivalent to that of an adolescent. They need some supervision, since they often have trouble foreseeing the consequences of their actions, but by taking advantage of special education programs many can hold a job and become self-supporting.

2. *Moderate retardation (an IQ of 35 to 49):* Moderately retarded adults, 10% of the retarded, reach a second-grade educational level. They are usually clumsy physically and have poor motor coordination, but with training they can take care of some of their needs and can achieve satisfactory social behavior.

3. *Severe retardation (an IQ of 20 to 34):* The severely retarded, who account for only 4% of the retarded, are called **dependent retarded.** They have extremely retarded motor and speech development and often sensory and motor disabilities as well. They may be able to perform simple tasks under close supervision, but they are always dependent on others for their care.

4. *Profound retardation (an IQ of less than 20):* Fewer than 1% of the retarded fall into this category. Speech is often absent; if present, it is rudimentary. These people are severely deformed, suffer from seizures, and require custodial care during their short life expectancy.

After reading this classification scheme you may be tempted to lump all retarded people in a particular level together. But not all people who fall within a particular IQ range are the same, just as all college students aren't the same. Thus, the behavior of mildly retarded people can range from being isolated and helpless to functioning well in the mainstream of society, depending on the characteristics of the individual and his or her living situation.

An example of how a living situation can affect the functioning of a mentally retarded person is provided by Cal, a 34-year-old mildly retarded man who had earned his high school diploma by attending special classes. Left alone after the death of his father, Cal became disoriented and unable to function. When he was placed in a group home facility, his functioning improved because most of his needs were taken care of by the staff; but he spent most of his time watching TV. Yet, after being trained in a semi-independent living program, he became a functioning member of society—he had a job and lived in a two-bedroom apartment with a girlfriend (Halpern, Close, & Nelson, 1986). Thus, instead of accepting a negative stereotype of retarded people as helpless and unaware, we must remember not only that a wide range of people are classified as mentally retarded, but that these people live in widely different environments that can have a great effect on their behavior and level of functioning.

The savant syndrome.   Although most people with mental retardation function at a level below that of people with normal or above-normal intelligence, there are some striking exceptions: people exhibiting the **savant syndrome,** who are classified as mentally retarded but who have exceptional skills in one area. Consider the following examples (Treffert, 1989):

- Tom has a vocabulary of fewer than 100 words but can flawlessly play any composition on the piano after hearing it only once.
- George can't figure out the change for a $10 bill from a $6 purchase and can't add, but he can remember 30 digits at a time. And if you give him any date within 40,000 years of the present, he can tell you the day of the week of that date.
- Kenneth is 38 years old but has a mental age of 11. Even though he has only 58 words in his general vocabulary, he can recite the population of every city and town in the United States with a population greater than

5000 and can tell you the names, number of rooms, and locations of 2000 leading hotels in the United States.

- David requires hospitalization because of his dangerous fits of rage and is seriously impaired in a number of areas. He has, however, memorized the bus system of Milwaukee, Wisconsin, so that if you give him the number of the bus pulling up in front of you and the time of day he can tell you on which corner you are standing.
- Nadia has extremely limited language functioning, has uncontrollable screaming fits, and avoids all eye contact and physical contact. Despite these crippling disabilities, she has been able to create amazingly realistic drawings since just 3 years of age (Figure 14.7) (Selfe, 1978).

These cases are fascinating because they pose a special problem for psychologists. How can an island of skill exist in an ocean of retardation? A possible explanation for the savant syndrome is that, during prenatal development, the left hemisphere of the brain is damaged. Damage is more likely in the left than the right hemisphere because it develops earlier and so is vulnerable to prenatal influences longer than the right hemisphere. This left-hemisphere damage not only causes retardation but also leads to an exaggerated development of the right hemisphere. The right hemisphere, therefore, dominates the person's behavior. This shift of functioning to the right hemisphere is consistent with the fact that most savants show decidedly "right-brain" talents, typically artistic or musical skills and memorization abilities (Schmidt, 1983; Treffert, 1989). This explanation is simply a hypothesis; we do not know whether it is correct. But what causes the vast majority of retardation in people who are not savants? We turn to those causes next.

Causes of mental retardation.   About 20% of mental retardation can be traced to biological causes: a mother's use of toxic agents such as alcohol during pregnancy, deficiencies in the mother's diet during pregnancy, trauma that occurs during the birth process, genetic abnormalities, and so on (Robinson & Robinson, 1976).

The importance of genetics is obvious from the fact that mental retardation tends to run in families and that some conditions have been linked to damage to a specific chromosome. One such condition is **Down's syndrome,** which affects 1 of 600 people in the United States. People afflicted with Down's syndrome have almond-shaped eyes, thick skin in their eyelids, a broad face and nose, and a short neck and fingers (Figure 14.8). They are usually moderately mentally retarded, with poor verbal and language skills but good spatial skills, suggesting that their problem may be localized in the left hemisphere of the brain. A well-established fact about Down's syndrome is that it is far more likely to occur when the mother is older. There is a 1 in 2000 chance of Down's syndrome if the mother is in her 20s, but a 1 in 50 chance if the mother is in her 40s.

Retardation has also been linked to environmental deprivation. This cause of retardation, which is often implicated when there is no obvious biological cause, results in what has been labeled **cultural-familial retardation.** It is typically seen in children who come from poverty-stricken families that provide little intellectual stimulation and much less touching and physical contact than in normal families. Three-quarters of mentally retarded children come from disadvantaged homes; since they don't develop vocabulary skills and have trouble following instructions, they are usually diagnosed as retarded when they begin having trouble in school.

The fact that most retardation may be caused by a disadvantaged home environment means that better living conditions or exposure to special training programs might prevent it. Thus, when children who live under deprived conditions because their mothers are retarded are exposed to special educational programs, their risk of becoming mentally retarded is greatly decreased (Landsman & Ramey, 1989).

FIGURE 14.8
Some mental retardation has genetic causes. Down's syndrome, for example, has been linked to a specific chromosome.

It is also important for retarded people to have the benefit of primary and secondary education, both to gain skills that may enable them to find employment and to give them the social skills necessary to get along with others. In the past, the retarded were educated either in institutions or in special education classes separated from other students in the school. Recently, however, *mainstreaming* has enabled retarded children to share classes with normal children across the United States. The issues involved in mainstreaming are explained in the following Interdisciplinary Dimension.

INTERDISCIPLINARY DIMENSION EDUCATION

Mainstreaming the Mentally Retarded

We were isolated. Symbolically—and appropriate to the prevailing attitudes—the "handicapped and retarded" classrooms were tucked away in the corner of the school basement. . . . Summing it up, the only contact we had with the "normal" children was visual. We stared at each other. On those occasions, I can report my own feelings: embarrassment. Given the loud, clear message that was daily being delivered to them, I feel quite confident that I can also report their feeling: YECH! We, the children in the "handicapped" class, were internalizing the "yech" message—plus a couple of others. We were in school because children go to school, but we were outcasts, with no future and no expectation of one. I, for one, certainly never contemplated my future. I could not even picture one, much less dream about it (Massachusetts Advocacy Center, 1987, pp. 4–5).

These are the words of a disabled person who was enrolled in "special education" classes. They capture the frustration some disabled students feel when they are separated from the other children in their school. But until recently it was standard practice to place students classified as disabled (mostly speech impaired, emotionally disturbed, and mentally retarded children) in these special education classes. The philosophy behind special education was that these students needed extra help, which could best be delivered in a special setting.

Special education classes were certainly a big improvement over the situation that existed at the turn of the century, when no schooling at all was available for the disabled, or the situation in the 1950s or 1960s, in which young children with noticeable disabilities usually stayed home with their mothers or were sent away to institutions (Odom & McEvoy, 1988).

But in the 1960s, as the civil rights movement was crusading against racial segregation, some educational leaders began arguing that students with disabilities, too, would be better off academically and socially if they weren't segregated from other students (Forest & Lusthaus, 1989; Stainback, Stainback, & Bunch, 1989). In response to pressure from these educational leaders and from parents and organizations representing the disabled, Congress passed Public Law 94-142, the Education for All Handicapped Children Act, in 1975. This law required the states to establish "procedures to assure that, to the maximum extent appropriate, handicapped children . . . are educated with children who are not handicapped" (PL 94-142, Section 612[5]).

This law legislated the procedure called **mainstreaming**—the placement of children with disabilities into educational programs designed for and attended by normally developing children.

Some of the arguments for mainstreaming were based on the many problems encountered in the old "dual" system (Stainback, Stainback, & Bunch, 1989)—problems such as the following:

- The dual system is inefficient, because two separate systems must be maintained.
- Students in special education classes become labeled as deviant and therefore have low expectations of themselves. As a mother of a child with Down's syndrome remarked about her son's experience in special classrooms, "I think he was trained to be retarded" (Flynn & Kowalczyk-McPhee, 1989).

- The dual system doesn't prepare students to live in the real world. When they leave school, there are not "regular" and "special" worlds. A student who was segregated in special classes throughout her school years puts it this way: "I graduated . . . completely unprepared for the real world. So I just stayed in the house all day, a shut-in, believing a job was out of the question. . . . Believe me, a segregated environment just will not do as preparation for an integrated life" (Massachusetts Advocacy Center, 1987, p. 4).

In addition, proponents of mainstreaming argued that it would provide the following advantages:

- Mainstreamed students would be exposed to a richer, more stimulating environment, which would enhance their academic performance.
- The regular students would serve as role models whom the retarded students could imitate.
- The mainstreamed students could interact socially with the regular students.

Has mainstreaming delivered on these promises? Its early proponents cited studies that compared the performance of students in mainstreaming programs with those in special education programs. Most of these early studies reported either no difference in the performance of children in the two programs or better performance by the mainstreamed students. Ironically, these studies, which provided the main scientific evidence favoring the passage of Public Law 94-142, turned out to be flawed because they did not randomly assign subjects to the mainstreaming and special education groups. Without this randomization, students with the most severe problems were usually placed in the special education groups, making comparisons of the performance of these two groups meaningless.

When we look at the results of more recent studies that have randomly assigned subjects to groups, we find little or no difference between the academic achievement of special education and mainstreamed students (Gottlieb, Alter, & Gottlieb, 1991; Odom & McEvoy, 1988).

Mainstreaming appears to be most advantageous in terms of its effects on social interactions between students. Clearly, if students aren't in contact they can't interact, so mainstreaming at least provides the possibility for interaction. Some studies show, however, that regular students tend to avoid interaction with retarded students (Gottlieb, 1981; Gottlieb et al., 1991; Gresham, 1982). Interaction is more likely to occur when special programs designed to promote interaction are used (Flynn & Kowalczyk-McPhee, 1989; Jenkins, Odom, & Speltz, 1989; Odom & McEvoy, 1988).

Although the results hoped for from mainstreaming—greater academic achievement and increased social integration and adjustment—haven't always been realized, proponents of mainstreaming argue that to realize its potential benefits we must do more than just place mentally retarded students in classes with regular students. They point out that retarded students have benefited greatly from programs in which (1) teachers are trained to deal with mainstreamed students, (2) the regular students are prepared for the entry of "different" students into their classes, and (3) teachers facilitate interactions between mainstreamed and regular students (Stainback, Stainback, & Bunch, 1989). In other words, just as educational effectiveness varies greatly in regular classrooms, so does the effectiveness of education for the mentally retarded. ∎

So far we have been using the behavioral level of analysis to look at how intelligence is measured and at the characteristics of people whose IQ scores fall at the extremes. Along the way, we have seen indications that intelligence may comprise more than a single quality—for example, Wechsler's scales, which identify different abilities, and savants, in whom high ability in certain areas exists side by side with low ability in others.

But is intelligence, in fact, composed of more than a single quality? If it is, how many qualities are there, and how do those qualities relate to one another? Questions such as these have led psychologists to propose a number of different models to represent the structure of intelligence.

The Structure of Intelligence: Maps of the Mind

The mind is a strange machine which can combine the materials offered to it in the most astonishing ways.

Bertrand Russell (1872–1970)
British philosopher

Should we describe intelligence with just one number, such as the IQ, or with many numbers, representing different kinds of intelligence? This question has been argued by two groups of psychologists, which Robert Sternberg (1990) describes as the *lumpers* and the *splitters*. The lumpers see intelligence as being global, so that one number should suffice to describe it. If they are correct, a person who is well endowed intellectually should perform equally well in a wide variety of areas.

The splitters see intelligence as made up of a number of specific mental faculties. According to this idea, a person might be intelligent in some areas yet not so intelligent in others. The argument between the lumpers and the splitters is, therefore, about the basic structure of intelligence: is it global or is it splintered?

One of the first psychologists to address this question was Charles Spearman (1904, 1927). Spearman noticed that the scores on most tests of ability correlate with one another. That is, a person who does well on test A is also likely to do well on tests B and C. Based on this observation, he proposed that there is a general factor, **g,** which he called **general mental ability,** that underlies people's performance on all of these tests (Figure 14.9). Spearman also noticed, however, that the correlations between these tests were not perfect. The difference between performance on the various tests must, Spearman reasoned, be due to abilities specific to each test, so he proposed that in addition to the general factor people also possess specific abilities related to the material on different tests.

Spearman's proposed structure, which is called the **two-factor theory,** contains components of both the lumper and splitter philosophies. Later psychologists proposed structures that more clearly favor the splitters' idea of numerous specific factors. For example, L. L. Thurstone (1938) analyzed the results of a number of different intelligence tests using a technique called factor analysis. (See Measurement & Methodology, "Factor Analysis.") He concluded that intelligence can be described in terms of the following seven **primary mental abilities**:

1. *Numerical ability,* measured by arithmetic word problems
2. *Reasoning ability,* measured by analogies ("LAWYER is to CLIENT as DOCTOR is to _?_ ") or series completions (2, 4, 7, 11, ?)
3. *Verbal fluency,* measured by how fast people can produce words ("What are 50 words that start with the letter *s*?")
4. *Verbal comprehension,* measured by vocabulary tests and tests of reading comprehension
5. *Spatial visualization,* measured by tests requiring mental manipulation of pictorial representations ("How many sides does this solid figure have?")
6. *Perceptual ability,* measured by testing for rapid recognition of symbols ("Cross out the letter *s* every time it appears in this sentence.")
7. *Memory,* measured by testing for recall of words, sentences, or picture-word pairs

Other psychologists have proposed even more specialized abilities. J. J. Guilford (1967) proposed 120 elementary abilities (Figure 14.10), with no *general*

FIGURE 14.9
Spearman proposed that a general mental ability, g, underlies people's performance on tests for specific abilities. This general factor is represented here by the overlapping area of the three abilities shown in this diagram.

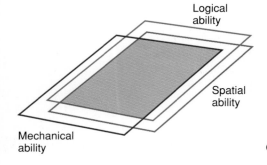

Logical ability

Spatial ability

Mechanical ability

quality of "intelligence" apart from those abilities. In a similar vein, Howard Gardner (1983), in his book *Frames of Mind: The Theory of Multiple Intelligences*, states that his goal is to "undermine the common notion of intelligence as a general capacity or potential which every human being possesses to a greater or lesser extent" (p. ix). Gardner proposes the following seven basic types of intelligence:

1. *Linguistic intelligence* is the ability to use words.
2. *Logical-mathematical intelligence* is the ability to reason logically and solve number problems.
3. *Spatial intelligence* includes the abilities involved in finding your way around the environment and forming mental images.

MEASUREMENT & METHODOLOGY

Factor Analysis

Factor analysis is a mathematical technique to simplify the interpretation of complex data. We can understand how it works by imagining that we are giving a number of tests to a group of people, with each test focusing on a specific ability. For example, we might give tests to measure the person's reading comprehension, vocabulary, mathematical problem-solving ability, logical reasoning ability, and knowledge of general information. We could then use factor analysis to investigate how the scores on those tests are related. For example, we would expect that people who do well on the reading comprehension test might also do well on the vocabulary test—that is, the scores on these tests would be *highly correlated*. By determining how the results in different tests are correlated, factor analysis can enable us to group together tests that measure common abilities. If we applied factor analysis to our five tests we might end up with two factors: one that groups reading, vocabulary, and general knowledge (we might call this a *verbal ability factor*) and one that groups mathematical problem-solving and logical reasoning abilities (we might call this a *problem-solving factor*).

Researchers in the areas of intelligence and personality have used factor analysis to simplify complex arrays of test scores into simpler, smaller sets of factors. In this way they gain insight into the attributes that may underlie a number of diverse test results.

The number in each box is a correlation between the scores on the two tests that intersect in this box. By determining correlations between all pairs of tests, we find that reading, vocabulary, and general knowledge all correlate highly with each other (verbal ability factor) and that mathematical reasoning and problem solving correlate highly with each other (the problem solving factor).

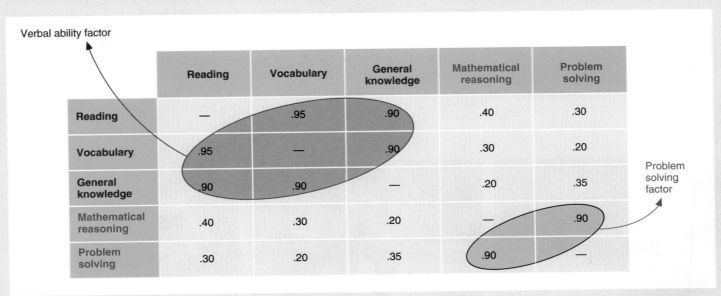

	Reading	Vocabulary	General knowledge	Mathematical reasoning	Problem solving
Reading	—	.95	.90	.40	.30
Vocabulary	.95	—	.90	.30	.20
General knowledge	.90	.90	—	.20	.35
Mathematical reasoning	.40	.30	.20	—	.90
Problem solving	.30	.20	.35	.90	—

Verbal ability factor

Problem solving factor

FIGURE 14.10

Guilford's model of intelligence proposes 120 different intellectual abilities. Each ability is based on a combination of factors representing (1) one of five types of mental operations; (2) one of four types of contents on which the mental operations are performed; and (3) one of six products or outcomes of applying the operations to the contents. For our purposes, the important feature of Guilford's model is his contention that intelligence consists of so many different abilities.

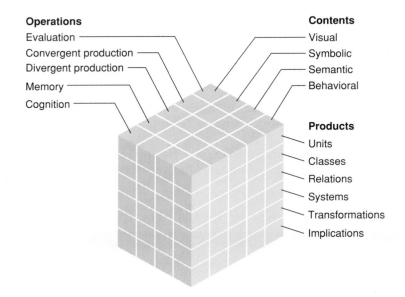

Operations
- Evaluation
- Convergent production
- Divergent production
- Memory
- Cognition

Contents
- Visual
- Symbolic
- Semantic
- Behavioral

Products
- Units
- Classes
- Relations
- Systems
- Transformations
- Implications

4. *Musical intelligence* is the ability to perceive and create pitch and rhythm patterns.
5. *Body-kinesthetic intelligence* is the ability to carry out motor movements, such as might be practiced by a surgeon or a dancer.
6. *Interpersonal intelligence* is the ability to understand other people.
7. *Intrapersonal intelligence* is the ability to understand oneself and to develop a sense of one's own identity.

Gardner's proposal of these different "intelligences" is in harmony with the splitter philosophy, which affirms that intelligence is made up of a number of specific abilities. Gardner goes beyond this idea, however, by including items—such as musical abilities, motor abilities, and the ability to understand people—that aren't usually accounted for by intelligence tests. Gardner argues that these abilities are just as important as the traditional verbal and mathematical skills that now dominate intelligence tests. He is therefore challenging the traditional way that psychologists have defined and measured intelligence, an idea we will return to at the end of this chapter.

What can we say about the models? Currently no single model enjoys unanimous support. However, we can say that the weight of the evidence gathered from intelligence tests favors the idea that intelligence has several components, or that there are several types of intelligence. This is reflected in practical terms by the Wechsler test, which measures performance on a number of scales.

Some of Gardner's seven types of intelligence. Architects use spatial intelligence, dancers use body-kinesthetic intelligence, and counselors use interpersonal intelligence.

If all scales yielded the same score, they wouldn't be necessary. The fact that they don't supports the idea of multiple components of intelligence.

In addition to working at the behavioral level to create models of intelligence, psychologists also work at the cognitive level to ask another question: "What kinds of mental processes underlie intelligence?"

The Mechanisms of Intelligence: Looking at Mental Processes

Intelligence is quickness to apprehend as distinct from ability,
which is capacity to act wisely on the thing apprehended.

Alfred North Whitehead (1861–1947)
British philosopher

In previous chapters we have seen how cognitive psychologists have investigated the mental processes involved in memory and cognition. This idea of looking at mental processes has also been embraced by cognitive psychologists to explore the nature of intelligence. Researchers using the information-processing approach ask questions like these:

8   THINKING

1. Is there a relationship between the speed of mental processing and intelligence?
2. Is there a way, using information-processing principles, to measure the intelligence of infants?
3. What cognitive processes occur as people solve a specific problem?

Processing Speed and Adult Intelligence

The information-processing approach to the measurement of intelligence is based on the hypothesis that intelligence is related to the speed at which the mind can process information (Vernon, 1983). This hypothesis, which is rooted in the biological level of analysis, states that more intelligent people should have more rapidly functioning physiological mechanisms, and that this increased physiological speed will be reflected in faster reaction times. Furthermore, these faster reaction times should be reflected in better performance on traditional intelligence tests. P. A. Vernon and his co-workers (1985) put it this way: "To the extent that speed-of-processing is a factor underlying intelligence, it would be expected that persons who can process information quickly (as evidenced by their reaction time) should . . . be able to answer more questions correctly during an intelligence test" (p. 370).

When expressed in this way, Vernon's suggestion that reaction time might be related to intelligence sounds reasonable. However, 100 years earlier James Cattell failed to find a relationship between reaction time and college grades. Why would present day psychologists propose using reaction time as a measure when it didn't work for Cattell? We can answer this question by looking at the difference between the reaction times Cattell measured and the ones measured by the information-processing psychologists. Cattell measured simple reaction times to simple stimuli by determining how quickly people reacted to a brief tone or flashing light. Present day psychologists measure choice reaction times to more complex stimuli. For example, in one choice reaction time task, subjects push the "home" button in the apparatus shown in Figure 14.11. This activates three of the eight lights, two being closer to each other than the third. The subject's task is to press the button next to the more distant light as rapidly as possi-

FIGURE 14.11
Apparatus used to measure choice reaction time. When a trial starts, the subject pushes the home button and three of the lights are lit, two close together and the third farther away. The subject then pushes the button under the light that is farther away. In this example, the correct answer would be the third light from the right.

FIGURE 14.12
Results of Ackerman's experiment. Each data point represents the reaction time of people who scored within a particular range on an intelligence test. People with higher scores on the test tend to have faster reaction times.

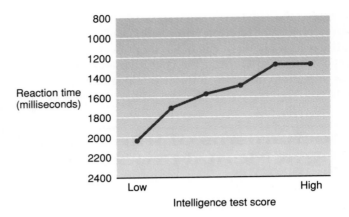

In another experiment, Phillip Ackerman (1986) combined choice reaction time with meaningful stimuli. He presented subjects with three categories such as *bird*, *tree*, and *time* and then, after a pause, presented three words such as *boat*, *hour*, and *rain*. The subjects' task was to choose which of the second group of words fit into one of the first three categories by pushing the correct button as rapidly as possible (the correct answer is *hour*, in this case). He presented many such problems to a group of people, and when he plotted their reaction times versus their scores on a conventional intelligence test, he found that those with faster reaction times tended to score higher on the intelligence test (Figure 14.12). This relationship between information-processing speed and IQ is consistent with the assumption that rapid physiological mechanisms underlie good performance on intelligence tests (see Eysenck, 1982). This principle has been applied not only to the problem of understanding adult intelligence but also to a problem that has baffled psychologists for years—how to measure infant intelligence.

Measuring Infant Intelligence

9   DEVELOPMENT

The problem with measuring infant intelligence has been that infants' IQs determined through conventional intelligence tests were poorly related to their IQs measured later in childhood (Bayley, 1949; McCall, Hogarty, & Hurlburt, 1972) (Table 14.1). We can understand the reason for this poor relationship between infant and later IQs by considering what the infant tests measured. Conventional infant intelligence tests assessed motor capacities such as the ability to sit, walk, and manipulate objects. However, tests for children and adults emphasized verbal ability and reasoning skill (Lecuyer, 1989). It is no wonder, therefore, that the IQ measured between 1 and 6 months, based largely on motor performance, is

TABLE 14.1
Correlations between infant IQ scores and later IQ scores

Age at First Testing	Age at Follow-Up		
	3–4 Years	5–7 Years	8–18 Years
1–6 months	.23	.01	.01
7–12 months	.33	.06	.20
13–18 months	.47	.30	.21
19–30 months	.54	.41	.49

Source: McCall, Hogarty, and Hurlburt, 1972.

poorly related to later IQ, but that the IQ measured between 13 and 30 months, based on the child's rapidly growing verbal abilities, begins to show a relationship to IQ scores measured later (McCall et al., 1972; Vernon, 1979).

Information-processing psychologists have tackled this problem by devising ways to measure intelligence that focus on mental processes. This poses a special challenge, because of young infants' inability to use language. Psychologists solved this problem by using the following two measures, which reflect mental processes but don't depend on language: (1) recognition memory for visual stimuli and (2) the rate of habituation to visual stimuli.

Recognition memory refers to the infant's ability to recognize a stimulus that was presented previously. Joseph Fagan (1984a) measured recognition memory in 7-month-olds by first familiarizing them with a picture of a face and then showing them that face together with another one they had never seen. When he did this, the infants tended to look longer at the novel face, indicating that they must have recognized the original face. When Fagan measured the IQ of these same children at 5 years of age, he found the correlation between IQ and the amount of time they looked at the novel face to be .40. In other words, greater recognition memory at 7 months predicts a higher IQ at 5 years (also see Fagan, 1984b; Fagan & Singer, 1983).

7   MEMORY

Habituation, another way to measure infant intelligence, refers to an infant's tendency to look less and less at a stimulus that is presented repeatedly. When Alan Slater and his co-workers (1989) measured how fast 4½-month-old children habituated to pictures and then measured their IQ when they were 8½ years old, they found correlations of about .60 to .70 between the speed of habituation and IQ. Faster habituation at 4½ months was associated with higher intelligence at 8½ years (also see Sigman et al., 1991).

Why should better recognition memory and faster habituation in infancy be associated with higher IQ years later? The answer is similar to that proposed for adults: faster information processing is associated with higher intelligence. Applying this idea to infant habituation, psychologists believe rapid habituation reflects faster information processing—the infant who rapidly takes in the information in a stimulus becomes bored sooner and decreases her or his looking time. Psychologists have also linked superior recognition memory in infants to efficient processing of information by hypothesizing that good memory is associated with the efficient encoding and storage of characteristics of the face stimuli. The fact is, we don't know exactly what is behind these relationships and we must always be cautious about drawing conclusions based on these results. (See Measurement & Methodology, "Tall Myopes Have Higher IQs: What Is the Cause?") However, whatever the mechanisms involved, there is no doubt that these new ways of assessing infant intelligence vastly improve our ability to predict adult intelligence from infant tests.

Our description of the information-processing approach so far has emphasized speed of processing as a factor that underlies intelligence. Information-processing psychologists have also sought other factors in intelligence by studying how adults go about solving the kinds of problems found on intelligence tests.

Information Processing During Problem Solving

How do people actually go about solving the problems on intelligence tests? This question has been asked by a number of researchers (Glaser & Pellegrino, 1987; Mullholland, Pellegrino, & Glaser, 1980; Pellegrino, 1985; Sternberg, 1977) for verbal and geometrical **analogy problems** like the ones shown in Figure 14.13. They have focused on analogies because they are used so extensively on intelligence tests. The strategy of research on analogies is (1) to determine how subjects go about solving these problems and (2) to identify differences between how low-ability and high-ability subjects solve them.

8   THINKING

Complete each sequence with one of the choices. Try these problems before reading the caption.

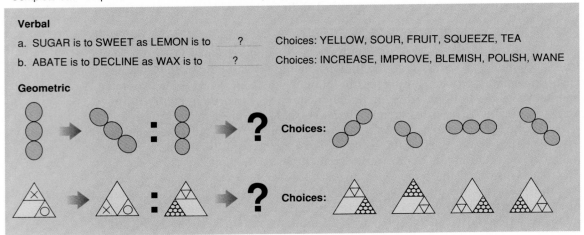

Verbal

a. SUGAR is to SWEET as LEMON is to ___?___   Choices: YELLOW, SOUR, FRUIT, SQUEEZE, TEA

b. ABATE is to DECLINE as WAX is to ___?___   Choices: INCREASE, IMPROVE, BLEMISH, POLISH, WANE

Geometric

FIGURE 14.13
Verbal and geometrical analogy problems.
The answers to the verbal problems are (a)
sour and (b) wane. The answer to both
geometrical problems is the fourth choice.

One way to determine how people are solving a problem is to ask them to verbalize their thoughts while they are solving it, as described in the Measurement & Methodology in Chapter 8 titled "Thinking Aloud Protocols." For example, consider the following narration produced by a subject in an experiment conducted by Joan Heller (1979; see Glaser & Pellegrino, 1987).

Problem: TEA is to COFFEE as BREAD is to ___?___

Narration (before seeing the choices below): "Tea is to coffee as bread is to . . . rolls, because tea and coffee, they're both drinks, and they're about the same thing, just two different names for two different drinks, and bread and a roll would be about the same—two different names for the same thing."

Reaction to choices

MILK	(Reject)	"That doesn't fit. It's a drink."
BUTTER	(Reject)	"Butter is something you put on bread, that doesn't fit."
ROLLS	(Accept)	"That's good."
JAM	(Reject)	"It's like butter, something you put on bread. It wouldn't fit because you don't put coffee on tea or in tea."

By collecting many of these descriptions, Heller was able to determine that high- and low-ability individuals use different problem-solving strategies. She found that low-ability individuals more often stay with an incorrect hypothesis, whereas high-ability individuals use the more effective strategy of modifying their incorrect hypothesis when they see it isn't working.

Another way to study analogy solutions is to present problems of varying complexity such as the geometrical analogies shown in Figure 14.14. The analogy in the first problem contains only one element (a circle) and one transformation (the large circle becomes a smaller one), whereas the one in the second problem contains two elements (a circle and some pluses), which undergo two transformations (the circle gets smaller and the number of pluses is reduced).

By comparing the time it takes for subjects to solve problems of varying complexity, researchers have been able to break these problems into a sequence of operations. For example, for most people the first step in solving the second problem in Figure 14.14 is *encoding:* the subject identifies the stimuli on the left side of the analogy: circles containing pluses. The next step is *inferring the transformation:* the subject determines that the large circle is changed to a small one and that the two pluses are reduced to one. The subject then encodes the stimulus on the right and applies the transformation rule to that stimulus: the sur-

Complete these sequences. Try these problems before reading the caption.

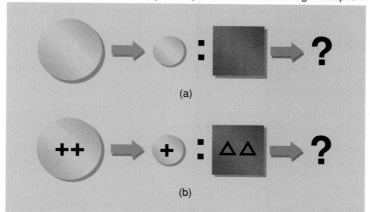

(a)

(b)

FIGURE 14.14
Geometrical analogies in which no choices
are given and the subject has to create the
correct answer. In (a) the answer is a small
square. In (b) the answer is a small square
with one Δ.

rounding figure is reduced in size, and the internal elements are reduced from
two to one. The result is the missing stimulus.

Tim Mullholland and his co-workers (1980) found that highly skilled analogy solvers often spend more time on the initial encoding than do less highly
skilled analogy solvers. Apparently, more time spent at the beginning of the
process pays off in faster overall performance. Similar results have been obtained using verbal analogies (Sternberg, 1977).

The information-processing studies described here represent an important
attempt to achieve a major goal of modern intelligence research—an understanding of the relationship between cognitive processes and intelligent behavior. Another goal of modern intelligence research is to determine the roles played
by heredity and the environment in shaping intelligence. We now turn to research at the biological, behavioral, and contextual levels of analysis that is designed to unravel the relative contributions of genetics and environmental influences to people's measured intelligence.

The Sources of Intelligence:
The Roles of Heredity and the Environment

*The intellect, character and skill possessed by any man are the product of certain
original tendencies and the training which they have received.*

Edward Thorndike (1914)

The early psychologists' discussions of how heredity and the environment contribute to a person's abilities often took place within the context of the *nature versus nurture debate*. This debate pitted researchers who believed that the most important factor in determining a person's ability was nature (heredity) against
those who believed it to be nurture (the environment). For example, Francis Galton argued for the primacy of heredity, whereas behaviorists such as John Watson and B. F. Skinner argued for the importance of the environment.

When we introduced basic developmental issues in Chapter 9, however,
we saw that the debate pitting hereditarians against environmentalists is a thing
of the past. Psychologists now see heredity and environment not as competing
influences but as interacting forces that are jointly responsible for determining a
person's abilities. The important question as far as present day psychologists are
concerned is not whether heredity or environment is more important, but how

heredity and environment determine *differences* between people. When we say that one person is more intelligent than another, how much of that difference is due to the genes inherited from the two sets of parents and how much is due to the environment in which each was raised?

The Role of Heredity

3   BIOLOGY

One way to sort out the contributions of heredity and environment to intelligence is by conducting family studies that compare the intelligence of family

MEASUREMENT & METHODOLOGY

Tall Myopes Have Higher IQs: What Is the Cause?

In interpreting psychological research we have to guard constantly against interpreting a correlation between two variables as a cause-and-effect relationship. Consider, for example, the following two relationships:

1. People who are myopic (nearsighted) have higher intelligence scores than people who are not myopic (Rosner & Belkin, 1987; Teasdale, Fuchs, & Goldschmidt, 1988). This relationship (Figure A) was determined from visual acuity and intelligence measurements made on 18,800 18-year-old draftees into the Danish army. So does nearsightedness cause a higher IQ?

2. Tall children have higher IQs than shorter children (Scott, 1962; Wilson et al., 1986). This relationship (Figure B) was determined from height and IQ data collected from 13,900 children by the U.S. National Center for Health Statistics. Does being tall raise your IQ? (Or does being smart make you taller?)

The point of these examples is to reinforce a lesson introduced in Chapter 2: *correlation is not causation*. This lesson is especially pertinent to intelligence, because you may often encounter claims that one variable or another is "associated with" higher intelligence. As the examples of myopia and height illustrate, good evidence of a *relationship* between variables is not the same as evidence that one variable *causes* the other.

FIGURE A

Relationship between intelligence-test scores of Danish army recruits and their degrees of myopia. Recruits who have greater myopia are more likely to have higher IQs.

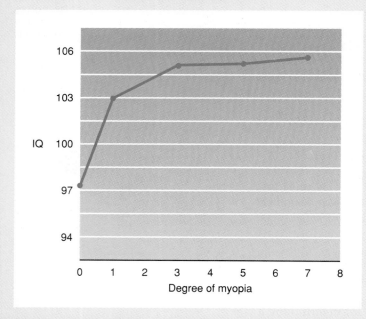

FIGURE B

Relationship between American children's IQ scores and their heights. Taller children are more likely to have higher IQs.

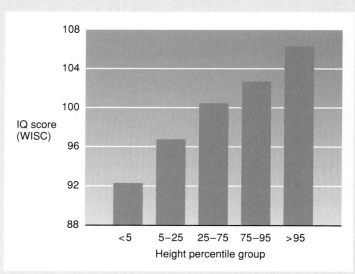

members who are genetically related in different degrees. Psychologists carry out these studies by collecting IQ scores from large numbers of families and calculating correlations between members related in the following ways:

- Identical twins, who trace their development to the same zygote (a single fertilized egg, split to form two genetically identical fertilized eggs). They are called **monozygotic (MZ) twins,** and share 100% of their genes.
- Fraternal twins, who trace their origins to two different zygotes (two separate eggs, fertilized by different sperm). They are called **dizygotic (DZ) twins,** and share, on the average, 50% of their genes.

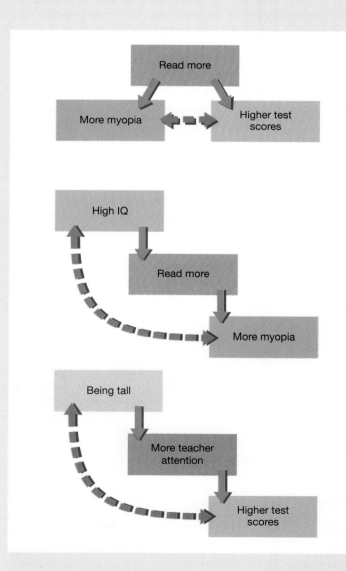

Consider some possible explanations for the observed relationship between intelligence and myopia and height. Although myopia is determined primarily by genetics, there is evidence that close work, such as reading, can cause an increase in myopia (Walraven, Turkel, & Trachtman, 1978; Young, 1961). Thus, people who read a lot might be more prone to myopia. At the same time, the knowledge they gain from reading might increase their test scores. Or perhaps people who have higher IQs in the first place tend to read more, which in turn makes them more prone to myopia (Figure C).

When considering why taller children have higher IQs, we can look to biological causes such as early childhood diet (since poor nutrition could affect both IQ and physical growth). More subtly, we could investigate behavioral causes by asking whether teachers pay more attention to taller students, thereby increasing both their learning and their motivation to obtain higher test scores.

It is clear that we should be cautious before inferring that a specific variable *causes* higher intelligence (or any other phenomenon). Correlational evidence can sometimes suggest where to look for possible causes, but it cannot by itself establish that a causal relationship exists.

FIGURE C

Three possible explanations for the apparent correlations between myopia, height, and IQ. Note that according to these explanations the relationships between IQ and myopia and between IQ and height are *correlational* relationships (indicated by a dashed arrow), *not* cause-and-effect relationships.

Sandra Scarr, a developmental psychologist from the University of Virginia, has done extensive research on the effects of heredity and environment on intelligence.

- Siblings born at different times, who share 50% of their genes.
- Siblings who are not genetically related to each other, such as in a family with both adopted and natural children.

The combined results of a number of family studies are shown in Figure 14.15. These data contain the following evidence supporting the role of genetics in determining intelligence:

- The correlation between the IQs of MZ twins reared together is .86; that of DZ twins reared together is .60 (Bouchard & McGue, 1981). The higher correlation for MZ twins reflects their genetic similarity (Scarr & Carter-Saltzman, 1982).
- The correlation between the IQs of biologically related siblings reared together is .47, of nonbiologically related siblings, .31. The shared genes of the biologically related siblings increase the correlation between their IQ scores.

Another way of using family members to investigate the role of genetics in determining a person's characteristics is to compare *individual* pairs of MZ and DZ twins. In Chapter 9 we saw that the changes in IQ that occur when we test children beginning at 3 months and continuing to 6 years are remarkably similar for the MZ twins, but the changes are not as similar for the DZ twins. Genetic programming apparently accounts for the greater similarity in intelligence scores over time observed in the MZ twins (Wilson, 1983).

Further evidence for the role of heredity comes from adoption studies. Sandra Scarr and Richard Weinberg (1983) compared the IQs of adopted children with the IQs of their biological parents as well as their adoptive parents. They found a moderate relationship (a correlation of .30 to .45) between the IQs of the children and their biological parents but only a low correlation between the children's IQs and those of their adoptive parents (a correlation of .10). Thus, even though adopted children share the environment of their adoptive parents, their IQ score is more closely related to that of their biological parents, whom they may never have seen.

The Role of the Environment

Looking again at Figure 14.15, we can also find evidence supporting the role of environment in determining IQ. Consider, for example, the fact that the correla-

FIGURE 14.15
Correlations of intelligence scores between siblings with different degrees of relatedness. The amount of black in the figures on the left indicates the degree of genetic overlap. Greater genetic overlap and being reared together are both associated with higher correlations between IQ scores, indicating that both genetic and environmental factors play roles in determining the IQ.

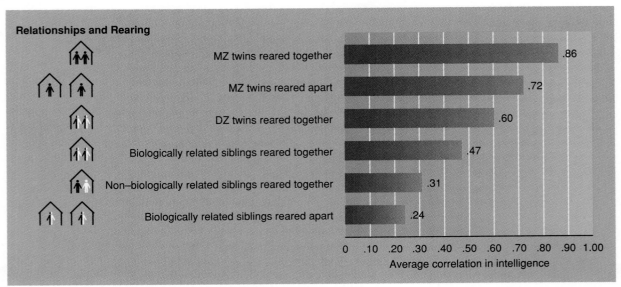

tion for MZ twins is .86. As impressive as this correlation is, it would be 1.00 if heredity were the *only* factor controlling intelligence, because MZ twins are genetically identical. Also, notice that when MZ twins experience different environments by being reared apart, the correlation between their IQs drops from .86 to .72. Similarly, the correlation for siblings drops from .47 if they are reared together to .24 if they are reared apart.

We can also compare DZ twins with nontwin siblings. Although they all share 50% of their genes, the DZ twins' IQs are more closely related—presumably because twins, whose ages match, experience more similar environments than do nontwin siblings, whose ages are different. Finally, even if children are biologically unrelated, just growing up in the same household results in a correlation of .31—evidence that environment affects intelligence.

The importance of environment to intelligence has also been demonstrated in studies in which children are moved from a deprived environment to an enriched one. For example, Scarr and Weinberg (1976) found that a group of African-American children who were adopted by white middle-class families had average IQs of 110, about 15 to 20 points higher than children raised in the deprived community from which they were adopted.

In another adoption study, done in France, researchers located a number of working-class mothers who had let one of their children be adopted by a middle-class professional family but had kept another. When they compared the children's IQ scores and failure rates in school, they found that the adopted children had higher IQs and lower school failure rates than the children who remained in the working-class environment (Schiff et al., 1978) (Figure 14.16). As in the Scarr and Weinberg study, these children's IQs increased when they were placed in families of higher socioeconomic status.

What are the implications of the fact that both genetics and the environment influence intelligence? Every individual inherits a set of genes that determines her or his abilities. There is not, however, a single "intelligence gene." Intelligence is determined by a large number of different genes that determine a person's basic potential. The person's actual level of intelligence is, however, determined by the interplay of this potential with the environmental conditions the person experiences during development.

It is important that we not overlook the social significance of this last statement. Intelligence is one of the determinants of a person's ability to obtain schooling and jobs and therefore helps determine the person's position in society. Thus, when people grow up in a deprived environment, they are handicapped not only by their lack of money, possibly dangerous living conditions, and poor health care, but also by the lack of opportunity to develop their full intellectual potential.

The environment in which a person lives can have other implications for intelligence, as well. Someone who grows up in a culture other than the one in which an intelligence test was developed may have normal intelligence but perform poorly on the test because of a lack of knowledge of the test's "culture." In such situations, intelligence tests will not accurately reflect people's capabilities. This is a serious problem, which we consider further here and in the Follow-Through at the end of the chapter.

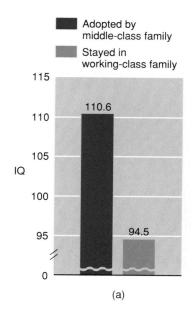

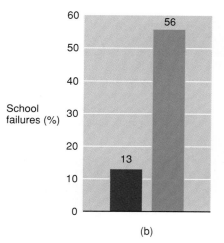

FIGURE 14.16
Results of a French adoption study. Working-class children adopted by middle-class families had (a) higher IQs and (b) lower school-failure rates than their siblings who remained in working-class families.

Intelligence and Society: The Uses and Abuses of Intelligence Tests

Testing is one of psychology's most visible contributions to our society. Millions of people take tests every year, and the scores they earn on those tests often play an important role in determining which grade school and high school classes they are assigned to, which colleges they can attend, and which jobs they will be offered. Some of these tests are **achievement tests**—tests designed to measure mastery of specific areas such as reading, mathematics, foreign languages, and science. Others are **aptitude tests**—such as the College Entrance Examination Board's Scholastic Aptitude Test (SAT), designed to predict future performance. Intelligence tests are aptitude tests designed to measure general mental ability. Other aptitude tests are designed to measure ability in specific areas.

Because of the importance of these tests in people's lives, it is critical that they be designed to accurately reflect a person's capabilities. Do intelligence tests accomplish this? We can approach this question in a number of ways. First we will introduce the concepts of reliability and validity; after that we will consider the specific problem of whether intelligence tests developed in one culture can accurately measure the IQs of people from another.

Test Reliability and Validity

For scores on either achievement or aptitude tests to be meaningful, the test must be both *reliable* and *valid*. **Reliability** refers to *consistency*—the extent to which a measuring device yields the same result when measurements are repeated under similar conditions. A bathroom scale is reliable if it registers the same weight when a person is weighed twice within a short period of time. A test is reliable if it produces the same score when a person is tested at two different times (Figure 14.17a).

One way to test for reliability is the **test-retest method,** in which a large group of people are tested and then retested later. A *reliability coefficient*, calculated by determining the correlations between the two sets of scores, indicates how replicable the scores are from one testing session to the next. A reliability coefficient of 1.00 means that the test is very consistent; a coefficient of 0 means it is

FIGURE 14.17
(a) High reliability: People earn similar scores when tested twice. Low reliability: People earn different scores when tested twice. (b) High predictive validity: Scores on the test predict scores on another measure. Low predictive validity: Scores on the test do not predict scores on the other measure.

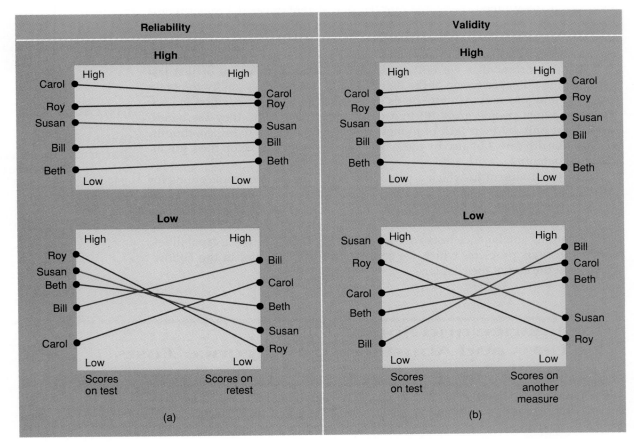

totally inconsistent. All the intelligence tests in regular use today are highly reliable, with reliability coefficients of .90 and above (Graham & Lilly, 1984).

Validity refers to whether a test measures what it is supposed to measure. One way to determine this is to verify the test's **predictive validity**—its ability to predict the characteristic the test is supposed to measure (Figure 14.17b). Psychologists usually measure predictive validity by determining the correlation between people's test scores and a particular behavior. We would expect, for example, people who score well on a test of mathematical ability to get high grades in mathematics courses. We would also expect that the scores on the SAT, which is supposed to predict college grades, would correlate highly with college grades. The actual correlation between SAT scores and college grades is about .42, indicating a moderate degree of predictive validity (Ramist, 1984).

Another way to determine validity is to measure **content validity**—the extent to which the test questions are relevant to the ability being tested and are an accurate cross section of possible questions relevant to that ability. For example, a test of mathematical ability should not include questions that require knowledge of unrelated topics such as biology or physics. Also, a test of mathematical ability that contained only simple addition problems would lack content validity because it didn't cover other areas of mathematics.

So far we have discussed tests designed to measure precisely defined skills (mathematics ability) or aptitudes (college grades). Being able to precisely define what a test is supposed to measure makes it easier to determine its validity. Establishing validity becomes more difficult, however, for tests designed to measure a difficult-to-define construct such as intelligence. **Construct validity** refers to how well the test results reflect the quality or trait that the test was designed to measure. Thus, content validity is one type of construct validity, since it is concerned with the appropriateness of the test questions.

Researchers can go further in assessing construct validity by considering what other qualities are *associated* with the quality being measured. One quality usually associated with intelligence, for example, is the ability to do well in academic subjects in school. Thus, one way to determine the construct validity of an intelligence test is to measure the correlation between IQ scores and school grades. Or we might give our test to two groups that we would predict would differ in intelligence, such as successful inventors and unskilled laborers. If our test is valid, the inventors should score higher than the laborers.

It should be clear from our discussion that a test can be extremely reliable yet completely invalid. For example, if we determined intelligence by measuring people's shoe sizes, our measurement would be highly reliable—it would be the same every time it was taken—but it would not be valid, because the size of people's feet is unrelated to their intelligence. Another way a test could be invalid is if it were designed by people in one culture but taken by people in another. Such a test could result in scores that tell us little about a person's actual intelligence.

Intelligence as a Cultural Construct

We have see that experts on intelligence haven't succeeded in agreeing on a definition of intelligence. This inability to define intelligence has not, however, stopped psychologists from constructing tests to measure it. This means that for practical purposes intelligence is defined by the items included on those tests.

The implications of this definition-by-test-items approach to intelligence become clear when we consider that intelligence tests are designed to predict school performance. Since in our society the material covered in school is determined by white, middle-class culture, the items on intelligence tests reflect that culture. It is not inaccurate, therefore, to say that both intelligence tests and our conception of intelligence itself are constructs of our culture.

If intelligence is a construct of culture, isn't it possible that cultures other than ours have different conceptions of intelligence? Cross-cultural studies indicate that this is so. A comparison of Australian and Chinese conceptions of intelligence shows that both value creativity, problem solving, and accumulated knowledge; but whereas Australians place particular value on language and communication skills, Chinese emphasize carefulness and correctness of thinking (Keats, 1982).

Looking at cultures less similar to our own, we find that the Mashona people of Zimbabwe feel that one aspect of intelligence is being cautious in social relations, and that the Bagandau people of Uganda value persistence and mental order (Irvine, 1969, 1970; Wober, 1974). Different conceptions of intelligence in different cultures mean that someone considered intelligent in one culture might not be in another. When members of the Kpelle tribe in Western Africa are tested using translated versions of our intelligence tests, their scores are often equivalent to those of a Western-culture grade-schooler. However, observation of the Kpelle's accomplishments and their way of relating to people shows clearly that their intelligence is far above that level (see the Follow-Through in Chapter 8, "Thinking in Traditional Cultures"). What this means is that tests may be valid only for members of the culture that designed the test. We consider this issue further in the Follow-Through at the end of this chapter, "Measuring Intelligence in Minority Groups."

8   THINKING

The Uses of Intelligence Tests

Psychologists have taken great pains to construct unbiased tests that contain questions that are not more difficult for a particular group and that predict future school performance equally well for all groups. But even if all biases were eliminated from intelligence tests, we would still need to consider the social implications of how the test scores are used.

Consider, for example, the fact that intelligence tests are routinely used to place children in classes according to their ability. This procedure, which is called *tracking*, has its supporters and detractors. Those who favor tracking point out that it is important for individual students to be in classes that are challenging yet not so hard as to be frustrating. According to this reasoning, tracking benefits both high- and low-ability students because they will be assigned to classes in which the level of instruction matches their intellectual capacities (Brophy, 1983; Kulik & Kulik, 1982; Scarr, 1981).

Those against tracking argue that once a child is perceived as having low ability, he or she is doomed to remain in the slow track, with little encouragement to advance (Rist, 1970; Warren, 1988). One mechanism that may cause this to happen is that teachers develop different expectations for children they perceive to have high or low ability and then unconsciously treat them differently.

Is carving masks a sign of intelligence? Probably not in American culture, but in countries such as Sri Lanka, where masks are an important part of the culture, the reverse is likely to be true.

Research has shown that teachers give "low-ability" students less time to answer questions (Allington, 1980), criticize them more often for failure, praise them less frequently for success (Babad, Inbar, & Rosenthal, 1982), pay less attention to them (Adams & Cohen, 1974; Rist, 1970), seat them farther back in the room (Rist, 1970), smile less at them, and make less eye contact with them (Chaiken, Sigler, & Derlega, 1974). If some teachers do treat low-ability students in this way, it is likely to make it harder for them to do well, thereby increasing the chances that they will remain in the slow track. This would be particularly damaging if a student whose potential was underestimated by an IQ score measured at an early age were erroneously assigned to a slow track.

In addition to being used for tracking in schools, IQ tests and other aptitude tests are used to determine college admissions and qualification for scholarships. The SAT, in particular, has been criticized because the lower scores earned by some groups make it more difficult for members of those groups to gain admission to colleges and to win scholarships. This concern is reflected in the 1989 decision of a U.S. federal court judge that the New York Board of Regents could not rely solely on SAT scores to determine the awarding of state scholarships (Glaberson, 1989; Holden, 1989).

The judge's reasoning in this case is particularly important, because he did not say that the SAT was biased. (In fact, many experts testified that the SAT was *not* biased.) He based his decision on the fact that females' lower scores on portions of the test prevented them from receiving their fair share of scholarships.

By reasoning in this way, the judge was taking into account a possible bias introduced not by the particular test but by growing up in our culture. Since females receive less encouragement to go into fields like mathematics and science, they receive less instruction and therefore score more poorly in those areas, on the average, than do males (Kimball, 1989). A similar effect occurs for African Americans, whose lower scores on the SAT may be attributable to the poorer preparation they receive in high school. Considered in this way, the issue of testing becomes more complex than simply determining whether a particular test is biased.

This discussion illustrates the importance of being aware of how intelligence and aptitude tests may restrict people's opportunities. We also need to be realistic about what test scores show. Intelligence tests and the SAT focus on testing language skills and mathematical and reasoning abilities that are associated with success in school. But other skills, ignored by the tests—such as creativity or the ability to get along with others—are more important for nonacademic life. We examine this issue in the next section, by considering some of the things that traditional intelligence tests *don't* measure.

Real-World Intelligence

> *Wisdom consists not so much in knowing what to do*
> *in the ultimate as in knowing what to do next.*
>
> Herbert Hoover (1874–1964)
> 37th president

Are intelligence test scores relevant to real life? Although IQ scores are related to grades in school, there is more to life than high school or college grades. One clue that there may be more to succeeding in the real world than the skills measured by intelligence tests is that the correlation between occupational performance and IQ is only about .20 (Wigdor & Garner, 1982). According to Seymour Epstein, a psychologist who has developed a test that measures the ability to deal effectively with life, "IQ and success in living have little to do with each other. Being intellectually gifted does not predict you will earn the most money or achieve the most recognition" (Goleman, 1988). Epstein also argues that "emotional intelligence" is an important factor in how well people use their intellectual ability. A person with a high IQ who solves problems well in quiet surroundings but can't think well in a group may be ineffective at work.

It has also been observed, at the other end of the IQ continuum, that low IQ is a poor predictor of a person's ability to achieve in the world outside the classroom. Our opening example of Paul O'Brien, who didn't excel in school but achieved success in the "real" world, is representative of such cases. "Street smarts" and good social skills may mean more in the real world than being able to solve math problems or analyze poetry (Landsman & Ramey, 1989).

The idea that intelligence goes beyond what is usually measured in intelligence tests is in harmony with the movement to place increased emphasis on practical intelligence. Norman Frederiksen (1986) points out that real-life problems are rarely posed in multiple-choice form, and that there is a big difference between answering a multiple-choice question and developing a strategy for solving a research problem or selling a product. One test developed by Frederickson is the "Formulating Hypothesis" test, in which senior psychology majors who are going on to graduate school are presented with a description of real psychological investigation, along with a graph or table showing the results. The students' task is to devise hypotheses that might explain the finding.

When Frederiksen compared the students' scores on this test with their performance in graduate school a few years later, he found that the number of hypotheses offered and the unusualness of the hypotheses were better predictors of accomplishments such as doing independent research, authoring a paper, or designing laboratory equipment than were the students' Graduate Record Examination (GRE) scores. As might be expected, however, the GRE was better at predicting first-year grades in graduate school.

This distinction between real-world knowledge and academic knowledge is illustrated by Robert Sternberg's (1984, 1985) **triarchic theory of intelligence** (Figure 14.18). Sternberg's theory is called triarchic because it consists of three subtheories, each describing a different aspect of intelligence:

1. The **componential aspect** refers to a person's ability to learn new things, to think analytically, and to solve problems. This aspect of intelligence is demonstrated by high performance on standard intelligence tests, which require general knowledge and ability in areas such as mathematics and vocabulary.
2. The **experiential aspect** refers to a person's ability to combine different experiences in unique and creative ways. It is responsible for original thinking and creativity in both the arts and the sciences.
3. The **contextual aspect** refers to a person's ability to deal with practical aspects of the environment and to adapt to new and changing contexts. This aspect of intelligence is sometimes called "street smarts."

These three aspects of intelligence are present in each of us, though one aspect is usually dominant. To illustrate this, Sternberg describes three idealized graduate students, each of whom is very strong in one of the aspects (see Trotter, 1986). Read the following descriptions and try to match each student with one of Sternberg's aspects.

Barbara had average grades and low GRE scores, but her letters of recommendation emphasized her capacity for original thinking and skill as a researcher. Her graduate school career confirmed that assessment: she did excellent original research in graduate school.

Alice had almost a 4.0 grade point average as an undergraduate, extremely high GRE scores, and excellent letters of recommendation. She got excellent grades in her first year in graduate school, but later in her graduate career had problems thinking of good ideas for research projects.

FIGURE 14.18

The three aspects of intelligence described in Sternberg's triarchic theory of intelligence.

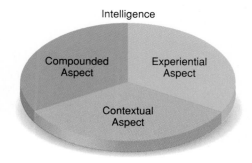

Intelligence

Compounded Aspect

Experiential Aspect

Contextual Aspect

Celia had good grades, GRE scores, and letters of recommendation and performed at an average level in both her graduate courses and research. However, after receiving her Ph.D. she was the easiest of all her peers to place in a good job.

Barbara is an example of a person with a strong experiential aspect, as indicated by her ability to be creative in the research laboratory. Alice has a strong componential aspect. Her strength is in analytical thinking, but without a strong experiential aspect, she lacks the creativity to do well in research. Celia has a strong contextual aspect. Although not as smart academically as Barbara or Alice, Celia is "street smart." She picks the right projects to work on and submits her papers to the right professional journals. (Notice that according to these examples, the key to success in graduate school and beyond lies not in having a high IQ, but in being able to think creatively and to relate to the environment.)

Many other tasks do not necessarily depend on having a high IQ. For example, when Stephen Ceci and Jeffrey Liker (1986) studied the handicapping abilities of 30 men who regularly attended a race track, they found no correlation between success in picking winning horses and IQ. Four of the subjects who were among the best handicappers had IQs in the low to mid-80s, whereas one subject among the worst handicappers had an IQ of 118.

If success at real-world tasks—ranging from functioning in a research laboratory to predicting the odds at a race track—is not related to IQ, what *is* successful performance of these tasks related to? Richard Wagner and Robert Sternberg (1986; Sternberg & Wagner, 1993) have proposed that people use **tacit knowledge**—knowledge that is not taught directly—in dealing with many real-world situations. The rules of how to function in a psychology laboratory or in a business setting may not be taught in school, but they are "picked up" by people who become successful in those fields. One test for this tacit knowledge is Wagner and Sternberg's test for business managers, which contains questions such as the one in Figure 14.19.

Robert Sternberg of Yale University has written extensively about intelligence as well as about the nature of love.

Your first year on the job has been generally favorable. Performance ratings for your department are at least as good as they were before you took over, and perhaps even a little better. You have two assistants. One is quite capable. The other just seems to go through the motions but to be of little real help. You believe that although you are well liked, there is little that would distinguish you in the eyes of your superiors from the nine other managers at a comparable level in the company. Your goal is rapid promotion to the top of the company. The following is a list of things you are considering doing. Rate the importance of each:

   a. Find a way to get rid of the "dead wood," e.g., the less helpful assistant and three or four others.

   b. Participate in a series of panel discussions to be shown on the local public television station.

   c. Find ways to make sure your superiors are aware of your important accomplishments.

   d. Accept a friend's invitation to join the exclusive country club that many higher-level executives belong to.

   e. When making decisions, give a great deal of weight to the way your superiors like things done.

Answer: According to Sternberg, the preferred ranking of the choices is e, a, c, b, d.
Source: Copyright ©1988 by the New York Times Company. Reprinted by permission.

FIGURE 14.19
A question from Wagner and Sternberg's tacit knowledge test

FIGURE 14.20
Which of these couples is actually in a relationship?

Is this test valid? Evidence that it has some validity for measuring business savvy is provided by the fact that the correlation between the subjects' test scores and their job titles and salaries is between .35 and .40.

Another example of the application of real-world intelligence is the use of nonverbal cues to determine relationships between individuals. Try this yourself by looking at the pictures in Figure 14.20. One of these couples is actually involved in a romantic relationship, and the other is not. Try picking the couple you think is involved in a romantic relationship. You'll find the answer on the next page.

How successful were you in this test of one aspect of "social intelligence"? Sternberg and Craig Smith (1985) found that paying attention to the following nonverbal cues helps distinguish the genuine couples from the "fakes":

- *Relaxation:* Genuine couples look, on the average, more relaxed with each other.
- *Angle of bodies:* Genuine couples tend to lean toward each other more.
- *Positioning of arms and legs:* Genuine couples position their arms and legs more naturally.
- *Tenseness of hands:* Fake couples' hands tend to reveal tension and discomfort.
- *Match in socioeconomic class:* Genuine couples are a better match in terms of socioeconomic class.
- *Distance between bodies:* Fake couples maintain a greater distance from each other.
- *Amount of physical contact:* Genuine couples show more physical contact.
- *General similarity:* Genuine couples are more similar in appearance.

The idea of real-world intelligence has led Wagner and Sternberg (1984) to conclude that current theories of intelligence, which assess intelligence as it relates to the *internal environment* of the individual, are inadequate because they ignore the relation between intelligence and the *external environment* in which intelligence functions. According to these researchers, "If our understanding of intelligence is to have any relevance for understanding the interface between the individual and his world, it will have to study the functioning of the individual in his world, rather than merely in a laboratory or on a standardized test" (p. 187).

If Wagner and Sternberg are right, future research will become more concerned with practical intelligence—the application of intelligence in everyday settings. This concern with practical intelligence, combined with new ideas that take an information-processing approach, promises to revolutionize our ideas about what intelligence is, how it should be measured, and how the measurements should be used.

Reprise: Intelligence—A Socially Relevant Construct

Throughout this chapter, we have seen that psychologists' work on intelligence has been driven largely by social concerns. The impetus for designing the first workable intelligence test was the French government's need for a way to determine which students should be placed in remedial classes. The impetus for designing the first group test of intelligence was the U.S. Army's need to determine how to assign jobs to its recruits. The impetus for developing the SAT was colleges' need for a standardized way to evaluate the qualifications of high school students.

In meeting the needs of school systems, the military, and colleges, psychologists have created a conception of intelligence that taps primarily that portion of human capabilities associated with academic success. Our somewhat narrow definition of intelligence has, therefore, been partly determined by the fact that psychologists have done a good job of meeting the needs of those who *requested* the tests.

Our definition of intelligence has also been determined by the fact that school-based knowledge is much easier to measure than other kinds of ability, such as social skills, business sense, and artistic talent. Thus, ease of measurement has done its part to establish that the ability to excel academically is what we mean when we say "intelligence."

Intelligence is also defined by the nature of the society within which intelligence tests are developed. Tests devised in one culture may not be valid for a person who comes from another, a fact that becomes particularly significant whenever we consider that the scores people earn on tests can have a large impact on their lives.

The problem we've experienced in both measuring and arriving at a satisfactory definition of intelligence occurs in other areas of psychology as well. In the next chapters we will discuss personality, mental illness, and psychological disorders—topics that have something in common with intelligence, in that they are all *psychological constructs,* concepts created by psychologists. As we explore these constructs we will confront some of the same questions that we have grappled with in this chapter: "How do we define these constructs?" "How do we measure them?" "How are they relevant to people's lives?"

ANSWER TO FIGURE 14.20
The top couple is involved in a romantic relationship.

Measuring Intelligence in Minority Groups

It is 1917. You are an Italian passing through Ellis Island, hoping to be admitted as an immigrant to the United States. As part of the procedure you are asked a number of questions by an English-speaking examiner. You do the best you can, but since your command of English is poor, you understand only a few of the questions and do poorly on the test.

This was the experience of many potential immigrants who, as they entered the United States early in the century, took an intelligence test developed by psychologist Henry Goddard (1917). On the basis of his test—which could hardly be understood by many of those taking it—Goddard concluded that 79% of Italians, 80% of Hispanics, and 83% of Jews were feebleminded!

In the same year, recruits in the U.S. Army were taking the army's Alpha intelligence test. When Stephen Gould (1981) analyzed the results of this test many years later, he found that the most common score on some sections of the test was zero. Perhaps, suggests Gould, the reason was that many recruits were unable to read.

Clearly, scores on these early intelligence tests were meaningless if the test-takers couldn't understand the questions. More recently, Diana, a Mexican-American girl whose primary language is Spanish, received a score of 30 on an IQ test given by an English-speaking examiner. Based on this score she was placed in an elementary school class for the "educable mentally retarded." But Diana's parents knew she wasn't mentally retarded, so they had her retested in Spanish. When she scored 79 on that test, Diana became eligible for regular classes (Kaplan, 1985). Cases like Diana's have led many states to pass legislation requiring that children be given IQ tests in their primary language.

A person who grows up in a Spanish-speaking neighborhood may be at a disadvantage if required to take an intelligence test written in English.

Immigrants who arrived in America at Ellis Island were tested in English—a language they often did not speak or understand.

Giving an intelligence test in a language unfamiliar to the test-taker clearly defeats the purpose of the test. But IQ tests can also discriminate against people in certain cultural groups, because of the nature of the test questions. For example, the question "Where does one put petrol?" might be difficult for an American child but would be easily answered by a British child, to whom the word *petrol* means "gasoline." The American child's inability to answer the question would be due not to low intelligence, but to lack of specific cultural experience. A question such as this on an IQ test designed to be taken by both American and British children would, therefore, penalize the American children unfairly and result in an erroneously low measurement of their IQ.

A number of psychologists have used these kinds of arguments to explain racial differences in IQ scores in the United States. African-American children test 15 IQ points lower, on the average, than white children (Loehlin, Lindzey, & Spuhler, 1975). Rather than jump to the conclusion that this reflects a racial difference in intelligence, many researchers say, we should see it as reflecting a difference in cultural background (Kaplan, 1985; Williams, 1974). For example, consider these questions: "Why is it better to pay bills by check than by cash?" "What does C.O.D. mean?" "What is the color of rubies?" These have all been used on IQ tests, and might easily be missed by African-American inner-city children simply because of their lack of exposure to the white middle-class experiences from which these questions are drawn.

One way to check for bias in intelligence tests is to analyze the way white children and minority children respond to the specific items on a test. If minority children have more difficulty with particular questions, then those items may unfairly discriminate against them. Jonathan Sandoval (1979) used this approach when he analyzed the responses of white, African-American, and Mexican-American children to specific items on the Wechsler Intelligence Scale for Children. He found that minority children scored lower than white children, overall, but that the items most difficult for the minority groups were generally also the most difficult for the white group. Sandoval therefore concluded that the lower minority scores were not caused by specific "bad" items.

Another way of checking to see whether a test is fair to different groups is to determine how well the test scores predict a person's performance on another measure, such as grades in school or job performance. Analysis of intelligence tests has shown that test scores predict school grades and employment performance as well for African Americans as they do for whites (Cole, 1981). Thus, when judged on their predictive power, current intelligence tests do not appear to be biased against minorities (Cleary et al., 1975; Schmidt, Berner, & Hunter, 1973).

If current intelligence tests are not biased in terms of bad items or predictive power, why are there differences in scores among ethnic groups? A possible answer is that some groups may not have had the training or experiences needed to do well on the tests. For example, females' lower scores on mathematics tests compared with males' scores can be traced to the fact that females take fewer math courses. When males and females take the same number of mathematics courses, the difference between the average male and female scores tends to disappear (Basow, 1992). We can apply this reasoning to minority groups by returning to the study described earlier, which showed that the IQs of African-American children who were adopted by white middle-class families increased by 15 to 20 points. Does this increase occur because of the generally enriched environment provided by the families who adopted the children, or does it occur because these children learn specific things that are associated with both the dominant white culture and the material on IQ tests? (Mercer, 1972, 1979).

Most likely, the answer is that both general enrichment and specific learning are involved. But whatever the exact reasons for the increase in IQ associated with growing up in an enriched environment, the fact remains that *not* experiencing such an environment is associated with lower scores. A number of approaches have been proposed to deal with this problem. One approach, the System of Multicultural Pluralistic Assessment (SOMPA), calculates a "correction factor" to take into account the lowering of IQ scores that may occur due to a person's low socio-economic status or poor health. Sociologist Jane Mercer (1979), who developed SOMPA, argues that the corrected scores indicate people's true learning potential.

Another system that has been developed is the Kaufman Assessment Battery for Children (K-ABC) (Kaufman & Kaufman, 1983; Kaufman, Kamphares, & Kaufman, 1985). This test measures a person's information-processing ability with items that test two kinds of mental processes: (1) processes that are performed sequentially (the subject repeats a series of numbers in the correct order or points to a sequence of pictures) and (2) processes that are performed simultaneously (the subject recalls the location of a number of pictures on a page).

The K-ABC is less affected by cultural differences among children than is the Stanford-Binet or the WISC-R. The difference between the average IQ scores of African American and white children on the K-ABC is only 7 points (95 and 102, respectively)—less than half the difference measured with the traditional intelligence tests. Hispanic subjects have an average score of 99 (Kaplan, 1985).

Of the new tests that have been proposed to eliminate possible cultural bias in IQ tests, the K-ABC test appears to be the most promising. Whether this test becomes widely used depends on the results of research designed to determine its reliability and validity.

Test scores depend not only on biological heritage but also on environment and amount of schooling.

The Measurement of Intelligence: Quantifying the Mind

- Psychologists have had difficulty defining intelligence. This difficulty reflects the fact that intelligence is a psychological construct and therefore can be measured only indirectly.

- Early ways of measuring intelligence included Broca's craniometry and Galton's sensory ability tests. These measurements were later shown to be invalid and were replaced by Binet's intelligence tests, which were based on a person's ability to reason and use judgment.

- Intelligence is now expressed as an intelligence quotient (IQ), which was first defined as mental age divided by chronological age times 100. Modern IQs are deviation IQs, which indicate a person's standing relative to the overall population.

- Group intelligence tests were developed during World War I. Today, both individual and group tests are used to measure intelligence. Some of the more recent individually administered intelligence tests include a number of scales to measure different kinds of abilities.

The Range of Intelligence: Giftedness and Mental Retardation

- At the high end of the distribution of IQ scores are people considered gifted. Giftedness is usually defined by a combination of high IQ and high achievement.

- About 7 million people in the United States are classified as mentally retarded. The four levels of retardation are mild, moderate, severe, and profound. Savants are people defined as retarded who have exceptional skills in one area.

- Mental retardation can be caused by biological factors ranging from the mother's use of toxic substances during pregnancy to genetic abnormalities. Retardation caused by environmental deprivation is called cultural-familial retardation.

- Mainstreaming is the placement of children with disabilities into educational programs for and with normally developing children. There is little difference between the academic achievement of special education and mainstreamed students, but mainstreaming provides an opportunity for retarded students to gain social skills and to practice functioning in the real world.

The Structure of Intelligence: Maps of the Mind

- Some psychologists (the "lumpers") see intelligence as a global quality that can be defined by one number. Others (the "splitters") see intelligence as consisting of multiple components.

- Theorists have constructed a number of models of intelligence. Spearman proposed a combination of general mental ability and specific abilities, a "two-factor theory." Thurstone described intelligence in terms of seven primary mental abilities. Guilford proposed 120 elementary abilities. Gardner proposes seven different types of intelligence. Although no one model of intelligence enjoys universal support, most evidence favors the idea that intelligence consists of a number of components.

The Mechanisms of Intelligence: Looking at Mental Processes

- Psychologists using the information-processing approach have demonstrated a relationship between choice reaction time and conventionally measured intelligence. They stress a connection between rapid physiological functioning and intelligence.

- Rapid habituation and high recognition memory in infants are associated with higher intelligence scores measured later in childhood.

- People with high ability for solving the analogy problems that appear on intelligence tests are quick to modify hypotheses that are not working. The first two steps in solving an analogy problem are encoding and inferring the transformation; the problem is solved by applying the inferred transformation rule to the stimuli. Highly skilled analogy solvers spend more time on the encoding step than others do.

The Sources of Intelligence: The Roles of Heredity and the Environment

- Family studies that compare the intelligence of people who are genetically related in varying degrees provide evidence supporting the roles of both genetics and the environment in determining intelligence. Additional evidence for the role of the environment comes from studies in which children placed in enriched environments show an increase in intelligence.

Intelligence and Society: The Uses and Abuses of Intelligence Tests

- For test scores to be meaningful the test must be both reliable and valid. There are a number of different types of validity: predictive validity, content validity, and construct validity.

- Intelligence tests are cultural constructs. Since different cultures have different conceptions of intelligence, someone considered intelligent in one culture might not be considered intelligent in another.

- Intelligence tests and other aptitude tests are used for purposes that include placing children in classes according to their ability, determining college admissions, and awarding scholarships. Although tests may not be biased, they sometimes favor one group over another because of societal advantages enjoyed by the favored group.

Reprise: Intelligence—A Socially Relevant Construct

- Psychologists' work on intelligence has been driven and shaped by societal concerns and the demands of those groups requesting the tests. The current practical definition of intelligence reflects the decision to focus on school-based knowledge, as well as on the characteristics of the society in which the test is developed.

Follow-Through/Diversity: Measuring Intelligence in Minority Groups

- If an intelligence test is given to a person with a limited command of the language, that person's score is meaningless. These tests may discriminate against people in cultural groups that do not share the cultural experience reflected in the test.

Key Terms

achievement tests
analogy problems
aptitude tests
componential aspect
construct validity
content validity
contextual aspect
cultural-familial retardation
dependent retarded
dizygotic (DZ) twins
Down's syndrome
experiential aspect
general mental ability (g)
implicit theory of intelligence

intelligence quotient (IQ)
mainstreaming
monozygotic (MZ) twins
normal distribution
predictive validity
primary mental abilities
psychological construct
reliability
savant syndrome
tacit knowledge
test-retest method
triarchic theory of intelligence
two-factor theory
validity

CHAPTER

15

The Psychodynamic Approach
Freud's Psychosexual Theory of Development
The Id, Ego, and Superego, and People's Responses to Anxiety
Evaluating Freud's Approach
Other Psychodynamic Theorists

The Humanistic Approach
Self-Actualization and Positive Regard
Evaluating Rogers's Approach

The Behaviorist Approach

The Trait Approach
Gordon Allport: Focusing on the Individual
Raymond Cattell: Applying Factor Analysis to Traits
Hans Eysenck: Basic Personality Dimensions
The Five-Factor Model: The Big Five Personality Dimensions
The Origin of Traits: The Role of Heredity and the Environment
The Trait-Situation Controversy
Interactionism: Considering Both Person and Situation

Interdisciplinary Dimension: History
Psychobiography

The Cognitive Approach
Personal Constructs
Locus of Control
Perceived Self-Efficacy
Self Schemas
Possible Selves

Personality Assessment
Objective Personality Tests
Projective Personality Tests

**Reprise: Theories and Multiple
Theoretical Approaches**

Follow-Through/Diversity
Freud and Women

Personality

There is an invisible garment woven around us from our earliest years; it is made of the way we eat, the way we walk, the way we greet people, woven of tastes and colors and perfumes which our senses spin in childhood.

Jean Giraudoux (1882–1944)
French playwright

Imagine that last week you took a "personality test"—a questionnaire that elicited your interests, likes, dislikes, and information about various aspects of your life. The results of this test are now available, and you have received them, sealed in an envelope with your name on it. You open the envelope and read the following description:

> You have a strong need for other people to like and admire you. You tend to be critical of yourself. You have a great deal of unused capacity that you have not turned to your advantage. Although you have some personality weaknesses, you are generally able to compensate for them. Your sexual adjustment has presented some problems for you. Disciplined and controlled on the outside, you tend to be a worrier and insecure inside. At times you have serious doubts about whether you have made the right decision or done the right thing. You prefer a certain amount of change and variety and become dissatisfied when hemmed in by restrictions and limitations. You pride yourself on being an independent thinker and do not accept others' opinions without satisfactory proof. You have found it unwise to be too frank in revealing yourself to others. At times you are extraverted, affable, and sociable, but at other times you are introverted, wary, and reserved. Some of your aspirations tend to be pretty unrealistic.

What do you think of this description? Does it accurately describe *you*?

In fact, this "personality assessment" would be regarded as accurate by many people. This was demonstrated when Roger Ulrich and his co-workers (1963) gave their students a personality test and then, a week later, gave *all* of them an "assessment" worded like the one you have just read. Not realizing that everyone received the same assessment—regardless of their responses on the test—92% of the students rated their assessment as excellent or good; when asked for additional comments, many replied with statements like "On the nose! Very good. I wish you had said more, but what you did mention was all true without a doubt" and "It appears to me that the results of this test are unbelievably close to the truth. For a short test of this type, I was expecting large generalizations for results, but this was not the case."

The students' enthusiastic acceptance of Ulrich's phony personality assessment shows that people have a lot in common. Apparently many people want others to like them, are critical of themselves, and are sociable sometimes but introverted at others. Yet the notion of "personality" implies that people *aren't* all the same. When we say that people have different personalities, we mean that they have unique combinations of qualities that set them apart from others. More formally, to psychologists **personality** is the dynamic organization of sys-

Although people in the same family are genetically related and have many shared experiences, each is also an individual with unique qualities.

tems inside each person that creates the person's characteristic patterns of behavior, thoughts, and feelings (Carver & Scheier, 1992).

This definition of personality has some important implications. First, it points to the fact that personality is a *construct*, something that is presumed to underlie many observable qualities but that is not itself observable. As we saw in our discussion of intelligence in Chapter 14, constructs can be slippery to measure and study, since we can get at them only indirectly. The fact that so many students in Ulrich's study could accept the same personality assessment as highly accurate for them illustrates the difficulty of precisely describing a personality. Clearly, a description that applies to almost all the subjects in a study tells us nothing at all about what makes those individuals *different*.

Second, psychologists' definition of personality implies the following specific things about human behavior:

- A person's behavior is *consistent*. Saying that a person has a characteristic pattern of behavior, thoughts, and feelings means that his or her behavior will be characteristic of that person in different situations and at different times.
- People are *distinctive*. Each person has a unique characteristic pattern of behavior, thoughts, and feelings.
- To the extent that personality explains behavior, behavior arises from *within*. Whatever causes a person's characteristic patterns of behavior exists inside the person.

The study of personality, then, is the study of the consistencies in an individual's behavior, the uniqueness of each individual, and the inner processes that create that consistency and uniqueness. This means that if psychologists are to learn anything useful about personality, they need to go beyond descriptions that fit most people and find ways to capture what is unique about individuals.

Historically, a number of psychologists have approached the study of personality by proposing general theories of personality or general approaches to its description and measurement. In this chapter we will survey those theories and approaches, including contemporary research that tends to be focused on more specific questions than those addressed by earlier theories. We will also examine the various measurement tools with which psychologists have attempted to assess, or describe, people's distinctive personalities.

As you read this chapter, you may wonder about the variety of approaches psychologists have adopted to study personality and about the striking disagreements among personality theorists. As with other subfields of psychology, the concept of levels of analysis can help us make sense of these complexities. One reason for the multiplicity of personality theories is that different theorists have tended to emphasize one or another level of analysis in their study of personality. In fact, personality can be usefully explored at all four levels.

At the behavioral level of analysis, we can describe people's observable characteristics and patterns of behavior. At the biological level, we can ask how individuals' genetic makeup influences personality characteristics such as emotionality and cautiousness. At the cognitive level, we can ask how the way people interpret situations and think about themselves influences their distinctive patterns of behavior. And at the contextual level, we can ask how those patterns are influenced by the social and cultural settings in which they find themselves (Figure 15.1).

We begin with one of the earliest general approaches to personality, the psychodynamic theory of Sigmund Freud (1856–1939). Because Freud was concerned with the structure of the mind and how mental processes—especially unconscious processes—determine behavior, his approach works primarily at the cognitive level of analysis.

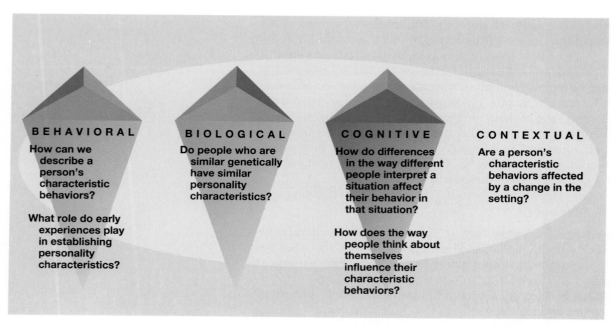

FIGURE 15.1
Questions we can ask about personality at each level of analysis

The Psychodynamic Approach

*Our unconscious is like a vast subterranean factory with intricate machinery
that is never idle, where work goes on day and night from the time we are born
to the moment of our death.*

Milton Sapirstein (1955, p. 8)

An exploration of the psychodynamic approach to personality takes us on a journey into Sigmund Freud's startling and influential conception of the mind (1933, 1900/1953, 1901/1960). This conception evolved from insights Freud had while treating patients for physical ailments that had no obvious physical cause. In searching for a mental explanation of these ailments, Freud began asking his patients to remember events from their childhood that might explain their symptoms. He suspected that the true explanation for their difficulties might lie in some formative experience they had while growing up.

Freud found that his patients were often unable to remember the disturbing events he believed must have occurred; he therefore concluded that their memory for those events must be hidden from their conscious awareness. Freud therefore developed the picture of the mind shown in Figure 15.2. In this conception, the conscious contents of the mind—what we are readily aware of—are symbolized by the tip of an iceberg jutting out of the water. Hidden "below" consciousness are the *unconscious* contents of the mind—what we are not aware of at any given moment—symbolized by the bulk of the iceberg, submerged below water. The unconscious is further divided into the **preconscious,** containing material that we can easily retrieve from our memory, and the **unconscious,** containing material that is locked away and therefore not easy to retrieve. As the iceberg metaphor suggests, Freud believed that the greater part of the mind—including most of the powerful forces that determine behavior and therefore personality—is beyond consciousness.

This claim was profoundly disturbing to Freud's contemporaries, because it implied that people are not in control of much of their behavior. Freud's theory

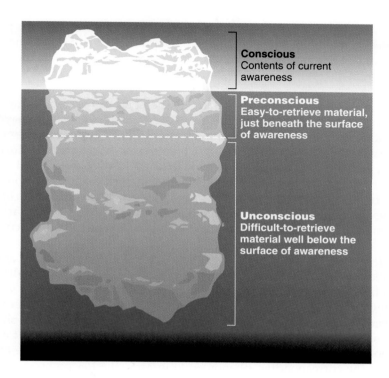

Conscious
Contents of current awareness

Preconscious
Easy-to-retrieve material, just beneath the surface of awareness

Unconscious
Difficult-to-retrieve material well below the surface of awareness

FIGURE 15.2
According to Freud, we are conscious of only a small portion of the contents of our mind, symbolized here by the "tip of the iceberg" above the water.

also introduced a number of other key assumptions about the structure of the mind and the nature of the forces that shape people's characteristic patterns of behavior. In addition to the role of the unconscious, Freud proposed the idea that the mind, or *psyche*, is a system within which **psychic energy** flows. A major source of that energy is the *libido*, which supplies energy for sexual urges. Freud's identification of that sexual energy led him to formulate the **pleasure principle**—the idea that, at a fundamental level of the psyche, people are driven to seek out pleasure. With these concepts in hand, we are ready to consider Freud's ideas about how individuals' personalities develop.

Freud's Psychosexual Theory of Development

According to Freud, our personalities are shaped by our experiences during the first five or six years of our lives. His theory is referred to as a *psychosexual* theory of development because it focuses on parts of the body that are connected with sexuality. Freud described this development in terms of a series of stages, much as Jean Piaget used stages in his description of cognitive development. However, whereas Piaget's emphasis was on cognitive development, Freud's was on the connection between development and sexuality.

9   DEVELOPMENT

Freud proposed that development proceeds through five stages. Of these five stages the first three, which extend from birth to about age 6, are the most important, because it is during these stages that the pleasure principle focuses children's psychic energy on their *erogenous zones*—parts of the body such as the mouth, anus, and genitals that are connected with sexuality. Freud believed that childhood experiences associated with these erogenous zones play a key role in shaping adult personality. In particular, a failure to resolve the conflict presented by each stage can explain characteristics that become evident in later life.

The oral stage (birth to 18 months).   During the **oral stage,** the infant's two primary behaviors are taking in and spitting out. The developmental conflict of this stage is weaning—shifting feeding away from the mother's breast or the bottle to drinking from a cup. If the child's oral needs are not met or if the child experiences difficulty in weaning, this can, according to Freud, cause the child to develop an *oral fixation*. Such a person would emphasize oral activities such as eating, drinking, kissing, and smoking later in life.

The anal stage (18 months to 3 years).   The crisis of the **anal stage** is toilet training, or the parents' demand that the child control her or his elimination. According to Freud, the way that demand is handled, by both parents and child, can shape the child's future personality. Children who have difficulty during this stage can develop an *anal fixation*, which in their adult behavior could manifest itself as an *anal-expressive personality*, exhibiting aggressive, messy, disorderly, or perhaps creative behavior. Another manifestation might be an *anal-retentive personality*, exhibiting compulsively neat and fastidious behavior. We will ask why a person might develop one of these types of personality later in our discussion.

The phallic stage (4 to 5 years).   By age 4, gender differences are apparent: children know that they are either boys or girls. As they enter the **phallic stage,** children begin to focus on their genitals and sometimes—often at the most embarrassing moments for their parents—engage in an early form of masturbation, manipulating their genitals. (Doing this while riding in a supermarket shopping cart is a sure way to get a parent's attention.) But the most important event of this period is the emergence (in boys) of something Freud called the Oedipus complex. (The corresponding phenomenon in girls, the Electra complex, is described in this chapter's Follow-Through, "Freud and Women.")

The Oedipus complex was named for the king in an ancient Greek legend who unwittingly murdered his father and married his mother. When a boy develops the **Oedipus complex,** therefore, he becomes sexually attracted to his mother and views his father as a rival for her attentions. However, the boy soon realizes that his father is too powerful to be eliminated. That realization leads to the development of **castration anxiety:** the fear that, angered by his son's competition, the father will cut off his son's penis. In response to this anxiety, the boy *resolves* his crisis by joining forces with his father and identifying with him. According to Freud, resolving the Oedipus complex is an important part of healthy personality development, because the boy's identification with his father strengthens his identity as a male.

The latency stage (6 to 12 years).   During the **latency stage,** little of significance transpires in terms of psychosexual development. With the crises of weaning, toilet training, and the Oedipus or Electra complex over, the developmental drama subsides for a while as the child makes his or her way through elementary school.

The genital stage.   With the onset of puberty, the situation changes dramatically. Now sexuality reappears, and the focus of psychic energy is again on the genitals as the adolescent enters the **genital stage**. This time, however, in healthy development the energy driving behavior is channeled into heterosexual outlets and eventually toward a committed adult relationship.

Freud's theory pictures events that happen during the first three stages of development as playing a crucial role in shaping adult personality. This linking of development to childhood sexuality was shocking to the Victorian society of his day. It was one of the reasons that Freud's theories were viewed with suspicion and alarm and were simply rejected by many people, including other psychologists. Freud persisted, however, in treating patients and developing his theory.

In addition to maintaining that an individual's personality is largely in place following the first three stages of psychosexual development, Freud proposed that an important manifestation of personality is the way a person charac-

According to Freud, the strong bond that often develops between a young boy and his mother sets the stage for the emergence of the Oedipus complex in the phallic stage of development.

teristically deals with anxiety. To understand this aspect of Freud's theory, we need to introduce the three components of the conscious and unconscious mind postulated by Freud: the *id, ego,* and *superego.*

The Id, Ego, and Superego, and People's Responses to Anxiety

We have already seen that Freud divided the mind into the conscious, preconscious, and unconscious. In addition, he also subdivided it into the id, the ego, and the superego.

The id.   The most primitive of the mind's components, the **id** is the only one present in animals and newborns. This is the part of the psyche that is ruled by the pleasure principle—the principle that the major purpose in life is the immediate satisfaction of needs. This property led Arthur Rieber (1985) to describe the id as "the ultimate hedonist." The id, however, is "blind"; it has no way of dealing effectively with the outside world. It depends on the ego for that.

The ego.   The ego is the component of the mind that is in contact with the outside world. It operates on the **reality principle,** which states that behavior should satisfy our needs in a realistic way so that we don't get into trouble. Developmentally, the reality principle starts operating when a young child begins to recognize the demands of the environment and learns to interact effectively with it. For example, the id may want food to satisfy hunger, but—because it lacks the ability to interact with the world—it can only fantasize about food, an ineffective way of coping with hunger. It is up to the ego to determine ways of actually obtaining the food (for example, by making plans to raid the refrigerator, go shopping, or go to a restaurant). The ego, therefore, acts as an interface between the id and the real world, translating the id's primitive impulses into more practical and socially acceptable behaviors.

The superego.   The last of the three components to develop, the **superego,** appears when the child is 2 or 3 years old. By this time, aided by the parents' teachings and admonitions about correct behavior, the child begins to develop the superego's subcomponents, the *conscience* and the *ego ideal.* The **conscience** contains information about behavior that is considered to be "bad" and punishes that behavior with feelings of shame or guilt. The **ego ideal** contains information about behavior that is "good" and rewards that behavior with feelings of pride. Thus, behavior that might be planned by the ego—such as stealing food if it's possible to get away with it—may be prevented by the moral sense embodied in the superego.

Figure 15.3 shows how we can combine Freud's two ways of dividing up the mind. As depicted in the figure, the id functions entirely at an unconscious level, whereas the ego and superego also operate at an unconscious level but are partly open to conscious awareness.

The important thing to remember about the id, ego, and superego is that they interact with each other in a dynamic way (hence the label psycho*dynamic* for Freud's approach). In this interaction (pictured in Figure 15.4), the ego, which generates behavior by interfacing with the environment, must mediate among three forces: (1) the id, which says "Do whatever you have to do to get what you want," (2) the superego, which says "Don't do the wrong thing (conscience); do the right thing (ego ideal)," and (3) reality, which defines what is possible given the circumstances.

How do these three components of personality interact with each other when we are faced with a challenging situation that might cause anxiety? It depends on the kind of anxiety. Freud proposed the following three types of anxiety, each of which involves the id, ego, and superego in different ways:

16   DISORDERS

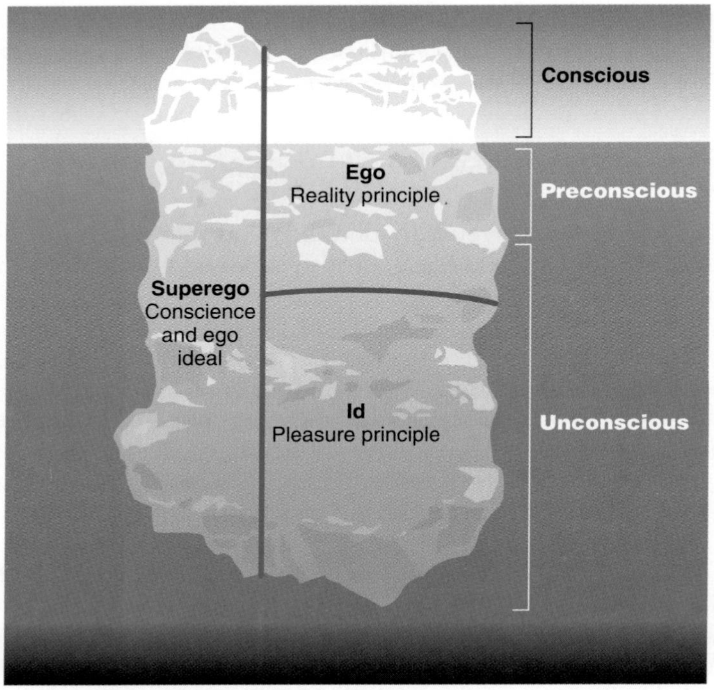

FIGURE 15.3
When we superimpose the id, ego, and superego onto the iceberg of Figure 15.2, we can see that we have some awareness of the workings of the ego and superego but that the id is totally shielded from conscious awareness.

Conscious

Ego
Reality principle

Preconscious

Superego
Conscience
and ego
ideal

Id
Pleasure principle

Unconscious

FIGURE 15.4
Forces operating on the ego. The ego is influenced by input from the id, superego, and the environment ("reality").

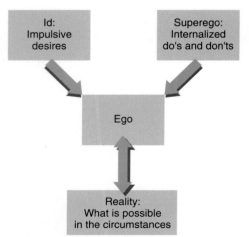

1. *Reality anxiety* is based on realistic fears about threats that actually exist in your environment. Anxiety caused by threats of physical attack or the possibility that you might get fired from your job because you have received poor performance ratings are examples of reality anxiety. Reality anxiety can, therefore, be seen as caused by a conflict between reality, which is posing a problem to be solved, and the ego, which is responsible for solving the problem (Figure 15.5).
2. *Moral anxiety* is felt when you have violated or feel you may violate your moral standards. Since this type of anxiety involves the conscience, it is usually felt as shame or guilt. The basis of moral anxiety is a conflict between the id, which is pushing you to violate your standards, and the superego, the repository of your standards.
3. *Neurotic anxiety* is based on the fear that your id impulses will lead you to do something that you will be punished for. It is therefore a conflict between the id, the source of the bad impulses, and the ego, the ultimate controller of your behavior.

How do we cope with these three types of anxiety? The answer directly implicates the ego, because if the ego were doing its job perfectly, we would never experience anxiety. Consider reality anxiety, which arises from real external dangers. A perfectly functioning ego would find a way to deal with those dangers by taking appropriate action. For example, the ego might avoid a feared physical attack by directing you to walk around a dangerous neighborhood rather than through it. Similarly, a perfectly functioning ego would be able to avoid moral or neurotic anxiety by holding the id under control.

Unfortunately, however, the ego usually does not function perfectly, and most people do experience anxiety. When this happens, the ego can respond in one of two ways. First, conscious problem solving may be employed to figure out ways to deal with some of the anxiety. This works best in dealing with low or moderate levels of reality anxiety. Second, **defense mechanisms,** unconscious tactics that help the ego deal with high levels of anxiety, may be called on. Some of the more important defense mechanisms are described in Table 15.1.

Are any of the behaviors in the list of defense mechanisms familiar to you? Using defense mechanisms is a normal part of life. Most people use them to various degrees to help reduce the anxieties produced by the stresses of daily living. According to Freud, however, overusing them can drain people's psychic energy, leaving them less able to deal pragmatically with the stresses of everyday life and more vulnerable to developing psychological problems.

Evaluating Freud's Approach

Freud's psychodynamic approach to personality development has been tremendously influential. As we will see, it has served as the starting point for a number of other psychodynamically oriented theories, and it is the basis of a method of treatment for psychological difficulties called psychoanalysis, which will be detailed in Chapter 17. Freud himself was not bashful about proclaiming the importance of his theory. He placed himself in the company of no less than Copernicus and Darwin in taking humankind down a notch: as he pointed out, Copernicus showed that the earth isn't the center of the universe; Darwin showed that humans are descended from mere animals, and he himself showed that we are not in charge of ourselves but rather are controlled by unconscious and uncontrollable forces in our minds (Gay, 1988, p. 449). Although this self-evaluation may seem immodest, it is not inaccurate.

Perhaps more than any other theory of behavior, Freud's has contributed ideas that have found their way into our everyday discourse. Statements such as "He has a big ego" or "I think you're repressing something" come directly from Freud's theory, and most people have heard of "Freudian slips"—mistakes in speaking such as that made by the student who, in asking her professor for an extension on a paper, said, "Last night my grandmother lied . . . I mean died!" (Motley, 1987). According to Freud (1901/1960), these slips expose our unconscious thoughts to public view (as in our example, where the student's slip may have been due to a fabricated excuse).

Although Freud's theory has been widely influential and has become integrated into our culture, it has also been criticized on a number of grounds. Some of the most important criticisms are as follows:

The theory is based on observations of just a few people, who were not representative of the general population.　　Freud's theory is based on his observations of his patients and his analysis of himself. Because Freud selected his patients carefully, they were all above average in intelligence and had high incomes. And the very fact that they were being treated by Freud meant that they had mental problems serious enough to require therapy. Is it valid, ask Freud's critics, to base a theory of personality that is supposed to hold for everyone on a selected population of people with psychological problems? Furthermore, the critics point out, Freud's population was not only selective but small. Freud describes only 12 cases in detail in all of his writings.

Freud's observations may have been biased.　　Biased observations are a danger in all of science. The possibility that therapists' assessment of patients can be biased was investigated by Ellen Langer and Robert Abelson (1974). They had therapists watch videotapes of people being interviewed who were randomly assigned labels of "patient" or "job applicant." After viewing the tapes the therapists concluded that the "patients" were more disturbed than the "job applicants." Since all therapists observed the same behaviors, their assessments must have been biased by the labels assigned to the people. In a similar way, Freud's belief in his theory may have influenced him to interpret most of his patients' behaviors in terms of sexual desires and unconscious motivations. Imagine, for example, how a Freudian therapist might react on first meeting with a fat, drunken, talkative patient with a cigar in his mouth. "Aha," the therapist might

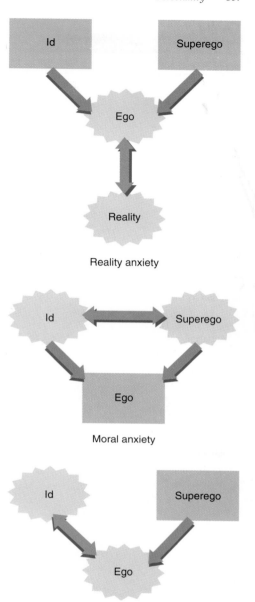

FIGURE 15.5

According to Freud, there are three types of anxiety: reality anxiety, involving conflict between the ego and reality; moral anxiety, involving conflict between the superego and id; and neurotic anxiety, involving conflict between the ego and id.

TABLE 15.1
Examples of defense mechanisms

Mechanism	Description	Example
Repression	The major defense mechanism, which pushes unpleasant or anxiety-provoking thoughts out of consciousness.	If you have done something you are ashamed of, or have had a traumatic experience, repression can protect you by burying your memory of that experience. People who have been sexually abused as children often repress all memory of the abuse and do not remember it as adults (Lew, 1988; Weiner, 1988).
Denial	A refusal to believe that an event has occurred.	A rejected boyfriend may say "She still loves me, but she just doesn't realize it," or a mother may refuse to believe a report that her daughter has just died in an automobile accident.
Projection	The transfer of unacceptable impulses in yourself to another person.	A husband who is tempted to be unfaithful to his wife might accuse his wife of being unfaithful.
Regression	Engaging in behaviors typical of an early period of development.	Smoking, fingernail biting, and excessive drinking are regressions to the oral stage of development.
Reaction formation	Emphasizing the opposite of an unacceptable impulse.	A person who feels hostility toward another might, instead of expressing that hostility, appear to be overflowing with love for that person.
Sublimation	The transformation of an id impulse into a more acceptable or practical action.	A sexually frustrated artist might deal with his frustration by channeling his sexual energy into the creation of a painting.
Displacement	Shifting an impulse from a dangerous target to a less dangerous one.	After taking abuse from your boss all day you don't tell him what you think of him; instead, you go home and yell at your children or the dog.
Rationalization	Finding an excuse for unacceptable events or behaviors.	After being rejected by the college of your choice, you decide it wasn't a very good school anyway.

think, "An oral fixation if I've ever seen one." From that point on, the therapist might tend to fit subsequent observations and interview questions into his or her preestablished theory of personality.

Patients may also be guilty of a similar type of bias. Consider a patient who has become intimately familiar with Freudian theory after six months of therapy. Because of this familiarity, the patient is more likely to bring up sexual material, thereby seeming to confirm the theory.

Freud didn't consider alternative explanations.   The common observation that 4-year-old boys are attracted to their mothers is explained by Freud in terms of the sexual longing of the Oedipus complex. This is, however, only one of many possible explanations. There are also nonsexual hypotheses that might explain why 4-year-olds pay attention to their mothers; we describe one of them in the Follow-Through at the end of this chapter.

The theory's basic concepts are not precisely defined or easily measurable. Concepts such as unconscious motivation, id, ego, and superego are only vaguely defined, with different definitions appearing throughout Freud's writings. If something is hard to define it is hard to measure, and although some researchers have devised ways to measure a person's "ego strength" or "unconscious needs," there is no commonly accepted way to measure these basic components of Freud's theory. In fact, it is sometimes difficult to tell when a particular concept is present. Consider, for example, Emily's apparent friendship with her mother-in-law. Is her courtesy real, or is it a result of the defense mechanism of reaction formation? Could it be that Emily actually dislikes her mother-in-law, but reaction formation makes her behave as if she likes her? How can we tell?

The theory cannot be disproved. It may seem strange to criticize a theory for being so good that we can't disprove it. However, one of the requirements of a good theory is that it should be *possible* to state the observations that would disprove it. Freud's theory, however, is so flexible that it can explain anything. For example, it seems reasonable to explain the behavior of a man with an anal-expressive personality (aggressive, creative, and messy) by pointing to the fact that his mother was relaxed about toilet training, so he "let it all out" as a child. However, Freud's theory could equally well explain the same behavior if his mother was very strict and made him "hold it in": in that case, he would be viewed as rebelling against his mother's strict demands. If a theory can explain all results, even contradictory ones, does it really explain anything?

These criticisms have led some psychologists to reject many of Freud's ideas. One idea, however, that is widely accepted is the centerpiece of Freud's theory—the idea that our behavior is strongly influenced by unconscious processes.

The presence of unconscious processes has been acknowledged for centuries because of phenomena like the *eureka* (or *incubation*) *effect.* You have experienced this effect if you have ever worked on a problem with little or no success and then, after putting it aside for days or weeks, come back to it and solved it easily (Anderson, 1985; Kihlstrom, 1988). Evidently a part of your mind outside of consciousness came up with the solution that all your conscious effort failed to produce.

Although phenomena like the eureka effect seem to be quite common, it wasn't until recently that the idea of the unconscious became widely researched and accepted by experimental psychologists. One example of a laboratory demonstration of unconscious processes is Anthony Marcel's (1983) experiment, in which he flashed on a screen a target word such as *lamp* followed by an intense random dot pattern. The intensity of the dot pattern masked the target word from view, so the subject was unable to name the word. After "seeing" the target word, the subject was asked to pick from two new words the one most closely related to the meaning of the target word. For example, for the target word *lamp,* those words might be *light* and *land.* Even though the subjects claimed they didn't know the target word, they were able to pick the word most closely related to it with better-than-chance accuracy. This result, which has been called *unconscious perception,* supports the idea that information in the subjects' unconscious is influencing their behavior.

Of course, the mechanism of unconscious perception may be very different from Freud's hypothesized workings of the id. Yet experiments like Marcel's and dozens of others that show that people are often completely unaware of the true causes of their behavior, have convinced many psychologists that unconscious forces can influence our behavior (Kihlstrom, 1987; Silverman, 1976). Thus, though many psychologists do not endorse the specific dynamics proposed by Freud, they do agree that processes of great importance occur in the unconscious.

Other Psychodynamic Theorists

Whether or not Freud's theory is correct, his influence has been tremendous. One reflection of that influence is that his ideas were taken as the starting point by other theories of personality. We will look briefly at the ideas of three theorists who were influenced by Freud and then went on to develop their own theories. These theories differ from Freud's in placing more emphasis on the roles of conscious processes and social influences in determining behavior.

Carl Jung: The collective unconscious. Carl Jung and Freud were extremely close when Jung began his studies with Freud in 1907. In fact, Freud picked Jung as his "crown prince," believing that he would succeed him as the major

Carl Jung

TABLE 15.2
The major Jungian archetypes

Archetype	Description
anima	The feminine side of the male
animus	The masculine side of the female
mother	Caregiving and fertility
shadow	The unconscious part of ourselves that is negative; the "dark half" of our personality
self	The organizing and unifying archetype, which allows us to feel a sense of unity or oneness

spokesperson for the psychodynamic approach. But this was not to be, since Jung soon began developing ideas that diverged from Freud's. Two of Jung's departures from Freudian theory were that (1) he believed that middle age—not early childhood—was the key period of personality development, and (2) he believed that Freud overemphasized the pleasure principle. Because of this divergence in theory, plus some other personal disagreements, Freud and Jung parted ways in 1913.

Jung's (1933) depiction of personality emphasized the dimensions of **extraversion** (personal qualities associated with being outgoing and social) and **introversion** (personal qualities associated with being inwardly directed). According to Jung, extraverts are likely to spend time with other people and, under stress, to gravitate toward others. In contrast, introverts tend to be shy and to prefer solitary activities; under stress, they withdraw. As we will see later in this chapter, these dimensions of personality played an important part in later research that was not tied to Jung's theory.

Another concept central to Jung's theory is that of the **collective unconscious**—"species" memories shared by all human beings. Jung inferred the existence of the collective unconscious from observing that very different cultures have quite similar symbols, myths, beliefs, and fears. For example, the mandala symbol (Figure 15.6) occurs in the artifacts of many cultures. Similarly, beliefs in supreme beings and irrational fears of insects, the dark, and open spaces occur in virtually all cultures. To Jung, such universal products of the mind were evidence of a collective unconscious distinct from the *personal unconscious* unique to each individual.

Jung proposed that the contents of the collective unconscious were expressed in **archetypes** that influence personality and behavior. Some of the more important archetypes identified by Jung are listed in Table 15.2. The most important archetype, the self (which is represented by the mandala), can't emerge until all the others develop. According to Jung, the self emerges in middle age and is often accompanied by a *midlife crisis*—a term he coined to describe the turmoil that sometimes surfaces during this transition.

FIGURE 15.6
Mandalas, geometric designs often having religious significance, are found in cultures throughout the world. Jung considered such universal artifacts as evidence of a collective unconscious.

Alfred Adler: Striving for superiority.   Alfred Adler was also associated with Freud early in his career, but like Jung veered away to establish his own theory of personality. Perhaps because of his own childhood experiences with illness and other challenges, Adler's theory emphasizes that people's ultimate goal is a **striving for superiority.** We can see why he developed this idea by stepping back to the beginning of Adler's career as a physician practicing general medicine. His medical training led him to examine a concept called organ inferiority, the idea that diseases often attack the weaker organs of the body (Adler, 1917). Adler applied this idea to psychology by noting that people with organic deficiencies may develop feelings of inferiority that in turn lead to a striving for superiority calculated to turn their deficiencies into strengths. The movie actor Arnold Schwarzenegger is an example of this striving. Schwarzenegger, a weakling as a child, gained strength through an extensive body building program and eventually became Mr. Universe and the star of movies such as *Terminator 2.*

Evidence for the idea that early deficiencies can lead to a striving for superiority comes from a study by Robert Helmreich and his co-workers (1972), who found that undersea divers who performed best on a demanding task had suffered the most illnesses during their childhood.

This striving for superiority that grows out of inferiority is normal, according to Adler, and occurs for everyone, since we all begin life in the inferior position of a weak and helpless child. However, if a person develops excessive *feelings* associated with their inferiority, they develop an **inferiority complex,** a conviction that they are inferior to others. This occurs if a person is spoiled or—at the other extreme—neglected when young and sometimes leads to a compensatory **superiority complex,** an exaggerated and unrealistic feeling of being better than others. Like Freud, Adler emphasized the importance of early experiences in shaping personality, but his theory called attention to a different set of factors than those stressed by Freud.

Karen Horney: Basic anxiety.   Karen Horney (pronounced "horn-eye") was not a direct student of Freud's, but she did study and practice psychoanalysis during his lifetime. She disagreed profoundly with the Freudian depiction of women (described in this chapter's Follow-Through) and also believed that traditional psychodynamic theory badly underestimated the role of social factors in determining personality characteristics. Uppermost in her list of influential social factors was relationships between people. The dynamics of relationships, particularly those from childhood, cause what Horney (1939, 1950) called **basic anxiety**—feelings of insecurity, isolation, or helplessness.

According to Horney, basic anxiety originates in relationships that don't meet a person's needs. For example, if a young girl is rejected by her mother, that rejection causes basic anxiety. To cope with the helplessness associated with basic anxiety, the daughter as an adult woman may employ one or more of three responses, which Horney called **neurotic trends**:

1. *Moving toward*: The woman strives to receive approval and acceptance by becoming unselfish, undemanding, and self-sacrificing.
2. *Moving against*: The woman denies any need for others and attempts to appear "tough."
3. *Moving away*: The woman becomes emotionally separated from others.

Horney postulated that problems arise both from excessive reliance on one of these trends (if, for example, our hypothetical daughter is too focused on moving toward, she might submerge her adult life in living up to others' expectations) and from conflicts among them during attempts to deal with basic anxiety. In this way, early relationships become a significant determinant of adult personality.

Even when breaking with Freud, psychodynamic theorists shared Freud's concern with the unconscious, early childhood experiences, and defense mechanisms. A more radical difference is evident in the next approach to personality that we consider, one that stands in contrast to Freud's rather dark view of human nature. Whereas Freud saw personality as seething with conflict, as the id, ego, and superego battle for control—often with negative effects on the psyche—the humanists' view of personality is based on the premise that people are basically good and have the potential for positive growth and development.

The Humanistic Approach

A musician must make music, an artist must paint, a poet must write, if he is to be ultimately at peace with himself. What a man can be, he must be.

Abraham Maslow (1954)

The development of the humanistic approach can be seen as a reaction to the negative view that human nature is at the mercy of unconscious forces and conflicts between id, ego, and superego. Abraham Maslow, one of the major humanistic psychologists, characterized Freud's approach as a "cripple psychology," since his theory was based on the study of patients in therapy. In reaction to this "cripple psychology," Maslow focused his attention on healthy, well-adjusted, fully functioning people. As we saw in Chapter 11, on motivation, Maslow proposed that people work toward satisfying a series of needs leading to the ultimate goal of self-actualization. Maslow's positive view of human nature was shared by Carl Rogers, the other leading humanistic psychologist. In this chapter we will use Rogers's ideas to illustrate the humanistic approach to personality.

In contrast to the psychodynamically oriented theorists we've considered, who all began their careers as medical doctors, Carl Rogers first studied to become a minister and then got his Ph.D. in clinical psychology. Although his training was different from that of the psychodynamically oriented therapists, Rogers began his career using therapies based on Freud's psychodynamic theory. The reason for this was simple: When Rogers began his career, in the 1930s, no alternative forms of therapy were available. Rogers was not, however, comfortable with a therapy technique that had as its premise such a negative view of people. In reaction, he developed the first alternative to psychodynamically oriented therapy.

This theory, which Rogers (1961b, 1980) developed over a number of years beginning in the 1940s, is based on two fundamental assumptions:

1. People naturally strive toward *self-actualization*.
2. To develop in a healthy way, people need *positive regard*: acceptance, warmth, respect, and love.

Let's look at how Rogers's thoughts about human behavior follow from these assumptions.

11   MOTIVATION

Carl Rogers

Self-Actualization and Positive Regard

According to Rogers, **self-actualization** is an innate tendency that people have to develop their capacities in ways that will enhance their functioning. This means that people will normally seek out complexity, independence, and social responsibility and will strive to become open to experiencing and trusting their feelings. How do we know whether a particular course of action is self-actualizing? According to Rogers, by using *organismic valuing*, an innate mechanism that enables us to determine the degree to which experiences and actions are self-actualizing.

Positive regard, the second key idea in Rogers's system, is predicated on the concept of the self—the idea that we view ourselves as having an identity separate from others, are aware of our own characteristics, and are able to evaluate them. According to Rogers, there are two ways to think of the self. The *actual self* is the perception we have of ourselves, and the *ideal self* is how we would like to see ourselves. Rogers has used a method called the **Q-sort** (see Measurement & Methodology, "Q-Sort: Measuring Actual and Ideal Selves") to measure a person's actual and ideal selves and how those selves change with time and experience. As a person comes closer to achieving self-actualization, the actual and ideal selves become more similar.

MEASUREMENT & METHODOLOGY

Q-Sort: Measuring Actual and Ideal Selves

How can we evaluate a person's real and ideal selves? Carl Rogers accomplished this using a testing technique called the Q-sort (Stephenson, 1953). The Q-sort test consists of 100 cards, each inscribed with a phrase such as "a talkative individual" or "behaves in an assertive fashion." The subject's task is to sort the cards into nine categories ranging from "extremely uncharacteristic" to "extremely characteristic." A limit on how many cards can be placed in each category forces the subject to distribute the cards into all nine categories.

Rogers used the Q-sort technique to measure the effects of therapy. He first had his clients sort the cards to represent their self-evaluations. The resulting distribution is a profile of each client's self-concept. Rogers then had them sort the cards to represent their "ideal" self—whom they would like to be. Comparing the two profiles makes it possible to see how far the real self is from the ideal self. As therapy progresses, additional Q-sorts are done to evaluate whether the self-concept is changing.

In the Q-sort technique, subjects must place cards that contain descriptive phrases into categories, according to how closely the description applies to themselves. The number of cards that must be placed in each category is indicated here by the number of cards in each pile.

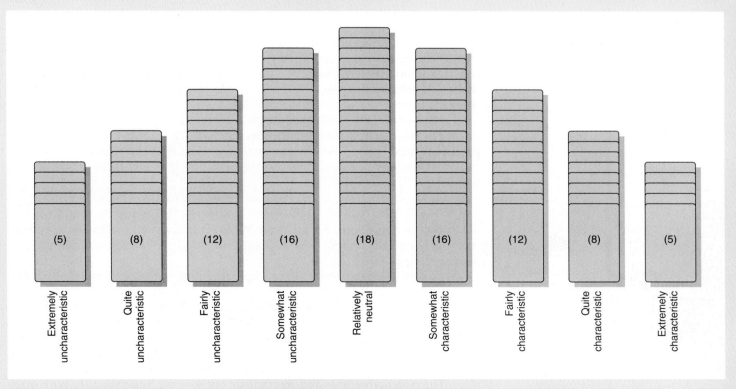

| (5) | (8) | (12) | (16) | (18) | (16) | (12) | (8) | (5) |

Extremely uncharacteristic · Quite uncharacteristic · Fairly uncharacteristic · Somewhat uncharacteristic · Relatively neutral · Somewhat characteristic · Fairly characteristic · Quite characteristic · Extremely characteristic

According to Rogers, our conception of self is based to a large extent on our ability to obtain **positive regard** from others in the form of acceptance, warmth, respect, and love. There are two ways to obtain positive regard.

1. We can receive *unconditional positive regard* simply for being ourselves. Unconditional positive regard has "no strings attached." Parents are demonstrating unconditional positive regard for their children when they continue to express their love even when the children misbehave. "I still love you, even though I don't like what you just did" is an expression of unconditional positive regard.

2. We can receive *conditional positive regard* for behaving in specific ways. Conditional positive regard is typified by the statements "I'll love you if . . ." and "If you do what I want, I'll reward you." Statements such as these are based on what Rogers calls *conditions of worth,* the conditions under which a person becomes worthy of positive regard. For example, a person who pursues a particular career because of family pressure is being influenced by the family's conditions of worth. "We will approve of you if you become a doctor like everyone else in the family" is an expression of conditional positive regard.

If people modify their behavior to satisfy someone else's conditions of worth, they are doing so not because they want to behave that way but to receive conditional positive regard. Eventually they may begin to apply others' conditions to themselves, which can lead to *conditional self-regard*—valuing *themselves* only if they live up to those conditions.

For Rogers, therefore, our personalities are shaped by the nature of the positive regard we receive as we grow up and on the expectations we place on ourselves as adults. How does this relate to your own behavior? Do you have certain expectations of yourself? If so, where did those expectations come from? If your expectations for yourself come primarily from others, this can, according to Rogers, stand in the way of achieving self-actualization.

Evaluating Rogers's Approach

The humanistic theory of Carl Rogers is one of the most influential approaches to the study of individual psychology. In a survey of 679 psychologists (Gilgen, 1982), Rogers was ranked as the fourth most influential psychologist in the first half of the 20th century (B. F. Skinner was the first, Freud second, and Jean Piaget third).

Most of Rogers's influence stems from the *client-centered therapy* that grew from his theory (Rogers, 1951). In this method, the therapist extends unconditional positive regard to clients, enabling them to reestablish their natural progress toward self-actualization. We will examine this form of therapy in greater detail in Chapter 17.

As we saw in the case of Freud, however, any theory—no matter how influential—is open to criticism. Like Freud's, Rogers's theory has been criticized for its imprecise definitions. For example, the exact nature of the organismic valuing process is unclear, and Rogers has never provided a clear way to measure self-actualization.

Rogers has also been criticized for depending almost exclusively on a person's own self-reports and for ignoring unconscious processes. Many psychologists believe that self-reports are inherently inaccurate, and even psychologists who don't fully agree with the psychodynamic view argue that unconscious processes do play some role in our behavior. To his credit, Rogers has encouraged research that tests his ideas (Rogers, 1959, 1961a, 1964; Rogers & Sanford, 1985).

The psychodynamic and humanistic approaches to personality both operate at the cognitive level of analysis. The psychodynamic approach focuses on unconscious cognitive processes, and an important concern of the humanistic approach is how people think about themselves. As we have seen in earlier chapters, such events "inside the mind" were explicitly rejected as fit subjects for scientific study by the behaviorists, who were committed to working exclusively at the behavioral level of analysis. In fact, to behaviorists the very idea of "personality" was suspect. How, then, did they account for the consistency and distinctiveness of individual behavior? We consider this question next.

The Behaviorist Approach

The behaviorist approach to personality traces its roots to Pavlov, Watson, and Skinner, whose classical and operant conditioning experiments were described in Chapter 6. For proponents of operant conditioning such as Skinner, the kinds of internal factors proposed by both psychodynamic and humanistic theorists are neither scientifically respectable nor necessary in explaining patterns of behavior. They would argue that our behavior is cued by discriminative stimuli that precede behavior and maintained by reinforcing stimuli that follow behavior (Figure 15.7). For a rat in a Skinner box, the discriminative stimulus might be the illumination of a light above the bar (indicating that pressing the bar will result in a reinforcement); the reinforcing stimulus is the presentation of food after the bar pressing.

Human behavior, too, is often maintained by reinforcers—those of a social nature. Thus, in an interaction between two people, John might provide a discriminative stimulus to Sally by smiling. This cue might lead Sally to smile back and attempt to strike up a conversation, which is then reinforced if John reciprocates.

Following the logic that behavior is controlled by reinforcers, behaviorally oriented psychologists maintain that the characteristic way a person relates to others is shaped by the individual's reinforcement history in social situations. According to this view, a highly aggressive person may have developed that pattern of behavior by being reinforced for acting aggressively as a child. Similarly, a shy person may have been reinforced for being passive or perhaps punished as a child for speaking out. Such different reinforcement histories are often cited to explain group as well as individual variations. For example, differences in the way boys (who are reinforced for aggressive behavior) and girls (who are reinforced for nurturing behavior) are raised lead to the prevalence of behaviors typically associated with men (aggression) and women (nurturance).

In addition to seeing a person's characteristics as being shaped by reinforcement history, the behaviorists believed that characteristics are influenced by observational learning. According to this idea, we observe and imitate the behavior of others—especially our parents or other caregivers—who are our most important role models during infancy and early childhood.

The behaviorists also considered classical conditioning to be an important mechanism for shaping behavior—especially our emotional reactions. For example, Little Albert, the infant conditioned by John Watson, might have grown up being anxious around furry objects because of his experience in which a white rat was paired with a loud noise. When we examine therapy techniques in Chap-

6 LEARNING

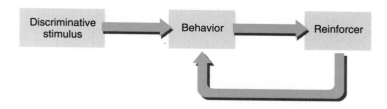

FIGURE 15.7
According to the behaviorist approach, behavior is triggered by a discriminative stimulus (for example, another person's smile triggers our smile back). If this behavior is reinforced (the other person says "hello"), we are more likely to repeat it.

12   EMOTION

ter 17, we will see that operant and classical conditioning have been used to eliminate undesirable emotions, some of which may have been established by conditioning in the first place.

As we saw when we introduced the principles of conditioning in Chapter 6, psychologists appreciated the importance of conditioning but recognized that conditioning and observational learning provide incomplete explanations of why we behave as we do. Many psychologists, therefore, looked to both biological and cognitive factors to provide a more complete description of human behavior. Similar considerations apply to personality. The behaviorist approach is seen as incomplete, so a number of theorists have developed explanations of personality based on a cognitive approach. However, before describing this cognitive approach, we will consider another way that personality has been studied at the behavioral level of analysis—an approach called the trait approach, which explains personality in terms of people's predispositions to behave in certain ways.

The Trait Approach

The more peculiarly his own a man's character is, the better it fits him.

Cicero (106–43 B.C.)
Roman statesman

The basic assumption of the **trait approach** is that we can classify people as having certain behavioral tendencies. This idea is an ancient one, as we can see from the following description of what we would now call a "cheapskate," taken from the writings of Theophrastus, a philosopher from the third century B.C.:

> Penuriousness is economy carried beyond all measure. A Penurious Man is one who goes to a debtor to ask for his interest before the end of the month. At dinner where expenses are shared, he counts the number of cups each person drinks, and he makes a smaller libation to Artemis than anyone. . . . If his wife drops a copper, he moves furniture, beds, chests, and hunts in the curtains. . . . (quoted in Allport, 1937, p. 57).

Although the origins of the trait approach may be ancient, it plays a prominent role in modern conceptions of personality. The trait approach focuses particularly on the following two behavioral factors:

1. *Consistency*: Each person has certain **traits**—predispositions to respond in a certain way—and if we know a person's traits we will be able to predict his or her behavior in a number of different situations. Thus, when we say people are neat, or shy, or aggressive, we are labeling them with traits that describe how they may have behaved in the past and how we expect them to behave in the future.

2. *Individual differences*: The differences between people reflect the fact that people have unique sets of traits.

There are a number of different versions of the trait approach, each reflecting the proposals of a particular theorist. Every theorist, however, asks two questions: (1) "Can we specify a limited number of basic traits that we can use to accurately describe people's personalities?" and (2) "If these basic traits exist, what are they?"

Gordon Allport: Focusing on the Individual

Gordon Allport (1961) describes people in terms of three types of traits. In rare cases, a person has a **cardinal trait,** one overriding trait that dominates his or her

Ebenezer Scrooge, the character in Charles Dickens's "A Christmas Carol," is an example of a person with the trait of "miserliness."

personality. Some people are remembered for a single trait (for example, Don Juan for amorousness and Mother Teresa for altruism), but most people's behavior cannot be described by one overriding trait. It is more common to describe people in terms of **central traits**—about half a dozen characteristic traits such as honesty, creativity, or punctuality that are readily observable in a person's day-to-day life—and **secondary traits**—characteristics that appear more rarely and only in specific circumstances. For example, musicality is a central trait for Mary, who is an opera singer, but a secondary trait for Susan, whose enthusiastic singing is limited to the shower.

Allport's approach is called *ideographic* (meaning "relating to the individual")—it considers each person to be unique, so that no two people have exactly the same characteristics. This means that even if two people share the same trait—for example, "aggressiveness"—it will be manifested differently in each of them. For example, John and Sam, both "aggressive," may *express* their aggression differently: John verbally, Sam physically. And even if their way of expressing aggression were the same, the inner, unobservable feelings connected with their aggression might be very different. Allport puts it this way: "Even the acts and concepts that we apparently 'share' with others, are at bottom individual" (ibid., p. 29).

How can we determine this individuality? Allport did this by analyzing personal documents such as letters and diaries. In his *Letters from Jenny* (1965), he analyzed the contents of 301 letters written by a woman over a number of years. The result, a detailed description of Jenny's personal characteristics, is an interesting illustration of the ideographic approach. Most personality researchers feel, however, that the ideographic approach is an extremely cumbersome way to study personality. Although they agree that each individual may be unique, they believe it is more profitable to discover principles that apply to people in general. A number of researchers, using a procedure called factor analysis (see Measurement & Methodology, "Factor Analysis," in Chapter 14), have sought to determine basic traits that can be used to describe all people's personalities.

Raymond Cattell: Applying Factor Analysis to Traits

Raymond Cattell (1965) began his search for basic traits with a list of 18,000 trait names developed by Allport and H. S. Odbert (1936). He first reduced this enormous list, which accounts for almost 5% of the words in the English language, to 171 trait names by eliminating irrelevant words and synonyms. Then, using the technique of factor analysis, he reduced that list to 16 basic personality factors. He did this by giving several different types of tests to a large number of people and determining the correlations between each of the questions on the tests. Groups of questions that correlated highly with one another defined a *factor*. For example, if there was a high probability that people answering "True" to the statement "I am often afraid when walking alone at night" will also answer "True" to the statement "I sometimes feel that other people are out to get me," the correlation between these two items will be high, and they, along with others, may define a trait we could label "fearfulness."

Cattell's 16 factors, shown in Table 15.3, are called **source traits.** These traits, which are the building blocks of personality, give rise to **surface traits,** which are the many behaviors we observe in different people. The 16 source traits, which apply to everyone, represent a *nomothetic* approach—one that, in contrast to the ideographic approach, looks for laws general enough to apply to everyone. This approach is used by most modern personality researchers; it assumes that everyone has the same traits but in differing amounts. It is as if everyone were created according to the same recipe but with varying amounts of each ingredient (Figure 15.8). Another theorist subscribing to the nomothetic approach is Hans Eysenck.

TABLE 15.3

Cattell's sixteen personality factors, in pairs of opposing traits

Reserved	outgoing
Less intelligent	more intelligent
Stable, strong ego	emotional, neurotic
Humble	assertive
Sober	happy-go-lucky
Expedient	conscientious
Shy	venturesome
Tough-minded	tender-minded
Trusting	suspicious
Practical	imaginative
Forthright	shrewd
Placid	apprehensive
Conservative	experimenting
Group-dependent	self-sufficient
Undisciplined	controlled
Relaxed	tense

FIGURE 15.8
According to some versions of trait theory, different people have varying amounts of each trait. This graph shows hypothetical trait strengths for a person who tends to be shy and for one who is more outgoing.

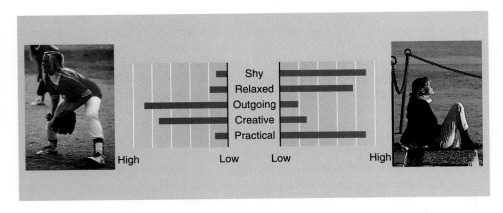

Shy
Relaxed
Outgoing
Creative
Practical

High   Low   Low   High

Hans Eysenck: Basic Personality Dimensions

Hans Eysenck (1952b) also used factor analysis to determine clusters of traits that would describe an individual's personality. Eysenck first proposed two *personality dimensions, introversion-extraversion* and *neuroticism-stability*, each consisting of a number of traits (Figure 15.9).

An extraverted person is outgoing and uninhibited, has many friends, and likes attending parties. In contrast, an introverted person is quiet, retiring, and reserved and would prefer reading books to being with large groups of people. A person high on the neuroticism scale tends to be highly emotional and has trouble returning to normal after an emotional outburst. In contrast, someone who is at the stable end of this scale is even-tempered, calm, and reliable.

In addition to the two dimensions in Figure 15.9, Eysenck later proposed a third, *psychoticism*. A person high in this dimension tends to be egocentric, aggressive, cold, and lacking in concern for others.

Eysenck's classification scheme is, like other trait systems, an example of the behavioral level of analysis because it describes behaviors. However, Eysenck also approaches traits from the biological level, because in contrast with other trait theorists who see a person's environment as playing an important role in determining traits, he believes that traits are biologically determined. For ex-

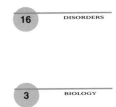

16   DISORDERS

3   BIOLOGY

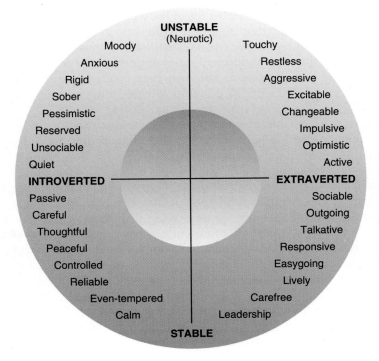

UNSTABLE
(Neurotic)

Moody   Touchy
Anxious   Restless
Rigid   Aggressive
Sober   Excitable
Pessimistic   Changeable
Reserved   Impulsive
Unsociable   Optimistic
Quiet   Active

INTROVERTED ———————— **EXTRAVERTED**

Passive   Sociable
Careful   Outgoing
Thoughtful   Talkative
Peaceful   Responsive
Controlled   Easygoing
Reliable   Lively
Even-tempered   Carefree
Calm   Leadership

STABLE

FIGURE 15.9
The traits associated with Eysenck's introverted-extraverted and unstable-stable personality dimensions.

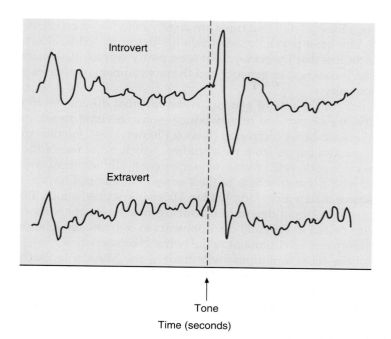

Tone

Time (seconds)

FIGURE 15.10
The electrical response to a tone, recorded by electrodes placed over the auditory cortex of an introverted subject and an extraverted subject. The introvert's response occurs more rapidly and is larger—a result consistent with Eysenck's idea that the introvert's nervous system is more easily aroused than the extravert's.

ample, he traces differences between extraverts and introverts to differences in the operation of their nervous systems. According to Eysenck, the introvert's nervous system is more easily aroused than the extravert's. Introverts, therefore, seek out quiet activities that minimize the chances of overexciting their nervous system. The nervous systems of extraverts, in contrast, are less easily aroused, so they seek out stimulation to keep from becoming bored.

Eysenck's hypothesis is supported by research that shows that when introverts and extraverts are given a choice of the intensity of a noise they will hear over earphones during a learning task, the extraverts choose a higher-intensity noise. In addition, when presented with a tone of a given intensity, introverts have a higher pulse rate than extraverts, just as Eysenck would predict (Geen, 1984). More recent research has also shown that the brain's electrical response to sounds is larger and more rapid in introverts than in extraverts, as shown in Figure 15.10 (Bullock & Gilliland, 1993; Stelmack, 1990).

The Five-Factor Model: The Big Five Personality Dimensions

Though Eysenck and Cattell both used the factor analysis approach, there is an important difference between their conclusions: Cattell proposed sixteen personality factors, whereas Eysenck proposed only three. Beginning in the 1980s a number of researchers, using the results of a number of factor analytic studies, have concluded that just five basic factors can describe personality. These factors, which have been called the **Big Five personality dimensions,** are detailed in Table 15.4. Two of the five factors, extraversion and emotionality, are very similar to Eysenck's two original factors. The additional factors of the Big Five model provide added dimensions with which to describe a person's personality.

Some of the enthusiasm among personality researchers for the Big Five can be traced to the results of cross-cultural studies, which show that the same five factors occur in other cultures, including those of Canada, Germany, Finland, Poland, Japan, and the Philippines (Digman, 1990; Paunonen et al., 1992).

The Origin of Traits:
The Role of Heredity and the Environment

How do people develop different patterns of traits? In particular, how do heredity and the environment contribute to the establishment of a person's traits? We

TABLE 15.4
The Big Five personality dimensions

Dimension	Representative Traits
extraversion	assertive, open to expressing impulses, energetic
agreeableness	nurturing, altruistic, giving emotional support, likable
conscientiousness	planning, striving toward goals, having the will to achieve
emotionality	anxious, neurotic
intelligence	perceptive, curious, impatient, open to new ideas, verbal

FIGURE 15.11
The "Jim twins" were reared apart, but nonetheless are amazingly similar in their behaviors, illustrating that genetics plays a large role in personality development.

have seen that Eysenck felt that traits are largely inherited, a conclusion that was not accepted by most psychologists when he first proposed it. However, recent evidence indicates that Eysenck was at least partly correct. Personality is determined by the interaction of genetics and the environment, with genetics playing an important role.

Evidence for the role of genetics is the fact that differences in the trait of emotionality are observable in newborns—some become upset quite easily, whereas others are easily comforted (Buss & Plomin, 1984). Further evidence for the role of genetics comes from twin studies, which make use of the difference between monozygotic (MZ) twins, who are genetically identical, and dizygotic (DZ) twins, who share only 50% of their genes. We saw in Chapter 14 that MZ twins' IQ scores match more closely than DZ twins' scores, which illustrates the importance of genetics in determining intelligence. Researchers have also studied MZ twins reared in different environments to estimate the relative contributions of heredity and environment to the twins' characteristics.

One of the most ambitious twin studies, the Minnesota Study of Twins Reared Apart, used this technique. This study, which was carried out at the University of Minnesota by Thomas Bouchard and his co-workers (1990), located more than 100 sets of MZ twins who had been reared apart and measured their IQs, personality traits, physical characteristics, attitudes, and personal habits. This research uncovered similarities between some of these twins that were amazing. For example, the "Jim twins," Jim Lewis and Jim Springer, were separated as infants and reunited at the age of 39. Despite having had no contact since infancy, both had dogs named Toy, served as sheriff's deputies, drove Chevrolets, chain-smoked the same brand of cigarette, and had built a circular bench around a tree in their yard (Figure 15.11). Other twins located in Bouchard's study exhibited equally striking similarities (Holden, 1980), suggesting that genetics plays an important role in shaping personality.

Another study that was part of the Minnesota research was carried out by Auke Tellegen and his co-workers (1988), who gave the same personality tests to MZ twins reared together, MZ twins reared apart, DZ twins reared together, and

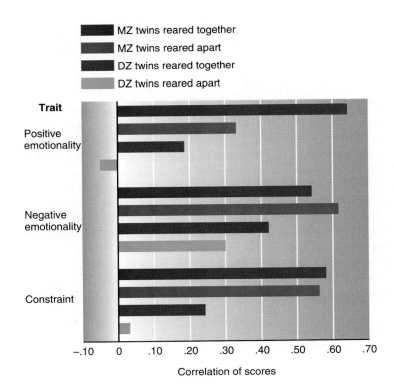

FIGURE 15.12
Correlations between personality traits of identical (MZ) and fraternal (DZ) twins, indicating strong influences of both genetics and the environment

DZ twins reared apart. The twins completed personality questionnaires that assessed the following three personality traits:

1. *Positive emotionality*: A person with this trait reports active, pleasurable transactions with the environment.
2. *Negative emotionality*: A person with this trait reports being stressed and harassed and having strong negative emotions such as anger and anxiety.
3. *Constraint*: A person with this trait is restrained and cautious, avoids activities that will cause excitement or thrills, and is generally conventional in his or her behavior.

The results of these tests, presented as correlations between the scores of the twin pairs, are shown in Figure 15.12. (The higher the number, the more similar are the scores.) The fact that the MZ twins are more similar than the DZ twins supports the idea that these personality traits are influenced by genetics. That environment is also a factor is clear from the higher correlations for DZ twins reared together than for DZ twins reared apart.

These results should be no surprise. We already know from Chapters 3 and 14 that genetics and the environment both play a role in determining personality and intelligence. But Tellegen's study goes one step further than previous twin studies. By analyzing the twins' data using special statistical techniques, Tellegen was able to calculate the influence of the environment that everyone in the family would share simply by virtue of living together. We might expect that sharing similar experiences while growing up in the same family would cause people to have personality traits in common. But this isn't what Tellegen found. His results, shown in Figure 15.13, show that a shared family environment contributes little to personality. The two major factors that determine personality are genetics and environmental experiences that are unique—experiences that occur outside of the family. The influence of shared family environment is limited to a small effect on positive emotionality. The finding that growing up in the same family has little effect on negative emotionality or constraint led Tellegen to conclude that "the common environment generally plays a very modest role in the determination of many personality traits" (Tellegen et al., 1988, p. 1037). Environment does count, but its effect is apparently to create personality *differences* among family members exposed to different social environments.

The Trait-Situation Controversy

Although the trait approach to personality, in the form of the Big Five, is currently popular among many personality psychologists, it has faced its share of controversy. At the center of this controversy, which raged in the 1970s and early 1980s, is the idea that traits should predict a person's behavior in a wide range of settings or situations. Walter Mischel (1968) proposed that this was not, in fact, the case. He supported this assertion by showing that the correlations between a person's behavior in different situations were usually only about .30. Mischel concluded that knowing a person's behavior in one situation (Barbara is shy at parties) gives us little clue to whether that behavior will occur in other situations (Barbara is not shy with her friends). Mischel's criticism led to the proposal of **situationism**—the idea that people's behavior is primarily determined not by stable personality traits but by the situations in which they find themselves.

In rebuttal, supporters of the trait position have pointed out that one reason for the low correlations reported by Mischel is that the studies he considered did not take into account that individuals differ in how strongly they are affected by a situation. When Daryl Bem and Andrea Allen (1974) compared subjects describing their behavior as varying in different situations with subjects describing their behavior as more consistent, they found low correlations between the "variable" subjects' behaviors in different situations but much higher correlations for the "consistent" subjects' behaviors (Figure 15.14).

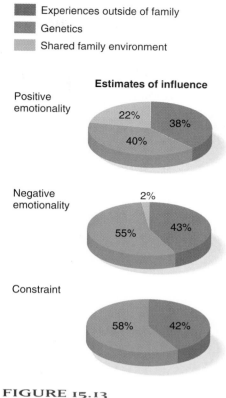

FIGURE 15.13
Tellegen's study shows that genetics and experiences outside of the family are the major factors that determine emotionality and constraint.

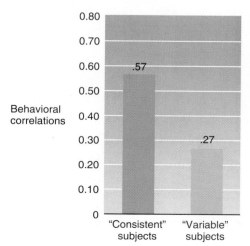

FIGURE 15.14
Bem and Allen's study looked at the behaviors of subjects who described themselves as behaving consistently and variably across different situations. The subjects' self-descriptions did, in fact, predict the variability of their behavior.

An additional defense of the trait approach was proposed by Seymour Epstein (1979). He argued that just as we wouldn't base our assessment of a person's intelligence on a one-question test, we shouldn't base our evaluation of a person's traits on behavior observed during a single event. It is more appropriate, Epstein suggested, to analyze people's behavior over a number of different situations so that we can detect consistencies that aren't so obvious when their behavior is observed in only a few situations.

Trait theorists and situationists alike could claim impressive evidence for their views. As so often happens in such debates, eventually a third alternative emerged that combined elements of both positions.

Interactionism: Considering Both Person and Situation

Recently, the debate between the trait theorists and the situationists has largely been resolved in an approach called **interactionism,** whose proponents reason that to understand people's behavior we need to consider both the person *and* the situation. One way to illustrate the interaction between people and situations is to consider the following ways that people can affect situations:

- People *choose* the situation they will be in. This again is the concept of the *behavioral niche* introduced in Chapter 3: People seek out situations that fit their characteristics. Susan's athletic skills point her toward the basketball team, whereas Kevin's mechanical skill leads him to choose to work on cars.
- People *alter* the situation. For example, an aggressive child's behavior will probably elicit either aggression or retreat in other children. Similarly, one person's competitiveness may bring out the competitiveness in others.
- People *interpret* the situation. A situation that appears threatening to one person (Kevin fears water because he can't swim) may appear inviting to another (Susan likes swimming and is good at it).

Thus, since people's traits affect the situations they find themselves in, it is an oversimplification to consider traits and situations separately.

We can also understand how people and situations interact by considering that the nature of the situation affects the extent to which specific traits influence behavior. Some situations, such as being in the army or attending church, exert a powerful control over behavior. In these situations most people act very similarly, despite their different personality traits. Other situations, however, such as

18   SOCIAL

FIGURE 15.15
The extent to which individuals' traits influence their behavior depends on the situation. Highly controlling situations, such as Marine boot camp, leave little latitude for individual expression, whereas less structured situations, such as a party, offer more room for people to express their individuality.

going on vacation or spending time with friends, exert a much weaker influence. In these situations, personality traits have a greater chance to influence a person's behavior (Figure 15.15).

The interaction between people and situations is also illustrated by individual differences in how much people are affected by the situation. We encountered this idea in Bem and Allen's research on high- and low-variability subjects, but it is also illustrated by research done by Mark Snyder on a personality characteristic called **self-monitoring** (Snyder, 1974; Snyder & Gangestad, 1986; Snyder & Monson, 1975).

Snyder found that people can be classified by how easily they are influenced by social situations. *High self-monitors* are concerned about how they appear to other people and so are easily influenced by the social situation. They tend to agree with this statement: "In different situations and with different people, I often act like a very different person." *Low self-monitors*, in contrast, are more concerned with living up to their own values and are less influenced by the situation. They tend to agree with this statement: "My behavior is usually an expression of my true inner feelings." Thus, to understand people's behavior, we need to consider both the situation and the extent to which the particular person is influenced by the situation.

Interactionism is another example of the nomothetic approach to personality, which attempts to formulate general laws of behavior that apply to large groups of people. Although most psychologists use this approach, others continue to believe that the ideographic approach—studying individual lives—is a valid and valuable avenue to understanding personality traits. An intriguing example of the ideographic approach combines the disciplines of psychology and history, as described in the following Interdisciplinary Dimension.

INTERDISCIPLINARY DIMENSION HISTORY

There are few things more fascinating or informative than learning about the experiences of other conscious beings as they make their way through the world.

William Runyan (1982, p. 3)

Psychobiography

In the subfield of personality psychology called **psychobiography**, psychologists use personality theory to make psychological sense of the stories of people's lives. We have seen that most psychologists believe that studying individual lives isn't useful unless it can lead to general laws that apply to all people. Arguing against this view, William Runyan (1982) starts from Kluckholn and Murray's (1953) dictum that every person is in certain respects

- like all other people
- like some other people
- like no other people

Runyan then states that the goals of personality psychology are to describe these factors:

- what is true of *all* human beings
- what is true of specified *groups* of human beings (distinguished by sex, race, culture, and so on)
- what is true of *individual* human beings

In naming these three goals, Runyan is saying that we can learn about personality by study at each of three levels—the general level, the group level, and the individual level (Figure 15.16). He observes that if we want to understand an individual life we can't simply rely on universal generalizations about human behavior but must take into account such considerations as an individual's reasons for acting in a particular way. Psychobiography, by working at the individual level, amplifies our understanding of individual lives and, in doing so, sometimes results in insights about general laws of behavior.

In "Portrait of the Artist" by Vincent van Gogh, a bandage covers the mutilated ear.

FIGURE 15.16

Most personality researchers study behavior at the general level, by looking for laws to explain the behavior of specific groups. Psychobiographers, however, study behavior at the individual level, by focusing on one particular person.

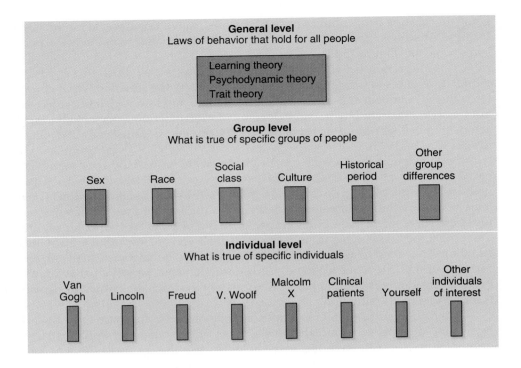

Psychobiography has focused on analyzing the personalities of historical figures and famous people. This creates a challenge for psychobiographers because their subjects, being either deceased or famous, are not available in person. Thus, data about these people must be collected indirectly by reading biographies, letters, speeches, and—in the case of contemporary figures—by gathering information from friends and acquaintances. The psychobiographer's first task, therefore, is to construct an accurate description of the events in a person's life. This is often difficult, especially in the case of historical figures, but once it is accomplished the psychobiographer can attempt to make psychological sense of the person's behavior. This poses another challenge: how to choose among alternative explanations.

We can illustrate this problem by looking at psychologists' attempts to understand a single well-known act by the painter Vincent van Gogh. On December 23, 1888, he "cut off the lower half of his left ear and took it to a brothel, where he asked for a prostitute named Rachel and handed the ear to her, asking her to 'keep this object carefully'" (Runyan, 1981, p. 78). Over a dozen explanations proposed to explain this extraordinary act have been gathered together in an article by Runyan titled "Why Did van Gogh Cut Off His Ear?" Three of those explanations follow.

1. In the months preceding van Gogh's self-mutilation there were 15 articles in the local paper about the notorious British murderer Jack the Ripper who, after killing prostitutes, sometimes cut off their ears. Perhaps Vincent was emulating these crimes. The psychobiographer who advanced this idea hypothesized that "As a masochist instead of a sadist, however, it is conceivable that he would reverse Jack's act by mutilating himself and bringing the ear to a prostitute" (Lubin, 1972, p. 159).

2. Van Gogh experienced auditory hallucinations during his psychotic attacks. He had speculated that these hallucinations were due to a disease of nerves in the ear. Perhaps he cut off his ear during one of his attacks to silence the disturbing sounds.

3. Van Gogh had an extremely close relationship with his brother Theo. He was both financially and emotionally dependent on him and often spent time with him over the Christmas holidays. Van Gogh had learned, however, that Theo was going to spend this Christmas with his new fiancée and her family. Fearing that Theo would care less for him once he was married, van Gogh may have cut off his ear to gain his attention, perhaps even hoping that he would leave his fiancée to take care of him.

TABLE 15.5
Strength of motivations for some American presidents

President	Date Assumed Office	Motivation		
		Achievement	*Intimacy-Affiliation*	*Power*
George Washington	1789	39	54	41
John Adams	1797	39	49	42
Thomas Jefferson	1801	49	51	51
John F. Kennedy	1961	50	85	77
Lyndon Johnson	1965	55	59	49
Richard Nixon	1969	66	76	53
Jimmy Carter	1977	75	59	59
Ronald Reagan	1981	60	51	63

Source: Winter, 1987.

How are we to choose among these explanations and the many others that have been proposed? According to Runyan, we need to look at the evidence supporting each one, much as we would consider the pros and cons of arguments in a court case. This evaluation requires the skills of both the historian and the psychologist. In analyzing the three explanations of van Gogh's self-mutilation, Runyan rejects the first as unlikely because there is no objective evidence that van Gogh even knew that Jack the Ripper cut off his victims' ears. This fact was mentioned in only 2 of the 15 newspaper stories that van Gogh might have read, and even if he did notice this detail, we would still have to assume that it made an impression on him and influenced him the night he cut off his ear.

The idea that van Gogh cut off his ear to silence auditory hallucinations is more likely, since we know that hallucinations were one of the symptoms that caused him to be admitted to a sanatorium, and because we have written evidence that he thought the hallucinations were due to diseased nerves of the ear.

However, the third explanation is the most convincing, according to Runyan, since van Gogh had a history of self-mutilation when threatened by the loss of love or support. Seven years earlier, van Gogh had visited the house of a woman he was in love with. Told that she had left the house to avoid seeing him, he placed his hand in the flame of a lamp and said "Let me see her for as long as I can keep my hand in the flame" (Tralbaut, 1969, p. 79).

As the example of van Gogh illustrates, it may not be possible for psychobiographers to provide definitive explanations for their subjects' every behavior. As in court decisions, it is a question of reaching the best conclusion possible from the evidence available.

Another approach to psychobiography has been taken by David Winter (1987), who has proposed that we can explain individuals' behaviors by analyzing their motives. When we discussed achievement motivation in Chapter 11, we saw that one method of measuring motivation is to analyze stories that people tell in response to ambiguous pictures. Thus, every time such a story mentions a concern for excellence or working toward achieving a goal adds a point to the subject's achievement motivation score. Winter has used a similar procedure by analyzing the inaugural addresses of American presidents to determine the strength of their achievement motivation as well as of their intimacy-affiliation motivation (concern for close relationships with others) and power motivation (concern for impact and prestige). Winter's results, shown in Table 15.5 for three early presidents and five recent ones, show interesting differences. Jimmy Carter and Richard Nixon score high on achievement motivation, John F. Kennedy and Ronald Reagan score high on power motivation, and Kennedy and Nixon score high on intimacy-affiliation motivation. But do these differences help explain the presidents' behavior? According to Winter, their scores *are* related to the presidents' actions while in office. For example, presidents high in power motivation were more likely to make more historically significant decisions and to lead the country into war.

Psychobiography is fascinating because it deals with famous people whose behavior we may wonder about. We should, however, keep in mind the speculative nature of many of the conclusions reached by psychobiographers. The challenge for psychobiography researchers continues to be to find objective, scientifically valid ways to study their subjects. ■

According to David Winter's analysis of presidential acceptance speeches, John Kennedy possessed high-power and intimacy-affiliation motivation and Ronald Reagan possesses high-power motivation.

The Cognitive Approach

The behaviorist approach and most trait approaches to personality work largely or exclusively at the behavioral level of analysis. Psychologists who favor the cognitive approach go beyond simply describing personality in terms of a person's reinforcement history or measurable traits. In this section we look at a number of cognitively oriented approaches that seek to explain both the consistencies in a particular person's behavior and individual behavioral differences among people by examining how people think about themselves and the world around them. One of the earliest cognitive approaches was proposed by George Kelly (1955), who introduced the idea of *personal constructs.*

Personal Constructs

8   THINKING

Kelly proposed that each individual possesses a set of **personal constructs** that shapes the way he or she views and interprets events in the environment. According to this idea, these constructs act as a "lens" or "filter" through which people experience the world; since each person has different constructs, people react differently to the same situation.

This idea is demonstrated by an experiment done by E. Tory Higgins, Gilliam King, and Gregory Mavin (1982), in which they asked "How do personal constructs influence the way one person views another's personality?" The first step in answering that question is to determine the nature of the "lens"—the personal construct—through which a person views others. Higgins did this by asking each of his subjects to write a list of traits that they use to evaluate other people. The traits at the top of their list—the ones they thought of first—were assumed to belong to their personal constructs, the primary traits they would pay attention to when evaluating others.

Several days later, Higgins's subjects returned and were asked (1) to read a description of a "target person," (2) to engage in a distracting task designed to disrupt their memory for the description, and (3) to remember as much as they could about the target person. The result of this memory test supported Kelly's theory: subjects were more likely to remember traits that were part of their personal constructs. How we see others is thus influenced by the "lens" through which we see them.

The importance of Kelly's approach is that it was one of the first to consider how people's thoughts determine their behavior. The Higgins experiment demonstrates how this occurs for one specific situation, evaluating another person's personality. Most of our behavior, according to Kelly, is influenced by how our personal constructs shape our view of the world, and differences in personal constructs can thus lead to the characteristic differences in behavior that we call personality. Following Kelly's lead, other psychologists began incorporating the role of thinking into their theories of personality. Another concept that focuses on how people's thoughts influence their behavior is that of locus of control.

Locus of Control

Figure 15.17 is a scale that measures a personality characteristic called **locus of control**—the degree to which people feel that the things that happen to them are due to qualities within themselves, as opposed to the external situation. Answer the questions in this figure yourself before reading further.

A recent sample of college students averaged about 52 on this scale (Burger, 1993). If you scored substantially above that average, you tend to have an *internal locus of control.* You usually give yourself credit for your success and take responsibility for your failures. If you scored considerably below average,

FIGURE 15.17
Locus of control scale

For each item below indicate the extent to which the statement applies to you, using the following scale:

1 Disagree strongly   5 Agree slightly
2 Disagree   6 Agree
3 Disagree slightly   7 Agree strongly
4 Neither agree nor disagree

_____ 1. When I get what I want it's usually because I worked hard for it.

_____ 2. When I make plans I am almost certain to make them work.

_____ 3. I prefer games involving some luck over games requiring pure skill.

_____ 4. I can learn almost anything if I set my mind to it.

_____ 5. My major accomplishments are entirely due to my hard work and ability.

_____ 6. I usually don't set goals, because I have a hard time following through on them.

_____ 7. Competition discourages excellence.

_____ 8. Often people get ahead just by being lucky.

_____ 9. On any sort of exam or competition I like to know how well I do relative to everyone else.

_____ 10. It's pointless to keep working on something that's too difficult for me.

Scoring: Reverse the point values for items 3, 6, 7, 8, and 10 ($1 = 7$; $2 = 6$; $3 = 5$; $4 = 4$; $5 = 3$; $6 = 6$; $7 = 1$). Then add the point values for each of the ten items.

Source: From Burger, 1993, and Paulhus, 1983.

you tend to have an *external locus of control* and feel that things happen to you largely because of forces over which you have little or no control.

This idea of locus of control, which was developed by Julian Rotter (1966), is important because it says that our reactions to events are influenced by the way we think about the outcomes of our actions. If we think we have little control over our fate, we may feel helpless, tend to remain passive, and become more easily depressed. In fact, research has shown that people with an external locus of control are more likely to become depressed (Benassi et al., 1988). Similarly, research has shown that people with an internal locus of control tend to get better grades (Findley & Cooper, 1983). Perhaps these people are more motivated to study because they believe that studying will make a difference. Generalized across many situations, locus of control could explain significant differences in personality.

Another cognitive approach to personality that focuses on people's perception of the outcome of their actions is Albert Bandura's idea of *perceived self-efficacy.*

Perceived Self-Efficacy

How well can you drive a car on a mountain road? Answer questions on a calculus test? Reach into a cage and pick up a snake? Your answers to these questions are a statement of your **perceived self-efficacy (PSE)**—your judgment of your ability to accomplish specific tasks (Bandura, 1977, 1992). PSE is important because it helps determine how well you actually perform those tasks. According to Bandura's theory of perceived self-efficacy, your performance on a particular task is a function of two factors: (1) your ability and (2) your perceived self-efficacy for that task. The higher your ability and the higher your PSE, the more likely it is that you will successfully complete the task.

PSE may sound very much like a personality trait. There are, however, important differences between PSE and traits.

- Traits like honesty, neatness, and aggressiveness hold steady across a number of situations. PSE judgments, on the other hand, are always made relative to a specific task. For example, you may feel confident about driving on city streets (high PSE) but be very wary of negotiating a curving mountain road (low PSE).
- PSE refers to a *cognitive* act—the way you think about a particular task. This cognitive nature of PSE is its most important characteristic, because if it is true that our performance of a specific task depends on PSE, this means that a judgmental process can affect our performance.

If PSE plays a role in performance, it would be of great practical value to know what causes it. Bandura cites a number of factors:

- *Past accomplishments*: Doing well on a task is one of the most powerful ways to increase PSE for that task.
- *Vicarious experience*: Watching someone else do a task can increase individuals' belief that they can do it, especially if they perceive their own capacities as similar to those of the person they are watching.
- *Verbal persuasion*: Being encouraged by other people can increase perceived self-efficacy.
- *Emotional arousal*: Feeling calm and relaxed before doing a task tends to increase people's expectations that they will succeed on the task.

11   MOTIVATION

Experimental evidence has begun to accumulate in support of the idea that PSE is a powerful determinant of behavior. For example, when Collins (1982) tested two groups of children who had equal math ability but different levels of PSE, he found that the children with high PSE solved more problems—and reworked more that they originally answered incorrectly—than did the children with low PSE. PSE, therefore, determines not only how well we do but also how persistently we will strive toward a goal (Cervone & Peake, 1986).

Self Schemas

7   MEMORY

Chapter 7 introduced the idea of schemas—mental structures about particular topics that guide the way people organize and process information about that topic. Recall, for example, that people who read a story from another culture about a battle between two tribes tended to change the story as they recalled it to fit what they knew about battles from their own culture.

A person can have many possible schemas, and they will differ from person to person. For example, people interested in automobile racing will have a strong automobile-racing schema, which might include their knowledge about cars, engines, and driving techniques. The presence of this schema will influence how they attend to and remember information in their environment. For example, they will be more likely to notice high-performance automobiles and announcements of racing events than will individuals without an automobile-racing schema.

Personality psychologists tend to focus on **self schemas**—the aspects of behavior that are most important to you and that guide the way you process information about yourself (Markus, 1977, 1983). A person's self schema might look like Figure 15.18: Things that are very important to this person overlap the self, whereas those less important are connected but at a greater distance, and those not part of the self schema are totally unconnected.

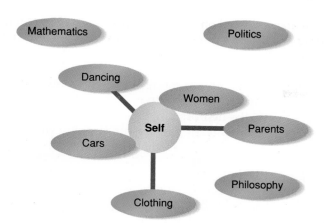

At the contextual level of analysis, the idea that schemas determine the way we see and react to the world has been applied in cross-cultural studies to explain differences in the way people of different cultures behave (Markus & Kitayama, 1991). Consider, for example, how the self is viewed in the United States and in Japan and other Asian countries. People who grow up in the United States are socialized to accept an independent view of the self, so they develop self schema qualities such as independence and autonomy. In contrast, people who grow up in Japan and other Asian countries are socialized to accept an interdependent view of the self, so they develop a self schema that closely embraces others (Figure 15.19).

These differences are reflected in the folk sayings of these cultures. Compare the American "truth" that "the squeaky wheel gets the grease" with the Japanese idea that "the nail that stands out gets pounded down." The interdependent value system responsible for the Japanese saying also operates in China, where a premium is placed on collective welfare and on showing sympathetic concern for others. Similarly, in Hispanic culture, a valued quality of being *simpático* refers to a person's ability to respect and share another's feelings.

How do these cultural effects on self schemas affect a person's behavior? In interdependent cultures, people generally restrain their feelings of anger and are much less likely to express negative emotions such as anger than are Westerners (Bond, 1986). Japanese rarely express anger to close relations, probably because they don't want to act negatively toward the people who form the core of their interdependent social network. In contrast, Westerners, who see anger as a way of asserting their independence, often express anger to close relations (Matsumoto et al., 1988).

Cultural differences also surface in the way people approach achievement. Americans associate achievement with asserting themselves as individuals, with pushing ahead and gaining control over their surroundings. In contrast, Japanese achievement is seen not so much in terms of the individual but in terms of its importance to the individual's group. One of the major reasons a Japanese child works to get into a top university is to enhance the family's social status (Maehr & Nicholls, 1980). By nurturing the development of specific types of self schemas, cultures create consistencies in the behavior of its members, whereas differences in values among cultures help create individual differences among people of different cultures.

Possible Selves

In addition to considering how people's self schemas influence their behavior, personality psychologists have begun to look at how people's thoughts about their future influence their behavior. Consider the following situation: David and Larry both get poor grades in a mathematics course. David isn't happy with

a. Independent view of self

b. Interdependent view of self

his grade, but he doesn't dwell on it. He is more interested in planning his activities for the summer. Larry, on the other hand, is distraught and considers retaking the course to get a better grade. Clearly, the same outcome has very different meanings to David and Larry.

12   EMOTION

This example becomes more meaningful when we realize that for David, an English major, the course was the only math course he would have to take, whereas for Larry it was the first of many math courses in his engineering curriculum. Thus, the two students' different aspirations for the future influenced their reaction to their grade. Behavior is, therefore, influenced by thoughts about what we might become someday. Thoughts about the kind of people we may become are called **possible selves** by personality psychologists (Markus & Nurius, 1986).

11   MOTIVATION

As we have seen from this example, possible selves help direct people's future behavior. Larry's subsequent decision to retake the math course is based on his feeling that getting a better grade will help him achieve his possible self. Possible selves also influence how we interpret things that happen to us. For example, a woman who has a history of cancer in her family, and so envisions a possible self as a cancer patient, might react differently to small changes in her health than would a person who does not have that possible self (Burger, 1993).

Our review of the cognitive approach to personality demonstrates that although psychological theories of personality date back to Freud's proposals made at the turn of the century, personality psychology is a dynamic and evolving field. Research in this field is presently focused on further developing the Big Five trait approach, as psychologists test the universality of these traits in various cultures, and on expanding the cognitive approach, as they search for ways to explain behavior in terms of the way people think about others, themselves, and their futures.

Personality Assessment

This chapter opened with a bogus personality evaluation that was supposedly derived from a personality test. We saw that this description was not a good one because in applying to almost everyone, it failed to uncover the unique traits of particular individuals.

Arriving at valid descriptions of unique personalities is the task of **personality assessment.** Psychologists have developed tests designed to measure both the characteristics shared by many people and individual uniqueness. These tests have been used by personnel departments to help match people and jobs and by clinical psychologists to identify people's psychological problems. Personality tests are of two kinds, objective and projective. Objective tests usually ask questions that can be answered "True"/"False" or "Agree"/"Disagree" or by using a rating scale. These tests can be scored simply and objectively. Projective tests ask subjects to interpret an ambiguous stimulus. These tests are more difficult to score because the tester has to interpret the subject's responses.

Objective Personality Tests

Objective personality tests focus on determining a person's traits. One of the most widely used methods of determining traits is **self-report tests,** in which a person responds to questions or statements. One of the earliest self-report tests was the Personal Data Sheet developed by Robert Woodworth (1919) at the beginning of World War I to help the U.S. Army weed out emotionally unstable people from their almost 2 million recruits. This test—which included questions such as "Do you wet your bed?"—was constructed using a commonsense approach. That is, Woodworth made up questions based on his own ideas about

16   DISORDERS

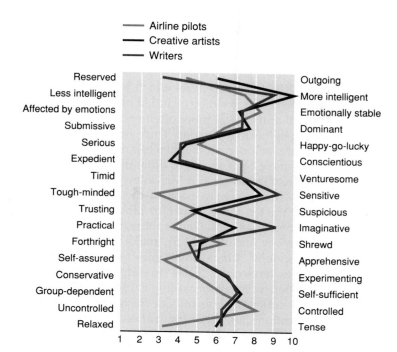

Airline pilots
Creative artists
Writers

	1	2	3	4	5	6	7	8	9	10	
Reserved											Outgoing
Less intelligent											More intelligent
Affected by emotions											Emotionally stable
Submissive											Dominant
Serious											Happy-go-lucky
Expedient											Conscientious
Timid											Venturesome
Tough-minded											Sensitive
Trusting											Suspicious
Practical											Imaginative
Forthright											Shrewd
Self-assured											Apprehensive
Conservative											Experimenting
Group-dependent											Self-sufficient
Uncontrolled											Controlled
Relaxed											Tense

FIGURE 15.20
Personality profiles measured by the 16PF test for airplane pilots, creative artists, and writers. Note that the groups are similar for many traits, but that the airline pilots tend to be more tough-minded, practical, self-assured, and relaxed than the writers and artists.

what answers would differentiate well-adjusted from emotionally unstable recruits. He also talked with army generals about their requirements and with psychiatrists about their experiences with patients. For example, if he felt a statement such as "I often feel people are watching me" would be endorsed by an unstable person but not by a stable person, he included it in his inventory.

Most of the tests that came after Woodworth's went beyond simply using common sense to select questions. Raymond Cattell (1965) selected questions for his **16 Personality Factor (16PF) Test** by noting how subjects responded to the questions he used in his factor analysis procedure that established the 16 personality factors discussed earlier (see Table 15.3). To be included in the 16PF, an item had to have demonstrated, by the way people responded to it, that it belonged with other questions that tested for a specific factor. For example, the three items in Table 15.6 all test for the *reserved-outgoing* factor, with answers on the left adding points for "reserved" and answers on the right adding points for "outgoing."

If we look at personality profiles created by the 16PF we can see that creative artists' and writers' profiles are similar to each other but different from the profile for airline pilots (Figure 15.20). Results such as these show that the 16PF test is able to differentiate types of people. For that reason, this test is often used by company personnel departments to help select people for specific jobs.

The most widely used self-report personality test is the **Minnesota Multiphasic Personality Inventory (MMPI).** This test, developed by the University of Minnesota's Starke Hathaway, a psychologist, and J. C. McKinley, a psychiatrist, was designed to identify people with psychological problems (Hathaway & McKinley, 1943). The MMPI is important not only because it is widely used (in 46 countries and 124 languages), but because of the way it was constructed.

Hathaway and McKinley started with over 1,000 items—statements such as "I like taking long walks"—that a person responds to by answering "True," "False," or "Can't say." They arrived at these initial items in much the same way that Woodworth did when he constructed his Personal Data Sheet more than 20 years earlier. They constructed items that, based on their experiences in dealing with people with psychological disturbances, would be answered one way by psychologically disturbed people and another way by nondisturbed people. But after creating their questions, Hathaway and McKinley took an important additional step: they gave the test to people who had already been diagnosed as hav-

TABLE 15.6
Questions on the 16PF

Statement	Reserved Answer	Outgoing Answer
I trust strangers	sometimes	almost always
I would rather work as	an engineer	a social science-teacher
I could stand being a hermit	true	false

TABLE 15.7
MMPI scales and their meanings

Scale	Characteristics of High Scorers
hypochondriasis	cynical, defeatist, overconcerned with physical health
depression	despondent, distressed, depressed
hysteria	reporting frequent symptoms with no apparent organic cause
psychopathic deviation	adventurous, showing disregard for social and moral standards
paranoia	guarded, suspicious, feeling persecuted
psychasthenia	anxious, rigid, tense, worrying
schizophrenia	showing social alienation or bizarreness in thinking
hypomania	emotionally excitable, impulsive, hyperactive
social introversion	shy, withdrawn, uninvolved in social relationships
masculinity/ femininity	indicates level of "traditional" male/female interests

ing various psychiatric disorders (such as depression, hypochondriasis, and schizophrenia, which we will describe in the next chapter) as well as to normal subjects. They then picked out the questions that actually differentiated between the two groups.

Hathaway and McKinley's procedure, which is called **empirical keying,** sometimes caused unexpected items to be included on the test. For example, the item "I like to tease small animals" is more often endorsed by people suffering from schizophrenia than by normal persons. Thus, in the empirical keying procedure, some questions are included on the final test not because they sound reasonable but because they have been shown to differentiate well.

Using this procedure, Hathaway and McKinley retained only about half of their original questions. The present version of the MMPI has 550 questions, which result in scores on the ten scales shown in Table 15.7. In addition, the test has a number of supplementary scales. One of these, the lying scale, is designed to detect people who answer untruthfully to "make themselves look good." A typical item on a lying scale is "I have sometimes told white lies." Since most people have told white lies, answering "False" to statements like this sends a signal to the tester that the person is not answering truthfully. This lying scale plus the other supplementary scales, such as the one designed to detect people who don't understand the questions, are major innovations introduced by the MMPI.

As you can see from Figure 15.21, the MMPI, like the 16PF, results in a personality profile. In evaluating this profile, the tester looks for scores that deviate from normal and uses the overall pattern to determine a person's specific problem.

Another common self-report personality test is the **California Personality Inventory (CPI).** This test is like the MMPI in having a number of scales, but differs in being designed primarily to measure the personality characteristics of people without psychiatric problems. This test, therefore, has scales that measure qualities like leadership, aggression, assertiveness, and sociability.

Projective Personality Tests

The second type of personality test is used primarily by therapists to uncover characteristics of a person that may be hidden in the unconscious. When we discuss psychoanalysis in Chapter 17, we will describe methods such as free association and dream analysis used by Freud and other psychoanalysts to uncover unconscious material. Another way of getting at this material is by using **projective tests,** which present ambiguous stimuli that can be interpreted in a number of ways.

FIGURE 15.21
In these MMPI personality profiles, the normal subject's scores fall within the normal range of 50–65, but the depressed and schizophrenic subjects have elevated scores on a number of scales.

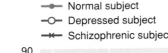

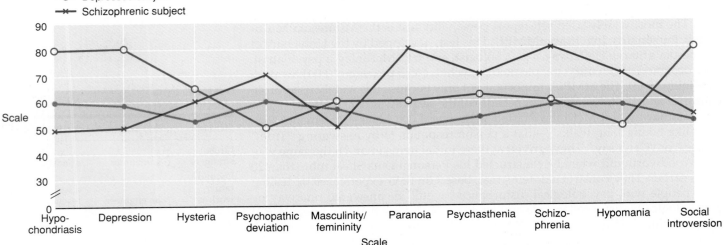

The rationale for projective tests is that subjects will *project* their unconscious wishes, conflicts, and needs onto ambiguous stimuli when asked to describe them. Figure 15.22 is an example of an ambiguous stimulus that can be interpreted in several ways. (Decide what you think it is: then see the figure caption for some interpretations.) The stimuli used in projective tests are even more ambiguous than this one, because they can be interpreted in a large number of ways.

In the **Thematic Apperception Test (TAT),** which we discussed in Chapter 11, people are asked to tell a story about pictures like the one in Figure 15.23. The assumption is that the subject will identify with the main character in the picture (so different sets of pictures are used for males and females and for adults and children) and that the feelings, thoughts, and actions attributed to that character will reflect the subject's own feelings about himself or herself (Morgan & Murray, 1935).

Another projective test is the **Rorschach test.** The "inkblot" stimulus shown in Figure 15.24 is typical of the stimuli used in this test, which was introduced in 1921 by the Swiss psychiatrist Hermann Rorschach. A person taking this test is presented with a series of ten nearly symmetrical inkblots—five in black and shades of gray, and five containing colors. The subject is asked to describe what he or she sees in each inkblot as a whole or in any part of it. After the subject reacts to each inkblot, the examiner elicits an explanation of those responses by asking questions like "Where did you see the man in this inkblot?" and "What is it about the inkblot that makes it look like a man?"

Scoring the Rorschach is complicated, and there are a number of different scoring systems. In one system (Klopfer & Davidson, 1962), the examiner focuses on three factors: (1) the *location* of the response (the part of the blot that elicited the response), (2) the *determinant* of the response (qualities such as form, color, and perceived movement that led to the response), and (3) the *content* of the response (what the response is about). Examples of interpretations in each of these three categories are shown in Table 15.8.

Although projective tests such as the Rorschach and TAT are widely used and have a loyal following among some psychologists and psychiatrists, attempts to determine whether they reliably measure aspects of personality have yielded mixed results. Early studies failed to find differences in Rorschach responses of creative and noncreative people (Zubin, 1954; Zubin, Eron, & Shumer, 1965). Another study showed that the correlation between assessments made using the Rorschach and assessments based on interviews was only .21 (Little & Shneidman, 1959).

Improvements in administering and scoring the Rorschach have increased

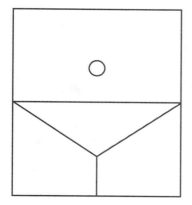

FIGURE 15.22
What is this? Some possibilities are a wine glass with a bubble escaping or an olive falling into it, a person in a bathing suit, or a three-dimensional geometric figure jutting out of the picture.

FIGURE 15.23
TAT picture for boys

TABLE 15.8
Interpreting Rorschach inkblots

Category	Response	Possible Interpretation
Location	"The whole blot looks like a car."	Suggests an ability to organize and integrate material, since the response is based on the whole blot.
	"That detail looks like a rabbit's ears."	Suggests a need to be exact and precise, since the response is based on a detail.
Determinant	"The colors remind me of flowers."	Suggests emotionality, since the response is based on colors.
Content	"That's two people fighting."	Suggests anxiety about hostile feelings, since the response refers to aggression.

FIGURE 15.24
A black and white stimulus for the Rorschach test. What does this look like to you?

TABLE 15.9
Theoretical approaches to personality

Approach	Basic Assumption	Strategy
Psychodynamic	People's behavior is controlled by inner forces of which they are unaware. The nature of the unconscious forces in each person depends largely on childhood experiences.	Identify the unconscious forces in a person and show how they explain specific patterns of behavior.
Humanistic	People are basically good at birth but may acquire a poor self-image if they grow up in a nonsupportive environment.	Determine the person's self-image and how it influences his or her behavior.
Behaviorist	People's behavior is controlled by their history of reinforcements and punishments: behaviors that have been reinforced are more likely to recur, those punished less likely to recur.	Determine how behavioral patterns are controlled by reinforcements and punishments.
Trait	People have a number of characteristics or traits such as honesty, aggressiveness, or anxiousness that control specific types of behavior. According to Eysenck, a person's biological heritage is an important determinant of those traits.	Measure people's traits and determine how well those characteristics describe their day-to-day behavior.
Cognitive	People's behavior is affected by cognitive processes such as interpreting the characteristics of a particular situation and holding beliefs about locus of control and self-efficacy.	Determine ways in which people's unique patterns of thought influence their patterns of behavior.

the test's reliability, so that two examiners giving the test are now more likely to reach similar conclusions (Exner, 1986). However, the test's validity is still controversial, and some research shows that it is difficult to identify particular clinical problems based on responses to the Rorschach inkblots (Vincent & Harman, 1991).

The TAT is open to similar criticisms of low reliability and validity. The TAT has, however, been used successfully to measure some motives (see the discussion on achievement motivation in Chapter 11) and does apparently reflect the issues that the person is concerned with at the time of taking the test (Lundy, 1985). The TAT may, however, be of less value for determining the enduring qualities of a person's personality.

Reprise: Theories and Multiple Theoretical Approaches

The study of personality, more than any of the areas in psychology we have described so far, is dominated by theoretical approaches (summarized in Table 15.9). Having studied a number of theories of personality in this chapter, we can appreciate that not all theories are created equal. Some theories boast an extensive network of concepts, such as Freud's psychodynamic theory, which includes the conscious, preconscious, and unconscious; the id, ego, and superego; a number of defense mechanisms; and many assumptions about how all these constructs interact with one another.

Other ways of looking at personality, such as the behaviorist approach, are so simple that they may not even deserve to be called theories. If the approach proposed by champions of operant conditioning is a theory, it is a stripped-down one, consisting primarily of the concept of reinforcement and a few associated principles such as discriminative cues. In fact, Skinner was against the idea of theories. He felt it was more productive to simply collect data about behavior than to create networks of assumptions and concepts to explain behavior.

We've also seen that different theories explain different aspects of behavior. The psychodynamic approach sets out to explain the workings of the unconscious and tends to emphasize problems in living, whereas the humanistic approach stresses people's efforts to grow. Trait theories focus on specific types of behavior, and cognitive theories probe for mental processes that underlie behavior.

Why are there so many different and varied theories of personality? This multiplicity can be interpreted in two ways. We can accept the reasoning of a physician friend of mine, who pointed out that if a number of cures is listed for a specific disease it usually means that none is totally effective and that we don't really know how to cure the disease. In contrast, diseases that have been "conquered" often have a single cure that works. If we draw an analogy between the field of personality and this way of thinking about medicine, we might be tempted to say that the multiplicity of personality theories means that we don't really understand personality.

There may be an element of truth to this analogy, because personality is extremely complex and difficult to understand. However, it is also reasonable to explain the diversity of personality theories by acknowledging that in its complexity personality can only be fully understood by marshaling a number of psychology's approaches, with each one contributing its own truths to our understanding. According to this view, it is correct to say that people are influenced by unconscious forces, by the situations they are in, by learned or inborn traits, by reinforcements, and by thoughts and feelings. This way of thinking about personality does not mean, however, that everything every theorist says about personality is correct. It is, for example, difficult to simultaneously accept Freud's dark view of human nature and Rogers's optimistic view.

What all this means is that we can acknowledge that we don't totally understand personality while also realizing that to fully understand it many approaches, working at different levels of analysis, are necessary. And in fact the age of all-encompassing personality theories seems to be past. Today personality psychologists tend to work on more narrowly focused areas of research, even if they draw their primary inspiration from one approach or another. As we explore abnormal behavior, in Chapter 16, we will again encounter the value of multiple approaches, employing various levels of analysis to explain complex human behavior.

Freud and Women

Everything we know of feminine early development appears to me unsatisfactory and uncertain.

Sigmund Freud (quoted in Gay, 1988, p. 501)

One of the issues we have been pursuing throughout this book is the extent to which psychological theory and research can either (1) be generalized to all human beings or (2) contribute to our understanding of human diversity. Sigmund Freud's theory of personality development is a good example of a theory that has been criticized for doing neither. In particular, it has been termed inadequate for its treatment of half of the human race—the female half.

The relationship between Freud and women is actually paradoxical. On one hand he fought for women's right to practice psychoanalysis (Freud's method of therapy, which we will discuss in Chapter 17) and to be admitted to the Vienna Psychoanalytic Society. On the other hand, he was against the feminist movement of his time, which was seeking equal rights for women. In addition, in a number of ways Freud's theory depicts women in an unfavorable light.

In this Follow-Through we will focus on Freud's views of how a girl develops during the phallic stage. We have seen that one of the events that causes boys to resolve their Oedipus complex in this stage is castration anxiety. The boy's fear of his father's anger and punishment, plus his awareness of the father's power, causes him to abandon competition and to identify with his father instead. The net result is positive for the boy: not only does he gain his father as a role model, but the "resolved" Oedipus complex contributes to the formation of a strong superego. (Freud is not clear about how resolving the Oedipus complex results in a strong superego, but this idea is an important part of Freud's explanation of differences between males and females, as we will see.)

According to Freud, a girl's development unfolds in a different order than a boy's, since the girl experiences a version of castration anxiety first when, on seeing a naked boy, she realizes that she doesn't have a penis. This leads to the development of **penis envy**—her feeling that she is missing something by not having a penis. In Freud's words, "When she makes a comparison with a playfellow of the other sex, she perceives that she has 'come off badly' and she feels this as a wrong done to her and as a ground for inferiority" (quoted in Gay, 1988, p. 665). Statements such as this one make it clear that Freud himself considered the possession of a penis to be a sign of superiority and the lack of one a sign of inferiority. This inferior status is not lost on the girl; because of her lack she "begins to share the contempt felt by men for a sex which is the lesser in so important a respect" (ibid., p. 674). Penis envy, therefore, causes girls to have contempt for themselves.

After the girl has developed penis envy she develops the Electra complex, which causes her to reject her mother (whom she blames for her lack of a penis) and to decide she wants to be impregnated by her father and have his baby (which would make up for her lack of a penis).

Clearly, in Freud's theory, girls fare much worse than boys.

Whereas boys succeed in resolving their Oedipus complex and emerge both having joined forces with the father and possessing a strong superego, girls are not given a satisfactory way of resolving their Electra complex (Figure 15.25). A girl is left wanting her father's baby (certainly an unsatisfactory wish) and feeling negatively toward her mother (which is painful, because of the girl's early intense attachment to her). The girl's failure to resolve the Electra complex deprives her of the building blocks necessary for forming a strong superego, thus leaving her with a weak conscience and ego ideal.

Freud saw girls' inability to form a strong superego as having effects that last into their adult life. According to Freud, women's underdeveloped superego leads to moral inferiority: "For women the level of what is ethically normal is different from what it is in men" (ibid., p. 677). To this failing he attributed "feminine" character traits such as being more easily influenced by feelings of affection or hostility, being less ready to deal with the difficulties of life, and having a weaker sense of justice than men.

Psychologists have criticized Freud's version of female development on a number of grounds. For one thing, it is seen as phallocentric—it is based on the assumed superiority of the male's penis. Girls feel bad about their lack of a penis, and boys are afraid they may lose theirs. But psychologists point out that there is no empirical evidence that penis envy is common in girls or women. What *is* common is women's envy of men's position in society.

FIGURE 15.25

The development of boys and girls during the phallic stage, according to Freud

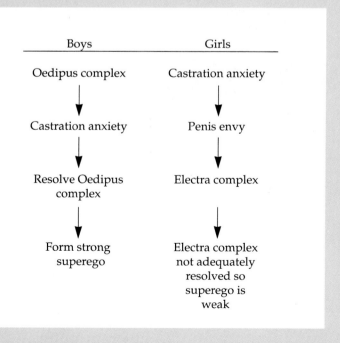

Clara Thompson (1942) states that what women want is not a penis, but the power and privileges enjoyed by men.

An experiment that supports this interpretation of penis envy examined the contents of women's dreams in different cultures and found that reflections of penis envy in their dreams depended on the status of women in the culture. In cultures in which the woman's status was higher, fewer signs of penis envy were detectable (Nathan, 1981).

Psychiatrist Karen Horney (1945, 1967) was a follower of Freud but then developed her own "feminine psychology" that abandoned Freud's negativity toward women. She turned the tables on Freud by suggesting that if girls suffer from penis envy, it is just as likely that boys suffer from **womb envy**—a desire to be able to have babies (Hyde, 1991). But it is more likely, states Horney, that the events of the phallic period have nothing to do with sexual longing for the mother or father. A simpler and more likely explanation is that the fears and jealousies of this period are caused by the basic anxiety that both boys and girls experience whenever they feel insecure.

Perhaps the main message of Freud's ideas about women is that Freud, like everyone else, was a product of his culture. In creating a system to "explain" women's inferiority, Freud was echoing the attitudes of the Viennese culture of which he was a part.

Victorian and modern images of women. In Freud's time, women were expected to restrict their activities to "womanly" pursuits. Contemporary women, in contrast, now engage in pursuits that were previously open only to men. If Freud had been a product of the second half of the 20th century, it is likely that his attitudes toward women would have been different.

Karen Horney, who wrote a series of influential papers in the 1920s and 1930s challenging the Freudian view of women

Freud's stance against the feminist campaign for equal rights was based, in part, on values common in 1920s Vienna, which judged a woman's proper place to be in the home and her proper role to be a wife and a mother. Commenting on women's aspirations to work outside of the house, Freud stated that "nature" had destined women "through beauty, charm, and sweetness, for something else" (quoted in Gay, 1988, p. 39). A woman's job, according to Freud, was to make a man's life more pleasant (Gay, 1988). With attitudes such as these, it is no wonder that Freud created a theory of behavior in which women generally appear to be inferior to men. We can only speculate about how his theory would have differed had he lived in a culture in which women's "inferiority" was not a "fact" needing explanation.

CHAPTER FIFTEEN SUMMARY

The Psychodynamic Approach

- Freud divided the mind into the unconscious, preconscious, and conscious. Two important concepts in his theory are psychic energy and the pleasure principle.

- Freud's theory of psychosexual development consists of five stages: oral, anal, phallic, latent, and genital. Personality is formed during the first three stages: the phallic stage, during which the Oedipus complex occurs, is especially important.

- Three further divisions of the mind are the id, the ego, and the superego. These three constructs interact with each other, particularly when a person is confronted with an anxiety-producing situation. Defense mechanisms are unconscious tactics that help the ego deal with high levels of anxiety.

- Freud's approach has been extremely influential, even in fields outside of psychology. However, it has also been criticized on a number of grounds. One of the most serious criticisms of Freud's theory is that it is difficult to test or disprove.

- Other early psychodynamic theorists include Carl Jung (the collective unconscious), Alfred Adler (striving for superiority), and Karen Horney (basic anxiety).

The Humanistic Approach

- The humanistic approach, pioneered by Carl Rogers and Abraham Maslow, contends that people strive toward self-actualization. It emphasizes the role of positive regard in the development of a healthy personality.

The Behaviorist Approach

- The behaviorist approach explains personality in terms of learning. Different reinforcement histories explain individuals' characteristically distinct behaviors.

The Trait Approach

- According to the trait approach, we can classify people as having certain behavioral tendencies that predict how they will behave in a wide variety of situations.

- Some of the major trait theorists are Gordon Allport (cardinal, central, and secondary traits; the ideographic approach); Raymond Cattell (16 traits derived by factor analysis); and Hans Eysenck (three basic personality dimensions). The modern version of trait theory, called the five-factor model or the Big Five, proposes five basic factors that describe the structure of personality. Most of the current trait approaches are nomothetic.

- Twin studies indicate that personality traits are determined by both genetics and environmental influences. Analysis of twin data indicates that the environment shared by people in a family contributes little to personality; experiences that are unique to each member and that occur outside the family environment, however, have a large effect on personality.

- The trait-situation controversy pitted psychologists who believed traits can predict a person's behavior over a wide range of settings against those who believed a person's behavior is determined primarily by the situation. Many psychologists currently subscribe to the idea of interactionism, which takes into account both person and situation.

- In psychobiography, psychologists use personality theory to make psychological sense of the stories of people's lives. It has been applied to historical figures as well as to well-known contemporary figures.

The Cognitive Approach

- The cognitive approach explains personality differences by looking at the characteristic ways in which different individuals think about themselves and their environment.

- According to George Kelly, personal constructs shape the way a person views and interprets events in the environment.

- Locus of control is a measurement of the degree to which people feel the things that happen to them are due to their internal qualities or to the external situation.

- Perceived self-efficacy is a person's judgment of his or her ability to accomplish specific tasks. An individual's level of self-efficacy with respect to a specific behavior helps determine the likelihood that he or she will engage in that behavior.

- Self schemas are mental structures about topics and events that are important to a particular person. These schemas help determine how people see and react to the world.

- Possible selves are an individual's thoughts about the kind of person she or he may become. The nature of a person's possible selves influences how she or he interprets events, and it influences future-oriented behavior.

Personality Assessment

- Personality assessment is used to help match people and jobs and to identify people's psychological problems. Personality can be assessed by objective tests—such as the 16PF test or the Minnesota Multiphasic Personality Inventory—which focus on traits, or by projective tests—such as the Rorschach test and the Thematic Apperception Test—which are designed to reveal unconscious material.

Reprise: Theories and Multiple Theoretical Approaches

- The study of personality has been dominated by theories, each of which focuses on different aspects of behavior. The complexity of personality can be fully understood only by marshaling a number of these approaches.

Follow-Through/Diversity: Freud and Women

- Freud's theory hypothesizes that boys and girls experience different processes during the phallic stage of development. Whereas boys succeed in resolving their Oedipus complex, girls do not resolve their Electra complex. The result, according to Freud, is a negative outcome for girls. Freud's theory has been criticized as being biased against women.

Key Terms

anal stage
archetypes
basic anxiety
Big Five personality
  dimensions
California Personality
  Inventory (CPI)
cardinal trait
castration anxiety
central traits
collective unconscious
conscience
defense mechanisms
denial
displacement
ego
ego ideal
empirical keying
extraversion
genital stage
id
inferiority complex
interactionism
introversion
latency stage
locus of control
Minnesota Multiphasic
  Personality Inventory
  (MMPI)
neurotic trends
objective personality tests
Oedipus complex
oral stage
penis envy
perceived self-efficacy (PSE)
personal constructs
personality

personality assessment
phallic stage
pleasure principle
positive regard
possible selves
preconscious
projection
projective tests
psychic energy
psychobiography
Q-sort
rationalization
reaction formation
reality principle
regression
repression
Rorschach test
secondary traits
self-actualization
self-monitoring
self-report tests
self schemas
situationism
16 Personality Factor (16PF)
  Test
source traits
striving for superiority
sublimation
superego
superiority complex
surface traits
Thematic Apperception Test
  (TAT)
trait approach
traits
unconscious
womb envy

CHAPTER

16

What Are Psychological Disorders?
Deviance
Maladaptiveness
Distress

Classifying Psychological Disorders

Levels of Analysis and the Search for Etiology

Anxiety Disorders
Types of Anxiety Disorder
The Search for Etiology: Anxiety Disorders

Dissociative Disorders
Types of Dissociative Disorder
The Search for Etiology: Dissociative Disorders

Interdisciplinary Dimension: Criminal Justice
The Expert Witness and Abnormal Behavior

Somatoform Disorders
Types of Somatoform Disorder
The Search for Etiology: Somatoform Disorders

Mood Disorders
Types of Mood Disorder
The Search for Etiology: Mood Disorders

Schizophrenia
Characteristics of Schizophrenia
Types of Schizophrenia
The Search for Etiology: Schizophrenia

Personality Disorders
Types of Personality Disorder

Reprise: Battling Misconceptions

Follow-Through/Diversity
Gender Differences in the Prevalence of Psychological Disorders

Psychological Disorders

Sanity is very rare: every man . . . and every woman has a dash of madness.

Ralph Waldo Emerson (1803–1882)
American essayist and poet

What do you think of when you hear the term *psychological disorder*? People locked up in the back wards of mental hospitals? Aggressive people? The brilliant student who became depressed and killed himself? Homeless people on the streets? Each of these images may contain a grain of truth while at the same time distort the basic nature of what psychologists define as abnormal behavior. In reality, it is often difficult to distinguish the behavior of most people diagnosed with a psychological disorder from the behavior of a "normal" person. Having such a disorder does not make one any more likely to be violent, even though the media publicity given to isolated cases of violent ex-patients may give that impression. And most people with psychological disorders are not found in mental hospitals or living on the street. They are more likely to be living in a home or apartment near you and working at a full-time job.

One of the purposes of this chapter is to describe the range of psychological disorders, so that you can understand what they are and what might contribute to them. You will see that although the symptoms of some disorders may fit your image of strange behavior or being out of touch with reality, many other symptoms are close relatives of behaviors you are quite familiar with. Consider, for example, the following examples:

> After leaving the house and driving a few blocks, John wonders if he locked his front door. He's pretty sure he did, but the thought keeps recurring that maybe he didn't. He feels compelled to go back to check. He returns home only to find that he had, in fact, locked the door.

> Susan has been feeling "down" for a few days now. She thinks she knows why—because she has been under a lot of stress lately at her job. She has too many projects to do and not enough time to do them, and she is having trouble dealing with the pressure.

> Raphael has always wanted to be included in the group of guys who hang around together after school. He is fairly shy, however, and has a hard time making friends. Besides, he sometimes wonders if Charlie, one of the guys in the group, talks about him behind his back.

If any of these descriptions seem familiar to you, you are acquainted with behaviors similar to symptoms of psychological illness (Goleman, 1989). As you read this chapter you will see that it is plausible that many abnormal behaviors simply represent "a distortion or exaggeration of normal functions" (Andreasen, 1988) or that "abnormal behaviors may be only the extreme form of quite ordinary states of behavior" (Eysenck, 1986). In fact, one of the key issues in the study of abnormal behavior is defining exactly what constitutes "abnormality" and "psychological disorders."

632

Although it can be difficult to say exactly when a pattern of behavior becomes abnormal, there is no denying the human and economic costs associated with significant psychological problems. Contrary to what many people believe, abnormal behavior is extremely prevalent—so prevalent, in fact, that it is very likely that you know several people who will at some point be diagnosed as exhibiting a psychological disorder.

A comprehensive survey of a cross section of the population of five U.S. cities (Baltimore, New Haven, St. Louis, Durham, and Los Angeles) found that the **lifetime prevalence** of psychological disorders—the percentage of people who at some time in their lives could be thus labeled—is about 32% (Robins & Regier, 1991). Translated into total population, this means that over 70 million Americans will experience a psychological disorder during their lifetime.

About 2 million people a year are admitted to U.S. mental hospitals and psychiatric units (U.S. Bureau of the Census, 1989), and many more are treated by community mental health units or outpatient counseling. Some 10 to 15 million people per year experience depression, and many more will suffer at least one episode of depression in their lifetime (Brody, 1992; Robins & Regier, 1991). Clearly, some degree of problematic behavior and mental distress affects many more people than is generally recognized.

There is no easy way to measure the suffering represented by these numbers. Nor is it easy to translate them into economic costs. It has been estimated that direct care costs for treating mental disorders reach $36 billion a year in the United States—and that figure does not include the income lost by the people who are incapacitated by their problems. Another estimate, which does take into account losses in productivity, estimates the economic cost of depression alone at $16.3 billion a year (Brody, 1992).

These statistics appear particularly striking when we consider that, according to a CBS–*New York Times* poll, only 1% of Americans think mental illness is a major health problem, and fewer than half of us think of depression as a health problem at all (Brody, 1992; Holden, 1986). Clearly this perception is incorrect, and if the statistics cited thus far aren't convincing enough, consider that 40% of all long-term hospital beds are filled by persons diagnosed as schizophrenic.

Abnormal behavior, then, is a subject with enormous practical and human implications. It is also of considerable theoretical interest, because probing the sources of abnormal behavior can help us understand the sources of *normal* behavior, much as investigations of physical disease have led to many discoveries about the normal functioning of our bodies.

Before we begin our discussion, however, a word of caution is in order. As you read about psychological disorders in this chapter, you may recognize certain symptoms as feelings you have experienced. This makes sense, in view of

Mental illness is sometimes obvious, as in the case of someone who seems to be out of touch with reality. In other cases, however, the signs may be less obvious, as with a person who is depressed.

our observation that many problematic behaviors are simply exaggerated or extreme forms of normal behavior. On recognizing these resemblances, you may be tempted to think that you have one or more of the disorders we will cover. This phenomenon, known as **medical student's syndrome** after medical students' tendency to believe they have many of the diseases they are studying, can also surface in studying psychological disorders.

As we will see, however, "odd" behaviors are usually not considered to signal a disorder *unless they begin seriously interfering with a person's life and are beyond that person's control.* So if you sometimes experience some of the things described in the following pages, keep in mind that occasional symptoms are normal and not, in themselves, a sign that you are suffering from anything more than the human condition.

Given the similarity between many psychological disorders and normal experiences, our first task in this chapter is to ask how psychologists decide when a psychological disorder is present. As we will see, the answer is not straightforward. We will then consider how psychological disorders are diagnosed and classified before describing the major types and probing how psychologists have investigated them at different levels of analysis to discover their **etiology**—the factors responsible for them.

What Are Psychological Disorders?

Consider the following descriptions of behavior:

> Warren, age 23, thinks he is God, hears voices that tell him what to do, suffers from bouts of depression, and talks incoherently. He is frequently distressed and has trouble holding a job and maintaining close relationships.

> Sheila, age 22, is a member of a religious sect that requires that she wear no makeup, dress in a style fashionable about 100 years ago, and eat only vegetables, fruits, and grains. She complains to her boyfriend that she is frequently ridiculed by people at work, who are not members of her sect.

Do these people have psychological disorders? Clearly the answer is "Yes" for Warren, but what about Sheila? Many people might consider her behavior strange. However, her behavior is similar to that of others in her sect and, at least outwardly, it doesn't seem to interfere with such normal activities as holding a job or maintaining a relationship with her boyfriend. Warren, on the other hand, cannot hold onto either a job or friends for long and is often desperately unhappy. Is it this maladjustment that makes it easier to label Warren's behavior as "disordered"? What if Sheila did not belong to a religious group but exhibited all the same behaviors? Would we then begin to think that perhaps something is wrong with her?

Clearly, the question of when a disorder is present is a complex one. We can appreciate this complexity by looking at three possible dimensions for defining psychological disorders: deviance, maladaptiveness, and distress.

Deviance

One possible indication that behavior is disordered could be the presence of "deviance"—behavior that is markedly different from normal behavior. But how do we define what is "normal" and consequently what is "deviant"? One objective way to define deviance is to use statistical criteria, as illustrated in Figure 16.1. This curve, which is a hypothetical distribution of speaking rates, indicates that the most common rate is about 200 words per minute. The area indicating people who speak at 350 words per minute or more could be said to reflect deviance, statistically speaking. These people fall in the top 1% of speakers, which (along

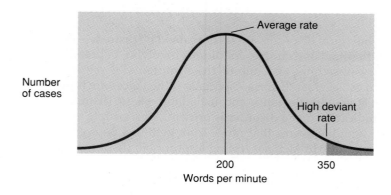

FIGURE 16.1
In this hypothetical distribution, the average speaking rate is around 200 words per minute. Those who speak much more slowly or much more rapidly than this can be classified as statistically deviant, but this is not enough to determine the existence of a psychological disorder.

with the bottom 1%) could be a reasonable definition of abnormality. (We will, in fact, see later in this chapter that extremely rapid speech is often typical of persons in the manic phase of bipolar disorder.)

But relying strictly on statistical deviance for our definition of psychological disorder won't work, because a purely statistical definition of disorder would include people who fall at the high end of a distribution because they are highly intelligent or creative, or at the low end because they have a physical disability. Clearly, being highly intelligent or physically disabled is not what we mean by "disordered" in the psychological sense.

We can refine our definition of deviance by adding the criterion that the behavior in question violates cultural norms. **Cultural norms,** the rules we live by, usually go unnoticed until they are broken. If you saw a man in the street wearing a dress, or with his face painted purple, or talking gibberish to himself, you would immediately recognize that he was not merely engaging in unusual behavior but was violating a cultural norm. But when considering cultural norms, we need to remember that, by definition, cultural norms differ across cultures. A man wearing a kilt is not unusual in Scotland, but his "skirt" would seem out of place to most people in Topeka. Moreover, norms differ across groups even within the same culture. Sheila, for example, complies with the norms of her sect, even though they are at variance with the norms of her larger society.

Thus, the idea of deviance alone is not a sufficient criterion for defining psychological disorder. As the distinction between Sheila and Warren suggests, we usually think of a disorder as being in some way problematic for the individual or for others. This leads to a second possible criterion: maladaptiveness.

Maladaptiveness

Maladaptive behavior impairs a person's ability to deal effectively with the environment, to reach reasonable goals, and to interact with other people. An example of maladaptive behavior would be disordered thought processes that make it impossible for a person to hold any job requiring logical thinking or planning, or that make it difficult for a person to relate to others.

Unfortunately maladaptiveness, like deviance, is not a foolproof definition of psychological disorder. What about Adam, who often spends more money than he earns and has therefore run up a huge balance on his credit card? His behavior may be maladaptive, but most people would not be willing to say that Adam has a psychological disorder based solely on his excessive spending. Similarly, members of Sheila's sect may sometimes have trouble relating to people outside of their group who consider them strange, but that doesn't mean that the members themselves experience serious problems in living. Perhaps, then, we need to go beyond simply describing people's behavior to capture what we mean by psychological disorder. Perhaps we need to consider how these people feel. After all, we go to the doctor when a physical disorder makes us feel bad. Wouldn't it be reasonable to include feelings such as distress among our criteria for psychological disorders?

If this scene were occurring in your neighborhood, you would probably think these two men were seriously deranged. However, within the context of their own culture, there is nothing abnormal about their behavior.

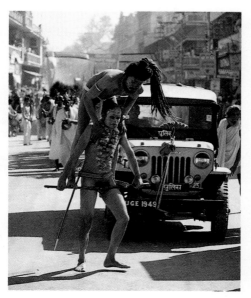

Distress

Many psychological disorders are accompanied by distress—a feeling of discomfort and suffering. For example, conditions involving depression or severe anxiety are very upsetting, and one of the symptoms of schizophrenia—hearing voices—can cause great distress, especially if the voices are hostile.

But just as with deviance and maladaptiveness, distress is not by itself a foolproof indication that a disorder is present. Most people feel distressed when confronted with life events that range from getting a poor grade on an exam to losing a loved one. In fact, *not* feeling appropriate distress in certain situations might be considered abnormal. (Not feeling distress is, in fact, one of the characteristics of antisocial personality disorder, in which a person may rob or even kill others and experience no remorse.)

As you can see, there is no straightforward formula for defining a behavior as disordered. But by evaluating a person's behavior and feelings according to all three criteria, taking into account exceptions like those mentioned, and considering the severity of the effect on each dimension, it is often possible to place a person on a continuum that ranges from effective to severely impaired functioning.

Let's see how our three criteria apply to the two examples presented at the beginning of this section. Taking all the criteria into account, we can probably agree that Warren has a severe disorder. His behavior is both deviant and maladaptive, and in addition he experiences significant distress. But how would we characterize Sheila? Her behavior is mildly deviant compared with that of society as a whole, but it is not deviant by the standards of her own group. Within the group, her behavior seems adaptive and causes her distress only in terms of the reaction of those outside the group. Consequently, we could place her at the "effective functioning" end of our continuum. Yet even in this example, the picture may not be so clear-cut. For example, what if Sheila in fact feels a great deal of distress when she is ridiculed by people outside of her religious group, and thus finds if difficult to function in the larger society? If you were a counselor, would you consider Sheila abnormal?

As we will see, professionals concerned with diagnosing and treating psychological disorders frequently have to wrestle with such questions. There is no foolproof definition that allows us to neatly characterize every individual or every problem of behavior.

Moreover, not all disorders are the same. One person may hear voices and another may be afraid of leaving the house; one person may worry excessively and another may feel depressed. It is likely that these different behaviors all have different causes and require different treatment. So even if we can agree on severe or extreme cases of disorder, we still are faced with the task of distinguishing different forms of psychological disorders if we are to understand and find treatments for them. Let's consider now how psychologists currently classify psychological disorders.

Classifying Psychological Disorders

Having seen the difficulties in determining how to define psychological disorders in general, we can appreciate the problem faced by a clinical psychologist or psychiatrist who, when confronted with a person suffering from psychological symptoms, must determine the nature of the person's problem and then classify it in order to specify a treatment.

We can draw an analogy between the psychologist's task and that of a doctor of internal medicine. The doctor asks the patient to describe the symptoms, takes a medical history, performs a physical examination, and may order diagnostic tests such as X rays or blood tests. Based on this information, the doctor determines a diagnosis and, based on the diagnosis, prescribes treatment.

Early in this century there was some hope that psychological disorders could be classified in the same way as physical disorders. This hope was provided by the German bacteriologist August von Wassermann, who developed a blood test that determined the presence of syphilis, a venereal disease that causes, among other symptoms, progressive mental deterioration. Wassermann's blood test provided an objective way to diagnose syphilis, and within three years a cure was discovered. Unfortunately, however, with the exception of a few types of psychological problems known to be caused by organic brain damage, there are no biological tests analogous to the physician's that can provide objective evidence for the presence of a specific disorder.

The psychologist, therefore, arrives at a diagnosis based on the patient's description of symptoms, information obtained from an interview, observation of the patient's behavior, and the results of intelligence and personality tests. Using these data, the psychologist classifies the patient using the classification system in the ***Diagnostic and Statistical Manual of Mental Disorders* (DSM)**, published by the American Psychiatric Association.

The *Diagnostic and Statistical Manual of Mental Disorders*

The first edition of the *Diagnostic and Statistical Manual* (DSM) appeared in 1952; it listed 60 different disorders and their symptoms. The DSM-II appeared in 1968, listing additional disorders. These first two versions of the DSM suffered from low reliability, meaning that two people using the system to diagnose the same patient would often arrive at different conclusions. This problem was solved in part in 1980 with the introduction of DSM-III, the first version of the manual to use a criterion-based, multiaxial approach. To illustrate what this means, let's look at examples from the most recent version of the manual, DSM-IV, introduced in 1994.

Criterion based.   Highly specific criteria must be met before a person's problem can be assigned to a category. For example, we can see from Table 16.1,

TABLE 16.1

Comparative descriptions of a manic episode: DSM-II and DSM-IV

DSM-II	*DSM-IV*
Manic episodes are characterized by excessive elation, irritability, talkativeness, flight of ideas, and accelerated speech and motor activity (APA, 1968, p. 36).	A "manic episode" is defined as including criteria A, B, and C, below. [*Note:* This is an excerpt; the actual description is longer.] A. A distinct period of abnormality and persistently elevated, expansive, or irritable mood lasting at least one week (or any duration if hospitalization is necessary). B. During the period of mood disturbance, at least three of the following symptoms have persisted (four if the mood is only irritable) and have been present to a significant degree: • Inflated self-esteem or grandiosity • Decreased need for sleep (for example, feels rested after only three hours of sleep) • More talkative than usual or feeling pressure to keep talking • Flight of ideas or subjective experience that thoughts are racing • Distractibility (that is, attention too easily drawn to unimportant or irrelevant external stimuli) • Increase in goal-directed activity (either socially, at work or school, or sexually) or psychomotor agitation • Excessive involvement in pleasurable activities having a high potential for painful consequences (such as unrestrained buying sprees, sexual indiscretions, or foolish business investments) C. Mood disturbance is sufficiently severe as to cause marked impairment in occupational functioning or in usual social activities or relationships with others, or to necessitate hospitalization to prevent harm to self or others (adapted from APA, 1993, p. J:6).

which compares the descriptions of manic disorders provided by the DSM-II and the DSM-IV, that the latter lists the symptoms for making this diagnosis in a much more specific way.

Multiaxial.   Instead of simply classifying a person as having a particular disorder, the diagnosis includes additional information about the individual's condition, presented on the following five axes:

- *Axis I, major syndrome:* This refers to the person's symptoms, such as depression, anxiety, sleep problems, or eating problems.
- *Axis II, personality disorders:* Personality disorders differ from the major syndromes listed on Axis I. Personality disorders are usually milder and not as debilitating as the major syndromes. For example, an Axis II disorder such as paranoid personality disorder might be the diagnosis if a person is overly suspicious of people but otherwise functions relatively normally. In contrast, an Axis I diagnosis such as paranoid schizophrenia indicates that the person is suspicious of other people and, in addition, suffers from more serious symptoms such as hallucinations or difficulty in thinking, which make normal functioning difficult.
- *Axis III, general medical conditions:* Conditions such as chronic illness, injury, or paralysis that are potentially relevant to the understanding or management of the case. For example, knowing that a person recently suffered a paralyzing injury or was diagnosed with cancer could help explain why the person is depressed. Knowing about medical conditions also helps assure that a person will receive medications for that condition in conjunction with treatment for the psychological problem.
- *Axis IV, psychosocial and environmental problems:* Negative life events such as a death in the family, financial difficulties, relationship problems, homelessness, or lack of social support that may affect the diagnosis, treatment, or course of an Axis I or II disorder.
- *Axis V, global assessment of functioning:* This is a rating of the person's overall level of functioning. The person is rated on a scale of 10 (persistent danger of severely hurting self or others) to 100 (superior functioning; no symptoms).

As you can see, the multiaxial system provides a much fuller description of a particular person's problem than simply stating the major syndrome, as was done in DSM-II. Notice, too, that this system takes into account the kinds of distress and maladaptiveness the person is experiencing.

The DSM system has become more useful as each revision makes it possible to classify disorders with greater reliability, so different researchers or therapists are more likely to come to similar diagnoses. This increase in accuracy helps psychologists classify patients both for research purposes and for determining treatment. It also makes it easier for psychologists to communicate with each other about abnormal behavior.

Despite these advantages, the DSM system has been criticized—not only for imperfect reliability but for the very assumptions on which it is based. The system reflects a medical model of classification, which places people into categories based on their symptoms. Thus, just as a physician uses physical symptoms to detect an underlying disease, so psychologists following the DSM use behavioral symptoms to detect an underlying psychological disorder. But many question whether a problematic behavioral pattern should be equated with a "disease." One drawback to this approach is that it can imply that a particular problem is located solely within the person, as a physical disease is. But psychological disorders and their treatment are more complicated than that. To understand and treat these problems we must take into account not only factors within the person but also outside influences such as the person's environment, family, and society. For example, if an entire family's patterns of behavior are dysfunctional, locating one member's difficulties within that person can be extremely misleading and counterproductive. It may be the family "system," not a "sickness" within the one member, that creates and maintains the patient's problematic behavior.

Yet in spite of these objections, the DSM classification system remains the standard in professional practice, and we will use it to provide a way of organizing our discussion of psychological disorders. As we look at each major type of disorder, we will examine the major symptoms of the disorder, as described in the DSM-IV, and probe what is currently known about the disorder's etiology. (The related topic of therapies to treat these disorders is discussed in the next chapter.) Our approach to etiology will use the concept of levels of analysis to describe how psychologists have gone beyond simply describing and classifying symptoms to searching for causes. Before looking at specific disorders, though, let's briefly consider how the levels of analysis approach can be applied to this search for the causes of psychological disorders.

Levels of Analysis and the Search for Etiology

A major goal of research on psychological disorders is to determine the etiology, or origins, of these disorders. One reason that determining causation is important is that it may help the process of classification. For example, it would be useful to distinguish between two disorders that have similar symptoms but different etiologies. Another reason that psychologists are interested in etiology is that knowing what causes a disorder may help them devise treatments for it.

Psychologists have searched for etiology by studying disorders at all four of our levels of analysis. Let's look at the tactics they use at each level.

Behavioral

When psychologists describe the behavior typifying a particular disorder, they are working at the behavioral level. The DSM classification system operates at this level when describing disorders in terms of behavioral symptoms. In terms of the search for etiology, work at the behavioral level can reveal the role of learning in creating and maintaining some disorders. For example, we will see how phobias—fears of particular situations or stimuli—can be explained in terms of classical conditioning.

Biological

The biological level of analysis has become a powerful tool in the hands of researchers seeking to determine etiology. The basic assumption of their approach is that many psychological disorders are evidence of biological processes gone awry. Some of the work done at this level has been a search for evidence that some disorders are genetically inherited. Accordingly, a number of researchers have devised studies comparing members of families to see to what degree they share the same diagnosis. Others have conducted biochemical research that looks for defects at the level of chromosomes and genes that can be linked to the occurrence of specific disorders.

Another facet of the biological approach is the search for problems in the brain that may or may not be the product of genetic inheritance. A few psychological disorders have been linked to obvious damage to brain tissue, but for most this damage, if it exists, is not obvious. The purpose of this branch of research has been to study neurotransmitters in the brain and to look for structural and functional differences between the brains of people with and without a given disorder. As we will see, many disorders are accompanied by either too little or too much of a particular neurotransmitter and by abnormalities in brain structure.

Cognitive

Psychologists have searched for etiology at the cognitive level in two very different ways. One is the psychodynamic approach pioneered by Sigmund Freud (see Chapter 15). Although Freud was not a cognitive psychologist in the contemporary sense, he did work at the cognitive level by hypothesizing that disorders were due to unconscious mental processes. As we will see in the next chapter, the goal of Freud's method of therapy, psychoanalysis, is to uncover the thoughts hidden in the unconscious that he believed were responsible for psychological disorders.

Present day psychologists have also applied the cognitive level of analysis to psychological disorders by using an information-processing approach to learn how processes such as thinking, memory, attention, and language operate in them. For instance, the modern cognitive approach has been applied to the study of depression by showing how depressed people think in more negative terms than do nondepressed people. And the DSM-IV operates at the cognitive level when it describes the thinking processes associated with a given disorder.

Contextual

The context in which a person lives—his or her family, neighborhood, social and economic class, and society and culture—can play a role in psychological disorders. For example, one of the factors that determines whether a person with schizophrenia must be hospitalized is the atmosphere in the person's family. Another example of context's significance is the fact that some disorders occur only in certain cultures. *Anorexia nervosa*, the disorder in which people—primarily women—starve themselves to lose weight, is found overwhelmingly in prosperous Western countries, particularly in the United States. Another disorder, *Taijin Kyofusho*, is characterized by an excessive concern about offending other people by being awkward in social situations. It is prevalent mainly in Japan (Kirmayer, 1991; Yap, 1951). Thus, behaviors that are categorized as signs of psychological disorder develop within a context that can help shape the particular form the disorder takes.

Figure 16.2 summarizes the foregoing description of how levels of analysis can be applied to the search for the etiology of psychological disorders. As we

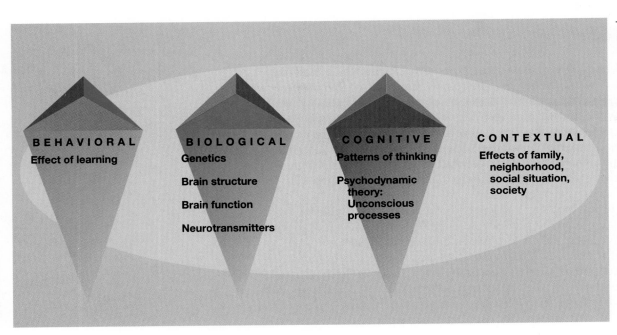

LEVELS OF ANALYSIS

FIGURE 16.2
Psychologists' search for the etiology of psychological disorders has extended to all four levels of analysis.

survey the various types of disorders in the rest of this chapter, we will use the levels of analysis concept to organize the information about etiology presented for each one. We begin our discussion of specific disorders with the most prevalent type: anxiety disorders.

Anxiety Disorders

Anne Watson, a 45-year-old woman, was returning home from work one evening when she suddenly felt that she couldn't catch her breath. Her heart began to pound and she broke into a cold sweat. Things began to seem unreal; her legs felt leaden, and she became sure she would die or faint before she reached home. She asked a passerby to help her get a taxi and went to a nearby hospital emergency room. At the emergency room the doctors found that her heart rate was initially somewhat elevated, but it returned to normal within 20 minutes. Having recovered, Anne was able to return home on her own. However, four weeks later she had a second attack, and within the next several weeks she had four more (adapted from Spitzer et al., 1983, pp. 7–8).

Types of Anxiety Disorder

When Anne Watson experienced physical symptoms and then became afraid she was going to die or pass out, she was experiencing a **panic attack**—a symptom of an anxiety disorder known as panic disorder. This disorder and other **anxiety disorders** share in common the disruptive experience of anxiety—an uncomfortable feeling of apprehension, fear, or confusion, usually accompanied by physiological signs such as increased heart rate, rapid breathing, and autonomic nervous system activation.

12   EMOTION

Anxiety is something most people have experienced, often in situations such as being lost in an unfamiliar neighborhood at night, performing in a play, or preparing for a job interview. But in anxiety disorders, this normal anxiety becomes so magnified that the anxiety becomes disruptive to the person's life. There are a number of different types of disorders in this group, which, as a whole, has a prevalence of about 12 to 18% in the United States (Robins et al., 1984; Robins & Regier, 1991). The specific types follow.

Panic disorder.   **Panic disorder** strikes about 1.5% of the population. Its symptoms, including shivering, pounding heart, perspiration, and a feeling of imminent disaster, usually overtake the person suddenly and without warning. Thus, a panic attack consists of both physical symptoms and feelings of anxiety.

Agoraphobia.   **Agoraphobia** means "fear of the marketplace" in Greek, but it actually specifies a condition in which a person is afraid of being in any place or situation from which escape might be difficult or embarrassing in the event of a panic or anxiety attack. The connection between agoraphobia and panic attacks is illustrated by this further description of Anne Watson's case.

She continued having panic attacks and found herself constantly thinking about her anxieties as attacks continued; she began to dread leaving the house alone for fear she would be stranded, helpless and alone, by an attack. She began to avoid going to movies, parties, and dinners with friends for fear she would have an attack and be embarrassed by her need to leave. . . . She also began walking the 20 blocks to her office to avoid the possibility of being trapped in a subway car between stops when an attack occurred (Spitzer et al., 1983, p. 8).

TABLE 16.2
Some common phobias

Fear of	Name
heights	acrophobia
open spaces	agoraphobia
enclosed spaces	claustrophobia
dirt, germs	mysophobia
snakes	ophidiophobia
stage fright	topophobia
animals	zoophobia

Agoraphobics, who are more likely to be women than men, tend to avoid confined places such as public transportation, tunnels, bridges, restaurants, and movie theaters. In some cases the problem becomes so severe that a person becomes a virtual prisoner inside the house, refusing to go outside for any reason. Although agoraphobia is often accompanied by panic attacks, some people who have agoraphobia do not suffer from panic attacks, but simply become anxious when faced with confining situations. The incidence of agoraphobia is about 3 to 6%.

Phobias.   **Phobias** are worries about or fears of a particular stimulus or situation that is out of proportion to its real danger. When confronted with that stimulus or situation the person becomes anxious, and for that reason will often avoid contact with it. For example, people who have a phobia for snakes become extremely anxious not only when near or in contact with a snake—which in some cases could be dangerous—but also when seeing snakes that are safely behind glass at the zoo or even in magazine photographs. They may, therefore, avoid backpacking, visiting the reptile section in the zoo, and reading articles about snakes. Phobias are relatively common, affecting 10 to 15% of the population (Robins et al., 1984; Robins & Regier, 1991).

Some of the more common phobias are listed in Table 16.2. Many of them do not greatly disrupt a person's life, because the person simply avoids the situation that causes them anxiety. Most people can easily function without having contact with snakes, for example. However, some phobias can be extremely inconvenient; a member of the Pittsburgh Steelers who is afraid to fly will have difficulty getting to next week's game with the San Francisco 49ers; since sportscaster John Madden refuses to travel by air, he must take buses and trains constantly to reach his coast-to-coast assignments.

Generalized anxiety disorder.   A person with **generalized anxiety disorder** experiences anxiety without having to be in contact with a specific object or situation, a condition that has been called "free-floating anxiety." The symptoms include shakiness, a relatively constant state of tension, and difficulty concentrating. People with generalized anxiety disorder are apprehensive and anxious even when things seem to be going well.

Obsessive-compulsive disorder.   Most of us do things we know are not entirely rational: stepping over cracks, walking around ladders. Or consider the person described at the beginning of this chapter, who felt compelled to return home to see if his doors were locked, even though he was pretty sure he had locked them. Behaviors such as this do little harm if they are only occasional. Problems begin when these behaviors become so magnified that they disrupt a person's life. According to Steve Rasmussen, director of the Butler Obsessive Disorder Clinic in Providence, Rhode Island, people with **obsessive-compulsive disorder (OCD)** are "worry-warts magnified a thousand times. They do unnatural things over and over, even when they know their actions are crazy. They devote hours to their rituals every day, sometimes arising at 4:00 A.M. just to get to work on time. In its most severe form, OCD can be "among the most crippling of all psychiatric illnesses" (Diffily, 1988, p. 26).

The compulsive behavior of Marie, a middle-aged woman, was described by her husband as follows:

> I recall Marie preparing Sunday dinner, a magnificent roast beef surrounded by potatoes. She was about to serve it when she noticed that the meat thermometer was still in the meat. The thought struck her that the mercury might have escaped and contaminated the roast. So she threw the whole dinner away. When Marie's illness was at its height, she had to clean the house, and herself, constantly. I was working at home and I could hear the shower running all day. She would shower until her skin was red and

raw, start to dry herself, and a minute later she'd be back in the shower again (ibid., p. 25).

Marie's compulsive behavior was associated with her irrational fear of germs. A similar fear haunted Howard Hughes, the millionaire industrialist, movie producer, and test pilot (Figure 16.3). Hughes feared germs so much that he made people who worked for him wash their hands repeatedly and wear multiple pairs of cotton gloves if they were going to handle documents he would touch (Fowler, 1986).

OCD, a disorder with a lifetime prevalence of about 2.5%, affects over 2 million people in the United States. It consists of two components: *obsessions*, which are persistent and repetitive thoughts and impulses, and *compulsions*, which are the behaviors that result from those obsessions. Some of the most common obsessions are a fear of harming others or of being responsible for something terrible happening; a fear of dirt, germs, and environmental hazards like radiation or toxic wastes; and an excessive need for neatness and perfection. There are two major classes of compulsions:

1. *Checking compulsions*: for example, checking appliances over and over to be sure they are turned off; circling the same route endlessly in a car to be sure no pedestrians have been hit; constant checking to see whether the door is locked (Goleman, 1988a).
2. *Contamination compulsions*: for example, continual hand and body washing and other grooming rituals; continual house cleaning.

Other common compulsions that don't fall into these two categories are continually counting to ward off disaster, being sure to walk through the exact center of doorways, and constantly rearranging objects in a room or on a desk.

OCD differs from panic attacks and phobias in an apparent absence of anxiety: enacting the compulsion frequently prevents the anxiety from being felt.

Posttraumatic stress disorder.   A headline in the *New York Times* on July 22, 1989, read "Relief giving way to despair as horror of crash sinks in." The crash referred to was that of United Airlines Flight 232, which plunged into a cornfield outside of Sioux City, Iowa, killing over a hundred passengers.

The report went on to say that mental health experts predicted that the 184 survivors would suffer "long-term psychological consequences." Those consequences would in many cases be diagnosed as **posttraumatic stress disorder,** caused by exposure to traumatic experiences such as airplane crashes, natural disasters, wartime experiences, and rape. The symptoms of this disorder include persistent and disturbing recollections of the event, upsetting dreams, "flashbacks" (reliving the event unexpectedly), irritability, difficulty concentrating, difficulty sleeping, depression, and a feeling of detachment from others.

These types of symptoms have been widely observed in veterans returning from combat. In one study, 43% of a sample of Vietnam War veterans experienced the disorder (Frye & Stockton, 1982). That study and others indicated that soldiers who experienced more intense combat or saw their friends killed in action were more likely to suffer from the disorder (Breslau & Davis, 1987).

The Search for Etiology: Anxiety Disorders

Anxiety disorders are clearly diverse. Understandably, therefore, a number of explanations, derived from the behavioral, biological, cognitive, and contextual levels of analysis, have been proposed for them. In examining these explanations we will focus on phobias, panic disorder, and OCD, though many of the principles introduced here hold for other anxiety disorders as well.

The behavioral approach.   The behavioral approach to explaining anxiety disorders is based on conditioning experiments similar to John Watson and

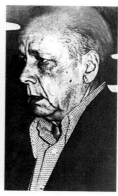

FIGURE 16.3
Howard Hughes, in his days as a millionaire, inventor, industrialist, and playboy, and in later years, showing the ravages of obsessive-compulsive disorder

Many people suffer from posttraumatic stress disorder after experiencing traumatic events such as Hurricane Andrew, which struck Florida in 1992.

Rosalie Rayner's "Little Albert" experiment, described in Chapter 6. In that experiment, a white rat, the neutral stimulus (NS), was paired with a loud noise, the unconditioned stimulus (US), which elicited fear, the unconditioned response (UR). After a few pairings, the rat alone had become a conditioned stimulus (CS), which elicited fear, the conditioned response (CR).

Classical conditioning has often been cited as an explanation for phobias. To illustrate how this process would work to establish a phobia, consider the case described by Stuart Agras (1985) of a woman with claustrophobia so severe that, although she lived in the severe climate of upstate New York, she slept with the door open and with every window removed from her bedroom and drove her car with all the windows open while holding the door partially open with one hand. The woman traced the cause of her fear of being in enclosed places to a childhood incident in which, on a dare, she got into a coffin in an undertaker's display room and her friends sat on the lid, ignoring her terrified screams. In this incident, a closed space (the CS) was associated with an inability to escape (the US), leading to fear (Figure 16.4). From then on, the woman was claustrophobic.

Consider, also, how this model might explain the development of agoraphobia. If a person's initial panic attacks occur in a crowded supermarket, the supermarket may become a conditioned stimulus through the pairing of place and attack. The person may avoid visiting the supermarket from then on. Eventually, if enough pairings occur between panic and other situations outside the home, the person may cease leaving the house altogether.

If we grant that an early frightening experience can establish a phobia via classical conditioning, we still need to explain why the fear can potentially persist unabated throughout a person's life. Why doesn't the fear response extinguish, like most classically conditioned responses? We can answer this question by reviewing what happens during the normal process of extinction. In classical conditioning, the conditioned stimulus, if presented repeatedly in the absence of the unconditioned stimulus, eventually stops eliciting the conditioned response. Thus, Watson and Rayner could have extinguished Little Albert's response by repeatedly presenting the rat without the loud noise. (Unfortunately, his mother removed him from the laboratory before extinction could be attempted.)

Now consider the behavior of a person with agoraphobia. If, after the initial traumatic experience, that person totally avoids similar experiences, she or

Conditioning

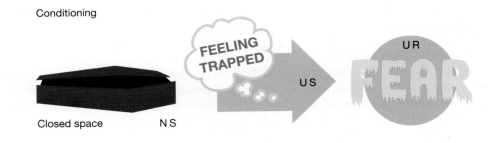

After conditioning

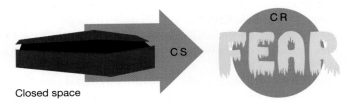

FIGURE 16.4
According to the classical conditioning explanation of phobias, a phobia can occur when a previously neutral object or situation is paired with a fearful situation. For example, pairing a closed space with the feeling of being trapped, as shown here, can cause the previously neutral closed space to become a fearful stimulus.

he will never find out that being in public places is not always associated with being trapped. This avoidance response is actually operant conditioning, like the avoidance procedure described in Chapter 6, in which a dog learns to jump to the other side of a shuttle box so it won't receive the shock presented shortly after a warning light. Once this learning has occurred, the dog jumps every time it sees the light, even if the shock has been turned off. We could say, therefore, that the dog has developed a phobia for staying on one side of the box once the warning light comes on. Since the dog never sticks around to find out whether the shock has been turned off, extinction does not occur and jumping continues indefinitely. Avoidance responses and phobias are, therefore, very difficult to extinguish.

This combination of classical conditioning and avoidance behavior also explains compulsive behavior such as hand washing. The reasoning that "as long as I wash my hands for five hours a day, no germs will get me" is never proved wrong, because the person always washes her hands for five hours a day. We will see in the next chapter that the principle behind one method of behavioral therapy is to force clients into contact with their phobic stimulus or to stop their compulsive behavior so they can observe that dire consequences do not necessarily occur. Extinction can then take place. **17** THERAPY

What about situations in which people cannot identify the pairing of a specific experience and fear? The behaviorist's answer is that in some cases phobias and obsessions can be established through observational learning. For example, Howard Hughes's OCD, in which he was extremely fearful of germs, could have been partly due to his mother's constant and unnecessary expression of worries about his health. Perhaps Hughes observed his mother's obsessive behavior as a child and then took it on as an adult (Fowler, 1986).

Though the behavioral model may explain some cases of phobias, simple conditioning can't be the whole story. Why, for example, are certain phobias such as the fear of spiders, closed spaces, heights, and the dark extremely common, even in the absence of any traumatic experiences or observational learning? Some researchers suggest that humans have evolved so that they are biologically predisposed to develop these specific phobias. We can understand how, from an evolutionary point of view, it would be beneficial to be afraid of and to avoid heights, the dark, closed spaces, and spiders. This idea is consistent with the concept of *preparedness* described in Chapter 6: some animals are biologically *prepared* to become more easily conditioned to fear some types of stimuli than others. **3** BIOLOGY

The biological approach. As we've seen, one way to explore the possibility of a genetic basis for a disorder is to determine *concordances* for a disorder among people who are genetically related to varying degrees. A **concordance** for a disorder is the percentage of people who, given a certain relationship to someone with a disorder, would be expected to develop the same disorder. For example, if the concordance for a particular disorder is 60% for identical (MZ) twins, this means that if one twin has the disorder there is a 60% chance that the other one will have it. Or, expressed in another way, if the concordance is 60% for MZ twins, in 60 out of 100 twin pairs, both twins will have the disorder.

To determine whether there is a genetic basis for anxiety disorders, Sven Torgersen (1983) carried out a survey of twin siblings with panic attacks, phobic disorder, and obsessive-compulsive disorder. He found that the concordance was 45% for identical (MZ) twins but only 15% for nonidentical (DZ) twins. The higher concordance in the more closely related twins argues for a genetic contribution to panic attacks. However, the fact that the concordance in MZ twins, who are genetically identical, is far less than 100% means that factors other than genetics play an important role in anxiety disorders.

Another biological approach has shown that some people who are prone to panic attacks have an overresponsive sympathetic nervous system (Agras, 1985;

Nutt, 1989). This causes the nervous system to respond with an exaggerated response to a perceived threat, a situation called *increased biological reactivity*. Thus, the fact that Sam "jumps out of his skin" when taken by surprise may be due to his overly responsive sympathetic nervous system. This exaggerated biological responsiveness makes it easier for the cognitive or behavioral mechanisms we will describe next to cause panic attacks.

Researchers taking a biological approach to anxiety disorders have also studied brain activity. By using positron emission tomography (PET) scans to create pictures of the brain, they have found evidence of heightened frontal lobe activity in the brains of patients with obsessive-compulsive disorder. (See Measurement & Methodology, "Is Brain Activity the 'Cause' of a Disorder?")

8   THINKING

The cognitive approach.   Cognitive factors can also play a role in anxiety disorders. For example, David Clark (1986) hypothesizes that panic attacks result from the misinterpretation of bodily symptoms. Thus, when a person misinterprets sensations such as dizziness or breathlessness as signaling a threat, apprehension results. The anxiety associated with apprehension triggers even more heightened bodily sensations, which are in turn interpreted as catastrophic, and the panic attack begins (Figure 16.5). We can see how this cognitive mechanism might interact with the proposal that people prone to panic attacks have high biological reactivity. If a person's bodily response is exaggerated, this might increase the chances of it being perceived as threatening, thereby triggering the "vicious circle" of misinterpretation of body sensations.

Another explanation at the cognitive level of analysis, very different from Clark's approach, was proposed near the turn of the century by Sigmund Freud, whose psychodynamic approach placed great emphasis on events in early childhood. It is here that the seeds of anxiety disorders are planted, according to Freud. Freud's model, which is based on principles we described in Chapter 15, can be applied to phobias and to OCD. We will illustrate his approach with OCD, which Freud conceived of as occurring in a three-step process.

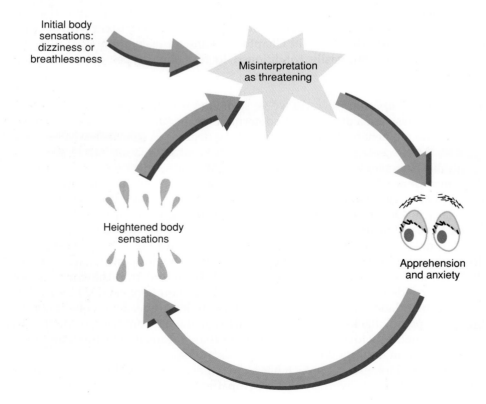

FIGURE 16.5
According to Clark, panic attacks result from the misinterpretation of bodily symptoms. The misinterpretation of a sensation such as dizziness can cause apprehension, which in turn intensifies the dizziness, which is misinterpreted further, and so on. The result is a full-blown panic attack.

1. The person experiences an unacceptable wish during childhood. For example, a boy might wish that he could kill his father. This wish is unacceptable, because it violates the standards of the superego.

2. The wish is repressed. Since the wish conflicts with the standards of the superego, the ego uses the defense mechanism of repression to prevent the wish from reaching consciousness. The wish now resides, in repressed form, in the unconscious.

3. The wish reappears, in disguise, as an obsession accompanied by anxiety. This occurs later in the person's life if his defense mechanisms are no longer strong enough to keep the wish repressed. If the child's repressed wish was to kill his father, the resulting obsession, a disguised version of the wish, may be to harm other people. In the next chapter we will see that one goal of Freud's method of therapy is to go back into the person's childhood to flush out the unacceptable childhood wish.

Our survey of the search for the etiology of anxiety disorders has revealed a number of different proposals derived at different levels of analysis. Of all the mechanisms we discussed, Freud's psychodynamic approach is the most problematic for many psychologists, since it is based largely on assumptions that are difficult to test (Chapter 15). However, most psychologists would agree that mechanisms derived at different levels can work together, as we saw in the case of the interaction between increased biological reactivity (biological level) and the misinterpretation of body sensations (cognitive level). These two mechanisms can work together to produce panic attacks, which in turn often lead to the avoidance (behavioral level) of certain stimuli or situations (contextual level).

The anxiety disorders are among the most common of the mental disorders. In contrast, the next group of disorders we will discuss, dissociative disorders, are quite rare yet can also involve anxiety.

MEASUREMENT & METHODOLOGY

Is Brain Activity the "Cause" of a Disorder?

Discovering brain differences between people with and without a disorder provides important information about the operation of the disorder. This information does not, however, necessarily indicate the *cause* of a disorder. Consider, for example, these PET scans of a normal control and a person with schizophrenia (Weinberger & Kleinman, 1986). The red area in the scan marked "schizo" indicates lower-than-normal activity in the frontal lobe—an area involved in behaviors that are deficient in schizophrenia, such as abstract thinking and focusing attention. Although this deficit in frontal-lobe activity is correlated with the behavioral symptoms of people with schizophrenia, we are still left with such questions as "What causes this greater frontal-lobe activity?" "Is it due to learning?" "To a genetic defect?" "To environmental influences during the process of fetal development?" Although a change in brain activity may be a sign of the disorder, it is not necessarily what is actually causing it. Only when we can answer questions about other possible causes can we say that we understand the etiology of a disorder.

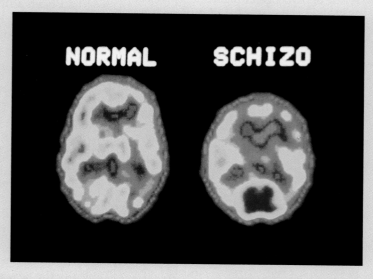

Dissociative Disorders

Sue Ellen Wade was admitted to the county psychiatric hospital for the first time when she was 37 years old. She complained of depression over her inability to control "impulses to self-destruct" that was forced upon her by someone she referred to as "Ellen." Over the previous six months Ellen had tried to kill her on more than one occasion—once making her swallow a large quantity of tranquilizers, and another time making her fall down the stairs of her house. Ms. Wade complained that she had been struggling for many years against Ellen, whom she described as "another self." Ellen periodically "took over" the patient's "real self" and made her do "horrible things." Ms. Wade said that Ellen had been going out with other men, spending afternoons away from home in motel rooms, and flaunting her promiscuity in front of her husband. Ms. Wade said that her real self, Sue, was a very diligent and conscientious mother, homemaker, and part-time secretary (Spitzer et al., 1983, p. 37).

Types of Dissociative Disorder

Dissociative disorders are characterized by a disturbance of a person's consciousness and identity. This means that people may lose their memories for parts of their lives and may also take on new identities. These disorders, such as Sue Ellen Wade's case of multiple personality, are rare. Until the 1970s only a few hundred cases of multiple personality had ever been reported, although this number has increased appreciably in recent years. The other dissociative disorder we will describe, psychogenic fugue, is also rare, accounting for only a fraction of a percent of all mental disorders.

7   MEMORY

Psychogenic fugue.   **Psychogenic fugue** is a disturbance of memory in which a person vanishes from home and turns up somewhere else with a new identity. Timmy's case is a typical example.

> Timmy, a 15-year-old high school student, was teased mercilessly by his fellow students, was doing poorly in his schoolwork, and fought constantly with his parents. One spring afternoon, he went home from school extremely disturbed and threw his books down on the porch in disgust. A year passed before his parents saw him again. Now in the army, Timmy had been admitted to a military hospital with severe stomach cramps and convulsions. He awoke the next morning wondering where he was and unable to explain how he got there. His last memory was throwing his books down on the porch in disgust (adapted from Laughlin, 1967, pp. 862–863, and Rosenhan & Seligman, 1989, p. 259).

A case of psychogenic fugue. In September 1980, this woman was found starving in a state park in Florida, unable to remember who she was or how she got there. Although she was eventually reunited with her parents, she could not recall anything about her identity or her past.

The circumstances in Timmy's case—traumatic or disturbing life events followed by disappearance and amnesia—are typical of psychogenic fugue. The condition appears to be a way to escape from unpleasant events that cause anxiety in the person's life. It occurs most often during wartime or after natural disasters (American Psychiatric Association, 1987). In a milder form of the disorder, **psychogenic amnesia,** the person suddenly loses memory for important personal events but does not travel to a new location or take on a new identity.

Multiple personality.   Sue Ellen Wade, whose case is described at the beginning of this section, is an example of a person with **multiple personality disorder (MPD).** People with MPD typically report that one or more other "personalities" take over their body and do things that they would never do themselves. Typically the new personality knows about the original one, but the original personality may, at least initially, not be aware of the new one. A fictional account similar to multiple personality disorder is described in Robert Lewis Stevenson's

Joanne Woodward played each of Chris Sizemore's three very different personalities in the film *The Three Faces of Eve.*

story "The Strange Case of Dr. Jekyll and Mr. Hyde," in which Dr. Jekyll, a quiet physician, is transformed into the murderous Mr. Hyde at night.

One of the most celebrated actual cases of MPD is that of Chris Sizemore, who was the subject of a book, *The Three Faces of Eve,* and a film of the same title, for which Joanne Woodward won an Oscar (Thigpen & Cleckley, 1954). Ms. Sizemore had problems with blackouts and rapid mood swings for years before beginning treatment as an adult. This selection from her autobiography describes the therapy session during which her second personality emerged.

> After several months of irregular visits to the doctor, the discovery was made. As she sat in the chair, drooped, head bent, eyes downcast, answering his questions in a barely audible voice, her head began to ache. . . . slowly, the head raised, straight and proud: "Hello Doc," she chirped, changing the tired droop of her body to a sensuous slouch with one almost imperceptible wiggle.
>
> "H-Hello," the doctor answered, treading on unsure ground. . . ."Who are *you*?" "I'm me," she flipped. "And what is your name?" he pursued. . . . "I'm Chris Costner." "Why are you using that name instead of Chris White (her married name)?" She straightened her skirt, hitching it up her leg, and tossing her head, "Because Chris White is her," she stated pointing off vaguely, "not me" (Sizemore & Pittillo, 1977, p. 255).

The Search for Etiology: Dissociative Disorders

We can only speculate as to the cause of psychogenic fugue, and exactly how MPD occurs is not clear. However, an important clue regarding MPD is the finding that 60 to 80%—or more—of these patients had been sexually or physically abused in childhood, were victims of incest, or had witnessed the violent death of a parent or sibling (Coons & Milstein, 1986; Putnam et al., 1986; Ross, Norton, & Wozney, 1989). This history of childhood trauma has led to the hypothesis that the multiple personalities developed as a way to cope with the situation, often while the trauma was happening. The victim creates another personality who takes the abuse, leaving the original personality able to feel that "this isn't happening to me."

This explanation depends on the defense mechanism of repression (see Chapter 15), which reduces anxiety by keeping the memory of the abuse and the various personalities from the person's consciousness. Many therapists who deal with MPD accept this explanation, although the main evidence supporting it is that most people with MPD have been abused. This explanation is, therefore, a hypothesis, and it is not accepted by everyone. (See Measurement & Methodology, "Are Multiple Personalities Created by the Therapist?")

At present, psychologists know little about the role of biology or conscious cognitive processes in dissociative disorders. In the case of MPD, this lack of knowledge extends to uncertainty about how to diagnose it, an issue that has been a central focus in some murder trials whose defendants claim to have MPD. In such cases, the court may bring in expert witnesses to present evidence regarding their diagnoses, as described in the following Interdisciplinary Dimension. This use of experts raises a number of issues at the intersection of law and psychology.

INTERDISCIPLINARY DIMENSION CRIMINAL JUSTICE

The Expert Witness and Abnormal Behavior

Kenneth Bianchi, known as the "Hillside Strangler," was on the witness stand during his trial for the brutal rapes and murders of at least a dozen women in Los Angeles and in Washington State. His defense—not guilty on the basis of insanity—was based on his claim that he had multiple personality disorder (MPD) and that his other personality, "Steve," had committed the murders. Was Bianchi telling the truth, or did he create Steve especially for his trial, to escape being incarcerated?

Mental health professionals—usually psychologists or psychiatrists—are often called into court to answer questions such as these that require a knowledge of psychological disorders. (Note, however, that "insanity" is a legal concept, not a psychological one. Ultimately it is a judge or jury that decides whether a defendant's psychological condition renders him or her insane—and therefore not criminally responsible—in the eyes of the law.) In the Bianchi case, the court heard the opinions of six experts. Four of the six diagnosed Bianchi as having MPD (Watkins, 1984). The other two said he had antisocial personality disorder, a condition in which people can commit crimes yet feel no guilt or remorse (Orne et al., 1984). The court agreed with the minority diagnosis and rejected the insanity defense. Bianchi was found guilty and sentenced to life imprisonment.

This example illustrates a common occurrence: it is not unusual for a number of psychological experts to offer conflicting testimony in the same case (Faust & Ziskin, 1988; Shah & McGarry, 1986). Often, for instance, one expert at a parole hearing testifies that it is probable that a prisoner will commit violent acts if released, whereas another states that the inmate poses no threat to society.

How can experts disagree so completely? According to critics of expert witness testimony, the state of psychological science is simply not equal to the difficult tasks experts are asked to perform (Faust & Ziskin, 1988). After all, the critics point out, when asked whether a prisoner will be dangerous, the expert is being asked to predict the future. When asked whether a defendant is legally sane, the expert is being asked to determine whether the person could distinguish right from wrong at the time of the crime—an event that may have taken place months or even years earlier. (The legal definition of insanity differs from state to state. Most states define it by referring to the idea that the defendant could not distinguish right from wrong.)

With the difficulties inherent in predicting the future or reconstructing the past in mind, critics of the expert witness system have marshaled a number of lines of evidence to show that expert testimony should often be viewed skeptically. David Faust and Jay Ziskin (1988) point to studies showing that when experts are asked to predict future violence, they are wrong twice as often as they are correct. For example, Henry Steadman found that of a group of 480 patients in mental hospitals who had been labeled dangerous by psychologists and psychiatrists, only 26 had committed violent acts while still confined to the hospital, four years later. While this low number may underestimate the violent behavior that might have occurred had these patients been released into the community (Klassen & O'Connor, 1988), it is generally established that mental health professionals show a consistent bias in favor of overpredicting dangerousness.

This overprediction makes sense when we consider the *base rate problem* facing the clinician. The base rate is the number of people who have a particular characteristic. If, for example, the base rate for violence is only 1 out of 100, then it would be very difficult for the psychologist to pick that one violent person out of a group of 100. If, however, the psychologist were to pick 50 people as possibly being violent, she stands a fairly good chance of picking the one violent person—while unfortunately labeling 49 others as vio-

Kenneth Bianchi, the "Hillside Strangler," claimed to have MPD.

lent. In practice this is what occurs, so many people are labeled dangerous who are not. Thus, both the American Psychological Association (1978) and the American Psychiatric Association (1974) have stated that psychologists or psychiatrists cannot accurately predict the violence of the people in their care.

A more specific problem facing experts who are asked to diagnose a defendant is that of the potentially biasing effect of knowing the person may have committed a crime. This biasing effect was demonstrated in the experiment by Ellen Langer and Robert Abelson (1974) that we described in Chapter 15. In that experiment, therapists were shown a videotape of an ordinary-looking man being interviewed. Half of the therapists were told that the man was a "job applicant" and half were told he was a "patient." When the therapists were asked to describe the person based on their viewing of the tape, those who believed he was a job applicant described him as ingenious, open, candid, upstanding, straightforward, and ordinary; in contrast, many of those who believed he was a patient described him as rigid, impulsive, conflicted over his homosexuality, dependent, and passive-aggressive. It is possible that a similar bias could prevail when a therapist is asked by the court to evaluate a person labeled as a "suspect."

Problems of potential bias aside, expert witnesses also face the usual problem: accurate diagnosis of psychological disorders is often difficult. Although the reliability of the *Diagnostic and Statistical Manual* has increased with each revision, it is still not unusual for two clinicians using it to arrive at different diagnoses of the same patient (Faust & Ziskin, 1988). This is one of the reasons that judges and juries sometimes hear testimony from experts for the defense and for the prosecution who confidently state opposite opinions.

MEASUREMENT & METHODOLOGY

Are Multiple Personalities Created by the Therapist?

We have seen that it is often not easy to diagnose psychological disorders accurately. This problem becomes particularly apparent when we consider multiple personality disorder (MPD). The fact that some therapists have seen 50 or more cases of multiple personality, whereas the vast majority have seen none throughout their whole careers, has led psychologists like Nicholas Spanos to question the validity of this diagnosis (Spanos, Weekes, & Bertrand, 1985).

Spanos not only finds it interesting that a few therapists have seen most of the reported cases of multiple personality, but also that most of the cases have occurred within the last 10 to 15 years. Why should this diagnosis, which was almost unknown before the 1960s, suddenly become more prevalent? Spanos suggests that its "popularity" may be due in part to the publicity MPD has received from recent movies and books. Because of this publicity, the symptoms of multiple personality are widely known. A person with psychological problems might, therefore, begin therapy with some knowledge of this disorder.

But only a minuscule fraction of people who have read books or seen movies about MPD become diagnosed as having it. One of the contributors to this diagnosis, says Spanos, may be the therapist's suggestion during the course of treatment that the person possesses another personality. For example, suppose a patient is having trouble remembering a sexual scene from her past and the therapist instructs her as follows: "Close your eyes and speak to the one who carried out the act." Based on this suggestion, the patient might begin referring to herself by a different name. The therapist may then validate the "other" personality simply by having conversations with it and taking those conversations quite seriously.

Consider the patient's situation. The therapist, whom the patient wants to please, is suggesting that there may be another person in there and talks with this other person when he or she appears. The patient's desire to please the therapist sets up a *demand characteristic* (discussed in Chapter 2) to behave as if another personality is present. Furthermore, being diagnosed as having a multiple personality has other advantages. The patient may know that people with MPD often become the center of attention. And having MPD also relieves people from taking responsibility for their actions. The idea that "I didn't do it; my 'bad' personality is responsible" has been used as a defense in murder trials such as the "Hillside Strangler" case referred to in the Interdisciplinary Dimension.

Is Spanos's idea—that the diagnosis of MPD can be created by the therapist's methods—accepted by other psychologists? Although his arguments are reasonable, most psychologists involved with MPD feel that the terrible sexual and physical abuse reported by most people with MPD is a persuasive argument that this disorder is created not by the therapist but by the victimized child, who created these personalities for protection. Nonetheless, it is important to keep in mind the possibility that demand characteristics of the therapeutic situation may, in some cases, lead to the creation of "multiple personalities" that may not have existed before therapy.

But it is important to point out that it is just as common in other fields for experts to disagree—two physicians, for example, often disagree about the diagnosis of a disease. Martin Orne, one of the psychiatrists who testified in the Bianchi case, points out that "The battle of experts is as profound in all medical specialties as it is in psychology and psychiatry. You find battling experts even in the reconstruction of an auto accident. It's intrinsic to the adversarial trial system" (quoted in Goleman, 1988b).

Others point out that mental health experts who testify in court actually agree with each other more than they disagree. A study of all criminal cases tried in Alaska between 1977 and 1981 indicated that clinicians who testified as expert witnesses agreed with each other 79% of the time (Phillips & Wolf, 1988). Despite the controversy over expert witnesses and recognition of the limitations to what they can explain, clinicians testify in over 1 million court cases annually, because judges and juries feel that they can often provide useful information that would otherwise not be available (Goleman, 1988b). ■

Somatoform Disorders

Eddie Evans was referred to a mental health clinic by his neurologist because his left arm and hand had been paralyzed for a year. He was able to move his fingers and hold on to objects but could not raise his arm without assistance. Extensive neurological testing had revealed no nerve or brain damage to account for the paralysis. He had received physical exercise therapy twice a week during the past year, with little improvement. The paralysis occurred after an auto accident during which he sustained some cuts on his leg and strained muscles in his neck (whiplash). He was driving to work, experienced a "blackout," lost control of the car, and hit a highway guardrail.

Types of Somatoform Disorder

Eddie's case is an example of a **somatoform disorder**, in which physical symptoms occur without any organic basis, usually following a stressful situation. The word *somatoform* comes from the Greek *soma*, which means "body." We will describe three representative forms of somatoform disorder: conversion disorder, hypochondriasis, and somatization disorder. All involve physical symptoms that have no organic basis, but each has its own characteristics.

Conversion disorder.   In **conversion disorders** a physical complaint is accompanied by no organic damage, as in the example of Eddie Evans. Symptoms may involve paralysis of part of the body, blindness, loss of hearing, or loss of feeling in part of the body. Even though many of these symptoms are extremely serious, the patient remains calm and expresses little anxiety.

3   BIOLOGY

When first seeing a patient with these symptoms, the doctor's task is to determine whether the cause is psychological or organic. In some cases this can be deduced from the parts of the body that are affected. Figure 16.6 shows an example of *glove anesthesia*, in which the patient reports a loss of sensation in the entire hand from the wrist to the tips of the fingers. Given the network of nerves in the hand, however, it is not possible for loss of sensitivity to occur in that pattern, so the phenomenon must be psychological.

Diagnosing conversion disorders is, however, often extremely difficult. In one study, 25% of patients diagnosed as having a conversion disorder were contacted 10 years later and found to have been rediagnosed and treated for an organic problem (Watson & Buranen, 1979). Other studies have found even higher rates of actual physiological problems (Gould et al., 1986). Sometimes, then, when physiological problems are difficult to detect, conversion disorder is assumed.

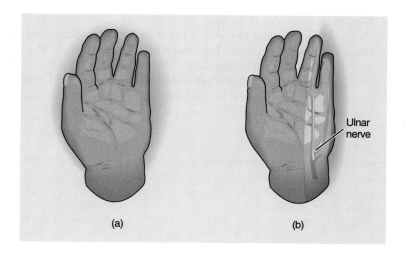

FIGURE 16.6
A person with a conversion disorder might report a loss of sensation in the entire hand, as shown in (a). However, this situation, called "glove anesthesia," is physiologically unlikely, since the hand is innervated by three separate nerves. For example, the ulnar nerve, shown in (b), innervates one side of the hand. Thus, we would expect the loss of sensation to be restricted to one part of the hand.

Somatization and hypochondriasis.   These two conditions are closely related. In **somatization disorder**, a person reports recurring physical symptoms, usually involving many different complaints. The following were reported by at least 60% of patients in one study (Perley & Guze, 1962).

Nervousness	Dizziness	Joint pain
Abdominal pain	Back pain	Constipation
Extremity pain	Depressed feelings	Palpitations
Excessive crying	Labored breathing	Anxiety attacks
Chest pain	Headache	Weakness
Fatigue	Visual blurring	
Abdominal bloating	Nausea	

Patients typically report their symptoms in dramatic, exaggerated fashion and visit many different physicians as each one fails to find an organic problem. Patients with somatization disorder are often anxious and depressed.

In **hypochondriasis** the patient can also be anxious and depressed about the possibility of disease. These patients focus their attention on specific symptoms and then exaggerate their importance. For example, they may think that an occasional cough is signaling the onset of a life-threatening disease. Thus, in hypochondriasis "symptoms" may actually be present, but their significance is overestimated. In somatization disorder, the symptoms themselves are much more diffuse and may be completely psychological in origin.

The Search for Etiology: Somatoform Disorders

Sigmund Freud pioneered the description and treatment of conversion disorder. He believed it was an anxiety disorder in which the loss of function was linked to an unacceptable repressed wish. In the anxiety disorders we discussed earlier, the repressed wish eventually resurfaces in the form of a disguised symptom that is accompanied by anxiety. In the case of conversion disorder, the repressed wish is *converted* into a physical symptom. Thus, the patient, although suffering from a serious problem such as paralysis, feels no anxiety.

Freud and others have also hypothesized that there is an element of **secondary gain** behind these disorders. Secondary gain refers to the positive aspects of having a disability or illness. Other people are often sympathetic, and, if the illness is serious enough, the person is cared for by others and can escape from responsibilities such as school, work, or caring for others. This situation can reinforce the person's feelings of illness. Note that this explanation is consistent with a behaviorist approach, in that gaining other people's sympathy and escaping responsibilities are positive reinforcers.

Like dissociative disorders, somatoform disorders are extremely rare, accounting for only a fraction of a percent of cases of psychological disorders. The etiology of these disorders, too, is highly speculative, since little is known about their biological or cognitive mechanisms.

We now turn to a group of disorders called mood disorders. These are very common and, as we will see when we consider their etiology, we can point to possible causes at each of our levels of analysis.

Mood Disorders

My nights were sleepless. I lay with dry, staring eyes gazing into space. I had a fear that some terrible calamity was about to happen. I grew afraid to be left alone. The most trivial duty became a formidable task. Finally, mental and physical exercises became impossible; the tired muscles refused to respond, my "thinking apparatus" refused to work, ambition was gone. . . . Life seemed utterly futile (Reid, 1910, pp. 612–613).

Types of Mood Disorder

12   EMOTION

Reid's description of his own depression emphasizes a defining characteristic of **mood disorders**—disorders that involve states of intense positive or negative emotion. His description also indicates that his depression affected not only his mood but also many other aspects of his functioning. There are two major types of mood disorders, **depressive disorders** and **bipolar disorders**.

Depressive disorders.   Depression is so widespread that it has been called the "common cold" of psychological disorders. Lee Robins and his co-workers (1984), in a survey of three American cities, found that at any given time 4 to 7% of the population suffers from **major depression**—the major defining characteristics of which are prolonged depressed mood or loss of interest or pleasure in most daily activities—and that 2 to 4% suffer from milder symptoms (called **dysthymia**). According to the National Institute of Mental Health, depression strikes 15 million Americans each year (Brody, 1992).

Symptoms typically associated with depression are hopelessness, despair, low self-esteem, guilt, feelings of worthlessness, loss of interest in everyday activities, lack of appetite, disturbed sleep, and inability to experience pleasure. Depressive episodes typically last between two weeks and six months and may recur a number of times during the person's life. Between episodes, the person can function normally, which accounts for the fact that suffering from depression does not always prevent a person from leading a productive life.

In fact, if you have been depressed you are in good company. Many famous people, such as Abraham Lincoln, Robert E. Lee, Winston Churchill, and Emily Dickinson, have been stricken with major depression. To some extent, depression is inherent in the human condition—just about everyone experiences unhappiness or depression at some point, usually in response to day-to-day events or grief over the loss of a loved one. What distinguishes major depression is that it often lasts longer and is more extreme than the normal feelings of depression that most people experience.

The extreme negative feelings experienced in the midst of a major depression are captured by the opening quote in this section and by the fact that many suicides can be traced to depression. About 15% of people with mood disorders end their lives by suicide, a rate over 30 times greater than that in the general population (Guze & Robins, 1970; Jamison, 1986), and about 60% of people who commit suicide are depressed (Wilson, O'Leary, & Nathan, 1992).

Bipolar disorders.   These disorders may also involve depression, but the defining characteristic of bipolar disorder is the manic episode—which can include euphoria, elated mood, hyperactivity, inability to sleep, extreme talkativeness, rapid flights of ideas, and increased agitation. (See Table 16.1 for a portion of the DSM-IV description of a manic episode.) It is also usual for the manic episode to alternate with depression: the person cycles from feeling depressed to feeling the exultation of manic behavior. Sometimes, however, bipolar disorder includes only manic episodes, and there is no depression.

Bipolar disorder is much rarer than major depression: just 1% of the population exhibits bipolar disorder at some point (Boyd & Weissman, 1981; Robins & Regier, 1991). Before DSM-III, bipolar disorder was known as **manic-depressive disorder**, and many still use this more descriptive term. A milder form of bipolar disorder, called **cyclothymia**, has a lifetime prevalence of between 0.4 and 3.5% (American Psychiatric Association, 1987, p. 227).

The following description illustrates the compulsive and sometimes foolish business-related behaviors often associated with this disorder:

> Terrence O'Reilly, a single 39-year-old transit authority clerk, was brought to the hospital in May 1973 by the police after his increasingly hyperactive and bizarre behavior and nonstop talking alarmed his family. He loudly proclaimed that he was not in need of treatment, and threatened legal action against the hospital and police. The family reported that a month prior to admission Mr. O'Reilly took a leave of absence from his civil service job, purchased a large number of cuckoo clocks and then an expensive car which he planned to use as a mobile showroom for his wares, anticipating that he would make a great deal of money. He proceeded to "tear around town" buying and selling the clocks and other merchandise, and when he was not out, he was continuously on the phone making "deals.". . . At the time of admission he was $3,000 in debt and had driven his family to exhaustion with his excessive activity and overtalkativeness. He said, however, that he felt "on top of the world." . . . Six years later he committed suicide in his apartment (Spitzer et al., 1983, p. 115).

Although bipolar disorder is dangerous and frightening, those suffering from it describe some aspects of the manic phase as positive. Men report the most important or enjoyable changes during the manic phase (in order of importance) as increased outgoingness and social ease, increased creativity, and increased sensitivity and alertness. Women report increased sexual intensity (number 5 on the male list), greater productivity, and increased outgoingness and social ease (Jamison et al., 1980).

That some of those positive aspects are productivity and creativity isn't surprising when we consider the extent to which bipolar disorder is associated with creative people. Poets Robert Lowell, Anne Sexton, and Sylvia Plath; novelists Virginia Woolf and Ernest Hemingway; and composers Robert Schumann and George Frederick Handel all suffered from bipolar disorder (Handel wrote *The Messiah* during a manic episode), and studies have shown that writers as a group are more prone to mood disorders than is normal (Andreasen & Powers, 1975), with poets heading the list.

What are the etiologies of mood disorders? Focusing mainly on depression, we will see that evidence for possible causes can be found at all four levels of analysis.

The Search for Etiology: Mood Disorders

We begin our discussion by examining work at the biological level of analysis that indicates that genetic inheritance plays a role in mood disorders and that depression is linked to a neurotransmitter imbalance in the brain.

Both Sylvia Plath (1932–1963), poet and novelist, and Ernest Hemingway (1899–1961), winner of the Nobel Prize for literature, suffered from depression and ended their lives by committing suicide.

3   BIOLOGY

The biological approach.   Figure 16.7 shows the concordances for three categories of mood disorder among MZ and DZ twins, derived from a number of studies (Gottesman & Shields, 1982). These figures agree with a more recent report of concordance rates of 67% for MZ twins and 20% for DZ twins for depression and bipolar disorder combined (Wender et al., 1986). The message of these data is that genetics is important (especially so for bipolar disorder, with its extremely high 72% concordance), but it is not the whole explanation, since the concordance rate does not reach the 100% level we would expect for the genetically identical MZ twins if genetics alone were responsible.

Another way of determining the influence of genetics on mood disorders is through biochemical experiments that look for defects at the level of the gene. A large amount of research has been dedicated to finding these genetic defects, and numerous papers appearing in the 1980s claimed to have found defects in specific genes of people with bipolar disorder, schizophrenia, and alcoholism. However, one by one, the results from these research studies have been withdrawn, as researchers have reanalyzed their data using more rigorous techniques (Barinaga, 1989). Researchers now feel that these disorders are so complex that they probably involve not a single genetic defect, as was originally thought, but the malfunctioning of a number of different genes (Angier, 1993).

Meanwhile, researchers working with brain chemistry have linked depression with lower-than-normal concentrations of *norepinephrine (NE)* and *serotonin,* neurotransmitters thought to be important in motivation. Evidence supporting this idea originated in a fortuitous observation by researchers searching for a drug to cure tuberculosis (TB). When they gave the drug iproniazid to TB patients they found that, though it did not cure their TB, it made them feel euphoric. Observing this, researchers gave iproniazid to depressed patients and found that it made them feel better also.

Why did these results occur? Iproniazid belongs to a class of drugs called *monoamine oxidase (MAO) inhibitors.* Monoamine oxidase is one of the enzymes that, as part of the process of synaptic transmission, breaks down NE and serotonin after they have acted at the synapse (Figure 16.8). MAO inhibitors block MAO from doing this, so the NE and serotonin are not broken down. Presumably, the reason for the TB patients' brightened mood was that the inactivation of MAO caused an increase in the effective concentration of NE. Other drugs that have the effect of increasing NE and serotonin concentrations are also effective in combating depression (Schildkraut, Green, & Mooney, 1985).

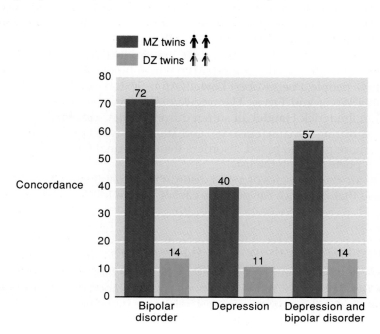

FIGURE 16.7

Evidence for a genetic contribution to mood disorders indicates that both twins in a pair of MZ (identical) twins are much more likely to be diagnosed as having bipolar disorder or depression than are both twins in a pair of DZ (fraternal) twins.

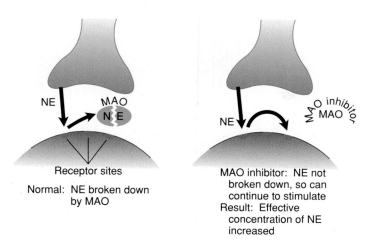

FIGURE 16.8
Monoamine oxidase inhibitors (MAO inhibitors) help treat symptoms of depression by increasing the effective concentration of norepinephrine at the synapse. This occurs when the MAO inhibitor inactivates the MAO that usually breaks down the norepinephrine, enabling the norepinephrine to stimulate more receptor sites.

The cognitive approach. Along with the evidence implicating biological mechanisms in mood disorders, there is also evidence suggesting that cognitive processes can play a role in causing or perpetuating depression. Cognitive theories of depression propose that a depressed person thinks about things in a different way from a nondepressed person. The two major cognitive theories of depression are Aaron Beck's cognitive theory and the learned helplessness theory.

8 THINKING

Beck's cognitive theory. Beck's (1967) theory of depression has two basic components: the *cognitive triad* and *cognitive distortions*.

The **cognitive triad** refers to Beck's assertion that people who are depressed experience automatic negative thoughts—thoughts that appear to pop into their head. These negative thoughts are about (1) *themselves* ("I can't do anything right"), (2) *the world or their environment* ("My job is terrible"), and (3) *the future* ("Things aren't going to get any better"). This negative way of thinking is illustrated in the following example, which focuses on the first element of the cognitive triad.

> A patient reported the following sequence of events occurring within a period of half an hour: His wife was upset because the children were slow in getting dressed. He thought, "I'm a poor father because the children are not better disciplined." He then noticed a leaky faucet, and thought that this showed he was also a poor husband. While driving to work, he thought "I must be a poor driver or other cars would not be passing me." As he arrived at work, he noticed some other personnel had already arrived. He thought, "I can't be very dedicated or I would have come earlier." When he noticed folders and papers piled up on his desk he concluded, "I'm a poor organizer because I have so much work to do" (Beck, 1967).

The second component of Beck's theory, **cognitive distortions,** are specific errors in thinking that can lead to erroneous conclusions. Two examples of cognitive distortion are as follows:

1. *Selective abstraction*: picking out one insignificant detail and ignoring the rest of a situation. For example, when Janet received a work evaluation that praised her performance profusely, recommended a raise, and pointed out that she might benefit from paying less attention to small details, she ignored the predominantly positive feedback, focused on the small suggestion for improvement, and considered herself a failure.
2. *Overgeneralization*: a tendency to draw global conclusions from scanty evidence. For example, the man described earlier saw a leaky faucet and drew the global conclusion that he was a bad husband (there are other dimensions to being a good husband than fixing dripping faucets!).

FIGURE 16.9

People in a bad mood who rated videotapes of themselves noticed more negative and fewer positive behaviors than people who were in a good mood.

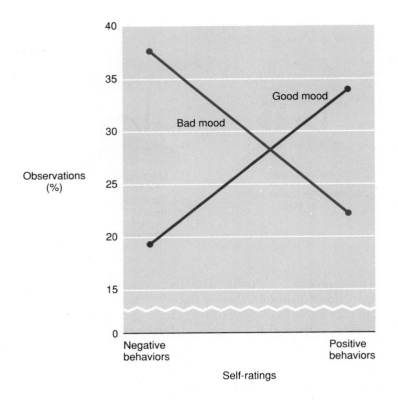

Substantial research supports the idea that depressed people perceive things more negatively than others do. For example, Joseph Forgas and his co-workers (1984) conducted an experiment in which they suggested either a good or bad mood to hypnotized subjects. The subjects then watched videotapes of themselves being interviewed. Asked to rate their own performance, those "in a bad mood" rated themselves much more negatively than those "in a good mood" (Figure 16.9).

Other studies have shown that people who are depressed tend to rate themselves more negatively than do nondepressed people (Lewinsohn et al., 1980). In a related study, Peter Lewinsohn and Michael Rosenbaum (1987) asked people who used to be depressed and people who were presently depressed to rate their parents. They found that the presently depressed people gave their parents lower ratings.

There is no question that depressed people see things more negatively than nondepressed people. In addition, comparing the thinking of depressed people with that of people with anxiety disorders reveals an interesting difference (Table 16.3). Depressed people tend to brood on negative aspects of themselves and the future. In contrast, people with anxiety disorder brood on possibilities of danger, sickness, or injury (Beck et al., 1987). When we consider therapy in the next chapter, we will see how Beck translated his ideas about depressed people's thinking into a powerful form of therapy.

Learned helplessness.   The **learned helplessness theory of depression** reflects depressed people's typical expectation that desired outcomes are unlikely to occur, that undesired outcomes are likely to occur, and that nothing they can do will change things (Abramson, Seligman, & Teasdale, 1978).

This theory traces its roots directly to the results of animal learning experiments. The experiment that led to the discovery of learned helplessness was conducted with dogs (Maier & Seligman, 1976; Maier, Seligman, & Solomon, 1969). The procedure was as follows:

6   LEARNING

TABLE 16.3
Thoughts of people with depression and anxiety disorder

Depression	Anxiety Disorder
I'm worthless.	What if I become sick and become an invalid?
I'm not worthy of other people's attention or affection.	I am going to be injured.
I'm a social failure.	What if no one reaches me in time to help?
I don't deserve to be loved.	I might be trapped.
Life isn't worth living.	I'm going to have an accident.
No one cares whether I live or die.	Something might happen that will ruin my appearance.
I have become physically unattractive.	I'm losing my mind.

Source: Adapted from Beck et al., 1987.

A dog was strapped into a hammock and subjected to moderately painful but not physically harmful shocks that were inescapable. That is, there was no way the dog could turn them off or escape from them. After resting for 24 hours, the dog was then placed in a shuttle box like the one shown in Figure 16.10 and again presented with the shocks. Even though the dog could escape the shocks by jumping to the other side of the shuttle box, it lay down on the grid and passively accepted them. Dogs in a control group that had not received the inescapable shocks behaved differently in the shuttle box. They easily learned to escape the shocks by jumping to the other side.

The results of this experiment led to the coining of the term *learned helplessness* to refer to situations in which animals learn to be helpless by being exposed to unpleasant, inescapable situations. Experiments using a similar rationale have shown that learned helplessness also occurs in humans. For example, D. S. Hiroto (1974) subjected people to an inescapable noise heard through earphones. When these people were put in a situation in which they could turn off the noise by moving their hand from one side of a small "human shuttle box" to another, they remained passive. People in control groups who had been exposed to noise they could turn off or to no noise at all easily learned to turn off the noise when given the shuttle box task.

Applied to depression, the learned helplessness theory says that when people experience unavoidable failure they give up and become depressed. But why do some people react to failure by becoming depressed and others by trying

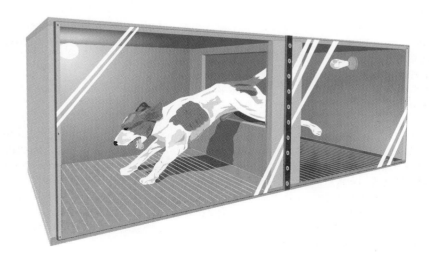

FIGURE 16.10
Shuttle box used to demonstrate learned helplessness. Dogs normally learn to avoid getting shocked by jumping across the barrier to safety. However, dogs who are first subjected to inescapable shocks feel helpless and do not jump to safety.

18   SOCIAL

harder to succeed? To address this question, Abramson and his co-workers (1978) proposed the **attribution model of helplessness,** which traces the likelihood of depression to people's *attributional styles.* Attributional styles are the way people explain things (Figure 16.11). When faced with failure, people with a negative attributional style tend to explain it in terms of *internal causes* within themselves ("I failed the exam because I am dumb") and to *stable causes* that will continue in time ("I will always be dumb"). This leads to a lowering of self-esteem (one of the symptoms of depression) and a belief that their failure and resulting helpless feelings will continue. In addition, people with a negative attributional style also tend to make *global attributions,* predicting from their failure at one task future failures at a wide range of others ("I'll probably fail my other course, too").

What happens when a person with a negative attributional style succeeds? According to the attribution model, he will tend to attribute his success to an *external cause,* outside of himself ("The exam was easy") and to an *unstable cause* that is temporary ("I was lucky"). He may also make *specific attributions,* seeing his success as being limited to the one particular situation ("I did well on that test, but it doesn't mean I'll do well on the others"). Thus, a negative attributional style increases feelings of helplessness, since the person attributes failures to personal qualities and successes to external factors that are beyond the person's control.

Research designed to test the attributional model of helplessness has shown that people who are depressed do, in fact, have negative attributional styles (Robins, 1988; Seligman et al., 1979; Sweeney, Anderson, & Bailey, 1986). Although this research does show that depression and the kind of thinking associated with a negative attributional style are correlated, it is still not clear which is cause and which effect. Does depression, perhaps triggered by biological predisposition, cause negative thinking, or does negative thinking cause depression (Figure 16.12)? Part of the answer may lie in the suggestion that there are a number of subtypes of depression. Some types may be caused more by biological factors and some more by cognitive factors (Abramson, Metalsky, & Alloy, 1988; Abramson, Seligman, & Teasdale, 1978).

6   LEARNING

The behavioral approach.   The learned helplessness theory we've described exemplifies a collaboration between the behavioral (animal learning) and cognitive (attributions) levels of analysis. We now turn to an approach that focuses ex-

FIGURE 16.11
According to the attribution model of helplessness, people with a negative attributional style tend to explain failure in terms of internal, stable, and global causes and success in terms of external, unstable, and specific causes. Both ways of thinking increase people's feelings of helplessness because they see failure as due to their personal qualities and don't give themselves credit for their success.

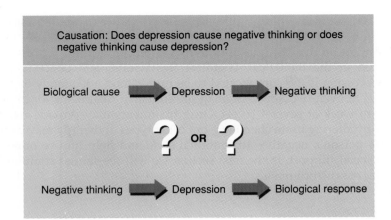

clusively on the behavioral level of analysis by considering the role reinforcers play in depression. Peter Lewinsohn (1974) has suggested that depression occurs in response to a low level of positive reinforcers. We can appreciate the basis for his idea by considering what happens when we stop reinforcing a rat for pressing a bar in a Skinner box. The rat's rate of bar pressing slows and eventually stops altogether. Eliminating reinforcement decreases the animal's rate of responding.

According to Lewinsohn, a similar thing happens in humans. When people lose positive reinforcers, perhaps because of a long illness, or the departure or death of a friend or family member, or the difficulty in meeting people in a new town, they may become inactive—perhaps choosing to stay in bed or at home more than usual. This inactivity further decreases the availability of positive reinforcers, resulting in even more inactivity and thus a vicious cycle (Figure 16.13) that leads to depression.

We can carry the behavioral analysis of depression a step further by considering what happens when our now inactive and depressed person receives visitors—friends who have come over to cheer the person up. Rather than alleviating the problem, this attention might reinforce the person's inactivity and thus prolong the depressed behavior.

The contextual approach.   How does a person's social environment affect depression? For one thing, environmental conditions that lead to stress—living in poverty, being unemployed, or experiencing other stressful life events—increase the chances of being depressed (Billings, Cronkite, & Moos, 1983). Lack of social support is also associated with depression. People with less social support—those who are divorced or separated, who have few friends, or who do not participate in social activities—are more likely to be depressed than those with adequate social support (Barnett & Gotlib, 1988). Conversely, good social support is often an antidote to depression. Understanding and treating depression means looking at the social context of the depressed person's behavior.

An experiment by James Coyne (1976; Strack & Coyne, 1983) has important implications for people's ability to get support from others once they are depressed. Coyne asked a group of nondepressed people to have a phone conversation with another person as part of an experiment on the "acquaintanceship process." Some of these people called depressed patients, some called nondepressed patients, and some called a nonpatient control group. Based on the responses to a questionnaire filled out after the phone call, those who had spoken with the depressed people were themselves more depressed, anxious, and hostile and expressed less desire to meet their new acquaintance in person than those who had spoken with people from the two nondepressed groups. Obviously, being depressed can drive others away, causing a loss of social support. Depressed people are therefore trapped in a vicious circle: being depressed

FIGURE 16.13
According to the behavioral approach to depression, losing positive reinforcers decreases a person's activity level, which in turn further decreases access to positive reinforcers. The result is a vicious circle that leads to depression.

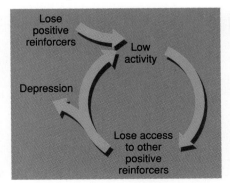

reduces social support, which in turn contributes further to the depression (Figure 16.14).

We have seen that the question "Why do people become depressed?" can be answered at the biological, cognitive, behavioral, and contextual levels. Clearly, depression is too complicated to be understood adequately by examining just one, or even two, levels of analysis. Similarly, treatments for depression may need to work at several levels. Drug treatments may provide relief from symptoms by altering brain chemistry, but other types of therapy may be needed to alter the person's negative attributional style and help him reconnect with sources of social support. In the next section we will see similar complexities in the disorder of schizophrenia.

Schizophrenia

Police took Rick Wheeler off an airplane at International Airport "Probably because I was in another dimension" and brought him to the hospital. . . . On admission he stated that he is Jesus Christ, that he can move mountains, that the devil wants to kill him and his food contains ground-up corpses, and that he had been born from his father's sexual organs. His speech is quite difficult to follow. For example, he plans to leave this city "because things happen here I don't approve of. I approve of other things but I don't approve of the other things. And believe me it's worse for them in the end" (Spitzer et al., 1983, p. 153).

Many people have erroneous conceptions of what schizophrenia is. Fully 62% of the people responding to one survey equated schizophrenia with a "multiple personality" (Wahl, 1987). A similar conception of schizophrenia is reflected by newspaper stories that use phrases like "he leads a schizophrenic existence" to describe a person who has two extremely different jobs or who has secretly been married to two people. Although the word *schizophrenia* does mean "split mind," the split referred to is not a split of personality but a splitting of the mind's thought processes. As we will see, one of the prominent characteristics of schizophrenia is disorganized thinking.

Psychologists define **schizophrenia** as a severe psychological disorder that is characterized by symptoms such as delusions (false and illogical beliefs), hallucinations (seeing visions or hearing sounds that are not actually there), illogical thinking, incoherent speech, and bizarre behavior. Although not the most prevalent psychological disorder—schizophrenia affects 1 out of every 100 people—its victims occupy 40% of the long-term hospital beds in the United States. Schizophrenia is likewise a costly and devastating illness in terms of human suffering, both for the afflicted and for their families, who must bear a dual burden—seeing someone they love become unable to function independently and, in many cases, having to care for the person at home.

Characteristics of Schizophrenia

People who become schizophrenic are often initially normal, bright, and functional. Then either suddenly or gradually the disorder manifests itself, usually in late adolescence or early adulthood. The following are some of the most prominent characteristics of schizophrenia; however, since every case is different, not all those exhibiting schizophrenia will have all of these symptoms.

Delusions and thought disorders.   **Delusions** are false beliefs that do not mesh with reality. For example, a woman may believe that external events such as an international summit conference or a plane crash 3000 miles away are related to her personally. **Thought disorders** are a breakdown in the way the person's thoughts are organized. The following example illustrates delusions (the

FIGURE 16.14
People's depression is often further exacerbated by their inability to receive social support when they are depressed.

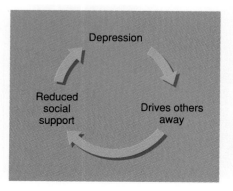

patient thinks she is in contact with many famous personalities) and thought disorder (her thoughts are strung together loosely and often illogically):

> I'm going to marry Geraldo Rivera. I think we're going to get married in Madison Square Garden, just like Sly Stone did. Mick Jagger wants to marry me. If I have Mick Jagger, I don't have to covet Geraldo Rivera. Mick Jagger is St. Nicholas and the Maharishi is Santa Claus. I want to form a gospel rock group called the Thorn Oil, but Geraldo wants me to be the music critic on "Eyewitness News," so what can I do? Got to listen to my boyfriend. Teddy Kennedy cured me of my ugliness. I'm pregnant with the son of God (Sheehan, 1982, p. 104).

8   THINKING

Breakdown in attention.   Schizophrenic patients often experience a breakdown in their attentional processes that makes it difficult for them to focus on just one idea at a time. This breakdown is described by one patient as follows:

> My mind's away. I have lost control. There are too many things coming into my head at once and I can't sort them out (McGhie & Chapman, 1961, p. 108).

People with schizophrenia therefore find it difficult to select relevant stimuli from all the other stimuli around them. One test of attention, called the *span of apprehension test,* requires a person to decide whether either a T or an F is present in arrays of briefly flashed letters. This task is easy when only a T or an F is presented, but it becomes more difficult when large numbers of other letters are introduced (Figure 16.15). Measuring the span of apprehension in both schizophrenic patients and normal subjects indicates that both groups do well when only a few letters are presented, but that schizophrenic patients do much more poorly as the need for selective attention increases with the addition of more irrelevant letters (Asarnow et al., 1978).

Distorted perception.   Distorted perceptions take a number of forms, from changes in sensations that occur when perceiving the environment, to **hallucinations**—perceptions that occur in the absence of actual stimulation. These hallucinations are usually auditory (hearing voices) but sometimes involve touch, vision, taste, or smell. One patient describes his changed sensations as follows:

4   PERCEPTION

> Colors seem to be brighter now, almost as if they are luminous. When I look around me it's like a luminous painting. I'm not sure if things are solid until I touch them (McGhie & Chapman, 1961, p. 105).

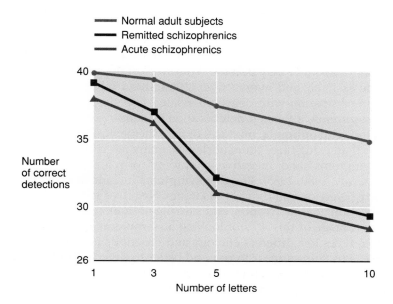

FIGURE 16.15
When many letters are presented in the span of an apprehension test, schizophrenic subjects do not perform as well as normal subjects. Interestingly, subjects who have recovered from their schizophrenic symptoms continue to show the lowered performance typical of those still suffering from schizophrenia.

Or consider the following conversation, in which the patient refers to both his hallucinations (false sensory impressions) and his delusions (false beliefs).

I: Who brought you here?

P: The police is what brought me to the hospital and that's all I know.

I: And no one's ever told you why?

P: I began seeing visions in the wall and things like that. Although it didn't prove to be mental illness, it could be religion.

I: Have you ever heard voices?

P: Yes, all the time. It started ten years ago this month, really, and I have heard voices ever since. I believe there are people really speaking to me. I believe I have extrasensory perception or something. I don't believe it is hallucinations.

I: What sort of things do you hear?

P: I hear people talking to me and I talk to other people. I hear two kinds of voices, really. I have conferences with people about religion and things like that, and then on the other hand I get beaten up by the voices of other people. I have always had this counterbalance with voices.

I: How can you be beaten up by voices?

P: Oh, it's what they say, they say horrible things.

I: About you?

P: Yes, and they ask questions. They interrogate me. Interrogation is painful (Shean, 1978, pp. 72–73).

---

11 — MOTIVATION — *Poor adaptive behavior and withdrawal from others.*   Patients with schizophrenia often lose motivation, maintain poor personal hygiene, and violate cultural norms of how to behave in public—talking to themselves or acting immodestly, for example. In addition, many people with schizophrenia seem to be living in their own private world and so have little to do with others.

12 — EMOTION — *Disturbed emotions.*   Schizophrenia often produces a flattening of emotions, as described by the patient who said "I am starting to feel pretty numb about everything because I am becoming an object and objects don't have feelings" (McGhie & Chapman, 1961, p. 109).

Another kind of emotional disturbance is shown by patients who respond with emotions that are inappropriate to the situation, such as smiling when in pain, crying while watching TV comedies, or laughing wildly when hearing about the death of a close relative.

Types of Schizophrenia

Eugen Bleuler (1911), the Swiss psychiatrist who coined the term *schizophrenia,* actually used the plural, *schizophrenias,* because he believed that the disorder exists in a number of different forms. The DSM-IV captures the diversity of the schizophrenias by differentiating between four types: (1) **catatonic schizophrenia,** in which the patient may become "frozen" into the same pose for hours or may become excitable and hyperactive; (2) **paranoid schizophrenia,** characterized by a preoccupation with delusions related to a single theme; (3) **disorganized schizophrenia,** a general deterioration of adaptive behavior; and (4) **undifferentiated schizophrenia,** mixtures of the other symptoms.

Rather than using these four subclasses, many researchers have focused on "positive symptoms" and "negative symptoms" of schizophrenia (Andreasen, 1982, 1985; Crow, 1980, 1985). **Positive symptoms** include delusions, hallucinations, bizarre behavior, and thought disorders. **Negative symptoms** include flattening of emotion, low motivation, and slowing of thinking and behavior.

The advantage of this way of looking at symptoms is that some evidence links the two types to a different etiology and prognosis for recovery. For example, positive symptoms appear to respond better to drug therapy than do negative ones. This difference in prognosis may be linked to differences in etiology: positive symptoms may be associated with malfunctioning chemical reactions

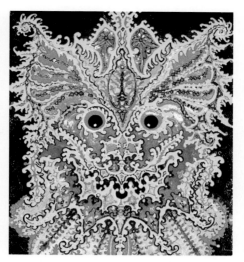

Paintings by the artist Louis Wain, who, in the later part of his life, was diagnosed as having some schizophrenic elements in his personality. Since we don't know when these pictures were executed, we can't say whether there is any connection between Wain's disorder and the appearance of these pictures. We do know, however, that schizophrenia can affect both perceptions and the creative process.

in the brain, whereas negative ones may be associated with deterioration of parts of the brain. This division of schizophrenic symptoms into positive and negative, though a promising approach, is by no means the final answer to the problem of classification. For one thing, many patients have both positive and negative symptoms, their proportions changing during the course of the disorder.

The Search for Etiology: Schizophrenia

The search for the etiology of schizophrenia has been dominated by biological research into genetic influences and the functioning of the brain. In addition, researchers working at the contextual level of analysis have probed the role of the family environment in creating or maintaining the disorder.

The biological approach.   We begin looking at the biology of schizophrenia by considering evidence pointing to the involvement of genetics.

③   BIOLOGY

Genetics.   The results of studies comparing the concordances of people with different degrees of relatedness are shown in Figure 16.16 (Nicol & Gottesman, 1983). The concordance of 46% for MZ (identical) twins compared with 14% for DZ (fraternal) twins supports a genetic basis for schizophrenia. So does the fact that there is a 46% chance that the children of two parents with schizophrenia will have the disorder, but a 13% chance when only one parent has it.

As was the case for the anxiety and mood disorders, however, the concordance for MZ twins, who share 100% of their genes, is less than 100, so genetics can't be the whole story. Furthermore, by themselves even the high concordances associated with greater biological similarity do not point unambiguously to genetic causes, because twins share not only genes but similar environments. Similarly, children of parents with schizophrenia might inherit a tendency to become schizophrenic, but they are also subject to the stresses of growing up with the schizophrenic parents. Thus, the data conceivably could be explained by environmental rather than biological factors.

How do we disentangle these possibilities? Researchers have uncovered three kinds of findings that rule out environment as the explanation for the high concordance rates for MZ twins and children of schizophrenics:

1. MZ twins who are reared apart are just as likely to have schizophrenia as MZ twins reared together (ibid.).
2. Children of schizophrenics who are adopted and grow up in normal households become schizophrenic at much higher rates than children of

FIGURE 16.16
Concordances for schizophrenia are higher for people who are closely related to one another.

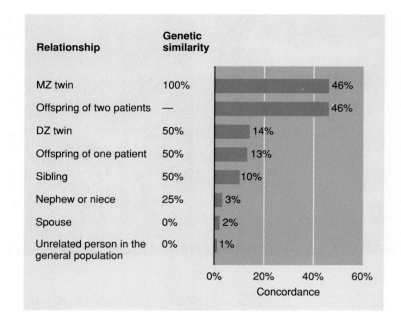

Relationship	**Genetic similarity**	Concordance
MZ twin	100%	46%
Offspring of two patients	—	46%
DZ twin	50%	14%
Offspring of one patient	50%	13%
Sibling	50%	10%
Nephew or niece	25%	3%
Spouse	0%	2%
Unrelated person in the general population	0%	1%

normal parents who are adopted and grow up in normal households (Gottesman & Shields, 1982; Nicol & Gottesman, 1983).

3. Children of normal parents who are adopted by people who subsequently become schizophrenic are no more likely than others to become schizophrenic (Wender et al., 1974).

These results strengthen the case for a genetic cause. But since schizophrenia is only partly determined by genetics, we can still ask "What, other than genetics, distinguishes a person with schizophrenia from one without it?" The search for the answer to this question has led brain researchers to discover differences in neurotransmitters, brain structure, and brain functioning between the two groups.

Neurotransmitters.   Just as researchers looked to a possible neurotransmitter imbalance as an explanation for depression, they looked for a similar explanation for schizophrenia. One result of that search is the **dopamine hypothesis.** According to this hypothesis, the symptoms of schizophrenia are associated with an excess of the excitatory neurotransmitter dopamine. One source of evidence supporting this idea is the effects of a class of drugs called phenothiazines, which alleviate the symptoms of schizophrenia in some patients. These drugs, which include Thorazine and Mellaril, block the action of dopamine at the synapse and thereby effectively reduce its concentration in the brain.

Some research supports the dopamine hypothesis, but other research points to a more complex etiology than simply an excessive amount of one transmitter. Most researchers believe that a neurotransmitter imbalance is involved in schizophrenia, but the exact nature of this imbalance is still not clear.

Brain structure and function.   In addition to looking at neurotransmitters in the brain, researchers have also looked at the structure and functioning of the brain itself. Using a technique called magnetic resonance imaging (MRI, described in Chapter 3), John Kelsoe and his co-workers (1988) were able to measure the size of the *ventricles,* the liquid-filled spaces inside the brain. Kelsoe's result, shown in Figure 16.17, shows that schizophrenic patients generally have slightly larger-than-normal ventricles (also see Pfeffenbaum et al., 1988).

Other research has shown that some structures in the left temporal lobe of

FIGURE 16.17
The fact that the ventricles of schizophrenics tend to be larger than the ventricles of normal subjects suggests to researchers that some degeneration of brain cells may have occurred in the schizophrenic subjects.

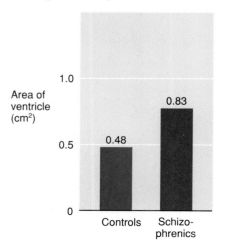

schizophrenics are smaller than normal (McCarley et al., 1993), and that in some people with schizophrenia the microscopic structure of cells in some areas of the temporal and frontal lobes is abnormal (Akbarian et al., 1993a, 1993b). What does all this mean? Perhaps schizophrenia causes the degeneration of brain cells. But a more intriguing possibility is the suggestion that the brain of schizophrenics may not develop normally in the first place (Bloom, 1993). The only thing we can be sure of at this point is that there are differences between the brains of schizophrenics and normal persons. Exactly how these differences occur remains to be determined.

The new techniques of brain imaging have not only yielded images of the brain that reveal its structure, they have also enabled researchers to create images of the brain's activity as it produces thoughts or behavior (Andreasen, 1988). It has been shown that the frontal lobes of schizophrenics are activated less than normal in response to tasks that usually elicit frontal lobe activity, as shown in the Measurement & Methodology on page 647 (Weinberger & Kleinman, 1986). This is particularly significant because the frontal lobe is important for abstract thinking, expressing language, "reading" social situations, forming emotional attachments, focusing attention, and adapting to the environment—all behaviors that are deficient in people with schizophrenia.

We have seen that there is a large amount of evidence for the involvement of biological mechanisms in schizophrenia. But we still don't know what causes the differences in the biology of schizophrenics compared with normal persons. And since the concordance is less than 100% in MZ twins, we know that factors other than genetics are involved. Some researchers have, therefore, focused on the contextual level of analysis and asked how the environment within which a person develops might influence the chances of becoming schizophrenic.

The contextual approach.   The major context within which a person develops is the family, and it is here that most researchers have focused their attention. In the 1940s and 1950s and even into the 1960s, schizophrenia was thought to be caused primarily by the patient's mother: the term *schizophrenogenic mother* was coined to refer to the cold, aloof, and domineering mothers who were supposed to cause schizophrenia in their children (Fromm-Reichman, 1948). This idea has now been abandoned, because it was supported by little evidence (but imagine the guilt it must have caused countless mothers who were blamed for causing the disorder in their children!). Instead, researchers have focused on communication and the emotional climate within families as a whole.

There is some evidence linking schizophrenia to faulty communication patterns within a family. In some families, a pattern called **communication deviance (CD)** arises in which the parents do not focus on what the child is saying and attack the child personally rather than offer constructive suggestions regarding his or her behavior. They may also subject the child to **double-bind communications,** which transmit two incompatible messages. The following describes such a communication:

> A young man who had fairly well recovered from an acute schizophrenic episode was visited in the hospital by his mother. He was glad to see her and impulsively put his arm around her shoulders whereupon she stiffened. He withdrew his arm and she asked, "Don't you love me anymore?" He then blushed and she said, "Dear, you must not be so easily embarrassed and afraid of your feelings." The patient was able to stay with her only a few minutes more and following her departure he assaulted an aide (Bateson et al., 1956, p. 251).

The double bind in this communication is the mother's freezing up in response to her son's affection and then criticizing him for not loving her.

In one study, Michael Goldstein (1985, 1987a, 1987b) compared a group of 20 troubled adolescents who had parents high in communication deviance with

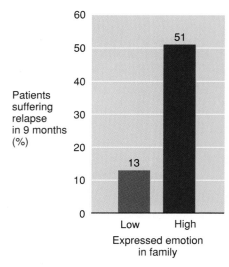

FIGURE 16.18
Schizophrenic patients in high EE families are almost four times more likely to be readmitted to the hospital than those in low EE families.

a group of 12 troubled adolescents whose parents were low in CD. He found that 10 of the 20 from the high-CD group were diagnosed as having schizophrenia or a related disorder 15 years later, whereas only 1 of the 12 in the low-CD group received that diagnosis. Thus, an atmosphere of negativity and confused communication appears to increase the likelihood of developing schizophrenia (Goldstein & Strachan, 1987).

In addition to examining the effects of CD in families, researchers have studied emotional communication in another way. They have looked at how the overall emotional climate in the family can affect the chances that patients returning from the hospital will suffer a worsening of their schizophrenic symptoms. A family in which there is an emotional climate of criticism, hostility, and overprotectiveness of the patient is said to be high in **expressed emotion (EE).** As shown in Figure 16.18, patients in these families are much more likely to suffer a relapse than are patients whose families are not critical, hostile, or overprotective (Rodnick et al., 1984; Vaughn & Leff, 1976; Vaughn et al., 1984). (See Measurement & Methodology, "The Expressed Emotion Interview.")

What do these results mean for the role of families in schizophrenia? Evidence from the adoption studies described earlier shows that schizophrenia depends more on whether the child's parents were schizophrenic than on the actual family in which the child was raised. This argues against the idea that problematic families "cause" schizophrenia. However, the evidence from studies of communication deviance and expressed emotion indicate that the stress created by poor family dynamics may increase the chances that people who are pre-

MEASUREMENT & METHODOLOGY

The Expressed Emotion Interview

A patient who returns home to a family with high expressed emotion (EE) is more likely to have a relapse than a patient who returns to a family with low EE. Expressed emotion is measured by a long interview with the family. The procedure is based on the observation that in the course of a lengthy interview people will sponta-

Family members' spontaneous expressions of negative feelings about the patient are scored by raters after the interviews.

neously express negative feelings that they may have denied in response to a direct question. The interviewer asks questions such as "What activities do you enjoy doing with him?" and "How does he get along with your husband?" The interview lasts for one and a half to two hours and is audiotaped for later scoring on the following scales:

- Criticism: total critical comments made about the patient. Both the content of the remark ("I resent cooking a meal for her only to have her leave it untouched on the table") and the tone of voice are taken into account. In contrast to the critical comments made by a high-EE relative, a low-EE relative might say something like "Whatever she does suits me" or "I just tend to let it go, because I know that when she wants to speak she will speak" (Hooley, 1985).
- Hostility: a more general criticism, usually reflecting an overall attitude about the patient. For example, "He is stupid. Everything he does is stupid" or "The farther I am away from him, the better." This is rated on a three-point scale.
- Emotional overinvolvement: remarks like "I'm devoting my life to Johnnie because I think he needs me." This is rated on a five-point scale.

Raters are typically trained for about one month before they are qualified. Once trained, two raters independently scoring the same interview usually agree quite closely: correlations between their ratings are typically between .8 and .9 (Hooley, 1985).

disposed to schizophrenia will actually develop it, or that people who are already schizophrenic will suffer a relapse and have to return to the hospital. This idea of an interaction between genetic predisposition and environmental stress is central to the diathesis-stress model of schizophrenia, which we discuss next.

The diathesis-stress model.   Although we still do not know the specific causes of schizophrenia, there is general agreement that there are multiple contributors. This has led to the **diathesis-stress model** of schizophrenia. The word *diathesis* refers to a constitutional susceptibility to a disorder, and *stress* refers to stressors in the environment. According to the diathesis-stress model, a person becomes vulnerable to schizophrenia because of his or her genetic inheritance or some other factor (for example, biological damage caused by a difficult birth) but actually becomes schizophrenic only if subjected to stresses that are too much to deal with (Gottesman, McGuffin, & Farmer, 1987; Zubin & Spring, 1977). Thus, the diathesis-stress model pictures the biological and contextual levels as interacting to produce schizophrenia, which in turn creates symptoms that are expressed as behavioral and cognitive differences from the norm.

13   STRESS & HEALTH

Personality Disorders

Jeff, a 40-year-old construction worker, believes that his coworkers do not like him and fears that someone might let his scaffolding slip in order to cause him injury on the job. This concern arose recently following a disagreement on the lunch line, in which the patient thought that a coworker was sneaking ahead and complained to him. He began noticing his new "enemy" laughing with the other men, and often wondered if he were the butt of their mockery. He thought of confronting them, but reasoned that the entire issue might just be all in his mind and that he might bring more trouble onto himself by taking any action (Spitzer et al., 1981, p. 37).

Types of Personality Disorder

When we discussed personality in Chapter 15, we introduced the idea of trait-specific attributes such as honesty, aggressiveness, and sensitivity that we can use to describe a person's central characteristics. **Personality disorders** have been described as the extremes of those normal basic traits (Frances, 1980). Thus, a person like Jeff, who has a paranoid personality disorder and thinks people are out to get him, may have exaggerated traits of suspiciousness, jealousy, and sensitivity. People with other types of disorders may have exaggerated traits of perfectionism (*compulsive personality disorder*), emotionality (*histrionic personality disorder*), or lack of self-esteem (*dependent personality disorder*). Table 16.4 summarizes the personality disorders described in the DSM-III-R.

15   PERSONALITY

Exaggerated traits become a personality disorder when they lead to inflexible patterns of behavior that impair the person's functioning. These disorders are usually not, however, as serious as the major disorders we have been reviewing. For example, Jeff may think other people are out to get him, but he does not exhibit the breakdown in thought processes and the bizarre behavior of a person with paranoid schizophrenia. Nonetheless, it has been said that people with personality disorders typically cause as much difficulty to others as they do to themselves (Carson & Butcher, 1992).

Others who deal with people exhibiting personality disorders often find them exasperating, unpredictable, and difficult to deal with. It is, therefore, not surprising that personality disorders cause those afflicted great difficulty in establishing personal relationships. This is particularly true of *borderline personality disorder*, so called because it has some features of personality disorders as well as some of the more extreme mood disorders and schizophrenia. People exhibit-

19   SOCIAL

TABLE 16.4
Personality disorders

Personality Disorder	Description
Antisocial	Engages in behaviors destructive to self and others, often impulsively, without remorse or shame. Is unable to sustain consistent work behavior. Is irritable or aggressive, often getting into fights or assaulting others. Steals, destroys property, engages in an illegal occupation.
Borderline	Has difficulty in interpersonal relationships; exhibits wildly flexible moods, shifting from normal to depressed or irritable. Demonstrates unpredictable and impulsive behavior; inappropriate, intense anger; and recurrent suicidal threats or self-mutilating behavior. Reports feelings of emptiness or boredom.
Compulsive	Strives for perfection; is preoccupied with trivial details, rules, schedules, and lists. Often has poor interpersonal relations because of demands that everything be done one way.
Dependent	Exhibits lack of self-confidence and a helpless or stupid self-image, depending on others to make decisions. Often defers to others and puts up with abusive relationships. Has difficulty initiating projects or doing things alone; volunteers to do unpleasant tasks to win other people's favor.
Histrionic	Is overly dramatic and emotional; always trying to draw attention to self. May be inappropriately seductive in appearance or behavior. Is self-centered and has no tolerance for the frustration of delayed gratification. Is uncomfortable if not the center of attention.
Narcissistic	Has a grandiose view of own importance and abilities. Demands others' attention but reacts strongly to criticism; takes advantage of others. Believes own problems to be unique; is preoccupied with fantasies of unlimited success, power, brilliance, or beauty.
Obsessive-compulsive	Is overly perfectionistic, so fails to complete tasks. Is preoccupied with details, rules, lists, or schedules. Is excessively devoted to work, to the exclusion of leisure activities and friendships. Is indecisive and exhibits restricted expression of affection.
Paranoid	Expects, without sufficient basis, to be exploited or harmed by others. Questions, without justification, the loyalty or trustworthiness of friends and the fidelity of spouse or sexual partner. Bears grudges or is unforgiving of insults or slights.

Gary Gilmore was executed in 1977 for two murders. His inability to follow rules from an early age, his intentional cruelty to others, and his lack of remorse for his crimes are all characteristics of a person with antisocial personality.

ing borderline personality disorder are usually aware of their surroundings, but they may experience short episodes of being out of contact with reality, have delusions, and hold paranoid beliefs (O'Connell et al., 1989). One of the things that makes them so difficult to get along with is their impulsiveness. At one moment they seem stable and peaceful and then, often without provocation, become intensely angry.

Antisocial personality disorder is among the most common of personality disorders, having a prevalence of 3% in males and less that 1% in females. People with this disorder, who are often popularly called sociopaths or psychopaths, engage in behaviors that are destructive not only to themselves but also to others. People with antisocial personality disorder can often be extremely charming and witty yet capable of taking advantage of others' trust and engaging in criminal behaviors ranging from stealing to harassment to murder. Perhaps the most frightening aspect of this disorder is the capacity for destructive impulsiveness combined with a lack of remorse about how a behavior affects others. The sociopath Gary Gilmore, who was executed for murder, described one of his robberies as follows:

> I pulled up near a gas station. I told the service station guy to give me all of his money. I then took him to the bathroom and told him to kneel down and then I shot him in the head twice. The guy didn't give me any trouble but I just felt like I had to do it (Spitzer et al., 1983).

When asked why he did this he said "I don't know, man. I'm impulsive. I don't think" (Mailer, 1979, p. 778). Other impulsive activities, such as poorly planned crimes or marrying a woman met hours earlier can be destructive to the sociopath himself.

Because personality disorders are difficult to diagnose and were not officially recognized as disorders until 1952, determining their etiology has been difficult. The two most researched personality disorders are the borderline and antisocial disorders. There is some evidence that genetic factors are important in developing borderline personality disorder (Loranger, Oldham, & Tulis, 1982) and that abuse in childhood may be involved. Ogata and his co-workers (1990) found that 71% of patients with borderline disorder had been abused as children. Similarly, both biological factors and disturbed family life have been linked with antisocial personality disorder (Hare, 1970).

Reprise: Battling Misconceptions

Psychological disorders are misunderstood by many because people often make baseless assumptions such as "Psychological health is not a serious problem," "All psychological disorders are bizarre and crippling," and "People with psychological disorders are often to blame for their problem." Such popular misconceptions often have serious social consequences, because politicians and the public may use them to decide social issues such as allocating public funds for mental health services or dealing with the needs of mentally ill homeless people. This chapter has recounted a number of facts that counter these misconceptions.

Are psychological disorders a serious problem? Both the statistics and the descriptions of disorders presented in this chapter say "Yes." We have seen these problems are far more common than many people believe and that they entail huge costs, both to society and to the afflicted individuals. Those who suffer from the most crippling forms of schizophrenia, who lose their former personalities and ability to function, represent lives lost—not only to themselves but to their families and to society. And for someone who has serious depression, the pain of the disorder is intense. In his description of his own nine-month bout of depression, Pulitzer Prize–winning author William Styron states that "the pain of severe depression is quite unimaginable . . . and it kills in many instances because its anguish can no longer be borne (Styron, 1992, p. 33). Descriptions such as this and the fact that the majority of the nation's 30,000 yearly suicides are linked to depression (Fawcett et al., 1987) make a strong argument for the seriousness of mental health problems.

We have also seen that not all psychological disorders are bizarre and permanently crippling. Although schizophrenia can be a crippling disorder, only 10% of schizophrenics deteriorate so far as to be profoundly disabled. About one-third recover (meaning no symptoms in five years), and 60% have varying degrees of disability. In the case of depression, the great majority of people recover from a depressive episode within less than a year even without therapy; and therapy can greatly hasten recovery as well as prevent relapses. The prognosis for less severe disorders such as anxiety and panic disorders is also quite good, especially given treatment. Psychological disorders are not all the same, remember, and even within classifications there is great diversity.

Finally, we have seen that people who suffer from psychological disorders do not "bring it on themselves." For instance, though more than two out of five people in the general public view depression as a "weakness" (Brody, 1992), in fact it can be linked to an imbalance in neurotransmitters in the brain, to genetic factors, and to external events and social influences. Similar considerations apply to many other disorders. Thus, in the next chapter, when we describe ways of treating psychological disorders, we will see that the starting point for therapy is a person's very real problems—which brought him or her to the therapeutic situation in the first place—and the therapist's sympathetic attitude and commitment to helping the person deal with these problems.

Sportscaster John Madden has dealt with his potentially crippling fear of flying by traveling in a van and arranging his schedule appropriately.

Gender Differences in the Prevalence of Psychological Disorders

Who have more psychological problems, males or females? Recent data reveal only small differences in the overall incidence of psychological disorders between males and females (Robins & Regier, 1991). But there are large differences in the prevalence of specific disorders between males and females.

Figure 16.19, which shows the lifetime prevalence of the major disorders, indicates that the only ones in which prevalences are similar for males and females are schizophrenia and bipolar disorder. Males have a higher prevalence of alcohol and drug abuse and antisocial personality disorder, and females have a higher prevalence of depression and anxiety disorders. In addition, females also have a much higher incidence of eating disorders, accounting for about 95% of the cases of anorexia nervosa and bulimia.

Why are there gender differences in psychological disorders? There is little evidence to support the idea that biological causes such as hormones explain gender differences (Basow, 1992; Janowsky & Rausch, 1985); however, it is likely that the explanation lies in the way boys and girls are socialized and in the demands that society places on them as adults.

Let's first consider why so many more males than females become addicted to alcohol and other drugs. One reason may be that males are socialized to be especially independent. Men who learn not to seek support from others when they have problems may turn to drinking as a way of coping. Getting drunk not only represents an "independent" way of dealing with their problems but also meets an expectation of the male gender role: males, almost by definition, drink—often to excess (Landrine, Bardwell, & Dean, 1988).

Turning to females, let's consider why depression is so much more prevalent in females than in males. Just as drinking is linked to the male gender role, behaviors related to depression are linked to the female gender role. Females are often socialized to feel and act helpless, even when they are not. These feelings of helplessness are sometimes confirmed by life events such as domestic abuse, sexual harassment, and rape, which tend to make women more aware of their disadvantage in size and strength, and may engender hopelessness rather than combativeness. More generally, females must deal with the fact that they are paid less and have a harder time advancing in the workplace than do males. The possibility that job inequality could contribute to depression is supported by a study in which employed women were matched with employed men of the same age, job classification, and educational background. If these women were earning the same salary as the men, then gender differences in depression disappeared (Maffeo, Ford, & Favin, 1990).

Another possible cause of females' higher incidence of depression is the different ways males and females cope with depres-

FIGURE 16.19

Lifetime prevalence of psychological disorders in males and females. The disorders on the left are more prevalent in males and the ones on the right are more prevalent in females. Only schizophrenia and bipolar disorder have about the same prevalence in both sexes.

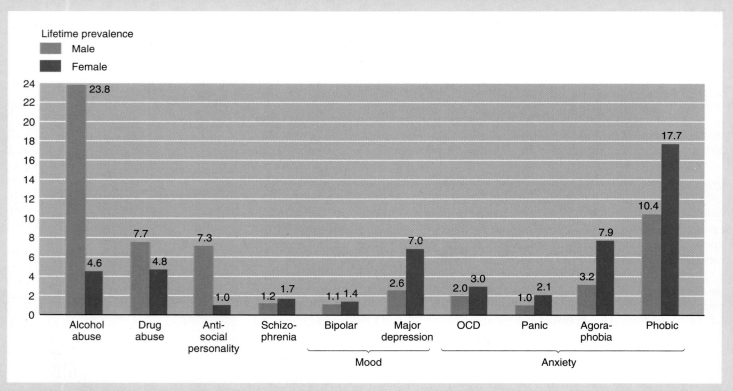

Drinking is part of the stereotypical male role, which may be one reason for the higher incidence of alcoholism among males than among females.

sion. When male and female college students were asked how likely they were to engage in various behaviors that "people do when depressed," males scored higher on items such as "I avoid thinking of reasons why I am depressed," "I do something physical," and "I take drugs." Females scored higher on items such as "I try to determine why I am depressed," "I talk to other people about my feelings," and "I cry to reduce the tension" (Nolen-Hoeksema, 1987). Thus, males are more likely to engage in behaviors that distract them from their depression, females to focus on their feelings. Whereas the male strategy might serve to break the cycle in which thinking about depression leads to deeper depression, the female strategy might serve to prolong depression by keeping attention focused on it.

Finally, depression has been linked to marital status. Among people who are single, divorced, or widowed, females have a lower incidence of depression than males (Walker et al., 1985;

Females tend to dwell on their depressed feelings; males are more likely to engage in behaviors that distract them from their depression.

Weissman & Klerman, 1977). However, married women are much more likely to be depressed than married men. We can understand why this might occur by comparing what typically happens to males and females when they get married.

For males, marriage means an increase in social support and the presence of someone to look after them. Men also gain an outlet for expressing their feelings, which they may not have had with their male friends. In terms of careers the male doesn't miss a step, continuing with his career as soon as the honeymoon is over. Females, on the other hand, may put their careers on hold, especially if children are planned. Career or not, marriage usually leads to an increase in housework for females, since husbands do much less of the family housework—only 14% if their wives are not employed, 24% if they are (Berardo, Shehan, & Leslie, 1987).

Females also become responsible for taking care of others—at first just their husbands, but then children as well. This caregiving role can be rewarding, but it can also mean that the wife sacrifices her own needs to those of others. It is therefore not surprising that women who are undergoing therapy for depression often express the idea that they have lost something by being married. Consider, for example, the following statement, made during a therapy session by a 30-year-old woman with two children.

And I do know that in the seven years we've been married, I've lost a great deal of myself, as far as, well you know, when you put so much of your energy and you're so consumed . . . with babies and being a mother and a wife and a homemaker. . . . You tend to kind of put off your own goals and your own achievements and your own talents and your own self, in a way (Jack, 1991, pp. 31–32).

One solution to this feeling of loss of self is employment outside of the home. Although adding the role of worker to the roles of wife and mother can create additional stress, research on working mothers shows that employment generally has beneficial effects on a woman's mental health (Pietromonaco, Manis, & Markus, 1987; Repetti, Matthews, & Waldron, 1989).

All of the evidence taken together indicates that gender roles are the probable explanation why certain disorders are more likely to surface in males and others in females. This is true not only of alcoholism and depression, but of other disorders as well. For example, as we discussed in Chapter 10, eating disorders are primarily seen in females because of societal pressures for them to be slim and attractive. Antisocial personality disorder, in contrast, occurs mainly in males—in part because of the male's biologically determined aggressiveness, but also because of the way male aggressiveness and violence are reinforced in our society.

One message in this discussion is that the "common wisdom" about abnormal behavior and about differences between groups of people is often highly simplistic. For example, you may hear it said that women are more likely to be depressed "because that's the way women are," but we have seen that if the context of socialization were the same for men and for women, some apparent differences between them might be diminished or even disappear. When we ask why people differ, we need to seek the answer at all levels of analysis: behavioral, biological, cognitive, and contextual.

What Are Psychological Disorders?

- Psychological disorders are serious problems, measured in terms of both human suffering and monetary cost.

- Psychological disorders are difficult to define. One approach is to describe a person's behavior in terms of deviance, maladaptiveness, and distress.

Classifying Psychological Disorders

- Psychological disorders are classified according to the *Diagnostic and Statistical Manual of Mental Disorders*, which describes people's psychological symptoms, physical condition, and life stresses on five axes.

Levels of Analysis and the Search for Etiology

- Etiology, the cause or origins of a disorder, can be determined by studying the disorder at all four levels of analysis—behavioral, biological, cognitive, and contextual. More distinct descriptions of causation may aid in determining treatment.

Anxiety Disorders

- Anxiety disorders include panic disorder, agoraphobia, phobias, generalized anxiety disorder, obsessive-compulsive disorder, and posttraumatic stress disorder.

- The etiology of anxiety disorders has been explained in terms of (1) the behavioral approach, especially the explanation of phobias as a result of classical conditioning; (2) the biological approach, which has found evidence of a genetic basis for some disorders, has hypothesized increased biological reactivity in people with panic disorder, and has measured abnormal brain activity in people with obsessive-compulsive disorder; and (3) the cognitive approach, based either on the misinterpretation of bodily symptoms or on Freud's psychodynamic approach, which explains anxiety disorders in terms of repressed childhood wishes.

Dissociative Disorders

- Dissociative disorders such as pychogenic fugue and multiple personality disorder involve a disturbance of a person's consciousness or identity. It has been suggested that multiple personalities are formed as a defense to deal with traumatic experiences in early childhood.

- When mental health professionals are asked to testify as expert witnesses at a trial, they face a number of difficulties: (1) it is difficult to judge mental states from an earlier period; (2) they are subject to bias because they know the person may have committed a crime; and (3) accurate diagnoses of psychological disorders are difficult to achieve in any circumstances.

Somatoform Disorders

- Somatoform disorders, which include conversion disorder, somatization, and hypochondriasis, all involve physical symptoms that have no organic basis. Explanations of the etiology of these disorders are speculative, but Freud linked conversion disorder to a repressed wish that is converted into a physical symptom.

Mood Disorders

- The two major types of mood disorder are depression and bipolar disorder. Depression is characterized by symptoms such as hopelessness, lack of appetite, and despair; whereas bipolar disorder is characterized by manic behavior, often alternating with depressive symptoms.

- The etiology of depression has been explained in terms of (1) the biological approach, which has linked depression to genetics and to a neurotransmitter imbalance at the synapse; (2) the cognitive approach, in the form of Beck's theory and the learned helplessness theory; (3) the behavioral approach, which links depression to a lack of positive reinforcement; and (4) the contextual approach, which links depression to stress and lack of social support.

Schizophrenia

- Schizophrenia is a severe mental disorder characterized by disruptions of thought processes such as delusions, hallucinations, disordered thought, and incoherent speech.

- There are four classes of schizophrenia: catatonic, paranoid, disorganized, and undifferentiated. Researchers have also distinguished between positive and negative symptoms of schizophrenia.

- The etiology of schizophrenia has been explained in terms of (1) the biological approach, which has found evidence for genetic involvement, neurotransmitter imbalance, and differences in brain structure and function compared with normal persons, and (2) the contextual approach, which has linked schizophrenic behaviors to communication problems and the emotional climate in families.

- The diathesis-stress model of schizophrenia sees it as caused by an interaction between biological factors and environmental influence.

Personality Disorders

- Personality disorders are extremes of normal personality traits. The resulting behaviors may cause problems for both the person with the disorder and others. People with antisocial personality disorder can harm others without feeling any remorse for their actions.

Reprise: Battling Misconceptions

- Psychological disorders are widely misunderstood because of popular misconceptions. On one hand people minimize the problem of psychological disorders when in fact it is quite serious. On the other hand, they have a stereotypical and often inaccurate view of people who have these disorders. Such misconceptions are important to correct, because they affect both individual behaviors and public policy.

Follow-Through/Diversity: Gender Differences in the Prevalence of Psychological Disorders

- Although the overall incidence of psychological disorders is similar for males and females, the genders differ in their vulnerability to specific disorders. Males have a higher prevalence of alcohol and drug abuse and of antisocial personality disorder; females have a higher prevalence of depression, anxiety disorders, and eating disorders. These gender differences seem to reflect differences in socialization and learned gender roles, rather than biological dissimilarity.

Key Terms

agoraphobia
antisocial personality disorder
anxiety disorders
attribution model of helplessness
bipolar disorders
borderline personality disorder
catatonic schizophrenia
cognitive distortions
cognitive triad
communication deviance
compulsive personality disorder
concordance
conversion disorders
cultural norms
cyclothymia
delusions
dependent personality disorder
depressive disorders
Diagnostic and Statistical Manual of Mental Disorders (DSM)
diathesis-stress model
disorganized schizophrenia
dissociative disorders
dopamine hypothesis
double-bind communications
dysthymia
etiology
expressed emotion (EE)
generalized anxiety disorder
hallucinations
histrionic personality disorder

hypochondriasis
learned helplessness theory of depression
lifetime prevalence
major depression
manic-depressive disorder
medical student's syndrome
mood disorders
multiple personality disorder (MPD)
narcissistic personality disorder
negative symptoms
obsessive-compulsive disorder (OCD)
obsessive-compulsive personality disorder
panic attack
panic disorder
paranoid personality disorder
paranoid schizophrenia
personality disorders
phobias
positive symptoms
posttraumatic stress disorder
psychogenic amnesia
psychogenic fugue
schizophrenia
secondary gain
somatization disorder
somatoform disorder
thought disorders
undifferentiated schizophrenia

CHAPTER

17

How Therapy Evolved
Therapy as Expelling Evil Spirits
Therapy as Treating Illness
The Birth of Psychotherapy
Therapy Today: The Diversity of Approaches

Psychodynamic Therapies
Freudian Psychoanalysis
Contemporary Psychodynamic Therapies

Interdisciplinary Dimension: Art
Art Therapy with Children

Client-Centered Therapies

Cognitive Therapies
Rational-Emotive Therapy
Beck's Cognitive Therapy

Behavior Therapies
Therapies Based on Classical Conditioning
Therapies Based on Operant Conditioning

Group Therapy

Biomedical Therapies
Drug Therapies
Electroconvulsive Therapy

Issues in Therapy
The Trend Toward Eclecticism
How Effective Is Psychotherapy?
The Issue of Institutionalization

Reprise: Levels of Analysis and the Treatment of Psychological Disorders

Follow-Through/Diversity
Cultural Issues in Therapy

Therapy

Canst thou not minister to a mind diseased,
Pluck from the memory a rooted sorrow,
Raze out the written troubles of the brain,
And with some sweet oblivious antidote
Cleanse the stuff'd bosom of that perilous stuff
Which weighs upon the heart?

William Shakespeare, Macbeth

"Canst thou not minister to a mind diseased . . .?" The anguished question asked by Shakespeare's Macbeth has, in one form or another, been posed throughout recorded time. In the last chapter, we surveyed the many types of psychological distress and maladaptive behaviors that psychologists have identified and sought to understand. Now we look at what can be done to respond to that psychological suffering—at how therapists apply the knowledge gained from both research and practice to the treatment of psychological disorders.

When you hear a word like *psychotherapy*, what image comes to mind? Here are a few possibilities:

- A business executive lies on a couch, looking at the ceiling and relating memories of his early childhood as a therapist sits quietly by, taking notes and looking very wise.
- A school counselor and his 8-year-old client sit face to face in comfortable chairs, talking about the events that have taken place in the boy's life during the last week.
- A woman struggling to balance her career with her family's demands is startled when her counselor says sharply, "What makes you think you need to be perfect all the time?"
- A young man who is fearful of heights imagines standing on the observation deck of a high-rise building; meanwhile, his therapist instructs him in systematic relaxation techniques.
- A psychiatrist writes out a prescription for an antidepressant drug and instructs her patient on how to take it and what to expect.

Each of these images captures a different aspect of therapy for psychological disorders. The first four are examples of *psychological* procedures, called **psychotherapy,** intended to improve a person's mental, emotional, or behavioral well-being. The last one is an example of a *biomedical therapy*—treating psychological symptoms through physiological interventions such as drugs. All are valid forms of therapy when carried out by trained professionals.

Just as many people have misconceptions about psychological disorders, so do they have inaccurate or incomplete pictures of therapy. Therapy isn't just for people who are severely disturbed, "crazy," or institutionalized. Those who seek therapy do not necessarily have "something wrong with them." Though much of therapy is intended to help people with debilitating psychological symptoms or severe behavioral problems, many people consult therapists out of a desire to live a fuller, richer, happier life. Nor do most therapists fit the stereotype of the "all-knowing doctor" who listens sagely to a patient reclining on a couch. As we will see in this chapter, both therapy and therapist take a number

Interactions between therapist and client can take a number of forms, not all of which correspond to the image of a patient lying on a couch.

of forms, to suit a variety of human needs. To appreciate what therapy is, we will first look at how it evolved into its present, diverse form. Then we'll consider the principal types of therapy in use today.

Toward the end of the chapter we'll look at three special issues: combining therapies, how effective therapy is, and the social problem of meeting the needs of people with severe psychological disorders.

How Therapy Evolved

Over the centuries, what we now consider to be psychological disorders have been viewed in very different ways, from the standpoint of quite varied belief systems. As a result, treatments for psychological problems have also varied dramatically. It is worth taking a brief look at how therapy has evolved, because a little historical perspective can help us to appreciate a basic point—that the ways in which people try to treat or "cure" psychological disorders depends to a large degree on how they see the nature and causes of psychological problems.

Therapy as Expelling Evil Spirits

Most ancient civilizations treated what we consider to be psychological disorders with methods based on a shared cultural assumption about etiology: that people's aberrant behavior was due to demons or evil spirits inhabiting their bodies. This assumption led to treatments that were harsh, painful, and generally ineffective in relieving symptoms. One such treatment—practiced as long as 10,000 years ago—was trepanning, in which holes were drilled in the sufferer's skull to let the evil spirits escape (Figure 17.1).

As early as the fifth century B.C., the Greek physician Hippocrates (460?–377? B.C.) protested this idea and argued instead that psychological disorders were due to natural bodily processes gone awry. Great strides were made in the diagnosis and treatment of mental illnesses during the enlightened Greco-Roman era. However, the "evil spirit" theory resurfaced in Christian guise after the fall of Rome in the fifth century, and the ancient, crude method of trepanning was again employed, along with other means of exorcising the devil.

In Medieval Europe, human life was seen as a battleground between good and evil forces; it was perhaps natural, therefore, to try to "treat" people who acted bizarrely with prayer. If that didn't work, more drastic methods were used to make the body an inhospitable place for evil spirits. People were fed vile-tasting liquids to make them vomit or to give them diarrhea ("purging"). There blood was "let," or drained; their bodies were flogged; they were immersed in water or immobilized. Still worse, people whose behavior was viewed as abnormal were often assumed to have made a compact with the devil, and even into the 1700s thousands of people—particularly women—died horribly by burning at the stake after being condemned as witches. Many of these unfortunates were probably simply ill.

One solution for aberrant behavior, then, was to rid people of evil spirits; another, later solution was to separate them from the rest of society by placing them in institutions. One such hospital in London, St. Mary's of Bethlehem, began admitting "lunatics" in 1403. (The word *lunatic* comes from the Latin for "moon," because some forms of psychological disorder were supposed by early peoples to fluctuate according to the moon's phases.) The treatment these people received was not, however, what we associate with hospitals. Inmates were chained, tortured, and exhibited to the public for its entertainment. Like many "asylums" that followed it, the hospital was a place of noisy uproar, filled with the screams of its unfortunate inhabitants. In fact, our modern word *bedlam*

FIGURE 17.1
In the ancient treatment called trepanning, holes were drilled in the skull to allow evil spirits to escape.

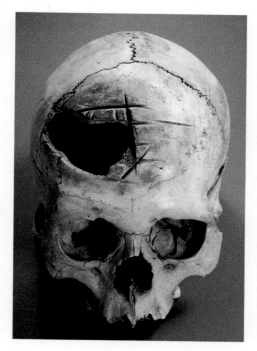

originates in the Middle English pronunciation of the name of this early London hospital.

Although attitudes toward the mentally ill were slow to change, occasionally someone would speak out against the inhumane practices followed in asylums. One court physician, Johann Weyer (1515–1588), suggested that aberrant behavior was due not to possession or witchcraft but to mental illness, and that people afflicted with psychological problems should be treated as patients. Today Weyer is recognized as the father of psychiatry, but in his own time people were not ready to accept his views, and his work was condemned and suppressed by the church. It was not until the 1800s that society began to see psychological problems as illnesses having natural causes. This important shift in how people viewed mental problems ushered in new forms of treatment.

Therapy as Treating Illness

A leading figure in the movement to redefine psychological problems as illness was Philippe Pinel (1745–1826), who, in 1793, was appointed director of the La Bicêtre mental hospital in Paris. Pinel believed in a medical etiology for abnormal behavior, which required a much more humane approach to treating mental patients. According to Pinel, "The mentally ill, far from being guilty people deserving of punishment, are sick people whose miserable state deserves all the consideration that is due to suffering humanity. One should try with the most simple methods to restore their reason" (quoted in Zilboorg & Henry, 1941, pp. 323–324).

Pinel's attitude toward mental illness led him to do something that was radical for its time—he unchained the patients and let them walk around the grounds. He found that this simple liberation, even with no further therapy, allowed some patients to recover enough to be discharged. In this way he stumbled on a result familiar to modern therapists: even people with serious disorders sometimes recover without treatment.

Pinel and others pioneered what was described in Chapter 16 as the "medical model" of abnormal behavior. But even as this new attitude about mental illness was taking hold, treatments were still primitive. For example, Benjamin Rush (1745–1813), the "father of American psychiatry," theoretically favored a medical model for the treatment of mental patients and advocated a soothing environment to calm them. Yet he continued using contemporary treatments such as dunking them in hot or cold water, severely restraining them, or spinning them at great speeds, which often resulted in unconsciousness (Figure 17.2). Some of these methods were intended to induce sudden, intense fright, which was thought to have a beneficial effect on certain conditions. Thus, even though by the 1800s attitudes toward mental illness were changing, knowledge about the sources of abnormal behavior remained scanty, and the methods used to treat these disorders were often extremely distressing and even fatal to the patient. Nevertheless, redefining psychological abnormality as an illness instead of a supernatural phenomenon was an important step on the way to more effective treatment.

The Birth of Psychotherapy

We can trace the beginnings of modern therapeutic methods to events that were taking place in Vienna and Paris in the late 1700s. Anton Mesmer, the pioneer hypnotist discussed in Chapter 5, developed a rather bizarre treatment for physical symptoms lacking any apparent origin in actual physical impairment—the condition called hysteria at that time and now classified as a conversion disorder (Chapter 16). Mesmer hypothesized that these disorders were caused by planetary influences on the distribution of a "magnetic fluid" in patients' bodies. He therefore touched them with an iron rod while staring intently at them, in order to transmit "animal magnetism" and effect a redistribution of this fluid.

FIGURE 17.2
An 18th-century water cure for mental illness

Although Mesmer's theory had no scientific foundation, strangely enough his method did seem to cure some people—probably through the power of suggestion. Mesmer's method is therefore considered to be an early example of treating psychological problems through hypnosis. Subsequently Jean Charcot (1825–1893), a brilliant Parisian neurologist, began demonstrating the relationship between hypnosis and hysteria and passed his knowledge along to an obscure young medical resident, Sigmund Freud.

The appearance of Freud (1856–1939) marks a turning point in the history of psychotherapy. Armed with the technique of hypnosis, the young neurologist began private practice in Vienna, treating patients with nervous disorders and hysterical symptoms. An earlier and now-famous case of his colleague and co-author Josef Breuer gave Freud the inspiration for much of his future theory. Breuer's patient, called by the pseudonym Anna O in his case study (1895), had a multitude of puzzling symptoms: paralysis of the legs, right arm, and right side; excessive squinting and coughing; difficulty swallowing liquids; hallucinations; and various speech disorders, including at times the inability to speak her native German, responding instead in English or Italian (Figure 17.3).

Breuer had treated "Anna" by listening to her talk about troubling past events, sometimes using hypnosis to encourage her. He found that she could thereby produce the original source of each physical symptom (for instance, her inability to swallow was traced to her strong feeling of disgust upon seeing a dog drink from a glass), which then caused the symptom to disappear. Anna called this "the talking cure," a phrase that has since been used to describe any therapy based primarily on patients talking about their symptoms and experiences. Breuer's description of the case of Anna O was responsible for one of Freud's earliest and most enduring insights: symptoms have *meanings,* and the key to relieving them is to discover what those meanings are.

Freud's reflections on the case of Anna O went beyond Breuer's, however, in elaborating the talking cure and in hypothesizing an underlying sexual component common to all hysterics' symptoms. Seeing a dog drinking from a glass, for instance, might seem insufficiently disturbing to produce a fear of drinking—Freud reasoned that there must be a stronger, more primitive association behind that symptom that had gone unexplored. Breuer and Freud ultimately parted ways over Freud's insistence on a sexual etiology for hysteria—a pattern that was to be repeated many times with other colleagues during Freud's career.

Freud's psychoanalysis, which we will describe further in this chapter, represented a new way of understanding and treating psychological problems. Other types of therapy, proposed after psychoanalysis, have been based on different assumptions about the sources of psychological difficulties and the ways to treat them.

FIGURE 17.3
Breuer's patient, "Anna O," coined the term "the talking cure." Her case helped Freud deduce principles that led to the development of psychoanalysis. Anna O, whose real name was Bertha Pannenheim, went on to found the League of Jewish Women and also became the world's first social worker.

Therapy Today: The Diversity of Approaches

Since Freud's time, hundreds of forms of treatment have been proposed for problems ranging from mild anxiety to extremely debilitating disorders such as schizophrenia. This diversity of approaches is a testament to the complexity of human behavior and to the wide variety of disorders from which people seek relief. To make sense of the main types of therapy described in this chapter, let's look at some basic principles that underlie contemporary treatments.

Basic principles of contemporary therapy. The goal of modern day therapy is to help people change their maladaptive behaviors, emotions, or thoughts. A person may, for example, feel depressed or anxious, hear voices, or engage in compulsive rituals or obsessive thinking. Most forms of therapy ask how these maladaptive practices originated and how they can be changed and normal functioning restored.

The different types of therapy can be distinguished by their underlying assumptions and preferred methods of treatment. We can appreciate how they differ from one another by examining Figure 17.4, in which the various processes involved in behavior are diagramed. This figure depicts a person as containing biological mechanisms, feelings, and thoughts, including memories of past experiences and unconscious thoughts. External to the person—in the sense that they can be directly observed—are overt behaviors (including emotional responses), stimuli in the environment, and the overall context in which the person's behavior takes place.

If this description sounds familiar, it should: it is essentially the picture of behavior that was sketched when you first encountered the levels of analysis concept in Chapter 1. Just as behavior in general can be understood by looking at this picture from different angles, so different types of therapy can change maladaptive behavior by focusing on different components of this scheme. For example, three types of therapy focus on different aspects of the person's thoughts: Freudian therapy focuses on conscious and unconscious thoughts, as the therapist strives to help the client understand the role of specific past experiences in causing the problem; client-centered therapy focuses on the thoughts caused by the conflict between the standards people set for themselves and their actual feelings and behaviors, as the therapist encourages them to accept themselves as they are; and cognitive therapies focus on illogical or unrealistic thought patterns that cause maladaptive behaviors and on changing these problematic thought patterns.

In contrast to the preceding types of therapy, which focus on a person's thoughts, behavior therapies focus directly on modifying behavior. Behavior therapists believe it is unnecessary to address factors within a person such as thoughts, biological processes, or past experiences in order to significantly change inappropriate behavior. Instead, maladaptive behaviors can be changed by using techniques of operant and classical conditioning.

The last group of therapies in use today, biomedical therapies, focuses on physiological mechanisms—particularly on the functioning of the brain. The assumption is that disorders are caused by physiological processes gone awry, just as Hippocrates believed millennia ago. These therapies use drugs or other biological interventions to modify those physiological processes and thereby ease the patient's symptoms or even effect a cure.

FIGURE 17.4
Different types of therapy operate on different aspects of a person. Cognitive, client-centered, and psychodynamic therapies operate on a person's thoughts in various ways, with psychodynamic therapies focusing also on past experiences. Biological therapies operate on physiological processes. Behavioral therapies focus on overt behavior. Each of these approaches has proven effective, some more effective for specific disorders.

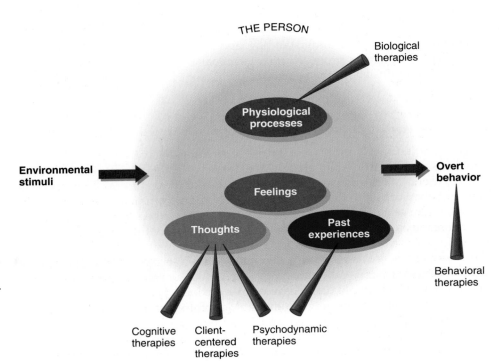

Which approach to therapy is "best"? There is no simple answer—just as there is no simple explanation for most behavior. By now you know that we need to look at behavior from all levels of analysis to understand why people behave as they do—though some levels are more pertinent than others to specific behaviors. Similarly, there is a diversity of treatments for psychological disorders because each addresses an important piece of the puzzle—though some therapies are more effective than others for specific problems. And often the "best" treatment is some combination of therapies, a point we will return to when we describe the trend toward eclecticism near the end of this chapter. Thus, present day providers of psychological services may draw from several "schools" of therapy rather than practicing within one narrow spectrum.

Contemporary therapy is also diverse in the types and qualifications of the professionals who deliver psychological services. Before looking in detail at the various therapies, let's briefly review the range of mental health professionals.

Types of therapists.   People seeking help with psychological problems today have a wide range of professional therapists to choose from. In addition to differences in therapeutic approach, there are wide differences in training among therapists.

- **Clinical psychologists** usually earn a Ph.D. in a department of psychology, during which they are trained in the diagnosis and treatment of psychological disorders. They also receive extensive training in research methods and are often the professionals most heavily involved in research on disorders and therapy.
- **Psychiatrists** are medical doctors (M.D.'s) who specialize in psychological disorders. They, too, are trained in diagnosing and treating psychological disorders, but as medical residents they may have had more training with institutionalized patients, and they are more likely than psychologists to be found working in hospital settings. As physicians, they are also trained in the administration and monitoring of drugs and other medical treatments such as the electroconvulsive therapy discussed later in this chapter. Psychiatrists are the only therapists licensed to prescribe medications.
- **Psychiatric social workers** usually have earned a master's degree in social work and are called M.S.W.'s, though some go on to earn doctorates. When employed in hospitals, they typically play an important role in helping patients utilize social support services in the community. M.S.W.'s may also offer therapy in private practice.
- **Psychiatric nurses** have either a B.A. or an M.A. in nursing, with a specialization in psychiatry. They collaborate with psychologists and psychiatrists in providing treatment, usually in a hospital setting.
- **Counselors** usually have a master's degree in counseling. They are often employed by school systems and social service agencies, though many are also in private practice. When counselors provide therapy, they typically focus on adjustment problems, vocational counseling, and marital and family counseling.

What differentiates these mental health professionals from one another, besides their degrees? Obviously, you would choose a psychiatrist if you sought drug therapy or were interested in the interaction of a medical and a psychological problem. But as far as providing psychotherapy, all of these professionals offer valuable services. As we will see when we consider factors that determine the effectiveness of therapy, the personal characteristics of the therapist—warmth, empathy, and understanding—are frequently more important than the approach used or the therapist's educational background. This means that skilled and caring people at many levels of training are capable of providing effective therapy.

But what exactly do therapists do? And what are their methods based on? To answer these questions, in the bulk of this chapter we will explore the major types of therapy in use today, beginning with the category of treatment pioneered by Sigmund Freud: psychodynamic therapies.

Psychodynamic Therapies

Life is a strange machine which can combine the materials offered to it in the most astonishing ways.

Bertrand Russell (1872–1970)
British philosopher

Psychodynamic therapies originated with Freud's theory of personality (Chapter 15) and the method of therapy based on it, which Freud called **psychoanalysis.** Although most contemporary psychodynamic therapists use methods that differ in many ways from those of psychoanalysis, they are descended from Freud's original method and share some of its features. We will therefore first examine psychoanalysis as practiced by Freud and then look at some ways in which modern adaptations of it diverge.

Freudian Psychoanalysis

The basic assumption behind Freud's therapy is that disorders develop because of conflicts early in a person's life (Freud, 1901/1960). Specifically, some event occurs—usually in childhood—that leads the child to wish for something that is unacceptable to his or her basic values or that is too fearful to contemplate. For example, a young boy who wishes to eliminate his father as a rival for his mother's attention finds that wish threatening and pushes it from his awareness via the defense mechanism of repression. However, the wish surfaces later in a disguised form in the young man's symptoms. Thus, the repressed wish "kill father" may become a neurotic symptom such as the obsessional thought "kill others." The goal of psychoanalysis, therefore, is to help the patient gain insight into the repressed material that is the real origin of his or her symptoms. Once that insight is achieved, *catharsis* occurs—the pent-up impulse is exposed to consciousness and thereby eliminated. The person can then redirect the energy that was required for repressing the wish toward dealing with life in a more well-adjusted manner.

But how can patients gain access to their unconscious thoughts and wishes? Let's look in on a psychoanalytic session with a patient named Sally. Sally reclines on a couch to relax; the therapist—called an *analyst* in this system—is sitting out of sight so as not to distract her. In this particular session, the analyst tells Sally to use **free association**—to say whatever enters her head in a completely candid, uncensored manner. In making this request the analyst is asking Sally to observe the **fundamental rule of psychoanalysis**—to reveal whatever comes up, no matter how shocking, revealing, or seemingly irrelevant.

As the session proceeds, Sally describes a dream she had, and the analyst encourages her to free-associate about some of its content. As we discussed in Chapter 5, on consciousness, Freud saw dreams as having two types of content: *manifest* (what happened in the dream) and *latent* (what the dream symbolizes, or is really about). Sally relates dreaming of riding a horse with a childhood friend (the manifest content), which the analyst interprets as a desire to see that person again and have a sexual relationship with him (the latent content). The analyst draws that inference from her knowledge that the horse is a common symbol of sexuality and from Sally's free associations, which link the now-married friend with other, more accessible men in her life.

Sigmund Freud

As the analyst listens to Sally's dream and associations she makes few, if any, comments. The rationale for this relative silence is that therapy is based on *Sally's* experience, to which only Sally has access. The analyst's job is to provide an occasional interpretation to help Sally discover for herself the hidden motives that are causing her distress. To interfere too much—even by asking too many questions—would be to block Sally's flow of thoughts and possibly to influence their direction.

The original psychoanalytic couch, in Freud's Vienna study

How, given this minimal intervention, does the analyst arrive at her interpretation? One way is to pay close attention to the connections between Sally's thoughts. Even though Sally's utterances may appear to be random, the analyst infers subtle connections between them based on their order or on recurring themes among them. Sally may use the same phrase or tone of voice as she mentions two seemingly unrelated persons or events, for instance. The analyst also listens for sudden silences, topic switches, or the omission of a logical step in a series, perhaps dismissed by Sally with "That isn't important." These behaviors signal that Sally may be approaching potentially "dangerous" and therefore important information. (Freud called these unconscious attempts to avoid confronting "threatening" topics **resistance.**) Thus, the analyst is like a detective, using all available clues to figure out what lies behind her patient's symptoms.

Another important aspect of psychoanalysis is the patient's relationship with the analyst. Patients often develop very strong reactions to their analyst. These reactions may be positive—for instance, when the client "falls in love" with the analyst as an atmosphere of trust develops—or negative—typically, when sensitive material is surfacing and therapy has become challenging.

Freud called these positive and negative reactions **transference.** He explained that the patient uses the analyst as a "stand-in" for a parent or other significant person in her or his life, "transferring" earlier, powerful emotions to the therapeutic situation. The patient thereby unconsciously role-plays a real-life drama from the past with a person whom the analyst comes to represent; this often enables the patient to "work through" a relationship by proxy. Freud thought it was important to observe the form that the transference takes, because the nature of patients' role playing reveals important information about their interpersonal problems and patterns. The following excerpt from a session with a 50-year-old male illustrates the transference phenomenon:

> *Patient:* I really don't feel like talking today.
> *Analyst* (*remains silent for several minutes, then*): Perhaps you'd like to talk about why you don't feel like talking.
> *Patient:* There you go again, making demands on me, insisting I do what I just don't feel up to doing. (*Pause*) Do I always have to talk here, when I don't feel like it? (*Voice becomes angry and petulant.*) Can't you just get off my back? You don't really give a damn how I feel, do you?
> *Analyst:* I wonder why you feel I don't care.
> *Patient:* Because you're always pressuring me to do what I feel I can't do.
> (Adapted from Davison & Neale, 1986, p. 479)

In this exchange, the patient—a successful business executive who is significantly older than the analyst—acts as though he feels weak and incompetent. Based on information gained through earlier sessions, the analyst interprets this exchange as an instance of transference. The patient's anger is actually an expression of his resentment toward his father, who was extremely critical of him as a child and was never satisfied with his efforts. In later sessions, analyst and patient were able to work directly on that relationship.

Freud's psychoanalysis is extremely intensive and time-consuming, with the patient often attending four or five sessions a week. Psychoanalysis in its strict form is rarely practiced today, but its offspring are numerous and related to the original to varying degrees; like Freud's, they are *psychodynamic* therapies.

Contemporary Psychodynamic Therapies

Present day psychodynamic therapies share a number of features with psychoanalysis, but they also differ from it significantly. Taken as a group, they tend to differ from Freud's methods in the following ways:

- Current psychodynamic therapy is shorter and less intensive than Freud's. In fact, some therapists have proposed an approach called time-limited psychotherapy, which consists of treatments limited to 12 to 30 sessions (Mann, 1973; Strupp, 1981; Strupp & Binder, 1984).

- Current therapists are less concerned with the unconscious, with psychosexual development, and with childhood experiences. Instead, they tend to focus on how the client copes with current situations and relationships. There is also more awareness of the role of environmental influences and less insistence on internal factors in psychological problems.

- Contemporary therapists take a more active role in the therapeutic interaction and are warmer toward the client (note the significant change of labels, for one thing: *analyst* and *patient* are now *therapist* and *client*). For example, one therapist, Helmut Kohut (1971), bases his work on the idea that many problems are due to low self-esteem caused by a lack of parental warmth. Therefore, though he uses traditional Freudian tools such as free association and dream analysis as he helps clients uncover crucial events in their childhood, he does so while relating to them in a warm, supportive, and sympathetic manner.

Although psychodynamic therapies began with the Freudian system, they have been reshaped to match new social realities and new conceptions of personality, as well as to make therapy accessible to a larger number of people. Freud's original clientele were primarily wealthy, well-educated persons of culture often suffering from dramatic somatoform or dissociative disorders (Chapter 16). Today's beneficiaries of the "talking cure" come from a much wider range of socioeconomic strata, though they must still have the intellectual and emotional capacity to reflect introspectively on their problems.

Another way in which therapists have been able to help a wider range of the population is by devising methods that rely on clients' ability to visualize thoughts and feelings. Especially in the case of children, relying on words may not always be the best way to gain access to clients' experiences. The following Interdisciplinary Dimension describes how some therapists have used the power of art as a therapeutic tool.

INTERDISCIPLINARY DIMENSION ART

Art Therapy with Children

> *The process of art therapy is based on the recognition that man's most fundamental thoughts and feelings, derived from the unconscious, reach expression in images rather than in words.*
>
> Margaret Naumburg (1958, p. 511)

With these words Margaret Naumburg, considered to be the founder of the field of **art therapy** in the United States, sets forth one of the basic principles of art therapy: art can succeed where words fail to express thoughts and feelings. Art therapists typically have training in art as well as in psychology and work with both adults and children. Here we will focus on some of the ways art therapy has been used with children.

One example of how art can be used in therapy with children is provided by Roger Arguile (1992). After asking children to draw a picture of their house, he says, "I wonder what's in there." Children typically respond by describing their siblings and parents in an unself-conscious and revealing manner, enabling him to explore the source of their problems.

A specialized application of art therapy to the problems of children is in treating children who have been sexually abused. This is a topic that is naturally difficult for children to talk about, and art provides an outlet for revealing the abuse. In examples provided by Harriet Wadeson, a 6-year-old girl drew the picture on the left in Figure 17.5 and described it as "Daddy's hand on my vagina." The picture of the Easter bunny, on the right, was also drawn by a 6-year-old girl, who asked the therapist's help in coloring the lower torso. When the therapist said, "That's a special area, isn't it?" the child agreed and then described how her father had fondled her "down there" (Wadeson, 1987).

Therapists who use art to facilitate communication and to generate information about children's inner lives treat their drawings or sculptures as a projective test like the Rorschach inkblot test (Chapter 15). In this way therapists can sometimes infer the children's unconscious wishes, conflicts, and needs.

However, interpreting pictures is not easy, because art is open to many more possible "readings" than words are. For example, before hearing the little girl's description of her drawing (Figure 17.5, left), a clinic staff member described it as "a tulip in an egg" (Wadeson, 1987). Nonetheless, some therapists have proposed "formulas" for determining the meaning of children's art. For example, it has been suggested that when a child draws a picture of a house, the door symbolizes the child's accessibility—an open door, according to the formula, signals that the child has a strong need for emotional warmth (Jolles, 1964).

As there is little evidence to validate such general interpretations, many art therapists are cautious about making too much of the contents of one picture. Wadeson created a quiz to demonstrate the reason for this caution. Look at the two pictures in Figure 17.6 and decide which one was drawn by a person with a psychological disorder. (The house was drawn by a 6-year-old boy and the tree was drawn by a woman in her early 20s.) After deciding, check your choice against the answer at the end of the paragraph. Whether or not you guessed correctly, you'll probably agree with Wadeson that "It is difficult if not impossible to make diagnostic determinations on the basis of the art alone" (Wadeson, 1987, p. 106). Art is therefore usually used in conjunction with other information. (In Figure 17.6, the house was drawn by a normally functioning boy and the tree by a depressed woman who committed suicide a month after drawing the picture.)

Art therapy is not so much a "school" of treatment as an approach that can be used with many types of therapies. Perhaps its greatest strength is that it provides clients with an alternative means of expression that can give client and therapist alike access to material that is difficult to verbalize. At least on occasion, a picture may be worth the proverbial 1000 words. ∎

FIGURE 17.5
Drawings by sexually abused children, from Wadeson's *The Dynamics of Art Psychotherapy*

FIGURE 17.6
Can you tell which of these pictures was drawn by a person with a psychological disorder? Wadeson's quiz points out the difficulty of diagnosing disorders on the basis of art alone.

Client-Centered Therapies

Contrary to those therapists who see depravity at man's core, who see man's deepest instincts as destructive, I have found that when man is truly free to actualize his nature as an organism capable of awareness, then he clearly appears to move towards wholeness and integration.

Carl Rogers (1966, p. 193)

In the 1930s, when Carl Rogers began working as a clinical psychologist in Rochester, New York, he used Freud's techniques—for the simple reason that they were the only therapeutic technique available. However, Rogers became disenchanted with psychoanalysis because he didn't agree that people are ruled by unconscious forces—nor that the therapist should direct the process of therapy. Neither did he share Freud's dark view of human nature. Like Abraham Maslow, whose view of personality was explored in Chapter 15, Rogers believed that people have an innate tendency to grow in a healthy way. To unlock his clients' own inner wisdom, he structured sessions to give clients more control over their direction—hence the term **client-centered therapy.**

Rogers (1951) assumes that people have a natural ability to heal themselves. The purpose of therapy is to remove the obstacles that keep this from happening and thus free clients to attain self-actualization. More specifically, the goal of therapy is to free the client from what Rogers calls a state of **incongruence**—a condition that exists when there is a discrepancy between the standards people set for themselves and their actual feelings and behavior.

For example, a woman who believes that she shouldn't have negative feelings toward others but nonetheless feels angry and hostile toward her husband is in a state of incongruence. Being in this state is unhealthy because it can lead the woman to deny her angry feelings—and denying them in turn can cause her to lose touch with her own genuine experience of reality. The major goal of Rogers's approach is therefore to resolve this incongruence by helping clients clarify their feelings and accept themselves as they truly are.

How does the therapist help clients free themselves from incongruence? The key is to help them become aware of the standards they set for themselves and to shift those standards so that they more closely match the clients' actual feelings and experiences. According to Rogers, this can best be done if the therapist creates a nonthreatening atmosphere of acceptance in which clients feel safe exploring their own feelings. To create this atmosphere, the therapist must display three basic attitudes.

1. *Genuineness:* The therapist is open and "real," honestly expressing his or her own emotions and thoughts. This openness and self-disclosure not only creates an atmosphere of trust but also serves to model those qualities for the client.
2. *Empathy:* The ability to see the world through the client's eyes is central to the process of therapy.
3. *Unconditional positive regard:* Rogers coined this phrase to describe an ability to express warmth and caring for the *client* even when the therapist doesn't approve of the client's *behavior.*

Given these definitions of the client's problem and the therapist's necessary attitudes, how does the therapist interact with the client? The key to this interaction is contained in the name of the therapy: client-centered. With the client at the center of the process, it is the therapist's job to create an environment that enables the client to get in touch with the nature of the problem. The therapist facilitates this process by interacting with the client in a *nondirective* manner.

We can see what Rogers means by nondirective in the following exchange between a client and her therapist:

Alice: I was thinking about this business of standards. I somehow developed a sort of a knack, I guess, of—well—habit—of trying to make people feel at ease around me, or to make things go along smoothly. . . .

Counselor: In other words, what you did was always in the direction of trying to keep things smooth and to make other people feel better and to smooth the situation.

Alice: Yes, I think that's what it was. Now the reason why I did it probably was—I mean, not that I was a good little Samaritan going around making other people happy, but that was probably the role that felt easiest for me to play. I'd been doing it around home so much, I just didn't stand up for my own convictions, until I don't know whether I have any convictions to stand up for.

Counselor: You feel that for a long time you've been playing the role of kind of smoothing out the frictions or differences or what not . . .

Alice: M-hm.

Counselor: Rather than having any opinion or reaction of your own in the situation. Is that it?

Alice: That's it. Or that I haven't been really honestly being myself, or actually knowing what my real self is, and that I've been just playing a sort of false role. Whatever role no one else was playing, and that needed to be played at the time, I'd try to fill it in. (Rogers, 1951, pp. 152–153)

Notice the close relationship between what the client says and the therapist's response. This kind of responding, in which the client's statement is not interpreted but rather is repeated in a slightly different or clearer form, is called **reflection.** By reflecting the client's statements without seeming to pass judgment on them, the therapist encourages the client to be more in touch with his or her feelings and to talk in a more emotional and honest way. According to Rogers, this process leads naturally to insight into the problem and to a shifting of the self-concept toward the client's real experiences.

Client-centered therapy has been an extremely influential form of therapy, but it is rarely practiced in the totally nondirective way specified by Rogers in any of its numerous forms. For example, its current practitioners may go beyond simply restating or clarifying the client's thoughts by offering an insight that has remained hidden from the client after a number of sessions spent discussing the same topic (Carson & Butcher, 1992).

The two types of therapy we have described so far, client-centered therapy and psychodynamic therapy, are based on different premises about human behavior and use different procedures. Both, however, share the goal of giving the client insight: psychodynamic focuses on insights about the client's early experiences, whereas client-centered focuses on insights about incongruence between the client's standards and actual feelings and behavior. The next type of therapy we will cover shares this goal of achieving insight but focuses specifically on the connection between the client's thought processes and the symptoms.

Cognitive Therapies

There is nothing either good or bad, but thinking makes it so.

William Shakespeare, *Hamlet*

The rationale behind cognitive therapies is that people's emotions and behavior are determined by how they cognitively structure their experience. For example, the same event can elicit anxiety or excitement, depending on whether the person interprets it as threatening or stimulating. The goal of cognitive therapy is to give people insight into how their thinking influences their behavior, and to help them eliminate their problems by changing their thinking.

Albert Ellis, whose rational-emotive therapy is based on the idea that irrational beliefs are at the root of psychological problems

To illustrate how cognitive therapies work, we'll look at two types: Albert Ellis's rational-emotive therapy and Aaron Beck's cognitive therapy for depression. Both share the goal of changing the client's pattern of thinking, but they propose slightly different ways of achieving that goal.

Rational-Emotive Therapy

Rational-emotive therapy, developed by Albert Ellis (1970, 1987), is based on the idea that psychological problems arise because of people's irrational beliefs. Ellis has created a list of irrational beliefs that people commonly hold. Two of the most common are "I should always be loved and appreciated by people who are important to me" and "I should be totally competent and successful in all things that I do." Since few, if any, of us are *always* loved and *always* competent, these beliefs are irrational, and holding them leads to irrational thinking. In turn, that irrational thinking leads to problematic psychological symptoms.

Ellis describes this process as an *A-B-C sequence*, in which A is an Activating event, B a Belief, and C the emotional Consequence. For example, when a client named Harold becomes depressed because his son fails a college course, the following sequence occurs:

TABLE 17.1
Some common irrational beliefs

Category	Example of Belief
having my own way	"I *must* have my way, and my plans must always work out."
being hurt	"People who do anything wrong—especially those who harm me—are evil and should be punished."
being problemless	"Things should not go wrong in life, and if by chance they do, there should be quick and easy solutions."
being a victim	"Other people and outside forces are responsible for any misery I experience."
being in danger	"If anything or any situation is dangerous in any way, I must be anxious and upset about it."
avoiding	"It is easier to avoid facing life's difficulties than to develop self-discipline; making demands of myself should not be necessary."
tyranny of the past	"What I did, and especially what happened to me in the past, determines how I act and feel today."
passivity	"I can be happy by avoiding, by being passive, by being uncommitted, and by just enjoying myself."
catastrophizing	"If any of the above principles is violated in my life, it is terrible, awful, and catastrophic. And, as everyone knows, catastrophes are beyond our control" (Egan, 1990, p. 197).

A: Activating event	Harold's son fails a college course.
B: Belief	"If my children don't succeed in everything they do, I am a bad parent."
C: Consequence	Harold feels anxious and depressed.

8   THINKING

The therapist's goal is to make Harold aware of his irrational thinking by directly confronting his beliefs. The therapist accomplishes this by interacting actively in sessions with Harold—openly challenging his logic with questions like "What does your son's poor performance have to do with your value as a father?" or "Why do you feel that you have to be perfect?" These confrontations are combined with homework assignments such as verbalizing "self-statements" (for example, "My worth as a father does not depend on my son's success.") to eliminate irrational beliefs and patterns of thinking. Look at Ellis's list of some other common beliefs in Table 17.1; do any of them strike you as familiar?

Beck's Cognitive Therapy

Aaron Beck's (1976, 1987) **cognitive therapy** was originally developed to treat depression, but it is now also used for anxiety disorders. Beck's therapy is based on the idea that disorders such as depression and anxiety are tied to a type of irrational thinking called *cognitive distortions*. You will remember that we encountered two of these distortions—selective abstraction (choosing to focus on one negative aspect of a generally positive experience) and overgeneralization (drawing global conclusions from one minor negative event)—when we looked at Beck's theory of depression in Chapter 16. Here are two more:

1. *Magnification* refers to blowing a single event out of proportion. For example, a student may believe that receiving a poor grade on one test in one course means that she will flunk out of college.
2. *Absolutist thinking* is thinking in "black and white." This is the favored distortion of perfectionists, who believe that anything less than perfection means failure. Thus, a music recital in which one wrong note was played means the performance was a disaster.

The goal of cognitive therapy is to make the client aware of cognitive distortions and to substitute more accurate and constructive thinking and behavior.

Beck calls this process of changing the person's thinking **cognitive restructuring**. It is accomplished through an active collaboration between therapist and client. They act as a detective team, first determining how the client thinks irrationally and then devising conscious mental exercises to change that way of thinking. The following interchange illustrates the first step in this collaboration: identifying a cognitive distortion the client holds about the quality of his help with a neighbor's wallpapering job.

> *Therapist:* Just how far off was the alignment of the flowers?
> *Client* (*holds out fingers about one-eighth of an inch apart*): About that much.
> *Therapist:* On each strip of paper?
> *Client:* No . . . on two or three pieces.
> *Therapist:* Out of how many?
> *Client:* About 20 or 25.
> *Therapist:* Did anyone else notice it?
> *Client:* No. In fact, my neighbor thought it was great.
> *Therapist:* Did your wife see it?
> *Client:* Yeah, she admired the job.
> *Therapist:* Could you see the defect when you stood back and looked at the whole wall?
> *Client:* Well . . . not really.
> *Therapist:* So you've selectively attended to a real but very small flaw in your effort to wallpaper. Is it logical that such a small defect should entirely cancel the credit you deserve?
> *Client:* Well, it wasn't as good as it should have been.
> *Therapist:* If your neighbor had done the same quality job in your kitchen, what would you say?
> *Client:* . . . pretty good job! (Beck et al., 1979, p. 131).

From this excerpt we can see how the therapist made the client aware that he was selectively attending to only part of the job and how, when confronted with the facts, the client was forced to reconsider his original assessment of his performance.

Cognitive therapists not only challenge clients' pictures of reality during their sessions together, but they also have clients engage in *reality-testing exercises* outside of the sessions, to determine whether their irrational beliefs are actually valid. For example, a client with the belief "If I count my change in front of the cashier, the cashier will disapprove and will make a negative comment" is encouraged to test this belief by actually carrying out the action. Usually—because these beliefs are irrational—the client finds they aren't valid.

The therapist also assigns homework designed to combat depression or anxiety and to help the client see the fallacy of his or her irrational thinking. One such assignment might be to keep a diary of upsetting events and the thoughts connected with them, in order to clarify the connection between thought processes and emotions. Or the therapist might encourage a depressed client to schedule specific activities such as shopping, working around the house, or exercising. These activities combat the lethargy that is often characteristic of depression and also increase the chances that the client will have some rewarding experiences.

Both cognitive therapy and rational-emotive therapy aim at replacing the client's irrational beliefs with more rational ones. The major difference between them is in the style of the therapists. Practitioners of rational-emotive therapy tend to be more confrontational, whereas cognitive therapists tend to work in a more reasoned way as they collaborate with clients to discover their distorted thinking and then test it.

So far we have discussed therapies that strive to give clients insight into their problems. We now turn to a class of therapies that takes a radically different approach. Instead of changing the client's *thoughts*, these types of therapies directly target problematic *behaviors*. Instead of seeing symptoms as *clues* to the underlying problem, they see symptoms as the problem *itself*.

Behavior Therapies

Behavior therapists generally avoid delving into the client's past, instead focusing on the here and now. **Behavior therapy** typically tackles one problem at a time and resolves it before considering the next. For that reason, it is most frequently employed for disorders with observable symptoms, such as phobias, obsessive-compulsive disorder, and panic disorder, rather than for generalized anxiety or depression. Both types of conditioning—classical and operant—are applied to achieve a measurable improvement in behavior.

Therapies Based on Classical Conditioning

6   LEARNING

In Chapter 6 we saw how the kind of learning discovered by Pavlov applies especially to reflexes and emotional responses. Studies of this type of learning focus on how responses can be either elicited or extinguished through classical conditioning. Therapies based on the assumption that maladaptive behavior has been learned, aim to get the client to "unlearn" that behavior. Four procedures for accomplishing this are *systematic desensitization*, *implosive therapy*, *flooding*, and *aversion therapy*.

Systematic desensitization.   As described in Chapter 6, systematic desensitization is typically used to decrease anxiety in specific situations, and is therefore most often used to treat panic disorders and to eliminate phobic fears. Remember that phobias are often "conditioned," or learned, through the pairing of a neutral stimulus—such as heights—with a stimulus that arouses fear—such as once narrowly escaping a fall. The rationale behind desensitization is that these same phobias can be "deconditioned" by pairing relaxation and the fear-producing stimulus (Figure 17.7). The process is called systematic because it typically pro-

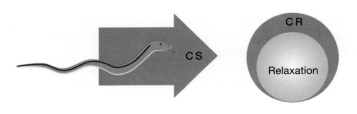

FIGURE 17.7
The principle of desensitization. During conditioning, the snake, a source of anxiety, is paired with relaxation training, which counters the tension associated with anxiety. After conditioning, the snake elicits relaxation and, therefore, no longer causes anxiety.

ceeds in a series of steps. For example, a person with a phobia for snakes might first relax while imagining writing the word "snake" and then, later in the process, relax while imagining seeing a snake in a zoo. (Refer back to Chapter 6 for a description of how desensitization was actually used to eliminate a snake phobia.)

Implosive therapy and flooding.   Whereas systematic desensitization is based on conditioning a new response to a familiar stimulus, implosive therapy and flooding are based on the principle of extinction. In **implosive therapy**, the client imagines the anxiety-producing situation with the help of the therapist, who may dramatically describe the situation in order to increase the client's anxiety. Instead of relaxing, as in the desensitization procedure, the client experiences a massive "implosion" of anxiety. Though this may seem counterproductive, the fact that the anxiety is experienced in the safety of the therapist's company and with no actual harmful consequences means that after numerous repetitions the conditioned response is extinguished.

In **flooding**, the client is repeatedly placed in the actual anxiety-producing situation until the conditioned fear is extinguished. For example, a woman with a fear of heights might be assigned to visit the tops of tall buildings. Research has shown that the more realistic flooding tends to be superior to implosion therapy in resolving phobias, though both have a good success rate (Barlow, 1988).

Flooding is also used to treat obsessive-compulsive disorder by preventing clients from carrying out their compulsive rituals. Thus, a man who washes his hands 25 times a day is forbidden to wash them at all, thereby creating a great deal of anxiety. But when the terrible consequences imagined by the client—such as becoming ill from contact with germs—fail to materialize, extinction should eventually occur.

Aversion therapy.   The goal of the methods discussed so far has been to eliminate undesirable or excessive anxiety from certain situations. The technique of *aversion therapy* seeks the opposite: to link aversive stimuli—fear or discomfort—with behaviors targeted for elimination, such as smoking or drinking (Figure 17.8). The basic classical conditioning procedure is used to do this; for instance,

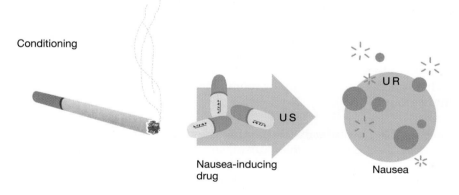

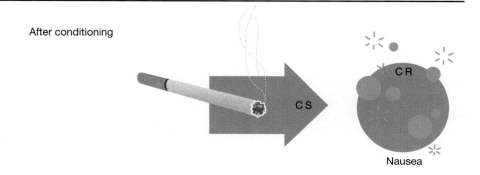

FIGURE 17.8
Aversion therapy for cigarette smoking. During conditioning, smoking a cigarette is paired with a drug that causes sickness. If conditioning is effective, smoking the cigarette eventually causes sickness.

drinking alcohol might be paired with electric shocks, or drugs might be prescribed that induce nausea in combination with alcohol. Aversion therapy can succeed in eliminating undesirable behaviors, but relapses are common.

Closely related to classical conditioning therapy is therapy based on operant conditioning. You'll recall that a main characteristic of operant conditioning is that people *operate* on their environments by behaving in such a way as to gain a future reward or avoid a future punishment.

Therapies Based on Operant Conditioning

Remember Thorndike's law of effect (Chapter 6)? Therapies based on operant conditioning make use of the first half of the law of effect: behaviors that are followed by satisfying effects are more likely to occur again. Thus, operant procedures use positive reinforcers to increase the frequency of a desired behavior. Three such procedures are *shaping and reinforcement*, *token economies*, and *biofeedback*.

Shaping and reinforcement.   We saw in Chapter 6 that shaping and reinforcement are particularly powerful procedures when used with retarded or autistic children. Lovaas (1987) used these tools to teach autistic children to speak by rewarding them with M&M candies. First he reinforced their production of speechlike sounds; then he shaped their learning gradually until they articulated actual words. Eventually, children who had never spoken were able to carry on conversations.

Positive reinforcement and shaping have also been used to train clients—individually or in groups—to be more assertive, to develop social skills, and to control their weight. These techniques have also been able to solve many day-to-day behavioral problems at work sites, in classrooms, and in institutional settings such as prisons, juvenile detention centers, and halfway houses.

Token economies.   Closely related to shaping and reinforcement is the use of a **token economy,** which employs secondary reinforcers—"tokens" that can be exchanged for primary reinforcers such as food or free time. Every time a desirable behavior occurs—studying, being kind to others, doing chores—each member earns a specified number of tokens that can be exchanged for primary reinforcers. Obviously, this system works only in structured environments in which everyone agrees on the "rules." But participants needn't be there involuntarily; such a system could be set up by roommates, for example, or by a weight-loss or study group.

In a biofeedback session, electrodes monitor tension in the client's facial muscles. Her task is to activate a tone that sounds when her muscle tension decreases.

Biofeedback.   **Biofeedback training** provides a way for people to gain control over their own physiological functions, such as muscle tension or brain waves. It has therefore proved useful in treating people who suffer from tension headaches (Blanchard et al., 1982) or simply from excessive anxiety. Biofeedback works by monitoring a physiological function and providing feedback to the client regarding that function. For instance, clients who suffer from severe headaches might have the muscle tension in their foreheads monitored electronically through suction cups attached to wires (similar to an EEG or EKG). The "feedback" is a tone that sounds when muscle tension is decreased; the clients' task is to keep that tone sounding steadily. After learning to control their tension in the laboratory or office, sufferers can employ what they've learned during or after stressful situations that occur in everyday life.

The techniques of behavior therapy covered here are most useful when a well-defined problem, such as "gets headaches" or "experiences anxiety in elevators," is presented. They have an advantage over the insight therapies in not relying on the client's intelligence or verbal skills, and they tend to require less time to achieve a positive outcome.

Our description of the different kinds of therapy up to this point has focused on situations in which the therapist and client have a one-on-one relationship. But therapy can also be conducted in a group setting. This way of conducting therapy, which is called group therapy, brings some unique characteristics and advantages to the process.

Group Therapy

In **group therapy**, typically one or two therapists meet with five to nine clients at a time (Ettin, 1992). Even larger groups are possible, as witnessed by the success and popularity of self-help groups that focus on specific shared problems: alcohol and drug abuse, overeating, underassertiveness, single parenting, and spousal abuse, among others. Such groups are usually led by people who have themselves profited from that type of therapy. We will focus here on the group therapy situation in which a trained therapist meets with a small number of group members.

 19   SOCIAL

What kinds of therapy are practiced in the group setting? It depends on the therapist leading the group. A psychodynamically oriented therapist might focus on transference patterns among the participants, looking at how their relationships within the group mirror their relationships outside of the group. A client-centered therapist would emphasize the expression of genuine feelings and the acceptance of others in the group—in this case, not only by the therapist but by each of the group's clients. A behaviorally oriented therapist might have everyone together learn a particular technique such as systematic desensitization. But all groups are alike in that the therapist proper is not the only helper: each member ideally helps the others—sometimes to the extent that the therapist plays an "invisible" role.

A main advantage of group therapy is that it is less costly than individual psychotherapy. But there are other advantages as well, which would be unavailable in one-on-one therapy. Irwin Yalom (1975, 1985), one of the pioneers of group psychotherapy, cites the following characteristics of groups that enhance the effectiveness of therapy:

• *Instillation of hope:* Clients who believe they will improve by undertaking therapy tend to have a better chance of benefiting from it. Since at least one or two people in a group show marked improvement as the group progresses, their example can instill hope in the others.

• *Recognition of universality:* Many people enter therapy thinking they are alone in their misery. By hearing other people's stories, members realize that their problems are not unique.

• *Opportunity to help others:* Supporting others in the group can be therapeutic in itself. In fact, when giving advice to one another clients may discover that their insights apply to themselves as well.

• *Recapitulation of the family:* Many problems are traceable to past or present interactions with a person's family. As the group evolves, clients often begin interacting with the leaders and each other as they did with their parents and siblings. A woman might, for example, begin to feel ignored by others in the group and then realize that this is how she felt when growing up in her family.

• *Improvement of social interactions:* As people interact within the group, they often display the same maladaptive social behaviors that don't work for them outside of the group. Unlike people on the "outside," however, who are likely to simply withdraw from relationships with a problematic personality, the group can provide feedback regarding the way the person is relating. For example, they might point out that a particular person avoids looking others in the eye when speaking to them, tries to manipulate others, or comes across as arrogant. This acting out of maladaptive interpersonal behaviors in the relatively safe social environment of the group is, according to Yalom, the "keystone upon which the entire approach to group therapy rests" (1975, p. 30).

• *Development of group cohesiveness:* Group members—who are usually strangers at the beginning of therapy—often develop very close relationships, expressed as genuine caring for one another and resulting in a feeling of group cohesiveness. The development of this cohesiveness is a major intermediate goal of group therapy, because often it enhances the likelihood that therapy will be successful for all.

Because of the many benefits of group therapy, it is widely used; for example, a substantial proportion of depressed clients in therapy eventually work in a group setting (Luby & Yalom, 1992). Sometimes its benefits are especially pronounced for clients who insist they are not "joiners": group therapy may offer them their first positive group experience. But group therapy is not for everyone, nor for every problem. People who want the attention of an individual therapist, or who cannot bring themselves to divulge their problems to a group, may be more comfortable with individual therapy. (Often clients do both, by meeting individually with the same therapist who leads their group.) For other clients, neither individual psychotherapy nor group therapy may be the sole answer. These clients obtain help not from talking with a therapist or sharing their experiences with a group, but through the use of drugs or other *biomedical* interventions. We will examine this type of therapy next.

Biomedical Therapies

3   BIOLOGY

Biomedical therapies are interventions intended to ease the symptoms associated with psychological disorders by modifying physiological processes such as brain chemistry. These therapies are based on the assumption that physiological problems are a root cause of at least some disorders. As we saw in Chapter 16, there is considerable evidence for this idea, especially in regard to some of the more severe disorders such as schizophrenia.

In a sense, in discussing these therapies we've come full circle from the early "cures" attempted for mental illness. Trepanning the skull, letting blood, and purging the digestive system were treatments that assumed a physiological cause for psychological aberrations. More recently, a brain operation called a *prefrontal lobotomy* was in vogue as a means of tranquilizing seriously disturbed mental patients (Shutts, 1982). This operation, developed by the Portuguese neurologist Antonio Egas Moniz, was introduced to the United States in the 1930s. It involves cutting the nerve fibers that connect the prefrontal cortex to the rest of the cortex. The intention was originally to calm patients with severe disorders by neutralizing their emotional responses and introspective behaviors. Early patients typically suffered from schizophrenia, but increasingly other major and minor disorders became a target for this procedure.

Unfortunately, lobotomies were often ineffective, and they also caused numerous undesirable side effects such as loss of memory, impaired intelligence, overexcitability, and a lessening of the ability to feel emotions (Stuss & Benson, 1984). These problems raised serious questions about whether lobotomies ought to be performed. Thus, when new biological therapies to treat depression and schizophrenia became available in the mid-1950s, the use of lobotomies was essentially abandoned (Lesse, 1984). Today's biomedical therapies are far more effective and have fewer side effects. Nevertheless, given the complexity of human physiology and the high likelihood of side effects in any biomedical treatment, all such therapy must be handled with care. We will look next at two contemporary biomedical treatments: drug therapy, which has been applied to a wide range of disorders, and electroconvulsive therapy, which has been used very selectively to deal with cases of severe depression.

Drug Therapies

Drug therapies are treatments that use medication to alter a patient's physiological processes and to provide relief from debilitating symptoms. The main types of medication used in treating psychological disorders are antipsychotic drugs, antidepressant drugs, lithium carbonate, and antianxiety drugs.

Antipsychotic drugs.   In 1955, a family of **antipsychotic drugs** called phenothiazines became available in the United States, ushering in a revolution in the treatment of serious disorders such as schizophrenia. One account of this revolution describes the maximum security ward of a mental hospital before and after the introduction of these drugs. The "before" picture fit the stereotype of a madhouse: patients exhibited bizarre behavior such as walking around nude, screaming, and sometimes threatening others with violence. A month after the trial of the new drugs, the "after" picture showed a much more orderly ward, with therapists able to converse with formerly inaccessible patients (Carson & Butcher, 1992).

These drugs, which included chlorpromazine (better known by its trade name, Thorazine), acted on the symptoms of schizophrenia: they eliminated hallucinations for many patients, helped them become more in touch with reality, and restored their cognitive powers. Although these drugs did not work on all patients, their net effect was to transform the lives of many and to dramatically alter the institutional scene. The results of a study of 463 schizophrenics who received either a phenothiazine drug or an inactive placebo are shown in Figure 17.9 (Davis, 1978).

Antipsychotic drugs act by impeding the release of dopamine from presynaptic neurons and by blocking dopamine receptors at the synapse. (Remember from Chapters 3 and 16 that the symptoms of schizophrenia have been linked to excessive activity by the neurotransmitter dopamine at the synapse.) Antipsychotic drugs accomplish this blocking because their chemical structure is similar to that of dopamine.

As effective as the antipsychotic drugs are, they are sometimes accompanied by serious side effects. Some patients begin exhibiting symptoms similar to

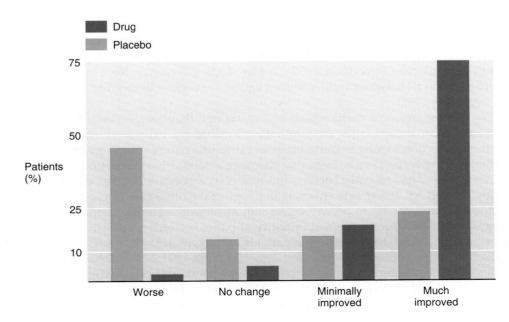

FIGURE 17.9
Results of an early study on the effectiveness of phenothiazine drugs in treating the symptoms of schizophrenia; 75% of patients who received the drug were much improved, whereas less than 25% of the patients who received the placebo were much improved.

those typical of Parkinson's disease: an extreme sensitivity to light, blurred vision, a dry mouth, peculiar posture, a shuffling gait, and tremors of the extremities. This makes sense when we realize that Parkinson's disease is thought to be caused by too little dopamine activity at the synapse (Miller & DeLong, 1988). Thus, when these antipsychotic drugs reduce dopamine concentrations, they eliminate symptoms of schizophrenia but activate those of Parkinson's disease.

Another serious side effect of these drugs is *tardive dyskinesia*, symptoms of which are teeth grinding, grimacing, and lip licking. Among patients receiving these drugs, 15 to 20% develop tardive dyskinesia (Bergen et al., 1989). To date there is no cure for this condition once it begins, so patients typically are given other drugs to combat these side effects.

The story of antipsychotic drugs, then, is one of great early success followed by some disappointment as their side effects appeared. The story of the next category of drugs is also one of success, but with a much lower incidence of subsequent side effect discoveries.

Antidepressant drugs.   There are three types of **antidepressant drugs:** (1) *tricyclics*, such as imipramine, marketed as Tofranil; (2) *monoamine oxidase inhibitors (MAOIs)*; and (3) *serotonin reuptake blockers*, of which fluoxetine, marketed as Prozac, is the first to be made available. All three work on brain chemicals, or neurotransmitters, that occur naturally in the brain (Chapter 3), but their effects occur in slightly different ways. The first two categories act to maintain the neurotransmitters serotonin and norepinephrine at the synaptic gap for a longer period of time, the tricyclics by blocking their reuptake, and the MAOIs by inhibiting an enzyme that inactivates those chemicals. The third and newest category selectively blocks the reuptake of serotonin alone, as its name implies (Figure 17.10).

The chemical actions of these drugs support the idea that lower levels of serotonin in the brain are responsible for depression. Although this may be part of the story, research has shown that it is more complex than that—the biology of depression can't be fully explained in terms of how much of a particular neurotransmitter is present at the synapse (Delgado et al., 1992).

How effective are antidepressant drugs? Early studies of antidepressants indicated that they relieved the symptoms of over one-half of depressed patients. However, many of the early studies were flawed: they didn't compare the improvement for those taking the drug with the improvement for those taking a placebo. Since a certain percentage of depressed people improve without any treatment at all, a placebo group must be included in any study testing the effectiveness of antidepressants. When this has been done, a number of studies have shown that about 65% of patients improve on antidepressants compared with 30% on a placebo (Goodwin, 1992). A few studies, however, have reported no difference at all between antidepressant and placebo groups (Brughta et al., 1992; Greenberg, 1992).

Antidepressants do have side effects, though they are generally less problematic than those of the antipsychotics. MAOIs are usually avoided unless other drugs don't work, because they can cause side effects such as hypertension if taken with certain foods, including cheese or alcohol. Fluoxetine, first available in the 1980s, has recently become the first choice because it takes effect more quickly and has fewer side effects than drugs in the other two categories. Some studies found reason to prescribe and monitor it with caution, claiming that it causes suicidal urges in a small minority of patients (Teicher et al., 1991). However, other studies have found that patients run no greater risk of suicide on Fluoxetine than on other antidepressant drugs (Hoover, 1991; Mann & Kapur, 1991).

Different people respond better to one or another of these drugs, depending on their own complex physiological makeup. The important thing is that they do work for many people. An example of a particularly successful use of

FIGURE 17.10

Serotonin reuptake blockers, such as fluoxetine, prevent serotonin from being taken back into the presynaptic neuron. This decreases depression by increasing the effective concentration of serotonin at the synapse.

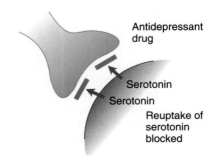

Antidepressant drug

Serotonin

Serotonin

Reuptake of serotonin blocked

drugs to treat depression is illustrated in the following case study of a man suffering from moderate levels of depression.

> Derek had probably suffered from depression all of his adult life but was unaware of it for many years. . . . Derek called himself a night person even though he was often awake by 4:00 A.M. He tried to schedule his work as editorial writer for a small-town newspaper so that it was compatible with his depressed mood at the beginning of the day. Therefore, he scheduled meetings for the mornings; talking with people got him moving. He saved writing and decision making for later in the day. . . .
>
> He often failed to answer people when they spoke to him. Sometimes they were surprised to hear his slow, soft-spoken reply 20 or 30 seconds later. . . . Derek's private thoughts were rarely cheerful and self-confident. He felt that his marriage was a mere business partnership. He provided the money, and she provided a home and children. Derek and his wife rarely expressed affection for each other. Occasionally, he had images of his own violent death in a bicycle crash, in a plane crash, or in a murder by an unidentified assailant.
>
> Derek might have continued living his battleship-gray life had it not been for a course called "The Use and Abuse of Psychoactive Drugs" at a local college. When the professor listed the symptoms of affective disorders on the blackboard, Derek had a flash of recognition. Perhaps he suffered from depression with melancholia. (Depression with melancholia is a type of major depression in which the person is incapable of feeling pleasure, awakens early, and feels worst in the morning.)
>
> Derek then consulted with a psychiatrist, who confirmed his suspicion and prescribed imipramine. A week later, Derek was sleeping until his alarm went off. Two weeks later, at 9:00 A.M. he was writing his column and making difficult decisions about editorials on sensitive topics. Writing was more fun than it had been in years. His images of his own violent death disappeared. His wife found him more responsive. He conversed with her enthusiastically and answered her questions without the long delays that had so tried her patience. (Adapted from Lickey & Gordon, 1983, pp. 168–170)

Not everyone responds as dramatically as Derek, and antidepressant drugs are not necessarily a substitute for other types of therapy for depression. They may, however, enable clients to make far better use of psychodynamic or cognitive therapies, for instance, by relieving the worst of the symptoms.

A drug for bipolar disorder.   In Chapter 16 we saw that bipolar disorder, formerly called manic-depressive disorder, is a relatively rare combination of depression alternating with periods of frenzied activity. The major drug for treating bipolar disorder is *lithium carbonate*, a naturally occurring salt. The story of the discovery of **lithium** as a treatment for bipolar disorder is set in Australia in the 1950s. Psychiatrist John Cade had a hypothesis that uric acid could control excitable behavior in manic patients. To test this hypothesis, he injected guinea pigs with the compound lithium urate and found that they indeed became calm. However, further testing showed it was the lithium—used to dissolve the uric acid—that had the calming effect!

Lithium has so many effects on the human organism that we still don't know *why* it works on bipolar disorder. But it has since been the standard treatment, boasting a success rate of about 70 to 80% (Black et al., 1988). Its dosage has to be monitored carefully to prevent lithium poisoning, which affects the brain and can lead to convulsions, coma, and death. Thus, patients on lithium therapy have the concentration of lithium in their blood checked frequently to prevent an overdose. The following description of the case of Anna illustrates lithium's beneficial effect:

Anna experienced three weeks of mild depression during her sophomore year in college. A few months later she became very hyperactive and increasingly upset, acting very unlike her usual sedate self and getting into conflicts with her parents over a variety of issues. She eventually reached a point at which her behavior was quite bizarre, exhibiting rapid speech, a constant flight of ideas, rhyming, punning, and outbursts of anger and physical aggressiveness. She was hospitalized and improved enough to return to school, but she then became depressed and withdrew from school again. When she was readmitted to the hospital her behavior was extremely manic. She talked and moved incessantly, her verbal production too rapid to be recorded in detail. Her thought content was grandiose, paranoid, angry, threatening, and filled with sexual themes.

When Anna was placed on lithium carbonate therapy for the first time, her manic behavior decreased greatly. When the lithium was withdrawn, this behavior returned. She was placed on a daily dose of lithium carbonate and discharged from the hospital. She returned to college, graduated, and had no recurrence of mania or depression over a two-and-a-half-year period following her discharge. (Adapted from Bunney et al., 1968)

Although benefits such as those experienced by Anna are common, recent research has questioned the long-term efficacy of lithium, based on findings of a relapse rate of 40% within 20 months (Harrow et al., 1990). Nonetheless, lithium is still the drug of choice for treating bipolar disorder.

Antianxiety drugs. Also called minor tranquilizers, **antianxiety drugs** are the most widely prescribed drugs in the United States. Drugs such as Valium, Librium, and Xanax, from the benzodiazepine family, act at the synapse to reduce overall nerve firing (Hayward, Wardle, & Higgitt, 1989). These drugs are prescribed for people suffering the symptoms of anxiety disorders as well as for those who are simply overly nervous or tense.

Taken in normally prescribed doses, drugs like Valium and Xanax may have undesirable side effects such as drowsiness, lightheadedness, and digestive problems for certain susceptible people. More serious problems occur if continued usage leads to tolerance, so that the person has to take more and more of the drug to achieve the same level of relief. Unfortunately this tolerance, which can show up within as little as several months, is accompanied by physical dependence (Baldessarini & Cole, 1988). At that point, the person must gradually discontinue use of the drug—a process that is complicated, however, by withdrawal symptoms that include the original symptom of anxiety. Buspar, a recently introduced drug in this category, has fewer side effects and is less likely to create dependence (Gorman & Davis, 1989).

In the 1960s and 1970s, Valium in particular was very widely prescribed, for a broad range of complaints including everyday stress and nervousness; after much negative publicity and criticism concerning overprescription, its use has decreased (Lickey & Gordon, 1983). Patients complaining of milder levels of anxiety today are more likely to receive counseling regarding changes in diet, exercise, and other lifestyle patterns than a long-term prescription.

Our survey of drug therapy indicates that it is often effective, but not always. In cases of severe depression that respond to neither drug treatment nor psychotherapy, a technique called *electroconvulsive therapy* is sometimes used.

Electroconvulsive Therapy

Electroconvulsive therapy (ECT) employs electric shock to produce a seizure in the cerebral cortex of the brain. ECT should be used as a last resort only, to treat severe depression when drugs and psychotherapy have been ineffective—especially when suicide seems likely. Treatment is simple but dramatic. The pa-

5   CONSCIOUSNESS

tient is sedated, and then a 150-volt current is passed through the patient's head for a fraction of a second. During the resultant brief seizure, the patient usually loses consciousness and about a minute later goes into convulsions. (Before muscle relaxant drugs became available, these convulsions could be strong enough to cause broken bones!) ECT is typically given in a series of 4 to 12 sessions, on an inpatient basis for safety and observation (Sackeim et al., 1987).

This treatment has long been controversial, and there has been considerable debate over how or even whether ECT works. Its side effects are disorientation—which usually subsides shortly after treatment—and some memory loss—which may persist for hours. In some cases, memory impairment can extend for months or longer (Breggin, 1979; Squire, Slater, & Chase, 1975). In addition to worrying about the side effects, many people recoil at the idea of passing an electric current through the brain—and at the convulsions caused by this treatment. Nevertheless, ECT is still widely used because of its purported effectiveness in alleviating depressive symptoms and preventing suicide (Sackeim, 1985).

Our consideration of biomedical therapies has demonstrated how they have helped people with serious psychological disorders lead productive lives. At the same time we have seen that, though a particular drug may effectively treat certain symptoms in one person, it may be ineffective in treating similar symptoms in another person. Although the effectiveness of drug therapy will almost certainly improve as we learn more about the biochemistry of psychological disorders, it is important to realize that psychologically based therapy, used either alone or in conjunction with drug therapy, may often be the treatment of choice for many psychological disorders.

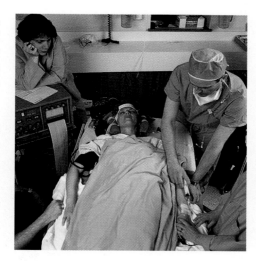

Although many people view electroconvulsive therapy negatively, it is still widely used for the treatment of severe depression.

Issues in Therapy

Having explored a number of different psychological and biological approaches to therapy, we can now consider some issues that cut across both. The first is the trend toward eclecticism—using different therapeutic approaches in conjunction. Second is the question of whether therapy actually accomplishes what it claims to do—effectively treat psychological disorders. The last issue is the way society has dealt with a problem that has important implications both for the individuals affected and for society as a whole—the problem of treating people whose disorders are so serious that institutionalization is required.

The Trend Toward Eclecticism

In our survey of therapies we have noted significant differences in both the underlying philosophies and the therapeutic methods of various types of treatment for psychological disorders. Despite this variety of assumptions and methods, recent years have seen a trend among therapists toward **eclecticism**—using several types of treatment, either together or in succession. What does it mean to be an eclectic therapist? In some cases it means that the therapist selects a method that he or she believes most closely fits a particular client's problem. In other cases it means that the therapist uses principles and techniques from a number of different approaches with the same client (Wolfe & Goldfried, 1988). For example, a therapist might use behavioral techniques to help a person eliminate a dysfunctional behavior such as sexual deviance, yet also use psychodynamic techniques to give the person some insight into why that behavior developed (Arkowitz & Messer, 1984; Wachtel, 1988). Similarly, therapists may treat depression by combining cognitive therapy with a biomedical treatment such as an antidepressant drug.

We can see why an eclectic approach might be valuable by comparing it with the levels of analysis approach taken in this text in general. If it makes sense to use several levels of analysis to achieve a more complete understanding of behavior—whether normal or abnormal—then it is plausible that therapists might achieve a better outcome by treating a client's problem in a number of ways, on a number of levels. Increasingly, too, therapists see many disorders as involving the family and social context surrounding the behavior—not just the patient in isolation.

The trend toward eclectic treatment is evident in surveys of practicing therapists. When asked to describe their approach, 31 to 58% of therapists responding to various surveys have called themselves eclectic. The approach named most often after that was psychodynamic, at 12 to 30%—then the cognitive, client-centered, and behavioral approaches (Norcross & Prochaska, 1982a, 1982b; Sammons & Gravitz, 1990; Smith, 1982).

How Effective Is Psychotherapy?

In 1952 Hans Eysenck published a paper called "The Effects of Psychotherapy: An Evaluation" that sent shock waves through the therapeutic community. Eysenck compared three groups of people: (1) those who were being treated by psychotherapy; (2) those who were on a waiting list to receive therapy; and (3) those who received no therapy at all. He found that all three groups showed improvement, and that the therapy group did no better than the others. Eysenck and others interpreted these results as showing that psychotherapy was of little use. Although not everyone accepted Eysenck's methods or conclusions as valid, his study triggered many additional investigations calculated to answer the question "Is psychotherapy effective?"

A more recent survey by Mary Lee Smith, Gene Glass, and Thomas Miller (1980) made use of a statistical technique called *meta-analysis* to combine the results of 475 studies of psychotherapy's effectiveness. (See Measurement & Methodology, "Meta-Analysis.") They concluded that psychotherapy was in fact effective, and that people who had been treated were better off than 80% of those who had similar problems but had gone untreated. Other studies have come to the same conclusion (Andrews & Harvey, 1981; Landman & Dawes, 1982).

As we have seen, however, psychotherapy comes in many forms. Is there a difference in the effectiveness of different kinds of therapies? When Smith and her co-workers considered this question, they found that the different types of therapy were essentially similar in effectiveness. Some studies suggest, however, that behavior therapy and cognitive therapy may be slightly superior for certain kinds of problems (Lambert et al., 1986). For example, behavior therapy is well suited for treating schizophrenia and the phobias, whereas cognitive therapies do well in treating depression.

The fact that the different types of therapy are similarly effective may seem surprising, because of the large differences in both theoretical bases and methods used in the therapy sessions. However, the different therapies do have some features in common. For example, clients generally enter any type of therapy *expecting* improvement, and as we saw in Chapter 13, on stress and health, simply maintaining a positive attitude can have a healing effect.

13   STRESS & HEALTH

Another thing different therapies have in common is that therapists from different schools all offer support, reassurance, suggestions, attention, and credibility. Since a number of studies have shown that these therapist qualities are among the variables associated with positive outcomes in therapy (Orlinsky & Howard, 1986), the similarity in effectiveness of the different kinds of therapy becomes less surprising.

We can find a possible explanation for this latter commonality among different therapies by noting that when therapists of all persuasions were asked to name the most influential *therapist*, Carl Rogers was ranked highest (Albert Ellis and Sigmund Freud were second and third), even though only a small minority call themselves client-centered therapists (Smith, 1982). Rogers's large influence is most likely due to the fact that all types of therapists have accepted his emphasis on the importance of empathy and of establishing a good client/therapist relationship. Thus, even behavior therapists, whose therapy methods have been described as "technical" and "mechanical," are often perceived by their clients as being warm and empathetic (Emmelkamp & van der Hout, 1983; Esse & Wilkins, 1978). It appears that qualities of the therapist may be as important for the outcome of therapy as the specific type of therapy used.

The idea that the success of therapy depends at least as much on the qualities of the therapist as on the specific therapeutic technique has been supported by a number of studies (Lambert, 1989). A dramatic example of how individual therapists can affect the outcome of therapy is found in a study that looked at how extremely disturbed adolescent boys who were undergoing therapy in a child guidance center turned out as adults (Ricks, 1974). These boys were treated by one of two therapists: therapist A, who had a high success rate and was called "supershrink" by one of the boys, and therapist B, who had a lower success rate. The differences between these two therapists show up most dramatically in the percentage of their patients who became schizophrenic: 27% of supershrink's cases became schizophrenic as adults, compared with 84% of therapist B's cases.

What was the difference between the two therapists? Supershrink spent more time with his most disturbed cases, was firm and direct with parents, and

MEASUREMENT & METHODOLOGY

Meta-Analysis

How do researchers draw an overall conclusion from the results of many different studies that have investigated the same question? This was the problem facing Mary Lee Smith and her co-workers (1980) as they sifted through the results of 475 studies of psychotherapy's effectiveness. Fortunately, a statistical technique called **meta-analysis** (meaning "more comprehensive" analysis) made it possible to combine those results. The first step in a meta-analysis of the results of many studies is to use a set formula to determine the *effect size,* or degree of positive outcome, for the target variable in each study. If the target variable is, for example, the score on a test designed to measure a particular symptom, the formula looks like this:

$$ES = \frac{M_{therapy} - M_{control}}{SD}$$

where

ES   is the effect size;
$M_{therapy}$ is the mean score for the group that received the therapy;
$M_{control}$ is the mean score for the control group, which received no therapy; and
SD   is the standard deviation of all the scores, from both groups.

The scores, M, indicate what happened to the people during the study. For therapy designed to treat depression, the score would reflect the decrease in the level of depression; for therapy designed to treat anxiety, the score would reflect the decrease in the level of anxiety; and so on.

The standard deviation, SD, is a measure of variability; in other words, it records how consistently grouped the individual scores are in any given study. Remember from Chapter 2 that a large standard deviation number indicates a large amount of variability, or scatter, in the scores. The higher the number, therefore, the less consistent (and reliable) the scores. Look again at the formula. You can see that the effect size will be larger if there is a large difference in the means of the groups and if the standard deviation is small. And the larger the effect score, the more significant the result.

To combine the results of their 475 studies of psychotherapy's effectiveness, Smith, Glass, and Miller averaged the effect sizes of all the studies by adding all the effect sizes and dividing by the number of studies. This number, which is called the *average effect size,* indicates the average effectiveness of all the therapies taken together. Based on their calculations, these researchers concluded that therapy is generally effective. By carrying out similar calculations for each individual type of therapy, they concluded that there is little difference between the different types of therapy in terms of effectiveness.

helped support his boys' ability to deal with situations in everyday life. In contrast, the other therapist pushed his boys too rapidly into dealing with deep material they were not prepared to handle. Other studies have also demonstrated large differences in therapist effectiveness, even when all the therapists use the same methods (Luborsky et al., 1985; also see Orlinsky & Howard, 1980).

One other variable also matters. Some research has shown that qualities of the client are important in determining the outcome of therapy. Patients who are more open to having a meaningful relationship with the therapist are more likely to get something out of therapy than patients who are not open to such a relationship (Strupp, 1980a, 1980b).

The Issue of Institutionalization

Although mental illness was once nearly synonymous with "being in an institution," today therapy for psychological disorders takes place in many settings. People may visit therapists in private offices, in clinics or schools, or even in the workplace when employers make these professionals available. Most people who visit therapists in such settings live at home, are employed, have friends and family, and function well in many areas of their lives. Only those whose psychological disorders disable them to the point at which they can no longer function in society become inpatients in institutions.

The history of mental institutions in the United States reveals some dramatic shifts in the way society has responded to the problem of severe disorders. In 1830 there were only four public mental hospitals, housing a total of fewer than 200 patients. Most people with disabling mental conditions lived with their families, ended up in jail, or became beggars who lived in "poorhouses." However, as mentally ill persons became more concentrated in America's expanding cities, a movement to build public mental hospitals for them grew. Beginning in the 1840s, many state mental hospitals were established, and by 1880 there were 75 public mental hospitals housing 36,780 patients. These mental institutions (or insane asylums, as they were popularly called) were usually built on large country estates, far from cities. These country locations were championed by some as being therapeutic, suggesting that peace and quiet were thought to be curative.

But the idealistic vision of mental hospitals as refuges from the city, where patients could benefit from walking about pleasant grounds, was doomed to failure. A rapid rise in the number of patients soon turned these hospitals into overcrowded warehouses providing little more than custodial care. To make matters worse, beginning in the 1880s the population in the hospitals skyrocketed, reaching over 150,000 by 1904 and continuing its upward course well into the 20th century (Torrey, 1988).

Then a striking reversal occurred. Figure 17.11, which documents the rapid rise in admissions that began in 1880, looks much like a very steep roller coaster, with hospital population steadily climbing to a peak in 1955, then crashing downward at a rapid rate: 80% of the beds in mental hospitals were eliminated between 1955 and 1984 (Torrey, 1988).

Why this sudden plunge in the number of people institutionalized with mental disorders? One reason was the appearance in 1961 of a congressional report that was highly critical of the mental health system in the United States (U.S. Congress, Joint Commission on Mental Illness and Health, 1961). The report cited the deplorable conditions in public mental hospitals, in which patients often lived under dehumanizing conditions. The commission's solution to this problem was to recommend integrating mental hospital patients into the community—a goal that, on paper, looked promising. The proposed program, which was called **deinstitutionalization,** involved placing patients in jobs and housing within the community while supporting them with a network of community mental health facilities that would provide counseling and monitor their drug therapies.

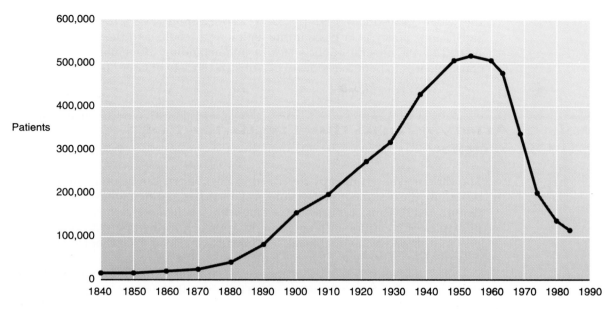

FIGURE 17.11
The number of patients in mental hospitals between 1840 and 1984. The availability of antipsychotic drugs and deinstitutionalization led to a large decrease in the number of patients in mental hospitals, beginning in the 1960s.

This plan would not have been conceivable had antipsychotic drugs not become available starting in 1955. These drugs made it possible to control the symptoms of many patients formerly exhibiting bizarre behavior, thereby qualifying them for release. Unfortunately, the plan to provide adequate care for these patients in the community was never realized. E. Fuller Torrey, a leading researcher on schizophrenia, put it this way:

> The seriously mentally ill were dumped out of mental hospitals into communities with few facilities and little aftercare. And as soon as they were gone, the hospitals were closed down so that they could not return. Rather than deinstitutionalization, which implied that alternative community facilities would be provided, what took place was simply depopulation of the state hospitals (1988, p. 4).

In short, people with severe disorders, unaccustomed to living independently, were returned to their communities and left to fend for themselves.

One result of the failure to provide adequate community-based services is that many patients do not take their prescribed drugs and therefore begin experiencing their symptoms again soon after discharge. If their symptoms get bad enough, they might be admitted to a hospital for a short stay until they "stabilize," then released again, only to discontinue taking their medications once more. Thus, a "revolving door" has been established that keeps hospital admissions high even though the number of long-term inpatients stays low.

Another result of deinstitutionalization without adequate community support has been a large increase in the number of persons with severe psychological disorders living in the streets. It has been estimated that perhaps one-third of the approximately 2 million homeless people in the United States are severely mentally ill (Greenblatt, 1992; Rossi, 1990; Torrey, 1988).

We seem to have come full circle from the situation of the early 1800s, prior to the advent of mental institutions. Once again, these unfortunate people are adrift in our communities, especially in urban areas.

What can be done to solve the problem of the severely mentally ill? As is the case for most large-scale problems, solutions are not easy. Among the ideas that have been proposed are making shelter more available for the homeless in general, establishing (and funding) better community mental health systems, and devising better ways of ensuring that those who need drugs receive them. But how, exactly, can these goals be accomplished? It is the difficulty of achieving these goals, perhaps, that has led some to recommend reinstitutionalization: "the return of the seriously mentally ill to the hospitals and clinics from which

Almost one-third of the homeless people in the United States are severely mentally ill.

they came" (Greenblatt, 1992, pp. 53–54; also see Shore & Cohen, 1992). As yet no satisfactory policy is in place in the nation as a whole, and the situation is not helped by the general public's lack of understanding of mental illness and its consequences to both the afflicted persons and society at large.

Reprise: Levels of Analysis and the Treatment of Psychological Disorders

The various types of therapy described in this chapter can be understood as approaching the treatment of psychological disorders at different levels of analysis (Figure 17.12). Thus, it is easy to see that behavior therapies, which are based on principles of conditioning, represent an approach to therapy that looks at the person from the behavioral level. It is equally clear that drug therapy and electroconvulsive therapy work at the biological level of analysis.

The therapies listed under the cognitive level differ from one another in several ways, but they have one thing in common: their goal is to provide people with *insight*. It is precisely that emphasis on a thought process that groups these very different kinds of therapy in the "Cognitive" column.

Freud's psychoanalytic approach, listed under "Cognitive," might also go under "Biological," because of the great weight he gave to instinctual drives. When Freud described the oral, anal, and phallic stages of psychosexual development (Chapter 15), he was envisioning biologically programmed behaviors that play an important role in determining a person's personality. It was this biological model that influenced Freud to focus his therapeutic system on his patients' early childhood experiences. However, in practice Freud's "talking cure" worked at the cognitive level.

Finally, moving to the contextual level of analysis, effective therapy often must take into account people's environments, including their family dynamics,

LEVELS OF ANALYSIS

FIGURE 17.12
Levels of analysis applied to treatment of psychological disorders

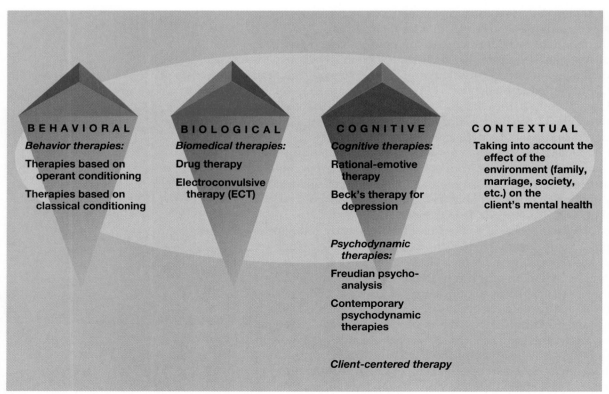

BEHAVIORAL

Behavior therapies:

Therapies based on operant conditioning

Therapies based on classical conditioning

BIOLOGICAL

Biomedical therapies:

Drug therapy

Electroconvulsive therapy (ECT)

COGNITIVE

Cognitive therapies:

Rational-emotive therapy

Beck's therapy for depression

Psychodynamic therapies:

Freudian psycho-analysis

Contemporary psychodynamic therapies

Client-centered therapy

CONTEXTUAL

Taking into account the effect of the environment (family, marriage, society, etc.) on the client's mental health

socioeconomic status, and neighborhood characteristics. Some types of therapy focus directly on contextual factors: family therapy, for instance, takes into account the nature of interactions among all the members of a family, frequently having them meet together for therapy sessions. (Remember from our discussion of schizophrenia in Chapter 16 that the emotional climate in the patient's family may determine whether she or he must be hospitalized or can be treated while living at home.) In the Follow-Through for this chapter we will examine another issue involving the contextual level: how cultural factors can affect interactions between clients and therapists.

Of course, the distinctions we have just drawn are not always so clear-cut in practice. The interaction among levels of analysis as a way of understanding behavior is mirrored in the growing eclecticism of practicing therapists. Though this complexity may seem frustrating, it is an advance over earlier, more simplistic views of psychological disorders and their treatment. When people believed that bizarre behavior was the work of demons, it was perhaps easier to confidently prescribe the appropriate "treatment," regardless of the exact nature of the problem. Our pronouncements today may be less certain and less simple, but in part that is because looking at behavior from multiple perspectives has given us a greater appreciation of the enormous complexity of human beings, their behavior, and their pain.

Cultural Issues in Therapy

In reading about different types of therapy, you may have noticed that the principal theorists discussed have represented white, Western culture. In fact the development of therapy, beginning with Freud, reflects Western values and behavioral norms.

What do these cultural roots of therapy mean for someone who comes from a culturally different background? According to Derald Wing Sue and David Sue (1990), authors of *Counseling the Culturally Different*, most therapists may ignore important characteristics of people from other cultures and therefore may not provide them with the service they need. Evidence that the dominant forms of therapy may not be meeting the needs of cultural minorities is provided by the dropout rates of these clients. Fewer than 30% of white clients terminate therapy after one contact, but over 50% of minority clients do (Sue & Sue, 1990).

Why is the dropout rate of minorities so high? Some of the resistance to therapy can perhaps be traced to cultural values such as those held by many Asians, who feel that having a psychological problem shames their family (Goleman, 1989). However, a more significant factor may be that most therapists have been insufficiently sensitive to the distinctive needs and values of culturally different clients, or to the special issues that arise in cross-cultural counseling.

We can appreciate a basic problem that may exist for many minority clients by imagining how a white, middle-class therapist would strike such a client on first meeting. As we have seen, an honest and trusting relationship is central to almost all forms of therapy. Yet a minority client may approach the therapist with the following kinds of thoughts: "What makes you any different from all the whites out there who have oppressed me?" "Before I open up to you, I want to know where you are coming from." and "Can you really understand what it is like to be Asian, Black, Hispanic, or any other race?" (Sue, 1990, p. 430). Imagine a client with these questions in mind being asked to do almost all of the talking and to reveal highly personal thoughts, feelings, and experiences while the therapist silently watches and listens. It may be, suggests Sue, that this client will resist disclosing anything of value until the therapist self-discloses first.

In addition to this basic problem of mistrust, the most well-meaning therapist may simply not understand the values and practices of other cultures. We have seen that therapists are often like detectives or puzzle solvers, having to infer the client's patterns and interpret his or her words to create a meaningful pattern. Without a good knowledge of the client's culture, the therapist may misinterpret hesitations, body language, and statements by referring to the norms of the majority culture. Consider, for example, the following potential sources of poor communication and misunderstanding in cross-cultural therapy.

Different Perceptions of "Openness"

Therapists generally expect clients to be open and to talk freely about their feelings and experiences. A client who does not self-disclose may be considered uncooperative, resistant, or "repressed." However, Japanese people tend to show respect by being silent.

Hispanic and Asian-American cultures associate wisdom and maturity with an ability to control feelings. Thus, being open about thoughts and feelings—especially with a therapist, who is a stranger—is not something that a person from such a background feels comfortable doing. An insensitivity to this fact can damage the relationship between counselor and client. Consider, for example, the following exchange between an Asian-American client and a white counselor:

> *Client:* It's hard for me to talk about these issues. My parents and friends . . . they wouldn't understand . . . if they ever found out I was coming here for help . . .
>
> *Counselor:* I sense it's difficult to talk about personal things. How are you feeling right now?
>
> *Client:* Oh, all right.
>
> *Counselor:* That's not a feeling. Sit back and get in touch with your feelings. [*Pause*] Now tell me, how are you feeling right now?
>
> *Client:* Somewhat nervous.
>
> *Counselor:* When you talked about your parents' and friends' not understanding and the way you said it made me think you felt ashamed and disgraced at having to come. Was that what you felt? (Sue & Sue, 1990, p. 88).

In this exchange the therapist keeps returning to the client's feelings, thereby demonstrating ignorance of or insensitivity to the fact that many Asian Americans do not share his assumption that "openness" is essential to therapy. The result is that the client becomes increasingly nervous as the session progresses.

Different Values Regarding "Insight"

One of the major goals of many "talk" therapies is for clients to achieve insight into themselves and their problems. However, this kind of self-knowledge is not valued in every culture. Attaining insight may seem irrelevant to an African-American single mother who is struggling to pay the rent or put food on the table. In another culture, insight may even be seen as harmful. For example, a troubled Chinese woman would be likely to receive the following advice from an elder in her culture about solving a psychological problem: "Avoid morbid thoughts," "Don't think about it," or "Think of your family." Often, therefore, a culturally different client is seeking not insight but concrete advice about handling practical problems. A cognitive or behavioral approach on the part of the therapist might be a greater service in such instances.

Different Concepts of the Self in Relation to Others

In Chapter 15 we distinguished between independent and interdependent views of the self, stressing that the U.S. culture values independence and the ability to succeed on one's own. A great deal of professional and popular writing on "good" adjustment and successful living reflects this cultural value, and many therapists

Different cultural views regarding the relationship of the self to others may require different approaches to therapy.

may take it for granted that their clientele share it. But in most Asian and Hispanic cultures, people share an interdependent view of the self—they see themselves in the context of their connections with family, friends, and their larger culture and history. Thus, if a Hispanic client says he can't decide about something without talking with his family, he is simply acting in accordance with his view of himself as inseparable from his social context. The insensitive majority-culture therapist might interpret such behavior as indicative of a pathological dependency.

Differences in Communicative Style

In recent years scholars who study interpersonal communication have described a number of cultural differences in communicative style. In Asian culture, for example, subtlety and indirectness are highly prized communicative skills. The direct and confrontive techniques employed by rational-emotive and some other therapists might therefore be perceived by an Asian-American client as

disrespectful, insensitive, or rude. Another communicative style clash involves how people perceive and use personal space. Hispanics, African Americans, Arabs, and the French, among others, stand closer together and touch each other more often during conversation than do most white Americans. Hence, when a Mexican-American client moves her chair closer to her therapist or touches him while making a point and the therapist leans away, she might see him as being distant and uncaring.

The examples cited here illustrate just some of the potential problems in cross-cultural therapy. More subtle problems can arise when the therapist is overly concerned about cultural differences—as when a white therapist avoids discussing the contribution of racism to an African-American client's problems for fear of seeming to be harping on the topic (Oltmanns, Neale, & Davison, 1986, pp. 45–47). Sue and Sue (1990) have suggested that the first place to tackle cross-cultural problems in therapy is in training programs for mental health professionals, and in fact many states already require this training before granting a license to practice therapy.

The American men shown on the left face outward as they relate to one another. In contrast, the Bedoins illustrate the touching and physical closeness that occurs during conversations in their culture.

How Therapy Evolved

- Early treatments for psychological disorders were often based on the assumption that afflicted persons harbored evil spirits. These treatments frequently were painful, harmful, or even fatal.

- The first mental hospitals were often inhumane places primarily designed to isolate the mentally ill. A few enlightened physicians, such as Philippe Pinel, argued that "lunatics" actually suffered from illnesses and should be treated as patients—but this idea did not become widespread until the 19th century.

- Modern treatments can be traced to nineteenth-century European applications of hypnosis to the treatment of mental problems. In Vienna the young Sigmund Freud, who was convinced that physical symptoms had a psychological meaning, used hypnosis and other techniques to gain access to the "unconscious" of his patients with nervous disorders. Through conversations with his colleague Josef Breuer about the latter's patient "Anna O.," Freud deduced many of his early ideas about psychoanalysis, which changed the course of psychological treatment.

- The goal of contemporary therapy is to change a person's maladaptive behaviors, feelings, or thoughts. The many different therapies attain this goal by focusing on different aspects of a person. Freudian (psychodynamic) therapy emphasizes early experiences and clients' conscious and unconscious thoughts about those experiences. Client-centered therapy aims to reconcile people to their authentic selves. Cognitive therapies focus more directly on the person's current problematic thought patterns. Behavior therapies attempt to modify behavior directly, and biomedical therapies stress the role of physiological mechanisms in their diagnosis and treatment.

- Several categories of professionals deliver psychological health services; they include clinical psychologists, psychiatrists, psychiatric social workers, psychiatric nurses, and counselors.

Psychodynamic Therapies

- The goal of Freudian psychoanalysis is to help patients gain insight into the repressed childhood wishes and conflicts that have caused their symptoms. To reveal repressed material, the analyst uses such techniques as free association and dream analysis. The patient is encouraged to obey the fundamental rule of psychoanalysis: to reveal whatever comes to mind, no mater how shocking or seemingly trivial. His or her transference to the analyst and resistance to certain interpretations or topics also provide information about unconscious contents.

- Contemporary psychodynamic therapies differ from Freud's in several ways: (1) they require fewer sessions; (2) they are less concerned with the unconscious, with childhood experience, and with sexual development; and (3) the therapist takes a more active role in therapy and may relate to the client in a warmer fashion.

- Art therapy has been used to supplement verbal communication with the therapist—especially in cases of sexual abuse, which children have particular trouble talking about. Interpreting such drawings is difficult, however, and must always be done in conjunction with other information about the client.

Client-Centered Therapies

- Client-centered therapy as developed by Carl Rogers assumes that people have an innate ability to heal themselves. The therapy process is designed to free clients from a state of incongruence: conflict between their personal standards and actual feelings and behaviors. Therapists should, according to Rogers, maintain an attitude of genuineness, empathy, and unconditional positive regard, and they should interact with clients in a reflective and nondirective manner.

Cognitive Therapies

- The rationale behind cognitive therapy is that people's emotions and behavior are determined by their thoughts about their experiences. The goals of this therapy are to give people insight into their problematic thought patterns and to help them eliminate their problems by changing their thinking.

- Rational-emotive therapy, as developed by Albert Ellis, is based on the idea that psychological problems develop because of people's irrational beliefs. The therapist works to change those beliefs by confronting the client about them when they surface in conversation and by assigning homework that combats those beliefs.

- Aaron Beck's cognitive therapy is used for depression and for anxiety disorders; it assumes that psychological disorders are caused by a type of irrational thinking called cognitive distortions. The therapist works to make clients aware of their irrational thinking and to show them how to substitute more constructive thinking and behavior. In addition to work in the office, homework exercises are common.

Behavior Therapies

- Behavior therapies are often based on the principles of classical conditioning. In systematic desensitization, for example, the client learns to pair a relaxation response with an anxiety-provoking situation. In implosive therapy, the client repeatedly and vividly imagines such a situation until the anxiety response is extinguished. Flooding is similar, except that the client actually experiences the anxiety-producing situation rather than imagining it.

- Other behavior therapies are based on operant conditioning principles. In aversion therapy a behavior to be eliminated is paired with an aversive stimulus. Shaping and reinforcement have also been used to establish desirable behaviors. Token economies award tokens as secondary reinforcers in exchange for desirable behavior. Biofeedback training allows clients to control their physiological responses to avoid a negative stimulus.

Group Therapy

- Therapy practiced in small groups is less costly than individual therapy. The therapist may have a less prominent role than is typical in individual therapy: he or she may serve a facilitating role, encouraging group members to identify with and help one another.

- Some unique and advantageous characteristics of group therapy are the instillation of hope through the example of others, the recognition of the universality of problems, the opportunity to help others, the recapitulation of family issues through intergroup transference, the improvement of social interactions, and the development of group cohesiveness

Biomedical Therapies

- A common form of biomedical therapy is the use of drugs to alter physiological functioning. The principal types of drugs used to treat psychological disorders are (1) antipsychotics, (2) antidepressants, (3) lithium carbonate, and (4) antianxiety drugs.

- Another type of biomedical intervention is electroconvulsive therapy, in which an electric charge is passed through the brain to induce a brief seizure. This controversial procedure is used to treat severe depression, but only when drugs and psychotherapy have been ineffective.

Issues in Therapy

- Many contemporary therapists identify themselves as being eclectic in their approach—they use a variety of methods, either to address different aspects of a person's problem or to treat a wide variety of problems, some of which respond best to a particular approach.

- A number of studies have been designed to answer the question "Is psychotherapy effective?" Using the technique of meta-analysis, researchers have combined all those results and found that it is effective, but that there is little difference among the types of therapy in terms of effectiveness. One reason for this is that qualities of the therapist may be as important as the type of therapy used in determining the outcome of treatment. In addition, the client's attitude can be an important determinant of the success of any type of therapy.

- Therapy in institutional settings began to grow in the 1800s and burgeoned in the first decades of the 20th century. However, concern about these hospitals' overcrowded condi-

tions, coinciding with the discovery of antipsychotic drugs, prompted the deinstitutionalization of patients in the mid-1950s. Deinstitutionalization has brought new problems, however, including the large number of people with severe disorders who are homeless and the "revolving door" phenomenon.

Reprise: Levels of Analysis and the Treatment of Psychological Disorders

- The principal types of therapy can be seen as working at different levels of analysis. Behavior therapies work at the behavioral level, biomedical therapies at the biological level. Psychodynamic therapy, client-centered therapy, and cognitive therapy all work at the cognitive level, though psychodynamic therapy also has biological components. Contextual factors are emphasized in several therapies, including family therapy, and are often important in determining the success of any treatment.

Follow-Through/Diversity: Cultural Issues in Therapy

- Cultural differences between therapist and client can prevent the establishment of trust and can cause both parties to misinterpret the other's statements and actions. Therapists need specific training, therefore, to develop the sensitivity and flexibility needed to effectively serve members of other cultures.

Key Terms

antianxiety drugs	free association
antidepressant drugs	fundamental rule of
antipsychotic drugs	psychoanalysis
art therapy	group therapy
aversion therapy	implosive therapy
behavior therapy	incongruence
biofeedback training	lithium
biomedical therapy	meta-analysis
client-centered therapy	psychiatric nurses
clinical psychologists	psychiatric social workers
cognitive restructuring	psychiatrists
cognitive therapy	psychoanalysis
counselors	psychotherapy
deinstitutionalization	rational-emotive therapy
eclecticism	reflection
eclectroconvulsive therapy	resistance
(ECT)	token economy
flooding	transference

CHAPTER

18

What Is Social Cognition?

Person Perception: Forming Impressions of Others
Picking Up Cues: The Power of First Impressions
Paying Attention to Appearance
Schemas
The In-Group/Out-Group Dynamic

Attribution: Cognitions About Causes
Why Do We Make Attributions?
Types of Attributions
Kelley's Model of Attribution: Taking Consensus, Distinctiveness, and
    Consistency into Account
Attributional Errors and Biases

The Self: Knowing and Accepting Ourselves
Representing the Self
Self-Verification and Self-Handicapping

Attitudes: Evaluating Objects, Events, and People
What Are Attitudes?
When Do Attitudes Predict Behavior?
How Are Attitudes Acquired?
How and When Do Attitudes Change?

Interdisciplinary Dimension: Marketing
The Social Psychology of Advertising

**Reprise: Processing Information About Ourselves
and Others**

Follow-Through/Diversity
Prejudice and Racism

Social Cognition
and Attitudes

There is really no such creature as a single individual; he has no more life of his own than a cast-off cell marooned from the surface of your skin.

Lewis Thomas, The Lives of a Cell (1974)

What is the longest time you've been totally isolated from other people? Most of us find it difficult to remember any occasions when we were totally alone for more than a few hours. But even if you have experienced such a time, it is likely that you were still deeply connected to others. For example, a friend of mine recently spent a week camping by herself in the Maine woods. Although she was physically alone, she was very much preoccupied with people who were hundreds of miles away. Thoughts of a recently ended relationship, her friends, and her family accompanied her into the solitude of the woods. In fact, our social world is in some ways like the atmosphere around us, like the ocean is to a fish. It permeates our thoughts and our behavior so completely that it is difficult to imagine how we would act or what we would be thinking about if it were not for the other people in our lives.

Social psychology—the subject of this chapter and the next—is the part of psychology that tries to isolate and understand how this immersion in our social reality influences our behavior. In the words of Gordon Allport (1985), social psychology is "an attempt to understand and explain how the thought, feeling and behavior of individuals are influenced by the actual, imagined, or implied presence of others" (p. 3). Whereas in everyday life we often see other people's behavior as being a product of their personal traits and characteristics, social psychologists zero in on the ways in which behavior is influenced by the *situations* in which people find themselves. The key insight of social psychology is that we cannot fully understand why people behave the way they do without looking at how their social situation affects their thoughts, feelings, and actions.

When you consider how much of your behavior involves interactions with others—from crowds on the street to the people you work with to your family and close friends—you can appreciate the variety of social situations that occur during your day-to-day life as an individual and as a member of society. Here are just some of the questions that social psychologists have asked about these social situations:

- What circumstances affect whether two people are attracted to each other? For example, do we tend to be attracted to people who are very different from us, or who are very similar? Do we sometimes like people simply because they are nearby, or because they are familiar?
- Why would bystanders seeing a person suddenly become ill on the street fail to help that person? Under what circumstances would people be more likely to offer help to a stranger?
- Why are people sometimes aggressive? Does watching violence on television, for example, make children more aggressive?
- What determines whether people will go along with pressure to conform to the wishes of a group, comply with a friend's request for a favor, or obey an order from an authority figure?

Questions like these are concerned with *interpersonal* relations—that is, behavior directed toward others. We explore these and other issues in Chapter 19.

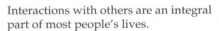
Interactions with others are an integral part of most people's lives.

But social psychology involves not only how we behave in interpersonal situations, but also the inner side of our social world—our thoughts and attitudes about ourselves and others. It is these *intrapersonal* processes that we address in this chapter on social cognition and attitudes. Thus we will be concerned with questions such as the following:

- How do we decide what other people are really like? What information do we use in forming our impressions of others, and how do we sometimes go wrong in making those judgments?
- Why is prejudice such a common feature of social life? What cognitive processes are involved in forming derogatory judgments about entire groups of people?
- When we observe others' behavior, how do we typically decide what causes them to act the way they do? In what ways do our judgments tend to be biased, and why?
- What thought processes typically occur as we form impressions of ourselves? How do our self-concepts affect the way we perceive other people and behave toward them? How much does the situation affect the self we present to others?
- How do we acquire our attitudes toward people, products, events, and issues? When others try to change our attitudes, what factors determine whether they will be successful?

As you might suspect from the nature of these questions, much of our attention in this chapter will be focused on the cognitive level of analysis, as we study the thought processes relevant to social behavior. Of course all social psychology, by definition, involves looking at behavior in its social context and therefore using the contextual level of analysis to understand behavior.

We begin our exploration of social psychology with the thought processes involved in processing and understanding our social world—what psychologists term *social cognition*.

What Is Social Cognition?

As Lynda approaches the restaurant, she wonders why she agreed to this blind date. Blind dates are, after all, for losers, and she has every expectation that it is a loser who at this very moment is waiting to meet her. She wonders vaguely whether it logically follows that she is a loser, too; but before she has a chance to ponder this possibility, she finds herself face to face with Roger. Disarmed by his shy smile and good looks, Lynda asks herself whether Roger is such a loser after all. As they talk over dinner she discovers he is a writer—he is excited about a short story that a magazine is considering for publication. Because he is a writer she begins to think that he must be intelligent, creative, and perhaps sensitive as well—all qualities Lynda associates with writers. She also notices that with a little encouragement Roger is quite a conversationalist, whose interests seem to include everything from baseball to ballet. Is he really so versatile, she wonders, or is he just trying to impress her?

It is almost time for dessert when Lynda realizes that Roger has been doing almost all of the talking. She begins to wonder whether he is naturally talkative or whether he might be a bit self-centered. Or perhaps she isn't doing enough to hold up her end of the conversation, and Roger is simply filling the vacuum. "He must think I'm dull," she frets to herself, and at the first opportunity she begins talking about her own projects and hobbies. After all, she wants Roger to know that she is a unique and interesting person, too.

As Lynda's experience with Roger illustrates, a relatively simple social situation—in this case meeting someone for the first time—can be accompanied by a great deal of cognitive activity. Social psychologists refer to this mental activity as **social cognition,** which is defined by Susan Fiske and Shelly Taylor (1991) as "how people make sense of other people and themselves" (p. 14) and by Robert Baron and Donn Byrne (1991) as "the process by which we notice, interpret, remember and use information about the social world" (p. 91).

If this last definition sounds familiar, it is because it describes the same processes discussed in Chapter 7, on memory, and Chapter 8, on thought and language. Those chapters introduced the information-processing approach, which is concerned with how people encode, store, manipulate, and retrieve information. Here we will focus specifically on the processing of *social* information: information about people, including ourselves.

What makes the study of social cognition fascinating and important is that the way we process social information can affect the accuracy of our social judgments as well as our subsequent behavior. Consider, for instance, how often people make instantaneous judgments about an individual based on nothing more than the person's age, gender, sexual orientation, attractiveness, ethnic identity, or affiliation with a certain religion or social group. For example, on seeing that Roger is good-looking, Lynda immediately decides that he isn't a loser after all. Whether positive or negative, such judgments are founded not on a real knowledge of the person but rather on a cognitive "shortcut" that frequently leads to inaccuracy ("He's so muscular; he must be dumb") and even to tragedy ("The only good _____ is a dead _____"—fill in the blanks).

How and why do we make such judgments? More generally, what processes underlie our cognitions about others and ourselves? To what extent do these processes incline us toward biases and errors in social judgments? These are the questions we will explore while discussing social cognition. We begin with the processes involved in person perception—that is, the cognitive influences at work when we form impressions of others. We will then look at how we arrive at our judgments of the causes of people's behavior, and finally at how we understand ourselves and present ourselves to others.

8 THINKING

Person Perception: Forming Impressions of Others

As Lynda begins to talk about herself, Roger's responses reinforce her feeling that he is intelligent and creative. He asks sharp questions about her sociology project, even though he has never had a course in the subject, and he even suggests an idea for offering students an incentive to complete the survey she is designing. He also has a nice way of hedging his suggestion, so that he defers politely to her own expertise. Lynda is surprised to learn, however, that Roger is a member of the campus ROTC and that he is thinking of a military career. To Lynda, that just doesn't seem to go with the other qualities she has been inferring. She'd never thought of ROTC "types" as literate, creative, and sensitive. Well, she thinks, maybe I'm just a bit prejudiced in that regard. I'll try to keep an open mind.

4 PERCEPTION

As Lynda continues to fill out her picture of Roger, she engages in a process very similar to the one we discussed in Chapter 4, on perception. That chapter introduced the idea that in perceiving the physical world we are like detectives who actively create an image based on many kinds of clues. But this detection process is not infallible; the way we go about making inferences about the world sometimes biases us toward perceptual errors.

Similarly, as we amass clues to form our *social* perceptions, we may arrive at a distorted image of social reality. One of the most immediate problems in evaluating social reality is determining what other people are like from the evidence presented to our senses. As the story of Lynda and Roger illustrates, we use many different types of clues to "deduce" the qualities of a person we are meeting for the first time. The nature of these clues, and the way we process them, is the concern of **person perception,** the study of how we form impressions of others.

Although our perception of people and of physical objects involves some of the same general processes, person perception is more complex, for at least three reasons. First, in forming impressions of others we try to "perceive" qualities that we cannot observe directly but must infer from their appearance and behavior. Whether or not Roger is "really" intelligent and sensitive, for example, is something Lynda tries to decide from observing his verbal and nonverbal behavior. Second, we see other people as *causal agents*—that is, as having motives and intentions that underlie their observed behavior. Consequently, in person perception we often invest substantial energy in trying to determine what those motives and intentions might be. Finally, we know that, unlike inanimate objects, persons can try to manipulate our impressions of them and even deceive us. For these reasons, the detective work involved in person perception is especially subtle and challenging.

As they have for the perception of objects, psychologists have been able to identify a number of processes—and errors—that influence our social detective work. We begin with a basic principle: Our impressions of other people are strongly influenced by the *first* information—or cues—that we take in about them.

Picking Up Cues: The Power of First Impressions

We look at a person and immediately a certain impression of his character forms itself in us. A glance, a few spoken words are sufficient to tell us a story about a highly complex matter. We know that such impressions form with remarkable rapidity and great ease. Subsequent observations may enrich or upset our first view, but we can no more prevent its rapid growth than we can avoid perceiving a given visual object or hearing a melody.

Solomon Asch (1946, p. 258)

According to Solomon Asch, simply seeing a person triggers a process that leads rapidly to an assessment of that person's character. In fact, when people are asked to rate the personality characteristics of strangers they have met only minutes before, they are able to make judgments about a number of the strangers' characteristics. Moreover, those judgments compare surprisingly well with the strangers' description of themselves. For example, a correlation of .41 has been reported between strangers' self-descriptions and the judgments of new acquaintances for the trait of extraversion, .53 for exhibitionism, and .44 for sociability (Albright, Kenny, & Malloy, 1988; Paunonen, 1989; Watson, 1989).

How do we infer the personal characteristics of people we have just met? We use *cues* based on attributes that are immediately apparent, such as talkativeness, grooming, smiling, gender, and general appearance. Of course, longer exposure allows us to become aware of additional cues and to refine our first impression (Paunonen, 1991). Thus, Lynda's initial assessment of Roger might be based on his appearance and his apparent friendliness; as she learns more about him—for example, that he writes short stories, talks a lot, and is in ROTC—she modifies her impression based on this new information.

This process sounds straightforward enough, but our description so far conceals an important fact: not all incoming information about a person counts equally as we form our impressions. In particular, our first impressions have an especially powerful influence on our perception of others, and they can color our

What impression do you have of this man and why do you have it? We usually try to figure out new acquaintances on the basis of easily observed characteristics.

perceptions of subsequent information. Consider, for example, what would have happened to Lynda's impression of Roger if he had told her about being in ROTC before talking about his writing and other interests. Given her picture of ROTC "types" as not particularly intelligent, creative, or sensitive, this information might well have colored her perception of his other disclosures (perhaps Roger is a different sort of writer from the kind she usually envisions). Yet Roger is the same person, no matter in what order he presents facts about himself.

Research confirms that we give more weight to the early information we absorb about others than to later information. Asch (1946) demonstrated this **primacy effect** by presenting subjects with one of the following descriptions of a hypothetical person:

intelligent, industrious, impulsive, critical, stubborn, envious

or

envious, stubborn, critical, impulsive, industrious, intelligent

These two lists contain the same traits, but one goes from positive to negative traits, the other from negative to positive. When Asch's subjects described this hypothetical person, the ones who read the description beginning with "intelligent" saw the person as being more happy, sociable, and humorous than the people who read the description beginning with "envious."

Subsequent research has confirmed Asch's conclusion that information presented first can bias our judgments (Burnstein & Schul, 1982; Kruglanski & Freund, 1983). For example, being exposed first to a description such as "intelligent" may lead us to interpret an adjective such as "critical" in a positive light ("Intelligent people often look at things with a critical eye"), whereas once a person has been described as "envious," we might interpret "critical" in a negative light ("Envious people are often unjustly critical of others").

The power of the cues we receive first about a person becomes particularly apparent when we consider the most obvious cue of all: physical appearance.

Paying Attention to Appearance

Bishop walked through my office door one day and said he wanted to work in my lab. Judging from the length of his beard I figured he was the kind of free spirit who would do well.

Dr. Harold Varmus, 1989 Nobel Laureate, describing his first meeting with Dr. Michael Bishop, fellow Nobel Laureate

Is this attractive woman also talented, intelligent, and interesting? Most people assume that people who are physically beautiful also possess other positive characteristics.

When meeting others for the first time, we pay particular attention to their appearance. In the case of Michael Bishop and Harold Varmus, who won the 1989 Nobel Price in physiology and medicine for their work on the causes of cancer, Varmus's positive reaction to Bishop's facial hair helped launch the collaboration of two future Nobel Prize winners.

As we will see in the next chapter, appearance is particularly important to people who are meeting a potential mate, as Lynda and Roger are. But physical appearance—especially a person's perceived attractiveness—plays a large role in all kinds of first impressions, and not simply because people appreciate good looks. Among college students, 90% believe that the face is an important guide to character (Liggett, 1974), and people in general feel that attractive people are happier, more intelligent, warmer, more poised, more sociable, more interesting, and have a better character than unattractive people (Berscheid & Walster, 1974; Cash & Janda, 1984; Feingold, 1989). In short, whether or not these qualities are *actually* associated with attractive people, people *believe* that they are, and therefore use attractiveness as a cue to predict them. In actuality, though attractive people do tend to have better-than-average social skills and to be more popular, they don't do any better on any of the other dimensions in which they are supposed to excel (Feingold, 1990). Attractiveness is thus a cognitive cue that can often lead to incorrect judgments.

Another example of such a cue is a "baby face" (large, round eyes and a short nose). Baby-faced adults are judged to be physically weaker and more submissive than other adults, but also more honest, warm, and kind (Berry & McArthur, 1986, 1988). Perhaps this is why violent criminals with those features, such as the 1930s gangster "Baby-Face" Nelson, are especially chilling—they violate our perceptual expectations.

Physical features aside, one way everyone can improve the first impression they make is to smile. No matter what their appearance, smiling causes others to see them as more attractive, sincere, sociable, and competent than people who don't smile (Reis et al., 1990). Once again, we see a perceptual rule of thumb at work that may or may not lead to accurate judgments. Have you ever felt "taken in" by someone who smiled a lot initially and then turned out to be a much less friendly person than you had assumed?

Schemas

So far we have been considering processes involved in inferring other people's specific traits on the basis of the cues we pick up. As we pick up these cues, another cognitive process comes into play—the activation of our social *schemas*.

We encountered the concept of schemas in Chapter 7, on memory. As you may recall, a schema is a cognitive structure that organizes our knowledge about specific categories of objects. The schemas at work in person perception contain information about the characteristics of people whom we perceive as members of a particular category. For example, our "politician" schema may consist of the information that politicians tend to be well dressed, outgoing, argumentative, power loving, and socially skilled (Anderson & Klatzky, 1987).

7   MEMORY

Once a schema has been formed, it can influence both what you perceive and what you remember. Thus, given your politician schema, simply identifying a new acquaintance as a politician can lead you to assign characteristics such as "outgoing" and "power loving" to that person. You may tend to notice and remember the acquaintance's behaviors that are consistent with your schema, while filtering out or forgetting information that doesn't fit your schema.

An example of how a "race" schema can affect how a person is perceived is provided by Birt Duncan (1976), who had white college students view a videotape of a discussion between two males, one white and one African American, that escalates into a heated argument and ends with one of them shoving the other. At that point in the interaction, the subjects were asked to judge what was going on during the shoving incident. One group of subjects viewed a tape in which the shover was African American, and the other saw a tape in which the shover was white.

The point of Duncan's procedure was to discover whether the white students would perceive the same incident differently depending on who was doing the shoving. The results showed clear differences in perception. When the shover was white, the subjects described his behavior as due more to the situation than to his personal characteristics and described the shoving as "dramatizing" or "playing around." In this condition fewer than one in five of the subjects labeled the shoving "violent." If, however, the shover was the African American, subjects tended to describe his behavior as due to his personality, and fully three-quarters of them labeled the shoving as "violent" (Figure 18.1). Apparently, the subjects' "black person" schema included "violent behavior", and that schema, when activated, influenced their perception of the shoving incident.

Schemas are important because they affect not only the way we think about

FIGURE 18.1
In Duncan's experiment, white subjects judged the violence of a shoving incident in which either a white person or a black person did the shoving.

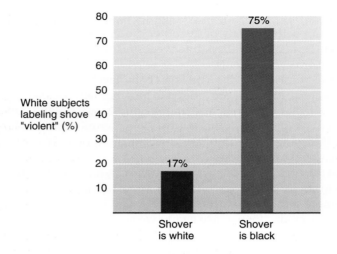

things but also how we behave. For example, someone whose "elderly person" schema includes the idea that the elderly are slow and unaware of what is going on around them might treat them in a condescending manner, perhaps even avoiding contact with them altogether. Interestingly enough, when people behave in this way, they may increase the chances that the other person will respond so as to confirm their schema. This is called a **self-fulfilling prophecy**—something happens because we expect it to happen.

To illustrate how self-fulfilling prophecies might work, let's consider an experiment designed by Mark Snyder and his co-workers (1977), in which male subjects had phone conversations with females they had never met. The women had been randomly designated as either attractive or unattractive by the experimenter, and this information was provided to the subjects. When talking to a female they thought was attractive, the subjects spoke with more warmth and were friendlier than when speaking with a female they thought was unattractive. This result, which is not surprising, was accompanied by another that isn't quite so predictable: the females who were labeled more attractive spoke to the males with more warmth and humor than the ones who were labeled as unattractive. Since these women had no idea what the males knew about them, their added warmth and humor must have occurred in response to the way the males related to them.

What might you conclude about attractive women if you were one of the males? You might come away feeling that they are warmer and more humorous than unattractive women—a result that, in fact, fits your schema for attractive women. Schemas therefore, in affecting how we relate to others, may even set in motion a process by which they confirm and thereby perpetuate themselves.

The importance of schemas becomes even more evident when we realize their relationship to stereotypes. **Stereotypes** are beliefs, shared by many people, that certain characteristics can be assigned to members of a group based solely on their group membership. The ideas that wealthy people are snobbish or that manual laborers drink beer and go bowling, for example, are stereotypes.

What is the relation between stereotypes and schemas? A stereotype is a schema about members of a group (Hamilton, 1979). Thus, some of the schemas we have been describing are also stereotypes. For example, the subjects in Duncan's experiment, who saw African Americans as more violent than whites, were being influenced by their stereotype of African Americans. Since stereotypes are usually negative and are often erroneous, especially when applied to a specific individual, they can work against forming good relationships between people in different groups. We will consider this effect of stereotyping in more detail when we discuss prejudice and racism in the Follow-Through at the end of this chapter. We will also return to schemas later in the chapter, when we look at how we apply them to ourselves.

The In-Group/Out-Group Dynamic

As the process of stereotyping illustrates, schemas can be activated when we identify a person as belonging to a specific group. Another related phenomenon, called the **in-group/out-group dynamic,** refers to our tendency to see people differently depending on whether they are members of our in-group (that is, any group we belong to). Not only do we tend to favor members of the in-group, but we tend to see members of the out-group (any group we don't belong to) differently in other ways. Whereas we may see in-group members as unique individuals with diverse qualities, we may see out-group members as being similar to one another.

Are all of these bare-chested, beer-drinking men alike? According to the in-group/out-group dynamic, we see other groups as homogeneous and our own group as consisting of unique individuals.

   In a study demonstrating this effect, Bernadette Park and Myron Rothbart (1982) asked people to estimate the percentage of males and the percentage of females who would subscribe to statements that were stereotypically male ("I often seek out competitive challenges—whether intellectual or athletic") or stereotypically female ("I would like to care for a small baby as a way to express my love"). Both males and females saw the other group in more stereotypical terms than their own group. For example, women described men as likely to subscribe to the masculine statements, but described women as more likely to subscribe to both masculine and feminine statements. The fact that the in-group tends to see itself as more complex than the out-group—even though males and females have a great deal of contact with each other in our society—demonstrates the power of the in-group/out-group dynamic. We would expect even greater perceptions of in-group/out-group differences when comparing groups such as different races or nationalities—groups that have less contact and therefore share less information about each other.

   From the principles described here—the power of first impressions; a person's appearance; and the way schemas, stereotypes, and the in-group/out-group dynamic help shape relations with others—you can see that forming impressions of others is complicated. It is a process in which information about people passes through cognitive filters that influence you to see that information in a certain way. Your initial view of a person is the starting point of your impression of him or her, but you may, based on further information, modify that initial impression. For example, you might see your psychology professor as a serious, intellectual person. If, however, you happened to observe your professor at a party and discovered that he or she was a wild dancer, you might change your impression based on this new information. Thus, person perception is an ongoing, dynamic process even though at the same time early impressions can be resistant to change because of the influence of the processes that helped form them in the first place.

   The process of "figuring people out" includes not only creating an impression of their characteristics, but also making judgments about why they behave as they do. In the next section we consider cognitive processes that affect the way we interpret the causes of people's actions, including our own.

15   PERSONALITY

Attribution: Cognitions About Causes

By the time Lynda's dinner with Roger is over, she feels she knows him surprisingly well, considering that she met him only two hours earlier. In many ways Roger seems to be an "open book"—he talks about his thoughts and feelings much more freely than most of the other men Lynda knows. At the same time, something about him puzzles her. For instance, there was his description of a violent argument he had had earlier that day with his roommate, Paul. The whole thing sounded rather trivial to Lynda, yet Roger still seemed angry as he talked about it, blaming the episode mostly on Paul. Then, too, she noticed at one point that Roger became more irritated with the waiter over the leisurely service than seemed justified. Was Roger just easily angered? The thought disturbed Lynda, because everything else about him seemed so nice. Maybe, she reflected, there was something going on in his life that was making him more tense and irritable than usual.

As Lynda's experience of Roger grows, her new questions represent another dimension of impression formation. Lynda is now speculating about the *causes* of his behavior. Because she wants to like Roger, it is important to her to ask such questions. After all, the answers may tell her a great deal about what he is really like.

How will Lynda go about creating explanations for Roger's behavior? One way to understand how she does this (and how we do, as well) is to examine **causal attribution**—the process by which people determine the causes of events. As with person perception, research on causal attribution has disclosed specific mechanisms that come into play when we try to figure out why people do the things they do. Notice that social psychologists' focus is not on the *real* causes of people's behavior, but rather on the way we form *judgments* about those causes in everyday life. To understand this process, we begin by asking what functions it serves.

Why Do We Make Attributions?

Think about a time when someone did something you didn't understand. Perhaps a casual acquaintance gave you a lavish gift, or you observed a friend lose her temper for no apparent reason, or you read a newspaper story about a senseless killing. Chances are that you asked yourself "Why did that happen?" and perhaps tried to figure it out. At such times you were making attributions about others.

You also make attributions about your own behavior. When you say that you flunked the math exam because you were tense (or didn't study, or were feeling ill that day), you are assigning a cause to your own behavior. As we will see, the way you make these attributions depends to some extent on whether you are making attributions about others' behavior or your own.

Making attributions is clearly commonplace in social life. One reason for this is that making attributions serves important functions. According to Susan Fiske and Shelly Taylor (1991), we make attributions because of a need to predict the future and exert some control over events. Understanding why things happen places us in a better position to achieve our goals. If you decide Larry became angry with you because you inadvertently mentioned his old girlfriend, you will avoid talking about her in the future, in order to get along with him. Similarly, making the judgment that you failed an exam because you waited too long to begin studying for it enables you to take steps to avoid a similar outcome next time.

Attributions, then, help us understand and predict behavior, and we often make them without even realizing it (Lupfer, Clark & Hutcherson, 1990). For example, when your mother sends you a check for your birthday you may not stop to speculate consciously about why she did it, because her gift confirms some things that you already know, such as "She's a thoughtful person" or "She likes to show that she cares about me." However, attribution becomes conscious and deliberate when a situation surprises us or we don't have enough facts about what is happening. For example, Lynda isn't sure why Roger fought with Paul or scolded the waiter. What information is she likely to use in arriving at an attribution, and how does she go about drawing conclusions from this information? These are the questions addressed by **attribution theory**—a general explanation of how people use information to arrive at judgments about the causes of behavior. Attribution theorists have tried to specify the kinds of attributions we make, the information we use to make those attributions, and the errors and biases that tend to influence the process. Let's look at each of these points.

Types of Attributions

Attribution theory began with Fritz Heider's book *The Psychology of Interpersonal Relations* (1958). In that book, Heider explored the "naive psychology" people use in thinking about others. Heider concluded that we assign two general kinds of causes to behavioral events. **Internal causes** of behavior are within the person. If Lynda concludes that Roger fought with Paul because Roger is an argumentative person, she is making an internal attribution about Roger's behavior. **External causes** of behavior are outside the person, in the environment. If Lynda decides that Roger fought with Paul because Paul acted badly, or because something was happening in Roger's life that made him especially tense and irritable, she is making an external attribution.

We also apply these two types of attributions to ourselves. If you explain a failing grade on a math test by telling yourself that you're not very smart when it comes to math, you are making an internal attribution—one that locates the cause in one of your own personal characteristics. If, on the other hand, you explain your performance in terms of the difficulty of the test or the professor's failure to prepare the class properly, you are making an external attribution—one that locates the cause outside of yourself, in the environment.

Choosing between these two basic types of attributions is important because of the way we use attributions to understand and predict events. Lynda's behavior toward Roger is likely to be different depending on whether she sees his anger as caused by an unattractive internal characteristic or by an external circumstance. Similarly, how you explain your performance on an exam is likely to influence how you approach similar exams in the future.

How do we go about determining whether the cause of a behavior is external or internal? According to Harold Kelley (1967), we follow the same steps used by a good detective or scientist: we sift through the available information and, through a process of reasoning, come to a conclusion. But Kelley went further: he tried to identify the *kinds* of information and reasoning we use in making attributional judgments.

Kelley's Model of Attribution: Taking Consensus, Distinctiveness, and Consistency into Account

Kelley introduced the idea that we arrive at causal attributions by asking three types of questions about a specific behavior; he called these the *consensus, distinctiveness*, and *consistency* questions.

The consensus question: How does the person's behavior compare with that of other people in the same situation?   For example, in trying to decide why Roger fought with Paul, Lynda might ask how other people relate to Paul. If not only Roger but also Harry, Sally, Jim, and Renaldo get into arguments with Paul, consensus is high. If only Roger gets into arguments with Paul, consensus is low (top panel of Figure 18.2).

The distinctiveness question: How does the person's behavior vary across situations or with other people?   Does Roger get angry with other people besides Paul? If Roger fights with Paul but not with Harry, Sally, Jim, and Renaldo, distinctiveness is high. If Roger fights not only with Paul but also with Harry, Sally, Jim, and Renaldo, distinctiveness is low (middle panel of Figure 18.2).

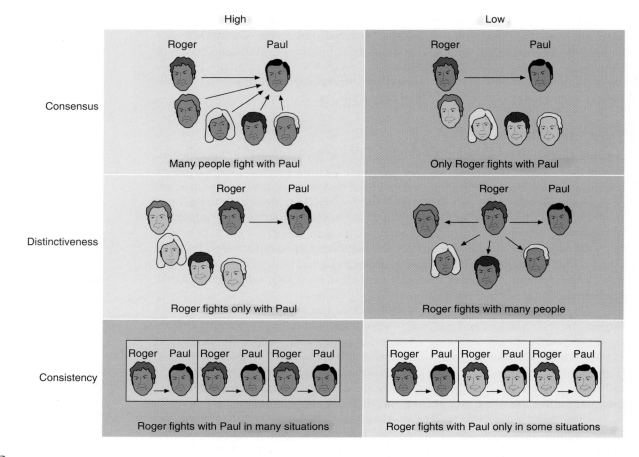

High

Low

Consensus

Many people fight with Paul

Only Roger fights with Paul

Distinctiveness

Roger fights only with Paul

Roger fights with many people

Consistency

Roger fights with Paul in many situations

Roger fights with Paul only in some situations

FIGURE 18.2

We apply Kelley's model of attribution by focusing on one person—Roger—and asking questions about consensus, distinctiveness, and consistency as applied to him. The left and right sections of each panel, respectively, illustrate high and low consensus, distinctiveness, and consistency.

The consistency question: How does the person behave at different times and in different situations?   Does Roger fight with Paul at different times and in different situations? If Roger frequently has trouble with Paul, no matter what situation they are in, consistency is high. If Roger has trouble with Paul only at specific times or in certain situations, then consistency is low (bottom panel of Figure 18.2). For example, perhaps Roger and Paul fight only when they talk about politics, or only when they are in the room they share.

According to Kelley, we arrive at either internal or external attributions by weighing all three of these factors. Let's imagine how this might work for Lynda's attribution about Roger's fight with Paul.

Example 1: High consensus, high distinctiveness, and high consistency.

- Many other people besides Roger have problems with Paul (high consensus).
- Roger rarely fights with others, but has problems with Paul (high distinctiveness).
- Roger has problems with Paul in many situations (high consistency).

What do you think Lynda would conclude from this information? Is the cause of the argument internal or external to Roger? In general, given the pattern above, most people would make an *external* attribution: the cause of the argument is not Roger, but something about Paul.

Example 2: Low consensus, low distinctiveness, and high consistency.

- Roger is the only one who has problems with Paul (low consensus).
- Roger fights with lots of people in addition to Paul (low distinctiveness).
- Roger has problems with Paul in many situations (high consistency).

What would Lynda's conclusion be in this case? In general, this pattern leads people to favor an *internal* attribution: something about Roger caused the argument.

Example 3: Low consensus, high distinctiveness, and high consistency.

- Roger is the only one who has problems with Paul (low consensus).
- Roger rarely fights with others, but has problems with Paul (high distinctiveness).
- Roger has problems with Paul in many situations (high consistency).

What would Lynda decide on the basis of this pattern? In this case the most logical attribution is less clear. On one hand, since Roger is the only one who has arguments with Paul, it is tempting to make an internal attribution. On the other hand, Roger gets along well with other people, which suggests that Roger may not be the problem. Perhaps, in this case, Lynda might decide that the problem lies in the *combination* of Roger and Paul. Neither Roger nor Paul is particularly argumentative—but put them together, and the sparks fly.

Kelley's proposed process is appealing because it suggests that our attributions make perfectly good sense. And, in fact, there is evidence that people do often think this way in making attributions (McArthur, 1972; Zuckerman, 1978). However, the job of weighing consensus, distinctiveness, and consistency is complex and time-consuming. Given the number of attributions we make in the course of a day, it seems unlikely that we go through such an elaborate process every time. Again, we tend to reserve this deliberate attribution process for situations in which events are unexpected or have an unpleasant outcome (Weiner, 1985; Wong & Weiner, 1981). For example, if Lynda judges Roger to be mild mannered, she isn't going to be surprised when she sees him get along with people. For this expected result, her attribution is so automatic that she is hardly aware of it. But if mild-mannered Roger gets into a fight, the unexpectedness of his behavior will trigger the more deliberate process of attributional reasoning.

Often, however, we avoid complex attribution processes even when events are unexpected or have an unpleasant outcome by taking cognitive "shortcuts." Thus, we sometimes associate certain behaviors automatically with external or internal causes (Hansen, 1980; Lupfer, Clark, & Hutcherson, 1990). For example, we may habitually attribute success in difficult endeavors to an internal cause such as ability or effort, even when we're surprised by someone's success. When Susan, who has always been shy, gives a moving speech, we attribute it to hidden talent we never knew she had. Similarly, people usually attribute laughing to an external cause such as hearing a joke or witnessing something funny. If someone laughs out loud, we normally assume something funny has occurred, even if we didn't see it ourselves. We can appreciate this attribution for laughing by realizing that people who often laugh for no apparent reason are likely to be considered strange.

Another of our attributional "rules of thumb" is that behavior is caused internally—by the person's traits—unless we see an external motive. Consider Arie Kruglanski's (1970) experiment in which he gave subjects the task of monitoring the output of two factory workers. Worker A was monitored during nine out of ten work periods, worker B during only two out of ten. Although there was no difference in the two workers' production, worker B was rated as more trustworthy than worker A. What's going on here? Kruglanski concluded, based on additional results, that the subjects attributed worker A's productivity to an external motive since worker A was aware he was almost constantly under surveillance. However, they attributed worker B's productivity to the fact that he was trustworthy—since he produced even though he wasn't watched much.

The behavior of Kruglanski's subjects is interesting because their attribution is not necessarily correct. It is entirely possible that worker A was at least as trustworthy as worker B. Our other shortcut, which says that success is usually

Is this woman reading because she loves to read or because she is being compelled to do it? The answer could be either (or both), but chances are your attribution would be different if you were told (a) she has an exam tomorrow or (b) it's summer vacation.

due to ability or effort, is also not always true—sometimes good fortune or the help of others plays a role.

⑧   THINKING

The shortcuts people use in making attributions are, in fact, *heuristics* (like the ones we discussed in Chapter 8, on thought and language). Heuristics, you may remember, are rules that help us make decisions or solve problems more rapidly but that do not necessarily result in the correct answer. Specifically, heuristics may introduce biases that cause us to make poor decisions or to solve problems erroneously. Let's consider now how such biases or errors can also cloud our ability to make correct attributions.

Attributional Errors and Biases

Social psychologists have found that attributional errors and biases sometimes lead to inaccurate judgments about whether the cause of a behavior is internal or external. In some situations these biases push us toward making erroneous internal attributions, in others toward erroneous external attributions.

The fundamental attribution error.   The **fundamental attribution error** is the widespread tendency for people to *overestimate internal factors* such as a person's traits or attitudes and to *underestimate situational factors* in explaining behavior (Heider, 1958; Ross, 1977). Thus, we may assume that a student who received poor grades in all of his courses is unintelligent or lazy, while overlooking possible environmental explanations such as family problems that have made it difficult for him to study.

In a sense, much of social psychology is a corrective to the fundamental attribution error. Whereas in our everyday attributions we tend to emphasize people's traits as the causes of their actions, social psychology has repeatedly demonstrated that situational influences can powerfully affect behavior. Remember, from Chapter 2, Stanley Milgram's famous obedience experiments, in which subjects were commanded by an experimenter to deliver what they believed to be painful and even dangerous electric shocks to another person?

When my students read about Milgram's study, which showed that 65% of his subjects delivered the maximum-intensity shock, they often want to attribute the subjects' behavior to internal traits—perhaps the subjects were unusually obedient or even sadistic people. Yet the powerful lesson of Milgram's studies is that most normal people, placed in the same situation, would obey the experimenter. To understand this result, we need to ask what forces were at work *in the situation* that account for the subjects' behavior. In short, we have to overcome the bias that predisposes us to look for internal rather than external causes of behavior.

As you read about other research in social psychology, you might keep the fundamental attribution error in mind. In the next chapter, for instance, we will see how situational factors affect a variety of interpersonal events and behaviors, from attraction to helping behavior to conformity and obedience—all behaviors that in everyday life we are prone to attribute to internal causes because of the fundamental attribution error. There is, however, an interesting qualification to our tendency to give undue credit to internal factors in assigning causes to behavior. Research has shown that our bias shifts depending on whether we are observing others' behavior or explaining our own—a phenomenon called the *actor-observer effect.*

The actor-observer effect.   The **actor-observer effect** is the tendency for the actor (the person performing a behavior) to attribute the behavior to the *situation* and for the observer (the person watching the actor behave) to attribute the same behavior to the actor's *disposition* (Jones & Nisbett, 1971; Nisbett et al., 1973). In other words, our bias in favor of internal causes—the fundamental attribution error—is stronger when we are explaining others' behavior rather than our own.

If you trip and fall while walking down the street, an observer is more likely than you are to conclude that you're clumsy or uncoordinated (an internal cause); you are more likely, however, to look for some external cause such as the condition of the sidewalk.

This tendency to give different explanations depending on whether we are actors or observers is illustrated by an experiment in which Richard Nisbett and his co-workers (1973) asked male subjects to describe why they liked *their* girlfriends and why a friend liked *his* girlfriend. The subjects described their own reasons for liking their girlfriends in terms of the *girlfriend's* wonderful qualities ("She's a relaxing person") but their friends' reasons in terms of the *friend's* qualities ("He is looking for someone who is relaxing"). Thus, when in the role of the actor, the subjects focused on the external situation (their girlfriends), whereas in the role of the observer they focused on the actors' (the friend's) personality traits.

Why does the actor-observer effect occur? The following two reasons have been proposed:

1. *Information*: We have more information about ourselves than we have about others, or than observers have about us. For example, we are aware of our actions in many different situations, whereas observers see us only in selected situations. Thus, although your tripping on the sidewalk may appear clumsy to others, you are aware that in most situations you are not clumsy at all. Consequently, you attribute your tripping to the sidewalk rather than to clumsiness.

2. *Perspective*: Actors and observers have different perceptual views of the same behavior. The actor in a given situation focuses on the environment around him or her, whereas an observer of behavior focuses on the actor (Figure 18.3).

4 PERCEPTION

Does the actor's greater access to information about himself or herself explain the actor-observer effect? Nisbett and his co-workers tested this explanation indirectly by having subjects make attributions regarding both people they had a lot of information about, such as their fathers or best friends, and people they knew little about, such as a new acquaintance. Although the "information" explanation of the actor-observer effect implies that subjects would make more situational attributions about people they knew well, there was no difference between the number of situational attributes made for the friend, father, or acquaintance. Other experiments have, however, offered some support for the information explanation. For example, spending more time with a friend, and thus presumably gaining more information about the person, increases the tendency to make situational attributions (Goldberg, 1981). In general, however, support for the information explanation is weak (Watson, 1982). It appears that merely having access to information does not mean that we will *use* that information in making attributions.

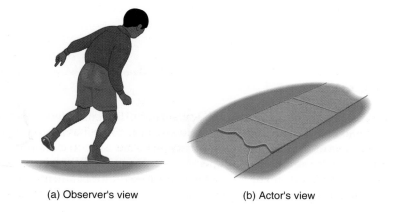

(a) Observer's view   (b) Actor's view

FIGURE 18.3
Two perspectives of the situation just before a person trips on the sidewalk. The observer views the actor tripping, whereas the actor views the cracked sidewalk.

Perspective, the second explanation of the actor-observer effect, appears to be more promising. Its operation was demonstrated in an experiment by Michael Storms (1973), who switched the perceptions of actor and observer by showing actors videotapes of their behavior from the observer's point of view (Figure 18.3a), and vice versa (Figure 18.3b). The result of this switching of perceptions was that the usual actor-observer effect was reversed: actors' attributions of their own behaviors shifted to more internal, dispositional causes, and observers' attributions of the actors' behaviors shifted to more situational causes.

Blaming the victim.   A third type of attributional bias occurs when we try to explain unfortunate events that happen to others, such as being mugged, raped, or fired from a job. Circumstances such as these intensify the tendency to look for internal causes, an effect called **blaming the victim**. For example, a blaming-the-victim reaction to the report of a rape is that "it was her fault because she dressed and acted provocatively."

Why do we tend to blame victims for their own misfortunes? One possible reason is that it protects us from the thought that those bad things could just as easily happen to us (Thornton, 1984). Also, blaming the victim allows people to maintain their belief in the **just world hypothesis**—the idea that life is basically fair, so that good things happen to good people and bad things happen to bad people. To acknowledge that victims do not "deserve" their misfortune is to call the just world belief into question—a threatening prospect. By blaming victims, we allow ourselves to think that because we do not share their attributes, we will escape similar misfortunes (Lerner & Miller, 1978).

The self-serving bias.   A fourth cognitive tendency applies to attributions we make about ourselves: the **self-serving bias.** This is the tendency to distort attributions about our behavior to make ourselves look good (Miller & Ross, 1975). We accomplish this by giving ourselves credit for good outcomes ("I did well on the test because I'm smart") and by blaming the situation for poor outcomes ("I did poorly because the test was unfair"). Self-serving bias is an especially powerful effect in intimate relationships, in which people often take credit for positive things about the relationship but blame their partner for negative ones (Harvey, 1987).

Why do we slant our attributions to favor ourselves? One obvious motive is to protect our self-esteem by allowing us to see ourselves in a positive light. A second reason is that self-serving biases allow us to present ourselves favorably to others (Miller, 1978). As we see in the next section, self-presentational strategies are an important topic in social-psychological research on the self.

We have seen that the attributions we make about ourselves and others give us the feeling that we understand why people are behaving the way they are, even though our explanations aren't always accurate because we lack adequate information or because of the operation of errors or biases. In addition to wanting to understand why other people do things, we also want to feel we understand ourselves. Let's explore how we think about ourselves and present ourselves to others.

The Self: Knowing and Accepting Ourselves

Lynda enjoyed her first date with Roger, but the evening left her with some mixed feelings as well. Roger also seemed to enjoy himself, and he had complimented Lynda on her appearance and her taste in clothes. Lynda appreciated these comments, up to a point—she usually did take care to dress well, and she did think of herself as attractive, if not beautiful. But she was less sure Roger had noticed other qualities that she felt were much more important, such as her interest in political issues and her determination to have a meaningful career in social work. Even though she had told Roger about some of her interests and ambitions, she doubted that his picture of her really agreed with her image of herself as a bright and independent individual who was not traditionally feminine in most ways. "Maybe," she mused," I played down that part of myself just a bit because I wasn't sure how he would react. I think I'll ask *him* out next time, and take a chance on showing more of what I'm really like."

Lynda's reactions to her date with Roger include a number of thoughts about herself—such as the qualities that she thinks of as being "the real me"—and about whether she always projects those qualities to others. All of us have impressions of ourselves, which we introduced in Chapter 10 as the **self-concept**. Much of the time we probably think of the self-concept as something private and independent of other people's reactions to us. If you think of yourself as bright and ambitious, then you assume you have those attributes whether or not other people always perceive them.

⓪19 SOCIAL

⓪10 DEVELOPMENT

In fact, however, one of the interesting discoveries of social psychologists is the extent to which the "self" is really a *social* creation. Even in what is most private to us—our thoughts about ourselves—we are inextricably linked to other people. For example, in order to define herself as "attractive," "bright," or "not traditionally feminine," Lynda compares herself with others whom she perceives as more or less attractive, bright, or feminine than she is. Thus, these self-descriptions are social, in the sense that they refer to other people. Moreover, if other people did not reinforce Lynda's impressions of herself—for instance, by complimenting her on her looks or intelligence—chances are that she would come to question those impressions. And, to some extent, the way Lynda presents herself to others depends on the situation and on whom she is with. At least to some degree, she is a "different person" with Roger than she is with some of her other friends, just as Roger probably projects somewhat different qualities to his fellow ROTC cadets than he does to Lynda. In many ways, then, the self is both a product of social interactions and a factor in how we interact with others.

We touched on this social aspect in the development chapters (Chapters 9 and 10), where we looked at how the self-concept is formed in a social context (for example, how children develop a view of themselves based in part on the way others, especially parents, respond to them). Now we extend our exploration of the self by looking at the interchange between our cognitions about our self and our behavior in social situations. Let's consider first how we envision our self in our own minds and then how our self-concept influences the way we perceive others and relate to them.

Representing the Self

How do people think about themselves, and in what ways do cognitions about the self differ from cognitions about others? One way to answer these questions is to ask people to write descriptions of themselves and others. When they describe themselves, they often include much more personal and "privileged" information than when they write about other people. Consider, for example, the following two excerpts written by a female college student about herself and about an acquaintance (Prentice, 1990, p. 381).

Description of Herself
At the present time, I am going through a very bad stint of the "Who Am I Freshman Blues." Lately, I have been very depressed and anxious but those things seem to be calming down. I consider myself very sensitive or at least hope I am. I have a lot of trouble accepting criticisms and very often I take things too personally or seriously. I am used to being very dependent on

other people: my mother, and boyfriend, and those bonds have proved very painful to break.

Description of Another Person

Eric is a very humorous person. At first, I was very intimidated by him because of his constant humor which borders on sarcasm. However, I believe he really is just a basic "happy-go-lucky" type character and just uses humor to get through rather than to hurt anyone else. He wears basically the same clothes everyday until they become so worn that he has to change to a new outfit.

If we look at these descriptions and count the number of references to personal qualities such as "depressed" or "humorous," we find that the student has included many more of them in her description of herself than in her description of Eric. One reason people include more personal information in their self-descriptions is simple, and perhaps obvious. We know a great deal more about ourselves than about others, since we are able to observe not only our own behavior but also our private thoughts and feelings (McGuire & McGuire, 1986; Prentice, 1990).

We use this knowledge of ourselves to create self schemas—knowledge structures that describe our conception of ourselves and that help us process information in social situations (Markus & Sentis, 1982).

10 DEVELOPMENT   ***The nature of self schemas.***   As we learned in Chapter 10, infants lack self schemas. In fact, they don't even become aware that they are separate from others until about 18 to 24 months of age, when they begin to recognize themselves in the mirror and to describe their actions in terms of personal pronouns such as "I" and "me."

As we get older, our interactions with others and our growing knowledge of the world enables us to create the self schemas that define us as individuals. These self schemas are cognitive representations of our physical characteristics, our attitudes and preferences, and our typical behaviors. Thus, we possess a gender schema and other schemas for family roles, relationships with others, and our body image (Markus, Hamill, & Sentis, 1987). These schemas are of different strength in different people. For example, some people may develop very strong gender schemas. These people are usually very masculine or very

7 MEMORY   feminine and tend to pay more attention to aspects of the environment associated with gender, as we saw in the Follow-Through to Chapter 7.

Our self schemas help us define our selves. But, in addition, they serve another function: they influence how we process social information and therefore how we relate to others.

How self schemas influence information processing.   We can appreciate how our self schemas influence the way we process information by looking at the behavior of people with strong gender schemas. We saw in the Follow-Through in Chapter 7 that when people with strong gender schemas are asked to recall a list of words, they recall them in gender-similar groups. Results such as these indicate that people with strong gender schemas see the world through "gender-colored glasses"—that is, they notice and seek out features of the world that are relevant to gender. Thus, Lynda might be perceived quite differently by acquaintances who have stronger or weaker gender schemas. A person with a strong gender schema might tend to notice whether she is wearing a dress or jeans and a shirt, whereas a person with a weaker gender schema might pay more attention to how intelligent or ambitious she is. The interesting point here is that these contrasting perceptions may be rooted in these people's self schemas—that is, the frames of reference they use in thinking about *themselves* (Figure 18.4).

Similar effects have been reported for other self schemas. For example, Hazel Markus, Ruth Hamill, and Keith Sentis (1987) find that some people have

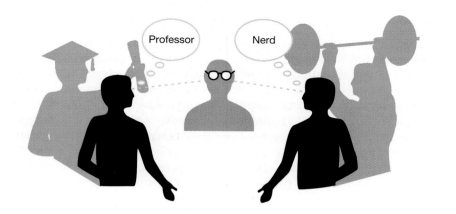

FIGURE 18.4
A person's self schema (how they view themselves) can influence how they view others. The person on the left, who has a strong "academic" self schema, sees the person with glasses as a professor. However, the person on the right, who has a strong "macho" self schema, sees the person with glasses as a nerd.

particularly strong body weight schemas. Such people pay a great deal of attention to body weight, tending to think they are overweight even if they aren't and to be very aware of food, eating, their own weight, and the weight of others.

The fact that people with strong body weight schemas pay attention to the weight of others illustrates one way in which schemas influence social information processing. Just as people notice characteristics of their environment that are related to their own schemas, they also seek out characteristics of other people that are relevant to their own schemas. This means that the impressions we form of others are shaped not only by their actual characteristics but also by our own characteristics. We can appreciate how our own qualities can affect the impressions we form of others by looking at the following descriptions of "Martha," written by two fellow students in her social psychology class (Park, 1986, p. 910).

Student A's Description of Martha
Self-centered and domineering. Martha spends so much time assuring herself that she is the center of attention that she forgets about the feelings of others. She is wealthy and egotistical, which makes for great fashion sense and good looks. She spends much time and takes much pride in her appearance. She is very intelligent, but classes serve only as a showcase to display her talents. She disturbs class by being loud and boisterous.

Student B's Description of Martha
She enjoys parties, people. She likes music; the-more-the-merrier type of person. She probably likes going out to dinner, clothes. I think she is a very "social" person; gregarious, outgoing. I would say that she has many friends/acquaintances. She reminds me of one of my cousins. I think she is intelligent but pretends that nothing is too important.

There are many similarities in the two descriptions, but the differences are especially noteworthy. Student A reacts negatively to Martha's outgoing nature, but student B seems to enjoy it. Since both students have observed Martha in the same context, it is likely that the differences in their descriptions of her reflect differences between them. Perhaps student A's negative reaction is because she is a shy person, and outgoing behavior such as Martha's makes her feel part of the background. Student B's more positive reaction may be related to the fact that Martha reminds her of a cousin she is especially fond of.

Differences in observers' characteristics lead not only to differences in the impressions they form of others but also to differences in the way they behave toward them. For example, when Susan Anderson and Sandra Bem (1981) asked subjects to have telephone conversations with strangers who were described as either attractive or unattractive, subjects with strong gender schemas were more attentive to subjects they thought were attractive, especially if they were of the opposite gender (also see McKenzie-Mohr & Zanna, 1990).

Self-Verification and Self-Handicapping

We have seen that the way you see yourself can influence the way you perceive others and the way you relate to them. The way you see yourself also influences your behavior in another way—it helps determine the kinds of experiences you seek out. An example of this influence is provided by a phenomenon called **self-verification**—doing things to verify your self-concept (Brown, 1986; Swann, 1983). William Swann (1983) hypothesizes that we tend to seek out experiences that confirm our self-concept because we prefer what is predictable and familiar and reduces uncertainty. Do you see the analogy between this idea and that of the *niche building* that we discussed in Chapter 9, on development? According to the idea of niche building, people tend to seek out environments and experiences that fit their abilities. Similarly, people tend to seek out environments and experiences that verify rather than threaten their self-concepts.

9   DEVELOPMENT

In our everyday lives, people we regularly come in contact with—friends, business associates, family members—know us well enough so that their interactions with us usually verify our conception of ourselves. When I walk into the psychology department office I am not surprised when one of the secretaries comments on my forgetfulness (I often leave my keys there), an attribute that is part of my own self-concept. But in many situations, verification of the self-concept is not so readily available. Consider, for example, a woman who sees herself as a professional and an expert in her field. She may have to work to gain confirmation of this view of herself. First, she chooses to attend professional conferences—a good venue for establishing her seriousness and expertise. In work-related situations, she seeks out men and women who show an interest in her ideas and avoids men who seem mostly interested in her as a sex object—all behaviors that work to verify her self-concept.

If we tend to behave so as to verify and thus maintain our view of ourselves, what happens if we view ourselves negatively? According to Swann (1992), people with negative self-concepts tend to seek out negative feedback. He demonstrated this via an experiment in which people who saw themselves either positively or negatively were told that they had been evaluated by two people. They were shown these evaluations (which were actually made up by the experimenter), one of which was positive and one negative, and were asked to pick the evaluator they would like to interact with. You might suppose that anyone would prefer interacting with people who see them positively, yet this was true only for people with positive self-concepts. People with negative self-concepts tended to pick the evaluator they thought had made negative comments about them. This occurred, according to Swann, because we prefer *congruent* partners—people whose views about us agree with our self-concept. Does this mean that people with negative self-concepts are simply gluttons for punishment? Not necessarily. Many of the subjects in Swann's study experienced conflict over their choice, stating that they liked the favorable feedback of the one evaluator but picked the other to interact with because that person "seems to know more about me."

Results like this show that, to some degree, we create our own social world, manipulating our social reality so that it matches our self-evaluations. We can also manipulate our social reality by the way we present ourselves to others. An example is the process called **self-handicapping**—creating an impediment to success that can be used as an excuse in case of failure (Arkin & Baumgardner, 1985; Jones & Berglas, 1978; Shepperd & Arkin, 1989). For example, if you go out partying the night before the big exam and then do poorly on the exam, you can attribute your poor performance to lack of studying (and perhaps to your hangover) rather than to lack of intelligence.

The reason people do this is to protect their self-esteem, and particularly to protect the image they project to others. James Shepperd and Robert Arkin

(1989) found that self-handicapping is more likely to occur if the handicapping activity (like partying before an exam) is public. If the point is to protect the person's public image, it is necessary that others be aware of the handicapping activity.

One of the themes of our discussion of the self has been that our thoughts about our selves often influence our behavior. Another thing that influences our behavior is the way we evaluate events, objects, and people. In the next section, we will look at characteristics of those evaluations (which we call attitudes), focusing on how they affect behavior, how they are formed, and how they can be changed.

Attitudes: Evaluating Objects, Events, and People

As Lynda and Roger begin seeing more of each other, they come to know more about each other's qualities. Lynda appreciates Roger's willingness to share his feelings, and Roger appreciates the thoughtful way Lynda approaches problems. But new issues arise as well. For example, Lynda discovers that she and Roger have different attitudes about politics and social issues. One way this difference has manifested itself is in their behavior toward homeless people. Roger brushes past the homeless people they encounter on the street and only glares when he is asked for spare change. He feels that most homeless people are basically lazy or they wouldn't be out on the street. Lynda, on the other hand, is compassionate toward them because she feels that many are unfortunate victims of society who are not to blame for their situation. The one time she and Roger argued about this issue, they both stuck steadfastly to their positions. Since Lynda has become quite fond of Roger, this difference in their beliefs upsets her. And it isn't just homeless people that they differ about; Roger seems more conservative than her in many ways. She wonders why she and Roger have such opposite attitudes, and whether either of them is likely to change.

Lynda and Roger have a problem: faced with the same social situation, they respond with quite different judgments and behaviors, and their differences may turn out to be a constant source of conflict because they involve more than just abstract disagreement. Roger and Lynda have different **attitudes**—evaluations of other people, objects, and issues that involve not only cognitions but also feelings and behavior.

Attitudes are a central concept in social psychology because they play an important role in influencing many different behaviors—including attraction to others, discrimination, and prejudice—as well as our choices when we make purchases, set priorities in our lives, or decide for whom we are going to vote. But exactly what are attitudes?

Attitudes often motivate people's behavior. This man's prejudiced attitudes are motivating his participation in a white-power group.

What Are Attitudes?

Early theorists identified three basic components of attitudes: (1) cognitive, our thoughts about an issue; (2) affective, the emotions associated with the issue; and (3) behavioral, how we behave with respect to the issue. Thus, in explaining your opposition to the waste incinerator that has been proposed for your community, you might state various arguments against it (cognitive component); you might get rather angry when you think about it (affective component); and you might help circulate petitions against it (behavioral component).

Although this three-component description does describe attitudes in many cases, some theorists have pointed out that emotions or actions do not necessarily accompany all attitudes (Fazio, 1990; Tesser & Shaffer, 1990). Another way to describe attitudes is by considering the following characteristics:

- Attitudes are *evaluations*. They involve positive or negative responses such as liking or disliking (Fishbein & Ajzen, 1975; Oskamp, 1977). These evaluations can, however, be more complex than that: for example, Lynda's attitude about homeless people includes thoughts about how society may have created their situation.

- Attitudes are *learned*. Lynda and Roger certainly had no thoughts about society, politics, or homeless people when they were infants. They acquired their attitudes about these and other things through socialization and other learning processes.

- Attitudes serve important *functions* (Shavitt, 1990). For example, they help us process information about the world. Thus, your political attitudes help you interpret information, which helps you decide which levers to pull in the voting booth. Attitudes may also serve a protective function. For example, Roger's attitude toward homeless people might serve to bolster his own self-concept.

- Attitudes are *enduring*. Unlike moods or emotions, which can change rapidly, attitudes tend to be relatively stable over time. In this respect they are like personality traits (Ajzen, 1987). Although they can change, it is not unusual for people to hold certain attitudes such as liberal or conservative political views—or "pro-choice" or "pro-life" views about abortion—throughout their lives.

- Attitudes influence a person's *behavior*. If Lynda sees that Roger avoids making eye contact with the homeless people he encounters, she attributes his behavior to his attitude. Similarly, people interested in changing others' behavior often try to influence the attitudes thought to underlie their behavior. Public health organizations try to influence our attitudes toward smoking or unsafe sex; advertisers try to create positive responses to their products; civil rights activists

6   LEARNING

MEASUREMENT & METHODOLOGY

Eliciting Honest Responses to Attitude Scales: The Bogus Pipeline Method

When researchers investigate people's attitudes toward particular groups, they are often interested in the negative qualities people associate with those groups. But they quickly run into a problem if people believe that society deems it "incorrect" to have less-than-favorable attitudes toward a particular group. This situation can create a demand characteristic that influences subjects to give responses that do not reflect their true feelings, hence distorting the results.

To solve this problem, Edward Jones and Harold Sigall (1971) created a device consisting of some phony electrical gear and "electrodes" attached to the subjects' forearms, which purported to be able to measure people's attitudes by measuring electrical potentials in their muscles. They called this device the *bogus pipeline*, because it was supposed to provide a pipeline to the subject's attitudes but was actually phony, or "bogus."

The reasoning behind the bogus pipeline is that if subjects believe it is real they will be more likely to give truthful responses, because they think the machine will be able to detect lies. To test this idea, Sigall and Richard Page (1971) had two groups of white subjects rate "Negroes" on traits such as honesty, intelligence, stupidity, and laziness. One group recorded those ratings by assigning numbers ranging from –3 (uncharacteristic) to +3 (characteristic) for each trait. The other group was hooked up to the machine and told to try to predict the numbers the machine would come up with. The results confirmed Sigall and Page's hypothesis: subjects hooked up to the machine reported more negative stereotypes than those not hooked up to the machine.

The results of this study make an important point: the attitudes people report may be influenced by their desire to present themselves in a favorable light. Thus, when asking people to indicate their attitudes, researchers must take precautions—such as promising subjects that their responses will remain anonymous—to ensure accurate reporting.

try to reduce discrimination by changing prejudicial attitudes. As we will see, the relationship between attitudes and behavior is more complex than many people assume, but there is no question that this relationship is one of the driving forces behind social psychologists' interest in attitudes.

When Do Attitudes Predict Behavior?

The assumption that attitudes influence behavior is a major reason that their study has become a central area in social psychology. If a person dislikes certain groups of people or favors a particular cause, we assume that she or he will behave accordingly (Fishbein & Ajzen, 1974). Yet this presumed connection between attitudes and behavior hasn't always been supported by research results. In fact, one classic study called into question whether people behave in accordance with their attitudes at all. This study was carried out by R. T. LaPiere (1934), who toured the United States in the 1930s with a Chinese couple, visiting over 250 hotels and restaurants. At the time, prejudice against Chinese people was sufficiently strong that LaPiere could expect to run into considerable discrimination. In fact, however, in only one case did an establishment refuse to serve the couple. Yet when LaPiere wrote to these same establishments several months later and asked them "Will you accept members of the Chinese race in your establishment?" 92% of those who replied (about half of the total visited) answered "No." These establishments expressed attitudes toward Chinese people that did not match the way they had behaved when actually confronted with the Chinese couple. Subsequently, other researchers found a similar lack of correlation between attitudes and behavior. By 1969, the literature seemed to indicate that despite our usual assumptions, attitudes and behavior are only weakly related (Wicker, 1969).

The story did not end there, however. Later researchers reexamined the attitude/behavior question and were able to show a stronger connection than earlier researchers had. Why had the connection been so elusive? The answer lies in how early researchers went about measuring the relationship between attitudes and behavior. We can gain an appreciation of the subtleties of the attitude/behavior connection by examining some of the ways in which earlier research may have obscured it.

Looking at isolated behavior.   Early attitude researchers may have oversimplified the relationship between attitudes and behavior by looking at isolated behaviors. This tactic ignored the fact that different people express similar attitudes differently. For example, Sebastian and Susan both have positive attitudes about religion, but Sebastian expresses his attitude by attending church and praying before meals, whereas Susan donates money to church-supported causes and works on humanitarian projects organized by her minister. Thus, when psychologists measure the connection between "attitude toward religion" and behavior, they cannot consider just one behavior such as attending church, because it is not necessarily relevant to everyone who is religious. Instead, researchers need to use measures that allow for a variety of behaviors related to a given attitude. This idea was confirmed by Martin Fishbein and Icek Ajzen (1974) when they found a very low correlation between people's attitude toward religion and single behaviors, such as "attending church," but a much higher correlation between attitude toward religion and 100 religion-related behaviors considered all together (Figure 18.5). Attitudes appear to correspond more closely with behavior, then, if people are given ample ways to demonstrate them.

Poor match between the imagined attitude object and the actual object.   To understand this point, consider LaPiere's study, in which the Chinese couple were served in establishments whose proprietors said they wouldn't admit Chinese people. The restaurateurs who responded to LaPiere's survey may have said they would refuse to serve Chinese people because they *imagined* barefoot

FIGURE 18.5
Fishbein and Ajzen found that the correlation between individuals' attitudes toward religion and their behavior is much higher if the attitude was compared to a number of behaviors rather than to a single behavior.

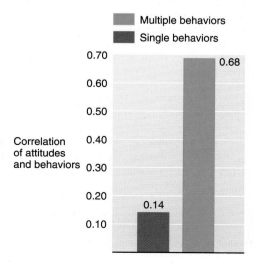

laborers in pigtails and coolie hats (a stereotype of Chinese people that still existed in the 1930s). Since LaPiere's well-dressed Chinese couple (the "actual object") did not match the coolie stereotype (the "imagined attitude object"), the couple may have been served because they weren't even perceived as being Chinese (Lord, Lepper, & Mackie, 1984).

The attitude object wasn't personally relevant to the subject.   We can illustrate this situation by looking at the result of John Sivacek and William Crano's (1982) study, in which they asked students whether they would help campaign against a proposed state law that would raise the legal drinking age from 18 to 20. Although almost all of the students were opposed to the proposed law, only those younger than 20 expressed any interest in actively campaigning against it. Thus, the connection between attitudes and behaviors is stronger when the person has a personal interest in the issue.

The insights provided by this more recent research suggest that the connection between attitudes and behavior is both stronger and more complex than earlier research had revealed. The present view of social psychologists is that attitudes do influence behavior. It is clear that this view is also shared by advertisers and politicians, who spend large sums of money trying to change people's attitudes and the behaviors linked with them. In the next two sections we consider some of the ways in which attitudes can be acquired and changed.

How Are Attitudes Acquired?

Where do attitudes come from? Although we may believe that our own attitudes are rational and based on solid evidence (for example, both Roger and Lynda believe that their attitudes about the homeless are justified by the "facts"), a number of other influences combine to shape our attitudes. Research at the behavioral level of analysis has focused on the processes of conditioning and modeling, as well as on the role of direct experience in shaping attitudes.

Classical conditioning.   A young child is walking down the street with her mother, when suddenly the mother sees members of another racial group approaching. With an anxious frown, the mother picks up her child and hurriedly crosses to the other side of the street. This behavior creates anxiety in the child, and after a number of pairings of this anxiety with the presence of members of other racial groups, the child starts to feel anxious in response to these people, even in the absence of her mother. This is the familiar classical conditioning mechanism introduced in Chapter 6: a previously neutral stimulus (the group members) is paired with an unconditioned stimulus (the mother's anxiety) that elicits an unconditioned response (anxiety) in the child. Eventually, the presence of the group members becomes a conditioned stimulus eliciting the conditioned response of anxiety (Figure 18.6). In this way the child may acquire an attitude of fear and prejudice toward members of other racial groups.

Can attitudes really be acquired in such a mechanical way? Arthur and Carolyn Staats (1958) demonstrated the classical conditioning of attitudes by training subjects to remember words that were arbitrarily paired with different nationalities, such as French/*blue*; Dutch/*gift*; Swedish/*pain*. One of these nationalities was always paired with a positive word, as in the case of Dutch/*gift*, and another was always paired with a negative word, such as Swedish/*pain*. After presenting these pairs, as well as some nationalities paired with neutral words, Staats and Staats asked their subjects how they felt about each nationality. The results, shown in Figure 18.7, indicate that pairing a nationality with negative words resulted in more negative attitudes, whereas pairing nationalities with positive words resulted in more positive attitudes. If a brief laboratory study can cause these effects, imagine how powerful such conditioning can be when applied repeatedly over a period of years as a child grows up.

6   LEARNING

Conditioning

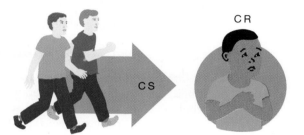

After
conditioning

Operant conditioning.   Operant conditioning, the mechanism by which getting reinforced for a particular behavior increases the probability that the behavior will occur again, can also play a role in shaping attitudes. Such conditioning occurs, for example, every time a child is reinforced for expressing an opinion. Thus, when John's father answers "That's right" every time John says something positive about his father's favorite football team, he is increasing the probability that John will display positive responses toward that team.

Modeling.   As we saw in Chapter 6, on learning, another mechanism through which behavior can be acquired is modeling—observing and repeating the behaviors of other people. When John observes his father cheering wildly as he watches his team score a touchdown on TV, he may learn to adopt that behavior as his own. Similarly, he may learn to denigrate opposing teams.

Modeling exerts a powerful influence on attitudes, not only through watching parents but also through the media images that children are exposed to

FIGURE 18.6
Classical conditioning of anxiety toward members of another racial group. The white males are initially a neutral stimulus (NS) to the child. However, when they are paired with the mother's anxiety (US), which causes the child to become anxious (UR), white males become a conditioned stimulus that elicits anxiety, a conditioned response (CR), in the child.

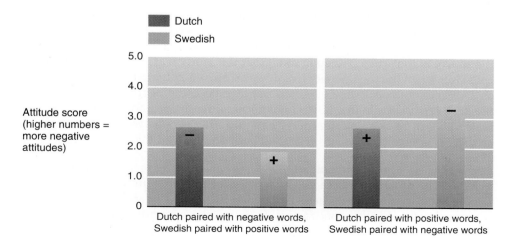

FIGURE 18.7
Results of the Staats and Staats experiment, which shows that attitudes can be influenced by pairing the names of nationalities with negative or positive words.

Observation of adult behavior by children can lead not only to the mimicking of behaviors but to the development of attitudes as well.

on TV. As children watch role models on TV—characters who act out male and female roles, "typical" families in situation comedies, or members of different racial and ethnic groups—they incorporate those depictions into attitudes toward those groups (Basow, 1992). The potential power of this source of models becomes especially obvious when we realize that grade school children watch an average of 30 hours of TV a week (Tangney & Feshbach, 1988).

Direct exposure.   One of the most effective mechanisms of attitude formation is through personal experience. Many of our attitudes evolve from evaluating our experiences—we find that we enjoy certain kinds of music or certain types of food by experiencing those kinds of music and food.

Attitudes formed through direct experience are more confidently held and more resistant to change than are attitudes formed indirectly (Fazio et al., 1982; Fazio & Zanna, 1978; Wu & Shaffer, 1987). Thus, our actual interactions with members of a particular group are a more powerful determinant of attitudes toward that group than feelings that might have been elicited through an indirect method such as conditioning.

How and When Do Attitudes Change?

We have seen that attitudes are acquired through experience and, once established, tend to be relatively enduring. How, then, would you go about getting others to change their attitudes so that they would buy a product, vote a certain way, eat healthfully, or avoid drinking and driving? This question has long interested social psychologists, who have studied factors that influence deliberate attempts to change attitudes through persuasion. In addition, researchers have investigated ways in which people's perception of their own behavior can lead them to change their attitudes.

Factors affecting persuasion: The communicator, the message, and the audience. Much early research on persuasion focused on such elements as the characteristics of the person doing the persuading, the nature of the message being delivered, and the audience receiving the message. Each of these elements—*who* says *what* to *whom*?—has an effect on persuasion.

Expertise and credibility of the communicator.   As we might expect, communicators who are considered more expert and more credible are better persuaders. This principle is often used in advertising: doctors (or actors posing as doctors) advertise health products, and race-car drivers advertise automobile tires.

A classic study that illustrates the importance of communicator credibility was carried out by Carl Hovland and W. Weiss (1951), who had subjects read an article designed to persuade people that it was possible to build a nuclear-powered submarine (which did not exist at that time). For one group of subjects, J. Robert Oppenheimer, the well-known physicist, was listed as the author of the article. For another group of subjects, the Soviet newspaper *Pravda* was listed as the source of the article. (Keep in mind that this study was conducted during the cold war, when the then–Soviet Union was seen as a potential enemy and *Pravda* as a vehicle of propaganda.) As you might expect, the people who were given the high-credibility source (Oppenheimer) had more favorable views about the feasibility of nuclear submarines than did the people who read the low-credibility source (*Pravda*), even though both groups read the identical article.

Attractiveness of the communicator.   We have already seen that people pay a great deal of attention to attractiveness when forming first impressions of others. People are also more likely to be persuaded by physically attractive or popular communicators than by unattractive or unpopular communicators (Chaiken & Eagly, 1983; Kiesler & Kiesler, 1969). Once again, advertising provides countless examples of this principle. How often do you see products associated with celebrities and good-looking men and women, even though the communicator's celebrity status and good looks are completely irrelevant to the product's value?

One- and two-sided messages.   What would be the most effective way to persuade someone to adopt a favorable attitude toward higher salaries for college professors? Should you present arguments only in support of higher salaries (a one-sided argument), or should you also mention some of the arguments against raising salaries (a two-sided argument)? Research has shown that the answer depends on your audience's existing attitudes. People who are already favorably inclined toward a proposition are generally more persuaded by a one-sided argument (that simply confirms what they believe). However, people who initially are not in favor of your proposition would be more persuaded by a two-sided argument (Hovland, Lumsdaine, & Sheffield, 1949). Apparently people who are initially skeptical will be more open to changing their point of view if presented with a more balanced argument.

Emotionally arousing messages.   Is arousing fear an effective way to persuade people? Will people become more likely to stop smoking, eat lower-cholesterol foods, or practice safe sex if they are exposed to fearful messages about what might happen to them if they don't? Sometimes using fear can backfire—especially if it is aroused without giving the person a way to deal with it. If, however, the message presents a way to cope with the fearful negative consequences, then arousing fear can be an effective way to change people's attitudes and thus their behavior (Leventhal, 1970; Leventhal, Singer, & Jones 1965; Rogers, 1983). When Margaret Robberson and Ronald Rogers (1988) compared the effects of a negative message about the dangers of not exercising with the effects of a positive message about the benefits of exercising, they found that the negative message was more effective in convincing people to exercise.

> **12**   EMOTION

Repeated messages.   Have you ever wondered why advertisers present identical messages over and over? One reason is the **mere exposure effect**—the fact that merely being exposed repeatedly to a stimulus, at least up to a point, can cause you to like that stimulus more. This effect has been demonstrated for such stimuli as words, sounds, and people (Moreland & Zajonc, 1982; Zajonc, 1968). Thus, simply hearing the word *Coke* repeatedly and seeing the Coke logo on billboards and in magazines may make you feel positively about Coke.

The audience's personality characteristics.   So far we have concentrated on characteristics of the communicator and the message. But the target of persuasive efforts also matters, because not everyone can be persuaded with equal ease or in the same way.

> **15**   PERSONALITY

One personality characteristic that is related to persuasion is the **need for cognition**. People with a high need for cognition like to try to understand new information and to engage in actually processing it. People with a low need for cognition tend to take mental shortcuts and to think only as much as necessary (Cacioppo & Petty, 1982). How do differences in need for cognition affect the ways in which people can be persuaded? People who have a high need for cognition tend to be more influenced by strong arguments, which present a large number of facts, and less influenced by weak arguments, which present few facts, than people with a low need for cognition. Apparently, in thinking about the arguments, people with a strong need for cognition are more likely to see the merit in the strong arguments and spot the weaknesses in the weak arguments (Cacioppo, Petty, & Morris, 1983; Petty & Cacioppo, 1986). As we will see in the Interdisciplinary Dimension, the personality characteristic called *self-monitoring* also affects the types of arguments to which people are receptive.

The audience's mood.   In addition to stable characteristics like need for cognition, audiences may be affected by temporary moods. People in a good mood are

> **12**   EMOTION

FIGURE 18.8
The Yale model of persuasion focused on the "Who," "What," and "To Whom" of persuasion by asking how the communicator, the message, and the audience influence persuasion.

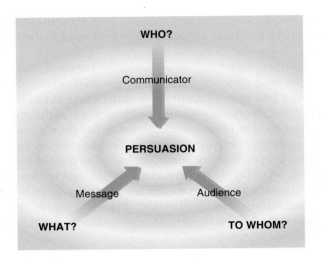

easier to persuade than people in a bad mood. For this reason, some of the most effective TV advertisements have humorous or upbeat messages (Bless et al., 1990).

The research we have just described is summarized in Figure 18.8. It is often called the Yale model of persuasion, because a great deal of the research on how communicator, message, and audience variables influence persuasion was done at Yale. This research focused on the process of persuasive communication rather than on the cognitive activity taking place within the individual. Thus, this line of research sheds light on when attitude change occurs and how to produce it, but it does not tell us *why* the attitude change is occurring. Another line of research on persuasion has focused on the cognitive level of analysis, asking what thinking processes are involved in persuasion. One of the ideas that has come out of this cognitive approach is that persuasion can occur along two pathways: central and peripheral.

Central and peripheral routes to persuasion.   The cognitive approach states that we can understand persuasion by realizing that it is not the message per se that is responsible for attitude change, but the thinking that occurs in response to the message. According to the **elaboration likelihood model** of attitude change,

FIGURE 18.9
Examples of the central and peripheral routes to persuasion. The tractor advertisement, which mentions characteristics of the product, uses the central route. Actor Michael J. Fox's endorsement of Diet Pepsi is an example of the peripheral route.

our response to a persuasive message depends on the degree to which we elaborate the message by consciously and actively processing it (Petty & Cacioppo, 1986). This model states that our response will follow one of two different routes. In one case the message results in *low elaboration*, in which little or no thoughtful consideration of the information and arguments contained in the message occurs. Low elaboration represents the **peripheral route to persuasion**. In this case, attitude change is based on simple persuasion cues such as the attractiveness or credibility of the communicator or the repeated presentation of the message.

The other route of persuasion results in *high elaboration*, or deliberate processing of information and arguments. High elaboration represents the **central route to persuasion.** In this case, attitude change is based more on the intrinsic quality of the arguments presented. Examples of stimuli that result in these two routes to persuasion are provided by the two advertisements in Figure 18.9. Since the advertisement on the left presents information about the product's characteristics, it illustrates the central route to persuasion. In contrast, Michael J. Fox's endorsement of Diet Pepsi provides no information about the product.

The fact that advertisements are a particularly potent form of persuasion has led social psychologists to study them, both in terms of the different routes to persuasion that they may take and in terms of how different types of advertisements appeal to people with different personality characteristics.

INTERDISCIPLINARY DIMENSION MARKETING

The Social Psychology of Advertising

One of the central facts of marketing is that advertisements do not affect all people in the same way. Some people may respond enthusiastically to a particular advertisement while others ignore it. These differences in individuals' responses to ads can occur for a number of reasons, two of which are (1) the consumer's degree of interest, or "involvement," in a product and (2) his or her personality characteristics. As we will see, the effect that each of these factors has depends on the nature of the advertisement.

We first look at research that shows that a person's degree of involvement with a product affects the kinds of advertising that will be more effective with that person. Richard Petty and his co-workers (1983) conducted an experiment in which subjects looked at ads and were then tested to measure their overall impression of the advertised products and how likely they would be to purchase them.

Although the subjects saw ads for a dozen different products, the experimenters focused their attention on one in particular, the "EDGE disposable razor." Two ads for the razor were presented. In the "strong-argument" ad, the razor was portrayed as "scientifically designed" and was described with phrases such as "special chemically formulated coating eliminates nicks and cuts and prevents rusting" and "new advanced honing method creates unsurpassed sharpness." In the "weak-argument" ad, the razor was portrayed as "designed for beauty" and described with phrases such as "floats in water with a minimum of rust" and "comes in various sizes, shapes, and colors."

Subjects in the high-involvement group were told that at the end of the experiment they would get to select a razor to keep and that they would see a razor advertised that would soon be available for purchase in their area. Subjects in the low-involvement group were told that they would get to select another of the advertised products and were told that the advertised razor would not be marketed in their area.

The subjects' reactions to the ads depended on their degree of involvement and the content of the ads. The results show that subjects more highly involved with the product were favorably impressed by the strong-argument ad but reacted negatively to the weak-argument ad. The low-involvement subjects also responded positively to the strong-argument ad, but did not react negatively to the weak-argument ad (Figure 18.10).

Petty and his co-workers interpreted their results in terms of the elaboration likelihood hypothesis. They concluded that, because the high-involvement subjects were more interested in razors, they elaborated the information in the ad more fully and their attitude about the razors was, therefore, determined by the central route to persuasion. In contrast, the low-involvement subjects paid less attention to the arguments in the ads, so

FIGURE 18.10

A person who is highly involved with a product responds positively to advertisements that present a strong argument but negatively to advertisements that present a weak argument. A person who is not very involved with a product responds positively to both kinds of arguments, although less positively to the advertisement with the weak argument.

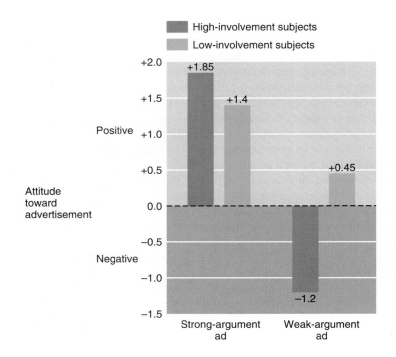

their attitudes were determined by the peripheral route to persuasion. This conclusion is supported by the result of an additional experiment that showed that low-involvement subjects rated the razors more positively if they were endorsed by a celebrity. The attitudes of the high-involvement subjects were, however, not affected by the celebrity endorser.

These results have practical implications for advertisers. If people are highly interested in a purchase—as would be likely if the item were particularly important to the targeted audience or required a large investment—then the ad should contain more informative detail about the product, and celebrity endorsers might make little difference.

15   PERSONALITY

Other research has shown that the effectiveness of an advertisement also depends on the personality characteristic of self-monitoring. In Chapter 15 we saw that people who are high self-monitors are concerned with how they appear to others. These people are therefore easily influenced by the social situation. In contrast, low self-monitors are more concerned with expressing their own values and are not as influenced by the social situation.

Mark Snyder and Kenneth DeBono (1985) presented two types of advertisements to subjects they had classified as high or low self-monitors based on their responses to a personality test. They tested advertisements for a number of products, but we will focus on the ads for Canadian Club whiskey. The ads showed a bottle of Canadian Club with one of two phrases: (1) "You're not just moving in, you're moving up" (an image-oriented ad) or (2) "When it comes to great taste, everyone draws the same conclusion" (a product-oriented ad). After the subjects were shown both ads, they were asked to compare them—picking the one they liked best, the one they thought would be more successful, and so on. High self-monitors (who are more concerned with how they appear to others) gave higher ratings to the image-oriented ads, whereas low self-monitors (who are more concerned with their own values) gave higher ratings to the product-oriented ads. The high self-monitors' preference for image-oriented advertising and the low self-monitors' preference for product-oriented advertising has been demonstrated not just for Canadian Club but also for food products, clothing (Lennon, Davis, & Fairhurst, 1988), and automobiles (DeBono & Snyder, 1989; Zuckerman, Gioioso, & Tellini, 1988).

The fact that image-oriented advertising appeals to one segment of consumers whereas product-oriented advertising appeals to another means that if advertisers want to reach the entire market, they need to use both kinds of ads. But these results go beyond their implications for advertisers; they also have implications for understanding the nature of attitudes in general. According to Snyder and DeBono, these results provide evidence that attitudes serve different functions for different types of people. For example, high self-monitors' attitudes toward consumer products serve a social function, which fits their need to present themselves favorably in social situations. In contrast, low self-monitors' attitudes toward products serve to express their basic values, with less concern for what other people will think.

Having looked at the cognitive approach to attitude change, we can now return to a number of our observations of attitude formation and change and ask whether they take the central or peripheral routes. Mechanisms such as conditioning and modeling, communicator traits such as credibility and attractiveness, and message characteristics such as repeated exposure all involve superficial processing; they therefore take the peripheral route to persuasion. These peripheral processes, since they involve less thinking, result in weaker and less enduring attitudes that are less likely to predict behavior.

In contrast, mechanisms that involve active processing, such as the thoughtful consideration of arguments, would take the central route. Attitude change based on this kind of processing tends to be stronger and more enduring (Petty & Cacioppo, 1986). Moreover, attitudes that are formed or changed via the central route tend to predict behavior better than those based on the peripheral route (Petty, Cacioppo, & Schumann, 1983).

To this point our consideration of how attitudes change has focused on how people respond to the appeals of a "communicator" (the Yale research) and on their cognitive responses to those appeals. Another line of research has investigated ways in which people's attitudes may change because of their awareness of their own thoughts, feelings, and behavior. One of the principal theories that has emerged from this work is called *cognitive dissonance theory*.

Cognitive dissonance: Changing our own attitudes. Consider the situation facing Lynda as she discovers that she likes Roger but that his political and social views are more conservative than hers. Lynda finds herself engaging in voluntary actions such as seeing Roger more often and getting emotionally involved with him but at the same time believing that Roger is really too conservative for her. This inconsistency between Lynda's actions and her doubts about their compatibility makes her feel uncomfortable—the feeling called cognitive dissonance. According to Leon Festinger (1957), **cognitive dissonance** is the unpleasant state of arousal that occurs when we discover inconsistencies in our beliefs—or between our beliefs and our behavior.

Festinger argued that cognitive dissonance is a type of drive state, like being thirsty. Once we are aware of dissonance, we are motivated to do something to reduce it, just as thirst motivates us to drink. Thus, Lynda is motivated to reduce the dissonance she experiences in connection with Roger. Unless she changes the way she *thinks* about her behavior—for example, by deciding that people who are in a relationship don't have to agree on everything—there are just two basic ways she can reduce her dissonance (Figure 18.11):

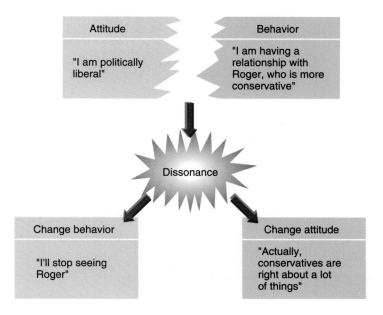

FIGURE 18.11
Lynda can reduce the dissonance she feels in her relationship with Roger in two ways: She can change her behavior to match her attitude or she can change her attitude to match her behavior.

1. She can change her *behavior*, by ending her relationship with Roger.
2. She can change her *attitudes*—for example, those about homeless people—to more closely match Roger's.

Notice that one way of reducing dissonance is to change an attitude so that it is more consistent with our behavior. Although Lynda may choose not to change her attitudes, there are many situations in which cognitive dissonance does result in attitude change. Such a situation is illustrated by a classic experiment by Leon Festinger and James Carlsmith (1959). In this experiment subjects were required to do a dull task: placing spools on a board, removing them, and then repeating the task many times. After completing the task they were told that they would be given $1 to tell another subject that the task was enjoyable. This sets up the dissonance-producing situation shown in Figure 18.12, in which there is a conflict between behavior (telling the person the task was enjoyable) and attitude (the task is boring).

One way to reduce the dissonance would be to refuse to tell others that the task is interesting. But, assuming that subjects feel obliged to follow the experimenter's instructions, another possibility is to change their attitude about the task. Subjects might reason, for example, that the task could be interesting to someone who was mechanically inclined. In fact, there was evidence that some process like this occurred for these subjects. After telling others that the task was interesting, subjects actually rated the task more positively than did control subjects who simply did the task and then rated it.

Festinger and Carlsmith were not satisfied, however, simply to demonstrate that cognitive dissonance can lead to attitude change. They set up another experimental group, in which subjects were paid $20 instead of $1 to describe the task as interesting. What do you suppose happened to subjects in this group? Did they come to feel that the task was even more enjoyable, because they had been paid more? On the contrary: as shown in Figure 18.13, the subjects who earned $20 felt more negatively about the task than the subjects who were paid only $1.

Although this result often surprises people, it is perfectly consistent with dissonance theory. The people who were paid just $1 to lie experienced *greater* dissonance, because the small sum didn't provide much justification for lying. The $20 group, however, experienced less dissonance, because the $20 payment gave them ample justification for their behavior, reducing their feeling of inconsistency between their behavior and their attitude about the task. Since they had

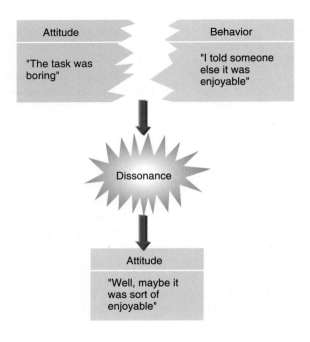

FIGURE 18.12

How subjects reduced dissonance in the Festinger and Carlsmith experiment, which demonstrated that dissonance can cause a change in a person's attitude

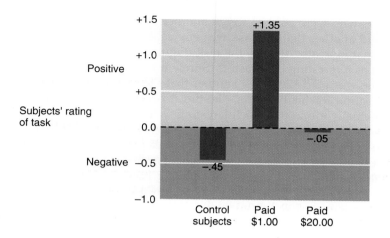

an alternative way of accounting for their behavior, they didn't find it necessary to change their attitude. Dissonance thus seems to produce the greatest attitude change when there is no external justification available for the inconsistency between people's behavior and their attitude.

Another prediction of dissonance theory is that you will value a goal more the harder you have to work to achieve it. What if, for example, you undergo a brutal initiation to join a college fraternity, but after being accepted as a member you realize that the fraternity isn't that great after all? This sets up a conflict between your behavior (undergoing the difficult initiation) and your attitude (the fraternity isn't that great.) Because you can't change the behavior, you change your attitude and decide that there are a number of positive aspects to the fraternity. Many experiments have confirmed this **effort justification effect:** people will be more likely to change their attitudes if they invest a large amount of effort or expense toward achieving a goal.

Dissonance theory, then, holds that attitudes sometimes change to reduce a conflict between behavior and an existing attitude. This change in attitude occurs not because of an outside "commentator" but because of forces within the person whose attitude is changed. Another explanation of such internally triggered attitude change is that we sometimes form or change attitudes based on our observation of our own behavior, a phenomenon called self-perception.

Self-perception theory: Inferring our attitudes from our behavior.   We usually infer other people's attitudes from observing their behavior. If we saw Roger brushing past homeless people on the streets and embracing a campaign to jail panhandlers, we would *infer* that Roger dislikes homeless people. In contrast, we usually *know* our own attitudes, so we don't have to infer them by observing our own behavior—right?

Not according to Daryl Bem's (1965, 1972) **self-perception theory**, which states that we often draw conclusions about our own attitudes after observing our own behavior. To see how this might work, let's consider an experiment by Stuart Valins (1966) in which he showed males pictures of scantily clad women and had them judge the women's attractiveness as they listened through earphones to a sound they thought was their own heartbeat. The "heartbeat" was not, however, actually being recorded from the subjects but was rather a prerecorded tape. A normal heartbeat was played as the subjects viewed half of the photographs, a speeded-up heartbeat as they viewed the others. Valins's subjects tended to rate women as more attractive if their pictures were accompanied by the faster heartbeats. Thus, they based their attitudes about the women on a perception of their own behavior: in this case, sounds they believed to be their own heartbeat.

According to Bem, self-perception theory is another way of explaining the results observed in dissonance studies. For instance, consider how self-perception theory might explain the apparent change in attitude experienced by

FIGURE 18.14
According to self-perception theory, when an attitude is weak or nonexistent, people determine their attitudes by observing their own behavior.

the subjects who were paid $1 to tell another that a boring task was enjoyable. Having told another that the task was enjoyable, a subject might *infer* from his behavior that he really did like the task (Figure 18.14). After all, why would he describe it as interesting if it wasn't? (Surely not just to receive $1!) In contrast, a subject who was paid $20 to tell another that the task was interesting has a perfect explanation for his behavior—he did it because he was paid well, not because he actually found the task interesting.

Thus, whereas dissonance theory explains apparent attitude change as a response to an unpleasant state of arousal, self-perception theory explains the same result in terms of logical information processing. More generally, self-perception theory offers a way of explaining how at least some attitudes are formed: we "discover" what our attitudes are by observing how we behave. (Also see Measurement & Methodology, "How Measuring Attitudes Can Create Them.")

This does not mean that self-perception theory has completely replaced other accounts of attitude formation and change, including dissonance theory. Instead, research suggests that self-perception theory is most applicable when attitudes are nonexistent, weak, or ambiguous (Fazio, 1987). This makes sense, if we consider that when we hold strong attitudes we don't need to examine our own behavior for clues. Thus, when Lynda votes for a political candidate who vows to help the homeless, chances are it is her attitude toward this issue and toward the candidate that determines her behavior, rather than the other way around. She doesn't vote for the candidate first and afterward think "I voted for that candidate, so I must like her and what she stands for."

MEASUREMENT & METHODOLOGY

How Measuring Attitudes Can Create Them

Imagine the following situation. People in your city are debating whether to allow a block of houses in your neighborhood to be torn down to make room for a new shopping center. You really haven't thought about the issue or followed the debate. But one

Sometimes answering questions on a survey triggers a process that causes people to develop attitudes regarding the questions they were asked.

day you receive a survey in the mail, sent out by the city to those residents who would be most affected by the proposal, soliciting their attitudes. After filling out the survey, you realize that you are opposed to the project.

How did you arrive at that realization? According to the self-perception theory of attitude formation, we can infer our attitudes by observing our behavior. This idea leads to an interesting question: could the behavior of filling out a survey designed to measure attitudes actually *create* attitudes that were not previously present?

The results of an experiment by Russell Fazio and his co-workers (1982) suggest that the answer is "Yes." These researchers had subjects solve a number of different puzzles. Afterward, some subjects were asked to fill out a rating scale to indicate their interest in each type of puzzle. The rest were not asked to fill out the rating scale. Then both groups were asked to respond as rapidly as possible to questions about how interesting each type of puzzle was. The key variable here was the *speed* of response, which the researchers used as a measure of the strength of the subjects' attitudes. The results showed that subjects who had previously filled out the survey responded more rapidly than those who had not. According to Fazio, answering questions on the survey had strengthened their attitudes, enabling them to respond more rapidly to the questions. The implication is that a survey may both measure attitudes and help shape them—at least in cases in which, as explained by self-perception theory, attitudes were weak or nonexistent to begin with.

Reprise: Processing Information About Ourselves and Others

Dear Mom and Dad,

I only have time for a quick note—I'm on my way to pick up Roger. The sweet guy bought us tickets to an expensive concert for my birthday. Thanks so much for the check and the cute card. And no, I don't know whether this thing with Roger is serious or not, but for now it's fun. We still argue a great deal, but I like the fact that he genuinely listens to my point of view. It's funny, isn't it, how two people looking at the same facts can have such different attitudes about them? I wonder why that's so. Speaking of seeing things differently, some of my friends have been riding me about Roger. They can't get past his being a "military type" who is more conservative about a lot of things than they are. But I don't think of him as a "type," and he's more open-minded than they give him credit for. They just don't know him like I do.

Well, gotta run. Talk to you soon!

Love, Lynda

This chapter has introduced an interesting application of research into cognitive processes. We have been dealing not with numbers, words, or solving problems, as we did in Chapters 7 and 8, but with our perceptions, beliefs, and attitudes about other people and ourselves. We have an important stake in the outcome of the processes of social cognition and attitude formation and change, for they determine the people we decide to associate with or to avoid, how we feel about ourselves, and what we believe in.

We have seen that these cognitive and attitudinal processes share a key characteristic with other forms of perception and information processing: in processing information about social reality we are sometimes logical, but we are also prone to bias and error. The interesting and significant thing about the biases and errors in social cognition is that they occur because of the functions they serve for us. Thus, our tendency to attribute victims' misfortunes to internal causes—whether true or not—serves a self-protective function. It allows us to think that we can escape similar calamities ourselves and that we live in a just world.

Of course, we don't always make errors in judging others and ourselves. We often size up other people correctly and fashion our own behavior to match our abilities. But it is important to note that the self-serving nature of some of the errors we do make, though perhaps good for our self-esteem, may be unfair to others. When this is true, our cognitive biases can produce negative effects not only for our neighbors but for society at large. For example, consider what happens when we succumb to the tendency to assume that others are personally to blame for their misfortune, without taking into account the severe situational pressures they face. In such circumstances we may not only judge people unfairly but also support ineffective public policy that fails to address the real causes of complex problems such as poverty, unemployment, crime, drug abuse, or homelessness.

In the next chapter we will move beyond social thinking and attitudes to look at behaviors such as helping, aggression, conformity, and compliance—all of which play important roles in the structure of our society. We will see that one reason research into these behaviors is important is that the knowledge we gain may suggest ways of changing social behavior to the benefit of ourselves and of society as a whole.

Prejudice and Racism

Prejudice is a negative attitude toward other people based on their membership in a particular group. A common form of prejudice in our society is **racism,** which has been defined as "any attitude, action or institutional structure which subordinates a person because of his or her color" (U.S. Commission on Civil Rights, 1969, p. 1). A number of psychologists have explored the nature and sources of racial prejudice, and what they have discovered can shed light on prejudice in general.

How prevalent is racial prejudice? Although the responses of white Americans to survey questions appear to reflect less prejudice over the years, there is evidence that racism still exists in many people under the surface. (See Measurement & Methodology, "Eliciting Honest Responses to Attitude Scales.") David Frey and Samuel Gaertner (1986) illustrated this more subtle form of racism in an experiment on helping behavior, in which either a white or an African American requested help on a puzzle from white subjects. The subjects were equally willing to help either the white or the African American if they were led to believe that help was needed because the task was difficult. If, however, they were led to believe that help was requested because the person was not trying hard, they were much less likely to help the African American (Figure 18.15).

Why did the white subjects act in a nonprejudicial manner under some conditions but not others? Frey and Gaertner suggest that people who consider themselves nonprejudiced may in fact discriminate if they can find a way to explain their behavior as something other than racism. In this experiment, subjects explained their lack of helping as reflecting not prejudice against

Racism involves perceiving members of another race as inferior.

African Americans but rather their unwillingness to help lazy people. (Yet they helped "lazy" white people!) From these and other results showing that prejudice is sometimes expressed in subtle ways (Rogers & Prentice-Dunn, 1981), we can conclude that racial prejudice may be more prevalent than is initially apparent.

What causes prejudice? For one thing, cognitive processes such as stereotyping and the in-group/out-group dynamic provide mental mechanisms that allow us to see members of an out-group as being "all alike" and as inferior to ourselves. These mechanisms, however, do not work in isolation. They are supplemented by behavioral and contextual factors such as early learning and economic and political forces.

Children begin acquiring stereotypes before they are old enough to be able to evaluate whether they are true or not (Devine, 1989). Although some stereotypes have positive components (such as the "female" stereotype, which includes traits like "nurturing" and "gentle"), the stereotype that many white children learn about African Americans is overwhelmingly negative. When Patricia Devine (1989) asked white adults to list characteristics of the common stereotype of "blacks," over half the subjects listed the following traits: "poor," "aggressive" or "hostile," "criminal," "low intelligence," "uneducated," "lazy," "sexually perverse," and "athletic." Children learn this stereotype from parents and other adults as well as from their peers. And these stereotypes are reinforced by the media, which until recently have depicted African Americans in a largely unfavorable light and still emphasize the most threatening components of the stereotype: aggressiveness and criminality.

The development of prejudice can also be traced to economic and political forces. When jobs are scarce or economic times are bad, prejudice, discrimination, and negative stereotyping increase (Allport, 1954)—and not only toward racial minorities. A classic study conducted by John Dollard in 1938 described a small American town that initially showed no evidence of prejudice against

FIGURE 18.15

Results of Frey and Gaertner's experiment showing a subtle expression of racial prejudice

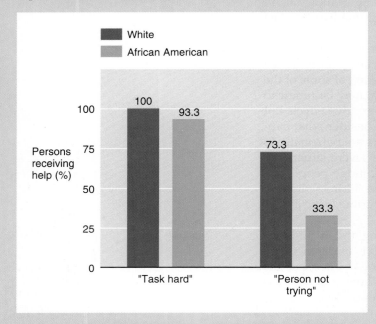

Germans. However, as German immigrants began competing with long-term residents for jobs in local manufacturing plants, anti-German prejudice grew.

One way of looking at the effects of political and economic forces is in terms of *scapegoating*, in which a particular person or group—usually one with little power—is blamed for a problem. A long-familiar cultural joke describes an office worker who, after being reprimanded by his boss, comes home and yells at his wife, who in turn is cross with the children, who react by taking out their frustrations on younger siblings or the dog. Although this example is humorous, scapegoating has often had tragic consequences. In the 1930s the Nazi party used Jews as scapegoats to ease people's frustration over Germany's rampant inflation and unemployment—a tactic that led ordinary citizens to attack Jewish people long before the Nazis embarked on their program of organized mass murder. And in the United States between 1882 and 1930, economic depression in the South (as measured by downturns in the price of cotton) was accompanied by an increase in lynchings of African Americans (Hovland & Sears, 1940).

Prejudice, then, is caused by multiple factors, only a few of which are described here. But once it is established, how is it maintained? Thomas Pettigrew (1979) has suggested that one way prejudice is perpetuated is through a cognitive bias called the *ultimate attribution error*. As you recall, the *fundamental attribution error* is overemphasizing personal traits, as opposed to external factors, in explaining others' behaviors. Pettigrew defines the "ultimate" attribution error as follows: When prejudiced people see what they regard as a negative act by an out-group member, they are more likely to attribute that act to the person's traits—often implying that they are "genetically determined"—than they are when the same act is performed by an in-group member. A good example of this is Birt Duncan's (1976) experiment described earlier in this chapter, in which white students watched videos of persons of different races first arguing then pushing. The subjects applied the ultimate attribution error in assessing the African American as more inherently violent and the white person as more affected by the situation.

But what happens when prejudiced people observe a member of an out-group engaging in a positive behavior that contradicts their negative stereotype? Pettigrew suggests that they use special techniques to "explain away" the unexpected behavior. For example, two such techniques are (1) saying the out-group member is a special case, or an exception to the rule, and (2) attributing unusual achievement to high motivation on the part of the out-group member, which overcomes the person's assumed inferiority. Techniques such as these allow prejudiced people to interact positively with specific members of an out-group while retaining their overall prejudice.

Given these mechanisms for perpetuating prejudice, are any methods likely to be effective in combating it? One potential technique for doing so is based on the **intergroup contact hypothesis,** which states that bringing equal-status persons together in pursuit of a common goal reduces prejudice (Allport, 1954). The classic example of the application of this hypothesis was an experiment carried out by Muzafer Sherif and his co-workers (1961), which is now called the Robber's Cave experiment. The subjects were a group of white, middle-class boys attending a summer camp at Robber's Cave State Park in Oklahoma. When they arrived at camp, they were arbitrarily divided into two groups, the Rattlers and the Eagles, which engaged in a series of competitions to win various prizes. As competition grew more and more fierce over time, hostility between the groups increased until the boys began raiding each others' cabins and the counselors had to intervene.

Having manipulated the boys into two groups that disliked each other, the psychologists then manufactured various situations in which boys from both groups had to cooperate to achieve a common goal. For example, the boys worked together to discover a leak in the camp's water supply, and they all pitched in to pull a truck out of some mud. After the boys had accomplished a number of goals through cooperation, the hostility between the groups began to diminish. By the end of camp, members of the two groups had become friends and had begun doing things together.

If bringing warring campers together to work cooperatively can help eliminate their negative feelings toward each other, would bringing different racial groups together under similar conditions do the same? Research indicates that it would: prejudice decreases among students when they are members of interracial sports teams (Slavin & Madden, 1979), and school programs in which students work in interracial cooperative learning groups also help reduce prejudice (Gaertner et al., 1989; Goleman, 1989). The success of such programs is encouraging, but it is also important to be realistic about conditions in our society as a whole that make the fight against racism difficult. Prejudice in the United States is fueled by large political and economic disparities between whites and some minorities. These inequities—combined with the largely segregated living arrangements that exist in most cities and people's natural tendency to stereotype and see those in out-groups as inferior—pose a great challenge to those seeking to eliminate racism.

Interracial contact helps to reduce prejudice, especially if races work together in pursuit of a common goal.

CHAPTER EIGHTEEN SUMMARY

What Is Social Cognition?

- Social cognition refers to the way in which people make sense of others and of themselves. It affects not only our thinking but our behavior as well.

Person Perception:
Forming Impressions of Others

- Social perception is the process through which we evaluate social reality. We use clues about people we have just met to determine their qualities. This process is called person perception.

- People are able to discern others' personality characteristics with some accuracy after a brief meeting, depending largely on cues that are immediately apparent. In general, the information we receive first tends to have more influence than the information we receive later. This is called the primacy effect.

- Appearance is a particularly important cue for forming first impressions, especially since many people believe that the face provides an important guide to character. Physically attractive people are generally predicted to have other positive traits, though only good social skills are actually correlated with good looks.

- Schemas can influence what we perceive and remember about people and also how we behave toward others. The effect of our schemas on our behavior can lead to the creation of self-fulfilling prophecies that confirm those schemas. Stereotypes—schemas about the characteristics of members of a group—have similar effects.

- The in-group/out-group dynamic refers to people's tendency to see others differently depending on whether they are in the in-group or the out-group. Out-groups are usually seen as having less favorable qualities and as being more homogeneous than in-groups.

Attribution: Cognitions About Causes

- When we make causal attributions about the behavior of others or ourselves, we are attempting to explain why that behavior occurred.

- The two general kinds of causes we assign to behavioral events are external and internal. According to Kelley, we take into account consensus, distinctiveness, and consistency as we decide whether to attribute a person's behavior to external or internal causes. We are most likely to use this approach to explain unexpected or unpleasant events.

- We often use cognitive "shortcuts" in making attributions: heuristics or rules that help us make attributions more rapidly. Sometimes those shortcuts lead to errors, some categories of which are the fundamental attribution error, the actor-observer effect, blaming the victim, and the self-serving bias.

The Self: Knowing and Accepting Ourselves

- When we describe ourselves, we include more personal qualities than when we describe others. We use our knowledge of ourself to create self schemas that help us define ourselves, influence how we process information about others, and determine how we behave toward others.

- We seek out environments and experiences that verify our self-concept. We also use a process called self-handicapping to protect our self-esteem and the image we project to others.

Attitudes: Evaluating Objects, Events, and People

- Attitudes have been described as having three components: cognitive, affective, and behavioral. They have also been described as being evaluative and learned, as serving important functions, as being enduring, and as influencing behavior.

- Early attempts to determine the connection between attitudes and behavior failed to find much connection, because the experimental designs were flawed in a number of ways. Later attempts demonstrated a connection by using multiple measures of behavior and by making sure the attitude in question was personally relevant to the subjects.

- Attitudes are acquired through classical conditioning, operant conditioning, modeling, and direct exposure.

- The Yale approach to studying persuasion and attitude change considers characteristics of (1) the communicator (expertise and credibility, attractiveness), (2) the message (one- or two-sided, emotionality, repetition), and (3) the audience (personality characteristics, moods).

- The cognitive approach to attitude change looks at thought processes and the way people process information. According to the elaboration likelihood model, attitude change can occur either via central or peripheral routes.

- The effectiveness of advertising depends on the consumer's degree of involvement with the product, his or her personality characteristics, and the nature of the advertisement. If product involvement is high, advertisements that include more detailed information are more effective. People who are high self-monitors respond to image-oriented ads, whereas low self-monitors respond to product-oriented ads.

- Two explanations of why we sometimes change our own attitudes are cognitive dissonance theory, which states that we try to resolve conflicts between our attitudes and our behaviors, and self-perception theory, which states that we infer our attitudes from our own behavior.

Reprise: Processing Information
About Ourselves and Others

- Social cognition and attitudes share a characteristic of other forms of information processing, in that people are sometimes logical and at other times prone to error. Many of the errors we make may serve important functions for us personally while being harmful to others or to society as a whole.

Follow-Through/Diversity: Prejudice and Racism

- Racism has by some measures been decreasing in the United States, though more subtle forms of racism can be detected even in those who consider themselves nonprejudiced. The cognitive mechanisms of stereotyping and the in-group/out-group dynamic help explain why prejudice occurs. In addition, prejudice develops through learning processes and through the operation of economic and political forces in society. Once established, prejudice can be maintained through cognitive processes such as the ultimate attribution error and "explaining away" the positive behaviors of out-group members. One way to reduce prejudice is to bring different racial groups together in pursuit of a common goal.

Key Terms

actor-observer effect
attitudes
attribution theory
blaming the victim
causal attribution
central route to persuasion
cognitive dissonance
effort justification effect
elaboration likelihood model
external causes
fundamental attribution error
in-group/out-group dynamic
intergroup contact hypothesis
internal causes
just world hypothesis
mere exposure effect

need for cognition
peripheral route to persuasion
person perception
prejudice
primacy effect
racism
self-concept
self-fulfilling prophecy
self-handicapping
self-perception theory
self-serving bias
self-verification
social cognition
social psychology
stereotypes

CHAPTER

19

Attraction: Liking and Loving Others
Sources of Attraction
From Liking to Loving

Prosocial Behavior: Helping Others
When Do People Help in an Emergency?
Why Do People Help Others?

Aggression: Hurting Others
Biological Level: Instinct and Biology
Behavioral Level: Learning Mechanisms
Contextual Level: Environmental Influences
Cognitive Level: Attributions and Arousal
Combining Context, Behavior, and Cognition: The Case of Sexual
    Violence Against Women

Conformity: Keeping in Step with Others
Asch's Conformity Experiment
When Do People Conform?

Interdisciplinary Dimension: Sociology
Conformity, Deviance, and Social Bonds

Compliance and Obedience:
Bowing to Pressure from Others
Compliance: Bowing to Requests
Obedience: Bowing to Authority

Groups: Behaving in Conjunction with Others
Working in Groups
Making Decisions in Groups
Deindividuation

Reprise: Social Psychology and Social Change

Follow-Through/Diversity
Communication Between Women and Men About Sex

Interpersonal
Relations

Chapter 18 introduced the central premise of social psychology: that much of our behavior is strongly affected by our relationships with other people. In that chapter we focused primarily on cognitive and attitudinal processes within individuals. We saw that cognitive processes guide the way we form impressions of others, how we think about ourselves and others, and how we make causal attributions about behavior. The cognitive level of analysis was also featured prominently in our discussion of how attitudes are formed and changed and how they affect behavior. We now broaden our perspective on social behavior by looking specifically at *interpersonal* behaviors and at how the situations we find ourselves in influence our interactions with others.

Of course, we interact with others in countless ways, but some kinds of interactions have received special attention from social psychologists. To begin with, they have looked at how we form relationships. What draws people to each other so they become friends, lovers, or lifelong partners? Is it all a matter of "chemistry," or are there general principles that can help explain why we form the relationships we do?

Often our cherished beliefs about topics like friendship and love reflect our ideals and wishes as much as they do reality. The same may be true of the next topic in this chapter, prosocial behavior. No doubt we would like to feel that we can count on the help of our fellow human beings when we are in need, and that we ourselves would be ready to respond to someone in distress. But are we really as likely to help one another as we would like to think? Is there more to helping behavior than individual kindness? As you will see, social psychologists investigating these questions have come up with some surprising answers.

People's willingness to help others is an important subject in this largely urbanized society, in which most of us are strangers even to our neighbors. Another social relations topic with larger implications is aggression. What circumstances make it likely that people will deliberately hurt others? Once again, the answer is less straightforward than we might imagine. You will see that psychologists need to work at all four levels of analysis to draw a complete picture of the factors involved in human aggression.

The three topics mentioned so far all concern our behavior toward others in specific social situations. Another important area of concern to social psychologists is interpersonal influence, or how our behavior is affected by the presence of others and by others' deliberate attempts to modify that behavior. This area of research investigates such issues as when and why people conform (that is, match their behavior to that of others), comply with others' requests, and obey authority figures. Here again you may find that reality doesn't always match our ideals. Although many of us—especially in the United States—pride ourselves on our independence, social influence exerts a powerful yet subtle control over much of our behavior.

When people are part of a group, they may behave differently than they do when alone.

Finally, social psychologists have studied how individuals' behavior changes when they are part of a group. They have shown how a group is—to borrow a phrase from Gestalt psychology—more than the sum of its parts. When groups come into being, so, too, do group processes that affect the group members' behavior.

Clearly, social psychologists get involved in a wide variety of issues. What all these disparate lines of research have in common is a concern with how the processes at work in social situations—whether they involve one other person or many people—affect individual behavior. Social psychologists thus do much of their work at the behavioral and contextual levels of analysis, though—as always—we find that the biological and cognitive levels have their own contributions to make. We begin our discussion of interpersonal relations by considering the kinds of interactions between two people that may lead from acquaintance to friendship or even romance.

Attraction: Liking and Loving Others

There is no hope of joy, except in human relations.

Antoine de Saint-Exupéry (1900–1944)
French writer

What makes life meaningful? For many people, the answer is "Relationships." Most people feel that their relationships with family, friends, partners, and children are more important to them than their money, career, or religion (Argyle, 1987; Duck, 1985).

As important as relationships are, psychologists have only recently begun studying them. And when research on relationships began increasing in the 1970s, some people were less than enthusiastic. One of them was William Proxmire, then senator from Wisconsin. Proxmire made the following comments as he announced his "Golden Fleece Award"—given to scientific projects that the senator thought were a waste of taxpayers' money—to an $84,000 project on the study of love that had been funded by the National Science Foundation:

I object to this not only because no one—not even the National Science Foundation—can argue that falling in love is a science; not only because

I'm sure that even if they spend $84 million or $84 billion they wouldn't get an answer that anyone would believe. I'm also against it because I don't want the answer. I believe that 200 million other Americans want to leave some things in life a mystery, and right at the top of things we don't want to know is why a man falls in love with a woman and vice versa. . . .

Despite the belief of people like Senator Proxmire that love should be left a mystery, such a central part of human relating was bound to attract attention from psychologists committed to using scientific investigation to widen our understanding of relationships. But what about his objection that such research could not produce answers that anyone would believe? Are liking and loving truly just mysterious happenings—the products of an indefinable "chemistry"? Or will they prove to be understandable, at least in part, if they are looked at psychologically? Let's see what social psychologists have discovered in answer to these questions, beginning where relationships themselves begin—with attraction.

Sources of Attraction

Why do we form relationships with certain people? What factors are involved in becoming attracted to someone else? Before answering "Chemistry," consider some more mundane influences that we often overlook, including perhaps the most obvious but underrated of all, physical proximity.

Proximity.   Bill Clinton and Hillary Rodham met when Hillary caught Bill staring at her in the Yale law school library. "I decided this was ridiculous," Hillary Clinton recalled. "So I got up and walked up to him and waited until he finished, and I said, 'You know, if you're going to keep looking at me and I'm going to keep looking back, we at least ought to know each other.'" (Ifill, 1992).

This meeting of the future president and first lady illustrates a basic finding about interpersonal attraction: whom you are attracted to depends in part on **proximity,** or physical nearness. Another illustration of the power of proximity is the case of a husband and wife described by Robert Baron and Donn Byrne (1991). The couple, who donated a large amount of money to New York University, mentioned that they had met in an economics class there. And it wasn't just that they had shared a class—their names were Edward *George* and Francis *Gildea,* and seating in the class was alphabetical! Although you may not marry the person seated in front of you, research has shown that in classes with alphabetical seating, students usually get to know other students whose last names begin with a letter near theirs (Segal, 1974).

Many other studies have demonstrated the link between physical proximity and attraction. Leon Festinger and his co-workers (1950), for example, found that most of the close friends of married students living in M.I.T. graduate student apartments lived in the same building. Even within buildings, students were more likely to befriend others who lived near them on the same floor. Moreover, the most "popular" students tended to live in either a floor's middle apartments or end apartments near staircases—two locations that made casual interaction more likely (Figure 19.1) (also see Ebbesen et al., 1976; Hays, 1985; Priest & Sawyer, 1967).

Thus, being in the same place at the same time as someone else increases the chances that attraction will occur. Proximity is, however, rarely sufficient by itself. Other factors come into play as well, including physical attractiveness, perceived similarity, and a feeling that liking is returned. Let's explore these additional influences on attraction, beginning with appearance.

Physical attractiveness.   We already know from Chapter 18 that physical attractiveness can play a large role in the first impressions we form of others, and that attractive people tend to be viewed more positively in many ways than less

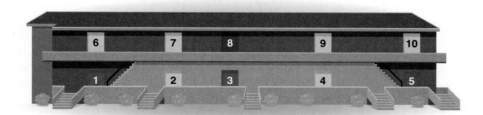

FIGURE 19.1
The effect of proximity on liking. Students who lived in apartments 1 and 5 near the staircases and in apartments 3 and 8 in the middle of each floor were the most popular because many people passed by apartments 1 and 5 on their way to and from the stairs and because apartments 3 and 8 had two neighbors on either side.

attractive people (Cash & Janda, 1984; Feingold, 1989). That would seem to give attractive people an advantage over others when it comes to being liked, no matter how much we might say that "Beauty is only skin deep" and "You can't tell a book by its cover"—and research bears this out.

Elaine Walster and her co-workers (1966) provided early evidence for the importance of attractiveness in a "real-world" setting by setting up a "computer-match" dance for freshmen at the University of Minnesota. Before the dance, students filled out questionnaires about their attitudes and interests, which they assumed would be analyzed by a computer to determine their date. In reality, dates were assigned randomly. After students at the dance had been with their dates for a few hours, they filled out another questionnaire that explored how they felt about their dates. The main finding from this questionnaire was that scholastic aptitude, personality traits, and the date's attitudes had no effect at all on whether the students liked their date, but that attractiveness did—the more physically attractive their dates were, the more the students liked them.

A number of follow-up studies confirmed the basic findings of the Walster research. Yet other studies have shown that when people are asked what qualities are important in potential mates, physical attractiveness is not at the top of the list. Traits such as "kind and understanding," "exciting personality," and "pleasing disposition" outrank physical attractiveness in importance for both men and women (Buss & Barnes, 1986; Buss et al., 1990; deRaad & Doddema-Winsemius, 1991). What's going on here?

One way to think about this question is to acknowledge the importance of attractiveness, which has been documented in a large number of studies, and to assume that each person is seeking the most attractive partner available. Although an ordinary-looking person might want to pair up with a highly attractive person, the attractive person, who also has the same desire, will be more likely to succeed in pairing up with another highly attractive person. Thus, in general, the best partner available to the ordinary-looking person is another person of similar attractiveness. And this is exactly what research shows. Both same-sex and opposite-sex pairs tend to be *matched* in attractiveness, and this is true not only for romantic couples but for friends (McKillip & Reidel, 1983). Although attractiveness is still important to people once they are in a relationship, they also come to appreciate other traits such as personality, kindness, and understanding. Thus, as we saw in Chapter 10, people rate "emotional security" as the most important component in their satisfaction with their relationship (Berry & Williams, 1987).

Although most couples are matched in attractiveness, some aren't. What is your reaction when you see a very attractive woman with a less attractive, perhaps much older, man? Do you find yourself speculating about what the man brings to the relationship? This is the starting point for **exchange theory,** which states that we choose relationships that are "profitable," and that relationships tend to be stable when both people receive equal profits (Homans, 1961, 1974). When people are similar in attractiveness (or other attributes), there is a balanced exchange between them, at least with respect to those qualities. Applying

Beauty and the Beast, a couple poorly matched in attractiveness. According to exchange theory, this relationship will work only if the Beast brings something extra to the relationship to make up for his appearance.

this idea to our "mismatched" couple, in which the woman is not receiving as much "attractiveness" as she is contributing, would lead us to hypothesize that the woman is receiving something else that redresses the imbalance. Perhaps the man is unusually loving, has a rare personality, or is very rich. Thus, both the rule (that people tend to be matched in attractiveness) and the exceptions (the "mismatches") can be seen as illustrating the basic idea that we tend to pursue relationships that we find equitable. This may also explain another important factor in attraction—similarity not only in attractiveness but in other qualities.

Similarity.   Do "opposites attract"? Think, for a moment, about your friends' ages, attitudes, beliefs, and ethnic and religious backgrounds. Chances are that you and your friends share many similarities. You may know dissimilar people who are in relationships, but the general rule is that the people who become our friends and partners are similar to us in many ways, including their attitudes and beliefs.

Research shows that the more attitudes people share, the more they like each other (Byrne & Nelson, 1965); that friends tend to share social, educational, and religious backgrounds (Laumann, 1969); and that dating couples are more likely to stay together if they are similar in age, intelligence, and physical attractiveness (Hill, Rubin, & Peplau, 1976). Eleanor Smith (1989) also found that dating couples have similar views about gender roles. Thus, men who are very macho—who see violence, risk taking, and conquering women as manly pursuits—and women who are very feminine—who define themselves in terms of their relationship with a man and who see sexuality as one of their primary assets—tend to be attracted to one another.

Why do we like people who are similar to ourselves? One reason may be that their attitudes and beliefs confirm and therefore validate our own. Another reason is that people with similar interests will tend to reinforce each other's behavior. If your friend provides positive reinforcement when the two of you go skydiving together, and you do the same, you're more likely to repeat that behavior in the future. But similarity may also promote a sense of balance or equity in the relationship, in keeping with the "fair exchange" idea introduced a moment ago. A final factor, which also relates to this idea of equity, is *reciprocity*.

Reciprocal liking.   How do you feel about another person if you find out that she likes you? A common response is **reciprocal liking,** or "returning the feeling"—you decide that you also like her. The idea of reciprocal liking can be phrased as "If you like me, then I'll like you back." Rebecca Curtis and Kim Miller (1988) have shown that it can also mean "If I *think* you like me, I'll behave in a way that will make you like me." That is, simply believing that we are liked encourages us to act in more likable ways. Curtis and Miller demonstrated this by telling subjects that they were each going to have a conversation with a "partner" who had been given either *false positive* information about them (so the partner would feel positively toward them) or *false negative* information about them (so the partner would feel negatively toward them). In other words, the researchers manipulated the subjects' *beliefs* about how their partners would view them. In reality, the partners received no information about the subjects and didn't even know that the subjects had been "set up" by the experimenter to think they had.

After a ten-minute conversation between subject and partner, the partner was asked to indicate how much he or she liked the subject. What do you suppose happened? As indicated in Figure 19.2, subjects who thought their partner had received positive information about them got higher "likableness" ratings than subjects who didn't.

Why this result? Curtis and Miller answered this question by observing how the subjects interacted with their partners. They saw that subjects who thought the partner was predisposed to like them had a better attitude, used a

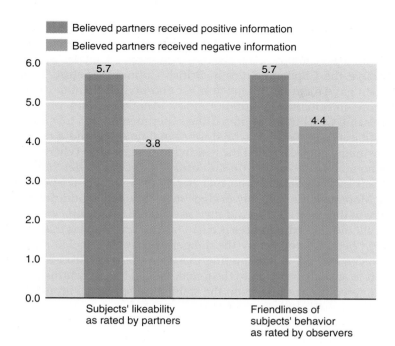

FIGURE 19.2
When subjects believe that another person feels positively about them, they are actually rated as more likeable than if they believe the person feels negatively about them (left pair of bars). Why does this occur? When subjects think others feel positively about them, they are friendlier (right pair of bars).

more friendly tone of voice, and revealed more about themselves than subjects who expected to be disliked. The message of this result is clear: if you *think* someone likes you, you relate to him or her in more likable ways and increase the chances that you will be liked. By the same token, if you *think* you are disliked, you may act in ways that make the person dislike you.

The factors we have covered so far help explain how we select people to have relationships with, from friendships to committed love relationships. However, the relative importance of those factors differs somewhat in friendship and in love. When Arthur Aron and his co-workers (1989) asked people how their friendship and love relationships began, they found that the beginnings of love tended to depend on physical attractiveness, desirable personality traits, and reciprocal liking, whereas friendships depended much more on proximity and similarity.

At least in our culture, we see romantic or love relationships as distinguished from other kinds of liking by the presence of sexual attraction. But love has other characteristics as well. This brings up questions such as "How does sexual attraction come about?" and "What are some other characteristics of love, in addition to sexual attraction?" We turn to these questions next.

From Liking to Loving

If sexual attraction is one of the hallmarks of romantic relationships, how does that attraction develop? Although this is just the kind of question Senator Proxmire said could not be answered scientifically, psychologists have succeeded in identifying a number of factors that contribute to sexual attraction. One approach views sexual attraction as a state of intense physiological arousal that we *attribute* to the presence of another. As you recall from Chapter 18, attributions are the explanations we give for events, including our own behavior. To say that sexual attraction involves an attribution is to say that we *perceive* the cause of the arousal to be the person to whom we feel attracted.

Why this emphasis on the process of attribution? Don't we *know* what causes our arousal when we feel sexually attracted to someone? Not according to a famous study by D. G. Dutton and A. P. Aron (1974), which we will call the "wobbly bridge" experiment.

12   EMOTION

The "wobbly bridge": Irrelevant arousal and sexual attraction.   In this experiment, male subjects were recruited by an attractive female researcher to make up stories "for a psychology study" as they crossed a suspension bridge swaying 230 feet above the Capilano River in British Columbia (Figure 19.3). The researcher then gave them her phone number and invited them to call her if they wanted more information about the study. Another group of subjects was treated the same way but encountered the experimenter on a low, stable bridge. Later the subjects' stories were scored for sexual imagery, and a tabulation was kept of how many subjects called the researcher. The results? Whereas only a few subjects who met the researcher on the sturdy bridge called her "for more information," half of the subjects who met her on the wobbly suspension bridge called her. Moreover, the "wobbly bridge" men included significantly more sexual imagery in their stories than did the "sturdy bridge" group.

Why should these differences occur? One interpretation is that the "wobbly bridge" men became aroused by the danger as they swung 230 feet above the river. However, instead of interpreting their physiological arousal as fear, they attributed it to sexual attraction to the female researcher. In contrast, the subjects who encountered the researcher on the stable bridge had no arousal to explain and so felt less sexual attraction to her.

This explanation hypothesizes that sexual attraction can be caused by a *misattribution* of arousal: arousal caused by one stimulus (the wobbly bridge, in our example) is mistakenly attributed to another stimulus (the woman). Other researchers offer different explanations. J. B. Allen and his co-workers (1989) have hypothesized that the effects of arousal aren't due to misattribution, but rather are caused by a process called **response facilitation,** in which arousal increases the intensity of whatever the person is already feeling. For example, suppose a man is exercising at his health club. Although he is aware that his increased heart rate is due to the exercise, his rapidly beating heart nonetheless increases his sexual attraction to a woman he meets right after finishing the exercise. According to Allen, therefore, a normal response of attraction is simply facilitated by the arousal caused by the exercise.

Whichever explanation of the effects of arousal on sexual attraction is correct, both propose that something unconnected with the target of the attraction contributes to the experience of sexual passion. Of course, passion also occurs without the aid of wobbly bridges, strenuous exercise, or other arousing conditions. But the fact that arousal brought on by danger or excitement can increase sexual feelings suggests that our everyday explanations of passionate attraction may not always supply the whole story.

Moreover, though we may use the word *love* to refer to all or most romantic and committed relationships, in reality love is far more complex. "Love" may mean one thing to one person and something totally different to another (Dion & Dion, 1975; Hendrick & Hendrick, 1986; Lee, 1988; Sternberg, 1988). Many people associate love with powerful emotions, but others associate it more with quiet contentment or meaningful intimacy. Thus, if we ask people about their experiences with love, their answers may reflect quite different conceptions of what love is.

The fact that love has many facets has made it more difficult to study. An important step in the study of love has therefore been to define more precisely the different types of love, so that each type can be studied separately. Robert Sternberg (1988) has tried to accomplish this in devising his triangular model of love.

Sternberg's model of romantic love.   According to Sternberg, we can make sense of the different meanings of love by distinguishing three main components of romantic love:

11   MOTIVATION

12   EMOTION

FIGURE 19.3

Male subjects interviewed by an attractive female on this suspension bridge, which swayed 230 feet above the river, were more likely to feel attracted to the interviewer than were subjects who were interviewed on a more stable bridge.

1. *Intimacy*: a close, connected, and bonded feeling in a relationship. Signs of intimacy include giving and receiving emotional support in time of need, sharing personal feelings, and experiencing feelings of happiness together (Sternberg & Grajek, 1984).
2. *Passion*: a sexually and emotionally charged feeling, associated with romance and physical attraction.
3. *Commitment*: the commitment to stay in the relationship.

These three basic *components* of love can be combined to create seven *kinds* of love, as shown in Figure 19.4. Thus, whereas Barbara's conception of love may be high on intimacy and passion—what Sternberg would call romantic love—David's might be more focused on passion alone—what Sternberg would call infatuation.

In addition to allowing us to define different kinds of love, breaking love into components enables us to look at each component, with its unique characteristics, separately. For example, Sternberg hypothesizes that each of these components has a different time course (Figure 19.5). In a sustained relationship intimacy develops slowly, passion peaks rapidly before falling to an intermediate level, and commitment gradually builds and then accelerates.

How well does Sternberg's theory describe the actual course of romantic love? Not enough research on Sternberg's model has been done to answer this question. However, Figure 19.6 shows the results of a study that measured how

The great love story of Romeo and Juliet focuses on the passionate component of the lovers' relationship.

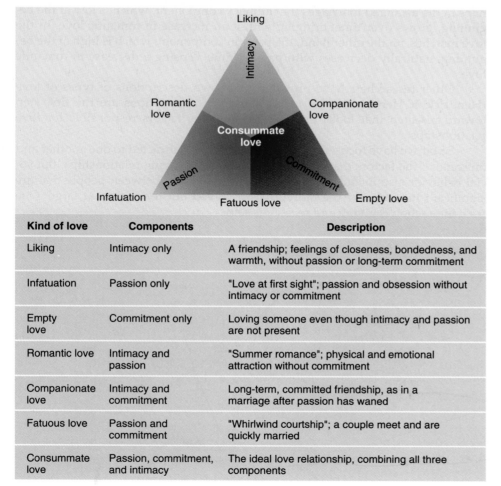

Kind of love	Components	Description
Liking	Intimacy only	A friendship; feelings of closeness, bondedness, and warmth, without passion or long-term commitment
Infatuation	Passion only	"Love at first sight"; passion and obsession without intimacy or commitment
Empty love	Commitment only	Loving someone even though intimacy and passion are not present
Romantic love	Intimacy and passion	"Summer romance"; physical and emotional attraction without commitment
Companionate love	Intimacy and commitment	Long-term, committed friendship, as in a marriage after passion has waned
Fatuous love	Passion and commitment	"Whirlwind courtship"; a couple meet and are quickly married
Consummate love	Passion, commitment, and intimacy	The ideal love relationship, combining all three components

FIGURE 19.4
Sternberg's three *components* of love—passion, intimacy, and commitment—are shown inside the triangle. The seven *kinds* of love are created from these three components.

FIGURE 19.5
Time course of the three components of love, according to Sternberg. These curves are hypothetical; they are not based on actual data.

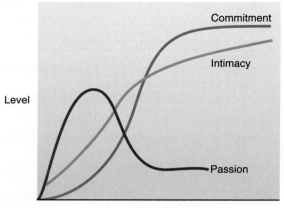

romantic love changed over the course of marriage in two types of couples in India. The first type comprised couples whose marriages were arranged by their families instead of being based on free choice. The second type comprised love matches, in which the spouses chose their own partners. As we would expect, the results showed that in the years just after marriage romantic love was higher in the love matches. However, with the passage of time, romantic love declined in the love matches and increased in the arranged matches. We can speculate, based on the idea that different components of love change over time, that perhaps in the arranged marriages the intimacy component, which is low at the beginning, grows over time, bringing with it an increase in romantic love. In the love matches, on the other hand, the passion component, which is high at the beginning, naturally decreases with passing time, causing a decrease in romantic love.

Other researchers have provided their own descriptions of types of love (Hendrick & Hendrick, 1986; Lee, 1973). Such descriptions are the first step toward research that looks more deeply into the factors responsible for love relationships.

So far we have focused on how people become attracted to one another and on some of the factors that contribute to liking and loving relationships. But social behavior also includes other types of interactions between people that are significant not only for the individuals involved but for society at large. One such interaction is giving and receiving help.

FIGURE 19.6
How romantic love changes in love marriages and arranged marriages in India. After about five years of marriage, the level of romantic love becomes higher in the arranged marriages than in the love marriages.

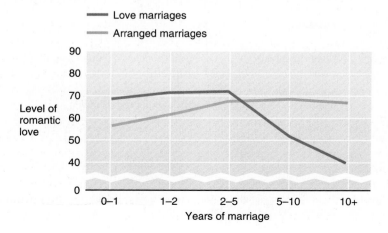

Prosocial Behavior: Helping Others

As often as we do good, we sacrifice.

Thomas Fuller (1654–1734)
English physician and writer

An important area of research for social psychologists is **prosocial behavior,** in which individuals help one another, often at some expense to themselves. Why should psychologists study helping behavior? One immediate reason is the realization that we can't take helping behavior for granted. In fact, it was a notorious case of people *not* helping someone in dire need that provoked social psychologists to ask "Under what conditions are people more—and less—likely to help others?" As you will see, the answers to this question proved surprising.

When Do People Help in an Emergency?

We often hear of acts of kindness and even heroism in response to emergencies—of people who dive into a river to rescue a stranger from drowning or who run into a burning building to rescue someone trapped inside. Yet sometimes those who desperately need help don't receive it. One such case occurred in New York City in the early morning hours of March 13, 1964, as Kitty Genovese, returning home from her job as a restaurant manager, was attacked by a man with a knife as she approached her apartment building. She screamed for help as she tried to escape. Although it was later documented that her screams were heard for over 30 minutes by at least 38 of her neighbors who came to their windows in the nearby apartment building, not one person so much as called the police as Kitty was stalked and eventually killed by her attacker.

The circumstances of Kitty Genovese's death shocked the nation—and inspired social psychologists to carry out numerous studies exploring the conditions that facilitate or inhibit helping behavior in emergencies. To chalk up Kitty Genovese's death to big-city apathy or callous neighbors, as many commentators did, seemed overly simplistic to these researchers. They suspected that the situations in which people find themselves might play a key role in their decision to help or not to help, and they began designing experiments that could isolate those influences.

In one such experiment (Latané & Rodin, 1969), subjects were asked to fill out a questionnaire in a small room while their female experimenter left for a few minutes, ostensibly to get some supplies. A few minutes later the subjects heard a scream, then a crash, followed by the experimenter crying "Oh, my God, my foot . . . I . . . I . . . can't move it. Oh, my ankle . . . I . . . can't get this . . . thing . . . off me."

Imagine that you are a subject in this experiment. What determines whether you will go to the experimenter's aid? In this situation the answer turned out to be *the number of subjects who were sitting in the room.* When only one subject was present, the experimenter received help 70% of the time. However, when two people were present, the experimenter received help only 40% of the time! Many similar experiments led to the same conclusion, which came to be called the **bystander intervention effect**: the *more* people who are present in an emergency situation, the *less* likely it is that a given person will offer to help.

One reason that more people leads to less helping is a phenomenon called **diffusion of responsibility**—the tendency for people to feel less personally responsible for helping when in the presence of others. Other reasons that people are inhibited about helping in the presence of others are that they don't want to seem out of control or to look foolish. In addition, people often fail to help because they decide that, since others aren't responding, there is actually no emergency. Thus, an important basis of the bystander intervention effect is that people take their cues from others around them when defining reality.

Although the major result of the research that followed the Kitty Genovese attack was the conclusion that the presence of more people inhibits helping, other research has shown that the presence of more people may increase helping if (1) it is obvious that there is an emergency, (2) the people in the group know each other and can easily read each other's reactions to the situation, or (3) members of the group have special skills, such as CPR, which they have learned to use specifically to deal with emergencies (Cramer et al., 1988; Piliavin, Rodin, & Piliavin, 1969; Rutkowski, Gruder, & Romer, 1983; Solomon, Solomon, & Stone, 1978). Thus, the bystander intervention effect occurs primarily when the situation is ambiguous and when the bystanders are strangers who can't easily tell how others are reacting.

We have seen that the likelihood that people will help in an emergency depends at least to some extent on characteristics of the situation: how many people are present, the relations between those people, and their skills relative to the situation. When we extend our discussion beyond emergencies, we find that social psychologists have identified some other basic principles to explain why people do or do not help.

Why Do People Help Others?

Let's first consider social exchange theory, which was introduced in our discussion of attraction. This theory analyzes helping behavior on the cognitive level, by considering how people think about the costs and benefits of helping.

Social exchange theory.   People decide to help, according to **social exchange theory,** by considering the helping situation as an exchange of social "goods" from which they can potentially receive some benefit. The potential benefit is calculated by the **minimax principle,** which states that we will behave so as to *minimize* costs and *maximize* rewards.

Let's look at how this might operate for the simple helping behavior of giving blood. Think of how you have reacted when asked to donate blood. Did you feel it was something you should do? Did the idea of giving blood as a way of helping others appeal to you? Did the idea of having your blood drawn make you feel queasy? According to the minimax principle, we decide whether or not to help in a particular situation by looking at the pluses and minuses of a particular action.

Thus, when deciding whether or not to give blood, you might take into account that donating blood would make you feel good about helping and give you access to blood if you needed a transfusion later. On the minus side, donating blood takes time, may be uncomfortable, and may make you feel tired later. *Not* donating would enable you to save time and avoid discomfort, but you might feel guilty for not helping (Piliavin, Evans, & Callero, 1982). Each individual, according to social exchange theory, comes to a decision that *for that person* minimizes the negative outcomes and maximizes the positive outcomes. In some cases this leads to helping behavior; in other cases it does not.

Social norms.   **Social norms**—the explicit or implicit rules of a group about how a member ought to behave—are powerful motivators of helping behavior. One of the most powerful norms of our society is **reciprocity.** We introduced reciprocal liking when we discussed attraction; in that context, it was phrased as "If you like me, I'll like you back." Applied to helping, the norm of reciprocity states "If you do something for me, I'll do something for you." This rule becomes especially powerful if someone provides you with an unexpected favor or makes a great sacrifice for you. Thus, when Sharon lends Bill $50 even though she is short of money herself, she increases the chances that Bill might help her at some later time.

Another norm, **social responsibility,** dictates that people should help others who are in need, without regard to social exchange. Caring for our children and donating money or time to charity are helping behaviors typically associated with social responsibility.

The social norm approach provides an example of how influences operating at the contextual and cognitive levels of analysis can work together. On one hand, context is important because culture-specific norms specify the rules of "proper" behavior. In another society, different rules might lead to different behaviors. For example, Ronald Cohen (1978) describes his observations in an African village as follows:

> In Africa I soon learned that feeling for others was not always considered a profitable or even a proper way to behave. Upon expressing my concern over the fate and feeling of a newcomer to my little village, the leaders of the town said, "Why are you doing all this: after all, this is just a person!" The implication was very clear. In their culture, relationships, especially kinship and hierarchical (patron-client) relations, are the most important things in life. A mere individual outside such relations—as this man was—is of no importance, nor is his fate, whatever it might be (p. 95).

Cohen's experience beautifully illustrates how we need to take cultural context into account to understand helping behavior (or the lack of it). We can combine this perspective with analysis at the cognitive level by looking at how people's thought processes influence their helping behavior. When we do this we see that in practice people tend to apply the cultural rule of social responsibility selectively. They are more likely to help those they believe to be victims of external circumstances than those who are "to blame" for their misfortune. People are more likely to help those whose houses are washed away by a flood than to help those that they believe are homeless because they are too lazy to look for work (Meyer & Mulherin, 1980; Reisenzein, 1986; Weiner, 1980).

One of the main messages of this discussion is that helping is influenced by the person's context—the situation within which helping does or does not occur—and by the person's cognitions about the situation. We now turn to aggression, which is also heavily influenced by context and cognition as well as having powerful behavioral and biological components. We will see that explaining aggression involves all the levels of analysis.

Aggression: Hurting Others

> *To knock a thing down, especially if it is cocked at an arrogant angle,*
> *is a deep delight to the blood.*
>
> George Santayana (1863–1952)
> American philosopher and poet

Aggression—behavior intended to harm or injure another person (Krebs & Miller, 1985)—is one of the most pervasive and troubling behaviors in human society. In the United States alone there are 20,000 homicides, 90,000 rapes, and 1,000,000 cases of child abuse every year (*World Almanac*, 1988). When we consider the world as a whole, violence—in the form of torture, killing, and war—is constantly in the news. In addition there are other, milder, forms of aggression, such as verbal harassment and threatening behaviors that do not lead to actual physical harm. It is tempting to conclude, as some have, from this prevalence of aggression that aggressive behavior is an instinctive, biologically determined behavior that is therefore an inevitable fact of life. However, as we will see, the causes of aggression are more complex than this.

As we ask "What causes aggression?" at each level of analysis, we will see that some of the biological processes involved in aggression have been identified, but that aggression is also influenced by factors such as learning, cognition, and the context in which such behavior occurs.

Biological Level: Instinct and Biology

Men are not gentle creatures who want to be loved. . . . They are, on the contrary, creatures among whose instinctual endowments is to be reckoned a powerful share of aggressiveness.

Sigmund Freud (quoted in Gay, 1988, p. 549)

As we have seen in earlier chapters, the concept of biological forces played a large role in the thinking of Sigmund Freud. To Freud, aggressive behavior was as fundamental as sex—an instinctive behavior that is built into the organism and that therefore requires no learning and resists cultural attempts to control it. The well-known ethologist Konrad Lorenz (1966, 1974) also viewed aggressive behavior as instinctual, citing not only the long history of human aggression, but also the aggression observed in animals. Based on his observations of instinctively determined aggressive behavior in animals, Lorenz concluded that humans share that instinct. Sociobiologists also view aggression as instinctive, reasoning that those who are more aggressive will be more successful in obtaining mates and will therefore be better able to pass on their genes to future generations (Thornhill & Thornhill, 1992).

Although these arguments that aggression is instinctive may seem reasonable, especially in view of the prevalence of aggression, most social psychologists reject them—for the same reason that motivation theorists abandoned explanations based on instincts (Chapter 11). They point out that arguments in favor of an instinctive explanation of aggression are basically circular arguments that look like this:

Question:	Why are people so aggressive?
Answer:	Because of their aggressive instinct.
Question:	How do you know people have an aggressive instinct?
Answer:	Because people are so aggressive.

In short, such explanations don't really *explain*; they simply restate the premise that people are aggressive.

Although they reject the idea that human aggression can be explained simply by calling it instinctive, social and physiological psychologists do believe there is an important biological *component* to aggression. For example, twin studies have shown that the correlation between aggressiveness of identical twins, who share all of their genes, is .40, whereas the correlation for fraternal twins, who share only half of their genes, is only .04 (Rushton et al., 1986). This result argues for a genetic component to aggression.

Another way to examine aggression at the biological level is to search for areas of the brain that might be responsible for it. Evidence that two nuclei—the hypothalamus and the amygdala—are implicated in causing aggression comes from studies showing that electrical stimulation of those areas in cats and monkeys can cause them to behave aggressively, especially if another animal is present as a target for their aggression (Figure 19.7). Further evidence comes from cases in which increased aggression occurs because of brain injury at birth (Mednick, Brennan, & Kandel, 1988) or brain tumors in adults.

Another possible biological mechanism of aggression is hormone action. The hormone testosterone is associated with aggression in animals (Brain, 1979;

FIGURE 19.7
The aggressive display caused by stimulation of this cat's hypothalamus is evidence of the presence of a biological component of aggression.

Mayer, 1974) and exists in high concentrations in human males. It has been suggested that testosterone is responsible for the higher level of aggression in human males compared with females. Studies such as those showing that male prison inmates with higher testosterone levels have committed more violent crimes (Dabbs et al., 1987) also support this link. But because these are correlational relationships, we can't be sure whether high testosterone is causing higher aggression (maybe aggression is caused by another hormone that we aren't measuring) or whether aggressive behavior causes high testosterone, rather than the other way around. Whatever the role of testosterone, there is no question that hormones and brain mechanisms play some role in aggression. As we will see below, however, learning, cognition, and context must also be considered.

Behavioral Level: Learning Mechanisms

One of the most convincing arguments against the claim that aggression is instinctive is that it can be influenced by learning. Evidence of this is provided by cultures such as those of the Hutterites and Amish, the Hopi and Zuni Indians, and the Tahitian Islanders who, by strongly discouraging aggression, have essentially banished if from their societies (Montagu, 1976).

Just as aggression can be reduced through learning, it can be increased in the same way. The mechanisms responsible for learned aggression are familiar to us from Chapter 6: operant conditioning and modeling.

Operant conditioning.   As you'll recall from earlier discussions of learning, operant conditioning is based on the principle of reinforcement. When rats are deprived of water, they will learn to attack other rats if their aggression is reinforced with a drink of water (Ulrich et al., 1963). Humans also increase their aggressive behavior if it is reinforced with money, food, or social approval (Buss, 1971; Gaebelein, 1973). Children who successfully retaliate against another child's aggression—and hence are reinforced for acting aggressively—become more aggressive in the future (Patterson, Littman, & Bricker, 1967). With aggression, as with so many other behaviors, responses that are followed by reinforcement tend to be repeated (Figure 19.8).

Modeling.   Modeling is the learning of a response by watching it. In a classic study of modeling, Albert Bandura, Dorothea Ross, and Sheila Ross (1961) placed a nursery-school child and an adult in a playroom. In the nonaggressive condition, the child and adult played quietly, the adult building a structure with Tinker Toys. In the aggressive condition, the adult viciously punched a large plastic Bobo doll and yelled phrases like "Sock him in the nose!" When the children were taken to another room containing both aggressive and nonaggressive

6   LEARNING

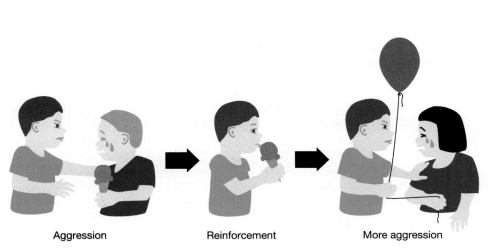

Aggression   Reinforcement   More aggression

FIGURE 19.8
The principle of operant conditioning can be applied to aggression; reinforcing aggressive behavior encourages further aggression.

FIGURE 19.9
Aggression also can be reinforced by modeling. Children who observed aggressive behavior toward the Bobo doll subsequently acted aggressively themselves.

12   EMOTION

toys, those who had seen the aggressive adult played much more aggressively than those who had seen the nonaggressive adult or than children in a control group who had seen no adult at all (Figure 19.9).

If watching aggression can cause an increase in aggression, does this mean that watching violence on TV and in movies can increase children's aggressiveness? Voluminous research indicates that it does (Pearl et al., 1982). For example, second- and third-grade boys were shown excerpts from an actual TV program in which violence was glorified (the "good guys" were admired for their violent behavior). The boys whom teachers had previously rated as being aggressive in class played much more violently after watching this program than they did after watching a nonviolent program (Josephson, 1987). This research, as well as studies like the one discussed in Chapter 2, which showed that children become more aggressive after playing violent video games (Schutte et al., 1988), leads to the conclusion that learning can powerfully influence aggressive behavior.

Contextual Level: Environmental Influences

This discussion of the effects of televised violence and violent video games on aggression illustrates the link between the behavioral and contextual levels of analysis. Although learning principles work at the behavioral level, it is no coincidence that researchers chose TV and video games to demonstrate the link between learning and aggression—both forms of media are consumed in vast amounts by children and adults alike in our society. Our societal context, therefore, provides a generous supply of aggressive stimuli through which people can learn to be aggressive.

Here are a few more examples of the connection between environmental context and aggression:

• Aggression occurs as a response to aggression (Ohbuchi & Kambara, 1985). Thus, a person growing up in a violent neighborhood potentially becomes a participant in a cycle of attacks by one group and counterattacks by another.

• Levels of aggression differ drastically among different cultures. We have already mentioned cultures that have created peaceful societies by strongly discouraging aggression. Another way to appreciate such differences in aggression is to compare the homicide rates of different cultures. Richard Nisbett (1990) points out that homicide rates in Iceland and Israel, for instance, are so low that homicides are "aberrations of extreme rarity," whereas homicides in inner cities in the United States are everyday occurrences.

• Aggression increases when the temperature rises. Riots, violent crimes, and family violence increase in hot weather (Anderson, 1987; Carlsmith & Anderson, 1979; Cotton, 1986; Rotton & Frey, 1985).

In addition to these contextual influences, the environment can contribute to aggressive behavior by providing conditions that create frustration. Frustration is the psychological state that results when a person is blocked from reaching a desired goal. Thus, people who lose money in a vending machine have been known to take out their frustration on the machine, and drivers caught in traffic jams may lose their temper with their passengers or other drivers.

Early research on the relationship between frustration and aggression proposed the **frustration-aggression hypothesis** (Dollard et al., 1939). The original hypothesis stated that frustration *always* leads to aggression, and that aggression is *always* caused by frustration. However, like most plausible and appealingly simple ideas, this one turned out to be *too* simple. Later research showed that aggression is not always preceded by frustration and that not every frustration leads to aggression. A more recent reformulation of the hypothesis states that frustration leads to aggression indirectly, by causing people to experience pain and anger (Berkowitz, 1989). Since not every frustration leads to negative emotions, we don't always respond to frustration by becoming aggressive (Figure

(a) Original frustration-aggression hypothesis   (b) Modified hypothesis

FIGURE 19.10
The original frustration-aggression hypothesis (a) stated that frustration always lead to aggression. In the modified hypothesis (b), frustration leads to aggression only if it results in negative emotional arousal.

19.10). Why do some frustrations lead to anger, whereas others do not? In part the answer lies in how we think about the frustrating situation. This brings us to the role of thought processes in aggression, and to the cognitive level of analysis.

Cognitive Level: Attributions and Arousal

Imagine that you are rushing to see a movie that starts soon, and you don't want to miss the beginning. Your emotions are running high, especially because you have just been ensnarled in a traffic jam that tried your patience to the limit. When you arrive at the theater in the nick of time, you find yourself fidgeting in the ticket line as the unbelievably slow person in front of you fumbles for her change purse and laboriously counts out her money.

In this scenario, in which you are emotionally aroused as you approach the ticket counter and are then faced with a frustrating situation, will you experience the negative emotions that lead to aggression? According to Zillman (1988), the answer depends on the *attribution* you make for your arousal. If you attribute your arousal to the current situation (the woman fumbling for her change), you are more likely to feel negative emotions and to behave aggressively. If, however, you realize that you are aroused mainly because of the traffic jam you experienced earlier, it is less likely that you will be aggressive. Thus, whether or not frustration leads to aggression depends on your cognitive response to the situation.

To cite another example of how cognitive processes mediate aggression, you may feel like being aggressive toward the woman counting out her change if you attribute her slowness to the fact that she isn't paying attention and is chatting with her friends. If, however, you realize that she is visually impaired and attribute her slowness to that cause, you will be less likely to be aggressive. In sum, the way we *think* about frustrating situations interacts with our physiological arousal in determining whether our response will be aggressive.

The phenomenon of aggression is a perfect example of how applying a number of levels of analysis can lead to a more complete understanding of a behavior (Figure 19.11). It is clear that looking at aggression from only one angle—whether biological, behavioral, contextual, or cognitive—tells us only part of the story about why people become aggressive. Thus, a person who is biologically prone to aggression but who grows up in a supportive, nonaggressive environment might never behave aggressively. Another person with the same disposition growing up in a hostile environment, in which aggression is rewarded, might behave aggressively enough to end up in jail. The next section applies three of our levels of analysis to a particularly prevalent form of aggression—sexual violence against women.

Combining Context, Behavior, and Cognition: The Case of Sexual Violence Against Women

Having looked at how aggression can be studied at all four levels of analysis, let's turn to a specific kind of aggression that involves three of them. Violence

12   EMOTION

8   THINKING

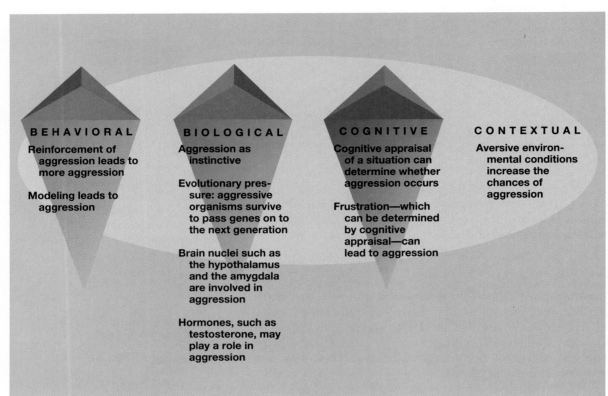

FIGURE 19.11
Levels of analysis applied to aggression. To fully explain aggression, we need to consider all four levels of analysis.

against women is one of the most serious problems in our society: about one in four women are raped during the course of their lifetime, and many others experience attempted rape (Allgeier, 1987; Russell, 1984). Many factors contribute to this alarming statistic, but we will focus on how males' viewing of media depictions of sexual violence against women may increase the likelihood that they will rape or attempt rape.

To begin at the contextual level of analysis, it is easy to see that people in our society are bombarded with media depictions of sexual violence against women. All we have to do is watch television, go to the movies, or read magazines. On TV soap operas, for example, the second-most-frequent sexual interaction is aggressive sexual contact between men and women (erotic touching between unmarried persons is the most frequent) (Lowry, Love, & Kirby, 1981). In movies, widely advertised and attended R-rated slasher films portray high levels of aggression against women, often in a sexual context.

A theme of many of these depictions is that when violence against women does occur, it is not always bad for the woman. This widely circulated "rape myth" even implies that rape may be "liberating" for the victim, who may be acting out what she secretly desires (Donnerstein & Linz, 1992). Thus, scenes of rape and violence on TV and in movies often depict rape as having a positive outcome. For example, a number of episodes of the daytime soap opera "General Hospital" were devoted to a story in which a well-liked female character was raped by a popular male character. Although the woman's initial reaction was one of extreme distress, all ended well: she ended up marrying the man who raped her!

At the cognitive level, researchers have investigated the effects of media presentations of this "woman-enjoys-rape" myth by using the Rape Myth Acceptance scale to determine whether viewing such films changes subjects' attitudes about rape. (See Measurement & Methodology, "Attitude Scales and Rape Myths.") These experiments show that after males view films that portray

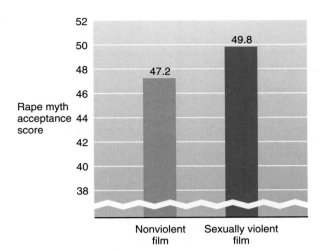

women as eventually having a positive reaction to being raped, their attitude shifts toward a greater acceptance of rape myths (Malamuth, 1984) (Figure 19.12).

The results of this research tell us that the media depictions prevalent in our society can have negative effects. By perpetuating the myth that women enjoy sexual aggression, they create an atmosphere in our society that makes rape seem more acceptable. (In the Follow-Through at the end of this chapter, we will look at the effects of another closely related myth prevalent in our society— that when a woman says "No" to a sexual advance, she really means "Yes.")

But what about the behavioral level? Do media depictions actually cause

MEASUREMENT & METHODOLOGY

Attitude Scales and Rape Myths

Martha Burt (1980) wanted to measure the connection between people's acceptance of rape myths and their attitudes about violence, sexuality, and male and female roles. To achieve this, she constructed a number of scales. For each scale she created a list of items that had good content validity—that is, the items were related to the characteristic to be measured by that scale. For example, all the items on her "acceptance of interpersonal violence scale" were about how people felt about using violence. She tested those items by presenting them to subjects and asking them to respond on a seven-point scale ranging from "Strongly agree" to "Strongly disagree." She then eliminated items to which the subjects' responses correlated poorly with their overall responses to the other items in that scale. The five scales she constructed, along with a sample item from each, are as follows:

1. *Rape myth acceptance scale* (example: "Any healthy woman can successfully resist a rapist if she really wants to.")
2. *Sex-role stereotyping scale* (example: "A man should fight when the woman he's with is insulted by another man.")
3. *Adversarial sexual beliefs scale* (example: "In a dating relationship a woman is largely out to take advantage of a man.")

4. *Sexual conservatism scale* (example: "A woman who initiates a sexual encounter will probably have sex with anybody.")
5. *Acceptance of interpersonal violence scale* (example: "Sometimes the only way a man can get a cold woman turned on is to use force.")

When Burt presented the completed scales to a random sample of subjects, her results indicated a high incidence of acceptance of rape myths in the population: over half of the subjects agreed with statements in the rape myth acceptance scale such as "In the majority of rapes, the victim was promiscuous or had a bad reputation." In addition, she found that this acceptance of rape myths was correlated with high scores on each of the other four scales. Thus, people who hold stereotypical sex-role beliefs and adversarial sexual beliefs, who are sexually conservative, and who accept interpersonal violence also tend to believe in rape myths.

Burt's study illustrates how using attitude scales can elucidate connections among different attitudes. Her Rape Myth Acceptance scale has since been used by other researchers to study the psychological factors involved in rape.

changes in males' behavior? The answer appears to be "Yes," at least as measured in laboratory situations. A large number of experiments have shown that after males view films depicting sexual violence toward women, they become more aggressive toward females but not toward males (Donnerstein, 1984; Malamuth, 1984).

In our discussion of the topics that follow we will continue looking at how the lessons we learn in our society influence our behavior by considering the forces that encourage us to conform, to obey others, and to be influenced by our membership in groups.

Conformity: Keeping in Step with Others

Trumpet in a herd of elephants;
Crow in the company of cocks;
Bleat in a flock of goats.

Malay proverb

If you've ever been in an urban business district during lunch hour, it may have struck you that many businesspeople dress amazingly alike. But before mocking them for being such "conformists," look around you at the students on your campus. They may display somewhat more diversity than businesspeople do, but you'll probably find that students have their "dress code," too. In fact, the vast majority of us are, in various ways and to various degrees, conformists.

Conformity refers to the way individuals alter their behavior to satisfy group standards because of real or imagined pressure from the group. Sometimes group standards are expressed in written rules, such as a code of ethical conduct or dormitory regulations. But many powerful standards are unwritten rules—for example, the rule that you shouldn't stare at a stranger, or that you should leave a tip for your waiter or waitress.

Although people are fond of criticizing conformity, social rules often serve a useful purpose. Dressing in a certain way for business can help create the desired image for a company, and sitting quietly during a lecture enables others to hear the speaker. On the other hand, most of us in this culture believe that people should also be individuals who are free to form their own opinions, follow their own tastes, and—within reasonable limits—behave as they wish. Moreover, most of us probably like to think that we don't conform just for the sake of conforming (we really *like* the clothes we wear, even if all our peers happen to like them, too), and that we can always choose to behave as distinct individuals—especially when we think everyone else is wrong.

But are we really as free as we think? A classic demonstration of conformity, created in the psychological laboratory of Solomon Asch, suggested that the pressure to conform is far more subtle and powerful than we might imagine.

Asch's Conformity Experiment

That we have found the tendency to conformity in our society so strong that
reasonably intelligent and well-meaning young people are willing
to call white black is a matter of concern. It raises questions about
our ways of education and about the values that guide our conduct.

Solomon Asch (1955, p. 34)

Imagine yourself sitting at a table and viewing the stimulus shown in Figure 19.13. Your task is to decide which of the three comparison lines matches the standard line. This is an easy task, and you confidently respond "Number two." Now imagine that a number of other people are sitting at the table with you and that these people, who have stated their answers before you, also said "Number two."

As the experiment continues with other, similar stimuli, each of the people before you gives the correct answer, and so do you. But then something strange happens. All of the other people begin answering incorrectly. It is obvious to you that the correct answer on a particular trial is "Number three," but everyone else is answering "Number one." How do you answer when it is your turn?

This was the dilemma facing the subject in Solomon Asch's experiment, who did not know that all the other "subjects" were actually confederates of the experimenter. Do you feel sure that if you were in that situation, you would stick with the right answer even though no one else agreed with you? Asch's results suggest otherwise. After several other people had given the wrong answer, 76% of the subjects in Asch's experiment responded with an incorrect answer at least once. Since only 5% of the subjects in a control group committed the same errors when they performed the task alone, Asch's result is an impressive demonstration of how others' behavior can influence us to conform.

Why did Asch's subjects respond in this way? Did the others' responses cause them to doubt the evidence of their own eyes, or even to *see* the lines differently? Or did they respond with answers that they knew were incorrect? To determine this, Asch (1957) designed a variation on his original experiment: subjects heard everyone else in the room answer out loud but were told to give their own responses in writing. When subjects were allowed to respond in this way, without having to publicly announce their answers, their conformity dropped by two-thirds. This result supports the interpretation that the subjects in Asch's original experiment were reporting answers that they knew were wrong, as opposed to being persuaded by others' responses. Even though no one was actively persuading them to conform, the subjects were willing to "call white black" rather than differ publicly with the group.

This demonstration of conformity in a line-matching experiment may seem relatively innocuous. However, in other situations conformity can be dangerous. Consider, for example, the teenager who conforms to the behavior of his peers by doing drugs with them or by drinking recklessly in order to fit in. Or consider what happens when large numbers of people conform to repressive laws, customs, or political systems. Conformity, along with prejudice and other factors, can help explain such social inequities as racial segregation in the United States, whether it is enforced by law or—more subtly—by whites conforming to the unwritten "rules" of their club, business, or neighborhood.

When Do People Conform?

What influences our readiness to change our behavior to conform to the behavior of others in a group? We saw in Asch's experiments that conformity de-

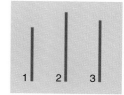

FIGURE 19.13
A stimulus similar to the one used in Asch's conformity experiment. The subject's task is to decide which of the comparison lines matches the standard line in the top panel.

The subject in Asch's experiment (center) reacting when other "subjects" provided the wrong answers to the line-judgment task

creased when the subjects' answers were private. Thus, the situation affects the likelihood that people will conform. Research has uncovered a number of other influential situational factors—among them the degree of cohesiveness of the group, the size of the group, and the amount of social support available to the individual.

Group cohesiveness.   Group cohesiveness refers to the degree to which people in a group like each other and the degree to which a member wants to be accepted by the others. High group cohesiveness tends to foster greater conformity. For example, imagine that you have joined a health club. One of the first things you notice is that a major topic of conversation is politics. You also notice that the majority of the club members express views considerably more conservative (or liberal) than yours. Do you change your views to match theirs? It depends on how attractive you find the group and how important it is to you that the other members like and accept you. If you are content to use the club as a place to work out and are not that interested in interacting with the other members, it is unlikely that your political views will be influenced by the group. If, however, you joined the club to make connections with other people, and you find that you enjoy these people's company, you will be more likely to shift your political views—or at least statements—to more closely match theirs.

The power of group cohesiveness has been demonstrated by a number of researchers. In a classic study, Theodore Newcomb (1943) measured the political and economic attitudes of five classes of students at Bennington College, a small women's college in Vermont. He found that the views of entering students in all five years were fairly conservative, reflecting the values of their wealthy and politically conservative families. However, with each passing year at school the students' views became more and more liberal, reflecting the liberal attitudes of the faculty and older students (Figure 19.14). Newcomb found that this effect was more pronounced for students who were more involved in school activities, and that the students' changed attitudes were still present 20 years later (Newcomb, 1963).

Similar effects have been demonstrated in other organizations. For example, Christian Crandall (1988) demonstrated how binge eating—the consump-

FIGURE 19.14
In the study of Bennington College women, Newcomb found that the students' views became more liberal with each year in school.

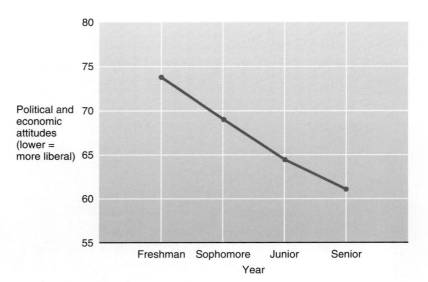

tion of tremendous amounts of food in one sitting—developed in college sororities over the course of a year. New members tended to steadily increase their binge eating, so that by the end of the year their behavior more closely matched that of their "sisters." The power of groups such as sororities and fraternities is enhanced by the fact that conformity is often rewarded by the formation of close relationships, and failure to conform may lead to rejection. Leon Festinger and his co-workers (1950) make this point as follows:

> The power of a group may be measured by the attractiveness of the group for its members. If a person wants to stay in a group, he will be susceptible to influences coming from the group, and he will be willing to conform to the rules which the group set up (p. 91).

Group size.   Does adding more people to a group of people who agree with each other increase the chances that others will conform as well? The answer is "Yes, up to a point." Asch (1955) found that conformity increases up to a group size of three or four and then levels off or even decreases as more people are added (Figure 19.15). Why? Wouldn't adding more and more people increase the pressure on the individual to conform? The answer to this question has to do with how people explain why the members of such a large group all had the same opinion. Subjects may become suspicious of the unanimity and conclude that the other subjects were colluding with one another (Insko et al., 1985), or they may decide that all the other people are themselves conforming to the responses of the first few. This idea was brought up by one of Asch's (1956) subjects, who stated, "I thought the mob was following the first man. . . . Yes, people tend to follow the leader."

Social support.   Asch (1956) found that when a person has an ally—another person who is willing to go against the majority opinion—conformity becomes less likely. Interestingly enough, this person doesn't have to agree with the subject—he or she just has to choose *not* to go along with the rest of the group.

We can understand why this might occur by considering two kinds of social pressure. *Normative social influence* occurs when subjects conform to gain

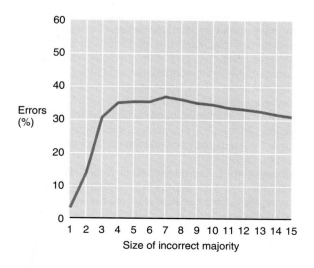

FIGURE 19.15
The effect of adding people to the "incorrect majority" in Asch's conformity experiment

rewards and avoid punishments from the group. *Informational social influence* occurs when people use the group to gain accurate information. In Asch's original experiment, the subjects were probably being affected by normative social influence—they sometimes gave incorrect answers in order to be accepted by the others in the group. Now suppose there is one other dissenter in the group. The subject's observation that nothing terrible happens to that person may make the subject less likely to be prey to normative social influence. In addition, if informational social influence was causing the subject to doubt the correctness of his or her answer, then the presence of a dissenting ally might make him or her feel less certain that the majority was right.

Does the fact that normative and informational social influences push us toward conformity mean that we always conform? Not necessarily. We also want to be seen as individuals and to feel that we can exert control over our lives—two needs that work against conformity. Since conformity is influenced by sometimes competing needs that may differ in different people, it is no wonder that people vary in their level of conformity. For example, in Asch's experiment 24% of the subjects didn't conform on any of the 12 "conformity" trials; 18% conformed on 7 to 9 of the trials; and 11% conformed on 10 to 12 of the trials (Asch, 1957).

In exploring the reasons for individual differences in people's tendency to conform, psychologists have searched for personality characteristics that might be correlated with conformity. Research has shown that in some situations people who are timid and need approval tend to conform more (McDavid & Sistrunk, 1964), and that women conform more than men if they are being observed by others (Eagly, 1978). However, these effects are weak ones that depend to some extent on the specific situation (Eagly & Chrvala, 1986). As you will see in the following Interdisciplinary Dimension, sociologists have taken another approach to how differences among people might influence conformity, by looking at this behavior in terms of the person's place in society.

INTERDISCIPLINARY DIMENSION SOCIOLOGY

Conformity, Deviance, and Social Bonds

Social psychologists are not the only researchers who study conformity. Sociologists also study conformity, but they take a somewhat different approach. One difference between the two disciplines' approaches is the kinds of behaviors they study. Psychologists have typically studied behaviors like the ones we just considered: making perceptual judgments, forming political views, and engaging in eating behavior. Much sociological research on conformity has focused instead on such behaviors as delinquency or criminal acts—behaviors that have broad social significance. This reflects sociology's interest in how individual behaviors are determined by conditions in society. The sociological approach, therefore, looks at conformity and at its opposite—deviance (the term favored by sociologists for *nonconformity*)—at the contextual level of analysis, and often from a more global perspective on that level. Thus, while psychologists may conduct experiments to study how others' behavior influences an individual's behavior, sociologists are more interested in how membership in specific social groups affects the chances that a person will deviate from society's rules. For example, a sociologist would be likely to consider how people's age, marital status, or socioeconomic class affects the chances that they will engage in deviant behavior.

Sociology, like psychology, has developed several different theories to explain aspects of people's behavior. One such approach to explaining deviance, called *control theory,* is worth considering here, both because it is well researched and because it focuses on a topic central to psychology: how rewards influence behavior. As a sociological approach, however, control theory looks at the relationship between rewards and behavior in terms of a person's situation in society.

6   LEARNING

Control theory focuses on explaining deviant behavior—behavior that violates the cultural norms specifying how a person in a particular culture should behave. A basic assumption of control theory is that "life is a vast cafeteria of temptation" (Stark, 1992, p. 187), and that deviant actions are rewarding for those who engage in them. Thus, stealing a car can provide the rewards of fun and the use of a vehicle; taking drugs can cause a pleasurable "high"; and robbing a bank yields that most tangible of rewards—money. The basic principle of control theory is that people conform only when they have more to gain by conforming than by being deviant.

What makes conforming worthwhile? Control theory answers that question in terms of *social bonds,* connections that bind individuals to groups. Simply put, control theory states that strong social bonds lead to conformity, and weak social bonds lead to deviance. There are four types of social bonds: attachment, investment, involvement, and beliefs (Stark & Bainbridge, 1981). Let's look at what control theory has to say about each one.

1. *Attachments:* Attachments are relations with others, such as lovers, friends, family, teachers, and co-workers. Research indicates that the more closely people are attached to others, the less likely they are to commit acts of delinquency (Hirschi, 1969; Liska, 1981). Thus, people who are married are less likely to be arrested than those who are single, divorced, or separated (Stark, 1992, p. 189) (Figure 19.16).

2. *Investments:* Investments are the costs we have expended to get where we are. We invest time, money, and effort to achieve such things as education, material possessions, and successful careers. The greater that investment, the more we have to lose by deviating from cultural norms. Thus a derelict, who has little invested in education, possessions, or a career, has little to lose if he gets caught robbing a bank and thus would be more likely to do so than a successful businessman, whose investment is high and who has more to lose (career, reputation, access to material goods) if he is caught. (Of course, another factor operating here might be that the derelict needs the money more than the businessman.) Control theory also explains the decrease in deviance that occurs as people get older in terms of older people's larger investments compared with younger people's.

3. *Involvements:* Involvements are the amount of time and energy we devote to our activities. A person high in involvement—for example, someone participating in school, clubs, sports, and a job—has little time to be delinquent, whereas someone who has little to do but hang around is more likely to fill time with delinquency (Hirschi, 1969).

4. *Beliefs:* Beliefs about what behavior is "correct" or the "right thing to do" are contained in *internalized norms,* or what we think of as conscience. A person with strong internalized norms might be likely to refrain from a delinquent behavior because he or she would feel bad about having done it even if no one else ever found out.

According to control theory, involvement in constructive work helps prevent socially deviant behaviors.

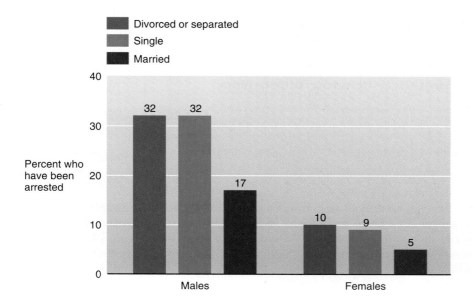

FIGURE 19.16
Married males and females are less likely to have been arrested than those who are single, divorced, or separated.

Control theory is not the only way in which sociologists have looked at the relations between individuals, society, and conformity. Other theories explore how the type of people one associates with affects the likelihood of engaging in deviant behavior (delinquents often hang out with other delinquents), how labeling people as deviant increases the chances that they will have trouble fitting into society (being an "ex-convict" or "ex–mental patient" makes it harder to get a job), and the relationship between a society's characteristics and deviance in that society (crime is higher in cities that people move in and out of frequently) (Crutchfield, Geerken, & Gove, 1983).

By identifying some of the societal factors associated with a person's likelihood of conformity or deviance, the sociological approach enables us to step back and look at conformity from a wider perspective than the psychological studies that investigate how specific conditions created in the laboratory influence people's likelihood of conforming. An important difference between the psychological and sociological approaches is that the latter—dealing as it does with the characteristics of large groups or even entire societies—uses less experimentation and more correlational procedures. Although this correlational research may not enable us to draw conclusions about cause and effect, combining the sociological and psychological approaches results in a more complete understanding of conformity than does either approach alone.   ■

In this section we have been considering the operation of social influence by looking at how people often modify their behavior and sometimes their beliefs simply to match the behavior and beliefs of people around them. Now we turn to a second kind of social influence, one that involves deliberate attempts to change our behavior through requests or commands.

Compliance and Obedience: Bowing to Pressure from Others

Reginald agrees to do a favor for Florence even though he doesn't really have the time. An executive does something she considers unethical because her boss told her to do it. In both cases, a person is acting in response to pressure from another. The first is an example of **compliance**—doing something in response to a request by another person. The second is an example of **obedience**—doing something in response to a demand, usually from a person with authority or power. Somewhat different processes are at work in these two kinds of behaviors. We first consider some of the factors that persuade people to comply.

Compliance: Bowing to Requests

He that complies against his will
Is of his own opinion still.

Samuel Butler (1612–1680)
English poet and satirist

We have all complied with another's request at one time or another. We comply when we do a favor for a friend, when we donate to a charity in response to a phone solicitation, or when, in response to a door-to-door salesperson, we buy a subscription to a magazine we hadn't really planned to subscribe to. People who seek our compliance use several common techniques to get us to accede to their requests. Let's see when and how some of those techniques work.

Ingratiation.   We have already seen that liking is a powerful force. If we think someone likes us, we may like them back and may also respond more positively to their requests. Therefore, one way that people try to gain our compliance is to flatter us, agree with us, and listen attentively to what we have to say (Byrne, Rasche, & Kelley, 1974; Cialdini, 1988). This technique, which is called **ingratiation,** is also used when the ingratiator attempts to make a good impression on the person she or he is trying to influence. If we perceive a person as attractive, sincere, and honest, that increases the chances that we will listen to that person's request.

Techniques based on reciprocity.   When we discussed prosocial behavior we saw that reciprocity is a powerful social norm. Reciprocity elicits prosocial behavior from others if they follow the rule "Because you helped me, I'll help you." Another way to state this norm is "If I do you a favor, you should do one for me." Stated in this way, reciprocity becomes a tool for gaining compliance. For example, some organizations mail out unsolicited colorful stamps or return address stickers imprinted with the recipient's name and address, along with a request for a donation. Even though the recipient didn't request the stamps or stickers, this technique works on people who feel compelled, by the norm of reciprocity, to make a contribution.

A special technique based on reciprocity is called the **door-in-the-face technique** (Cialdini, 1988). A solicitor starts off by making a large request that is usually rejected (we could describe this rejection as the door being slammed in the person's face). He or she then scales down the request to something more reasonable. This technique is often used by people asking for contributions on the phone. I recently received such a call, which began with a request for a $1,000 contribution to the university I attended. I rejected this request immediately, at which point my caller suggested that perhaps a contribution of $100 or $50 might work better for me. I went for the $50 contribution, an amount that I'm sure my caller was pleased to receive. Would I have given $50 if he had started out by asking for that amount? Perhaps not.

Robert Cialdini and his co-workers (1975) demonstrated the door-in-the-face technique by asking college students to commit to working two hours a week counseling juvenile delinquents for a period of at least two years. Needless to say, this presumptuous request was rejected by everyone. If, however, the researchers followed that request with a more reasonable one—that the students help chaperone a group of juvenile delinquents on a day-trip to the zoo—50% of them agreed. When another group of students was asked to make the day-trip without first being asked for the two-year commitment only 17% of them agreed.

How is the door-in-the-face technique related to reciprocity? The key to this technique is that the person making the request is perceived to have done the other person a favor by compromising on the original request: "I scaled down my request, so now you should be willing to compromise also."

Another technique based on reciprocity is the **that's-not-all technique.** This is similar to the door-in-the-face technique, but it happens faster. A salesperson presents you with a product costing, say, $10. Before you have a chance to react to her proposal, she says ". . . but you can have it for $8.50." Research on the that's-not-all technique has found that when two groups of people are offered an item at the same price, more people in the group that was first told the price was higher buy the product (Burger, 1986).

Techniques based on commitment.   Once people are committed to a cause, a product, or a behavior, they are more likely to be open to requests to support that cause, buy that product, or engage in that behavior. One of the techniques based on commitment is called the **foot-in-the-door technique.** This technique involves first making a small request that the person agrees to and then following it with a larger one. To illustrate how this works, let's consider an experiment by Jonathan Freedman and Scott Fraser (1966). Freedman and Fraser asked homeowners if they would place a 3-inch-square sign in their window that read "Be a Safe Driver." Two weeks later, another person increased the request by asking the homeowners if they would place a large, unattractive "Drive Carefully" sign on their front lawn. If they had earlier agreed to place the small card in the window, 76% of them said "Yes"; but only 17% agreed if they had not previously been asked to display the card (also see Beaman et al., 1983).

The foot-in-the-door technique is based on the idea that in making the original small commitment, the homeowners may have come to believe in the cause they were asked to support—in this case, safe driving. Once committed, they were then willing to support the cause. Making such a commitment could also encourage them to see themselves as "helpful," making them more willing to help when asked again.

Another technique based on commitment is called the **lowball technique.** One person gets another to commit to what appears to be a very good deal (for example, a good price on a new car), but later informs the person that the deal isn't as good as originally advertised (for example, the car is still available, but some of the options originally promised aren't part of the deal). Although making the deal worse turns some prospective buyers off, many people will still go ahead with the deal. Apparently, the act of making the commitment is a powerful inducement to stay with the commitment, even under adverse conditions (Cialdini, 1988).

As you were reading about these techniques for gaining compliance, what did you think? Did you wonder why people would fall for them? Or did you think of times when you actually did comply in response to one of these methods? Whatever your personal reaction to these techniques, the fact that they often do work is a testament to one of the central principles of social psychology: Behavior is affected by the situation more than we might suppose. In the next section, on obedience, we will see a chilling example of just how much situation can affect behavior.

Obedience: Bowing to Authority

Obedience
Bane of all genius, virtue, freedom, truth,
Makes slaves of men, and, of the human frame,
A mechanized automaton.

Percy Bysshe Shelley (1792–1822)
English poet

Is this German SS trooper, who is escorting Jews to a concentration camp, illustrating a German character trait of unquestioning obedience of authority? Milgram originally thought so but, when he tested Americans in his experiment, they behaved as he thought the Germans would.

Why did so many Germans obey Adolf Hitler's commands to assist in expelling and ultimately exterminating the Jewish people? Yale psychologist Stanley Milgram thought he knew the answer to this question—he believed it had to do with the German national character. To test this hypothesis he designed an experiment in which people would be ordered to give painful electrical shocks to another person. Would Germans obey as Milgram thought they would? As it turned out, Milgram's question about whether Germans had a special propensity to obey authority became almost irrelevant, because pilot experiments done in the United States showed that *American* men behaved exactly as Milgram thought the Germans would—they obeyed commands to give intense shocks to another person (Lippa, 1990).

Let's look in detail at Milgram's (1963, 1974) procedure, which has already been described in Chapter 2. A subject in Milgram's experiment was given the role of "teacher," with the task of reading a list of words to a "learner" and testing the learner's memory for the list. After the subject was introduced to the "learner"—who was actually a confederate of the experimenter—he watched him be taken to another room and strapped into a device resembling an electric chair. The subject was then seated in front of a "shock machine" with an impressive panel showing various levels of shocks up to "450 Volts XXX Danger."

When it was time for the learner to be tested, the experimenter told the subject to administer the memory test and to deliver a shock every time the learner answered incorrectly. With each incorrect answer, the subject was to increase the shock by one level. As you can imagine, the experimenter's commands made many subjects uncomfortable. Of course, the "learner" was not really being shocked at all, but the subject didn't know that.

As the learner's "mistakes" continued and the shocks reached the level labeled "Intense," the subject heard the learner pound on the wall and demand to be let out. At still higher levels, the learner began screaming "Let me out, let me out, I can't take it anymore!" Whenever a subject became upset and told the experimenter that he didn't want to continue, the experimenter responded by saying "You must continue. It is important that we complete the experiment." The question was, would subjects continue to obey the experimenter's instructions when they believed they were delivering painful and even dangerous levels of shock?

The results of Milgram's experiment surprised not only Milgram himself but also a large group of psychiatrists, who had predicted that fewer than 1% of the subjects would follow the experimenter's orders to go all the way to the 450-volt level (Milgram, 1965). No less than 65% of the subjects obeyed totally, going to the maximum level on the shock machine. Other subjects stopped before reaching this level, but most of them continued beyond the level marked "Intense."

These results were both disturbing and provocative. Evidently, placing ordinary people in a situation that elicits obedience causes them to do things they would not normally do. But what exactly was it about the situation that caused subjects to obey? To find out, Milgram carried out further experiments, systematically changing the experimental conditions to discover what factors affected people's willingness to obey. He found that obedience decreased if (1) the learner was in the same room as the subject (40% went to the maximum in this condition); (2) the subject had to touch the learner, forcing his hand onto a metal shock plate (30%); or (3) the experimenter was not in the same room with the subject (21%). In addition, one of the most powerful ways to influence obedience was to add another "teacher." If this person (another accomplice of the experimenter) refused to continue delivering the shocks, the subject's willingness to go to the maximum shock level fell to 10%. If, on the other hand, the other teacher obeyed the experimenter's commands, obedience actually rose to 93%.

Why did Milgram's subjects obey? Were the ones who delivered high-intensity shocks sadists, who enjoyed shocking their victims? Not at all. Most of the subjects were visibly upset by their situation. Although few of them would have predicted beforehand that they would deliver intense shocks to a loudly protesting person, they did not anticipate the strong pressure they would feel in the situation in which they were placed. What were the pressures? Our previous discussion provides some clues. First, the subjects were influenced by the social norm that they should obey authority figures. In addition, the experimental design made them prey to the foot-in-the-door technique. They began by giving low-intensity shocks that were not supposed to be painful, so by the time the shock level had increased substantially, they were committed to both giving shocks and following instructions. In the experiments in which another teacher was added, conformity pressures evidently operated as well.

Milgram's result, which has been replicated using subjects in a number of different countries (Kilham & Mann, 1974; Mantell, 1971; Shanab & Yahya, 1977),

"Shock machine" used in Milgram's obedience experiment. Although the subjects thought they were presenting shocks with this machine, they actually weren't.

generated a good deal of controversy. We described this controversy in Chapter 2, as well as the ethical problems raised by this experiment and the precautions Milgram took to ensure the welfare of his subjects. Despite those precautions, it is doubtful that a university ethics committee would approve an experiment like Milgram's today. Nonetheless, the results of his experiment stand as a monument to the power of the social situation to influence behavior. An implication of the study is that people may, because of the social situation they find themselves in, engage in destructive behavior that they would ordinarily abhor. At the end of this chapter we will discuss some ways people can decrease the effects of the situation.

Groups: Behaving in Conjunction with Others

Observe any meetings of people, and you will always find their eagerness and impetuosity rise or fall in proportion to their numbers

Lord Chesterfield (1694–1773)
English statesman

Workers in a microchip factory working independently but in the presence of others

Consider the following groups:

- People waiting at a bus stop
- People picking up trash on the beach
- People in a symphony orchestra

Although we have called these three examples "groups," social psychologists would not consider the first one a group like the other two examples. That is because social psychologists are interested in the processes that come into play when people *act* in conjunction with others. Accordingly, they define a **group** as two or more people who interact and communicate with each other over a period of time (Lippa, 1990). Thus, a group in this sense is more than a temporary conglomeration of people standing at a bus stop. At the same time, a group may be informal and relatively short-lived—like a group of volunteers working to clean up a beach—or formal and relatively enduring—like a symphony orchestra.

Groups are an important part of our lives. We join groups because they meet psychological needs such as the need to belong and to receive affection; because they make it possible to perform tasks that would be difficult or impossible to perform alone; and because belonging to a group is a source of social identity. But groups also introduce their own dynamics and processes that affect our thinking and behavior. Let's look at some of the principal ways in which group processes interact with individual behavior.

Working in Groups

There are two types of situations in which people work in the presence of others. In one, people work independently on their own task but with other people present; in the other, people work together to accomplish a group task.

An example of the first kind of work situation is a person working on a puzzle in a room full of other people. In this example, the person and the others present may not form a group in the sense defined earlier, because the people are working independently and do not necessarily bear any relation to one another. Nevertheless, the situation does affect the behavior of the individual worker. This kind of work situation has been studied by social psychologists since the late 1800s, beginning with Norman Triplett (1897), who showed that children wound in fishing lines faster when standing next to each other than when alone. This study, and many that followed, indicated that working in the presence of others enhances an individual's performance, a phenomenon called **social facilitation.** Further research indicated that for more difficult tasks, the presence of others can impair a person's performance. Both of these effects—better performance in the presence of others for easy tasks and worse performance for harder tasks—have been traced to arousal caused by the presence of others (Zajonc, 1965, 1980). Apparently, being aroused energizes people to do well on simple tasks but makes it more difficult for them to concentrate on hard tasks.

An example of the second kind of work situation is a group of people pulling on a rope, as in a tug-of-war. In this type of work situation, in which each person's work contributes to the performance of the whole group, a phenomenon called **social loafing** occurs—individuals exert less effort when their efforts are combined with others' than when they work alone (Latané, Williams, & Harkins, 1979; Shepperd, 1993).

The classic social loafing experiment was carried out by Max Ringelmann (1913), a French agricultural engineer. Ringelmann had single individuals and groups of various numbers of people pull on a rope as hard as they could while he measured the force they exerted. He found that as people were added to the group, the individual members *decreased* their effort (Figure 19.17). Thus, when pulling in a group of four people, an individual pulls only 75% as hard as he pulled when alone. Other researchers have reported similar results for the rope-pulling task (Ingham et al., 1974). These researchers have concluded that the decrease in the efficiency of the group, compared with that of the individual, could be accounted for by two factors: (1) loss of coordination (for example, everyone pulling in a tug-of-war may not pull in exactly the same direction at the same moment, causing some cancellation of effort) and (2) social loafing (each person exerts less effort).

How can we be sure that the decrease in group effort observed in the rope-pulling task isn't all due to loss of coordination? Alan Ingham and his co-workers (1974) answered this question by blindfolding people and giving them the impression they were pulling either by themselves or with other people, even though in all cases they were pulling alone. Ingham's subjects pulled less hard when they thought they were pulling with others than when they thought they were pulling alone. Thus, the decrease in group effectiveness cannot be explained by coordination losses alone. People loaf when they are working as part of a group—and even when they *think* they are working as part of a group.

Why do people loaf? Perhaps because when people work in groups their efforts become lost in the crowd. Since there is no way to evaluate how hard an

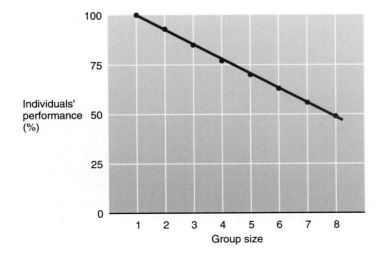

FIGURE 19.17
Data from Max Ringelmann's experiment show that adding people to a group pulling a rope causes a systematic decrease in the amount of effort exerted by each individual.

11   MOTIVATION

individual is working within the group, the person loafs. To test this explanation, experimenters have led subjects to believe that their individual output could be measured while they worked as part of a group. When they did this, social loafing vanished (Williams, Harkins, & Latané, 1981).

Both social facilitation and social loafing show that the presence of others can influence an individual's work performance. A person's behavior can also be affected by others when a group is making decisions.

Making Decisions in Groups

When people get together to discuss an issue or make a decision, how does the process of group discussion affect the views of individuals in the group? We can answer this question by describing an experiment conducted by David Myers and George Bishop (1970), in which they had two groups of high school students discuss their attitudes about race. The students in the *high-prejudice group* began the discussion with prejudicial attitudes about race. The students in the *low-prejudice group* were not as prejudiced. As you can see from the results (Figure 19.18), discussion within a like-minded group tended to make the views of the individual members more extreme—those who were prejudiced became more prejudiced; those who were less prejudiced became even less prejudiced.

The Myers and Bishop result is an example of **group polarization,** in which individuals who participate in a group shift their views toward more extreme positions. Thus, interactions between like-minded people strengthen their views—liberals become more liberal, conservatives more conservative.

Why does group polarization occur? Psychologists point to the following two explanations:

1. *Social comparison*: As the person determines the consensus of the group, he or she may begin to feel that it is "correct" and also feels social pressure from the group to conform. This is similar to normative social influence, which was introduced in our discussion of conformity: people shift their views to gain others' approval (Goethals & Zanna, 1979).
2. *Informal influence*: Exposure to persuasive arguments, such as those that people in a like-minded group have access to, can influence members' opinions so that they become more extreme (Isenberg, 1986).

8 THINKING

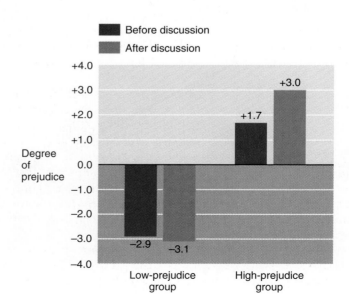

FIGURE 19.18
Group polarization. Discussing prejudice reinforced the views of subjects in both low- and high-prejudice groups, with the effect being more pronounced in the high-prejudice group.

What does group polarization imply for the effectiveness of group discussions in making decisions? It has both positive and negative effects. The consensus and cohesiveness provided by polarization can lead to effective, concerted group action. Thus, the goal of a successful political convention is polarization, so that all the party faithful will rally around the nominee and devote their energy to the campaign. On the negative side, by strengthening the initial majority viewpoint, polarization can make it difficult for dissenters (who, after all, may be right) to be heard. For example, juries typically achieve a consensus because the minority eventually accepts the majority viewpoint (Kaplan & Miller, 1987; Kerr, 1981). The lesson for decision-making groups is that understanding the processes that typically operate in groups can lead to higher-quality decisions.

We have seen that pressure from others can alter our performance in a work setting and can also influence how we arrive at our views about issues. In both cases we might say that a person loses some of her or his individuality by being in the group. This occurs in a more extreme form when people feel anonymous as part of a crowd or camouflage their individual identity in some other way. The result is *deindividuation*.

During jury deliberations, group processes may influence individuals to conform to a group consensus.

Deindividuation

Deindividuation occurs when a person feels submerged in the group and so loses a sense of personal identity. In such cases, the person may ignore his or her own standards and go along with a group's behavior. Consider, for example, the following description of the spectators' response to a suicide attempt, reported in the June 8, 1964, *New York Times*.

> A Puerto Rican handyman perched on a 10th floor ledge for an hour yesterday morning as many persons in a crowd of 500 on upper Broadway shouted at him in Spanish and English to jump. Even as cries of "Jump!" and "Brinca!" rang out, policemen pulled the man to safety from the narrow ledge . . .

Leon Mann (1981) analyzed reports of suicides and attempted suicides and found a number of instances like the one in New York, in which large crowds urged a person to jump, jeered when the person was rescued, and even threw stones and debris at the rescue squad. Mann found that these instances of "crowd baiting" were more likely to occur under the following conditions: (1) when the crowd was large; (2) when lighting was dim or dark; (3) when the victim was not physically close to the crowd.

All these conditions have something in common—they all contribute to the feeling of anonymity. The idea that anonymity fosters deindividuation has been supported by many experiments. For example, when Philip Zimbardo (1970) dressed women in lab coats and hoods, so that they resembled members of the Ku Klux Klan (Figure 19.19), they delivered longer shocks to victims than did women wearing name tags and their own clothes.

Zimbardo also carried out another experiment, which shares with Milgram's the distinction of being one of the more frightening examples of how context can encourage people to engage in destructive behavior (Haney et al., 1973). Zimbardo carried out a "prison simulation" experiment in which male subjects were randomly assigned roles as "prisoners" or "jailers" and were instructed to play out those roles in a jail constructed in the basement of Stanford University's psychology department. Deindividuation was achieved by assigning the prisoners serial numbers and having them wear identical uniforms and nylon stocking caps (to simulate having their heads shaved). The guards wore uniforms and reflective sunglasses, which made them more anonymous.

The prison simulation soon got out of hand, as the prisoners and guards began taking their roles seriously. Most distressing was the behavior of the guards, who treated prisoners brutally if they broke prison rules. As the experi-

FIGURE 19.19
The hooded women in Zimbardo's experiment

ment progressed, the guards increased their abuse of the prisoners, and a number of the prisoners became depressed and suffered breakdowns. Although the experiment was originally scheduled to last for two weeks, it had to be terminated after six days.

Zimbardo's study, though a "simulation," points to the power of situational context to influence behavior. And these contexts do exist in the real world—not only in prisons but also in the military and during riots.

Other people—whether they are just standing around, are part of a group cooperating to accomplish something, or are part of a riot—clearly have the ability to affect an individual's behavior. Groups create a special kind of situation that influences individuals to behave differently than they would if they were alone.

Reprise: Social Psychology and Social Change

It is fitting to have ended this chapter by describing Zimbardo's prison experiment and speculating that processes such as deindividuation play a role in the mob violence increasingly observed in our cities. These examples are important not simply because of their dramatic nature, but because they emphasize the connection between social psychology and events in the real world. We can also appreciate the relevance of social psychology on a more individual level simply by glancing back over the topics covered in this chapter. Love, helping, aggression, conformity, compliance, and group participation are all behaviors that commonly occur in our lives.

The importance of social psychology lies not only in helping us understand common behaviors but in helping us prevent some of the negative ones from occurring. Consider, for example, Milgram's obedience experiments, which showed that normal people can be induced to engage in destructive behavior if ordered to by an authority figure. The very unmasking of this phenomenon, which even the experts failed to predict, is the first step toward minimizing it. Being aware of the ways that authority can be abused can lead people to question authority and take more responsibility for their own actions (Powers & Geen, 1972). Research shows, in fact, that simply knowing about experiments such as Milgram's can increase people's ability to resist authority (Sherman, 1980). Similar findings have been reported for other behaviors. For example, learning about the Kitty Genovese incident and the bystander effect in psychology courses increases the chances that people will help others in emergencies (Beaman et al., 1978). Similarly, knowing about the techniques used to gain compliance can lead to clearer thinking the next time you find yourself the target of a salesperson using one of them (Cialdini, 1988).

We have been talking about individual behaviors—how *you* can resist obedience, become more likely to help others, and not be tricked into compliance— but what does all of this mean for society as a whole? We can approach this question in two ways. The first is to acknowledge that since society is made up of individuals, one way to create a better society is to educate its individual members. The second way is to remember that contexts inherent in our society create the situations that lead to many of the undesirable behaviors described in this chapter. Thus, though we know that aggression has biological, behavioral, and cognitive causes, we also know that one way to decrease aggression would be to change the harsh environmental conditions that provide the context of many people's lives.

Psychology plays an important role in pointing out these solutions. But actually implementing them in the real world is an extremely complex and difficult endeavor. Although psychologists may be able to identify an undesirable situation, it is not so simple to change it. It was easy for Zimbardo to solve the problems he observed in his simulated prison—he had the ability simply to terminate the experiment. But we can't just close down prisons, undesirable neighborhoods, or warring countries. Thus, changing social conditions involves political and economic questions that extend far beyond psychology. At the same time, psychological theory and research can provide insights into some of the causes of social problems and point the way toward promising solutions.

Communication Between Women and Men About Sex

Consider the following situation: A man and woman are out on a date. In response to the man's sexual advances, the woman says "No." The man ignores her and continues. Even after the woman pushes the man away, he persists. Why does he continue this behavior in the face of her negative response? Perhaps he doesn't really care what the woman wants. But in many cases the man's behavior is based on the assumption that even though the woman is saying "No," she really means "Yes." This assumption is often a serious error—one that, if pursued, can result in rape. Since as many as 80 to 90% of all rapes are committed by someone the woman knows, and half of all rapes occur in her house (Allgeier, 1987; Russell, 1984), it is likely that communication problems play a role in at least some instances of rape.

Recent research has shed some light on the process of communication between females and males in potentially sexual situations. Several studies have shown that males tend to misinterpret females' friendly behavior as sexual invitation. Antonia Abbey (1982) relates the following incident that occurred when she was a graduate student at Northwestern University. She and some female friends were sharing a table at a crowded campus bar with two males they didn't know. During one of the band's breaks the women struck up a friendly conversation with the males, but they quickly found themselves the target of unwanted sexual advances and had to leave the table. The men had apparently interpreted the women's friendly conversation as an expression of sexual interest.

To investigate this phenomenon in the laboratory, Abbey asked a male and a female student (the "actors") to have a five-minute conversation about their experiences at school while another male and female (the "observers") watched their interaction through a one-way mirror. Following the conversation, both the observers and the actors filled out a questionnaire. Their answers to the questionnaire indicated that (1) male observers rated the female actor as more seductive and promiscuous than did female observers, and (2) male actors' level of sexual attraction to their female partners was higher than the female actors' level of sexual attraction to their male partners. In addition, male observers also rated the male actor as being more flirtatious and seductive than the female observers did. These results led Abbey to conclude that "men are more likely to perceive the world in sexual terms and to make sexual judgments than women are" (p. 236).

Other experiments using similar procedures have led to similar conclusions. Catherine Johnson and her co-workers (1991) found that when viewing a male-female interaction, male observers saw the female actor in more sexual terms than did female observers (Figure 19.20). Johnson concluded that "men are more likely than women to misperceive women's interpersonal behaviors" (p. 475).

What are the implications of these results? If a man perceives that a woman is acting sexually or is signaling a desire for sex when she isn't, this could lead to unwanted advances like the ones experienced by Abbey's friends in the bar or, worse, sexual aggression like that described at the beginning of this Follow-Through. We will return to these results shortly, but first let's consider another, related, communication problem. In this case, the situation is more overtly sexual than in the Abbey and Johnson experiments.

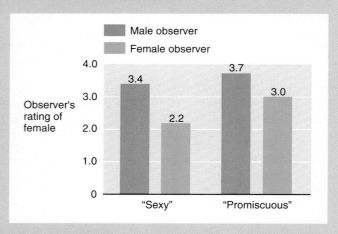

FIGURE 19.20

When male and female observers rated the woman in a male-female interaction, the males rated the woman as sexier and more promiscuous than did the females. This result, among others, supports the idea that males tend to perceive the world more in sexual terms than females do.

A male and female—let's call them Richard and Sally—are on their third or fourth date, and Richard makes advances that indicate he is interested in having sex with Sally. Sally likes Richard and is interested. But even though she does not personally believe it would be wrong to have sex with him, she hesitates to say "Yes."

Why does Sally hesitate even though she would like to have sex with Richard? For many women, the answer might be found in their personal moral or religious beliefs. But other women in this situation report fearing that accepting a man's advances too early in a relationship may lead the man to lose respect for her. He may, in fact, think that she is promiscuous, even though he doesn't think of himself this way (Muehlenhard & McCoy, 1991). The basis for this feeling is the **sexual double standard.** According to the sexual double standard, men are allowed more sexual freedom than women. This difference is reflected in the language used to describe men who are very sexually active ("studs") and women who engage in exactly the same behavior ("sluts").

If a woman doesn't want to be considered "cheap" or "easy" but would like to have sex, what is she to do? One course of action, called the **scripted refusal,** is based on the following sexual script: The male makes sexual advances. → The woman resists. → The male continues his advances. → The woman gives in and, in fact, responds positively. This script, which is often depicted in films and on television, is based on the idea that when a woman says "No" to sex, she really means "Yes."

Most of the time, however, when women say "No" they really mean it. When women *do* engage in scripted refusal, the reason they cite most frequently is that they do not want to appear promiscuous (Muehlenhard & Hollabaugh, 1988). When Charlene Muehlenhard and Marcia McCoy (1991) surveyed 403 women at the University of Kansas, they found that over a third of them had engaged in scripted refusal at least once with a new partner. In addition, over half of the women reported that in a similar situation (a male they had never had sex with made advances), they had openly acknowledged wanting to have sex with him.

What explains why women would say "Yes" to some men but use scripted refusal with others? Muehlenhard and McCoy hypothesized that if scripted refusal is a product of the sexual double standard, then women are more likely to use that tactic if they believe the male subscribes to the double standard. To test their hypothesis, they had all the women in the study complete the Sexual Double Standard Scale, which measured the extent of their belief in the sexual double standard. They then asked them to fill out the scale as if they were the male with whom they had engaged in scripted refusal or the male to whom they had openly acknowl-

edged their desire to have sex. The answers to the scale showed no difference in personal acceptance of the double standard among the women. However, the women who had used scripted refusal recorded their male partners as being more accepting of the double standard than did the women who had openly acknowledged their willingness to have sex. Although this result is correlational, it suggests the possibility that the womens' behavior in the scripted refusal situation may have been at least partly determined by what they thought the men would think of them if they had simply said "Yes."

If we consider this research on scripted refusal in conjunction with the research on males' sexualized perception of women, we can see a connection. If males have had experiences with scripted refusal—a woman says "No" when she doesn't mean it—then those experiences, combined with the tendency to view women's behavior in sexual terms, could lead them to interpret females as wanting sex even when their words and behavior say they don't. Although it is true that most women have never engaged in scripted refusal (Muehlenhard & Hollabaugh, 1988), males have also seen the scripted refusal situation modeled in films and on TV. Furthermore, experiences in which a male's persistence has led his date to agree to have sex even though she didn't really want to allow him to interpret the outcome in terms of the no-means-yes scenario.

The research described here, on communication about sex, is yet another example of how difficult clear communication is between people with different backgrounds, socialization, and cognitive schemas. We saw in Chapter 10 that men and women often have difficulty communicating in nonsexual situations, and in the Follow-Through for Chapter 17 that a therapist and a client from different cultures may communicate poorly because of differences in their upbringing. Differences in upbringing also play a role in the miscommunications described here. In our society, males are socialized to be sexually aggressive, and females are socialized to be relatively passive sexually. These differences, combined with the sexual double standard learned by both males and females, can lead to miscommunication that in turn can result in serious negative consequences for both the male and female. Given the seriousness of those consequences, the message of this research for males is that when a woman says "No," he should believe her. As Muehlenhard and McCoy state at the end of their paper, "Even if a man is certain that a woman's no really means yes, if she does mean no and he has sex with her, *it is rape*" (p. 406).

Attraction: Liking and Loving Others

- Attraction between two people depends on many factors, including proximity, physical attractiveness, similarity, and reciprocal liking.

- People in couples tend to be matched in attractiveness. According to exchange theory, when a couple is mismatched in attractiveness, the less attractive person has to bring something additional to the relationship in order for both people to derive equal "profit" from it.

- Irrelevant arousal may contribute to sexual attraction. One explanation of the results of the "wobbly bridge" experiment is that attraction can be caused by the misattribution of arousal. Another explanation, response facilitation, proposes that attraction can be caused by arousal magnifying normal feelings.

- Sternberg's model of romantic love distinguishes three components—intimacy, passion, and commitment—and seven kinds of love made up of combinations of those components.

Prosocial Behavior: Helping Others

- The Kitty Genovese incident stimulated researchers to conduct experiments designed to determine why people sometimes do not help in an emergency. Their conclusions are formulated as the bystander intervention effect: the more people present in an emergency, the less likely it is that at least one person will help.

- According to social exchange theory, people consider the helping situation to be an exchange of "goods" from which they can potentially receive some benefit. Helping behavior is also fostered by the social norms of reciprocity and social responsibility.

Aggression: Hurting Others

- Aggression has been studied at all four levels of analysis: (1) At the biological level, Freud and the ethologists proposed that aggression is instinctive. Although psychologists tend to reject this explanation as inadequate, there is support for the idea that genetics plays a role in predisposing certain people to be aggressive. From the physiological standpoint, the hypothalamus and amygdala are important brain structures involved in aggression, and hormones such as testosterone may also be involved. (2) At the behavioral level, aggression can be learned through operant conditioning and modeling. (3) At the contextual level, a person's neighborhood and culture—as well as temporary conditions like hot weather—can influence the likelihood of aggression. Aggression can also occur in response to environmental conditions that result in frustration (the frustration-aggression hypothesis), although the effects of frustration may depend on the emotions aroused by the situation. (4) At the cognitive level, aggression can depend on the attribution a person makes to explain her or his negative emotions.

- Rape and other forms of aggression against women have been linked to media depictions of sexual violence. Research indicates that viewing such depictions increases males' aggression toward women in laboratory experiments and can increase their acceptance of rape myths. Belief in those myths is correlated with sex-role stereotyping, sexual conservativism, and an acceptance of interpersonal violence.

Conformity: Keeping in Step with Others

- Asch's conformity experiments show that some people alter their perceptual judgments to conform to those of others in a group, even if the majority's judgments are in error. This effect occurs because of normative social influence and informational social influence.

- Factors that influence conformity are group cohesiveness, group size (conformity increases up to a size of three or four), and social support (the presence of a nonconforming person makes conformity less likely).

- According to the sociological concept of control theory, conformity occurs if social bonds are strong, and deviance occurs if they are weak. Social bonds are a function of a person's attachments, investments, involvements, and beliefs.

Compliance and Obedience: Bowing to Pressure from Others

- Techniques for gaining compliance include ingratiation; techniques based on reciprocity, such as the door-in-the-face technique and the that's-not-all technique; and techniques based on commitment, such as the foot-in-the-door and lowball techniques.

- Milgram's obedience experiments showed that most people will obey an authority figure's commands, even if they involve morally questionable behaviors. This result illustrates the power of situational factors in determining behavior.

Groups: Behaving in Conjunction with Others

- When people work independently but in the company of others, the arousal caused by the presence of the other people can enhance their performance on simple tasks—an effect called social facilitation. For more complex tasks, the presence of others can cause a decrease in performance.

- When people work together to reach a goal, individuals exert less effort than if they were working alone—an effect called social loafing. One reason for social loafing is that the presence of the group makes it difficult to calculate the output of the individual.

- When people get together to discuss an issue or make a decision, individuals often shift their views to more extreme positions—an effect called group polarization. This effect occurs because of social comparison and informational influence.

- Deindividuation occurs when being in a group causes a person to feel a loss of personal identity and hence to become anonymous. When this happens, people are more likely to behave as they normally wouldn't to conform with the group.

Reprise: Social Psychology and Social Change

- By pointing out the situational factors that affect behavior, social psychology helps us understand common behaviors helps individuals resist pressure from others, when appropriate, and provides information that may be helpful in solving real-world problems.

Follow-Through/Diversity: Communication Between Women and Men About Sex

- A number of factors contribute to miscommunication between women and men about sex, including men's cognitive schemas, socialization differences between the genders, the sexual double standard, and the phenomenon of scripted refusal, which men may observe directly or through media portrayals.

Key Terms

aggression
bystander intervention effect
compliance
conformity
control theory
deindividuation
diffusion of responsibility
door-in-the-face technique
exchange theory
foot-in-the-door technique
frustration-aggression
  hypothesis
group
group polarization
ingratiation
lowball technique

minimax principle
obedience
prosocial behavior
proximity
reciprocal liking
reciprocity
response facilitation
scripted refusal
sexual double standard
social exchange theory
social facilitation
social loafing
social norms
social responsibility
that's-not-all technique

Glossary

academic psychologists Psychologists engaged in research and teaching, usually in a college or university setting

accommodation As suggested by Piaget, the process of modifying an existing scheme to deal with new challenges

achievement motivation The desire to accomplish something difficult, to overcome obstacles, and to attain a high standard

achievement tests Tests to measure mastery of specific areas such as reading, mathematics, foreign languages, and science

action potential The rapid increase in positive charge inside an axon as an electrical message is conducted down the axon

actor-observer effect The tendency for a person performing a behavior (the actor) to attribute the behavior to the situation and for a person watching the behavior (the observer) to attribute the same behavior to the actor's disposition

adaptation As suggested by Piaget, the process that occurs when changes in schemes are made as a result of experience

adolescence The developmental period beginning with puberty and ending with young adulthood

adolescent egocentrism Adolescents' belief that other people share their own preoccupation with themselves

aggression Behavior intended to harm or injure another organism

agoraphobia A condition in which people are afraid of being in any place or situation from which they feel escape might be difficult in the event of an anxiety attack

alarm stage The first stage of Hans Selye's general adaptation syndrome in which the autonomic nervous system and endocrine system release hormones into the bloodstream, which energizes the body to deal with stress

algorithms Procedures that are guaranteed to result in the solution of a problem, such as the procedures for multiplication and division

alpha waves Rhythmical, 10- to 12-cycle-per-second brain waves that occur in people who are relaxed but awake

altruistic behavior Behavior that is good for the survival of the group but not for the survival of the individual

Ames room A distorted room constructed by Adelbert Ames that causes people to misperceive the sizes of objects by creating misleading depth information

amygdala Subcortical nucleus that is important for emotional behavior and memory storage

analogy problems Problems of the type: A is to B as C is to D

anal stage The second stage in Freud's theory of psychosexual development (18 months to 3 years) during which toilet training occurs

animism The attribution of conscious life to inanimate objects; occurs in children during Piaget's preoperational stage of development

antianxiety drugs Also called minor tranquilizers; used to treat people suffering from anxiety disorders as well as those who are overly nervous or tense

antidepressant drugs Drugs, including tricyclics, monoamine oxidase inhibitors, and serotonin reuptake blockers, used to treat depression by altering brain chemistry

antipsychotic drugs Drugs used to treat serious psychological disorders such as schizophrenia

anxiety Apprehension, fear, or confusion; usually accompanied by physiological reactions

anxiety hierarchy The technique used in systematic desensitization in which the patient develops a list of 20 situations ordered according to the severity of the anxiety associated with them

aphagia The condition in rats with a lateral hypothalamus lesion; the animals simply stop eating and will die unless force-fed

aptitude tests Tests, such as the SAT, designed to predict future performance

archetypes Images found in cultures throughout the world that influence personality and behavior; identified by Carl Jung

artificial intelligence (AI) An interdisciplinary field that combines the work of cognitive psychologists and computer scientists

art therapy The use of art to allow patients to express their unconscious thoughts and feelings

assimilation The process of applying existing schemes to new situations; suggested by Piaget

attachment The bond established between infant and caregiver; typically measured by the strange-situation test

attitudes Evaluations of other people, objects, and issues that involve not only cognition but feelings and behavior

attribution A judgment about the causes of our own behavior and the behavior of others

attribution model of helplessness The idea that depression can be traced to the way people explain things

attribution theory Any theory that explains how we assign causes to our own behavior or to the behavior of others

audibility curve The relation between the threshold for hearing a tone versus its frequency

auditory canal A small tube in the ear whose function is to protect the delicate structures inside the ear from the hazards of the outside world

auditory cortex Part of the cortex in the temporal lobe of the brain involved in hearing

autonomic nervous system Responsible for communicating between the brain and the body's internal organs

availability heuristic Events that are easily remembered are judged to be more probable than events less easily remembered

aversion therapy Therapy that links aversive stimuli, such as fear or discomfort, with behaviors targeted for elimination

axon A neural fiber that conducts electrical signals

backward conditioning Conditioning technique in which the neutral stimulus is presented after the unconditioned stimulus

bait shyness Phenomenon in which a rat eats a piece of poisoned bait, gets sick but lives, and learns to avoid any bait with the same taste

baseline level In operant conditioning, the rate of response prior to the introduction of reinforcement

basic anxiety According to Karen Horney, the feelings of insecurity, isolation, or helplessness that are produced from the dynamics of childhood relationships

basic rule of experimentation In order to determine a cause-and-effect relationship, change one variable while keeping every other relevant variable constant

basilar membrane The membrane that runs down the middle of the cochlea; its vibration in response to a sound stimulus leads to stimulation of the hair cells

behavioral level of analysis Research that focuses on measuring observable behavior

behavioral medicine Field of health psychology that involves collaboration between psychologists, physicians, and biomedical scientists

behaviorism Viewpoint made popular by John B. Watson; argued that psychology should focus on behavior that could be publicly observed

behavior therapy Therapy based on the principles of conditioning

Big Five personality dimensions Five basic factors that have been used to describe personality: extraversion, agreeableness, conscientiousness, emotionality, and intelligence

binocular depth cue Allows us to see depth because of a difference in the location of images on each retina

biofeedback training A way for people to gain control over their own physiological functions

biological clock A "clock" in our bodies that controls our circadian rhythms

biological level of analysis Research that emphasizes the relationships among the brain, nervous system, and behavior

biomedical model States that all diseases or physical disorders can be explained by disturbances of physiological processes, such as infection, injury, or inborn abnormality

biomedical therapies Interventions intended to ease the symptoms associated with psychological disorders by modifying physiological processes such as brain chemistry

bipolar disorder A mood disorder characterized by depression and bouts of mania

blaming the victim The tendency to explain unfortunate events that happen to others as being caused by characteristics of the victims

blind interviewing procedure Research technique in which the interviewer does not know the groups to which individual subjects have been assigned

blind scoring procedure A research technique in which the scorer is unaware of which condition the subject received

blocking The prevention of the conditioning of one stimulus pair by the prior conditioning of another stimulus

brain The complex network of neurons contained in the skull that directs behavior; creates perceptions, emotions, and thoughts; and oversees bodily functions

brain lesioning Destroying a brain structure

brain stem The base of the brain, just above the spinal cord, that contains the medulla

brain stimulation Presenting an electrical or chemical stimulus to a brain structure

Broca's area Part of the cerebral cortex, usually in the left frontal lobe, that is involved in speech

buffering hypothesis The idea that social support provides a buffer that protects people against high levels of stress

bystander intervention effect The more people who are present in an emergency situation, the less likely a given person will offer to help

California Personality Inventory (CPI) Self-report personality test designed to measure the personality characteristics of people without psychiatric problems

Cannon-Bard theory An emotion-producing stimulus stimulates the thalamus, which in turn activates the cortex and the autonomic nervous system, causing emotional feelings and bodily responses

cardinal trait According to Gordon Allport, the overriding trait that dominates one's personality

case study In-depth observations of the history and behavior of an individual subject

castration anxiety A boy's fear that his father will cut off his penis because he is a rival for his mother; occurs during Freud's phallic stage of development (4–5 years)

catatonic schizophrenia Type of schizophrenia in which the patient may become frozen into the same pose for hours or become excitable and hyperactive

categories Groups of objects or events having similar properties

causal attribution The process by which people determine the causes of events

cause-and-effect relationship A situation in which one variable causes another variable; determined experimentally by following the basic rule of experimentation

cell body Part of the neuron that contains the nucleus and the other metabolic mechanisms needed to keep the cell alive

central nervous system The neurons that comprise the brain and spinal cord

central route to persuasion When messages are given high elaboration or deliberate processing of information and arguments

central trait According to Gordon Allport, the type of trait that is readily available in a person's day-to-day life

cerebellum The small, wrinkled structure nestled under the back of the brain that controls coordinated movement

cerebral cortex A thin layer of neurons covering the brain; contains mechanisms that enable us to coordinate our movements, perceive the environment, and carry out higher mental functions, such as language, problem solving, and planning for the future

chunking Memory aid that involves combining a number of small units to make a larger one that is easier to remember

circadian rhythm Internal bodily rhythms that operate on a 24-hour cycle

classical conditioning A procedure in which a previously neutral stimulus is paired with one that elicits a response so that the neural stimulus also comes to elicit the response

client-centered therapy Developed by Carl Rogers, a type of psychotherapy based on the idea that people have an innate tendency to grow in a healthy way; the therapist creates an accepting environment and interacts with the client in a nondirective manner

clinical psychologists Usually earn a Ph.D. and are trained in the diagnosis and treatment of psychological disorders; may also do research

cochlea Bony, snail-like structure in the inner ear that is filled with liquid and contains the receptors for hearing

cognitive appraisal An assessment of the significance of a particular situation for a person's well-being; involved in the creation of emotions, according to Richard Lazarus

cognitive dissonance The unpleasant state of arousal that occurs when we discover inconsistencies in our beliefs or between our beliefs and our behavior

cognitive distortions Beck's cognitive therapy suggests these are errors in thinking that can lead to erroneous conclusions

cognitive level of analysis Research that explores the study of mental processes such as memory

cognitive map A map of the environment to be formed during exploration of an area, suggested by Edward Tolman

cognitive psychology The study of such mental processes as memory, problem solving, language, and decision making

cognitive restructuring One of the goals of Aaron Beck's cognitive therapy; involves changing a person's thinking to remove cognitive distortions

cognitive therapy Type of psychotherapy developed by Aaron Beck and used to treat depression and anxiety disorders; works to change the way the client thinks about his or her life experiences

cognitive triad Refers to Beck's assertion that people who are depressed experience automatic negative thoughts about themselves, the environment, and the future

collective unconscious The type of *species* memories shared by all human beings, independent of culture; suggested by Carl Jung after he observed universal products of the mind, such as myths, beliefs, and fears

color matching Experiment used to test people's observable response to colors by having them match the color of one wavelength of light by combining two or more other wavelengths

common fate, law of Gestalt law of perception that states that we tend to group together things moving in the same direction

communication deviance (CD) Pattern of family communication in which the parents attack the child personally and do not focus on what the child is saying

compliance Doing something in response to a request by another person

componential aspect One of the three components of Robert Sternberg's triarchic theory of intelligence; refers to a person's ability to learn new things, to think analytically, and to solve problems

computerized axial tomography (CAT) scan Most widely used brain imaging technique; combines X-ray technology with computer processing in order to visualize the living brain

concordance The percentage of people who, given a certain relationship to someone with a disorder, would be expected to develop the same disorder

concrete operations stage One of the stages of Piaget's theory of cognitive development during which children begin to think logically

conditioned drug tolerance A classical conditioning explanation of drug tolerance; suggests that the decrease in a drug's effect on the body is the result of a compensatory response in the body triggered by familiar surroundings (conditioned stimuli)

conditioned emotional response An emotional response elicited by a previously neutral stimulus after it has been associated with an aversive stimulus

conditioned response (CR) In classical conditioning, the reaction that has been conditioned to occur in response to a conditioned stimulus

conditioned stimulus In classical conditioning, a previously neutral stimulus that comes to elicit a conditioned response after being paired with an unconditioned stimulus

conditioned suppression (CS) Occurs when a stimulus that has gained negative properties because of its association with an aversive unconditioned stimulus suppresses ongoing behavior

conditioned taste aversion Phenomenon in which conditioning produces a link between sickness and a flavor so that the flavor is avoided

cones Receptors for vision responsible for color vision and detailed vision

conformation bias The tendency to look selectively for information that confirms a hypothesis and to overlook information that argues against it

conformity The way individuals alter their behavior to satisfy group standards because of real or imagined pressure from the group

conjunction fallacy Violation of the conjunction rule

conjunction rule States that the probability of a conjunction of two events (A and B) cannot be more than the probability of the single constituents (A alone or B alone)

conscience Part of the mind that contains information about behavior that is considered to be bad and punishes that behavior with feelings of shame or guilt

consciousness What a person is aware of and what is accessible at any given moment

conservation The understanding that the physical properties of objects remain the same (as long as nothing is added or taken away), even though their appearances change

consolidation hypothesis States that structural changes in the brain need to remain undisturbed for a period of time before long-term memories become firmly established

consolidation period Period of time necessary for structural changes in the brain to establish long-term memory

constructive nature of memory The idea that recall is not a mental photograph of reality but is constructed from a combination of information stored in memory and other information on hand

construct validity Refers to how well test results reflect the quality or trait that a test was designed to measure

content validity The extent to which test questions are relevant to the ability being tested and are an accurate cross-section of possible questions relevant to that ability

contextual aspect One of the three components of Robert Sternberg's triarchic theory of intelligence; refers to a person's ability to deal with practical aspects of the environment and to adapt to new and changing contexts

contextual level of analysis Research that focuses on how behavior is influenced by the overall physical and social context in which it occurs

contiguity hypothesis The idea that classical conditioning would work with any neutral stimulus as long as it occurs about the same time as the unconditioned stimulus

continuity vs. discontinuity A basic issue in the study of development, involving the question of whether development is a smooth, continuous process or a sequence of distinct stages

continuous reinforcement schedule (CRF) In operant conditioning, the pattern of reinforcement in which every response is reinforced

control group The group in an experiment that does not experience the independent variable

control theory A sociological theory that focuses on explaining deviant behavior or behavior that violates cultural norms

conversational rule Used by a listener to determine the real meaning of a sentence

conversion disorder Condition in which a loss of physical function occurs without any organic damage

Coolidge effect The finding that a sexually gratified male rat or hamster will become aroused when a new female is presented

cornea The transparent front of the eye through which light passes

coronary heart disease (CHD) Consists of a number of conditions that result from the narrowing or blocking of arteries that serve the heart

corpus callosum A bundle of nerve fibers that connects the left and right hemispheres of the brain

correlation Occurs when two variables are related to each other so that specific values of one are associated with specific values of the other

correlation coefficient A number that indicates the strength of the relationship between two variables

counselors Have a master's degree in counseling and are often employed by school systems and social service agencies

counterconditioning A procedure in which a new response, such as relaxation, is conditioned to a stimulus that arouses anxiety or fear

cross-sectional method Research method in which the same behavioral characteristics of a number of groups of people, each differing in age, are compared

crystallized intelligence Intelligence based on abilities gained from previous experiences, such as vocabulary skills or historical knowledge

cultural norms The rules of behavior that are developed by a society

cultural-familial retardation Retardation that has been linked to environmental deprivation

cumulative record Used in conditioning research, a record of an animal's cumulative responses versus time

cyclothymia A mild form of bipolar disorder

deception Research technique used to hide the real purpose of a study

deduction Type of reasoning; when certain assertions are true, a conclusion must follow

deductive reasoning Type of reasoning using deduction

deep processing Processing the meaning of a stimulus and relating it to other things we know

defense mechanisms Unconscious tactics, such as denial and displacement, that help the ego deal with high levels of anxiety

deindividuation Occurs when a person feels submerged in a group and loses a sense of personal identity

deinstitutionalization The program involving releasing patients from mental hospitals, placing them in jobs and housing within the community, and supporting them with a network of community mental health facilities

delay conditioning A conditioning procedure in which the neutral stimulus is presented first and remains present while the unconditioned stimulus is presented

delta waves Large, low-frequency brain waves that appear in stage three sleep

delusions False beliefs that do not mesh with reality

demand characteristics Characteristics of an experimental situation that suggest how a subject should behave

dendrite Part of the neuron that branches out from the cell body to receive electrical signals from other neurons

dependent retarded The severely retarded who are always dependent on others for their care

dependent variable The variable that is hypothesized to change as a result of manipulations of the independent variable

depressive disorder A type of mood disorder

depth cues Properties of visual stimuli that provide the information that creates the perception of depth

descriptive statistics Statistics that summarize and organize data

developmental psychologists Psychologists who study the process of human development

Diagnostic and Statistical Manual of Mental Disorders **(DSM)** A book published by the American Psychiatric Association, used by psychologists to assign diagnoses to patients

diathesis-stress model The idea that a person becomes vulnerable to schizophrenia because of his or her genetic inheritance but actually becomes schizophrenic only if subjected to stresses that are too much to manage

differential reinforcement A process in which a behavior is reinforced in the presence of one stimulus and extinguished in the presence of another

diffusion of responsibility The tendency for people to feel less personally responsible for helping when in the presence of others

discrimination training A procedure in which a response is conditioned to one stimulus while simultaneously being extinguished to another stimulus

discriminative stimulus A stimulus that signals whether a response will be followed by a reinforcer

disorganized schizophrenia Type of schizophrenia characterized by a general deterioration of adaptive behavior

display rules Rules that specify when it is appropriate to display certain emotions

dissociation A psychological disorder in which a set of activities becomes separated from the rest of the person's mind and functions independently

dissociative disorders Psychological disorders characterized by a disturbance of a person's consciousness and identity

dizygotic (DZ) twins Fraternal twins who are the result of two different zygotes fertilized by different sperm

dominant hemisphere Thought to be the left hemisphere because language is predominantly located there

door-in-the-face technique Used to gain compliance by making a large request and, when it is denied, offering a more reasonable request

dopamine Brain neurotransmitter that is involved in controlling voluntary movements; implicated in Parkinson's disease and schizophrenia

dopamine hypothesis The idea that the symptoms of schizophrenia are associated with an excess of the excitatory neurotransmitter dopamine

double-bind communications A type of communication that transmits two incompatible messages; seen in families with communication deviance

double-blind procedure Situation in which neither the subject nor the experimenter knows which group a research subject is in

double standard An unwritten rule of society in which females are held to different standards than males

Down's syndrome A genetic condition characterized by almond-shaped eyes, a broad face and nose, short neck and hands, moderate mental retardation, poor verbal and language skills, and good spatial skills

dream work According to Freud, the process by which dangerous material in the unconscious is distorted to a form that appears in a dream; the distortion protects us from becoming aware of the dangerous material

drive An internal state of tension buildup

drive reduction The satisfaction of a drive

dual-center hypothesis The idea that the ventromedial hypothalamus and the lateral hypothalamus are centers in the brain that control hunger and feeding behavior

dysthymia A depressive disorder with symptoms milder than major depression

echoic memory The brief sensory memory for auditory stimuli

eclecticism The use of various therapeutic approaches in conjunction with each other

effort justification effect The finding that people will be more likely to change their attitudes if they invest a large amount of effort or expense toward achieving a goal

ego According to Freud, the part of the mind that is in contact with the outside world

egocentric Interpreting the world in terms of one's own vantage point, without taking another person's point of view into account

ego ideal According to Freud, the part of the mind that contains information about behavior that is good and rewards that behavior with feelings of pride

elaboration likelihood model Model of attitude change that suggests our response to a persuasive message depends on the degree to which we elaborate the message by consciously and actively processing it

elaborative rehearsal Rehearsal in which meaningful associations are formed between new information to be remembered and information already in long-term memory

electrical stimulation of the brain (ESB) Technique in which a weak electrical current is passed through an electrode in the brain of an animal in order to elicit a specific behavior

electroconvulsive therapy (ECT) Use of electric shock to produce a seizure in the cerebral cortex; used in the treatment of severe depression

electroencephalogram (EEG) Brain waves measured by electrodes attached to the scalp

electromagnetic spectrum The entire range of electromagnetic energy, including X-rays, radio waves, microwaves, and visible light

electromyogram (EMG) Electrical activity of the muscles

electrooculogram (EOG) Electrical response used to measure eye movements during sleep

elimination by aspects A decision-making strategy in which a choice is eliminated if it does not meet a minimum requirement for some consideration

embryonic period Period of prenatal development lasting from the second through the eighth week

emotion A complex experience involving subjective feelings, observable behavior, and physiological responses, all taking place in the context of a specific event or situation

empirical keying A procedure in which a test is given to two groups and the questions that differentiate the groups are selected for inclusion on the test

empiricism Refers to making observations

empty-nest syndrome A period of stress during which the mother is unhappy because her children have left home

encoding Stage in memory in which an object, sound, or event to be remembered is transformed into a mental representation

endocrine glands Glands of the endocrine system that secrete hormones into the bloodstream

endocrine system Comprised of the seven major endocrine glands; communicates with the body through the release of hormones into the bloodstream

epidermis The outer layer of the skin consisting of tough, dead skin cells

episodic memory Memory that stores the kinds of information you would include in your life story, such as the names of the schools you attended

escape-avoidance training A procedure used to measure how a negative reinforcer can increase the frequency of a behavior; often involves the use of a dog in a shuttle box

estrogen Hormone, primarily found in females, that is involved in sexual differentiation

ethologists Group of biologists who study behavior from a genetic point of view by studying the behavior of animals in their natural settings

etiology The factors that cause a disorder

Eve principle The situation in which a female develops unless testosterone is present; refers to the idea that, in a sense, the male is derived from the female

evolution The process by which organisms have changed from their ancient ancestors into their present form

evolutionary theory of sleep Theory that proposes sleep as an adaptive response of a particular species to its environment

exchange theory States that we choose relationships that are profitable and that relationships tend to be stable when both people receive equal profits

excitatory center Label given to the lateral hypothalamus because it seems to turn on eating behavior

excitatory postsynaptic potential (EPSP) A small increase in the positive charge inside a neuron; leads to the generation of an action potential if it becomes large enough

excitatory transmitter Transmitters that generate excitatory postsynaptic potentials

exhaustion stage Stage of Hans Selye's general adaptation syndrome in which stress lasts too long and the organism becomes exhausted and dies

expectancy-value model of achievement Proposes that achievement motivation results from two tendencies, one to approach success and another to avoid failure

experiential aspect One of the three components of Robert Sternberg's triarchic theory of intelligence; refers to a person's ability to combine different experiences in unique and creative ways

experimental design The basic plan of an experiment

experimental group The group of subjects in an experiment who experience the independent variable

experimentation A method in which observations are made under controlled conditions designed to test specific ideas about causal relationships

expressed emotion (EE) Exists in families in which there is an emotional climate of criticism, hostility, and overprotectiveness; usually used to describe families of patients with schizophrenia

external causes Causes of behavior that are outside the person (in the environment)

external desynchronization When the body's biological clock is out of sync with the external environment

externality hypothesis Schachter's idea that obese people's eating is controlled by external cues, such as the presence of food

extinction In classical conditioning, the decrease in response to the conditioned stimulus when it is repeatedly presented in the absence of the unconditioned stimulus; in operant conditioning, the decrease in responding that occurs when reinforcement is terminated

extraneous variable Variable in addition to the independent variable that could influence the results of the experiment

extraversion Personal qualities associated with being outgoing and social

extrinsic motivation Type of motivation that leads a person to perform some activity to gain external rewards

facial feedback hypothesis Idea that we sense various emotions through feedback from the patterns of facial muscles that are relaxed and tensed

familiarity, law of Gestalt law of perception that states we are more likely to perceive things together if they create a familiar or meaningful figure

feature detectors Cortical neurons that respond best to specific features of visual stimuli

fetal period Period of prenatal development lasting from the second month to birth

field experiment A study that uses the experimental method to observe events as they take place in the natural environment

fixed interval schedule (FI) In operant conditioning, a schedule of reinforcement in which reinforcers become available after a specific time interval

fixed ratio schedule (FR) In operant conditioning, a schedule of reinforcement in which reinforcers are delivered after the organism makes a certain number of responses

flashbulb memories Memories people have of where they were and what they were doing when they heard of shocking and emotionally charged events

flooding Therapy in which the client is repeatedly placed in the actual anxiety-producing situation until a conditioned fear is extinguished

fluid intelligence Intelligence based on abilities such as reproducing designs or manipulating numbers; usually declines as a person's physical abilities decline

foot-in-the-door technique A technique used to gain compliance in which a small request is made and, when it is granted, a larger request is then substituted

formal operations stage The last stage of Piaget's theory of cognitive development, in which children begin to think abstractly and hypothetically

fovea Small area on the retina that contains only cone receptors

free association Technique used in psychoanalysis in which the patient is instructed to say whatever enters his or her head, in a completely candid, uncensored manner

free running cycle Circadian rhythm cycle that occurs in the absence of environmental cues

frequency Number of times per second the pressure in a sound wave goes through one cycle, from one peak to the next

frequency distribution A way of describing results that indicate how many scores fall within narrow ranges of scores

frontal lobe The part of the cerebral cortex involved in thinking, planning, and motor coordination

frustration-aggression hypothesis States that frustration always leads to aggression

functional fixedness Preconceived notions about an object's function that can cause its other possible uses to be ignored in a problem-solving situation

fundamental attribution error The tendency for people to overestimate internal factors and to underestimate situational factors in explaining the behavior of others

fundamental rule of psychoanalysis To reveal whatever comes up during therapy, no matter how shocking, revealing, or seemingly irrelevant

gate control theory of pain Theory that cognition can control a "gate" that determines the proportion of signals, generated in response to painful stimulation, that are transmitted to the brain

gender constancy The knowledge that one's gender is permanent

gender identity The knowledge that we are male or female

gender roles The behaviors considered appropriate for males and females in a society

gender schema Schema about what it is like to be male or female

gender segregation The fact that boys and girls often play in separate groups; leads to the establishment of two different cultures with different environments and rules for boys and girls

gender socialization The teaching of rules about how males and females should behave

general adaptation syndrome Hans Selye's three stages describing the body's reaction to long-term stress

generalization Occurs when a conditioned response is elicited by stimuli that are similar to the original conditioned stimulus

generalized anxiety disorder Characterized by experiencing anxiety without having to be in contact with a specific object

general mental energy The general factor of intelligence (the g factor); proposed by Spearman

genes Molecules of DNA found on chromosomes that determine a person's characteristics by controlling the synthesis of proteins

genital stage The fifth stage in Freud's theory of psychosexual development; characterized by adolescence and a refocusing on the genitals

genotype The genetic blueprint that creates a person's physical and behavioral characteristics

germinal period First period of prenatal development during which cells of the zygote begin to divide

gestalt psychology The approach to the study of perception made popular by Max Wertheimer; argues that perception cannot be explained by the addition of elementary sensations

given-new contract Agreement between speaker and listener that demands that the speaker construct sentences containing both given information that the listener already knows and new information that the listener is hearing for the first time

goal state The last condition of a problem space in problem solving

good continuation, law of Gestalt law of perception; states that points that result in straight or smoothly curving lines when connected are perceived as belonging together and that lines are seen in such a way as to create the smoothest possible path

group Two or more people who interact and communicate with each other over a period of time

group polarization Occurs when individuals in a group shift their views toward more extreme positions

hair cells Tiny auditory receptors located adjacent to the basilar membrane; responsible for generating electrical signals in response to sound stimuli

hallucinations Perceptions that occur in the absence of actual stimulation

hardy personality Personality characteristics that include being committed to work, relationships, and activities; taking control of situations; and seeing change as a challenge and opportunity for personal growth

hassles Daily events that are negative in nature

health psychology The field concerned with how psychological knowledge can contribute to promoting health and to preventing and treating illness

heterosexuality Sexual attraction to people of the other sex over a significant period of time

heuristics "Rules of thumb" that are often helpful in decision making or problem solving but sometimes do not lead to the correct answer; often result in faster decisions or solutions to the problem

hidden observer According to Hilgard, the part of the mind that watches a person under hypnosis carry out the hypnotist's commands

hierarchy of needs Maslow's idea that motivation occurs within a context of needs ranging from basic survival to higher psychological needs; lower needs must be met before higher ones can be satisfied

hippocampus Subcortical brain structure involved in memory and emotion

homeostasis The body's tendency to keep its internal environment constant

homophobia Negative feelings toward homosexuals

homosexuality Sexual attraction to people of a person's own sex over a significant period of time

homunculus The "map" on the somatosensory cortex that illustrates the amount of cortical area allotted to various parts of the body

hormones Chemicals secreted into the bloodstream from endocrine glands

humanistic approach Made popular by Carl Rogers and Abraham Maslow; looks at people as naturally good and striving to reach their full potential

hunger motivation Motivation that induces a person to eat

hyperphagia Condition in rats with lesions of the ventromedial nucleus of the hypothalamus; the animals eat large quantities of food and become extremely obese

hypnosis A social interaction in which one person experiences alterations in perceptions, memory, and voluntary action in response to suggestions offered by another person

hypochondriasis Condition in which a person becomes anxious and depressed about the possibility of disease, focusing attention on specific symptoms and then exaggerating their importance

hypothalamus Subcortical brain structure consisting of groups of neurons that regulate temperature, hunger, thirst, sexual arousal, and the emotions

hypothesis A precise statement of the predicted outcome of an experiment

iconic memory Brief sensory memory for visual stimuli

id According to Freud, the most primitive part of the mind; ruled by the pleasure principle

identity achievement Type of identity status in which a person has gone through a decision-making process and has defined his or her occupational and ideological goals

identity crisis Occurs when a person is struggling with the decision-making process in forming his or her identity

identity diffusion Occurs when a person has not yet defined his or her occupational or ideological identity

identity foreclosure Occurs when a person has settled on occupational and ideological goals that have been defined by others, usually the parents

identity moratorium Type of identity status in which a person has an identity crisis

immune system The system that protects the body from disease-carrying microorganisms

immunosuppressants Substances that decrease the efficiency of the immune system

implicit theory of intelligence The commonsense concept of what it means to be intelligent

implosive therapy Type of therapy in which a client imagines an anxiety-producing situation with the help of the therapist in order to extinguish the fear in the safety of the therapist's company

incentive value The degree of anticipated pride in succeeding or shame in failing that can influence achievement motivation

incongruence A condition that exists when there is a discrepancy between the standards people set for themselves and their actual feelings and behavior; the goal of Carl Rogers's client-centered therapy is to reduce incongruence

independent variable The variable controlled by the experimenter in order to observe what happens when that variable is changed

indirect statements Statements whose literal meaning is not the meaning the speaker is trying to convey

induction Conclusion reached through inductive reasoning

inductive reasoning The process of drawing the conclusion that a given statement is probable, based on past experiences

inferential statistics Statistical methods for interpreting data and drawing conclusions from them

inferiority complex A personality trait consisting of the conviction that one is inferior to others

information processing Taking information in, transforming it, and analyzing it

ingratiation When people use flattery and agree with others to gain their compliance

in-group/out-group dynamic The tendency to evaluate people in other groups more negatively than those in groups to which one belongs

inhibitory postsynaptic potential (IPSP) A small increase in the negative charge inside a neuron; inhibits the generation of action potentials

inhibitory transmitter A neurotransmitter that generates inhibitory postsynaptic potentials

initial state The first condition of the problem space; occurs at the beginning of a problem

inner ear Portion of the ear that consists of the bony, snail-like structure called the cochlea

insecurely attached: ambivalent Type of attachment in which the infant seems angry with the mother when she reenters the room in the strange situation test

insecurely attached: avoidant Type of attachment in which the infant avoids the mother when she reenters the room in the strange situation test

insecurely attached: disorganized Type of attachment in which the infant's behavior toward the mother when she reenters the room in the strange situation test is confused, sometimes positive and sometimes negative

insight The sudden realization of the solution to a problem; demonstrated by Köhler with chimpanzees

insomnia An inability to get enough sleep to feel rested

instinctive drift Situations in which biologically built-in behaviors interfere with conditioning

instincts Behavior that is programmed genetically and requires no learning

intelligence quotient (IQ) A measure of intelligence calculated by dividing mental age by chronological age and multiplying by 100

interactionism Considering both the person and the situation to understand behavior

interference Information that prevents rehearsal and therefore disrupts memory

intermediate states The various conditions that exist along the pathways between the initial and goal states of a problem-solving task

internal causes Causes of behavior that are within the person, such as personality traits

internal desynchronization When bodily rhythms, such as the sleep/wakefulness cycle and temperature, are out of sync with each other

intrinsic motivation Type of motivation that leads a person to perform some activity for the satisfaction of doing the activity itself

introspection The technique practiced by the structuralists; relies on a person's description of the sensations and feelings experienced in response to specific stimuli

introversion Personal qualities associated with being inwardly directed

inventory Similar to a survey; permits data collection from large numbers of people about their attitudes and behavior

ions Molecules that carry an electrical charge. Positive and negative ions are responsible for the resting potential and action potential

James-Lange theory The idea that we feel emotions because of feedback from activity in the autonomic nervous system

jet lag The desynchronization of circadian rhythms caused by changing time zones; usually results in fatigue and performance deficits

just world hypothesis The idea that life is basically fair

kin selection The sociobiological principle stating that behaviors survive selectively if they increase the chances of survival of the animal's relatives

labeled line theory Theory of taste perception suggesting that each of the four basic taste qualities (sour, salty, sweet, and bitter) is signaled by activity in specific nerve fibers

Language acquisition device (LAD) Device in the brain proposed by Chomsky to be specially adapted to language learning

latency stage Fourth stage in Freud's theory of psychosexual development (approximately 6 years to puberty) during which little of significance transpires

latent dream The deeper meaning of a dream; consists of the unconscious thoughts that underlie the dream we remember

lateral geniculate nucleus (LGN) Part of the thalamus involved in transmitting visual information to the visual cortex

lateralization of function The idea that some behavioral functions are based in either the left or right hemisphere

lateral nucleus of the hypothalamus (LH) Brain structure hypothesized to be involved in the control of eating

law of effect Law stating that behaviors followed by satisfying effects are strengthened and therefore more likely to occur again; behaviors followed by unsatisfying effects are weakened and therefore less likely to occur again

laws of organization Gestalt laws describing what perceptions will occur, given certain stimulus arrangements

learned helplessness Occurs when an organism has learned to be helpless in one situation and remains helpless in a new situation, even though it may have the ability to control the situation

learned helplessness theory of depression Suggests that depressed people typically expect that desired outcomes are unlikely to occur, that undesired outcomes are likely to occur, and that nothing they can do will change things

learning Relatively long-lasting changes in behavior that are based on past experience

left hemisphere The left half of the brain

lens Part of the eye located just behind the cornea; involved in focusing light onto the retina

levels of analysis A way of simplifying the multiplicity of approaches in psychology by looking at behavior from various perspectives

levels of processing theory Idea that memory depends on the way information is programmed into the mind, with deep processing resulting in good memory and shallow processing resulting in poor memory

lifetime prevalence The percentage of people who at some time in their lives will have a psychological disorder

linguistic relativity hypothesis States that the structure of a culture's language influences the way people in that culture think and how they perceive the world

lithium The major drug used in the treatment of bipolar disorder

lobes Four areas of the cerebral cortex

localization of function The idea that various behavioral functions are located in specific brain areas

locus of control The degree to which people feel that the things that happen to them are caused by qualities within themselves or by the external situation

longitudinal method Research method used by developmental psychologists in which particular behaviors are measured at an early age and then at other ages as the subjects become older

long-term potentiation (LTP) An enhanced response in neural firing after repeated stimulation; has been proposed as a physiological mechanism of memory

love or belongingness needs In Maslow's hierarchy of needs; defined as the need to feel affection from others and to feel part of a group

low ball technique Convincing a person to commit to what appears to be a very good deal but later changing the deal; often the person still agrees to the deal

magnetic resonance imaging (MRI) Creates pictures of the brain by placing the patient in a strong magnetic field and sending radio waves through the brain

main effect hypothesis The idea that a person's social network provides benefits both during stress and when there is no stress

maintenance rehearsal Rehearsal by mere repetition; memory following this type of rehearsal is poorer than memory following elaborative rehearsal

major depression Condition in which a person suffers from a prolonged depressed mood or loss of interest or pleasure in most daily activities

manic-depressive disorder Another name for bipolar disorder; the patient suffers from depression and manic episodes

manifest dreams The meaning or content of a dream as we would describe it

mean One type of measure of central tendency; calculated by dividing the sum of the scores by the total number of scores

means-end analysis Strategy of problem solving, the primary goal of which is to reduce the difference between the initial and goal states

measures of central tendency Single numbers that represent an entire set of scores; for example, the mean, median, and mode

measures of variability Measures, such as the range and standard deviation, that indicate how scattered or variable a set of scores are

median One type of measure of central tendency; the middle score in a set of scores that are listed in order from highest to lowest

medical student's syndrome Medical students' tendency to believe they have many of the diseases they are studying; may also be seen in students studying abnormal psychology

medulla The group of neurons in the brain stem that control vital functions such as breathing, heart rate, salivation, coughing, and sneezing

memory code The form in which an actual object, sound, or event is represented in the mind

menarche The first menstruation period for girls

mental set The tendency to respond in a particular manner or from a particular perspective; can interfere with problem solving by limiting the strategies used to solve the problem

mere exposure effect The fact that merely being exposed repeatedly to a stimulus can cause a person to like that stimulus more

meta-analysis Statistical technique that makes it possible to combine and analyze the results of many studies

microelectrode Thin glass or metal probe used to stimulate or lesion brain structures

midbrain reticular formation Part of the reticular formation just below the thalamus; involved in attention and sleep

middle ear Part of the ear containing the ossicles; located between the outer and inner ear

midlife crisis Hypothesized to occur around the age of 40–45; men, and perhaps women, question their lives and change their views of themselves

mind-body dualism The philosophical position that the mind and the body function separately

minimax principle States that we will help others in ways that minimize our costs and maximize our rewards

Minnesota Multiphasic Personality Inventory (MMPI) The most widely used self-report personality test; designed to identify people with psychological problems

mnemonic device Technique to aid memory by associating material to be remembered with something meaningful and familiar

modeling *See* observational learning

monozygotic (MZ) twins Identical twins who are the result of the same zygote splitting to form two genetically identical zygotes

mood congruity effect The finding that memory is better for events that match one's mood

mood disorder Disorders, such as depression, that involve states of intense positive or negative emotion

moon illusion The moon appears larger when it is near the horizon than when it is higher in the sky

motivation The process that drives an organism to act and that determines what direction the action takes

motive to avoid failure Factor in achievement motivation in which a person strives to avoid failure

motor cortex The area of the cortex that results in movement by sending nerve impulses from the brain to the muscles

movement parallax Objects that are closer to an observer move across the observer's field of view more rapidly in response to the observer's movement; used as a cue to depth

multiple personality disorder (MPD) Dissociative disorder in which a person has a number of distinct personalities that function independently of each other

multistore model Model of memory that proposes three types of memory stores (sensory memory, short-term memory, and long-term memory), each of which holds information for different periods of time

narcolepsy A condition causing numerous daytime "sleep attacks" during which a person falls asleep and sometimes goes completely limp

naturalistic observation Research method in which a researcher systematically observes behavior without intervening directly in it

natural selection Darwin's theory that characteristics that increase an organism's chances of survival increase the chances that the organism will reproduce; these characteristics are therefore more likely to be passed on to the next generation

nature and nurture A basic issue in development; involves the question of whether behavior is affected more by genetic inheritance or environment

nearness, law of Gestalt law of perception; states that items near to each other are grouped together

need for cognition The need for some people to try to understand new information and to engage in processing it

need to achieve (nAch) A personality characteristic related to achievement motivation

negative correlation A relationship between two variables in which increases in one variable are associated with decreases in the other

negative reinforcer A stimulus that, when removed after a response, increases the rate of the response above baseline

negative symptoms The flattening of emotion, low motivation, and slowing of thinking and behavior found in schizophrenia

nervous system One of the body's communication networks; consists of billions of neurons

neurons Cells in the nervous system involved in the transmission of information in the form of neural impulses called action potentials

neurotic trends Behaviors that help cope with basic anxiety; Karen Horney described three types: moving toward, moving against, and moving away

neurotransmitter The chemical released at the synapse as a result of an action potential

neutral stimulus (NS) In classical conditioning, a stimulus that does not elicit the unconditioned response

niche building Occurs when people select the part of the environment they want to experience

normal distribution A bell-shaped, symmetrical curve derived from a specific mathematical rule

obedience Doing something in response to a demand, usually from a person with authority or power

obesity An excess of weight, frequently resulting in an impairment of health

object permanence A child's realization that an object still exists when it is not being perceived; occurs at about 14–18 months of age, during the sensorimotor stage in Piaget's theory of cognitive development

objective personality test A personality test that can be scored quantitatively and objectively; usually focuses on determining a person's traits

observational learning A change in behavior that occurs after observing someone else's behavior

obsessive-compulsive disorder (OCD) An anxiety disorder in which people repeat behaviors over and over, even when they know the actions are irrational

occipital lobe Part of the cerebral cortex involved in vision

oculomotor cues The depth cues of convergence (turning the eyes inward to see an object) and accommodation (changing the shape of the lens to focus on an object)

Oedipus complex Freud's term for the conflict that occurs when a boy becomes sexually attracted to his mother and views his father as a rival

olfactory bulb Brain structure that receives nerve fibers from the olfactory receptors

olfactory mucosa Moist surface in the nose that contains the receptors for smell

operant behavior Behavior in which an animal operates on its environment

operant conditioning Behavior in which an animal operates on its environment to gain rewards or avoid negative stimuli

operational definition A statement of the procedures used to create the independent variable or to measure the dependent one

operators In the information-processing approach to problem solving, the permissible moves that can be made toward the solution of a problem

opponent-process theory of color vision States that there are opponent mechanisms in the retina that respond in opposite ways to blue and yellow and to red and green

oral stage First stage in Freud's theory of psychosexual development, lasting from birth to 18 months; the primary behavior of the child is taking in and spitting out

organization The formation of more complex schemes by combining simple ones

ossicles Tiny bones in the middle ear (the malleus, incus, and stapes) that bridge the gap between the tympanic membrane and the inner ear

outer ear The pinna (or earlobe) and the auditory canal

overextension The overinclusion of objects to a particular category that occurs during a child's development of language; for example, when the child calls all four legged animals "dogs"

overregularization The tendency of children to apply rules of language to all words, even the exceptions, for example, adding "ed" to all past tense words, as in "goed"

panic attack A symptom of an anxiety disorder involving strong physiologic reactions and strong feelings of anxiety

panic disorder Type of anxiety disorder involving shivering, pounding heart, perspiration, and a feeling of imminent disaster

papillae Ridges and valleys on the tongue where taste buds are located

paradoxical intention Tactic used by sleep therapists in which the patient is instructed to go to bed and try to remain awake

parallel processing Processing in the brain that simultaneously processes different types of information

paranoid schizophrenia Type of schizophrenia characterized by a preoccupation with delusions related to a single theme

parasympathetic division Part of the autonomic nervous system that maintains bodily functions at a normal level of activity (homeostasis)

parietal lobe Part of the cerebral cortex involved in touch

Parkinson's disease A condition characterized by difficulty in initiating voluntary movements

partial reinforcement In operant conditioning, presenting the reinforcer following only some responses

perceived self-efficacy (PSE) The judgment of one's ability to accomplish specific tasks

perception The process that creates our sensory experiences

perceptual consciousness The perceptions, thoughts, and feelings we are experiencing (what we are aware of)

peripheral nervous system The system of neurons outside the brain and spinal cord that carries nerve impulses between the brain and the sensory receptors, muscles, and internal organs

peripheral retina Area of the retina outside the fovea

peripheral route to persuasion Occurs when a message results in low elaboration of the information and when attitude change is based on simple persuasion cues, such as attractiveness or credibility of the communicator

personal constructs Ideas possessed by individuals that shape the way they view and interpret events in the environment; part of George Kelly's cognitive approach to the description of personality

personal fable The idea that one's own experiences and thoughts are unique; typical of adolescents but also may be held by adults

personality The dynamic organization inside each person that creates the person's characteristic patterns of behavior, thought, and feelings

personality assessment Measurement of the characteristics of a person's personality

person perception The study of how we form impressions of others

phallic stage Third stage in Freud's theory of psychosexual development (from 4 to 5 years), in which children focus on their genitals

phenotype The expression of a person's genetic blueprint; the characteristics and behaviors that actually develop from the genotype

phobias Fears of specific stimuli or situations that are out of proportion to their true danger

physical dependence Occurs when the use of a drug causes changes in the body's cells so that the cells must have periodic doses of the drug to function normally and to avoid withdrawal symptoms

physiological needs One of the needs in Maslow's hierarchy; defined as survival needs, such as satisfying hunger and thirst

pictorial cues Depth cues, such as overlap, that can be represented in a flat picture like the one formed on the retina

pitch The perception of "highness" or "lowness" of tones that depends primarily on the frequency of the sound stimulus

placebo A pill with no active ingredients

place theory of pitch perception A theory of pitch perception that proposes that each frequency causes maximal vibration of a particular place along the basilar membrane and maximal neural firing of the hair cells located at that place

pleasure principle Freud's idea that at the fundamental level of the psyche (the id), people are driven to seek out pleasure

Ponzo illusion Also known as the railroad track illusion; occurs when a picture of two equally sized rectangles superimposed on two lines that converge into the distance are perceived as different in size

population The group of people to which an experimenter wants to apply the results of a study

positive correlation A relationship between two variables in which increases in one variable are associated with increases in the other

positive regard Acceptance, warmth, respect, and love we obtain from other people; Rogers encouraged the therapist's use of positive regard in client-centered therapy

positive reinforcer A stimulus that maintains or increases the rate of the response when presented after a response

positive symptoms The delusions, hallucinations, bizarre behavior, and thought disorders in schizophrenia

Positron Emission Tomography (PET) scan Imaging technique used to measure the biochemical activity of the brain as a person behaves

possible selves Thoughts about the kinds of people we may become

post-formal operations stage Stage of cognitive development beyond formal operations that involves dialectical thinking

postsynaptic neuron The neuron that receives neurotransmitters at the synapse from the presynaptic neuron

posttraumatic stress disorder A disorder caused by exposure to a traumatic event; the person may experience flashbacks of the event, have nightmares, and endure bouts of depression

preconscious According to Freud, the part of the unconscious that we can easily retrieve from our memory

predictive validity A test's ability to predict the characteristic the test is supposed to be measuring

prefrontal cortex Part of the frontal lobe involved in thinking, problem solving, and planning for the future

prejudice A negative attitude toward other people based on their membership in a particular group

Premack principle States that any response can be reinforced by a more preferred response

prenatal sexual differentiation The differentiation of the fetus into male or female that occurs in the womb prior to birth

preoperational stage The first stage of Piaget's theory of cognitive development (from 2–7 years) characterized by such cognitive processes as animism and egocentrism

preparedness The idea that animals are biologically prepared to associate certain pairings of neutral and unconditioned stimuli

presynaptic neuron The neuron that releases neurotransmitters at the synapse

primacy effect *In memory research:* Occurs when memory for information presented at the beginning of a sequence is superior; can be observed when data is plotted on a serial position curve. *In social psychology:* The finding that we give more weight to the early information we absorb about others than to later information

primary emotions Pure emotions that do not result from a combination of other emotions; examples proposed by Plutchik are fear and sadness

primary mental abilities The seven basic abilities used by Thurstone to define intelligence

primary reinforcer A reinforcer that is unlearned, such as food, water, access to sex, and painful stimuli

proactive interference Occurs when learning from the past interferes with new learning

problem space In the information processing approach to problem solving, the various elements of a problem: the initial, intermediate, and goal states

procedural memory Type of memory that stores skills and procedures

progressive muscle relaxation A technique in which people relax each part of the body in turn; used in systematic desensitization therapy

projective tests Personality tests that present ambiguous stimuli that can be interpreted in a number of ways

prosocial behavior Behavior in which individuals help one another, sometimes at some expense to themselves

proximity A factor that can influence interpersonal attraction; we are more likely to form relationships with people who are physically near us than those farther away

pseudodialogues Interactions between infant and caregiver in which the infant vocalizes, the adult responds, the infant vocalizes back, and so on; occurs before the infant can produce actual words

pseudoinsomnia A person's belief that they have insomnia even though they get a full night's sleep

pseudomemories Events a hypnotized person "remembers" as having happened but that never actually did happen

psychiatric nurses Have either a B.A. or M.A. in nursing, with a specialization in psychiatry

psychiatric social workers Usually have earned a master's degree and typically help patients utilize social support services in the community

psychiatrists Medical doctors who specialize in treating psychological disorders

psychic energy Flow of energy within the mind

psychoactive drug Any chemical that alters the workings of the human mind

psychoanalysis The method of therapy based on Freud's theory of personality

psychobiography Subfield of personality psychology in which personality theory is used to make psychological sense of the stories of individual people's lives

psychogenic amnesia Type of dissociative disorder in which the person suddenly loses memory for important personal events but does not take on a new identity or travel to a new location

psychogenic fugue Type of dissociative disorder involving memory loss accompanied by vanishing from home and taking a new identity

psychological anthropology Subfield within anthropology that focuses on how people think, feel, and perceive the world in various cultures

psychological construct An abstract attribute that is inferred rather than observed directly, such as motivation, intelligence, and personality

psychoneuroimmunology The study of the effects of stress and psychological factors on the physiological functioning of the body, with special emphasis on the immune system

psychophysics The study of quantitative relationships between physical stimuli and the psychological responses to these stimuli

psychosocial theory of development Erik Erikson's theory of development; postulates that people must deal with a series of "crises" as they pass through several stages from birth to death

psychotherapy Psychological procedures carried out by mental health professionals that are intended to improve a person's mental, emotional, or behavioral well-being

puberty Developmental period during which the reproductive organs become functional

punishment When presentation or removal of a stimulus after a response decreases the rate of response

pure tone Tone in which the air-pressure changes follow a sine wave pattern

Q-sort The method used by Carl Rogers to measure actual and ideal selves

racism Any attitude, action, or institutional structure that subordinates a person because of his or her color

random assignment Procedure for assigning subjects to groups in an experiment so that each person in the sample has an equal chance of being in the experimental or control group

random sampling A procedure that ensures that any person in the population is equally likely to be chosen for the experiment

range The simplest measure of variability, which is the difference between the highest and lowest score in a data set

raphe system Part of the medulla that plays a role in sleep and wakefulness

rapid eye movement (REM) sleep Fifth stage of sleep; characterized by observable eye movements and rapid, disorganized waves. When people are awakened during REM sleep, they report they were dreaming

rational emotive therapy Type of psychotherapy developed by Albert Ellis; based on the idea that psychological problems arise because of people's irrational beliefs

reasoning Thinking; usually implies a logical process

recall test Test that requires the person to supply the answer without seeing any alternatives

recency effect Occurs when memory is superior for information presented at the end of a sequence; can be observed when data is plotted on a serial position curve

receptor A neuron that responds to environmental stimuli, such as light, pressure, chemicals, or sound waves

receptor sites Small areas on the postsynaptic neuron that are sensitive to specific neurotransmitters

reciprocal liking Liking someone when you find out they like you

reciprocity In the context of helping, refers to *"If you do something for me, I'll do something for you."*

recognition test Test that requires the person to pick the correct answer from a list of alternatives, as in a multiple-choice test

reflection Method used in client-centered therapy in which the client's statement is not interpreted but is repeated by the therapist in a slightly different or clearer form

reflective consciousness Our awareness that perceptual consciousness is occurring

reflex arc Spinal cord mechanism that produces a reflexive response without traveling to the brain first

regional cerebral blood flow (RCBF) Brain-imaging technique used to measure activity in the cerebral cortex

reinforcer A stimulus that, when presented or removed after a response, raises the rate of that response above its baseline level

reliability The extent to which a measuring device yields the same results when measurements are repeated under similar conditions

REM rebound The occurrence of more REM periods than usual following REM deprivation

replicate To repeat an experiment using other subjects

representativeness heuristic When events are judged to be more likely because they more closely match a prototype; for example, a man who reads a lot and wears glasses might be judged to be a librarian because he matches a person's concept of a librarian

repression Occurs when the mind pushes dangerous material into the unconscious

resistance Unconscious attempts to avoid confronting threatening topics that come up during psychoanalysis

resistance stage The second stage of Selye's general adaptation syndrome during which the body continues to fight the stress

response facilitation Occurs when physiological arousal increases the intensity of whatever a person is already feeling; used to explain sexual attraction

resting metabolic rate The amount of energy the body needs to maintain itself when at rest

resting potential The electrical charge of a neuron that is not generating an electrical signal; typically about −70 mV

restorative theory of sleep The idea that we need sleep to recharge and repair the body and brain

reticular formation The part of the medulla involved in sleep, wakefulness, and attention

retina Thin layer of neurons lining the eye; contains the receptors for vision

retrieval Process of transferring information from long-term memory to short-term (or working) memory

retrieval cue Cue that provides information

that helps us retrieve other information from memory

retroactive interference When new learning interferes with memory from the past

reuptake The process by which neurotransmitters are taken back into the presynaptic neuron

reversibility Occurs when a child realizes that a situation can be reversed to a previous state, for example, that water poured from a wide glass into a tall glass can be poured back into the wide glass

right hemisphere The right half of the brain

risk-aversion strategy In decision making, a cautious decision that may be made when a choice is framed in terms of gain

risk-taking strategy In decision making, a hazardous decision that may be made when a choice is framed in terms of loss

rods Receptors for vision responsible for vision in low illumination

Rorschach test A type of projective test using inkblot stimuli

safety needs One of the needs in Maslow's hierarchy; defined as needs such as living in a secure environment

satiety center Label given to the ventromedial hypothalamus because evidence suggested that it turned off eating behavior

satiety signal A signal that turns off hunger; high glucose levels in the blood is an example

savant syndrome Occurs in people who are classified as mentally retarded but who have exceptional skills in one area

scalloping The characteristic graph of the cumulative record of an animal on a fixed interval schedule, which is flat immediately after presentation of the reinforcer and then becomes steeper as the time for the next reinforcement approaches

schema Ways of interpreting information about particular concepts; for example, a gender schema would contain information about what it means to be male or female

scheme According to Piaget, an organized pattern of actions that guides children's interactions with the environment

schizophrenia A severe psychological disorder that is characterized by such symptoms as delusions, hallucinations, illogical thinking, incoherent speech, or bizarre behavior

scientific empiricism Involves making observations that are objective, systematic, and replicable

script Sequences of actions that describe common activities, such as going to a restaurant or to a doctor's office

scripted refusal Occurs when a woman who doesn't want to be considered *cheap* or *easy* initially resists sexual advances by a man, but ultimately gives in

secondary emotions Emotions produced by a combination of primary emotions; according to Plutchick, examples are love and submission

secondary gain The positive aspects of having a disability or illness, such as being cared for by others and escaping responsibilities

secondary reinforcer A reinforcer that has been learned because it has been paired with obtaining primary reinforcers

secondary trait According to Gordon Allport, a characteristic of a person that occurs rarely and only in specific circumstances

second-order conditioning Using one conditioned stimulus to create another

securely attached An infant who reacts positively to his or her mother when she reenters the room in the strange-situation test

self-actualization The highest need in Maslow's hierarchy; consists of a person's desire to attain his or her full potential

self-awareness An awareness of the boundaries that separate yourself from others

self-concept A sense of who you are and what your unique qualities are

self-esteem The overall value you assign to the elements that make up your identity

self-esteem needs One of the needs in Maslow's hierarchy; consists of the need to feel positively about oneself and to be esteemed by others

self-fulfilling prophecy When something happens because you expect it to happen

self-handicapping Creating an impediment to success that can be used as an excuse in case of failure

self-monitoring The tendency to be influenced by how others may perceive you in a social situation

self-perception theory States that we often draw conclusions about our own attitudes after observing our own behavior

self-recognition The ability to recognize oneself that develops in the second year; test is to notice how children react to seeing their images in a mirror

self-report tests Personality tests in which people respond to questions or statements about themselves

self schemas The aspects of behavior that are most important to you and that guide the way you process information about yourself

self-serving bias The tendency to distort attributions about our behavior to make ourselves look good

self-verification Doing things that verify your self-concept

semantic memory Type of memory for storing knowledge of words, rules for putting them together, and all the facts, ideas, and concepts you have learned about the world

sensorimotor stage The first stage in Piaget's theory of cognitive development (birth to 2 years), in which sensory and motor capabilities develop rapidly

sensory coding How the information contained in nerve impulses represents different qualities of the environment

sensory memory Stage of memory that automatically registers any stimulus striking the sensory receptors and that holds stimulus information for a few seconds or fractions of a second

sensory reinforcers Reinforcers that gain their value because they involve sensory stimulation

seriation Ability to arrange objects in order along quantitative dimensions such as weight, length, or size

set point The weight toward which the body naturally gravitates

sexual dimorphism The physical differences between males and females

sexual double standard A standard by which men are allowed more sexual freedom than women

sexual motivation The motivation to engage in sexual behavior

shallow processing Processing of a stimulus only in terms of its superficial characteristics

shape constancy The tendency for our perception of an object's shape to remain constant, even when we view it from different angles

shaping A technique of establishing a desired behavior by rewarding successive approximations of the behavior

short-term memory (STM) Type of memory in which a small amount of information currently in use is stored

shuttle box A two-sided apparatus used to teach an animal to jump from one side to another to avoid shock

similarity, law of Gestalt law of perception; states that we perceive similar items as being grouped together

simplicity, law of Gestalt law of perception; states that stimulus patterns are seen in such a way that the resulting structure is as simple as possible

simultaneous conditioning Classical conditioning procedure in which the neutral stimulus and unconditioned stimulus are presented together

situationism The idea that behavior is primarily determined not by stable personality traits but by the situations in which people find themselves

16 Personality Factor (16PF) A test developed by Raymond Catell; evaluates a person's personality in terms of 16 factors

size constancy The tendency for our perception of an object's size to remain fairly constant independent of its distance from the observer or the size of its retinal image

size-distance scaling Mechanism by which we arrive at perceived size by taking into account both an object's retinal size and its perceived distance

Skinner box A box designed by B. F. Skinner; contains a response apparatus and a way to present reinforcers, typically a bar protruding from the wall of the box

sleep apnea A condition in which a person's breathing is repeatedly interrupted during sleep

sleep spindles Rapid brain waves indicative of stage two sleep

slow wave sleep (SWS) Stages of sleep other than rapid eye movement sleep; so named because of the slowness of their EEG waves

social cognition How people think about other people and themselves

social exchange theory States that people decide to help by considering the helping situation as an exchange of social goods from which they can receive some potential benefit

social facilitation The idea that working in the presence of others influences an individual's performance, usually enhancing it

socialization The process by which children are taught the values, rules of behavior, and social roles deemed appropriate by their culture

socializing agents People or institutions that teach children the behaviors deemed appropriate in a particular culture

social loafing The idea that individuals exert less effort when they work with others than when they work alone

social norms The explicit or implicit rules of a group about how a member should behave

social readjustment rating scale (SRRS) A self-report scale that is supposed to measure stress by tabulating the life events experienced by a person

social referencing Occurs when an infant in an uncertain situation refers to an adult's emotional expression before determining a course of action

social reinforcers Category of reinforcers especially important to humans, such as praise and attention

social responsibility A social norm; dictates that people should help others who are in need, without regard to social exchange

social support The resources provided to us through our interactions with other people

sociobiology A recently developed branch of evolutionary biology that applies evolutionary theory to the explanation of social behavior

somatic nervous system Division of the peripheral nervous system responsible for communicating between the brain and the senses and skeletal muscles

somatization disorder Condition in which a person reports recurring physical symptoms, usually involving many different complaints

somatoform disorder Condition in which physical symptoms occur without any organic basis

somatosensory cortex Area on the parietal lobe that is specialized to respond to touch

sound wave Pattern of air pressure changes generated by an auditory stimulus

source traits According to Gordon Allport, the traits that are the building blocks of personality and are found in everyone

species-specific defense reactions The ways in which specific kinds of animals deal with unpleasant stimuli

speech segmentation The perception of breaks between spoken words

spinal cord The roughly cylindrical tube that transmits signals from the sense organs and muscles below the head to the brain

split-brain operation Procedure in which a patient's left and right brain hemispheres are separated by cutting the corpus callosum

spontaneous recovery The reappearance of a previously extinguished conditioned response after a rest period, during which the conditioned stimulus was not presented

stability vs. instability A basic issue in development; considers whether or not personal characteristics are stable across the lifespan

stage four sleep Deepest stage of sleep; dominated by delta waves

stage one sleep First stage of sleep; characterized by waveforms smaller, faster, and less rhythmical than alpha waves

stage three sleep Stage of sleep characterized by delta waves

stage two sleep Second stage of sleep; characterized by sleep spindles

standard deviation A measure of variability; calculated by a mathematical formula that takes into account the extent to which each score in a group differs from the group mean

Stanford hypnotic susceptibility scale Scale that measures how susceptible a person is to hypnosis

state-dependent learning The idea that recall is better if a person is in the same mental state or setting during encoding and recall

statistically significant A difference between two groups that is unlikely to be due to chance

stereotypes Beliefs, shared by many people, that certain characteristics can be assigned to members of a group based solely on their group membership

storage Where information is placed if we are to remember it later

strange situation The standard procedure for measuring infant-caregiver attachment; a child is separated from his or her caregiver and the child's reactions are noted when they are reunited

stressors Stressful stimuli

striving for superiority According to Alfred Adler, the ultimate goal of all people, particularly those with early deficiencies

structuralism School of psychology that believed that the mind could be broken down into elementary elements; introspection was one research tool used to study the structure of the mind

Structured Interview A method to assess impatience, hostility, and aggression; a series of questions are asked about the individual's behavior and his or her emotional reactions are noted

subcortical nuclei Nuclei (places where many neurons synapse) located beneath the cerebral cortex

superego According to Freud, the part of the mind that contains the conscience and the ego ideal

superiority complex A personality trait consisting of an exaggerated and unrealistic feeling of being better than others

superstitious behavior Behavior that is related to reinforcement by chance, but which is believed to cause the delivery of reward

suprachiasmatic nucleus (SCN) A small nucleus in the hypothalamus; regulates the sleep/wakefulness cycle

surface traits According to Gordon Allport, the many behaviors we observe in different people

survey A research method similar to an inventory; permits data collection from large numbers of people about their attitudes and behavior

survival of the fittest Principle of evolution; suggests that organisms who possess behaviors that increase their chance of survival are more likely to reproduce and pass these characteristics to their offspring

susceptibility The depth of hypnosis achieved under standard conditions of hypnotic induction

sympathetic division The part of the autonomic nervous system that mobilizes the body for emergencies

synapse The place where one neuron communicates with another neuron

synaptic vesicles Structures in the presynaptic neuron that store neurotransmitter

syntax How words are combined to form grammatically correct sentences

systematic desensitization A technique in which a phobia is eliminated by training a subject to relax in the presence of stimuli similar to the feared stimulus

taste buds Receptors for taste located in papillae on the tongue

telegraphic speech The use of shorthand sentences by children

temporal lobe A lobe on the side of the cerebral cortex, part of which is involved in hearing

teratogens Substances that are harmful to prenatal development

terminal buttons The portion of the neuron at the end of the axon that contains neurotransmitters

testosterone A sex hormone found in high concentrations in males and involved in sexual differentiation

test-retest method Method of testing reliability in which a large group of people are tested and then retested later

thalamus The brain structure that serves as the switching station for sensory information

that's-not-all technique A technique used to gain compliance; an item is quoted at a price and then immediately offered at a lower price

Thematic Apperception Test (TAT) A projective test in which a person tells a story about an ambiguous picture

theory A model of the universe and a set of rules that relates quantities in the model to observations that are made

think aloud protocol Procedure in which people solving a problem dictate what they are doing into a tape recorder

thinking The active transformation of existing knowledge to create new knowledge that can be used to achieve a goal

thought disorders A breakdown in the way a person's thoughts are organized; occurs in disorders such as schizophrenia and bipolar disorder

tip-of-the-tongue (TOT) effect The inability to recall information although you feel as if the answer is on "the tip of your tongue"

token economy The use of secondary reinforcers to shape and reinforce desired behaviors; often tokens are accumulated and then exchanged for primary reinforcers

tolerance A state of progressively decreasing responsiveness to a drug, so a user requires more of it to achieve the same effect

trace conditioning Conditioning procedure in which the neutral stimulus is presented and then terminated before the unconditioned stimulus is presented

trait approach Claims that people can be classified as having certain traits or behavioral tendencies

traits Predispositions to respond in a certain way

trance logic State created during hypnosis that enables subjects to be oblivious to paradoxes that they would recognize immediately in everyday experience

transduction Process through which receptors transform environmental energy into electrical energy

transference Positive and negative reactions that patients may develop toward their therapist

transitivity The ability to recognize relations among a number of ordered objects; for example: If Susan is taller than Ruth and Ruth is taller than Grace, then Susan must also be taller than Grace

triarchic theory of intelligence Sternberg's theory of intelligence; describes intelligence as having three aspects

trichromatic theory of color vision Hypothesizes that color vision results from the action of three receptors that respond best to light in different regions of the electromagnetic spectrum

two-factor theory Schachter and Singer's theory that emotion is caused by physiological arousal and cognition

tympanic membrane Also called the eardrum; divides the middle and outer ear

Type-A Behavior Pattern (TABP) Characterized by such things as high competitiveness, difficulty relaxing, and a sense of urgency and impatience

unconditioned reflex Response that occurs before any conditioning takes place

unconditioned response (UR) The response that occurs automatically to an unconditioned stimulus

unconditioned stimulus (US) A stimulus that automatically elicits an unconditioned response

unconscious According to Freud, the part of the mind hidden from awareness

underextension The use of a category name to refer to only one object when other objects should also be included in the category; for example, when a child calls all dogs "Spot"

undifferentiated schizophrenia Type of schizophrenia characterized by mixtures of other symptoms

uplifts Daily events that are positive in nature

validity Refers to whether a test measures what it is supposed to measure

variable interval schedule (VI) In operant conditioning, a schedule of reinforcement in which reinforcers become available at different time intervals

variable ratio schedule (VR) In operant conditioning, a schedule of reinforcement in which reinforcers are delivered after a certain number of responses, with this number varying from reinforcement to reinforcement

vascular theory of emotional efference (VTEE) Theory of emotion suggesting that blood flow in facial muscles alters brain chemistry involved in emotion

ventromedial nucleus of the hypothalamus (VMH) A brain structure suggested to be involved in the control of eating

visible light The light we can see from the sun, from biological sources, and from artificial sources; the wavelength of visible light ranges from 350 to 750 nanometers

visual cortex Cortical area in the occipital lobe that is involved in vision

visual receiving area The part of the occipital lobe that receives signals originally generated in the retina

wish fulfillment Part of Freud's theory of dreaming; suggests that dreams represent wishes that the dreamer would like to see fulfilled

withdrawal symptoms Nausea, disorientation, hallucinations, or convulsions associated with stopping drug use

womb envy A desire to be able to have babies; proposed by Karen Horney

working memory Another name for short-term memory

zeitgebers German word for "time givers"; involved in setting the body's biological clock that controls circadian rhythms

zygote The result of the union of a sperm and an egg

References

ABADINSKY, H. (1989). *Drug use: An introduction.* Chicago: Nelson–Hall.

ABBEY, A. (1982). Sex differences in attributions for friendly behavior: Do males misperceive females' friendliness? *Journal of Personality and Social Psychology, 42,* 830–838.

ABRAMSON, E. (1982). Behavioral approaches to the treatment of obesity. In B. Wolman (Ed.), *Psychological aspects of obesity* (pp. 207–224). New York: Van Nostrand.

ABRAMSON, L. Y. (1989). Hopelessness depression: A theory-based subtype of depression. *Psychological Review, 96,* 358–372.

ABRAMSON, L. Y., METALSKY, G. I., & ALLOY, L. B. (1988). The hopelessness theory of depression: Does the research test the theory? In L. Y. Abramson (Ed.), *Social cognition and clinical psychology: A synthesis* (pp. 33–65). New York: Guilford.

ABRAMSON, L. Y., SELIGMAN, M. E. P., & TEASDALE, J. (1978). Learned helplessness in humans: Critique and reformulation. *Journal of Abnormal Psychology, 87,* 32–48.

ACKERMAN, D. (1990). *A natural history of the senses.* New York: Vintage.

ACKERMAN, P. L. (1986). Individual differences in information processing: An investigation of intellectual abilities and task performances during practice. *Intelligence, 10,* 101–139.

ACTON, W. (1871). *The functions and disorders of the reproductive organs in childhood, youth, adult age and advanced life, considered in their physiological, social and moral relations* (5th ed.). London: Churchill.

ADAMAKOS, H., RYAN, K., ULLMAN, D. G., & PASCOE, J. (1986). Material social support as a predictor of mother-child stress and stimulation. *Child Abuse & Neglect, 10,* 463–470.

ADAMS, D. B., GOLD, A. R., & BURT, A. D. (1978). Rise in female-initiated sexual activity at ovulation and its suppression by oral contraceptives. *New England Journal of Medicine, 299,* 1145–1150.

ADAMS, G. R., ABRAHAM, K. G., & MARKSTROM, C. A. (1987). The relations among identity development, self-consciousness, and self-focusing during middle and late adolescence. *Developmental Psychology, 23,* 292–297.

ADAMS, G. R., & COHEN, A. S. (1974). Children's physical and interpersonal characteristics that affect student-teacher interactions. *Journal of Experimental Education, 43,* 1–5.

ADAMS, J. A., MAURER, D., & DAVIS, M. (1986). Newborns' discrimination of chromatic from achromatic stimuli. *Journal of Experimental Child Psychology, 41,* 267–281.

ADAMS, P. R., & ADAMS, G. R. (1984). Mount Saint Helen's ashfall. *American Psychologist, 39,* 252–260.

ADAMSON, R. E. (1952). Functional fixedness as related to problem solving. *Journal of Experimental Psychology, 44,* 288–291.

ADER, R., & COHEN, N. (1975). Behavioral conditioned immunosuppression. *Psychosomatic Medicine, 37,* 333–340.

ADER, R., & COHEN, N. (1984). Behavior and the immune system. In W. D. Gentry (Ed.), *Handbook of Behavioral Medicine* (pp. 117–173). New York: Guilford.

ADER, R., & COHEN, N. (1985). CNS-immune system interactions: Conditioning phenomena. *Behavioral and Brain Sciences, 8,* 379–395.

ADER, R., & COHEN, N. (1993). Psychoneuroimmunology: Conditioning and stress. *Annual Review of Psychology, 44,* 53–85.

ADERMAN, D., & BERKOWITZ, L. (1970). Observational set, empathy, and helping. *Journal of Personality and Social Psychology, 14,* 141–148.

ADLER, A. (1917). *Study of organ inferiority and its physical compensation.* New York: Nervous and Mental Diseases Publishing.

ADLER, A. (1936). On the interpretation of dreams. *International Journal of Individual Psychology, 2,* 3–16.

AGRAS, W. S. (1985). Stress, panic and the cardiovascular system. In A. H. Tuma & J. Maser (Eds.), *Anxiety and the anxiety disorders* (pp. 363–368). Hillsdale, NJ: Erlbaum.

AINSWORTH, M. D. S. (1982). Attachment: Retrospect and prospect. In C. M. Parkes & J. Stevenson-Hinde (Eds.), *The place of attachment in human behavior* (pp. 3–30). New York: Basic Books.

AINSWORTH, M. D. S., & WITTIG, B. A. (1969). Attachment and exploratory behavior of one-year-olds in a strange situation. In B. M. Foss (Ed.), *Determinants of infant behavior* (Vol. 4, pp. 111–136). London: Methuen.

AJZEN, I. (1987). Attitudes, traits, and actions: Dispositional prediction of behavior in personality and social psychology. In L. Berkowitz (Ed.), *Advances in experimental social psychology* (Vol. 20, pp. 1–64). San Diego: Academic Press.

AKBARIAN, S., BUNNEY, W. E., POTKIN, S. G., WIGAL, S. B., HAGMAN, J. O., SANDMAN, C. A., & JONES, E. G. (1993a). Altered distribution of nicotinamide-adenine dinucleotide phosphate-diphorase cells in frontal lobe of schizophrenics implies disturbances of cortical development. *Archives of General Psychiatry, 50,* 227–230.

AKBARIAN, S., VIÑUELA, A., KIM, J. J., POTKIN, S. G., BUNNEY, W. E., & JONES, E. G. (1993b). Distorted distribution of nicotinamide-adenine dinucleotide phosphate-diphorase neurons in temporal lobe of schizophrenics implies anomalous cortical development. *Archives of General Psychiatry, 50,* 178–187.

AKERS, R. L. (1985). *Deviant behavior: A social learning approach* (3rd ed.). Belmont, CA: Wadsworth.

AKERS, R. L. (1992). *Drugs, alcohol, and society.* Belmont, CA: Wadsworth.

ALAGNA, S. W., & HAMILTON, J. A. (1986). Social stimulus perception and self evaluation: Effects of menstrual cycle phase. *Psychology of Women Quarterly, 10,* 327–338.

ALBRIGHT, L., KENNY, D. A., & MALLOY, T. E. (1988). Consensus in personality judgments at zero acquaintance. *Journal of Personality and Social Psychology, 55,* 387–395.

ALLEN, J. B., KENRICK, D. T., LINDER, D. E., & McCALL, M. A. (1989). Arousal and attraction: A response-facilitation alternative to misattribution and negative-reinforcement models. *Journal of Personality and Social Psychology, 57,* 261–270.

ALLEN, L. S., HINES, M., SHRYNE, E., & GORSKI, R. A. (1989). Two sexually dimorphic cell groups in the human brain. *Journal of Neuroscience, 9,* 497–506.

ALLGEIER, E. R. (1987). Coercive versus consensual sexual interactions. In V. P. Makosky (Ed.), *The G. Stanley Hall Lecture Series* (Vol. 7, pp. 11–63). Washington, DC: American Psychological Association.

ALLINGTON, R. (1980). Teacher interruption behaviors during primary-grade oral reading. *Journal of Educational Psychology, 72,* 371–377.

ALLISON, T., & CHICHETTI, D. (1976). Sleep in mammals: Ecological and constitutional correlates. *Science, 194,* 732–734.

ALLPORT, G. W. (1937). *Personality: A psychological interpretation.* New York: Holt.

ALLPORT, G. W. (1954). *The nature of prejudice.* Reading, MA: Addison-Wesley.

ALLPORT, G. W. (1961). *Pattern and growth in personality.* New York: Holt.

ALLPORT, G. W. (1965). *Letters from Jenny.* New York: Harcourt, Brace & World.

ALLPORT, G. W. (1985). The historical background of social psychology. In G. Lindsey & E. Aronson (Eds.), *Handbook of social psychology* (3rd Ed.). (Vol. 1, pp. 1–46). New York: Random House.

ALLPORT, G. W., & ODBERT, H. S. (1936). Traitnames: A psycho-lexical study. *Psychological Monographs, 47* (Whole No. 211).

AMERICAN ASSOCIATION OF UNIVERSITY WOMEN. (1991). *Shortchanging girls, shortchanging America.* Washington, DC: The Greenberg-Lake Analysis Group.

AMERICAN MEDICAL ASSOCIATION. (1986). Council report: Scientific status of refreshing recollection by the use of hypnosis. *International Journal of Clinical & Experimental Hypnosis, 34,* 1–12.

AMERICAN PSYCHIATRIC ASSOCIATION. (1968). *Diagnostic and statistical manual of mental disorders* (2nd ed.). Washington, DC: Author.

AMERICAN PSYCHIATRIC ASSOCIATION. (1974). *Clinical aspects of the violent individual.* Washington, DC: Author.

AMERICAN PSYCHIATRIC ASSOCIATION (1987). *Diagnostic and statistical manual of mental disorders* (3rd ed., rev.). Washington, DC: Author.

AMERICAN PSYCHIATRIC ASSOCIATION. (1993). DSM-IV draft criteria. Washington, DC: American Psychiatric Association.

AMERICAN PSYCHOLOGICAL ASSOCIATION. (1978). Report of the Task Force on the Role of Psychology in the Criminal Justice System. *American Psychologist, 33,* 1099–1113.

AMERICAN PSYCHOLOGICAL ASSOCIATION. (1981). *Ethical principles of psychologists.* Washington, DC: Author.

ANAND, B. K., & BROBECK, J. R. (1951). Localization of a feeding center in the hypothalamus of the rat. *Journal of the Society of Experimentation and Medicine, 77,* 323–324.

ANASTASI, A. (1988). *Psychological testing* (6th ed.). New York: Macmillan.

ANDERSON, A. (1982, December). How the mind heals. *Psychology Today,* pp. 51–56.

ANDERSON, C. A. (1987). Temperature and aggression: Effects on quarterly, yearly, and city rates of violent and nonviolent crime. *Journal of Personality and Social Psychology, 52,* 1161–1173.

ANDERSON, E. S. (1977). *Learning to speak with style.* Unpublished doctoral dissertation, Stanford University, Stanford, CA.

ANDERSON, J. (1985). *Cognitive psychology and its implications.* New York: W. H. Freeman.

ANDERSON, J. R., & BOWER, G. G. (1973). *Human associative memory.* Washington, DC: V. H. Winston.

ANDERSON, N. B. (1989). Racial differences in stress-induced cardiovascular reactivity and hypertension: Current status and substantive issues. *Psychological Bulletin, 105,* 89–105.

ANDERSON, N. B., & JACKSON, J. S. (1986). Race, ethnicity, and health psychology: The example of essential hypertension. In G. C. Stone, S. M. Weiss, J. D. Matarazzo, N. E. Miller, J. Rodin, C. D. Belar, M. J. Follick, & J. E. Singer (Eds.), *Health psychology.* Chicago: University of Chicago Press.

ANDERSON, N. B., LANE, J. D., MURANAKA, M., WILLIAMS, R. B., JR., & HOUSEWORTH, S. J. (1988). Racial differences in blood pressure and forearm vascular responses to the cold face stimulus. *Psychosomatic Medicine, 50,* 57–63.

ANDERSON, S. M., & BEM, S. L. (1981). Sex typing and androgyny in dyadic interaction: Individual differences in responsiveness to physical attractiveness. *Journal of Personality and Social Psychology, 41,* 74–86.

ANDERSON, S. M., & KLATZKY, R. L. (1987). Traits and social stereotypes: Levels of categorization in person perception. *Journal of Personality and Social Psychology, 53,* 235–246.

ANDREASEN, N. C. (1982). Negative vs. positive schizophrenia: Definition and validation. *Archives of General Psychiatry, 39,* 789–794.

ANDREASEN, N. C. (1985). Positive vs. negative schizophrenia: A critical evaluation. *Schizophrenia Bulletin, 11,* 380–389.

ANDREASEN, N. C. (1988). Brain imaging: Applications in psychiatry. *Science, 239,* 1381–1388.

ANDREASEN, N. C., & POWERS, P. S. (1975). Creativity and psychosis: An examination of conceptual style. *Archives of General Psychiatry, 32,* 70–73.

ANDREWS, G., & HARVEY, R. (1981). Does psychotherapy benefit neurotic patients? A reanalysis of the Smith, Glass, and Miller data. *Archives of General Psychiatry, 38,* 1203–1208.

ANGIER, N. (1993, January 13). Gene for mental illness proves elusive. *New York Times,* p. B7.

ANISFELD, M. (1984). *Language development from birth to three.* Hillsdale, NJ: Erlbaum.

ANREP, G. V. (1923). The irradiation of conditioned reflexes. *Proceedings of the Royal Society of London, 94B,* 404–426.

ANTONI, M. H., BAGGETT, L., IRONSON, G., LAPIERRIERE, A., AUGUST, S., KLIMAS, N., SCHNEIDERMAN, N., & FLETCHER, M. A. (1991). Cognitive-behavioral stress management intervention buffers distress responses and immunologic changes following notification of HIV-1 seropositivity. *Journal of Consulting and Clinical Psychology, 59,* 906–915.

ARGUILE, R. (1992). Art therapy with children and adolescents. In. D. Waller & A. Gilroy (Eds.), *Art therapy: A handbook* (pp. 140–154). Philadelphia: Open University Press.

ARGYLE, M. (1987). *The psychology of happiness.* London: Methuen.

ARKIN, R. M., & BAUMGARDNER, A. H. (1985). Self-handicapping. In J. H. Harvey & C. Weary (Eds.), *Attribution: Basic issues and applications.* New York: Academic Press.

ARKOWITZ, H., & MESSER, S. (Eds.). (1984). *Psychoanalytic therapy and behavior therapy: Is integration possible?* New York: Plenum.

ARMSTEAD, C. A., LAWLER, K. A., GORDEN, G., CROSS, J., & GIBBONS, J. (1989). Relationship of racial stressors to blood pressure responses and anger expression in black college students. *Health Psychology 8,* 541–556.

ARMSTRONG, S. L., GLEITMAN, L . R., & GLEITMAN, H. (1983). What some concepts might not be. *Cognition, 13,* 263–308.

ARON, A., DUTTON, D. G., ARON, E. N., & IVERSON, A. (1989). Experiences of falling in love. *Journal of Social and Personal Relationships, 6,* 243–257.

ASARNOW, R. F., STEFFY, R. A., MacCRIMMON, D. J., & CLEGHORN, J. M. (1978). An attentional assessment of foster children at risk for schizophrenia. In L. C. Wynne, R. L. Cromwell, and S. Matthysse (Eds.), *The nature of schizophrenia.* New York: Wiley.

ASCH, S. E. (1946). Forming impressions of personality. *Journal of Abnormal and Social Psychology, 41,* 258–290.

ASCH, S. E. (1955, November). Opinions and social pressure. *Scientific American,* pp. 31–35.

ASCH, S. E. (1956). Studies of independence and conformity: I. A minority of one against a unanimous majority. *Psychological Monographs, 70* (9, Whole No. 416).

ASCH, S. E. (1957). An experimental investigation of group influence. In Walter Reed Army Institute of Research (Ed.), *Symposium on preventive and social psychiatry.* (pp. 17–24) Washington, DC: U.S. Government Printing Office.

ASERINSKY, E., & KLEITMAN, N. (1953). Regularly occuring periods of eye motility and concomitant phenomena during sleep. *Science, 118,* 273–274.

ASHCRAFT, M. H. (1982). The development of mental arithmetic: A chronometric approach. *Developmental Review, 2,* 213–236.

ASHCRAFT, M. H., KELLAS, G., & NEEDHAM, S. (1975). Rehearsal and retrieval processes in free recall of categorized lists. *Memory and Cognition, 3,* 506–512.

ATCHLEY, R. C. (1980). *The social forces in later life* (3rd ed.). Belmont, CA: Wadsworth.

ATKINSON, J. W. (1957). Motivational determinants of risk-taking behavior. *Psychological Review, 64,* 359–372.

ATKINSON, J. W. (1964). *An introduction to motivation.* Princeton: Van Nostrand.

ATKINSON, R., & SHIFFRIN, R. (1971, August). The control of short term memory. *Scientific American,* 82–90.

ATKINSON, R. C., & SHIFFRIN, R. M. (1968). Human memory: A proposed system and its control processes. In K. W. Spence & J. T. Spence (Eds.), *The psychology of learning and motivation: Advances in research and theory* (Vol. 2, pp. 89–195). New York: Academic Press.

AUGUSTINE, ST. (1919). *Confessions* (William Watts, Trans.). London: Heinemann.

AUGUSTINE, ST. (1948). *Soliloquies* (Thomas F. Gilligan, Trans.). New York: Cima.

AYOUB, D. M., GREENOUGH, W. T., & JURASKA, J. M. (1983). Sex differences in dendritic structure in the preoptic area of the juvenile macaque monkey brain. *Science, 219,* 197–198.

AZRIN, N. H. (1960). Effects of punishment intensity during variable-interval reinforcement. *Journal of the Experimental Analysis of Behavior, 3,* 123–142.

AZRIN, N. H., & HOLZ, W. C. (1966). Punishment. In W. K. Honig (Ed.), *Operant behavior: Areas of research and application* (pp. 380–447). New York: Appleton-Century-Crofts.

BABAD, E. Y. (1986). The Israeli case: Minority status and politics. In K. R. Scherer, H. G. Wallbott, & A. B. Summerfield (Eds.), *Experiencing emotion: A cross-cultural study.* (pp. 246–255) Cambridge: Cambridge University Press.

BABAD, E., INBAR, J., & ROSENTHAL, R. (1982). Pygmalion, Galatea and the Golem: Investigations of biased and unbiased teachers. *Journal of Educational Psychology, 74,* 459–474.

BABLADELIS, G. (1987). Young persons' attitudes toward aging. *Perceptual and Motor Skills, 65,* 553–554.

BADDELEY, A. D. (1988). Cognitive psychology and human memory. *Trends in Neuroscience, 11,* 176–181.

BADDELEY, A. D. (1990). *Human memory: Theory and practice.* Needham Heights, MA: Allyn & Bacon.

BADDELEY, A. D. (1992). Working memory: The interface between memory and cognition. *Journal of Cognitive Neuroscience, 4,* 281–288.

BADDELEY, A. D., & HITCH, G. L. (1974). Working memory. In G. H. Bower (Ed.), *The psychology of learning and motivation* (Vol. 8, pp. 47–89). New York: Academic Press.

BAER, P. E., GARMEZY, L. B., MCLAUGHLIN, R. J., POKORNY, A. D., & WERNICK, M. J. (1987). Stress, coping, family conflict and adolescent alcohol use. *Journal of Behavioral Medicine, 10,* 449–466.

BAHRICK, H. P. (1984). Semantic memory content in permastore: Fifty years of memory learned in school. *Journal of Experimental Psychology: General, 113,* 1–26.

BAHRICK, H. P., BAHRICK, P. O., & WITTLINGER, R. P. (1975). Fifty years of memory for names and faces: A cross-sectional approach. *Journal of Experimental Psychology: General, 104,* 54–75.

BAHRICK, H. P., & PHELPS, E. (1987). Retention of Spanish vocabulary over 8 years. *Journal of Experimental Psychology: Learning, Memory, and Cognition, 13,* 344–349.

BAILEY, J. M. & PILLARD, R. C. (1991). A genetic study of male sexual orientation. *Archives of General Psychiatry, 48,* 1089–1096.

BAILEY, J. M., PILLARD, R. C., NEALE M. C., & AGYEI, Y. (1993). Heritable factors influence sexual orientation in women. *Archives of General Psychiatry, 50,* 217–223.

BALDESSARINI, R. J., & COLE, J. O. (1988). Chemotherapy. In A. M. Nicholi, Jr. (Ed.), The new Harvard guide to psychiatry. Cambridge, MA: Harvard University Press.

BANCROFT, J. (1987). A physiological approach. In J. H. Geer & W. T. O'Donohue (Eds.), Theories of human sexuality. (pp. 411–421) New York: Plenum.

BANDURA, A. (1965). Influence of model's reinforcement contingencies on the acquisition of imitative responses. *Journal of Personality and Social Psychology, 1,* 589–595.

BANDURA, A. (1977). Self-efficacy: Toward a unifying theory of behavioral change. *Psychological Review, 84,* 191–215.

BANDURA, A. (1992). Exercise of personal agency through the self-efficacy mechanism. In R. Schwarzer (Ed.), *Self efficacy: Thought control of action.* (pp. 3–38) Washington, DC: Hemisphere.

BANDURA, R., ROSS, D., & ROSS, S. A. (1961). Transmission of aggression through imitation of aggressive models. *Journal of Abnormal and Social Psychology, 63,* 575–582.

BANDURA, A., ROSS, D., & ROSS, S. A. (1963). Imitation of film-mediated aggressive models. *Journal of Abnormal and Social Psychology, 66,* 3–11.

BANDURA, A., & WALTERS, R. (1963). *Social learning and personality development.* New York: Holt, Rinehart & Winston.

BANKS, J. K., & GANNON, L. R. (1988). The influence of hardiness on the relationship between stressors and psychosomatic symptomatology. *American Journal of Community Psychology, 16,* 25–37.

BANKS, M. S., & SALAPATEK, P. (1978). Acuity and contrast sensitivity in 1-, 2-, and 3-month-old human infants. *Investigative Ophthalmology & Visual Science, 17,* 361–365.

BARASH, D. P. (1977). *Sociobiology and behavior.* New York: Elsevier.

BARD, P. (1929). The central representation of the sympathetic nervous system as indicated by certain physiologic observations. *Archives of Neurological Psychiatry, 22,* 230–246.

BAREFOOT, J. C., DAHLSTROM, W. G., & WILLIAMS, R. B. (1983). Hostility, CHD incidence, and total mortality: A 25-year follow-up study of 225 physicians. *Psychosomatic Medicine, 45,* 59–63.

BAREFOOT, J. C., SIEGLER, J. C., NOWLIN, J. B., PETERSON, B. L., HANEY, T. L., & WILLIAMS, R. B. (1987). Suspiciousness, health, and mortality: A follow-up study of 500 older adults. *Psychosomatic Medicine, 49,* 450–457.

BARINAGA, M. (1989). Manic depression gene put in limbo. *Science, 246,* 886–887.

BARLOW, D. H. (1988). *Anxiety and its disorders.* New York: Guilford.

BARNETT, P. A., & GOTLIB, I. (1988). Psychosocial functioning and depression: Distinguishing among antecedents, concomitants, and consequences. *Psychological Bulletin, 104,* 97–126.

BARON, R. A., & BYRNE, D. (1991). *Social psychology* (6th ed.). Boston: Allyn & Bacon.

BARON, R. S., CUTRONA, C. E., HICKLIN, D., RUSSELL, D. W., & LUBAROFF, D. M. (1990). Social support and immune function among spouses of cancer patients. *Journal of Personality and Social Psychology, 59,* 344–352.

BARTLETT, F. C. (1932). *Remembering.* Cambridge: Cambridge University Press.

BARTOSHUK, L. M. (1971). The chemical senses: I. Taste. In J. W. Kling & A. A. Riggs (Eds.), *Experimental psychology* (3rd ed.) (pp. 169–192) New York: Holt, Rinehart & Winston.

BARTOSHUK, L. M. (1978). Gustatory system. In R. B. Masterson (Ed.), *Handbook of behavioral neurobiology: Vol I. Sensory integration* (pp. 503–567). New York: Plenum.

BASOW, S. A. (1992). *Gender: Stereotypes and roles* (3rd ed.). Pacific Grove, CA: Brooks/Cole.

BATESON, G., JACKSON, D. D., HALEY, J., & WEAKLAND, J. (1956). Toward a theory of schizophrenia. *Behavior Science, 1,* 251–264.

BATESON, G., & MEAD, M. (1942). *Balinese character.* New York: Academy of Sciences.

BATH, J. A., & LEWIS, E. C. (1962). Attitudes of young female adults toward some areas of parent-adolescent conflict. *Journal of Genetic Psychology, 100,* 241–253.

BATSON, C. D., & SHAW, L. L. (1991). Evidence for altruism: Toward a pluralism of prosocial motives. *Psychological Inquiry, 2,* 107–122.

BAUM, A., GATCHEL, R. J., & SCHAEFFER, M. A. (1983). Emotional, behavioral and physiological effects of chronic stress and Three Mile Island. *Journal of Consulting and Clinical Psychology, 51,* 565–572.

BAUMRIND, D. (1964). Some thoughts on ethics of research: After reading Milgram's "Behavioral study of obedience." *American Psychologist, 19,* 421–423.

BAUMRIND, D. (1979). IRB's and social science research: The cost of deception. *IRB: A Review of Human Subjects Research, 1,* 1–4.

BAUMRIND, D. (1985). Research using intentional deception: Ethical issues revisited. *American Psychologist, 40,* 165–174.

BAUMRIND, D. (1986). Sex differences in moral reasoning: Response to Walker's (1984) conclusion that there are none. *Child Development, 57,* 511–521.

BAXTER, L. R., PHELPS, M. E., MAZIOTTA, J. C., GUZE, G. H., SCHWARTZ, J. M., & SELIN, C. E. (1987). Local cerebral glucose metabolic rates in obsessive-compulsive disorder: A comparison with rates in unipolar depression and normal controls. *Archives of General Psychiatry, 44,* 211–218.

BAYLEY, N. (1949). Consistency and variability in the growth of intelligence from birth to eighteen years. *Journal of Genetic Psychology, 65,* 175–196.

BEAMAN, A. L., BARNES, P. J., KLENTZ, B., & McQUIRK, B. (1978). Increasing helping rates through information dissemination: Teaching pays. *Personality and Social Psychology Bulletin, 4,* 406–411.

BEAMAN, A. L., COLE, M., PRESTON, M., KLENTZ, B., & STEBLAY, N. M. (1983). Fifteen years of the foot-in-the-door research: A meta-analysis. *Personality and Social Psychology Bulletin, 9,* 181–186.

BECK, A. T. (1964). Thinking and depression: II. Theory and therapy. *Archives of General Psychiatry, 9,* 561–571.

BECK, A. T. (1967). *Depression: Clinical, experimental, and theoretical aspects.* New York: Harper & Row.

BECK, A. T. (1987). Cognitive models of depression. *Journal of Cognitive Psychotherapy, 1,* 5–37.

BECK, A. T., BROWN, G., STEER, R. A., EIDELSON, J. I., & RISKIND, J. H. (1987). Differentiating anxiety and depression: A test of the cognitive content-specificity hypothesis. *Journal of Abnormal Psychology, 96,* 179–183.

BECK, A. T., RUSH, A. J., SHAW, B. F., & EMERY, G. (1979). *Cognitive therapy of depression.* New York: Guilford.

BEE, H. (1992). *The developing child.* New York: Harper Collins.

BEECHER, H. K. (1972). The placebo effect as a nonspecific force surrounding disease and the treatment of disease. In R. Janzen, W. D. Kerdel, A. Herz, C. Steichele, J. P. Payne, & P. Burt (Eds.), *Pain: Basic principles, pharmacology, and therapy.* Stuttgart, West Germany: Georg Thiene.

BEHRICK, H. P., & PHELPS, E. (1987). Retention of Spanish vocabulary over 8 years. *Journal of Experimental Psychology: Learning, Memory and Cognition, 13,* 344–349.

BÉKÉSEY, G. VON (1960). *Experiments in hearing.* New York: McGraw-Hill.

BELL, A. P., WEINBERG, M. S., & HAMMERSMITH, S. L. (1981). *Sexual preference: Its development in men and women.* Bloomington: Indiana University Press.

BELLOC, N. D., & BRESLOW, L. (1972). Relationship of physical health status and family practices. *Preventive Medicine, 1,* 409–421.

BELSKY, J., GILSTRAP, B., & ROVINE, M. (1984). The Pennsylvania infant and family development project: I. Stability and change in mother-infant and father-infant interaction in a family setting at 1, 3 and 9 months. *Child Development, 55,* 692–705.

BEM, D. J. (1965). An experimental analysis of self-persuasion. *Journal of Experimental Social Psychology, 1,* 199–218.

BEM, D. J. (1972). Self perception theory. In L. Berkowitz (Ed.), *Advances in experimental social psychology* (Vol. 6, pp. 2–62). New York: Academic Press.

BEM, D. J., & ALLEN, A. (1974). On predicting some of the people some of the time: The search for cross-situational consistencies in behavior. *Psychological Review, 81,* 506–520.

BEM, S. L. (1981). Gender schema theory: A cognitive account of sex typing. *Psychological Review, 88,* 354–364.

BEM, S. L. (1985). Androgyny and gender schema theory: A conceptual and empirical integration. In T. B. Sonderegger (Ed.), *Nebraska Symposium on Emotion, 32* (pp. 179–226). Lincoln: University of Nebraska Press.

BENASSI, V. A., SWEENEY, P. D., & DUFOUR, C. L. (1988). Is there a relationship between locus of control orientation and depression? *Journal of Abnormal Psychology, 97,* 357–367.

BENNETT, E. L., DIAMOND, M. C., DRECH, N., & ROSENZWEIG, M. R. (1964). Chemical and anatomical plasticity of brain. *Science, 146,* 610–619.

BENNETT, P., WEINMAN, J., & SPURGEON, P. (Eds.). (1990). *Current developments in health psychology.* Chur, Switzerland: Harwood.

BERARDO, D. H., SHEHAN, C. L., & LESLIE, G. R. (1987). A residue of tradition: Jobs, careers, and spouses' time in housework. *Journal of Marriage and the Family, 49,* 381–390.

BERGEN, J. A., EYLAND, E. A., CAMPBELL, J. A., JENKINS, P., KELLEHEAR, K., RICHARDS, A., & BEAUMONT, P. J. V. (1989). The course of tardive dyskinesia in patients on long-term neuroleptics. *British Journal of Psychiatry, 154,* 523–528.

BERGIN, A. E., & SUINN, R. M. (1975). Individual psychotherapy and behavior therapy. *Annual Review of Psychology, 26,* 509–556.

BERKMAN, L. F., & SYME, S. L. (1979). Social networks, host resistance and mortality: A nine-year follow-up study of Alameda County residents. *American Journal of Epidemiology, 109,* 186–204.

BERKOWITZ, L. (1989). Frustration-aggression hypothesis: Examination and reformulation. *Psychological Bulletin, 106,* 59–73.

BERLIN, B., & KAY, P. (1969). *Basic color terms: Their universality and evolution.* Berkeley: University of California Press.

BERMANT, G. (1976). Sexual behavior: Hard times with the Coolidge Effect. In M. H. Siegel & H. P. Ziegler (Eds.), *Psychological research: The inside story* (pp. 76–103). New York: Harper & Row.

BERMOND, B., NIEUWENHUYSE, B., FASOTTI, L., & SCHUERMAN, J. (1991). Spinal cord lesions, peripheral feedback, and intensities of emotional feelings. *Cognition and Emotion, 5,* 201–220.

BERNARD, C. (1957). *An introduction to the study of experimental medicine* (H. C. Greene, Trans.). New York: Dover. (Original work published 1865)

BERNSTEIN, D. A., AND BORKOVEC, T. C. (1973). *Progressive relaxation training.* Champaign, IL: Research Press.

BERRY, D. S., & McARTHUR, L. Z. (1986). Perceiving character in faces: The impact of age-related craniofacial changes on social perception. *Psychological Bulletin, 100,* 3–18.

BERRY, D. S., & ZEBROWITZ-McARTHUR, L. (1988). What's in a face? Facial maturity and the attribution of legal responsibility. *Personality and Social Psychology Bulletin, 14,* 23–33.

BERRY, R. E., & WILLIAMS, F. L. (1987). Assessing the relationship between quality of life and marital and income satisfaction: A path analytic approach. *Journal of Marriage and the Family, 49,* 107–116.

BERSCHEID, E., DION, K., WALSTER, E., & WALSTER, G. W. (1971). Physical attractiveness and dating choice: A test of the matching hypothesis. *Journal of Experimental Social Psychology, 7,* 173–189.

BERSCHEID, E., & WALSTER, E. (1974). A little bit about love. In T. L. Huston (Ed.), *Foundations of interpersonal attraction* (pp. 356–382). New York: Academic Press.

BERTHENTHAL, B. I., CAMPOS, J. J., & BARRETT, K. C. (1984). Self-produced locomotion: An organizer of emotional, cognitive, and social development in infancy. In R. N. Emde & R. J. Harmon (Eds.), *Continuities and discontinuities in development* (pp. 175–210). New York: Plenum.

BERTONCINI, J., BIJELAC-BABIC, B., JUSCZYK, P. W., KENNEDY, L. J., & MAHLER, J. (1988). An investigation of young infants' perceptual representation of speech sounds. *Journal of Experimental Psychology: General, 117,* 21–33.

BEST, J. B. (1989). *Cognitive psychology* (2nd ed.). St. Paul, MN: West.

BIEDERMAN, I. (1981). On the semantics of a glance at a scene. In M. Kubovy & J. Pomerantz (Eds.), *Perceptual organization* (pp. 213–253). Hillsdale, NJ: Erlbaum.

BILLINGS, A. G., CRONKITE, R. C., & MOOS, R. H. (1983). Social-environmental factors in unipolar depression: Comparisons of depressed patients and nondepressed controls. *Journal of Abnormal Psychology, 92,* 119–133.

BINET, A., & HENRI, V. (1895). La psychologie individuelle. *L'Année Psychologique, 2,* 411–465.

BIRDWHISTELL, R. L. (1970). *Kinesics and context.* Philadelphia: University of Pennsylvania Press.

BJORKLUND, D. F. (1989). *Children's thinking.* Pacific Grove, CA: Brooks/Cole.

BLACK, D. W., WINOKER, G., BELL, S., NASRUALLAH, A., & HULBERT, J. (1988). Complicated mania: Comorbidity and immediate outcome in the treatment of mania. *Archives of General Psychiatry, 45,* 232–236.

BLAKEMORE, C., & GREENFIELD, S. (Eds.). (1987). *Mindwaves.* Oxford: Blackwell.

BLANCHARD, E. B., ANDRASIC, F., NEFF, D. F., ARENA, J. G., AHLES, T. A., JURISH, S. E., PALLMEYER, T. P., SAUNDERS, N. L., & TEDERS, S. J. (1982). Biofeedback and relaxation training with three kinds of headache: Treatment effects and their prediction. *Journal of Consulting and Clinical Psychology, 50,* 562–575.

BLANCHARD, E. B., KOLB, L. C., PALLMEYER, T. P., & GERARDI, R. J. (1986). Cardiac response to relevant stimuli as an adjunctive tool for diagnosing post-traumatic stress disorder in Vietnam veterans. *Behavior Therapy, 17,* 592–606.

BLASS, E. M., & TEICHER, H. M. (1980). Suckling. *Science, 210,* 15–22.

BLESS, H., BOHNER, G., SCHWARTZ, N., & STRACK, F. (1990). Mood and persuasion: A cognitive response analysis. *Personality and Social Psychology Bulletin, 16,* 331–345.

BLEULER, E. (1911). *Dementia praecox, or the group of schizophrenies* (J. Zinkin and N. D. C. Lewis, Trans.) New York: International Universities Press, 1950.

BLISS, T., & GARDNER-MEDWIN, A. (1973). Long lasting potentiation of synaptic transmission in the dentate area of unanesthetized rabbit following stimulation of the perforant path. *Journal of Physiology, 232,* 357–374.

BLOCK, J. H. (1973). Conceptions of sex-roles: Some cross-cultural and longitudinal perspectives. *American Psychologist, 28,* 512–526.

BLOOM, B. L., & CALDWELL, R. A. (1981). Sex differences in adjustment during the process of marital separation. *Journal of Marriage and the Family, 43,* 693–701.

BLOOM, F. E. (1993). Advancing a neurodevelopmental origin for schizophrenia. *Archives of General Psychiatry, 50,* 224–227.

BLOOM, L., LIGHTBOWN, P., & HOOD, L. (1975). Structure and variation in child language. *Monographs of the Society for Research in Child Development, 40* (Serial No. 160).

BOESCH, C. (1991). Teaching in wild chimpanzees. *Animal Behavior, 41,* 530–532.

BOESCH-ACKERMAN, H., & BOESCH, C. (1993). Tool use in wild chimpanzees: New light from dark forests. *Current Directions in Psychological Science, 2,* 18–21.

BOLLES, R. C. (1970). Species-specific defense reactions and avoidance learning. *Psychological Review, 77,* 32–48.

BOLTON, P. J. (1983). Drugs of abuse. In D. F. Hawkins (Ed.), *Drugs and Pregnancy: Human teratogens and related problems* (pp. 128–154). Edinburgh: Churchill Livingstone.

BOND, C. F., JR., & BROCKETT, D. R. (1987). A social context–personality index theory of memory for acquaintances. *Journal of Personality and Social Psychology, 52,* 1110–1112.

BOND, M. H. (1986). *The psychology of the Chinese people.* New York: Oxford University Press.

BOORSTIN, D. J. (1983). *The Discoverers.* New York: Random House.

BORBELY, A. A., BAUMANN, F., BRANDEIS, D., STRAUCH, I., & LEHMANN, D. (1981). Sleep deprivation: Effect on sleep stages and EEG power density in man. *Electroencephalography and Clinical Neurophysiology, 51,* 483–493.

BORING, E. G. (1915). Processes referred to alimentary and urinary tracts. *Psychological Review, 22,* 316–319.

BORKE, H. (1975). Piaget's mountains revisited: Changes in the egocentric landscape. *Developmental Psychology, 11,* 240–243.

BORNSTEIN, M. H. (1989). Information processing (habituation) in infancy and stability in cognitive development. *Human Development, 32,* 129–136.

BOTVIN, G. L., & MURRAY, F. B. (1975). The efficacy of peer modeling and social conflict in the acquisition of conservation. *Child Development, 46,* 796–799.

BOUCHARD, C., TREMBLAY, A., DESPRÉS, J-P., NADEAU, A., LUPIEN, P. J., THERAULT, G., DUSSAULT, J., MOORJANI, S., PINAULT, S., & FOURNIER, G. (1990). The response to long-term overfeeding in identical twins. *New England Journal of Medicine, 322,* 1477–1482.

BOUCHARD, T. J., LYKKEN, D. T., McGUE, M., SEGAL, N. L., & TELLEGEN, A. (1990). Sources of human psychological differences: The Minnesota study of twins reared apart. *Science, 250,* 223–228.

BOUCHARD, T. J., & McGUE, M. (1981). Familial studies of intelligence: A review. *Science, 212,* 1055–1058.

BOURGUIGNON, E. (1979). *Psychological anthropology.* New York: Holt.

BOWER, G. (1981). Mood and memory. *American Psychologist, 36,* 129–148.

BOWER, G. H., BLACK, J. B., & TURNER, T. J. (1979). Scripts in memory for text. *Cognitive Psychology, 11,* 177–220.

BOWER, G. H., CLARK, M., WINENZ, D., & LESGOLD, A. (1969). Hierarchical retrieval schemes in recall of categorized word lists. *Journal of Verbal Learning and Verbal Behavior, 8,* 323–343.

BOWER, G. H., & SPRINGSTON, F. (1970). Pauses as recording points in letter series. *Journal of Experimental Psychology, 83,* 421–430.

BOWER, G. H., & WINENZ, D. (1970). Comparison of associative learning strategies. *Psychonomic Science, 20,* 119–120.

BOWLBY, J. (1969). *Attachment and loss: Vol. 1. Attachment.* New York: Basic Books.

BOWLBY, J. (1973). *Attachment and loss: Vol. 2. Separation, anxiety, and anger.* New York: Basic Books.

BOWLBY, J. (1980). *Attachment and loss: Vol. 3. Sadness and depression.* New York: Basic Books.

BOWLING, A. (1987). Mortality after bereavement: A review of the literature on survival periods and factors affecting survival. *Social Science & Medicine, 24,* 117–124.

BOYD, J. H., & WEISSMAN, M. M. (1981). Epidemiology of affective disorders. *Archives of General Psychiatry, 38,* 1039–1046.

BOYLE, P. C., STORLIEN, L. H., & KEESEY, R. E. (1978). Increased efficiency of food utilization following food loss. *Physiology and Behavior, 21,* 261–264.

BRAIN, P. F. (1979). Steroidal influences on aggressiveness. In J. Obiols, C. Ballús, E. González Monclús, & J. Pujol (Eds.), *Biological psychiatry today* (pp. 1204–1208). Amsterdam: Elsevier/North Holland Biomedical Press.

BRANSFORD, J., & JOHNSON, M. (1972). Contextual prerequisites for understanding: Some investigations of comprehension and recall. *Journal of Verbal Learning and Verbal Behavior, 61,* 717–726.

BRANSFORD, J., & STEIN, B. S. (1984). *The ideal problem solver: A guide for improving thinking, learning and creativity.* New York: W. H. Freeman.

BRAY, D. W., & HOWARD, A. (1983). The AT&T longitudinal studies of managers. In K. W. Schaie (Ed.), *Longitudinal studies of adult psychological development* (pp. 266–312). New York: Guilford.

BRAY, G. A. (1986). Effects of obesity on health and happiness. In K. D. Brownell & J. P. Foreyt (Eds.), *Handbook of eating disorders* (pp. 3–44). New York: Basic Books.

BREGGIN, P. R. (1979). *Electroshock, its brain-disabling effects.* New York: Springer.

BREGMAN, A. S., & CAMPBELL, J. (1971). Primary auditory stream segregation and perception of order in rapid sequence of tones. *Journal of Experimental Psychology, 89,* 244–249.

BRELAND, K., & BRELAND, M. (1961). The misbehavior of organisms. *American Psychologist, 16,* 681–684.

BRELAND, K., & BRELAND, M. (1966). *Animal behavior.* New York: Macmillan.

BRESLAU, N., & DAVIS, G. C. (1987). Posttraumatic stress disorder: The etiologic specificity of wartime stressors. *American Journal of Psychiatry, 144,* 578–583.

BRESLOW, L. (1983). The potential of health promotion. In D. Mechanic (Ed.), *Handbook of health, health care, and the health professions* (pp. 50–66). New York: Free Press.

BRESLOW, L. (1993) Health practices and disability: Some evidence from Alameda County. *Preventive Medicine, 22,* 86–95.

BREUER, J., & FREUD, S. (1957). *Studies in hysteria.* New York: Basic Books. (Original work published 1895)

Brian Boitano Proves to Be a Grand and Classy Champion. (1988, February 22). *The PRESS-Enterprise* (Riverside, CA), p. 3.

BRIGGS, J. L. (1970). *Never in anger: Portrait of an Eskimo family.* Cambridge, MA: Harvard University Press.

BROCA, P. (1861). Sur le volume et la forme du cerveau suivant les individus et suivant les races. *Bulletin Société d'Anthropologie Paris, 2,* 139–207, 301–321, 441–446.

BRODY, J. E. (1983, May 24). Emotions found to influence nearly every human ailment. *New York Times,* pp. C1, C8.

BRODY, J. E. (1992, September 30). Personal health: Depression often isn't recognized and myriad masks hide its epidemic. *New York Times,* p. B6.

BRODY, J. E. (1993, May 12). 7 deadly sins of living linked to illness as well as mortality. *New York Times,* p. B6.

BROPHY, J. E. (1983). Research on the self-fulfilling prophecy and teacher expectations. *Journal of Educational Psychology, 75,* 631–661.

BROWN, A. M., DOWELL, R. C., & CLARK, G. M. (1987). Clinical results for postlingually deaf patients implanted with multichannel cochlear prosthestics. *Annals of Otology, Rhinology, and Laryngology, 96* (Suppl. 128), 127–128.

BROWN, J. D. (1986). Evaluations of self and others: Self-enhancement biases in social judgments. *Social Cognition, 4,* 353–376.

BROWN, P. K., & WALD, G. (1964). Visual pigments in single rods and cones of the human retina. *Science, 144,* 45–52.

BROWN, R. (1958). *Words and things.* Glencoe, IL: Free Press.

BROWN, R., & KULICK, J. A. (1977). Flashbulb memories. *Cognition, 5,* 73–99.

BROWN, R. W., & LENNEBERG, E. H. (1954). A study of language and cognition. *Journal of Abnormal and Social Psychology, 49,* 454–462.

BROWN, R. W., & McNEIL, D. (1966). The "tip-of-the-tongue" phenomenon. *Journal of Verbal Learning and Verbal Behavior, 5,* 325–337.

BRUCE, C., DESIMONE, R., & GROSS, C. G. (1981). Visual properties of neurons in a polysensory area in the superior temporal sulcus of the macaque. *Journal of Neurophysiology, 46,* 369–384.

BRUGHTA, T. S., BEBBINGTON, P. W., MacCARTHY, B., & STUART, E. (1992). Antidepressants may not assist recovery in practice: A naturalistic prospective survey. Acta *Psychiatra Scandinavica, 86,* 5–11.

BRUNER, J. (1983). *Child's talk: Learning to use language.* New York: Norton.

BRUNER, J. S., GOODNOW, J., & AUSTIN, G. A. (1956). *A study of thinking.* New York: Wiley.

BUCHSBAUM, M. S., & HAIER, R. J. (1987). Psychopathology: Biological approaches. *Annual Review of Psychology, 34,* 401–430.

BUCKHOUT, R. (1975). Nearly 2000 witnesses can be wrong. *Social Action and the Law, 2,* 7.

BUELL, S. J., & COLEMAN, P. D. (1979). Dendritic growth in the aged human brain and failure of growth in senile dementia. *Science, 206,* 854–856.

BUGELSKI, B. R., & ALAMPAY, D. A. (1961). The role of frequency in developing perceptual sets. *Canadian Journal of Psychology, 15,* 205–211.

BULLOCK, W. A., & GILLILAND, K. (1993). Eysenck's arousal theory of introversion-extraversion: A converging measures investigation. *Journal of Personality and Social Psychology, 64,* 113–123.

BULLOUGH, V. L. (Ed.). (1976). *Sex, society and history.* New York: Science History.

BULLOUGH, V. L. (1980). *Sexual variance in society and history.* Chicago: University of Chicago Press.

BULLOUGH, V. L. (1987). A historical approach. In J. H. Geer & W. T. O'Donohue (Eds.), *Theories of human sexuality.* New York: Plenum.

BUNNEY, W. E., GOODWIN, F. K., DAVIS, J. M., & FAWCETT, J. A. (1968). A behavioral-biochemical study of lithium treatment. *American Journal of Psychiatry, 125,* 91–104.

BURGER, J. M. (1986). Increasing compliance by improving the deal: The that's-not-all technique. *Journal of Personality and Social Psychology, 51,* 277–283.

BURGER, J. M. (1989). Negative reactions to increases in perceived personal control. *Journal of Personality and Social Psychology, 56,* 246–256.

BURGER, J. M. (1993). *Personality* (3rd ed.). Pacific Grove, CA: Brooks/Cole.

BURNSTEIN, E., & SCHUL, Y. (1982). The informational basis of social judgments: Operations in forming an impression of another person. *Journal of Experimental Social Psychology, 18,* 217–234.

BURT, M. R. (1980). Cultural myths and supports for rape. *Journal of Personality and Social Psychology, 38,* 217–230.

BUS, A. G., & van IJZENDOORN, M. H. (1988). Attachment and early reading: A longitudinal study. *Journal of Genetic Psychology, 149,* 199–210.

BUSS, A. H. (1971). Aggression pays. In J. L. Singer (Ed.), *The control of aggression and violence.* New York: Academic Press.

BUSS, A. H., & PLOMIN, R. (1984). *Temperament: Early developing personality traits.* Hillsdale, NJ: Erlbaum.

BUSS, D. M. (1985). Human mate selection. *American Scientist, 73,* 47–51.

BUSS, D. M., ABBOTT, M., ANGLEITNER, A., ASHERIAN, A., et al. (1990). International preferences in selecting mates: A study of 37 cultures. *Journal of Cross-Cultural Psychology, 21,* 5–47.

BUSS, D. M., & BARNES, M. (1986). Preferences in human mate selection. *Journal of Personality and Social Psychology, 50,* 559–570.

BUSSE, E. W., & MADDOX, G. L. (1985). *The Duke longitudinal studies of normal aging: 1955–1980.* New York: Springer.

BUTLER, R. H. (1954). Incentive conditions which influence visual exploration. *Journal of Experimental Psychology, 48,* 19–23.

BYRNE, D., & NELSON, D. (1965). Attraction as a linear proportion of positive reinforcements. *Journal of Personality and Social Psychology, 1,* 659–663.

BYRNE, D., RASCHE, L., & KELLEY, K. (1974). When "I like you" indicates disagreement. *Journal of Research in Personality, 8,* 207–217.

CACIOPPO, J. T., & PETTY, R. E. (1982). The need for cognition. *Journal of Personality and Social Psychology, 42,* 116–131.

CACIOPPO, J. T., PETTY, R. E., & MORRIS, K. J. (1983). Effects of need for cognition on message evaluation, recall, and persuasion. *Journal of Personality and Social Psychology, 45,* 805–818.

CAIN, W. S. (1979). To know with the nose: Keys to odor identification. *Science, 203,* 467–470.

CAIN, W. S. (1980). Sensory attributes of cigarette smoking. In Gori, G. B., & Bock, F. G. (Eds.), *Banbury Rep, A safe cigarette?* (pp. 239–249). Cold Spring Harbor, NY: Cold Spring Harbor Laboratory.

CAIN, W. S. (1988). Olfaction. In R. A. Atkinson, R. J. Herrenstein, G. Lindzey, & R. D. Luce (Eds.), *Stevens' handbook of experimental psychology* (Vol 1, pp. 409–459). New York: Wiley.

CANNON, W. B. (1927). The James-Lange theory of emotions: A critical examination and an alternative theory. American Journal of Psychology, 39, 106–124.

CANNON, W. B., & WASHBURN, A. L. (1912). An explanation of hunger. *American Journal of Physiology, 29,* 441–454.

CARANI, C., ZINI, D., BALDINI, A., DELLA CASA, L., GHIZZANI, A., & MARRAMA, P. (1990). Effects of androgen treatment in impotent men with normal and low levels of free testosterone. *Archives of Sexual Behavior, 19,* 223–234.

CAREY, S. (1978). The child as word learner. In M. Halle, J. Bresnan, and G. A. Miller (Eds.), *Linguistic theory and psychological reality* (pp. 264–293). Cambridge, MA: MIT Press.

CARLSMITH, J. M., & ANDERSON, C. A. (1979). Ambient temperature and the occurrence of collective violence: A new analysis. *Journal of Personality and Social Psychology, 37,* 337–344.

CARLSON, M., CHARLIN, V., & MILLER, N. (1988). Positive mood and helping behavior: A test of six hypotheses. *Journal of Personality and Social Psychology, 55,* 211–227.

CARROLL, J. L., VOLK, K. D., & HYDE, J. S. (1985). Differences between males and females in motives for engaging in sexual intercourse. *Archives of Sexual Behavior, 14,* 131–139.

CARSKADON, M. A., & DEMENT, W. C. (1989). Normal sleep and its variations. In M. H. Kryger, T.

Roth, & W. C. Dement (Eds.), *Principles and practice of sleep medicine* (pp. 3–13). Philadelphia: Saunders.

CARSON, R. C., & BUTCHER, J. N. (1992). *Abnormal psychology and modern life* (9th ed.). New York: Harper Collins.

CARTER, B. (1991, May 1). Children's TV, where boys are king. *New York Times*, pp. A1, C18.

CARTER, D. B., & LEVY, G. D. (1988). Cognitive aspects of early sex-role development: The influence of gender schemas on preschoolers' memories and preferences for sex-typed toys and activities. *Child Development, 59*, 782–792.

CARTWRIGHT, R. D. (1977). *Nightlife: Explorations in dreaming.* Englewood Cliffs, NJ: Prentice-Hall.

CARTWRIGHT, R. D. (1978). *A primer on sleep and dreaming.* Reading, MA: Addison-Wesley.

CARVER, C. S., & SCHEIER, M. F. (1988). *Perspectives on personality.* Boston: Allyn & Bacon.

CARVER, C. S., & SCHEIER, M. F. (1992). *Perspectives on personality* (2nd ed.). Boston: Allyn & Bacon.

CASH, T. F., & JANDA, L. H. (1984, December). The eye of the beholder. *Psychology Today*, pp. 46–52.

CATTELL, R. B. (1965). *The scientific analysis of personality.* Baltimore: Penguin.

CAVANAUGH, J. C. (1993). *Adult development and aging* (2nd ed.). Pacific Grove, CA: Brooks/Cole.

CECI, S. J., & LIKER, J. K. (1986). A day at the races: A study of IQ, expertise, and cognitive complexity. *Journal of Experimental Psychology: General, 115*, 255–266.

CENTERS FOR DISEASE CONTROL (1991). Mortality attributable to HIV infection/AIDS—United States, 1981–1990. *Morbidity and Mortality Weekly Reports, 40*, 41–44.

CENTERS FOR DISEASE CONTROL (1993a). *AIDS information: Statistical projections/trends, January 1, 1993.* Atlanta: Author.

CENTERS FOR DISEASE CONTROL (1993b). *AIDS information: International projections/statistics, January 1, 1993.* Atlanta: Author.

CERVONE, D., & PEAKE, P. K. (1986). Anchoring, efficacy, and action: The influence of judgmental heuristics and self-efficacy judgments and behavior. *Journal of Personality and Social Psychology, 50*, 492–501.

CHAIKEN, A. L., SIGLER, E., & DERLEGA, V. J. (1974). Nonverbal mediators of teacher expectancy effects. *Journal of Personality and Social Psychology, 30*, 144–149.

CHAIKEN, S., & EAGLY, A. H. (1983). Communication modality as a determinant of persuasion: The role of communicator salience. *Journal of Personality and Social Psychology, 45*, 241–256.

CHAPMAN, W. P., SCHROEDER, H. R., GEYER, G., BRAZIER, M. A. B., FAGEN, C., POPPEN, J. L., SOLOMON, A. H. C., & YAKOVLEV, P. I. (1954). Physiological evidence concerning importance of amygdaloid nuclear region in the integration of circulatory function and emotion in man. *Science, 120*, 949–950.

CHASE, W. G., & SIMON, H. A. (1973). The mind's eye in chess. In W. G. Chase (Ed.), *Visual information processing* (pp. 215–282). New York: Academic Press.

CHI, M. T., FELTOVITCH, P. J., & GLASER, R. (1981). Representation of physics knowledge by novices and experts. *Cognitive Science, 5*, 121–152.

CHI, M. T., GLASER, R., & REES, E. (1982). Expertise in problem solving. In R. Sternberg (Ed.), *Advances in the psychology of human intelligence* (Vol. 1, pp. 7–75). Hillsdale, NJ: Erlbaum.

CHIRIBOGA, D. A. (1982). Adaptation to marital separation in later and earlier life. *Journal of Gerontology, 37*, 109–114.

CHOMSKY, N. (1959). Review of Verbal *Behavior* by B. F. Skinner. *Language, 35*, 26–58.

CHRIST, M. A. G., LAHEY, B. B., FRICK, P. J., RUSSON, M. F., McBURNETT, K., LOEBER, R., STOUTHAMER-LOEBER, M., & GREEN, S. (1990). Serious conduct problems in the children of adolescent mothers: Disentangling confounded correlations. *Journal of Consulting and Clinical Psychology, 58*, 840–844.

CHRISTIANSEN, L. (1988). Deception in psychological research: When is its use justified? *Personality and Social Psychology Bulletin, 14*, 664–675.

CHWALISZ, K., DIENER, E., & GALLAGHER, D. (1988). Autonomic arousal feedback and emotional experience: Evidence from the spinal cord injured. *Journal of Personality and Social Psychology, 54*, 820–828.

CIALDINI, R. B. (1988). *Influence: Science and practice* (2nd ed.) Glenview, IL.: Scott, Foresman/Little, Brown.

CIALDINI, R. B. (1991). Altruism or egoism? That is (still) the question. *Psychological Inquiry, 2*, 124–126.

CIALDINI, R. B., VINCENT, J. E., LEWIS, S. K., CATALAN, J., WHEELER, D., & DARBY, B. L. (1975). Reciprocal concessions procedure for inducing compliance: The door-in-the-face technique. *Journal of Personality and Social Psychology, 31*, 206–215.

CLANCY, W. J., & LETSINGER, R. (1981) NEOMYCIN: Reconfiguring a rule-based expert system for application to teaching. *Proceedings of the IJCAI 1981.* Menlo Park, CA: American Association for Artificial Intelligence.

CLAPAREDE, E. (1951). Recognition and me-ness. In D. Rapaport (Ed.), *Organization and pathology of thought* (pp. 58–75). New York: Columbia University Press. (Original work published 1911)

CLARK, D. M. (1986). A cognitive approach to panic. *Behavior Research and Therapy, 24*, 461–470.

CLARK, H. H., & CLARK, E. V. (1977). *Psychology and language: An introduction to psycholinguistics.* New York: Harcourt Brace Jovanovich.

CLARK, H. H. & LUCY, P. (1975). Understanding what is meant from what is said. A study in conversationally conveyed requests. *Journal of Verbal Learning and Verbal Behavior, 14*, 56–72.

CLARK, W. C., & CLARK, S. B. (1980). Pain responses in Nepalese porters. *Science, 209*, 410–412.

CLARKE, A. E., & RUBLE, D. N. (1978). Young adolescents' beliefs concerning menstruation. *Child Development, 49*, 231–234.

CLAYTON, P. J. (1990). Bereavement and depression. *Journal of Clinical Psychology, 51*, 34–40.

CLEARY, T. A., HUMPHREYS, L. G., KENDRICK, S. A., & WESMAN, A. (1975). Educational uses of tests with disadvantaged students. *American Psychologist, 30*, 15–41.

CLIFFORD, M. M. (1975). Physical attractiveness and academic performance. *Child Study Journal, 5*, 2201–2209.

COBB, S., & ROSE, R. M. (1973). Hypertension, peptic ulcer, and diabetes in air traffic controllers. *Journal of the American Medical Association, 224*, 489–492.

COCHLEAR CORPORATION. (1989). Brochure for Nucleus 22 Channel Cochlear Implant System. Englewood, CO: Author.

COCHRAN, S. D., MAYS, V. M., CIARLETTA, J., CARUSO, C., & MALLON, D. (1992). Efficacy of the theory of reasoned action in predicting AIDS-related sexual risk reduction among gay men. *Journal of Applied Social Psychology, 22*, 1481–1501.

COHEN, C. I., & THOMPSON, K. S. (1992). Homeless mentally ill or mentally ill homeless? *American Journal of Psychiatry, 149*, 816–823.

COHEN, D. B. (1979). *Sleep and dreaming: Origins, nature, and functions.* New York: Pergamon Press.

COHEN, R. (1978). Altruism: Human, cultural, or what? In L. Wispe (Ed.), *Altruism, sympathy, and helping: Psychological and sociological principles.* New York: Academic Press.

COHEN, S. (1988). Psychosocial models of the role of social support in the etiology of physical disease. *Health Psychology, 7*, 269–297.

COHEN, S., EVANS, G. W., STOKOLS, D., & KRANTZ, D. S. (1986). *Behavior, health, and environmental stress.* New York: Plenum.

COHEN, S., & WILLIAMSON, G. (1991). Stress and infectious disease in humans. *Psychological Bulletin, 109*, 5–24.

COHEN, S., & WILLS, T. A. (1985). Stress, social support, and the buffering hypothesis. *Psychological Bulletin, 98*, 310–357.

COHN, D. A. (1990). Child-mother attachment of six-year-olds and social competence at school. *Child Development, 61*, 151–162.

COILE, D. C., & MILLER, N. E. (1984). How radical animal activists try to mislead humane people. *American Psychologist, 39*, 700–701.

COLBY, A., KOHLBERG, L., GIBBS, J., & LIEBERMAN, M. (1983). *A longitudinal study of moral judgment. Monographs of the Society for Research in Child Development, 48* (Serial No. 200).

COLE, M. (1977). An ethnographic psychology of cognition. In P. N. Johnson-Laird & P. C. Wason (Eds.), *Thinking: Readings in cognitive science* (pp. 468–482). Cambridge: Cambridge University Press.

COLE, M., & SCRIBNER, S. (1974). *Culture and thought: A psychological introduction.* New York: Basic Books.

COLE, N. S. (1981). Bias in testing. *American Psychologist, 36*, 1067–1077.

COLEMAN, R. M. (1986). *Wide awake at 3 A.M.* New York: W. H. Freeman.

COLES, C. D., PLATZMAN, K. A., SMITH, I., & JAMES, M. E. (1992). Effects of cocaine and alcohol use in pregnancy on neonatal growth and neurobehavioral status. *Neurotoxicology and Teratology, 14*, 23–33.

COLLINS, A. M., & LOFTUS, E. F. (1975). A spreading-activation theory of semantic processing. *Psychological Review, 82*, 407–428.

COLLINS, A. M., & QUILLIAN, M. R. (1969). Retrieval time from semantic memory. *Journal of Verbal Learning and Verbal Behavior, 8*, 240–247.

COLLINS, J. L. (1982). Self efficacy and ability in achievement behavior. Paper presented at the meeting of the American Educational Research Association, New York.

COMAS-DIAZ, L. (1991). Feminism and diversity in psychology. *Psychology of Women Quarterly, 15*, 597–609.

COMSTOCK, G., CHAFFEE, S., KATZMAN, N., McCOMB, M., & ROBERTS, D. (1978). *Television and human behavior.* New York: Columbia University Press.

CONDRY, J., & DYER, S. (1976). Fear of success: Attribution of cause to the victim. *Journal of Social Issues, 32*, 63–83.

CONGER, R., McCARTY, J., YLANG, R., LAHEY, B., & KROPP, J. (1984). Perception of child, child-rearing values, and emotional distress as mediating links between environmental stressors and observed maternal behavior. *Child Development, 54*, 2234–2247.

CONRAD, R. (1964). Acoustic confusion in immediate memory. *British Journal of Psychology, 55*, 75–84.

CONWAY, T. L., VICKERS, R. R., WARD, H. W., & RAHE, R. H. (1981). Occupational stress and variation in cigarette, coffee, and alcohol consumption. *Journal of Health and Social Behavior, 22*, 155–165.

COOK, M., & MINEKA, S. (1989). Observational conditioning of fear to fear-relevant versus fear-irrelevant stimuli in rhesus monkeys. *Journal of Abnormal Psychology, 98*, 448–459.

COOK, M., & MINEKA, S. (1990). Selective associations in the observational conditioning of fear in rhesus monkeys. *Journal of Experimental Psychology: Animal Behavior Processes, 16*, 372–389.

COONS, P. M., & MILSTEIN, V. (1986). Psychosexual disturbances in multiple personality: Characteristics, etiology, and treatment. *Journal of Clinical Psychology, 47*, 106–110.

COOPERSMITH, S. (1967). *The antecedents of self esteem.* New York: W. H. Freeman.

CORKIN, S. (1984). Lasting consequences of bilateral medial temporal lobectomy: Clinical course and experimental findings in H. M. *Seminars in Neurology, 4*, 249–259.

COTTINGTON, E. M., & HOUSE, J. S. (1987). Occupational stress and health: A multivariate relationship. In A. Baum & J. E. Singer (Eds.), *Handbook of psychology and health* (Vol. 5, pp. 295–342). Hillsdale, NJ: Erlbaum.

COTTON, J. L. (1986). Ambient temperature and violent crime. *Journal of Applied Social Psychology, 16*, 786–801.

COUSINS, N. (1979). *Anatomy of an illness.* New York: Norton.

COYNE, J. C. (1976). Toward an interactions description of depression. *Psychiatry, 39*, 28–40.

CRAIGHEAD, L. W., STUNKARD, A. J., & O'BRIEN, R. M. (1981). Behavior therapy and pharmacotherapy for obesity. *Archives of General Psychiatry, 38*, 763–768.

CRAIK, F. I. M., & LOCKHART, R. S. (1972). Levels of processing: A framework for memory research. *Journal of Verbal Learning and Verbal Behavior, 11*, 671–684.

CRAIK, F. I. M., & TULVING, E. (1975). Depth of processing and the retention of words in episodic memory. *Journal of Experimental Psychology: General, 104*, 268–294.

CRAIK, F. I. M., & WATKINS, M. J. (1973). The role of rehearsal in short term memory. *Journal of Verbal Learning and Verbal Behavior, 12*, 599–607.

CRAMER, R. E., MCMASTER, M. R., BARTELL, P. A., & DRAGNA, M. (1988). Subject competence and minimization of the bystander effect. *Journal of Applied Social Psychology, 18*, 1133–1148.

CRANDALL, C. S. (1988). Social contagion of binge eating. *Journal of Personality and Social Psychology, 55*, 588–598.

CRATTY, B. (1979). *Perceptual and motor development in infants and preschool children.* Englewood Cliffs, NJ: Prentice-Hall.

CRAWFORD, J. D. (1991). Sex recognition by electric cues in a sound-producing mormyrid fish. *Brain, Behavior, and Evolution, 38*, 20–38.

CROCKENBERG, S. (1981). Infant irritability, mother responsiveness, and social support influences on the security of infant-mother attachment. *Child Development, 52*, 857–865.

CROSS, J. H., & ALLEN, J. G. (1970). Ego identity status, adjustment, and academic achievement. *Journal of Consulting and Clinical Psychology, 34*, 288.

CROW, T. J. (1980). Molecular pathology of schizophrenia: More than one disease process? *British Medical Journal, 280*, 1–9.

CROW, T. J. (1985). The two-syndrome concept: Origins and current status. *Schizophrenia Bulletin, 11*, 471–486.

CRUTCHFIELD, R., GEERKEN, M., & GOVE, W. R. (1983). Crime rates and social integration. *Criminology, 20*, 467–478.

CURTIS, R. C., & MILLER, K. (1986). Believing another likes or dislikes you: Behaviors making the beliefs come true. *Journal of Personality and Social Psychology, 51*, 284–290.

CUTRONA, C. E. (1986). Behavioral manifestations of social support: A microanalytic investigation. *Journal of Personality and Social Psychology, 51*, 201–208.

DABBS, J. M., JR., FRADY, R. L., CARR, T. S., & BESCH, N. F. (1987). Saliva testosterone and criminal violence in young adult prison inmates. *Psychosomatic Medicine, 49*, 174–182.

DAMASIO, A. R. AND DAMASIO, H. (1992, September). Brain and language. *Scientific American,* pp. 89–95.

D'ANDRADE, R. G. (1961). Anthropological studies of dreams. In F. L. K. Hsu (Ed.), *Psychological anthropology* (pp. 296–332). Homewood, IL: Dorsey Press.

DANFORTH, E., & SIMS, E. A. H. (1992). Obesity and efforts to lose weight. *New England Journal of Medicine, 327*, 1947–1948.

DARWIN, C. (1959). *On the origin of the species by means of natural selection.* Philadelphia: University of Pennsylvania Press. (Original work published 1859)

DARWIN, C. (1965). *The expression of the emotions in man and animals.* New York: Appleton. (Original work published 1872)

DARWIN, C. T., TURVEY, M. T., & CROWDER, R. G. (1972). An auditory analogue of the Sperling partial report procedure: Evidence for brief auditory storage. *Cognitive Psychology, 3*, 255–267.

DASEN, P. R. (1977). Are cognitive processes universal? A contribution to cross-cultural Piagetian psychology.

DASEN, P. R. (1982). Cross-cultural data on operational development: Asymptotic development curves. In T. G. Bever (Ed.), *Regressions in mental development: Basic phenomena and theories* (pp. 221–232). Hillsdale, NJ: Erlbaum.

DASEN, P. R., & HERON, A. (1981). Cross-cultural tests of Piaget's theory. In H. Triandis & A. Heron (Eds.), *Handbook of cross-cultural psychology: Vol. 4. Developmental psychology.* Boston: Allyn & Bacon.

DASEN, P. R., NGINI, L., & LAVELEE, M. (1979). Cross-cultural training studies of concrete operations. In L. H. Eckenberger, W. J. Lonner, & Y. H. Poortinga (Eds.), *Cross-cultural contributions to psychology.* Amsterdam: Swets & Zeilinger.

DAVIDSON, R. J. (1984). Hemispheric asymmetry and emotion. In K. R. Scherer and P. Ekman (Eds.), *Approaches to emotion* (pp. 39–57). Hillsdale, NJ: Erlbaum.

DAVIS, J. A., & SMITH, T. (1987). *General social surveys 1972–1987: Cumulative data.* Storrs, CT: Roper Center for Public Opinion Research.

DAVIS, J. M. (1978). Dopamine theory of schizophrenia: A two-factor theory. In L. C. Wynne, R. L. Cromwell, & S. Matthysse (Eds.), *The nature of schizophrenia: New approaches to research and treatment.* (pp. 105–115) New York: Wiley.

DAVIS, K. E. (1985, February). Near and dear: Friendship and love compared. *Psychology Today,* pp. 22–30.

DAVISON, G. C., & NEALE, J. M. (1986). *Abnormal psychology* (4th ed.). New York: Wiley.

DAVITZ, J. R. (1969). *The language of emotion.* New York: Academic Press.

DEAUX, K., & HANNA, R. (1984). Courtship in the personals column: The influence of gender and sexual orientation. *Sex Roles, 5*, 571–580.

DeBONO, K. G., & SNYDER, M. (1989). Understanding consumer decision-making processes: The role of form and function in product evaluation. *Journal of Applied Social Psychology, 19*, 416–424.

DeCASPER, A. J., & FIFER, W. P. (1980). Of human bonding: Newborns prefer their mothers' voices. *Science, 208*, 1174–1175.

DeCASPER, A. J., & SPENCE, M. J. (1986). Prenatal maternal speech influences newborn's perception of speech sounds. *Infant Behavior and Development, 9*, 133–150.

DeCHARMS, R., & CARPENTER, V. (1968). Measuring motivation in culturally disadvantaged school children. In H. J. Klausmeirer & G. T. O'Hearn (Eds.), *Research and development toward the improvement of education* (pp. 31–41). Madison WI: Educational Research Services.

DeCHICK, J. (1988, July 19). Most mothers want a job, too. *USA Today,* p. D1.

DECI, E. L. (1975). *Intrinsic motivation.* New York: Plenum.

DECI, E. L. (1978). Applications of research on the effects of rewards. In M. Lepper & D. Greene (Eds.), *The hidden cost of rewards.* New York: Erlbaum.

DE GROOT, A. (1965). *Thought and choice in chess.* The Hague: Mouton.

DeLaCOSTE-UTAMSING, C., & HOLLOWAY, R. L. (1982). Gonadal hormones induce dendritic growth in the human corpus callosum. *Science, 216*, 1431–1432.

DELGADO, J. (1969). *Physical control of the mind.* New York: Harper & Row.

DELGADO, P. L., PRICE, L. H., HENINGER, G. R., & CHARNEY, D. S. (1992). Neurochemistry. In E. S. Paykel (Ed.), *Handbook of affective disorders* (pp. 219–254). London: Churchill Livingstone.

DeLONGIS, R., COYNE, J. C., DAKOF, G., FOLKMAN, S., & LAZARUS, R. S. (1982). Relationship of daily hassles, uplifts and major life events to health states. *Health Psychology, 1*, 119–136.

DeMARIA, T. (1986). Psychologists are functioning as family practitioners. Ninety-third annual convention of the American Psychological Association: The need to train psychologists as family practitioners. *Psychotherapy in Private Practice, 4*, 19–22.

DEMBROSKI, T. M., & CZAJKOWSKI, S. M. (1989). Historical and current developments in coronary-prone behavior. In A. W. Siegman & T. M. Dembroski (Eds.), *In search of coronary-prone behavior: Beyond Type A* (pp. 21–39). Hillsdale NJ: Erlbaum.

DEMENT, W., & WOLPERT, E. (1958). Relation of eye movements, body motility and external stimuli. *Journal of Experimental Psychology, 55*, 543–553.

DEMENT, W. C. (1972). *Some must watch while some must sleep.* San Francisco: W. H. Freeman.

DEMENT, W. C. (1976). *Some must watch while some must sleep.* San Francisco: San Francisco Book Co.

DEMENT, W. C. (1992). *The sleepwatchers.* Stanford, CA: Portable Stanford Books Series.

DEMENT, W. C., CARSKADON, M. A., & LEY, R. (1973). The prevalence of narcolepsy, *Sleep Research, 2*, 147.

DEMENT, W. C., & KLEITMAN, N. (1957). Cyclic variations in EEG during sleep and their relation to eye movements, body motility, and dreaming. *EEG and Clinical Neurophysiology, 9*, 673–690.

DEMENT, W. C., ZARCONE, V., VARNER, V., ET AL. (1972). The prevalence of narcolepsy. *Sleep Research, 1*, 148.

DEMPSTER, F. N., & FARRIS, R. (1990). The spacing effect: Research and practice. *Journal of Research and Development in Education, 23*, 97–101.

DENNIS, W. (1960). Causes of retardation among institutional children: Iran. *Journal of Genetic Psychology, 96*, 47–59.

DeRAAD, B., & DODDEMA-WINSEMIUS, M. (1992). Factors in the assortment of human mates: Differential preferences in Germany and the Netherlands. *Personality and Individual Differences, 13*, 103–114.

DEREGOWSKI, J. B. (1980). *Illusions, patterns and pictures: A cross-cultural perspective.* New York: Academic Press.

DES JARLAIS, D. C., & FRIEDMAN, S. (1987). HIV infection among intravenous drug users: Epidemiology and risk reduction (editorial review). *AIDS, 1*, 67–76.

DESOR, J. A., & BEAUCHAMP, G. K. (1974). The human capacity to transmit olfactory information. *Perception and Psychophysics, 16*, 551–556.

DeVALOIS, R. L., & JACOBS, G. H. (1968). Primate color vision. *Science, 162,* 533–540.

DeVALOIS, R. L., & JACOBS, G. H. (1984). Neural mechanisms of color vision. In J. M. Brookhart & V. B. Mountcastle (Eds.), *Handbook of physiology, the nervous system* (Vol. 3, pp. 425–456). Bethesda, MD: American Physiological Society.

DEVINE, P. G. (1989). Stereotypes and prejudice: Their automatic and controlled components. *Journal of Personality and Social Psychology, 56,* 5–18.

DIAMOND, E. L. (1982). The role of anger and hostility in essential hypertension and coronary heart disease. *Psychological Bulletin, 92,* 410–433.

DICKSTEIN, S., & PARKE, R. D. (1988). Social referencing in infancy: A glance at fathers and marriage. *Child Development, 59,* 506–511.

DIENER, C. I., & DWECK, C. S. (1980). An analysis of learned helplessness: II. The processing of success. *Journal of Personality and Social Psychology, 39,* 940–952.

DIFFILY, A. (1988, December). Obsessed. *Brown Alumni Monthly,* pp. 24–30.

DIGMAN, J. M. (1990). Personality structure: Emergence of the five-factor model. *Annual Review of Psychology, 41,* 417–440.

DiMATTEO, M. R. (1991). *The psychology of health, illness, and medical care.* Belmont, CA: Wadsworth.

DION, K. K., & DION, K. L. (1975). Self-esteem and romantic love. *Journal of Personality, 43,* 39–57.

DOBSON, V., & TELLER, D. (1978). Visual acuity in human infants: Review and comparison of behavioral and electrophysiological studies. *Vision Research, 18,* 1469–1483.

DOLLARD, J. (1938). Hostility and fear in social life. *Social Forces, 17,* 15–26.

DOLLARD, J., DOOB, J., MILLER, N., MOWRER, O., & SEARS, R. (1939). *Frustration and aggression.* New Haven: Yale University Press.

DOMINICK, J. R. (1984). Videogames, television violence and aggression in teenagers. *Journal of Communication, 34,* 134–147.

DONNERSTEIN, E. (1984). Pornography: Its effect on violence against women. In. N. M. Malamuth and E. Donnerstein (Eds.), *Pornography and sexual aggression.* New York: Academic Press.

DONNERSTEIN, E., & LINZ, D. (1992). Mass media sexual violence and male viewers: Current theory and research. In M. S. Kimmel & M. A. Messner (Eds.), *Men's lives* (2nd ed.) (pp. 466–479). New York: Macmillan.

DORNER, G., SCHENK, B., SCHMIEDEL, B., & AHRENS, L. (1983). Stressful events in prenatal life of bi- and homosexual men. *Experimental and Clinical Endocrinology, 81,* 83–87.

DORNER, G., GEIER, T., AHRENS, L., KRELL, L., MUNX, G., SIELER, H., KITTNER, E., & MULLER, H. (1980). Prenatal stress and possible aetiogenetic factor homosexuality in human males. *Endokrinologie, 75,* 365–368.

DOVIDIO, J. F. (1991). The empathy-altrusim hypothesis: Paradigm and promise. *Psychological Inquiry, 2,* 123–158.

DREISTADT, R. (1971). How dreams are used in creative behavior. *Psychology, 8,* 24–50.

DUCK, S. (1985). Social and personal relationships. In M. L. Knapp and G. R. Miller (Eds.), *Handbook of interpersonal communication* (pp. 655–686). Beverly Hills, CA: Sage.

DUCLAUX, R., & KENSHALO, D. R. (1980). Response characteristics of cutaneous warm fibers in the monkey. *Journal of Neurophysiology, 43,* 1–15.

DUNCAN, B. L. (1976). Differential social perception and attribution of intergroup violence: Testing the lower limits of stereotyping of blacks. *Journal of Personality and Social Psychology, 34,* 590–598.

DUNCKER, K. (1945). On problem solving (L. S. Lees, Trans.). *Psychological Monographs, 58* (Whole No. 270).

DUNN, J., & KENDRICK, C. (1982). Interaction between young siblings: Association with the interaction between mother and firstborn child. *Developmental Psychology, 17,* 336–343.

DUNNING, D., MILOJKOVIC, J. H., & ROSS, L. (1989). The overconfidence effect in social prediction. *Journal of Personality and Social Psychology, 58,* 568–581.

DUTTON, D. G., & ARON, A. P. (1974). Some evidence for heightened sexual attraction under conditions of high anxiety. *Journal of Personality and Social Psychology, 30,* 510–517.

DYWAN, J., & BOWERS, K. (1983). The use of hypnosis to enhance recall. *Science, 222,* 184–185.

EAGLY, A. H. (1978). Sex differences in influenceability. *Psychological Bulletin, 85,* 86–116.

EAGLY, A. H., & CHRVALA, C. (1986). Sex differences in conformity: Status and gender-role interpretations. *Psychology of Women Quarterly, 10,* 203–220.

EBBESEN, E. B., KJOS, G. L., & KONECNI, V. J. (1976). Spatial ecology: Its effects on the choice of friends and enemies. *Journal of Experimental Social Psychology, 12,* 505–518.

EBBINGHAUS, H. (1964). *Memory: A contribution to experimental psychology* (H. A. Ruger & E. R. Bussemius, Trans.). New York: Dover. (Original work published 1885)

EDRIDGE-GREEN, F. W. (1900). *Memory and its cultivation.* New York: Appleton.

EDWARDS, B. (1989). *Drawing on the right side of the brain* (rev. ed.). Los Angeles: Tarcher.

EGAN, D., & SCHWARTZ, B. (1979). Chunking in recall of symbolic drawings. *Memory and Cognition, 8,* 157–173.

EGAN, G. (1990). *The skilled helper* (4th ed.). Pacific Grove, CA: Brooks/Cole.

EGGAN, D. (1961). Dream analysis. In B. Kaplan (Ed.), *Studying personality cross-culturally* (pp. 551–578). Evanston, IL: Row, Peterson.

EGGER, M. D., & FLYNN, J. P. (1963). Effects of electrical stimulation of the amygdala on hypothalamically elicited attack behavior in cats. *Journal of Neurophysiology, 26,* 705–720.

EHRENREICH, B., & ENGLISH, D. (1978). *For her own good* New York: Anchor.

EHRHARDT, A. A., MEYER-BAHLBURH, H. F. L., ROSEN, L. R., FELDMAN, J. F., VERDIANO, N. P., ZIMMERMAN, I., & McEWEN, B. S. (1985). Sexual orientation after prenatal exposure to exogenous estrogen. *Archives of Sexual Behavior, 14,* 57–77.

EIBL-EIBESFELDT, I. (1972). *Love and hate: The natural history of behavior patterns* (G. Strachan, Trans.). New York: Holt, Rinehart & Winston.

EIBL-EIBESFELDT, I. (1973). *Der vorprogrammierte Mensch* [The preprogrammed human]. Vienna: Fritz Molden.

EICHENBAUM, H. (1992). The hippocampal system and declarative memory in animals. *Journal of Cognitive Neuroscience, 4,* 217–231.

EINSTEIN, A. (1936). *Physics and reality.*

EISENBERG, N., CIALDINI, R. B., McCREATH, H., & SHELL, R. (1987). Consistency-based compliance: When and why do children become vulnerable? *Journal of Personality and Social Psychology, 52,* 1174–1181.

EKMAN, P. (1972). Universals and cultural differences in facial expressions of emotion. In J. K. Cole (Ed.), *Nebraska Symposium on Motivation* (pp. 207–283). Lincoln: University of Nebraska Press.

EKMAN, P. (1992). Facial expressions of emotion: New findings, new questions. *Psychological Science, 3,* 34–38.

EKMAN, P., DAVIDSON, R. J., & FRIESEN, W. V. (1990). The Duchenne smile: Emotional expression and brain physiology II. *Journal of Personality and Social Psychology, 58,* 342–353.

EKMAN, P., & FRIESEN, W. V. (1971). Constants across cultures in the face and emotion. *Journal of Personality and Social Psychology, 17,* 124–129.

EKMAN, P., FRIESEN, W. V., & O'SULLIVAN, M. (1988). Smiles when lying. *Journal of Personality and Social Psychology, 54,* 414–420.

EKMAN, P., FRIESEN, W. V., O'SULLIVAN, M., CHAN, A., DIACOYANNI-TARLATZIS, I., HEIDER, K., KRAUSE, R., LeCOMPTE, W., PITCAIRN, T., RICCI-BITTI, P., SCHERER, K., TOMITA, M., & TZAVARAS, A. (1987). Universals and cultural differences in the judgments of facial expressions of emotion. *Journal of Personality and Social Psychology, 53,* 712–717.

EKMAN, P., LEVENSON, R. W., & FRIESEN, W. V. (1983). Autonomic nervous system activity distinguishes among emotions. *Science, 221,* 1208–1210.

ELDER, G. (1974). *Children of the great depression.* Chicago: University of Chicago Press.

ELDER, G., CASPI, A., & NGUYEN, T. (1986). Resourceful and vulnerable children: Family influence in hard times. In R. K. Silbereisen, K. Eyferth, & G. Rudinger (Eds.), *Development as action in context* (pp. 167–186). New York: Springer.

ELDER, G., LIKER, J., & CROSS, C. (1984). Parent-child behavior in the Great Depression: Life course and intergenerational influences. In P. Baltes & O. Brim (Eds.), *Life-span development and behavior* (Vol. 6, pp. 109–158). Orlando, FL: Academic Press.

ELKIND, D. (1967). Egocentrism in adolescence. *Child Development, 38,* 1025–1034.

ELLIOTT, D. S., HUIZINGA, D., & AGETON, S. (1985). *Explaining delinquency and drug use.* Beverly Hills, CA: Sage.

ELLIS, A. (1965). *Homosexuality: Its causes and cure.* New York: Lyle Stuart.

ELLIS, A. (1970). *The essence of rational psychotherapy: A comprehensive approach to treatment.* New York: Institute for Rational Living.

ELLIS, A. (1987). *The practice of rational emotive therapy.* New York: Springer.

ELLIS, H. (1903). Variation in man and woman. *Popular Science Monthly, 62,* 237–253.

ELLIS, L., & AMES, M. A. (1987). Neurohormonal functioning and sexual orientation: A theory of homosexuality-heterosexuality. *Psychological Bulletin, 101,* 233–258.

EME, R., MAISIAK, R., & GOODALE, W. (1979). Seriousness of adolescent problems. *Adolescence, 14,* 93–99.

EMERY, C. F., & BLUMENTHAL, J. A. (1991). Effects of physical exercise on psychological and cognitive functioning of older adults. *Annals of Behavioral Medicine, 13,* 99–107.

EMMELKAMP, P. M. G., & van der HOUT, A. (1983). Failure in treating agoraphobia. In E. B. Foa & P. M. G. Emmelkamp (Eds.), *Failures in behavior therapy.* New York: Wiley.

EPSTEIN, S. (1979). The stability of behavior: On predicting most of the people much of the time. *Journal of Personality and Social Psychology, 37,* 1097–1126.

ERDELYI, M. H. (1985). *Psychoanalysis: Freud's cognitive psychology.* New York: W. H. Freeman.

ERICKSON, R. P. (1963). Sensory neural patterns and gustation. In Y. Zotterman (Ed.), *Olfaction and taste* (Vol. 1, pp. 205–213). Oxford: Pergamon Press.

ERICKSON, R. P. (1982). The across-fiber pattern theory: An organizing principle for molar neural function. In W. D. Neff (Ed.), *Contributions to sensory physiology* (Vol. 6, pp. 79–109). New York: Academic Press.

ERICSSON, K. A., CHASE, W. G., & FALOON, S. (1980). Acquisition of a memory skill. *Science, 208,* 1181–1182.

ERICSSON, K. A., & SIMON, H. A. (1980). Verbal reports as data. *Psychological Review, 87*, 215–251.

ERIKSON, E. H. (1963). *Childhood and society* (2nd ed.). New York: Norton.

ERIKSON, E. H. (1980). *Identity and the life cycle.* New York: Norton.

ERIKSON, M. F., SROUFE, L. A., & EGELAND, B. (1985). The relationship between the quality of attachment and behavior problems in preschool in a high-risk sample. In I. Bretherton and E. Waters (Eds.), Growing points of attachment theory and research. *Monographs of the Society for Research in Child Development, 50,* (1–2, Serial No. 209).

ERKUT, S. (1983). Exploring sex differences in expectancy, attribution, and academic achievement. *Sex Roles, 9,* 217–231.

ERNST, M. L., & LOTH, D. (1948). *American sexual behavior and the Kinsey report.* New York: Greystone Press.

ERON, L. D. (1982). Parent-child interaction, television violence, and aggression of children. *American Psychologist, 37,* 197–211.

ERON, L. D. (1987). The development of aggressive behavior from the perspective of a developing behaviorism. *American Psychologist, 42,* 425–442.

ESSE, J. T., & WILKINS, W. (1978). Empathy and imagery in avoidance behavior reduction. *Journal of Consulting and Clinical Psychology, 46,* 202–203.

ESSEX, M. J., & NAM, S. (1987). Marital status and loneliness among older women. *Journal of Marriage and the Family, 49,* 93–106.

ESTES, W. K., & SKINNER, B. F. (1941). Some quantitative properties of anxiety. *Journal of Experimental Psychology, 29,* 390–400.

ETTIN, M. F. (1992). *Foundations and applications of group psychotherapy: A sphere of influence.* Boston: Allyn & Bacon.

EXNER, J. E., JR. (1986). *The Rorschach: A comprehensive system* (2nd ed.). New York: Wiley.

EYSENCK, H. J. (1952a). The effects of psychotherapy: An evaluation. *Journal of Consulting Psychology, 16,* 319–324.

EYSENCK, H. J. (1952b). *The scientific study of personality.* New York: Macmillan.

EYSENCK, H. J. (1982). Introduction. In H. J. Eysenck (Ed.), *A model for intelligence* (pp. 1–10). Berlin: Springer.

EYSENCK, H. J. (1986). A critique of contemporary classification and diagnosis. In T. Millon & G. Kleinman (Eds.) *Contemporary directions in psychopathology* (pp. 73–98) New York: Guilford.

FAGAN, J. F. (1976). Infants' recognition of invariant features of faces. *Child Development, 47,* 627–638.

FAGAN, J. F. (1984a) The relationship of novelty preferences during infancy to later intelligence and later recognition memory. *Intelligence, 8,* 31–36.

FAGAN, J. F. (1984b). The intelligent infant: Theoretical implications. *Intelligence, 8,* 1–9.

FAGAN, J. F., AND SINGER, L. T. (1983). Infant recognition memory as a measure of intelligence. In L. P. Lipsett (Ed.), *Advances in infancy research* (Vol. 2, pp. 31–78). Norwood, NJ: Ablex.

FAGOT, B. I. (1984). Teacher and peer reactions to boys' and girls' play styles. *Sex Roles, 11,* 691–702.

FAGOT, B. I. (1985a). A cautionary note: Parents' socialization of boys and girls. *Sex Roles, 12,* 471–476.

FAGOT, B. I. (1985b). Beyond the reinforcement principle: Another step toward understanding sex-role development. *Developmental Psychology, 21,* 1097–1104.

FAGOT, B. I. (1985c). Changes in thinking about early sex role development. *Developmental Review, 5,* 83–98.

FARRELL, M. P., & ROSENBERG, S. D. (1981). *Men at midlife.* Boston: Auburn House.

FAUST, D., & ZISKIN, J. (1988). The expert witness in psychology and psychiatry. *Science, 241,* 31–35.

FAUSTO-STERLING, A. (1985). *Myths of gender.* New York: Basic Books.

FAWCETT, J., SHEFNER, W., CLARK, D., HEDEKER, D., GIBBONS, R., & CORYELL, W. (1987). Clinical predictors of suicide in patients with major affective disorders: A controlled prospective study. *American Journal of Psychiatry, 144,* 35–40.

FAY, R. E., TURNER, C. F., KLASSEN, A. D., & GAGNON, J. H. (1989). Prevalence and patterns of same-gender sexual contact among men. *Science, 243,* 338–348.

FAZIO, R. H. (1987). Self perception theory: A current perspective. In M. Zanna, J. M. Olson, & C. P. Herman (Eds.), *Social influence: The Ontario symposium* (Vol. 3, pp. 129–150). Hillsdale, NJ: Erlbaum.

FAZIO, R. H. (1990). Multiple processes by which attitudes guide behavior: The MODE model as an integrative framework. *Advances in Experimental Social Psychology, 23,* 75–109.

FAZIO, R. H., CHEN, J., McDONEL, E. C., & SHERMAN, S. J. (1982). Attitude accessibility, attitude-behavior consistency and the strength of the object-evaluation association. *Journal of Experimental Social Psychology, 18,* 339–357.

FAZIO, R. H., & ZANNA, M. P. (1978). Attitudinal qualities relating to the strength of the attitude-behavior relationship. *Journal of Experimental Social Psychology, 14,* 398–408.

FEINGOLD, A. (1989). *Gender differences in effects of attractiveness and similarity on opposite-sex attraction: Integration of self-report and experimental findings.* Unpublished manuscript, Yale University, New Haven, CT.

FEINGOLD, A. (1990). *Good-looking people are not what we think: An integration of the experimental literature on physical attractiveness stereotyping with the literature on correlates of physical attractiveness.* Unpublished manuscript, Yale University, New Haven, CT.

FELDHAUSEN, J. F. (1986). A conception of giftedness. In R. J. Sternberg & J. E. Davidson (Eds.), *Conceptions of giftedness* (pp. 112–127). Cambridge: Cambridge University Press.

FERSTER, C. B., CULBERTSON, S., & BOREN, M. (1975). *Behavior principles* (2nd ed.). New York: Prentice-Hall.

FESTINGER, L. (1957). *A theory of cognitive dissonance.* Evanston, IL: Row, Peterson.

FESTINGER, L., & CARLSMITH, J. M. (1959). Cognitive consequences of forced compliance. *Journal of Abnormal and Social Psychology, 58,* 203–210.

FESTINGER, L., SCHACHTER, S., & BACK, K. W. (1950). *Social pressures in informal groups.* New York: Harper.

FIELD, T. (1990). *Infancy.* Cambridge, MA: Harvard University Press.

FINDLEY, M. J., & COOPER, H. M. (1983). Locus of control and academic achievement: A literature review. *Journal of Personality and Social Psychology, 44,* 419–427.

FISCHBACH, G. D. (1992, September). Mind and brain. *Scientific American,* pp. 48–57.

FISHBEIN, M., & AJZEN, I. (1974). Attitudes towards objects as predictors of single and multiple behavioral criteria. *Psychological Review, 81,* 59–74.

FISHBEIN, M., & AJZEN, I. (1975). *Belief, attitude, intention and behavior: An introduction to theory and research.* Reading, MA: Addison-Wesley.

FISHER, H. E. (1987, Oct.). The four-year itch. *Natural History, 96,* 22–33.

FISHER, W. A., & BYRNE, D. (1978). Sex differences in response to erotica? Love versus lust. *Journal of Personality and Social Psychology, 36,* 117–125.

FISKE, S. T., & TAYLOR, S. E. (1991). *Social cognition* (2nd ed.). New York: McGraw-Hill.

FITCH, S. A., & ADAMS, G. R. (1983). Ego identity and intimacy status: Replication and extension. *Developmental Psychology, 19,* 839–845.

FITZGERALD, F. T. (1981). The problem of obesity. *Annual Review of Medicine, 32,* 221–231.

FLAVELL, J. H. (1963). *The developmental psychology of Jean Piaget.* New York: Van Nostrand.

FLEMING, J. (1984). *The impact of college environments on Black students.* San Francisco: Jossey-Bass.

FLYNN, G., & KOWALCZYK-McPHEE, B. (1989). A school system in transition. In S. Stainback, W. Stainback, and Marsha Forest (Eds.), *Educating all students in the mainstream of regular education* (pp. 29–42). Baltimore: Paul H. Brookes.

FOA, E. B., FESKE, U., MURDOCK, T. B., KOZAK, M. J., & McCARTHY, P. R. (1991). Processing of threat-related information in rape victims. *Journal of Abnormal Psychology, 100,* 156–162.

FOA, E. B., & KOZAK, M. J. (1986). Emotional processing of fear: Exposure to corrective information. *Psychological Bulletin, 99,* 20–35.

FOLDS, T. H., FOOTO, M. M., GUTTENTAG, R. E., & ORNSTEIN, P. A. (1990). When children mean to remember: Issues of content specificity, strategy effectiveness, and intentionality in the development of memory. In D. F. Bjorklund (Ed.), *Children's strategies* (pp. 67–91) Hillsdale, NJ: Erlbaum.

FONER, A., & SCHWAB, K. (1981). *Aging and retirement.* Monterey, CA: Brooks/Cole.

FORER, B. R. (1949). The fallacy of personal validation: A classroom demonstration of gullibility. *Journal of Abnormal and Social Psychology, 44,* 118–123.

FOREST, M., & LUSTHAUS, E. (1989). Promoting educational equality for all students: Circles and maps. In S. Stainback, W. Stainback, and Marsha Forest (Eds.), *Educating all students in the mainstream of regular education* (pp. 43–58). Baltimore: Paul H. Brookes.

FORGAS, J. P., & BOWER, G. H. (1987). Mood effects on person-perception judgments. *Journal of Personality and Social Psychology, 53,* 53–60.

FORGAS, J. P., BOWER, G. H., & KRANTZ, S. E. (1984). The influence of mood on perceptions of social interactions. *Journal of Experimental Social Psychology, 20,* 497–513.

FOULKES, D. (1985). *Dreaming: A cognitive-psychological analysis.* Hillsdale, NJ: Erlbaum.

FOWLER, R. D. (1986, May). Howard Hughes: A psychological autopsy. *Psychology Today,* pp. 22–33.

FOX, R., ASLIN, R. N., SHEA, S. L., & DUMAIS, S. T. (1980). Stereopsis in human infants. *Science, 207,* 323–324.

FOY, D. W., DONAHOE, C. P., CARROLL, E. M., GALLERS, J., & RENO, R. (1987). Posttraumatic stress disorder. In L. Michelson & L. M. Ascher (Eds.), *Anxiety and stress disorders* (pp. 361–378). New York: Guilford.

FRANCES, A. (1980). The DSM-III personality disorders section: A commentary. *American Journal of Psychiatry, 137,* 1050–1054.

FRANCIS, P. L., & McCROY, G. (1983). *Bimodal recognition of human stimulus configurations.* Paper presented at the biennial meeting of the Society for Research in Child Development.

FRANK, F. (1973). An analysis of hamster afferent taste nerve response functions. *Journal of General Physiology, 61,* 588–618.

FRANZ, C. E., McCLELLAND, D. C., & WEINBERGER, J. (1991). Childhood antecedents of conventional social accomplishment in midlife adults: A 36-year prospective study. *Journal of Personality and Social Psychology, 60,* 586–594.

FREARSON, W., BARRETT, P., & EYSENCK, H. J. (1988). Intelligence, reaction time and the effects of smoking. *Personality and Individual Differences, 9,* 497–517.

FREDERIKSEN, N. (1986). Toward a broader conception of human intelligence. In R. J. Sternberg & R. K. Wagner (Eds.), *Practical intelligence: Nature and origins of competence in the everyday world* (pp. 84–116). Cambridge: Cambridge University Press.

FREDRIKSON, M. (1986). Racial differences in reactivity to behavioral challenge in essential hypertension. *Journal of Hypertension, 4,* 325–331.

FREEDMAN, J., & FRASER, S. (1966). Compliance without pressure: The foot-in-the-door technique. *Journal of Personality and Social Psychology, 4,* 195–202.

FREIBERG, P. (1991). Self-esteem gender gap widens in adolescence. *APA Monitor, 22,* 29.

FREUD, S. (1933). *New introductory lectures on psychoanalysis.* New York: W. W. Norton.

FREUD, S. (1949). Instincts and their vicissitudes (J. Riviere, Trans.). In *Collected papers of Sigmund Freud.* (Vol. 4, pp. 60–83). (Original work published 1915)

FREUD, S. (1953). The interpretation of dreams. In J. Strachy (Ed. and Trans.), *The standard edition of the complete psychological works of Sigmund Freud* (Vols. 4 and 5). London: Hogarth Press. (Original work published 1900)

FREUD, S. (1960). Psychopathology of everyday life. In J. Strachy (Ed. and Trans.), *The standard edition of the complete psychological works of Sigmund Freud* (Vol. 6). London: Hogarth Press. (Original work published 1901)

FREY, D. L., & GAERTNER, S. L. (1986). Helping and the avoidance of inappropriate interracial behavior: A strategy that perpetuates a nonprejudiced self-image. *Journal of Personality and Social Psychology, 50,* 1083–1090.

FREY, K. S., & RUBLE, D. N. (1985). What children say when the teacher is not around: Conflicting goals in social comparison and performance assessment in the classroom. *Journal of Personality and Social Psychology, 48,* 550–562.

FRIEDMAN, H. S., & MILLER-HERRINGER, T. (1991). Nonverbal display of emotion in public and private: Self-monitoring, personality, and expressive cues. *Journal of Personality and Social Psychology, 61,* 766–775.

FRIEDMAN, M., & POWELL, L. H. (1984). The diagnosis and quantitative assessment of Type A behavior: Introduction and description of the videotaped structured interview. *Integrative Psychiatry, 2,* 123–129.

FRIEDMAN, M., & ROSENMAN, R. H. (1974). *Type A behavior and your heart.* New York: Knopf.

FRIESEN, W. V. (1972). *Cultural differences in facial expression in a social situation: An experimental test of the concept of display rules.* Unpublished doctoral dissertation, University of California, San Francisco.

FRITSCH, G., & HITZIG, E. (1960). On the electrical excitability of the cerebrum. In G. von Bronin (Ed.), *The cerebral cortex.* Springfield, IL: Charles C Thomas.

FROMM-REICHMANN, F. (1948). Notes on the development of treatment of schizophrenics by psychoanalytic psychotherapy. *Psychiatry, 11,* 263–273.

FRYE, J. S., & STOCKTON, R. A. (1982). Discriminant analysis of post traumatic stress disorder among a group of Vietnam veterans. *American Journal of Psychiatry, 139,* 52–56.

GAEBELEIN, J. W. (1973). Third-party instigation of aggression: An experimental approach. *Journal of Personality and Social Psychology, 27,* 389–395.

GAERTNER, S. L., MANN, J., MURREL, A., & DOVIDIO, J. F. (1989). Reducing intergroup bias: The benefits of recategorization. *Journal of Personality and Social Psychology, 57,* 239–249.

GALLUP, G. G. (1970). Chimpanzees: Self recognition. *Science, 167,* 86–87.

GALTON, F. (1883). *Inquiries into human faculty and development.* London: Macmillan.

GANSTER, D. C., & VICTOR, B. (1988). The impact of social support on mental and physical health. *British Journal of Medical Psychology, 61,* 17–36.

GARCIA, J., ERVIN, F. R., & KOELLING, R. A. (1966). Learning with prolonged delay of reinforcement. *Psychonomic Science, 5,* 121–122.

GARCIA, J., HANKINS, W. G., & RUSINIAK, K. W. (1974). Behavioral regulation of the milieu interne in man and rat. *Science, 185,* 824–831.

GARCIA, J., & KOELLING, R. A. (1966). Relation of cue to consequence in avoidance learning. *Psychonomic Science, 4,* 123–124.

GARCIA-COLL, C. T., KAGAN, J., & RESNICK, J. S. (1984). Behavioral inhibitions in young children. *Child Development, 55,* 1005–1019.

GARDNER, H. (1976). *The shattered mind.* New York: Random House.

GARDNER, H. (1983). *Frames of mind: The theory of multiple intelligences.* New York: Basic Books.

GARNER, D. M., GARFINKEL, P. E., SCHWARTZ, D., & THOMPSON, M. (1980). Cultural expectations of thinness in women. *Psychological Reports, 47,* 483–491.

GARVEY, C. (1984). *Children's talk.* Cambridge, MA: Harvard University Press.

GASTIL, J. (1990). Generic pronouns and sexist language: The oxymoronic character of masculine generics. *Sex Roles, 23,* 629–643.

GAY, P. (1988). *Freud: A life for our time.* New York: Norton.

GAZZANIGA, M. S., & LeDOUX, J. E. (1978). *The integrated mind.* New York: Plenum.

GAZZANIGA, M. S., STEEN, D., & VOLPE, B. T. (1979). *Functional neuroscience.* New York: Harper & Row.

GEEN, R. G. (1984). Preferred stimulation levels in introverts and extraverts: Effects on arousal and performance. *Journal of Personality and Social Psychology, 46,* 1303–1312.

GELIEBTER, A., WESTREICH, S., HASHIM, S. A., & GAGE, D. (1987). Gastric balloon reduces food intake and body weight in obese rats. *Physiology and Behavior, 39,* 399–402.

GELLER, G. (1984). Aspirations of female high school students. *Resources for Feminist Research, 13,* 17–19.

GELMAN, R., & SHATZ, M. (1978). Appropriate speech adjustments: The operation of conversational constraints on talk to two-year olds. In M. Lewis & L. A. Rosenblum (Eds.), *Interactive conversation and the development of language* (pp. 27–61). New York: Wiley.

GENTRY, W. D., CHESNEY, A. P., GARY, H. E., HALL, R. P., & HARBURG, E. (1982). Habitual anger-coping styles: I. Effect on mean blood pressure and risk for essential hypertension. *Psychosomatic Medicine 44,* 195–202.

GENTRY, W. D., CHESNEY, A. P., HALL, R. P., KENNEDY, C. D., GARY, H. E., & HARBURG, E. (1983). The relation of demographic attributes and habitual anger-coping styles. *Journal of Social Psychology, 121,* 45–50.

GEORGOTAS, A., & McCUE, R. E. (1986). Benefits and limitations of major pharmacological treatment for depression. *American Journal of Psychotherapy, 40,* 370–376.

GESHWIND, N. (1979, Sept.). Specializations of the human brain. *Scientific American,* pp. 108–119.

GESCHWIND, N., & MILLER, J. (1983). The organization of the living brain. In J. Miller (Ed.), *States of mind* (pp. 116–135). New York: Pantheon.

GETTYS, L. D., & CANN, A. (1981). Children's perceptions of occupational sex stereotypes. *Sex Roles, 7,* 301–308.

GIBSON, J. J. (1950). *The perception of the visual world.* Boston: Houghton Mifflin.

GIBSON, J. J. (1979). *The ecological approach to visual perception.* Boston: Houghton Mifflin.

GIBSON, R. A., & WALK, R. D. (1960, April). The "visual cliff." *Scientific American,* pp. 64–71.

GILFORD, R., & BENGSTON, V. (1979). Measuring marital satisfaction in three generations: Positive and negative dimensions. *Journal of Marriage and the Family, 41,* 387–398.

GILGEN, A. R. (1982). *American psychology since WW II: A profile of the discipline.* Westport, CT: Greenwood.

GILLIGAN, C. (1982). *In a different voice.* Cambridge, MA: Harvard University Press.

GLABERSON, W. (1989). Scholarships based on S.A.T.'s are unfair to girls, court rules. *New York Times,* p. 1.

GLADUE, B. A., GREEN, R., & HELLMAN, R. E. (1984). Neuroendocrine response to estrogen and sexual orientation. *Science, 225,* 1469–1499.

GLADWIN, E. T. (1970). *East is a big bird.* Cambridge, MA: Harvard University Press.

GLANZER, M., & CUNITZ, A. (1966). Two storage mechanisms in free recall. *Journal of Verbal Learning and Verbal Behavior, 5,* 351–360.

GLASER, R., & PELLEGRINO, J. W. (1987). Aptitudes for learning and cognitive processes. In F. Weinert & R. Kluwe (Eds.), *Metacognition, motivation, and understanding* (pp. 267–288). Hillsdale, NJ: Erlbaum.

GLASS, A. L., & HOLYOAK, K. J. (1986). *Cognition.* New York: Random House.

GLENBERG, A., & BRADLEY, M. M. (1979). Mental contiguity. *Journal of Experimental Psychology: Human Learning and Memory, 5,* 88–97.

GLENBERG, A., SMITH, S. M., & GREEN, C. (1977). Type I rehearsal: Maintenance and more. *Journal of Verbal Learning and Verbal Behavior, 16,* 339–352.

GLICK, P. C., & LIN, S. L. (1986). Recent changes in divorce and remarriage. *Journal of Marriage and the Family, 48,* 737–748.

GMELCH, G. (1978, Aug.). Baseball magic. *Human Nature,* 32–39.

GODDARD, G. V. (1980). Component properties of the memory machine: Hebb revisited. In P. W. Jusczyk & R. M. Klein (Eds.), *The nature of thought: Essays in honor of D. O. Hebb* (pp. 231–247) Hillsdale, NJ: Erlbaum.

GODDARD, H. H. (1917). Mental tests and the immigrant. *Journal of Delinquency, 2,* 243–277.

GODDEN, D. R., & BADDELEY, A. D. (1975). Context-dependent memory in two natural environments: On land and underwater. *British Journal of Psychology, 66,* 325–332.

GOETHALS, G. P., & ZANNA, M. P. (1979). The role of social comparison in choice shifts. *Journal of Personality and Social Psychology, 37,* 1469–1476.

GOLDBERG, L. R. (1981). Unconfounding situational attributions from uncertain, neutral, and ambiguous ones: A psychometric analysis of descriptions of oneself and various type of others. *Journal of Personality and Social Psychology, 41,* 517–552.

GOLDMAN-RAKIC, P. S. (1984). The frontal lobes: Uncharted provinces of the brain. *Trends in Neuroscience, 7,* 425–429.

GOLDMAN-RAKIC, P. S. (1987). Development of cortical circuitry and cognitive function. *Child Development, 58,* 601–622.

GOLDMAN-RAKIC, P. S. (1992, September). Working memory and the mind. *Scientific American,* pp. 111–117.

GOLDMAN-RAKIC, P. S., ISSEROFF, A., SCHWARTZ, M. L., & BUGBEE, N. M. (1983). The neurobiology of cognitive development. In P. M. Mussen (Ed.), *Handbook of child psychology* (4th ed.). (Vol. 2, pp. 281–344). New York: Wiley.

GOLDSTEIN, E. B. (1989). *Sensation and Perception* (3rd ed.). Belmont, CA: Wadsworth.

GOLDSTEIN, M.J. (1985). Family factors that antedate the onset of schizophrenia and related disorders: The results of a fifteen year prospective longitudinal study. *Acta Psychiatra Scandinavica, 71,* 7–18.

GOLDSTEIN, M.J. (1987a). The UCLA high-risk project. *Schizophrenia Bulletin, 13,* 505–514.

GOLDSTEIN, M.J. (1987b). Psychosocial issues. *Schizophrenia Bulletin, 13,* 157–171.

GOLDSTEIN, M. J., & STRACHAN, A. M. (1987a). The family and schizophrenia. In T. Jacob (Ed.), *Family interaction and psychopathology: Theories, methods, and findings* (pp. 481–508). New York: Plenum.

GOLEMAN, D. (1988a, April 5). New scales of intelligence measure talent for living. *New York Times,* p. 17.

GOLEMAN, D. (1988b, October 11). Psychologists' expert testimony called unscientific. *New York Times,* pp. A19, A23.

GOLEMAN, D. (1988c, December 13). Obsessive disorder: Secret toll is found. *New York Times.*

GOLEMAN, D. (1989a, March 7). From Tokyo to Tampa, different ideas of self. *New York Times,* pp. 17, 26.

GOLEMAN, D. (1989b, June 27). Delusion, benign and bizarre, is recognized as common. *New York Times.*

GOLEMAN, D. (1991, November 26). Doctors find comfort is a potent medicine. *New York Times,* pp. B5, B8.

GOLEMAN, D. (1992, February 12). Relaxation and aerobic exercise may slow pace of the AIDS virus. *New York Times.*

GOMBRICH, E. H. (1956). *Art and illusion.* Princeton, NJ: Princeton University Press.

GOODE, E. (1984). *Drugs in American society* (2nd ed.). New York: Knopf.

GOODE, E. (1989). *Drugs in American society* (3rd ed.) New York: Knopf.

GOODENOUGH, D. R. (1978). Dream recall: History and current status of the field. In A. M. Arkin, J. S. Antnobus, & S. J. Ellman (Eds.), *The mind in sleep: Psychology and psychophysiology* (pp. 113–142) Hillsdale, NJ: Erlbaum.

GOODENOUGH, F. L. (1932). Expression of the emotions in a blind-deaf child. *Journal of Abnormal and Social Psychology, 27,* 328–333.

GOODENOUGH, W. H. (1953). Native astronomy in the Central Carolines. *Museum Monographs.* Philadelphia: University Museum, University of Pennsylvania.

GOODMAN, N., DORNBUSCH, S. M., RICHARDSON, S. A., & HASTORF, H. H. (1963). Variant reactions to physical disabilities. *American Social Review, 28,* 429–435.

GOODWIN, G. M. (1992). Tricyclic and newer antidepressants. In E. S. Paykel (Ed.), *Handbook of affective disorders* (pp. 327–344) London: Churchill Livingstone.

GORDON, D., & LAKOFF, G. (1971). Conversational postulates. *Papers from the seventh regional meeting of the Chicago Linguistic Society.*

GORMAN, J. M., & DAVIS, J. M. (1989). Antianxiety drugs. In H. I. Kaplan & B. J. Sadock (Eds.), *Comprehensive textbook of psychiatry* (Vol. 4, pp. 1579–1590). Baltimore: Williams & Wilkins.

GORSKI, R. A., HARLAN, R. E., JACOBSON, C. D., SHRYNE, J. E., & SOUTHAM, A. M. (1980). Evidence for a morphological sex difference within the medial preoptic area of the rat brain. *Journal of Comparative Neurology, 193,* 529–539.

GOTTESMAN, I. I., MCGUFFIN, P., & FARMER, A. E. (1987). Clinical genetics as clues to the "real" genetics of schizophrenia. *Schizophrenia Bulletin, 13,* 23–47.

GOTTESMAN, I. I., & SHIELDS, J. (1982). *Schizophrenia: The epigenetic puzzle.* New York: Columbia University Press.

GOTTFREDSON, M., & HIRSCHI, T. (1990). *A general theory of crime.* Stanford, CA: Stanford University Press.

GOTTLIEB, J. (1981). Mainstreaming: Fulfilling the promise? *American Journal of Mental Deficiency, 86,* 115–126.

GOTTLIEB, J., ALTER, M., & GOTTLIEB, B. W. (1991). Mainstreaming mentally retarded children. In J. L. Matson & J. A. Mulick (Eds.), *Handbook of mental retardation* (2nd ed.) (pp. 63–73). New York: Pergamon Press.

GOULD, R. L. (1972). The phases of adult life: A study in developmental psychology. *American Journal of Psychiatry, 129,* 521–531.

GOULD, R. L. (1980). Transformations during early and middle adult years. In N. J. Smelser & E. H. Erikson (Eds.), *Themes of work and love in adulthood* (pp. 213–237). Cambridge, MA: Harvard University Press.

GOULD, R., MILLER, B. L., GOLDBERG, M. A., & BENSON, D. F. (1986). The validity of hysterical signs and symptoms. *The Journal of Nervous and Mental Disease, 174,* 593–597.

GOULD, S. J. (1981). *The mismeasure of man.* New York: Norton.

GRAEBER, R. C. (1989). Jet lag and sleep disruption. In M. H. Kryger, T. Roth, & W. C. Dement (Eds.), *Principles and practice of sleep medicine* (pp. 324–331). Philadelphia: Saunders.

GRAHAM, J. R., & LILLY, R. S. (1984). *Psychological testing.* Englewood Cliffs, NJ: Prentice-Hall.

GRAHAM, R. B. (1990). *Physiological psychology.* Belmont, CA: Wadsworth.

GREEN, R. F. (1969). Age-intelligence relationship between ages sixteen and sixty-four: A rising trend. *Developmental Psychology, 1,* 618–627.

GREENBERG, R. P. (1992). A meta-analysis of antidepressant outcome under "blinder" conditions. *Journal of Consulting and Clinical Psychology, 60,* 664–669.

GREENBLATT, M. (1992). Deinstitutionalization and reinstitutionalization of the mentally ill. In M. J. Robertson & M. Greenblatt (Eds.), *Homelessness* (pp. 47–56). New York: Plenum.

GREENE, E. (1986). Forensic hypnosis to lift amnesia: The jury is still out. *Behavioral Sciences and the Law, 4,* 65–72.

GREENFIELD, P. M. (1966). On culture and conservation. In J. S. Bruner, R. P. Olver, & P. M. Greenfield (Eds.), *Studies in cognitive growth.* New York: Wiley.

GREENO, J. G. (1974). Hobbits and orcs: Acquisition of a sequential concept. *Cognitive Psychology, 6,* 270–292.

GREENOUGH, W. T. (1984a). Possible structural substrate of plastic neural phenomena. In G. Lynch, J. L. McGaugh, & N. W. Weinberger (Eds.), *Neurobiology of learning and memory* (pp. 470–478). New York: Guilford.

GREENOUGH, W. T. (1984b). Structural correlates of information storage in the mammalian brain: A review and hypothesis. *Trends in Neuroscience, 7,* 229–233.

GREER, STEVEN. (1991). Psychological response to cancer and survival. *Psychological Medicine, 21,* 43–49.

GREGORY, R. L. (1966). *Eye and brain: The psychology of seeing.* New York: McGraw-Hill.

GREGORY, R. L. (1973). *Eye and brain* (2nd ed.). New York: McGraw-Hill.

GRESHAM, F. M. (1982). Misguided mainstreaming: The case for social skills training with handicapped children. *Exceptional Children, 48,* 422–433.

GRIFFIN. D. R. (1992). *Animal minds.* Chicago: University of Chicago Press.

GRIFFITH, R. M., MIYAGO, O., & TOGO, A. (1958). The universality of typical dreams: Japanese vs. Americans. *American Anthropologist, 60,* 1173–1179.

GRIFFITT, W. (1987). Females, males and sexual responses. In K. Kelley (Ed.), Females, males, and sexuality: *Theories and research* (pp. 141–173). Albany: State University of New York.

GRIFFITT, W., & HATFIELD, E. (1985). *Human sexual behavior.* Glenview, IL: Scott, Foresman.

GRIGGS, R. A., & COX, J. R. (1982). The elusive thematic-materials effect in Wason's selection task. *British Journal of Psychology, 73,* 407–420.

GROEN, G. J., & PARKMAN, J. M. (1972). A chronometric analysis of simple addition. *Psychological Review, 79,* 329–343.

GUILFORD, J. P. (1967). *The nature of human intelligence.* New York: McGraw-Hill.

GUILLEMINAULT, C. (1989). Narcolepsy syndrome. In M. Kryger, T. Roth, & W. C. Dement (Eds.), *Principles and practices of sleep medicine* (pp. 338–346). Philadelphia: Saunders.

GURN, S. M. (1985). Continuities and changes in fatness from infancy through adulthood. *Current Problems in Pediatrics, 15,* 1–27.

GUTHRIE, R. V. (1976). *Even the rat was white.* New York: Harper & Row.

GUTTMAN, N., & KALISH, H. I. (1956). Discrimination and stimulus generalization. *Journal of Experimental Psychology, 51,* 79–88.

GUZE, S. B., & ROBINS, E. (1970). Suicide among primary affective disorders. *British Journal of Psychiatry, 117,* 437–438.

HAGEN, M. A. (Ed.). (1979). *The perception of pictures* (Vols. 1 & 2). New York: Academic Press.

HAGEN, M. A. (1986). *Varieties of realism.* Cambridge: Cambridge University Press.

HAIST, F., SHIMAMURA, A. P., & SQUIRE, L. R. (1992). On the relationship between recall and recognition memory. *Journal of Experimental Psychology: Learning, Memory and Cognition, 18,* 691–702.

HALL, C. (1951, May). What people dream about. *Scientific American,* pp. 60–63.

HALL, C. (1963). *Dreams of college students.* Lawrence: University of Kansas Social Science Studies.

HALL, C., & VAN DE CASTLE, R. L. (1966). *The content analysis of dreams.* New York: Appleton-Century-Crofts.

HALL, E. G., & DAVIES, S. (1991). Gender differences in perceived intensity and affect of pain between athletes and nonathletes. *Perceptual and Motor Skills, 73,* 779–786.

HALPERN, A. S., CLOSE, D. W., & NELSON, D. J. (1986). *On my own.* Baltimore: Paul H. Brookes.

HALPERN, D. F. (1986). *Sex differences in cognitive abilities.* Hillsdale, NJ: Erlbaum.

HALPERN, D. F. (1989). *Thought and knowledge* (2nd ed.). Hillsdale, NJ: Erlbaum.

HALPERN, R. (1990). Poverty and early childhood parenting. *American Journal of Orthopsychiatry, 60,* 6–18.

HAMILTON, D. L. (1979). A cognitive-attributional analysis of stereotyping. *Advances in Experimental Social Psychology, 12,* 53–85.

HAMILTON, D. L. (Ed.). (1981). *Cognitive processes in stereotyping and intergroup behavior.* Hillsdale, NJ: Erlbaum.

HANEY, C., BANKS, W., & ZIMBARDO, P. (1983). Interpersonal dynamics in a simulated prison. *International Journal of Criminology, 1,* 69–97.

HANSEN, R. D. (1980). Common sense attribution. *Journal of Experimental Social Psychology, 17,* 398–411.

HARBURG, E. (1978). Skin color, ethnicity and blood pressure in Detroit blacks. *American Journal of Public Health, 68,* 1177–1183.

HARBURG, E., BLACKLOCK, E. H., & ROEPER, P. J. (1979). Resentful and reflective coping with arbitrary authority and blood pressure: Detroit. *Psychosomatic Medicine, 41,* 189–202.

HARE, R. D. (1970). *Psychopathology: Theory and research.* New York: Wiley.

HARKINS, S. G. (1987). Social loafing and social facilitation. *Journal of Experimental Social Psychology, 23,* 1–18.

HARLOW, H. (1958). The nature of love. *American Psychologist, 13,* 673–685.

HARLOW, H. & HARLOW, M. (1962, Nov.). Social deprivation in monkeys. *Scientific American,* pp. 136–146.

HARRELL, T. H., & STOLP, R. (1985). Effects of erotic guided imagery on female sexual arousal and emotional response. *Journal of Sex Research, 21,* 292–304.

HARRIS, R. L., ELLICOTT, A. M., & HOLMES, D. S. (1986). The timing of psychosocial transitions and changes in women's lives: An examination of women aged 45 to 60. *Journal of Personality and Social Psychology, 51,* 409–416.

HARRIS, W. (1982). *The harder we run: Black workers since the Civil War.* New York: Oxford Unversity Press.

HARRISON, J., CHIN, J., & FICARROTTO, T. (1992). Warning: Masculinity may be dangerous to your health. In M. S. Kimmel & M. A. Messner (Eds.), *Men's lives* (2nd ed.) (pp. 271–285) New York: Macmillan.

HARROW, M., GOLDBERG, J. F., GROSSMAN, L. S., & MELTZER, H. Y. (1990). Outcome in manic disorders: A naturalistic follow-up study. *Archives of General Psychiatry, 47,* 665–671.

HARTER, S. (1982). The perceived competence scale for children. *Child Development, 53,* 87–97.

HARVEY, J. H. (1987). Attributions in close relationships: Research and theoretical developments. *Journal of Social and Clinical Psychology, 5,* 420–434.

HARVEY, W. (1628). Exercitatio anatomica de mota cordis et sanguinis. In Animabilus, Frankfurt-am-Main, Germany.

HASS, A. (1979). *Teenage sexuality: A survey of teenage sexual behavior.* New York: Macmillan.

HATHAWAY, S. R., & McKINLEY, J. C. (1943). *The Minnesota Multiphasic Personality Inventory.* Minneapolis: University of Minnesota Press.

HAVILAND, J., & LELWICA, M. (1987). The induced affect response: 10-week-old infants' responses to three emotion expressions. *Developmental Psychology, 23,* 97–104.

HAVILAND, S. E., & CLARK, H. H. (1974). What's new? Acquiring new information as a process in comprehension. *Journal of Verbal Learning and Verbal Behavior, 13,* 512–521.

HAWKING, S. M. (1988). *A brief history of time.* New York: Bantam.

HAYES, J. R. (1978). *Cognitive psychology.* Homewood, IL: Dorsey Press.

HAYS, R. B. (1985). A longitudinal study of friendship development. *Journal of Personality and Social Psychology, 48,* 909–924.

HAYS, R. B., TURNER, H., & COATES, T. J. (1992). Social support, AIDS-related symptoms, and depression among gay men. *Journal of Consulting and Clinical Psychology, 60,* 463–469.

HAYWARD, P., WARDLE, J., & HIGGITT, A. (1989). Benzodiazepine research: Current findings and practical consequences. *British Journal of Psychiatry, 28,* 307–327.

HEATH, R. G. (1963). Electrical self-stimulation of the brain in man. *American Journal of Psychiatry, 120,* 571–577.

HEATH, R. G. (1981). The neural basis for violent behavior: Physiology and anatomy. In L. Valzelli & L. Mogese (Eds.), *Aggression & violence: A psychobiological and clinical approach* (pp. 176–194). Milan: Edizioni, St. Vincent.

HEBB, D. O. (1949). *Organization of behavior.* New York: Wiley.

HEBB, D. O. (1980). The structure of thought. In P. W. Jucscyk & R. M. Klein (Eds.), *The nature of thought* (pp. 19–35). Hillsdale, NJ: Erlbaum.

HEIDER, F. (1958). *The psychology of interpersonal relations.* New York: Wiley.

HEIMAN, J. R. (1975, November). The physiology of erotica: Women's sexual arousal. *Psychology Today,* pp. 90–94.

HELD, R., BIRCH, E. E., & GWIAZDA, J. (1980). Stereoacuity of human infants. *Proceedings of the National Academy of Sciences, 77,* 5572–5574.

HELLER, J. T. (1979). *Cognitive processing in verbal analogy solution.* Unpublished doctoral dissertation, University of Pittsburgh.

HELMHOLTZ, H. VON. (1852). On the theory of compound colors. *Philosophical Magazine, 4,* 519–534.

HELMREICH, R. L., LeFAN, J. H., BAKEMAN, R., WILHELM, J., & RADLOFF, R. (1972). The Tektite 2 human behavior program. JSAS Catalog of Selected *Documents in Psychology, 2,* 13 (Ms. No. 70).

HELSON, H. (1933). The fundamental propositions of Gestalt psychology. *Psychological Review, 40,* 13–32.

HELZER, J. E., ROBINS, L. N., & McEVOY, L. (1987). Post-traumatic stress disorder in the general population. *The New England Journal of Medicine, 317,* 1630–1634.

HENDRICK, C., & HENDRICK, S. (1986). A theory and method of love. *Journal of Personality and Social Psychology, 50,* 392–402.

HERDT, G. (Ed.). (1984). *Ritualized homosexuality in Melanesia.* Berkeley: University of California Press.

HERGENHAN, B. R. (1992). *An introduction to the history of psychology* (2nd ed.). Belmont, CA: Wadsworth.

HERING, E. (1878). *Zur lehr vom lichtsinne.* Vienna: Gerold.

HERING, E. (1964). *Outlines of a theory of the light sense.* (L. M. Hurvich & D. Jameson, Trans.). Cambridge, MA: Harvard University Press.

HERMAN, C. P., & MACK, D. (1975). Restrained and unrestrained eating. *Journal of Personality, 43,* 647–660.

HERRERO, S. (1985). *Bear attacks: Their causes and avoidance.* Piscataway, NJ: Winchester.

HERSKOVITS, M. J. (1934). A critical discussion of the "Mulatto hypothesis." *Journal of Negro Education, 401.*

HESSE-BIBER, S., & MARINO, M. (1991). From high school to college: Changes in women's self-concept and its relationship to eating problems. *The Journal of Psychology, 125,* 199–216.

HIGGINS, E. T., KING, G. A., & MAVIN, G. H. (1982). Individual construct accessibility and subjective impressions and recall. *Journal of Personality and Social Psychology, 43,* 35–47.

HILGARD, E. R. (1965). *Hypnotic susceptibility.* New York: Harcourt, Brace & World.

HILGARD, E. R. (1973). A neodissociation interpretation of pain reduction in hypnosis. *Psychological Review, 80,* 396–411.

HILGARD, E. R. (1986). *Divided consciousness: Multiple controls in human thought and action.* New York: Wiley. (Original work published 1977.)

HILGARD, E. R. (1987). *Psychology in America: A historical survey.* New York: Harcourt Brace Jovanovich.

HILGARD, E. R., & HILGARD, J. R. (1983). *Hypnosis in the relief of pain* (2nd ed.). Los Altos, CA: William Kaufmann.

HILGARD, E. R., & LOFTUS, E. F. (1979). Effective interrogation of the eye witness. *International Journal of Clinical and Experimental Hypnosis, 27,* 342–357.

HILL, C., RUBIN, Z., & PEPLAU, L. A. (1976). Break-ups before marriage: The end of 103 affairs. *Journal of Social Issues, 32,* 147–167.

HINELINE, P. N., & RACHLIN, H. (1969). Escape and avoidance of shock by pigeons pecking a key. *Journal of the Experimental Analysis of Behavior, 12,* 533–538.

HINES, M. (1982). Prenatal gonadal hormones and sex differences in human behavior. *Psychological Bulletin, 92,* 56–80.

HINES, M., DAVIS, F. C., COQUELIN, A., GOY, R. W., & GORSKI, R. A. (1985). Sexually dimorphic regions in the medial preoptic area and the bed nucleus of the stria terminalis of the guinea pig brain: A description and an investigation of their relationship to gonadal steroids in adulthood. *Journal of Neuroscience, 5,* 40–47.

HIROTO, D. S. (1974). Locus of control and learned helplessness. *Journal of Experimental Psychology, 102,* 187–193.

HIRSCH, J., & LEIBEL, R. L. (1988). New light on obesity. *New England Journal of Medicine, 318,* 509–510.

HIRSCHI, T. (1969). *Causes of delinquency.* Berkeley: University of California Press.

HOBSON, J. A., & McCARLEY, R. W. (1977). The brain as a dream state generator: An activation-synthesis hypothesis of the dream process. *American Journal of Psychiatry, 134,* 1335–1348.

HOCHBERG, J. E. (1971). Perception. In J. W. Kling & L. A. Riggs (Eds.), *Experimental psychology* (3rd ed.) (pp. 396–550). New York: Holt, Rinehart & Winston.

HODGES, K. K., BRANDT, D. A., & KLINE, J. (1981). Competence, guilt and victimization: Sex differences in attribution of causality in television dramas. *Sex Roles, 7,* 537–546.

HOEBEL, B. G., & TEITELBAUM, P. (1962). Hypothalamic control of feeding and self-stimulation. *Science, 135,* 375–377.

HOFFMAN, C., LAU, I., & JOHNSON, D. R. (1986). The linguistic relativity of person cognition: An English-Chinese comparison. *Journal of Personality and Social Psychology, 51,* 1097–1105.

HOKANSON, J., DeGOOD, D. E., FORREST, M., & BRITTON, T. (1971). Availability of avoidance behaviors in modulating vascular stress responses. *Journal of Personality and Social Psychology, 19,* 60–68.

HOLDEN, C. (1980). Identical twins reared apart. *Science, 207,* 1323–1325.

HOLDEN, C. (1986). Giving mental illness its research due. *Science, 232,* 1084–1085.

HOLDEN, C. (1989). Court ruling rekindles controversy over SATs. *Science, 243,* 885–887.

HOLLINGWORTH, L. S. (1914). Variability as related to sex differences in achievement. *American Journal of Sociology, 19,* 510–530.

HOLMES, T., & RAHE, R. (1967). The social readjustment rating scale. *Journal of Psychosomatic Research, 11,* 213–218.

HOLWAY, A. H., & BORING, E. G. (1941). Determinants of apparent visual size with distance variant. *American Journal of Physiology, 54,* 21–37.

HOMANS, G. C. (1961). *Social behavior: Its elementary forms.* New York: Harcourt, Brace & World.

HOMANS, G. C. (1974). *Social behavior: Its elementary forms* (rev. ed.). New York: Harcourt Brace.

HOOKER, E. (1957). The adjustment of the male overt homosexual. *Journal of Projective Techniques, 21,* 18–31.

HOOLEY, J. M. (1985). Expressed emotion: A review of the critical literature. *Clinical Psychology Review, 5,* 119–139.

HOOVER, C. B. (1991). Suicidal ideation not associated with fluoxetine. *American Journal of Psychiatry, 148,* 543.

HORN, J. L. (1982). The aging of human abilities. In B. B. Wolman (Ed.), *Handbook of developmental psychology.* Englewood Cliffs, NJ: Prentice-Hall.

HORN, J. L., & DONALDSON, G. (1976). On the myth of intellectual decline in adulthood. *American Psychologist, 31,* 701–719.

HORNER, M. S. (1970). Femininity and successful achievement: A basic inconsistency. In J. M. Bardwick, E. Bouvan, M. S. Horner, & D. Gutmann (Eds.), *Feminine personality and conflict* (pp. 45–76). Pacific Grove, CA: Brooks/Cole.

HORNEY, K. (1939). *New ways in psychoanalysis.* New York: Norton.

HORNEY, K. (1945). *Our inner conflicts.* New York: Norton.

HORNEY, K. (1950). *Neurosis and human growth.* New York: Norton.

HORNEY, K. (1967). *Feminine psychology.* New York: W. W. Norton.

HOTHERSALL, D. (1990). *History of psychology* (2nd ed.). New York: McGraw-Hill.

HOUSE, J. S., LANDIS, K. R., & UNBERSON, D. (1988). Social relationships and health. *Science, 241,* 540–545.

HOUSE, J. S., ROBBINS, C., & METZNER, H. L. (1982). The association of social relationships and activities with mortality: Prospective evidence from the Tecumseh Community Health Study. *American Journal of Epidemiology, 116,* 123–140.

HOUSTON, L. N. (1990). *Psychological principles and the Black experience.* New York: University Press of America.

HOUSTON-STEIN, A., & HIGGENS-TRENK, A. (1978). Development of females from childhood through adulthood: Career and feminine role orientations. In P. B. Baltes (Ed.), *Life-span development and behavior.* New York: Academic Press.

HOVLAND, C., & SEARS, R. (1940). Minor studies of aggression: Correlation of lynchings with economic indices. *Journal of Psychology, 9,* 301–310.

HOVLAND, C. I., LUMSDAINE, A. A., & SHEFFIELD, F. D. (1949). *Studies in social psychology in World War II: Vol. 3. Experiments on mass communication.* Princeton, NJ: Princeton University Press.

HOVLAND, C. I., & WEISS, W. (1951). The influences of source credibility on communication effectiveness. *Public Opinion Quarterly, 15,* 635–650.

HUBEL, D. H., & WIESEL, T. N. (1959). Receptive fields of single neurons in the cat's striate cortex. *Journal of Physiology, 148,* 574–591.

HUBEL, D. H., & WIESEL, T. N. (1961). Integrative action in the cat's lateral geniculate body. *Journal of Physiology, 155,* 385–398.

HUBEL, D. H., & WIESEL, T. N. (1965). Receptive fields and functional architecture in two non-striate visual areas (18 & 19) of the cat. *Journal of Neurophysiology, 28,* 229–289.

HUDSON, W. (1960). Pictorial depth perception in sub-cultural groups in Africa. *Journal of Social Psychology, 52,* 183–208.

HUDSON, W. (1967). The study of the problem of pictorial perception among unacculturated groups. *International Journal of Psychology, 2,* 89–107.

HUMPHREY, N. (1983). *Consciousness regained.* New York: Oxford University Press.

HUMPHREY, N. (1987). The inner eye of consciousness. In C. Blakemore and S. Greenfield (Eds.), *Mindwaves* (pp. 377–381). Oxford: Blackwell.

HUNT, P. J., & HILLERY, J. M. (1973). Social facilitation in a location setting: An examination of the effects over learning trials. *Journal of Personality and Social Psychology, 9,* 563–571.

HUSBAND, R. W. (1931). Analysis of methods in human maze learning. *Journal of Genetic Psychology, 39,* 258–277.

HUTCHINS, E. (1983). Understanding Micronesian navigation. In D. Gentner & A. Stevens (Eds.), *Mental models* (pp. 191–225) Hillsdale, NJ: Erlbaum.

HYDE, J. S. (1991). *Half the human experience* (4th ed.). Lexington, MA: Heath.

HYDE, T. S., & JENKINS, J. J. (1973). Recall for words as a function of semantic, graphic and syntactic orienting tasks. *Journal of Verbal Learning and Verbal Behavior, 12,* 471–480.

IFILL, G. (1992, July 16). Tenacity and change in a son of the South. *New York Times,* pp. A1, A14.

INCIARDI, J. A. (1986). *The war on drugs.* Palo Alto, CA: Mayfield.

INGHAM, A., LEVINGER, G., GRAVES, J., & PECKHAM, V. (1974). The Ringelmann effect: Studies of group size and group performance. *Journal of Experimental Social Psychology, 10,* 371–384.

INHELDER, B., & PIAGET, J. (1955/1958). *The growth of logical thinking from childhood to adolescence.* New York: Basic Books.

INSKO, C. A., SMITH, R. H., ALICKE, M. D., WADE, J., & TAYLOR, S. (1985). Conformity and group size: The concern with being right and the concern with being liked. *Personality and Social Psychology Bulletin, 11,* 41–50.

INTONS-PETERSON, M. J. (1988). *Children's concepts of gender.* Norwood, NJ: Ablex.

IRVINE, S. H. (1969). The factor analysis of African abilities and attainments: Constructs across cultures. *Psychological Bulletin, 71,* 20–32.

IRVINE, S. H. (1970). Affect and construct—A cross-cultural check on theories of intelligence. *Journal of Social Psychology, 80,* 23–30.

ISABELLA, R. A., & BELSKY, J. (1991). Interactional synchrony and the origins of infant-mother attachment. *Child Development, 62,* 373–384.

ISEN, A. M., & LEVIN, P. F. (1972). Effect of feeling good on helping. *Journal of Personality and Social Psychology, 21,* 384–388.

ISENBERG, D. J. (1986). Group polarization: A critical review and meta-analysis. *Journal of Personality and Social Psychology, 50,* 1141–1151.

IZARD, C. E. (1971). *The face of emotion.* New York: Appleton-Century-Crofts.

IZARD, C. E. (1977). *Human emotions.* New York: Plenum Press.

IZARD, C. E. (1982). *Measuring emotions in infants and children.* London: Cambridge University Press.

IZARD, C. E. (1984). Emotion-cognition relationships and human development. In C. E. Izard, J. Kagan, & R. B. Zajonc (Eds.), *Emotions, cognition and behavior.* Cambridge, England: Cambridge University Press.

IZARD, C. E. (1990). The substrates and functions of emotion feelings: William James and current emotion theory. *Personality and Social Psychology Bulletin, 16,* 626–635.

JACK, D. C. (1991). *Silencing the self: Women and depression.* Cambridge, MA: Harvard University Press.

JACKLIN, C. N., & MCBRIDE-CHANG, C. (1991). The effects of feminist scholarship on developmental psychology. *Psychology of Women Quarterly, 15,* 549–556.

JACOB, R. G., & CHESNEY, M. A. (1986). Psychological and behavioral methods to reduce cardiovascular reactivity. In K. A. Matthews, S. Weiss, T. Detre, T. Dembroski, B. Falkner, S. Manuck, & R. Williams, (Eds.), *Handbook of stress, reactivity and cardiovascular disease* (pp. 417–457). New York: Wiley.

JAHODA, G. (1980). Theoretical and systematic approaches in mass-cultural psychology. In H. C. Triandis & W. W. Lambert (Eds.), *Handbook of cross-cultural psychology* (Vol 1, pp. 69–142). Boston: Allyn & Bacon.

JAMES, S. A., HARTNETT, S. A., & KALSBEEK, W. (1983). John Henryism and blood pressure differences among black men. *Journal of Behavioral Medicine, 6,* 259–278.

JAMES, S. A., LaCROIX, A. Z., KLEINBAUM, D. G., AND STROGATZ, D. S. (1984). John Henryism and blood pressure differences among black men: II. The role of occupational stressors. *Journal of Behavioral Medicine 7,* 259–275.

JAMES, W. (1892). *Psychology: Briefer course.* New York: Holt.

JAMES, W. (1968). What is an emotion? In M. Arnold (Ed.), *The nature of emotion* (pp. 17–36). Baltimore: Penguin. (Original work published 1884)

JAMES, W. (1981). *The principles of psychology* (rev. ed.). Cambridge, MA: Harvard University Press. (Original work published 1890)

JAMES, W. T. (1937). An experimental study of the defense mechanisms in the oppossum, with emphasis on natural behavior and its relation to mode of life. *Journal of Genetic Psychology, 51,* 95–100.

JAMISON, K. R. (1986). Suicide and bipolar disorders. In J. J. Mann & M. Stanley (Eds.), Psychobiology of suicidal behavior. *Annals of the New York Academy of Sciences, 487,* 301–315.

JAMISON, K. R., GERNER, R. H., HAMMEN, C., & PADESKY, C. (1980). Clouds and silver linings: Positive experiences associated with the primary affective disorders. *American Journal of Psychiatry, 137,* 198–202.

JANET, J. (1889). *L'Automatisme psychologique.* Paris: Alcan.

JANOWSKY, D. S., & RAUSCH, J. (1985). Biochemical hypotheses of premenstrual tension syndrome. *Psychological Medicine, 15,* 3–8.

JEMMOTT, J. B., III, BORYSENKO, J. Z., BORYSENKO, M. L., McCLELLAND, D. C., CHAPMAN, R., MEYER, D., & BENSON, H. (1983). Academic stress, power motivation, and decrease in salivary secretory immunoglobulin A secretion rate. *Lancet, 1,* 1400–1402.

JEMMOTT, J. B., III, & LOCKE, S. E. (1984). Psychosocial factors, immunologic mediation, and human susceptibility to infectious diseases: How much do we know? *Psychological Bulletin, 95,* 78–108.

JEMMOTT, J. B., III, & MAGLOIRE, K. (1988). Academic stress, social support, and secretory immunoglobulin A. *Journal of Personality and Social Psychology, 55,* 803–810.

JENKINS, C. D., ROSENMAN, R. H., & FRIEDMAN, M. (1968). Replicability of rating the coronary-prone behavior pattern. *British Journal of Preventive Social Medicine, 22,* 16–22.

JENKINS, C. D., ROSENMAN, R. H., & ZYZANSKI, J. S. (1974). Prediction of clinical coronary heart disease by a test for the coronary-prone behavior pattern. *New England Journal of Medicine, 290,* 1271–1275.

JENKINS, J. J., & RUSSELL, W. A. (1952). Associative clustering during recall. *Journal of Abnormal and Social Psychology, 47,* 818–821.

JENKINS, J. R., ODOM, S. L., & SPELTZ, M. L. (1989). Effects of social integration on preschool children with handicaps. *Exceptional Children, 55,* 420–428.

JOHNSON, C. B., STOCKDALE, M. S., & SAAL, F. (1991). Persistence of men's misperceptions of friendly cues across a variety of interpersonal encounters. *Psychology of Women Quarterly, 15,* 463–475.

JOHNSON, E. H. (1987). Behavioral factors associated with hypertension in Black Americans. In S. Julius and D. R. Bassett (Eds.), *Handbook of hypertension: Vol. 9. Behavioral factors in hypertension.* Amsterdam: Elsevier.

JOHNSON, E. J., & TVERSKY, A. (1983). Affect, generalization, and the perception of risk. *Journal of Personality and Social Psychology, 45,* 20–31.

JOHNSON, M. K., BRANSFORD, J. D., & SOLOMON, S. (1973). Memory for tacit implications of sentences. *Journal of Experimental Psychology, 98,* 203–205.

JOHNSON, R. C., McCLEARN, C. G., YUEN, S., NAGOSHI, C. T., AHERN, F. M., & COLE, R. E. (1985). Galton's data a century later. *American Psychologist, 40,* 875–892.

JOHNSON, W., EMDE, R. N., PANNABECKER, B., STEINBERG, C., & DAVIS, M. (1982). Maternal perception of infant emotion from birth through 18 months. *Infant Behavior and Development, 5,* 313–322.

JOINT COMMISSION ON MENTAL ILLNESS AND HEALTH. (1961). *Action for mental health: Final report of the Joint Commission on Mental Illness and Health.* New York: Basic Books.

JOLLES, I. (1964). *A Catalogue for the Qualitative Interpretation of the HTP.* Beverly Hills, CA: Western Psychological Services.

JONES, A., WILKINSON, H. J., & BRADEN, I. (1961). Information deprivation as a motivational variable. *Journal of Experimental Psychology, 62,* 126–137.

JONES, E. E., & BERGLAS, S. (1978). Control of attributions about the self through self-handicapping strategies: The appeal of alcohol and the role of under-achievement. *Personality and Social Psychology Bulletin, 4,* 200–206.

JONES, E. E., & NISBETT, R. E. (1971). The actor and the observer: Divergent perceptions of the causes of behavior. In E. Jones, D. Kanouse, H. Kelley, R. Nisbett, S. Valins, & B. Weiner (Eds.), *Attribution: Perceiving the causes of behavior* (pp. 79–94). Morristown, NJ: General Learning Press.

JONES, E. E., & SIGALL, H. (1971). The bogus pipeline: A new paradigm for measuring affect and attitudes. *Psychological Bulletin, 76,* 349–364.

JONES, M. C. (1924). The elimination of children's fears. *Journal of Experimental Psychology, 7,* 382–390.

JONES, M. C. (1965). Psychological correlates of somatic development. *Child Development, 36,* 899–911.

JOSEPHSON, W. L. (1987). Television violence and children's aggression: Testing and priming, social script, and disinhibition predictions. *Journal of Personality and Social Psychology, 53,* 882–890.

JOUVET, M., & RENAULT, J. (1966). Insomnie persistante après lesions des noyaux du raphe chez le chat [Persistent insomnia after lesions of the raphe nuclei in the cat]. *Comptes Rendus des Séances de la Société de Biologie, 160,* 1461–1465.

JULIEN, R. M. (1981). *A primer of drug action* (3rd ed.). San Francisco: W. H. Freeman.

JUNG, C. G. (1933a). *Modern man in search of a soul.* New York: Harcourt, Brace & World.

JUNG, C. G. (1933b). *Psychological types.* New York: Harcourt, Brace & World.

JUNG, C. (1964). The meaning of psychology for modern man. In *Civilization in Transition* (Vol. 10, pp. 134–156). New York: Pantheon. (Original work published 1934)

JUNG, C. (1969). On the nature of dreams. In H. Read, M. Fordham, G. Adler, & W. McGure, (Eds.), *The collected works of C. G. Jung* (Vol. 8, pp. 281–300). Princeton, NJ: Princeton University Press.

JUNG, C. G. (1974). *Dreams.* Princeton, NJ: Princeton University Press.

KAGAN, J. (1984). *The nature of the child.* New York: Basic Books.

KAIL, R. (1991). Processing time declines exponentially during childhood and adolescence. *Developmental Psychology, 27,* 259–266.

KAITZ, M., MESCHULACH-SARFATY, O., & AVERBACH, J. (1988). A reexamination of newborns' abilty to imitate facial expressions. *Developmental Psychology, 24,* 3–7.

KALAT, J. W. (1992). *Biological psychology* (4th ed.). Belmont, CA: Wadsworth.

KALISH, R. A. (1985). The social context of death and dying. In R. H. Binstock & E. Shanas (Eds.), *Handbook of aging and the social sciences* (2nd ed.) (pp. 149–170). New York: Van Nostrand Reinhold.

KAMIN, L. J. (1969). Predictability, surprise, attention, and conditioning. In B. A. Campbell & R. M. Church (Eds.), *Punishment and aversive behavior* (pp. 279–293). New York: Appleton-Century-Crofts.

KAMIN, L. J. (1974). *The science and politics of IQ.* Hillsdale, NJ: Erlbaum.

KANDEL, E. (1976). *Cellular basis of behavior.* San Francisco: W. H. Freeman.

KANNER, A. D., COYNE, J. C., SCHAEFER, C., & LAZARUS, R. S. (1981). Comparisons of two modes of stress measurement: Daily hassles and uplifts versus major life events. *Journal of Behavioral Medicine, 4,* 1–39.

KAPLAN, H. B., MARTIN, S. S., JOHNSON, R. J., & ROBBINS, C. A. (1986). Escalation of marijuana use: Application of a general theory of deviant behavior. *Journal of Health and Social Behavior, 27,* 44–61.

KAPLAN, M. R., & MILLER, C. E. (1987). Group decision making and normative versus informational influence: Effects of type of issue and assigned decision rule. *Journal of Personality and Social Psychology, 11,* 470–477.

KAPLAN, N. M. (1986). *Clinical hypertension* (4th ed.). Baltimore: Williams & Wilkins.

KAPLAN, R. M. (1985). The controversy related to the use of psychological tests. In B. Wolman (Ed.), *Handbook of intelligence* (pp. 465–504). New York: Wiley.

KAPLAN, R. M., SALLIS, J. F., & PATTERSON, T. L. (1993). *Health and human behavior.* New York: McGraw-Hill.

KAPTEIN, A. A., VAN DER PLOEG, H. M., GARSSEN, B., SCHREURS, P. J. G., & BEUN-DERMAN, R. (Eds.). (1990). *Behavioral medicine.* Chichester, England: Wiley.

KAUER, J. S. (1987). Coding in the olfactory system. In T. E. Finger and W. L. Silver (Eds.), *Neurobiology of taste and smell* (pp. 205–231). New York: Wiley.

KAUER, J. S., & MOULTON, D. G. (1974). Responses of olfactory bulb neurons to odour stimulation of small nasal areas in the salamander. *Journal of Physiology, 243,* 717–737.

KAUFMAN, A. S., KAMPHARES, R. W., & KAUFMAN, N. L. (1985). New directions in intelligence testing. The Kaufman Assessment Battery for Children (K-ABC). In B. Wolman (Ed.), *Handbook of intelligence* (pp. 663–698). New York: Wiley.

KAUFMAN, A. S., & KAUFMAN, N. L. (1983). K-ABC Kaufman Assessment Battery for Children. Circle Pines, MN: American Guidance Service.

KAUFMAN, B., & WOHL, A. (1992). *Casualties of childhood.* New York: Brunner/Mazel.

KAUFMAN, L., & ROCK, I. (1962). The moon illusion I. *Science, 136,* 953–961.

KAUFMAN, L., & ROCK, I. (1962, July). The moon illusion. *Scientific American,* pp. 120–132.

KAUSLER, D. H. (1991). *Experimental psychology, cognition and human aging.* New York: Springer.

KAYE, D. B., POST, T. A., HALL, V. C., & DINEEN, J. J. (1986). The emergence of information retrieval strategies in numerical cognition: A developmental study. *Cognition and Instruction, 3,* 137–166.

KAZDIN, A. E. (1977). *The token economy: A review and evaluation.* New York: Plenum.

KEATS, D. M. (1982). Cultural bases of concepts of intelligence: A Chinese versus Australian comparison. *Proceedings: Second Asian Workshop on Child and Adolescent Development,* pp. 67–75.

KEESEY, R. E. (1980). The regulation of body weight: A set-point analysis. In A. J. Stunkard (Ed.), *Obesity* (pp. 144–165). Philadelphia: Saunders.

KEESEY, R. E. (1986). A set-point theory of obesity. In K. D. Brownell & J. P. Foreyt (Eds.), *Handbook of eating disorders* (pp. 63–87). New York: Basic Books.

KELLEHER, R. (1958). Fixed ratio schedules of conditioned reinforcement with chimpanzees. *Journal of the Experimental Analysis of Behavior, 3,* 281–289.

KELLER, H. (1910). From a letter to Dr. J. Kerr Love, March 31, 1910.

KELLEY, H. H. (1967). Attribution theory in social psychology. In D. L. Vine (Ed.), *Nebraska Symposium on Motivation* (pp. 192–241). Lincoln: University of Nebraska Press.

KELLMAN, P. I., & SHORT, K. R. (1987). Development of three-dimensional form perception. *Journal of Experimental Psychology: Human Perception and Performance, 13,* 545–557.

KELLY, G. A. (1955). *The psychology of personal constructs* (Vols. 1 & 2). New York: Norton.

KELLY, G. A. (1970). A brief introduction to personal construct theory. In D. Bannister (Ed.), *Perspectives in personal construct theory* (pp. 1–29). New York: Academic Press.

KELMAN, H. C. (1967). Human use of human subjects: The problem of deception in social psychological experiments. *Psychological Bulletin, 67,* 1–11.

KELSOE, J. R., CADET, J. L., PICAR, D., & WEINBERGER, D. R. (1988). Quantitative neuronanatomy in schizophrenia. *Archives of General Psychiatry, 45,* 533–541.

KENRICK, D. T., STRINGFIELD, D. O., WAGENHALS, W. L., DAHL, R. H., & RANSDELL, H. J. (1980). Sex differences, androgyny, and approach responses to erotica: A new variation on the old volunteer problem. *Journal of Personality and Social Psychology, 38,* 517–524.

KENSHALO, D. R. (1976). Correlations of temperature sensitivity in man and monkey, a first approximation. In Y. Zotterman (Ed.), *Sensory functions of the skin in primates, with special reference to man* (pp. 305–330). New York: Plenum.

KERR, N. L. (1981). Social transition schemes: Charting the group's road to agreement. *Journal of Personality and Social Psychology, 41,* 684–702.

KIECOLT-GLASER, J. (1986). Psychological influences on immunity. *Psychosomatics, 27,* 621–624.

KIESLER, C. A., & KIESLER, S. B. (1969). *Conformity.* Reading, MA: Addison-Wesley.

KIHLSTROM, J. F. (1985). Hypnosis. *Annual Review of Psychology, 36,* 385–418.

KIHLSTROM, J. F. (1987). The cognitive unconscious. *Science, 237,* 1445–1452.

KIHLSTROM, J. F. (1988). Letter to Science. *Science, 238,* 1638.

KIHLSTROM, J. F., & MCCONKEY, K. M. (1990). William James and hypnosis: A centennial reflection. *Psychological Science, 1,* 61–67.

KILHAM, W., & MANN, L. (1974). Level of destructive obedience as a function of transmitter and executant roles in the Milgram obedience paradigm. *Journal of Personality and Social Psychology, 29,* 696–702.

KIMBALL, M. (1989). A new perspective on women's math achievement. *Psychological Bulletin, 105,* 198–214.

KIMMEL, M. S., & LEVINE, M. P. (1992). Men and AIDS. In M. S. Kimmel & M. A. Messner (Eds.), *Men's lives* (2nd ed.) (pp. 318–329) New York: Macmillan.

KIMURA, D. (1973). The asymmetry of the human brain. *Scientific American,* pp. 70–78.

KIMURA, D. (1992, September). Sex differences in the brain. *Scientific American,* pp. 119–125.

KIMZEY, S. L., JOHNSON, P. C., RITZMAN, S. E., & MENGEL, C. E. (1976). Hematology and immunology studies: The second manned skylab mission. *Aviation, Space, and Environmental Medicine, 47,* 383–390.

KINSEY, A. C., POMEROY, W. B., & MARTIN, C. E. (1948). *Sexual behavior in the human male*. Philadelphia: Saunders.

KINSEY, A. C., POMEROY, W. B., MARTIN, C. E., & GEBHARD, P. H. (1953). *Sexual behavior in the human female*. Philadelphia: Saunders.

KINTSCH, W., & BUSCHKE, H. (1969). Homophones and synonyms in short-term memory. *Journal of Experimental Psychology, 80*, 403–407.

KIRMAYER, L. J. (1991). The place of culture in psychiatric nosology: Taijin Kyofusho and DSM-III-R. *Journal of Nervous and Mental Disorders, 179*, 19–28.

KLAHR, D. (1982). Non monotone assessment of monotone development: An information processing analysis. In S. Strauss (Ed.), *U-shaped behavioral growth* (pp. 63–99). New York: Academic Press.

KLASSEN, D., & O'CONNOR, W. A. (1988). Predicting violence in schizophrenic and non-schizophrenic patients: A prospective study. *Journal of Community Psychology, 16*, 217–227.

KLATZKY, R. L. (1980). *Human memory*, 2nd ed. San Francisco: W. H. Freeman.

KLEINBERG, O. (1935). *Race differences*. New York: Harper & Row.

KLEINBERG, O. (1938). Emotional expression in Chinese literature. *Journal of Abnormal and Social Psychology, 33*, 517–520.

KLEITMAN, N. (1963). *Sleep and wakefulness* (rev. ed). Chicago: University of Chicago Press.

KLOPFER, B., & DAVIDSON, H. H. (1962). *The Rorschach technique: An introductory manual*. New York: Harcourt, Brace & World.

KLUCKHOLN, C., & MURRAY, H. A. (1953). Personality formation: The determinants. In C. Kluckhohn, H. Murray, & D. Schneider (Eds.), *Personality in nature, society and culture* (pp. 3–49). New York: Knopf.

KLÜVER, H., & BUCY, P. C. (1938). An analysis of certain effects of bilateral temporal lobectomy in the rhesus monkey with special reference to "psychic blindness." *Journal of Psychology, 5*, 33–54.

KOBASA, S. C. (1979). Stressful life events, personality and health: An inquiry into hardiness. *Journal of Personality and Social Psychology, 37*, 1–11

KOBASA, S. C., MADDI, S. R., & KAHN, S. (1982). Hardiness and health: A prospective study. *Journal of Personality and Social Psychology, 42*, 168–177.

KOBASA, S. C., MADDI, S. R., PUCCETTI, M. C., & ZOLA, M. A. (1985). Effectiveness of hardiness, exercise and social support as resources against illness. *Journal of Psychosomatic Research, 29*, 525–533.

KOHLBERG, L. (1963). Development of children's orientation towards a moral order: Part I. Sequence in the development of moral thought. *Vita Humana, 6*, 11–36.

KOHLBERG, L. (1966). A cognitive-developmental analysis of children's sex-role concepts and attitudes. In E. E. Maccoby (Ed.), *The development of sex differences* (pp. 82–173). Stanford, CA: Stanford University Press.

KOHLBERG, L. (1981). *Essays on moral development: Vol. 1. The philosophy of moral development*. New York: Harper & Row.

KOHLBERG, L. (1984). *Essays on moral development: Vol. 2. The psychology of moral development*. New York: Harper & Row.

KÖHLER, W. (1925). *The mentality of apes* (E. Winter, Trans.). New York: Harcourt Brace. (Original work published 1917)

KÖHLER, W. (1927). *The mentality of apes* (rev. ed.). London: Routledge & Kegan Paul.

KOHLSTROM, J. F. (1987). The cognitive unconscious. *Science, 237*, 1445–1452.

KOHN, R. R. (1977). Heart and cardiovascular system. In C. E. Finch & L. Hayflick (Eds.), *Handbook of the biology of aging*. New York: Van Nostrand Reinhold.

KOHUT, H. J. (1971). The analysis of the self. *Monograph series of the psychoanalytic study of the child*. New York: International Universities Press.

KOLATA, G. (1992, September 1). Linguists debate study classifying language as innate human skill. *New York Times*, p. B6.

KOLB, B., & WHISHAW, I. Q. (1985). *Fundamentals of human neuropsychology* (2nd ed.). New York: W. H. Freeman.

KOSAMBI, D. D. (1967). Living prehistory in India. *Scientific American*, p. 105.

KRAMER, D. A. (1989). A developmental framework for understanding conflict resolution processes. In J. D. Sinnott (Ed.), *Everyday problem solving: Theory and applications* (pp. 138–152). New York: Praeger.

KRANTZ, D. S., & DECKEL, A. W. (1983). Coping with coronary heart disease and stroke. In T. G. Burish & L. A. Bradley (Eds.), *Coping with chronic disease: Research and applications* (pp. 85–112). New York: Academic Press.

KREBS, D. L., & MILLER, D. T. (1985). Altruism and aggression. In G. Lindzey & E. Aronson (Eds.), *Handbook of social psychology* (3rd ed.) (Vol 2, pp. 1–72). New York: Random House.

KREIGER, N. (1990). Racial and gender discrimination: Risk factors for high blood pressure? *Social Science and Medicine, 30*, 1273–1281.

KRIPKE, D. F., & SIMONS, R. N. (1976). Average sleep, insomnia, and sleeping pill use. *Sleep research, 5*, 110.

KROGER, W. S., & DOUCE, R. G. (1979). Hypnosis in criminal investigation. *International Journal of Clinical and Experimental Hypnosis, 27*, 358–374.

KROLL, N. E. A., PARKS, T. E., PARKINSON, S. R., BIEBER, S. L., & JOHNSON, A. L. (1970). Short-term memory while shadowing: Recall of visually and aurally presented letters. *Journal of Experimental Psychology, 85*, 220–224.

KRUGLANSKI, A. W. (1970). Attributing trustworthiness in supervisor-worker relations. *Journal of Experimental Social Psychology, 6*, 214–232.

KRUGLANSKI, A. W., & FREUND, T. (1983). The freezing and unfreezing of lay-inferences: Effects on impressional primacy, ethnic stereotyping, and numerical anchoring. *Journal of Experimental Social Psychology, 19*, 448–468.

KUBLER-ROSS, E. (1969). *On death and dying*. New York: Macmillan.

KUBOVY, M. (1986). *The psychology of perspective and Renaissance art*. Cambridge: Cambridge University Press.

KUIPER, N. A., & ROGERS, T. B. (1979). Encoding of personal information: Self-other differences. *Journal of Personality and Social Psychology, 37*, 499–514.

KULIK, C., & KULIK, J. (1982). Effects of ability groups on secondary school students. A meta-analysis of evaluation findings. *American Educational Research Journal, 190*, 415–418.

KUPFERMAN, I. (1981). Localization of higher functions. In E. Kandel & J. Schwartz (Eds.), *Principles of neural function* (pp. 580–592). New York: Elsevier.

LABARRE, W. (1947). The cultural basis of emotions and gestures. *Journal of Personality, 16*, 49–68.

LABORATORY OF COMPARATIVE HUMAN COGNITION. (1983). Culture and cognitive development. In P. Mussen (Ed.), *Handbook of child psychology* (Vol. 1, pp.295–356). New York: Wiley.

LABOUVIE-VIEF, G. (1985). Intelligence and cognition. In J. E. Birren & K. W. Schaie (Eds.), *Handbook of the psychology of ageing* (2nd ed.) (pp. 500–530). New York: Van Nostrand Reinhold.

LABOUVIE-VIEF, G., & BLANCHARD-FIELDS, F. (1982). Cognitive aging and psychological growth. *Ageing and Society, 2*, 183–209.

LABOV, W. (1975). The boundaries of words and their meanings. In C. J. N. Bailey & R. W. Shuy, (Eds.), *New ways of analyzing variations in English*. Washington, DC: Georgetown University Press.

LAIRD, J. D. (1974). Self-attribution of emotion: The effects of expressive behavior on the quality of emotional experience. *Journal of Personality and Social Psychology, 29*, 475–486.

LAIRD, J. D. (1984). The real role of facial response in the experience of emotion: A reply to Tourangeau and Ellsworth, and others. *Journal of Personality and Social Psychology, 47*, 909–917.

LAMB, M. E. (1977). Father-infant and mother-infant interaction in the first year of life. *Child Development, 48*, 167–181.

LAMBERT, M. J. (1989). The individual therapist's contribution to psychotherapy process and outcome. *Clinical Psychology Review, 9*, 469–485.

LAMBERT, M. J., SHAPIRO, D. A., & BERGIN, A. E. (1986). The effectiveness of psychotherapy. In S. L. Garfield and A. E. Bergin (Eds.), *Handbook of psychotherapy and behavior change*, 3rd ed. New York: Wiley.

LANDMAN, J. T., & DAWES, R. M. (1982). Psychotherapy outcome: Smith and Glass' conclusions stand up under scrutiny. *American Psychologist, 38*, 504–516.

LANDRINE, H., BARDWELL, S., & DEAN, T. (1988). Gender expectations for alcohol use: A study of the significance of the masculine role. *Sex Roles, 19*, 703–712.

LANDSMAN, S., & RAMEY, C. (1989). Developmental psychology and mental retardation: Integrating scientific principles with treatment practices. *American Psychologist, 44*, 409–415.

LANG, P., & LAZOVIK, A. D. (1963). Experimental desensitization of a phobia. *Journal of Abnormal and Social Psychology, 66*, 519–525.

LANGE, C. G. (1922). *The emotions*. Baltimore: Williams & Wilkins. (Original work published 1885)

LANGER, E. J. (1989). *Mindfulness*. Reading, MA: Addison-Wesley.

LANGER, E., & ABELSON, R. (1974). A patient by any other name . . . : Clinical group differences in labeling bias. *Journal of Consulting and Clinical Psychology, 42*, 4–9.

LANGLOIS, J. H., & DOWNS, A. C. (1980). Mothers, fathers and peers as socializing agents of sex-typed play behaviors in young children. *Child Development, 51*, 1217–1247.

LAPIERE, R. T. (1934). Attitudes and actions. *Social Forces, 13*, 230–237.

LASSEN, N. A., INGUAR, D. H., & SKINHØS, E. (1978, Oct.). Brain function and blood flow. *Scientific American*.

LATANÉ, B., & DARLEY, J. M. (1970). *The unresponsive bystander: Why doesn't he help?* New York: Appleton-Century-Crofts.

LATANÉ, B., & RODIN, J. (1969). A lady in distress: Inhibiting effects of friends and strangers on bystander intervention. *Journal of Experimental Social Psychology, 5*, 189–202.

LATANÉ, B., WILLIAMS, K., & HARKINS, S. (1979). Many hands make light the work: The causes and consequences of social loafing. *Journal of Personality and Social Psychology, 37*, 822–832.

LAUGHLIN, H. P. (1967). *The neuroses*. Washington, DC: Butterworth.

LAUMANN, E. O. (1969). Friends of urban men: An assessment of accuracy in reporting their socioeconomic attributes, mutual choice, and attitude development. *Sociometry, 32*, 54–69.

LAURENCE, J.-R., & PERRY, C. (1983). Hypnotically created memory among highly hypnotizable subjects. *Science, 222*, 523–524.

LAURENCE, J.-R., PERRY, C., & KIHLSTROM, J. F. (1983). "Hidden observer" phenomena in hypnosis: An experimental creation? *Journal of Personality and Social Psychology, 44,* 163–169.

LAVIE, P., & HOBSON, J. A. (1986). Origin of dreams: Anticipation of modern theories in the philosophy and physiology of the eighteenth and nineteenth centuries. *Psychological Bulletin, 100,* 229–240.

LAZARUS, R. S. (1982). Thoughts on the relations between emotion and cognition. *American Psychologist, 37,* 1019–1024.

LAZARUS, R. S. (1984). On the primacy of cognition. *American Psychologist, 39,* 124–129.

LAZARUS, R. S. (1991a). Cognition and motivation in emotion. *American Psychologist, 46,* 352–367.

LAZARUS, R. S. (1991b). Progress on a cognitive-motivational-relational theory of emotion. *American Psychologist, 46,* 819–834.

LAZARUS, R. S., & COHEN, J. B. (1977). Environmental stress. In L. Altman & J. F. Wohlwill (Eds.), *Human behavior and the environment: Current theory and research* (Vol. 2, pp. 90–127). New York: Plenum.

LAZARUS, R. S., COYNE, J. C., & FOLKMAN, S. (1982). Cognition, emotion, and motivation: The doctoring of Humpty-Dumpty. In R. W. J. Newfeld (Ed.), *Theories of emotion* (pp. 189–217). New York: Academic Press.

LAZARUS, R. S., & FOLKMAN, S. (1984). *Stress, appraisal and coping.* New York: Springer.

LEACH, E. (1972). The influence of the cultural context on nonverbal communication in man. In R. Hinde (Ed.), *Nonverbal communication* (pp. 315–344). London: Cambridge University Press.

LECUYER, R. (1989). Habituation and attention, novelty and cognition: Where is the continuity? *Human Development, 32,* 148–157.

LeDAIN, G. (ED.). (1970). *Interim drug report of the commission of inquiry into the nonmedical use of drugs.* Ottawa: Information Canada.

LeDOUX, J. E. (1989). Cognitive-emotional interactions in the brain. *Cognition and Emotion, 3,* 267–289.

LEE, J. A. (1973). *The colors of love: An exploration of the ways of loving.* Don Mills, Ontario: New Press.

LEE, J. A. (1988). Love-styles. In R. J. Sternberg & M. L. Barnes (Eds.), *The psychology of love* (pp. 38–67). New Haven, CT: Yale University Press.

LEIGH, B. C. (1989). Reasons for having and avoiding sex: Gender, sexual orientation, and relationship to sexual behavior. *Journal of Sex Research, 26,* 299–309.

LEINER, H. C., LEINER, A. L., & DOW, R. S. (1989). Reappraising the cerebellum: What does the hindbrain contribute to the forebrain? *Behavioral Newscience, 103,* 998–1008.

LEMPERS, J. D., CLARK-LEMPERS, D., & SIMONS, R. L. (1989). Economic hardship, parenting, and distress in adolescence. *Child Development, 60,* 25–39.

LENNON, S. J., DAVIS, L. L., & FAIRHURST, A. (1988). Evaluations of apparel advertising as a function of self-monitoring. *Perceptual and Motor Skills, 66,* 987–996.

LERNER, M. J., & MILLER, D. T. (1978). Just world research and the attribution process: Looking back and ahead. *Psychological Bulletin, 85,* 1030–1051.

LERNER, R. M., & GELLERT, E. (1969). Body build identification, preference and aversion in children. *Developmental Psychology, 5,* 456–462.

LERNER, R. M., OROLOS, J. B., & KNAPP, J. R. (1976). Physical attractiveness, physical effectiveness, and self-concept in late adolescents. *Adolescence, 11,* 313–326.

LESERMAN, J., PERKINS, D. O., & EVANS, D. L. (1992). Coping with the threat of AIDS: The role of social support. *American Journal of Psychiatry, 149,* 1514–1520.

LESSE, S. (1984). Psychosurgery. *American Journal of Psychotherapy, 38,* 224–228.

LESTER, B. M. (1984). A biosocial model of infant crying. In L. P. Lipsitt (Ed.), *Advances in infancy research* (Vol. 3, pp. 168–212). Norwood, NJ: Ablex.

LESTER, B. M., CORWIN, M. J., SPEKOSKI, C., SEIFER, R., PEUCKER, M., McLAUGHLIN, S., & GOLUB, H. L. (1991). Neurobehavioral syndromes in cocaine-exposed newborn infants. *Child Development, 62,* 694–705.

LESTER, G. L., & GORZALKA, B. B. (1988). Effect of novel and familiar mating partners on the duration of sexual receptivity in the female hamster. *Behavioral and Neural Biology, 49,* 398–405.

LETTIERI, D. J., SAYERS, M., & PEARSON, H. W. (Eds.). (1980). *Theories on drug abuse* (NIDA Research Monograph 30). Rockville, MD: National Institute on Drug Abuse.

LeVAY, S. (1991). A difference in hypothalamic structure between heterosexual and homosexual men. *Science, 253,* 1034–1037.

LEVENSON, R. W. (1992). Autonomic nervous system differences among emotions. *Psychological Science, 3,* 23–27.

LEVENSON, R. W., EKMAN, P., & FRIESEN, W. V. (1990). Voluntary facial action generates emotion-specific autonomic nervous system activity. *Psychophysiology, 27,* 363–384.

LEVENSON, R. W., EKMAN, P., HEIDER, K., & FRIESEN, W. V. (1992). Emotion and autonomic nervous system activity in the Minangkabau of West Sumatra. *Journal of Personality and Social Psychology, 62,* 972–988.

LEVENTHAL, H. (1970). Findings and theory in the study of fear communications. In L. Berkowitz (Ed.), *Advances in experimental social psychology* (Vol. 5, pp.120–182). New York: Academic Press.

LEVENTHAL, H. (1984). A perceptual-motor theory of emotion. *Advances in Experimental Social Psychology, 17,* 117–182.

LEVENTHAL, H., SINGER, R., & JONES, S. (1965). The effects of fear and specificity of recommendation upon attitudes and behavior. *Journal of Personality and Social Psychology, 2,* 20–29.

LEVINE, F. M., & SANDEEN, E. (1985). *Conceptualization in psychotherapy: The models approach.* Hillsdale, NJ: Erlbaum.

LeVINE, R. A. (1966). *Dreams and deeds: Achievement motivation in Nigeria.* Chicago: University of Chicago Press.

LEVINSON, D. J. (1990). A theory of life structure development in adulthood. In C. N. Alexander & E. J. Langer (Eds.), *Higher states of human development* (pp. 35–53). New York: Oxford University Press.

LEVINSON, D. J., DARROW, C. N., KLEIN, E. B., LEVINSON, M. H., & MCKEE, B. (1978). *The seasons of a man's life.* New York: Knopf.

LEW, M. (1988). *Victims no longer: Men recovering from incest and other sexual child abuse.* New York: Nevraumont.

LEWIN, M., & WILD, C. L. (1991). The impact of the feminist critique on tests, assessment, and methodology. *Psychology of Women Quarterly, 15,* 581–596.

LEWINSOHN, P. M. (1974). A behavioral approach to depression. In R. J. Friedman & M. M. Katz (Eds.), *The psychology of depression: Contemporary theory and research* (pp. 157–186). New York: Halsted.

LEWINSOHN, P. M., MISCHEL, W., CHAPLIN, W., & BARTON, R. (1980). Social competence and depression: The role of illusory self-perceptions. *Journal of Abnormal Psychology, 89,* 203–212.

LEWINSOHN, P. M., & ROSENBAUM, M. (1987). Recall of paternal behavior by acute depressives, remitted depressives, and nondepressives. *Journal of Personality and Social Psychology, 52,* 611–619.

LEWIS, C. (1987). Early sex-role socialization. In D. J. Hargreaves and A. M. Colley (Eds.), *The psychology of sex roles* (pp. 95–117). New York: Hemisphere.

LEWIS, M. (1987). Social development in infancy and early childhood. In J. D. Osofsky (Ed.), *Handbook of infancy* (2nd ed.) (pp. 419–493). New York: Wiley.

LEWIS, M., & BROOKS-GUNN, J. (1979). *Social cognition and the acquisition of self.* New York: Plenum.

LEWIS, M., FIERING, C., McGUFFY, C., & JASKIR, J. (1984). Predicting psychopathology in six-year-olds from early social relations. *Child Development, 55,* 123–136.

LICHTENSTEIN, S., SLOVIC, P., FISCHHOFF, B., LAYMAN, M., & COMBS, J. (1978). Judged frequency of lethal events. *Journal of Experimental Psychology: Human Learning and Memory, 4,* 551–578.

LICHTMAN, S. W., PISARSKA, K., BERMAN, E. R., PESTONE, M., DOWLING, H., OFFENBACHER, E., WEISER, H., HESHKA, S., MATTHEWS, D. E., & HEYMSFIELD, S. B. (1992). Discrepancy between self-reported and actual caloric intake and exercise in obese subjects. *New England Journal of Medicine, 327,* 1893–1898.

LICKEY, M. E., & GORDON, B. (1983). *Drugs for mental illness.* New York: W. H. Freeman.

LIEBERMAN, D. A. (1990). *Learning: Behavior and cognition.* Belmont, CA: Wadsworth.

LIEBERT, R. M., WICKS-NELSON, R., & KAIL, R. V. (1986). *Developmental psychology* (4th ed.). Englewood Cliffs, NJ: Prentice-Hall.

LIEBOWITZ, H., BRISLIN, R., PERLMUTTER, L., & HENNESSY, R. (1969). Ponzo perspective as a manifestation of space perception. *Science, 166,* 1174–1176.

LIEBOWITZ, H., & PICK, H. (1972). Cross-cultural and educational aspects of the Ponzo perspective illusion. *Perception and Psychophysics, 12,* 430–432.

LIEBOWITZ, H., SHINA, K., & HENNESSY, H. R. (1972). Oculomotor adjustments and size constancy. *Perception and Psychophysics, 12,* 497–500.

LIGGETT, J. C. (1974). *The human face.* New York: Stein & Day.

LIKER, J. K., & ELDER, G. H., JR. (1983). Economic hardship and marital relations in the 1930s. *American Sociological Review, 48,* 343–359.

LIPPA, R. A. (1990). *Introduction to social psychology.* Belmont, CA: Wadsworth.

LIPS, H. (1993). *Sex and gender* (2nd ed.). Mountain View, CA: Mayfield.

LISKA, A. E. (1981). *Perspectives on deviance.* Englewood Cliffs, NJ: Prentice-Hall.

LITTLE, K. B., & SCHNEIDIMAN, E. S. (1959). Congruencies among interpretations of psychological test and anamnestic data. *Psychological Monographs, 73* (Whole No. 476).

LIVINGSTONE, M. S., & HUBEL, D. H. (1984). Anatomy and physiology of a color system in the primate visual cortex. *Journal of Neuroscience, 4,* 309–356.

LIVINGSTONE, M. S., & HUBEL, D. H. (1987). Psychophysical evidence for separate channels for the perception of form, color, movement and depth. *Journal of Neuroscience, 7,* 3416–3468.

LIVINGSTONE, M. S., & HUBEL, D. H. (1988). Segregation of form, color, movement, and depth: Anatomy, physiology, and perception. *Science, 240,* 740–749.

LOCKE, J. (1974). *An essay concerning human understanding* (A. D. Woozley, Ed.). New York: New American Library. (Original work published 1706)

LODICO, M. G., GHATALA, E. S., LEVIN, J. R., PRESSLEY, M., & BELL, J. A. (1983). The effects of strategy-monitoring on children's selection of effective memory strategies. *Journal of Experimental Child Psychology, 35,* 263–277.

LOEHLIN, J. C., LINDZEY, G., & SPUHLER, J. N. (1975). *Race differences in intelligence.* San Francisco: W. H. Freeman.

LOFTUS, E. F. (1979). *Eyewitness testimony.* Cambridge, MA: Harvard University Press.

LOFTUS, E. F. (1992). When a lie becomes memory's truth: Memory distortion after exposure to misinformation. *Current Directions in Psychological Science, 1,* 121–123.

LOFTUS, E. F., & LOFTUS, G. R. (1980). On the permanence of stored information in the human brain. *American Psychologist, 35,* 409–420.

LOFTUS, E. F., MILLER, D. G., & BURNS, H. J. (1978). Semantic integration of verbal information into a visual memory. *Journal of Experimental Psychology: Human Learning and Memory, 4,* 19–31.

LOFTUS, E. F., & PALMER, J. C. (1974). Reconstruction of automobile destruction: An example of the interaction between language and memory. *Journal of Verbal Learning and Verbal Behavior, 13,* 585–589.

LONG, J. M., LYNCH, J. J., MACHIRAN, N. M., THOMAS, S. A., & MALINOW, K. L. (1982). The effect of status on blood pressure during verbal communications. *Journal of Behavioral Medicine, 5,* 165–172.

LoPRESTO, C. T., SHERMAN, M. F., & SHERMAN, N. C. (1985). The effects of a masturbation seminar on high school males' attitudes, false beliefs, guilt, and behavior. *Journal of Sex Research, 21,* 142–156.

LORANGER, A. W., OLDHAM, J. M., & TULIS, E. H. (1982). Familial transmission of DSM-III borderline personality disorder. *Archives of General Psychiatry, 39,* 795–799.

LORD, C. G., LEPPER, M. R., & MACKIE, D. (1984). Attitude prototypes as determinants of attitude-behavior consistency. *Journal of Personality and Social Psychology, 46,* 1254–1266.

LORD, C. G., ROSS, L., & LEPPER, M. (1979). Biased assimilation and attitude polarization: The effects of prior theories on subsequently considered evidence. *Journal of Personality and Social Psychology, 37,* 2098–2109.

LORENZ, K. (1957). The past twelve years in the comparative study of behavior. In C. H. Schiller (Ed.), *Instinctive behavior* (pp. 288–310). New York: International Universities Press. (Original work published 1952)

LORENZ, K. (1966). *On aggression.* New York: Harcourt, Brace & World.

LORENZ, K. (1974). *Civilized man's eight deadly sins.* New York: Harcourt Brace Jovanovich.

LOVAAS, O. I. (1987). Behavioral treatment and normal educational and intellectual functioning in young autistic children. *Journal of Consulting and Clinical Psychology, 55,* 3–9.

LOVAAS, O. I., & SIMMONS, J. Q. (1969). Manipulation of self-destruction in three retarded children. *Journal of Applied Behavior Analysis, 2,* 143–157.

LOWENSTEIN, L. F. (1991). Teacher stress leading to burnout: Its prevention and cure. *Education Today, 41,* 12–16.

LOWRY, D. T., LOVE, G., & KIRBY, M. (1981). Sex on the soap operas: Patterns of intimacy. *Journal of Communication, 31,* 90–96.

LUBIN, A. (1972). *Stranger on the earth: A psychological biography of Vincent Van Gogh.* New York: Holt, Rinehart & Winston.

LUBORSKY, L., MCLELLAN, T., WOODY, G. E., O'BRIEN, C. P., & AUERBACH, A. (1985). Therapist success and its determinants. *Archives of General Psychiatry, 42,* 602–611.

LUCHINS, A. S. (1942). Mechanization in problem solving. *Psychological Monographs, 54* (6, Whole No. 248).

LUH, C. W. (1922). The conditions of retention. *Psychological Monographs, 31* (Whole No. 142).

LUNDY, A. (1985). The reliability of the thematic apperception test. *Journal of Personality Assessment, 49,* 141–145.

LUPFER, M. B., CLARK, L. F., & HUTCHERSON, H. W. (1990). Impact of context on spontaneous trait and situational attributions. *Journal of Personality and Social Psychology, 58,* 239–249.

MACCOBY, E. E., & JACKLIN, C. N. (1974). *The psychology of sex differences.* Stanford, CA: Stanford University Press.

MACCOBY, E., & JACKLIN, C. N. (1987). Gender segregation in childhood. *Advances in Child Development and Behavior, 20,* 239–287.

MACKAY-SIM, A., SHAMAN, P., & MOULTON, D. (1982). Topographic coding of olfactory quality. Odorant-specific patterns of epithelial responsivity in the salamander. *Journal of Neurophysiology, 48,* 584–596.

MADDOX, G. L., BACK, K., & LIEDERMAN, V. (1968). Overweight as social deviance and disability. *Journal of Health and Social Behavior, 9,* 287–298.

MAEHR, M., & NICHOLLS, J. (1980). Culture and achievement motivation: A second look. In N. Warren (Ed.), *Studies in cross-cultural psychology* (Vol. 2, pp. 221–267). New York: Academic Press.

MAES, S., SPIELBERGER, C. D., DEFARES, P. B., & SARASON, I. G. (Eds.). (1988). *Topics in health psychology.* New York: Wiley.

MAFFEO, P. A., FORD, T. W., & LAVIN, P. F. (1990). Gender differences in depression in an employment setting. *Journal of Personality Assessment, 55,* 249–262.

MAIER, N. R. F. (1931). Reasoning in humans: II. The solution of a problem and its appearance in consciousness. *Journal of Comparative Psychology, 12,* 181–194.

MAIER, S. F., & SELIGMAN, M. E. P. (1976). Learned helplessness: Theory and evidence. *Journal of Experimental Psychology, 105,* 3–46.

MAIER, S. F., SELIGMAN, M. E. P., & SOLOMON, R. L. (1969). Pavlovian fear conditioning and learned helplessness: Effects on escape and avoidance behavior of (a) the CS-US contingency and (b) the independence of the US and voluntary responding. In B. Campbell & R. Church (Eds.), *Punishment and aversive behavior* (pp. 299–342). New York: Appleton.

MAIER, S. F., SHERMAN, J. E., LEWIS, J. W., TERMAN, G. W., & LIEBESKIND, J. C. (1983). The opioid/nonopioid nature of stress-induced analgesia and learned helplessness. *Journal of Experimental Psychology: Animal Behavior, 9,* 80–90.

MAILER, N. (1979). *The executioner's song.* Boston: Little, Brown.

MAIN, M., & GEORGE, C. (1985). Responses of abused and disadvantaged toddlers to distress in agemates: A study in the day care setting. *Developmental Psychology, 21,* 407–412.

MAIN, M., & SOLOMON, J. (1990). Procedures for identifying infants as disorganized/disoriented during the Ainsworth Strange Situation. In M. T. Greenberg, D. Cicchetti, & E. M. Cummings (Eds.), *Attachment in the preschool years: Theory, research, and intervention* (pp. 121–160). Chicago: University of Chicago Press.

MAJORS, R., & BILLSON, J. M. (1992). *Cool pose: The dilemmas of black manhood in America.* Lexington, MA: Lexington Books.

MALAMUTH, N. M. (1984). Aggression against women: Cultural and individual causes. In N. M. Malamuth and E. Donnerstein (Eds.), *Pornography and sexual aggression* (pp. 19–52). New York: Academic Press.

MALATESTA, C. Z., & HAVILAND, J. M. (1982). Learning display rules: The socialization of emotion expression in infancy. *Child Development, 53,* 991–1003.

MANN, J. (1973). *Time-dated psychotherapy.* Cambridge, MA: Harvard University Press.

MANN, J. J., & KAPUR, S. (1991). The emergence of suicidal ideation and behavior during antidepressant therapy. *Archives of General Psychiatry, 48,* 1027–1033.

MANN, L. (1981). The baiting crowd in episodes of threatened suicide. *Journal of Personality and Social Psychology, 41,* 703–709.

MANTELL, D. M. (1971). The potential for violence in Germany. *Journal of Social Issues, 27,* 101–112.

MARCEL, A. J. (1983). Conscious and unconscious perception: An approach to the relations between phenomenal experience and perceptual processes. *Cognitive Psychology, 15,* 238–300.

MARCIA, J. E. (1966). Development and validation of ego identity status. *Journal of Personality and Social Psychology, 3,* 551–558.

MARCIA, J. E. (1980). Identity in adolescence. In J. Adelson (Ed.), *Handbook of adolescent psychology* (pp. 159–187). New York: Wiley.

MARKUS, H. (1977). Self-schemata and processing information about the self. *Journal of Personality and Social Psychology, 51,* 443–450.

MARKUS, H. (1978). The effect of mere presence on social facilitation: An unobtrusive test. *Journal of Experimental Social Psychology, 14,* 389–397.

MARKUS, H. (1983). Self-knowledge: An expanded view. *Journal of Personality, 51,* 543–565.

MARKUS, H., HAMILL, R., & SENTIS, K. P. (1987). Thinking fat: Self-schemas for body weight and the processing of weight relevant information. *Journal of Applied Social Psychology, 17,* 50–71.

MARKUS, H., & KITAYAMA, S. (1991). Culture and the self: Implications for cognition, emotion and motivation. *Psychological Review, 98,* 224–253.

MARKUS, H., & NURIUS, P. (1986). Possible selves. *American Psychologist, 41,* 954–969.

MARKUS, H., & SENTIS, K. (1982). The self in social information processing. In J. Suls (Ed.), *Social psychological perspectives on the self* (pp. 41–70). Hillsdale, NJ: Erlbaum.

MARLATT, A. G., & ROHSENOW, D. J. (1981, December). The think-drink effect. *Psychology Today,* pp. 60–69, 93.

MARSHALL, G. D., & ZIMBARDO, P. G. (1979). Affective consequences of inadequately explained physiological arousal. *Journal of Personality and Social Psychology, 37,* 970–988.

MARSHALL, J. F., & TEITELBAUM, P. (1974). Further analysis of sensory inattention following lateral hypothalamic damage in rats. *Journal of Comparative and Physiological Psychology, 86,* 375–395.

MARTIN, C. L., & HALVERSON, C. F., JR. (1983). Gender constancy: A methodological and theoretical analysis. *Sex Roles, 9,* 775–790.

MARTIN, G., & PEAR, J. (1983). *Behavior modification.* Englewood Cliffs, NJ: Prentice-Hall.

MASLACH, C. (1979). Negative emotional biasing of unexplained arousal. *Journal of Personality and Social Psychology, 37,* 953–969.

MASLOW, A. H. (1943). A theory of motivation. *Psychological Review, 50,* 370–396.

MASLOW, A. H. (1954). *Motivation and personality.* New York: Harper & Row.

MASLOW, A. H. (1973). Theory of human motivation. In R. J. Lowry (Ed.), *Dominance, self-esteem, self-actualization: Germinal papers of A. H. Maslow.* Pacific Grove, CA: Brooks/Cole.

MASSACHUSETTS ADVOCACY CENTER (1987). *Out of the mainstream.* Boston: Author.

MASTERS, W. H., JOHNSON, V. E., & KOLODNY, R. C. (1988). *Human sexuality* (3rd ed.). Glenview, IL: Scott, Foresman.

MATSUMOTO, D. (1990). Cultural similarities and differences in display rules. *Motivation and Emotion, 14,* 195–214.

MATSUMOTO, D., KUDOH, T., SCHERER, K., & WALLBOTT, H. (1988). Antecedents of and reactions to emotions in the United States and Japan. *Journal of Cross-Cultural Psychology, 19,* 267–286.

MAYO, C., & LAFRANCE, M. (1978). On the acquisition of nonverbal communication: A review. *Merrill Palmer Quarterly, 24,* 213–228.

McARTHUR, L. A. (1972). The how and what of why: Some determinants and consequences of causal attribution. *Journal of Personality and Social Psychology, 22,* 171–193.

McCALL, R. B. (1979). *Infants.* Cambridge, MA: Harvard University Press.

McCALL, R. B., HOGARTY, P. S., & HURLBURT, N. (1972). Transitions in infant sensorimotor development and the prediction of childhood IQ;. *American Psychologist, 27,* 728–748.

McCANN, I. L., & HOLMES, D. S. (1984). Influence of aerobic exercise on depression. *Journal of Personality and Social Psychology, 46,* 1142–1147.

McCARLEY, R. W., SHENTON, M. E., O'DONNELL, B. F., FAUX, S. F., KIKINIS, R., NESTOR, P. G., & JOLESZ, F. A. (1993). Auditory P300 abnormalities and left posterior superior temporal gyrus volume reduction in schizophrenia. *Archives of General Psychiatry, 50,* 190–197.

McCAULEY, C. (1989). The nature of social influence in groupthink: Compliance and internalization. *Journal of Personality and Social Psychology, 57,* 250–260.

McCLELLAND, D. C. (1985a). The social mandate of health psychology. *American Behavioral Science, 28,* 451–467.

McCLELLAND, D. C. (1985b). *Human motivation.* Glenview, IL: Scott, Foresman.

McCLELLAND, D. C., ATKINSON, J. W., CLARK, R., & LOWELL, E. L. (1953). *The achievement motive.* New York: Appleton-Century-Crofts.

McCLOSKEY, M., WIBLE, C. G., & COHEN, N. J. (1988). Is there a special flashbulb-memory mechanism? *Journal of Experimental Psychology: General, 117,* 171–181.

McCORMICK, D. A., & THOMPSON, R. F. (1984). Cerebellum: Essential involvement in classically conditioned eyelid response. *Science, 223,* 296–298.

McCRAE, R. R., & COSTA, P. T., JR. (1984). *Emerging lives, enduring dispositions.* Boston: Little, Brown.

McCRAE, R. R., & COSTA, P. T., JR. (1990). *Personality in adulthood.* New York: Guilford.

McDAVID, J. W., & SISTRUNK, F. (1964). Personality correlates of two kinds of conformity behavior. *Journal of Personality, 32,* 421–435.

McDOUGALL, W. (1908). *Social psychology.* New York: Putnam.

McDOUGALL, W. (1932). *The energies of men.* London: Methuen.

McFARLAND, C., ROSS, M., & DECOURVILLE, N. (1989). Women's theories of menstruation and biases in recall of menstrual symptoms. *Journal of Personality and Social Psychology, 57,* 522–531.

McFARLANE, J., MARTIN, C. L., & WILLIAMS, T. M. (1988). Mood fluctuations: Women versus men and menstrual versus other cycles. *Psychology of Women Quarterly, 12,* 201–223.

McGHIE, A., & CHAPMAN, J. (1961). Disorders of attention and perception in early schizo-phrenia. *British Journal of Medical Psychology, 34,* 103–116.

McGUIRE, W. J., & McGUIRE, C. V. (1986). Differences in conceptualizing self versus conceptualizing other people as manifested in contrasting verb types used in natural speech. *Journal of Personality and Social Psychology, 51,* 1135–1143.

McKENNA, R. J. (1972). Some effects of anxiety level and food cues on the eating behavior of obese and normal subjects. *Journal of Personality and Social Psychology, 22,* 311–319.

McKENZIE-MOHR, D., & ZANNA, M. (1990). Treating women as sexual objects: Look to the (gender schematic) male who has viewed pornography. *Personality and Social Psychology Bulletin, 16,* 296–308.

McKILLIP, J., & REIDEL, S. L. (1983). External validity of matching on physical attractiveness for same

and opposite sex couples. *Journal of Applied Social Psychology, 13,* 328–337.

McKINNEY, M. E., HOFSCHIRE, P. J., BUELL, J. C., & ELIOT, R. S. (1984). Hemodynamic and biochemical responses to stress: The necessary link between Type A behavior and cardiovascular disease. *Behavioral Medicine Update, 6,* 16–21.

McKOON, G., RATCLIFFE, R., & DELL, G. S. (1986). A critical evaluation of the semantic-episodic distinction. *Journal of Experimental Psychology: Learning, Memory and Cognition, 12,* 295–306.

McLOYD, V. C. (1990). The impact of economic hardship on black families and children: Psychological distress, parenting, and socioemotional development. *Child Development, 61,* 311–346.

McNALLY, R. J., KASPI, S. P., RIEMANN, B. C., & ZEITLIN, S. B. (1990). Selective processing of threat cues in posttraumatic stress disorder. *Journal of Abnormal Psychology, 99,* 398–402.

McNEILL, D. (1966). Developmental psycholinguistics. In F. Smith & G. A. Miller (Eds.), *The genesis of language.* Cambridge, MA: MIT Press.

McTAVISH, D. G. (1971). Perceptions of old people: A review of research, methodologies and findings. *The Gerontologist, 11,* 90–101.

MEAD, M. (1935). *Sex and temperament.* New York: Morrow.

MEDNICK, S. A., BRENNAN, P., & KANDEL, E. (1988). Predisposition to violence. *Aggressive Behavior, 14,* 25–33.

MEECE, J. L., ECCLES-PARSON, J., KACZAIA, C. M., GOFF, S. B., & FUTTERMAN, R. (1982). Sex differences in math achievement: Toward a model of academic choice. *Psychological Bulletin, 91,* 324–448.

MEFFORD, I. N., BAKER, T. L., BOEHME, R., FOUTZ, A. S., CIARANELLO, R. D., BARCHAS, J. D., AND DEMENT, W. C. (1983). Narcolepsy: Biogenic amine deficits in an animal model. *Science, 220,* 629–632.

MELTZOFF, A. N., & MOORE, M. K. (1989). Imitation in newborn infants: Exploring the range of gestures imitated and the underlying mechanisms. *Developmental Psychology, 25,* 954–962.

MELZAK, R. (1973). *The puzzle of pain.* New York: Basic Books.

MELZAK, R., & WALL, P. D. (1983). *The challenge of pain.* New York: Basic Books.

MERCER, J. R. (1972). Anticipated achievement: Computerizing the self-fullfilling prophecy. Paper presented at the meeting of the American Psychological Association, Honolulu.

MERCER, J. R. (1979). In defense of racially and culturally non-discriminatory assessment. *School Psychology Digest, 8,* 89–115.

MERVIS, C. B., & ROSCH, E. (1981). Categorization of natural objects. *Annual Review of Psychology, 32,* 89–115.

MERZENICH, M. M., RECANZONE, G., JENKINS, W. M., ALLARD, T. T., & NUDO, R. J. (1988). Cortical representational plasticity. In P. Rakic & W. Singer (Eds.), *Neurobiology of the neocortex* (pp. 41–67). Dahlem, West Germany: S. Bernhard.

MESQUITA, B., & FRIJDA, N. H. (1992). Cultural variations in emotions: A review. *Psychological Bulletin, 112,* 179–204.

MEUDELL, P. (1983). The development and dissolution of memory. In A. Mayes (Ed.), *Memory in animals and humans* (pp. 83–133). Workingham, England: Van Nostrand Reinhold.

MEYER, A. S., & BOCK, K. (1992). The tip of the tongue phenomenon: Blocking or pretrial activation? *Memory and Cognition, 20,* 715–726.

MEYER, J. P., & MULHERIN, A. (1980). From attribution to helping: An analysis of the mediating effects of affect and expectancy. *Journal of Personality and Social Psychology, 39,* 201–210.

MEYER, P. (1970, Feb.). If Hitler asked you to electrocute a stranger, would you? *Esquire, 73,* pp. 72–73, 128, 130, 132.

MILES, L. E. M., RAYNAL, D. M., & WILSON, M. A. (1977). Blind man living in normal society has circadian rhythms of 24.9 hours. *Science, 198,* 421–423.

MILGRAM, S. (1963). Behavioral study of obedience. *Journal of Abnormal and Social Psychology, 67,* 371–378.

MILGRAM, S. (1965). Liberating effects of group pressure. *Journal of Personality and Social Psychology, 1,* 127–134.

MILGRAM, S. (1974). *Obedience to authority: An experimental view.* New York: Harper & Row.

MILLER, D. T. (1978). What constitutes a self-serving attributional bias? A reply to Bradley. *Journal of Personality and Social Psychology, 36,* 1211–1223.

MILLER, D. T., & ROSS, M. (1975). Self-serving biases in the attribution of causality: Fact or fiction? *Psychological Bulletin, 82,* 213–225.

MILLER, G. A. (1956). The magic number seven, plus or minus two: Some limits of our capacity for processing information. *Psychological Review, 63,* 81–97.

MILLER, G. A. (1981). *Language and speech.* New York: W. H. Freeman.

MILLER, G. A., & GILDEA, P. M. (1987, September). How children learn words. *Scientific American,* pp. 94–99.

MILLER, N. (1985). The value of behavioral research on animals. *American Psychologist, 40,* 423–440.

MILLER, W. C., & DeLONG, M. R. (1988). Parkinsonian symptomatology: An anatomical and physiological analysis. *Annals of the New York Academy of Sciences, 515,* 287–302.

MILNER, B. (1965). Memory disturbances after bilateral lesions. In P. Milner & S. Glickman (Eds.), *Cognitive processes and the brain* (pp. 104–105). Princeton, NJ: Van Nostrand.

MILNER, B., CORKIN, S., & TEUBER, H. L. (1968). Futher analysis of the hippocampal amnesic syndrome: 14-year follow-up study of H.M. *Neuropsychologica, 6,* 215–234.

MINEKA, S., & COOK, M. (1988). Social learning and the acquisition of snake fear in monkeys. In T. Zentall & B. Galef (Eds.), *Social learning: Psychological and biological perspectives* (pp. 51–73). Hillsdale, NJ: Erlbaum.

MINGAY, D. J. (1987). The effects of hypnosis on eyewitness memory: Reconciling forensic claims and research findings. *Applied Psychology: An International Review, 36,* 163–183.

MISCHEL, W. (1968). *Personality and assessment.* New York: Wiley.

MISHKIN, M. (1986, January 24). Two visual systems. Talk presented at the Western Psychiatric Institute and Clinic, Pittsburgh, PA.

MISHKIN, M., & APPENZELLER, T. (1987, June). The anatomy of memory. *Scientific American,* pp. 80–89.

MISHKIN, M., UNGERLEIDER, L. G., & MACKO, K. A. (1983). Object vision and spatial vision: Two central pathways. *Trends in Neuroscience, 6,* 414–417.

MITLER, M. M., BOYSEN, B. G., CAMPBELL, L., & DEMENT, W. C. (1974). Narcolepsycataplexy in a female dog. *Experimental Neurology, 45,* 322–340.

MITLER, M. M., GUILLEMINAULT, C., OREM, J., ZARCONE, V. P., & DEMENT, W. C. (1975). Sleeplessness, sleep attacks, and things that go wrong in the night. *Psychology Today,* pp. 45–50.

MOFFITT, T. E., CASPI, A., BELSKY, J., & SILVA, P. A. (1992). Childhood experience and the onset of menarche: A test of a sociobiological model. *Child Development, 63,* 47–58.

MONEY, J. (1987). Sin, sickness, or status? Homosexual gender identity and psychoneuroendocrinology. *American Psychologist, 42,* 384–399.

MONTAGU, A. (1976). *The nature of human aggression.* New York: Oxford University Press.

MONTEMAYOR, R. (1982). The relationship between parent-adolescent conflict and the amount of time adolescents spend alone and with parents and peers. *Child Development, 53,* 1512–1519.

MONTEMAYOR, R. (1983). Parents and adolescents in conflict. *Journal of Early Adolescence, 3,* 83–103.

MONTEMAYOR, R., & EISEN, M. (1977). The development of self-conceptions from childhood to adolescence. *Developmental Psychology, 13,* 314–319.

MORALES, A. (1982). The Mexican American gang member: Evaluation and treatment. In R. M. Becerra, M. Karno, & J. I. Escabear (Eds.), *Mental health and Hispanic Americans* (pp. 139–155). New York: Grune & Stratton.

MORAWSKI, J. G., & AGRONICK, G. (1991). A restive legacy. *Psychology of Women Quarterly, 15,* 567–579.

MORELAND, R. L., & ZAJONC, R. B. (1982). Exposure effects in person perception: Familiarity, similarity, and attraction. *Journal of Experimental Social Psychology, 18,* 395–415.

MORGAN, C. D., & MURRAY, H. A. (1935). A method for investigating fantasies: The Thematic Apperception Test. *Archives of Neurology and Psychiatry, 34,* 289–306.

MOROKOFF, P. J. (1986). Volunteer bias in the psychophysiological study of female sexuality. *Journal of Sex Research, 22,* 35–51.

MORRIS, R. G. M. (1981). Spatial localization does not require the presence of local cues. *Learning and Motivation, 12,* 239–260.

MORUZZI, G., & MAGOUN, H. W. (1949). Brain stem reticular formation and activation of the EEG. *Electroencephalography and Clinical Neurophysiology, 1,* 455–473.

MOSKOWITZ, A. B. (1978, Nov.). The acquisition of language. *Scientific American,* pp. 92–98, 103–108.

MOTLEY, M. T. (1987, February). What I meant to say. *Psychology Today,* pp. 24–28.

MOUNTCASTLE, V. B. (1978). An organizing principle for cerebral function: The unit module and the distributed system. In B. M. Edelman and V. B. Mountcastle (Eds.), *The mindful brain* (pp. 7–50). Cambridge, MA: MIT Press.

MOYER, K. E. (1974). Sex differences in aggression. In R. C. Friedman, R. M. Richart, & R. L. VandeWiele (Eds.), *Sex differences in behavior* (pp. 335–372). New York: Wiley.

MOYER, K. E. (1976). *The psychobiology of aggression.* New York: Harper & Row.

MUEHLENHARD, C. L., & HOLLABAUGH, L. C. (1988). Do women sometimes say no when they mean yes? The prevalence and correlates of women's token resistance to sex. *Journal of Personality and Social Psychology, 54,* 872–879.

MUEHLENHARD, C. L., & MCCOY, M. L. (1991). Double standard/double bind: The sexual double standard and women's communication about sex. *Psychology of Women Quarterly, 15,* 447–461.

MULLHOLLAND, T. M., PELLEGRINO, J. W., & GLASER, R. (1980). Components of geomet-ric analogy solution. *Cognitive Psychology, 12,* 252–284.

MURDOCK, B. B. (1962). The serial position effect in free recall. *Journal of Experimental Psychology, 64,* 484–488.

MURPHY, K. R., AND DAVIDSHOFER, C. O. (1988). *Psychological testing.* Englewood Cliffs, NJ: Prentice-Hall.

MURRAY, H. A. (1938). *Explorations in personality.* New York: Oxford University Press.

MUUSS, R. E. (1982). *Theories of adolescence* (4th ed.). New York: Random House.

MUUSS, R. E. (1986). Adolescent eating disorder: Bulimia. *Adolescence, 21,* 257–267.

MUUSS, R. E. (1990). Adolescent eating disorders: Anorexia nervosa and bulimia. In R. E. Muuss (Ed.), *Adolescent behavior and society* (4th ed.) (pp. 320–333). New York: McGraw-Hill.

MYERS, D. G., & BISHOP, G. D. (1970). Discussion effects on racial attitudes. *Science, 169,* 778–779.

NADEL, L., & WILLNER, J. (1980). Context and conditioning: A place for space. *Physiological Psychology, 8,* 218–228.

NASH, M. (1987). What, if anything, is regresed about hypnotic age regression? A review of the empirical literature. *Psychological Bulletin, 102,* 42–52.

NATHAN, S. (1981). Cross-cultural perspectives on penis envy. *Psychiatry, 44,* 39–44.

NATIONAL INSTITUTE OF HEALTH. (1985). Consensus Development Panel on the Health Implications of Obesity. *Annals of Internal Medicine, 103,* 1073–1077.

NATSOULAS, T. (1978). Consciousness. *American Psychologist, 33,* 435–450.

NATSOULAS, T. (1988). The intentionality of retroawareness. *Journal of Mind and Behavior, 9,* 549–574.

NAUMBURG, M. (1958). Art therapy: Its scope and function. In E. F. Hammer (Ed.), *Clinical applications of projective drawings.* Springfield, IL: Charles C Thomas.

NEIMARK, E. D. (1982). Adolescent thought: Transition to formal operations. In B. B. Wolman (Ed.), *Handbook of human development.* Englewood Cliffs, NJ: Prentice-Hall.

NEISSER, U., & WINOGRAD, E. (1988). *Remembering reconsidered—ecological and traditional approaches to the study of memory.* Cambridge: Cambridge University Press.

NELSON, K. (1973). Structure and strategy in learning to talk. *Monographs of the Society for Research in Child Development, 38* (Serial No. 149).

NELSON, K. (1988). The ontogeny of memory for real events. In U. Neisser & E. Winograd (Eds.), *Remembering reconsidered: Ecological and traditional approaches to the study of memory* (pp. 244–276). Cambridge: Cambridge University Press.

NELSON, R. J., SUR, M., FELLERMAN, D. J., & KAAS, J. H. (1980). Representations of the body surface in postcentral parietal cortex of macaca fasicularis. *Journal of Comparative Neurology, 192,* 611–643.

NEWCOMB, T. M. (1943). *Personality and social change.* New York: Dryden.

NEWCOMB, T. M. (1963). Persistence and regression of changed attitudes: A long range study. *Journal of Social Issues, 19,* 3–14.

NEWELL, A. (1990). *Unified theories of cognition.* Cambridge, MA: Harvard University Press.

NEWELL, A., & SIMON, H. A. (1972). *Human problem solving.* Englewood Cliffs, NJ: Prentice-Hall.

NICOL, S. E., & GOTTESMAN, I. I. (1983). Clues to the genetics and neurobiology of schizophrenia. *American Scientist, 71,* 398–404.

NISBETT, R. E. (1990). Evolutionary psychology, biology, and cultural evolution. *Motivation and Emotion, 14,* 255–263.

NISBETT, R. E., CAPUTO, C., LEGANT, P., & MARECK, J. (1973). Behavior as seen by the actor and as seen by the observer. *Journal of Personality and Social Psychology, 27,* 154–164.

NISBETT, R. E., & WILSON, T. D. (1977). Telling more than we can know: Verbal reports on mental processes. *Psychological Review, 84,* 231–259.

NOLEN-HOEKSEMA, S. (1987). Sex differences in unipolar depression: Evidence and theory. *Psychological Bulletin, 101,* 259–282.

NORCROSS, J. C., & PROCHASKA, J. O. (1982a). A national survey of clinical psychologists: Charac-

teristics and activities. *The Clinical Psychologist, 35(2),* 1, 5–8.

NORCROSS, J. C., & PROCHASKA, J. O. (1982b). A national survey of clinical psychologists: Affiliations and orientations. *The Clinical Psychologist, 35(3),* 1, 4–6.

NOVIN, D., & VANDERWEELE, D. A. (1977). Visceral involvement in feeding: There is more to regulation than the hypothalamus. In J. M. Sprague & A. N. Epstein (Eds.), *Progress in psychobiology and physiolgoical psychology* (Vol. 7, pp. 193–241). New York: Academic Press.

NUTT, D. J. (1989). Altered central alpha-2-adrenoceptor sensitivity in panic disorder. *Archives of General Psychiatry, 46,* 165–169.

NYITI, R. M. (1982). The validity of "cultural differences explanations" for cross-cultural variation in the rate of Piagetian cognitive development. In D. Wagner & H. Stevenson (Eds.), *Cultural perspectives on child development* (pp. 146–165). New York: W. H. Freeman.

O'CONNELL, M., COOPER, S., PERRY, J. C., & HOKE, L. (1989). The relationship between thought disorder and psychotic symptoms in borderline personality disorder. *Journal of Nervous and Mental Disorders, 177,* 273–278.

O'NEIL, C. W. (1965). A cross-cultural study of hunger and thirst motivation manifested in dreams. *Human Development, 8,* 181–193.

ODOM, S. L., & MCEVOY, M. A. (1988). Integration of young children with handicaps and normally developing children. In S. Odom & M. Karnes (Eds.), *Early intervention for infants and children with handicaps: An empirical base* (pp. 241–268). Baltimore: Paul H. Brookes.

OFFER, D. (1969). *The psychological world of the teenager.* New York: Basic Books.

OFFER, D., OSTROV, E., & HOWARD, K. I. (1981). The mental health professional's concept of the normal adolescent. *Archives of General Psychiatry, 38,* 149–152.

OGATA, S. N., SILK, K. R., GOODRICH, S., & LOHR, N. E. (1990). Childhood sexual and physical abuse in adult patients with borderline personality disorder. *American Journal of Psychiatry, 147,* 1008–1013.

OHBUCHI, K., & KAMBARA, T. (1985). Attacker's intent and awareness of outcome, impression management, and retaliation. *Journal of Experimental Social Psychology, 21,* 321–330.

OLDS, J. L., ANDERSON, M. L., MCPHIE, D. L., STATEN, L. D., & ALKON, D. L. (1989). Imaging of memory-specific changes in the distribution of protein kinase C in the hippocampus. *Science, 245,* 866–869.

OLDS, J. L., & MILNER, P. (1954). Positive reinforcement produced by electrical stimulation of septal area and other regions of the rat brain. *Journal of Comparative and Physiological Psychology, 47,* 419–427.

OLDS, M. E., & OLDS, J. L. (1963). Approach-avoidance analysis of rat diencephalon. *Journal of Comparative Neurology, 120,* 259–295.

OLTMANNS, T. F., NEALE, J. M., & DAVISON, G. C. (1986). *Case studies in abnormal psychology.* New York: Wiley.

OLTON, D. S. (1979). Mazes, maps, and memory. *American Psychologist, 34,* 583–596.

ORLINSKY, D. E., & HOWARD, K. I. (1986). Process and outcome in psychotherapy. In S. L. Garfield & A. E. Bergin (Eds.), *Handbook of psychotherapy and behavior change* (pp. 311–381). New York: Wiley.

ORLOFSKY, J. L., MARCIA, J. E., & LESSER, I. M. (1973). Ego identity status and the intimacy versus isolation crisis of young adulthood. *Journal of Personality and Social Psychology, 27,* 211–219.

ORNE, M. T. (1951). The mechanisms of hypnotic age regression: An experimental study. *Journal of Abnormal and Social Psychology, 46,* 213–225.

ORNE, M. T. (1979). The use and misuse of hypnosis in court. *International Journal of Clinical and Experimental Hypnosis, 27,* 311–341.

ORNE, M. T., DINGES, D. F., & ORNE, E. C. (1984). On the differential diagnosis of multiple personality in the forensic context. *The International Journal of Clinical and Experimental Hypnosis, 32,* 118–169.

OSKAMP, S. (1977). *Attitudes and opinions.* Englewood Cliffs, NJ: Prentice-Hall.

OSLER, W. (1892). *Lectures on angina pectoris and allied states.* New York: Appleton.

OSTERTAG, P. A., & McNAMARA, J. R. (1991). "Feminization" of psychology. *Psychology of Women Quarterly, 15,* 349–369.

OWENS, E. (1989). Present status of adults with cochlear implants. In E. Owens & D. K. Kessler (Eds.), *Cochlear implants in young deaf children* (pp. 25–52). Boston: Little, Brown.

PALLMEYER, T. P., BLANCHARD, E. B., & KOLB, L. C. (1986). The psychophysiology of combat-induced post-traumatic stress disorder in Vietnam veterans. *Behavioral Research Therapy, 24,* 645–652.

PALMORE, E. (1952). Published reactions to the Kinsey report. *Social Forces, 31,* 165–170.

PALUMBO, S. R. (1978). *Dreaming and memory: A new information processing model.* New York: Basic Books.

PARK, B. (1986). A method for studying the development of impressions of real people. *Journal of Personality and Social Psychology, 51,* 907–917.

PARK, B., & ROTHBART, M. (1982). Perception of out-group homogeneity and levels of social categorization: Memory for the subordinate attributes of in-group and out-group members. *Journal of Personality and Social Psychology, 42,* 1051–1068.

PARK, K. A., AND WATERS, E. (1989). Security of attachment and preschool friendships. *Child Development, 60,* 1076–1081.

PARKE, R. D. (1979). Perspectives on father-infant interaction. In J. D. Osofsky (Ed.), *Handbook of infant development* (pp. 549–590). New York: Wiley.

PARKE, R. D. (1981). *Fathers.* Cambridge, MA: Harvard University Press.

PARKER, E. S., BIRNBAUM, I. M., & NOBLE, E. P. (1976). Alcohol and memory: Storage and state dependency. *Journal of Verbal Learning and Verbal Behavior, 15,* 691–702.

PARKER, S. P. (1982). *Work and retirement.* Boston: George Allen & Unwin.

PATTERSON, G. R., LITTMAN, R. A., & BRICKER, W. (1967). Assertive behavior in children: A step toward a theory of aggression. *Monographs for the Society for Research in Child Development, 32* (Serial No. 113).

PATTISON, E. M. (1977). The dying experience—retrospective analysis. In E. M. Pattison (Ed.), *The experience of dying* (pp. 303–315). Englewood Cliffs, NJ: Prentice-Hall.

PAULHUS, D. (1983). Sphere-specific measures of perceived control. *Journal of Personality and Social Psychology, 44,* 1253–1265.

PAUNONEN, S. V. (1989). Consensus in personality judgments: Moderating effects of target-rater acquaintanceship and behavior observability. *Journal of Personality and Social Psychology, 56,* 823–833.

PAUNONEN, S. V. (1991). On the accuracy of ratings of personality by strangers. *Journal of Personality and Social Psychology, 58,* 471–477.

PAUNONEN, S. V., JACKSON, D. N., TZEBINSKI, J., & FORSTERLING, F. (1992). Personality structure across cultures: A multimethod evaluation.

Journal of Personality and Social Psychology, 62, 447–456.

PAVLOV, I. P. (1927). *Conditioned reflexes.* New York: Oxford University Press.

PEALE, N. V. (1952). *The power of positive thinking.* New York: Prentice-Hall.

PEARL, D., BOUTHILET, L., & LAZAR, J. (Eds.), (1982). Television and behavior: *Ten years of scientific progress and implications for the eighties: Vol. 2. Technical reviews.* Washington, DC: U.S. Government Printing Office.

PELLEGRINO, J. W. (1985). Inductive reasoning ability. In R. J. Sternberg (Ed.), *Human abilities: An information processing approach* (pp. 195–225). New York: W. H. Freeman.

PELLEGRINO, J. W. (1985, October). Anatomy of analogy. *Psychology Today,* pp. 49–54.

PENFIELD, W., & RASMUSSEN, T. (1950). *The cerebral cortex of man.* New York: Macmillan.

PERKY, C. W. (1910). An experimental study of imagination. *American Journal of Psychology, 21,* 422–52.

PERLBERG, M. (1979, April). Trauma at Tenerife: The psychic aftershocks of a jet disaster. *Human Behavior,* pp. 49–50.

PERLEY, M. J., & GUZE, S. B. (1962). Hysteria—the stability and usefulness of clinical criteria. *New England Journal of Medicine, 266,* 421–466.

PERLMUTTER, M. (1986). A life-span view of memory. In Baltes, P. B., Featherman, D. L., & Lerner, R. M. (Eds.), *Life-span development and behavior* (Vol. 7). Hillsdale, NJ: Erlbaum.

PERRY, B. D., SOUTHWICK, S. M., & GILLER, E. L. (1990). Adrenergic receptor regulation in posttraumatic stress disorder. In E. Giller (Ed.), *Biological assessment and treatment in P.T.S.D.* (pp. 89–114). Washington, DC: APA Press.

PERRY, W. G., JR. (1970). *Forms of intellectual and ethical development in the college years: A scheme.* New York: Holt, Rinehart & Winston.

PERRY, W. G., JR. (1981). Cognitive and ethical growth: The making of meaning. In A. W. Chickering (Ed.), *The modern American college: Responding to the new realities of diverse students and a changing society* (pp. 76–116). San Francisco: Jossey-Bass.

PETERSEN, A. C. (1987, September). Those gangly years. *Psychology Today,* pp. 28–34.

PETERSEN, A. C. (1988). Adolescent development. *Annual Review of Psychology, 39,* 583–607.

PETERSON, L. R., & PETERSON, M. J. (1959). Short-term retention of individual verbal items. *Journal of Experimental Psychology, 58,* 193–198.

PETRI, H. L. (1991). *Motivation.* Belmont, CA: Wadsworth.

PETTIGREW, T. F. (1979). The ultimate attribution error: Extending Allport's cognitive analysis of prejudice. *Personality and Social Psychology Bulletin, 5,* 461–476.

PETTY, R. E., & CACIOPPO, J. T. (1986). *Communication and persuasion: Central and peripheral routes to attitude change.* New York: Springer.

PETTY, R. E., CACIOPPO, J. T., & SCHUMANN, D. (1983). Central and peripheral routes to advertising effectiveness: *The moderating role of involvement. Journal of Consumer Research, 10,* 134–148.

PFAFFENBARGER, R. S., HYDE, R. T., WING, A. L., & HSIEH, C. (1986). Physical activity, all—cause mortality and longevity of college alumni. *New England Journal of Medicine, 314,* 605–613.

PFEFFENBAUM, A., ZIPURSKY, R. B., LIM, K. O., ZATZ, L. M., STAHL, S. M., & JERNIGAN, T. L. (1988). Computed tomographic evidence for generalized sulcal and ventricular enlargement in schizophrenia. *Archives of General Psychiatry, 45,* 633–640.

PFUNGST, O. (1911). *Clever Hans.* New York: Holt.

PHELPS, M. E., & MAZZIOTTA, J. C. (1985). Positron emission tomography: Human brain function and biochemistry. *Science, 228,* 799–809.

PHILLIPS, M. R., & WOLF, A. S. (1988). Psychiatry and the criminal justice system: Testing and myths. *American Journal of Psychiatry, 145,* 605–610.

PHILLIPS, S. (1982). Career exploration in adulthood. *Journal of Vocational Behavior, 20,* 129–140.

PIAGET, J. (1929). *The child's conception of the world.* New York: Harcourt Brace.

PIAGET, J. (1952). *The origins of intelligence in children* (M. Cook, Trans.). New York: International Universities Press. (Original work published 1936)

PIAGET, J. (1954). *The construction of reality in the child.* New York: Basic Books. (Original work published 1937)

PIAGET, J. (1962). *Judgement and reasoning in the child* (M. Warden, Trans.). London: Routledge and Paul. (Original work published 1928)

PIAGET, J. (1970). Piaget's theory. In P. H. Mussen (Ed.), *Carmichael's manual of child psychology* (Vol. 1, pp. 703–732). New York: Wiley.

PIAGET, J., & INHELDER, B. (1957). *The child's conception of space.* London: Routledge & Kegan Paul.

PICKERING, T. G., AND FRIEDMAN, R. (1991). The white coat effect: A neglected role for behavioral factors in hypertension. In P. McCabe, N. Schneiderman, T. Field, & J. Skyles (Eds.), *Stress, coping and disease* (pp. 35–49). Hillsdale, NJ: Erlbaum.

PIETROMONACO, P. R., MANIS, J., & MARKUS, H. (1987). The relationship of employment to self-perception and well-being in women: A cognitive analysis. *Sex Roles, 17,* 467–477.

PIFER, A., & BRONTE, L. (Eds.), (1986). *Our aging society: Paradox and promise.* New York: Norton.

PILIAVIN, I. M., RODIN, J., & PILIAVIN, J. A. (1969). Good Samaritanism: An underground phenomenon? *Journal of Personality and Social Psychology, 13,* 289–299.

PILIAVIN, J. A., EVANS, D. E., & CALLERO, P. (1982). Learning to "Give to unnamed strangers": The process of commitment to regular blood donation. In E. Staub, D. BarTal, J. Karylowski, & J. Reykawski (Eds.), *The development and maintenance of prosocial behavior: International perspectives.* New York: Plenum.

PINEL, J. P. J. (1993). *Biopsychology* (2nd ed.). Boston: Allyn & Bacon.

PIRSIG, R. (1974). *Zen and the art of motorcycle maintenance.* New York: Morrow.

PI-SUNYER, X., KISSILEFF, H. R., THORNTON, J., & SMITH, G. P. (1982). C-terminal occtapeptide of cholecystokinin decreases food intake in obese men. *Physiology & Behavior, 29,* 627–630.

PLUTCHIK, R. (1980, February). A language for the emotions. *Psychology Today,* pp. 68–78.

PLUTCHIK, R. (1984). Emotions: A general psychoevolutionary theory. In K. Scherer & P. Ekman (Eds.), *Approaches to emotion.* Hillsdale, NJ: Erlbaum.

POINCARÉ, J. H. (1913). Quoted in B. Russell, *Science and method* (G. B. Halsted, Trans.).

POPE, K. S. (1978). How gender, solitude, and posture influence the stream of consciousness. In K. S. Pope and J. L. Singer (Eds.), *The stream of consciousness* (pp. 259–269). New York: Plenum.

POSNER, M. I., & KEELE, S. W. (1967). Decay of visual information from a single letter. *Science, 158,* 137–139.

POWER, T. (1981). Sex typing in infancy: The role of the father. *Infant Mental Health Journal, 2,* 226–240.

POWERS, P. C., & GEEN, R. G. (1972). Effects of the behavior and perceived arousal of a model on instrumental aggression. *Journal of Personality and Social Psychology, 23,* 175–184.

PRATT, J. (Ed.) (1991). *The biological bases of drug tolerance and dependence.* New York: Academic Press.

PREMACK, D. (1959). Toward empirical behavior laws: Part 1. Positive reinforcement. *Psychological Review, 66,* 219–233.

PREMACK, D. (1962). Reversibility of the reinforcement relation. *Science, 136,* 235–237.

PRENTICE, D. A. (1990). Familiarity and differences in self-and-other representations. *Journal of Personality and Social Psychology, 59,* 369–383.

PRESSLEY, M. A., & LEVIN, J. R. (1977). Developmental differences in subjects' associative learning strategies and performance: Assessing a hypothesis. *Journal of Experimental Child Psychology, 24,* 431–439.

PRIEST, R. F., & SAWYER, J. (1967). Proximity and peership: Bases of balance in interpersonal attraction. *American Journal of Sociology, 72,* 633–649.

PUTNAM, F. W., GUROFF, J. J., SILBERMAN, E. K., BARBAN, L., & POST, R. M. (1986). The clinical phenomenology of multiple personality disorder: Review of 100 recent cases. *Journal of Clinical Psychiatry, 47,* 285–293.

RABKIN, J. G., & STREUNING, E. L. (1976). Life events, stress, and illness. *Science, 194,* 1013–1020.

RACHMAN, S., & WILSON, T. G. (1980). *The effects of psychological therapy.* New York: Pergamon Press.

RADKE-YARROW, M., ZAHN-WAXLER, C., & CHAPMAN, M. (1983). Children's pro-social dispositions and behavior. In P. Mussen (Ed.), *Carmichael's manual of child psychology* (4th ed.) (Vol. 4). New York: Wiley.

RAMIST, L. (1984). Predictive validity of the ATP tests. In. T. F. Donlon (Ed.), *The College Board technical handbook for the Scholastic Aptitude Test & Achievement Tests.* New York: College Entrance Examination Board.

RAPHAEL, B. (1976). *The thinking computer.* New York: W. H. Freeman.

RATCLIFFE, R., & MCKOON, G. (1986). More on the distinction between episodic and semantic memories. Journal of Experimental Psychology: *Learning, Memory and Cognition, 12,* 312–313.

RAVUSSIN, E., LILLIOJA, S., KNOWLER, W. C., CHRISTIN, L., FREYMOND, D., ABBOTT, W. G. H., BOYCE, V., HOWARD, B. V., & BOGARDUS, C. (1988). Reduced rate of energy expenditure as a risk factor for body-weight gain. *New England Journal of Medicine, 318,* 467–472.

RAY, O. (1978). *Drugs, society and human behavior* (2nd ed.). St. Louis, MO: C. V. Mosby.

RECHTSCHAFFEN, A., WOLPERT, E. A., DEMENT, W. C., MITCHELL, S. A., & FISHER, C. (1963). Nocturnal sleep of narcoleptics. *Electroencephalography and Clinical Neurophysiology, 15,* 599–609.

REEDY, M. N., BIRREN, J. E., & SCHAIE, K. W. (1981). Age and sex differences in satisfying love relationships across the adult life span. *Human Development, 24,* 52–66.

REIBER, A. (1985). The Penguin dictionary of psychology. New York: Penguin.

REID, E. C. (1910). Autopsychology of the manic-depressive. *Journal of Nervous and Mental Disorders, 37,* 606–620.

REINISCH, J. M. (1981). Prenatal exposure to synthetic progestins increases potential for aggression in humans. *Science, 211,* 1171–1173.

REINKE, B. J., HOLMES, D. S., & HARRIS, R. L. (1985). The timing of psychosocial changes in women's lives: The years 25 to 45. *Journal of Personality and Social Psychology, 48,* 1353–1364.

REIS, H. T., WILSON, I. M., MONESTERE, C., BERNSTEIN, S., CLARK, K., SEIDL, E., FRANCO, M., GIOSO, E., FREEMAN, L., & RADOANE, K. (1990). What is smiling is beautiful and good. *European Journal of Social Psychology, 20,* 259–267.

REISCHAUER, R. (1986, Fall). The prospects for welfare reform. *Public Welfare,* pp. 4–11.

REISENZEIN, R. (1983). The Schachter theory of emotion: Two decades later. *Psychological Bulletin, 94,* 239–264.

REISENZEIN, R. (1986). A structural equation analysis of Weiner's attribution-affect model of helping behavior. *Journal of Personality and Social Psychology, 50,* 1123–1133.

REISER, M. F., REEVES, R. B., AND ARMINGTON, J. (1958). Effects of variations in laboratory procedure and experimenter upon the ballistocardiogram, blood pressure and heart rate in healthy young men. *Psychosomatic Medicine, 17,* 185–199.

REISS, B. F. (1980). Psychological tests in homosexuality. In J. Marmor (Ed.), *Homosexual behavior* (pp. 296–311). New York: Basic Books.

REISSLAND, N. (1988). Neonatal imitation in the first hour of life: Observations in rural Nepal. *Developmental Psychology, 24,* 464–469.

REITMAN, J. S. (1976). Skilled perception in Go: Deducing memory structures from inter-response times. *Cognitive Psychology, 8,* 336–356.

RENZULLI, J. S. (1986). The three-ring conception of giftedness: A developmental model for creative productivity. In R. J. Sternberg & J. E. Davidson (Eds.), *Conceptions of giftedness* (pp. 53–92). Cambridge: Cambridge University Press.

REPETTI, R. L., MATTHEWS, K. A., & WALDRON, I. (1989). Employment and women's health: Effects of paid employment on women's mental and physical health. *American Psychologist, 44,* 1394–1401.

RESCORLA, R. A. (1966). Predictability and number of pairings in Pavlovian fear conditioning. *Psychonomic Science, 4,* 383–384.

RESCORLA, R. A. (1968). Probability of shock in the presence and absence of CS in fear conditioning. *Journal of Comparative and Physiological Psychology, 66,* 1–5.

RESCORLA, R. A. (1972). Informational variables in Pavlovian conditioning. In G. H. Bower (Ed.), *Psychology of learning and motivation* (Vol. 6, pp. 1–46). New York: Academic Press.

RESCORLA, R. A. (1981). Simultaneous associations. In P. Harzem & M. D. Zeiler (Eds.), *Predictability, correlation, and contiguity.* New York: Wiley.

RESCORLA, R. A. (1988). Pavlovian conditioning: It's not what you think it is. *American Psychologist, 43,* 151–159.

REST, J. R., & THOMA, S. J. (1985). Relation of moral judgment development to formal education. *Developmental Psychology, 21,* 709–714.

REZNICK, S. L., KAGAN, J., SNIDMAN, N., GERSTEN, M., BACK, K., & ROSENBERG, A. (1986). Inhibited and uninhibited children: A follow-up study. *Child Development, 57,* 660–680.

RHEINGOLD, H., & COOK, H. (1975). The contents of boys' and girls' rooms as an index of parents' behavior. *Child Development, 46,* 459–463.

RHYNE, D. (1981). Basis of marital satisfaction among men and women. *Journal of Marriage and the Family, 43,* 941–955.

RICKS, D. F. (1974). Supershrink: Methods of a therapist judged successful on the basis of adult outcomes of adolescent patients. In D. F. Ricks, M. Roff, & A. Thomas (Eds.), *Life history research in psychopathology* (Vol. 3, pp. 275–297). Minneapolis: University of Minnesota Press.

RILEY, V. (1975). Mouse mammary tumors: Alteration of incidence as an apparent function of stress. *Science, 189,* 465–468.

RILEY, V. (1981). Psychoneuroendocrine influences on immunocompetence and neoplasia. *Science, 212,* 1100–1109.

RINGELMANN, M. (1913). Recherches sur les moteurs animes: Travail de l'homme. *Annales de l'Institut National Agronomique, 2e serie, 12,* 1–40.

RIPS, L. J. (1983). Cognitive processes in propositional reasoning. *Psychological Review, 90,* 38–71.

RIPS, L. J., & MARCUS. S. L. (1977). Supposition and the analysis of conditional sentences. In M. A. Just & P. A. Carpenter (Eds.), *Cognitive processes in comprehension.* Hillsdale, NJ: Erlbaum.

RIST, R. C. (1970). Student social class and teacher expectations: The self-fullfulling prophecy in ghetto education. *Harvard Educational Review, 40,* 411–451.

RITVO, E. R., FREEMAN, B. J., PINGREE, C., MASON-BROTHERS, A., JORDE, L., JENSON, W. R., MCMAHON, W. M., PETERSON, P. B., MO, A., & RITVO, A. (1989). The UCLA-University of Utah epidemiologic survey of autism: Prevalence. *American Journal of Psychiatry, 146,* 194–199.

ROBBERSON, M. R., & ROGERS, R. W. (1988). Beyond fear appeals: Negative and positive persuasive appeals to health and self-esteem. *Journal of Applied Social Psychology, 18,* 277–287.

ROBERTS, J. M., & ROWLAND, N. E. (1981). Hypertension in adults 25–74 years of age: United States, 1971–1975. Vital and Health Statistics, series 11, no. 221 (DHHS Publication No. PHS 81-1671). Washington, DC: U.S. Government Printing Office.

ROBINS, C. J. (1988). Attributions and depression: Why is the literature so inconsistent? *Journal of Personality and Social Psychology, 54,* 880–889.

ROBINS, L. N., HELZER, J. E., WEISSMAN, M. M., ORVASCHEL, H., GRUENBERG, E., BURKE, J. D., & REGIER, D. A. (1984). Lifetime prevalence of specific psychiatric disorders in three sites. *Archives of General Psychiatry, 41,* 949–958.

ROBINS, L. N., & REGIER, D. A. (Eds.). (1991). *Psychiatric disorders in America.* New York: Free Press.

ROBINSON, F. P. (1970). *Effective study.* New York: Harper & Row.

ROBINSON, N. M., & ROBINSON, H. B. (1976). *The mentally retarded child* (2nd ed.). New York: McGraw-Hill.

RODIN, J. (1981). Current status of the internal-external hypothesis for obesity. *American Psychologist, 36,* 361–372.

RODIN, J. (1982). Obesity: Why the losing battle? In B. B. Wolman (Ed.), *Psychological aspects of obesity* (pp. 30–87). New York: Van Nostrand Reinhold.

RODIN, J. (1985). Insulin levels, hunger and food intake: An example of feedback loops in body weight regulation. *Health Psychology, 4,* 1–18.

RODIN, J., SILBERSTEIN, L., & STRIEGEL-MOORE, R. (1984). Women and weight: A normative discontent. In T. B. Sonderegger (Ed.), *Nebraska Symposium on Motivation* (pp. 267–307). Lincoln: University of Nebraska Press.

RODIN, M. J. (1987). Who is memorable to whom: A study of cognitive disregard. *Social Cognition, 5,* 144–165.

RODNICK, E. H., GOLDSTEIN, M. J., LEWIS, J. M., & DOANE, J. A. (1984). Parental communication style, affect, and role as precursors of offspring schizophrenia-spectrum disorders. In F. Watt, E. J. Anthony, L. C. Wynn, & J. E. Rolf (Eds.), *Children at risk for schizophrenia: A longitudinal perspective* (pp. 81–92). Cambridge: Cambridge University Press.

ROEDER, K. (1963). *Nerve cells and insect behavior.* Cambridge, MA: Harvard University Press.

ROEDER, K. D., & TREAT, A. E. (1961). The detection and evasion of bats by moths. *American Scientist, 49,* 135–148.

ROGERS, C. R. (1951). *Client-centered therapy: Its current practice, implications and theory.* Boston: Houghton Mifflin.

ROGERS, C. R. (1959). A theory of therapy, personality, and interpersonal relationships, as developed in the client-centered framework. In S. Koch (Ed.), *Psychology: A study of a science* (Vol. 3, pp. 184–256). New York: McGraw-Hill.

ROGERS, C. R. (1961a). A tentative scale for the measurement of process in psychotherapies. In M. P. Stein (Ed.), *Contemporary psychotherapies* (pp. 113–127). New York: Free Press.

ROGERS, C. R. (1961b). *On becoming a person: A therapist's view of psychotherapy.* Boston: Houghton Mifflin.

ROGERS, C. R. (1964). Toward a sense of the person. In T. W. Wann (Ed.), *Behaviorism and phenomenology* (pp. 109–133). Chicago: University of Chicago Press.

ROGERS, C. R. (1966). Client-centered therapy. In S. Arieti (Ed.), *American handbook of psychiatry* (Vol. 3, pp. 183–200). New York: Basic Books.

ROGERS, C. R. (1980). *A way of being.* Boston: Houghton Mifflin.

ROGERS, C. R., & SANFORD, R. C. (1985). Client centered therapy. In H. I. Kaplan & B. J. Sadock (Eds.), *Comprehensive textbook of psychiatry* (4th ed.) (pp. 1374–1388). Baltimore: Williams & Wilkins.

ROGERS, R. W. (1983). Cognitive and physiological processes in fear appears and attitude change: A revised theory of protection motivation. In J. Cacioppo & R. Petty (Eds.), *Social psychophysiology.* New York: Guilford.

ROGERS, R. W., & PRENTICE-DUNN, S. (1981). Deindividuation and anger-mediated interracial aggression: Unmasking regressive racism. *Journal of Personality and Social Psychology, 41,* 63–73.

ROLAND, P. E. (1984). Metabolic measurements of the working frontal cortex in man. *Trends in Neuroscience, 7,* 430–435.

ROLAND, P. E., & FRIBERG, L. (1985). Localization of cortical areas activated by thinking. *Journal of Neurophysiology, 53,* 1219–1243.

RORSCHACH, H. (1921). *Psychodiagnostik.* Bern, Switzerland: Bircher.

ROSCH, E. (1973). On the internal structure of perceptual and semantic categories. In T. E. Moore (Ed.), *Cognitive development and the acquisition of language.* New York: Academic Press.

ROSCH, E. (1975). Cognitive representations of semantic categories. *Journal of Experimental Psychology: General, 3,* 192–233.

ROSCH, E. (1977). Classification of real-world objects: Origins and representation in cognition. In P. N. Johnson-Laird & P. C. Wason (Eds.), *Thinking: Readings in cognitive science* (pp. 212–222). Cambridge: Cambridge University Press.

ROSCH, E., & MERVIS, C. B. (1975). Family resemblances: Studies in the internal structure of categories. *Cognitive Psychology, 7,* 573–605.

ROSE, J. E., BRUGGE, J. F., ANDERSON, D. J., & HIND, J. E. (1967). Phase locked response to low frequency tones in single auditory nerve fibers of the squirrel monkey. *Journal of Neurophysiology, 30,* 769–793.

ROSEN, D. H. (1974). *Lesbianism: A study of female homosexuality.* Springfield, IL: Charles C Thomas.

ROSENHAN, D. L., SALOVEY, P., & HARGIS, K. (1981). The joys of helping: Focus of attention mediates the impact of positive affect on altruism. *Journal of Personality and Social Psychology, 40,* 899–905.

ROSENHAN, D. L., & SELIGMAN, M. E. P. (1989). *Abnormal psychology.* New York: W. W. Norton.

ROSENMAN, R. H. (1978). The interview method of assessment of the coronary-prone behavior pattern. In T. M. Dembroski, S. Weiss, J. Shields, S. G. Haynes, & M. Feinleib (Eds.), *Coronary-prone behavior* (pp. 55–69). New York: Springer.

ROSENMAN, R. H., SWAN, G. E., & CARMELLI, D. (1988). Definition, assessment, and evolution of the Type A behavior pattern. In B. K. Houston and C. R. Snyder (Eds.), *Type A behavior: Research, theory, and intervention* (pp. 8–31). New York: Wiley.

ROSENTHAL, R. (1966). Experimenter effects in behavioral research. New York: Appleton-Century-Crofts.

ROSENZWEIG, M. R. (1984). Experience, memory and the brain. *American Psychologist, 39,* 365–376.

ROSENZWEIG, M. R. (1986). Interrelationships between experimental and physiological psychology in the study of memory. In F. Klix & H. Hagendorg (Eds.), *Human memory and cognitive capabilities, Part B* (pp. 559–578). Amsterdam: Elsevier.

ROSENZWEIG, M. R., & BENNETT, E. L. (1984). Basic processes and modulatory influences in the stages of memory formation. In G. Lynch, J. L. McGaugh, & N. M. Weinberger (Eds.), *Neurobiology of learning and memory* (pp. 263–288). New York: Guilford.

ROSENZWEIG, M. R., BENNETT, E. L., & DIAMOND, M. C. (1972, February). Brain changes in response to experience. *Scientific American,* pp. 22–29.

ROSNER, M., & BELKIN, M. (1987). Intelligence, education and myopia in males. *Archives of Ophthalmology, 105,* 1508–1511.

ROSS, C. A., NORTON, G. R., & WOZNEY, K. (1989). Multiple personality disorder: An analysis of 236 cases. *Canadian Journal of Psychiatry, 34,* 413–418.

ROSS, E. D., & MESULAM, M. M. (1979). Dominant language functions of the right hemisphere? Prosody and emotional gesturing. *Archives of Neurology, 36,* 144–148.

ROSS, L. (1977). The intuitive psychologist and his shortcomings: Distortions in the attribution process. In L. Berkowitz (Ed.), *Advances in experimental social psychology* (Vol. 10, pp. 174–221). New York: Academic Press.

ROSS, S. M., & ROSS, L. E. (1971). Comparison of trace and delay classical conditioning as a function of interstimulus interval. *Journal of Experimental Psychology, 91,* 165–167.

ROSSI, P. H. (1990). The old homeless and the new homelessness in historical perspective. *American Psychologist, 45,* 954–959.

ROTTER, J. B. (1966). Generalized expectancies for internal versus external control of reinforcement. *Psychological Monographs, 80,* (1, Whole No. 609).

ROTTON, J., & FREY, J. (1985). Air pollution, weather, and violent crimes: Concomitant time-series analysis of archival data. *Journal of Personality and Social Psychology, 49,* 1207–1220.

ROVEE-COLLIER, C., GREISLER, P. C., & EARLEY, L. A. (1985). Contextual determinants of retrieval in three-month-old infants. *Learning and motivation, 16,* 139–157.

RUBIN, J. Z., PROVENZANO, F. J., & LURIA, Z. (1974). The eye of the beholder: Parents' views on sex of newborns. *American Journal of Orthopsychiatry, 44,* 512–519.

RUBIN, V., & COMITAS, L. (1976). *Ganja in Jamaica: The effects of marijuana use.* Garden City, NY: Anchor/Doubleday.

RUMBACK, R. B., & CARR, T. S. (1984). Schema guided information search in stereotyping the elderly. *Journal of Applied Social Psychology, 14,* 57–68.

RUNDUS, D. (1971). Analysis of rehearsal processes in free recall. *Journal of Experimental Psychology, 89,* 63–77.

RUNYAN, W. M. (1981). Why did Van Gogh cut off his ear? The problem of alternative explanations in psychobiography. *Journal of Personality and Social Psychology, 40,* 1070–1077.

RUNYAN, W. M. (1982). *Life histories and psychobiography: Explorations in theory and method.* New York: Oxford University Press.

RUSAK, B., & GROOS, G. (1982). Suprachiasmatic stimulation phase shifts rodent circadian rhythms. *Science, 215,* 1407–1409.

RUSAK, B., & ZUCKER, I. (1979). Neural regulation of circadian rhythms. *Physiological Reviews, 59,* 449–526.

RUSHTON, J. P. (1989). Genetic similarity, human altruism, and group selection. *Behavioral and Brain Sciences, 12,* 503–559.

RUSHTON, J. P. (1991). Is altruism innate? *Psychological Inquiry, 2,* 141–143.

RUSHTON, J. P., FULKER, D. W., NEALE, M. C., NIAS, D., K. B., & EYSENCK, H. J. (1986). Altruism and aggression: The heritability of individual differences. *Journal of Personality and Social Psychology, 50,* 1192–1198.

RUSSELL, D. E. H. (1984). *Sexual exploitation: Rape, child sexual abuse, and workplace harassment.* Beverly Hills, CA: Sage.

RUSSO, N. F., & DENMARK, F. L. (1987). Contributions of women to psychology. *Annual Review of Psychology, 38,* 279–298.

RUTKOWSKI, G. K., GRUDER, C. L., & ROMER, D. (1983). Group cohesiveness, social norms, and bystander intervention. *Journal of Personality and Social Psychology, 44,* 545–552.

RUTTER, M., GRAHAM, P., CHADWICK, O. F. D., & YULE, W. (1976). Adolescent turmoil: Fact or fiction? *Journal of Child Psychology and Psychiatry, 17,* 35–56.

SAARNI, C. (1989). Children's understanding of strategic control of emotional expression in social transactions. In C. Saarni & P. L. Harris (Eds.), *Children's understanding of emotion.* Cambridge: Cambridge University Press.

SAARNI, C. (1990). Emotional competence: How emotions and relationships become integrated. In R. A. Thompson (Ed.), *Nebraska Symposium on Motivation.* Lincoln: University of Nebraska Press.

SACHS, J. (1987). Young children's language use in pretend play. In S. U. Philips, S. Steele, & C. Tanz (Eds.) *Language, gender, and sex in comparative perspective.* Cambridge: Cambridge University Press.

SACHS, J. S. (1967). Recognition memory for syntactic and semantic aspects of connected discourse. *Perception and Psychophysics, 2,* 437–442.

SACKEIM, H. A. (1985, June). The case for ECT. *Psychology Today,* pp. 36–40.

SACKEIM, H. A., DECINA, P., KANZLER, M., KERR, B., & MALITZ, S. (1987). ECT. In S. Malitz & H. A. Sackheim (Eds.), *American Journal of Psychiatry, 144,* 1449–1455.

SACKS, O. (1984, February 16). The lost mariner. *The New York Review,* pp. 14–19.

SACKS, O. (1987). *The man who mistook his wife for a hat.* New York: Harper & Row.

SADKER, M., & SADKER, D. (1985, March). Sexism in the schoolroom of the '80s. *Psychology Today,* pp. 54–55, 57.

SAGY, S. (1990). Explaining life satisfaction in later life: The sense of coherence and activity theory. *Behavior, Health, & Aging, 1,* 11–25.

SALE, K. (1990). *The conquest of paradise.* New York: Plume.

SALTZMAN, A. (1991, June 17). Trouble at the top. *U.S. News and World Report,* pp. 40–48.

SAMMONS, M. T., & GRAVITZ, M. A. (1990). Theoretical orientations of professional psychologists and their former professors. *Professional Psychology: Research and Practice, 21,* 131–134.

SAMOVAR, L. A., & PORTER, R. E. (1991). *Communication between cultures.* Belmont, CA: Wadsworth.

SANDOVAL, J. (1979). The WISC-R and interval evidence of test bias with minority groups. *Journal of Consulting and Clinical Psychology, 47,* 919–927.

SANFORD, E. C. (1991). A sketch of a beginner's course in psychology. *Journal of Genetic Psychology, 152,* 430–436. (Original work published 1906)

SANNA, L. J., & SHOTLAND, R. L. (199). Valence of anticipated evaluation and social facilitation. *Journal of Experimental Social Psychology, 26,* 82–92.

SAPIRSTEIN, M. R. (1955). *Paradoxes of everyday life.* New York: Random House.

SARAFINO, E. P. (1990). *Health psychology: Biopsychosocial interactions.* New York: Wiley.

SATTLER, J. M. (1988). *Assessment of children* (3rd ed.). San Diego: Author.

SCARR, S. (1981). Testing for children. *American Psychologist, 36,* 1159–1166.

SCARR, S. (1992). Developmental theories for the 1990s: Development and individual differences. *Child Development, 63,* 1–19.

SCARR, S., & CARTER-SALTZMAN, L. C. (1982). Genetics and intelligence. In R. J. Sternberg (Ed.), *Handbook of human intelligence.* Cambridge: Cambridge University Press.

SCARR, S., & McCARTNEY, K. (1983). How people make their own environments. *Child Development, 54,* 425–435.

SCARR, S., & WEINBERG, R. A. (1976). IQ test performance of black children adopted by white families. *American Psychologist, 31,* 726–739.

SCARR, S., & WEINBERG, R. A. (1983). The Minnesota adoption studies. *Child Development, 54,* 260–267.

SCHACHTER, D. L., HARBLUK, J. L., & McLACHLAN, D. R. (1984). Retrieval without recollection: An experimental analysis of source amnesia. *Journal of Verbal Learning and Verbal Behavior, 23,* 593–611.

SCHACHTER, J., KERR, L. L., WIMBERLY, F. C., & LACHIN, J. M. (1974). Heart rate levels of black and white newborns. *Psychosomatic Medicine, 36,* 513–524.

SCHACHTER, S. (1971). Some extraordinary facts about obese humans and rats. *American Psychologist, 26,* 129–144.

SCHACHTER, S., & SINGER, J. E. (1962). Cognitive, social and physiological determinants of emotional state. *Psychological Review, 69,* 379–399.

SCHAFFER, H. R. (1979). Acquiring the concept of the dialogue. In M. H. Bornstein & W. Kessen (Eds.), *Psychological development from infancy: Image to intention* (pp. 279–305). Hillsdale, NJ: Erlbaum.

SCHAIE, K. W. (1977). Quasi-experimental designs in the psychology of aging. In J. E. Birren & K. W. Schaie (Eds.), *Handbook of the psychology of aging.* New York: Van Nostrand Reinhold.

SCHAIE, K. W. (1981). Psychological changes from midlife to early old age: Implications for the maintenance of mental health. *Journal of Orthopsychiatry, 51,* 199–218.

SCHANK, R. C., & ABELSON, R. (1977). *Scripts, plans, goals, and understanding.* Hillsdale, NJ: Erlbaum.

SCHEIER, M. F., MAGOVERN, G. J., ABBOTT, R. A., MATTHEWS, K. A., OWENS, J . F., LEFEBRE, R. C., & CARVER, C. S. (1989). Dispositional optimism and recovery from coronary artery bypass surgery: The beneficial effects on physical and psychological well-being. *Journal of Personality and Social Psychology, 57,* 1024–1040.

SCHIEDEL, D. G., & MARCIA, J. E. (1985). Ego identity, intimacy, sex role orientation, and gender. *Developmental Psychology, 21,* 149–160.

SCHIFF, M., DUYME, M., DUMARET, A., STEWART, J., TOMKIEWICZ, S., & FEINGOLD, J. (1978). Intellectual status of working-class children adopted early into upper-middle-class families. *Science, 200,* 1503–1504.

SCHILDKRAUT, J. J., GREEN, A. I., & MOONEY, J. J. (1985). Affective disorders: Biochemical aspects. In H. I. Kaplan & B. J. Sadock (Eds.), *Comprehensive textbook of psychiatry: V.* Baltimore: Williams & Wilkins.

SCHMIDT. (1983, July 12). Gifted retardates: The search for clues to mysterious talent. *New York Times.*

SCHMIDT, F. L., BERNER, J. G., & HUNTER, J. E. (1973). Racial differences in validity of employment tests: Reality or illusion? *Journal of Applied Psychology, 58,* 5–9.

SCHMIDT, S. R., & BOHANNON, J. N. (1988). In defense of the flashbulb-memory hypothesis: A comment on McClosky, Wible and Cohen. *Journal of Experimental Psychology: General, 117,* 332–334.

SCHMITT, B. H., GILOVICH, T., GOORE, N., & JOSEPH, L. (1986). Mere exposure and social facilitation: One more time. *Journal of Experimental Social Psychology, 22,* 242–248.

SCHNEIDER, W., & PRESSLEY, M. (1989). *Memory development between 2 and 20.* New York: Springer.

SCHROEDER, D. H., & COSTA, P. T., JR. (1984). Influence of life event stress on physical illness: Substantive effects or methodological flaws? *Journal of Personality and Social Psychology, 46,* 853–863.

SCHUTTE, N. S., MALOUFF, J. M., POST-GORDEN, J. C., & RODASTA, A. L. (1988). Effects of playing videogames on children's aggressive and other behaviors. *Journal of Applied Social Psychology, 18,* 456–460.

SCHWARTZ, D. M., THOMPSON, M. G., & JOHNSON, C. L. (1985). Anorexia nervosa and bulimia: The sociocultural context. In S. W. Emmett (Ed.), *Theory and treatment of anorexia nervosa and bulimia.* (pp. 95–112). New York: Brunner/Mazel.

SCHWARTZ, W. J., & GAINER, H. (1977). Suprachiasmatic nucleus: Use of 14C-labeled deoxyglucose uptake as a functional marker. *Science, 197,* 1089–1091.

SCHWARZER, R. (Ed.). (1992). *Self efficacy: Thought control of action.* Washington, DC: Hemisphere.

SCOTT, J. A. (1962). Intelligence, physique, and family size. *British Journal of Prevention, Society of Medicine, 16,* 165.

SCOVILLE, W. B. & MILNER, B. (1957). Loss of recent memory after bilateral hippocampal lesions. *Journal of Neurology, Neurosurgery and Psychiatry, 20,* 11–21.

SCRIBNER, S. (1977). Modes of thinking and ways of speaking: culture and logic reconsidered. In Johnson-Laird, P. N., & Wason, P. C. (Eds.), *Thinking: Readings in cognitive science* (pp. 483–500). Cambridge: Cambridge University Press.

SEARS, R. R., MACCOBY, E. E., & LEVIN, H. (1951). Patterns of child-rearing. Evanston, IL: Row, Peterson.

SEGAL, M. W. (1974). Alphabet and attraction: An unobtrusive measure of the effect of propinquity in a field study. *Journal of Personality and Social Psychology, 30,* 654–657.

SELFE, L. (1978). *Nadia: A case of extraordinary drawing ability in an autistic child.* New York: Academic Press.

SELIGMAN, M. E. P. (1970). On the generality of the laws of learning. *Psychological Review, 77,* 406–418.

SELIGMAN, M. E. P., ABRAMSON, L. Y., SEMMEL, A., & VON BAEYER, C. (1979). Depressive attributional style. *Journal of Abnormal Psychology, 88,* 242–247.

SELIGMAN, M. E. P., & YELLEN, A. (1987). What is a dream? *Behavior Research and Therapy, 25,* 1–24.

SELYE, H. (1956). *The stress of life.* New York: McGraw-Hill.

SELYE, H. (1978). *The stress of life* (rev. ed.). New York: McGraw-Hill.

SEM-JACOBSEN, C. W. (1968). *Depth-electrographic stimulation of the human brain and behavior.* Springfield, IL: Charles C Thomas.

SERBIN, L. A., & O'LEARY, K. D. (1975, December). How nursery schools teach girls to shut up. *Psychology Today,* pp. 57–58, 102–103.

SERBIN, L. A., O'LEARY, K. D., KENT, R. N., & TRONICK, J. J. (1973). A comparison of teacher response to the preacademic and problem behavior of boys and girls. *Child Development, 44,* 796–804.

SHAFFER, D. R. (1989). *Developmental pyschology: Childhood and adolescence.* Pacific Grove, CA: Brooks/Cole.

SHAH, S., & McGARRY, A. (1986). Legal psychiatry and psychology: Review of programs, training and qualifications. In W. Curran, A. McGarry, & S. Shah (Eds.), *Forensic psychiatry and psychology* (pp. 7–42). Philadelphia: Davis.

SHANAB, M. E., & YAHYA, K. A. (1977). A behavioral study of obedience in children. *Journal of Personality and Social Psychology, 35,* 530–536.

SHAPIRO, C. M., BORTZ, R., MITCHELL, D., BARTEL, P., & JOOSTE, P. (1981). Slow wave sleep: A recovery period after exercise. *Science, 214,* 1253–1254.

SHAVITT, S. (1990). The role of attitude objects in attitude functions. *Journal of Experimental Social Psychology, 26,* 124–148.

SHEA, S. L., FOX, R., ASLIN, R., & DUMAIS, S. T. (1980). Assessment of stereopsis in human infants. *Investigative Ophthalmology and Visual Science, 19,* 1400–1404.

SHEAN, G. (1978). *Schizophrenia: An introduction to research and theory.* Cambridge, MA: Winthrop.

SHEEHAN, S. (1982). *Is there no place on earth for me?* Boston: Houghton Mifflin.

SHEPARD, R. N., & METZLER, J. (1971). Mental rotation of three-dimensional objects. *Science, 171,* 701–703.

SHEPPERD, J. A. (1993). Productivity loss in performance groups: A motivation analysis. *Psychological Bulletin, 113,* 67–81.

SHEPPERD, J. A., & ARKIN, R. M. (1989). Self-handicapping: The moderating roles of public self-consciousness and task importance. *Personality and Social Psychology Bulletin, 15,* 252–265.

SHERIDAN, C. L., & RADMACHER, S. A. (1992). *Health psychology: Challenging the biomedical model.* New York: Wiley.

SHERIF, M., HARVEY, O. J., WHITE, B. J., HOOD, W. E., & SHERIF, C. W. (1961). *Intergroup conflict and cooperation: The Robber's Cave experiment.* Norman, OK: University of Oklahoma Book Exchange.

SHERMAN, J. A. (1982). Mathematics, the critical filter: A look at some residues. *Psychology of Women Quarterly, 6,* 428–444.

SHERMAN, S. J. (1980). On the self-erasing nature of errors of prediction. *Journal of Personality and Social Psychology, 39,* 211–221.

SHIELDS, P. J., & ROVEE-COLLIER, C. (1992). Long-term memory for context-specific category information at six months. *Child Development, 63,* 245–259.

SHIELDS, S. A. (1975). Functionalism, Darwinism, and the psychology of women. *American Psychologist, 30,* 739–755.

SHIRLEY, M. M. (1933). *The first two years.* Minneapolis: University of Minnesota Press.

SHORE, M. F., & COHEN, M. D. (1992). Homelessness and the chronically mentally ill. In M. J. Robertson & M. Greenblatt (Eds.), *Homelessness: A national perspective.* New York: Plenum.

SHORTLIFFE, E. H. (1976). *Computer-based medical consultations, MYCIN.* New York: Elsevier.

SHUTTS, D. (1982). *Lobotomy: Resort to the knife.* New York: Van Nostrand Reinhold.

SIEBER, J. E. (1982). Deception in social research: I. Kinds of deception and the wrongs they may involve. *IRB: A Review of Human Subjects Research, 4,* 1–6.

SIEGEL, S. (1984). Pavlovial conditioning and heroin overdose: Reports by overdose victims. *Bulletin of the Psychonomic Society, 22,* 428–430.

SIEGEL, S. (1986). Morphine tolerance acquisition as an associative process. In N. A. Marlin (Ed.), *Directed readings for the principles of learning and behavior* (2nd ed.) (pp. 53–65). Pacific Grove, CA: Brooks/Cole.

SIEGEL, S., HINSON, R. E., KRANK, M. D., & McCULLY, J. (1982). Heroin "overdose" death: Contribution of drug-associated environmental cues. *Science, 216,* 436–437.

SIEGEL, S., KRAUK, M. D., & MINSON, R. E. (1987). Anticipation of pharmacological and nonpharmacological events: Classical conditioning and addictive behavior. *Journal of Drug Issues, 17,* 83–110.

SIEGEL, S., & MacRAE, J. (1984). Environmental specificity of tolerance. *Trends in Neuroscience, 7,* 140–143.

SIEGLER, R. S. (1976). Three aspects of cognitive development. *Cognitive Psychology, 8,* 481–520.

SIEGLER, R. S. (1986). *Children's thinking.* Englewood Cliffs, NJ: Prentice-Hall.

SIEGLER, R. S. (1987). The perils of averaging data over strategies: An example from children's addition. *Journal of Experimental Psychology: General, 116,* 250–264.

SIEGLER, R. S., LIEBERT, D. E., & LIEBERT, R. M. (1973). Inhelder and Piaget's pendulum problem: Teaching preadolescents to act as scientists. *Developmental Psychology, 9,* 97–101.

SIGALL, H., & PAGE, R. (1971). Current stereotypes: A little fading, a little faking. *Journal of Personality and Social Psychology, 18,* 247–255.

SIGMAN, M., COHEN, S. E., BECKWITH, L., ASARNOW, R., & PARMELEE, A. H. (1991). Continuity in cognitive abilities from infancy to 12 years of age. *Cognitive Development, 6,* 47–57.

SILVERMAN, L. H. (1976). Psychoanalytic theory: "The reports of my death are greatly exaggerated." *American Psychologist, 31,* 621–637.

SILVERSTEIN, B., PERDUE, L., PETERSON, B., & KELLY, E. (1986). The role of the mass media in promoting a thin standard of bodily attractiveness for women. *Sex Roles, 14,* 519–532.

SIMMONS, J. A. (1971). The sonar receiver of the bat. *Annals of the New York Academy of Sciences, 188,* 161–174.

SIMMONS, J. A. (1979). Perception of echo phase information in bat sonar. *Science, 204,* 1336–1338.

SIVACEK, J., & CRANO, W. D. (1982). Vested interest as a moderator of attitude-behavior consistency. *Journal of Personality and Social Psychology, 43,* 210–221.

SIZEMORE, C. C., & PITTILLO, E. S. (1977). *I'm Eve.* New York: Doubleday.

SKINNER, B. F. (1948). "Superstition" in the pigeon. *Journal of Experimental Psychology, 38,* 168–172.

SKINNER, B. F. (1953). *Science and human behavior.* New York: Macmillan.

SKINNER, B. F. (1957). *Verbal behavior.* Englewood Cliffs, NJ: Prentice-Hall.

SKINNER, B. F. (1979). *The shaping of a behaviorist.* New York: Knopf.

SLATER, A., COOPER, R., ROSE, D., & MORISON, V. (1989). Prediction of cognitive performance from infancy to early childhood. *Human Development, 32,* 137–147.

SLATER, A., MORISON, V., & ROSE, D. (1984). Habituation in the newborn. *Infant Behavior and Development, 7,* 183–200.

SLAUGHTER, D. T. (1988). Editor's notes. *New Directions for Child Development, 42,* 1–7.

SLAVIN, R. E., & MADDEN, N. A. (1979). School practices that improve social relations. *American Education Research Journal, 16,* 169–180.

SLOVIC, P. (1987). Perception of risk. *Science, 236,* 280–285.

SLOVIC, P., FISCHOFF, B., & LICHTENSTEIN, S. (1976). Cognitive processes in societal risk taking. In J. S. Cernoll & J. W. Payne (Eds.), *Cognition and societal behavior.* Hillsdale, NJ: Erlbaum.

SMITH, A. C., & KLEINMAN, S. (1989). Managing emotions in medical school: Students' contacts with the living and the dead. *Social Psychology Quarterly, 52,* 56–69.

SMITH, D. (1982). Trends in counseling and psychotherapy. *American Psychologist, 37,* 802–809.

SMITH, E. R. (1989). *Interpersonal attraction as a function of similarity and assumed similarity in traditional gender role adherence.* Unpublished doctoral dissertation, State University of New York at Albany.

SMITH, J. E., WALDORF, V. A., & TREMBATH, D. L. (1990). "Single white male looking for thin, very attractive . . . " *Sex Roles, 23,* 675–685.

SMITH, M. B. (1989). A path analysis of an adolescent drinking behavior model derived from problem behavior theory. *Journal of Studies in Alcoholism, 50,* 128–142.

SMITH, M. L., GLASS, G., & MILLER, T. (1980). *The benefits of psychotherapy.* Baltimore: Johns Hopkins University Press.

SMITH, S. M. (1979). Remembering in and out of context. Journal of Experimental Psychology: *Human Learning and Memory, 5,* 460–471.

SMITH, S. M., GLENBERG, A., & BJORK, R. A. (1978). Environmental context and human memory. *Memory and Cognition, 6,* 342–353.

SNAREY, J. R. (1985). Cross-cultural universality of social-moral development: A critical review of Kohlbergian research. *Psychological Bulletin, 97,* 202–232.

SNYDER, M. (1974). The self-monitoring of expressive behavior. *Journal of Personality and Social Psychology, 30,* 526–537.

SNYDER, M., BERSCHEID, E., & GLICK, P. (1985). Focusing on the exterior and the interior: Two investigations of the initiation of personal relationships. *Journal of Personality and Social Psychology, 48,* 1427–1439.

SNYDER, M., & DEBONO, K. G. (1985). Appeals to images and claims abut quality: Understanding the psychology of advertising. *Journal of Personality and Social Psychology, 49,* 586–597.

SNYDER, M., & GANGSTEAD, S. (1986). On the nature of self-monitoring: Matters of assessment, matters of validity. *Journal of Personality, 51,* 497–516.

SNYDER, M., & MONSON, T. C. (1975). Persons, situations and the control of social behavior. *Journal of Personality and Social Psychology, 32,* 637–674.

SNYDER, M., TANKE, E. D., & BERSCHEID, E. (1977). Social perception and interpersonal behavior: On the self-fulfilling nature of social stereotypes. *Journal of Personality and Social Psychology, 35,* 656–666.

SOLOMON, L. Z., SOLOMON, H., & STONE, R. (1978). Helping as a function of number of bystanders and ambiguity of emergency. *Personality and Social Psychology Bulletin, 4,* 318–321.

SOLOMON, P. R., SOLOMON, S. C., SCHARF, E. V., & PERRY, H. E. (1983). Altered activity in the hippocampus is more detrimental to classical conditioning than removing the structure. *Science, 220,* 329–331.

SOLOMON, R. L., & WYNNE, L. (1953). Traumatic avoidance learning: Acquisition in normal dogs. *Psychological Monographs, 67,* (4, Whole No. 354).

SOLOMON, Z., MIKULINCER, M., & HOBFOLL, S. E. (1987). Objective versus subjective measurement of stress and social support: Combat-related reactions. *Journal of Consulting and Clinical Psychology, 55,* 577–583.

SORCE, J. F., EMDE, R. N., CAMPOS, J. J., & KLINNERT, M. D. (1985). Maternal emotional signaling: Its effect on the visual cliff behavior of one-year olds. *Developmental Psychology, 20,* 195–200.

SPANOS, N. P. (1986). Hypnotic behavior: A social-psychological interpretation of amnesia, analgesia and "trance logic." *Behavioral and Brain Sciences, 9,* 449–502.

SPANOS, N. P., DEGROOT, H. P., TILLER, D. K., WEEKS, J. R. & BERTRAND, L. D. (1985). Trance logic, duality, and hidden observer responding in hypnotic, imagination control, and simulating subjects: A social psychological analysis. *Journal of Abnormal Psychology, 94,* 611–623.

SPANOS, N. P., RADTKE, H. L., & BERTRAND, L. D. (1985). Hypnotic amnesia as a strategic enactment: Breaching amnesia in highly susceptible subjects. *Journal of Personality and Social Psychology, 47,* 1155–1169.

SPANOS, N. P., WEEKES, J. R., & BERTRAND, L. D. (1985). Multiple personality: A social psychological perspective. *Journal of Abnormal Psychology, 94,* 362–376.

SPEAR, N. E. (1978). *The processing of memories: Forgetting and retention.* Hillsdale, NJ: Erlbaum.

SPEARMAN, C. (1904). "General intelligence," objectively determined and measured. *American Journal of Psychology, 15,* 201–293.

SPEARMAN, C. (1927). *The abilities of man.* London: Macmillan.

SPENCE, J. R., & HELMREICH, R. L. (1983). Achievement-related motives and behaviors. In J. T. Spence (Ed.), *Achievement and achievement motives* (pp. 7–74). New York: W. H. Freeman.

SPERLING, G. A. (1960). The information available in brief visual presentations. *Psychological Monographs, 74* (Whole No. 498).

SPERRY, R. W. (1966). Brain bisection and consciousness. In J. Eccles (Ed.), *Brain and conscious experience* (pp. 24–58). New York: Springer.

SPITZER, R. L., SKODOL, A. E., GIBBON, M., & WILLIAMS, J. B. W. (1981). *DSM-III casebook.* Washington, DC: American Psychiatric Association.

SPITZER, R. L., SKODOL, A. E., GIBBON, M., & WILLIAMS, J. B. W. (1983). *Psychopathology: A casebook.* New York: McGraw-Hill.

SPRINGER, S. P., & DEUTSCH, G. (1989). *Left brain, right brain* (3rd ed.). New York: W. H. Freeman.

SQUIRE, L. R. (1977). ECT and memory loss. *American Journal of Psychiatry, 134,* 997–1001.

SQUIRE, L. R. (1986). Mechanisms of memory. *Science, 232,* 1612–1619.

SQUIRE, L. R. (1987). *Memory and the brain.* New York: Oxford University Press.

SQUIRE, L. R., & COHEN, N. J. (1979). Memory and amnesia: Resistance to disruption develops for years after learning. *Behavioral and Neural Biology, 25,* 115–125.

SQUIRE, L. R., SLATER, P. C., & CHASE, P. M. (1975). Retrograde amnesia: Temporal gradient in very long-term memory following electroconvulsive therapy. *Science, 187,* 77–79.

SQUIRE, L. R., & ZOLA-MORGAN, S. (1988). Memory: Brain systems and behavior. *Trends in Neuroscience, 11,* 170–175.

SROUFE, L. A., FOX, J. N., & PANCAKE, V. (1983). Attachment and dependency in developmental perspective. *Child Development, 54,* 1615–1627.

STAATS, A. W., & STAATS, C. K. (1958). Attitudes established by classical conditioning. *Journal of Abnormal and Social Psychology, 57,* 37–40.

STAINBACK, W., STAINBACK, S., & BUNCH, G. (1989). A rationale for the merger of regular and special education. In S. Stainback, W. Stainback, and M. Forest (Eds.), *Educating all students in the mainstream of regular education* (pp. 15–28). Baltimore: Paul H. Brookes.

STANLEY, S. M., LYNN, S. J., & NASH, M. R. (1986). Trance logic, susceptibility screening, and the transparency response. *Journal of Personality and Social Psychology, 50,* 447–454.

STANOVICH, K. E. (1989). *How to think straight about psychology* (2nd ed.). Glenview, IL: Scott, Foresman.

STARK, R. (1992). *Sociology* (4th ed.). Belmont, CA: Wadsworth.

STARK, R., & BAINBRIDGE, W. S. (1981). American-born sects: Initial findings. *Journal for the Scientific Study of Religion, 20,* 130–149.

STAUB, E. (1991). Altruistic and moral motivations for helping and their translation into action. *Psychological Inquiry, 2,* 150–153.

STAUDENMAYER, H. (1975). Understanding conditional reasoning with meaningful propositions. In R. J. Falmaye (Ed.), *Reasoning: Representation and process in children and adults.* Hillsdale, NJ: Erlbaum.

STEFANIS, C., DORNBUSH, R., & FINK, M. (1977). *Hashish: Studies of long-term use.* New York: Raven.

STEINBERG, L. (1987). Impact of puberty on family relations: Effects of pubertal status and pubertal timing. *Developmental Psychology, 23,* 451–460.

STELMACK, R. M. (1990). Biological bases of extraversion: Psychophysiological evidence. *Journal of Personality, 58,* 293–311.

STEPHENSON, W. (1953). *The study of behavior: Q-technique and its methodology.* Chicago: University of Chicago Press.

STERIADE, M., & MCCARLEY, R. W. (1990). *Brainstem control of wakefulness and sleep.* New York: Plenum.

STERNBERG, R. J. (1977). *Intelligence, information processing and analogical reasoning.* Hillsdale, NJ: Erlbaum.

STERNBERG, R. J. (1984). Toward a triarchic theory of human intelligence. *Behavior and Brain Sciences, 7,* 269–315.

STERNBERG, R. J. (1985). Human intelligence: The model is the message. *Science, 230,* 1111–1118.

STERNBERG, R. J. (1986a). A triangular theory of love. *Psychological Review, 93,* 119–135.

STERNBERG, R. J. (1986b). Haste makes waste versus a stitch in time? A reply to Vernon, Nador, and Kantor. *Intelligence, 10,* 265–270.

STERNBERG, R. J. (1986c). *Intelligence applied.* New York: Harcourt Brace Jovanovich.

STERNBERG, R. J. (1988). Triangulating love. In R. J. Sternberg & M. L. Barnes (Eds.), *The psychology of love* (pp. 119–138). New Haven, CT: Yale University Press.

STERNBERG, R. J. (1990). *Metaphors of mind.* Cambridge: Cambridge University Press.

STERNBERG, R. J., CONWAY, B. E., KETRON, J. L., & BERNSTEIN, M. (1981). People's conceptions of intelligence. *Journal of Personality and Social Psychology, 41,* 37–55.

STERNBERG, R. J., & DETTERMAN, D. K. (Eds.). (1986). *What is intelligence?* Norwood, NJ: Ablex.

STERNBERG, R. J., & GRAJEK, S. (1984). The nature of love. *Journal of Personality and Social Psychology, 47,* 312–329.

STERNBERG, R. J., & SMITH, C. (1985). Social intelligence and decoding skills in nonverbal communication. *Social Cognition, 2,* 168–192.

STERNBERG, R. J., & WAGNER, R. K. (1993). The g-ocentric view of intelligence and job performance is wrong. *New Directions in Psychological Science, 2,* 1–4.

STERNBERG, S. (1966). High speed scanning in human memory. *Science, 153,* 652–654.

STEVENS-LONG, J. (1988). *Adult life* (3rd ed.). Mountain View, CA: Mayfield.

STONE, G. C. (1987). The scope of health psychology. In G. C. Stone, S. M. Weiss, J. D. Martarazzo, N. E. Miller, J. Rodin, C. D. Belar, M. J. Follick, & J. E. Singer (Eds.), *Health psychology: A discipline and a profession* (pp. 27–40). Chicago: University of Chicago Press.

STORMS, M. D. (1973). Videotape and the attribution process: Reversing actors' and observers' points of view. *Journal of Personality and Social Psychology, 27,* 165–175.

STRACK, F., MARTIN, L. L., & STEPPER, S. (1988). Inhibiting and facilitating conditions of the human smile: A nonobtrusive test of the facial feedback hypothesis. *Journal of Personality and Social Psychology, 54,* 768–777.

STRACK, S., & COYNE, J. C. (1983). Social confirmation of dysphoria: Shared and private reactions to depression. *Journal of Personality and Social Psychology, 44,* 798–806.

STRAUSS, M. E., LESSEN-FIRESTONE, J. K., STARR, R. H., & OSTREA, E. M., JR. (1975). Behavior of narcotics-addicted newborns. *Child Development, 46,* 887–893.

STREIB, G. (1983). The social psychology of retirement: Theoretical perspectives and research priorities. In J. E. Birren, J. M. A. Munnichs, H. Thomae, & M. Marois (Eds.), *Aging: A challenge to science and society* (Vol. 3, pp. 202–213). Oxford: Oxford University Press.

STRUPP, H. H. (1980a). Success and failure in time-limited psychotherapy: A systematic comparison of two cases—comparison 1. *Archives of General Psychiatry, 37,* 595–603.

STRUPP, H. H. (1980b). Success and failure in time-limited psychotherapy: A systematic comparison of two cases—comparison 2. *Archives of General Psychiatry, 37,* 708–716.

STRUPP, H. H. (1980c). Success and failure in time-limited psychotherapy: With special reference to a lay counselor. *Archives of General Psychiatry, 37,* 831–841.

STRUPP, H. H. (1981). Toward a refinement of time-limited dynamic psychotherapy. In S. H. Budman (Ed.), *Forms of brief therapy* (pp. 219–242). New York: Guilford.

STRUPP, H. H., & BINDER, J. L. (1984). *Psychotherapy in a new key: A guide to time-limited dynamic psychotherapy.* New York: Basic Books.

STUNKARD, A. J. (1958). The management of obesity. *New England Journal of Medicine, 58,* 79–87.

STUNKARD, A. J., HARRIS, J. R., PEDERSEN, N. L., & MCCLEARN, G. E. (1990). The body-mass index of twins who have been reared apart. *New England Journal of Medicine, 332,* 1483–1487.

STUSS, D. T., & BENSON, D. F. (1984). Neuropsychological studies of the frontal lobes. *Psychological Bulletin, 95,* 3–28.

STYRON, W. (1990). *Darkness visible: A memoir of madness.* New York: Random House.

SUE, D. (1990). Culture-specific strategies in counseling: A conceptual framework. *Professional Psychology: Research and Practice, 21,* 423–433.

SUE, D. W., & SUE, D. (1990). *Counseling the culturally different* (2nd ed.). New York: Wiley.

SUPER, D. E. (1957). *The psychology of careers.* New York: Harper & Row.

SUPER, D. E. (1980). A life span, life space approach to career development. *Journal of Vocational Behavior, 16,* 282–298.

SURBEY, M. K. (1990). Family composition, stress, and human menarche. In T. E. Ziegler & F. B. Bercovitch (Eds.), *Socioendocrinology of primate reproduction* (pp. 11–32). New York: Wiley.

SUSSER, M., HOPPER, K., & RICHMAN, R. (1983). Society, culture, and health. In D. Mechanic (Ed.), *Handbook of health, health care, and the health professions* (pp. 23–49). New York: Free Press.

SWAAB, D. F., & FLIERS, E. (1985). A sexually dimorphic nucleus in the human brain. *Science, 188,* 1112–1115.

SWANN, W. B. (1983). Self-verification: Bringing social reality into harmony with the self. In J. Suls & A. G. Greenwald (Eds.), *Psychological perspectives on the self* (Vol. 2, pp. 33–66). Hillsdale, NJ: Erlbaum.

SWANN, W. B. (1992). Seeking "truth," finding despair: Some unhappy consequences of a negative self-concept. *Current Directions in Psychological Science, 1,* 15–18.

SWEENEY, P. D., ANDERSON, K., & BAILEY, S. (1986). Attributional style in depression: A meta-analytic review. *Journal of Personality and Social Psychology, 50,* 974–991.

TAKAGI, S. F. (1980). Dual nervous systems for olfactory functions in mammals. In H. Van der Starre (Ed.), *Olfaction and taste* (Vol. 7, pp. 275–278). London: IRC Press.

TANGNEY, J. P., & FESHBACH, S. (1988). Children's television-viewing frequency: Individual differences and demographic correlates. *Personality and Social Psychology Bulletin, 14,* 145–158.

TANNEN, D. (1990). *You just don't understand: Women and men in conversation.* New York: Morrow.

TANNER, J. M. (1971). Sequence, tempo, and individual variation in growth and development of boys and girls aged twelve to sixteen. In R.E. Muuss (Ed.), *Adolescent behavior and society* (4th ed.) (pp. 39–50). New York: McGraw-Hill.

TANNER, J. M. (1978). *Fetus into man: Physical growth from conception to maturity.* Cambridge, MA: Harvard University Press.

TAVRIS, C., & OFFIR, C. (1977). *The longest war: Sex differences in perspective.* New York: Harcourt Brace Jovanovich.

TAYLOR, S. E., KEMENY, M. E., ASPINWALL, L. G., SCHNEIDER, S. G., RODRÍGUEZ, R., & HERBERT, M. (1992). Optimism, coping, psychological distress, and high-risk sexual behavior among men at risk for acquired immunodeficiency syndrome (AIDS). *Journal of Personality and Social Psychology, 63,* 460–473.

TEASDALE, T. W., FUCHS, J., & GOLDSCHMIDT, E. (1988). Degree of myopia in relation to intelligence and educational level. *The Lancet, 332,* 1351–1354.

Teen Sex: Not for Sale. (1989, May). *Psychology Today,* pp. 10, 12.

TEICHER, M. H., GLOD, C. C., & COLE, J. O. (1991). Emergence of intense suicidal preoccupation during fluoxetine treatment. *American Journal of Psychiatry, 147,* 207–210.

TEITELBAUM, P. (1955). Sensory control of hypothalamic hyperphagia. *Journal of Comparative and Physiological Psychology, 48,* 156–163.

TEITELBAUM, P. (1957). Random and food-directed activity in hyperphagic and normal rats. *Journal of Comparative and Physiological Psychology, 50,* 486–490.

TEITELBAUM, P., & STELLAR, E. (1954). Recovery from the failure to eat produced by hypothalamic lesions. *Science, 120,* 894–895.

TELLEGEN, A., LYKKEN, D. T., BOUCHARD, T. J., JR., WILCOX, K. J., SEGAL, N. L., & RICH, S. (1988). Personality similarity in twins reared apart and together. *Journal of Personality and Social Psychology, 54,* 1031–1039.

TERMAN, L. M. (1916). *The measurement of intelligence.* Boston: Houghton Mifflin.

TERMAN, L. M. (Ed.). (1925). *Genetic studies of genius* (Vol. I). Stanford, CA: Stanford University Press.

TERMAN, L. M., & ODEN, M. H. (1959). *Genetic studies of genius* (Vol. 5). Stanford, CA: Stanford University Press.

TESSER, A., & SHAFFER, D. R. (1990). Attitudes and attitude change. *Annual Review of Psychology, 41,* 479–523.

TEYLER, T. J., & DISCENNA, P. (1984). Long-term potentiation as a candidate mnemonic device. *Brain Research Reviews, 7,* 15–28.

THIGPEN, C. H., & CLECKLEY, H. M. (1954). *The three faces of Eve.* Kingsport, TN: Kingsport Press.

THOMAS, A., & CHESS, S. (1980). *The dynamics of psychological development.* New York: Brunner/Mazel.

THOMAS, G. S., & RUTLEDGE, J. H. (1986). Fitness and exercise for the elderly. In K. Dychtwaki (Ed.), *Wellness and health promotion for the elderly.* Rockville, MD: Aspen.

THOMPSON, C. (1942). Cultural pressures in the psychology of women. *Psychiatry, 5,* 331–339.

THOMPSON, C. H. (1934). The conclusion of scientists relative to racial differences. *Journal of Negro Education, 3*, 494–512.

THOMPSON, C. P. (1982). Memory for unique personal events: The roommate study. *Memory & Cognition, 10*, 324–332.

THOMPSON, D. A., & CAMPBELL, R. G. (1977). Hunger in humans induced by 2-deoxy D-glucose: Glucoprivic control of taste preference and food intake. *Science, 198*, 1065–1068.

THOMPSON, J. K. (1986, April). Larger than life. *Psychology Today*, pp. 39, 42, 44.

THOMPSON, R. F. (1985). *The brain*. New York: W. H. Freeman.

THOMPSON, R. F. (1986). The neurobiology of learning and memory. *Science, 233*, 941–947.

THORNDIKE, E. L. (1898). Animal intelligence: An experimental study of associative processes in animals. *Psychological Reviews Monograph, 2* (Suppl. 8).

THORNDIKE, E. L. (1914). *Educational psychology: Briefer edition*. New York: Teachers College Press.

THORNDIKE, E. L., ET AL. (1921). Intelligence and its measurement. *Journal of Educational Psychology, 12*.

THORNHILL, R., & THORNHILL, N. W. (1992). The evolutionary psychology of men's coercive sexuality. *Behavioral and Brain Sciences, 15*, 363–421.

THORNTON, B. (1984). Defensive attribution of responsibility: Evidence for an arousal-bound motivational bias. *Journal of Personality and Social Psychology, 46*, 721–734.

THOULESS, R. H. (1931). Phenomenal regression to the real object: I. *British Journal of Psychology, 21*, 339–359.

THURSTONE, L. L. (1938). *Primary mental abilities*. Chicago: University of Chicago Press.

TINBERGEN, N. (1951). *The study of instinct*. London: Oxford University Press.

TISCHENKEL, N. J., SAAB, P. G., SCHNEIDERMAN, N., NELESEN, R. A., PASIN, R. D., GOLDSTEIN, D. A., SPITZER, S. B., WOO-MING, R., & WEIDLER, D. J. (1989). Cardiovascular and neurohumoral responses to behavioral challenge as a function of race and sex. *Health Psychology, 8*, 503–524.

TISSOT, S. A. D. (1766). *Onanism, or a treatise upon the disorders of masturbation* (A. Hume, Trans.). London: J. Pridden.

TITCHENER, E. B. (1910). *A textbook of psychology*. New York: Macmillan.

TOLMAN, E. C. (1932). *Purposive behavior in animals and men*. New York: Appleton-Century-Crofts.

TOLMAN, E. C. (1948). Cognitive maps in rats and man. *Psychological Review, 55*, 189–208.

TOLMAN, E. C., & HONZIK, C. H. (1930). Introduction and removal of reward, and maze performance in rats. *University of California Publications in Psychology, 4*, 257–275.

TOMKINS, S. (1962). *Affect, imagery, consciousness* (Vol. 1). New York: Springer.

TOMKINS, S. S. (1980). Affect as amplification: Some modificatons in theory. In R. Plutchik & H. Kellerman (Eds.), *Emotion: Theory, research and experience* (Vol. 1). New York: Academic Press.

TORDOFF, M. G., NOVIN, D., & RUSSEK, M. (1982). Effects of hepatic denervation on the anorexic response to epinephrine, amphetamine, and lithium chloride: A behavioral identification of glucostatic afferents. *Journal of Comparative and Physiological Psychology, 96*, 361–375.

TORGERSEN, S. (1983). Genetic factors in anxiety disorders. *Archives of General Psychiatry, 40*, 1085–1089.

TORREY, E. F. (1988). *Nowhere to go: The tragedy of the homeless mentally ill*. New York: Harper & Row.

TRALBAUT, M. E. (1969). *Vincent Van Gogh*. New York: Macmillan.

TREFFERT, D. A. (1989). *Extraordinary people*. New York: Harper & Row.

TRESMER, D. W. (1977). *Fear of success*. New York: Plenum.

TRESMER, D. (1974, Oct.). Fear of success. Popular, but unproven. *Psychology Today*, p. 82.

TREVARTHEN, C. (1987). Brain development. In R. L. Gregory (Ed.), *The mind* (pp. 101–110). Oxford: Oxford University Press.

TRIESMAN, A. (1986 Nov.). Features and objects in visual processing. *Scientific American*, pp. 114–125.

TRIPLETT, N. (1897). The dynamogenic factors in pacemaking and competition. *American Journal of Psychology, 9*, 507–533.

TROTTER, R. J. (1986, August). Three heads are better than one. *Psychology Today*, pp. 56–62.

TULVING, E. (1983). *Elements of episodic memory*. London: Oxford University Press.

TULVING, E. (1984). Précis of elements of episodic memory. *Behavioral and Brain Sciences, 7*, 223–268.

TULVING, E. (1985). How many memory systems are there? *American Psychologist, 40*, 385–398.

TULVING, E. (1986). What kind of a hypothesis is the distinction between episodic and semantic memory? *Journal of Experimental Psychology: Learning, Memory, and Cognition, 12*, 307–311.

TULVING, E., & PSOTKA, J. (1971). Retroactive inhibition in free-recall: Inaccessibility of information available in the memory store. *Journal of Experimental Psychology, 87*, 1–8.

TULVING, E., & THOMSON, D. M. (1973). Encoding specificity and retrieval processes in episodic memory. *Psychological Review, 80*, 352–373.

TURNER, A. M., & GREENOUGH, W. T. (1983). Synapses per neuron and synaptic dimensions in occipital cortex of rats reared in complex, social, or isolation housing. *Acta Stereologica, 2*, 239–244.

TURNER, A. M., & GREENOUGH, W. T. (1985). Differential rearing effects on rat visual cortex synapses: I. Synaptic and neuronal density and synapses per neuron. *Brain Research, 329*, 195–203.

TVERSKY, A., (1972). Elimination by aspects: A theory of choice. *Psychological Review, 79*, 281–299.

TVERSKY, A., & KAHNEMAN, D. (1973a). Availability: A heuristic for judging frequency and probability. *Cognitive Psychology, 5*, 207–232.

TVERSKY, A., & KAHNEMAN, D. (1973b). On the psychology of prediction. *Psychological Review, 80*, 237–251.

TVERSKY, A., & KAHNEMAN, D. (1981). The framing of decisions and the rationality of choice. *Science, 211*, 453–458.

TVERSKY, A., & KAHNEMAN, D. (1990). Extensional versus intuitive reasoning: The conjunction fallacy in probability judgment. *Psychological Review, 90*, 293–315.

ULRICH, R. E., STACHNIK, T. J., & STAINTON, N. R. (1963). Student acceptance of generalized personality interpretations. *Psychological Reports, 13*, 831–834.

UNDERWOOD, B. J. (1961). Ten years of massed practice on distributed practice. *Psychological Review, 68*, 229–247.

UNDERWOOD, B. J. (1970). A breakdown of the total-time law in free-recall learning. *Journal of Verbal Learning and Verbal Behavior, 9*, 573–580.

UNGERLEIDER, L. G., & MISHKIN, M. (1982). Two cortical visual systems. In D. J. Ingle, M. A. Goodale, & R. J. W. Mansfield (Eds.), *Analysis of visual behavior* (pp. 549–586). Cambridge, MA: MIT Press.

UNITED STATES BUREAU OF THE CENSUS. (1989). *Statistical abstract of the United States: 1989*. Washington, DC: U.S. Government Printing Office.

UNITED STATES BUREAU OF THE CENSUS. (1991). *Statistical abstract of the United States: 1991*. Washington, DC: U.S. Government Printing Office.

UNITED STATES COMMISSION ON CIVIL RIGHTS. (1969). *Racism in America and how to combat it*. Washington, DC: U.S. Government Printing Office.

UNITED STATES DEPARTMENT OF HEALTH AND HUMAN SERVICES. (1987). *Sleep disorders* (DHHS Publication No. ADM 87-1541). Rockville, MD: National Institute of Mental Health.

UNITED STATES DEPARTMENT OF HEALTH AND HUMAN SERVICES. (1987). *Vital statistics of the United States, 1984: Life tables* (DHHS Publication No. PHS 87-1104). Washington, DC: U.S. Government Printing Office.

UNITED STATES DEPARTMENT OF LABOR, WOMEN'S BUREAU. (1988). *20 facts on women workers*. Washington, DC: Author.

UNITED STATES HOUSE OF REPRESENTATIVES, COMMITTEE ON WAYS AND MEANS (1985). *Children in Poverty*. Washington, DC: U.S. Government Printing Office.

U.S. NEWS AND WORLD REPORT (1989, December 18). Tooting your own horn, p. 82.

VAILLANT, G. E. (1977). *Adaptation to life*. Boston: Little, Brown.

VAILLANT, G. E., & McARTHUR, C. C. (1972). Natural history of male psychological health: The adult life cycle from eighteen to fifty. *Seminars in Psychiatry, 4*, 415–427.

VALINS, S. (1966). Cognitive effects of false heart-rate feedback. *Journal of Personality and Social Psychology, 4*, 400–408.

VAN DE CASTLE, R. L. (1971). *The psychology of dreaming*. New York: General Learning Corp.

VANESSEN, D. C. (1979). Visual areas of the mammalian cerebral cortex. *Annual Review of Neuroscience, 2*, 227–264.

VANESSEN, D. C., & MAVENSELL, J. H. R. (1983). Hierarchical organization and functional streams in the visual cortex. *Trends in Neuroscience, 6*, 370–375.

VAN IJZENDOORN, M. H., & KROONENBERG, P. M. (1988). Cross-cultural patterns of attachment: A meta-analysis of the strange situation. *Child Development, 59*, 147–156.

VAUGHN, C. E., & LEFF, J. P. (1976). The influence of family and social factors on the course of psychiatric illness: A comparison of schizophrenic and depressed neurotic patients. *British Journal of Psychiatry, 129*, 125–137.

VAUGHN, C. E., SNYDER, K. S., JONES, S., FREEMAN, W. B., & FALLOON, I. R. H. (1984). Family factors in schizophrenic relapse: A California replication of the British research on expressed eomtion. *Archives of General Psychiatry, 41*, 1169–1177.

VAUGHN, E. D. (1977). Misconceptions about psychology among introductory psychology students. *Teaching of Psychology, 4*, 138–141.

VERNON, P. E. (1979). *Intelligence, heredity and environment*. San Francisco: W. H. Freeman.

VERNON, P. E. (1983). Speed of information processing and general intelligence. *Intelligence, 7*, 53–70.

VERNON, P. E. (1990). An overview of chronometric measures of intelligence. *Social Psychology Review, 19*, 399–410.

VERNON, P. E., NADOR, S., & KANTOR, L. (1985). Reaction-times and speed of processing: Their relationship to timed and untimed measures of intelligence. *Intelligence, 9*, 357–374.

VICTOR, M., ADAMS, R. D., & COLLINS, G. H. (1971). *The Wernicke-Korsakoff syndrome*. Philadelphia: Davis.

VIGIL, J. D. (1988a). *Barrio gangs: Street life and identity in Southern California*. Austin: University of Texas Press.

VIGIL, J. D. (1988b). Group processes and street identity: Adolescent Chicano gang members. *Ethos, 16,* 421–445.

VINCENT, K. R., & HARMAN, M. J. (1991). The Exner Rorschach: An analysis of its clinical validity. *Journal of Clinical Psychology, 47,* 596–599.

VISINTAINER, M. A., VOLPICELLI, J. R., & SELIGMAN, M. E. P. (1982). Tumor rejection in rats after inescapable or escapable shock. *Science, 216,* 437–438.

VITALIANO, P. P., MAIURO, R. D., RUSSO, J., & MITCHELL, E. S. (1989). Medical student distress: A longitudinal study. *The Journal of Nervous and Mental Disease, 177,* 70–76.

VOLLMER, F. (1984). Sex differences in personality and expectancy. *Sex Roles, 11,* 1121–1139.

VON CRAMON, D. Y., HEBEL, N., & SCHURI, U. (1985). A contribution to the anatomical basis of thalamic amnesia. *Brain, 108,* 993–1008.

WACHTEL, P. (1988). *Action and insight.* New York: Guilford.

WADDEN, T. A., & STUNKARD, A. J. (1985). Social and psychological consequences of obesity. *Annals of Internal Medicine, 103,* 1062–1067.

WADESON, H. (1987). *The dynamics of art psychotherapy.* New York: Wiley.

WAGENAAR, W. A. (1986). My memory: A study of autobiographical memory over six years. *Cognitive Psychology, 18,* 225–252.

WAGNER, R. K., & STERNBERG, R. J. (1984). Alternative conceptions of intelligence and their implications for education. *Review of Educational Research, 54,* 179–223.

WAGNER, R. K., & STERNBERG, R. J. (1986). Tacit knowledge and intelligence in the everyday world. In R. J. Sternberg & R. K. Wagner (Eds.), *Practical intelligence* (pp. 51–83). Cambridge: Cambridge University Press.

WAHL, O. (1987). Public vs. professional conceptions of schizophrenia. *Journal of Community Psychology, 15,* 285–291.

WALDROP, M. M. (1987). The workings of working memory. *Science, 237,* 1564–1567.

WALDROP, M. M. (1988a). Toward a unified theory of cognition. *Science, 241,* 27–29.

WALDROP, M. M. (1988b). Soar: A unified theory of cognition? *Science, 241,* 296–298.

WALK, R. D., & HOMAN, C. P. (1984). Emotion and dance in dynamic light displays. *Bulletin of the Psychonomic Society, 22,* 437–440.

WALKER, E., BETTES, B. A., KAIN, E. L., & HARVEY, P. (1985). Relationship of gender and marital status with symptomatology in psychotic patients. *Journal of Abnormal Psychology, 94,* 42–50.

WALKER, L. J. (1984). Sex differences in the development of moral reasoning: A critical review. *Child Development, 55,* 677–691.

WALLACH, L., & WALLACH, M. A. (1991). Why altruism, even though it exists, cannot be demonstrated by social psychological experiments. *Psychological Inquiry, 2,* 153–155.

WALLRAVEN, J., TURKEL, J., & TRACHTMAN, J. (1978). Extreme myopia produced by modest change in early visual experience. *Science 201,* 1249–1251.

WALSTER, E., ARONSON, E., ABRAHAMS, D., & ROTTMAN, L. (1966). Importance of physical attractiveness in dating behavior. *Journal of Personality and Social Psychology, 4,* 508–516.

WALTERS, G. C., & GRUSEC, J. E. (1977). *Punishment.* San Francisco: W. H. Freeman.

WARREN, W. J. (1988, December 21). Grouping students by ability comes under fire. *New York Times.*

WASON, P. C. (1960). On the failure to eliminate hypotheses in a conceptual task. *Quarterly Journal of Experimental Psychology, 12,* 129–140.

WASON, P. C. (1968). Reasoning about a rule. *Quarterly Journal of Experimental Psychology, 20,* 273–281.

WATKINS, J. G. (1984). The Bianchi (L.A. Hillside Strangler) case: Sociopath or multiple personality? *The International Journal of Clinical and Experimental Hypnosis, 32,* 67–101.

WATSON, C. G., & BURANEN, C. (1979). The frequency and identification of false positive conversion reactions. *Journal of Nervous and Mental Disorders, 167,* 243–247.

WATSON, D. (1982). The actor and the observer: How are their perceptions of causality divergent? *Psychological Bulletin, 92,* 682–700.

WATSON, D. (1989). Strangers' ratings of the five robust personality factors: Evidence of a surprising convergence with self-reports. *Journal of Personality and Social Psychology, 57,* 120–128.

WATSON, J. B. (1913). Psychology as the behaviorist sees it. *Psychological Review, 20,* 158–177.

WATSON, J. B. (1925). *Behaviorism.* New York: Norton.

WATSON, J. B. (1926). What the nursery has to say about instincts. In C. Murchison (Ed.), *Psychologies of 1925* (pp. 1–34). Worchester, MA: Clark University Press.

WATSON, J. B., & RAYNER, R. (1920). Conditioned emotional reactions. *Journal of Experimental Psychology, 3,* 1–14.

WAUGH, N. C., & NORMAN, D. A. (1965). Primary memory. *Psychological Review, 72,* 89–104.

WEBB, W. B. (1974). Sleep as an adaptive process. *Perceptual & Motor Skills, 38,* 1023–1027.

WEBB, W. B., & AGNEW, H. W. JR. (1967). Sleep cycling within 24 hour periods. *Journal of Experimental Psychology, 74,* 158–160.

WECHSLER, D. (1939). *The measurement of adult intelligence.* Baltimore: Williams & Wilkins.

WECHSLER, D. (1949). *Wechsler Intelligence Scale for Children.* New York: Psychological Corporation.

WECHSLER, D. (1958). *The measurement and appraisal of adult intelligence.* Baltimore: Williams & Wilkins.

WEIDNER, G., SEXTON, S., MCLELLARN, R., CONNOR, S. L., & MATARAZZO, J. D. (1987). The role of the Type A behavior and hostility in an elevation of plasma lipids in adult women and men. *Psychosomatic Medicine, 49,* 450–457.

WEINBERGER, D. R., & KLEINMAN, J. E. (1986). Observation on the brain in schizophrenia. In A. J. Frances & R. E. Hales (Eds.), *American Psychiatric Association, Annual Review* (Vol. 5.). Washington, DC: American Psychiatric Association.

WEINBERGER, M., HINER, S. L., & TIERNEY, W. M. (1987). In support of hassles as a measure of stress in predicting health outcomes. *Journal of Behavioral Medicine, 10,* 19–31.

WEINER, B. (1972). *Theories of motivation: From mechanism to cognition.* Chicago: Markham.

WEINER, B. (1974a). An attributional interpretation of expectancy-value theory. In B. Weiner (Ed.), *Cognitive views of human motivation.* New York: Academic Press.

WEINER, B. (Ed.). (1974b). *Cognitive views of human motivation.* New York: Academic Press.

WEINER, B. (1980). A cognitive (attribution) emotion-action model of motivated behavior: An analysis of judgments of helpgiving. *Journal of Personality and Social Psychology, 39,* 186–200.

WEINER, B. (1985a). "Spontaneous" causal thinking. *Psychological Bulletin, 97,* 74–84.

WEINER, B. (1985b). *Human motivation.* New York: Springer.

WEINER, B., & KUKLA, A. (1970). An attributional analysis of achievement motivation. *Journal of Personality and Social Psychology, 15,* 1–20.

WEINER, L. J. (1988). Issues in sex therapy with survivors of intrafamily sexual abuse. *Women and Therapy, 7,* 253–264.

WEINGARTEN, H. P. (1983). Conditioned cues elicit feeding in sated rats: A role for learning in meal initiation. *Science, 220,* 431–433.

WEINGARTNER, H., GRAFMAN, J., BOUTELLE, W., KAYE, W., & MARTIN, P. R. (1983). Forms of memory failure. *Science, 221,* 380–382.

WEISENBERG, M. (1977). Pain and pain control. *Psychological Bulletin, 84,* 1008–1044.

WEISMAN, A. D. (1972). *On dying and denying.* New York: Behavioral Publications.

WEISS, J. M. (1968). Effects of coping responses on stress. *Journal of Comparative and Physiological Psychology, 65,* 251–260.

WEISSMAN, M., & KLERMAN, G. (1977). Sex differences and the epidemiology of depression. *Archives of General Psychiatry, 34,* 98–111.

WEITZ, R. (1991). Uncertainty and the lives of persons with AIDS. In A. Monat & R. S. Lazarus (Eds.), *Stress and coping* (3rd ed.) (pp. 352–369). New York: Columbia University Press.

WEITZENHOFFER, A. M., & HILGARD, E. R. (1959). *Stanford Hypnotic Susceptibility Scales, Forms A and B.* Palo Alto, CA: Consulting Psychologists Press.

WEITZENHOFFER, A. M., & HILGARD, E. R. (1962). *Stanford Hypnotic Susceptibility Scales, Form C.* Palo Alto, CA: Consulting Psychologists Press.

WEITZENHOFFER, A.M., & HILGARD, E. R. (1963). *Stanford Profile Scales of Hypnotic Susceptibility, Forms 1 and 2.* Palo Alto, CA: Consulting Psychologists Press.

WEITZMAN, L. J. (1985). *The divorce revolution: The unexpected social and economic consequences for women and children in America.* New York: Free Press.

WELDON, E., & GARGANO, G. M. (1988). Cognitive loafing: The effects of accountability and shared responsibility on cognitive effort. *Personality and Social Psychology Bulletin, 14,* 159–171.

WELLS, G. L. (1984). Do the eyes have it? More on expert eyewitness testimony. *American Psychologist, 39,* 1064–1065.

WENDER, P. H., KETY, S. S., ROSENTHAL, D., SCHULSINGER, F., ORTMAN, J., & LUNDE, I. (1986). Psychiatric disorders in the biological and adoptive families of adopted individuals with affective disorders. *Archives of General Psychiatry, 43,* 923–929.

WENDER, P. H., ROSENTHAL, D., KETY, S. S., SCHULSINGER, F., & WELNER, J. (1974). Cross-fostering: A research strategy for clarifying the role of genetic and experiential factors in the etiology of schizophrenia. *Archives of General Psychiatry, 310,* 121–128.

WERTHEIMER, M. (1923). Untersuchungen zur lehre von der gestalt: 2. *Psychologische Forschung 4,* 301–350.

WHITE, C. (1973). The effects of viewing film of different arousal content on the eating behavior of obese and normal weight subjects. *Dissertation Abstracts International, 34,* 2324B.

WHITE, H. R., BATES, M., & JOHNSON, V. (1990). Social reinforcement and alcohol consumption. In M. Cox (Ed.), *Why people drink.* New York: Gardner.

WHITE, J. (1968). *The birth and rebirth of pictorial space* (2nd ed.). London: Faber & Faber.

WHITING, B. B. (Ed.) (1963). *Six cultures: Studies of child rearing.* New York: Wiley.

WHITING, B. B., & WHITING, J. W. M. (1975). *Children of six cultures: A psychocultural analysis.* Cambridge, MA: Harvard University Press.

WHORF, B. (1956). *Language, thought, and reality.* Cambridge, MA: MIT Press.

WICKELGREN, W. A. (1965). Acoustic similarity and intrusion errors in short-term memory. *Journal of Experimental Psychology, 70,* 102–108.

WICKER, A. W. (1969). Attitudes versus actions: The relationship of verbal and overt behavioral responses to attitude objects. *Journal of Social Issues, 25,* 41–78.

WICKWARE, F. S. (1948, August 2). Report on the Kinsey report. *Life*, pp. 86–90.

WIDNALL, S. E. (1988). AAAS Presidential lecture: Voices from the pipeline. *Science, 241*, 1740–1745.

WIGDOR, A. K., & GARNER, W. R. (Eds.). (1982). *Ability testing: Uses, consequences and controversies.* Washington, DC: National Academy Press.

WILCOX S., & UDRY, J. R. (1986). Autism and accuracy in adolescent perceptions of friends' sexual attitudes and behavior. *Journal of Applied Social Psychology, 16*, 361–374.

WILCOXON, H. C., DRAGOIN, W. B., & KRAL, P. A. (1971). Illness-induced aversions in rat and quail: Relative salience of visual and gustatory cues. *Science, 171*, 826–828.

WILLIAMS, J. E., & BENNETT, S. M. (1975). The definition of sex stereotypes via the adjective check list. *Sex Roles, 1*, 327–337.

WILLIAMS, K., HARKINS, S., & LATANÉ, B. (1981). Identifiability as a deterrent to social loafing: Two cheering experiments. *Journal of Personality and Social Psychology, 40*, 303–311.

WILLIAMS, P. S. (1974). Scientific racism and IQ: The silent mugging of the black community. *Psychology Today*, pp. 32–41.

WILSON, D. M., HAMMER, L. D., DUNCAN, P. M., DORNBUSCH, S. M., RITTER, P. L., HINTZ, R. L., GROSS, R. T., & ROSENFELD, R. G. (1986). Growth and intellectual development. *Pediatrics, 78*, 646–650.

WILSON, E. O. (1975). *Sociobiology, the new synthesis.* Cambridge, MA: Harvard University Press.

WILSON, G. T. (1982). Adult disorders. In G. T. Wilson & C. M. Franks (Eds.), *Contemporary behavior therapy: Conceptual and empirical foundations* (pp. 505–562). New York: Guilford.

WILSON, G. T., O'LEARY, K. D., & NATHAN, P. (1992). *Abnormal psychology.* Englewood Cliffs, NJ: Prentice-Hall.

WILSON, R. S. (1978). Synchronies in mental development: An epigenetic perspective. *Science, 202*, 939–948.

WILSON, R. S. (1983). The Louisville twin study: Developmental synchronies in behavior. *Child Development, 54*, 298–316.

WING, R. R., & JEFFERY, R. W. (1979a). The effect of two behavioral techniques and social context on food consumption. *Addictive Behavior, 4*, 71–72.

WING, R. R., & JEFFERY, R. W. (1979b). Outpatient treatments of obesity: A comparison of methodology and clinical results. *International Journal of Obesity, 3*, 261–279.

WINTER, D. G. (1987). Leader appeal, leader performance, and the motive profiles of leaders and followers: A study of American presidents and elections. *Journal of Personality and Social Psychology, 52*, 196–202.

WOBER, M. (1974). Toward an understanding of the Kiyanda concept of intelligence. In J. W. Berry & P. R. Dasen (Eds.), *Culture and cognition: Readings in cross-cultural psychology.* London: Methuen.

WOLFE, B. E., & GOLDFRIED, M. R. (1988). Research on psychotherapy integration: Recommendations and conclusions from an NIMH workshop. *Journal of Consulting and Clinical Psychology, 56*, 448–451.

WOLFE, J. B. (1936). Effectiveness of token-rewards for chimpanzees. *Comparative Psychology Monographs, 12*, 1–72 (Serial No. 60).

WONG, P. T. P., & WEINER, B. (1981). When people ask "why" questions, and the heuristics of attributional search. *Journal of Personality and Social Psychology, 40*, 650–663.

WOODWORTH, R. S. (1919). *Personal data sheet (Psychoneurotic inventory).* Chicago: Stoelting.

WOODWORTH, R. S. (1920). *Personal data sheet.* Chicago: Stoelting.

WOODWORTH, R. S., & SELLS, S. B. (1935). An atmosphere effect in formal syllogistic reasoning. *Journal of Experimental Psychology, 18*, 457–460.

WOOLSEY, C. N., MARSHALL, W. H., & BARD, P. (1942). Representation of cutaneous tactile sensibility in the cerebral cortex of the monkey as indicated by evoked potentials. *Bulletin of the Johns Hopkins Hospital, 70*, 399–441.

THE WORLD ALMANAC. (1988). New York: Pharos Books.

WORRINGHAM, C. J., & MESSICK, D. M. (1983). Social facilitation of running: An unobtrusive study. *Journal of Social Psychology, 121*, 23–29.

WU, C., & SHAFFER, D. R. (1987). Susceptibility to persuasive appeals as a function of source credibility and prior experience with the attitude object. *Journal of Personality and Social Psychology, 52*, 677–688.

WUNDT, W. (1904). *Principles of physiological psychology* (E. Titchener, Trans.). London: Swan Sonnenschein. (Original work published 1874)

WYERS, E. J., PEEKE, H. V. S., & HERZ, M. J. (1973). Behavioral habituation in invertebrates. In H. V. S. Peeke & M. J. Herz (Eds.), *Habituation* (Vol. 1, pp. 1–57). New York: Academic Press.

YALOM, I. D. (1975). *The theory and practice of group psychotherapy*, 2nd ed. New York: Basic Books.

YALOM, I. D. (1985). *The theory and practice of group psychotherapy*, 3rd ed. New York: Basic Books.

YAP, P. M. (1951). Mental diseases peculiar to certain cultures: A survey of comparative psychiatry. *Journal of Mental Science, 87*, 313.

YOUNG, F. A. (1961). The effects of restricted visual space on the primate eye. *American Journal of Ophthalmology, 52*, 799–806.

YOUNG, T. (1802). On the theory of light and colours. *Philosophical Transactions of the Royal Society of London, 92*, 12–48.

YUM, J. O. (1991). The impact of Confucianism on interpersonal relationships and communication patterns in East Asia. In L. A. Samovar & R. E. Porter (Eds.), *Intercultural communication* (6th ed.) (pp. 66–78). Belmont, CA: Wadsworth.

ZAJONC, R. B. (1965). Social facilitation. *Science, 149*, 269–274.

ZAJONC, R. B. (1968). Attitudinal effects of mere exposure. *Journal of Personality and Social Psychology* [Monograph] Suppl. 9, 1–27.

ZAJONC, R. B. (1980). Compresence. In P. B. Paulus (Ed.), *Psychology of group influence.* Hillsdale, NJ: Erlbaum.

ZAJONC, R. B. (1984). On the primacy of affect. *American Psychologist, 39*, 117–123.

ZAJONC, R. B. (1985). Emotion and facial efference: A theory reclaimed. *Science, 228*, 15–21.

ZAJONC, R. B., MURPHY, S. T., & INGLEHART, M. (1989). Feeling and facial efference: Implications of the vascular theory of emotion. *Psychological Review, 96*, 395–416.

ZARAGOZA, M. S., & McCLOSKEY, M. (1989). Misleading postevent information and the memory impairment hypothesis: Comment on Belli and reply to Tversky and Tuchin. *Journal of Experimental Psychology: General, 118*, 92–99.

ZEKI, S. (1992, September). The visual image in mind and brain. *Scientific American*, pp. 69–76.

ZESKIND, P. S., & MARSHALL, T. R. (1988). The relation between variations in pitch and maternal perceptions of infant crying. *Child Development, 59*, 193–196.

ZHANG, G., & SIMON, H. A. (1985). STM capacity for Chinese words and idioms: Chunking and acoustical loop hypothesis. *Memory and Cognition, 13*, 193–201.

ZILBOORG, G., & HENRY, G. W. (1941). *A history of medical psychology.* New York: Norton.

ZILLMANN, D., & BRYANT, J. (1974). Effect of residual excitation on the emotional response to provocation and delayed aggressive behavior. *Journal of Personality and Social Psychology, 30*, 782–791.

ZILLMAN, D. (1988). Cognition-excitation interdependencies in aggressive behavior. *Aggressive Behavior, 14*, 51–64.

ZIMBARDO, P. G. (1970). The human choice: Individuation, reason, and order versus deindividuation, impulse, and chaos. In W. J. Arnold & D. Levine (Eds.), *Nebraska Symposium on Motivation* (pp. 237–308). Lincoln: University of Nebraska Press.

ZIMMERMAN, D. W. (1957). Double secondary reinforcement: Method and theory. *Psychological Review, 64*, 373–383.

ZOLA-MORGAN, S., SQUIRE, L. R., & AMARAL, D. (1986). Human amnesia and the medial temporal region: Enduring memory impairment following a bilateral lesion limited to the CA1 field of the hippocampus. *Journal of Neuroscience, 6*, 2950–2967.

ZUBIN, J. (1954). Failures of the Rorschach technique. *Journal of Projective Techniques, 18*, 303–315.

ZUBIN, J., ERON, L. D., & SHUMER, F. (1965). *An experimental approach to projective techniques.* New York: Wiley.

ZUBIN, J., & SPRING, B. (1977). Vulnerability—a new view of schizophrenia. *Journal of Abnormal Psychology, 86*, 103–126.

ZUCKERMAN, M. (1978). Actions and occurrences in Kelley's cube. *Journal of Personality and Social Psychology, 36*, 647–656.

ZUCKERMAN, M., GIOIOSO, C., & TELLINI, S. (1988). Control orientation, self-monitoring, and preference for image versus quality approach to advertising. *Journal of Research in Personality, 22*, 89–100.

NAME INDEX

Abadinsky, H., 207
Abbey, Antonia, 788
Abelson, Robert, 310, 597, 651
Abraham, K. G., 422
Abramson, E., 459
Abramson, L. Y., 658, 660
Ackerman, Diane, 127, 138, 140, 146, 148
Ackerman, Phillip, 568
Acton, William, 463
Adamakos, H., 523
Adams, D. B., 462
Adams, G. R., 455, 525, 579
Adams, J. A., 376
Adams, P. R., 525
Adams, R. D., 101
Adamson, Robert, 337
Ader, Robert, 54, 530–532
Aderman, D., 48, 49
Adler, A., 194
Adler, Alfred, 601
Ageton, S., 208
Agnew, 188
Agras, Stuart, 644, 645
Agronick, G., 29
Ainsworth, Mary, 412
Ajzen, Iceky, 734, 735
Akbarian, S., 667
Akers, R. L., 207, 208
Alagna, S. W., 68
Alampay, D. A., 166
Albright, L., 717
Allen, Andrea, 611
Allen, J. B., 760
Allen, J. G., 422
Allen, Laura, 120
Allgeier, E. R., 770, 788
Allington, R., 579
Allison, T., 188
Alloy, L. B., 660
Allport, Gordon W., 606–607, 714,
    748, 749
Alter, M., 563
Amaral, D., 101, 305
American Association of University
    Women, 422, 423
American Psychiatric Association, 469,
    648, 651, 655
American Psychological Association, 19,
    65, 559, 651
Ames, Adelbert, 163
Ames, Ashley, 470
Anand, B. K., 102
Anderson, A., 532

Anderson, C. A., 768
Anderson, D. J., 143
Anderson, E. S., 428
Anderson, J. R., 299
Anderson, K., 660
Anderson, N. B., 546, 547
Anderson, S. M., 719
Anderson, Susan, 731
Andreasen, N. C., 599, 632, 655, 664, 667
Andrews, G., 702
Angier, N., 656
Anrep, G. V., 232
Antoni, M. H., 532
Appenzeller, T., 101, 110, 305
Arguile, Roger, 686–687
Argyle, M., 755
Aries, 434
Aristotle, 9, 10, 331
Arkin, Robert M., 732
Arkowitz, H., 701
Armstead, Cheryl, 546–547
Armstrong, S. L., 325
Aron, Arthur P., 759
Asarnow, R. F., 663
Asch, S. E., 718
Asch, Solomon, 772–773, 775, 776
Aserinsky, Eugene, 37, 183–185
Ashcraft, M. H., 294, 392
Atkinson, 471
Atkinson, John, 473
Atkinson, Richard, 278, 287–288
Augustine, Saint, 463
Austin, G. A., 323
Ayoub, D. B., 120
Azrin, N. H., 255, 259

Babad, E., 579
Babad, Elisha, 511
Back, K., 455
Bacon, Roger, 68
Baddeley, A. D., 281, 298
Baer, P. E., 527
Bahrick, Harry, 306–307
Bailey, 470
Bailey, S., 660
Bainbridge, W. S., 777
Baldessarini, R. J., 700
Bancroft, J., 461
Bandura, Albert, 43, 265, 617–618, 767
Banks, J. K., 539
Banks, M. S., 111
Barash, D. P., 117

Bard, P., 100
Bard, Philip, 502–503
Bardwell, S., 672
Barefoot, J. C., 537
Barlow, D. H., 693
Barnes, M., 757
Barnett, P. A., 661
Baron, Robert, 716, 756
Baron, Robert S., 532
Barrett, K. C., 507
Bartlett, F. C., 308–310, 311
Bartoshuk, L. M., 149, 150
Basow, S. A., 61, 269, 380, 422, 423, 462,
    585, 672, 738
Bates, M., 208
Bateson, G., 667
Bateson, Gregory, 511
Bath, J. A., 419
Baum, A., 525
Baumgardner, A. H., 732
Baumrind, D., 62, 426
Baxter, L. R., 647
Bayley, N., 568
Beaman, A., 786
Beauchamp, G. K., 151
Beck, Aaron T., 657–658, 689, 690–692
Bee, Helen, 436
Beecher, H. K., 147
Békésy, Georg von, 142–143, 145
Belkin, M., 572
Bell, Alan, 470
Belloc, Nedra, 519
Belsky, J., 268, 414
Bem, Daryl, 611, 745–746
Bem, Sandra L., 316, 731
Bennett, E. L., 111–112, 304
Bennett, P., 519
Bennett, S. M., 269
Benson, D. F., 696
Berardo, D. H., 673
Bergen, J. A., 698
Berglas, S., 732
Berkman, Lisa, 534–535
Berkowitz, L., 48, 49, 768
Berlin, Brent, 355–356
Bermant, G., 464
Bermond, B., 504
Bernard, Claude, 38
Berner, J. G., 585
Bernstein, D. A., 543
Berry, D. S., 719
Berry, R. E., 429, 757
Berscheid, E., 380, 718

Berthenthal, B. I., 507
Bertonici, J., 377
Bertrand, L. D., 651
Bertrand, Lorne, 203
Best, J. B., 329
Bianchi, Kenneth, 650
Biederman, Irving, 166
Billings, A. G., 661
Billson, Janet, 421
Billson, J. M., 421, 422
Binder, J. L., 686
Binet, Alfred, 555–556, 557
Birch, E. E., 377
Birdwhistell, R. L., 510
Birnbaum, I. M., 298
Birren, J. E., 429
Bishop, George, 784
Bishop, Michael, 718
Bjorklund, D. F., 382
Black, D., 699
Blacklock, E. H., 547
Blakemore, C., 175
Blanchard, E. B., 113, 694
Blanchard-Fields, F., 381
Blass, E. M., 448
Bless, H., 740
Bleuler, Eugen, 664
Bliss, T., 303
Block, J. H., 269
Bloom, B. L., 430
Bloom, F. E., 667
Blumenthal, J. A., 381
Bock, K., 296
Boerhaave, Hermann, 463
Boesch, C., 222
Boesch-Ackerman, H., 222
Bohannon, J. N., 308
Boitano, Brian, 492–493
Bolles, Robert, 256–257
Bolton, P. J., 375
Bond, M. H., 619
Boorstin, D. J., 7
Borbely, A. A., 188
Boren, M., 253
Boring, E. G., 11, 160
Borke, Helene, 390
Borkovec, T. C., 543
Botvin, G. L., 390
Bouchard, Claude, 456
Bouchard, T. J., 574, 610
Bourguignon, E., 216
Bower, G. G., 299
Bower, G. H., 283

Bower, Gordon, 291–292, 294, 310, 311, 487, 489
Bowers, Kenneth, 204
Bowlby, J., 410
Bowling, A., 532
Boyd, J. H., 655
Boyle, P. C., 457
Braden, I., 248
Bradley, M. M., 291
Braid, James, 198
Brain, P. F., 766
Brandt, D. A., 268
Bransford, J., 336
Bransford, John, 295, 296, 352
Bray, Douglas, 431
Bray, G. A., 454
Breggin, P. R., 701
Bregman, A. S., 153
Breland, Keller, 261–263
Breland, Marian, 261–263
Brennan, P., 766
Breslau, N., 643
Breslow, Lester, 519
Breuer, Josef, 681
Bricker, W., 767
Bridgman, Percy W., 358
Briggs, J. L., 511
Brobeck, J. R., 102
Broca, Paul, 96, 103–104, 109, 111, 554
Brody, J. E., 525, 633, 654, 671
Brooks-Gunn, Jeanne, 415
Brophy, J. E., 578
Brown, A. M., 145
Brown, P. K., 136
Brown, Roger, 308
Brown, R. W., 296, 355
Brugge, J. F., 143
Brughta, T. S., 698
Bruner, J., 408
Bruner, J. S., 323
Bryant, 507
Buckhout, R., 312
Bucy, P. C., 103
Bugelski, B. R., 166
Bullock, W. A., 609
Bullough, Vince, 463
Bunch, G., 562, 563
Bunney, W. E., 700
Buranen, C., 652
Burger, J. M., 616, 617, 619, 779
Burnstein, E., 718
Burt, A. D., 462
Burt, Martha, 771
Bus, Adriana, 413
Buschke, H., 290
Buss, A. H., 610, 767
Buss, D. M., 757
Butcher, J. N., 114, 669, 671, 689, 697
Butler, R. H., 248
Butler, Samuel, 778
Byrne, D., 466, 779
Byrne, Donn, 716, 756, 758

Cacioppo, J. T., 739, 741, 743
Cade, John, 699
Cain, William S., 149, 151–152
Cajal, Santiago Ramón y, 80
Caldwell, R. A., 430
Calkins, Mary, 28
Callero, P., 764
Campbell, J., 153
Campbell, R. G., 451
Campos, J. J., 507
Cann, A., 269
Cannon, Walter, 449–450, 452, 502–503
Carani, C., 462

Carey, S., 407
Carlsmith, James M., 744, 745, 768
Carlson, M., 489
Carmelli, D., 538
Carpenter, V., 473
Carroll, Janell, 465–466
Carroll, J. L., 465
Carskadon, M. A., 185
Carson, R. C., 114, 669, 671, 689, 697
Carter, B., 268
Carter, Bruce, 317
Carter-Saltzman, L. C., 574
Cartwright, R. D., 194
Carver, C. S., 590
Cash, T. F., 718, 757
Caspi, A., 437
Cattell, James, 554–555, 567
Cattell, Raymond, 607, 609, 620
Cavanaugh, J. C., 396, 429
Ceci, Stephen, 581
Centers for Disease Control, 517
Cervone, D., 618
Chaiken, A. L., 579
Chaiken, S., 738
Chapman, J., 663, 664
Chapman, M., 415
Chapman, W. P., 103
Charcot, Jean, 681
Charlin, V., 489
Chase, P. M., 701
Chase, William, 284–285
Chesney, M. A., 543
Chi, Michilen, 345
Chichetti, D., 188
Chomsky, Noam, 404, 407–408
Christiansen, L., 65
Chrvala, C., 776
Chwalisz, Kathleen, 503–504
Cialdini, Robert B., 779, 780, 786
Clancey, W. J., 347
Claparede, E., 290
Clark, David, 646
Clark, E. V., 168
Clark, G. M., 145
Clark, Herbert H., 352–353, 354
Clark, H. H., 168
Clark, Kenneth, 29
Clark, L. F., 722, 725
Clark, S. B., 406
Clark, W. C., 406
Clarke, A. E., 68
Clark-Lempers, D., 437
Classman, 698
Clayton, P. J., 532
Cleary, T. A., 585
Cleckley, H. M., 649
Clifford, M. M., 455
Close, D. W., 560
Cobb, Sidney, 526
Cochlear Corporation, 144
Cochran, S. D., 518
Cohen, 306
Cohen, A. S., 455, 579
Cohen, D. B., 188
Cohen, J. B., 520–521
Cohen, M. D., 706
Cohen, Nicholas, 530–532
Cohen, N. J., 308
Cohen, Ronald, 765
Cohen, S., 523, 532, 535
Cohn, 413
Coile, D. C., 65
Colby, A., 426
Cole, J. O., 700
Cole, M., 355
Cole, Michael, 358

Cole, N. S., 585
Coleman, R. M., 177, 181, 189
Coles, C. D., 375
Collins, Allan, 298–299
Collins, A. M., 299
Collins, G. H., 101
Collins, J. L., 618
Comas-Diaz, L., 29
Comitas, L., 207
Comstock, G., 43
Condry, J., 479
Conger, R., 437
Conrad, R., 282
Conway, T. L., 527
Cook, H., 268
Cook, Michael, 495–496
Coons, P. M., 649
Cooper, H. M., 617
Coopersmith, S., 416
Copernicus, Nicolaus, 40, 68
Corkin, S., 304
Costa, Paul, 432–433
Costa, P. T., Jr., 525
Cottington, E. M., 527
Cotton, J. L., 768
Cousins, Norman, 533
Cox, J. R., 341
Coyne, James C., 661
Coyne, J. C., 507
Craighead, Linda, 459
Craik, Fergus, 291, 292, 293
Cramer, R. E., 764
Crandall, Christian, 775
Crano, William, 736
Cratty, B., 378
Crawford, J. D., 138
Crockenberg, Susan, 413
Cronkite, R. C., 661
Cross, C., 437
Cross, J. H., 422
Crow, T. J., 664
Crutchfield, R., 778
Culbertson, S., 253
Cunitz, Anita, 288
Curtis, Rebecca, 758–759
Cutrona, Carolyn, 535
Cutshall, J. L., 313
Czajkowski, S. M., 537

Dabbs, J. M., Jr., 767
Damasio, A. R., 98
Damasio, H., 98
D'Andrade, Roy, 216, 217
Danforth, E., 458
Darley, John M., 6
Darwin, Charles, 13, 35–38, 68, 116–117, 444, 485, 496–497
Darwin, C. T., 280
Dasen, Pierre, 398, 399
Davidson, H. H., 623
Davidson, R. J., 491
Davies, Simon, 169
Da Vinci, Leonardo, 25
Davis, 698
Davis, G. C., 643
Davis, J. A., 468
Davis, J. M., 697, 700
Davis, M., 376
Davison, G. C., 685
Davison, J. M., 709
Davitz, J. R., 485
Dawes, R. M., 702
Dax, Marc, 104
Dean, T., 672
Deaux, K., 423
DeBono, Kenneth G., 742
DeCasper, Anthony, 375, 382

deCharms, Richard, 473
DeChick, J., 432
Deci, Edward L., 474
Deckel, A. W., 526
De Courville, N., 68
de Groot, A., 285
deLaCoste-Utamsing, C., 120
Delgado, J., 504
Delgado, P. L., 698
Dell, G. S., 290
DeLong, M. R., 698
Delongis, R., 524
de Mairan, Jean, 177
Dembroski, T. M., 537
Dement, W., 37
Dement, William C., 177, 181, 183, 184, 185, 187, 191, 193
Dempster, F. N., 314
Denmark, F. L., 28
Dennis, Wayne, 376
deRaad, B., 757
Deregowski, J. B., 168
Derlega, V. J., 579
Descartes, René, 9, 516–517
Des Jarlais, D. C., 518
Desor, J. A., 151
Detterman, D. K., 553
Deutsch, G., 108
DeValois, R. L., 136
Devine, Patricia, 748
Diamond, M. C., 112, 304
Dickstein, Susan, 412
Diener, Carol, 475
Diffily, A., 642
Digman, J. M., 609
DiMatteo, M. R., 242
DiMatteo, Robin, 538
Dion, K. K., 760
Dion, K. L., 760
Dipboyle, 455
Discenna, P., 304
Dobson, V., 111
Doddema-Winsemius, M., 757
Dollard, J., 768
Dollard, John, 748
Dominick, J. R., 43
Donaldson, G., 394
Donnerstein, E., 770, 772
Dornbush, R., 207
Dorner, 461
Dorner, G., 470
Douce, R. C., 203
Dowell, R. C., 145
Downs, A. C., 268
Doyle, Arthur Conan, 126
Dragoin, W. B., 238
Dreistadt, R., 194
Duck, S., 755
Duclaux, R., 147
Duncan, Birt, 719, 749
Duncker, Karl, 337
Dunn, J., 415
Dunning, D., 5
Dutton, D. G., 759
Dweck, Carol, 475
Dyer, S., 479
Dywan, Jane, 204

Eagly, A. H., 738, 776
Ebbesen, E. B., 756
Ebbinghaus, Hermann, 275–276, 301, 306
Edwards, B., 103
Egan, D., 346
Egan, G., 690
Eggan, D., 216

Egger, M. D., 103
Ehrenreich, B., 28
Ehrhardt, A. A., 470
Eibl-Eibesfeldt, Irenaus, 57, 445
Eichenbaum, H., 305
Einstein, Albert, 66–67
Eisen, M., 415
Eisle, 423
Ekman, Paul, 491, 499, 501, 510, 511
Elder, Glen, 437
Elkind, D., 389
Elliot, 99
Elliott, A. M., 429
Elliott, D. S., 208
Ellis, A., 469
Ellis, Albert, 689–690, 702
Ellis, H., 68
Ellis, Lee, 470
Eme, R., 423
Emery, C. F., 381
Emmelkamp, P. M. G., 703
English, D., 28
Epstein, Seymour, 579–580, 612
Erdelyi, M. H., 16
Erickson, R. P., 150
Ericsson, K. A., 284, 344
Erikson, Erik, 409, 416
Erikson, M. F., 413
Erkut, S., 478
Ernst, M. L., 464
Eron, L. D., 5, 623
Ervin, F. R., 238
Esse, J. T., 703
Estes, William, 495
Ettin, 695
Evans, D. E., 764
Evans, D. L., 518
Exner, J. E., Jr., 623
Eysenck, Hans J., 567, 608–609, 632, 702

Fagan, J. F., 378
Fagan, Joseph F., 569
Fagot, B. I., 268, 416, 417
Fairhurst, A., 742
Faloon, S., 284
Farland, C., 68
Farmer, A. E., 669
Farrell, Michael, 432
Farris, R., 314
Faust, David, 650, 651
Fausto-Sterling, A., 69
Favin, P. F., 673
Fawcett, J., 671
Fazio, Russell H., 734, 738, 746
Feingold, A., 718, 719, 757
Feldhausen, John, 559
Feltovich, P. J., 345
Ferster, C., 253
Feshbach, S., 738
Festinger, Leon, 743–744, 745, 756, 775
Field, T., 376
Fifer, William, 375, 382
Findley, M. J., 617
Fink, M., 207
Fischbach, G. D., 80, 87
Fishbein, Martin, 734, 735
Fisher, 430
Fisher, W. A., 466
Fiske, Susan, 716, 722
Fitzgerald, F. T., 454, 458
Fliers, E., 461
Flynn, G., 562, 563
Flynn, J. P., 103
Foa, Edna, 489–490
Folds, T. H., 392
Folkman, Susan, 507, 522

Ford, T. W., 673
Forest, M., 562
Forgas, Joseph, 489, 658
Foulkes, D., 194
Fowler, R. D., 643, 645
Fox, J. N., 413
Fox, R., 377
Foy, D. W., 113
Frances, A., 669
Francis, P. L., 377–378
Frank, F., 150
Franz, Carol, 427
Fraser, Scott, 780
Frearson, W., 567
Fredericksen, Norman, 580
Fredrickson, M., 546
Freedman, Jonathan, 780
Freiberg, L., 99
Freiberg, P., 478
Freud, Sigmund, 16, 40, 195–197, 216,
    443, 446–447, 469, 470, 591–599,
    624, 625, 626–627, 640, 646–647, 653,
    681, 684–686, 702, 706, 766
Freund, T., 718
Frey, David, 748
Frey, J., 768
Frey, K. S., 416
Friedman, Howard, 492
Friedman, Meyer, 536–538
Friedman, Richard, 529
Friedman, S., 518
Friesen, Wallace, 491, 499, 510, 511
Frijda, N. H., 511
Fritsch, Gustav, 101
Fromkin, 455
Fromm-Reichman, F., 667
Frye, J. S., 643
Fuchs, J., 572

Gaebelein, J. W., 767
Gaertner, Samuel, 748, 749
Gainer, H., 178
Galilei, Galileo, 7, 68, 167
Gall, Franz Joseph, 94–95
Gallup, George, 415
Galton, Francis, 554–555, 571
Gangstead, S., 613
Gannon, L. R., 539
Ganster, D. C., 535
Garcia, John, 236–237, 238
Garcia-Coll, C. T., 367
Gardner, H., 97
Gardner, Howard, 565–566
Gardner-Medwin, A., 303
Garner, D. M., 423
Garner, W. R., 580
Garvey, Catherine, 407, 408
Gastil, John, 356–357
Gatchel, R. J., 525
Gay, P., 597, 626, 627
Gazzaniga, Michael, 108, 212–213
Geen, R. G., 609, 786
Geerken, M., 778
Geliebter, Allan, 451–452
Geller, G., 479
Gellert, E., 455
Gelman, R., 390
Gentry, W. D., 547
George, Carol, 41–42, 51, 53, 54
Geschwind, Norman, 96
Gettys, L. D., 269
Gibson, J. J., 158
Gibson, R. A., 412
Gildea, P. M., 407
Gilgen, A. R., 604
Giller, E. L., 113

Gilligan, Carol, 426
Gilliland, K., 609
Gioioso, C., 742
Glaberson, W., 579
Gladue, Brian, 470
Gladwin, E. T., 399
Glanzer, Murray, 288
Glaser, R., 344, 345, 569, 570
Glass, A. L., 322, 329
Glass, Gene, 702, 703
Gleitman, H., 325
Gleitman, L. R., 325
Glenberg, A. M., 291
Glick, P. C., 430
Gmelch, George, 250
Goddard, G. V., 303
Goddard, Henry, 584
Godden, D. R., 298
Goethals, G. P., 784
Gold, A. R., 462
Goldberg, L. R., 727
Goldberger, Joseph, 38, 39, 44, 51, 329
Goldfried, M. R., 701
Goldman-Rakic, Patricia S., 99, 101–102,
    111, 405
Goldschmidt, E., 572
Goldstein, E. B., 101, 165, 169, 225, 323
Goldstein, Michael J., 667–668
Goleman, D., 535, 580, 632, 643, 652,
    708, 749
Golgi, Camillo, 77, 80
Gombrich, E. H., 164–165
Goodale, W., 423
Goode, E., 205, 206, 207, 211
Goodenough, D. R., 192
Goodenough, W. H., 399
Goodman, N., 455
Goodnow, J., 323
Goodwin, G. M., 698
Gordon, B., 699, 700
Gordon, D., 354
Gorman, J. M., 700
Gorski, R. A., 120
Gorzalka, B. B., 464
Gotlib, I., 661
Gottesman, I. I., 656, 665, 666, 669
Gottfredson, M., 208
Gottlieb, J., 563
Gould, R. L., 432, 554, 652
Gould, Stephen, 584
Gove, W. R., 778
Graeber, R. C., 176, 180
Graham, 577
Graham, R. B., 84
Grajek, S., 761
Gravitz, M. A., 702
Green, A. I., 656
Green, R. F., 366
Greenberg, R. P., 698
Greenblatt, M., 705, 706
Greene, E., 204
Greenfield, S., 175
Greeno, J. G., 345
Greenough, W. T., 112, 120, 304
Greer, Steven, 542
Gregory, Richard L., 160, 163, 168
Griffin, D. R., 175, 222
Griffit, W., 462
Griffith, R. M., 194
Griggs, R. A., 341
Groen, G., 392
Groos, G., 178
Gruder, C. L., 764
Grusec, J. E., 259
Guilford, J. J., 564
Guilleminault, C., 191

Gurn, S. M., 456
Guthrie, R. V., 29, 68
Guttman, N., 254
Guze, S. B., 653, 654
Gwiazda, J., 377

Hagen, M. A., 157
Haist, F., 307
Hall, C., 174, 192
Hall, Calvin, 193–194
Hall, Evelyn, 169
Hall, G. Stanley, 28
Halpern, A. S., 560
Halpern, D. F., 61, 334
Halpern, R., 437
Halverson, C. F., Jr., 316
Hamill, Ruth, 730–731
Hamilton, D. L., 720
Hamilton, J. A., 68
Haney, C., 785
Hankins, W. G., 236
Hanna, R., 423
Hansen, R. D., 725
Harbluk, J. L., 290
Harburg, E., 546, 547
Hargis, K., 489
Harkins, S., 783, 784
Harlow, Harry, 409–410
Harlow, Margaret, 409–410
Harman, M. J., 623
Harrell, T. H., 466
Harris, R. L., 429, 430
Harris, W., 546
Harrison, James, 520
Harrow, 700
Harrow, M., 700
Harter, Susan, 416
Hartnett, S. A., 547
Harvey, J. H., 728
Harvey, R., 702
Harvey, William, 536
Hass, A., 465
Hastie, 312
Hatfield, E., 462
Hathaway, Starke, 621–622
Haviland, Jeanette, 411
Haviland, Jeannette, 494
Haviland, Susan E., 352–353
Hawking, Stephen, 38–40
Hayes, J. R., 340
Hays, R. B., 756
Hays, Robert, 534
Hayward, P., 700
Heath, R. G., 103
Hebb, Donald, 111, 355
Hebel, N., 101
Heider, F., 726
Heider, Fritz, 723
Heiman, Julia, 466–468
Held, R., 377
Heller, Joan, 570
Helmholtz, Hermann von, 10–11, 133,
    135, 137
Helmreich, R. L., 473
Helmreich, Robert, 601
Helson, H., 153
Helzer, J. E., 113
Hendrick, C., 760, 762
Hendrick, S., 760, 762
Hennessy, H. R., 157
Henri, V., 555
Henry, G. W., 680
Herdt, G., 464
Hergenhahn, B. R., 167
Hering, Ewald, 134–135, 137
Herman, Peter, 453

Heron, A., 398
Herrero, S., 449
Herskovits, M. J., 68
Herz, M. J., 224
Hesse-Biber, S., 422, 423
Higgens-Trenk, A., 420
Higgins, E. Tory, 616
Higgitt, A., 700
Hilgitt, E. R., 17, 199, 202, 204
Hilgard, J. R., 199, 202
Hill, C., 758
Hind, J. E., 143
Hineline, P. N., 257
Hiner, S. L., 524
Hines, M., 120
Hinson, R. E., 241
Hippocrates, 679
Hiroto, D. S., 659
Hirsch, J., 457
Hirschi, T., 777
Hirshi, T., 208
Hitch, G. L., 281
Hitzig, Eduard, 101
Hobfoll, N. E., 536
Hobson, Allen, 194
Hochberg, J. E., 153
Hodges, K. K., 268
Hoebel, B. G., 102
Hoffman, Albert, 206–207
Hoffman, C., 357
Hogarty, P. S., 568
Hokanson, Jack, 541
Holden, C., 579, 610, 633
Hollabaugh, L. C., 788, 789
Hollingworth, L. S., 68
Holloway, R. L., 120
Holmes, David, 543
Holmes, D. S., 430
Holmes, J. S., 429
Holmes, Thomas, 523–524
Holway, A. H., 160
Holyoak, K. J., 322, 329
Holz, W. C., 259
Homan, Carolyn, 491
Homans, G. C., 757
Honzik, C. H., 263
Hooker, Evelyn, 469
Hooley, J. M., 668
Hoover, C. B., 698
Hopper, K., 526
Horn, J. L., 394
Horner, Matina, 478–479
Horney, Karen, 601–602, 627
Hothersall, D., 12
House, James, 534
House, J. S., 527
Houston, L. N., 29
Houston-Stein, A., 420
Hovland, C., 749
Hovland, Carl, 738
Hovland, C. I., 739
Howard, Ann, 431
Howard, K. I., 380, 702, 704
Hubel, D. H., 110, 191
Hudson, W., 168
Huesmann, L. Rowell, 368
Hughes, Howard, 643, 645
Huizinga, D., 208
Humphrey, N., 175
Hunter, B., 789
Hunter, J. E., 585
Hurlburt, N., 568
Hutcherson, H. W., 722, 725
Hutchins, E., 399
Hyde, J. S., 61, 62, 69, 260, 268, 417,
　465, 627

Hyde, T. S., 293
Ifill, G., 756
Inbar, V., 579
Inciardi, James, 208
Ingham, Alan, 783
Inglehart, M., 502
Inguar, 109
Inhelder, B., 385
Insko, 775
Intons-Peterson, M. J., 417
Irvine, S. H., 578
Isabella, R. A., 414
Isen, Alice, 48, 50, 488
Isenberg, D. J., 784
Izard, Caroll E., 410, 486, 487, 499

Jacklin, C. N., 29, 269
Jacklin, J. N., 417
Jackson, J. S., 547
Jacob, R. G., 543
Jacobs, G. H., 136
Jahoda, G., 399
James, S. A., 547
James, William, 12, 175, 276–277, 296,
　497–498, 503, 504
James, W. T., 256
Jamison, K. R., 655
Janda, L. H., 718, 757
Janet, J., 202
Janowsky, D. S., 672
Jeffery, Robert, 452, 459
Jemmott, J. B., III, 520, 532
Jenkins, C. D., 538
Jenkins, James, 294
Jenkins, J. J., 293
Jenkins, J. R., 563
Johnson, Catherine, 788
Johnson, C. L., 423
Johnson, D. R., 357
Johnson, E. H., 546
Johnson, Eric, 488
Johnson, Marcia, 295, 352
Johnson, V., 208
Johnson, V. E., 464
Johnson, W., 411
Jolles, I., 687
Jones, A., 248
Jones, Edward, 734
Jones, E. E., 726, 732
Jones, Mary Cover, 239
Jones, M. C., 380
Jones, S., 739
Josephson, W. L., 768
Julien, R. M., 206, 211
Jung, Carl, 192, 599–600
Juraska, J. M., 120

Kagan, Jerome, 366–367
Kahneman, D., 332, 333, 334–335
Kail, Robert, 393
Kail, R. V., 406
Kalat, J. W., 449, 462, 476
Kalish, H. I., 254
Kalsbeck, W., 547
Kambara, T., 768
Kamin, L. J., 62
Kamin, Leon, 235–236, 238, 260–261
Kamphares, R. W., 585
Kandel, E., 222, 224, 766
Kanner, A. D., 524
Kanner, Allen, 523, 524
Kant, Immanuel, 10
Kaplan, M. R., 785
Kaplan, N. M., 546
Kaplan, R. M., 208, 520, 584, 585
Kaptein, A. A., 519

Kapur, S., 698
Kauer, J. S., 149, 151
Kaufman, A. S., 585
Kaufman, Lloyd, 164–165
Kaufman, N. L., 585
Kay, Paul, 355–356
Kaye, D. B., 392
Kazdin, A. E., 259
Keats, D. M., 578
Keele, S. W., 282
Keesey, Richard, 457
Kellas, G., 294
Keller, Breland, 261–263
Keller, Helen, 138
Keller, Marian, 261–263
Kelley, Harold, 723–726
Kelley, K., 779
Kellman, P. I., 377
Kelly, George, 616
Kelman, H. C., 62
Kelsoe, John, 666
Kendrick, C., 415
Kendrick, D. T., 466
Kenny, D. A., 717
Kenshalo, D. R., 147
Kerr, N. L., 785
Kiecolt-Glaser, J., 532
Kiesler, C. A., 738
Kiesler, S. B., 738
Kihlstrom, J. F., 198, 202, 599
Kilham, W., 781
Kimball, M., 579
Kimmel, Michael, 518
Kimura, D., 104
Kimura, Doreen, 120, 121
Kimzey, S. L., 532
King, Gilliam, 615
Kinsey, A. C., 43, 465, 468
Kinsey, Alfred, 463–464
Kintsch, W., 290
Kirby, M., 770
Kirmayer, L. J., 640
Kitayama, S., 618
Klahr, David, 391
Klassen, D., 650
Klatzky, 289
Klatzky, R. L., 719
Kleinberg, O., 68, 510
Kleinman, J. E., 667
Kleinman, Sheryl, 493–494
Kleitman, Nathaniel, 37, 181, 183–185
Klerman, G., 673
Kline, J., 268
Klopfer, B., 623
Kluckholn, C., 613
Klüver, H., 103
Kobasa, Suzanne, 539
Koelling, R. A., 238
Kohlberg, Lawrence, 424–427, 435
Köhler, Wolfgang, 17, 264–265, 355
Kohn, R. R., 381
Kohut, Helmut, 686
Kolata, G., 408
Kolb, B., 305
Kolb, L. C., 113
Kolodny, R. C., 464
Kosambi, D. D., 169
Kowalczyk-McPhee, B., 562, 563
Kozak, Michael, 489
Kral, P. A., 238
Kramer, D. A., 396
Krank, M. D., 241
Krantz, D. S., 526
Krebs, D. L., 765
Kripke, D. F., 189
Kroger, W. S., 203

Kroll, N. E. A., 282
Kruglanski, Arie W., 718, 725–726
Kübler-Ross, Elizabeth, 433–434
Kubovy, M., 157
Kuiper, N. A., 292
Kulick, James, 308
Kulik, C., 578
Kulik, J., 578
Kupferman, I., 104

LaBarre, W., 510
Laboratory of Comparative Human
　Cognition, 399
Labouvie-Vief, Giesela, 381, 395
Labov, W., 324
LaFrance, M., 492
Laird, James D., 499, 500
Lakoff, G., 354
Lamb, Michael, 414
Lambert, M. J., 702, 703
Landman, J. T., 702
Landrine, H., 672
Landsman, S., 559, 561, 580
Lang, Peter, 239–240
Lange, David, 498, 503, 504
Langer, E. J., 337
Langer, Ellen, 597, 651
Langlois, J. H., 268
LaPiere, R. T., 735–736
Lassen, 109
Latané, Bibb, 6, 763, 783, 784
Lau, I., 357
Laughlin, H. P., 648
Laumann, E. O., 758
Lavie, 194
Laurence, Jean-Roche, 204
Lazarus, Richard S., 507, 508, 520–521,
　522, 525
Lazovik, David, 239–240
Leach, E., 510
Lecuyer, R., 568
LeDain, G., 206
LeDoux, Joseph, 108, 504
Lee, J. A., 762
Leff, J. P., 668
Leibel, R. L., 457
Leinen, 89
Lelwica, Mary, 411
Lempers, J. D., 437
Lenneberg, E. H., 355
Lennon, S. J., 742
Lepper, M. R., 736
Lerner, M. J., 728
Lerner, Richard, 423
Lerner, R. M., 455
Leslie, G. R., 673
Lesse, S., 696
Lesser, I. M., 422
Lesserman, J., 518
Lester, B. M., 375, 411
Lester, G. L., 464
Letsinger, R., 347
Lettieri, D. J., 208
Levenson, Robert W., 499, 500, 511
Leventhal, 499
Leventhal, H., 739
Levin, H., 427
Levin, Joel, 393
Levin, Paula, 48, 50, 488
Levine, F. M., 239
Levine, Martin, 518
LeVine, Robert, 216–217
Levinson, D. J., 380, 432
Levy, Gary, 317
Lewin, M., 29
Lewinsohn, Peter, 658, 661

Lewis, 268
Lewis, E. C., 419
Lewis, M., 410
Lewis, Michael, 415
Lia, S. L., 430
Lichtenstein, S., 332
Lichtman, Steven, 458
Lichtman, S. W., 454
Lickey, M. E., 699, 700
Lieberman, D. A., 248, 264
Liebert, Diane, 390
Liebert, R. M., 406
Liebert, Robert, 390
Liebowitz, H., 157
Liebowitz, Hershel, 168
Liederman, V., 455
Liggett, J. C., 718
Liker, J., 437
Liker, Jeffrey, 581
Lilly, 577
Lindzey, G., 584
Linz, D., 770
Lippa, 780, 782
Lips, Hillary, 478
Liska, A. E., 777
Little, K. B., 623
Littman, R., 767
Livingstone, M. S., 110, 137
Locke, John, 9, 16
Locke, S. E., 520
Lockhart, R. S., 292
Lodico, M. G., 393
Loehlin, J. C., 584
Loftus, Elizabeth F., 204, 297, 299, 311, 312
Loftus, G. R., 297
LoPresto, C. T., 465
Loranger, 671
Lord, C. G., 736
Lord, Charles, 330
Lorenz, K., 445
Lorenz, Konrad, 766
Loth, D., 464
Lovaas, O. I., 257–259, 694
Love, G., 770
Lowenstein, L. F., 527
Lowry, D. T., 770
Lubin, A., 614
Luborsky, L., 704
Luby, 696
Luchins, A. S., 338
Lucy, Peter, 354
Luh, C. W., 307
Lumsdaine, A. A., 739
Lundy, A., 623
Lupfer, M. B., 722, 725
Lusthaus, E., 562
Lynn, S. J., 201

McArthur, C. C., 432
McArthur, L. A., 725
McArthur, L. Z., 719
McBride-Chang, C., 29
McCall, R. B., 376, 568, 569
McCann, Lisa, 543
McCarley, Robert, 194
McCarley, R. W., 667
McCartney, Kathleen, 371
McClelland, David C., 471–473, 474, 476
McClelland, D. C., 517
McCloskey, M., 297, 308
Maccoby, E., 269, 417, 427
McConkey, K. M., 202
McCormick, D. A., 305
McCoy, Marcia, 788–789
McCrae, Robert, 432–433

McCroy, G., 377–378
McCully, J., 241
McDavid, J. W., 776
McDougall, William, 444
McEvoy, L., 113
McEvoy, M. A., 562, 563
McFarland, C., 68
McFarlane, J., 68
McGarry, A., 650
McGhie, A., 663, 664
McGue, M., 574
McGuffin, P., 669
McGuire, C. V., 730
McGuire, W. J., 730
Mack, Deborah, 453
MacKay, A., 151
McKenna, R. J., 458
McKenzie-Mohr, D., 731
Mackie, D., 736
McKillip, 757
McKinley, J. C., 621–622
McKinney, M. E., 528
Macko, K. A., 110, 133
McKoon, G., 290
McLachlan, J. R., 290
McLoyd, Vonnie, 437
McNally, Richard, 490
McNamara, J. R., 29
McNeil, D., 296
McNeill, D., 408
MacRae, J., 241
Madden, 749
Maddox, G. L., 455
Maehr, M., 619
Maes, S., 519
Magloire, K., 532
Magoun, H. W., 185
Maier, N. R. F., 542
Maier, S. F., 338, 658
Mailer, Norman, 670
Main, M., 412
Main, Mary, 41–42, 51, 53, 54
Maisiak, R., 423
Majors, R., 421, 422
Majors, Richard, 421
Malamuth, N. M., 770, 772
Malatesta, Carol, 494
Malloy, T. E., 717
Mann, J., 686
Mann, J. J., 698
Mann, L., 781
Mann, Leon, 785
Mantell, D. M., 781
Marcel, Anthony, 599
Marcia, James, 418, 419
Marcia, J. E., 422
Marcus, Sandra, 328
Marino, M., 422, 423
Markstrom, C. A., 422
Markus, H., 618, 619
Markus, Hazel, 730–731
Marlatt, Alan, 211
Marshall, J. F., 451, 506
Marshall, Timothy, 410
Marshall, W. H., 100
Martin, C. E., 43
Martin, C. L., 68, 316
Martin, G., 240
Martin, Leonard, 500
Maslach, C., 506
Maslow, Abraham, 16, 17, 443, 447–448, 602, 687
Massachusetts Advocacy Center, 562, 563
Masters, W. H., 464
Matsumoto, David, 511, 619

Matteo, P. A., 673
Maurer, D., 376
Mavensell, J. H. R., 110
Mavin, Gregory, 616
Mayer, 767
Mayo, C., 492
Mazziotta, J. C., 99
Mead, Margaret, 269, 511
Mechel, 68
Mednick, S. A., 766
Meece, J. L., 260
Meltzoff, A. N., 376
Melzak, R., 169
Melzak, Ronald, 148
Mercer, Jane, 585
Mervis, C. B., 325
Merzenich, M. M., 112
Mesmer, Anton, 198, 680–681
Mesquita, B., 511
Messer, S., 701
Mesulam, M. M., 105
Metalsky, G. I., 660
Metzler, J., 282
Metzner, Helen, 534
Meudell, P., 300
Meyer, A. S., 296
Meyer, J. P., 765
Mikulincer, M., 536
Miles, L. E. M., 178
Milgram, Stanley, 62–65, 726, 780–781, 786
Miller, C. E., 785
Miller, D. T., 728, 765
Miller, George A., 283, 407
Miller, Kim, 758–759
Miller, N., 489
Miller, Neal, 64–66
Miller, Thomas, 702, 703
Miller, W. C., 698
Miller-Herringer, Terry, 492
Milner, B., 101, 304
Milner, P., 103 Milojkovic, J. H., 5
Milstein, V., 649
Mineka, Susan, 495–496
Mingay, D. J., 204
Minson, R. E., 241
Mischel, Walter, 611
Mishkin, M., 101, 110, 133, 305
Mitler, M. M., 191
Moffitt, T. E., 397
Money, J., 464
Moniz, Antonio Egas, 696
Monson, T. C., 613
Montagu, A., 767
Montemayor, Richard, 415, 419
Mooney, J. J., 656
Moore, M. K., 376
Moos, R. H., 661
Morales, A., 420
Morawski, J. G., 29
Moreland, R. L., 739
Morokoff, Patricia, 467
Morris, K. J., 739
Morris, R. G. M., 264
Morrison, V., 225
Moruzzi, G., 185
Moskowitz, Arlene, 405
Motley, M. T., 597
Moulton, D., 151
Moulton, D. G., 151
Mountcastle, V. B., 87
Moyer, K. E., 103
Muehlenhard, Charlene L., 788–789
Mulherin, A., 765
Mullholland, Tim M., 569, 571
Murdock, B. B., 288

Murphy, S. T., 502
Murray, F. B., 390
Murray, H. A., 471, 613
Muuss, R. E., 391, 422, 423
Myers, 356
Myers, David, 784

Nadel, L., 298
Nash, 201
Nash, M. R., 201
Nathan, P., 654
Nathan, S., 627
National Institutes of Health, 454
Natsoulas, T., 175
Naumburg, Margaret, 686
Neale, G. C., 709
Neale, J. M., 685
Needham, S., 294
Neimark, E. D., 391
Neisser, V., 306
Nelson, D., 758
Nelson, D. J., 560
Nelson, K., 300
Nelson, R. J., 100
Newcomb, Theodore, 774
Newell, Alan, 342–343, 347
Nguyen, T., 437
Nicholls, J., 619
Nicol, S. E., 665, 666
Nisbett, Richard, 768
Nisbett, Richard E., 6, 726, 727
Noble, E. P., 298
Nolen-Hoeksema, S., 673
Norcross, J. C., 702
Norman, D. A., 287
Norton, G. R., 649
Nutt, D. J., 646
Novin, D., 450, 451
Nurius, P., 619
Nyiti, Raphael, 399

O'Brien, Paul, 580
O'Connell, M., 670
O'Connor, W. A., 650
Odbert, H. S., 607
Oden, M. H., 559
Odom, S. L., 562, 563
Offer, D., 380, 419
Offir, Carole, 466
Ohbuchi, K., 768
Oldham, 671
Olds, J. L., 103, 304
Olds, M. E., 103
O'Leary, K. D., 654
O'Leary, R. D., 417
Oltmanns, T. F., 709
O'Neil, C. W., 197
Oppenheimer, J. Robert, 738
Orlinsky, D. E., 702, 704
Orlofsky, J. L., 422
Orne, Martin T., 200, 203, 204, 652
Orne, M. T., 650
Oskamp, S., 734
Osler, William, 536–537
Ostertag, P. A., 29
Ostrov, E., 380
O'Sullivan, Maureen, 491
Owens, E., 145

Page, Richard, 734
Pallmeyer, T. P., 113
Palmer, J. C., 312
Palmore, E., 464
Palumbo, S. R., 194
Pancake, V., 413

Pannenheim, Bertha, 681
Park, B., 731
Park, Bernadette, 721
Park, K. A., 413
Parke, R. D., 268
Parke, Ross, 412
Parker, E. S., 298
Parker, S. P., 433
Parkman, J., 392
Patterson, G. R., 767
Patterson, T. L., 520
Pattison, E. M., 434
Paulhus, 616
Paunonen, S. V., 609, 717
Pavlov, Ivan, 15, 224, 226–228, 232, 233, 238, 243, 357, 692
Peake, P. K., 618
Peale, Norman Vincent, 540
Pear, J., 240
Pearl, D., 768
Pearlmutter, Marion, 394
Pearson, H. W., 208
Peeke, H. V. S., 224
Pellegrino, J. W., 569, 570
Penfield, Wilder, 100
Peplau, L. A., 758
Perkins, D. O., 518
Perky, Cheves, 57
Perley, M. J., 653
Perry, B. D., 113
Perry, C., 204
Perry, William, 395–396
Petersen, A. C., 378, 380, 423
Peterson, Lloyd, 286
Peterson, Margaret, 286
Petri, H. L., 448
Petty, Richard E., 739, 741, 743
Pfaffenbarger, R. S., 381
Pfeffenbaum, A., 666
Pfungst, Oscar, 54
Phelps, 307
Phelps, M. E., 99
Phillips, M. R., 652
Phillips, Susan, 430–431
Piaget, Jean, 42, 369, 382–391, 398–399, 426–427
Pick, H., 168
Pickering, Thomas, 529
Pietromonaco, P. R., 432
Piliavin, J. A., 764
Pillard, 470
Pinel, John, 449
Pinel, Philippe, 680
Pi-Sunyer, X., 451
Pittillo, E. S., 649
Plato, 9
Plomin, R., 610
Plutchik, Robert, 485, 486–487
Poincaré, Jules-Henri, 7
Pomeroy, W. B., 43
Pope, K. S., 174
Porter, R. E., 168
Posner, M. I., 282
Powell, L. H., 538
Power, T., 268
Powers, P. C., 786
Powers, P. S., 655
Premack, David, 256
Prentice, D. A., 729–730
Prentice-Dunn, S., 748
Pressley, M., 392
Pressley, Michael, 393
Priest, R. F., 756
Prochaska, J. O., 702
Ptolemy, Claudius, 39, 40
Putnam, F. W., 649

Quillian, Ross, 299

Rabkin, J. G., 525
Rachlin, H., 257
Rachman, S., 258
Radke-Yarrow, M., 415
Radmacher, S. A., 519, 533
Radtke, Lorraine, 203
Rahe, Richard, 523–524
Ramey, C., 559, 561, 580
Ramist, L., 577
Raphael, B., 343
Rasche, L., 779
Rasmussen, Steve, 642
Rasmussen, Theodore, 100
Ratcliffe, R., 290
Rausch, J., 672
Ravussin, E., 457
Raynal, D. M., 178
Rayner, Rosalie, 15–16, 228, 229, 232, 495, 643–644
Rechtschaffen, A., 191
Reedy, M. N., 429
Rees, E., 344
Regier, D. A., 633, 641, 642, 672
Reid, E. C., 654
Reidel, 757
Reinisch, June, 120
Reinke, B. J., 430
Reis, H. T., 719
Reischauer, R., 437
Reisenzein, R., 507, 765
Reiser, M. F., 529
Reiss, B. F., 469
Reissland, N., 376
Reitman, J. S., 346
Renzulli, Joseph, 559
Repetti, R. L., 432
Rescorla, R. A., 234–235, 238, 260–261
Resnick, J. S., 367
Reznick, S. L., 367
Rheingold, H., 268
Rhyne, D., 429
Richman, R., 526
Ricks, D. F., 703
Rieber, Arthur, 595
Riley, Vernon, 521, 523
Rips, Lance, 328
Rist, R. C., 579
Ritvo, E. R., 257
Robberson, Margaret, 739
Robbins, Cynthia, 534
Robins, C. J., 660
Robins, E., 654
Robins, L. N., 113, 633, 641, 642, 672
Robinson, Francis, 312
Robinson, H. B., 561
Robinson, N. M., 561
Rock, Irving, 164–165
Rodin, J., 423, 455, 458, 763, 764
Rodnick, E. H., 668
Roeder, K., 118, 138
Roeper, P. J., 547
Rogers, Carl, 16, 17, 602–605, 625, 687–689, 702–703
Rogers, Ronald, 739
Rogers, R. W., 748
Rogerts, T. B., 292
Rohsenow, Damaris, 211
Roland, P. E., 99
Romer, D., 764
Rorschach, Hermann, 623
Rose, D., 225
Rose, J. E., 143
Rose, Robert, 526

Rosen, D. H., 469
Rosenbaum, Michael, 658
Rosenberg, Stanley, 432
Rosenhan, 648
Rosenhan, D. L., 489
Rosenman, Ray, 536–538
Rosenthal, R., 55, 579
Rosenzweig, Mark, 304
Rosenzweig, Michael, 111–112
Rosner, M., 572
Ross, C. A., 649
Ross, D., 43, 265
Ross, Dorothea, 767
Ross, E. D., 105
Ross, L., 5, 726
Ross, L. E., 230
Ross, M., 68
Ross, S. A., 43, 265
Ross, Sheila, 767
Ross, S. M., 230
Rossi, P. H., 705
Rothbart, Myron, 721
Rotter, Julian, 617
Rotton, J., 768
Rovee-Collier, Carolyn, 298
Rubin, J. Z., 268
Rubin, V., 207
Rubin, Z., 758
Ruble, D. N., 68, 416
Rundus, D., 289
Runyan, William, 613–614
Rusak, B., 178
Rush, Benjamin, 680
Rushton, J. P., 766
Rusiniak, K. W., 236
Ruskin, John, 129
Russek, M., 451
Russell, Bertrand, 564
Russell, Diana E. H., 770, 788
Russell, Wallace, 294
Russo, N. F., 28
Rutkowski, G. K., 764
Rutledge, J. A., 381
Rutter, M., 419

Saarni, C., 417
Sachs, Jacqueline, 290–291, 308, 428
Sachs, O., 274
Sackheim, H. A., 701
Sacks, Oliver, 74–75
Sadker, D., 417
Sadker, M., 417
Salapatek, P., 111
Sale, K., 442, 443
Sallis, J. F., 520
Salovey, P., 489
Saltzman, A., 268
Sammons, M. T., 702
Samovar, L. A., 168
Sandeen, E., 239
Sandoval, Jonathan, 584–585
Sanford, E. C., 4
Sanford, R. C., 604
Sarafino, 205
Sattler, J. M., 557
Sawyer, J., 756
Sayers, M., 208
Scarr, Sandra, 371, 574, 575, 578
Schachter, J., 546
Schachter, Stanley, 457–458, 505–506
Schacter, D. L., 290
Schaeffer, M. A., 525
Schaffer, H. R., 406
Schaie, K. W., 366, 394, 429
Schank, Roger, 310
Scheier, M. F., 590

Scheier, Michael, 540
Schiff, M., 575
Schildkraut, J. J., 656
Schmalz, 468
Schmidt, 561
Schmidt, F. L., 585
Schmidt, S. R., 308
Schneider, W., 392
Schneidiman, E. S., 623
Schroeder, D. H., 525
Schul, Y., 718
Schumann, D., 743
Schuri, U., 101
Schutte, N. S., 43, 44, 45, 46, 47, 49, 50, 51, 768
Schwartz, B., 346
Schwartz, D. M., 423
Schwartz, W. J., 178
Scott, J. A., 572
Scoville, W. B., 304
Scribner, Sylvia, 355, 358–359
Sears, R., 749
Sears, R. R., 427
Segal, M. W., 756
Selfe, L., 561
Seligman, 648
Seligman, Martin, 237
Seligman, M. E. P., 195, 523, 658, 659
Selye, Hans, 528–529
Sem-Jacobson, C. W., 504
Sentis, Keith, 730–731
Serbin, L. A., 259, 417
Shaffer, 368
Shaffer, D. R., 734, 738
Shah, S., 650
Shaman, P., 151
Shanab, 781
Shapiro, Colin, 186
Shatz, M., 390
Shavitt, S., 734
Shean, G., 663–664
Sheehan, S., 663
Sheffield, F. D., 739
Shehan, G., 673
Shepard, R. N., 282
Shepperd, James A., 732, 783
Sheridan, C. L., 519, 533
Sherman, J. A., 260
Sherman, M. F., 465
Sherman, N. C., 465
Shields, J., 656, 666
Shields, S. A., 68
Shiffrin, Richard, 278, 287–288
Shimamura, A. P., 307
Shina, K., 157
Shore, M. F., 706
Short, K. R., 377
Shortliffe, E. H., 347
Shotland, R. L., 789
Shumer, F., 623
Shutts, D., 696
Sieber, J. E., 62
Siegel, Shepard, 241–242
Siegler, Robert S., 390, 391, 392, 393
Sigall, Harold, 734
Sigler, E., 579
Sigman, M., 569
Silberstein, L., 423, 455
Silverman, L. H., 599
Silverstein, B., 423
Simmons, J. A., 138
Simmons, James, 258–259
Simon, 344
Simon, H. A., 344
Simon, Herbert, 282–283, 284–285, 342–343

Simon, Theodore, 382
Simons, R. L., 437
Simons, R. N., 189
Sims, E. A. H., 458
Singer, Jerome, 505–506
Singer, R., 739
Sistrunk, F., 776
Sivacek, John, 736
Sizemore, Chris C., 649
Skinhos, 109
Skinner, B. F., 4, 7, 16, 223, 224, 244–246, 249–250, 261, 263, 322, 407, 495, 571, 605, 624, 661
Slater, A., 225
Slater, Alan, 569
Slater, P. C., 701
Slaughter, D. T., 437
Slavin, 749
Slovic, Paul, 332
Smith, Allen, 493–494
Smith, Craig, 582
Smith, D., 702
Smith, Eleanor, 758
Smith, J. E., 423
Smith, Mary Lee, 702, 703
Smith, T., 468
Snarey, J. R., 426
Snyder, Mark, 613, 720, 742
Solomon, J., 412
Solomon, L. Z., 764
Solomon, P. R., 102
Solomon, R. L., 247, 658
Solomon, Susan, 352
Solomon, Z., 536
Sorce, James, 412
Southwick, S. M., 113
Spanos, Nicholas P., 200, 203, 651
Spear, N. E., 298
Spearman, Charles, 564
Speltz, M. L., 563
Spence, J. R., 473
Spence, Melanie J., 375
Sperling, George, 279–280
Sperry, Roger, 106, 108
Spitzer, R. L., 641, 648, 655, 662, 669, 670
Spring, B., 669
Springer, S. P., 108
Springston, F., 283
Spuhler, J. N., 584
Spurgeon, P., 519
Squire, L. R., 101, 112, 305, 306, 307, 701
Sroufe, L. A., 413
Staats, Arthur, 736–738
Staats, Carolyn, 736–738
Stainback, S., 562, 563
Stainback, W., 562, 563
Stanley, S. M., 201
Stanovich, K. E., 8, 38
Stark, R., 777
Staudt, 461
Steen, Diana, 212–213
Stefanis, C., 207
Stein, B. S., 296, 336
Steinberg, L., 418
Stellar, E., 451
Stelmack, R. M., 609
Stephenson, W., 603
Stepper, Sabine, 500
Stern, William, 556–557
Sternberg, R. J., 552, 553, 569, 571
Sternberg, Robert, 564, 580–581, 582, 760–761
Sternberg, Saul, 286, 287
Stevens-Long, J., 434
Stockton, R. A., 643
Stolp, R., 466

Stone, 240
Storlieu, L. H., 457
Storms, Michael, 728
Strachan, A. M., 668
Strack, Fritz, 500
Strack, S., 661
Streib, G., 433
Streuning, E. L., 525
Striegel-Moore, R., 423, 455
Strupp, H. H., 686, 704
Stunkard, Albert J., 456, 458–459
Stuss, D. T., 696
Styron, William, 671
Sue, David, 708, 709
Sue, Debra Wing, 708, 709
Sumner, Francis, 28–29
Super, Donald, 430–431
Surbey, M. K., 397
Susser, M., 526
Swaab, D. F., 461
Swan, G. E., 538
Swann, William, 732
Sweeney, P. D., 660
Syme, Leonard, 534–535

Takagi, S. F., 151
Tangney, J. P., 738
Tannen, Deborah, 350, 428–429
Tanner, J. M., 377
Tavris, Carol, 466
Taylor, S. E., 518
Taylor, Shelly, 716, 722
Teasdale, J., 658, 660
Teasdale, T. W., 572
Teicher, H. M., 448
Teicher, M. H., 698
Teitelbaum, P., 102, 451
Tellegen, Auke, 610–611
Teller, D., 111
Tellini, S., 742
Terman, Lewis, 556–557, 559
Tesser, A., 734
Teuber, H.-L., 304
Teyler, T. J., 304
Thigpen, C. H., 649
Thomas, G. S., 381
Thompson, C. H., 68
Thompson, Clara, 627
Thompson, C. P., 308
Thompson, D. A., 451
Thompson, Kevin, 455
Thompson, M. G., 423
Thompson, R. F., 26, 87, 305
Thorndike, Edward L., 243–244, 246, 357, 553, 693
Thornhill, N. W., 766
Thornhill, R., 766
Thornton, B., 728
Thouless, R. H., 161
Thurstone, L. L., 564
Tierney, W. M., 524
Tinbergen, N., 445
Tischenkel, N. J., 546
Tissot, S. A. D., 463
Titchener, Edward, 12, 18, 214
Tolman, E. C., 17
Tolman, Edward, 263–264
Tomkins, Silvan, 486–487, 499
Tordoff, M. G., 451
Torrey, E. Fuller, 704, 705
Trachtman, J., 573
Tralbaut, M. E., 614
Treat, A. E., 118
Treffert, D. A., 560, 561
Trembath, D. L., 423
Tresemer, D. W., 479

Trevarthen, C., 111
Triplett, Norman, 782–783
Trotter, R. J., 580
Tulis, 671
Tulving, Endel, 289–290, 293
Turkel, J., 573
Turner, A. M., 112
Tversky, A., 331, 332, 333, 334–335
Tversky, Amos, 488

Udry, J. R., 477
Ulrich, R. E., 767
Ulrich, Roger, 590, 591
Underwood, B. J., 314
Ungerleider, L. G., 110, 133
U.S. Commission on Civil Rights, 748
U.S. Congress, Joint Commission on Mental Illness and Health, 704
U.S. Department of Health and Human Services, 191, 517
U.S. Department of Labor, 431
U.S. House of Representatives, Committee on Ways and Means, 437
U.S. News and World Report, 5

Vaillant, G. E., 432
Valins, Stuart, 745
Van de Castle, R. L., 192
van der Hout, A., 703
VanderWeele, D. A., 450
VanEssen, D. C., 110
van Gogh, Vincent, 614
van Ijzendoom, Marinus, 413
Varmus, Harold, 718
Vaughn, C. E., 668
Vaughn, Eva, 5
Vernon, P. A., 567–568, 569
Victor, M., 101
Victor, P., 535
Vigil, James Diego, 420
Vincent, K. R., 623
Visintainer, Madelon A., 523, 541–542
Volk, K. D., 465
Vollmer, F., 478
Volpe, B., 212–213
Volpicelli, J. R., 523
von Cramon, D. Y., 101
von Wasserman, August, 637

Wachtel, P., 701
Wadden, T. A., 458
Wadeson, H., 687
Wagenaar, Willem, 297, 308
Wagner, Richard, 581
Wahl, O., 662
Wald, G., 136
Waldorf, V. A., 423
Waldrop, M. M., 281, 336, 347
Walk, R. D., 412
Walk, Richard, 491
Walker, E., 673
Walker, L. J., 426
Wall, Patrick, 148
Wall, P. D., 169
Walls, 311
Walraven, J., 573
Walster, E., 718
Walters, G. C., 259
Wardle, J., 700
Warren, W. J., 579
Washburn, A. L., 450
Washburn, Margaret, 28
Wason, P. C., 329–330, 341
Waters, E., 413
Watkins, J. G., 650
Watkins, Michael, 291

Watson, C. G., 652
Watson, D., 727
Watson, John B., 14–15, 15–16, 176, 223, 224, 228–230, 232, 263, 357, 369, 495, 571, 605, 643–644
Waugh, N. C., 287
Webb, 188
Weber, Ernst, 10
Weber, Max, 11
Wechsler, D., 557
Weekes, J. R., 651
Weidner, G., 537
Weinberg, R. A., 371
Weinberg, Richard, 574, 575
Weinberger, D. R., 667
Weinberger, M., 524
Weiner, B., 725, 765
Weiner, Bernard, 474–475
Weingarten, Harvey, 452
Weingartner, H., 300
Weinman, J., 519
Weisenberg, M., 54, 530
Weisman, A. D., 434
Weiss, J. M., 541
Weiss, W., 738
Weissman, M., 673
Weissman, M. M., 655
Weitz, R., 518
Weitzenhoffer, A. M., 199
Weitzman, L. J., 430
Wender, P. H., 656, 666
Wernicke, Carl, 96–97, 109
Wertheimer, Max, 13
Weyer, Johann, 680
Whishaw, I. Q., 305
White, C., 458
White, H. R., 208
White, J., 157
Whiting, Beatrice B., 372–373
Whiting, John W. M., 372–373
Whorf, Benjamin, 355
Wiback, 455
Wible, C. G., 308
Wickelgren, W. A., 282
Wicker, A. W., 735
Wicks-Nelson, R., 406
Wickware, F. S., 464
Widnall, S. E., 422
Wiesel, Thorsten, 131
Wigdor, A. K., 580
Wikler, 240
Wilcox, S., 477
Wilcoxon, H. C., 238
Wild, C. L., 29
Wilkins, W., 703
Wilkinson, H. J., 248
Williams, F. L., 429, 757
Williams, J. E., 269
Williams, K., 783, 784
Williams, P. S., 584
Williams, T. M., 68
Williamson, G., 532
Willner, J., 298
Wills, T. A., 535
Wilson, D. M., 572
Wilson, E. D., 117
Wilson, G. T., 240, 654
Wilson, M. A., 178
Wilson, R. S., 370, 574
Wilson, T. G., 258
Wilson, Timothy, 6
Wing, Rena, 452
Wing, R. R., 459
Winograd, E., 306
Winter, David, 614–615
Winzenz, David, 291–292

Wittig, B. A., 412
Wober, M., 578
Wolf, A. S., 652
Wolfe, B. E., 701
Wolfe, J. B., 248
Wolpe, Joseph, 239
Wolpert, Edward, 193
Wong, P. T. P., 725
Woodworth, Robert, 620
Woolsey, C. N., 100
Wozney, K., 649

Wu, C., 738
Wundt, Wilhelm, 11, 12, 18, 175, 214
Wyers, E. J., 224
Wynne, L., 247

Yahya, 781
Yalom, Irwin, 695–696
Yap, P. M., 640
Yellen, A., 195
Young, F. A., 573
Young, Thomas, 133, 135, 137
Yum, J. O., 354

Zahn-Wexler, C., 415
Zajonc, R. B., 739, 783
Zajonc, Robert B., 501, 502, 508
Zanna, M., 731
Zanna, M. P., 738, 784
Zaragoza, M. S., 297
Zeki, S., 110
Zeskind, Philip, 410
Zhang, Guojun, 282–283

Zilboorg, G., 680
Zillman, 507
Zillman, D., 769
Zimbardo, P. G., 506
Zimbardo, Philip, 785–786, 787
Zimmerman, Donald, 260
Ziskin, Jay, 650, 651
Zola-Morgan, S., 101, 305
Zubin, J., 623, 669
Zucher, I., 178
Zuckerman, M., 725, 742
Zyzanski, J. S., 538

SUBJECT INDEX

Absolutist thinking, 690
Accommodation, 383
Achievement motivation, 471–476, 478–479
Achievement tests, 576
Acquired immunodeficiency syndrome. *See* AIDS
Action potential, 78–80
Actor-observer effect, 726–728
Adaptation, 383
Adler's theory of personality, 601
Adolescence, 379–380, 389, 418–423
Adolescent egocentrism, 389
Adoption studies, 574, 575
Adulthood, 393–396, 427–434. *See also specific topics*
Advertising, 741–742
African Americans. *See* Race
Aggression, 367–368, 765–772
Agoraphobia, 641–642
AIDS, 517–519, 534
Alarm stage, 528
Alcohol, 206, 209, 211, 371
Algorithms, 331–332
Alpha waves, 183
Altruism. *See* Prosocial behavior
American Psychological Association (APA), 19, 28–29, 66
American Psychological Society, 19
Ames room, 162–163
Amnesia, 648
Amphetamines, 205, 209
Amygdala, 87, 101, 103
Analogy problems, 569–570
Anal stage, 594
Animal research, 65–67, 102. *See also specific topics*
Animism, 386
Anonymity, 785
Anthropology, 372–373, 420–421
Antianxiety drugs, 700
Antidepressant drugs, 698–699
Antipsychotic drugs, 697–698
Antisocial personality disorder, 670–671
Anxiety, 595–597, 601
  disorders, 641–647, 700
APA. *See* American Psychological Association
Aphagia, 450–451
Aphasia, 95–96
Aptitude tests, 576
Arousal, 505–506, 739, 760
Art, 25, 686–687
Artificial intelligence, 347–349
Assimilation, 383
Attachment, 409–414, 436–437
Attention, 663
Attitudes, 733–746

acquisition of, 736–738
  and behavior, 735–736, 745–746
  changes in, 738–746
  nature of, 733–735
Attraction, 755–762
  sources of, 756–759
Attribution, 474–476, 660, 721–728
Audibility curve, 139–140
Auditory canal, 140
Auditory cortex, 100–101
Autism, 257–259
Autonomic nervous system, 90
Availability heuristic, 332
Aversion therapy, 693
Axon, 77

Bait shyness, 237
Barbiturates, 206, 209, 211
Baseline level, 246
Basic anxiety, 601
Basilar membrane, 140
Behavioral level of analysis, 23
Behaviorism, 14–16, 224–263, 266–267
  and aggression, 767–768
  and attitudes, 736–738
  classical conditioning, 224, 226–242
  and consciousness, 176
  and development, 369
  and emotions, 495–496
  habituation, 224, 225
  and language, 407
  operant conditioning, 242–263
  and personality, 605–606
  and psychological disorders, 639, 643–645, 660–661
  and therapy, 239–240, 692–695
Behavior therapy, 239–240, 459–460
Bias, 5, 68–69
  and Freudianism, 597–598
  and research methods, 54–57
Big Five personality dimensions, 609
Binocular cues, 158–159
Biofeedback training, 694
Biological clocks, 177–178
Biological level of analysis, 22
Biology, 74–121
  and aggression, 766–767
  development, 373–382
  and dreams, 194–195
  and drug use, 208, 209, 210
  and emotions, 103, 104–106, 485, 496–505
  endocrine system, 91–94
  evolution, 116–119

and gender, 118–119, 120–121
  heredity, 115–116
  and hunger, 449–452
  and memory, 101–102, 303–306
  and motivation, 444–446
  nervous system, 87–91
  neurons, 76–86, 131–133
  and operant conditioning, 256–257
  and psychological disorders, 639, 645–646, 656, 665–667
  and sexuality, 461–462
  and stress, 527–533
  and weight, 455–457
  See also Brain; *specific topics*
Biomedical therapy, 696–701
Bipolar disorders, 655, 699–700
Blaming the victim, 728
Blind interviewing procedures, 55
Blind scoring procedures, 55
Blocking, 235–236
Body-kinesthetic intelligence, 566
Body language, 491
Bogus pipeline method, 734
Borderline personality disorder, 669–670
Brain, 87, 94–110
  changes in, 110–114
  computer imaging, 98–99
  and drug use, 209, 210
  and emotions, 103, 104–106, 502–505
  and gender, 461
  lateralization of function, 103–109
  lesioning, 102
  localization of function, 94–103, 304–305, 450–451
  parallel processing, 109–110
  and perception, 100–101, 127–128, 130
  and schizophrenia, 666–667
  and sleep, 178–180, 185
  stimulation, 102
  as system, 109
  See also Biology
Brain stem, 90
Bridging assumption, 353
Broca's area, 96
Brown v. *Board of Education,* 29
Buffering hypothesis of social support, 535
Bystander intervention effect, 763

Caffeine, 205
California Personality Inventory (CPI), 622
Camouflage, 155
Cannon-Bard theory of emotion, 502–504, 505
Cardinal trait, 606–607
Case studies, 42–43

Castration anxiety, 594
CAT (Computerized Axial Tomography) scan, 98
Catatonic schizophrenia, 664
Categorization, 323–326
Catharsis, 684
Causal attribution, 722
Causation, 38, 50–53
CCK. *See* Cholecystokinin
Cell body, 77
Cells, 76–77
Central nervous system, 87–90
Central route to persuasion, 741
Central traits, 607
Cerebellum, 89
Cerebral cortex, 87
CHD. *See* Coronary heart disease
Children. *See* Development; Parenting
Cholecystokinin (CCK), 451
Christiansen, 65
Chunking, 283–285, 348
Cigarette smoking, 242
Circadian rhythms, 176–181
Classical conditioning, 224, 226–242
    and attitudes, 736–737
    elements of, 230–234
    modern approaches to, 234–238
    and operant conditioning, 244, 260–263
    Pavlov, 226–228
    and public health, 240–242
    and therapy, 239–240, 692–693
    Watson, 228–230
    See also Behaviorism
Client-centered therapy, 17, 604, 687–689
Cocaine, 205, 209
Cochlea, 140, 143
Cochlear implant, 144–145
Cognitive appraisal, 507–508, 522
Cognitive approaches, 17–18
    and achievement motivation, 474–476
    and aggression, 769
    and dreams, 194
    and drug use, 211
    and emotions, 505–508
    and language, 408
    and learning, 263–266
    and personality, 615–620
    and psychological disorders, 640, 646–647,
        657–660
    and therapy, 689–692
    See also Cognitive development; Intelligence;
        Memory; Thinking
Cognitive development, 382–396
    adulthood, 393–396
    information-processing approach, 391–393
    Piagetian theory, 382–391
Cognitive dissonance, 743–745
Cognitive distortions, 657–658
Cognitive level of analysis, 22
Cognitive maps, 263–264
Cognitive restructuring, 691
Cognitive therapy, 690–691
Cognitive triad, 657
Collective unconscious, 600
Color, 133–137
Common fate, law of, 154
Communication
    cultural differences, 709
    deviance, 667–668
    and gender, 428–429, 788–789
    See also Language
Compliance, 778–780
Componential aspect of intelligence, 580
Concordance, 645
Concrete operations stage, 386–388, 424
Conditional reasoning, 327–328
Conditioned drug tolerance, 241

Conditioned emotional response, 495
Conditioned response (CR), 227, 495. *See also*
    Behaviorism
Conditioned stimulus (CS), 227. *See also* Behaviorism
Conditioned suppression, 234, 260–261
Conditioned taste aversion, 237
Cones, 130
Confirmational bias, 329–330
Conformity, 772–778
Conjunction rule, 333
Conscience, 595
Consciousness, 174–217
    circadian rhythms, 176–181
    and description of experience, 212–214
    and drugs, 176, 205–212
    hypnosis, 197–205
    sleep, 176, 181–191
    study of, 175–176
Consensus question, 723
Conservation, 385–387
Consistency question, 724
Consolidation hypothesis, 305–306
Constructive nature of memory, 311
Construct validity, 577
Content validity, 577
Contextual approaches, 23
    and aggression, 768–769
    and psychological disorders, 640–641, 661–662,
        667–669
Contextual aspect of intelligence, 580
Contiguity hypothesis, 234–238
Continuity vs. discontinuity, 368–369
Continuous reinforcement schedule (CRF), 250
Control, 540–542
Control theory, 776–778
Conversational rule, 354
Conversion disorders, 652
Coolidge effect, 464
Cornea, 130
Coronary heart disease (CHD), 526–527, 538
Corpus callosum, 87
Correlation, 50–53
Counterconditioning, 239–240
CPI. *See* California Personality Inventory
CR. *See* Conditioned response
Craniometry, 554
CRF. *See* Continuous reinforcement schedule
Criminal justice
    and hypnosis, 203–204
    and memory, 311–312
    and psychological disorders, 650–652
Cross-sectional method, 365, 366
Crystallized intelligence, 394
CS. *See* Conditioned stimulus
Cultural differences
    and development, 372–373, 398–399, 436–437
    and dreams, 216–217
    and emotions, 492–493, 494, 510–511 and intelli-
        gence, 577–578
    and perception, 162, 164, 168–169
    and psychological disorders, 635
    and sexuality, 464
    and therapy, 708–709
    and thinking, 355–356, 358–359
    See also Race
Cultural-familial retardation, 561
Cultural norms, 635
Cyclothymia, 655

Death, 433–434
Decentration, 387
Deception, 56
Decision making, 330–335, 784–785
Deductive reasoning, 327–329
Deep processing, 292–293
Defense mechanisms, 596, 598, 649

Deindividuation, 785–786
Deinstitutionalization, 704–706
Delay conditioning, 230
Delta waves, 183
Delusions, 662–663
Demand characteristics, 56–57, 202–203, 500, 734
Dendrites, 77
Dependent retarded, 560 Dependent variable, 44
Depressants, 206, 209
Depression, 654, 698–699
Depth cues, 156
Depth perception, 156–160, 168
Descriptive statistics, 58
Development, 364–399
    cognition, 382–396
    continuity vs. discontinuity, 368–369, 393
    cultural differences, 372–373, 398–399
    language, 370, 404–408
    links among areas, 434–435
    nature vs. nurture, 369–372
    physical/perceptual, 373–382
    social, 408–434
    stability vs. instability, 365–368
Deviance, 634–635, 776–778
Deviation IQ, 557, 558
Diagnostic and Statistical Manual of Mental Disorders
    (DSM), 637–639, 651
Diathesis–stress model of schizophrenia, 669
Dieting, 452–453
Differential reinforcement, 254
Diffusion of responsibility, 763–764
Discrimination, 232–233
Discriminative stimuli, 254
Disorganized schizophrenia, 664
Display rules, 492–493, 494
Dissociation, 202
Dissociative disorders, 648–652
Distinctiveness question, 723
Distress, 636
Diversity. *See* Cultural differences; Gender; Race
Divorce, 430
Dizygotic (DZ) twins, 573–575
Dominant hemisphere, 104–105
Door-in-the-face technique, 779
Dopamine, 85–86, 666
Double-bind communications, 667
Double-blind procedure, 56
Dreams, 184–185, 192–197
    cultural differences, 216–217
    Freudian theory of, 195–197
Drives, 445–446
Drugs
    and consciousness, 176, 205–212
    and insomnia, 189–190
    therapies using, 697–700
    tolerance, 208–209, 240–242
    types of, 205–208
    See also specific topics
DSM. *See Diagnostic and Statistical Manual of Mental
    Disorders*
Dual-center hypothesis, 451
Duchenne smiles, 491
Dysthymia, 654
DZ twins. *See* Dizygotic (DZ) twins

Ear, 142
Eating disorders, 423
Eclecticism, 701–702
ECT. *See* Electroconvulsive therapy
Education, 562–563
EE. *See* Expressed emotion
EEG. *See* Electroencephalogram
Efference, 501
Effort justification effect, 745
Ego, 595
Egocentrism, 385, 388

Ego ideal, 595
Elaboration likelihood model of attitude change, 740–741
Elaborative rehearsal, 291–292
Electrical stimulation of the brain (ESB), 504
Electroconvulsive therapy (ECT), 700–701
Electroencephalogram (EEG), 182, 183
Electromagnetic spectrum, 130
Eletromyogram (EMG), 182
Elimination by aspects, 331
Embryonic period, 374
EMG. *See* Eletromyogram
Emotional support, 534
Emotions, 484–511
   and attitude change, 739
   behavioral effects of, 487–490
   behavioral explanations of, 495–496
   and biology, 103, 104–106, 485, 496–505
   cognitive approaches, 505–508
   cultural differences, 492–493, 494, 510–511
   expression, 490–495, 510–511
   nature of, 484–487
   and schizophrenia, 664
   and social development, 410–412
Empirical keying, 621
Empiricism, 8
Empty nest syndrome, 430
Encoding, 278–279, 282–283, 290–291, 391–392, 570–571
Endocrine system, 91–94
Environment, objects in, 152–156
Epidermis, 146
Episodic memory, 290
ESB. *See* Electrical stimulation of the brain
Esteem support, 534
Estrogen, 120, 461
Ethics, 229
Ethological approach to motivation, 445
European Americans. *See* Race
Eve principle, 461
Evolution, 116–119
   and emotions, 496–497, 510
   and functionalism, 12–13
   and motivation, 444
   and observation, 35–37
   and sleep, 190–191
Exchange theory, 757–758
Excitatory center, 451
Excitatory transmitters, 81
Exercise, 186, 543
Exhaustion stage, 528–529
Expectancy-value theory, 473–474
Expectations, and perception, 165–167
Experiential aspect of intelligence, 580
Experimental groups, 45–46
Experimental methods, 43–49
Experimentation, 37–38
Expressed emotion (EE), 668
External causes, 723
External desynchronization, 180
Externality hypothesis, 458
Extinction, 231–232, 249, 253
Extraneous variables, 46
Extraversion, 600
Extrinsic motivation, 474

Facial feedback hypothesis, 498–502
Factor analysis, 565, 607
Familiarity, law of, 155
Feature detectors, 132–133
Feedback loop, 449
Fetal period, 374
FI. *See* Fixed-interval (FI) schedule of reinforcement
Field experiments, 48–49
Fixed-interval (FI) schedule of reinforcement, 252
Fixed-ratio (FR) schedule of reinforcement, 250–251

Flashbulb memories, 307–308
Flooding, 693
Fluid intelligence, 394
Focal colors, 355–356
Foot-in-the-door technique, 779–780
Forgetting, 286, 300–302
Formal operations stage, 388–389
Fovea, 130
FR. *See* Fixed-ratio (FR) schedule of reinforcement
Framing effects, 334–335
Free association, 684
Frequency distribution, 59
Freudianism, 16
   and aggression, 766
   and dreams, 195–197
   and motivation, 446–447
   and personality, 592–598, 626–627
   and sexuality, 469–470
   and therapy, 681, 682, 684–685
   and women, 626–627
Frontal lobe, 87
Frustration-aggression hypothesis, 768–769
Functional fixedness, 337–338
Functionalism, 12–13
Fundamental attribution error, 726, 749
Fundamental rule of psychoanalysis, 684
Gate control theory of pain, 148
Gender
   and achievement motivation, 478–479
   and biology, 118–119, 120–121
   and health, 519–520
   and history of psychology, 28–29
   identification, 416–417
   and language, 356–357
   learning, 268–269
   and memory, 316–317
   and methodology, 68–69
   and parenting, 414
   and personality, 626–627
   and physical develop ment, 379–380, 461
   and psychological disorders, 672–673
   schemas, 316–317
   and sexuality, 428–429, 464–468
   and social development, 414, 420, 422–423, 426, 430, 431–432
   socialization, 268–269, 316, 417–418, 428
   violence against women, 769–772
   and weight, 455
   and work, 431–432
   See also Diversity
Gender segregation, 417
General adaptation syndrome, 528
Generalization, 232, 254–255
Generalized anxiety disorder, 642
General mental ability, 564
Genes, 115
Genetics. *See* Biology; Nature-nurture debate; Physical development
Genital stage, 594–595
Genotype, 115–116
Germinal period, 374
Gestalt psychology, 13–14, 153–156
Giftedness, 558–559
Given-new contract, 352–353
Good continuation, law of, 154, 156
Group cohesiveness, 774–775
Group polarization, 784–785
Groups, 782–786
Group therapy, 695–696

Habituation, 224, 225, 377
Hair cells, 140
Hallucinations, 663
Hallucinogens, 206–207
Hardy personality, 539, 542
Hassles and uplifts scale, 523, 524–525

Health, 516–547
   AIDS, 517–519, 534
   and behavior, 519–520
   and race, 526, 546–547
   and social suppport, 533–536
   See also Stress
Hearing, 100–101, 138–145
   and brain specialization, 100–101
   development, 377
   medical treatment, 144–145
   and perception of objects, 153–154
   sensory codes for, 142–143
   stimulus for, 138–141
   system structure, 141, 142
Helplessness, learned, 542, 658–660
Heredity, 115–116. *See also* Nature-nurture debate
Heroin, 206, 242
Heterosexuality, 468
Heuristics, 331–334
Hierarchy of needs, 447–448
High blood pressure. *See* Hypertension
Hippocampus, 87, 101, 103, 304–305
History, field of, 463–464, 613–615
History of psychology, 8–21
   behaviorism, 14–16
   cognitive approach, 17–18
   contemporary approaches, 19–21
   diversity in, 28–29
   Freudianism, 16
   functionalism, 12–13
   Gestalt psychology, 13–14
   humanistic approach, 17
   19th century physiology, 10–11
   philosophy, 8–10
   structuralism, 11–12
   technological advances, 18
   therapy, 679–684
   See also specific topics
Homeostasis, 240–241
Homophobia, 468
Homosexuality, 464, 468–471
Homunculus, 100 Hormones, 91–94, 120–121
Horney's theory of personality, 601
Humanistic approach, 17
   and motivation, 447–448
   and personality, 602–605
Humor, 494
Hunger, 448–460
   and biology, 449–452
   psychological influences, 452–453
   See also Weight
Hyde, 62
Hyperphagia, 450
Hypertension, 526–527, 529, 546–547
Hypnosis, 197–205
   alterations in behavior during, 198–200
   and criminal justice, 203–204
   paradox of, 200–201
   study of, 198
   theories of, 201–203
Hypochondriasis, 653
Hypothalamus, 88, 93, 103, 450–451
Hypothesis, 43–44

Id, 595
Identity formation, 418–421
Immune system, 528–532
Immunosuppressants, 529
Implicit theory of intelligence, 552
Implosive therapy, 693
Incongruence, 688
Independent variable, 44
Indirect statements, 353–354
Inductive reasoning, 329–330
Inferences, 352–353
Inferential statistics, 60–62

Inferiority complex, 601
Informational support, 534
Information processing, 277
    cognitive development, 391–393
    and problem solving, 342–345, 569–571
    and social cognition, 730–731
Ingratiation, 779
In-group/out-group dynamic, 721
Inhibitory transmitters, 81
Inner ear, 142
Insomnia, 189–190
Instinct approach to motivation, 444
Instinctive drift, 262–263
Insulin, 451
Intelligence, 552–585
    and cultural differences, 358–359
    and development, 367, 394–395
    measurement of, 553–557, 575–579, 584–585
    processes of, 567–571
    and race, 584–585
    range of, 557–563
    real-world, 579–582
    sources of, 571–575
    structure of, 564–567
Intelligence quotient (IQ), 556–557, 558
Interactionism, 612–613
Interdisciplinary connections, 25–26
    attitudes, 741–742
    behaviorism, 240–242
    biology, 117–119
    conformity, 776–778
    emotions, 493–494
    hearing, 144–145
    hypnosis, 203–204
    intelligence, 562–563
    memory, 311–312
    personality, 613–615
    problem solving, 347–349
    psychological disorders, 650–652
    sexuality, 463–464
    social development, 420–421
    stress, 530–532
    therapy, 686–687
Intergroup contact hypothesis, 749
Internal causes, 723
Interpersonal intelligence, 566
Interpersonal relations, 754–789
    aggression, 765–772
    attraction, 755–762
    communication, 428–429, 709, 788–789
    compliance, 778–780
    conformity, 772–778
    groups, 782–786
    obedience, 778, 780–782
    prosocial behavior, 488–489, 763–765
Interval schedule of reinforcement, 250
Intrapersonal intelligence, 566
Intrinsic motivation, 474
Introspection, 11, 12
Introversion, 600
Inventories, 43
IQ. *See* Intelligence quotient

James-Lange theory of emotion, 497–498, 503–504, 505
Jet lag, 180
John Henryism, 547
Jung's theory of personality, 599–600
Just noticeable difference, 10, 11
Just world hypothesis, 728

Kaufman Assessment Battery for Children (K–ABC), 585
Kin selection, 118

Labeled line theory of taste, 150
LAD. *See* Language acquisition device

Language
    and brain, 95–98, 107
    development, 370, 404–408
    and emotions, 486
    and problem solving, 350–354
    and thinking, 350–357
    See also Communication
Language acquisition device (LAD), 408
Latency stage, 594
Latent dream, 195
Lateral geniculate nucleus (LGN), 130, 131
Lateralization of function, 103–109
Lateral nucleus of the hypothalamus (LH), 450–451
Learned helplessness, 542, 658–660
Learning, 222–224
    and cognition, 263–266
    and emotions, 494
    gender roles, 268–269
    and performance, 223
    See also Behaviorism
Left hemisphere, 87
Lens, 130
Lesioning, 102
Levels of analysis, 21–24
Levels of processing theory of memory, 292–293
LGN. *See* Lateral geniculate nucleus
LH. *See* Lateral nucleus of the hypothalamus
Librium, 206
Lifetime prevalence of psychological disorders, 633
Linguistic intelligence, 565
Linguistic relativity hypothesis, 355
Literature, 25
Lithium, 699–700
Little Albert experiment, 228–230
Lobotomy, 696
Localization of function, 94–103
Locus of control, 616, 617
Logical-mathematical intelligence, 565
Longitudinal method, 366–367
Long-term memory (LTM), 281, 287–303
    encoding, 290–291
        forgetting, 300–302
        retrieval, 296–299
        short-term memory transfer, 287–289
        storage, 291–296
Long-term potentiation (LTP), 303–304
Love, 759–762
Love/belongingness needs, 447
Lowball technique, 780
LSD, 206–207
LTM. *See* Long–term memory
LTP. *See* Long–term potentiation
Lysergic acid diethylamide. *See* LSD

Magnification, 690
Main effect hypothesis of social support, 535
Mainstreaming, 562–563
Maintenance rehearsal, 291
Major depression, 654
Maladaptiveness, 635, 664
Manic-depressive disorder, 655
Manifest dream, 195
Marijuana, 207–208
Marketing, 741–742
Marriage, 429–430, 673
Maturation, and brain, 110–111
MBRF. *See* Midbrain reticular formation
Means-end analysis, 343–345
Measurement. *See* Methodology and measurement; *specific topics*
Measures of central tendency, 58–59
Measures of variability, 59–60
Medical student's syndrome, 634
Medicine, 144–145, 493–494
Medulla, 90
Memory, 274–317

and biology, 101–102, 303–306
and criminal justice, 311–312
and dreams, 192
and emotions, 487–488
and gender schemas, 316–317
information-processing model, 278–279
long-term, 281, 287–303
real-world, 306–311
research history, 275–277
sensory, 279–280
short-term, 280–289, 303
and studying, 312–315
Memory code, 279
Menarche, 379
Men. *See* Gender
Mental retardation, 559–563
Mental set, 338–340
Mere exposure effect, 739
Mescaline, 206, 207
Meta-analysis, 702, 703
Metabolism, 457
Methodology and measurement, 7, 24–25, 40–57
    aggression, 771
    attitudes, 734, 746
    and bias, 54–57, 467
    and brain, 98–99, 102, 105
    causation and correlation, 50–53
    correlation coefficient, 52–53
    development, 366–367
    and diversity, 68–69
    emotions, 500
    experimental, 43–49
    habituation, 225
    hypnosis, 199
    intelligence, 558, 565, 572–573
    memory, 287, 307
    observational, 41–43, 57
    operant conditioning, 245
    operational definitions, 45
    perception, 140, 145, 164
    personality, 603
    problem solving, 344, 392
    psychological disorders, 647, 651, 668
    sexuality, 467
    sleep, 182
    stress, 525, 529
    therapy, 703
    See also specific topics
Midbrain reticular formation (MBRF), 185
Middle ear, 140
Midlife crisis, 432–433
Mind-body dualism, 516–517
Minimax principle, 764
Minnesota Multiphasic Personality Inventory (MMPI), 620–622
Minorities. *See* Diversity
Mnemonic devices, 284, 315
Modeling, 265–266, 737–738, 767–768
Modus ponens, 327
Modus tollens, 327–328
Monozygotic (MZ) twins, 573–575
Mood disorders, 654–662
Moon illusion, 163, 164–165
Moral reasoning, 423–427
Morphine, 206
Motivation, 442–479
    achievement, 471–476
    hunger, 448–460
    multiple causes, 476–477
    sexual, 460–471
    theories of, 444–448
Motor cortex, 101
Movement-produced cues, 158
MPD. *See* Multiple personality disorder
MRI (Magnetic Resonance Imaging), 99
Multiple personality disorder (MPD), 648–649,

650–652
Multistore memory model, 278
Musical intelligence, 565
MZ twins. *See* Monozygotic (MZ) twins

nAch. *See* Need to achieve
Narcolepsy, 191
Naturalistic observation, 41–42
Natural selection, 12–13, 36–37, 117, 444
Nature-nurture debate, 369–372, 571–575, 609–611
Nearness, law of, 153–154
Need for cognition, 739
Need to achieve (nAch), 473. *See also* Achievement motivation
Negative correlation, 52
Negative reinforcement, 246–247, 255–256
Negative symptoms, 664–665
Nervous system, 87–91, 93–94
  and perception, 100–101, 127–128
  See also Biology; Brain
Neurons, 76–86, 131–133
Neurotic trends, 601
Neurotransmitters, 80, 209, 666. *See also* Biology; Brain
Neutral stimulus (NS), 226, 227, 230. *See also* Behaviorism
Nicotine, 205, 242
Normal distribution, 554
Normative social influence, 775–776
Nose, 150–151
NS. *See* Neutral stimulus

Obedience, 62–64, 778, 780–782
Obesity, 454–455. *See also* Weight
Observation, 35–37, 41–43, 57
Observational learning, 265–266, 269, 495–496
Obsessive-compulsive disorder (OCD), 642–643, 647
Occipital lobe, 87
OCD. *See* Obsessive-compulsive disorder
Oculomotor cues, 156–157
Oedipus complex, 594, 626
Olfactory bulb, 150
Olfactory mucosa, 150
Operant conditioning, 242–263
  and aggression, 767
  and attitudes, 737
  and classical conditioning, 244, 260–263
  elements of, 246–256
  refinements of, 256–257
  Skinner, 244–246
  and therapy, 257–260, 693–695
  Thorndike, 243–244
  See also Behaviorism
Operational definition, 44, 45
Opiates, 206
Opponent-process theory of color vision, 135–136
Oral stage, 593–594 Organization, 383–384
Ossicles, 140
Outer ear, 140
Overextension, 406
Overregularization, 406

Pain, 146–148, 168–169
Panic disorder, 641
Papillae, 149
Paradoxical intention, 190
Parallax, 158
Parallel processing, 109–110
Paranoid schizophrenia, 664
Parasympathetic division, 91
Parenting
  and adolescence, 419
  and adult development, 427–428
  and social development, 409–414, 429–430
Parietal lobe, 87
Parkinson's disease, 84–85
Partial reinforcement effect, 250, 253
Penis envy, 626–627

Perceived self-efficacy (PSE), 617–618
Perception, 126–169
  chemical senses, 148–152
  construction of, 129
  depth, 156–160
  development, 373–382
  and expectations, 165–167
  hearing, 100–101, 138–145
  misperception, 162–165
  and nervous system, 100–101, 127–128
  objects, 152–156
  and problem solving, 336–337
  shape constancy, 161
  size constancy, 160–161
  skin senses, 146–148
  vision, 100–101, 129–138, 152–167
Perceptual set, 165–167
Peripheral nervous system, 90–91
Peripheral retina, 130
Peripheral route to persuasion, 741
Personal constructs, 616
Personal fable, 389
Personality, 590–627
  assessment, 620–623
  behaviorist approach, 605–606
  cognitive approach, 615–620
  disorders, 669–671
  humanistic approach, 602–605
  pscyhobiography, 613–615
  psychodynamic approaches, 592–602, 626–627
  and stress, 536–539
  trait approach, 606–613
Person perception, 716–721
Persuasion, 738–743
PET (Positron Emission Tomography) scanner, 18, 99
Phallic stage, 594
Phenotype, 116
Philosophy, 8–10
Phobias, 239, 642
Phrenology, 95
Physical attractiveness, 423, 718–719
  and attitude change, 738–739
  and attraction, 756–758
  and weight, 455
Physical dependence, 208
Physical development, 373–382
Physiological needs, 447
Physiology, 10–11. *See also* Biology
Piagetian theory, 382–391
  and cultural differences, 398–399
  evaluation of, 389–391
  and moral reasoning, 424
Pictorial cues, 157–158
Placebo, 530
Place theory of pitch perception, 143
Pleasure principle, 593, 600
Ponzo illusion, 163–164
Positive correlation, 52
Positive regard, 603, 604
Positive reinforcement, 246–247
Positive symptoms, 664–665
Possible selves, 619–620
Post–formal operations stage, 395–396
Postsynaptic neuron, 80
Posttraumatic stress disorder (PTSD), 113–114, 489–490, 643
Preconscious, 592
Predictions, 5–6
Predictive validity, 577
Prefrontal cortex, 99
Prefrontal lobotomy, 696
Prejudice, 748–749. *See also* Racism; Stereotypes
Premack principle, 256
Prenatal sexual differentiation, 120
Preoperational stage, 384–385, 424
Preparedness, 237, 496

Presynaptic neuron, 80
Primacy effect, 288–289, 718
Primary emotions, 486
Primary mental abilities, 564
Primary qualities, 167
Primary reinforcers, 248
Proactive interference, 301
Problem solving, 335–350
  development, 391–392
  expert vs. novice, 344, 345–347
  and information processing, 342–345, 391–392, 569–571
  and language, 350–354
  obstacles to, 336–340
  and representation, 340–342
  and stress, 540
Problem space, 342–343
Procedural memory, 290
Progestins, 120
Progressive muscle relaxation, 543
Projective tests, 622–623
Proprioception, 376–377
Prosocial behavior, 118, 488–489, 763–765
Prototypes, 324–325
PSE. *See* Perceived self-efficacy
Pseudodialogues, 406
Pseudoinsomnia, 190–191
Psychedelic drugs, 206–207
Psychic energy, 593
Psychoactive drugs, 176, 205–212
Psychobiography, 613–615
Psychodynamic approaches to personality, 592–602
  Adler's theory, 601
  evaluating, 597–599
  Freudian theory, 592–599
  Horney's theory, 601
  Jung's theory, 599–600
  and women, 626–627
  See also Freudianism; Psychodynamic therapy
Psychodynamic therapy, 681, 682, 684–686
Psychogenic fugue, 648
Psychological anthropology, 216
Psychological construct, 553
Psychological disorders, 632–673
  anxiety disorders, 641–647
  classifying, 636–639
  dissociative disorders, 648–652
  and gender, 672–673
  misconceptions, 671
  mood disorders, 654–662
  nature of, 634–636
  personality disorders, 669–671
  schizophrenia, 662–669
  somatoform disorders, 652–654
Psychology
  challenge of, 26–27
  common knowledge of, 4–6
  integration of, 21–26
  interdisciplinary connections, 25–26
  as science, 6–8
  specializations, 19–21
  See also specific topics
Psychoneuroimmunology, 532
Psychophysics, 10–11
Psychosocial theory of development, 409
Psychotherapy. *See* Therapy
PTSD. *See* Posttraumatic stress disorder
Public health, 240–242
Punishment, 255–256, 259
Pure tones, 139

Q-sort, 603

Race
  and history of psychology, 28, 29
  and hypertension, 526, 546–547

and intelligence, 584–585
and methodology, 68–69
racism, 719, 748–749
and social development, 437
See also Cultural differences
Racism, 719, 748–749
Random assignment, 46
Random sampling, 44–45, 46
Range, 59
Rape, 769–772
Raphe system, 90
Rapid eye movement (REM) sleep, 184–185, 188, 189, 190, 193, 206
Rational-emotive therapy, 689–690
Ratio schedule of reinforcement, 250
Rat/man demonstration, 166
RCBF. *See* Regional cerebral blood flow
Reality principle, 595
Reasoning, 326–330
Recall, 307
Recency effect, 288
Receptors, 77
Receptor sites, 80
Reciprocal liking, 758–759
Reciprocity, 764–765, 779
Recognition, 307
Reflex arc, 83
Regional cerebral blood flow (RCBF), 99
Reinforcement, 246–248, 268, 693–694
Relaxation, 543
Reliability, 576–577, 623
REM sleep. *See* Rapid eye movement (REM) sleep
Representativeness heuristic, 333–334
Repression, 195
Research methods. *See* Methodology
Resistance, 685
Resistance stage, 528
Response facilitation, 760
Restorative theory of sleep, 185–188
Reticular formation (RF), 90, 185
Retina, 130
Retirement, 433
Retrieval, 279, 285–286, 296–299
Retroactive interference, 301–302
Reuptake, 80
Reversibility, 387
RF. *See* Reticular formation
Right hemisphere, 87
Risk aversion strategies, 334
Risk-taking strategies, 334–335
Rods, 130
Rorschach test, 622–623

Safety needs, 447
Satiety, 451
Savant syndrome, 560–561
Scalloping, 252
Scapegoating, 748–749
Schemas, 310, 316–317, 719–721
Schizophrenia, 662–669, 697–698
Scientific empiricism, 8
Scientific research, 7, 34–69
conclusions from, 57–62
ethical issues, 62–66
and everyday thinking, 66–67
logic of, 34–40
methods of, 7, 40–57
SCN. *See* Suprachiasmatic nucleus
Scripts, 310–311
Secondary emotions, 486
Secondary gain, 653
Secondary memory, 276–277
Secondary qualities, 167
Secondary reinforcers, 248, 260
Secondary traits, 607
Second-order conditioning, 233–234

Self, development of, 414–423
adolescence, 418–423
gender, 416–417
self-awareness, 414–415
self-concept, 415
self-esteem, 415–416, 422–423
Self-actualization, 447–448, 602
Self-concept, 415, 728–733
Self-esteem, 415–416, 422–423, 447
Self-fulfilling prophecy, 720
Self-handicapping, 732–733
Self-monitoring, 613
Self-perception theory, 745–746
Self-report tests, 620–622
Self schemas, 618–619, 730–731
Self-serving bias, 728
Self-verification, 732
Semantic memory, 290, 298–299
Senses. *See* Perception
Sensorimotor stage, 384
Sensory memory, 279–280
Sensory reinforcers, 248
Seriation, 387
Set point theory, 457
Sexual dimorphism, 120
Sexual double standard, 788
Sexuality, 460–471
and biology, 461–462
and communication, 788–789
development, 371, 379
and gender, 464–468
and violence against women, 769–772
See also Interpersonal relations
Sexual orientation, 464, 468–471
Shallow processing, 292
Shape constancy, 161
Shaping, 248, 693–694
Shock therapy. *See* Electroconvulsive therapy
Short-term memory (STM), 280–289, 303
SHSS. *See* Stanford Hypnotic Susceptibility Scale
Similarity, law of, 153
Simplicity, law of, 153
Situationism, 611–612
16 Personality Factor (16PF) Test, 620
Size constancy, 160–161
Size-distance scaling, 160–161
Skin, 146–148
Sleep, 176, 181–191
biological control of, 185
disorders, 189–191
dreams, 184–185, 192–197
functions of, 185–189
stages of, 182–185
Sleep apnea, 191
Slow-wave sleep (SWS), 184, 185, 186, 188
Smell, 150–152
Snoring, 191
Soar, 347–349
Social change, 786–787
Social cognition, 714–749
attitudes, 733–746
attribution, 721–728
person perception, 716–721
racism, 719, 748–749
and self, 728–733
Social development, 408–434
adulthood, 427–434
attachment, 409–414
moral reasoning, 423–427
psychosocial theory, 409
self, 414–423
Social exchange theory, 764
Social facilitation, 783
Social factors, 202–203, 208, 211. *See also* Social cognition
Socialization, 268–269, 316, 372–373, 417–418

Socializing agents, 417
Social learning theory, 208
Social loafing, 783
Social norms, 475, 764–765
Social Readjustment Rating Scale (SRRS), 523–525
Social referencing, 412
Social reinforcers, 248
Social responsibility, 765
Social support, 533–536, 775–776
Society for Neuroscience, 66
Sociobiology, 117–119
Socioeconomic status, 437. *See also* Race
Sociology, 776–778
Somatic nervous system, 90–91
Somatization disorder, 653
Somatoform disorders, 652–654
Somatosensory cortex, 100
Sound. *See* Hearing
Sound wave, 139
Source traits, 607
Spatial intelligence, 565
Species-specific defense reactions, 256–257
Spinal cord, 89–90
Split-brain research, 106–109, 212–213
Spontaneous recovery, 231–232
SQ3R method, 312–314
SRRS. *See* Social Readjustment Rating Scale
Stability vs. instability, 365–368
Stains, 76
Standard deviation, 59
Stanford-Binet test, 556–557, 585
Stanford Hypnotic Susceptibility Scale (SHSS), 199
State-dependent learning effect, 297–298
Statistical significance, 61
Stereotypes, 720–721, 735–736
Stimulants, 205, 209
STM. *See* Short-term memory
Storage, 279, 283–285, 291–296
Strange situation, 412–413
Stress, 520–533
biological effects, 527–533
coping with, 539–543, 544
measurement of, 523–527
nature, 520–522
and personality, 536–539
and social support, 535
Structuralism, 11–12, 20
Structured Interview, 538
Studying, 312–315
Subcortical nuclei, 87
Subject bias, 56–57
Superego, 595
Superiority complex, 601
Suprachiasmatic nucleus (SCN), 178–180, 185
Surface traits, 607
Surveys, 43
Survival of the fittest, 117
SWS. *See* Slow-wave sleep
Syllogism, 327
Sympathetic division, 91
Synapse, 80
Synaptic vesicles, 80
Systematic desensitization, 239–240, 692–693

TABP. *See* Type A behavior pattern
Tacit knowledge, 581
Tangible support, 534
Taste, 148–150
Taste buds, 149
TAT. *See* Thematic Apperception Test
Telegraphic speech, 96, 406
Temperature, 146–148
Temporal lobe, 87
Testosterone, 120, 461
Test-retest method, 576–577
Tests. *See* Intelligence

Thalamus, 88, 101
That's not all technique, 779
Thematic Apperception Test (TAT), 472–473, 478–479, 622, 623
Theories, 38–40
Therapy, 678–709
    art, 686–687
    behavioral approaches, 239–240, 692–695
    biomedical, 696–701
    and classical conditioning, 239–240
    client-centered, 17, 604, 687–689
    cognitive approaches, 689–692
    cultural differences, 708–709
    eclecticism, 701–702
    effectiveness, 702–704
    group, 695–696
    history of, 679–684
    institutionalization, 704–706
    and operant conditioning, 257–259
    professionals, 683
    psychodynamic, 681, 682, 684–686
Thinking, 322–359
    categorization, 323–326
    cultural differences, 355–356, 358–359
    decision making, 330–335
    development, 392–393
    and language, 350–357
    problem solving, 335–350
    reasoning, 326–330
Thorazine, 697
Thought disorders, 662–663
Tip-of-the-tongue (TOT) effect, 296
Token economies, 694
Tolerance, drug, 208–209, 240–242
Tongue, 149–150
TOT effect. *See* Tip-of-the-tongue (TOT) effect

Touch, 100, 146–148
Trace conditioning, 230
Tracking, 578–579
Trait approach to personality, 606–613
Tranquilizers, 206
Transduction, 77
Transference, 685
Transitivity, 387
Triarchic theory of intelligence, 580–581
Twin studies, 370, 470–471, 573–575
Two-factor theory, 506, 564
Tympanic membrane, 140
Type A behavior pattern (TABP), 537

Ultimate attribution error, 749
Unconditioned reflex, 226
Unconditioned response (UR), 226. *See also* Behaviorism
Unconditioned stimulus (US), 226, 227, 230. *See also* Behaviorism
Unconscious, 592, 599
Underextension, 406
Undifferentiated schizophrenia, 664
UR. *See* Unconditioned response
US. *See* Unconditioned stimulus

Validity, 577, 623
Valium, 206, 700
Variable-interval (VI) schedule of reinforcement, 252
Variable-ratio (VR) schedule of reinforcement, 251
Variables, 38, 44, 47
Vascular theory of emotional efference (VTEE), 501–502
Ventromedial nucleus of the hypothalamus (VMH), 450, 451
VI. *See* Variable-interval (VI) schedule of reinforce-ment

Visible light, 130
Vision, 100–101, 129–138
    development, 376–378
    sensory code for, 131–137
    system structure, 130
Vision. *See also* Perception
Visual cliff, 412
Visual cortex, 100–101
Visual receiving area, 130
VMH. *See* Ventromedial nucleus of the hypothalamus
Volunteer bias, 467
VR. *See* Variable-ratio (VR) schedule of reinforcement
VTEE. *See* Vascular theory of emotional efference

Wechsler Intelligence tests, 557, 585
Weight, 454–460
    psychological theories, 457–458
    and self-esteem, 423
    treatment, 458–460
Wernicke's area, 96–97
Whites. *See* Race
Women. *See* Gender
Work
    and circadian rhythms, 181
    and groups, 782–784
    and social development, 430–432
Working memory, 101–102

Yale model of persuasion, 740, 743

Zeitgebers, 177–178
Zygote, 374

CREDITS

These pages constitute an extension of the copyright page. We have made every effort to trace the ownership of all copyrighted material and to secure permission from copyright holders. In the event of any question arising as to the use of any material, we will be pleased to make the necessary corrections in future printings. Thanks are due to the following authors, publishers, and agents for permission to use the material indicated.

Figure and Table Credits

Chapter One: 19: Figure 1.6, From *Introduction to Psychology,* 3rd ed., by James W. Kalat, p. 11. Copyright © 1993 by Wadsworth, Inc.

Chapter Two: 62: Figure 2.18, From "Gender Differences in Mathematics Performance: A Meta-analysis," by J. S. Hyde, E. Fennema, and S. J. Lamon, 1990, *Psychological Bulletin, 107,* 139–155. Copyright © 1990 by the American Psychological Association. Reprinted by permission. 66: Figure 2.21, "Ethical Principles of Psychologists and Code of Conduct," *American Psychologist, 47,* 1597–1611. Copyright © 1992 by the American Psychological Association. Reprinted by permission.

Chapter Three: 74: Excerpt from "The Man Who Mistook His Wife for a Hat," by Oliver Sacks, pp. 25–26. Copyright © 1970, 1981, 1983, 1984, 1985 by Oliver Sacks. Reprinted by permission of Summit Books, a division of Simon & Schuster, Inc. 120: Figure 3.23, Adapted from "Prenatal Exposure to Synthetic Progestins Increases Potential for Aggression in Humans," by J. M. Reinisch, 1981, *Science, 211,* 1171–1173. Copyright © 1981 by the American Association for the Advancement of Science. Reproduced by permission. 121: Figure 3.24, Illustration on page 124 by Jared Schneidman, from "Sex Differences in the Brain," by Doreen Kimura, *Scientific American,* September 1992. Copyright © 1992 by Scientific American. All rights reserved. Reprinted by permission. 121: Figure 3.25, Illustration on page 122 by Johnny Johnson, from "Sex Differences in the Brain," by Doreen Kimura, *Scientific American,* September 1992. Copyright © 1992 by Scientific American. All rights reserved. Reprinted by permission.

Chapter Four: 134: Figure 4.7, From "Visual Properties of Neurons in a Polysensory Area in the Superior Temporal Sulcus of the Macaque," by C. Bruce, R. Desimone, and C. G. Gross, 1981, *Journal of Neurophysiology, 46,* 369–384. Reprinted by permission of the American Physiological Society. 135: Figure 4.8, Adapted from "Human Color Vision and Color Blindness," by G. Wald and P. K. Brown, 1965, *Cold Spring Harbor Symposia on Quantitative Biology, 30,* pp. 345–359. Used by permission. 136: Figure 4.10, From "Primate Color Vision," by R. L. DeValois and G. H. Jacobs, *Science, 162,* pp. 533–540, November 1, 1968. Copyright 1968 by the American Association for the Advancement of Science. Used by permission. 141: Figure 4.14, (b): Figure [4.2] from *Human Information Processing: An Introduction to Psychology,* 2nd ed., by Peter H. Lindsay and Donald A. Norman, copyright © 1977 by Harcourt Brace & Company, reproduced by permission of the publisher. 143: Figure 4.15, From "A Revised Frequency-Map of the Guinea-Pig Cochlea," by E. Culler, J. D. Coakley, K. Lowy, and N. Gross, 1943, *American Journal of Psychology, 56,* pp. 475–500. Used by permission of the University of Illinois Press. 144: Figure 4.16, (left) From "Shearing Motion in Scala Media of Cochlea Models," by J. Tonndorf, 1960, *Journal of the Acoustical Society of America, 32,* p. 238–244. Copyright © 1960 by the Acoustical Society of America. Reprinted by permission. 147: Figure 4.17, (b) Figure from *Fundamentals of Neurology: A Psychological Approach,* 6th ed. by Ernest Gardner, p. 222, copyright © 1975 by Saunders College Publishing, reproduced by permission of the publisher. 149: Figure 4.19, (center, right) Adapted from "The Anatomy and Ultrastructure of Taste Endings," by R. G. Murray and A. Murray. In G. E. W. Wolstenholme and J. Knight (Eds.), *Taste and Smell in Vertebrates.* J & A Churchill, 1970. Used by permission. 151: Figure 4.20, Drawing on page 43 of cross-section of head by Bunji Tagawa from "The Stereochemical Theory of Odor" by John E. Amoore, James W. Johnston, Jr. and Martin Rubin, *Scientific American,* February 1964. Copyright © 1964 by Scientific American, Inc. All rights reserved. Reprinted by permission. 166: Figures 4.41, 4.43, 4.44: From "The Role of Frequency in Developing Perceptual Sets," by B. R. Bugelski and D. A. Alampay, 1961, *Canadian Journal of Psychology, 15,* 205–211. Reprinted by permission. 167: Figure 4.44, From "On the Semantics of a Glance at a Scene," by I. Biederman, In *Perceptual Organization,* M. Kubovy and J. Pomerantz (Eds.), pp. 213–254, 1981. Lawrence Erlbaum & Associates. Used by permission.

Chapter Five: 177 and 178: Figures 5.1 and 5.2, From *Wide Awake at 3:00 A.M.,* by Richard M. Coleman, 1986, p. 18. W. H. Freeman & Company, Publishers. Copyright © 1986 by Richard M. Coleman. Reprinted by permission. 181: Figure 5.5, From *Wide Awake at 3:00 A.M.,* by Richard M. Coleman, 1986, p. 46. W. H. Freeman & Company Publishers. Copyright © 1986 by Richard M. Coleman. Reprinted by permission of the author. 199: Excerpts from *Hypnotic Susceptibility,* by E. R. Hilgard, 1965. Harcourt Brace & World. Copyright © 1965 by E. R. Hilgard. Reproduced by permission of the author. 207: Figure 5.2, From *Drugs, Alcohol and Society,* by R. L. Akers, 1992. Copyright © Wadsworth, Inc. 211: Figure 5.15, From *Drugs, Society and Human Behavior,* 5th ed. by O. Ray and C. Ksir, p. 169. Copyright © 1990 by Mosby-Year Book, Inc. Reproduced by permission. 213: Figure 5.17, From *The Integrated Mind,* by M. Gazzaniga and J. E. Le Doux, p. 149. Copyright Plenum Publishing Corp. Reprinted by permission.

Chapter Six: 231: Figure 6.5 Adapted from *Psychology: Themes and Variations,* 2nd ed., by W. Weiten. Copyright © 1992, 1989 by Wadsworth, Inc. 232: Figure 6.6, Adapted from "The Irradiation of Conditioned Reflexes," by G. V. Anrep, 1923, *Proceedings of the Royal Society of London, 94B,* 404–426. Adapted by permission of the Royal Society of London. 258: Figure 6.19, From "Manipulation of Self-Destruction in Three Retarded Children," by O. I. Lovaas and J. Q. Simmons, 1969, Journal of Applied Behavior Analysis, 2, 143–157. Copyright © Society for Experimental Analysis of Behavior.

Reproduced with permission. 263: Figure 6.21, From "Introduction and Removal of Reward and Maze Performance in Rats," by E. C. Tolman and C. H. Honzik, *University of California Publications in Psychology, 4*, 257–275. Copyright © 1930 by The Regents of the University of California. Reproduced by permission.

Chapter Seven: 282: Figure 7.8, Adapted from "STM Capacity for Chinese Words and Idioms: Chunking and Acoustical Loop Hypothesis," by G. Zhang and H. A. Simon, 1985, *Memory and Cognition, 13*, 193–201. Copyright © 1985 by the Psychonomic Society. Adapted by permission. 283: Figure 7.9, Adapted from "The Mind's Eye in Chess," by W. G. Chase and H. A. Simon. In *Visual Information Processing*, W. G. Chase (Ed.). Copyright © 1973 by Academic Press, Inc. Adapted by permission. 288: Figure 7.11, From "Short-Term Retention of Individual Verbal Items," by L. R. Peterson and M. J. Peterson, 1959, *Journal of Experimental Psychology, 58*, 193–198. Copyright © 1959 by the American Psychological Association. Reprinted by permission. 288: Figure 7.12, Data from "The Serial Position Effect in Free Recall," by B. B. Murdock, 1962, *Journal of Experimental Psychology, 64*, 484–488. Copyright © 1962 by the American Psychological Association. Used by permission. 294: Figure 7.16, Adapted from "Hierarchical Retrieval Schemes in Recall of Categorized Word Lists," by G. H. Gordon, M. C. Clark, A. M. Lesgold, and D. Winzenz, 1969, *Journal of Verbal Learning and Verbal Behavior, 8*, p. 324. Copyright © 1969 by Academic Press, Inc. Adapted by permission. 295: Figure 7.17, From "Contextual Prerequisites for Understanding: Some Investigations of Comprehension and Recall," by J. Bransford and M. Johnson, 1972, *Journal of Verbal Learning and Verbal Behavior, 61*, 717–726. Copyright © 1972 by Academic Press. Used by permission. 297: Figure 7.18, From *The Ideal Problem Solver*, by Barry S. Stein and John D. Bransford (pp. 142–143). Copyright © 1993 by W. H. Freeman and Company. Reprinted with permission. 299: Figures 7.20 and 7.21, From "Retrieval Time from Semantic Memory," by A. M. Collins and M. R. Quillian, 1969, *Journal of Verbal Learning and Verbal Behavior, 8*, 240–248. Copyright © 1969 by Academic Press, Inc. Used by permission. 207: Excerpt from "The Conditions of Retention," by C. W. Luh, 1922, *Psychological Monographs, 31*. Copyright © 1922 by the American Psychological Association. Adapted by permission. 308: Figure 7.26, From "Semantic Memory Content in Permastore: Fifty Years of Memory Learned in School," by H. P. Bahrick, 1984, *Journal of Experimental Psychology: General, 113*, 1–26. Copyright © 1984 by the American Psychological Association. Used by permission. 309: Figure 7.27, Excerpt from *Remembering: A Study in Experimental and Social Psychology*, by F. C. Barlett, p. 65, 1932, Cambridge University Press. Copyright © 1932. Reprinted with permission of Cambridge University Press. 310: Figure 7.28, Adapted from "Scripts in Memory for Text," by G. H. Bower, J. B. Black, and T. J. Turner, 1979, *Cognitive Psychology, 11*, 177–220. Copyright © 1979 by Academic Press, Inc. Adapted by permission.

Chapter Eight: 325: Figure 8.2, Adapted from "Family Resemblances: Studies in the Internal Structure of Categories," by E. Rosch and C. B. Mervis, 1975, *Cognitive Psychology, 7*, 573–605. Copyright © 1975 by Academic Press, Inc. Adapted by permission. 326: Figure 8.4, From "On the Internal Structure of Perceptual and Semantic Categories," by E. Rosch, 1973. In *Cognitive Development and the Acquisition of Language*, T. E. Moore (Ed.). Copyright © 1973 by Research Foundation SUNY. Used by permission. 328: Table 8.3 and Figure 8.5, Adapted from "Supposition and the Analysis of Conditional Sentences," by L. J. Rips and S. L. Marcus, 1977. In *Cognitive Processes in Comprehension*, M. A. Just and P. A. Carpenter (Eds.). Copyright © 1977 Lawrence Erlbaum Associates, Inc. Adapted by permission. 335: Figure 8.6, Adapted from *Introduction to Psychology*, 2nd ed., by James W. Kalat, p. 343. Copyright © 1990 Wadsworth, Inc. 337: Excerpt from Mindfulness, © 1989 by Ellen J. Langer, Ph.D. (pp. 9–10). Reprinted with permission of Addison-Wesley Publishing Company, Inc. 339: Figure 8.11, Adapted from "Reasoning in Humans II. The Solution of a Problem and Its Appearance in Consciousness," by N. R. F. Maier, 1931, *Journal of Comparative Psychology, 12*, 181–194. Copyright © 1931 by the American Psychological Association. Adapted by permission. 339: Figure 8.12, Adapted from "Mechanization in Problem Solving," by A. S. Luchins, 1942, *Psychological Monographs, 54*, 6. Whole No. 248. Copyright © 1942 by the American Psy-

chological Association. Adapted by permission. 340: Figure 8.13, From *Cognitive Psychology*, by J. R. Hayes, pp. 179–180. Copyright © 1978 by John R. Hayes. Adapted by permission. 348: Figure 8.21, Adapted from "Soar: A Unified Theory of Cognition," by M. M. Waldrop, 1988, *Science, 241*, 296–298. Copyright © 1988 by the American Association for the Advancement of Science. Adapted by permission. 348: Figure 8.22, Reprinted by permission of the publishers from *Unified Theories of Cognition*, by Allen Newell, p. 347, Cambridge, Mass.: Harvard University Press, Copyright © 1990 by the President and Fellows of Harvard College.

Chapter Nine: 368: Figure 9.1, From "Stability of Aggression Over Time and Generations" by L. R. Huesmann, L. D. Eron, M. M. Lefkowitz, and L. O. Walder, 1984, *Developmental Psychology, 20* (6), p. 1125. Copyright © American Psychological Association. Reprinted by permission of the author. 369: Figure 9.2, From tables 3.1 and 3.2 in the chapter "Social Psychology from a Social-developmental Perspective," by D. R. Shaffer. In C. Hendrick, *Perspectives on Social Psychology*. Copyright © 1977 by Lawrence Erlbaum Associations. Reprinted by permission. 376: Figure 9.8, From *A Child's World*, by Papalia and Olds, 5th ed., p. 161. Copyright © 1990 by McGraw-Hill Publishing, College Division. Reprinted by permission. 377: Figure 9.9, Adapted from *Of Children*, by Thomas Lefrancois, figure 5.3, p. 225. Copyright © Wadsworth, Inc. (based on data from Denver Developmental Screening Test Reference Manual: Revised 1975 Ed. by Frankenburg, Dodds, Fandal, Kazuk, and Cohrs, University of Colorado Medical Center.) 381: Figure 9.12, From *The Developing Person Through the Life Span*, 2nd ed., by Kathleen S. Berger, p. 528. Copyright © 1988 by Worth Publishers, Inc. Reprinted by permission. 385: Figure 9.15, Adapted from *The Child's Conception of Space*, by J. Piaget and B. Inhelder, p. 211. Copyright © 1957 by Routledge Kegan and Paul Ltd. Adapted by permission. 385 and 387: Figures 9.16 and 9.17, From *Psychology: Themes and Variations*, 2nd ed., by W. Weiten, p. 391. Copyright © 1992, 1989 by Wadsworth, Inc. 393: Figure 9.21, From "Processing Time Declines Exponentially During Childhood and Adolescence," by R. Kail, 1991, *Developmental Psychology, 27*, 259–266. Copyright © 1991 by the American Psychological Association. Reprinted by permission. 398: Figure 9.24, From "Cross-Cultural Tests of Piaget's Theory," by P. Dasen and A. Heron, 1981, p. 311. In H. Triandis and A. Herons (Eds.), *Handbook of Cross-Cultural Psychology: Vol. 4, Developmental Psychology*. Copyright © 1981 Allyn & Bacon. Reprinted by permission. 398: Figure 9.25, From "Cross-Cultural Training Studies of Concrete Operations," by P. Dasen, L. Ngini, and M. Lavelee, 1979. In L. H. Eckenberger, W. J. Lonner, and Y. H. Poortinga (Eds.), *Cross-Cultural Contributions to Psychology*. Copyright © 1979 by Swetsen Zeilinger. 399: Figure 9.26, Adapted from "The Validity of 'Cultural Differences Explanations' for Cross-Cultural Variation in the Rate of Piagetian Cognitive Development," by R. M. Nyiti, 1982. In D. Wagner and H. Stevenson (Eds.), *Cultural Perspectives on Child Development*. Copyright © 1982 by W. H. Freeman and Company. Adapted by permission.

Chapter Ten: 416: Figure 10.6, From "The Perceived Competence Scale for Children," by S. Harter, 1982, *Child Development, 53*, 87–97, Copyright © 1982 by The Society for Research in Child Development. Reprinted by permission. 418: Table 10.1, From "Gender Segregation in Childhood," by E. Maccoby and C. N. Jacklin, 1987, *Advances in Child Development and Behavior, 20*, 239–287. Copyright © 1987 by Academic Press, Inc. Reprinted by permission. 429: Figure 10.9, From "Age and Sex Differences in Satisfying Love Relationships Across the Adult Life Span," by M. N. Reedy, J. E. Birren, and K. W. Schaie 1981, *Human Development, 24*, 52–66. Copyright © 1981 by Ablex Publishing Corporation. Reprinted by permission. 431: Figure 10.11, From "The AT&T Longitudinal Studies of Managers," by D. W. Bray and A. Howard. In *Longitudinal Studies of Adult Psychological Development*, K. Warner Schaie (Ed.), p. 292. Copyright © 1983 by The Guilford Press. Reprinted by permission. 433: Figure 10.12, Adapted from *Personality in Adulthood*, by R. R. McCrae and P. T. Costa, Jr., 1990, p. 58. Copyright © 1990 by The Guilford Press. Adapted by permission. 436: Table 10.5, From "Cross-Cultural Patterns of Attachment: A Meta-Analysis of the Strange Situation," by M. H. van Ijzendoorn and P. M. Kroonenberg, 1988, *Child Development, 59*, 147–156. Copyright © 1988 by The Society for Research in Child Development. Reprinted by permission.

Chapter Eleven: 457: Figure 11.12, Adapted from *Physiology and Behavior, 21*, by P. Boyle, L. H. Storlien, and R. E. Keesey, "Increased Efficiency of Food Utilization Following Food Loss," 261–264, Copyright © 1978 with kind permission from Pergamon Press, Ltd., Headington Hill Hall, Oxford OX3 0BW, UK. 460: Figure 11.13, From "Behavior Therapy and Pharmacotherapy for Obesity," by L. W. Craighead, A. J. Stunkard, and R. M. O'Brien, 1981, *Archives of General Psychiatry, 38*, 763–768. Copyright © 1981 by the American Medical Association. Reprinted by permission. 462: Figure 11.14, From "Rise in Female-Initiated Sexual Activity at Ovulation and its Suppression by Oral Contraceptives," by D. B. Adams, A. R. Gold, and A. Burt, 1978, *New England Journal of Medicine, 299*, 1145–1150. Copyright © 1978 by the New England Journal of Medicine. Reprinted by permission. 466: Table 11.3, From *The Longest War: Sex Differences in Perspective,* by Carol Tavris and Carole W. Offir, p. 68, copyright © 1977 Harcourt Brace and Company, reprinted by permission of the publisher.

Chapter Twelve: 487: Figure 12.1, Based on art in "Language for Emotions," by R. Plutchik, 1980, *Psychology Today, 13* (9), 69–78. Reprinted by permission from *Psychology Today* magazine. Copyright © 1980 (Sussex Publishers, Inc.). 489: Figure 12.3, From "Mood Effects on Person-Perception Judgements," by J. P. Forgas and G. Bower, 1987, *Journal of Personality and Social Psychology, 53* (1), 53–60. Copyright © 1987 by the American Psychological Association. Reprinted by permission. 491: Figure 12.6, from experiment taken from "Emotion and Dance in Dynamic Light Displays," by R. D. Walk and C. P. Homan, 1984, *Bulletin of the Psychonomic Society, 22* (5), 437–440. Copyright © 1984 by the Psychonomic Society, Inc. Reprinted by permission. 493: Excerpt from "Managing Emotions in Medical School: Students' Contacts with the Living and the Dead," by A. C. Smith and S. Kleinman, 1989, *Social Psychology Quarterly, 52*, 56–69. Copyright © 1989 American Sociological Association. Reprinted by permission. 499: Figure 12.11, Adapted from "Self-Attribution of Emotion: The Effects of Expressive Behavior on the Quality of Emotional Experience," by J. D. Laird, 1974, *Journal of Personality and Social Psychology, 29*, 475–486. Copyright © 1974 by the American Psychological Association. Adapted by permission. 510: Table 12.1, From *Emotion in One Human Face: Guidelines for Research and an Integration of Findings,* by Paul Ekman, W. Friesen, and P. Elllsworth. Copyright © 1972 by Pergamon Press, Ltd. Reprinted by permission.

Chapter Thirteen: 519: Figure 13.2, Data from L. Breslow, "The Potential of Health Promotion." Reprinted with permission of The Free Press, a division of Macmillan, Inc. from D. Mechanic (Ed.), *Handbook of Health, Health Care, and the Health Professions.* Copyright © 1983 by The Free Press, a Division of Macmillan, Inc. 520: Table 13.1, From "Warning: Masculinity May Be Dangerous to Your Health," by J. Harrison, J. Chin, and T. Ficarrotto. Copyright © 1988 by James Harrison, James Chin, and Thomas Ficarrotto. Reprinted by permission of James B. Harrison, Director of Psychology, Black Mountain Center, North Carolina. 524: Table 13.2, Reprinted with permission from *Journal of Psychosomatic Research, 11*, by T. Holmes and R. Rahe, "The Social Readjustment Rating Scale," 1967, 213–218, Copyright © 1967 Pergamon Press, Ltd., Oxford, England. 524: Table 13.3, From "Comparisons of Two Modes of Stress Measurement: Daily Hassles and Uplifts Versus Major Life Events," by A. D. Kanner, J. C. Coyne, C. Schaefer, and R. S. Lazarus, 1981, *Journal of Behavioral Medicine, 4*, 1–39. Copyright © 1981 by Plenum Publishing Co. Reprinted by permission. 527: Figure 13.6, Data from "Hypertension, Peptic Ulcer, and Diabetes in Air Traffic Controllers," by S. Cobb and R. M. Rose, 1973. *Journal of the American Medical Association, 224*, 489–492. Copyright © 1973 by the American Medical Association. Reprinted by permission. 541: Figure 13.18, Adapted from "Availability of Avoidance Behaviors in Modulating Vascular Stress Responses," by J. E. Hokanson, D. E. DeGood, M. Forrest, and T. Brittain, 1971, *Journal of Personality and Social Psychology, 19*, 60–68. Copyright © 1971 by the American Psychological Association. Adapted by permission. 543: Figure 13.19, From "Influence of Aerobic Exercise on Depression," by I. L. McCann and D. S. Holmes, 1984, *Journal of Personality and Social Psychology, 46*, 1142–1147. Copyright © 1984 by the American Psychological Association. Reprinted by permission. 544: Figure 13.20, Reprinted by permission of The Hope Heart Institute of Seattle, Washington. Copyright © 1989 by the The Hope Heart Institute.

Chapter Fourteen: 558: Excerpt adapted from *Introduction to Psychology,* 2nd ed. by James Kalat, p. 356. Copyright © 1990 by Wadsworth, Inc. 559: Figure 14.6, Adapted from "The Three–Ring Conception of Giftedness," by J. S. Renzulli. In R. J. Sternberg and J. E. Davidson (Eds.), *Conceptions of Giftedness,* pp. 53–92. Copyright © 1986 Cambridge University Press. Adapted by permission. 568: Table 14.1, From "Transitions in Infant Sensoromotor Development and the Prediction of Childhood IQ," by R. B. McCall, P. S. Hogarty, and N. Hurlburt, 1972, *American Psychologist, 27*, 728–748. Copyright © 1972 by the American Psychological Association. Reprinted by permission. 570: Figure 14.13, From "An Anatomy of Analogy," by James W. Pelligrino in *Psychology Today*, October 1985, p. 50. Reprinted by permission of *Psychology Today* magazine. Copyright © 1985 (Sussex Publishers, Inc.). 572: (a): From "Degree of Myopia in Relation to Intelligence and Educational Level," by T. Teasdale, J. Fuchs, and E. Goldschmidt, 1988, *The Lancet, 332*, 1351–1354. Copyright © 1988 by Lancet, Ltd. Reprinted by permission. (b): From "Growth and Intellectual Development," by D. M . Wilson, L. D. Hammer, P. M. Duncan, S. M. Dornbush, P. L. Ritter, R. L. Hintz, R. T. Gross, and R. G. Rosenfeld, 1986, *Pediatrics.* Reproduced by permission of Pediatrics, Vol. 78, p. 646, copyright © 1986. 574: Figure 14.15, Adapted from "Familial Studies of Intelligence: A Review," by T. J. Bouchard and M. McGue, 1981, *Science, 212*, 1055–1059. Copyright © 1981 by the American Association for the Advancement of Science. Adapted by permission. 576: Figure 14.17, From *Psychology: Themes and Variations,* 2nd ed. by W. Weiten, pp. 304, 306. Copyright © 1992, 1989 by Wadsworth, Inc. 582: Figure 14.19, From "Practical Intelligence for Business," by Daniel Goleman. April 5, 1988, *The New York Times.* Copyright © 1988 by The New York Times Company. Reprinted by permission.

Chapter Fifteen: 608: Figure 15.9, Adapted from Eysenck and Eysenck, 1968. Reprinted by permission of H. J. Eysenck. 609: Figure 15.10, From "Extraversion and Individual Differences in Auditory Evoked Response," by R. M. Stelmack, E. Achorn, and A. Michaud, 1977, *Psychophysiology, 14* (4), p. 371. Copyright © 1977 by The Society for Psychophysiological Research. Reprinted by permission. 610 and 611: Figures 15.12 and 15.13, Adapted from "Personality Similarity in Twins Reared Apart and Together," by A. Tellegen, D. T. Lykken, T. J. Bouchard, Jr., K. J. Wilcox, N. L. Segal, and S. Rich, 1988, *Journal of Personality and Social Psychology, 54* (6), 1031–1039. Copyright © 1988 by the American Psychological Association. Adapted by permission. 614: Figure 15.16, From "Life Histories and Psychobiography: Explorations in Theory and Method," by W. M. Runyan, 1982. Copyright © 1982 by Oxford University Press. 615: Table 15.5, From "Leader Appeal, Leader Performance and the Motive Profiles of Leaders and Followers: A Study of American Presidents and Elections," by D. G. Winter, 1987, *Journal of Personality and Social Psychology, 52*, 196–202. Copyright © 1987 by the American Psychological Association. Reprinted by permission. 616 and 618: Figures 15.17 and 15.18, Adapted from *Personality,* 3rd ed., by J. M. Burger, 1993. Copyright © 1993 by Wadsworth, Inc. 619: Figure 15.19, From "Culture and the Self: Implications for Cognition, Emotion and Motivation," by H. R. Markus and Shinobu Kitayama, 1991, *Psychological Review, 98*, 224–253. Copyright © 1991 by the American Psychological Association. Reprinted by permission. 621: Table 15.7, from Minnesota Multiphasic Personality Inventory. Copyright © The University of Minnesota, 1942, 1943 (renewed 1970). MMPI scale names reproduced by permission of the publisher. 621: Figure 15.20, Adapted from Raymond B. Cattell, *Handbook for the Sixteen Personality Factors.* Copyright © 1970, 1988 by the Institute for Personality and Ability Testing, Inc. All rights reserved. Adapted by permission. 622: Figure 15.21, Adapted from Wayne Weiten, *Psychology: Themes and Variations,* 2nd ed., by W. Weiten, p. 459. Copyright © 1992, 1989 by Wadsworth, Inc.

Chapter Sixteen: 637: Table 16.1, From *The Diagnostic and Statistical Manual of Mental Disorders,* 3rd ed., revised. Copyright © 1987 American Psychiatric Association. Reprinted by permission. 638: Excerpt adapted with permission from *The Diagnostic and Statistical Manual of Mental Disorders,* 3rd ed., revised. Copyright © 1987 American Psychiatric Association. 641: Excerpts from *Psychopathology: A Casebook,* by R. L. Spitzer, A. E. Skodol, M. Gibbon, and J. B. W. Williams, 1983, pp. 7–8, 37, 115, 153, Copyright © 1983 by McGraw-Hill, Inc. Reprinted by permission. 646: Figure 16.15,

Reprinted from *Behavior Research and Therapy, 24*, by D. M. Clark, "Cognitive Approach to Panic, p. 463. Copyright © 1986 with kind permission from Pergamon Press, Ltd., Headington Hill Hall, Oxford OX3, UK. 657: Figure 16.8, Adapted from *Introduction to Psychology*, 3rd ed., by James W. Kalat, p. 47. Copyright © 1993 by Wadsworth, Inc. 658: Figure 16.9, From "The Influence of Mood on Perceptions of Social Interactions," by J. P. Forgas, G. H. Bowerand, S. E. Krantz, 1984, *Journal of Experimental Social Psychology, 20, 497–513*. Copyright © 1984 by Academic Press. Reprinted by permission. 663: Excerpt from *Schizophrenia: An Introduction to Research and Theory*, by G. Shean, 1978, p. 72–73. Copyright © 1978 Winthrop Publishing. By permission of Glenn Shean. 664: Figure 16.15, From "An Attentional Assessment of Foster Children at Risk in Schizophrenia," by R. F. Asarnow, R. A. Steffy, D. J. MacCrimmon, and J. M. Cleghorn, 1978, p. 124. In *The Nature of Schizophrenia*, L. C. Wynne, R. L. Cromwell, and S. Matthysse (Eds.). Copyright © 1978 by John Wiley & Sons, Inc. Reprinted by permission. 666: Figure 16.16, From "Clues to the Genetics and Neurobiology of Schizophrenia," by S. E. Nicol and I. I. Gottesman, 1983, *American Scientist, 71*, 398–404. Copyright © 1983 by the Scientific Research Society. Reprinted by permission.

Chapter Seventeen: 687: Figures 17.5 and 17.6, From *The Dynamics of Art Therapy* by Harriet Wadeson, 1980, John Wiley & Sons, pp. 95–96, *102, 104*. Copyright © 1980 by Harriet Wadeson. Reprinted by permission of Harriet Wadeson. 690: Table 17.1, From *The Skilled Helper*, 4th ed., by G. Egan, p. 197. Copyright © 1990 by Wadsworth, Inc. 697: Figure 17.9, From "Dopamine Theory of Schizophrenia: A Two-Factor Theory," by J. M. Davis. In L. C. Wynne, R. L. Cromwell, and S. Matthysse (Eds.), *The Nature of Schizophrenia: New Approaches to Research and Treatment*. Copyright © 1978 by John Wiley & Sons. Reprinted by permission of John M. Davis. 705: Figure 17.11, From *Nowhere to Go*, by E. Torrey, 1988, pp. 3, 140. Copyright © 1988 by HarperCollins Publishers. Reprinted by permission.

Chapter Eighteen: 737: Figure 18.7, From *Social Psychology*, by Richard Lippa, p. 233. Brooks/Cole Publishing Co. Copyright © 1990 by Wadsworth, Inc. (based on data from "Attitudes Established by Classical Conditioning," by A. W. Staats and C. K. Staats, 1958, *Journal of Abnormal and Social Psychology, 57*, 37–40.)

Chapter Nineteen: 757: Figure 19.1, Reprinted from *Social Pressures in Informal Groups*, by Leon Festinger, Stanley Schachter, and Kurt Back, with permission of the publisher, Stanford University Press. Copyright © 1950 by Leon Festinger, Stanley Schachter, and Kurt Back. 761: Figure 19.4, Adapted from "A Triangle Theory of Love," by R. J. Sternberg, 1986, Psychological Review, 93, 119–135. Copyright © 1986 by the American Psychological Association. Adapted by permission. 762: Figure 19.5, Adapted from *Psychology: Themes and Variations*, 2nd ed., by W. Weiten, p. 592. Copyright © 1992, 1989 by Wadsworth, Inc. 773 and 775: Figures 19.13 and 19.16, Adapted from "Opinion and Social Pressure," by Solomon Asch, *Scientific American*, November, 1955, from illustrations by Sara Love on pp. 32, 35. Copyright © 1955 by Scientific American, Inc. All rights reserved. 777: Figure 19.16, From *Sociology*, by R. Stark, 1992, 4th ed., p. 189. Copyright © 1992 by Wadsworth, Inc. 783: Figure 19.17, Adapted from "Ringelmann Rediscovered: The Original Article," by D. Kravitz and B. Martin, 1986, *Journal of Personality and Social Psychology, 50* (5), 936–941. Copyright © 1986 by the American Psychological Association. Adapted by permission.

Photo Credits

Chapter One: 3, Bob Daemmrich/The Image Works; 5, (top) Frank Siteman/Stock Boston; (bottom) Owen Franken/Stock Boston; 7, Brown Brothers; 9, Bridgeman Art Library; 10, Lawrence Migdale/Stock Boston; 11, Archives of the History of American Psychology, University of Akron; 12, National Library of Medicine; 13, UPI/Bettmann; 15, (top) Culver Pictures; (bottom) Archives of the History of American Psychology, University of Akron; 16, (top) Archive Collections; (bottom) National Library of Medicine; 17, Doug Land/Landmark Photo; 18, Robert Frerck/Odyssey; 19, Hank Morgan/Photo Researchers, Inc. 21, (left) Rhoda Sydney/PhotoEdit; (center) Peter Arnold Inc.; (right) Rick Friedman/Black Star; 23, (left) Richard Pasley/Stock Boston; (right) Alon Reininger/Contact Press; 25, (left) Alain Kubacsi/Photo Researchers, Inc.; 28, (top) Archives of the History of American Psychology, University of Akron; (bottom) Archives of the History of American Psychology, University of Akron; 29, (left) UPI/Bettmann; (top right) Archive Collections; (bottom right) Archives of the History of American Psychology, University of Akron.

Chapter Two: 35, (left) Bridgeman Art Library; (right) Brown Brothers; 36, (left to right) Tim Davis/Photo Researchers Inc.; Frans Lanting/Photo Researchers, Inc.; Tim Davis/Photo Researchers Inc.; 37, Phillipe Plailly/Science Photo Library/Custom Medical Stock Photography; 38, UPI/Bettmann; 41, David Young-Wolff/PhotoEdit; 42, Bill Anderson/Monkmeyer Press; 43, Arthur Tilley/Tony Stone Worldwide; 50, Doris De Witt/Tony Stone Worldwide; 54, Mary Evans Picture Library; 63, Archive Collections.

Chapter Three: 75, Shooting Star International; 77, Martin Rotker/Phototake; 80, Bettmann Archive; 85, Lynn Johnson/Black Star; 86, (left) David Young-Wolff/PhotoEdit; (right) James Holland/Stock Boston; 87, Dr. C. Chumbley/Photo Researchers Inc.; 95, Coco McCoy/Rainbow Photo; 96, Courtesy of Dr. L. Friberg; 97, (bottom left) David Madison/Duomo; (top right) Bill Aron/PhotoEdit; 98, (left) Grant LeDuc/Monkmeyer Press; (right) Ohio Nuclear Corp./Photo Researchers, Inc.; 99, Mehau Kulyk/Photo Researchers, Inc.; 112, Professor Mark R. Rosenzweig; 114, David Turnley/Black Star; 116, Paula Lerner/Woodfin Camp & Associates; 118, Richard R. Hansen/Photo Researchers Inc.

Chapter Four: 126, Bridgeman Art Library; 134, Peter Mensel/Stock Boston; 154, Bridgeman Art Library; 155, (top) Nicholas DeVore III/Photographers Aspen; (right) Skip Moody/Dembinsky Photo Associates; (bottom) "The Forest Has Eyes" by Bev Doolittle/The Greenwich Workshop; 157, (top) Kevin McCarthy/Offshoot Stock; (center) Peter Menzel/Stock Boston; (bottom) David Muench Photography; 158, (a) David Muench Photography; (b) "The Rest on the Flight into Egypt" by David Gerard, c.1510/Courtesy of the National Gallery of Art-Andrew Mellon Collection; (c) Fritz Polking/Peter Arnold, Inc.; (d) Russell Schleipman/Offshoot Stock; (e) David Muench Photography; 159, Dr. E. R. Degginger; 162, Baron Wolman/Woodfin Camp & Associates; 163, Dembinsky Photo Associates; 164, (top) Dr. E. R. Degginger; (bottom) M. L. Dembinsky Jr./Dembinsky Photo Associates; 169, Bettmann Archive.

Chapter Five: 175, (left) Ben Barnhart/Offshoot Stock; (center) Seth Resnick/Stock Boston; (right) John Cleare/Mountain Camera/Offshoot Stock; 178, Courtesy of NASA; 182, Michael Heron/Woodfin Camp & Associates; 188, Culver Pictures; 193, Salvador Dali, "The Persistence of Memory," 1931/Museum Of Modern Art; 198, Culver Pictures; 200, Bob Daemmrich/Stock Boston; 202, Reproduced with permission from "Hypnosis in the Relief of Pain" by E.R. C291-6; 205, Kal Muller/Woodfin Camp & Associates; 206, Lorran Meares/Tom Stack & Associates; 217, Pennie Tweedie/Woodfin Camp & Associates.

Chapter Six: 223, Takeshi Kawamoto/Offshoot Stock. 224, David Carter; 225, Hank Morgan/Photo Researchers Inc.; 237, (left) Tom McHugh/Photo Researchers, Inc.; (right) G. C. Kelley/Photo Researchers, Inc.; 238, Lev Nisnevith/Tony Stone Worldwide; 239, Archives of the History of American Psychology; 240, John Cancalosi/Stock Boston; 241, Jane Schreibman/Photo Researchers, Inc.; 248, Yerkes Regional Primate Research Center of Emory University; 252, Kenneth Jarecke/Contact Press Images; 254, Paul Chesley/Tony Stone Worldwide; 257, Photopress International; 262, Phil A. Dotson/Photo Researchers, Inc.; 265, Superstock; 269, (top) Margaret Miller/Photo Researchers, Inc.; (bottom) Karen Kasmauski/Woodfin Camp & Associates.

Chapter Seven: 273, Mike Yamashita/Woodfin Camp & Associates; 274, PhotoEdit; 279, Peter Menzel/Stock Boston; 281, Gerd Ludwig/Woodfin Camp & Associates; 289, (left) Denis Valentine/The Stock Market; (right) Blair Seitz/Photo Researchers, Inc.; (bottom) Lester Sloan/Woodfin Camp

& Associates; 298, Professor Carolyn Rovee-Collier; 308, Associated Press/Wide World Photos; 310, Nathan Benn/Woodfin Camp & Associates; 313, Andy Levin/Photo Researchers, Inc.; 316, Don Smetzer/Tony Stone Worldwide; 317, (left) Alon Reininger/Contact Press Images; (right) Robert Severt/Woodfin Camp & Associates.

Chapter Eight: 322, Dardelet/Photo Researchers, Inc.; 327, Bridgeman Art Library; 330, James Wilson/Woodfin Camp & Associates; 332, Art Wilkinson/Woodfin Camp & Associates; 333, Dale Durfee/Tony Stone Worldwide; 347, Shooting Star; 351, Fred Bodin/Offshoot Stock; 358, Robert Frerck/Odyssey; 359, (left) Goodsmith/The Image Works; (right) Robert Frerck/Odyssey.

Chapter Nine: 364, John Eastcott/VA Momatiuk/Woodfin Camp & Associates; 371, (left) Vanessa Vick/Photo Researchers, Inc.; (right) Paul Solomon/Woodfin Camp & Associates; 372, (top) H. Armstrong Roberts; (bottom) James P. Rowan/Tony Stone Worldwide; 374, (L-R) Petite Format-Nestle/Photo Researchers, Inc.; 375, Andy Levin/Photo Researchers, Inc.; 376, Walter Salinger/Photo property of Anthony DeCasper; 378, From A. N. Meltzoff & M. K. Moore; 379, Bob Daemmrich/Tony Stone Worldwide; 381, Jose Carillo/Stock Boston; 382, Archives of the History of American Psychology; 384, (top) Diana Raschf/Tony Stone Worldwide; (bottom) Doug Goodman/Monkmeyer Press; 388, (left) Chip Henderson/Tony Stone Worldwide; (bottom) Alan Carey/The Image Works; (right) Bob Daemmrich/Tony Stone Worldwide; 399, Gary Brettnacher/Tony Stone Worldwide.

Chapter Ten: 403, Alon Reininger/Woodfin Camp & Associates; 404, Frank Siteman/Stock Boston; 406, (top) Jeffry W. Myers/Stock Boston; (bottom) Robert Brenner/PhotoEdit; 410, (a) James Sugar/Black Star; (b) Margaret Miller/Photo Researchers, Inc.; (c) Elaine Rebman/Photo Researchers, Inc.; (bottom) Tony Stone Worldwide; 411, (a) Robert Fried; (b) Ariel Skelley/The Stock Market; (c) John Ficara/Picture Group; (d) David Young-Wolff/PhotoEdit; (bottom-right) Mary Kate Denny/PhotoEdit; (bottom-middle) Myrleen Fergusen/PhotoEdit; (bottom-left) Michael Newman/PhotoEdit; 412, Topham/The Image Works; 414, Cathlyn Melloan/Tony Stone Worldwide; 417, Gabe Palmer/The Stock Market; 419, Louis Fernandez/Black Star; 421, Tony O'Brien/Picture Group; 423, Tony Freeman/PhotoEdit; 424, McGlynn/The Image Works; 429, Amy Etra/PhotoEdit; 432, William Hill/The Image Works; 433, P. Davidson/The Image Works; 436, (right) Zev Radovan/PhotoEdit; (left) K. Newton/Woodfin Camp & Associates.

Chapter Eleven: 443, (top) Renee Lynn/Photo Researchers, Inc.; (bottom) Brown Brothers; 444, (top) Darlyne Murawski/Tony Stone Worldwide; (bottom) Rod Planck/Tony Stone Worldwide; 445, Julie Bruton/Photo Researchers, Inc.; 451, Courtesy of Dr. Miller; 452, Sylvian Grandadam; 455, (left) Erich Lessing/Art Resource; (right) Leonello Bertolucci/Sygma; 456, PhotoEdit; 462, (top) David Woodward/Tony Stone Worldwide; (bottom) Robert Frerck/Odyssey; 463, Bridgeman Art Library; 468, Elena Dorfman/Offshoot Stock; 471, Wally McNamee; 472, McClelland, Atkinson, Clark & Lowell; 473, Terry Wild Studio; 478, Tony Freeman/PhotoEdit; 479, Associated Press/Wide World.

Chapter Twelve: 483, Rob Swanson/Picture Group; 485, Dr. Paul Ekman/The Human Interaction Laboratory; 492, (top) Dr. Paul Ekman/The Human Interaction Laboratory; (bottom-left) Dorothy Littell/Stock Boston; (bottom-right) Gerd Ludwig/Woodfin Camp & Associates; 493, Dr. Paul Ekman/The Human Interaction Laboratory; 494, Custom Medical Stock Photo; 496, Robert Brenner/PhotoEdit; 499, Dr. Paul Ekman/The Human Interaction Library; 500, Elena Dorfman/Offshoot Stock.

Chapter Thirteen: 515, Tom Sobolik/Black Star; 516, Monkmeyer Press; 517, Jim Caccavo/Picture Group; 521, (left) David Madison/Duomo Photography; (right) Bill Anderson/Monkmeyer Press; 525, Neal Palumbo/Gamma Liaison; 526, Roger Werths/Woodfin Camp & Associ-

ates; 527, Ron Watts/Black Star; 528, Dr. A. Liepins/Science Photo Library/Photo Researchers, Inc.; 529, Ed Kashi; 534, Christopher Brown/Stock Boston.

Chapter Fourteen: 537, Ed Kashi; 542, Duomo Photography; 544, Alon Reininger/Woodfin Camp & Associates; 546, Mario Ruiz/Picture Group; 547, (top) Alexandra Avakian/Woodfin Camp & Associates; (bottom) Photo Researchers, Inc.; 560, (top) Charles Gupton; (bottom) Lorna Selfe, "Nadia, A Case of Extraordinary Drawing in an Autistic Child," Harcourt Brace & Company; 561, Mario Ruiz/Picture Group; 566, (left) Gabe Palmer/Stock Market; (center) Bob Shaw/Stock Market; (right) David E. Dempster/Offshoot Stock; 574, Courtesy of Sandra Scarr; 578, Robert Frerck/Odyssey; 581, Courtesy of Robert Sternberg; 582, Elena Dorfman/Offshoot Stock; 584, (left) Culver Pictures; (right) Chuck Fishman/Woodfin Camp & Associates; 585, Kenneth Jarecke/Woodfin Camp & Associates.

Chapter Fifteen: 590, Jeffrey Aaronson/Network Aspen; 594, Mitch Kezar/Black Star; 599, ARCHIVE/Photo Researchers, Inc.; 600, John Elk III; (top right) Eric Neurath/Stock Boston; (bottom right) Eric Carle/Stock Boston; 602, Bettmann Archive; 606, Northwind Picture Archive; 608, (left) Spencer Grant/Photo Researchers, Inc.; (right) Frank Clarkson/Liaison International; 610, D. Gorton/Time Life Picture Syndicate; 612, (left) Bob Krist/Black Star; (right) Catherine Karnow/Woodfin Camp & Associates; 613, The Bridgeman Art Library/Courtauld Institute Galleries/University of London; 615, (left) UPI/Bettmann; (right) Pamela Price/Picture Group; 623, (center) Dr. David McClelland; (bottom) Courtesy of Harvard University; 627, (bottom left) Courtesy of Dr. Marianne Eckardt; (top left) Offshoot Special Collections; (top right) Levinson/Monkmeyer Press.

Chapter Sixteen: 631, John Launois/Black Star; 633, Ed Kashi; 635, Peter Menzel/Stock Boston; 643, (left) Associated Press/Wide World Photos; (right) UPI/Bettmann; (bottom) Gamma Liaison; 647, NIH/Science Source/Photo Researchers, Inc.; 648, UPI/Bettmann; 649, (left) Museum of Modern Art/Film Stills Archive; (center) Springer/Bettmann Film Archive; (right) Springer/Bettmann Film Archive; 650, UPI/Bettmann; 655, UPI/Bettmann; 665, Guttmann-Maclay Collection; The Bethlem Royal Hospital & The Maudsley Hospital; 668, James Prince/Photo Researchers, Inc.; 670, UPI/Bettmann; 671, Associated Press/Wide World Photos; 673, (top) Bruce Ayres/Tony Stone Images; (bottom) Collins/Monkmeyer Press.

Chapter Seventeen: 677, Rob Nelson/Picture Group; 678, Goldberg/Monkmeyer Press; 679, J.W. Verano/The National Museum of Natural History; 680, Mary Evans Picture Library; 681, Mary Evans Picture Library; 684, Mary Evans Picture Library; 687, *The Dynamics of Art Psychotherapy*—Reproduced by permission of John Wiley/Interscience Publications; 688, Archive Collections; 694, Custom Medical Stock; 701, James D. Wilson/Woodfin Camp & Associates; 705, Larry Downing/Woodfin Camp & Associates; 709, (top left) David Stoecklein/The Stock Market; (top right) Mike Yamashita/Woodfin Camp & Associates; (bottom left) Craig Aurness/Woodfin Camp & Associates; (bottom right) Robert Azzi/Woodfin Camp & Associates.

Chapter Eighteen: 713, John Curtis/Offshoot Stock; 714, Steve Shapiro/Gamma Liaison; 717, Ed Kashi; 718, David Leifer/Offshoot Stock; 721, Gottlieb/Monkmeyer Press; 725, Ben Barnhart/Offshoot Stock; 733, Paul Brou/Picture Group; 738, Ariel Skelly/The Stock Market; 740, (left) Courtesy of John Deere; (right) Ed Kashi; 746, Michael Newman/PhotoEdit; 748. Gamma Liaison; 749, The Stock Market.

Chapter Nineteen: 755, Luis Villota/The Stock Market; 757, Carrington/Shooting Star; 760, Courtesy of Dr. Don Dutton; 761, Shooting Star; 768, Cary S. Wolinsky/Stock Boston; 773, Courtesy of the Soloman Asch Estate; 777, Bob Daemmrich/Stock Boston; 780, Shooting Star; 782, Chip Henderson/Tony Stone Worldwide; 785, (top) Jim Pickerell/Stock Boston; (bottom) Philip Zimbardo.

TO THE OWNER OF THIS BOOK:

I hope that I've been able to make this book likable. I'd like to learn your reactions to using this textbook. Only through your comments and advice and the comments and advice of others can I hope to improve the next edition of *Psychology*.

School: _____

Your instructor's name: _____

1. What did you like most about *Psychology*? _____

_____

_____

2. What did you like least about the book? _____

_____

_____

3. Were all the chapters of the book assigned for you to read? _____

   (If not, which ones weren't?) _____

4. How interesting did you find the Measurement & Methodology sections? _____

_____

_____

5. Did the chapters come across as a story that showed how scientists pursued a question and raised new questions, and how multiple perspectives lead to scientific progress? _____

_____

_____

6. How helpful was the levels of analysis concept in fostering an understanding of the complexity of human behavior? _____

_____

_____

7. In the space below, or on a separate sheet, please let me know what other comments about the book you'd like to make. (For example, did you like the Reprise sections or the Follow-Through/Diversity sections?) I'd be delighted to hear from you!

_____

_____

_____

Optional:

Your name: _____ Date: _____

May Brooks/Cole quote you, either in promotion for *Psychology* or in future publishing ventures?

Yes: _____ No: _____

Sincerely,

Bruce Goldstein

- FOLD HERE -

BUSINESS REPLY MAIL

FIRST CLASS   PERMIT NO. 358   PACIFIC GROVE, CA

POSTAGE WILL BE PAID BY ADDRESSEE

ATT: *Dr. Bruce Goldstein*

**Brooks/Cole Publishing Company
511 Forest Lodge Road
Pacific Grove, California 93950-9968**

- FOLD HERE -